Y0-EMQ-981

AMM

Customer Support Information

Plunkett's Entertainment & Media Industry Almanac 2008

Please register your book immediately...

if you did not purchase it directly from Plunkett Research, Ltd. This will enable us to fulfill your replacement request if you have a damaged product, or your requests for assistance. Also it will enable us to notify you of future editions, so that you may purchase them from the source of your choice.

If you are an actual, original purchaser but did not receive a FREE CD-ROM version with your book...*

you may request it by returning this form.

_____ YES, please register me as a purchaser of the book.
I did not buy it directly from Plunkett Research, Ltd.

_____ YES, please send me a free CD-ROM version of the book.
I am an actual purchaser, but I did not receive one with my book.
(Proof of purchase may be required.)

Customer Name _____

Title_____	_____	**Disk**	_____	**Video**	_____
Organization ___	_____	**Cassette**	_____	**CD**	_____
Address _____	_____	**Text**	_____	**Other**	_____

City_____ State_____ Zip_____

Country (if other than USA) _____

Phone_____ Fax _____

E-mail _____

Mail or Fax to: # Plunkett Research, Ltd.

Attn: FREE CD-ROM and/or Registration
P.O. Drawer 541737, Houston, TX 77254-1737 USA
713.932.0000 · Fax 713.932.7080 · www.plunkettresearch.com

* Only the original purchaser of the book is eligible to register. Use of CD-ROMs is subject to the terms of their end user license agreements.

PLUNKETT'S ENTERTAINMENT & MEDIA INDUSTRY ALMANAC 2008

The Only Comprehensive Guide to the Entertainment & Media Industry

Jack W. Plunkett

Published by:
Plunkett Research, Ltd., Houston, Texas
www.plunkettresearch.com

PLUNKETT'S ENTERTAINMENT & MEDIA INDUSTRY ALMANAC 2008

Editor and Publisher:
Jack W. Plunkett

Executive Editor and Database Manager:
Martha Burgher Plunkett

Senior Editors and Researchers:
Addie K. FryeWeaver
Christie Manck
John Peterson

Editors, Researchers and Assistants:
Devin Ayers
Andreea Balan
Brandon Brison
Lindsey Meyn
Kristen Morrow
Holly Scarpinato
Michael Sheehan
Kyle Wark
Suzanne Zarosky

E-Commerce Managers:
Mark Cassells
Heather M. Cook
Emily Hurley
Ian Markham
Lynne Zarosky

Information Technology Managers:
Wenping Guo

Cover Design:
Kim Paxson, Just Graphics
Junction, TX

Special Thanks to:
American Gaming Association
Association of American Publishers
Book Industry Study Group, Inc.
Editor & Publisher
International Federation of the Phonographic Industries (IFPI)
InternetWorldStats.com
National Association of Theatre Owners
National Cable & Telecommunications Association
Nielsen Media Research
Newspaper Association of America
PriceWaterhouseCoopers
Publishers Information Bureau
SNL Kagan
U.S. Bureau of Labor Statistics
U.S. Census Bureau
U.S. Federal Communications Commission (FCC)
Universal McCann
Veronis Suhler Stevenson
Video Business
Wireless Association (The)

Plunkett Research, Ltd.
P. O. Drawer 541737, Houston, Texas 77254, USA
Phone: 713.932.0000 Fax: 713.932.7080 www.plunkettresearch.com

Published by:

Plunkett Research, Ltd.

P. O. Drawer 541737

Houston, Texas 77254-1737

Phone: 713.932.0000

Fax: 713.932.7080

Internet: www.plunkettresearch.com

ISBN10 # 1-59392-103-9

ISBN13 # 978-1-59392-103-3

Disclaimer of liability
for use and results of use:

PLUNKETT'S ENTERTAINMENT & MEDIA INDUSTRY ALMANAC 2008

CONTENTS

Continued on the next page

Continued from the previous page

A Short Entertainment & Media Industry Glossary

1080p: A classification for high-definition video. 1080 refers to 1,080 lines of vertical resolution; p refers to progressive scan, meaning that the lines that comprise the video picture appear on the screen sequentially. This standard is used in the production of high definition film, high definition television (HDTV) and high definition digital video disc (HD DVD). 1080p is a superior technology to 1080i (i stands for interlaced) which delivers lines of video alternatively resulting in slight distortions in picture quality.

10-K: An annual report filed by publicly held companies. It provides a comprehensive overview of the company's business and its finances. By law, it must contain specific information and follow a given form, the "Annual Report on Form 10-K." The U.S. Securities and Exchange Commission requires that it be filed within 90 days after fiscal year end. However, these reports are often filed late due to extenuating circumstances. Variations of a 10-K are often filed to indicate amendments and changes. Most publicly held companies also publish an "annual report" that is not on Form 10-K. These annual reports are more informal and are frequently used by a company to enhance its image with customers, investors and industry peers.

802.11a (Wi-Fi5): A faster wireless network standard than 802.11b ("Wi-Fi"). 802.11a operates in the 5-GHz band at speeds of 50 Mbps or more. This standard may be affected by weather and is not as suitable for outdoor use. 802.11 standards are set by the IEEE (Institute of Electrical and Electronics Engineers).

802.11b (Wi-Fi): An extremely popular, Wi-Fi short-range wireless connection standard created by the IEEE (Institute of Electrical and Electronics Engineers). It operates at 11 Mbps and can be used to connect computer devices to each other. 802.11b competes with the Bluetooth standard. Its range is up to 380 feet, but 150 feet or so may be more practical in some installations.

802.11g: A recent addition to the series of 802.11 specifications for Wi-Fi wireless networks, 802.11g provides data transfer at speeds of up to 54 Mbps in the 2.4-GHz band. It can easily exchange data with 802.11b-enabled devices, but at much higher speed. 802.11g equipment, such as wireless access points, will be able to provide simultaneous WLAN connectivity for both 802.11g and 802.11b equipment. The 802.11 standards are set by the IEEE (Institute of Electrical and Electronics Engineers).

802.11n (MIMO): Multiple Input Multiple Output antenna technology. The new standard in the series of 802.11 Wi-Fi specifications for wireless networks. It has the potential of providing data transfer speeds of 100 to perhaps as much as 500 Mbps. 802.11n also boasts better operating distances than current networks. MIMO uses spectrum more efficiently without any loss of reliability. The technology is based on several different antennas all tuned to the same channel, each transmitting a different signal.

802.15: See "Ultrawideband (UWB)." For 802.15.1, see "Bluetooth."

802.16 (WiMAX): An advanced wireless standard with significant speed and distance capabilities, WiMax is officially known as the 802.16 standard. Using microwave technologies, it has the potential to broadcast at distances up to 30 miles and speeds of up to 70 Mbps. The 802.XX standards are set by the IEEE (Institute of Electrical and Electronics Engineers).

Advertising-On-Demand: Television advertising that viewers can watch voluntarily, in contrast to traditional television advertising, which is shown on the air without viewer choice. See "Demand-Driven Advertising."

Affiliate: A broadcast radio or television station that is an "affiliate" of a national network, such as NBC or CBS, contracts with the national network, which provides programming to the affiliate for all or part of each day. In return, the affiliate provides the network with an agreed-upon number of minutes of advertising time, which the network then resells to advertisers.

AM (Amplitude Modulation): Radio broadcasts in the range of 535 kHz to 1705 kHz.

American Research Bureau (ARB): One of several national firms that conduct audience research. ARB is the founder of Arbitron ratings.

Analog: A form of transmitting information characterized by continuously variable quantities. Digital transmission, in contrast, is characterized by discrete bits of information in numerical steps. An analog signal responds to changes in light, sound, heat and pressure.

Area of Dominant Influence (ADI): A market area established by Arbitron that places cities and/or parts of counties into groupings that are reached by the same local radio or television stations. It is similar to Nielsen's "Designated Market Area." For example, advertising on radio stations in Boston will reach listeners far outside of Boston within the surrounding ADI.

ARPU (Average Revenue Per User): A measure of the average monthly billing revenue of a wireless company on a per user basis.

ATM (Asynchronous Transfer Mode): A digital switching and transmission technology based on high speed. ATM allows voice, video and data signals to be sent over a single telephone line at speeds from 25 million to 1 billion bits per second (bps). This digital ATM speed is much faster than traditional analog phone lines, which allow no more than 2 million bps. See "Broadband."

Baby Boomer: Generally refers to people born in the U.S. and Western Europe from 1946 to 1964. In the U.S., the total number of Baby Boomers is about 78 million--one of the largest and most affluent demographic groups. The term evolved to include the children of soldiers and war industry workers who were involved in World War II. When those veterans and workers returned to civilian life they started or added to families in large numbers. As a result, the baby boom generation is one of the largest demographic segments in the U.S. Some baby boomers have already started reaching early retirement age. By 2011, millions will begin turning traditional retirement age (65), resulting in extremely rapid growth in the senior portion of the population.

Bandwidth: The data transmission capacity of a network, measured in the amount of data (in bits and bauds) it can transport in one second. A full page of text is about 15,000 to 20,000 bits. Full-motion, full-screen video requires about 10 million bits per second, depending on compression.

Basic Cable: Primary level or levels of cable service offered for subscription. Basic cable offerings may include retransmitted broadcast signals as well as local and access programming. In addition, regional and national cable network programming may be provided.

Blog (Web Log): A web site consisting of a personal journal, news coverage, special-interest content or other data that is posted on the Internet, frequently updated and intended for public viewing by anyone who might be interested in the author's thoughts. Short for "web log," blog content is frequently distributed via RSS (Real Simple Syndication). Blog content has evolved to include video files (VLOGs) and audio files (Podcasting) as well as text. Also, see "RSS (Real Simple Syndication)," "VLOG (Video Blog)," "Moblog," "Podcasting" and "User-Generated Content."

Bluetooth: An industry standard for a technology that enables wireless, short-distance infrared connections between devices such as cell phone headsets, Palm Pilots or PDAs, laptops, printers and Internet appliances. Compatible with the IEEE's 802.15 specification, Bluetooth is ideally suited for connecting devices that will remain close to each other (within 30 feet or less). Since its power consumption is very low, it is also ideally suited for battery-powered devices such as cell phones. See www.bluetooth.com. Data transmission speeds are up to 3 Mbps per second, vastly slower than Ultrawideband. See "Ultrawideband (UWB)." Bluetooth 2.0 offers three times the speed of Bluetooth 1.0 plus lower power consumption. The succeeding version, 3.0 will roll out by 2008 with enhanced encryption, better transmission of audio and video files and better "pairing" of Bluetooth devices for stronger connections. Version 3.0 may offer astonishing speeds of 12.5 to 50 Mbps.

Branded Entertainment: Entertainment programming or content whereby a brand's message, image or positioning is built into the content in a vital and relevant manner. The benefits may include an opportunity to break through the advertising "clutter"; a chance to align the brand with relevant stars, athletes, settings or scripts; or a new opportunity to reach target audiences in a meaningful and memorable way. Also, see "Embedded Advertising."

Branding: A marketing strategy that places a focus on the brand name of a product, service or firm in order to increase the brand's market share, increase sales, establish credibility, improve satisfaction, raise the profile of the firm and increase profits.

Broadband: The high-speed transmission range for telecommunications and computer data. Broadband refers to any transmission at 2 million bps (bits per second) or higher (much higher than analog speed). A broadband network can carry voice, video and data all at the same time. Internet users enjoying broadband access typically connect to the Internet via DSL line, cable modem or T1 line. Several wireless methods now offer broadband as well.

Broadcast: Electronic transmission of media by radio or television; generally refers to wireless methods.

Browser: A program that allows a user to read Internet text or graphics and to navigate from one page to another. The most popular browsers are Microsoft Internet Explorer and Netscape Navigator. Firefox is an open source browser introduced in 2005 that is rapidly gaining popularity.

B-to-B, or B2B: See "Business-to-Business."

B-to-C, or B2C: See "Business-to-Consumer."

Business Process Outsourcing (BPO): The outsourcing of non-mission-critical business processes that may include call centers, basic accounting or human resources management, depending on the industry involved. Also, see "ITES (IT-Enabled Services)."

Business-to-Business: An organization focused on selling products, services or data to commercial customers rather than individual consumers. Also known as B2B.

Business-to-Consumer: An organization focused on selling products, services or data to individual consumers rather than commercial customers. Also known as B2C.

Cable Modem: An interface between a cable television system and a computer or router. Most cable modems are external devices that connect to the PC through a standard 10Base-T Ethernet card and twisted-pair wiring. External Universal Serial Bus (USB) modems and internal PCI modem cards are also available. The cable modem enables a computer to access the Internet via a TV cable. Cable modem access can be very high-speed and is much faster than traditional "dial-up" access via a standard telephone line. Cable modem speeds vary, depending on the cable modem system and current traffic load. From the Internet to the computer, the modem may connect at speeds as high as 1 to 3 Mbps. From the computer to network, speeds typically run between 500 Kbps and 2.5 Mbps. Cable modem access competes with DSL access.

Cable TV: A television system consisting of a local television station that is equipped with an antenna or satellite dish. The antenna or dish receives signals from distant, central network stations and retransmits those signals via TV cable to the local subscriber.

Caching: A method of storing data in a temporary location closer to the user so that it can be retrieved quickly when requested.

Call Letters: Letters that identify a station, e.g., KTRU. Call letters are established by the Federal Communications Commission. Each broadcast station has unique letters. The letters may denote whether the station is in the eastern or western U.S.

Captive Offshoring: Used to describe a company-owned offshore operation. For example, Microsoft owns and operates significant captive offshore research and development centers in China and elsewhere that are offshore from Microsoft's U.S. home base. Also see "Offshoring."

CATV: Cable television.

CDF (Channel Definition Format): Used in Internet-based broadcasting. With this format, a channel serves as a web site that also sends an information file about that specific site. Users subscribe to a channel by downloading the file.

Circulation: The numerical distribution of print media such as magazines or newspapers. "Controlled circulation" refers to magazines that are generally sent to a defined subscriber base free-of-charge. "Audited circulation" refers to a subscription base that has been verified as to its size by an independent agency.

Click Through: In advertising on the Internet, click through refers to how often viewers respond to an ad by clicking on it. Also known as click rate.

Closed Circuit TV (CCTV): Programs or other material that limit the target audience to a specific group instead of the general public. For example, major retailers use such private TV systems, distributed via satellite, to provide training to employees at remote store locations.

Codec: Hardware or software that converts analog to digital and digital to analog (in both audio and video formats). Codecs can be found in digital telephones, set-top boxes, computers and videoconferencing equipment. The term is also used to refer to the compression of digital information into a smaller format.

Community Antenna Television: A community television system that is served through cable and is connected to a common set of antennae.

Compression: A technology in which a communications signal is squeezed so that it uses less bandwidth (or capacity) than it normally would. This saves storage space and shortens transfer time. The original data is decompressed when read back into memory.

Content Aggregator: A content aggregator collects content and distributes it to subscribers, network operators or other content companies.

Contract Manufacturer: A company that manufactures products that will be sold under the brand names of its client companies. For example, a large number of consumer electronics, such as laptop computers, are manufactured by contract manufacturers for leading brand-name computer companies such as Dell. Many other types of products are made under contract manufacturing, from apparel to pharmaceuticals. Also see "OEM (Original Equipment Manufacturer)" and "ODM (Original Design Manufacturer)."

Controlled (Qualified) Circulation: Restricting the circulation of an advertisement to target qualified customers (e.g., sending lock-pick catalogs only to certified locksmiths, or medical equipment brochures only to doctors and hospitals).

Controlled Circulation: See "Circulation."

Cookie: A piece of information sent to a web browser from a web server that the browser software saves and then sends back to the server upon request.

Cookies are used by web site operators to track the actions of users returning to the site.

Cost Per Click (CPC): Online advertising that is billed on a response basis. An advertiser sells a banner ad and is paid by the number of users who click on the ad.

Cost Per Thousand (CPM): A charge for advertising calculated on a fixed amount multiplied by the number of users who view an ad, computed in thousands.

CPC: See "Cost Per Click (CPC)."

CPM: See "Cost Per Thousand (CPM)."

CRM (Customer Relationship Management): The automation of integrated business processes involving customers, including sales (contact management, product configuration), marketing (campaign management, telemarketing) and customer service (call center, field service).

Cyberspace: Refers to the entire realm of information available through computer networks and the Internet.

DBA: Doing business as.

DBS (Direct Broadcast Satellite): A high-powered satellite authorized to broadcast television programming directly to homes. Home subscribers use a dish and a converter to receive and translate the TV signal. An example is the DirecTV service. DBS operates in the 11.70- to 12.40-GHz range.

Decompression: See "Compression."

Demand-Driven Advertising: Allows television viewers to choose which commercials to watch, how many to watch and when to watch them.

Demographics: The breakdown of the population into statistical categories such as age, income, education and sex.

Dendrimer: A type of molecule that can be used with small molecules to give them certain desirable characteristics. Dendrimers are utilized in technologies for electronic displays. See "OLED (Organic LED)."

Dial-Up Access: The connection of a computer or other device to a network through a modem and a public telephone network. The only difference between dial-up access and a telephone connection is that computers are at each end of the connection rather than people. Dial-up access is slower than DSL, cable modem and other advanced connections.

Digital: The transmission of a signal by reducing all of its information to ones and zeros and then regrouping them at the reception end. Digital transmission vastly improves the carrying capacity of the spectrum while reducing noise and distortion of the transmission.

Digital Millennium Copyright Act: The Digital Millennium Copyright Act is a U.S. law created in 1998. It was written in response to the rapid growth of content on the Internet. The act contains a "safe harbor" provision that enables Internet site publishers to promptly eliminate most faults or penalties of infringement if they promptly remove online content when notified by the proper owners of that content's copyright.

Digital Subscriber Line (DSL): A broadband (high-speed) Internet connection provided via telecommunications systems. These lines are a cost-effective means of providing homes and small businesses with relatively fast Internet access. Common variations include ADSL and SDSL. DSL competes with cable modem access and wireless access.

Direct Marketing: A form of non-store retailing in which customers are exposed to merchandise through catalogs, direct-mail brochures, telemarketing or television. Direct marketing may be used to generate direct-response purchases, store traffic, sales leads or a combination thereof.

Direct Selling: A form of marketing which involves manufacturing and then selling merchandise or services through direct mail or through salespeople who contact consumers directly or by telephone at home or place of work (e.g., Mary Kay cosmetics).

Distributor: An individual or business involved in marketing, warehousing and/or shipping of products manufactured by others to a specific group of end users. Distributors do not sell to the general public. In order to develop a competitive advantage, distributors often focus on serving one industry or one set of niche clients. For example, within the medical industry, there are major distributors that focus on providing pharmaceuticals, surgical supplies or dental supplies to clinics and hospitals.

DMA (Designated Market Area): A television market as delineated by AC Nielsen.

DOCSIS (Data Over Cable Service Interface Specification): Standards for transferring data over cable television.

DRM (Digital Rights Management): Enables control and maintenance of publishers' rights by delivering encrypted information and, instead of providing the key (or using the recipient's public key for encryption), in effect permitting the recipient to borrow the decryption key in a highly controlled fashion.

DS-1: A digital transmission format that transmits and receives information at a rate of 1,544,000 bits per second.

DSL: See "Digital Subscriber Line (DSL)."

Dub: A recorded copy of a TV or radio appearance on video or audiotape.

DVD (Digital Video Disc): Similar to music CDs, these discs can store more than seven times as much data. (DVDs store 4.7 gigabytes of data, compared to 650 megabytes on a CD.) They are commonly used to store full-length motion pictures.

DVR (Digital Video Recorder): A device that records video files, typically television programming including movies, in digital format to be replayed at a later time. The most commonly known PVR is the TiVo. DVRs encode video as MPEG files and save them onto a hard drive. DVRs are also known as PVRs (Personal Video Recorders).

Dynamic HTML: Web content that changes with each individual viewing. For example, the same site could appear differently depending on geographic location of the reader, time of day, previous pages viewed or the user's profile.

EC (European Community): See "EU (European Union)."

Echo Boomers: See "Generation Y."

E-Commerce: The use of online, Internet-based sales methods. The phrase is used to describe both business-to-consumer and business-to-business sales.

EDI (Electronic Data Interchange): An accepted standard format for the exchange of data between various companies' networks. EDI allows for the transfer of e-mail as well as orders, invoices and other files from one company to another.

Electronic Book (e-Book): An electronic method of storing and accessing books online or in portable e-book viewing machines (readers), so that consumers can purchase and read a digital copy of a book instead of a traditional print copy. Advantages include the ability to search by key word and the ability to store dozens of books in digital form on one portable device.

Electronic Paper Displays (EPD): Electronic paper is a term used to describe a recently developed type of high contrast, flexible display. The displays use low amounts of power and can be viewed in bright sunlight and at any angle. They are well suited for use as screens on mobile devices and may have broad applications in outdoor advertising.

ENPS (Electronic News Production System): A content management software application designed by broadcasters for use in television newsrooms. Introduced in 1997, the application addresses nearly all newsroom activities, including scripting, messaging, archiving, news wire management and text searching of news feeds.

Enterprise Resource Planning (ERP): An integrated information system that helps manage all aspects of a business, including accounting, ordering and human resources, typically across all locations of a major corporation or organization. ERP is considered to be a critical tool for management of large organizations. Suppliers of ERP tools include SAP and Oracle.

EU (European Union): A consolidation of European countries (member states) functioning as one body to facilitate trade. Previously known as the European Community (EC), the EU expanded to include much of Eastern Europe in 2004, raising the total number of member states to 25. In 2002, the EU launched a unified currency, the Euro. See europa.eu.int.

EU Competence: The jurisdiction in which the EU can take legal action.

EV-DO (CDMA 2000 1xEV-DO): A 3G (third generation) cellular telephone service standard that is an improved version of 1xRTT. The EV-DO (Evolution Data Optimized) standard introduced in 2004 allows data download speeds of as much as 2.4 Mbps. A version slated for 2006 allows up to 3.1 Mbps data download speeds. EV-DO is also known as CDMA 2000 1xEV-DO. EV-DO's capabilities will be used by the entertainment industry to enable video via cell phone.

Extensible Markup Language: See "XML (Extensible Markup Language)."

Extranet: A computer network that is accessible in part to authorized outside persons, as opposed to an intranet, which uses a firewall to limit accessibility.

FCC (Federal Communications Commission): See "Federal Communications Commission (FCC)."

Federal Communications Commission (FCC): The U.S. Government agency that regulates broadcast television and radio, as well as satellite transmission, telephony and all uses of radio spectrum.

Field Emission Display (FED): A self-luminescent display that can be extremely thin, draw very low power, and be very bright from all angles and in all types of light. The latest FEDs are based on carbon nanotubes. Samsung is a leader in this field. Early applications include high-end television and computer monitors.

FM (Frequency Modulation): Radio broadcasts in the range of 88 MHz to 108 MHz.

Frequency: The number of times that an alternating current goes through its complete cycle in one second. One cycle per second is referred to as one hertz; 1,000 cycles per second, one kilohertz; 1 million cycles per second, one megahertz; and 1 billion cycles per second, one gigahertz.

Frequency Band: A term for designating a range of frequencies in the electromagnetic spectrum.

FTTC: Fiber to the curb. See "FTTH (Fiber to the Home/Fiber to the Premises)."

FTTH (Fiber to the Home/Fiber to the Premises): Refers to the extension of a fiber-optic system through the last mile so that it touches the home or office where it will be used. This can provide Internet access at speeds of 5 to 50 Mbps, much faster than typical T1, DSL or cable modem access. FTTH is now commonly installed in new communities where telecom infrastructure is being built for the first time. Another phrase used to describe such installations is FTTP, or Fiber to the Premises.

FTTN (Fiber to the Node): Refers to the extension of a fiber-optic system through the last mile so that it touches a central neighborhood junction close to the home or office where it will be used. The remaining distance is covered by existing copper phone line that uses DSL (digital subscriber line) technology to speed data transfer.

FTTP: Fiber to the premises. See "FTTH (Fiber to the Home/Fiber to the Premises)."

FVOD (Free Video On Demand): VOD programming offered by a network operator free of charge. FVOD programming includes on-demand advertising and on-demand programming offered as part of a basic VOD package.

Gatekeeper: A person or persons controlling the flow of information. Individuals who allow information to pass through them to be disseminated to the public are referred to as gatekeepers. These include newspaper publishers, editors, reporters, television and radio producers, station owners and executives.

GDP (Gross Domestic Product): The total value of a nation's output, income and expenditures produced with a nation's physical borders.

General Magazines: Consumer magazines that are not aimed at special-interest audiences.

Generation Y: Refers to Americans born between 1977 and 1997, who number about 75 million. They are also known as Echo Boomers. These are children of the Baby Boomers are filling the U.S. work force as Baby Boomers retire.

Geostationary: A geosynchronous satellite angle with zero inclination, making a satellite appear to hover over one spot on the earth's equator.

GIF (Graphic Interchange Format): See "Graphic Interchange Format (GIF)."

Global Positioning System (GPS): A satellite system, originally designed by the U.S. Department of Defense for navigation purposes. Today, GPS is in wide use for consumer and business purposes, such as navigation for drivers, boaters and hikers. It utilizes satellites orbiting the earth at 10,900 miles to enable users to pinpoint precise locations using small, electronic wireless receivers.

Globalization: The increased mobility of goods, services, labor, technology and capital throughout the world. Although globalization is not a new development, its pace has increased with the advent of new technologies, especially in the areas of telecommunications, finance and shipping.

GNP (Gross National Product): A country's total output of goods and services from all forms of economic activity measured at market prices for one calendar year. It differs from GDP (Gross Domestic Product) in that GNP includes income from investments made in foreign nations.

GPS: See "Global Positioning System (GPS)."

Graphic Interchange Format (GIF): A widely used format for image files.

Gross Rating Points (GRPs): Measures the audience share of a television program's audience delivery. GRPs are the sum of individual ratings for all programs in a particular time slot. See "Ratings/Ratings Points/Ratings Share."

Haptics: Relates to virtual touch technology, using electronics to give people the sensation that they are touching and feeling solid objects.

HD Radio (High Definition Radio): A technology that enables station operators to slice existing radio spectrum into multiple, thin bands. Each band is capable of transmitting additional programming. One existing radio station's spectrum may be sliced into as many as eight channels.

HDMI (High-Definition Multi-Media Interface): HDMI is an industry-standard interface to conduct uncompressed, all-digital audio and video signals into high definition entertainment components including HDTV. The goal is to enable consumer entertainment devices to display high quality, high-definition content. HDMI is backward-compatible with earlier DVI equipment, so that HDMI can HDMI equipment can display video received from DVI products.

Headend: A facility that originates and distributes cable service in a given geographic area. Depending on the size of the area it serves, a cable system may be comprised of more than one headend.

Hertz: A measure of frequency equal to one cycle per second. Most radio signals operate in ranges of megahertz or gigahertz.

HFC: Hybrid Fiber Coaxial. A type of cable system.

High-Definition Television (HDTV): A type of television broadcasting that increases the resolution of the visual field contained by the image, making for a clearer and more movie-like viewing experience. HDTV requires advanced digital broadcasting and receiving equipment.

Homes Passed: Households that have the ability to receive cable service and may opt to subscribe.

Impressions: In Internet advertising, the total number of times an ad is displayed on a web page. Impressions are not the same as "hits," which count the number of times each page or element in a page is retrieved. Since a single complicated page on a web site could consist of five or more individual elements, including graphics and text, one viewer calling up that page would register multiple hits but just a single impression.

Impulse VOD: Affords television viewers the ability to order VOD programming without having to phone in an order to the content provider.

Infotainment: Programming which combines information with entertainment. It most often refers to television programming or web-based programming that informs the viewer while extolling the virtues of a product or service that is for sale.

Initial Public Offering (IPO): A company's first effort to sell its stock to investors (the public). Investors in an up-trending market eagerly seek stocks offered in many IPOs because the stocks of newly public companies that seem to have great promise may appreciate very rapidly in price, reaping great profits for those who were able to get the stock at the first offering. In the United States, IPOs are regulated by the SEC (U.S. Securities Exchange Commission) and by the state-level regulatory agencies of the states in which the IPO shares are offered.

Interactive: In entertainment, advertising and communications, interactive refers to systems that enable the viewer or user to interact via a response or two-way communication. For example, interactive television advertising may enable the viewer to respond via a set-top box, immediately purchasing the item being advertised.

Interactive TV (ITV): Allows two-way data flow between a viewer and the cable TV system. A user can exchange information with the cable system—for example, by ordering a product related to a show he/she is watching or by voting in an interactive survey.

Internet: A global computer network that provides an easily accessible way for hundreds of millions of users to send and receive data electronically when appropriately connected via computers or wireless devices. Access is generally through HTML-enabled sites on the World Wide Web. Also known as the Net.

Internet Appliance: A non-PC device that connects users to the Internet for specific or general purposes. A good example is an electronic game machine with a screen and Internet capabilities. It is anticipated that many types of Internet appliances will be of common use in homes in the near future.

Internet Sharing Programs: Internet networks that allow users to share files and programs, in spite of possible copyright restrictions (e.g., Napster, before the federal ruling that barred it from downloading music files free of charge).

Intranet: A network protected by a firewall for sharing data and e-mail within an organization or company. Usually, intranets are used by organizations for internal communication.

IP Number/IP Address: A number or address with four parts that are separated by dots. Each machine on the Internet has its own IP (Internet protocol) number, which serves as an identifier.

IP VOD: See "VOD-Over-IP."

IPTV: Internet Protocol Television. That is, television delivered by Internet-based means such as fiber to the home (FTTH) or a very high speed DSL. Microsoft is a leading provider of advanced IPTV software. SBC and BT are two leading telecom firms that are using Microsoft's new software to offer television services over high speed Internet lines.

ISP (Internet Service Provider): A company that sells access to the Internet to individual subscribers. Leading examples are MSN and AOL.

ITES (IT-Enabled Services): The portion of the Information Technology industry focused on providing business services, such as call centers, insurance claims processing and medical records transcription, by utilizing the power of IT, especially the Internet. Most ITES functions are considered to be back-office procedures. Also, see "Business Process Outsourcing (BPO)."

ITV: See "Interactive TV (ITV)."

IVOD (Interactive Video On Demand): An extension of VOD that offers many of the functions typically provided by VCRs, such as pause, fast forward and fast rewind. Through a set-top box, the IVOD customer can browse, select and purchase products; avoid or select advertisements; and investigate additional details about news events.

Java: A programming language developed by Sun Microsystems that allows web pages to display interactive graphics. Any type of computer or operating systems can read Java.

JPEG (Joint Photographic Experts Group): A widely used format for digital image files.

LAN (Local Area Network): A computer network that is generally within one office or one building. A LAN can be very inexpensive and efficient to set up when small numbers of computers are involved. It may require a network administrator and a serious investment if hundreds of computers are hooked up to the LAN. A LAN enables all computers within the office to share files and printers, to access common databases and to send e-mail to others on the network.

LBA (Location Based Advertising): The ability for advertisers and information providers to push information to mobile consumers based on their

locations. For example, GPS equipped cell phones have the potential to alert consumers on the go to nearby restaurants, entertainment attractions, and special sale events at retailers.

LED (Light Emitting Diode): A small tube containing material that emits light when exposed to electricity. The color of the light depends upon the type of material. The LED was first developed in 1962 at the University of Illinois at Urbana-Champaign. LEDs are important to a wide variety of industries, from wireless telephone handsets to signage to displays for medical equipment, because they provide a very high quality of light with very low power requirements. They also have a very long useful life and produce very low heat output when. All of these characteristics are great improvements over a conventional incandescent bulb. Several advancements have been made in LED technology. See "OLED (Organic LED)," "PLED (Polymer Light Emitting Diode)," "SMOLED (Small Molecule Organic Light Emitting Diode)" and "Dendrimer."

Linear Programming: See "Linear TV."

Linear TV: A type of television programming that is (1) standard non-PVR and non-VOD television service. (2) TV programming that the producers, broadcasters, etc. do not want the viewer leaving in any way, including visiting the program advertiser's website. (3) Programming that is dependent on programming that has already been presented. (4) Non-interactive TV.

Liquid Crystal Display (LCD): A digital screen composed of liquid crystal cells that change luminosity when exposed to an electric field. The newest LCDs have a higher resolution and use less power than conventional displays.

LMDS: Local Multipoint Distribution System.

Local Area Network (LAN): See "LAN (Local Area Network)."

Location-Based Entertainment: The use of entertainment themes and attractions to draw consumers to specific locations, such as shopping malls, casinos and restaurants.

LOHAS: Lifestyles of Health and Sustainability. A marketing term that refers to consumers who choose to purchase and/or live with items that are natural, organic, less polluting, etc. Such consumers may also prefer products powered by alternative energy, such as hybrid cars.

Long Form Advertisement: Usually takes the form of a lengthy television commercial with entertaining and/or educational elements. These advertisements may be offered with other commercials or as links for viewers to click on for more information about the advertised product or service.

M2M (Machine-to-Machine): Refers to the transmission of data from one device to another, typically through wireless means such as Wi-Fi. For example, a Wi-Fi network might be employed to control several machines in a household from a central computer. Such machines might include air conditioning and entertainment systems. In logistics and retailing, M2M can refer to the use of RFID tags to transmit information. See "RFID (Radio Frequency Identification.)"

MAN (Metropolitan Area Network): A data and communications network that operates over metropolitan areas and recently has been expanded to nationwide and even worldwide connectivity of high-speed data networks. A MAN can carry video and data.

Market Segmentation: The division of a consumer market into specific groups of buyers based on demographic factors.

Marketing: Includes all planning and management activities and expenses associated with the promotion of a product or service. Marketing can encompass advertising, customer surveys, public relations and many other disciplines. Marketing is distinct from selling, which is the process of sell-through to the end user.

Mass Media: Refers to all media that disseminate information throughout the world, including television, radio, film, print, photography and electronic media.

Mbps (Megabits per second): 1 million bits transmitted per second.

M-Commerce: Mobile e-commerce over wireless devices.

Media: Used loosely to refer to the entire communications system of reporters, editors, producers, print publications, broadcast programs, magazines and online publications.

Media Literacy: Refers to an individual's ability to read, analyze and evaluate media. If one is media literate, that person can recognize the rhetorical arguments and techniques used by the media to persuade audiences.

Media Outlet: A broadcast or publication that brings news and features to the public through a distribution channel.

Mega-Theater: A movie theater with as many as 30 screens and more frequent show times. Some also offer luxury seating, with amenities such as restaurant-style food, a wait staff and reservations.

Merchandising: Any marketing method utilized to foster sales growth.

Metropolitan Area Network (MAN): See "MAN (Metropolitan Area Network)."

Miles of Plant: The number of cable plant miles laid or strung by a cable system; the cable miles in place.

Moblog: Mobile blog. This is a blog created by cell phone or other mobile device. It often consists largely of photos taken by a cell phone's built-in camera. Also, see "Blog (Web Log)."

Modem: A device that allows a computer to be connected to a phone line, which in turn enables the computer to receive and exchange data with other machines via the Internet.

MOS (Media Object Server): An XML-based protocol designed to transfer information between newsroom automation systems and other systems, including media servers. The MOS protocol allows various devices to be controlled from a central device or piece of software, which limits the need to have operators stationed at multiple locations throughout the news studio.

MOST (Media Oriented Systems Transport): A standard adopted in 2004 by the Consumer Electronics Association for the integration of or interface with consumer electronics (such as iPods) into entertainment systems in automobiles.

MP3: A subsystem of MPEG used to compress sound into digital files. It is the most commonly used format for downloading music and audio books. MP3 compresses music significantly while retaining CD-like quality. MP3 players are personal, portable devices used for listening to music and audio book files. See "MPEG."

MPEG, MPEG-1, MPEG-2, MPEG-3, MPEG-4: Moving Picture Experts Group. It is a digital standard for the compression of motion or still video for transmission or storage. MPEGs are used in digital cameras and for Internet-based viewing.

MSO (Multiple System Operator): An individual or company owning two or more cable systems.

Multicasting: Sending data, audio or video simultaneously to a number of clients. Also known as broadcasting.

Multimedia: Refers to a presentation using several different media at once. For example, an encyclopedia in CD-ROM format is generally multimedia because it features written text, video and sound in one package.

Multipoint Distribution System (MDS): A common carrier licensed by the FCC to operate a broadcast-like omni-directional microwave transmission facility within a given city. MDS carriers often pick up satellite pay-TV programming and distribute it, via their local MDS transmitter, to specially installed antennas and receivers.

NAND: NAND memory is an advanced type of flash memory chip. It is popular for use in consumer electronics such as MP3 players and digital cameras.

Network: In computing, a network is created when two or more computers are connected. Computers may be connected by wireless methods, using such technologies as 802.11b, or by a system of cables, switches and routers.

Network Numbers: The first portion of an IP address, which identifies the network to which hosts in the rest of the address are connected.

Network Storage: See "Network-Based VOD."

Network-Based VOD: Involves a television content provider storing either all or most of its programming

content at its location, usually on its servers. Network-based VOD is more typical of cable TV than satellite TV.

New Media: A wide array of digital communication technologies, including Internet development tools and services, desktop and portable personal computers, workstations, servers, audio/video compression and editing equipment, graphics hardware and software, high-density storage services and video conferencing systems.

Newspaper Syndicate: A firm selling features, photos, columns, comic strips or other special material for publication in a large number of newspapers. For example, a typical fee charged by a syndicate to a daily newspaper for a popular comic strip is $10 per day. Generally, the syndicate splits the fee with the author.

Nielsen Ratings: Ratings created by ACNielsen, a company engaged in television audience ratings and other market research.

Nielsen Station Index (NSI): An index that rates individual television stations.

Nielsen Television Index (NTI): An index that rates national television network programming.

Non-Store Retailing: A form of retailing that is not store-based. Non-store retailing can be conducted through vending machines, direct-selling, direct-marketing, party-based selling, catalogs, television programming, telemarketing and Internet-based selling.

nPVR (Network Personal Video Recording): See "Server-Based SVOD Programming."

NVOD (Near Video On Demand): An alternative method of VOD television programming delivery. NVOD delivers only a small portion of the ordered programming to the customer before playback. This initial download serves as a buffer while the rest of the programming is viewed directly off the provider's server. In contrast, traditional VOD typically involves the delivery of the entire ordered programming to the customer for playback from the customer's hard drive.

ODM (Original Design Manufacturer): A contract manufacturer that offers complete, end-to-end design, engineering and manufacturing services. ODMs design and build products, such as consumer electronics, that client companies can then brand and sell as their own. For example, a large percentage of laptop computers, cell phones and PDAs are made by ODMs. Also see "OEM (Original Equipment Manufacturer)" and "Contract Manufacturer."

OEM (Original Equipment Manufacturer): A company that manufactures a product or component for sale to a customer that will integrate the component into a final product or assembly. The OEM's customer will distribute the end product or resell it to an end user. For example, a personal computer made under a brand name by a given company may contain various components, such as hard drives, graphics cards or speakers, manufactured by several different OEM "vendors," but the firm doing the final assembly/manufacturing process is the final manufacturer. Also see "ODM (Original Design Manufacturer)" and "Contract Manufacturer."

Offshoring: The rapidly growing tendency among U.S., Japanese and Western European firms to send knowledge-based and manufacturing work overseas. The intent is to take advantage of lower wages and operating costs in such nations as China, India, Hungary and Russia. The choice of a nation for offshore work may be influenced by such factors as language and education of the local workforce, transportation systems or natural resources. For example, China and India are graduating high numbers of skilled engineers and scientists from their universities. Also, some nations are noted for large numbers of workers skilled in the English language, such as the Philippines and India. Also see "Captive Offshoring" and "Outsourcing."

OLED (Organic LED): A type of electronic display based on the use of organic materials that produce light when stimulated by electricity. Also see "Polymer," "PLED (Polymer Light Emitting Diode)," "SMOLED (Small Molecule Organic Light Emitting Diode)" and "Dendrimer."

On-Demand Advertising: See "Advertising-On-Demand."

On-Demand Video Magazines: Video clips concerning a variety of subjects offered by content providers as part of a VOD programming package.

Original Design Manufacturer: See "ODM (Original Design Manufacturer)."

Original Equipment Manufacturer: See "OEM (Original Equipment Manufacturer)."

Out-of-Home Advertising: Advertising in public places through billboards, signs on buses, etc. Also referred to as outdoor advertising.

Outsourcing: The hiring of an outside company to perform a task otherwise performed internally by the company, generally with the goal of lowering costs and/or streamlining work flow. Outsourcing contracts are generally several years in length. Companies that hire outsourced services providers often prefer to focus on their core strengths while sending more routine tasks outside for others to perform. Typical outsourced services include the running of human resources departments, telephone call centers and computer departments. When outsourcing is performed overseas, it may be referred to as offshoring. Also see "Offshoring."

P2P (Peer-to-Peer): Refers to a connection between computers that creates equal status between the computers. P2P can be used in an office or home to create a simple computer network. However, P2P more commonly refers to networks of computers that share information online. For example, peer-to-peer music sharing networks enable one member to search the hard drives of other members to locate music files and then download those files. These systems can be used for legal purposes. Nonetheless, they became notorious as systems that enable members to collect music and videos for free, circumventing copyright and other legal restrictions. At one time Napster was widely known as a P2P music system that enabled users to circumvent copyright.

Palm Pilot: A handheld device in which data is stored and may also be transmitted. Data usually consists of address books, calendar information and e-mail. These small personal computers are known as PDAs. See "PDA (Personal Digital Assistant)."

Parental Guidelines: A rating system established by the television industry in 1997, which gives parents information about the content and age-appropriateness of television programming.

Pay Cable: A network or service available for an added monthly fee. Also called premium cable. Some services, called mini-pay, are marketed at an average monthly rate below that of full-priced premium.

Pay Cable Unit: Each premium service to which a household subscribes.

Pay-Per-View (PPV): A service that enables television subscribers, including cable and satellite viewers, to order and view events or movies on an individual basis. PPV programming may include sporting events.

PDA (Personal Digital Assistant): A handheld or pocket-size device containing address and calendar information, as well as e-mail, games and other features. A Palm Pilot is a PDA.

Peer-to-Peer: See "P2P (Peer-to-Peer)."

Periodical: A publication that changes on a regular publishing schedule, such as weekly or monthly. (In contrast, a book that does not change on a regular basis is referred to as a monograph.)

Personal Television (PTV): Television programming that has been manipulated to a viewer's personal taste. For example, the TiVo service allows viewers to eliminate commercials, watch programming stored in memory or watch selected real-time moments in slow motion.

Personalized VOD Entertainment: A VOD service that automatically detects household television viewing interests by monitoring the channel-surfing behavior of residents. The system uses this viewing data to select programming relevant to the household. The service can also deliver custom VOD libraries to PVRs.

PLED (Polymer Light Emitting Diode): An advanced technology that utilizes plastics (polymers) for the creation of electronic displays (screens). It is based on the use of organic polymers which emit light when stimulated with electricity. They are solution processable, which means they can be applied to substrates via ink jet printing.

Podcasting: The creation of audio files as webcasts. The name comes from the ability of these files to be used on iPods and portable MP3 players. They can also be listened to on personal computers. Podcasts can be anything from unique radio-like programming to sales pitches to audio press releases. Audio RSS

(Real Simple Syndication) enables the broadcast of these audio files to appropriate parties. Also see "RSS (Real Simple Syndication)," "VLOG (Video Blog)" and "Blog (Web Log)."

Portal: A comprehensive web site that is designed to be the first site seen when a computer logs on to the web. Portal sites are aimed at broad audiences with common interests and often have links to e-mail usage, a search engine and other features. Yahoo! and msn.com are portals.

Positioning: The design and implementation of a merchandising mix, price structure and style of selling to create an image of the retailer, relative to its competitors, in the customer's mind.

Powerline: A method of networking computers, peripherals and appliances together via the electrical wiring that is built in to a home or office. Powerline competes with 802.11b and other wireless networking methods.

PTV (Personal Television): See "Personal Television (PTV)."

Publication: A printed magazine or newspaper containing information, news or feature stories.

PVR (Personal Video Recorder): See "DVR (Digital Video Recorder)."

Ratings/Rating Points/Ratings Share: The rating of a medium is its audience size expressed as a percentage of the measured market, where one rating point is equivalent to 1% of the base. Ratings are often referred to as "percent coverage." A television show with a 22% share has 22 points, or 22% of the total TV audience within its market.

RDF (Resource Description Framework): A software concept that integrates many different software applications using XML as a syntax for the exchange of data. It is a core concept for development of the Semantic Web, an enhanced World Wide Web envisioned by W3C, the global organization that oversees development of the web. RDF may be useful for the syndication of news or the aggregation of all types of data for specific uses.

Reach: The geographic area inhabited by a potential audience. Also the number of readers, listeners or viewers that are able to access a given medium. A prime time television show on a national network such as ABC has nationwide reach.

Real Time: A system or software product specially designed to acquire, process, store and display large amounts of rapidly changing information almost instantaneously, with microsecond responses as changes occur.

Recommendation-Based VOD: See "Personalized VOD Entertainment."

Return on Investment (ROI): A measure of a company's profitability, expressed in percentage as net profit (after taxes) divided by total dollar investment.

RFID (Radio Frequency Identification): A technology that applies a special microchip-enabled tag to an individual item or piece of merchandise or inventory. RFID technology enables wireless, computerized tracking of that inventory item as it moves through the supply chain from factory to transport to warehouse to retail store or end user. Also known as radio tags.

RSS (Real Simple Syndication): Uses XML programming language to let web logs and other data be broadcast to appropriate web sites and users. Formerly referred to as RDF Site Summary or Rich Site Summary, RSS also enables the publisher to create a description of the content and its location in the form of an RSS document. Also useful for distributing audio files. See "Podcasting."

SACD (Super Audio Compact Disc): A technology that offers high-resolution digital audio.

Satellite Broadcasting: The use of Earth-orbiting satellites to transmit, over a wide area, TV, radio, telephony, video and other data in digitized format.

Semantic Web: The Semantic Web is an initiative started by the World Wide Web Consortium (W3C). This project is focused on improving the way we access databases and online content by adding semantic metadata to content that will clearly define the relationships between data. As a result, the user will get much better search results, and web site developers will be able to create pages that update results and content based on related data on-the-fly. Data will automatically be shared across applications and across organizations.

Server: A computer that performs and manages specific duties for a central network such as a LAN. It may include storage devices and other peripherals. Competition within the server manufacturing industry is intense among leaders Dell, IBM, HP and others.

Server-Based SVOD Programming: Programming that is delivered directly to the customer's TV from where it is stored on the content provider's servers. In contrast, non-server-based SVOD (satellite TV) needs a storage device at the customer's location (such as a PVR or DVR) to store and play VOD content for the viewer's TV. Server-based SVOD surpasses non-server-based SVOD in its ability to simultaneously send or receive more than one video stream to or from the customer.

Set-Top Box: Sits on top of a TV set and provides enhancement to cable TV or other television reception. Typically a cable modem, this box may enable interactive enhancements to television viewing. For example, a cable modem is a set-top box that enables Internet access via TV cable. See "Cable Modem."

Share: In broadcasting, the percentage of television households tuned into a particular program or category of programming. The higher the share, the larger the amount that can be charged for advertising on the program.

SMOLED (Small Molecule Organic Light Emitting Diode): A type of organic LED that relies on expensive manufacturing methods. Newer technologies are more promising. See "Organic Polymer" and "PLED (Polymer Light Emitting Diode."

Social Media (Social Networks): New outlets on the Internet for user-generated content. Such media include wikis, blogs and specialty web sites such as MySpace.com and Friendster.com. Social media are seen as powerful new online tools because all or most of the content is user-generated.

Spam: A term used to refer to generally unwanted, solicitous, bulk-sent e-mail. In recent years, significant amounts of government legislation have been passed in an attempt to limit the use of spam. Also, many types of software filters have been introduced in an effort to block spam on the receiving end. In addition to use for general advertising purposes, spam may be used in an effort to spread computer viruses or to commit financial or commercial fraud.

Specialty Publication: A trade or professional magazine that is industry- or audience-specific (e.g., Shopping Center World magazine).

Spot Revenue: Revenue from advertising placed on a cable system by a local or national advertiser.

Streaming Media: One-way audio and/or video that is compressed and transmitted over a data network. The media is viewed or heard almost as soon as data is fed to the receiver; there is usually a buffer period of a few seconds.

Subscriber: A term used interchangeably with household in describing cable, Internet access or telephone customers.

Subsidiary, Wholly-Owned: A company that is wholly controlled by another company through stock ownership.

Superstation: A local television station with a signal that is retransmitted via satellite to distant cable systems that cannot be reached by over-the-air signals.

Superstore: A large specialty store, usually over 40,000 square feet. Many superstores focus on a particular field of merchandise. For example, BestBuy is a consumer electronics superstore.

Supply Chain: The complete set of suppliers of goods and services required for a company to operate its business. For example, a manufacturer's supply chain may include providers of raw materials, components, custom-made parts and packaging materials.

SVOD (Subscription Video On Demand): Allows subscribers unlimited access to selected VOD television programming for a fixed monthly fee.

Syndicated: A report, story, television program, radio program or graphic that is sold to multiple media outlets simultaneously. For example, popular newspaper columns are commonly syndicated to various newspapers throughout the United States, but only one newspaper per market is allowed to participate.

System (Cable): A facility that provides cable television service in a given geographic area, consisting of one or more headends.

T1: A standard for broadband digital transmission over phone lines. Generally, it can transmit at least 24 voice channels at once over copper wires, at a high speed of 1.5 Mbps. Higher speed versions include T3 and OC3 lines.

T3: Transmission over phone lines that supports data rates of 45 Mbps. T3 lines consist of 672 channels, and such lines are generally used by Internet service providers. They are also referred to as DS3 lines.

Telecommunications: Systems of hardware and software used to carry voice, video and/or data between locations. This includes telephone wires, satellite signals, cellular links, coaxial cable and related devices.

Telescopic On-Demand PVR/VOD Advertising: Telescopic On-Demand PVR/VOD Advertising is a short television commercial that offers the viewer access to another longer, related commercial. The commercial is called telescopic because it can be made longer if the viewer so desires.

Third Screen: Refers to the cell phone as a viewing device that is beyond the two primary screens used by consumers--the TV and the computer monitor.

Time Shifting: Services that allow viewers to digitally record television programs for playback at a later, more convenient time. Such services include video-on-demand (VOD) and personal TV services. Time shifting will eventually make up a significant portion of all television viewing.

Time-And-Channel-Based TV: See "Linear TV."

TiVo: A digital recorder that allows customers to record television shows through a hard disk and computer schedule instead of a videotape or manual recording set-up.

Transactional VOD: Allows VOD customers to pay a single price for a single VOD program or a set of programs rather than paying a set fee for a set amount of VOD programming (as in SVOD services).

TV over IP: See "IPTV."

TVOD (True Video On Demand): Offers VOD customers seamless interaction with the VOD system. TVOD allows users to not only order programs, but perform VCR-like commands at VCR-like speeds on the VOD system.

UHF (Ultra High Frequency): The frequency band ranging from 300 MHz to 3,000 MHz, which includes TV channels 14 through 83.

Ultrawideband (UWB): A means of low-power, limited-range wireless data transmission that takes advantage of bandwidth set aside by the FCC in 2002. UWB encodes signals in a dramatically different way, sending digital pulses in a relatively secure manner that will not interfere with other wireless systems that may be operating nearby. It has the potential to deliver very large amounts of data to a distance of about 230 feet, even through doors and other obstacles, and requires very little power. Speeds are scalable from approximately 100 Mbps to 2Gbps. UWB works on the 802.15.3 IEEE specification.

User-Generated Content: Generally refers to data added by users of web sites. Such web sites can include wikis, blogs or social networking sites. Also see "Social Media (Social Networks)."

UWB: See "Ultrawideband (UWB)."

V-Chip: A system built into TV sets that helps parents screen out programs with questionable parental guideline ratings. Consumers can purchase a special set-top box that performs the same function.

Very Small Aperture Terminal (VSAT): A small Earth station terminal, generally 0.6 to 2.4 meters in size, that is often portable and primarily designed to handle data transmission and private-line voice and video communications.

VHF (Very High Frequency): The frequency band ranging from 30 MHz to 300 MHz, which includes TV channels 2 through 13 and FM radio.

VLOG (Video Blog): The creation of video files as webcasts. VLOGs can be viewed on personal computers and wireless devices that are Internet-enabled. They can include anything from unique TV-like programming to sales pitches to music videos, news coverage or audio press releases. Online video is one of the fastest-growing segments in Internet usage. Leading e-commerce companies such as

Microsoft, through its MSN service, Google and Yahoo!, as well as mainstream media firms such as Reuters, are making significant investments in online video services. RSS (Real Simple Syndication) enables the broadcasting of these files to appropriate parties. Also see "RSS (Real Simple Syndication)," "Podcasting" and "Blog (Web Log)."

VOD (Video On Demand): A system that allows customers to request programs or movies over cable or the Internet. Generally, the customer can select from an extensive list of titles. In some cases, a set-top device can be used to digitally record a broadcast for replay at a future date.

VOD-Over-IP: VOD (video on demand) television viewing that is distributed via the Internet.

WAP (Wireless Access Protocol): A technology that enables the delivery of World Wide Web pages in a smaller format readable by screens on cellular phones.

Web 2.0: Web 2.0 generally refers to the evolving system of advanced services available via the Internet. These services include collaborative sites that enable multiple users to create content such as wikis, sites such as photo-sharing services that share data among large or small groups and sites such as Friendster and MySpace that enable consumers to form groups of people with similar interests. Common features of Web 2.0 are tagging, social networks and folksonomies.

Web Page: A document on the World Wide Web that is identified by a URL.

Web Services: Self-contained modular applications that can be described, published, located and invoked over the World Wide Web or another network. Web services architecture evolved from object-oriented design and is geared toward e-business solutions. Microsoft Corporation is focusing on web services with its .NET initiative. Also see "XML (Extensible Markup Language)."

Web Site: A specific domain name location on the World Wide Web. Each site contains a homepage and usually consists of additional documents.

Weblog: See "Blog (Web Log)."

Webmaster: Any individual who runs a web site. Webmasters generally perform maintenance and upkeep.

Wi-Fi: A popular phrase that refers to 802.11b and other 802.11 specifications. See "802.11b (Wi-Fi)."

Wi-Fi5: A popular phrase that refers to 802.11a. See "802.11a (Wi-Fi5)."

Wiki: A web site that enables large or small groups of users to create and co-edit data. The best known example is Wikipedia, a high traffic web site that presents a public encyclopedia that is continuously written and edited by a vast number of volunteer contributors and editors who include both experts and enthusiasts in various subjects. (Also, see "User-Generated Content".)

WiMAX (802.16): A wireless standard with exceptional speed and distance capabilities, officially known as the 802.16 standard. See "802.16 (WiMAX)." Wi-Fi stands for "World Interoperability for Microwave Access."

Wire Service: An organization that sends news stories, features and other types of information by direct line to subscribing or member newspapers, radio stations and television stations. The Associated Press (AP) is a well-known wire service.

Wireless: Transmission of voice, video or data by a cellular telephone or other wireless device, as opposed to landline, telephone line or cable. It includes Wi-Fi, WiMAX and other local or long-distance wireless methods.

Wireless Cable: A pay television service that delivers multiple programming services to subscribers equipped with special antennae and tuners. It is an alternative to traditional, wired cable TV systems.

World Wide Web: A computer system that provides enhanced access to various sites on the Internet through the use of hyperlinks. Clicking on a link displayed in one document takes you to a related document. The World Wide Web is governed by the World Wide Web Consortium, located at www.w3.org. Also known as the web.

XML (Extensible Markup Language): A programming language that enables designers to add extra functionality to documents that could not otherwise be utilized with standard HTML coding. XML was developed by the World Wide Web Consortium. It can communicate to various software programs the actual meanings contained in HTML documents. For example, it can enable the gathering and use of information from a large number of databases at once and place that information into one web site window. XML is an important protocol to web services. See "Web Services."

xviiiPlunkett Research, Ltd.

INTRODUCTION

PLUNKETT'S ENTERTAINMENT & MEDIA INDUSTRY ALMANAC, the eighth edition of our guide to the entertainment and media field, is designed as a general source for researchers of all types.

The data and areas of interest covered are intentionally broad, ranging from the most important trends in the entertainment and media industry, to emerging technologies, to an in-depth look at the major firms (which we call "THE ENTERTAINMENT 400") within the many sectors that make up the entertainment and media industry, such as book, newspaper and magazine publishing; electronic games; gambling and casinos; retailers, such as bookstores, of entertainment and media products; radio; television, including broadcast, satellite and cable; movie production and distribution; movie theaters, publishers of databases and much more, including related services, hardware and software.

This reference book is designed to be a general source for researchers. It is especially intended to assist with market research, strategic planning, employment searches, contact or prospect list creation (be sure to see the export capabilities of the accompanying CD-ROM that is available to book and eBook buyers) and financial research, and as a data resource for executives and students of all types.

PLUNKETT'S ENTERTAINMENT & MEDIA INDUSTRY ALMANAC takes a rounded approach for the general reader. This book presents a complete overview of the entertainment and media field (see "How To Use This Book"). For example, the impact of the Internet upon entertainment is discussed in exacting detail, along with easy-to-use tables on all facets of entertainment and media in general, from the types of services involved to names and descriptions of the divisions and affiliates of the major firms within this industry.

THE ENTERTAINMENT 400 is our unique grouping of the biggest, most successful corporations in all segments of the entertainment and media industry. Tens of thousands of pieces of information, gathered from a wide variety of sources, have been researched and are presented in a unique form that can be easily understood. This section includes thorough indexes to THE ENTERTAINMENT 400, by geography, industry, sales, brand names, subsidiary names and many other topics. (See Chapter 4.)

Especially helpful is the way in which PLUNKETT'S ENTERTAINMENT & MEDIA INDUSTRY ALMANAC enables readers who have no business background to readily compare the financial records and growth plans of entertainment companies and major industry groups. You'll see the mid-term financial record of each firm, along with the impact of earnings, sales and strategic plans on each company's potential to fuel growth, to serve new markets and to provide investment and employment opportunities.

No other source provides this book's easy-to-understand comparisons of growth, expenditures, technologies, corporations and many other items of great importance to people of all types who may be studying this, one of the most rapidly evolving industries in the world today.

By scanning the data groups and the unique indexes, you can find the best information to fit your personal research needs. The major companies in entertainment are profiled and then ranked using several different groups of specific criteria. Which firms are the biggest employers? Which companies earn the most profits? These things and much more are easy to find.

In addition to individual company profiles, an overview of entertainment and media technology and its trends is provided. This book's job is to help you sort through easy-to-understand summaries of today's trends in a quick and effective manner.

Whatever your purpose for researching the entertainment and media field, you'll find this book to be a valuable guide. Nonetheless, as is true with all resources, this volume has limitations that the reader should be aware of:

- Financial data and other corporate information can change quickly. A book of this type can be no more current than the data that was available as of the time of editing. Consequently, the financial picture, management and ownership of the firm(s) you are studying may have changed since the date of this book. For example, this almanac includes the most up-to-date sales figures and profits available to the editors as of late 2007. That means that we have typically used corporate financial data as of mid-2007.

- Corporate mergers, acquisitions and downsizing are occurring at a very rapid rate. Such events may have created significant change, subsequent to the publishing of this book, within a company you are studying.

- Some of the companies in THE ENTERTAINMENT 400 are so large in scope and in variety of business endeavors conducted within a parent organization, that we have been unable to completely list all subsidiaries, affiliations, divisions and activities within a firm's corporate structure.

- This volume is intended to be a general guide to a vast industry. That means that researchers should look to this book for an overview and, when conducting in-depth research, should contact the specific corporations or industry associations in question for the very latest changes and data. Where possible, we have listed contact names, toll-free telephone numbers and World Wide Web site addresses for the companies, government agencies and industry associations involved so that the reader may get further details without unnecessary delay.

- Tables of industry data and statistics used in this book include the latest numbers available at the time of printing, generally through mid-2007. In a few cases, the only complete data available was for earlier years.

- We have used exhaustive efforts to locate and fairly present accurate and complete data. However, when using this book or any other source for business and industry information, the reader should use caution and diligence by conducting further research where it seems appropriate. We wish you success in your endeavors, and we trust that your experience with this book will be both satisfactory and productive.

Jack W. Plunkett
Houston, Texas
January 2008

HOW TO USE THIS BOOK

The two primary sections of this book are devoted first to the entertainment & media industry as a whole and then to the "Individual Data Listings" for THE ENTERTAINMENT 400. If time permits, you should begin your research in the front chapters of this book. Also, you will find lengthy indexes in Chapter 4 and in the back of the book.

THE ENTERTAINMENT & MEDIA INDUSTRY

Glossary: A short list of entertainment and media industry terms.

Chapter 1: Major Trends Affecting the Entertainment & Media Industry. This chapter presents an encapsulated view of the major trends that are creating rapid changes in the entertainment and media industry today, from mergers and acquisitions, to Internet delivery, to personal video recorders.

Chapter 2: Entertainment & Media Industry Statistics. This chapter presents in-depth statistics ranging from an industry overview, to sector-by-sector revenues, to the growing use of the Internet and much more.

Chapter 3: Important Entertainment & Media Industry Contacts – Addresses, Telephone Numbers and World Wide Web Sites. This chapter covers contacts for important government agencies, industry organizations and trade groups. Included are numerous important World Wide Web sites.

THE ENTERTAINMENT 400

Chapter 4: THE ENTERTAINMENT 400: Who They Are and How They Were Chosen. The companies compared in this book (the actual count is 391) were carefully selected from the entertainment and media industry, largely in the United States. 63 of the firms are based outside the U.S. For a complete description, see THE ENTERTAINMENT 400 indexes in this chapter.

    Individual Data Listings:

    Look at one of the companies in THE ENTERTAINMENT 400's Individual Data Listings. You'll find the following information fields:

    Company Name:

    The company profiles are in alphabetical order by company name. If you don't find the company you are seeking, it may be a subsidiary or division of one of the firms covered in this book. Try looking it up in the Index by Subsidiaries, Brand Names and Selected Affiliations in the back of the book.

Ranks:

Industry Group Code: An NAIC code used to group companies within like segments. (See Chapter 4 for a list of codes.)

Ranks Within This Company's Industry Group: Ranks, within this firm's segment only, for annual sales and annual profits, with 1 being the highest rank.

Business Activities:

A grid arranged into six major industry categories and several sub-categories. A "Y" indicates that the firm operates within the sub-category. A complete Index by Industry is included in the beginning of Chapter 4.

Types of Business:

A listing of the primary types of business specialties conducted by the firm.

Brands/Divisions/Affiliations:

Major brand names, operating divisions or subsidiaries of the firm, as well as major corporate affiliations—such as another firm that owns a significant portion of the company's stock. A complete Index by Subsidiaries, Brand Names and Selected Affiliations is in the back of the book.

Contacts:

The names and titles up to 27 top officers of the company are listed, including human resources contacts.

Address:

The firm's full headquarters address, the headquarters telephone, plus toll-free and fax numbers where available. Also provided is the World Wide Web site address.

Financials:

Annual Sales (2007 or the latest fiscal year available to the editors, plus up to four previous years): These are stated in thousands of dollars (add three zeros if you want the full number). This figure represents consolidated worldwide sales from all operations. 2007 figures may be estimates or may be for only part of the year—partial year figures are appropriately footnoted.

Annual Profits (2007 or the latest fiscal year available to the editors, plus up to four previous years): These are stated in thousands of dollars (add three zeros if you want the full number). This figure represents consolidated, after-tax net profit from all operations. 2007 figures may be estimates or may be for only part of the year—partial year figures are appropriately footnoted.

Stock Ticker, International Exchange, Parent Company: When available, the unique stock market symbol used to identify this firm's common stock for trading and tracking purposes is indicated. Where appropriate, this field may contain "private" or "subsidiary" rather than a ticker symbol. If the firm is a publicly-held company headquartered outside of the U.S., its international ticker and exchange are given. If the firm is a subsidiary, its parent company is listed.

Total Number of Employees: The approximate total number of employees, worldwide, as of the end of 2007 (or the latest data available to the editors).

Apparent Salaries/Benefits:

(The following descriptions generally apply to U.S. employers only.) A "Y" in appropriate fields indicates "Yes."

Due to wide variations in the manner in which corporations report benefits to the U.S. Government's regulatory bodies, not all plans will have been uncovered or correctly evaluated during our effort to research this data. Also, the availability to employees of such plans will vary according to the qualifications that employees must meet to become eligible. For example, some benefit plans may be available only to salaried workers—others only to employees who work more than 1,000 hours yearly. Benefits that are available to employees of the main or parent company may not be available to employees of the subsidiaries. In addition, employers frequently alter the nature and terms of plans offered.

NOTE: Generally, employees covered by wealth-building benefit plans do not *fully* own ("vest in") funds contributed on their behalf by the employer until as many as five years of service with that employer have passed. All pension plans are voluntary—that is, employers are not obligated to offer pensions.

Pension Plan: The firm offers a pension plan to qualified employees. In this case, in order for a "Y" to appear, the editors believe that the employer offers a defined benefit or cash balance pension plan (see discussions below).The type and generosity of these plans vary widely from firm to firm. Caution: Some employers refer to plans as "pension" or "retirement" plans when they are actually 401(k) savings plans that require a contribution by the employee.

- Defined Benefit Pension Plans: Pension plans that do not require a contribution from the employee are infrequently offered. However, a few companies, particularly larger employers in high-profit-margin industries, offer defined benefit pension plans where the employee is guaranteed to receive a set pension benefit upon retirement. The amount of the benefit is determined by the years of service with the company and the employee's salary during the later years of employment. The longer a person works for the employer, the higher the retirement benefit. These defined benefit plans are funded entirely by the employer. The benefits, up to a reasonable limit, are guaranteed by the Federal Government's Pension Benefit Guaranty Corporation. These plans are not portable—if you leave the company, you cannot transfer your benefits into a different plan. Instead, upon retirement you will receive the benefits that vested during your service with the company. If your employer offers a pension plan, it must give you a summary plan description within 90 days of the date you join the plan. You can also request a summary annual report of the plan, and once every 12 months you may request an individual benefit statement accounting of your interest in the plan.

- Defined Contribution Plans: These are quite different. They do not guarantee a certain amount of pension benefit. Instead, they set out circumstances under which the employer will make a contribution to a plan on your behalf. The most common example is the 401(k) savings plan. Pension benefits are not guaranteed under these plans.

- Cash Balance Pension Plans: These plans were recently invented. These are hybrid plans—part defined benefit and part defined contribution. Many employers have converted their older defined benefit plans into cash balance plans. The employer makes deposits (or credits a given amount of money) on the employee's behalf, usually based on a percentage of pay. Employee accounts grow based on a predetermined interest benchmark, such as the interest rate on Treasury Bonds. There are some advantages to these plans, particularly for younger workers: a) The benefits, up to a reasonable limit, are guaranteed by the Pension Benefit Guaranty Corporation. b) Benefits are portable—they can be moved to another plan when the employee changes companies. c) Younger workers and those who spend a shorter number of years with an employer may receive higher benefits than they would under a traditional defined benefit plan.

ESOP Stock Plan (Employees' Stock Ownership Plan): This type of plan is in wide use. Typically, the plan borrows money from a bank and uses those funds to purchase a large block of the corporation's

stock. The corporation makes contributions to the plan over a period of time, and the stock purchase loan is eventually paid off. The value of the plan grows significantly as long as the market price of the stock holds up. Qualified employees are allocated a share of the plan based on their length of service and their level of salary. Under federal regulations, participants in ESOPs are allowed to diversify their account holdings in set percentages that rise as the employee ages and gains years of service with the company. In this manner, not all of the employee's assets are tied up in the employer's stock.

Savings Plan, 401(k): Under this type of plan, employees make a tax-deferred deposit into an account. In the best plans, the company makes annual matching donations to the employees' accounts, typically in some proportion to deposits made by the employees themselves. A good plan will match one-half of employee deposits of up to 6% of wages. For example, an employee earning $30,000 yearly might deposit $1,800 (6%) into the plan. The company will match one-half of the employee's deposit, or $900 The plan grows on a tax-deferred basis, similar to an IRA. A very generous plan will match 100% of employee deposits. However, some plans do not call for the employer to make a matching deposit at all. Other plans call for a matching contribution to be made at the discretion of the firm's board of directors. Actual terms of these plans vary widely from firm to firm. Generally, these savings plans allow employees to deposit as much as 15% of salary into the plan on a tax-deferred basis. However, the portion that the company uses to calculate its matching deposit is generally limited to a maximum of 6%. Employees should take care to diversify the holdings in their 401(k) accounts, and most people should seek professional guidance or investment management for their accounts.

Stock Purchase Plan: Qualified employees may purchase the company's common stock at a price below its market value under a specific plan. Typically, the employee is limited to investing a small percentage of wages in this plan. The discount may range from 5 to 15%. Some of these plans allow for deposits to be made through regular monthly payroll deductions. However, new accounting rules for corporations, along with other factors, are leading many companies to curtail these plans—dropping the discount allowed, cutting the maximum yearly stock purchase or otherwise making the plans less generous or appealing.

Profit Sharing: Qualified employees are awarded an annual amount equal to some portion of a company's profits. In a very generous plan, the pool of money awarded to employees would be 15% of profits. Typically, this money is deposited into a long-term retirement account. Caution: Some employers refer to plans as "profit sharing" when they are actually 401(k) savings plans. True profit sharing plans are rarely offered.

Highest Executive Salary: The highest executive salary paid, typically a 2006 amount (or the latest year available to the editors) and typically paid to the Chief Executive Officer.

Highest Executive Bonus: The apparent bonus, if any, paid to the above person.

Second Highest Executive Salary: The next-highest executive salary paid, typically a 2006 amount (or the latest year available to the editors) and typically paid to the President or Chief Operating Officer.

Second Highest Executive Bonus: The apparent bonus, if any, paid to the above person.

Other Thoughts:

Apparent Women Officers or Directors: It is difficult to obtain this information on an exact basis, and employers generally do not disclose the data in a public way. However, we have indicated what our best efforts reveal to be the apparent number of women who either are in the posts of corporate officers or sit on the board of directors. There is a wide variance from company to company.

Hot Spot for Advancement for Women/Minorities: A "Y" in appropriate fields indicates "Yes." These are firms that appear either to have posted a substantial number of women and/or minorities to high posts or that appear to have a good record of going out of their way to recruit, train, promote and retain women or minorities. (See the Index of Hot Spots For Women and Minorities in the back of the book.) This information may change frequently and can be difficult to obtain and verify. Consequently, the reader should use caution and conduct further investigation where appropriate.

Growth Plans/ Special Features:

Listed here are observations regarding the firm's strategy, hiring plans, plans for growth and product development, along with general information regarding a company's business and prospects.

Locations:

A "Y" in the appropriate field indicates "Yes."

Primary locations outside of the headquarters, categorized by regions of the United States and by international locations. A complete index by locations is also in the front of this chapter.

Chapter 1

MAJOR TRENDS AFFECTING THE ENTERTAINMENT & MEDIA INDUSTRY

Major Trends Affecting the Entertainment & Media Industry:

1) Introduction to the Entertainment & Media Industry
2) Multimedia Hub Homes Slowly Become a Reality
3) DVR Market Evolves; Time-Shifting Hurts Advertisers
4) Apple's iPod Revitalizes the Music Industry
5) Internet Film Content Explodes
6) Netflix and Blockbuster Go Head to Head
7) Major Casino Expansion Continues in the U.S. and Macau
8) Reality TV Dominates Broadcast Programming/Networks Find New Ways to Distribute Content
9) New Platforms Revolutionize Electronic Games
10) "Cell" Chip Technology Sizzles in PS3
11) Satellite Radio Fails to Earn a Profit/Traditional Radio Faces Challenges
12) Radio Via IP Grows/The Era of Digital Radio Begins
13) Cable and Satellite TV Compete Fiercely for Market Share
14) Video-on-Demand (VOD) and Subscription Video-on-Demand (SVOD) Go Mass Market
15) TV over IP—Telecom Companies Enter the Television Market

16) TV over IP—TV Networks, Cable Companies and Web Sites Converge
17) High-Definition Grows—HDTV and HD-DVD
18) Movie Attendance Rallies/Film Companies Innovate with DVDs, IMAX and Big Budget Films
19) Last Mile Challenges Tumble; Mass Broadband Markets Emerge
20) Entertainment-Based Retailing, including Power Towns
21) Video Via Cell Phone Slowly Takes Off
22) Apple's iPhone Makes a Splash
23) Music Plays a Major Role in New Cell Phones
24) Rules for Digital TV Are Finalized
25) Daily Newspapers Combine Online with Print and Launch Weekly Specialty Papers

1) Introduction to the Entertainment & Media Industry

Total spending (including advertising) in the U.S. on media of all types was about $930 billion in 2007. U.S. advertising spending alone was about $284 billion.

Broadly measured, the entertainment and media industry spans multiple sectors, from America's 9,163 FM radio stations, to the 1.45 billion movie tickets sold each year in U.S. theaters. The gambling sector, with more than $60 billion in annual revenues, is often included when considering entertainment as a whole.

Today, new media of all types must be considered when considering the scope of the entertainment and media industry. The number of broadband Internet connections in the U.S. has reached true mass market in size, at about 80 million homes and businesses in 2007. Comcast (the cable TV provider) alone has more than 12 million high-speed Internet subscribers. Advertising on the Internet is now a $17 billion industry. Most recently, the "Third Screen" (cell phone-based entertainment including video and music) is becoming a major factor in entertainment and media.

Meanwhile, revenues are mixed at traditional entertainment and media segments. Book sales at retail were about $55 billion in the U.S. in 2007, according to the Book Industry Study Group, an increase of about 3.3%. The traditional, storefront video rental sector is suffering due to alternatives including Netflix, TiVo and video-on-demand services. Newspapers are finding it increasingly difficult to compete against Internet news and advertising rivals. Recorded music sales on CD-ROM continue to drop while sales of digital music files are soaring. Traditional radio broadcasting is hurting, finding it increasingly difficult to gather listeners for advertising-based radio programming due to such alternatives as satellite radio and digital MP3 players.

The burning issue affecting all sectors of the entertainment and media industry is maintaining control of content and audiences while taking advantage of myriad new electronic delivery venues. Competition in the entertainment sector is fierce. Gone are the days when television and radio programmers enjoyed captive audiences who happily sat through ad after ad, or planned their schedules around a favorite show. Consumers, especially consumers in younger demographics, now demand more and more control over what they watch, read and listen to.

Issues related to control include:

1) Pricing for content (including free-of-charge access; illegal downloads versus authorized downloads; and full ownership of a paid download versus pay-per-view).

2) Portability (including the ability for a consumer to download once, and then use a file on multiple platforms and devices including iPods and cell phones, or the ability to share a download with friends).

3) Delayed viewing or listening (such as viewing TV programming at the consumer's convenience via TiVo and similar personal video recorders).

The competition among entertainment delivery platforms has intensified; all sectors face daunting challenges from alternative delivery methods. For example, satellite radio delivery of subscription-based music and talk programming has hit its stride with multimillion subscriber counts for Sirius and its competitor XM. Another example: telecommunications companies such as AT&T and Verizon are now delivering television programming to the home via ultra high-speed Internet connections, battling cable and satellite TV firms for market share.

Today, electronic offerings such as DVDs, digital video recorders (DVRs), video-on-demand (VOD) and MP3 players have vastly altered the way consumers enjoy entertainment. People watch and listen according to their own desires and whims. Miss the finale to a favorite television show? Rent or buy it on DVD or record it to watch later. Interested in only one track from a recording artist's new CD? Buy and download just the one song via the Internet. Love a prime-time drama on a major network but hate commercials? Record the show while skipping over the commercials with a DVR.

The implications of these changes are staggering. The business models upon which most entertainment companies have traditionally run are becoming obsolete. Revenue from traditional advertising is in jeopardy while revenue from subscription-based business models is soaring. Online advertising is growing at supersonic speed. Television programming schedules are losing relevance while electronic program guides are becoming more and more vital. Traditional media are losing share while newer digital media are becoming the norm. Entertainment companies are forced to evolve in order to deal with new technologies and new demands from consumers.

Rapid changes in viewing habits are already occurring. Network TV news, radio news and newspapers all find that they have to compete fiercely against Internet-based news content. A large portion of sports programming has migrated away from "free" broadcasts on TV and onto paid cable channels and pay-per-view systems.

Meanwhile, platforms and delivery are evolving quickly. Multipurpose cell phones are now used for more and more entertainment purposes, including video and TV-like programming. Game machines are going multipurpose with the ability to connect to the Internet and play DVDs. Broadband to the home has matured into a true mass-market medium, while wireless broadband systems such as Wi-Fi are enhancing the mobility of entertainment and media access. A serious evolution of access and delivery methods will continue at a rapid-fire pace, and media companies will be forced to be more nimble than ever. The current battle for dominance of high definition (HD) video standards is part of this evolution.

Advanced technology is elevating entertainment to new heights. For example, Sony's new PlayStation 3 utilizes a supercomputer-like chip called "Cell" that has the potential to revolutionize the electronic games industry due to its ability to run highly realistic, advanced software at amazing speed. Meanwhile, Nintendo's Wii has added a virtual reality feature to game players that has been a stunning success. Another excellent example of the technology revolution at work in entertainment is today's level of special effects in movies.

Recommendation software that learns the habits and tastes of consumers will evolve and will do a better job of pushing appropriate entertainment choices toward audiences. Amazon.com has long been a leader in the use of such software. Netflix has created an admirable package of its own. Likewise, Apple's iTunes software is strong on recommending content to customers. Some interesting mergers might be driven by the potential to use extremely powerful recommendation software to attract and better serve consumers across multiple types of entertainment media.

The gambling sector remains strong, with massive new projects in Las Vegas, incredible growth in Macau and rebuilding, on a much bigger and better scale, of the Gulf Coast casinos that were wiped out by 2005's hurricanes. Native American-owned casinos across the U.S. are booming as well.

Advertising, long the main revenue source for much of the media industry, is rapidly moving to the Internet. This is well illustrated by the incredible financial success of Yahoo! and Google, among other search sites that offer advertising services.

You should count on continued, rapid changes: The revolution in new media continues, platforms will evolve quickly, consumers will obtain even greater control and competition will become even hotter.

2) Multimedia Hub Homes Slowly Become a Reality

Computer software and hardware companies have growing stakes in entertainment, and consumers are keenly interested in using a home PC to control all off a household's entertainment. Microsoft, after spending more than 10 years and billions of dollars on the development of its home entertainment empire, saw sales of more than 10 million of its Windows XP Media Center applications in 2006. The software, combined with specially configured PCs, plays and records television shows, manages music video and personal photo files, plays music files and burns CDs and DVDs, all by remote control. Today's version, which is part of the Vista operating system, includes Internet radio among its other entertainment features.

Designing computers to serve as electronic hubs of digital homes, routing music, movies, TV programming, e-mail and news between the web and PCs, television set-top boxes, stereo speakers and other gadgets, has long been the goal of Microsoft, as well as Sony, Gateway, HP, Apple and Digeo to name a few. Intel is also at the forefront of PC-controlled home entertainment, investing in ever-more-powerful chips capable of generating high-definition video images suitable for many video uses, including cutting-edge projection TVs.

Home entertainment centers now connect components such as TVs, sound systems, cable or satellite set-top boxes and, increasingly, PCs. On the fixed end, a home's network is tied to an Internet connection. Internet access for advanced entertainment is delivered by the consumer's choice of DSL, cable modem or satellite dish. The faster the download speed the better. In an increasing number of new neighborhoods, access is achieved by true fiber to the home (FTTH) networks capable of delivery at blazing speeds, enabling such Holy Grail media as video-on-demand and interactive TV. Verizon and AT&T are leaders in this field in the U.S.

Within the home, there are two schools of thought as to the best way to connect all of the entertainment components. Since Ethernet wire is prohibitively expensive, many electronics, cable and satellite companies are looking towards using either existing electrical wiring or coaxial cable. On the existing electrical wiring side, a standard called HomePlug AV carries up to 200 megabits of data per second over home electrical wiring. Devices can simply be plugged into electrical outlets to be connected. Proponents of this idea are members of the HomePlug Powerline Alliance (HPPA www.homeplug.org) and include companies such as Intel, Comcast, RadioShack and Sharp. Detractors claim that signal interference is a problem, but proponents say that many of the difficulties have been ironed out.

Coaxial cable has its own supporters, who have organized the Multimedia Over Coax Alliance (MoCA, www.mocalliance.org). This system uses coaxial cable, typically existing wire that has been installed by cable television companies. Devices are connected to cable outlets for data and programming delivered at up to 100 megabits per second. Participating companies in MoCA include Echostar, Panasonic and Motorola. While signal interference is not a problem, most homes have not been built with cable access in every room.

An additional option is ultrawideband (UWB) wireless, which can be used to beam data at up to 480 megabits per second across distances of up to 30 feet. UWB makes it possible to place that new plasma TV on a wall that doesn't have a cable outlet. UWB combined with coax has the potential to complete the multimedia home, making it possible to enjoy entertainment literally anywhere in the house—even in the backyard.

The HomePlug Powerline Alliance and MoCA have many of the same companies backing them. Intel, Motorola and RadioShack are all members of both alliances, since making and selling electronics and services that cater to both systems is relatively cheap.

Until recently, Microsoft's Media Center software claimed only a small percentage of the home computer market. Technical problems such as poor video quality plagued the software giant, and a hefty percentage of the home entertainment consumer base refused to watch video programming on computer monitors. Vista offers significantly enhanced TV quality, and is compatible with hardware featuring multiple TV tuners that receive up to three signals. Viewers can watch one program while recording another. The greatest breakthrough, however, is the release of the Media Center Extender, utilizing home Wi-Fi systems, as the missing link that beams content from a PC to TVs in up to five additional rooms. Microsoft projects that Media Center PCs equipped with its software will represent from 10% to 20% of the home computer market over the next few years. Media Center PCs reached 20 million total in October 2006. By May 2007, 40 million licenses to the new Windows Vista operating system had been sold in the first 100 days after its launch, 78% of which included Media Center functionality.

Many computer industry giants such as Gateway, Dell and Hewlett-Packard have been quick to join the party with their own versions of Media Center PC hardware. Prices start at about $1,400 and run up to about $3,000. Some, such as Alienware Hangar18,

are designed to be stacked in with other entertainment components and have sleek, living-room-worthy looks starting at $2,199 (see www.alienware.com). Competitor Niveus Media offers the top-of-the-line Denali Edition, which operates silently thanks to a fanless system. Silence appears to be golden, since the Denali's price can run $8,499.

Apple, Inc. (which changed its name from Apple Computer in 2007 to emphasize its focus on consumer electronics and entertainment as well as computers) has a secure place in the home media center arena thanks to its industry-changing iPod. Apple is hoping to have the same success with Apple TV. The moderately priced (starting at $299.00) Apple TV unit acts as an interface between a consumer's television, computer and iPod. For example, Apple TV will send digital entertainment that is stored on your computer directly to your TV. This is becoming increasingly important since widescreen home TVs are now standard equipment in many living rooms, and these widescreens are vastly superior to computer monitors for watching videos. Also, the Apple TV unit will send home videos, movies, TV shows, and photos from your video iPod to your TV.

Entertainment-Enabled Macs and PCs

Consumers now have the ability to manage virtually all of their home entertainment options via personal computer or Apple's Macintosh computers. For example, Microsoft's Windows Media Center running on a fully featured entertainment PC from makers such as Dell or Sony can offer:

- Television access, which can be connected to cable, antenna or satellite
- Electronic games
- Internet access
- Communication, including VoIP telephony and e-mail
- DVR (digital video recording of TV programs)
- Music recording, storage and management in formats such as MP3 or WMA, as well as conversion of music CDs into MP3 files
- Recording and playing of CDs and DVDs
- Multiple picture frames on one screen
- Digital photography management, including editing of still and video
- Integration with a wireless home network
- Internet-based radio

3) DVR Market Evolves; Time-Shifting Hurts Advertisers

Digital Video Recorders (DVRs, also known as Personal Video Recorders or PVRs) allow viewers to download broadcast television, satellite television and cable programs for later viewing. Viewers are typically able to store between 40 and 1,000 hours of programming for playback at their discretion. Programming can also be viewed and manipulated to skip commercials almost in real-time. (Or, in some cases, viewers can fast-forward through commercials.) Viewers can also playback key moments or watch in slow motion. This is all accomplished via a hard drive connected to a television set (often in addition to a cable box, satellite receiver box and/or video game equipment). The fact that very large hard drives are available at modest prices is accelerating the acceptance of DVRs.

TiVo was the first DVR to attract any serious market share. Simple, elegant and easy to use, TiVo had attracted a limited but rabidly loyal subscriber base of 4.1 million, as of the end of 2007. However, it's facing tough competition from Motorola, Digeo, ReplayTV, THOMSON and Akimbo, to name but a few. Despite the fact that TiVo was first and has achieved brand recognition, it is far from having a lock on the DVR market.

Costs for the boxes when they debuted in 2001 ran between $250 and $400, depending on recording capacity, plus a monthly service fee. New players by a host of manufacturers have driven the price down as low as $100 or so after rebates, while top-end units cost as much as $2,200.

DVRs have caught on in a big way. As of the end of 2007, one in five U.S. homes had these devices in the U.S., according to Leichtman Research Group. By 2010, 39% of U.S. households are expected to have DVRs. Within the television industry, recording and delayed viewing of programming is referred to as "time-shifting." Industry veterans expect time-shifting to account for 40% to 50% of all TV viewing over the long term.

The impact of these devices on the advertising industry, as well as ancillary businesses such as television networks and cable companies, is very great indeed. Television advertising has long been based on charging the most for ad time in and around the highest-rated shows. Fox's top-rated *American Idol*, for example, has commanded advertising rates of more than $1 million per 30-second spot for a season finale, and 30-second spots aired during the Super Bowl cost $2.6 million in 2007. It's not

surprising then, that advertisers cry foul over DVR viewers' ability to skip or fast-forward through their extremely expensive ads. A CBS news study found that 64% of DVR users skipped commercials entirely, while and additional 26% fast-forwarded though most ads.

The ad-skipping phenomenon is forcing advertising agencies to become more creative. One theory calls for getting viewers actively involved. For example, in mid-2006, Sony Corporation began running ads for its Bravia flat-panel TVs that encouraged viewers to choose an ending of the ad from two on-screen choices (viewers choose the desired ending using their remote controls).

Other alternative ad approaches such as "showcases" and "branded tags" are available to DVR users. TiVo now offers a setup screen in which advertising videos as well as film and television program previews are "showcased." Viewers must choose to view the showcase. Branded tags are advertising icons that appear while fast-forwarding through commercials while watching TiVo. Viewers can select the icon with their remotes to learn more information about the product. In yet another attempt to get DVR users accustomed to sitting through ads, KFC promoted an ad in 2006 in which a secret code word appeared in a single frame of a spot for its Buffalo Snacker sandwich. DVR users could slow or stop the ad to see the code and then go to the company's web site where that code could be entered for a free sandwich coupon. 103,000 viewers went to the KFC site and claimed the coupon. As an added dividend, news programs ran stories on the promotion and the fast food company enjoyed a 40% spike in traffic to its web site.

In late 2007, TiVo entered into a strategic partnership with NBC Universal to sell the DVR firm's interactive tag advertising. In addition, NBC Universal's TV networks, along with owned and operated stations, will subscribe to TiVo's Stop//Watch ratings service, which measures viewing behavior and ad campaigns on a second-by-second basis.

Cable companies, satellite services, electronics manufacturers and even entertainment PC manufacturers are building DVRs into their devices. For example, Time Warner offers a set-top cable box with DVR capabilities. Comcast offers a similar set-top box DVR option through its partnership with Motorola. Many users would rather purchase DVR access as part of cable or satellite services to avoid stacking yet another box on or near their TV sets, a preference these companies are attempting to capitalize on.

TiVo finally succeeded in its attempts to partner with Comcast in March 2005. The cable giant now offers its digital customers (which amount to about 12.7 million of its 24.2 million cable customers as of March 2007) TiVo service. The two companies were able to agree upon payment and control issues, with Comcast paying the DVR company a monthly fee for each subscriber. Satellite system DirecTV was a major distributor of TiVo, paying the DVR firm a nominal fee per month per customer, until 2005, when DirecTV stopped issuing set top boxes equipped with TiVo. (DirecTV's owner, Liberty Media, rolled out its own line of DVRs.) However, DirecTV and TiVo may yet have a future together since the satellite company announced that users of old TiVo-equipped boxes will receive updates in 2008 that include features such as web-based scheduling and a Recently Deleted Folder from which video can be reloaded.

The real future of TiVo, and subsequently all DVR companies, lies in expanded services and more sophisticated technology. Portability of recorded programming will become standard. New services will include the ability to watch recorded programming on PCs or portable devices. To accomplish this, TiVo is partnering with Microsoft, Sonic and AMD to provide a service called TiVoToGo, which allows both Microsoft Windows and Apple Mac users to watch downloaded programming and even burn it to DVD. Sonic Solutions has launched an enhanced version of its MyDVD Studio line that enables users to transfer TiVo programming to DVD for playback later on any DVD-equipped device. In 2006, the company teamed with Verizon Wireless to launch TiVo Mobile, which allows Verizon customers to schedule recordings from their cell phones. Watch for further shifts in DVR technology as the ability to download video programming from the Internet becomes widespread.

4) Apple's iPod Revitalizes the Music Industry

The sale of legal downloadable music via the Internet and Internet-enabled cell phones is finally gaining significant traction. This is due to several factors, including the growing clampdown on illegal downloads by court systems worldwide, the rising popularity of advanced features on cell phones, and the incredible popularity of Apple's iPod and the related iTunes music download site. Nielsen SoundScan reports that while album sales were down

4.9% in 2006 over the previous year, digital track sales increased by 65% with 582 million songs sold. Digital album sales more than doubled, reaching almost 33 million sold in 2006. PriceWaterhouseCoopers projected that overall music industry revenue would fall 1.3% to $35.62 billion in 2007. However, digital music sales continued to grow briskly throughout 2007.

Since the advent of sites such as Napster.com in the late-90s, tens of millions of Internet surfers have downloaded unlimited free music. Although the original Napster.com site was shut down by the court system for aiding copyright violations, the ruling did not curtail the bootleg traffic of music and video files, which continue to proliferate in cyberspace. Peer-to-peer (P2P) Internet sharing programs have enabled users to share files whether legal or not.

Consequently, global recorded music revenues declined significantly since 1998. Profit margins, once 15% to 20% in the 1980s, fell to 5% or so. Overall, music publishers lose about $4 billion to piracy each year. Music companies are forced to seek ways to safeguard digital music files against illegal download and distribution. At the same time, music makers are seeking ways in which to profit from music files downloaded by legal, authorized means from the Internet.

The saga continued in March 2005 when the U.S. Supreme Court found that file-sharing companies such as Grokster and Streamcast could be held liable for copyright infringement due to marketing and technical advice that induces customers to share files illegally. Courts in other nations have entered rulings against peer-to-peer software firms as well.

A big step forward for the music industry came in the form of the groundbreaking iTunes Music Store, a digital service provided by Apple Computer, Inc. Launched in the U.S. in April 2003, the service offers single track and album files for download from all five major U.S. music companies. Priced at $0.99 per song, with no subscription fees, Apple announced 2 million song downloads in the venture's first 16 days. Apple announced in July 2005 that the 500 millionth music download had been sold via iTunes. A few months later, in February 2006, the billionth song was sold. During 2007, iTunes captured about 70% of worldwide online digital music sales, and had strengthened its hold on the music download industry thanks to Apple's incredibly popular personal digital music player—the iPod. In late 2007, the iTunes Store topped 3 billion songs sold, as well as 100 million TV shows and over 2 million feature-length films sold since its launch.

The iPod started off slowly from a storage point of view, as early models were limited to 5 gigabytes (GB) of storage (the equivalent of less than 1,000 high-quality song recordings). However, iPod sales really took off when the firm introduced a 10-GB unit in March 2002. Even more powerful units are common today, enabling the latest iPods to download and display video as well as audio content. The iPod is an astonishing success. In 2006, 39.4 million iPods were sold. Apple has added to the iPod experience by partnering with a broad spectrum of companies that make iPod carrying cases, speakers and adapters that integrate iPod files into home and car sound systems. Everything from snappy Kate Spade leather carrying cases to powerful and portable Altec Lansing and Bose speakers are keeping consumers closely tied to the iPod brand, which holds approximately 66% of the digital music player market.

In 2007, Apple offered the ability to store and play video as well as music on its 30 GB and 80 GB models. Priced starting at $249, the units hold up to 20,000 songs, full-color album cover art and up to 25,000 photos, in addition to up to 100 hours of video on a 2.5-inch color display. Music-only aficionados can choose the $199, 2 GB, 4 GB or 8 GB iPod nano. By April 2007, more than 100 million iPods had been sold worldwide throughout the product's history.

Apple's online music service is simple to use and offers a truly broad selection of music. Users set up the iTunes "jukebox" with a quick download from the Apple site. Once installed, users merely click a button to view song selections. Thirty-second previews of any song may be heard for free, and purchases are made with one click. Once the songs are downloaded, users have virtually unlimited use of the purchased files. (The files are permanent and may be burnt onto CDs or downloaded onto MP3 players a total of 10 times, which limits mass reproduction.)

iTunes arrive in a format called AAC. The file format is relatively small (requiring minimal disk space), boasts sound quality superior to that of MP3 files and may be run on a standard computer or Apple's iPod. (The iTunes service was initially available only to Macintosh users, with a version for Windows-based computers available shortly after launch.) Apple is keeping its system proprietary, meaning that iTunes patrons can only listen to music on iPods. Competitors such as Microsoft's MSN Music, Yahoo!'s Musicmatch and the legally reborn Napster offer music than can be played on a variety of different devices by different manufacturers, with the exception of iPods. This is reminiscent of the VHS-Betamax format battle when videotapes were first introduced.

Listeners are happy with the iTunes system, as is evident from its continuing success. The music companies also stand to benefit, receiving about $0.65 in gross revenue per song. More importantly, the advent of iTunes is a watershed for the industry, enabling it for the first time to significantly limit music file piracy in a manner that is extremely popular with consumers.

Rival online music services, such as Rhapsody and the legal version of Napster.com, are betting on subscription services as opposed to iTunes' single-song/album purchase store. Subscription services typically charge between $7.95 and $15 per month for listening to an unlimited number of songs on a computer. The business model is especially attractive to the subscription providers because they pay far less per song to the music companies than the $0.65 paid by online stores like iTunes for an outright sale. Gross margins for music sale services are 10% to 15%, while for subscription services, those margins can be 40% to 50%. Subscribers have the option of burning CDs, listening on their PCs or listening on portable music players.

Consumers so far have firmly shown their preference for online music stores, largely because of the portability and flexibility of the downloads.

In an effort to remain competitive, many subscription services also offer song/album purchase as an additional service. However, subscription appears to be the service that most online music purveyors are backing. Thanks to the technology by Microsoft called Janus that allows devices such as MP3 players to play songs downloaded via subscription (songs are programmed to expire on a set date, but dates are automatically extended when users continue to subscribe), subscription services believe that consumer tastes will shift. Napster, Inc. introduced its Napster To Go subscription service in February 2005. This service utilizes the Microsoft software that makes it possible to listen to rented music on portable players in addition to PCs. RealNetworks offers similar services for listening on cell phones, computers and personal music players.

It will be interesting to see whether on not buyers will make that change from *a la carte* song purchases to monthly subscriptions, as well as how Apple will refine and expand its brand over the mid-term in an effort to retain its supremacy.

> **Plunkett's Law of Online Consumers:**
> Online consumer usage grows exponentially as broadband access prices decline (both fixed and mobile) and wireless Internet devices are adopted. This creates increased demand from online consumers, and leads to increased offerings of enhanced online services, entertainment and telephony at reasonable prices.

5) Internet Film Content Explodes

The music industry's plight over pirated music has proven a valuable lesson for filmmakers and distributors. Film files are far larger than music files and are best downloaded via very high-speed Internet. Since it took several years for fast broadband access to penetrate a large segment of the U.S. home market, film companies had the luxury of time to determine how to a) battle illegal copies of movies in digital form, and b) offer movie downloads for sale. Since 2005, the number of films and videos available for download via the Internet have increased dramatically, as film studios, electronics manufacturers, broadband providers and even cable TV companies all try to get a piece of the action.

Unfortunately, illegal downloads of movies via the Internet are also commonplace. In May 2005, when the last installment of the "*Star Wars*" films hit movie theaters, an illegal online version was posted on file-sharing site Elite Torrents, which was shut down by federal agents several days later. According to the Motion Picture Association of America, the film industry lost $6.1 billion to piracy in 2005 alone, and has therefore been keenly observing the effort made by the music industry to limit illegal downloads. Thanks to groundbreaking digital rights technology developed by Microsoft, video files can now be made more difficult to hack, and filmmakers have far greater control over how a file is shared and on how many devices.

The handful of web sites that currently offer legal movie downloads include Movielink, MovieFlix, Amazon's Unbox and CinemaNow, which offer pay-per-view downloads and rentals; and SuperPass from Real and Starz Vongo, which offer monthly subscription services.

Walt Disney Co. and its ABC subsidiary initiated a bold video download program in 2006 by offering 10 TV shows for download from its web site, free of charge. The company has sold brief advertising slots, alongside these programs, to companies including AT&T and Toyota Motor Corp. to pay for the venture.

The Yankee Group estimated that customers downloaded 5.8 million movies in 2005, generating revenues of $26.3 million for the companies that provide the films. Looking ahead to 2008, analysts project that downloads will exceed 37 million and generate $169.4 million in revenue.

For the time being, however, most users of movies paid for and legally downloaded from the Internet are tech-savvy college students or business travelers who want to watch a movie on their laptops while flying from meeting to meeting. (There is also a rapidly growing market for short film clips that are viewed on Internet-enabled cell phones. Meanwhile, there is also a vast audience for free video clips on sites such as YouTube.com.) For now, the selection of movies available remains low. In contrast, DVDs offer much greater depth of selection. For example, Netflix, the online service that delivers DVDs through the mail, offers more than 90,000 titles. Blockbuster offers 75,000 titles through its stores and mail delivery service. In 2007, Netflix began offering thousands of titles as movie downloads in addition to rentals through the mail.

In order for the legitimate movie download business to become truly profitable, the number of titles available must be significantly larger, and viewers must have an easy way to watch downloaded files on their TVs instead of on their computers. Many companies are scrambling to provide new products and services to make this possible. Intel, for example, offers Viiv, a platform that easily connects PCs and TVs. Likewise, Cisco Systems' subsidiary Linksys is promoting its KiSS 1600, a media player that links to the Internet. Apple, Inc. has its Apple TV unit, and Microsoft is pushing its Xbox 360 as a full media center in addition to a gaming console. Startup Vudu offers a slick black box for $400 with minimalist controls that hooks up to a TV and to an Ethernet cable or a WiFi signal. As of 2007, Vudu had a library of 5,000 movie titles, which cost $5 to $20 to buy or $1 to $4 to rent. The box can hold up to 50 movies on its 250-gigabyte hard drive.

Apple's iTunes site began selling various types of videos at $1.99 each in 2005. Programming for sale included short films from Pixar and selected TV shows from Disney, NBC Universal, the SciFi Channel and the USA Network. More than 1 million videos were sold in the first 20 days of the new service.

Apple's big news in 2007 was the announcement of a further entry into the video industry with the debut of a new device that makes downloaded movies more useful and more portable. The $299

Apple TV unit acts as an interface between a consumer's television, computer and iPod. For example, Apple TV will send digital entertainment that is stored on your computer directly to your TV. Also, the Apple TV unit will send home videos, movies, TV shows, and photos from your video iPod to your TV.

As part of this Apple TV strategy, Apple is boosting the amount of video content available for sale at iTunes. Apple has deals with Walt Disney, Paramount, MGM and Lionsgate for full-length movies , which will take approximately 30 minutes each to download (using a broadband connection) and cost between $9.99 and $14.99 each. One challenge is pricing, since retailers often sell the same titles on DVD at discounts. Wal-Mart, for example, currently accounts for approximately 40% of DVD sales in the U.S.

Amazon.com launched its Unbox service in 2006. When Unbox was launched, the service had no support for burning disks that will play in a DVD player. However, users can download directly to a TiVo. Unbox has been praised for very high quality resolution.

A digital video recorder called Akimbo stores up to 200 hours of programming downloaded from the Internet. The hardware is a set-top box, very similar to TiVo, which connects to the Internet and to TVs via wired or wireless home networks. The cost for the box is $199.99, and monthly service is about $10. Its limitations are many. Users cannot watch programming until it is fully downloaded. Available content is a fraction of what is available to cable subscribers. The latest Akimbo equipment is compatible with Microsoft Media Center. Other companies, such as TiVo, are attempting to offer customers similar systems with many of the same limitations.

Both the music and film industries have learned that paid options must equal the ease and depth of selection available in free, illegal Internet files. Over the mid-term, music firms and moviemakers will have to evolve to find ways of harnessing the power of the Internet rather than becoming a victim of it. Film companies will seek ways to sell digital movie files directly to the consumer, bypassing the middleman. In addition, the Motion Picture Association of America has launched an all-out campaign to boost awareness of the consequences of film piracy and has filed hundreds of suits against individuals as well as companies who are involved in illegal movie downloads.

SPOTLIGHT: Brightcove, Inc.

Founded in 2004, Brightcove (www.brightcove.com) is an Internet TV system that facilitates the offering of video and other content for download from the Internet. Headquartered in Cambridge, Massachusetts, Brightcove is a private company headed by management culled from entertainment firms such as Comcast, Lycos, News Corp. and Discovery Networks. The firm helps content owners, web publishers and advertisers (among others) create Internet TV channels, and also consults with existing channel operators to enhance their sites and increase revenue. Selected customers include Fox Entertainment Group, The New York Times, MarketWatch and SonyBMG. Not only is the company amassing an impressive clientele, it is backed by some of the biggest names in electronics and entertainment including AOL/Time Warner, InterActiveCorp/IAC, the Hearst Corporation and General Electric.

Major electronics companies including Sony, Sharp Corp., Toshiba Corp. and Hitachi Ltd. are banding together to establish standards for Internet-connected TVs in an attempt to compete with computer hardware makers. The electronics firms hope to standardize aspects of Internet TV such as the operating system, copyright protection, connectivity and security.

As the Internet provides more and more video entertainment, new issues arise regarding the rights of TV networks versus those of web sites, Internet providers and so forth. Take, for example, the broadcast of Major League Baseball (MLB) games. MLB has exclusive deals with local and regional TV stations for the broadcast of its games (each regional agreement earns MLB about $250 million per year). 2,400 games each season are also broadcast online to subscribers (which nets MLB another $265 million per year). In order to maintain the TV stations' exclusive airing rights, Internet subscribers' access to local games is blocked.

Meanwhile, video-on-demand and subscription-based video-on-demand, very rapidly growing services offered by cable and satellite TV systems, appears to be succeeding in a big way where Internet-based film services have found only modest results. For details, see "Video-on-Demand (VOD) and Subscription Video-on-Demand (SVOD) Go Mass Market."

6)   Netflix and Blockbuster Go Head to Head

Netflix.com, an online DVD rental service, was launched in 2002. Now the largest such service in the world, it offers its members access to more than 90,000 titles. For a typical monthly subscription fee of $16.99, users may keep up to three DVDs at any given time. A lower-level subscription plan at $9.99 monthly enables subscribers to have only one DVD on loan at a time (the company also offers several additional levels of membership). Users select the titles they wish to view, and the discs are mailed to them in paper envelopes. For return, subscribers tear off the top flap of the paper mailer, revealing a pre-addressed and postage-paid envelope ready for mailing back to Netflix. Users are encouraged to maintain a list, or queue, of desired DVDs. As soon as one is returned, the next available selection in the list is shipped out. One of the best selling points is the company's policy of no late fees. Users keep their rentals as long as they like, since there are never due dates for returns.

In 2007, Netflix launch its download service in which subscribers choose from more than 6,000 full-length movies and TV episodes. Playback starts a few seconds after download begins and the cost is included in subscribers' monthly memberships. Subscribers are allowed certain monthly limits on the number of hours they may spend watching downloaded media (for example, at the $16.99 level, users are allowed 17 hours of watching time per month).

Gauging by the number of subscribers, Netflix is catching on in a big way, with total membership exceeding 7 million as of late 2007. Its success has had a serious impact on rivals including Blockbuster. Total revenues at Netflix rose from $688 million in 2005 to $996.7 million in 2006, while profits rose from $41.9 million to $49.1 million.

Blockbuster has responded with both an in-store subscription program and an online service, which it combined in an offering called Total Access. Customers can select movies online, receive them by mail and then return by mail or in a Blockbuster store. Monthly subscription pricing runs between $9.99 and $17.99, depending on the number of movies rented at a time. If this model sounds familiar, it's only because Blockbuster had to totally redesign its business in order to stay competitive with Netflix, especially embracing the no late fee policy. Although Blockbuster's sales have fallen in recent years (2006 sales were $5.5 billion, down from 2005's $5.7 billion), it posted a profit in 2006 for the first time since 2002 (2006 profits were $54.7 million).

Striking yet another blow to Blockbuster, Netflix took over Wal-Mart's DVD rental business in May 2005 in return for the promotion of Wal-Mart's movie sales business on the Netflix web site.

Watch for increased competition in online video rental markets as Netflix attempts to maintain its momentum. Meanwhile, Netflix maintains significant competitive advantage due to the software that drives its online system. In a manner similar to the way that Amazon.com suggests book titles to customers, the Netflix system does a superb job of recommending movies to customers, based on their history on the site. Additionally, Netflix customers receive superior service, and they enjoy prompt, effortless delivery of movies thanks to the company's network of distribution centers in strategic locations nationwide.

Spotlight: Redbox Automated Retail LLC

Netflix and Blockbuster face another challenger in the form of vending machine DVD rentals. Redbox Automated Retail LLC is a leader in this field. Redbox is a venture owned by a subsidiary of McDonald's Corporation and Coinstar, Inc. There are 5,000 Redbox kiosks in locations such as 1,400 McDonald's restaurants, in addition to 2,600 supermarkets and other high traffic locations that offer a selection of about 500 DVDs each for a $1 rental fee. Redbox expects the self-service DVD rental market to grow to $3 billion by 2009, and it is positioning itself to have a major market share. Redbox is very user-friendly. For example, it charges no late fees. In September 2006, the company launched an online movie rental service that offers users the ability to select DVDs online and then pick them up at a Redbox location.

---

7)   Major Casino Expansion Continues in the U.S. and Macau

The U.S. gambling mecca of Las Vegas, along with other gambling outposts including Atlantic City and the rapidly growing Chinese coastal enclave of Macau, are experiencing phenomenal growth. For 2006, gaming revenues in Las Vegas alone topped $6.69 billion (an 11% increase over 2005) according to the Nevada Gaming Control Board; while Macau's revenues reached $6.95 billion (an enormous increase of 22% over 2005). Casino operators are scrambling to capitalize on the boom with even more casinos, hotels and resorts of ever-larger sizes.

MGM Mirage is planning a 66-acre, $7-billion CityCenter complex that is expected to include 6,800 hotel rooms and condos, as well as a 4,000-room hotel-casino designed by world-famous architect Cesar Pelli and high-end shops and spas. This project received a major boost when Dubai World invested $2.7 billion in the project during 2007, buying a 50% stake. This will most entice large numbers of visitors from the Middle East to this new resort.

Big developments elsewhere in Las Vegas include the recently opened, five star Wynn luxury hotel casino along with the adjoining Wynn Towers. Next door to the Wynn, the Las Vegas Sands (which owns the all-suite Venetian in Las Vegas and the Sands Macao in China) began accepting guest reservations for its new Palazzo in a soft opening in late 2007, followed by an official opening the first week in January 2008. The new Palazzo tower features 3,025 suites (in addition to the 4,049 suites next door at the Venetian), including a series of huge suites on the top floors and around the pool, ranging up to 11,000 square feet each, luxurious shops and restaurants plus a total of 450,000 square feet of meeting space.

In addition to acres of slot machines, black jack tables and roulette wheels, Las Vegas is teeming with new versions of famous restaurants, couture shopping boutiques and world-class entertainment including internationally known singers, dancers and comedians and several different permanent shows by the Cirque du Soleil troupe of acrobats, clowns and musicians. Las Vegas hotels and casinos make roughly one-half their net profits through non-gambling activities.

The MGM Mirage/Mandalay Resort merger in 2005 entrenched the empire run by billionaire investor Kirk Kerkorian as the dominant force on the Las Vegas strip, with holdings of more than half of the famous street's 72,000 hotel rooms. Top properties include Bellagio, Mandalay Bay, Luxor and New York-New York.

For the first time, Macau surpassed Las Vegas in revenue in 2006 according to some analysts. The former Portuguese colony, which reverted back to Chinese rule in 1999, claimed its gambling revenue rose 22% from 2005 to 2006, reaching $6.95 billion. Macau is the only place in China where gambling is legal, therefore attracting more than 22 million mostly Chinese visitors in 2006. Existing properties include the Sands Macau, Wynn Macau, MGM Macau, Venetian Macau and a Mandarin Oriental Hotel, while new projects include the Four Seasons

Macau, which is expected to open in early 2008; and the Sheraton Macau Hotel and the Macau Studio City slated for 2009 openings.

Gambling is still one of today's major growth industries, grossing more than $84 billion in 2005 in the U.S., according to the American Gaming Association, as casino/hotels, riverboat casinos, Native American reservation casinos, bingo halls and slot machine parlors continue to attract visitors by the millions. (This figure also includes lotteries, legal bookmaking and pari-mutuel betting. Commercial casinos alone enjoyed $30.3 billion in revenues that year.) Destinations such as Atlantic City and Biloxi, Mississippi are investing heavily in Las Vegas-style attractions such as upscale retailers, big name entertainment and swanky restaurants to lure customers. The Native American gaming industry has more than doubled since 2000, bringing in $25.5 billion in 2006 according to consulting firm Analysis Group.

Meanwhile, online gambling is growing at a tremendous rate. Although illegal in the U.S., Internet gambling sites are expected to net $24.5 billion in 2010 after paying out winnings, up from 2004's $8.2 billion, according to Christiansen Capital Advisory. All of these businesses are based outside the U.S., and are therefore largely beyond the jurisdiction of the U.S. Department of Justice. However, the U.S. government enacted the Unlawful Internet Gambling Enforcement Act in October 2006, which effectively shut down many up and coming international gambling sites that targeted players in the U.S.

Meanwhile, peer-to-peer betting, or wagering directly against another player as opposed to betting against the house, is flourishing outside the U.S. PartyGaming, based in Gibraltar, is one of the largest online gaming companies, with 768,000 real money players. (The company was forced to close its operations that related to U.S. customers in October 2006, mere days after the Unlawful Internet Gambling Enforcement Act took effect). The firm's sites include PartyPoker.com, PartyCasino.com, PartyBingo.com and PartyGammon.com for game players and PartyBets.com and Gamebookers.com (which was acquired from Trident Gaming in 2006) for sports betting. PartyGaming's head office and operations center is in Gibraltar, while its IT operations are in Hyderabad, India.

The next big thing in gambling may well be wireless hand-held gaming devices. In 2005, Nevada became the first state to allow the use of the devices, which afford gamblers the ability to play video poker, blackjack, roulette and other games on hand-held units in public areas of casinos such as bars, restaurants and pools. The devices are banned in hotel rooms and other private areas, and will require additional security and surveillance equipment in order for casinos to enforce the ban. Users rent the units from the casinos with proper identification and a deposit of funds into an electronic account.

8) Reality TV Dominates Broadcast Programming/Networks Find New Ways to Distribute Content

Reality TV programming began with the comic *Candid Camera* show in 1948. Host Allen Funt filmed unwitting people reacting to rigged situations such as talking mailboxes. Far less humorous but riveting television aired on PBS in 1973 when *An American Family* showed the unscripted breakdown of a marriage and the coming-out of a homosexual son. The show attracted 10 million viewers. More recently, unscripted life has been caught on videotape in shows such as MTV's *Real World* and Fox's *America's Most Wanted*. Other reality formats, including *Big Brother*, were pioneered in Europe during the late 1990s.

Today, reality shows such as *Survivor* and *American Idol* are changing the landscape of broadcast television. In the winter of 2007/2008, 15 reality shows were on the schedules of the four major U.S. broadcast networks (ABC, CBS, Fox and NBC). At the Fox network, as much as 60% of the primetime schedule is devoted to reality programs. With a major strike by TV scriptwriters who are members of the Writers Guild of America in 2007, reality programming got an even bigger boost since these programs typically script themselves.

One reason why this kind of programming is so popular with viewers is the suspense and drama inspired by challenges. Will the hopeful young singer, that viewers have come to know and love, win a record contract on *American Idol*? Which contestant will be voted-off the *Survivor* program after hours of grueling competition?

As a business model, shows of this ilk are providing advertisers with new means of reaching viewers with implanted advertising. This is vital since, with the advent of DVRs, viewers are fast-forwarding through ads or skipping them altogether. *Survivor* reaches as many as 28 million viewers who saw events such as a participant winning a Ford F350 truck as a prize in a reward challenge. NBC's *The Apprentice* challenged its teams to harvest and sell Sue Bee honey in a supermarket. This style of

advertising is called product placement. Other newly popular alternatives to classic 30- and 60-second commercials are advertiser sponsorships. For example, Ford, Coca-Cola and Cingular sponsor *American Idol*.

Analysts are reluctant to predict how long the reality TV craze will continue, but many question the proliferation and how it might kill off the genre by airing too much reality for viewers to swallow. The fifth season of *The Biggest Loser* was scheduled to air its first episode in January 2008, a mere three weeks after the finale from the previous season. Another limitation to reality TV is that it typically does not go into syndication, since the current nature of the shows is part of the appeal. Syndication allows many other types of programs to be produced at a loss, and then generate profits when aired again.

Meanwhile, TV production companies are expanding their distribution efforts for all types of programming. Faced by intense competition from the Internet for consumers' attention, networks are rightly concerned about keeping viewers tuned in. Production is hugely expensive, as a one-hour episode of a new series can cost between $1 million and $2 million or more. Advertising revenues and cable fees are often not enough to cover the costs, so the networks are looking for other avenues. Releasing programming on DVD, pay-per-view or on international markets are among ways to raise additional revenues, and more creative means are emerging as well. For example, *Desperate Housewives* reruns are now available for purchase by iPod users who have video-enabled units. CBS is selling replays of its *CSI* series and *Survivor* to Comcast barely hours after their first run. Several television programs are now available as pay-per-view on Internet-enabled cell phones.

Watch for more innovative ways in which television networks will attempt to stay profitable. NBC is especially intent on offering digital content to beef up its ratings. While attempts in 2007 to promote NBC shows on the broadband comedy channel (www.dotcomedy.com) were not successful; the network offers full episodes of many of its top shows on its web site in addition to previews and special features, as do its competitors. See "TV over IP—TV Networks and Web Sites Converge" in this chapter for more on the online TV phenomenon.

In January 2007, the CBS television network announced several new initiatives to make its content available online and on multiple platforms. One of the most interesting developments at CBS is a test with technology provider Slingbox to enable

Slingbox users to share clips of CBS programming with their friends by posting the clips to a CBS-branded website. (Slingbox is a technology firm that sells set-top boxes that enable users to watch TV programming on PCs or mobile devices.) Meanwhile, CBS extended its cooperation with YouTube (where users can already view CBS program clips) to include a contest where YouTube users submitted a 15-second video to be played during a SuperBowl 2007 TV ad.

9) New Platforms Revolutionize Electronic Games

Electronic games are an immense global business. Global revenues in 2007 for the video game industry were projected to rise 18.5% to $37.47 billion in 2007, according to PriceWaterhouseCoopers. The firm expects worldwide revenues to escalate to $55 billion by 2008. The big news is the release of ever-more-complex game machine technology. While Wii is the technical standout due to its remarkable virtual motion reality, all of today's advanced machines not only combine games with MP3 and DVD players, but offers full Internet access and interactive TV as well. Game players can find online opponents, check e-mail, shop online and download music and video entertainment with a single system. The future of games lies in one word: online.

Sony's Play Station 2, released in the fall of 2001, was the first unit to play DVDs and audio CDs while offering top-of-the-line high-tech gaming. By mid-2007, Play Station 2 had sold 115 million units worldwide, and the company dropped its retail price from $179 to $129, thereby extending the sales life of the unit.

Microsoft was hoping to break Sony's dominance in the market with its Xbox, which was released in November 2001 (with a $500-million marketing budget). Xbox is a major step in the company's attempt to revolutionize the home in the same way that PCs revolutionized the office. The unit is a combination of some of the functions of a high-end PC, complete with high-speed Internet port and a powerful graphics chip; a video game console; and ultimately a headset that will allow players to talk to other players down the street or in another country via the Internet.

Xbox Live, Microsoft's online gaming subscription service, was launched in November 2003 and had 6 million members by June 2007. It provides gamers with the ability to play against each other using the Internet and is becoming a key component to the video gaming experience. Xbox Live's popularity places the software giant in contention for the first time with top-rated Sony, long the number-one video game company in the world.

More news in the Sony-versus-Microsoft video game war was Sony's release of the PlayStation Portable, or PSP. Launched in late 2004 in Japan, and in mid-2005 in the U.S., the PSP was Sony's first hand-held portable game player. It boasts cutting-edge graphics and the ability to play MP3 music files as well as movies on a 4.3-inch-wide screen. Users can also access the Internet via built-in Wi-Fi connectivity and web browser.

Sony's PlayStation 3 (PS3) went on sale with great fanfare in November 2006. By the end of August 2007, Sony had sold 1.75 million units, according to NPD Group. Sony projects total worldwide sales of 11 million units by the end of its fiscal year in March 2008. For more about PS3, see "Cell" Chip Technology Sizzles in PSP3 below.

The debut of Microsoft's $4-billion baby, the Xbox 360, was a major milestone in video gaming. Released for sale at midnight, November 22, 2005, Xbox 360 is a completely redesigned game console, which, not surprisingly, continues to focus on games as part of Microsoft's complete home entertainment concept. In addition to the game console, it has a wireless controller, cables for TV connection, a DVD player, a removable 20 GB hard disk, a headset and a complimentary pass to Xbox Live (this is the setup for the $400 premium version, there is also a more basic system for $300 that does not include the connecting cables or headset and has a wired controller). The console includes ports for attaching digital cameras, portable MP3 music players (including Apple's iPod) or Microsoft's Windows Media Center PC. The software giant hopes that sales of its new game systems will spur further sales of its other home products. The Xbox 360, with its three-core 3.2-gigahertz custom chip from IBM, has been a big hit so far, with about 3 million units selling in the first 90 days alone. Hundreds of thousands of would-be Xbox owners were forced to place their names on waiting lists as initial supplies sold out immediately. The Xbox 360 Elite model features a massive 120GB hard drive.

Nintendo, the third key player in video game sets, has been outdoing its rivals in many ways. Its hand-held game player Nintendo DS (first released in 2004) was the best selling game machine in the U.S. at the end of 2007. Meanwhile, in a vigorous attempt to hold on to its top spot and to compete with Sony's PSP, Nintendo launched a super small player in 2005, the Game Boy Micro. Starting at $89.99, it is barely four inches wide and two inches tall. It has a leg up over other portable devices because it is compatible with more than 700 games designed for earlier Game Boy models.

Nintendo released its revolutionary game system, Nintendo Wii (pronounced "we"), in 2006, which has been a smashing success. Equipped with a state-of-the-art wireless controller and priced at $249, the system offers gamers new, sensory-enhanced playing. The controller communicates with sensors mounted near a television that respond to the player's hand and arm movements. A fishing game, for example, causes the controller to "tug" on the player's hand when a fish is hooked, and the player can then "jerk" on the controller like a fishing pole to reel the catch in. The new technology works with long-time game favorites including *Pokémon, Mario Bros.* and *The Legend of Zelda.* As of August 2007, Nintendo had sold 4 million Wii consoles in the U.S. since its launch compared to competitors' sales of 1.75 million PS3 units and 8.3 million Xbox 360s, according to NPD Group.

Not surprisingly, because of its lengthy history of dominating certain software segments, Microsoft maintains complete control over the licensing of its Xbox consoles and the games that can be played on it. Conversely, Sony allows almost any game developer to design games that can be run on Play Station 2 and on PS3 as well. This allows online interaction between Sony players without subscribing to an additional service such as Xbox Live.

Spotlight: Electronic Arts

In the world of video games, developer Electronic Arts (EA) is the undisputed megastar. Although the delayed release of Sony's PlayStation 3 posed some significant problems, EA still brought in more than $3 billion in 2007 revenues. It makes most of the top video games on the market, especially in genres such as sports, movies and action heroes. Top titles include *Madden NFL 08, NBA Live 08, Harry Potter and the Order of the Phoenix* and *Tiger Woods PGA TOUR 08.*

EA partners with leading film studios, sports franchises, publishers and recording artists to design games with cutting-edge style. Movie producers looking to market their new films are quick to license content to EA. For example, legendary director Steven Spielberg is collaborating with EA to develop three new original games. Likewise, recording artists are eager to have tracks from not-yet-released CDs included in EA games. The firm maintains an in-house creative team that is largely culled from the film and music industries. EA is a powerhouse that has the creative, marketing and financial ability to enable it to enter into exclusive agreements with such organizations as the NFL for development of new games.

Firmly committed to expanding its online gaming, EA offers its own Sports Nation network. Betting on its top-rated sports games, the company is offering tournament play, leagues, rankings, stats and laddering systems, as well as sweetening the pot with offers of prizes or cash payments for winners.

In late 2007, Vivendi SA announced plans to acquire rival U.S. videogame maker Activision, Inc. for about $8 billion, and merge it with its own gaming division to form Activision Blizzard. Assuming that the deal goes through, the new entity should give EA a run for its money.

As for online games, they have become one of the largest and fastest-growing sectors of the worldwide entertainment business. Online video games were expected to attract 40 million players in the U.S. alone by 2006, according to Jupiter Research.

Gaming has presented new ways of making money. Multi-player games (known as massively multiplayer online games or MMOGs) have sparked a new market in which players broker deals to buy and sell game currency, point-building online items and even winning players' online personas, which are called avatars. Many games, such as Sony Online Entertainment's EverQuest or Vivendi subsidiary

Blizzard Entertainment's phenomenally popular World of Warcraft are designed so that players must conquer a large number of challenges to win points and proceed to higher levels. Game masters reach the pinnacle by performing all tasks, which can number as many as 60 or 70. Gamers looking to cash in on the booming popularity of these games (World of Warcraft has 8 million subscribers worldwide) are finding ways to buy and sell virtual assets for real currency.

Second Life, a 3-D "virtual world" may not be a game exactly, but it is the leader in a category that utilizes game-like features such as avatars. Second Life is an world-like online platform where "members" create personalities, open businesses, create buildings and interact with each other—even to the point of getting married in a virtual, fantasy sort of way.

For a time, winning player avatars and other assets were traded on eBay (the auction site has since ceased to allow these kinds of items on its site), and numerous private buying and selling sites have sprung up, such as IGE (www.ige.com) to handle the demand. Some game companies are setting up real money trade (RMT) services of their own. In July of 2005, Sony created Station Exchange, which hosted $540,000 in RMTs in its first three months, charging a 10% commission on each transaction.

The potential for this new market is huge. IGE estimates that by 2009 the marketplace for virtual assets will reach $7 billion. The practice raises some sticky questions, however, about the true ownership of cyber-assets. Some game companies maintain that all currency, points, avatars and other assets are their property and not that of its players. Others disagree. As greater and greater sums are being made from virtual asset brokerage, the question becomes more important. Is a game company liable to its players for their cyber-assets should it discontinue the game or alter its rules? It is also possible that in the U.S., the Internal Revenue Service will begin taxing profits made selling these assets.

When most people think of video game enthusiasts, they picture kids and young men playing violent, action-packed titles such as *Counter-Strike* and *EverQuest*. However, 82.5 million people in the U.S. play "simple" online games such as checkers, mah jong and bridge, vastly larger than the number of people who play sophisticated titles. It's a market that earns $450 million per year for game companies, largely through advertising. Less than 2% of the players of these kinds of games pay to subscribe.

The average "simple" online player is female and between the ages of 35 and 54. Game playing is as much a social activity as a solitary pursuit, as many players connect online with opponents both known and unknown. Xfire (www.xfire.com), an advertiser-supported web site that tracks friends, browses servers, posts game statistics and provides instant messaging, is cashing in on the play-with-friends trend. It debuted in January 2004 with $5 million in venture funding and was acquired by Viacom in 2006. In late 2007, the site surpassed 8 million registered users.

Simple games such as hearts and pool not only attract more users, they are much cheaper and easier to produce. A major shoot 'em up action game can require dozens of computer coders and designers as well as budgets of between $5 million and $15 million. Simple games, such as Yahoo!'s hit pool game, take one developer and about $100,000 to put together. A typical Friday afternoon finds upwards of 36,000 people playing pool on Yahoo!'s gaming site.

Microsoft is capitalizing on the popularity of its video games as a way to gain a strong position in the entertainment industry. The firm's online gaming site, Zone.MSN.com, is extremely successful. However, it is facing tough competition from firms such as Electronic Arts, Yahoo! and Sony, who are all looking for the next smash (read simple) online game.

10)   "Cell" Chip Technology Sizzles in PS3
By releasing Xbox 360 in November 2005, Microsoft beat Sony's widely anticipated release of its PlayStation 3 (PS3), which was released in the U.S. a year later. By the early 2007, Sony had shipped 1.3 million of the consoles to U.S. retailers. Priced between $399 and up (depending on the size of the hard drive), PS3 includes a high-definition DVD player using the Sony standard called Blu-ray. This is a bold move since the entertainment industry is still undecided as to which DVD technology will be embraced by the buying public, and stand-alone Blu-ray players are expected to command a $1,000 price tag. Sony is actually taking a loss on the DVD player included in PS3 in order to market the new technology and soften the blow for movie watchers who will have to buy high-definition versions of their favorite DVDs.

Cell, Xbox 360, Pentium 4-840 Processor Speeds Compared		
Chip:	*Transistors:*	*Speed in gigaflops:*
Cell, PlayStation 3 (November 2006 release)		
	234 million	230
Xbox 360 (November 2005 release)		
	165million	77
Pentium 4 (Extreme Edition 840, 3.2 GHz, 2005 release)		
	230 million	26

The biggest innovation for PS3 is an extremely powerful seven-core, 3.2-gigahertz "Cell" microprocessor developed by IBM and Toshiba. This Cell chip represents a true revolution in technology for consumer devices, since it essentially packs the processing speed of a supercomputer. The PS3 can call on the Cell chip to crunch up to 2 trillion calculations per second. This means that game developers can create extremely realistic virtual characters and settings that move at blistering-fast speeds. To put the Cell chip into perspective, it runs at speeds nine-times as fast as a very high level Intel Pentium 4, dual-core chip.

While other firms are pursuing the Cell with high-speed chip designs of their own, the Cell's early lead will result in rapid adoption by game developers and by makers of other electronics devices. The fact that the Cell was forced to be created as a low-power consumption, lightweight, high-speed chip for use in a revolutionary game machine will lend it to creative use in other devices and multi-use platforms. Watch for the Cell to be used as an enabler for entertainment units of all kinds, with enriched media offerings such as real-time video chat and extremely evolved interactive TV on the go. Multi-use cell phones with vast numbers of entertainment offerings via fast wireless Internet access and high-definition color screens will become the biggest benefactors. Meanwhile, the games designed for PS3 will reach a new level of extreme virtual reality and virtual world immersion. Non-entertainment uses for Cell chip technology will evolve rapidly as well, including applications for engineering, research and aerospace.

11) Satellite Radio Fails to Earn a Profit/Traditional Radio Faces Challenges

Satellite broadcast radio provides yet another example of consumers seeking niche, often ad-free entertainment. There are two major players in this sector, XM Satellite Radio and Sirius. Each offers more than 130 themed radio channels in clear, CD-

quality sound. Both firms have signed up multimillion subscriber bases, although they are below their initial goals, while racking up huge losses.

XM Satellite Radio has an important leg-up on Sirius because it hit the market almost a year ahead in September 2001. It broadcasts more than 170 music, information and entertainment channels through two satellites with a small amount of advertising (many channels are completely ad-free). As of the end of 2007, XM had about 9 million subscribers (up from 3.2 million at the first of 2005) who pay $12.95 per month. The company had targeted 9 million users in 2006 but fell short.

Sirius, formerly known as CD Radio, was launched in July 2002. It transmits its more than 150 channels of news, information, entertainment and music from three satellites to any vehicle or home equipped with a Sirius receiver. Its mid 2007 subscriber total reached 7 million, and monthly subscription fees are the same $12.95 charged by XM.

Both companies face fierce opposition from traditional radio stations (terra stations) which form a powerful lobby known as the National Association of Broadcasters (NAB). Throughout satellite radio's development, the NAB has pushed through legislation that severely limits satellite radio's activity. FCC regulations require satellite firms to have paying subscribers (free, advertising-supported stations are forbidden), and air space is limited to 25 megahertz. In addition, the Digital Performance Right in Sound Recordings Act of 1995 frees terra radio from paying royalties to recording artists, while requiring that satellite stations do so. XM paid almost $20 million in royalties in its first two years on the air (17% of total revenue for that period).

The most difficult regulation of all for satellite radio is that it is banned from broadcasting local programming. No local traffic, weather or sports reporting may be beamed into specific markets. However, in 2004, XM found a loophole in the requirement and began broadcasting 20 localized feeds via satellite to particular channels. These channels are broadcast nationally so listeners across the U.S. can tune into traffic reports for a city such as New York or Los Angeles, but the audience for the channels is more likely to be local. In a further development, XM acquired WCS Wireless LLC, a Nevada wireless company that owns part of the broadcasting spectrum that is right next to XM's in 15 of the top 20 metropolitan markets. The new spectrum enables XM to target local markets with local programming.

Traditional radio is attempting to fight back by tinkering with its programming and formats. Many stations, including those owned by industry leader Clear Channel Communications, Inc., are cutting commercials and playing more music. Viacom's Infinity Broadcasting offers an open source format on one of its San Francisco AM stations. Instead of its standard talk radio programs, KYOU airs podcasts, which are submissions from its listeners with a wide variety of home-grown content. Clear Channel also offers podcasting channels as of mid-2005. Many traditional stations are also offering high-definition (HD) radio channels such as Clear Channel's Mother Trucker country and southern rock digital channel and Full Metal Racket heavy metal channel.

Meanwhile, satellite radio is scrambling to maintain its subscribership and cut costs. Many of the most expensive startup costs, such as the satellites and the design and manufacture of receivers, are behind the two companies, but both are facing unexpected new costs such as escalating contracts for on-air talent such as Sirius' $500-million, five-year contract with notorious disc jockey Howard Stern that began in January 2006.

Attempts to build subscriber revenue via agreements that each company has with various major automakers have created their own problems. Sirius has partnerships with a lengthy list of car makers, including Ford, Chrysler, Mercedes-Benz and BMW, allowing the car companies to equip new vehicles with their receivers. Part of the subscription revenue is paid as a royalty to the automaker during the full lifetime of the automobile. XM is partnering with GM and Honda (both automakers have stakes in XM), as well as with Toyota and Hyundai. These agreements do get the product in front of potential customers, but both XM and Sirius are finding that many drivers choose not to activate subscriptions. The firms countered by offering free trial access to car buyers starting in 2006, but are discovering that the rate of drivers who choose to keep the service once the trials run out is expected to be disappointingly low.

Satellite radio does offer an ever-increasing depth and variety of programming. XM has the rights to broadcast all Major League Baseball games. Sirius has the rights to broadcast National Football League games. With the plethora of channels available from both companies, coverage of sporting events can offer a dizzying variety of flavors. Take the 2006 Super Bowl, for example. XM covered the game on

at least six different channels. One favored the Pittsburgh Steelers, while another offered a pro-Seattle Seahawk slant. Moreover, other channels broadcast the game in languages from Spanish to Chinese to German.

Satellite radio is also beamed into homes, offices and even offshore, with service for everything from the living room to the tractor to the pleasure boat. The receivers cost between $100 and $200 and can be purchased through most major electronics retailers, including Best Buy, Circuit City and Wal-Mart. Newer receivers such as Sirius' S50 and XM's Nexus have the ability to record up to 750 songs or other programming and organize that material in playlists similar to the Apple iPod. Cost for these receivers is around $180.

Satellite radio does have the ability to broadcast content other than audio entertainment and news. Real-time weather content is now being broadcast to the yachting and shipping market. Also, Sirius has launched a few channels of children's video entertainment, aimed at back-seat screens in automobiles.

However, XM and Sirius have their work cut out for them if they are to continue to build subscribership and manage to finally make a profit. Watch for possible cost-cutting measures over the mid-term and new ways of seeking those elusive new subscribers who may prefer to stick to their iPods.

In February 2007, XM agreed to a merger of equals with Sirius Satellite Radio, Inc. The $13 billion merger is subject to massive regulatory oversight, which may derail the deal.

12) Radio Via IP Grows/The Era of Digital Radio Begins

It is now common for broadcast radio stations in markets across the U.S. to stream real-time programming on their web sites at the same time that the programming is on the air. This makes it possible for a listener to tune in via PC, even when thousands of miles away. It also enables the station to maintain a multimedia connection with the listener, since the web site can post ads, program schedules, DJ profiles and the like. Radio listenership over IP has grown to 29 million listeners per week, up from 20 million in 2004, according to Arbitron, Inc. and Edison Media Research.

Peer-to-peer (P2P) web sites that operate in a radio-like manner (but are not part of traditional radio stations) are proliferating at a rapid rate as well. Generally, such sites enable a listener to request a constant stream of either popular genres or very specific niche music. For example, a listener could receive a constant stream of reggae music, or jazz or classical music. Hundreds of thousands of listeners are tuning in through this method. On the programming end, thousands of amateur enthusiasts are packaging their favorite music, or commentary, and playing it via the web. For example, AOL offers such a service called Shoutcast, a free streaming MP3 music file server.

Other sites use simple streaming technology that is not P2P. Companies attempting to create revenues by enabling online listening include Live365 (www.live365.com). Yahoo! is in the business with its Launchcast service, as is RealNetworks with its Rhapsody service.

Another slant to radio over IP is music sharing with friends with similar musical tastes. Social fm is one such site which provides users with social distribution channels for listening on PCs or over mobile devices. In late 2007, the site launched social music applications for Facebook users.

The broadcast and satellite radio industry will watch these developments closely and may seek new ways to compete via IP delivery. These radio via IP services operate in a legal manner. Music is available for listening, but the files are streamed temporarily to listeners' PCs, not permanently downloaded. The real test for radio via IP is the ability to listen to the music on portable devices, especially those which can be listed to while on the road in cars and trucks. Startup firms Slacker, Inc. and Pandora Media, Inc. are raising investment money to do just that. Another firm, SanDisk Corp., already has a $249.99 Sansa Connect digital music player on the market that allows users in wireless Internet zones to hear online music from stations associated with Yahoo, Inc. (the player also stores a library of music for listening when away from WiFi hotspots).

A noteworthy radio industry innovation, digital radio, refers to technology that improves radio signals while increasing the number of channels available. By early 2007, HD multicast formats were available in all of the top 100 radio markets in the U.S. Automotive companies such as Ford and auto dealers David McDavid Automotive Group in Texas and Motor City Chevrolet in Michigan are providing HD receivers. Digital broadcasting offers several advantages. To begin with, the reception is higher quality, with clearer tones and less interference.

Next, utilizing digital technology enables broadcasters to get create extra stations from the same bandwidth. In this manner, extra stations,

typically called HD-2 and HD-3, can be broadcast that offer niche content. For example, a broadcaster that typically offers a wide variety of jazz on its main station could focus on Latin jazz on HD-2 and classic jazz of the 1940s on HD-3.

Currently, prices for digital receivers are high, starting at about $200, with offerings on the market from Kenwood, Polk Audio and others. However, prices will plummet if the receivers become widely popular. Meanwhile, these receivers are already available in a handful of new cars.

While digital radio broadcasting is in its infancy, it could easily become the standard of the future. In the same way that the FCC is requiring that all TV broadcasts become digital by February 17, 2009, similar rulings may eventually be passed regarding radio.

13) Cable and Satellite TV Compete Fiercely for Market Share

In the race for home media customers, cable companies and satellite firms are battling to offer the most services, the greatest convenience and, more importantly in today's market, more consumer control over what to view. Nielsen Media Research estimates that, as of late 2006, approximately 73 million U.S. households currently subscribe to cable service while about 23 million homes have satellite service (up from only 1.6 million in late 1997). Based on subscribers alone, cable appears to have the lion's share of the market. However, changes in technology, viewer tastes and habits are profoundly changing, creating more and more room in the market for satellite and its many components.

Satellite companies took millions of customers away from cable firms in recent years, but cable companies are using new bundled services to fight back. The reasons for satellite TV's success include lower prices and the widely spreading availability of local channels via satellite. Monthly cable subscription prices were notorious for rising abruptly. U.S. cable leader Comcast Corporation raised its rates by an average of 5.9% in 2004, after a 5.7% hike in 2003. However, in 2005, many cable companies including Comcast began offering discounts, which continued through 2006, thereby cutting into satellite's long-held advantage on monthly rates. The most important pricing issue today is the total cost to consumers of bundled services that include TV, Internet access, movie packages and telephone service.

Cable companies are faced with perhaps the toughest competition they've yet seen, and they are investing in new technology that may lure customers back from the satellite providers. Thanks to the approximately $100 billion spent by cable companies in the past decade on new high-speed fiber-optic lines and large numbers of localized servers that house movies and programs for fast download by nearby customers, new services offered today include Internet access, video-on-demand (VOD) and VOIP telephone service. Cable companies Time Warner, Inc. and Cablevision Systems Corp. are bundling these services together to entice customers with complete packages at discounted prices.

A newcomer to the cable-versus-satellite fray is AT&T, which launched a cable TV service called U-verse in 2005. The service, which offers up to 300+ channels and charges monthly fees of between $44 and $99, was first tested in San Antonio, Texas, and then spread to the San Francisco, New Haven and Hartford, Connecticut markets in early 2007. U-verse was available to 8 million households by the end of 2007.

Local programming is another significant issue in the battle between cable and satellite companies. Since 2001, the two major satellite companies, EchoStar and DirecTV have added enough satellite capacity to add local channels such as ABC, NBC, CBS, PBS and Fox affiliates to more than 92% of subscriber households. DirecTV, the leading satellite company in the U.S. with 16.3 million subscribers in 2007, is investing $1 billion to launch new satellites that offer local channels with high definition. Cable is quickly losing its local edge in most markets.

Now, cable providers face new competition from telephone companies such as AT&T, Inc. (formerly known as SBC Communications). Up until recently, cable's best competitive advantage over satellite was its ability to offer superior high-speed Internet connections and VOIP telephone service via cable. Comcast, the nation's largest cable company, is also the nation's largest provider of broadband Internet access, with 12.9 million Internet access subscribers as of the end of 2007. The competitive situation is changing, however, as major telecom companies, which have long been cable's competition in broadband access, now have the ability to deliver television programs through fiber-optic lines (see "TV over IP—Telecom Companies Enter the Television Market").

14) Video-on-Demand (VOD) and Subscription Video-on-Demand (SVOD) Go Mass Market
Cable companies such as Comcast, Time Warner Cable and Cablevision already have a presence in a vast number of U.S. homes. In a growing number of markets across the U.S., they offer video-on-demand (VOD), subscription video-on-demand (SVOD), high-speed Internet service and/or digital programming for HDTV. According to Leichtman Research Group, the percentage of cable subscribers who watch VOD almost doubled in 2006 to 65%. In 2007, Comcast announced that it had registered more than 6 billion on-demand views since 2003, and had 1 billion hours of on-demand content watched in 2007 with 250 million views each month and 100 views each second.

With regard to VOD, there are two ways in which digital cable watchers can access paid programming. The first way is to select a film or television show for a per-unit price (usually about $3.95). It is transmitted from the hundreds of films and television shows stored on hard drives in the cable company's offices, and the viewer can watch it as many times as they wish during a 24-hour period. The second way is to subscribe to unlimited access to a particular set of shows, such as an entire season of a favorite television show or selected programming from a particular network such as HBO. The price for this option is around $6.95 per month.

Satellite companies such as DirecTV and EchoStar Communications so far control only a small part of the high-speed Internet access market, and satellite-based VOD is limited because the two-way communication necessary between subscriber and provider is limited to telephone lines (cable utilizes broadband lines much better suited to two-way communication). Satellites can beam programming to TVs, but cannot easily receive data. However, satellite companies do have a competitive offering with DVRs. These recorders, of which TiVo is a major brand, can be included in satellite converter boxes. This is a plus for viewers who are tired of the excess of receiver boxes and other electronic equipment stacked around their television sets. Satellite companies are gambling that the record-now, watch-later, skip-over-advertising features inherent in DVRs are more than a match for VOD. Another plus for satellite companies is a decisive lead in HDTV programming.

Meanwhile, huge enhancements to the cable experience were launched during 2006 as set-top boxes got an upgrade. Microsoft, with its Foundation software, Digeo and SeaChange International are all vying to sell their advanced technology software to the cable providers. This software, along with improved set-top box hardware, will enable cable firms to provide the latest in VOD, digital video recording (providing TiVo with even more competition) and interactive services such as on-screen shopping.

An excellent example of the use of VOD is Comcast's "ON DEMAND" service. ON DEMAND includes hundreds of movies, programming for children, fitness programs, lifestyle programs, music videos, concerts and sports such as NFL game highlights. While most of the ON DEMAND programming is free, the firm uses the system to build revenue by selling access to movies for $3.95 for new releases and $2.95 for other movies, as well as fees for access to special programming such as concerts. It also makes popular series available via ON DEMAND, such as *CSI Crime Scene Investigation* and *Survivor*. Using On DEMAND, customers can play, fast-forward, rewind, pause and restart their selections as many times as they want during the 24 hours after they select the program. Comcast's customers watch more than 100 million ON DEMAND programs each month.

15)   TV over IP—Telecom Companies Enter the Television Market

At some point over the mid-term, however, TV over IP (IPTV) will become a serious threat. This is due to several reasons, including a) the cost and difficulty of digital production and distribution are plummeting, b) high-speed broadband access to the Internet in homes will become standard and c) the number of homes equipped with media PCs, capable of capturing TV programming from the web and sending it to high-tech monitors for display in the living room, will grow rapidly.

Some of the implications include the possibility of thousands of new "channels" of TV over the Internet. Independent producers will have a plethora of new outlets. Online program guides will be absolutely essential so that consumers can determine what channels to watch. The TV audience is already fragmented because of the vast number of satellite and cable channels. IPTV will increase this fragmentation, creating both challenges and opportunities for advertisers, producers and delivery platforms. The potential for highly targeted, niche audience ads will be immense. The future may see viewers faced with hundreds of Martha Stewart look-alikes offering cooking and decorating advice via Internet TV channels. At the same time, TV viewing will become much more portable, as mobile viewing platforms evolve and are made extremely useful via 3G cellular, WiMAX and other wireless networks. Broadcast, cable and satellite TV providers may

compete by positioning themselves with value-added content and services, such as enhanced interactive TV and expensive programming such as made-for-TV movies and major league sports coverage. IPTV is already growing rapidly in Asian markets such as Japan.

Telecom companies are now able to provide television programming in addition to phone service and high-speed Internet access. One tool, Microsoft TV Internet Protocol Television, digitally encodes and compresses TV signals so that they can be transmitted over phone lines. Customers have a set-top box that decodes and decompresses the signals for viewing. All programming is delivered as VOD (video-on-demand).

AT&T launched its Homezone service in 2006, and it is currently available throughout much of its service area. The service provides live, high definition (HD) satellite TV provided by EchoStar's Dish Network. The system also includes a built-in digital video recorder. Video-on-demand arrives via Movielink, an online video service. The monthly price for an entertainment package starts at about $70.

AT&T launched a faster, more ambitious service called U-verse in 2006, which provides digital TV via IP over its own proprietary high speed DSL network. By the end of 2007, U-verse was available to 8 million homes in the AT&T service area, and the company hopes to sign up 1 million subscribers by the end of 2008. Overall, AT&T is investing $6.5 billion in IPTV.

Verizon has invested $18 billion in IPTV and ultra high-speed Internet to the home. The firm already offers a full menu of TV channels (including HD channels) plus an on-demand library of thousands of titles starting at $32.99 per month, which is substantially cheaper than many premium monthly cable packages. The service, called FiOS, also provides premium channel packages for additional fees, as well as single or multi-room DVR. It provides subscribers with a very high speed 5 Mbps Internet access service for speedy downloads. Banc of America analysts predict that Verizon will have 2 million FiOS TV customers by the end of 2008.

The standard for IPTV was set in Hong Kong in 2003 by local phone company PCCW. It offers Now Broadband TV, which, as of mid-2007, enjoyed more than 800,000 subscribers in the Hong Kong market. In 2006, PCCW also launched a mobile TV service for 3G cell phone subscribers.

The prospect of IPTV is a boon to telecom companies, since it gives them a highly coveted entertainment service to add to their bundle of offerings. They will have the ability to bundle services that might include any or all of the following: Internet access, landline telephone, long-distance, VOIP telephony, cellular telephone and television via IP—all on one discounted bill. The major telephone service providers have been in a tough spot in the past few years, with revenues from landline customers declining as more consumers switch to cellular phones and VOIP as their standard methods of communication.

As for Microsoft, TV over IP technology is the firm's long-awaited break into the television market. Over several years, the software giant has invested $20 billion in cable companies and other TV-related activities. Some of those investments, such as WebTV and UltimateTV, were not great successes. With IPTV, Microsoft technology has an additional entrée not only into living rooms, but also onto devices such as cell phones and PDAs, which are expected to be able to provide TV programming once wireless speeds become fast enough. In June 2007, the company announced Mediaroom, its latest IPTV software platform. It features in-home personal music and photo sharing, multiple picture-in-picture capabilities and the Multimedia Application Environment, which enables service providers to deploy video-on-demand portals, games and interactive TV services.

Apple's TV unit, formerly called iTV was introduced in 2007, and was expected to revolutionize TV watching as the iPod did for music listening. However, Apple TV, as it has been renamed, has fallen far short of its lofty ambitions as of the end of 2007. Sales of the Apple TV box in its first six months were approximately 250,000. Film companies have proven reluctant to work with Apple, especially since Apple planned to download films for $9.99 or about half the price of a recent release DVD. Of the six major U.S. movie studios, only two have struck deals for content on Apple TV.

16) TV over IP—TV Networks, Cable Companies and Web Sites Converge

Internet portals, web sites and television networks are acutely aware of the potential afforded should television audiences truly turn to their PCs for entertainment. Many popular Internet sites are already producing programming, while television networks are finding ways to air their content online on their own sites. America Online (AOL) offers a selection of free programming kicked off with a bang with the Live 8 web cast of July 2005, which attracted an estimated 3 billion viewers worldwide. Viewers clicked between footage of performances in London, Paris, Philadelphia, Toronto, Rome and Berlin. As of late 2007, AOL offered nearly 40 live concert programs including performances by Bruce Springsteen, Beyoncé and the Dave Matthews Band.

Television stations such as CNN, MTV and Nickelodeon are airing programming on their web sites. CNN debuted its CNN Pipeline service (www.cnn.com/pipeline) in 2005, which offered users a choice of four live news video streams for $2.95 per month. The service has since been renamed CNN.com Live and made available free of charge. MTV has Internet video features, formerly called MTV Overdrive, which offer dozens of music and celebrity related programs, including a daily web cast of music news and events. There is no fee for the service, which is funded by online advertising. Unlike DVR programming on television, in which viewers can fast forward or skip advertising altogether, the ads on MTV bookend programming and also reside in separate windows that can't be closed. Lucrative online advertising is spurring many media companies to take hard looks at ways to diversify programming away from TV and toward the PC.

Portals such as Yahoo! are also getting into the IPTV act by providing video searches. Yahoo! Search (http://video.search.yahoo.com) offers a search engine for a wide variety of video on the web from an extensive list of sources including CBS, Warner Brothers, *BusinessWeek*, ESPN and many more. As programming proliferates, the need for efficient methods to search for content becomes critical.

Cable companies such as Comcast and Time Warner are also getting into the act by investing heavily in new technology that makes video content available on their web sites to all and sundry, not just to their subscribers. Subscribers may, however, route web site content to their TVs for high-quality viewing in comfort.

Search engine sites such as Yahoo! and Google have further expanded their businesses as well, including video content from a variety of sources. These sites enable movie studios, television networks and even sports associations such as Major League Baseball to sell content directly to consumers.

The latest news about TV related convergence is the 2007 announcement by NBC Universal and News Corp. of a joint venture that will go head to head with

Google, Inc.'s wildly popular YouTube site. The venture offers viewers access to programming on a variety of sites with huge market reach including AOL, MSN, MySpace and Yahoo, in addition to the new venture's own web site. Insiders are calling the project MySpace TV or NewTube. It will feature shared short clips from established TV shows, however, unlike YouTube, it will not air consumer-produced video.

17) High-Definition Grows—HDTV and HD-DVD

High-definition TV (HDTV) is a part of the category of TV known as digital television or DTV. The Consumer Electronics Association (CEA) estimates that 11 million HDTV sets were sold in 2006, and that annual sales will rise to 27 million in 2008. These sets have a minimum of 720 progressive scanning lines; a 16:9 ratio for wide screens and 4:3 ratio for standard screens; and Dolby digital audio or an equivalent sound system. (DTV sets have a minimum of 480 progressive scanning lines.) This technology also uses a 1080p standard. 1080 refers to 1,080 lines of vertical resolution; p refers to progressive scan, meaning that the lines that comprise the video picture appear on the screen sequentially. What that really means is that the video quality provided by these systems is the sharpest, clearest and richest ever produced, as much as 10 times sharper than analog TV.

There are three categories of HDTV sets: rear-projection, plasma and liquid-crystal displays (LCDs). Rear-projection systems are the cheapest, but are large, bulky units best watched in darkened rooms. As of 2007, rear-projection was being phased out by leading manufacturers. Plasma screens have significantly dropped in price to the point that they are generally affordable. Screens of up to 102 inches in size are available, although they vary in picture quality (the best being enhanced definition, or EDTV, which has the highest resolution). At the 2007 Consumer Electronics Show in Las Vegas, Sharp Electronics unveiled a 108-inch LCD TV. Not all plasma screens can display high-definition content. LCD sets are among the most expensive. They are lighter than plasma screens and more energy-efficient.

HDTV reception is achieved via special antenna, cable or satellite. The antennae receive free broadcasts from the major networks over the airwaves in major urban areas. Most cable companies offer a handful of HTDV channels as do satellite providers EchoStar and DirecTV.

Meanwhile, consumers can get high-definition in their DVDs as well as in their TV reception thanks to HD DVDs that contain films and other recorded programming. The future for high-definition DVDs is bright. High-definition DVDs debuted in early 2003 in Japan. This new disc format holds five times as much data and features high-definition video of up to 1,080 lines of vertical resolution on screen (in comparison to the 480 lines of standard DVDs). The difference in color and clarity is noticeable, but there's a catch to using the new discs. They only play on high-definition DVD players (which also play standard DVDs). The discs and their players hit the U.S. market in 2006. State-of-the-art systems feature a re-writeable optical disc with both play and record capabilities.

There is currently an intense rivalry in the consumer electronics industry as to what the leading standard will be for this technology. Sony, Dell, HP and an extensive list of other companies are backing a standard known as Blu-ray, which has six times the capacity of traditional DVDs and awe-inspiring clarity. Toshiba, NEC and Sanyo are pushing a standard called HD-DVD that has less capacity but is cheaper, since existing DVD plants can produce it. The conflict between the two camps continued through 2007, even though industry analysts expected an agreement as to which format was to be globally adopted by the end of 2005. The point may be moot, however, since consumers are already enjoying many of the benefits afforded by cutting-edge DVDs by watching high-definition VOD and using DVRs.

In 2007, "next generation" players hit the market, which play both Blu-ray and HD-DVD discs. Regardless of which format wins, the crystal-clear graphics and vivid color comes a much higher retail price than standard DVD. As of 2007, HD-DVD offers Paramount and Universal titles exclusively while Disney, Fox, Lionsgate, MGM and Sony back Blu-ray. Warner content is available in both formats.

> **Internet Research Tip:**
> For general information and a list of web sites pertaining to HDTV, see www.hdtv.com.

18) Movie Attendance Rallies/Film Companies Innovate with DVDs, IMAX and Big Budget Films

PriceWaterhouseCoopers projected overall 2007 movie industry revenue to grow by 3.8% to $84.29 billion. Box office receipts represent a small, but important, portion of total revenues. Additional revenue streams come from pay television, cable and broadcast TV, while the remaining 50% comes from video rentals, DVD sales and video-on-demand. U.S. box office ticket sales rallied in 2006, with receipts up 6.5% in 2006 over 2005, rising to a total of about $9.5 billion. (In contrast, sales were down by about 5% in 2005, to $9 billion, compared $9.4 billion in 2004.) 2006 attendance was also up by almost 5%. Approximately 1.44 million movie theater tickets were sold in the U.S. during 2006, up about 3% from the previous year. The industry's rise in profits and attendance is credited to the production of a broader range of films that appeal to a wider range of tastes and ages, and to continuing release of blockbuster sequels.

Studios have enjoyed a long string of successes. For example, with a total 2006 worldwide gross of $1.06 billion ($423 million in the US alone), *Pirates of the Caribbean: Dead Man's Chest* led the pack for 2006, followed by *The Da Vinci Code* with $756.6 million. Top movies for 2007 included *Spider-Man 3, Shrek the Third, Transfomers, Pirates of the Caribbean: At World's End, and Harry Potter and the Order of the Phoenix.* Four of the top five movies in 2007 were sequels.

Meanwhile, IMAX continues to grow in popularity, and many films are reformatted for IMAX viewing. *The Polar Express* earned about $195 million in revenues from its IMAX release in 2005.

According to numbers compiled by Rentrak, DVDs and VHS tapes had combined U.S. sales and rentals revenues of about $23.6 billion in 2006, a vital source of revenue. However, the DVD market has matured to the point that sales have hit a plateau.

Additional important income streams come from character licensing, international release, TV and cable release. To a growing extent, new formats such as video clips for iPod and cell phone will become very important as well.

Movie theater companies are investing heavily in a high-end new concept called Cinema De Lux (CDL) which outfits theaters with martini bars, Starbucks coffee counters, concierge desks, private party rooms, and theaters that boast luxurious leather reclining seats which are assigned (as opposed to open seating), live performances before showings and escorted seating service. National Amusements, a Massachusetts-based theater business with 1,500 screens, already has several CDLs in multiple states, including New York, Ohio, Connecticut and Virginia.

19) Last Mile Challenges Tumble; Mass Broadband Markets Emerge

A mass-market "tipping point" of consumer broadband access to the Internet occurred during the first quarter of 2004, when more than 26 million U.S. homes and businesses had broadband connections of one type or another. As high-speed Internet prices continue to fall, a large proportion of consumers accessing the Internet are choosing broadband methods over than dial-up. The Age of Convergence, between television, the Internet, telephones, entertainment systems and computers, has begun in earnest.

By 2007, broadband connections in the U.S. reached more than 80 million homes and businesses. Fueling this growth has been intense price competition between cable and DSL providers, with monthly service now starting as low as $14.95 (for new customers for the first year) in some markets. Dial-up users by the millions have converted to broadband at these low prices. If you add the number of wireless broadband users to the number above, the Internet is now reaching a vast U.S. market.

What will widespread use of fast Internet access mean to consumers? Here's a great example: Apple's booming iTunes site is the convergence between recorded music, video, the Internet, personal computers and personal electronic devices. Opportunities are endless, and the amount of entertainment, news and reference content repurposed to take advantage of broadband will grow rapidly. Likewise, more and more content, such as television news and sports coverage, is being reformatted to be viewed over state-of-the-art cell phones.

Adoption of broadband is supported by several factors: wider availability thanks to evolving technologies; reduced connection prices due to increased competition; and greatly improved content and web-based consumer services that will grow in relation to the number of people who have broadband.

By 2010 to 2012, Plunkett Research estimates that as many as 100 million U.S. homes and businesses will have high-speed, broadband Internet access. Broadband in the home will be essential for everyday activities ranging from children's homework to distance education for adults, from shopping to managing financial accounts, from renewing a driver's license to filing an insurance claim. Connections will be much faster. Online entertainment and information options will be vast. Some online services will seem indispensable, and always-on will become the accepted standard. The quality of streaming video and audio will be clear and reliable; making music and movie downloads possible in a matter of seconds, and allowing Internet telephone users to see their parties on the other end as if they were in the same room. Compression and caching techniques will have evolved, and distribution and storage costs will have plummeted. Consumers will accept pay-per-view or pay-per-use service offerings because of their convenience and moderate cost. A significant portion of today's radio, television and movie entertainment will migrate to the web.

> **Plunkett's Law of Convergence:**
> Online consumer usage grows exponentially as broadband access prices decline and more and more Internet devices are adopted—fixed and mobile. This increases demand for new online products and leads to increased offerings of high-value online services and entertainment at reasonable prices.

20) Entertainment-Based Retailing, including Power Towns

Since the earliest days of the marketplace, merchants have realized that entertainment draws crowds of people who linger and shop. Even during the Dark Ages, jugglers, storytellers and other entertainers were an integral part of public markets, helping to draw throngs of people who might purchase goods.

For the foreseeable future, entertainment's value as a drawing card for retail customers will be of paramount importance, especially for the retailing of goods beyond everyday staple items. In fact, the explosive growth of retailing over the Internet means that brick and mortar retailers must offer more than the mere availability of merchandise in order to lure shoppers out of their homes, away from their computer screens and web browsers and into the retail store. New shopping centers, especially those in urban areas, are devoting up to 40% of gross leaseable area (GLA) to entertainment, restaurants and movie theaters.

Yet consumers still want the convenience found in neighborhood centers. Consequently, many new shopping center developments will include the most desirable elements of both power centers and lifestyle centers, including dominant anchor tenants in large formats, dotted with smaller specialty retailers and a plethora of entertainment and dining facilities, all set in a pleasant outdoor environment with sidewalks, trees, lawns and ponds. In many ways, they will be the shopping center equivalent of the super-merchandiser stores.

Several of these new centers, sometimes called power towns, have already been built, including Desert Ridge in Scottsdale, Arizona; the Burbank Empire Center in Burbank, California; and Avon Common in Avon, Ohio. These centers sprawl over 80 to 100 acres and contain 600,000 to 1,000,000 square feet of retail space. Builders spent 25% to 30% more on these areas than on a comparable power center, sparing no expense to make the stores and surrounding areas as pleasant and attractive as possible. Though the costs of power towns might be intimidating, they have impressive drawing power for customers. Desert Ridge, for example, brings in shoppers from a 15-mile radius, with many people driving past other shopping centers just to go to there.

Beyond these initial projects, however, lies the potential for even more ambitious mixed-use projects. Developers are planning to make centers that not only provide entertainment but are also designed to be communities, with space for offices and residential areas. These projects may even include areas for post offices, day-care centers and community centers for performance theatres and galleries. An early form of this idea is found in the Easton Town Center, in Columbus, Ohio. Built for pedestrians instead of cars, the 1.7-million-square-foot retail center contains anchors such as Nordstrom, Barnes & Noble, a Trader Joe's and an AMC theatre, mixed in with a spa and fitness center, a comedy club and a mammography center. The retail center sits within a 1,300 acre, 12 million square foot mixed-use development overseen by The Georgetown Company and Limited Brands.

Another example is the massive $2-billion Meadowlands Xanadu center being built by Colony Capitol Acquisitions in New Jersey (the project was originally under the control of Mills Corp.). Beyond retail tenants, there will be a 780-foot ski slope for skiing and snowboarding called the Snow Dome; a Culinary Arts Center with live cooking demonstrations; an enormous ferris wheel with views of Manhattan; a simulated sky diving feature called Sky Venture; and a 60,000 square foot children's education district featuring Wannado City, an indoor, kid-size city promoting various careers. Developers are betting that Xanadu's entertainment features will draw enough shoppers to justify steeper than usual rent averages of $67.50 per square foot for its non-anchor space. Xanadu's entertainment features will open in 2008-2009.

21)   Video Via Cell Phone Slowly Takes Off

Cell phones with advanced technology have great potential as entertainment platforms. There are challenges here as well, such as the small screens and the fact that consumers often face cellular service disruptions. Nonetheless, cell phones are too big a market for media and entertainment firms to ignore. In 2006, an estimated 1 billion cell phones were sold worldwide—many of them having advanced 3G features. In fact, more cell phones are sold each year than any other type of consumer electronic. Of the 213 million mobile phone subscribers in 2006 in the U.S., 12 million watched video clips, 6 million watched live TV and 3 million paid for a video subscription service, according to Interpublic Group. Market intelligence firm IDC estimates that $3 billion in revenues will be generated by mobile-video subscriptions by 2009. Advertising and technology consulting firm Ovum predicts that there will be $1.26 billion in U.S. spending on cell-phone ads by 2009 as well.

Video via cell phone is rapidly becoming a major business, despite the fact that a relatively small percentage of cell phone users in the U.S. watch it. It is currently a $62 million market in the U.S., but is expected to swell to $500 million by 2010. Cell phone service provider Verizon already offers the V Cast video service on a subscription basis at about $15 monthly. V Cast uses Microsoft Windows Media software to stream short clips of entertainment, sports, news and weather to subscribers via their cell phone screens. Twentieth Century Fox Television is one of several companies producing one-minute entertainment episodes designed for the small screen. Other programs creating "mobisodes" for cell phone viewing include *Sesame Street, The Daily Show, Fox Sports, 24* and several reality shows. The technology has quite a way to go, however, since it can take between 30 and 90 seconds to load a one- to two-minute video clip. An uncompressed video clip download requires about 50 times the bandwidth used by a typical song download.

Verizon may have solved many of its problems with the early 2007 release of V Cast Mobile TV. The service offers true broadcast quality television service for cell phones using a technology called MediaFLO from QUALCOMM. MediaFLO operates as a dedicated broadcast network delivering signals to devices equipped with compatible receivers. The picture has the quality of normal broadcast TV, delivering 30 frames per second. Sprint and T-Mobile are testing the technology.

Cell phone video is already very popular in Japan, Korea and parts of Europe. In the U.S., in addition to Verizon's offering, Alltel, Cingular and Sprint Nextel are in the business with MobiTV, a subscription service that costs $9.99 monthly. In March 2007, MobiTV signed a deal with NBC Universal to make full-length prime time on demand programming available over U.S. wireless networks for the first time. Starting rates for the service are $1.99 for a 24-hour viewing period.

Other video content providers such as News Corporation, MTV and CBS Corporation are bypassing wireless companies and selling content directly to users. News Corporation's Mobizzo is a mobile entertainment store backed by a production studio that focuses strictly on content for cell phones. Programming is available on a piecemeal basis for between $1.99 and $2.99, and there are also two subscription plans for $5.99 per month each. CBS News to Go is a similar service available free of charge, and E.T. to Go, a service with programming from the television show *Entertainment Tonight,* is available for $3.99 per month. ESPN, despite discontinuing its pricey cell phone and service package called Mobile ESPN in 2006, is attracting 9 million visits to its cell phone web site each month.

22)   Apple's iPhone Makes a Splash

The big news in cell phones is the debut of Apple's iPhone at the Macworld Conference & Expo in San Francisco in early 2007. The unit features a touch screen that combines some features from the iPod with those of a highly advanced cell phone. The 8-GB unit that retails for $399. Included are widescreen iPod features and an Internet communications device with e-mail, web browsing, maps and searching capabilities, in addition to a cell phone that offers the ability to dial a number by touching a listing in the unit's address book. The phone syncs with PCs, Macs and Internet services for names, phone numbers and addresses.

The iPhone hit the retail market with great fanfare in June 2007. By September 10th, the firm had sold one million units. Early detractors claim that the AT&T "Edge" broadband network utilized by iPhone is too slow for Web browsing. Some users will also find iPhone's exclusive contract with AT&T a deal breaker since there are areas in the U.S. where AT&T service may not be as strong as that of Verizon Wireless, Sprint or T-Mobile. Another concern is the battery, which requires sending the unit back to the factory when it's time for replacement at a hefty cost and a wait of three business days. Promoters point out that the iPhones can offer faster Web browsing when using Wi-Fi hotspots. It must also be noted that Apple has a history of groundbreaking technology with the Mac computer and the iPod. The iPhone's elegant, usable touch screen makes using multiple functions easy, especially when compared to clumsy or complicated interfaces used by other handsets.

Regardless of early concerns, sales the first weekend were brisk. The firm had sold approximately 5 million iPhones by the end of 2007.

23) Music Plays a Major Role in New Cell Phones

Many new cell phones on today's market come equipped with software to play MP3 music files and can utilize stereo headphones with outlets for each ear, such as Motorola's Bluetooth Stereo Headset HT820 (less than $100). Many users are finding the sound quality to be similar to mobile devices such as iPods or portable CD players. Market research firm iSuppli Corp. estimates that the annual music-enabled cell phone market was about $44.6 billion as of 2006.

After a few initial sour notes, when the early music phones read MP3 files but not popular alternatives such as music downloaded from Apple's iTunes or RealNetworks' Rhapsody, new models are compatible with a wider variety of formats. For example, Motorola's RAZR V3i plays songs downloaded from Apple's iTunes jukebox with a somewhat limited storage capability of 100 songs. Nokia hopes to solve the storage problem with its N91 phone, which boasts a 4-gigabyte hard drive (capable of storing up to 1,000 songs). The N91 debuted in late 2005, and the N95m which has even greater storage capacity, was introduced in late 2006. Nokia invests approximately $1 billion each year on R&D for multi-media devices.

Radio is also part of the cell phone lexicon. Sprint Nextel offers a radio service from Sirius for $6.95 per month, in addition to regular subscriber fees, for commercial-free streaming music in a variety of genres. LM Ericsson and Napster, Inc. reached an agreement in June 2005 to provide a digital music service for cell phones, and began offering the service in early 2006. AT&T (formerly Cingular) teamed with Napster and Yahoo! in 2006 also, and the company now offers a music service on its cell phone network

Verizon launched V Cast Music, a music service offering up to 1.9 million songs in early 2007. Songs are priced at $1.99 each and can be downloaded directly to Verizon cell phones and also to a PC

(Sprint Nextel offers a similar service for $2.50 per song). Verizon charges a $15 per month subscription fee for the service (which also includes video clips and e-mail), which generates revenue for the company even if subscribers do not purchase music. Phones equipped to play these music files start at $99 and have 1-gigabyte memory cards that can hold up to 700 songs. Many analysts were watching V Cast closely as a competitor to the widely successful Apple iPod, but the debut of Apple's new iPhone may mean that all bets are off.

Ringtones Making Sweet Music

Music performing rights organization BMI projected that U.S. ringtone sales for cellular phones in 2006 exceeded $600 million, up from $500 million in 2005 and $245 million in 2004. This is at a time when sales of CDs, cassettes and videos fell 7.6% from 2004 to 2005. The tones cost between $2.50 and $3.50 to download, and record companies are enthusiastic about the new sources of revenue as well as their value as marketing tools. Warner Music Group released "Hung Up" by Madonna as a ringtone a month before the song was released to radio stations or available for sale online or in music stores. Sales appear to have spiked in 2006, however, as BMI projects revenues fell to $550 million in 2007.

---

24) Rules for Digital TV are Finalized

The era of the digital TV in the U.S. is building momentum. Federal regulations require that all television broadcasts move to digital format by February 17, 2009. This has many implications. To begin with, older televisions based on analog technology will not receive broadcasts unless retrofitted with a converter. However, since the change is for broadcast TV only, households that rely entirely on cable or satellite reception will see no effect, and this includes the vast majority of homes in the U.S.

The new rules are fueled by the Federal government's desire to open up vast amounts of spectrum currently reserved for analog television broadcast. The government will reap $10 billion or more by auctioning off this soon-to-be unused spectrum for other purposes. Meanwhile, all new television sets sold in the U.S. will eventually be required to be digital rather than analog. Watch for consumers to buy increasing numbers of very sophisticated, high-definition, digital-enabled TV sets as prices come down and volumes go up.

25) Daily Newspapers Combine Online with Print and Launch Weekly Specialty Papers

The print publication industry is undergoing changes of its own. With more people resorting to new media, particularly the Internet, for news and entertainment, many publications have been struggling to maintain their subscription and advertiser base. The most successful publications will be those that publish their material online in conjunction with their print editions. In the U.S., there are approximately 2,344 daily and Sunday newspapers. They generated about $49 billion in advertising fees in 2006, but a growing portion of their ads share visibility on newspaper web sites in conjunction with printed editions. Also, a growing percentage of those ad revenues are from new weekly community and "shopper" newspapers that are given to consumers at no charge. The Newspaper Association of America predicts that 2007 spending on ads on newspaper web sites increased 22% over 2006, but spending on print ads of the same papers increased just 1.2%.

Newspaper ad sales have been sluggish as well, both at the national and local levels. The rapidly growing use of specialty Internet sites like eBay, Monster.com and Autotrader.com is slicing market share from classified papers. Also, general interest sites like Craigslist.com are hurting classifieds in newspapers. Craigslist, an extremely popular, localized news and classified ads site with a grassroots feeling, has already expanded to 190 markets. Meanwhile, Microsoft and Google have established their own for localized sites that compete in the classified and local search field, adding an even greater threat to the core business of newspapers.

Newspapers are fighting back by putting more and more emphasis on their own local web sites. For example, most newspapers enable advertisers to write their own classified ads in an online form, and then preview and purchase the ad online. That classified ad is typically shown both in the printed newspaper and in the online edition. Other newspapers are improving online search at their web sites, so that consumers can easily find local services, stores and restaurants with a simple search. This puts the newspapers in direct competition with Yellow Pages publishers.

Newspapers have been able to make good profit margins and increase advertising prices during the recent strong economy. Nonetheless, the industry knows that business models must adapt to the digital age. The biggest indicator of changing times is the steady drop in circulation at daily newspapers, despite the rising U.S. population. For example, the Newspaper Association of America reports that daily circulation peaked in 1985 (the pre-Internet era) at 62.8 million, and by 2004 was only 54.6 million. The Internet isn't the only problem faced by newspapers. Changing demographics and intense competition are also in play. While older generations of Americans were hooked on daily newspapers as their primary source of news, newer generations have enjoyed much greater choices and have developed their own modern habits. For example, the extreme popularity of cable TV news coverage from CNN and weather coverage from The Weather Channel make newspapers less dominant.

The largest newspaper organizations have entered the weekly newspaper business in a huge way, in order to better appeal to audience segments that include non-English speakers, young people and consumers in affluent suburbs or revitalized downtown areas. These weeklies tend to be smaller, more fun to read, and given away to consumers for free. Advertising in them appeals to smaller businesses, because the cost of an ad may be one-fourth the rate of advertising in a higher-circulation daily paper. Some of these papers are aimed at Spanish-language speakers and other ethnic groups. Others are "shoppers," that is, they are filled with discount coupons and shopping tips.

One of the biggest events in the newspaper industry of late was the 2006 acquisition of Knight Ridder by The McClatchy Company for about $6.5 billion. McClatchy is now America's second-largest newspaper publishing firm in terms of daily circulation, after Gannett, and fourth in terms of annual revenues after Gannett, Tribune Co. and the New York Times Co. Milestones in 2007 included News Corp.'s acquisition of Dow Jones, the publisher of *The Wall Street Journal*, and the acquisition of Tribune Co. by private investors.

Chapter 2

ENTERTAINMENT & MEDIA INDUSTRY STATISTICS

Contents:

Entertainment & Media Industry Overview

	Amount	Unit	Date	Source
Total U.S. Media Spending	885.2	Bil. US$	2006	VSS
Total U.S. Media Spending	930	Bil. US$	2007	PRE
Annual U.S. Advertising Spending	284	Bil. US$	2007	UM
RADIO				
Full Service FM Radio Stations, Including Educational, U.S.	9,163		Sep-07	FCC
Licensed AM Radio Stations, U.S.	4,776		Sep-07	FCC
Radio Stations Authorized to Broadcast Digitally, U.S.	1,422		Dec-07	FCC
PRINT MEDIA				
U.S. Magazine Advertising Revenues, PIB Measured Magazines	24.0	Bil. US$	2006	PIB
Total Daily & Sunday Newspapers, U.S.	2,344		2006	E&P
Annual Newspaper Advertising Expenditures, U.S. (Print & Online)	49.3	Bil. US$	2006	NAA
Value of Books Sold, U.S. (Retail Consumer Purchases)	55.6	Bil. US$	2007	BISG
TELEVISION				
U.S. Households with Televisions (98.2%)	112	Mil.	2007	NMR
Broadcast TV Stations, Including Class A, U.S.	2,320		Sep. 2007	FCC
Basic Cable TV Subscribers, U.S.	65.3	Mil.	Jun-07	SNL
Digital Cable Subscribers, U.S.	36.2	Mil.	Sep-07	SNL
Cable High Speed Data Subscribers, U.S.	34.7	Mil.	Sep-07	SNL
Non-Cable Multichannel Video Program Subscribers, U.S.	32.0	Mil.	Jun-07	NCTA
Cable Telephony (VoIP) Customers, U.S.	13.7	Mil.	Sep-07	NCTA
Number of TiVo Subscribers, U.S.	4.1	Mil.	Nov-07	Tivo
Number of Global Mobile Phone TV Subscribers (Projection)	125	Mil.	2011	In-Stat
MUSIC				
Album Sales, U.S.*	588.2	Mil. Units	2006	NSS
Album Sales, U.S., First Half of Year*	271.6	Mil. Units	2007	NSS
Global Downloaded Music Sales, incl. Internet & Cell Phone	2.0	Bil. US$	2006	IFPI
Satellite Radio Subscribers, U.S.	16.3	Mil.	3Q 2007	PRE
Number of iPods Sold during the Fiscal Year ending Sep. 29	51.63	Mil.	2007	Apple
OTHER				
Cell Phone Subscribers, U.S.	250	Mil.	Nov-07	CTIA
Gambling Revenues, U.S. (includes all types of legal gambling)	84.65	Bil. US$	2005	AGA
Internet Users, Worldwide	1.24	Bil.	Sep-07	IWS
FILM				
U.S. Box Office Revenues	10.2	Bil. US$	2007	PRE
Number of Movie Tickets Sold, U.S.	1.45	Bil.	2006	NATO
Number of Movie Screens, U.S.	38,415		2006	NATO
Consumer Spending on DVD & VHS (Rental & Sales), U.S.	23.6	Bil. US$	2006	VB
ELECTRONIC GAMES				
Video Game Industry Revenues, U.S.	7.4	Bil. US$	2006	ESA
Video Game Industry Revenues, Worldwide	37.4	Bil. US$	2007	PWC

VSS = Veronis Suhler Stevenson; PRE = Plunkett Research estimate; FCC = Federal Communications Commission; PIB = Publishers Information Bureau; E&P = Editor & Publisher; NAA = Newspaper Association of America; BISG = Book Industry Study Group; NMR = Nielsen Media Research; SNL = SNL Kagan; NCTA = National Cable & Telecommunications Association; NSS = Nielsen SoundScan; IFPI = International Federation of the Phonographic Industry; CTIA = CTIA, The Wireless Association; AGA = American Gaming Association; IWS = InternetWorldStats.com; NATO = National Association of Theatre Owners; VB = Video Business; ESA = Entertainment Software Association, UM = Universal McCann; PWC = PriceWaterhouseCoopers

* Figure includes single track downloads which are converted into track-equivalent albums and added to total physical album sales.

Plunkett's Entertainment & Media Industry Almanac 2008

Estimated U.S. Information & Entertainment Sector Revenues by NAICS Code: 2004-2007

(In Millions of US$)

NAICS Code[1]	Kind of business	2007			2006	2005	2004
		3Q*	2Q	1Q			
51	**Information**	**281,685**	**280,689**	**270,579**	**1,048,329**	**1,004,367**	**955,083**
511	Publishing industries (except Internet)	72,993	71,652	69,813	275,884	271,144	256,301
51111	Newspaper publishers	11,523	12,003	11,245	48,861	49,723	48,366
51112	Periodical publishers	12,299	12,450	11,421	44,874	46,247	42,290
5111 pt	Book, directory & mailing list; & other publishers[2]	14,793	12,437	11,795	53,540	54,200	53,384
5112	Software publishers	34,378	34,762	35,352	128,609	120,974	112,261
512	Motion picture & sound recording industries	25,379	26,871	24,841	94,400	92,231	88,269
515	Broadcasting (except Internet)	24,385	25,068	23,615	94,872	88,911	83,466
5151	Radio & television broadcasting	13,453	14,598	14,054	56,435	53,308	52,093
5152	Cable & other subscription programming	10,932	10,470	9,561	38,328	36,297	35,599
516, 5181, 519	Internet publishing & broadcasting; Internet service providers & web search portals; & other information services	15,615	15,032	14,445	45,874	43,040	40,287
517	Telecommunications	125,414	123,566	120,477	467,236	446,090	429,430
5171	Wired telecommunications carriers	47,955	47,872	47,610	199,933	206,778	211,176
5172	Wireless telecommunications carriers (except satellite)	45,584	43,877	42,802	160,159	140,096	127,602
5175	Cable & other program distribution	25,720	25,739	24,151	88,724	80,493	73,317
517 pt	Other telecommunications[3]	6,155	6,078	5,914	18,420	18,723	17,335
5182	Data processing, hosting, & related services	17,899	18,500	17,388	70,063	62,951	57,330

Estimates have not been adjusted for seasonal variation, holiday or trading-day differences, or price changes. Estimates are based on data from the Quarterly Services Survey and have been adjusted using results of the 2005 Service Annual Survey. All estimates are based on the 2002 North American Industry Classification System (NAICS). Sector totals and subsector totals may include data for kinds of business not shown.

[1] For a full description of the NAICS codes used in this table, see www.census.gov/epcd/www/naics.html.
[2] Includes NAICS 51113 (book publishers), 51114 (database and directory publishers), and 51119 (other publishers).
[3] Includes NAICS 5173 (telecommunications resellers), 5174 (satellite telecommunications), and 5179 (other telecommunications).

* Preliminary estimate.

Source: U.S. Census Bureau

Plunkett's Entertainment & Media Industry Almanac 2008

Estimated Annual U.S. Advertising Expenditures: 2002-2008

(In Millions of US$)

Advertising Medium	2002[F]	2003[F]	2004[e]	2005[P]	2006[P]	2007[P]	2008[P]
Newspapers	**44,031**	**44,843**	**46,935**	**49,618**	**47,709**	**42,939**	**42,147**
National	6,806	7,357	7,762	8,290	7,241	6,624	6,558
Local	37,225	37,486	39,173	41,328	40,468	36,315	35,589
Magazines	**10,995**	**11,435**	**12,121**	**13,006**	**13,425**	**13,695**	**14,106**
Broadcast TV	**42,068**	**41,932**	**46,020**	**46,675**	**47,109**	**45,749**	**48,300**
Network	15,000	15,030	16,458	16,787	16,934	17,043	17,895
Spot (National)	10,920	9,948	10,943	10,834	11,144	10,870	11,957
Spot (Local)	13,114	13,520	14,670	14,967	14,973	14,440	15,018
Syndication[1]	3,034	3,434	3,949	4,087	4,058	3,396	3,430
Cable	**16,297**	**18,814**	**21,069**	**22,568**	NA	NA	NA
Cable Network	12,071	13,954	15,628	16,722	19,119	20,479	21,718
Spot (Local)	4,226	4,860	5,441	5,846	NA	NA	NA
Radio	**18,877**	**19,100**	**19,779**	**20,981**	NA	NA	NA
Network	775	798	852	924	NA	NA	NA
Spot (National)	3,340	3,540	3,575	3,782	4,411	4,307	4,350
Spot (local)	14,762	14,762	15,352	16,275	15,203	14,285	14,285
Yellow Pages	**13,776**	**13,896**	**14,035**	**14,499**	**14,372**	**14,538**	**14,705**
National	2,087	2,114	2,135	2,242	2,185	2,228	2,272
Local	11,689	11,782	11,900	12,257	12,187	12,310	12,433
Direct Mail	**46,067**	**48,370**	**52,240**	**57,203**	**59,912**	**60,988**	**63,732**
Business Papers	**3,976**	**4,004**	**4,094**	**4,252**	NA	NA	NA
Out of Home[2]	**5,175**	**5,443**	**5,790**	**6,080**	NA	NA	NA
National	2,061	2,298	2,440	2,584	NA	NA	NA
Local	3,114	3,145	3,350	3,496	NA	NA	NA
Internet	**4,883**	**5,650**	**7,062**	**8,828**	**9,317**	**10,920**	**12,722**
Miscellaneous	**30,730**	**31,990**	**34,554**	**36,907**	NA	NA	NA
National	23,414	24,550	26,735	28,713	NA	NA	NA
Local	7,316	7,440	7,819	8,194	NA	NA	NA
Total National	**145,429**	**152,482**	**165,994**	**178,254**	**184,696**	**188,197**	**198,542**
Total Local	**91,446**	**92,995**	**97,705**	**102,363**	**100,410**	**95,680**	**95,834**
Grand Total	**236,875**	**245,477**	**263,699**	**280,617**	**285,106**	**283,877**	**294,376**

[1] Syndication includes PAX, UPN & WB.

[2] Out Of Home replaces Billboards, to include billboards on buses, etc.

F = Final.   e = Estimate.   P = Projection.

Source: Prepared for Universal McCann by Robert J. Coen

Plunkett's Entertainment & Media Industry Almanac 2008

Personal Consumption Expenditures for Recreation, U.S.: 1990-2006

(In Billions of US$; Latest Year Available)

Type of product or service	1990	1995	2000	2001	2002	2003	2004	2005	2006
Total recreation expenditures	290.2	418.1	585.7	604.0	629.9	659.9	707.8	746.9	791.1
Percent of total personal consumption	7.6	8.4	8.7	8.6	8.6	8.6	8.6	8.6	8.6
Books & maps	16.2	23.2	33.7	34.6	37.1	38.7	40.4	41.8	43.4
Magazines, newspapers & sheet music	21.6	27.5	35.0	35.0	35.1	36.3	39.4	42.1	45.0
Nondurable toys & sport supplies	32.8	44.4	56.6	57.6	59.2	60.6	63.3	66.5	71.4
Wheel goods, sports & photographic equipment1	29.7	39.7	57.6	59.2	61.4	65.6	71.3	76.2	78.9
Video & audio products, computer equipment & musical instruments	53.0	81.5	116.6	115.5	120.0	123.1	133.3	142.3	151.5
Video & audio goods, including musical instruments	44.1	57.2	72.8	73.6	75.4	76.5	81.7	85.8	90.1
Computers, peripherals & software	8.9	24.3	43.8	42.0	44.6	46.6	51.6	56.5	61.4
Radio & television repair	3.2	3.6	4.2	4.0	4.1	4.1	4.6	4.8	5.4
Flowers, seeds & potted plants	10.9	14.0	18.0	18.0	18.0	17.9	18.3	19.2	19.9
Admissions to specified spectator amusements	15.1	21.1	30.4	32.2	34.8	36.0	37.6	38.7	39.9
Motion picture theaters	5.1	5.6	8.6	9.0	9.6	9.9	9.9	9.5	9.3
Legitimate theaters & opera & entertainments of nonprofit institutions[2]	5.2	8.1	10.3	10.9	11.7	11.9	12.5	13.2	13.4
Spectator sports[3]	4.8	7.4	11.5	12.4	13.5	14.3	15.3	16.0	17.2
Clubs & fraternal organizations except insurance4	13.5	17.4	19.0	20.0	21.1	22.2	22.3	23.7	23.9
Commercial participant amusements[5]	25.2	48.8	75.8	79.6	83.7	91.2	100.9	106.8	115.3
Pari-mutuel net receipts	3.5	3.7	5.0	5.1	5.3	5.2	5.7	6.2	6.6
Other[6]	65.4	93.4	133.9	143.2	150.0	158.9	170.8	178.7	190.0

[1] Includes boats and pleasure aircraft.

[2] Except athletic.

[3] Consists of admissions to professional and amateur athletic events and to racetracks, including horse, dog, and auto.

[4] Consists of current expenditures (including consumption of fixed capital) of nonprofit clubs and fraternal organizations and dues and fees paid to proprietary clubs.

[5] Consists of billiard parlors; bowling alleys; dancing, riding, shooting, skating, and swimming places; amusement devices and parks; golf courses; sightseeing buses and guides; private flying operations; casino gambling; and other commercial participant amusements.

[6] Consists of net receipts of lotteries and expenditures for purchases of pets and pet care services, cable TV, film processing, photographic studios, sporting and recreation camps, video cassette rentals, and recreational services, not elsewhere classified.

Source: Bureau of Economic Analysis

Plunkett's Entertainment & Media Industry Almanac 2008

U.S. Magazine Advertising Revenue & Pages
for PIB* Measured Magazines: 1960-2006

(Latest Year Available)

Year	Magazine Advertising Revenue	Magazine Advertising Pages	Number of Magazines Measured
1960	829,727,760	74,861	79
1965	1,048,765,191	80,147	86
1970	1,168,668,178	76,924	89
1975	1,336,313,425	80,735	94
1980	2,846,083,540	114,705	102
1985	4,919,948,386	152,566	142
1990	6,753,356,745	171,689	164
1991	6,538,195,541	156,650	170
1992	7,141,903,718	163,513	176
1993	7,625,491,794	176,973	179
1994	8,504,647,259	180,589	185
1995	10,114,898,726	208,378	201
1996	11,179,246,682	213,781	208
1997	12,754,950,695	231,371	216
1998	13,813,403,372	242,383	227
1999	15,508,357,011	255,383	238
2000	17,665,305,333	286,932	248
2001	16,213,541,737	237,612	250
2002	17,254,061,740	225,619	234
2003	19,216,085,358	225,831	228
2004	21,313,206,733	234,428	235
2005	23,068,182,388	243,305	244
2006	23,996,768,141	244,907	239

* PIB = Publishers Information Bureau.

Sunday supplements excluded.

Source: www.magazine.org

Plunkett's Entertainment & Media Industry Almanac 2008

Number of U.S. Magazines*: 1988-2006

(Latest Year Available)

Year	National Directory of Magazines	SRDS	ABC	BPA Worldwide	PIB
1988	13,541	1,723	559	NA	156
1989	12,797	1,795	585	196	166
1990	14,049	1,904	587	232	164
1991	14,256	2,000	600	244	170
1992	14,870	2,126	617	243	176
1993	14,302	2,256	631	245	179
1994	15,069	2,347	643	252	187
1995	15,996	2,428	668	273	201
1996	17,195	2,470	711	312	208
1997	18,047	2,513	751	311	216
1998	18,606	2,522	758	448	227
1999	17,970	2,520	750	485	238
2000	17,815	2,567	836	494	248
2001	17,694	2,600	817	505	250
2002	17,321	2,431	764	NA	234
2003	17,254	2,509	703	NA	228
2004	18,821	2,570	708	208	235
2005	18,267	2,640	718	NA	239
2006	19,419	2,790	741	NA	239

NA = Not available.

*There are several sources that provide the number of consumer magazines available in the U.S., some more comprehensive than others. The chart cites five of these sources: the National Directory of Magazines, Standard Rate and Data Service (SRDS), Audit Bureau of Circulations (ABC), BPA Worldwide and the Publishers Information Bureau (PIB).

Source: www.magazine.org

Plunkett's Entertainment & Media Industry Almanac 2008

Average Circulation of the Top 25 U.S. ABC* Magazines, Through June 2007

Rank	Publication Name	Subscriptions	Single Copy	Total
1	AARP THE MAGAZINE *	23,963,146	1,186	23,964,332
2	AARP BULLETIN *	23,361,340	-	23,361,340
3	READER'S DIGEST	9,662,514	384,171	10,046,685
4	BETTER HOMES AND GARDENS	7,433,077	242,833	7,675,910
5	NATIONAL GEOGRAPHIC	4,888,877	172,449	5,061,326
6	GOOD HOUSEKEEPING	4,078,468	661,305	4,739,773
7	LADIES' HOME JOURNAL	3,645,046	280,710	3,925,756
8	WOMAN'S DAY	3,333,864	584,667	3,918,531
9	FAMILY CIRCLE	2,974,498	941,749	3,916,247
10	AAA WESTWAYS *	3,754,704	-	3,754,704
11	PEOPLE	2,300,886	1,438,016	3,738,902
12	TIME-THE WEEKLY NEWSMAGAZINE	3,296,763	103,204	3,399,967
13	PREVENTION	2,983,511	413,249	3,396,760
14	TV GUIDE	3,043,289	221,900	3,265,189
15	SPORTS ILLUSTRATED	3,163,869	87,043	3,250,912
16	NEWSWEEK	3,038,797	100,092	3,138,889
17	COSMOPOLITAN	1,048,386	1,867,481	2,915,867
18	PLAYBOY	2,614,677	265,660	2,880,337
19	VIA MAGAZINE	2,836,029	-	2,836,029
20	SOUTHERN LIVING	2,623,325	189,791	2,813,116
21	MAXIM	2,085,058	483,281	2,568,339
22	AMERICAN LEGION MAGAZINE *	2,557,935	-	2,557,935
23	AAA GOING PLACES *	2,544,842	-	2,544,842
24	O, THE OPRAH MAGAZINE	1,548,867	887,836	2,436,703
25	AAA LIVING *	2,426,694	-	2,426,694

* ABC = Audit Bureau of Circulations.

** High proportion of titles' circulation attributed to membership benefits.

Source: www.magazine.org

Plunkett's Entertainment & Media Industry Almanac 2008

Periodical Publishers:
Estimated Sources of Revenue & Expenses, U.S.: 2004-2006

(In Millions of US$; Latest Year Available)

NAICS Code: 51112	2006	2005	2004	Percent Change	
				2006/05	2005/04
Total Operating Revenue	**44,874**	**46,247**	**42,290**	**-3.0**	**9.4**
General interest periodicals	25,111	25,110	23,371	Z	7.4
Subscription & sales	8,220	8,443	8,246	-2.6	2.4
Advertising space	16,891	16,667	15,385	1.3	8.3
Professional & academic periodicals	7,684	8,234	7,640	-6.7	7.8
Subscription & sales	4,328	4,614	4,220	-6.2	9.3
Advertising space	3,356	3,620	3,420	-7.3	5.8
Other periodicals	4,587	4,819	3,677	-4.8	31.1
Subscription & sales	2,283	2,417	2,143	-5.5	12.8
Advertising space	2,304	2,402	2,078	-4.1	15.6
Other operating revenue	7,491	8,086	6,983	-7.4	15.8
Printing services for others	832	936	972	-11.1	-3.7
Licensing of rights to content	405	301	233	34.6	29.2
All other operating revenue	6,254	6,849	5,777	-8.7	18.6
Breakdown of Revenue by Media Type					
Print periodicals	33,777	35,249	32,990	-4.2	6.8
Online periodicals	2,967	2,359	2,037	25.8	15.8
Other media periodicals	638	554	465	15.2	19.1
Operating Expenses					
Total	**36,105**	**37,685**	**34,614**	**-4.2**	**8.9**
Personnel costs	14,342	14,668	13,274	-2.2	10.5
Gross annual payroll	11,719	11,873	10,855	-1.3	9.4
Employer's cost for fringe benefits	2,159	2,282	1,946	-5.4	17.3
Temporary staff & leased employee expense	464	513	473	-9.6	8.5
Expensed materials, parts & supplies	1,368	1,535	1,435	-10.9	7.0
Expensed equipment	171	163	137	4.9	19.0
Expensed purchase of other materials, parts & supplies	1,198	1,372	1,298	-12.7	5.7
Expensed purchased services	7,725	7,537	6,936	2.5	8.7
Expensed purchases of software	174	212	242	-17.9	-12.4
Purchased electricity & fuels (except motor fuels)	115	117	93	-1.7	25.8
Lease & rental payments	1,036	1,104	985	-6.2	12.1
Purchased repair & maintenance	143	164	136	-12.8	20.6
Purchased advertising & promotional services	1,901	1,995	1,801	-4.7	10.8
Purchased printing services	4,356	3,945	3,678	10.4	7.3
Other operating expenses	12,669	13,955	12,969	-9.2	7.6
Depreciation & amortization charges	1,354	1,555	1,412	-12.9	10.1
Governmental taxes & license fees	135	148	139	-8.8	6.5
All other operating expenses	11,180	12,252	11,419	-8.7	7.3

Notes: Estimates are based on data from the 2006 Service Annual Survey and administrative data. Estimates for 2005 and prior years have been revised to reflect historical corrections to individual responses. Dollar volume estimates are published in millions of dollars; consequently, results may not be additive. Estimates have been adjusted using results of the 2002 Economic Census. Estimates cover taxable and tax-exempt firms and are not adjusted for price changes.
Z = Absolute value is less than 0.05.

Source: U.S. Census Bureau
Plunkett's Entertainment & Media Industry Almanac 2008

Newspaper Publishers:
Estimated Sources of Revenue & Expenses, U.S.: 2004-2006

(In Millions of US$; Latest Year Available)

NAICS Code: 51111	2006	2005	2004	Percent Change	
				2006/05	2005/04
Total Operating Revenue	**48,861**	**49,723**	**48,366**	**-1.7**	**2.8**
General newspapers	40,908	41,577	40,569	-1.6	2.5
Subscription & sales	8,658	8,626	8,623	0.4	Z
Advertising space	32,250	32,951	31,946	-2.1	3.1
Specialized newspapers	2,623	2,488	1,792	5.4	38.8
Subscription & sales	S	S	S	S	S
Advertising space	2,241	2,205	2,121	1.6	4.0
Other operating revenue	5,331	5,658	5,386	-5.8	5.1
Printing services	1,257	1,356	1,253	-7.3	8.2
Distribution services	1,971	2,088	2,017	-5.6	3.5
All other operating revenue	2,103	2,214	2,116	-5.0	4.6
Breakdown of Revenue by Media Type					
Print newspapers	40,979	41,550	40,705	-1.4	2.1
Online newspapers	2,128	2,135	1,869	-0.3	14.2
Other media newspapers	423	381	406	11.0	-6.2
Breakdown of Revenue by Advertising Revenue					
Classified advertising	11,354	11,728	11,121	-3.2	5.5
All other advertising	23,137	23,427	22,946	-1.2	2.1
Operating Expenses					
Total	**42,269**	**41,093**	**40,038**	**2.9**	**2.6**
Personnel costs	19,570	19,870	19,451	-1.5	2.2
Gross annual payroll	15,273	15,756	15,433	-3.1	2.1
Employer's cost for fringe benefits	4,056	3,884	3,766	4.4	3.1
Temporary staff & leased employee expense	241	230	251	4.8	-8.4
Expensed materials, parts & supplies	3,969	4,373	4,396	-9.2	-0.5
Expensed equipment	75	72	83	4.2	-13.3
Expensed purchase of other materials, parts & supplies	3,894	4,301	4,313	-9.5	-0.3
Expensed purchased services	3,587	3,313	3,104	8.3	6.7
Expensed purchases of software	96	88	79	9.1	11.4
Purchased electricity & fuels (except motor fuels)	355	340	298	4.4	14.1
Lease & rental payments	587	573	545	2.4	5.1
Purchased repair & maintenance	359	368	369	-2.4	-0.3
Purchased advertising & promotional services	675	670	616	0.7	8.8
Purchased printing services	1,515	1,274	1,198	18.9	6.3
Other operating expenses	15,142	13,537	13,047	11.9	3.8
Depreciation & amortization charges	2,004	1,868	1,849	7.3	1.0
Governmental taxes & license fees	414	386	378	7.3	2.1
All other operating expenses	12,724	11,284	10,820	12.8	4.3

Notes: Estimates are based on data from the 2006 Service Annual Survey and administrative data. Estimates for 2005 and prior years have been revised to reflect historical corrections to individual responses. Dollar volume estimates are published in millions of dollars; consequently, results may not be additive. Estimates have been adjusted using results of the 2002 Economic Census. Estimates cover taxable and tax-exempt firms and are not adjusted for price changes. Z = Absolute value is less than 0.05. D = Estimate in table is withheld to avoid disclosing data of individual companies; data are included in higher level totals.

S = Estimate does not meet publication standards because of high sampling variability (coefficient of variation is greater than 30%) or poor response quality (total quantity response rate is less than 50%). Unpublished estimates derived from this table by subtraction are subject to these same limitations and should not be attributed to the U.S. Census Bureau.

Source: U.S. Census Bureau

Plunkett's Entertainment & Media Industry Almanac 2008

Annual U.S. Newspaper Advertising Expenditures: 1990-2007

(In Millions of US$)

Year	NATIONAL		RETAIL		CLASSIFIED		PRINT TOTAL	
	$	% Change	$	% Change	$	% Change	$	% Change
1990	4,122	4.40%	16,652	0.90%	11,506	-3.50%	32,280	-0.30%
1991	3,924	-4.80%	15,839	-4.90%	10,587	-8.00%	30,349	-6.00%
1992	3,834	-2.30%	16,041	1.30%	10,764	1.70%	30,639	1.00%
1993	3,853	0.50%	16,859	5.10%	11,157	3.70%	31,869	4.00%
1994	4,149	7.70%	17,496	3.80%	12,464	11.70%	34,109	7.00%
1995	4,251	2.50%	18,099	3.40%	13,742	10.30%	36,092	5.80%
1996	4,667	9.80%	18,344	1.40%	15,065	9.60%	38,075	5.50%
1997	5,315	13.90%	19,242	4.90%	16,773	11.30%	41,330	8.50%
1998	5,721	7.70%	20,331	5.70%	17,873	6.60%	43,925	6.30%
1999	6,732	17.70%	20,907	2.80%	18,650	4.30%	46,289	5.40%
2000	7,653	13.70%	21,409	2.40%	19,608	5.10%	48,670	5.10%
2001	7,004	-8.50%	20,679	-3.40%	16,622	-15.20%	44,305	-9.00%
2002	7,210	2.90%	20,994	1.50%	15,898	-4.30%	44,102	-0.50%
2003	7,797	8.10%	21,341	1.70%	15,801	-0.60%	44,939	1.90%
2004	8,083	3.70%	22,012	3.10%	16,608	5.10%	46,703	3.90%
2005	7,910	-2.15%	22,187	0.79%	17,312	4.24%	47,408	1.51%
2006	7,505	-5.12%	22,121	-0.30%	16,986	-1.88%	46,611	-1.68%
2007 1Q	1,688	-2.80%	4,773	-2.20%	3,379	-13.20%	9,840	-6.40%
2007 2Q	1,839	-7.90%	5,241	-6.40%	3,435	-16.40%	10,515	-10.20%
2007 3Q	1,670	-2.50%	5,061	-4.90%	3,416	-17.00%	10,147	-9.00%

	ONLINE TOTAL		PRINT AND ONLINE TOTAL	
	$	% Change	$	% Change
2003	1,216	N/A	46,156	N/A
2004	1,541	26.70%	48,244	4.50%
2005	2,027	31.48%	49,435	2.47%
2006	2,664	31.46%	49,275	-0.32%
2007 1Q	750	22.30%	10,590	-4.80%
2007 2Q	796	19.30%	11,311	-8.60%
2007 3Q	773	21.10%	10,920	-7.40%

Source: Newspaper Association of America

Plunkett's Entertainment & Media Industry Almanac 2008

Book Publishers: Estimated Sources of Revenue, Inventories & Expenses, U.S.: 2004-2006

(In Millions of US$; Latest Year Available)

NAICS Code: 51113	2006	2005	2004	Percent Change 2006/05	Percent Change 2005/04
Total Operating Revenue	**28,192**	**27,994**	**27,904**	**0.7**	**0.3**
Books	24,272	24,239	24,398	0.1	-0.7
Textbooks	10,139	9,919	9,657	2.2	2.7
Children's books	3,094	3,073	3,162	0.7	-2.8
General reference books	1,136	1,144	1,520	-0.7	-24.7
Professional, technical & scholarly books	3,363	3,274	3,799	2.7	-13.8
Adult trade books	6,540	6,829	6,260	-4.2	9.1
Breakdown of Revenue by Media Type					
Print books	22,764	22,883	23,063	-0.5	-0.8
Online books	714	666	659	7.2	1.1
Other media books	795	690	675	15.2	2.2
Inventories at End of the Year					
Total	**4,336**	**4,538**	**4,457**	**-4.5**	**1.8**
Finished goods	3,657	3,791	3,748	-3.5	1.1
Work-in-process	511	574	531	-11.0	8.1
Materials, supplies, fuel, etc.	169	173	178	-2.3	-2.8
Operating Expenses					
Total	**16,268**	**16,754**	**16,024**	**-2.9**	**4.6**
Personnel costs	6,703	6,634	6,581	1.0	0.8
Gross annual payroll	5,336	5,301	5,244	0.7	1.1
Employer's cost for fringe benefits	1,121	1,118	1,125	0.3	-0.6
Temporary staff & leased employee expense	246	215	S	14.4	S
Expensed materials, parts & supplies	465	487	560	-4.5	-13.0
Expensed equipment	225	214	235	5.1	-8.9
Expensed purchase of other materials, parts & supplies	240	273	S	-12.1	S
Expensed purchased services	3,353	3,244	3,019	3.4	7.5
Expensed purchases of software	111	S	S	S	S
Purchased electricity & fuels (except motor fuels)	66	62	65	6.5	-4.6
Lease & rental payments	538	545	571	-1.3	-4.6
Purchased repair & maintenance	110	109	108	0.9	0.9
Purchased advertising & promotional services	911	935	923	-2.6	1.3
Purchased printing services	1,617	1,485	1,243	8.9	19.5
Other operating expenses	5,748	6,389	5,839	-10.0	9.4
Depreciation & amortization charges	1,050	978	899	7.4	8.8
Governmental taxes & license fees	74	80	83	-7.5	-3.6
All other operating expenses	4,624	5,332	4,857	-13.3	9.8

Notes: Estimates are based on data from the 2006 Service Annual Survey and administrative data. Estimates for 2005 and prior years have been revised to reflect historical corrections to individual responses. Dollar volume estimates are published in millions of dollars; consequently, results may not be additive. Estimates have been adjusted using results of the 2002 Economic Census. Estimates cover taxable and tax-exempt firms and are not adjusted for price changes.
S = Estimate does not meet publication standards because of high sampling variability (coefficient of variation is greater than 30%) or poor response quality (total quantity response rate is less than 50%). Unpublished estimates derived from this table by subtraction are subject to these same limitations and should not be attributed to the U.S. Census Bureau.

Source: U.S. Census Bureau
Plunkett's Entertainment & Media Industry Almanac 2008

Quantity of Books Sold, U.S.: 2004-2009

(In Millions)

Type of publication	2004	2005	2006[P]	2007[P]	2008[P]	2009[P]
Total	**2966.2**	**3078.9**	**3150.1**	**3171.2**	**3183.0**	**3228.2**
Trade	1613.1	1689.8	1747.3	1748.1	1747.5	1776.1
Adult	785.8	810.4	828.3	841.8	848.3	861.0
Hardback	396.9	406.4	413.8	419.2	421.0	424.7
Paperback	388.9	404.0	414.5	422.6	427.2	436.3
Juvenile	827.3	879.4	919.0	906.2	899.3	915.1
Hardback	253.4	273.0	274.7	277.4	302.8	279.5
Paperback	574.0	606.4	644.4	628.9	596.5	635.7

Mass market paperbacks, rack sized						
Religious	241.1	255.5	266.9	278.0	288.9	300.0
Hardback	85.3	91.0	97.1	101.2	105.2	109.2
Paperback	155.8	164.5	169.8	176.9	183.7	190.8
Professional	274.0	278.9	282.7	286.7	290.9	295.9
Hardback	97.8	99.2	100.0	101.0	96.9	96.2
Paperback	176.1	179.8	182.7	185.8	194.0	199.7

	2004	2005	2006	2007	2008	2009
University press	24.7	24.5	24.6	24.7	24.6	24.7
Hardback	9.3	9.1	9.2	9.3	9.3	9.3
Paperback	15.4	15.5	15.3	15.4	15.4	15.4
Elementary/High school text	159.5	179.8	181.6	189.6	194.2	199.0
Hardback	56.1	63.2	64.9	67.7	69.4	71.1
Paperback	103.4	116.6	116.8	121.9	124.9	127.9
College text	77.1	76.5	75.9	75.4	74.4	73.8
Hardback	34.2	33.8	33.5	33.3	32.8	32.6
Paperback	42.9	42.7	42.4	42.2	41.6	41.3

Represents net publishers' shipments after returns. Includes all titles released by publishers in the United States and imports which appear under the imprints of American publishers. Multivolume sets, such as encyclopedias, are counted as one unit. Due to changes in methodology and scope, these data are not comparable to those previously published.

P = Projected

Source: Book Industry Study Group, Inc.

Plunkett's Entertainment & Media Industry Almanac 2008

Books Sold: Value of U.S. Domestic Consumer Expenditures: 2004-2009

(In Millions of US$)

Type of publication	2004	2005	2006[P]	2007[P]	2008[P]	2009[P]
Total	**49,146.6**	**51,919.8**	**53,723.8**	**55,546.9**	**57,194.3**	**58,875.2**
Trade	23,394.4	24,571.1	25,362.6	25,992.3	26,553.2	27,086.2
Adult	14,952.1	15,532.4	15,937.2	16,370.1	16,670.0	16,985.4
Hardback	9,036.3	9,387.6	9,631.4	9,904.1	10,095.2	10,330.8
Paperback	5,915.8	6,144.8	6,305.8	6,466.0	6,574.8	6,654.6
Juvenile	5,369.3	5,883.0	6,185.9	6,298.4	6,500.5	6,643.7
Hardback	2,489.0	2,727.1	2,755.3	2,831.4	3,122.1	2,927.4
Paperback	2,880.3	3,155.9	3,430.6	3,467.0	3,378.4	3,716.3
Mass market paperbacks, rack sized	3,073.00	3,155.70	3,239.50	3,323.80	3,382.70	3,457.10
Religious	4104.0	4436.7	4725.7	5013.5	5322.2	5628.5
Hardback	2436.6	2634.1	2847.8	3018.2	3207.2	3391.7
Paperback	1667.4	1802.6	1877.9	1995.3	2115.0	2236.8
Professional	10275.3	10680.4	11046.6	11415.8	11798.1	12192.4
Hardback	6428.0	6695.8	6923.4	7175.8	7428.8	7553.5
Paperback	2791.9	2908.5	3017.5	3112.2	3218.9	3465.5
Subscription reference	1055.4	1076.1	1105.7	1127.8	1150.4	1173.4
University press	547.1	582.3	639.9	655.8	667.4	682.0
Hardback	267.4	279.5	305.8	310.9	315.7	320.5
Paperback	279.7	302.8	334.1	344.9	351.7	361.5
Elementary/High school text	4622.0	5320.0	5507.6	5892.9	6187.6	6493.7
Hardback	2307.3	2654.6	2793.4	2989.0	3138.5	3295.4
Paperback	2314.7	2665.4	2714.2	2903.9	3049.1	3198.3
College text	6203.8	6329.3	6441.4	6576.6	6665.8	6792.4
Hardback	4156.6	4221.5	4289.8	4379.9	4439.3	4523.7
Paperback	2047.2	2107.8	2151.6	2196.7	2226.5	2268.7

Includes all titles released by publishers in the United States and imports which appear under the imprints of American publishers. Due to changes in methodology and scope, these data are not comparable to those previously published.

P = Projected

Source: Book Industry Study Group, Inc.

Plunkett's Entertainment & Media Industry Almanac 2008

Television Broadcasting:
Estimated Sources of Revenue & Expenses, U.S.: 2004-2006

(In Millions of US$; Latest Year Available)

NAICS Code: 51512	2006	2005	2004	Percent Change	
				2006/05	2005/04
Total Operating Revenue	**38,328**	**36,297**	**35,599**	**5.6**	**2.0**
Air time	26,859	25,971	25,892	3.4	0.3
National/regional air time	16,456	16,211	16,233	1.5	-0.1
Local air time	10,403	9,760	9,659	6.6	1.0
Other operating revenue	S	10,326	9,707	S	6.4
Network compensation	S	6,321	5,765	S	9.6
Public & non-commercial programming services	1,550	1,337	1,371	15.9	-2.5
All other operating revenue	3,193	2,668	2,571	19.7	3.8
Operating Expenses					
Total	**29,892**	**28,805**	**27,992**	**3.8**	**2.9**
Personnel costs	7,884	7,570	7,176	4.1	5.5
Gross annual payroll	6,575	6,438	6,108	2.1	5.4
Employer's cost for fringe benefits	1,152	1,008	955	14.3	5.5
Temporary staff & leased employee expense	157	124	113	26.6	9.7
Expensed materials, parts & supplies	219	223	222	-1.8	0.5
Expensed equipment	58	57	61	1.8	-6.6
Expensed purchase of other materials, parts & supplies	161	166	161	-3.0	3.1
Expensed purchased services	2,149	2,003	1,897	7.3	5.6
Expensed purchases of software	47	39	33	20.5	18.2
Purchased electricity & fuels (except motor fuels)	421	343	330	22.7	3.9
Lease & rental payments	490	426	411	15.0	3.6
Purchased repair & maintenance	S	250	244	S	2.5
Purchased advertising & promotional services	888	945	879	-6.0	7.5
Other operating expenses	19,640	19,009	18,698	3.3	1.7
Broadcast rights & music license fees	12,802	12,036	11,710	6.4	2.8
Network compensation fees (networks only)	609	695	658	-12.4	5.6
Depreciation & amortization charges	1,458	1,385	1,413	5.3	-2.0
Governmental taxes & license fees	144	150	177	-4.0	-15.3
All other operating expenses	4,627	4,743	4,741	-2.4	Z

Notes: Estimates are based on data from the 2006 Service Annual Survey and administrative data. Estimates for 2005 and prior years have been revised to reflect historical corrections to individual responses. Dollar volume estimates are published in millions of dollars; consequently, results may not be additive. Estimates have been adjusted using results of the 2002 Economic Census. Estimates cover taxable and tax-exempt firms and are not adjusted for price changes.

S = Estimate does not meet publication standards because of high sampling variability (coefficient of variation is greater than 30%) or poor response quality (total quantity response rate is less than 50%). Unpublished estimates derived from this table by subtraction are subject to these same limitations and should not be attributed to the U.S. Census Bureau.

Z = Absolute value is less than 0.05.

Source: U.S. Census Bureau

Plunkett's Entertainment & Media Industry Almanac 2008

Cable & Other Subscription Programming:
Estimated Sources of Revenue & Expenses, U.S.: 2004-2006

(In Millions of US$; Latest Year Available)

NAICS Code: 5152	2006	2005	2004	Percent Change	
				2006/05	2005/04
Total Operating Revenue	**38,437**	**35,603**	**31,373**	**8.0**	**13.5**
Licensing of rights to broadcast specialty programming protected by copyright	18,266	16,788	15,395	8.8	9.0
Air time	15,185	14,574	12,877	4.2	13.2
Other operating revenue	4,985	4,242	3,100	17.5	36.8
Operating Expenses					
Total	**25,229**	**23,606**	**21,441**	**6.9**	**10.1**
Personnel costs	4,599	4,604	3,986	-0.1	15.5
Gross annual payroll	3,512	3,653	3,159	-3.9	15.6
Employer's cost for fringe benefits	653	623	544	4.8	14.5
Temporary staff & leased employee expense	434	328	283	32.3	15.9
Expensed materials, parts & supplies	318	276	267	15.2	3.4
Expensed equipment	50	55	60	-9.1	-8.3
Expensed purchase of other materials, parts & supplies	268	222	207	20.7	7.2
Expensed purchased services	2,593	2,299	1,977	12.8	16.3
Expensed purchases of software	54	46	39	17.4	17.9
Purchased electricity & fuels (except motor fuels)	52	50	52	4.0	-3.8
Lease & rental payments	463	515	448	-10.1	15.0
Purchased repair & maintenance	96	101	S	-5.0	S
Purchased advertising & promotional services	1,928	1,588	1,329	21.4	19.5
Other operating expenses	17,719	16,426	15,210	7.9	8.0
Program & production costs	12,964	12,051	11,625	7.6	3.7
Depreciation & amortization charges	1,382	1,399	1,369	-1.2	2.2
Governmental taxes & license fees	107	136	124	-21.3	9.7
All other operating expenses	3,267	2,840	2,093	15.0	35.7

Notes: Estimates are based on data from the 2006 Service Annual Survey and administrative data. Estimates for 2005 and prior years have been revised to reflect historical corrections to individual responses. Dollar volume estimates are published in millions of dollars; consequently, results may not be additive. Estimates have been adjusted using results of the 2002 Economic Census. Estimates cover taxable and tax-exempt firms and are not adjusted for price changes.

S = Estimate does not meet publication standards because of high sampling variability (coefficient of variation is greater than 30%) or poor response quality (total quantity response rate is less than 50%). Unpublished estimates derived from this table by subtraction are subject to these same limitations and should not be attributed to the U.S. Census Bureau.

Source: U.S. Census Bureau

Plunkett's Entertainment & Media Industry Almanac 2008

Cable Network Statistics, U.S.: 1986-2007

Average Monthly Price for Expanded Basic Programming Packages		Revenue From Advertising				Revenue From Customers		
		Cable Network Revenue	Local/Spot Revenue	Regional Sports Revenue	Total Ad Revenue	Basic Cable	Premium Cable	Total Customer Revenue
Year	Basic Price	*(In Millions of US$)*						
2007[e]	42.76	20,731	4,752	789	26,939	33,608	6,467	74,716
2006	41.17	18,210	4,296	724	23,757	32,274	6,414	68,233
2005	39.96	15,865	3,978	659	20,968	31,075	6,389	62,267
2004	38.23	13,873	3,807	588	18,602	30,336	5,871	57,600
2003	36.59	12,288	3,354	530	16,406	28,960	5,190	51,300
2002	34.52	10,790	3,294	490	14,718	28,492	5,533	49,427
2001	31.58	10,325	2,860	443	13,715	27,031	5,259	43,518
2000	30.08	10,444	2,879	425	13,802	24,445	4,949	40,855
1999	28.92	8,874	2,667	426	11,976	23,146	4,930	36,919
1998	27.81	7,188	2,233	317	9,738	21,830	4,857	33,503
1997	26.48	5,901	1,925	261	8,087	20,405	4,823	30,493
1996	24.41	4,911	1,662	225	6,799	18,395	4,757	27,706
1995	23.07	3,999	1,433	201	5,633	16,860	4,607	25,421
1994	21.62	3,293	1,204	169	4,666	15,170	4,394	23,134
1993	19.39	2,835	978	164	3,977	13,528	4,810	22,843
1992	19.08	2,426	818	140	3,384	12,433	5,108	21,079
1991	18.10	2,100	710	118	2,928	11,418	4,968	19,426
1990	16.78	1,821	634	103	2,557	10,174	4,882	17,582
1989	15.21	1,397	496	74	1,967	8,671	4,663	15,378
1988	13.86	1,135	374	52	1,561	7,345	4,308	13,409
1987	12.18	891	268	33	1,192	6,016	3,959	11,563
1986	10.67	748	195	22	965	4,887	3,767	9,955

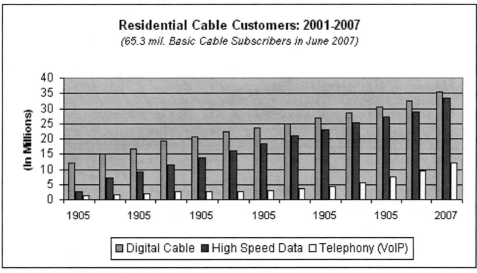

Residential Cable Customers: 2001-2007
(65.3 mil. Basic Cable Subscribers in June 2007)

Digital Cable ■ High Speed Data □ Telephony (VoIP)

e = Estimates

Sources: SNL Kagan; National Cable & Telecommunications Association (NCTA)

Plunkett's Entertainment & Media Industry Almanac 2008

Top 25 U.S. Cable MSOs* as of June 2007

Rank	MSO	Subscribers
1	Comcast Cable Communications	24,141,000
2	Time Warner Cable	13,391,000
3	Cox Communications	5,424,000
4	Charter Communications &	5,376,800
5	Cablevision Systems	3,139,000
6	Bright House Networks LLC (e)	2,327,100
7	Suddenlink Communications (e)	1,416,800
8	Mediacom Communications Corp.	1,344,000
9	Insight Communications	1,341,000
10	CableOne	696,700
11	WideOpenWest (e)	361,400
12	RCN Corp.	355,000
13	Bresnan Communications (e)	294,900
14	Service Electric (e)	288,700
15	Atlantic Broadband	285,700
16	Armstrong Group of Co.	232,500
17	Knology Holdings &	221,800
18	Midcontinent Communications &	199,100
19	Pencor Services (e)	183,400
20	Millennium Digital Media (e)	157,600
21	Buckeye CableSystem	147,300
22	MetroCast Cablevision	143,200
23	General Communication	142,200
24	Northland Communications Corporation	139,800
25	MidOcean Ptnrs. & Crestview Ptnrs.(e)	138,900

Note: Unless otherwise noted, counts include owned and managed subscribers.

* MSO = Multi-System Operator.

e = Estimate.

& = Counts include recent sale or acquisition.

Source: SNL Kagan. All rights reserved. Reprinted with permission (data released June 29, 2007); Data from Suddenlink Communications as of June 2007

Plunkett's Entertainment & Media Industry Almanac 2008

Number & Percent of U.S. Households (HH) with TV, Wired Cable, Pay Cable & VCRs: 1975-2007

(In Thousands)

Year	TV Households	% of Total HH	Wired Cable HH	% of TV HH	Pay Cable HH	% of TV HH	VCR HH	% of TV HH
1975	68,500	97.1	8,600	12.6%	140	0.2%	-	-
1976	69,600	97.4	10,100	14.5%	470	0.7%	-	-
1977	71,200	97.4	11,300	15.9%	980	1.4%	-	-
1978	72,900	97.6	12,500	17.1%	1,600	2.2%	200	0.3%
1979	74,500	97.7	13,600	18.3%	3,100	4.2%	400	0.5%
1980	76,300	97.9	15,200	19.9%	5,200	6.8%	840	1.1%
1981	79,900	98.1	17,830	22.3%	8,100	10.1%	1,440	1.8%
1982	81,500	98.1	24,290	29.8%	12,600	15.5%	2,530	3.1%
1983	83,300	98.1	28,320	34.0%	16,100	19.4%	4,580	5.5%
1984	83,800	98.1	32,930	39.3%	19,820	23.7%	8,967	10.7%
1985	84,900	98.1	36,340	42.8%	21,840	25.7%	17,744	20.9%
1986	85,900	98.1	39,160	45.6%	22,840	26.6%	30,924	36.0%
1987	87,400	98.1	41,690	47.7%	22,850	26.1%	42,564	48.7%
1988	88,600	98.1	43,790	49.4%	24,290	27.4%	51,388	58.1%
1989	90,400	98.2	47,770	52.8%	26,100	28.9%	58,398	64.6%
1990	92,100	98.2	51,900	56.4%	27,120	29.4%	63,181	68.6%
1991	93,100	98.2	54,860	58.9%	27,040	29.0%	66,939	71.9%
1992*	92,100	98.3	55,490	60.2%	25,990	28.2%	69,075	75.0%
1993	93,100	98.3	57,200	61.4%	25,850	27.8%	71,780	77.1%
1994	94,200	98.3	58,750	62.4%	26,070	27.7%	74,420	79.0%
1995	95,400	98.3	60,460	63.4%	27,100	28.4%	77,270	81.0%
1996	95,900	98.3	62,580	65.3%	30,360	31.7%	78,830	82.2%
1997	97,000	98.4	64,470	66.5%	31,620	32.6%	81,670	84.2%
1998	98,000	98.3	65,810	67.2%	34,090	34.8%	82,910	84.6%
1999	99,400	98.2	67,120	67.5%	39,100	39.3%	84,140	84.6%
2000	100,800	98.2	68,550	68.0%	31,760**	31.5%	85,810	85.1%
2001	102,200	98.2	69,490	68.0%	34,100	33.4%	88,120	86.2%
2002	105,500	98.2	73,230	69.4%	41,900	39.7%	96,190	91.2%
2003	106,700	98.2	74,430	69.8%	40,760	38.2%	97,630	91.5%
2004	108,400	98.2	73,860	68.1%	39,950	36.9%	98,400	90.8%
2005	110,200	98.2	73,930	67.5%	35,120	32.0%	98,860	90.2%
2006	111,400	98.2	73,210	66.4%	34,040	30.9%	97,690	88.6%
2007	112,800	98.2	71,390	64.1%	35,580	31.9%	95,210	85.5%

Note: Cable HH data is based on Wired Cable Homes only, and does not include alternative delivery systems (ADS).

* Reflects adjustments to conform to the 1990 census.

** Decline due to reclassification of the Disney channel.

Source: Nielsen Media Research

Plunkett's Entertainment & Media Industry Almanac 2008

Percent of U.S. Households with
Alternative Broadcast Delivery Systems: 1998-2007

Year	Quarter	SMATV	MMDS	Satellite Dish	DBS	Total ADS
1998	1st	1.1	1.0	1.5	4.7	8.3
	2nd	0.8	1.1	1.4	5.3	8.7
	3rd	0.7	1.1	1.4	5.7	8.8
	4th	0.8	1.0	1.6	5.9	9.1
1999	1st	0.9	0.8	1.4	6.2	9.2
	2nd	0.7	0.9	1.3	6.6	9.5
	3rd	0.7	0.9	1.1	6.7	9.3
	4th	0.7	0.8	0.9	6.9	9.3
2000	1st	0.8	0.7	1.0	7.4	9.9
	2nd	0.8	0.6	1.1	7.8	10.3
	3rd	0.8	0.6	1.2	9.1	11.5
	4th	0.8	0.6	1.0	9.2	11.4
2001	1st	0.8	0.6	0.8	9.8	11.8
	2nd	0.7	0.5	0.7	11.0	12.8
	3rd	0.6	0.5	0.7	12.0	13.6
	4th	0.6	0.4	0.7	12.4	14.1
2002	1st	0.7	0.4	0.5	13.2	14.8
	2nd	0.6	0.3	0.5	13.7	15.0
	3rd	0.6	0.3	0.5	14.2	15.4
	4th	0.6	0.3	0.5	15.1	16.3
2003	1st	0.6	0.3	0.4	15.6	16.7
	2nd	0.7	0.2	0.5	15.8	17.0
	3rd	0.5	0.2	0.3	16.4	17.3
	4th	0.5	0.2	0.4	17.3	18.2
2004	1st	0.5	0.1	0.5	17.6	18.6
	2nd	0.5	0.1	0.4	18.0	18.9
	3rd	0.5	0.1	0.3	18.0	18.8
	4th	0.5	0.0	0.3	18.6	19.3
2005	1st	0.4	0.0	0.2	19.1	19.6
	2nd	0.4	0.0	0.2	19.9	20.4
	3rd	0.4	0.0	0.2	19.9	20.4
	4th	0.5	0.1	0.2	20.2	20.8
2006	1st	0.5	0.1	0.1	20.9	21.5
	2nd	0.5	0.1	0.1	22.0	22.6
	3rd	0.5	0.1	0.1	22.9	23.5
	4th	0.5	0.0	0.1	23.8	24.3
2007	1st	0.5	0.0	0.1	25.1	25.6

SMATV = Satellite Master Antenna: In complexes or hotels, signals received via satellite, and distributed by coaxial cable.

MMDS = Microwave Multi Distribution System, "Wireless Cable": Distributes signals by microwave. Home receiver picks up signal, then distributes via internal wiring.

Satellite Dish (C-Band/KU Band), "Big Dish": Household receives transmissions from satellite, via a 1 to 3 meter dish.

DBS = Direct Broadcast Satellite: Satellite service delivers directly via household's own small (usually 18") dish.

Source: Nielsen Media Research

Plunkett's Entertainment & Media Industry Almanac 2008

Motion Picture & Sound Recording Industries: Estimated Revenue & Inventories, U.S.: 2004-2006

(In Millions of US$; Latest Year Available)	2006	2005	2004	Percent Change	
				2006/05	2005/04
Motion Picture & Sound Recording (NAICS Code 512)					
Total Operating Revenue	**94,400**	**92,231**	**88,269**	**2.4**	**4.5**
Total Inventories at End of Year	27,352	25,338	25,131	7.9	0.8
Finished goods	21,264	18,970	18,938	12.1	0.2
Work-in-process	5,816	6,115	5,965	-4.9	2.5
Materials, supplies, fuel, etc.	272	256	230	6.3	11.3
Motion Picture & Video Industries (NAICS Code 5121)					
Total Operating Revenue	**73,241**	**73,503**	**71,774**	**-0.4**	**2.4**
Total Inventories at End of Year	26,757	24,780	24,627	8.0	0.6
Finished goods	20,774	18,504	18,506	12.3	Z
Work-in-process	5,790	6,099	5,952	-5.1	2.5
Materials, supplies, fuel, etc.	194	180	170	7.8	5.9
Sound Recording Industries (NAICS Code 5122)					
Total Operating Revenue	**21,159**	**18,728**	**16,495**	**13.0**	**13.5**
Total Inventories at End of Year	595	558	504	6.6	10.7
Finished goods	490	466	432	5.2	7.9
Work-in-process	S	16	14	S	14.3
Materials, supplies, fuel, etc.	78	76	60	2.6	26.7

Notes: Estimates are based on data from the 2006 Service Annual Survey and administrative data. Estimates for 2005 and prior years have been revised to reflect historical corrections to individual responses. Dollar volume estimates are published in millions of dollars; consequently, results may not be additive. Estimates have been adjusted using results of the 2002 Economic Census. Estimates cover taxable and tax-exempt firms and are not adjusted for price changes.
S = Estimate does not meet publication standards because of high sampling variability (coefficient of variation is greater than 30%) or poor response quality (total quantity response rate is less than 50%). Unpublished estimates derived from this table by subtraction are subject to these same limitations and should not be attributed to the U.S. Census Bureau.
Z = Absolute value is less than 0.05.

Source: U.S. Census Bureau

Plunkett's Entertainment & Media Industry Almanac 2008

Motion Picture & Video Production & Distribution:
Estimated Sources of Revenue & Expenses, U.S.: 2004-2006

(In Millions of US$; Latest Year Available)

NAICS Code: 5121X	2006	2005	2004	Percent Change	
				2006/05	2005/04
Total Operating Revenue	**57,770**	**58,487**	**56,605**	**-1.2**	**3.3**
Domestic licensing of rights to motion picture films	13,801	12,890	12,538	7.1	2.8
Domestic licensing of rights to television programs	6,981	7,918	9,738	-11.8	-18.7
International licensing of rights to motion picture films	7,691	7,458	5,938	3.1	25.6
International licensing of rights to television programs	3,475	3,260	2,988	6.6	9.1
Audiovisual works speculatively produced for outright sale	S	S	S	S	S
Contract production of audiovisual works	5,018	4,676	4,750	7.3	-1.6
Domestic licensing of rights to others to distribute audiovisual works	2,597	2,623	2,960	-1.0	-11.4
International licensing of rights to others to distribute audiovisual works	S	1,148	1,015	S	13.1
Sale of audiovisual works for the wholesale, retail, and rental markets	7,843	8,516	6,803	-7.9	25.2
Other production services	5,206	5,506	5,354	-5.4	2.8
Merchandise licensing	448	444	589	0.9	-24.6
All other operating revenue	3,338	3,532	3,454	-5.5	2.3
Operating Expenses					
Total	**49,152**	**48,952**	**48,277**	**0.4**	**1.4**
Personnel costs	13,731	13,314	11,778	3.1	13.0
Gross annual payroll	12,189	11,805	10,354	3.3	14.0
Employer's cost for fringe benefits	961	948	942	1.4	0.6
Temporary staff & leased employee expense	582	560	482	3.9	16.2
Expensed materials, parts & supplies	790	741	748	6.6	-0.9
Expensed equipment	137	117	94	17.1	24.5
Expensed purchase of other materials, parts & supplies	653	623	654	4.8	-4.7
Expensed purchased services	6,994	6,668	6,809	4.9	-2.1
Expensed purchases of software	57	83	59	-31.3	40.7
Purchased electricity & fuels (except motor fuels)	72	67	72	7.5	-6.9
Lease & rental payments	1,579	1,406	1,353	12.3	3.9
Purchased repair & maintenance	202	202	211	Z	-4.3
Purchased advertising & promotional services	5,084	4,910	5,114	3.5	-4.0
Other operating expenses	27,638	28,199	28,942	-2.0	-2.6
Depreciation & amortization charges	2,411	2,206	3,149	9.3	-29.9
Governmental taxes & license fees	1,245	1,229	1,156	1.3	6.3
All other operating expenses	23,982	24,765	24,637	-3.2	0.5

Notes: Estimates are based on data from the 2006 Service Annual Survey and administrative data. Estimates for 2005 and prior years have been revised to reflect historical corrections to individual responses. Dollar volume estimates are published in millions of dollars; consequently, results may not be additive. Estimates have been adjusted using results of the 2002 Economic Census. Estimates cover taxable and tax-exempt firms and are not adjusted for price changes.

S = Estimate does not meet publication standards because of high sampling variability (coefficient of variation is greater than 30%) or poor response quality (total quantity response rate is less than 50%). Unpublished estimates derived from this table by subtraction are subject to these same limitations and should not be attributed to the U.S. Census Bureau.

Z = Absolute value is less than 0.05.

Source: U.S. Census Bureau

Plunkett's Entertainment & Media Industry Almanac 2008

Number of U.S. Movie Screens & Total Admissions: 1987-2006

(Latest Year Available)

Year	Indoor Screens	Drive-In Screens	Total Screens	Admissions (In Billions)
1987	20,595	2,084	22,679	1.09
1988	21,632	1,497	23,129	1.08
1989	21,907	1,014	22,921	1.26
1990	22,904	910	23,814	1.19
1991	23,740	899	24,639	1.14
1992	24,344	870	25,214	1.17
1993	24,789	837	25,626	1.24
1994	25,830	859	26,689	1.29
1995	26,995	848	27,843	1.26
1996	28,905	826	29,731	1.34
1997	31,050	815	31,865	1.39
1998	33,418	750	34,168	1.48
1999	36,448	683	37,131	1.47
2000	35,567	683	36,280	1.42
2001	34,490	683	35,173	1.49
2002	35,170	666	35,836	1.63
2003	35,361	634	35,995	1.57
2004	36,012	640	36,652	1.53
2005	37,092	648	37,740	1.40
2006	37,776	649	38,415	1.45

Indoor screen counts are for the last day of each year. Because many drive-ins are closed for the winter on Dec. 31, drive-in screen counts for each year are tallied the previous summer.

Figures do not include Puerto Rico screens.

Source: National Association of Theater Owners (NATO)

Plunkett's Entertainment & Media Industry Almanac 2008

Internet Publishing & Broadcasting:
Estimated Sources of Revenue & Expenses, U.S.: 2004-2006

(In Millions of US$; Latest Year Available)

NAICS Code: 516	2006	2005	2004	% Change 06/05
Operating Revenue				
Total Operating Revenue	**10,612**	**10,334**	**8,695**	**2.7**
Publishing & broadcasting of content on the Internet	5,889	5,307	4,416	11.0
Online advertising space	2,221	1,979	1,594	12.2
Licensing of rights to use intellectual property	506	422	393	19.9
All other operating revenue	1,997	2,640	2,268	-24.4
Breakdown of Revenue by Customer Type				
Government	S	S	341	S
Business firms & not-for-profit organizations	7,185	7,367	6,260	-2.5
Household consumers & individual users	2,783	2,491	2,094	11.7
Operating Expenses				
Total	**8,342**	**8,197**	**7,011**	**1.8**
Personnel costs	3,782	3,899	3,320	-3.0
Gross annual payroll	3,095	3,244	2,696	-4.6
Employer's cost for fringe benefits	473	462	434	2.4
Temporary staff & leased employee expense	214	193	190	10.9
Expensed materials, parts & supplies (not for resale)	247	249	211	-0.8
Expensed equipment	94	93	90	1.1
Expensed purchase of other materials, parts, & supplies	152	156	121	-2.6
Expensed purchased services	1,678	1,603	1,298	4.7
Expensed purchases of software	216	144	80	50.0
Purchased electricity & fuels (except motor fuels)	18	16	15	12.5
Lease & rental payments	271	276	278	-1.8
Purchased repair & maintenance	87	89	96	-2.2
Purchased advertising & promotional services	1,086	1,078	829	0.7
Other operating expenses	2,636	2,446	2,181	7.8
Depreciation & amortization charges	682	643	694	6.1
Governmental taxes & license fees	60	57	48	5.3
All other operating expenses	1,894	1,747	1,439	8.4

Notes: Estimates are based on data from the 2006 Service Annual Survey & administrative data. Estimates for 2005 & prior years have been revised to reflect historical corrections to individual responses. Dollar volume estimates are published in millions of dollars; consequently, results may not be additive. Estimates have been adjusted using results of the 2002 Economic Census. Estimates cover taxable & tax-exempt firms & are not adjusted for price changes.

S = Estimate does not meet publication standards because of high sampling variability (coefficient of variation is greater than 30%) or poor response quality (total quantity response rate is less than 50%). Unpublished estimates derived from this table by subtraction are subject to these same limitations & should not be attributed to the U.S. Census Bureau.

Source: U.S. Census Bureau

Plunkett's Entertainment & Media Industry Almanac 2008

Number of Business & Residential High Speed Internet Lines, U.S.: 2000-2006

(Latest Year Available)

Types of Technology[1]	Dec-00	Dec-01	Dec-02	Dec-03	Dec-04	June-05	Dec-05	Jun-06	Dec-06
ADSL	1,977,101	3,947,808	6,471,716	9,509,442	13,817,280	16,316,309	19,515,483	22,575,010	25,417,359
SDSL & Traditional Wireline	1,021,291	1,078,597	1,216,208	1,305,070	1,468,566	898,468	878,973	948,160	1,031,781
SDSL	-	-	-	-	-	411,731	368,782	337,438	344,510
Traditional Wireline	-	-	-	-	-	486,737	510,191	610,722	687,271
Cable Modem	3,582,874	7,059,598	11,369,087	16,446,322	21,357,400	24,017,442	26,558,206	28,861,965	32,097,223
Fiber[2]	63,206	91,921	108,541	116,390	159,653	315,651	448,257	700,083	1,030,119
Satellite & Wireless	112,405	212,610	276,067	367,118	549,621	965,068	3,812,655	11,872,309	22,966,393
Satellite	-	-	-	-	-	376,837	426,928	495,365	571,980
Fixed Wireless	-	-	-	-	-	208,695	257,431	360,976	484,073
Mobile Wireless	-	-	-	-	-	379,536	3,128,296	11,015,968	21,910,340
Power Line & Other	-	-	-	-	-	4,872	4,571	5,208	4,776
Total Lines	**6,756,877**	**12,390,534**	**19,441,619**	**27,744,342**	**37,352,520**	**42,517,810**	**51,218,145**	**64,962,735**	**82,547,651**

Note: High-speed lines are connections to end-user locations that deliver services at speeds exceeding 200 kbps in at least one direction. Advanced services lines, which are a subset of high-speed lines, are connections that deliver services at speeds exceeding 200 kbps in both directions. Line counts presented in this report are not adjusted for the number of persons at a single end-user location who have access to, or who use, the Internet-access services that are delivered over the high-speed connection to that location. For data through December 2004, only those providers with at least 250 lines per state were required to file.

[1] The mutually exclusive types of technology are, respectively: Asymmetric digital subscriber line (ADSL) technologies, which provide speeds in one direction greater than speeds in the other direction; symmetric digital subscriber line (SDSL) technologies; traditional wireline technologies "other" than ADSL and SDSL, including traditional telephone company high-speed services that provide equivalent functionality, and also Ethernet service if delivered to the subscriber's location over copper (as opposed to optical fiber) plant; cable modem, including the typical hybrid fiber-coax (HFC) architecture of upgraded cable TV systems; optical fiber to the subscriber's premises (e.g., Fiber-to-the-Home, or FTTH); satellite and fixed and mobile terrestrial wireless systems, which use radio spectrum to communicate with a radio transmitter; and electric power line.

[2] Fiber line counts included electric power line through December 2004. The June 2005 fiber counts reflect a downward correction by one or more filers. Fiber line counts prior to June 2005 have been adjusted to take into account this downward correction.

Source: U.S. Federal Communications Bureau (FCC)

Plunkett's Entertainment & Media Industry Almanac 2008

Number of Residential High Speed Internet Lines, U.S.: 2000-2006

(Latest Year Available)

Types of Technology[1]	Dec-00	Dec-01	Dec-02	Dec-03	Dec-04	June-05	Dec-05	Jun-06	Dec-06
ADSL	1,594,879	3,615,989	5,529,241	8,909,027	13,119,326	14,442,823	17,370,508	20,143,255	22,773,133
SDSL & Traditional Wireline	176,520	139,660	213,489	289,764	419,215	159,489	129,444	112,043	117,469
SDSL	-	-	-	-	-	153,978	122,220	102,631	104,773
Traditional Wireline	-	-	-	-	-	5,511	7,224	9,412	12,696
Cable Modem	3,294,546	7,050,709	11,342,512	16,416,364	21,270,158	23,578,060	25,714,461	28,068,716	31,230,519
Fiber[2]	1,994	4,139	14,692	19,830	34,959	83,293	213,479	442,027	758,137
Satellite & Wireless	102,432	194,897	256,978	341,864	422,623	428,367	532,704	1,839,368	3,359,952
Satellite	-	-	-	-	-	265,017	320,142	382,047	455,936
Fixed Wireless	-	-	-	-	-	160,775	203,179	301,153	424,127
Mobile Wireless	-	-	-	-	-	2,574	9,384	1,156,168	2,479,889
Power Line & Other	-	-	-	-	-	4,447	4,550	5,093	4,711
Total Lines	**5,170,371**	**11,005,396**	**17,356,912**	**25,976,850**	**35,266,281**	**38,696,480**	**43,965,147**	**50,610,502**	**58,243,921**

Note: High-speed lines are connections to end-user locations that deliver services at speeds exceeding 200 kbps in at least one direction. Advanced services lines, which are a subset of high-speed lines, are connections that deliver services at speeds exceeding 200 kbps in both directions. Line counts presented in this report are not adjusted for the number of persons at a single end-user location who have access to, or who use, the Internet-access services that are delivered over the high-speed connection to that location. For data through December 2004, only those providers with at least 250 lines per state were required to file. Small business lines were included in totals through December 2004.

[1] The mutually exclusive types of technology are, respectively: Asymmetric digital subscriber line (ADSL) technologies, which provide speeds in one direction greater than speeds in the other direction; symmetric digital subscriber line (SDSL) technologies; traditional wireline technologies "other" than ADSL and SDSL, including traditional telephone company high-speed services that provide equivalent functionality, and also Ethernet service if delivered to the subscriber's location over copper (as opposed to optical fiber) plant; cable modem, including the typical hybrid fiber-coax (HFC) architecture of upgraded cable TV systems; optical fiber to the subscriber's premises (e.g., Fiber-to-the-Home, or FTTH); satellite and fixed and mobile terrestrial wireless systems, which use radio spectrum to communicate with a radio transmitter; and electric power line.
[2] Fiber line counts included electric power line through December 2004. The June 2005 fiber counts reflect a downward correction by one or more filers. Fiber line counts prior to June 2005 have been adjusted to take into account this downward correction.

Source: U.S. Federal Communications Commission (FCC)

Plunkett's Entertainment & Media Industry Almanac 2008

Total Global Music Sales by Market:
First Half 2007

(In Millions of US$)

Country	US$	Local Currency		% Change	% Digital
US	2,486	USD	2,486	-11%	29%
Japan	1,611	JPY	193,431	-3%	14%
UK	740	GBD	378	-12%	11%
Germany	608	EUR	456	-7%	7%
France	446	EUR	334	-15%	7%
Canada	170	CAD	192	-18%	12%
Australia	158	AUD	196	-17%	10%
Italy	136	EUR	102	-17%	9%
Russia	130	RUB	3,380	-27%	0%
Spain	122	EUR	91	-12%	10%
Netherlands	101	EUR	76	-12%	5%
Switzerland	83	CHF	102	0%	
Mexico	80	MXP	874	-21%	8%
Belgium	79	EUR	60	2%	14%
South Korea	71	KRW	66,260	6%	63%
South Africa	60	ZAR	430	12%	2%
Austria	59	EUR	44	-2%	8%
India	55	INR	2,338	10%	12%
Brazil	54	BRL	111	-53%	10%
Sweden	54	SEK	374	-11%	8%
Other	551			-2%	13%
Total	**7,853**			**-9%**	**17%**

Notes: Physical sales include: audio formats (singles, LPs, cassettes, CDs, DVD Audio, SACD, MiniDisc) and music video formats (DVD, VHS, VCD). Digital sales include: single track downloads, album downloads, music video online downloads, streams, master recording ringtones, full track audio download to mobile, ringback tunes, music video downloads to mobile and subscription income. Excluded from these figures are monophonic and polyphonic ringtones and non-music content. Figures were collected from IFPI members (physical sales), major record companies (digital sales) and include an estimate for non-reported sales, effectively representing 100% of the market. Growths are based on fixed US$ values using IMF average monthly exchange rates. IFPI figures represent sales of recorded music in physical and digital formats. IFPI does not track revenue streams such as licensing income, synchronization or revenues generated from advertising-supported business models. Publicly reported national statistics are available on IFPI's website (statistics page).

Source: International Federation of the Phonographic Industry (IFPI)

Plunkett's Entertainment & Media Industry Almanac 2008

Estimated Export Revenue for Information Sector Firms, U.S.: 2004-2006

(In Millions of US$; Latest Year Available)

NAICS Code	Kind of business	2006	2005	2004	Percent Change 2006/05	Percent Change 2005/04
51	**Information**	**41,308**	**43,194**	**41,324**	**-4.4**	**4.5**
511	Publishing industries (except Internet)	17,782	17,516	16,612	1.5	5.4
5111	Newspaper, periodical, book, and directory publishers	2,037	2,515	2,083	-19.0	20.7
51111	Newspaper publishers	S	49	63	S	-22.2
51112	Periodical publishers	813	S	1,002	S	S
51113	Book publishers	686	612	624	12.1	-1.9
51114	Directory and mailing list publishers	328	305	244	7.5	25.0
51119	Other publishers	120	97	150	23.7	-35.3
511191	Greeting card publishers	40	46	76	-13.0	-39.5
511199	All other publishers	80	51	74	56.9	-31.1
5112	Software publishers	15,745	15,001	14,529	5.0	3.2
512	Motion picture and sound recording industries	14,838	14,894	14,627	-0.4	1.8
5121	Motion picture and video industries	14,700	14,757	14,487	-0.4	1.9
5121x	Motion picture and video production and distribution[1]	14,559	14,629	14,390	-0.5	1.7
5122	Sound recording industries	138	137	140	0.7	-2.1
515	Broadcasting (except Internet)	267	315	245	-15.2	28.6
5152	Cable and other subscription programming	228	292	224	-21.9	30.4
516	Internet publishing and broadcasting	142	123	148	15.4	-16.9
517	Telecommunications	2,290	5,273	5,726	-56.6	-7.9
5171	Wired telecommunications carriers	S	2,674	3,348	S	-20.1
5172	Wireless telecommunications carriers (except satellite)	S	507	409	S	24.0
517212	Cellular and other wireless telecommunications	414	498	399	-16.9	24.8
5174	Satellite telecommunications	D	1,631	1,608	D	1.4
5175	Cable and other program distribution	D	193	140	D	37.9
518	Internet service providers, web search portals & data processing svcs.	4,293	3,667	2,759	17.1	32.9
5181	Internet service providers & web search portals	2,357	1,559	882	51.2	76.8
518111	Internet service providers	D	S	S	D	S
518112	Web search portals	D	1,265	705	D	79.4
5182	Data processing, hosting & related services	1,936	2,108	1,877	-8.2	12.3
519	Other information services	1,696	1,406	1,207	20.6	16.5
51911	News syndicates	237	243	224	-2.5	8.5
51912	Libraries and archives	14	13	13	7.7	Z
51919	All other information services	1,445	1,150	970	25.7	18.6

Notes: Estimates are based on data from the 2006 Service Annual Survey and administrative data. Estimates for 2005 and prior years have been revised to reflect historical corrections to individual responses. Dollar volume estimates are published in millions of dollars; consequently, results may not be additive. Estimates have been adjusted using results of the 2002 Economic Census. Estimates cover taxable and tax-exempt firms and are not adjusted for price changes.

S = Estimate does not meet publication standards because of high sampling variability (coefficient of variation is greater than 30%) or poor response quality (total quantity response rate is less than 50%). Unpublished estimates derived from this table by subtraction are subject to these same limitations and should not be attributed to the U.S. Census Bureau.

D = Estimate in table is withheld to avoid disclosing data of individual companies; data are included in higher level totals.

Z = Absolute value is less than 0.05.

[1]Includes NAICS 51211 (motion picture and video production) and NAICS 51212 (motion picture and video distribution).

Source: U.S. Census Bureau

Plunkett's Entertainment & Media Industry Almanac 2008

U.S. Employment in Entertainment & Media Occupations: May 2006

(Latest Year Available)

Occupation Title	Number Employed[1]	Median Hourly	Mean Hourly	Mean Annual[2]	Mean RSE[3]
Art Directors	31,030	$32.74	$37.70	$78,420	1.10%
Multi-Media Artists & Animators	26,260	$24.69	$27.90	$58,030	2.80%
Fashion Designers	15,670	$30.10	$33.30	$69,270	3.10%
Set & Exhibit Designers	8,320	$20.11	$21.93	$45,620	2.00%
Actors	51,880	$11.61	$21.84	NA	4.90%
Producers & Directors	63,840	$27.07	$34.72	$72,210	3.20%
Dancers	16,010	$9.55	$13.86	NA	3.70%
Choreographers	16,340	$16.67	$18.42	$38,320	2.60%
Music Directors & Composers	9,470	$19.11	$25.63	$53,320	6.10%
Musicians & Singers	46,600	$19.73	$27.51	NA	3.40%
Radio & Television Announcers	40,020	$11.69	$17.36	$36,120	2.30%
Broadcast News Analysts	6,770	$22.46	$32.17	$66,910	2.20%
Reporters & Correspondents	53,060	$16.09	$20.14	$41,900	1.40%
Editors	100,170	$22.60	$26.50	$53,220	0.90%
Technical Writers	45,330	$27.91	$29.25	$60,850	0.70%
Writers & Authors	43,260	$23.38	$27.93	$58,080	1.90%
Interpreters & Translators	30,910	$17.10	$19.11	$39,750	1.30%
Audio & Video Equipment Technicians	40,360	$16.75	$18.61	$38,710	1.10%
Broadcast Technicians	32,070	$14.75	$17.09	$35,540	1.30%
Radio Operators	1,220	$18.22	$18.69	$38,870	2.70%
Sound Engineering Technicians	14,080	$20.68	$24.16	$50,260	2.30%
Photographers	60,300	$12.58	$15.30	$31,830	1.40%
Camera Operators, Television, Video, & Motion Picture	22,230	$19.26	$22.19	$46,150	3.80%
Film & Video Editors	17,380	$22.44	$27.93	$58,100	3.10%

[1] Estimates do not include self-employed workers.

[2] Annual wages have been calculated by multiplying the hourly mean wage by a "year-round, full-time" hours figure of 2,080 hours; for those occupations where there is not an hourly mean wage published, the annual wage has been directly calculated from the reported survey data.

[3] The relative standard error (RSE) is a measure of the reliability of a survey statistic. The smaller the relative standard error, the more precise the estimate.

NA = Wages for some occupations that do not generally work year-round, full time, are reported either as hourly wages or annual salaries depending on how they are typically paid.

Source: U.S. Bureau of Labor Statistics

Plunkett's Entertainment & Media Industry Almanac 2008

Chapter 3

IMPORTANT ENTERTAINMENT & MEDIA INDUSTRY CONTACTS

I. Advertising/Marketing Associations

Advertising Club, The
235 Park Ave. S., 6th Fl.
New York, NY 10003-1450 US
Phone: 212-533-8080
Fax: 212-533-1929
Web Address: www.theadvertisingclub.org
The Advertising Club strives to elevate the understanding of marketing and advertising communications in New York by providing a forum for members of the industry to address common interests.

Advertising Research Foundation (ARF)
432 Park Ave. S
New York, NY 10016 US
Phone: 212-751-5656
E-mail Address: *info@thearf.org*
Web Address: www.thearf.org
The Advertising Research Foundation (ARF), a
nonprofit corporate-membership association, is a
leading professional organization in the fields of
advertising, marketing and media research.

Advertising Women of New York (AWNY)
25 W. 45th St., Ste. 403
New York, NY 10036 US
Phone: 212-221-7969
Fax: 212-221-8296
E-mail Address: *awny@awny.org*
Web Address: www.awny.org
Advertising Women of New York (AWNY) provides
a forum for personal and professional growth, serves
as a catalyst for the advancement of women in the
communications field and promotes and supports
philanthropic endeavors through the AWNY
Foundation. The web site also provides content from
Women Executives in Public Relations (WERP),
such as its a dynamic job board.

American Advertising Federation, Inc. (AAF)
1101 Vermont Ave. NW, Ste. 500
Washington, DC 20005-6306 US
Phone: 202-898-0089
Fax: 202-898-0159
E-mail Address: *aaf@aaf.org*
Web Address: www.aaf.org
The American Advertising Federation, Inc. (AAF)
protects and promotes the well-being of advertising
through a nationally coordinated network of
advertisers, agencies, media companies, local
advertising clubs and college chapters.

**American Association of Advertising Agencies
(AAAA)**
405 Lexington Ave., 18th Fl.
New York, NY 10174-1801 US
Phone: 212-682-2500
Fax: 212-682-8391
Web Address: www.aaaa.org
The American Association of Advertising Agencies
(AAAA) is the national trade association representing
the advertising agency industry in the United States.

American Business Media (ABM)
675 3rd Ave.

New York, NY 10017-5704 US
Phone: 212-661-6360
Fax: 212-370-0736
E-mail Address: *info@abmmail.com*
Web Address: www.americanbusinessmedia.com
American Business Media (ABM) is the industry
association for business-to-business information
providers, including producers of magazines, CD-
ROMS, web sites, trade shows and other ancillary
products that build upon the printed product.

American Institute of Graphic Arts (AIGA)
164 5th Ave.
New York, NY 10010 US
Phone: 212-807-1990
Fax: 212-807-1799
Web Address: www.aiga.org
The purpose of the American Institute of Graphic
Arts (AIGA) is to further excellence in
communication design, both as a strategic tool for
business and as a cultural force.

American Marketing Association (AMA)
311 S. Wacker Dr., Ste. 5800
Chicago, IL 60606 US
Fax: 312-542-9001
Toll Free: 800-262-1150
Web Address: www.marketingpower.com
The American Marketing Association (AMA) serves
marketing professionals in both business and
education and serves all levels of marketing
practitioners, educators and students.

Arbitron
142 W. 57Th. St.
New York, NY 10019-3300 US
Phone: 212-887-1300
E-mail Address: *radioquestions@arbitron.com*
Web Address: www.arbitron.com
Arbitron, an international media and marketing
research firm, serves the radio, online radio, cable
and television industries, as well as advertising
agencies and advertisers in Europe and the U.S.

Art Directors Club, Inc. (ADC)
106 W. 29th St.
New York, NY 10001 US
Phone: 212-643-1440
Fax: 212-643-4266
E-mail Address: *info@adcglobal.org*
Web Address: www.adcglobal.org
The Art Directors Club (ADC) is an international
not-for-profit organization of creative leaders in

advertising, graphic design, interactive media, broadcast design, typography, packaging, environmental design, photography, illustration and related disciplines.

Association for Women In Communications (AWC)
3337 Duke St.
Alexandria, VA 22314 US
Phone: 703-370-7436
Fax: 703-370-7437
E-mail Address: *info@womcom.org*
Web Address: www.womcom.org
The Association for Women In Communications (AWC) is a professional organization that works for the advancement of women across all communications disciplines by recognizing excellence, promoting leadership and positioning its members at the forefront of the communications industry.

Association of Canadian Advertisers, Inc. (ACA)
95 St. Clair Ave. W., Ste.1103
Toronto, ON M4V 1N6 Canada
Phone: 416-964-3805
Fax: 416-964-0771
Toll Free: 800-565-0109
E-mail Address: *rlund@acaweb.ca*
Web Address: www.aca-online.com
The Association of Canadian Advertisers (ACA) is an organization that is expressly dedicated to representing the interests of companies that market and advertise their products in Canada.

Association of Independent Commercial Producers (AICP)
3 W. 18th St., 5th Fl.
New York, NY 10011 US
Phone: 212-929-3000
Fax: 212-929-3359
E-mail Address: *info@aicp.com*
Web Address: www.aicp.com
The Association of Independent Commercial Producers (AICP) represents the interests of U.S. companies that specialize in producing commercials in various media for advertisers and agencies.

Association of Independent Creative Editors (AICE)
308 W. 107th St., Ste. 5F
New York, NY 10025 US
Phone: 212-665-2679
E-mail Address: *info@aice.org*

Web Address: www.aice.org
The Association of Independent Creative Editors (AICE) is a national association serving the needs and interests of independent creative editorial companies.

Audit Bureau of Circulations (ABC)
900 N. Meacham Rd.
Schaumburg, IL 60173-4968 US
Phone: 847-605-0909
Fax: 847-605-0483
E-mail Address: *kammi.altig@accessabc.com*
Web Address: www.accessabc.com
The Audit Bureau of Circulations (ABC) is the leading third-party auditing trade organization for newspaper and magazine publishers in the U.S., as well as advertising agencies and advertisers, striving to conduct audits that set the industry standard for integrity, objectivity and accuracy.

BPA Worldwide
2 Corporate Dr., Ste. 900
Shelton, CT 06484 US
Phone: 203-447-2800
E-mail Address: *info@bpaww.com*
Web Address: www.bpaww.com
BPA Worldwide is a global provider of audited data to the marketing, media and information industries. Worldwide it serves over 2,500 media properties.

Business Marketing Association (BMA)
401 N. Michigan Ave., Ste. 1200
Chicago, IL 60611 US
Fax: 312-822-0054
Toll Free: 800-664-4262
Web Address: www.marketing.org
The Business Marketing Association (BMA) serves the professional, educational and career development needs of business-to-business marketers and their partner suppliers.

Cabletelevision Advertising Bureau (CAB)
830 3rd Ave., Fl. 2
New York, NY 10022 US
Phone: 212-508-1200
Fax: 212-832-3268
Web Address: www.onetvworld.org
The Cabletelevision Advertising Bureau (CAB) provides information and resources to the advertising community to support marketing and media planning; assists its industry members in maximizing advertising revenues; and promotes the use of cable

as an advertising medium locally, regionally and nationally.

Direct Marketing Association (DMA)

1120 Ave. of the Americas
New York, NY 10036-6700 US
Phone: 212-768-7277
Fax: 212-302-6714
E-mail Address: *customerservice@the-dma.org*
Web Address: www.the-dma.org
The Direct Marketing Association (DMA) is the oldest and largest trade association for users and suppliers in the direct, database and interactive marketing fields.

Intermarket Agency Network (IAN)

5307 S. 92nd St.
Hales Corners, WI 53130 US
Phone: 414-425-8800
Fax: 414-425-0021
E-mail Address: *bille@nonbox.com*
Web Address: www.intermarketnetwork.com
The Intermarket Agency Network (IAN) is a network of independent, full-service advertising agencies.

International Advertising Association (IAA)

275 Madison Ave., Ste. 2102
New York, NY 10016 US
Phone: 212-557-1133
Fax: 212-983-0455
E-mail Address: *membership@iaaglobal.org*
Web Address: www.iaaglobal.org
The International Advertising Association (IAA) is a strategic partnership that champions the common interests of disciplines across the full spectrum of the marketing communications industry.

International Association of Business Communicators (IABC)

1 Hallidie Plaza, Ste. 600
San Francisco, CA 94102 US
Phone: 415-544-4700
Fax: 415-544-4747
Toll Free: 800-776-4222
E-mail Address: *service_centre@iabc.com*
Web Address: www.iabc.com
The International Association of Business Communicators (IABC) is the leading resource for effective business communication practices.

International Public Relations Association (IPRA)

1 Dunley Hill Ct., Ranmore Common
Dorking, Surrey RH5 6SX UK
Phone: 44-1483-280-130
Fax: 44-1483-280-131
E-mail Address: *iprasec@btconnect.com*
Web Address: www.ipra.org
The International Public Relations Association (IPRA) is an international group of public relations practitioners that promotes the exchange of information and cooperation in the profession and creates development opportunities aimed at enhancing the role of public relations in management and international affairs.

Mailing & Fulfillment Service Association (MFSA)

1421 Prince St., Ste. 410
Alexandria, VA 22314 US
Phone: 703-836-9200
Fax: 703-548-8204
Toll Free: 800-333-6272
E-mail Address: *mfsa-mail@MFSAnet.org*
Web Address: www.mfsanet.org
Mailing & Fulfillment Service Association (MFSA), the national trade association for the mailing and fulfillment services industry, works to improve the business environment for mailing and fulfillment companies and to provide opportunities for the learning and professional development of the managers of these companies.

Marketing Agencies Association Worldwide (MAA)

460 Summer St.
Stamford, CT 06901 US
Phone: 203-978-1590
Fax: 203-969-1499
Web Address: www.maaw.org
Marketing Agencies Association Worldwide (MAA) is a global organization dedicated exclusively to the CEOs, presidents, managing directors and principals of top marketing services agencies.

Media Credit Association (MCA)

810 7th Ave., 24th Fl.
New York, NY 10019 US
Phone: 212- 872-3700
Web Address:
www.magazine.org/finance_and_operations/media_c
redit_association
Media Credit Association (MCA) is an association for consumer magazines that represents over 240 domestic publishing companies, over 80 international firms and over 100 associate members.

National Advertising Division of the Council of Better Business Bureaus, Inc. (NAD)
70 W. 36th St., 13th Fl.
New York, NY 10018 US
Phone: 212-705-0120
E-mail Address: *sharris@nad.bbb.org*
Web Address: www.nadreview.org
The National Advertising Division of the Council of Better Business Bureaus, Inc. (NAD) provides the advertising community with a system of self-regulation, minimizes government intervention and fosters public confidence in the credibility of advertising.

National Agri-Marketing Association (NAMA)
11020 King St., Ste. 205
Overland Park, KS 66210 US
Phone: 913-491-6500
Fax: 913-491-6502
E-mail Address: *agrimktg@nama.org*
Web Address: www.nama.org
The National Agri-Marketing Association (NAMA) connects those involved in marketing communications, public relations, products management and sales in the agribusiness industry.

New York American Marketing Association (NYAMA)
116 E. 27th St., 6th Fl.
New York, NY 10016 US
Phone: 212-687-3280
Fax: 212-557-9242
Web Address: www.nyama.org
The New York American Marketing Association (NYAMA) is an organization of marketing professionals from a wide range of industries who seek the knowledge to make themselves more effective marketers.

Outdoor Advertising Association of America, Inc. (OAAA)
1850 M St. NW, Ste. 1040
Washington, DC 20036 US
Phone: 202-833-5566
Fax: 202-833-1522
Web Address: www.oaaa.org
The Outdoor Advertising Association of America, Inc. (OAAA) is a leading trade association representing the outdoor advertising industry.

Point-of-Purchase Advertising Institute (POPAI)
1600 Duke St., Ste. 400
Alexandria, VA 22314 US

Phone: 703-373-8800
E-mail Address: *info@popai.org*
Web Address: www.popai.com
The Point-of-Purchase Advertising Institute (POPAI) is an international nonprofit trade association dedicated to serving the interests of advertisers, retailers, producers and suppliers of point-of-purchase products and services. POPAI has over 1,700 member companies.

Public Relations Society of America, Inc. (PRSA)
33 Maiden Ln., 11th Fl.
New York, NY 10038-5150 US
Phone: 212-460-1400
Fax: 212-995-0757
E-mail Address: *pr@pras.org*
Web Address: www.prsa.org
The Public Relations Society of America (PRSA) exists to unify, strengthen and advance the profession of public relations.

Television Bureau of Advertising (TVB)
3 E. 54th St.
New York, NY 10022-3108 US
Phone: 212-486-1111
Fax: 212-935-5631
E-mail Address: *info@tvb.org*
Web Address: www.tvb.org
The Television Bureau of Advertising (TVB) is the not-for-profit trade association of America's broadcast television industry, providing resources that enable advertisers to make the best use of local television.

Women in Direct Marketing International (WDMI)
Att: Barbara Lewis, c/o Wunderman
285 Madison Ave., 14th Fl.
New York, NY 10017 US
Phone: 732-469-5900 ext. 307
E-mail Address: *bladden@directmaildepot.com*
Web Address: www.wdmi.org
Women in Direct Marketing International (WDMI) is a network of direct marketers dedicated to connecting women in the field and to promoting excellence in direct marketing.

II. Advertising/Marketing Resources

USA TODAY ADTRACK
Web Address:
www.usatoday.com/money/advertising/adtrack/index_oldstyle.htm

USA TODAY ADTRACK is a web site that delivers the results of a weekly poll conducted by USA TODAY and Harris Interactive to determine the effectiveness of major advertising campaigns.

III.   Booksellers Associations

American Booksellers Association, Inc.
200 White Plains Rd., Ste. 600
Tarrytown, NY 10591 US
Fax: 914-591-2720
Toll Free: 800-637-0037
E-mail Address: *info@bookweb.org*
Web Address: www.bookweb.org
The American Booksellers Association is a nonprofit association representing independent bookstores in the United States.

Midwest Booksellers Association (MBA)
3407 W. 44th St.
Minneapolis, MN 55410 US
Phone: 612-926-5868
Fax: 612-926-6657
Toll Free: 800-784-7522
E-mail Address: *info@midwestbooksellers.org*
Web Address: www.midwestbooksellers.org
Midwest Booksellers Association (MBA) is a regional non-profit organization that promotes retail bookselling and supports professional independent booksellers throughout the Midwest.

National Association of College Stores (NACS)
500 E. Lorain St.
Oberlin, OH 44074 US
Fax: 440-775-4769
Toll Free: 800-622-7498
E-mail Address: *webteam@nacs.org*
Web Address: www.nacs.org
The National Association of College Stores (NACS) is the professional trade association representing college retailers and associate members who supply books and other products to college stores.

IV.   Broadcasting, Cable, Radio & TV Associations

Academy of Television Arts and Sciences
5220 Lankershim Blvd.
North Hollywood, CA 91601-3109 US
Phone: 818-754-2800
Fax: 818-761-2827
E-mail Address: *webmaster@emmys.org*

Web Address: www.emmys.org
The Academy of Television Arts and Sciences is a nonprofit corporation devoted to the advancement of telecommunications arts and sciences and to fostering creative leadership in the telecommunications industry. It is one of three organizations that administer the Emmy Awards. It is responsible for prime time Emmys.

Advanced Television Systems Committee (ATSC)
1750 K St. NW, Ste. 1200
Washington, DC 20006 US
Phone: 202-872-9160
Fax: 202-872-9161
E-mail Address: *lsheltongross@atsc.org*
Web Address: www.atsc.org
The Advanced Television Systems Committee (ATSC) is an international nonprofit membership organization that develops voluntary standards for the entire spectrum of advanced television systems.

Alliance for Community Media (ACM)
666 11th St. NW, Ste. 740
Washington, DC 20001-4542 US
Phone: 202-393-2650
Fax: 202-393-2653
E-mail Address: *rmccausland@alliancecm.org*
Web Address: www.ourchannels.org
The Alliance for Community Media (ACM) is a group committed to assuring universal access to electronic media.

American Federation of Television and Radio Artists (AFTRA)
260 Madison Ave., 7th Fl.
New York, NY 10016-2401 US
Phone: 212-532-0800
Fax: 212-545-1238
E-mail Address: *info@aftra.com*
Web Address: www.aftra.org
The American Federation of Television and Radio Artists (AFTRA) represents actors and other professional performers and broadcasters in television, radio, sound recordings, non-broadcast/industrial programming and new technologies such as interactive programming and CD-ROMs.

American Sportscasters Association (ASA)
225 Broadway, Ste. 2030
New York, NY 10007 US
Phone: 212-227-8080
Fax: 212-571-0556

E-mail Address: *Lschwa8918@aol.com*
Web Address: www.americansportscasters.com
The American Sportscasters Association (ASA) is a
professional organization for the promotion and
support of sports broadcasters. The ASA is also a
resource for those interested in becoming
sportscasters.

**American Women in Radio and Television, Inc.
(AWRT)**
8405 Greensboro Dr., Ste. 800
McLean, VA 22102 US
Phone: 703-506-3290
Fax: 703-506-3266
E-mail Address: *info@awrt.org*
Web Address: www.awrt.org
American Women in Radio and Television (AWRT)
is a national nonprofit organization dedicated to
advancing the role of women in electronic media and
related fields.

Association for International Broadcasting (AIB)
P.O. Box 141
Cranbrook, TN17 9AJ UK
Phone: 44-20-7993-2557
Fax: 44-20-7993-8043
E-mail Address: *contactaib@aib.org.uk*
Web Address: www.aib.org.uk
The Association for International Broadcasting (AIB)
aims to increase the scope and effectiveness of
international broadcasting, working on a global, co-
operative basis.

**Association for Maximum Service Television, Inc.
(MSTV)**
P.O. Box 9897
4100 Wisconsin Ave., N.W.
Washington, DC 20016 US
Phone: 202-966-1956
Fax: 202-966-9617
E-mail Address: *sbaurenfeind@mstv.org*
Web Address: www.mstv.org
Association for Maximum Service Television
(MSTV) is a national association of local television
stations dedicated to preserving and improving the
technical quality of free, universal, community-based
television service to the American public.

**Association of America's Public Television
Stations (APTS)**
666 11th St. NW, Ste. 1100
Washington, DC 20001 US
Phone: 202-654-4200

Fax: 202-654-4236
E-mail Address: *jeffrey@apts.org*
Web Address: www.apts.org
The Association of America's Public Television
Stations (APTS) is a nonprofit membership
organization formed to support the continued growth
and development of strong and financially sound
noncommercial television service for the American
public.

Association of Cable Communicators (ACC)
P.O. Box 75007
Washington, DC 20013-5007 US
Phone: 202-222-2370
Fax: 202-222-2317
Toll Free: 800-210-3396
E-mail Address: *services@cablecommunicators.org*
Web Address: www.cablecommunicators.org
Association of Cable Communicators (ACC) is the
only national professional organization specifically
addressing the issues, needs and interests of the cable
industry's public affairs professionals.

Broadcast Cable Credit Association, Inc. (BCCA)
550 W. Frontage Rd., Ste. 3600
Northfield, IL 60093 US
Phone: 847-881-8757
Fax: 847-784-8059
E-mail Address: *info@bccacredit.com*
Web Address: www.bccacredit.com
The Broadcast Cable Credit Association (BCCA)
exists to provide tools and services that allow its
members to perform their functions to the best of
their abilities and achieve a profitable bottom line.

**Broadcast Cable Financial Management
Association (BCFM)**
550 W. Frontage Rd., Ste. 3600
Northfield, IL 60093 US
Phone: 847-716-7000
Fax: 847-716-7004
E-mail Address: *mcollins@bcfm.com*
Web Address: www.bcfm.com
The Broadcast Cable Financial Management
Association (BCFM) exists to provide and maintain
open, intellectual exchange and create opportunities
to help its members grow professionally and
personally.

Broadcast Designers' Association, Inc. (BDA)
Promax & BDA
9000 W. Sunset Blvd., Ste. 900
Los Angeles, CA 90069 US

Phone: 310-788-7600
Fax: 310-788-7616
E-mail Address: *anush@promax.tv*
Web Address: www.promax.tv
Broadcast Designers' Association (BDA) is the
world's foremost organization working on behalf of
those involved in the promotion, marketing and
design of all electronic media.

Broadcast Education Association (BEA)
1771 N St. NW
Washington, DC 20036-2891 US
Phone: 202-429-3935
E-mail Address: *BEAMemberServices@nab.org*
Web Address: www.beaweb.org
The Broadcast Education Association (BEA) is the
professional association for professors, industry
professionals and graduate students interested in
teaching and research related to electronic media and
multimedia enterprises.

Broadcast Pioneers Library of American Broadcasting (LAB)
3210 Hornbake Library
University of Maryland
College Park, MD 20742 US
Phone: 301-405-9160
Fax: 301-314-2634
E-mail Address: *labcast@umd.edu*
Web Address: www.lib.umd.edu/lab/
The Broadcast Pioneers Library of American
Broadcasting (LAB) holds a wide-ranging collection
of audio and video recordings, books, pamphlets,
periodicals, personal collections, oral histories,
photographs, scripts and vertical files devoted
exclusively to the history of broadcasting.

Broadcasters' Foundation, Inc.
7 Lincoln Ave.
Greenwich, CT 06830 US
Phone: 203-862-8577
Fax: 203-629-5739
E-mail Address:
ghastings@broadcastersfoundation.org
Web Address: www.broadcastersfoundation.org
The Broadcasters' Foundation is the only
organization in radio and television that provides
anonymous financial assistance to fellow
broadcasters in acute need.

Cable & Telecommunications Association for Marketing (CTAM)
201 N. Union St., Ste. 440

Alexandria, VA 22314 US
Phone: 703-549-4200
E-mail Address: *info@ctam.com*
Web Address: www.ctamnetforum.com/eweb
The Cable & Telecommunications Association for
Marketing (CTAM) is dedicated to the discipline and
development of consumer marketing excellence in
cable television, new media and telecommunications
services.

Cable in the Classroom (CIC)
1724 Massachusetts Ave. NW, Ste. 100
Washington, DC 20001 US
Phone: 202-222-2335
Fax: 202-222-2336
Web Address: www.ciconline.org
The Cable in the Classroom (CIC) program provides
schools across the U.S. with free cable service and
over 540 hours per month of commercial-free
educational programming.

Cable Television Laboratories, Inc. (CableLabs)
858 Coal Creek Cir.
Louisville, CO 80027-9750 US
Phone: 303-661-9100
Fax: 303-661-9199
E-mail Address: *m.schwartz@cablelabs.com*
Web Address: www.cablelabs.com
Cable Television Laboratories (CableLabs) is a
nonprofit research and development consortium
dedicated to pursuing new cable telecommunications
technologies and to helping its cable operator
members integrate those technical advancements into
their business objectives.

Canadian Association of Broadcasters (CAB)
350 Sparks St., Ste. 306
Ottawa, ON K1R 7S8 Canada
Phone: 613-233-4035
Fax: 613-233-6961
E-mail Address: *tvandusen@cab-acr.ca*
Web Address: www.cab-acr.ca
The Canadian Association of Broadcasters (CAB) is
the collective voice of the majority of Canada's
private radio and television stations, networks and
specialty services.

Community Broadcasters Association (CBA)
3605 Sandy Plains Rd.
Ste. 240462
Marietta, GA 30066 US
Toll Free: 800-215-7655
E-mail Address: *amy@communitybroadcasters.com*

Web Address: www.dtvnow.org
The Community Broadcasters Association (CBA) is a national organization dedicated to enhancing and representing the diversity, vitality, localism, community service and economic survival of Class A and low-power television stations in the U.S.

Country Radio Broadcasters, Inc. (CRB)
819 18th Ave. S.
Nashville, TN 37203 US
Phone: 615-327-4487
Fax: 615-329-4492
Web Address: www.crb.org
Country Radio Broadcasters (CRB) brings together country radio broadcasters from around the world for the purpose of assuring the continued vitality of the country radio format.

Hollywood Radio & Television Society (HRTS)
13701 Riverside Dr.
Ste. 205
Sherman Oaks, CA 91423 US
Phone: 818-789-1182
Fax: 818-789-1210
E-mail Address: info@hrts.org
Web Address: www.hrts.org
The Hollywood Radio & Television (HRTS) is an organization of executives from west coast networks, stations, studios, production companies, advertisers, ad agencies, cable companies, media companies, legal firms, publicity agencies, talent and management agencies, performers, services, suppliers and allied fields.

International Federation of Television Archives (IFTA)
E-mail Address: office@fiatifta.org
Web Address: www.fiatifta.org
International Federation of Television Archives (IFTA) is an association of broadcast and national audiovisual archives and libraries involved in the collection and preservation of film and television images.

Jones/NCTI, Inc.
9697 E. Mineral Ave. Centennial
Centennial, CO 80112 US
Toll Free: 866-575-7206
Web Address: www.ncti.com
Jones/NCTI, Inc. provides workforce performance products, services and education to the broadband and cable television industry.

National Association of Black Owned Broadcasters, Inc. (NABOB)
1155 Connecticut Ave. NW, Ste. 600
Washington, DC 20036 US
Phone: 202-463-8970
Fax: 202-429-0657
E-mail Address: info@nabob.org
Web Address: www.nabob.org
National Association of Black Owned Broadcasters, Inc. (NABOB) is a trade organization representing the interests of African-American owners of radio and television stations in the U.S.

National Association of Broadcasters (NAB)
1771 N St. NW
Washington, DC 20036 US
Phone: 202-429-5300
Fax: 202-429-4199
E-mail Address: nab@nab.org
Web Address: www.nab.org
The National Association of Broadcasters (NAB) represents broadcasters for radio and television. The organization also provides benefits to employees of member companies and to individuals and companies that provide products and services to the electronic media industries.

National Association of Television Program Executives (NATPE)
5757 Wilshire Blvd., Penthouse 10
Los Angeles, CA 90036-3681 US
Phone: 310-453-4440
Fax: 310-453-5258
E-mail Address: info@natpe.org
Web Address: www.natpe.org
The National Association of Television Program Executives (NATPE) is the leading association for content professionals in the global television industry.

National Broadcasting Society (NBS)
PO Box 4206
Chesterfield, MO 63006 US
Web Address: www.nbs-aerho.org
The National Broadcasting Society (NBS), also known as Alpha Epsilon Rho, is a student and professional society of more than 85 chapters on college, university, community college and high school campuses.

National Cable and Telecommunications Association (NCTA)
25 Massachusetts Ave. NW, Ste. 100

Washington, DC 20001 US
Phone: 202-222-2300
E-mail Address: *webmaster@ncta.com*
Web Address: www.ncta.com
The National Cable and Telecommunications
Association (NCTA) is the principal trade association
of the cable television industry in the United States.

National Captioning Institute (NCI)

1900 Gallows Rd., Ste. 3000
Vienna, VA 22182 US
Phone: 703-917-7600
Fax: 703-917-9853
E-mail Address: *mail@ncicap.org*
Web Address: www.ncicap.org
The National Captioning Institute (NCI) is a
nonprofit organization that provides domestic and
international captioning, subtitling and described
video for broadcast and cablecast television
programs, TV commercials, home video programs,
government agencies and corporations.

National Religious Broadcasters (NRB)

9510 Technology Dr.
Manassas, VA 20110 US
Phone: 703-330-7000
Fax: 703-330-7100
E-mail Address: *info@nrb.org*
Web Address: www.nrb.org
National Religious Broadcasters (NRB) is an
international association of Christian communicators
with more than 1,400 member organizations.

National Television Academy (NTA)

111 W. 57th St., Ste. 600
New York, NY 10019 US
Phone: 212-586-8424
Fax: 212-246-8129
Web Address: www.emmyonline.org
The National Television Academy (NTA) is
dedicated to the advancement of the arts and sciences
of television and the promotion of creative leadership
for artistic, educational and technical achievements
within the television industry.

New York State Broadcasters Association (NYSBA)

1805 Western Ave.
Albany, NY 12203 US
Phone: 518-456-8888
Fax: 518-456-8943
E-mail Address: *info@nysbroadcasters.org*
Web Address: www.nysbroadcasters.org

New York State Broadcasters Association (NYSBA)
serves as the primary advocate and active
representative for New York State's broadcast
industry in state and national issues.

Parents Television Council (PTC)

707 Wilshire Blvd., Ste. 2075
Los Angeles, CA 90017 US
Phone: 213-403-1300
Fax: 213-403-1301
Toll Free: 800-882-6868
E-mail Address: *editor@parentstv.org*
Web Address: www.parentstv.org
The Parents Television Council (PTC) provides
reviews of television shows, screening for violence,
sexuality and language.

Public Radio News Directors, Inc. (PRNDI)

4200 James Ray Dr.
Grand Forks, ND 58203 US
Phone: 701-777-6505
Fax: 701-777-2339
E-mail Address: *chris@innovators.net*
Web Address: www.prndi.org
Public Radio News Directors (PRNDI) is a nonprofit
national service organization that encourages the
professional development and training of public radio
journalists.

Radio Advertising Bureau (RAB)

1320 Greenway Dr., Ste. 500
Irving, TX 75038-2510 US
Phone: 212-681-7205
Fax: 972-753-6727
Toll Free: 800-232-3131
E-mail Address: *rcassis@rab.com*
Web Address: www.rab.com
The mission of the Radio Advertising Bureau (RAB)
is to increase the awareness, credibility and salability
of radio by designing, developing and implementing
appropriate programs, research, tools and activities
for member stations.

Radio Marketing Bureau (RMB)

175 Bloor St. E.
Ste. 316, N. Tower
Toronto, ON M4W 3R8 Canada
Phone: 416-922-5757
Toll Free: 800-667-2346
E-mail Address: *info@rmb.ca*
Web Address: www.rmb.ca
The Radio Marketing Bureau (RMB) is a marketing
source for radio advertising in Canada, representing

stations generating over 80% of all Canadian radio revenue.

Radio Television News Directors Association (RTNDA Canada)
2175 Sheppard Ave. E., Ste. 310
Toronto, ON M2J 1W8 Canada
Phone: 416-756-2213
Fax: 416-491-1670
Toll Free: 877-257-8632
E-mail Address: *info@rtndacanada.com*
Web Address: www.rtndacanada.com
Radio Television News Directors Association (RTNDA Canada) offers a forum for open discussion and action in the broadcast news industry in Canada.

Radio Television News Directors Association (RTNDA)
1600 K St. NW, Ste. 700
Washington, DC 20006-2838 US
Phone: 202-659-6510
Fax: 202-223-4007
Toll Free: 800-807-8632
E-mail Address: *rtnda@rtnda.org*
Web Address: www.rtnda.org
The Radio Television News Directors Association (RTNDA) is the world's largest professional organization exclusively committed to professionals in electronic journalism.

Satellite Broadcasting & Communications Association of America (SBCA)
1730 M St. NW, Ste. 600
Washington, DC 20036 US
Phone: 202-349-3620
Fax: 202-349-3621
Toll Free: 800-541-5981
E-mail Address: *info@sbca.org*
Web Address: www.sbca.com
The Satellite Broadcasting & Communications Association of America (SBCA) is the national trade organization representing all segments of the satellite consumer services industry.

Syndication Network Television Association (SNTA)
630 5th Ave., Ste. 2320
New York, NY 10111 US
Phone: 212-259-3740
Fax: 212-259-3770
E-mail Address: *mburg@snta.com*
Web Address: www.snta.com

The Syndication Network Television Association (SNTA) is an organization of national and independent television stations that syndicate television shows.

Television Bureau of Canada (TVB)
160 Bloor St. E., Ste. 1005
Toronto, ON M4W 1B9 Canada
Phone: 416-923-8813
Fax: 416-413-3879
E-mail Address: *tvb@tvb.ca*
Web Address: www.tvb.ca
The Television Bureau of Canada (TVB) is a resource center for television stations, networks and their sales representatives.

The Cable Center
2000 Buchtel Blvd.
Denver, CO 80210 US
Phone: 303-871-4885
Fax: 303-871-4514
Web Address: www.cablecenter.org
The Cable Center supports communication in the business, technology and programming of cable telecommunications and provides education, training and research for all aspects of the industry.

Women in Cable & Telecommunications (WICT)
14555 Avion Pkwy., Ste. 250
Chantilly, VA 20151 US
Phone: 703-234-9810
Fax: 703-817-1595
E-mail Address: *mnorthern@wict.org*
Web Address: www.wict.org
Women in Cable & Telecommunications (WICT) exists to advance the position and influence of women in media through leadership programs and services at both the national and local level.

V. Canadian Government Agencies

Canadian Intellectual Property Office (CIPO)
50 Victoria St., Rm. C-114
Gatineau, QC K1A 0C9 Canada
Phone: 819-934-0544
Fax: 819-953-7620
Toll Free: 866-997-1936
E-mail Address: *cipo.contact@ic.gc.ca*
Web Address: strategis.gc.ca
The CIPO is the agency responsible for the administration and processing of intellectual property in Canada.

Canadian Radio-Television and Telecommunications Commission (CRTC)
CRTC
Ottawa, ON K1A 0N2 Canada
Phone: 819-997-0313
Fax: 819-994-0218
Toll Free: 877-249-2782
Web Address: www.crtc.gc.ca
The CRTC is the government agency responsible for the regulation of the Canadian broadcasting and telecommunications industries.

VI.   Careers-First Time Jobs/New Grads

Black Collegian Home Page
140 Carondelet St.
New Orleans, LA 70130 US
Phone: 504-523-0154
Web Address: www.black-collegian.com
Black Collegian Home Page features listings for job and internship opportunities. The site includes a list of the top 100 minority corporate employers and an assessment of job opportunities.

Collegegrad.com
576 N. Washington Ave.
Cedarburg, WI 53012 US
Phone: 262-375-6700
Web Address: www.collegegrad.com
Collegegrad.com offers in-depth resources for college students and recent grads seeking entry-level jobs.

Job Web
62 Highland Ave.
Bethlehem, PA 18017-9085 US
Phone: 610-868-1421
Fax: 610-868-0208
Toll Free: 800-544-5272
Web Address: www.jobweb.com
Job Web, owned and sponsored by National Association of Colleges and Employers (NACE), displays job openings and employer descriptions. The site also offers a database of career fairs, searchable by state or keyword, with contact information.

MBAjobs.net
Fax: 413-556-8849
E-mail Address: contact@mbajobs.net
Web Address: www.mbajobs.net
MBAjobs.net is a unique international service for MBA students and graduates, employers, recruiters and business schools.

MonsterTrak
11845 W. Olympic Blvd., Ste. 500
Los Angeles, CA 90064 US
Toll Free: 800-999-8725
E-mail Address: college.monstertrak@monster.com
Web Address: www.monstertrak.monster.com
MonsterTrak features links to hundreds of university and college career centers across the U.S. with entry-level job listings categorized by industry. Major companies can also utilize MonsterTrak.

National Association of Colleges and Employers (NACE)
62 Highland Ave.
Bethlehem, PA 18017-9085 US
Phone: 610-868-1421
Fax: 610-868-0208
Toll Free: 800-544-5272
Web Address: www.naceweb.org
The National Association of Colleges and Employers (NACE) is a premier U.S. organization representing college placement offices and corporate recruiters who focus on hiring new grads.

VII.   Careers-General Job Listings

America's Job Bank
Toll Free: 877-348-0502
E-mail Address: info@careeronestop.org
Web Address: www.jobsearch.org
America's Job Bank was developed by the U.S. Department of Labor as part of an array of web-based job tools. It offers an extensive list of searchable employment vacancies as well as other job resources for employers and job seekers.

Career Exposure, Inc.
805 SW Broadway, Ste. 2250
Portland, OR 97205 US
Phone: 503-221-7779
Fax: 503-221-7780
E-mail Address: feedback@CareerExposure.com
Web Address: www.careerexposure.com
Career Exposure, Inc. is an online career center and job placement service, with resources for employers, recruiters and job seekers.

CareerBuilder
200 N. LaSalle St., Ste. 1100
Chicago, IL 60631 US
Phone: 773-527-3600
Fax: 773-399-6313
Toll Free: 800-638-4212

Web Address: www.careerbuilder.com
CareerBuilder focuses on the needs of companies and also provides a database of job openings, called the Mega Job Search. Hundreds of thousands of job openings are posted. Resumes are sent directly to the company, and applicants can set up a special e-mail account for job-seeking purposes. CareerBuilder, Inc. is a joint venture of three newspaper giants: Knight Ridder, Gannett and Tribune Company.

HotJobs
45 W. 18th St., 6th Fl.
New York, NY 10011 US
Phone: 646-351-5300
Fax: 212-944-8962
Web Address: hotjobs.yahoo.com
HotJobs, designed for experienced professionals, employers and job seekers, is a Yahoo-owned site that provides company profiles, a resume posting service and a resume workshop. The site allows posters to block resumes from being viewed by certain companies and provides a notification service of new jobs.

HRS Federal Job Search
Web Address: www.hrsjobs.com
HRS Federal Job Search features a database of federal jobs available across the U.S. Most jobs are within the public sector. The job seeker creates a profile with desired job type, salary and location to receive applicable postings by e-mail.

JobCentral
9002 N. Purdue Rd., Quad III, Ste. 100
Indianapolis, IN 46268 US
Phone: 317-874-9000
Fax: 317-874-9100
Toll Free: 866-268-6206
E-mail Address: *info@jobcentral.com*
Web Address: www.jobcentral.com
JobCentral, operated by the nonprofit DirectEmployers Association, links users directly to hundreds of thousands of job opportunities posted on the sites of participating employers, thus bypassing the usual job search sites. This saves employers money and allows job seekers to access many more job opportunities.

LaborMarketInfo
7000 Franklin Blvd., Ste. 1100
Sacramento, CA 95823 US
Phone: 916-262-2162
Fax: 916-262-2352

Web Address: www.labormarketinfo.edd.ca.gov
LaborMarketInfo, formerly the California Cooperative Occupational Information System, is sponsored by California's Economic Development Office. The web site is geared to providing job seekers and employers a wide range of resources, namely the ability to find, access and use labor market information and services. It provides demographical statistics for employment on both a local and regional level, as well as career searching tools for California residents.

Mediabistro.com
494 Broadway, 4th Fl.
New York, NY 10012 US
Phone: 212-929-2588
Fax: 212-966-8984
Web Address: www.mediabistro.com
Mediabistro.com offers an array of employment resources, including job listings in the media industry.

Monster Worldwide, Inc.
622 3rd Ave., 39th Fl.
New York, NY 10017 US
Phone: 212-351-7000
Toll Free: 800-666-7837
Web Address: www.monster.com
Monster Worldwide, Inc. is an electronic career center that displays hundreds of thousands of job opportunities in 23 countries around the world. Job seekers can build and store a resume online and find job listings that match their profiles. Monster e-mails the results once per week.

Recruiters Online Network
Web Address: www.recruitersonline.com
The Recruiters Online Network provides job postings from thousands of recruiters, Careers Online Magazine, a resume database, as well as other career resources.

TrueCareers, Inc.
Web Address: www.truecareers.com
TrueCareers, Inc. offers job listings and provides an array of career resources. The company also offers a search of over 2 million scholarships.

Wall Street Journal - CareerJournal.com
P.O. Box 300
Princeton, NJ 08543-0300 US
Web Address: www.careers.wsj.com

The Wall Street Journal's executive career site, called CareerJournal.com, features a job database with more than 100,000 available positions. It provides a weekly career column and a range of articles about topics including diversity issues and promotion.

VIII.   Careers-Job Reference Tools

Newspaperlinks.com
E-mail Address: *sally.clarke@naa.org*
Web Address: www.newspaperlinks.com
Newspaperlinks.com, a service of the Newspaper Association of America, links individuals to local, national and international newspapers. Job seekers can search through thousands of classified sections.

Vault.com
150 W. 22nd St., 5th Fl.
New York, NY 10011 US
Phone: 212-366-4212
Web Address: www.vault.com
Vault.com is a comprehensive career web site for employers and employees, with job postings and valuable information on a wide variety of industries. Vault gears many of its features toward MBAs. The site has been recognized by Forbes and Fortune Magazines.

IX.   Computer & Electronics Industry Associations

HomePlug Powerline Alliance
Web Address: www.homeplug.org
The HomePlug Powerline Alliance's goal is to promote standards-based home networks that utilize existing electrical wiring to carry signals between personal computers, entertainment systems and other home devices.

Information Technology Association of Canada (ITAC)
2800 Skymark Ave., Ste. 402
Mississauga, ON L4W 5A6 Canada
Phone: 905-602-8345
Fax: 905-602-8346
E-mail Address: *nhelsberg@itac.ca*
Web Address: www.itac.ca
The ITAC seeks to promote the contribution of the IT, software, computer and telecommunications industry in Canada.

Korea Association of Information and Telecommunications (KAIT)
Dong-Ah Villat 2nd Town 2F
1678-2 Seocho-Dong, Seocho - Gu
Seoul, 137-070 Korea
Phone: 82-2-580-0580
Fax: 82-2-580-0599
E-mail Address: *webmaster@kait.or.kr*
Web Address: www.kait.or.kr
The KAIT was created to develop and promote the InfoTech, computer, consumer electronics, wireless, software and telecommunications sectors in Korea.

Multimedia Over Coax Alliance (MoCA)
E-mail Address: *help@mocalliance.org*
Web Address: www.mocalliance.org
Multimedia Over Coax Alliance (MoCA) is a standard body promoting networking of multiple streams of high definition video and entertainment using existing coaxial cable already in the home.

X.   Corporate Information Resources

bizjournals.com
120 W. Morehead St., Ste. 400
Charlotte, NC 28202 US
Web Address: www.bizjournals.com
Bizjournals.com is the online media division of American City Business Journals, the publisher of dozens of leading city business journals nationwide. It provides access to research into the latest news regarding companies small and large.

Business Wire
44 Montgomery St., 39th Fl.
San Francisco, CA 94104 US
Phone: 415-986-4422
Fax: 415-788-5335
Toll Free: 888-381-9473
Web Address: www.businesswire.com
Business Wire offers news releases, industry- and company-specific news, top headlines, conference calls, IPOs on the Internet, media services and access to tradeshownews.com and BW Connect On-line through its informative and continuously updated web site.

Edgar Online
50 Washington St., 11th Fl.
Norwalk, CT 06854 US
Phone: 203-852-5666
Fax: 203-852-5667
Toll Free: 800-416-6651

Web Address: www.edgar-online.com
Edgar Online is a gateway and search tool for
viewing corporate documents, such as annual reports
on Form 10-K, filed with the U.S. Securities and
Exchange Commission.

PRNewswire
810 7th Ave., 32nd Fl.
New York, NY 10019 US
Phone: 212-596-1500
Toll Free: 800-832-5522
E-mail Address: *information@prnewswire.com*
Web Address: www.prnewswire.com
PRNewswire provides comprehensive
communications services for public relations and
investor relations professionals ranging from
information distribution and market intelligence to
the creation of online multimedia content and
investor relations web sites. Users can also view
recent corporate press releases.

Silicon Investor
Web Address: www.siliconinvestor.com
Silicon Investor is focused on providing information
about technology companies. The company's web site
serves as a financial discussion forum and offers
quotes, profiles and charts.

XI.	Economic Data & Research

STAT-USA
U.S. Department of Commerce, Rm. H-4885
Washington, DC 20230 US
Phone: 202-482-1986
Fax: 202-482-2164
Toll Free: 800-742-8872
E-mail Address: *statmail@doc.gov*
Web Address: www.stat-usa.gov
STAT-USA is an agency in the Economics and
Statistics Administration of the U.S. Department of
Commerce. The site offers daily economic news,
statistical releases, and databases relating to export
and trade, as well as the domestic economy.

XII.	Engineering, Research & Scientific Associations

Association of Federal Communications Consulting Engineers (AFCCE)
Cohen, Dippell and Everist, P.C.
1300 L St. NW, Ste. 1100
Washington, DC 20005 US

Web Address: www.afcce.org
The Association of Federal Communications
Consulting Engineers (AFCCE) is a professional
organization of individuals who regularly assist
clients on technical issues before the Federal
Communications Commission (FCC).

Audio Engineering Society, Inc. (AES)
60 E. 42nd St., Rm. 2520
New York, NY 10165-2520 US
Phone: 212-661-8528
Fax: 212-682-0477
Web Address: www.aes.org
The Audio Engineering Society (AES) provides
information on educational and career opportunities
in audio technology and engineering.

Broadcast Technological Society (BTS) of the Institute of Electrical & Electronics Engineers, Inc.
445 Hoes Ln.
Piscataway, NJ 08854 US
Phone: 732-562-3906
E-mail Address: *bts@ieee.org*
Web Address:
www.ieee.org/organizations/society/bt/index.html
The Broadcast Technological Society (BTS) is the
arm of the Institute of Electrical & Electronics
Engineers (IEEE) devoted to devices, equipment,
techniques and systems related to broadcast
technology.

Society of Broadcast Engineers, Inc. (SBE)
9102 N. Meridian St., Ste. 150
Indianapolis, IN 46260 US
Phone: 317-846-9000
Fax: 317-846-9120
E-mail Address: *mclappe@sbe.org*
Web Address: www.sbe.org
The Society of Broadcast Engineers (SBE) exists to
increase knowledge of broadcast engineering and
promote its interests, as well as to continue the
education of professionals in the industry.

Society of Cable Telecommunications Engineers (SCTE)
140 Philips Rd.
Exton, PA 19341-1318 US
Phone: 610-363-6888
Fax: 610-363-5898
Toll Free: 800-542-5040
E-mail Address: *scte@scte.org*
Web Address: www.scte.org

The Society of Cable Telecommunications Engineers (SCTE) is a nonprofit professional association dedicated to advancing the careers and serving the industry of telecommunications professionals by providing technical training, certification and standards.

Society of Motion Picture and Television Engineers (SMPTE)
3 Barker Ave.
White Plains, NY 10601 US
Phone: 914-761-1100
Fax: 914-761-3115
Web Address: www.smpte.org
The Society of Motion Picture and Television Engineers (SMPTE) is the leading technical society for the motion imaging industry. The firm publishes recommended practice and engineering guidelines, as well the SMPTE Journal.

XIII. Entertainment & Amusement Associations

American Amusement Machine Association (AAMA)
450 E. Higgins Rd., Ste. 201
Elk Grove Village, IL 60007 US
Phone: 847-290-9088
Fax: 847-290-9121
Toll Free: 866-372-5190
E-mail Address: *information@coin-op.org*
Web Address: www.coin-op.org
The American Amusement Machine Association (AAMA) is an international nonprofit trade organization representing the manufacturers, distributors and suppliers of the coin-operated amusement industry.

Amusement and Music Operators Association (AMOA)
33 W. Higgins Rd., Ste. 830
S. Barrington, IL 60010 US
Phone: 847-428-7699
Fax: 847-428-7719
Toll Free: 800-937-2662
E-mail Address: *amoa@amoa.com*
Web Address: www.amoa.com
The Amusement and Music Operators Association (AMOA) serves the global, coin operated amusement, music, entertainment and vending industries.

Amusement Industry Manufacturers and Suppliers, International (AIMS)
Banco Business Park
1061 Main St., Bin #28
N. Huntingdon, PA 15642 US
Phone: 724-864-3862
Fax: 724-864-8035
E-mail Address: *info@aimsintl.org*
Web Address: www.aimsintl.org
Amusement Industry Manufacturers and Suppliers International (AIMS) is a nonprofit organization that represents amusement industry manufacturers and suppliers worldwide.

Entertainment Technology Center (ETC)
509 W. 29th St.
Los Angeles, CA 90007 US
Phone: 213-743-1600
Fax: 213-743-1803
E-mail Address: *info@etcenter.org*
Web Address: www.etcenter.org
The Entertainment Technology Center (ETC) exists to discover, research, develop and accelerate entertainment technology.

Game Manufacturers Association (GAMA)
280 N. High St., Ste. 230
Columbus, OH 43215 US
Phone: 614-255-4500
Fax: 614-255-4499
E-mail Address: *ops@gama.org*
Web Address: www.gama.org
The Game Manufacturers Association (GAMA) is an international nonprofit trade association serving the hobby games industry.

Information Display and Entertainment Association (IDEA)
1990 E. Lohman Ave., Ste. 122
Las Cruces, NM 88001-3116 US
Phone: 505-524-6876
Fax: 505-524-4813
Toll Free: 888-832-4332
E-mail Address: *info@ideaontheweb.org*
Web Address: www.ideaontheweb.org
The Information Display and Entertainment Association (IDEA) is a worldwide association of electronic display system and scoreboard operators.

International Association of Amusement Parks and Attractions (IAAPA)
1448 Duke St.
Alexandria, VA 22314 US

Phone: 703-836-4800
Fax: 703-836-9678
E-mail Address: *communications@iaapa.org*
Web Address: www.iaapa.org
The International Association of Amusement Parks
and Attractions (IAAPA) is dedicated to the
preservation and prosperity of the amusement
industry.

**International Association of Assembly Managers
(IAAM)**
635 Fritz Dr., Ste. 100
Coppell, TX 75019-4442 US
Phone: 972-906-7441
Fax: 972-906-7418
E-mail Address: *mike.meyers@iaam.org*
Web Address: www.iaam.org
The International Association of Assembly Managers
(IAAM) is an international trade organization
representing managers and suppliers of public
assembly facilities, such as arenas, amphitheaters,
auditoriums, convention centers/exhibit halls,
performing arts venues, stadiums and university
complexes.

International Laser Display Association (ILDA)
3721 SE Henry St.
Portland, OR 97202 US
Phone: 503-407-0289
E-mail Address: *david@laserist.org*
Web Address: www.ilda.wa.org
The International Laser Display Association (ILDA)
is a nonprofit organization dedicated to advancing the
use of laser displays in art, entertainment and
education.

International Special Events Society (ISES)
401 N. Michigan Ave.
Chicago, IL 60611-4267 US
Phone: 312-321-6853
Fax: 312-673-6953
Toll Free: 800-688-4737
E-mail Address: *info@ises.com*
Web Address: www.ises.com
The International Special Events Society (ISES) is a
society of special events professionals representing
the industry's diverse disciplines.

International Ticketing Association (INTIX)
330 W. 38th St., Ste. 605
New York, NY 10018 US
Phone: 212-629-4036
Fax: 212-629-8532

E-mail Address: *info@intix.org*
Web Address: www.intix.org
International Ticketing Association (INTIX) is a
nonprofit professional and trade organization for the
admission services industry, representing
professionals in the performing arts, theater,
entertainment, professional sports and college and
university athletics.

National Association of Theater Owners (NATO)
PO Box 77318
Washington, DC 20013 US
Phone: 202-962-0054
Fax: 202-962-0370
E-mail Address: *nato@natodc.com*
Web Address: www.natoonline.org
The National Association of Theater Owners
(NATO) is an exhibition trade organization
represents 29,000 movie screens in the U.S., and
additional cinemas in over 40 countries worldwide.

National Association of Ticket Brokers (NATB)
214 N. Hale St.
Wheaton, IL 60187 US
Phone: 630-510-4594
Fax: 630-510-4501
E-mail Address: *gadler@oconnorhannan.com*
Web Address: www.natb.org
The National Association of Ticket Brokers (NATB)
is a nonprofit trade organization representing the
ticket broker industry. The association promotes
consumer protection and the education of the public
concerning the ticket brokers industry.

World Waterpark Association (WWA)
8826 Santa Fe Dr., Ste. 310
Overland Park, KS 66212 US
Phone: 913-599-0300
Fax: 913-599-0520
E-mail Address: *memberservices@waterparks.org*
Web Address: www.waterparks.org
The World Waterpark Association (WWA) is an
international non-profit partnership of private and
public water leisure facility owners, managers,
suppliers and developers.

XIV. Film & Television Resources

Baseline, Inc.
3415 S. Sepulveda Blvd., Ste. 200
Los Angeles, CA 90034 US
Fax: 310-393-7799
Toll Free: 800-858-3669

E-mail Address: *contact@blssi.com*
Web Address: www.blssi.com
Baseline, Inc., which does business as Baseline StudioSystems, Baseline/FilmTracker and associated names and web sites, offers subscription database with information regarding the film and television industries. The Studio System is its flagship service. Baseline is a division of The New York Times Company.

Directors World
865 S. Figueroa St.
Los Angeles, CA 90017 US
Phone: 213-228-0381
E-mail Address: *news@creativeplanet.com*
Web Address:
www.uemedia.net/CPC/directorsworld/
DirectorsWorld is an Internet community for film and video professionals providing daily information on the art, technology and business of directing.

IFILM
1024 N. Orange Dr.
Hollywood, CA 90038 US
Phone: 323-308-3400
E-mail Address: *feedback@ifilm.com*
Web Address: www.ifilm.com
IFILM is a leading broadband entertainment content network for consumers and marketers.

Independent Feature Project (IFP)
104 W. 29th St., 12th Fl.
New York, NY 10001-5310 US
Phone: 212-465-8200
Fax: 212-465-8525
E-mail Address: *webmaster@ifp.org*
Web Address: www.ifp.org
The Independent Feature Project (IFP) exists to facilitate the professional development and exhibition of new work from a diverse community of American filmmakers.

Internet Movie Database (IMDB)
Web Address: www.imdb.com
Internet Movie Database (IMDB), a unit of Amazon.com, is a movie database that provides information on such topics as box office revenues and new DVD releases, in addition to production and cast details on thousands of movies and television shows.

Kidon Media-Link
E-mail Address: *media-link@kidon.com*

Web Address: www.kidon.com/media-link
Kidon Media-Link is an independent web directory of newspapers and other news sources on the Internet.

Movieweb
E-mail Address: *support@movieweb.com*
Web Address: www.movieweb.com
Movieweb is an Internet movie site featuring information on movies coming soon to theaters and available on home video.

Museum of Broadcast Communications (MBC)
400 N. State St., Ste. 240
Chicago, IL 60610 US
Phone: 312-245-8200
Fax: 312-245-8207
E-mail Address: *archives@museum.tv*
Web Address: www.museum.tv
Museum of Broadcast Communications (MBC) is a non-profit broadcast museum and home to the only National Radio Hall of Fame. It seeks to collect, preserve and present historic and contemporary radio and television content, as well as to inform, educate and entertain through its archives, public programs, exhibits, screenings, online access and publications.

Samuel French Theater and Film Bookshops
45 W. 25th St.
New York, NY 10010-2751 US
Phone: 212-206-8990
Fax: 212-206-1429
E-mail Address: *info@samuelfrench.com*
Web Address: www.samuelfrench.com
Samuel French seeks out the world's best plays and makes them available to a wide range of producing groups.

SCREENSite
E-mail Address: *webmaster@screensite.org*
Web Address: www.screensite.org
SCREENSite is a resource center for film and TV scholarship with an archive of course syllabi, e-mail listings of media scholars, conference information, school listings and job list.

Screenwriters Online
16752 Bollinger Dr.
Pacific Palisades, CA 90272 US
Phone: 310-459-5278
E-mail Address: *insider@leonardo.net*
Web Address: www.screenwriter.com

Screenwriters Online is a web site offering information on screenwriting, scriptwriting and creative writing software, books, supplies and contests.

The Palley Center for Media
25 W. 52nd St.
New York, NY 10019 US
Phone: 212-621-6800
Web Address: www.mtr.org
The Palley Center for Media, formerly The Museum of Television & Radio, leads the discussion about the cultural, creative and social significance of television, radio and emerging platforms for the professional community and media-interested public.

XV.   Film & Theater Associations

Academy of Interactive Arts & Sciences (AIAS)
23622 Calabasas Rd., Ste. 220
Calabasas, CA 91302 US
Fax: 818-876-0850
Toll Free: 818-876-0826 ext. 201
E-mail Address: info@interactive.org
Web Address: www.interactive.org
The Academy of Interactive Arts & Sciences (AIAS) is a nonprofit membership organization serving the interactive entertainment development community.

Academy of Motion Picture Arts and Sciences (AMPAS)
8949 Wilshire Blvd.
Beverly Hills, CA 90211-1972 US
Phone: 310-247-3000
Fax: 310-859-9619
Web Address: www.oscars.org
The Academy of Motion Picture Arts and Sciences (AMPAS) is a professional honorary organization, founded to advance the arts and sciences of motion pictures.

Alliance of Motion Picture and Television Producers (AMPTP)
15503 Ventura Blvd.
Encino, CA 91436 US
Toll Free: 818-995-3600
Web Address: www.amptp.org
The Alliance of Motion Picture and Television Producers (AMPTP) is the primary trade association with respect to labor issues in the motion picture and television industry.

American Cinema Editors (ACE)
100 Universal City Plaza, Verna Fields Bldg. 2282, Rm. 190
Universal City, CA 91608 US
Phone: 818-777-2900
Fax: 818-733-5023
E-mail Address: amercinema@earthlink.net
Web Address: www.ace-filmeditors.org
American Cinema Editors (ACE) is an honorary society of motion picture editors that seeks to advance the art and science of the editing profession.

American Society of Cinematographers (ASC)
1782 N. Orange Dr.
Hollywood, CA 90028 US
Phone: 323-969-4333
Fax: 323-882-6391
Toll Free: 800-448-0145
E-mail Address: office@theasc.com
Web Address: www.theasc.com
The American Society of Cinematographers (ASC) is a trade association for cinematographers in the motion picture industry.

Art Directors Guild (ADG)
11969 Ventura Blvd., 2nd Fl.
Studio City, CA 91604 US
Phone: 818-762-9995
Fax: 818-762-9997
E-mail Address: scott@artdirectors.org
Web Address: www.artdirectors.org
The Art Directors Guild (ADG) represents the creative talents that conceive and manage the background and settings for most films and television projects.

Association of Cinema and Video Laboratories (ACVL)
Web Address: www.acvl.org
The Association of Cinema and Video Laboratories (ACVL) is an international organization whose members are pledged to the highest possible standards of service to the film and video industries.

Association of Film Commissioners International (AFCI)
109 E. 17th St.
Cheyenne, WY 82001 US
Phone: 307-637-4422
Fax: 413-375-2903
E-mail Address: info@afci.org
Web Address: www.afci.org

The Association of Film Commissioners International (AFCI) is an association of government film contacts worldwide supporting video, television and film production.

Canadian Film and Television Production Association (CFTPA)
151 Slater St., Ste. 902
Ottawa, ON K1P 5H3 Canada
Phone: 613-233-1444
Fax: 613-233-0073
Toll Free: 800-656-7440
E-mail Address: *ottawa@cftpa.ca*
Web Address: www.cftpa.ca
The mission of the Canadian Film and Television Production Association (CFTPA) is to create a favorable national and international environment for the film industry and culture to prosper.

Casting Society of America (CSA)
606 N. Larchmont Blvd., Ste. 4-B
Los Angeles, CA 90004-1309 US
Phone: 323-463-1925
Fax: 323-463-5753
E-mail Address: *info@castingsociety.com*
Web Address: www.castingsociety.com
Casting Society of America (CSA) is an association of casting professionals in film, television and theater.

Directors Guild of America, Inc. (Los Angeles DGA)
7920 Sunset Blvd.
Los Angeles, CA 90046 US
Phone: 310-289-2000
Fax: 310-289-2029
Toll Free: 800-421-4173
Web Address: www.dga.org
The Directors Guild of America, Inc. (Los Angeles DGA) seeks to protect directorial teams' legal and artistic rights, contend for their creative freedom and strengthen their ability to develop meaningful and credible careers.

Directors Guild of America, Inc. (New York DGA)
110 W. 57th St.
New York, NY 10019 US
Phone: 212-581-0370
Fax: 212-581-1441
Toll Free: 800-356-3754
Web Address: www.dga.org
The Directors Guild of America, Inc. (New York DGA) seeks to protect directorial teams' legal and

artistic rights, contend for their creative freedom and strengthen their ability to develop meaningful and credible careers.

DirectorsNet
Web Address: www.directorsnet.com
DirectorsNet is the home of creative professionals focused on motion picture, television, music videos, corporate video and commercial production.

Film Arts Foundation (FAF)
145 9th St., Ste. 101
San Francisco, CA 94103 US
Phone: 415-552-8760
Fax: 415-552-0882
E-mail Address: *info@filmarts.org*
Web Address: www.filmarts.org
The Film Arts Foundation (FAF) is a nonprofit leader in the media arts field, providing comprehensive training, equipment, information, consultations and exhibition opportunities to independent filmmakers.

Hollywood Post Alliance (HPA)
225 E. 9th St., Ste. 299
Los Angeles, CA 90015 US
Phone: 213-614-0860
Fax: 213-614-0890
E-mail Address: *ekramer@hpaonline.com*
Web Address: www.hpaonline.com
The Hollywood Post Alliance (HPA) is an organization dedicated to serving the entertainment technology industry by bringing together the post-production community.

Independent Film & Television Alliance (IFTA)
10850 Wilshire Blvd., 9th Fl.
Los Angeles, CA 90024-4321 US
Phone: 310-446-1000
Fax: 310-446-1600
E-mail Address: *info@ifta-online.org*
Web Address: www.ifta-online.org
The Independent Film & Television Alliance (IFTA), formerly the American Film Marketing Association (AFMA), is a trade association whose mission is to provide the independent film and television industry with high-quality, market-oriented services and worldwide representation.

International Alliance of Theatrical Stage Employees (IATSE)
1430 Broadway, 20th Fl.
New York, NY 10018 US
Phone: 212-730-1770

Fax: 212-730-7809
E-mail Address: *webmaster@iatse-intl.org*
Web Address: www.iatse-intl.org
The International Alliance of Theatrical Stage
Employees (IATSE) is the labor union representing
technicians, artisans and crafts workers in the
entertainment industry, including live theater, film
and television production and trade shows.

International Animated Film Society (ASIFA-Hollywood)

2114 Burbank Blvd.
Burbank, CA 91506 US
Toll Free: 818-842-4691
E-mail Address: *info@asifa-hollywood.org*
Web Address: www.asifa-hollywood.org
International Animated Film Society (ASIFA-
Hollywood) is a nonprofit organization dedicated to
the advancement of the art of animation.

International Documentary Association (IDA)

1201 W. 5th St., Ste. M320
Los Angeles, CA 90017 US
Phone: 213-534-3600
Fax: 213-534-3610
E-mail Address: *sandra@documentary.org*
Web Address: www.documentary.org
The International Documentary Association (IDA) is
a nonprofit member service organization, providing
publications, benefits and a public forum to its
members for issues regarding nonfiction film, video
and multimedia.

International Quorum of Motion Picture Producers

810 Dominican Dr.
Nashville, TN 37228 US
Phone: 615-255-4000
Fax: 615-255-4111
Web Address: www.iqfilm.org
International Quorum of Motion Picture Producers is
a select group of filmmakers and video producers,
limited to 100 hand-picked members.

Motion Picture Association of America (MPAA)

1600 Eye St. NW
Washington, DC 20006 US
Phone: 202-293-1966
Fax: 202-296-7410
Toll Free: 818-995-6600
Web Address: www.mpaa.org

The Motion Picture Association of America (MPAA)
serves as the voice and advocate of the U.S. motion
picture, home video and television industries.

Motion Picture Editors Guild (MPEG)

7715 Sunset Blvd., Ste. 200
Hollywood, CA 90046 US
Phone: 323-876-4770
Fax: 323-876-0861
Toll Free: 800-705-8700
E-mail Address: *mail@editorsguild.com*
Web Address: www.editorsguild.com
The Motion Picture Editors Guild's (MPEG) web site
provides an online directory of editors, a discussion
forum and links to related magazines and other
organizations that serve the motion picture industry.

National Film Board of Canada (NFB)

Constitution Square, 360 Albert St., Ste. 1005
Ottawa, Ontario K1A 0M9 Canada
Phone: 514-283-9000
Toll Free: 800-267-7710
Web Address: www.nfb.ca
The National Film Board of Canada (NFB) produces
and distributes socially engaged documentaries,
auteur animations, alternative dramas and more.

National Film Preservation Board (NFPB)

101 Independence Ave. SE
Library of Congress (4690)
Washington, DC 20540 US
E-mail Address: *sleg@loc.gov*
Web Address: www.loc.gov/film
The National Film Preservation Board (NFPB) is a
federally-chartered organization that seeks to
preserve national film treasures.

National Film Preservation Foundation (NFPF)

870 Market St., Ste. 1113
San Francisco, CA 94102 US
Phone: 415-392-7291
Fax: 415-392-7293
E-mail Address: *info@filmpreservation.org*
Web Address: www.filmpreservation.org
The National Film Preservation Foundation (NFPF),
a non-profit organization created by the U.S.
Congress, supports activities that preserve American
films and improves film access for study education
and exhibition.

New York Screen Actors Guild (SAG New York)

360 Madison Ave., 12th Fl.
New York, NY 10017 US

Phone: 212-944-1030
Web Address: www.sag.org
The New York Screen Actors Guild (SAG New York) represents guild members in New York and serves as the east coast national headquarters.

Producers Guild of America (PGA)
8530 Wilshire Blvd., Ste. 450
Beverly Hills, CA 90211 US
Phone: 310-358-9020
Fax: 310-358-9520
E-mail Address: *info@producersguild.org*
Web Address: www.producersguild.org
The Producers Guild of America (PGA) is a nonprofit organization for career professionals who initiate, create, coordinate, supervise and control all aspects of the motion picture and television production processes.

Screen Actors Guild (SAG)
5757 Wilshire Blvd., 7th Fl.
Los Angeles, CA 90036-3600 US
Phone: 323-954-1600
Fax: 323-549-6603
Toll Free: 800-724-0767
Web Address: www.sag.org
The Screen Actors Guild (SAG) represents its members through negotiation and enforcement of collective bargaining agreements that establish equitable levels of compensation, benefits and working conditions for performers.

Stuntmen's Association of Motion Pictures (SAMP)
10660 Riverside Dr., 2nd Fl., Ste. E
Toluca Lake, CA 91602 US
Phone: 818-766-4334
Fax: 818-766-5943
E-mail Address: *info@stuntmen.com*
Web Address: www.stuntmen.com
The Stuntmen's Association of Motion Pictures (SAMP) is a nonprofit organization of top stuntmen in the motion picture and television industries.

Sundance Institute
8530 Wilshire Blvd., 3rd Fl.
Beverly Hills, CA 90211-3114 US
Phone: 310-360-1981
Fax: 310-360-1969
E-mail Address: *Institute@sundance.org*
Web Address: www.sundance.org

The Sundance Institute is dedicated to the development of artists involved in independent film and the exhibition of their work.

Women In Film (WIF)
8857 W. Olympic Blvd., Ste. 201
Beverly Hills, CA 90211-3605 US
Phone: 310-657-5144
Fax: 310-657-5154
E-mail Address: *info@wif.org*
Web Address: www.wif.org
Women In Film (WIF) strives to empower, promote and mentor women in the entertainment, communication and media industries through a network of contacts, educational programs and events.

XVI.   Gambling, Gaming Associations

American Gaming Association (AGA)
1299 Pennsylvania Ave. NW, Ste. 1175
Washington, DC 20004 US
Phone: 202-552-2675
Fax: 202-552-2676
E-mail Address: *info@americangaming.org*
Web Address: www.americangaming.org
The AGA, established in 1995, represents the commercial casino entertainment industry by addressing federal legislative and regulatory issues affecting its members and their employees and customers, such as federal taxation, regulatory issues, and travel and tourism matters.

National Indian Gaming Commission (NIGC)
1441 L Street NW, Ste. 9100
Washington, DC 20005 US
Phone: 202-632-7003
Fax: 202-632-7066
Web Address: www.nigc.gov
As an independent federal regulatory agency of the United States, the National Indian Gaming Commission was established pursuant to the Indian Gaming Regulatory Act of 1988. The Commission comprises a Chairman and two Commissioners, each of whom serves on a full-time basis for a three-year term. The Chairman is appointed by the President and must be confirmed by the Senate. The Secretary of the Interior appoints the other two Commissioners. The Commission maintains its headquarters in Washington, D.C., with five Regional Offices, located in Portland, Oregon; Sacramento, California; Phoenix, Arizona; St. Paul, Minnesota; and Tulsa, Oklahoma

XVII. Graphic Artists Associations

Graphic Arts Technical Foundation (GATF)
200 Deer Run Rd.
Sewickley, PA 15143 US
Phone: 412-741-6861
Fax: 412-741-2311
Toll Free: 800-910-4283
E-mail Address: *piagatf@piagatf.org*
Web Address: www.gain.net
Graphic Arts Technical Foundation (GATF) seeks to reposition print media as an integral part of the information technology sector.

Society of Illustrators (SI)
128 E. 63rd St.
New York, NY 10021-7303 US
Phone: 212-838-2560
Fax: 212-838-2561
E-mail Address: *info@societyillustrators.org*
Web Address: www.societyillustrators.org
The Society of Illustrators (SI) promotes the appreciation of illustration through exhibitions, lectures, education and open discussion.

XVIII. Human Resources Industry Associations

Society of Human Resource Management (SHRM)
1800 Duke St.
Alexandria, VA 22314 US
Phone: 703-548-3440
Fax: 703-535-6490
Toll Free: 800-283-7476
Web Address: www.shrm.org
The Society of Human Resource Management (SHRM) addresses the interests and needs of HR professionals through its resource materials.

XIX. Industry Research/Market Research

Adams Media Research
27865 Berwick Dr.
Carmel, CA 93923 US
Phone: 831-624-0303
Fax: 813-624-2190
E-mail Address: *info@adamsmediaresearch.com*
Web Address: www.adamsmediaresearch.com
Adams Media Research is a media industry source of market data and financial analysis in the filmed entertainment and interactive media markets.

Forrester Research
400 Technology Sq.
Cambridge, MA 02139 US
Phone: 617-613-6000
Fax: 617-613-5200
Web Address: www.forrester.com
Forrester Research identifies and analyzes emerging trends in technology and their impact on business. Among the firm's specialties are the financial services, retail, health care, entertainment, automotive and information technology industries.

Marketresearch.com
11200 Rockville Pike, Ste. 504
Rockville, MD 20852 US
Phone: 240-747-3000
Fax: 240-747-3004
Toll Free: 800-298-5699
E-mail Address:
customerservice@marketresearch.com
Web Address: www.marketresearch.com
Marketresearch.com is a leading broker for professional market research and industry analysis. Users are able to search the company's database of research publications including data on global industries, companies, products and trends.

Nielsen
770 Broadway
New York, NY 10003 US
Phone: 646-654-5000
Fax: 646-654-5002
E-mail Address: *GlobalC@nielsen.com*
Web Address: www.nielsen.com
The Nielson Company, provides market research, information and analysis for a number of industries.

Nielsen EDI
6255 Sunset Blvd.
19th Fl.
Hollywood, CA 90028 US
Phone: 323-860-4600
Fax: 323-860-4610
E-mail Address: *mike.marcell@nielsenedi.com*
Web Address: www.entdata.com
Nielsen EDI provides the film industry with instantaneous and comprehensive worldwide box office results.

Plunkett Research, Ltd.
P.O. Drawer 541737
Houston, TX 77254-1737 US
Phone: 713-932-0000

Fax: 713-932-7080
E-mail Address: *info@plunkettresearch.com*
Web Address: www.plunkettresearch.com
Plunkett Research, Ltd. is a leading provider of
market research, industry trends analysis and
business statistics. Since 1985, it has served clients
worldwide, including corporations, universities,
libraries, consultants and government agencies. At
the firm's web site, visitors can view product
information and pricing and access a great deal of
basic market information on industries such as
financial services, InfoTech, e-commerce, health care
and biotech.

Reuters Investor
Web Address: www.investor.reuters.com
Reuters Investor is an excellent source for industry
and company reports written by professional stock
and business analysts. It also offers news and advice
on stocks, funds and personal finance, and allows
users to screen a database of major corporations and
view pertinent financial and business data on selected
firms.

Simba Information
11200 Rockville Pike, Ste. 504
Rockville, MD 20852 US
Phone: 240-747-3091
Fax: 240-747-3004
Toll Free: 888-297-4622
E-mail Address:
customerservice@simbainformation.com
Web Address: www.simbanet.com
Simba Information is a leading authority for market
intelligence and forecasts in all aspects of the media
industry.

XX.   Internet & Online Business Resources

Media Rating Council (MRC)
370 Lexington Ave., Ste. 902
New York, NY 10017 US
Phone: 212-972-0300
Fax: 212-972-2786
E-mail Address: *staff@mediaratingcouncil.org*
Web Address: www.mediaratingcouncil.org
The Media Rating Council (MRC) is a nonprofit
regulatory agency that promotes secure, accurate
audience measurement services for the media
industry.

XXI.   Internet Business/Technology

World Teleport Association (WTA)
55 Broad St., 14th Fl.
New York, NY 10004 US
Phone: 212-825-0218
Fax: 212-825-0075
E-mail Address: *wta@worldteleport.org*
Web Address: www.worldteleport.org
The World Teleport Association (WTA) is a
nonprofit trade association representing the key
commercial players in satellite communications.

XXII.   Internet Industry Associations

**International Academy of Digital Arts and
Sciences (IADAS)**
41 Union Sq. W., Ste. 1131
New York, NY 10003 US
Phone: 212-675-3555
E-mail Address: *dmdavies@iadas.net*
Web Address: www.iadas.net
The International Academy of Digital Arts and
Sciences (IADAS) is dedicated to the progress of
new media worldwide.

World Wide Web Consortium (W3C)
Laboratory for Computer Science
32 Vassar St., Rm. 32-G515
Cambridge, MA 02139 US
Phone: 617-253-2613
Fax: 617-258-5999
Web Address: www.w3.org
The World Wide Web Consortium (W3C), housed at
the Laboratory for Computer Science on the MIT
campus, develops technologies and standards to
enhance the performance and utility of the World
Wide Web.

XXIII.   MBA Resources

MBA Depot
1781 Spyglass Ln., Ste. 198
Austin, TX 78746 US
Phone: 512-499-8728
Fax: 847-556-0608
Toll Free: 888-858-8806
E-mail Address: *contact@mbadepot.com*
Web Address: www.mbadepot.com
MBA Depot is an online community for MBA
professionals.

XXIV. Media Associations-Educational

Center for Communication, Inc.
110 E. 23rd St., Ste. 900
New York, NY 10010 US
Phone: 212-686-5005
Fax: 212-504-2632
E-mail Address: *info@cencom.org*
Web Address: www.cencom.org
The Center for Communication is a nonprofit
organization that encourages university students to
meet professionals in communications industries.

XXV. Media Industry Information

BIA Financial Network, Inc.
15120 Enterprise Ct., Ste. 100
Chantilly, VA 20151 US
Phone: 703-818-2425
Fax: 703-803-3299
Toll Free: 800-331-5086
E-mail Address: *info@bia.com*
Web Address: www.bia.com
The BIA Financial Network offers merchant banking
and financial and strategic advisory services for
media, telecommunications and related industries.

Caslon Analytics Pty Ltd.
P.O. Box 132
Braddon, ACT 2612 Australia
Phone: 02-6262-5445
Fax: 02-6230-6265
Web Address: www.caslon.com.au
Caslon Analytics Pty Ltd. Is a research firm with a
web site that offers a wealth of information on such
sectors as publishing, intellectual property and media
regulatory issues.

Ketupa.net
The Ketupa Project, P.O. Box 132
Braddon, ACT 2612 Australia
Web Address: www.ketupa.net
Ketupa.net offers resources for those interested in the
media industries and information economy.

SRDS Media Solutions
1700 Higgins Rd.
Des Plaines, IL 60018-5605 US
Phone: 847-375-5000
Fax: 847-375-5001
Toll Free: 800-851-7737
Web Address: www.srds.com

SRDS Media Solutions creates publications and
directories that unite the buyers and sellers of media
coverage throughout the nation.

Veronis Suhler Stevenson (VSS)
350 Park Ave.
New York, NY 10022 US
Phone: 212-935-4990
Fax: 212-381-8168
E-mail Address: *stevensonj@vss.com*
Web Address: www.vss.com
Veronis Suhler Stevenson (VSS) is a private equity
firm solely dedicated to the media, communications
and information industries. Its web site offers a
wealth of information about the media industry.

XXVI. News Organizations

Associated Press (AP)
450 W. 33rd St.
New York, NY 10001 US
Phone: 212-621-1500
E-mail Address: *info@ap.org*
Web Address: www.ap.org
The Associated Press (AP), a not-for-profit
organization owned by its 1,500 U.S. daily
newspaper members, is the leading provider of news,
video, graphics, photo and audio services to
newspaper, radio, television and online customers.

XXVII. Printers & Publishers Associations

American Book Producers Association (ABPA)
381 Park Ave. S.
New York, NY 10016 US
Phone: 212-645-2368
Fax: 212-802-2893
Toll Free: 800-209-4575
E-mail Address: *office@abpaonline.org*
Web Address: www.abpaonline.org
The American Book Producers Association (ABPA)
is the trade association for independent book
producers in the U.S. and Canada.

Associated Collegiate Press (ACP)
2221 University Ave. SE, Ste. 121
Minneapolis, MN 55414 US
Phone: 612-625-8335
Fax: 612-626-0720
E-mail Address: *info@studentpress.org*
Web Address: www.studentpress.org/acp

The Associated Collegiate Press (ACP) is an organization of college media outlets, offering a forum for discussion, networking and awards for publications through different categories.

Association for Suppliers of Printing, Publishing and Converting Technologies (NPES)
1899 Preston White Dr.
Reston, VA 20191-4367 US
Phone: 703-264-7200
Fax: 703-620-0994
E-mail Address: *npes@npes.org*
Web Address: www.npes.org
The Association for Suppliers of Printing, Publishing and Converting Technologies (NPES) is a trade association for companies that manufacture and distribute equipment, systems, software and supplies used in printing, publishing and converting printed material.

Association of Alternative Newsweeklies (AAN)
1250 Eye St. NW, Ste. 804
Washington, DC 20005 US
Phone: 202-289-8484
Fax: 202-289-2004
E-mail Address: *web@aan.org*
Web Address: www.aan.org
The Association of Alternative Newsweeklies (AAN) is the trade organization for the alternative newspaper industry.

Association of American Publishers, Inc. (AAP)
71 5th Ave., 2nd Fl.
New York, NY 10003-3004 US
Phone: 212-255-0200
Fax: 212-255-7007
E-mail Address: *dhuntington@publishers.org.*
Web Address: www.publishers.org
The Association of American Publishers (AAP) is the principal trade association of the book publishing industry.

Association of American University Presses, Inc. (AAUP)
71 W. 23rd St.
New York, NY 10010 US
Phone: 212-989-1010
Fax: 212-989-0275
E-mail Address: *info@aaupnet.org*
Web Address: www.aaupnet.org
The Association of American University Presses (AAUP) is a nonprofit group of scholarly publishers.

Association of Canadian Publishers (ACP)
174 Spadina Ave., Ste. 306
Toronto, ON M5T 2C2 Canada
Phone: 416-487-6116
Fax: 416-487-8815
E-mail Address: *admin@canbook.org*
Web Address: www.publishers.ca
The ACP is the national trade organization for English-language Canadian book publishers.

Association of Education Publishers (AEP)
510 Heron Dr., Ste. 201
Logan Township, NJ 08085 US
Phone: 856-241-7772
Fax: 856-241-0709
E-mail Address: *mail@AEPweb.org*
Web Address: www.aepweb.org
The Association of Education Publishers (AEP) supports the growth of educational publishing and its positive impact on learning and teaching. It tracks education and industry information and trends, provides professional development and promotes quality supplemental materials as essential learning resources.

Association of Free Community Papers (AFCP)
P.O. Box 1989
1630 Miner St., Ste. 204
Idaho Springs, CO 80452 US
Fax: 781-459-7770
Toll Free: 877-203-2327
E-mail Address: *afcp@afcp.org*
Web Address: www.afcp.org
The Association of Free Community Papers (AFCP) represents publishers of more than 3,000 free-circulation community papers, reaching nearly 40 million homes weekly.

Book & Periodical Council (BPC)
192 Spadina Ave., Ste. 107
Toronto, ON M5T 2C2 Canada
Phone: 416-975-9366
Fax: 416-975-1839
E-mail Address: *info@thebpc.ca*
Web Address: www.bookandperiodicalcouncil.ca
The Book & Periodical Council (BPC) is the umbrella organization for associations involved in the writing, editing, publishing manufacturing, distribution, selling and lending of books and periodicals in Canada.

Book Industry Study Group, Inc. (BISG)
370 Lexington Ave., Ste. 900

New York, NY 10017 US
Phone: 646-336-7141
Fax: 646-336-6214
E-mail Address: *info@bisg.org*
Web Address: www.bisg.org
Book Industry Study Group (BISG) is a nonprofit
corporation examining the business of print and
electronic media.

Book Manufacturers' Institute, Inc. (BMI)

2 Armand Beach Dr., Ste. 1B
Palm Coast, FL 32137-2612 US
Phone: 386-986-4552
Fax: 386-986-4553
E-mail Address: *info@bmibook.com*
Web Address: www.bmibook.com
The Book Manufacturers' Institute (BMI) is the
leading nationally recognized trade association of the
book manufacturing industry.

BookWire

R.R. Bowker
630 Central Ave.
New Providence, NJ 07974 US
Fax: 908-219-0073
Toll Free: 888-269-5372 ext. 0059
E-mail Address: *alex.stamatellos@bowker.com*
Web Address: www.bookwire.com
BookWire provides information on thousands of
titles, authors and publishers, as well as offering
news, reviews and bestseller lists.

Center for Book Arts, Inc.

28 W. 27th St., 3rd Fl.
New York, NY 10001 US
Phone: 212-481-0295
E-mail Address: *info@centerforbookarts.org*
Web Address: www.centerforbookarts.org
The Center for Book Arts is dedicated to preserving
the traditional crafts of book-making, as well as
exploring and encouraging contemporary
interpretations of the book as an art object.

City & Regional Magazine Association (CRMA)

4929 Wilshire Blvd., Ste. 428
Los Angeles, CA 90010 US
Phone: 323-937-5514
Fax: 323-937-0959
E-mail Address: *administrator@citymag.org*
Web Address: www.citymag.org
The City & Regional Magazine Association (CRMA)
is dedicated exclusively to the interests and concerns
of city and regional magazines.

Council of Literary Magazines & Presses (CLMP)

154 Christopher St., Ste. 3C
New York, NY 10014-9110 US
Phone: 212-741-9110
Fax: 212-741-9112
E-mail Address: *info@clmp.org*
Web Address: www.clmp.org
The Council of Literary Magazines & Presses
(CLMP) serves the independent publishers of fiction,
poetry and prose.

Evangelical Christian Publishers Association (ECPA)

9633 S. 48th St., Ste. 140
Phoenix, AZ 85044 US
Phone: 480-966-3998
Fax: 480-966-1944
E-mail Address: *info@ecpa.org*
Web Address: www.ecpa.org
The Evangelical Christian Publishers Association
(ECPA) is an international, non-profit trade
organization serving the Christian publishing
industry.

Evangelical Press Association (EPA)

P.O. Box 28129
Crystal, MN 55428 US
Phone: 763-535-4793
Fax: 763-535-4794
E-mail Address: *director@epassoc.org*
Web Address: www.epassoc.org
The Evangelical Press Association (EPA) is a
religious and educational nonprofit corporation that
seeks to promote the cause of evangelical Christianity
and enhance the influence of Christian journalism.

International Digital Enterprise Alliance (IDEAlliance)

1421 Prince St., Ste. 230
Alexandria, VA 22314-2805 US
Phone: 703-837-1070
Fax: 703-837-1072
E-mail Address: *info@idealliance.org*
Web Address: www.idealliance.org
The International Digital Enterprise Alliance
(IDEAlliance) is a not-for-profit membership
organization striving to advance user-driven, cross-
industry solutions for all publishing and content-
related processes by developing standards, fostering
business alliances and identifying best practices.

International Newspaper Financial Executives (INFE)
21525 Ridgetop Cir., Ste. 200
Sterling, VA 20166 US
Phone: 703-421-4060
Fax: 703-421-4068
E-mail Address: *infehq@infe.org*
Web Address: www.infe.org
The International Newspaper Financial Executives (INFE) is a professional association serving the newspaper financial management community.

International Newspaper Marketing Association (INMA)
10300 N. Central Expressway, Ste. 467
Dallas, TX 75231 US
Phone: 214-373-9111
Fax: 214-373-9112
Web Address: www.inma.org
The International Newspaper Marketing Association (INMA) is dedicated to strengthening the marketing of newspaper companies' products and approaching all activities with a global perspective.

International Prepress Association (IPA)
7200 France Ave. S., Ste. 223
Edina, MN 55435 US
Phone: 952-896-1908
Fax: 952-896-0181
Toll Free: 800-255-8141
E-mail Address: *info@ipa.org*
Web Address: www.ipa.org
The International Prepress Association (IPA) is comprised of premedia professionals within the corporate, creative, packaging, print publishing and in-plant sectors within the graphic communication industry. It is a forum of peer networking and a source of technical, business and management resources for graphic solutions providers.

International Publishers Association (IPA)
3 Ave. de Miremont
Geneva, 1206 Switzerland
Phone: 41-22-346-3018
Fax: 41-22-347-5717
E-mail Address:
secretariat@internationalpublishers.org
Web Address: www.internationalpublishers.org
The International Publishers Association (IPA) is a non-governmental global group representing all aspects of journal and book publishing worldwide through more than 60 organizations from over 50 countries.

International Publishing Management Association (IPMA)
710 Regency Dr., Ste. 6
Kearney, MO 64060 US
Phone: 816-902-4762
Fax: 816-902-4766
E-mail Address: *ipmainfo@ipma.org*
Web Address: www.ipma.org
The International Publishing Management Association (IPMA) is an exclusive not-for-profit organization dedicated to assisting in-house corporate publishing and distribution professionals.

International Regional Magazine Association, Inc. (IRMA)
E-mail Address: *us002848@earthlink.net*
Web Address: www.regionalmagazines.org
International Regional Magazine Association, Inc. (IRMA) exists to provide free and open communication among the publishers of North American regional publications.

Jewish Book Council (JBC)
520 8th Ave., 4th Fl.
New York, NY 10018 US
Phone: 212-201-2920
Fax: 212-532-4952
E-mail Address: *jbc@jewishbooks.org*
Web Address: www.jewishbookcouncil.org
The Jewish Book Council (JBC) is a non-profit organization dedicated solely to promoting Jewish-interest literature. It serves as a catalyst for the writing, publication, distribution, reading and public awareness of books that reflect the Jewish experience.

Magazine Publishers of America, Inc.
810 7th Ave., 24th Fl.
New York, NY 10019 US
Phone: 212-872-3700
E-mail Address: *mpa@magazine.org*
Web Address: www.magazine.org
Magazine Publishers of America is the industry association for consumer magazines.

Media Coalition, Inc.
275 7th Ave., Ste. 1504
New York, NY 10003 US
Phone: 212-587-4025
Fax: 212-587-2436
Web Address: www.mediacoalition.org
Media Coalition, Inc. is an association that defends the First Amendment right to produce and sell books,

magazines, movies, recordings, videotapes, DVDs and video games, as well as the American public's First Amendment right to have access to the broadest possible range of opinion and entertainment.

National Association of Independent Publishers Representatives (NAIPR)
111 E. 14th St., PMB 157
Zeckendorf Towers
New York, NY 10003 US
Fax: 800-416-2586
Toll Free: 888-624-7779
E-mail Address: *greatblue2@rcn.com*
Web Address: www.naipr.org
The National Association of Independent Publishers Representatives (NAIPR) is a trade association of book publishers' commission representatives, book publishers and other associate members.

National Association of Printers & Lithographers (NAPL)
75 W. Century Rd., Ste. 100
Paramus, NJ 07652-1408 US
Phone: 201-634-9600
Toll Free: 800-642-6275
E-mail Address: *information@napl.org*
Web Address: www.napl.org
The National Association of Printers & Lithographers (NAPL) focuses on helping graphic arts professionals increase their expertise.

National Newspaper Association (NNA)
129 Neff Annex
University of Missouri-Columbia
Columbia, MO 65211 US
Phone: 573-882-5800
Fax: 573-884-5490
Toll Free: 800-829-4662
Web Address: www.nna.org
The National Newspaper Association (NNA) represents the owners, publishers and editors of America's community newspapers.

National Press Foundation (NPF)
1211 Connecticut Ave. NW, Ste. 310
Washington, DC 20036 US
Phone: 202-663-7280
Fax: 202-530-2855
E-mail Address: *npf@nationalpress.org*
Web Address: www.nationalpress.org
The National Press Foundation (NPF) seeks to increase journalists' knowledge of complex issues in order to improve public understanding.

National Scholastic Press Association (NSPA)
2221 University Ave. SE, Ste. 121
Minneapolis, MN 55414 US
Phone: 612-625-8335
Fax: 612-626-0720
E-mail Address: *info@studentpress.org*
Web Address: www.studentpress.org/nspa
The National Scholastic Press Association (NSPA) is a non-profit educational association that provides journalism education services to students, teachers, media advisers and others worldwide.

New York Center for Independent Publishing (The) (NYCIP)
20 W. 44th St.
New York, NY 10036 US
Phone: 212-764-7021
Fax: 212-840-2046
E-mail Address: *info@smallpress.org*
Web Address: www.nycip.org
The New York Center for Independent Publishing (NYCIP), formerly the Small Press Center (SPC), provides information and draws public awareness to the offerings of smaller, independent publishers.

Newspaper Association of America (NAA)
4401 Wilson Blvd., Ste. 900
Arlington, VA 22203-1867 US
Phone: 571-366-1000
Fax: 571-366-1195
E-mail Address: *webmaster@naa.org*
Web Address: www.naa.org
The Newspaper Association of America (NAA) is a nonprofit organization representing the newspaper industry.

Newspaper Guild (The)
501 3rd St. NW, 6th Fl.
Washington, DC 20001-2797 US
Phone: 202-434-7177
Fax: 202-434-1472
E-mail Address: *guild@cwa-union.org*
Web Address: www.newsguild.org
The Newspaper Guild exists to advance the economic interests and improve the working conditions of its members, raise the standards of journalism and ethics in the industry and promote industrial unity.

Organization for the Advancement of Structured Information Standards (OASIS)
630 Boston Rd., Ste. M-102
Billerica, MA 01821 US
Phone: 978-667-5115

Fax: 978-667-5114
E-mail Address: *info@oasis-open.org*
Web Address: www.oasis-open.org
The Organization for the Advancement of Structured
Information Standards (OASIS) is a consortium
which drives the development and adoption of e-
business standards.

**Periodical & Book Association of America, Inc.
(PBAA)**
481 8th Ave., Ste. 826
New York, NY 10001 US
Phone: 212-563-6502
Fax: 212-563-4098
E-mail Address: *lscott@pbaa.net*
Web Address: www.pbaa.net
The Periodical & Book Association of America
(PBAA) is an organization that represents newsstand
publications to the retail community.

**Protestant Church-Owned Publishers Association
(PCPA)**
2850 Kalamazoo Ave. SE
Grand Rapids, MI 49560 US
Phone: 616-224-0795
E-mail Address: *mulder@pcpaonline.org*
Web Address: www.pcpanews.org
The Protestant Church-Owned Publishers
Association (PCPA) is an association of publishers
directly connected to their respective church
denominations and is devoted to the welfare of
official church-owned publishing houses.

Publishers Marketing Association (PMA)
627 Aviation Way
Manhattan Beach, CA 90266 US
Phone: 310-372-2732
Fax: 310-374-3342
E-mail Address: *info@pma-online.org*
Web Address: www.pma-online.org
The Publishers Marketing Association (PMA) is a
trade association of independent publishers.

R.R. Bowker LLC
630 Central Ave.
New Providence, NJ 07974 US
Phone: 908-286-1090
Toll Free: 888-269-5372
E-mail Address: *isbn-san@bowker.com*
Web Address: www.bowker.com
Bowker is a leading source for book, serial and
publishing data serving library, publishing and
bookselling professionals and their patrons

worldwide. The company is also the steward of the
U.S. International Standard Book Numbering (ISBN)
Agency.

Society for Scholarly Publishing (SSP)
10200 W. 44th Ave., Ste. 304
Wheat Ridge, CO 80033-2840 US
Phone: 303-422-3914
Fax: 303-422-8894
E-mail Address: *info@sspnet.org*
Web Address: www.sspnet.org
The mission of the Society for Scholarly Publishing
(SSP) is to facilitate learning, communication and the
advancement of appropriate technologies among
those involved in scholarly communication.

**Southern Newspaper Publishers Association
(SNPA)**
3680 N. Peachtree Rd., St. 300
Atlanta, GA 30341 US
Phone: 404-256-0444
Fax: 404-252-9135
E-mail Address: *edward@snpa.org*
Web Address: www.snpa.org
The Southern Newspaper Publishers Association
(SNPA) is a regional trade association representing
daily newspaper owners and publishers.

**Women's National Book Association, Inc.
(WNBA)**
2166 Broadway, Ste. 9-E
New York, NY 10024 US
Phone: 212-208-4629
Fax: 212-208-4629
E-mail Address: *publicity@bookbuzz.com*
Web Address: www.wnba-books.org
The Women's National Book Association (WNBA)
is the oldest organization open to women and men in
all occupations allied to the publishing industry.

World Association of Newspapers (WAN)
7 Rue Geoffroy St. Hilaire
Paris, 75005 France
Phone: 33-1-47-42-85-00
Fax: 33-1-47-42-49-48
E-mail Address: *contact_us@wan.asso.fr*
Web Address: www.wan-press.org
The World Association of Newspapers (WAN)
groups 73 national newspaper associations,
individual newspaper executives in 102 nations, 11
national and international news agencies, a media
foundation and nine affiliated regional and
worldwide press organizations. It defends and

promotes freedom of the press and represents 18,000 newspapers.

Yellow Pages Association (YPA)
200 Connell Dr., Ste. 1700
Connell Corporate Park
Berkeley Heights, NJ 07922-2747 US
Phone: 908-286-2380
Fax: 908-286-0620
E-mail Address: *neg.norton@ypassociation.org*
Web Address: www.ypassociation.org
The Yellow Pages Association (YPA) leads, serves and helps to foster the global print and electronic media industry focused on Yellow Pages publishers and other associated professionals.

XXVIII. Recording & Music Associations

American Composers Alliance (ACA)
648 Broadway, Rm. 803
New York, NY 10012 US
Phone: 212-362-8900
Fax: 212-925-6798
E-mail Address: *info@composers.com*
Web Address: www.composers.com
The American Composers Alliance (ACA) is a membership organization serving professional composers of concert music in America.

American Federation of Musicians
1501 Broadway, Ste. 600
New York, NY 10036 US
Phone: 212-869-1330
Fax: 212-764-6134
Web Address: www.afm.org
The American Federation of Musicians (AFM) is the largest union in the world for music professionals.

American Society of Composers, Authors & Publishers (ASCAP)
1 Lincoln Plaza
New York, NY 10023 US
Phone: 212-621-6000
Fax: 212-724-9064
E-mail Address: *info@ascap.com*
Web Address: www.ascap.com
American Society of Composers, Authors & Publishers (ASCAP) is a membership association of U.S. composers, songwriters and publishers of every kind of music with hundreds of thousands of members worldwide.

Broadcast Music, Inc. (BMI)
320 W. 57th St.
New York, NY 10019-3790 US
Phone: 212-586-2000
Web Address: www.bmi.com
Broadcast Music, Inc. (BMI) is an American performing rights organization that represents songwriters, composers and music publishers in all genres of music.

Canadian Recording Industry Association (CRIA)
85 Mowat Avenue
Toronto, ON M6K 3E3 Canada
Phone: 416-967-7272
Fax: 416-967-9415
E-mail Address: *info@cria.ca*
Web Address: www.cria.ca
The CRIA is the trade organization for the sound recording manufacturing and marketing sector in Canada.

Country Music Association, Inc. (CMA)
1 Music Cir. S.
Nashville, TN 37203 US
Phone: 615-244-2840
Fax: 615-726-0314
Web Address: www.cmaworld.com
The Country Music Association (CMA) is a trade association dedicated to promoting and guiding the development of country music throughout the world.

International Association of Audio Information Services (IAAIS)
Toll Free: 800-280-5325
Web Address: www.iaais.org
International Association of Audio Information Services (IAAIS) is an organization that provides audio access to information for people who are print-disabled.

International Federation of the Phonographic Industry (IFPI)
54 Regent Street
London, W1B 5RE UK
Phone: 44 (0)20 7878 7900
Fax: 44 (0)20 7878 7950
E-mail Address: *info@ifpi.org*
Web Address: www.ifpi.org
The International Federation of the Phonographic Industry (IFPI) represents recorded music publishers worldwide in 75 countries. Its goals include the fight against music piracy and the promotion of fair market access and adequate copyright laws. The IFPI

publishes extensive studies yearly regarding its industry.

International Recording Media Association

182 Nassau St., Ste. 204
Princeton, NJ 08542-7005 US
Phone: 609-279-1700
Fax: 609-279-1999
E-mail Address: *info@recordingmedia.org*
Web Address: www.recordingmedia.org
The International Recording Media Association is a worldwide trade association encompassing organizations involved in every facet of recording media.

Music Publisher's Association of the United States (MPA)

243 5th Ave., Ste. 236
New York, NY 10016 US
Phone: 212-327-4044
E-mail Address: *admin@mpa.org*
Web Address: www.mpa.org
The Music Publisher's Association of the United States (MPA) serves as a forum for publishers to deal with the music industry's vital issues and is actively involved in supporting and advancing compliance with copyright law, combating copyright infringement and exploring the need for further reform.

National Association of Recording Merchandisers (NARM)

9 Eves Dr., Ste. 120
Marlton, NJ 08053 US
Phone: 856-596-2221
Fax: 856-596-3268
Web Address: www.narm.com
The National Association of Recording Merchandisers (NARM) is a non-profit trade association that serves the music retailing community in the areas of networking, advocacy, education, information and promotion.

National Music Publisher's Association (NMPA)

101 Constitution Ave. NW, Ste. 705 E.
Washington, DC 20001 US
Phone: 202-742-4375
Fax: 202-742-4377
Web Address: www.nmpa.org
The National Music Publisher's Association (NMPA) seeks to protect, promote and advance the interests of music's creators.

Recording Academy (The)

3402 Pico Blvd.
Santa Monica, CA 90405 US
Phone: 310-392-3777
Fax: 310-399-3090
Web Address: www.grammy.com
The Recording Academy is the premier outlet for honoring achievements in the recording arts and supporting the music community. It is internationally known for the Grammy awards.

Recording Industry Association of America (RIAA)

1025 F St. NW, 10th Fl.
Washington, DC 20004 US
Phone: 202-775-0101
E-mail Address: *webmaster@riaa.com*
Web Address: www.riaa.com
The Recording Industry Association of America (RIAA) is the trade group that represents the U.S. recording industry.

Recording Industry of Association of Korea (RIAK)

3F Shinsung Bldg., 108-4
Sungsan-dong, Mapo-gu
Seoul, Korea
Phone: 82-2-322-1562-4
Fax: 82-2-322-2464
E-mail Address: *master@riak.or.kr*
Web Address: www.miak.or.kr
The RIAK, founded by the Korean Ministry of Culture & Information, represent the interests of its 133 member companies in the recorded music, video and gaming industries.

Society of Professional Audio Recording Services (SPARS)

9 Music Sq. S., Ste. 222
Nashville, TN 37203 US
Fax: 616-296-0386
Toll Free: 800-771-7727
E-mail Address: *spars@spars.com*
Web Address: www.spars.com
The Society of Professional Audio Recording Services (SPARS) is an organization for members of the recording industry to share practical business information about audio and multimedia facility ownership, management and operations.

Songwriters Guild of America

209 10th Ave. S, Ste. 321
Nashville, TN 37203 US

Phone: 615-742-9945
Fax: 615-742-9948
E-mail Address: *corporate@songwritersguild.com*
Web Address: www.songwritersguild.com
The Songwriters Guild of America is the nation's largest and oldest songwriters' organization, serving its members with information and programs to further their careers and understanding of the music industry.

XXIX. Research & Development, Laboratories

Electronics and Telecommunications Research Institute (ETRI)
138 Gajeong-Dong
Yuseong-gu
Daejeon, 305-700 Korea
Phone: 82-42-860-6114
Web Address: www.etri.re.kr
Established in 1976, ETRI is a non-profit government-funded research organization that promotes technological excellence. The research institute has successfully developed information technologies such as TDX-Exchange, High Density Semiconductor Microchips, Mini-Super Computer (TiCOM), and Digital Mobile Telecommunication System (CDMA). ETRI's focus is on information technologies, robotics, telecommunications, digital broadcasting and future technology strategies.

XXX. Retail Industry Associations

Entertainment Merchants Association (The) (EMA)
16530 Ventura Blvd., Ste. 400
Encino, CA 91436-4551 US
Phone: 818-385-1500
Fax: 818-385-0567
E-mail Address: *emaoffice@entmerch.org*
Web Address: www.vsda.org
The Entertainment Merchants Association (EMA), formerly the Video Software Dealer Association (VSDA), is the international trade organization that represents the home entertainment industry. The EMA was established in 2006 through the merger of the Interactive Entertainment Merchants Association (IEMA) and the VSDA.

XXXI. Software Industry Associations

Entertainment Software Association (ESA)
575 7th St. NW, Ste. 300

Washington, DC 20004 US
E-mail Address: *esa@theesa.com*
Web Address: www.theesa.com
The Entertainment Software Association (ESA) serves the business and public affairs needs of companies that publish video and computer games for consoles, personal computers and the Internet.

XXXII. Sports Industry Resources

American Bar Association (ABA) Forum on the Entertainment & Sports Industries
321 N. Clark St.
Chicago, IL 60610 US
Phone: 312-988-5000
Toll Free: 800-285-2221
E-mail Address: *tucok@staff.abanet.org*
Web Address:
www.abanet.org/forums/entsports/home.html
The American Bar Association (ABA) Forum on the Entertainment & Sports Industries, formed in 1977, seeks to educate attorneys in the transactional and legal principles of sports and entertainment law. The forum's quarterly newsletter is directed toward lawyers practicing entertainment, sports, arts and intellectual property law.

XXXIII. Toy Industry Associations

Toy Industry Association, Inc.
1115 Broadway, Ste. 400
New York, NY 10010 US
Phone: 212-675-1141
Fax: 212-633-1429
Web Address: www.toy-tia.org
The Toy Industry Association is a leading organization for manufacturers, designers, inventors and retailers of toys and games. It is the owner and manager of the American International Toy Fair held each year in the U.S.

XXXIV. Trade Associations-Global

World Trade Organization (WTO)
Rue de Lausanne 154, CH-1211
Geneva, 21 Switzerland
Phone: 41-22-739-51-11
Fax: 41-22-731-42-06
E-mail Address: *enquiries@wto.og*
Web Address: www.wto.org
The World Trade Organization (WTO) is a global organization dealing with the rules of trade between

nations. To become a member, nations must agree to abide by certain guidelines. Membership increases a nation's ability to import and export efficiently.

XXXV.   U.S. Government Agencies

Bureau of Economic Analysis (BEA)
1441 L St. NW
Washington, DC 20230 US
Phone: 202-606-9900
E-mail Address: *customerservice@bea.gov*
Web Address: www.bea.gov/index.htm
The Bureau of Economic Analysis (BEA), an agency of the U.S. Department of Commerce, is the nation's economic accountant, preparing estimates that illuminate key national, international and regional aspects of the U.S. economy.

Bureau of Labor Statistics (BLS)
2 Massachusetts Ave. NE
Washington, DC 20212-0001 US
Phone: 202-691-5200
Fax: 202-691-6325
Web Address: stats.bls.gov
The Bureau of Labor Statistics (BLS) is the principal fact-finding agency for the Federal Government in the field of labor economics and statistics. It is an independent national statistical agency that collects, processes, analyzes and disseminates statistical data to the American public, U.S. Congress, other federal agencies, state and local governments, business and labor. The BLS also serves as a statistical resource to the Department of Labor.

FCC-Common Carrier Bureau (CCB)
445 12th St. SW
Washington, DC 20554 US
Phone: 202-418-1500
Fax: 202-418-2825
E-mail Address: *fccinfo@fcc.gov*
Web Address: www.fcc.gov/wcb
The Common Carrier Bureau (CCB) is a unit of the Federal Communications Commission (FCC). It is responsible for administering the FCC's policies concerning companies that provide wireline telecommunications.

FCC-Mass Media Bureau
445 12th St. SW
Washington, DC 20554 US
Fax: 202-418-0232
Toll Free: 888-225-5322
E-mail Address: *mbinfo@fcc.gov*

Web Address: www.fcc.gov/mb
The Mass Media Bureau of the Federal Communications Commission (FCC) regulates broadcast television and radio stations in the United States for the FCC.

Federal Communications Commission (FCC)
445 12th St. SW
Washington, DC 20554 US
Fax: 866-418-0232
Toll Free: 888-225-5322
E-mail Address: *fccinfo@fcc.gov*
Web Address: www.fcc.gov
The Federal Communications Commission (FCC) is an independent U.S. government agency established by the Communications Act of 1934, and is responsible for regulating interstate and international communications by radio, television, wire, satellite and cable.

Federal Communications Commission (FCC)-International Bureau
445 12th St. SW
Washington, DC 20554 US
Fax: 866-418-0232
Toll Free: 888-225-5322
E-mail Address: *fccinfo@fcc.gov*
Web Address: www.fcc.gov/ib
The International Bureau of the Federal Communications Commission (FCC) exists to administer the FCC's international telecommunications policies and obligations.

Federal Communications Commission (FCC)-Office of Engineering & Technology (OET)
445 12th St. SW
Washington, DC 20554 US
Fax: 866-418-0232
Toll Free: 888-225-5322
E-mail Address: *fccinfo@fcc.gov*
Web Address: www.fcc.gov/oet
The Office of Engineering & Technology (OET) unit of the Federal Communications Commission (FCC) evaluates technologies and equipment.

Federal Communications Commission (FCC)-Wireless Telecommunications Bureau
445 12th St. SW
Washington, DC 20554 US
Fax: 202-418-0710
Toll Free: 888-225-5322
Web Address: wireless.fcc.gov

The Wireless Bureau of the Federal Communications Commission (FCC) handles nearly all FCC domestic wireless telecommunications programs and policies, including cellular and PCS phones, pagers and two-way radios. The bureau also regulates the use of radio spectrum for businesses, aircraft/ship operators and individuals.

FedWorld
5285 Port Royal Rd.
Springfield, VA 22161 US
Phone: 703-605-6000
E-mail Address: *helpdesk@fedworld.gov*
Web Address:
www.fedworld.gov/jobs/jobsearch.html
FedWorld, a program of the U.S. Department of Commerce, provides an annotated index of links to job-, labor- and management-related U.S. government web sites. Employment opportunities, labor statistics and links to other government information sites are also offered. The site is managed by the National Technical Information Service (NTIS).

Government Printing Office (GPO)
732 N. Capitol St. NW
Washington, DC 20401 US
Phone: 202-512-0000
Fax: 202-512-2104
E-mail Address: *contactcenter@gpo.gov*
Web Address: www.gpo.gov
The U.S. Government Printing Office (GPO) is the primary information source concerning the activities of Federal agencies. GPO gathers, catalogues, produces, provides, authenticates and preserves published information.

U.S. Business Advisor
Web Address: www.business.gov
U.S. Business Advisor offers a searchable directory of business-specific government information. Topics include taxes, regulations, international trade, financial assistance and business development. U.S. Business Advisor was created by the Small Business Administration in a partnership with 21 other federal agencies.

U.S. Census Bureau
4700 Silver Hill Rd.
Washington, DC 20233 US
E-mail Address: *pio@census.gov*
Web Address: www.census.gov

The U.S. Census Bureau is the official collector of data about the people and economy of the U.S. It provides official social, demographic and economic information.

U.S. Copyright Office
101 Independence Ave. SE
Washington, DC 20559-6000 US
Phone: 202-707-3000
Web Address: www.copyright.gov
The U.S. Copyright Office promotes the progress of the arts and protection for the works of authors.

U.S. Department of Commerce (DOC)
1401 Constitution Ave. NW
Washington, DC 20230 US
Phone: 202-482-2000
E-mail Address: *cgutierrez@doc.gov*
Web Address: www.doc.gov
The U.S. Department of Commerce (DOC) regulates trade and provides valuable economic analysis of the economy.

U.S. Department of Labor (DOL)
200 Constitution Ave. NW
Washington, DC 20210 US
Toll Free: 866-487-2365
Web Address: www.dol.gov
The U.S. Department of Labor (DOL) is the government agency responsible for labor regulations. This site provides tools to help citizens find out whether companies are complying with family and medical-leave requirements.

U.S. Patent and Trademark Office (PTO)
Dulany St., 1st Fl.
Alexandria, VA 22314 US
Phone: 571-272-1000
Fax: 571-273-8300
Toll Free: 800-786-9199
Web Address: www.uspto.gov
The U.S. Patent and Trademark Office (PTO) administers patent and trademark laws for the U.S. and enables registration of patents and trademarks.

U.S. Securities and Exchange Commission (SEC)
100 F St. NE
Office of Investor Education and Assistance
Washington, DC 20549 US
Phone: 202-551-6551
Toll Free: 800-732-0330
E-mail Address: *help@sec.gov*
Web Address: www.sec.gov

The U.S. Securities and Exchange Commission (SEC) is a nonpartisan, quasi-judicial regulatory agency responsible for administering federal securities laws. These laws are designed to protect investors in securities markets and ensure that they have access to disclosure of all material information concerning publicly traded securities. Visitors to the web site can access the EDGAR database of corporate financial and business information.

XXXVI. Wireless & Cellular Industry Associations

WiMedia Alliance
2400 Bishop Dr., Ste. 375
San Ramon, CA 94583 US
Phone: 925-275-6604
Fax: 925-886-3809
E-mail Address: *rranck@inventures.com*
Web Address: www.wimedia.org
The WiMedia Alliance is an open, nonprofit wireless industry association that promotes the adoption and standardization of ultrawideband (UWB) worldwide for use in the PC, CE and mobile market segments.

XXXVII. Writers, Photographers & Editors Associations

American Association of Sunday and Feature Editors (AASFE)
College of Journalism, 1117 Journalism Bldg.
University of Maryland
College Park, MD 20742-7111 US
Phone: 301-314-2631
E-mail Address: *kchadha@jmail.umd.edu*
Web Address: www.aasfe.org
The American Association of Sunday and Feature Editors (AASFE) is an organization and a network of creative editors in the U.S. and Canada dedicated to the quality of features in newspapers and to the craft of feature writing.

American Medical Writers Association (AMWA)
40 W. Gude Dr., Ste. 101
Rockville, MD 20850-1192 US
Phone: 301-294-5303
Fax: 301-294-9006
E-mail Address: *amwa@amwa.org*
Web Address: www.amwa.org
The American Medical Writers Association (AMWA) seeks to promote excellence in writing,

editing and producing printed and electronic biomedical communications.

American Society of Journalists and Authors, Inc. (ASJA)
1501 Broadway, Ste. 302
New York, NY 10036 US
Phone: 212-997-0947
Fax: 212-937-2315
E-mail Address: *director@asja.org*
Web Address: www.asja.org
The American Society of Journalists and Authors (ASJA) is of the nation's leading organizations of independent nonfiction writers.

American Society of Magazine Editors (ASME)
810 7th Ave., 24th Fl.
New York, NY 10019 US
Phone: 212-872-3700
E-mail Address: *mpa@magazine.org*
Web Address: www.magazine.org/editorial
The American Society of Magazine Editors (ASME) is a professional organization for editors of print and online magazines.

American Society of Media Photographers (ASMP)
150 N. 2nd St.
Philadelphia, PA 19106 US
Phone: 215-451-2767
Fax: 215-451-0880
E-mail Address: *dyson@asmp.org*
Web Address: www.asmp.org
The American Society of Media Photographers (ASMP) is a trade organization that promotes photographers' rights, educates photographers in better business practices and produces business publications for photographers.

American Society of Newspaper Editors (ASNE)
11690B Sunrise Valley Dr.
Reston, VA 20191-1409 US
Phone: 703-453-1122
Fax: 703-453-1133
E-mail Address: *asne@asne.org*
Web Address: www.asne.org
The American Society of Newspaper Editors (ASNE) is an association that brings together editors of daily newspapers and people directly involved with developing content for daily newspapers.

Associated Press Sports Editors (APSE)
Phone: 215-854-4545

E-mail Address: *jjenks@phillynews.com*
Web Address: apse.dallasnews.com
Associated Press Sports Editors (APSE) is a trade organization for professional sports reporters, editors, copy editors and designers.

Association for Women in Sports Media (AWSM)

P.O. Box F
Bayville, NJ 08721 US
E-mail Address: *info@awsmonline.org*
Web Address: www.awsmonline.org
The Association for Women in Sports Media (AWSM) is a global organization of over 600 women and men employed in sports writing, editing, broadcast and production, public relations and sports information.

Association of Writers & Writing Programs (AWP)

George Mason University, Mailstop 1E3
Fairfax, VA 22030-4444 US
Phone: 703-993-4301
Fax: 703-993-4302
E-mail Address: *awp@awpwriter.org*
Web Address: www.awpwriter.org
The Association of Writers & Writing Programs (AWP) exists to foster literary talent and achievement, to advance the art of writing as essential to a good education and to serve the makers, teachers, students and readers of contemporary writing.

Authors Guild

31 E. 32th St., 7th Fl.
New York, NY 10016 US
Phone: 212-563-5904
Fax: 212-564-5363
E-mail Address: *staff@authorsguild.org*
Web Address: www.authorsguild.org
The Authors Guild is a society of published authors and a leading advocate for fair compensation, free speech and copyright protection.

Authors Registry, Inc.

31 E. 32th St., 7th Fl.
New York, NY 10016 US
Phone: 212-563-6920
Fax: 212-564-5363
E-mail Address: *staff@authorsregistry.org*
Web Address: www.authorsregistry.org
The Authors Registry is a nonprofit organization formed to help expedite the flow of royalty payments and small re-use fees to authors, particularly for new-media uses. It was founded by the Authors Guild.

Editorial Freelancers Association (EFA)

71 W. 23rd St., 4th Fl.
New York, NY 10010 US
Phone: 212-929-5400
Fax: 212-929-5439
Toll Free: 866-929-5400
E-mail Address: *office@the-efa.org*
Web Address: www.the-efa.org
The Editorial Freelancers Association (EFA) is a national, nonprofit, professional organization of self-employed workers in the publishing and communications industries.

Education Writers Association (EWA)

2122 P St. NW, Ste. 201
Washington, DC 20037 US
Phone: 202-452-9830
Fax: 202-452-9837
E-mail Address: *ewa@ewa.org*
Web Address: www.ewa.org
The Education Writers Association (EWA) is the national professional organization of education reporters.

Football Writers Association of America (FWAA)

18652 Vista del Sol
Dallas, TX 75287 US
E-mail Address: *webmaster@sportswriters.net*
Web Address: www.footballwriters.com
The Football Writers Association of America (FWAA) consists of North American journalists, broadcasters and publishers who cover college football. The FWAA also includes executives in all areas that involve the game.

Garden Writers Association of America (GWAA)

10210 Leatherleaf Ct.
Manassas, VA 20111 US
Phone: 703-257-1032
Fax: 703-257-0213
Web Address: www.gwaa.org
The Garden Writers Association of America (GWAA) is an organization of over 1,800 professional communicators in the lawn and garden industry.

Horror Writers Association (HWA)

P.O. Box 50577
Palo Alto, CA 94303 US
E-mail Address: *hwa@horror.org*

Web Address: www.horror.org
The Horror Writers Association (HWA) is a
worldwide organization of writers and publishing
professionals dedicated to promoting the interests of
writers of horror and dark fantasy.

International Journalists' Network (IJNet)
International Center for Journalists
1616 H St. NW, 3rd Fl.
Washington, DC 20006 US
Phone: 202-737-3700
Fax: 202-737-0530
E-mail Address: *editor@icfj.org*
Web Address: www.ijnet.org
International Journalists' Network (IJNet) is an online
source for media news, journalism training
opportunities, reports on the state of media around
the world and media directories.

International Women's Writing Guild (IWWG)
Box 810, Gracie Station
New York, NY 10028-0082 US
Phone: 212-737-7536
Fax: 212-737-9469
E-mail Address: *dirhahn@aol.com*
Web Address: www.iwwg.com
The International Women's Writing Guild (IWWG)
is a network for the personal and professional
empowerment of women through writing.

Investigative Reporters & Editors, Inc. (IRE)
138 Neff Annex
Missouri School of Journalism
Columbia, MO 65211 US
Phone: 573-882-2042
Fax: 573-882-5431
E-mail Address: *info@ire.org*
Web Address: www.ire.org
Investigative Reporters & Editors, Inc. (IRE) is a
non-profit organization that provides educational
services to reporters, editors and others interested in
investigative journalism.

Media Communications Association International (MCAI)
2810 Crossroads Dr., Ste. 3800
Madison, WI 53718 US
Phone: 608-443-2464
Fax: 608-443-2474
E-mail Address: *execdirect@mca-i.org*
Web Address: www.mca-i.org
The Media Communications Association
International (MCAI) is the leading global

community for media communications professionals
seeking to drive the convergence of communications
and technology for the growth of the profession.

Mystery Writers of America (MWA)
17 E. 47 St., 6th Fl.
New York, NY 10017 US
Phone: 212-888-8171
Fax: 212-888-8107
E-mail Address: *mwa@mysterywriters.org*
Web Address: www.mysterywriters.org
Mystery Writers of America (MWA) is a non-profit
organization for mystery writers and other
professionals in the mystery field.

National Association of Black Journalists (NABJ)
8701-A Adelphi Rd.
Adelphi, MD 20783 US
Phone: 301-445-7100
Fax: 301-445-7101
Toll Free: 866-479-6225
E-mail Address: *nabj@nabj.org*
Web Address: www.nabj.org
The National Association of Black Journalists
(NABJ) is an organization of journalists, students and
media-related professionals that provides programs
and services to and advocates on behalf of black
journalists worldwide.

National Association of Hispanic Journalists (NAHJ)
1000 National Press Bldg., 529 14th St. NW
Washington, DC 20045-2001 US
Phone: 202-662-7145
Fax: 202-662-7144
Toll Free: 888-346-6245
E-mail Address: *nahj@nahj.org*
Web Address: www.nahj.org
The National Association of Hispanic Journalists
(NAHJ) is dedicated to the recognition and
professional advancement of Hispanics in the news
industry.

National Association of Science Writers, Inc. (NASW)
P.O. Box 890
Hedgesville, WV 25427 US
Phone: 304-754-5077
Fax: 304-754-5076
E-mail Address: *director@nasw.org*
Web Address: www.nasw.org
The National Association of Science Writers
(NASW) exists to foster the dissemination of

accurate information regarding science through all media devoted to informing the public.

National Collegiate Baseball Writers Association (NCBWA)
5201 N. O'Connor, Ste. 300
Irving, TX 75039 US
E-mail Address: *webmaster@sportswriters.net*
Web Address: www.ncbwa.com
The National Collegiate Baseball Writers Association (NCBWA) consists of writers, broadcasters and publicists of college baseball in the U.S.

National Conference of Editorial Writers (NCEW)
3899 N. Front St.
Harrisburg, PA 17110 US
Phone: 717-703-3015
Fax: 717-703-3014
E-mail Address: *ncew@pa-news.org*
Web Address: www.ncew.org
The National Conference of Editorial Writers (NCEW) strives to stimulate the conscience and quality of editorial writing.

National Federation of Abstracting & Information Services (NFAIS)
1518 Walnut St., Ste. 1004
Philadelphia, PA 19102 US
Phone: 215-893-1561
Fax: 215-893-1564
E-mail Address: *nfais@nfais.org*
Web Address: www.nfais.org
The National Federation of Abstracting & Information Services (NFAIS) serves groups that aggregate, organize and facilitate access to information and provides a forum for its members to address common interests through education and advocacy.

National Federation of Press Women (NFPW)
P.O. Box 5556
Arlington, VA 22205 US
Fax: 703-812-4555
Toll Free: 800-780-2715
E-mail Address: *presswomen@aol.com*
Web Address: www.nfpw.org
The National Federation of Press Women (NFPW) is an organization of professional journalists and communicators.

National Press Club (NPC)
529 14th St. NW, 13th Fl.
Washington, DC 20045 US

Phone: 202-662-7500
Web Address: npc.press.org
The National Press Club (NPC) provides people who gather and disseminate news with a center for the advancement of their professional standards and skills, the promotion of free expression, mutual support and social fellowship.

National Press Club of Canada
150 Albert St., 2nd Fl.
Ottawa, Ontario K1P 5G2 Canada
Phone: 613-233-5641
Fax: 613-233-3511
E-mail Address: *rosaleen@flora.org*
Web Address: www.pressclub.on.ca
The National Press Club of Canada provides a location for growth and discussion and a social home for reporters, editors and others involved in the news industry.

National Press Photographers Association, Inc. (NPPA)
3200 Croasdaile Dr., Ste. 306
Durham, NC 27705 US
Phone: 919-383-7246
Fax: 919-383-7261
E-mail Address: *info@nppa.org*
Web Address: www.nppa.org
National Press Photographers Association, Inc. (NPPA) seeks to advance, create, edit and distribute photojournalism in all news media.

National Society of Newspaper Columnists (NSNC)
PO Box 411532
San Francisco, CA 94141 US
Fax: 866-635-5759
Toll Free: 866-440-6762
Web Address: www.columnists.com
The National Society of Newspaper Columnists (NSNC) provides a forum for newspaper columnists to discuss the industry and common interests.

National Writers Union (NWU)
113 University Pl., 6th Fl.
New York, NY 10003 US
Phone: 212-254-0279
Fax: 212-254-0673
E-mail Address: *nwu@nwu.org*
Web Address: www.nwu.org
The National Writers Union (NWU) is a labor union that represents freelance writers in all genres, formats and media. It is committed to improving the

economic and working conditions of freelance writers.

Outdoor Writers Association of America (OWAA)
121 Hickory St., Ste. 1
Missoula, MT 59801 US
Phone: 406-728-7434
Fax: 406-728-7445
Toll Free: 800-692-2477
E-mail Address: *krhoades@owaa.org*
Web Address: www.owaa.org
The Outdoor Writers Association of America (OWAA) exists to improve the professional skills of its members, set the highest ethical and communications standards, encourage public enjoyment and conservation of natural resources and be mentors for the next generation of professional outdoor communicators.

Overseas Press Club of America (OPCA)
40 W. 45th St.
New York, NY 10036 US
Phone: 212-626-9220
Fax: 212-626-9210
Web Address: www.opcofamerica.org
The Overseas Press Club of America (OPCA) is an international association of journalists working in the United States and abroad.

Poetry Society of America
15 Gramercy Park
New York, NY 10003 US
Phone: 212-254-9628
E-mail Address: *brett@poetrysociety.org*
Web Address: www.poetrysociety.org
The Poetry Society of America provides a local meeting place for poets and information regarding readings, seminars, competitions, and other resources.

Reporters Committee for Freedom of the Press (RCFP)
1101 Wilson Blvd., Ste. 1100
Arlington, VA 22209 US
Phone: 703-807-2100
Toll Free: 888-336-4243
E-mail Address: *rcfp@rcfp.org*
Web Address: www.rcfp.org
The Reporters Committee for Freedom of the Press (RCFP) is a nonprofit organization dedicated to providing free legal help to journalists and news organizations.

Romance Writers of America (RWA)
16000 Stuebner Airline Rd., Ste. 140
Spring, TX 77379 US
Phone: 832-717-5200
Fax: 832-717-5201
E-mail Address: *info@rwanational.org*
Web Address: www.rwanational.org
Romance Writers of America (RWA) is the professional association for published and aspiring romance writers.

Science Fiction & Fantasy Writers of America, Inc. (SFWA)
P.O. Box 877
Chestertown, MD 21620 US
E-mail Address: *execdir@sfwa.org*
Web Address: www.sfwa.org
Science Fiction & Fantasy Writers of America (SFWA) is an organization for writers in the science fiction and fantasy genres, promoting dialogue and furthering the rights of its members.

Society for Technical Communication (STC)
901 N. Stuart St., Ste. 904
Arlington, VA 22203 US
Phone: 703-522-4114
Fax: 703-522-2075
E-mail Address: *stc@stc.org*
Web Address: www.stc.org
Society for Technical Communication (STC) is a membership organization dedicated to advancing the art and science of technical writing.

Society of American Business Editors & Writers (SABEW)
Missouri School of Journalism
385 McReynolds
Columbia, MO 65211-1200 US
Phone: 573-882-7862
Fax: 573-884-1372
E-mail Address: *sabew@missouri.edu*
Web Address: www.sabew.org
The Society of American Business Editors & Writers (SABEW) is a not-for-profit organization of business journalists in North America that promotes business journalism through education.

Society of American Travel Writers (SATW)
7044 S. 13th St.
Oak Creek, WI 53154 US
Phone: 414-908-4949
Fax: 414-768-8001
E-mail Address: *satw@satw.org*

Web Address: www.satw.org
The Society of American Travel Writers (SATW) promotes responsible journalism, provides professional support and development for members and encourages the conservation and preservation of travel resources worldwide.

Society of Children's Book Writers and Illustrators (SCBWI)
8271 Beverly Blvd.
Los Angeles, CA 90048 US
Phone: 323-782-1010
Fax: 323-782-1892
E-mail Address: *scbwi@scbwi.org*
Web Address: www.scbwi.org
The Society of Children's Book Writers and Illustrators (SCBWI) serves people who write, illustrate or share a vital interest in children's literature.

Society of Environmental Journalists (SEJ)
P.O. Box 2492
Jenkintown, PA 19046 US
Phone: 215-884-8174
Fax: 215-884-8175
E-mail Address: *sej@sej.org*
Web Address: www.sej.org
The Society of Environmental Journalists (SEJ) seeks to advance public understanding of environmental issues by improving the quality, accuracy and visibility of environmental reporting.

Society of Professional Journalists (SPJ)
Eugene S. Pulliam National Journalism Center
3909 N. Meridian St.
Indianapolis, IN 46208 US
Phone: 317-927-8000
Fax: 317-920-4789
E-mail Address: *bking@spj.org*
Web Address: www.spj.org
The Society of Professional Journalists (SPJ) is dedicated to the perpetuation of a free press.

United States Basketball Writers Association (USBWA)
1818 Chouteau Ave.
St. Louis, MO 63103 US
E-mail Address: *webmaster@sportswriters.net*
Web Address: www.sportswriters.net/usbwa/
The United States Basketball Writers Association (USBWA) is an organization representing writers who follow college and high school basketball in the U.S.

Western Writers of America, Inc. (WWA)
1012 Fair St.
Franklin, TN 37064 US
E-mail Address: *wwa@unm.edu*
Web Address: www.westernwriters.org
Western Writers of America, Inc. (WWA) exists to promote the literature of the American West.

Writers Guild of America East, Inc. (WGAE)
555 W. 57th St.
New York, NY 10019 US
Phone: 212-767-7800
Fax: 212-582-1909
E-mail Address: *info@wgaeast.org*
Web Address: www.wgaeast.org
The Writers Guild of America East (WGAE) is the east coast branch of WGA, a labor union that protects and defends the rights of television, radio and film writers.

Writers Guild of America West, Inc. (WGAW)
7000 W. 3rd St.
Los Angeles, CA 90048 US
Phone: 323-951-4000
Fax: 323-782-4800
Toll Free: 800-548-4532
Web Address: www.wga.org
The Writers Guild of America West (WGAW) is the west coast branch of the WGA, a labor union that protects and defends the rights of television and film writers.

Chapter 4

THE ENTERTAINMENT 400: WHO THEY ARE AND HOW THEY WERE CHOSEN

Includes Indexes by Company Name, Industry & Location, And a Complete Table of Sales, Profits and Ranks

The companies chosen to be listed in PLUNKETT'S ENTERTAINMENT & MEDIA INDUSTRY ALMANAC comprise a unique list. THE ENTERTAINMENT 400 (the actual count is 391 companies) were chosen specifically for their dominance in the many facets of the entertainment and media industry in which they operate. Complete information about each firm can be found in the "Individual Profiles," beginning at the end of this chapter. These profiles are in alphabetical order by company name.

THE ENTERTAINMENT 400 companies are from all parts of the United States, Canada, Europe and Asia. THE ENTERTAINMENT 400 includes companies that are deeply involved in the technologies, services and products that keep the entire industry forging ahead.

Simply stated, THE ENTERTAINMENT 400 contains 391 of the largest, most successful, fastest growing firms in entertainment and related industries in the world. To be included in our list, the firms had to meet the following criteria:

1) Generally, these are corporations based in the U.S., however, the headquarters of 63 firms are located in other nations.

2) Prominence, or a significant presence, in entertainment, media services and supporting fields. (See the following Industry Codes section for a complete list of types of businesses that are covered).

3) The companies in THE ENTERTAINMENT 400 do not have to be exclusively in the entertainment and media field.

4) Financial data and vital statistics must have been available to the editors of this book, either directly from the company being written about or from outside sources deemed reliable and accurate by the editors. A small number of companies that we would like to have included are not listed because of a lack of sufficient, objective data.

INDUSTRY LIST, WITH CODES

This book refers to the following list of unique industry codes, based on the 1997 NAIC code system (NAIC is used by many analysts as a replacement for older SIC codes because NAIC is more specific to today's industry sectors). Companies profiled in this book are given a primary NAIC code, reflecting the main line of business of each firm.

Entertainment

Toys, Sporting Goods & Miscellaneous Manufacturing
339000   Miscellaneous Manufacturing
Book & Magazine Distribution
422920   Books or Magazines Distribution
422921   Videos/Games/Software/Recorded Music
            Distribution
Publishing
511000   Publishing, General
511110   Newspapers, Publishing
511120   Magazines Publishing
511130   Books, Publishing
511140   Databases & Directories, Publishing
511191   Greeting Cards, Publishing
Film, Video & Music Recording
512110   TV/Video/Theatrical, Production
512131   Movie Theaters
512191   Film and Video Post-Production
512230   Music, Publishing
532230   Video Rental
Broadcasting
513111   Radio Broadcasting
513111A   Radio Broadcasting via Satellite
513120   Television Broadcasting
513120A   Television Broadcasting via the Internet or
            Wireless
513210   Cable TV Networks
513220   Cable & Satellite TV & Data Service
Entertainment Events & Sports
711211   Stadiums/Sports Teams
711310   Entertainment Events
Gambling & Recreation
713110   Theme Parks/Rides/Game Centers
713210   Casinos/Horse Racing, Gambling
713290   Gambling Equipment
713910   Golf Courses & Country Clubs
713920   Snow Skiing Facilities
713940   Fitness Centers/Health Clubs
713950   Bowling Facilities
713990   Games/Auto Racing/Misc. Recreation
Hotels & Accommodations
721110   Hotels/Resorts/Motels
721120   Casino Resorts

Financial Services

Financial Data
514100   Financial Data Publishing- Print & Online
Banking, Credit & Finance
522210   Credit Card Issuing
522220A   Financing--Business

Food & Restaurants

Food Service
722110   Restaurants

InfoTech

Computers & Electronics Manufacturing
334110   Computer Networking & Related Equipment, Manufacturing
334310   Audio & Video Equipment, Consumer Electronics
Software
511202   Computer Software, Content & Document Management
511204   Computer Software, Operating Systems, Languages & Development Tools
511208   Computer Software, Games & Entertainment
511209   Computer Software, Multimedia, Graphics & Publishing
Information & Data Processing Services
514199   Online Publishing, Services & Niche Portals
514199B   Search Engine Portals

Manufacturing

Food Products Manufacturing
311330   Chocolate & Confectionery Manufacturing
Beverage & Tobacco Manufacturing
312120   Beverages--Breweries
Printing Services
323000   Printing

Retailing

Computers & Electronics Stores
443110   Electronics, Audio & Appliance Stores
443110E   Electronics, Audio & Appliance Stores-Online
Sporting Goods, Hobbies, Books & Music Stores
451120   Toys/Hobbies/Games Stores
451211   Book Stores
451211E   Book Stores-Online
451220   Music Stores
451220E   Music Stores-Online
Miscellaneous Retailers
453220   Gift/Sundry Stores

Nonstore Retailers
454110A   Direct Selling, Including Mail Order & Misc. Online
454110B   TV Shopping

Services

Real Estate
525930   Real Estate Investment Trusts - REITs
Consulting & Professional Services
541800   Marketing Agencies & Related Services
541810   Advertising Services/Agencies
541810A   Advertising/Marketing--Online
541850   Advertising, Display & Billboards
541870   Advertising Material Distribution Services
541910   Market Research
Management
551110   Management of Companies & Enterprises

Telecommunications

Telecommunications
513300A   Telephone Service-Local Exchange Carrier & Diversified
514191   Internet Access Provider

INDEX OF RANKINGS WITHIN INDUSTRY GROUPS

Company	Industry Code	2006 Sales (U.S. $ thousands)	Sales Rank	2006 Profits (U.S. $ thousands)	Profits Rank
Advertising Material Distribution Services					
DG FASTCHANNEL	541870	68,667	1	-649	1
Advertising Services/Agencies					
INTERPUBLIC GROUP OF COMPANIES INC	541810	6,190,800	3	-31,700	3
OMNICOM GROUP INC	541810	11,376,900	2	864,000	2
WPP GROUP PLC	541810	11,436,000	1	934,266	1
Advertising, Display & Billboards					
CLEAR CHANNEL OUTDOOR	541850	2,897,721	1	153,072	1
LAMAR ADVERTISING CO	541850	1,120,091	2	43,899	2
Advertising/Marketing--Online					
24/7 REAL MEDIA INC	541810A	200,243	1	-8,622	2
DOUBLECLICK INC	541810A				
TRAFFIX INC	541810A	72,844	2	1,903	1
YAHOO! SEARCH MARKETING GROUP	541810A				
Agents, Performers, Models, Athletes					
CREATIVE ARTISTS AGENCY	711410				
ENDEAVOR AGENCY	711410				
FORD MODELS INC	711410				
IMG WORLDWIDE INC	711410				
INTERNATIONAL CREATIVE MANAGEMENT (ICM)	711410				
UNITED TALENT AGENCY INC	711410				
WILLIAM MORRIS AGENCY INC	711410				
Audio & Video Equipment, Consumer Electronics					
BOSE CORPORATION	334310	2,000,000	7		
CLARION CO LTD	334310	1,567,896	8	49,910	5
DIGEO INC	334310				
DIGITAL VIDEO SYSTEMS INC	334310				
DTS INC	334310	78,314	11	3,024	7
LOUD TECHNOLOGIES INC	334310	215,033	9	625	8
MATSUSHITA ELECTRIC INDUSTRIAL CO LTD	334310	75,601,800	1	1,312,500	2
PIONEER CORPORATION	334310	6,354,100	6	-715,270	11
SAMSUNG ELECTRONICS CO	334310	63,495,000	3	8,535,460	1
SANYO ELECTRIC COMPANY	334310	21,804,658	5	-1,757,786	12
SHARP CORPORATION	334310	24,113,009	4	764,405	4
SONY CORPORATION	334310	64,021,000	2	1,047,270	3
SRS LABS INC	334310	18,500	13	4,700	6
TIVO INC	334310	195,925	10	-34,398	10
TRANS-LUX CORPORATION	334310	53,911	12	-1,647	9
Beverages--Breweries					
ANHEUSER BUSCH COS INC	312120	15,717,000	1	1,965,200	1
Book Stores					
BARNES & NOBLE INC	451211	5,103,004	1	146,681	1
BOOKS A MILLION INC	451211	503,751	3	13,067	3

Company	Industry Code	2006 Sales (U.S. $ thousands)	Sales Rank	2006 Profits (U.S. $ thousands)	Profits Rank
BORDERS GROUP INC	451211	4,030,700	2	101,000	2
Book Stores-Online					
AMAZON.COM INC	451211E	10,711,000	1	190,000	1
BARNESANDNOBLE.COM INC	451211E				
Books or Magazines Distribution					
ANDERSON COS	422920				
EBSCO INDUSTRIES INC	422920	2,300,000	1		
Books, Publishing					
EDUCATIONAL DEVELOPMENT	511130	31,789	7	2,398	7
HARPERCOLLINS PUBLISHERS	511130				
HOUGHTON MIFFLIN CO	511130				
JOHN WILEY & SONS INC	511130	1,044,185	4	110,328	3
LERNER PUBLISHING GROUP	511130				
MARVEL ENTERTAINMENT INC	511130	351,798	5	58,704	5
MCGRAW HILL COS INC	511130	6,255,138	2	882,231	2
PEARSON PLC	511130	8,343,090	1	945,830	1
RANDOM HOUSE INC	511130				
SCHOLASTIC CORP	511130	2,283,800	3	68,600	4
SIMON & SCHUSTER INC	511130				
THOMAS NELSON INC	511130	253,057	6	20,977	6
Bowling Facilities					
AMF BOWLING WORLDWIDE	713950	499,149	1	-15,885	1
Cable & Satellite TV & Data Service					
BRITISH SKY BROADCASTING	513220	7,534,012	7	1,000,781	5
CABLEVISION SYSTEMS CORP	513220	5,927,462	9	-126,465	19
CHARTER COMMUNICATIONS	513220	5,504,000	10	-1,370,000	20
COMCAST CORP	513220	26,339,000	2	2,533,000	2
COX COMMUNICATIONS INC	513220				
DIRECTV GROUP INC	513220	14,755,500	3	1,420,100	4
ECHOSTAR COMMUNICATIONS	513220	9,818,486	5	608,272	8
HOT CABLE SYSTEMS MEDIA	513220				
I-CABLE COMMUNICATIONS	513220	327,600	17	24,500	13
INSIGHT COMMUNICATIONS COMPANY INC	513220	1,262,600	14	-36,600	16
ITV PLC	513220	4,270,800	11	434,700	9
KNOLOGY INC	513220	258,991	19	-39,505	17
LIBERTY GLOBAL INC	513220	6,487,500	8	706,200	6
LODGENET ENTERTAINMENT	513220	288,213	18	1,841	14
MEDIACOM COMMUNICATIONS	513220	1,210,400	15	-124,922	18
NASPERS LIMITED	513220	2,128,200	12	341,000	11
NTL: TELEWEST BUSINESS	513220				
ON COMMAND CORP	513220				
PRIMACOM AG	513220	167,160	20	-21,680	15
ROGERS COMMUNICATIONS	513220	7,583,888	6	669,318	7
SHAW COMMUNICATIONS INC	513220	2,122,630	13	395,520	10
SKY NETWORK TELEVISION LIMITED	513220	383,840	16	42,090	12
SUDDENLINK COMMUNICATIONS	513220				
TIME WARNER CABLE INC	513220	11,767,000	4	1,976,000	3
TIME WARNER INC	513220	44,224,000	1	6,552,000	1

Company	Industry Code	2006 Sales (U.S. $ thousands)	Sales Rank	2006 Profits (U.S. $ thousands)	Profits Rank
Cable TV Networks					
A&E TELEVISION NETWORKS	513210				
CABLE NEWS NETWORK LP	513210				
CROWN MEDIA HOLDINGS INC	513210	201,179	4	-388,972	4
CW NETWORK	513210				
DISCOVERY COMMUNICATIONS	513210				
ESPN INC	513210				
FOX BROADCASTING CO	513210				
FOX SPORTS NET INC	513210				
MTV NETWORKS	513210				
NBC UNIVERSAL	513210	16,188,000	2	2,919,000	2
RAINBOW MEDIA HOLDINGS	513210				
TURNER BROADCASTING SYSTEM	513210				
VIACOM INC	513210	11,466,500	3	1,592,100	3
WALT DISNEY COMPANY	513210	33,747,000	1	3,374,000	1
Casino Resorts					
AMERISTAR CASINOS INC	721120	1,000,298	8	59,565	8
AZTAR CORP	721120				
BOYD GAMING CORP	721120	2,192,634	4	116,778	5
DIAMONDHEAD CASINO CORP	721120				
HARRAH'S ENTERTAINMENT	721120	9,673,900	1	535,800	3
KERZNER INTERNATIONAL LIMITED	721120				
LAS VEGAS SANDS CORP (THE VENETIAN)	721120	2,340,178	3	442,003	4
MGM MIRAGE	721120	7,175,956	2	648,264	1
MTR GAMING GROUP INC	721120	382,610	10	4,446	9
PINNACLE ENTERTAINMENT INC	721120	912,357	9	76,886	7
RIVIERA HOLDINGS CORP	721120	200,944	11	-335	11
SANDS REGENT	721120	92,574	12	2,431	10
STATION CASINOS INC	721120	1,339,024	6	110,212	6
TRUMP ENTERTAINMENT RESORTS INC	721120	1,026,162	7	-18,507	12
WYNN RESORTS LIMITED	721120	1,432,257	5	628,728	2
Casinos/Horse Racing, Gambling					
CANTERBURY PARK HOLDING	713210	55,840	10	3,125	7
CENTURY CASINOS INC	713210	56,285	9	7,629	6
CHURCHILL DOWNS INC	713210	376,671	5	29,811	3
DOVER DOWNS GAMING & ENTERTAINMENT INC	713210	236,451	6	25,328	4
HERBST GAMING INC	713210				
ISLE OF CAPRI CASINOS INC	713210	987,400	3	-18,900	10
LAKES ENTERTAINMENT INC	713210	81,600	8	19,800	5
MAGNA ENTERTAINMENT CORP	713210	702,139	4	-87,351	12
MELCO PBL ENTERTAINMENT LIMITED	713210	36,101	11	-73,479	11
PENN NATIONAL GAMING INC	713210	2,244,547	1	327,088	1
RANK GROUP PLC (THE)	713210	1,076,200	2	233,000	2
TRANS WORLD CORP	713210	26,216	12	2,027	8
YOUBET.COM INC	713210	136,683	7	-2,031	9
Chocolate & Confectionery Manufacturing					
HERSHEY CO	311330	4,944,230	1	559,061	1

Company	Industry Code	2006 Sales (U.S. $ thousands)	Sales Rank	2006 Profits (U.S. $ thousands)	Profits Rank
Computer Hardware, Manufacturing					
APPLE INC	334111	19,315,000	1	1,989,000	1
CONCURRENT COMPUTER	334111	71,612	3	-9,345	3
NINTENDO CO LTD	334111	4,327,100	2	836,600	2
Computer Software, Content & Document Management					
MACROVISION CORP	511202	247,590	1	33,043	1
Computer Software, Electronic Games & Entertainment					
ACTIVISION INC	511208	1,468,000	3	40,251	4
ATARI INC	511208	206,796	7	-68,986	8
BIOWARE CORP	511208				
BRASH ENTERTAINMENT LLC	511208				
CONCRETE SOFTWARE INC	511208				
DIGITAL BRIDGES LIMITED	511208				
ELECTRONIC ARTS INC	511208	2,951,000	2	236,000	2
GLU MOBILE INC	511208	46,166	9	-12,310	7
HANDS-ON MOBILE	511208				
LUCASARTS ENTERTAINMENT COMPANY LLC	511208				
MIDWAY GAMES INC	511208	165,574	8	-77,783	9
NTN BUZZTIME INC	511208	32,985	10	-4,773	6
SEGA SAMMY HOLDINGS INC	511208	4,656,310	1	557,350	1
SHANDA INTERACTIVE ENTERTAINMENT LIMITED	511208	211,900	6	67,800	3
TAKE-TWO INTERACTIVE SOFTWARE INC	511208	1,037,840	4	-184,889	10
THQ INC	511208	806,560	5	34,269	5
VINDIGO INC	511208				
Computer Software, Multimedia, Graphics & Publishing					
AVID TECHNOLOGY INC	511209	910,578	1	-42,927	2
REALNETWORKS INC	511209	395,261	2	145,216	1
Computer Software, Operating Systems, Languages & Development Tools					
MICROSOFT CORP	511204	44,282,000	1	12,599,000	1
Credit Card Issuing					
AMERICAN EXPRESS CO	522210	27,136,000	1	3,707,000	1
Databases & Directories, Publishing					
DAG MEDIA INC	511140	232	3	-174	3
REED ELSEVIER GROUP PLC	511140	10,570,400	1	1,223,900	1
THOMSON CORP	511140	6,641,000	2	1,143,000	2
Direct Selling, Including Mail Order & Misc. Online					
TICKETMASTER	454110A				
Electronics, Audio & Appliance Stores					
BEST BUY CO INC	443110	30,848,000	1	1,140,000	1
CIRCUIT CITY STORES INC	443110	11,514,000	2	147,000	2
HARVEY ELECTRONICS INC	443110	36,028	6	-3,238	5
INTERTAN CANADA LTD	443110				
RADIOSHACK CORPORATION	443110	4,777,500	3	73,400	3
REX STORES CORP	443110	374,451	5	28,269	4
TWEETER HOME ENTERTAINMENT GROUP INC	443110	775,287	4	-16,483	6

Company	Industry Code	2006 Sales (U.S. $ thousands)	Sales Rank	2006 Profits (U.S. $ thousands)	Profits Rank
Electronics, Audio & Appliance Stores-Online					
BUY.COM INC	443110E				
Entertainment Events					
LIVE NATION INC	711310	3,691,559	1	-31,442	1
RENAISSANCE ENTERTAINMENT CORP	711310				
Film & Video Post-Production					
ASCENT MEDIA GROUP INC	512191				
LASERPACIFIC MEDIA CORP	512191				
Financial Data Publishing-Print & Online					
BLOOMBERG LP	514100	4,700,000	2	1,500,000	1
INTERACTIVE DATA CORPORATION	514100	612,403	3	93,362	3
MARKETWATCH INC	514100				
REUTERS GROUP PLC	514100	5,027,000	1	597,500	2
VALUE LINE INC	514100	85,186	4	23,439	4
XINHUA FINANCE LIMITED	514100				
Financing--Business					
GENERAL ELECTRIC CO (GE)	522220A	163,391,000	1	20,829,000	1
Fitness Centers/Health Clubs					
24 HOUR FITNESS USA	713940				
BALLY TOTAL FITNESS HOLDING CORPORATION	713940	1,059,051	1	43,067	2
CURVES INTERNATIONAL INC	713940				
GOLD'S GYM INTERNATIONAL	713940				
LIFE TIME FITNESS INC	713940	511,897	2	50,565	1
Gambling Equipment					
AMERICAN WAGERING INC	713290	12,524	12	419	9
ARISTOCRAT LEISURE LTD	713290	862,500	3	-32,200	11
BALLY TECHNOLOGIES INC	713290	547,144	5	-46,071	13
GAMETECH INTERNATIONAL	713290	49,289	11	4,383	7
GAMING PARTNERS INTERNATIONAL CORP	713290	73,954	9	5,129	6
GTECH HOLDINGS CORP	713290	1,304,806	2	211,045	2
INTERNATIONAL GAME TECHNOLOGY	713290	2,511,700	1	473,600	1
INTERNATIONAL LOTTERY & TOTALIZATOR SYSTEMS	713290	3,445	13	-2,344	10
MULTIMEDIA GAMES INC	713290	145,112	8	3,532	8
PROGRESSIVE GAMING INTERNATIONAL CORP	713290	69,509	10	-36,624	12
SCIENTIFIC GAMES CORP	713290	781,683	4	66,761	3
SHUFFLE MASTER INC	713290	163,468	7	6,802	5
WMS INDUSTRIES INC	713290	451,200	6	33,300	4
Games/Misc. Recreation Items					
AMERICAN COIN MERCHANDISING INC	713990				
Gift/Sundry Stores					
DELAWARE NORTH COMPANIES	453220	2,040,000	1		
Golf Courses & Country Clubs					
AMERICAN GOLF CORP	713910				
CLUBCORP INC	713910	1,020,000	1		

Company	Industry Code	2006 Sales (U.S. $ thousands)	Sales Rank	2006 Profits (U.S. $ thousands)	Profits Rank
Greeting Cards, Publishing					
AMERICAN GREETINGS CORP	511191	1,885,701	2	84,376	1
HALLMARK CARDS INC	511191	4,100,000	1		
Hotels/Resorts/Motels					
GAYLORD ENTERTAINMENT	721110	947,922	1	-79,435	1
SHUN TAK HOLDINGS LIMITED	721110				
Internet Access Provider					
AOL LLC	514191				
UNITED ONLINE INC	514191	522,654	1	42,272	1
Magazines, Publishing					
ADVANCE PUBLICATIONS INC	511120	7,700,000	1		
CONDE NAST PUBLICATIONS	511120				
DENNIS PUBLISHING LTD	511120				
EMAP PLC	511120	1,485,500	5	219,200	2
FORBES INC	511120				
INTERNATIONAL DATA GROUP	511120	3,020,000	2		
JOHNSON PUBLISHING COMPANY INC	511120	458,000	8		
LAGARDERE ACTIVE MEDIA	511120				
MARTHA STEWART LIVING OMNIMEDIA INC	511120	288,341	10	-16,995	6
MEREDITH CORP	511120	1,561,465	4	144,792	3
PENTON MEDIA INC	511120				
PLAYBOY ENTERPRISES INC	511120	331,142	9	2,285	5
PRIMEDIA INC	511120	849,309	7	38,252	4
READER'S DIGEST ASSOCIATION INC	511120	2,386,200	3	-117,400	7
RODALE INC	511120				
TIME INC	511120				
TRADER CLASSIFIED MEDIA NV	511120				
UNITED BUSINESS MEDIA PLC	511120	1,447,300	6	286,700	1
US NEWS AND WORLD REPORT	511120				
WENNER MEDIA LLC	511120				
ZIFF DAVIS MEDIA INC	511120				
Management of Companies & Enterprises					
BERKSHIRE HATHAWAY INC	551110	98,539,000	1	1,015,000	1
VULCAN INC	551110				
Market Research					
ARBITRON INC	541910	329,250	2	50,658	2
HARRIS INTERACTIVE INC	541910	212,184	3	9,460	3
NETRATINGS INC	541910	81,769	4	2,829	4
NIELSEN COMPANY BV	541910				
TAYLOR NELSON SOFRES PLC (TNS)	541910	2,000,120	1	79,470	1
Marketing Agencies & Related Services					
MDI ENTERTAINMENT INC	541800				
WASSERMAN MEDIA GROUP	541800				
Miscellaneous Manufacturing					
AMERICAN EDUCATIONAL PRODUCTS LLC	339000				
Movie Theaters					
AMC ENTERTAINMENT INC	512131	1,730,450	2	-188,762	4
CARMIKE CINEMAS INC	512131	495,499	3	-19,389	3

Company	Industry Code	2006 Sales (U.S. $ thousands)	Sales Rank	2006 Profits (U.S. $ thousands)	Profits Rank
CINEMARK INC	512131				
CINEMASTAR LUXURY THEATERS INC	512131				
IMAX CORPORATION	512131	20,730	4	-11,990	2
NATIONAL AMUSEMENTS INC	512131				
REGAL ENTERTAINMENT GROUP	512131	2,598,100	1	86,300	1
SIMEX-IWERKS	512131				
Music Stores					
CD WAREHOUSE INC	451220				
TRANS WORLD ENTERTAINMENT CORP	451220	1,238,486	1	609	1
WHEREHOUSE ENTERTAINMENT (RECORD TOWN INC)	451220				
Music Stores-Online					
AUDIBLE INC	451220E	82,178	2	-8,447	1
LIQUID DIGITAL MEDIA	451220E				
MP3.COM INC	451220E				
NAPSTER INC	451220E	94,691	1	-54,945	2
Music, Publishing					
COLUMBIA MUSIC ENTERTAINMENT INC	512230				
EMI GROUP PLC	512230	4,092,680	2	232,390	2
INTEGRITY MEDIA INC	512230				
SONY BMG MUSIC ENTERTAINMENT	512230				
UNIVERSAL MUSIC GROUP	512230				
VIVENDI SA	512230	26,522,143	1	3,458,838	1
WARNER MUSIC GROUP	512230	3,516,000	3	60,000	3
Newspapers, Publishing					
BELO CORP	511110	1,588,272	11	130,526	6
COMMUNITY NEWSPAPER HOLDINGS INC	511110				
COX ENTERPRISES INC	511110	13,200,000	1		
DAILY JOURNAL CORP	511110	32,369	20	2,438	12
DOW JONES & CO INC	511110	1,783,870	8	386,564	3
E W SCRIPPS CO	511110	2,498,077	7	353,220	4
FREEDOM COMMUNICATIONS	511110				
GANNETT CO INC	511110	8,033,354	2	1,160,782	1
GATEHOUSE MEDIA INC	511110	314,900	19	-1,600	14
HARTE-HANKS INC	511110	1,184,688	12	111,792	7
HEARST CORPORATION	511110	4,520,000	4		
HOLLINGER INC	511110	2,447	21	-16,590	16
JOURNAL COMMUNICATIONS	511110	671,853	16	64,373	10
JOURNAL REGISTER CO	511110	506,065	17	-6,238	15
LANDMARK COMMUNICATIONS	511110	1,750,000	9		
LEE ENTERPRISES INC	511110	1,128,648	13	70,832	9
MCCLATCHY COMPANY	511110	1,675,190	10	-155,577	17
MEDIA GENERAL INC	511110	983,189	14	79,042	8
MEDIANEWS GROUP INC	511110	835,900	15	1,100	13
METRO INTERNATIONAL SA	511110	416,534	18	12,975	11
MORRIS COMMUNICATIONS COMPANY LLC	511110				
NEW YORK TIMES CO	511110	3,289,903	6	-543,443	18
NEWS WORLD COMMUNICATIONS INC	511110				

Company	Industry Code	2006 Sales (U.S. $ thousands)	Sales Rank	2006 Profits (U.S. $ thousands)	Profits Rank
TRIBUNE CO	511110	5,517,708	3	593,995	2
WASHINGTON POST CO	511110	3,904,927	5	324,459	5
Online Publishing, Services & Niche Portals					
CNET NETWORKS INC	514199	387,376	2	6,836	4
DIALOG	514199				
GEMSTAR-TV GUIDE INTERNATIONAL INC	514199	571,254	1	72,464	1
GLAM MEDIA INC	514199				
HOLLYWOOD MEDIA CORP	514199	115,895	4	9,523	3
HOOVER'S INC	514199				
IGN ENTERTAINMENT	514199				
IVILLAGE INC	514199				
JUPITERMEDIA CORP	514199	137,530	3	13,124	2
SALON MEDIA GROUP INC	514199	6,500	5	-1,100	5
Printing					
COURIER CORP	323000	269,051	2	28,380	2
R R DONNELLEY & SONS CO	323000	9,316,600	1	400,600	1
Publishing, General					
BERRY COMPANY	511000				
XINHUA FINANCE MEDIA LIMITED	511000				
Radio Broadcasting					
BEASLEY BROADCAST GROUP	513111	125,190	11	10,134	8
CBS RADIO	513111				
CITADEL BROADCASTING CORP	513111	432,930	5	-48,014	13
CLEAR CHANNEL COMMUNICATIONS INC	513111	7,066,957	1	691,517	1
CORUS ENTERTAINMENT INC	513111	630,060	2	30,770	6
COX RADIO INC	513111	440,468	4	-24,447	10
CUMULUS MEDIA INC	513111	334,321	8	-44,588	12
EMMIS COMMUNICATIONS	513111	387,381	6	357,771	2
ENTERCOM COMMUNICATIONS	513111	440,485	3	47,981	4
GRUPO RADIO CENTRO SA DE CV	513111	73,677	13	38,792	5
RADIO ONE	513111	367,017	7	-6,730	9
REGENT COMMUNICATIONS	513111	85,033	12	-26,597	11
SALEM COMMUNICATIONS	513111	227,769	9	18,999	7
SPANISH BROADCASTING SYSTEM INC	513111	176,931	10	49,870	3
Radio Broadcasting via Satellite					
SIRIUS SATELLITE RADIO	513111A	637,235	2	-1,104,867	2
XM SATELLITE RADIO HOLDINGS INC	513111A	933,417	1	-718,872	1
Real Estate Investment Trusts - REITs					
ENTERTAINMENT PROPERTIES TRUST	525930	195,500	1	70,432	1
Restaurants					
LANDRY'S RESTAURANTS INC	722110	1,134,301	1	-21,770	1
Search Engine Portals					
GOOGLE INC	514199B	10,604,917	1	3,077,446	1
YAHOO! INC	514199B	6,425,679	2	751,391	2
Snow Skiing Facilities					
AMERICAN SKIING COMPANY	713920	307,810	2	-65,653	2
BOOTH CREEK SKI HOLDINGS	713920				
BOYNE USA RESORTS	713920				

Company	Industry Code	2006 Sales (U.S. $ thousands)	Sales Rank	2006 Profits (U.S. $ thousands)	Profits Rank
VAIL RESORTS INC	713920	838,852	1	45,756	1
Stadiums/Sports Teams					
ANSCHUTZ ENTERTAINMENT GROUP	711211				
Telephone Service--Local Exchange Carrier & Diversified					
AT&T INC	513300A	63,055,000	2	7,356,000	1
RCN CORP	513300A	585,476	3	-11,856	3
VERIZON COMMUNICATIONS	513300A	88,144,000	1	6,197,000	2
Television Broadcasting					
ABC INC	513120	14,638,000	3		
ACME COMMUNICATIONS INC	513120	34,789	20	-4,179	14
BERTELSMANN AG	513120	25,458,500	1	3,198,000	1
BRITISH BROADCASTING CORPORATION (BBC)	513120	6,966,700	6	6,300	13
CANWEST GLOBAL COMMUNICATIONS	513120	2,484,570	8	154,210	7
CBS CORP	513120	14,320,200	4	1,660,500	3
ENTRAVISION COMMUNICATIONS CORP	513120	291,752	14	-134,599	17
FISHER COMMUNICATIONS INC	513120	135,691	19	16,836	10
FOX ENTERTAINMENT GROUP	513120				
GRANITE BROADCASTING	513120				
GRAY TELEVISION INC	513120	332,137	13	11,711	12
GRUPO TELEVISA SA	513120	3,406,340	7	771,055	5
HEARST-ARGYLE TELEVISION	513120	785,402	10	98,723	8
ION MEDIA NETWORKS	513120	228,896	16	-173,744	18
LIN TV CORP	513120	426,100	12	-234,500	19
MODERN TIMES GROUP MTG AB	513120				
NEWS CORP	513120	25,327,000	2	2,314,000	2
NEXSTAR BROADCASTING GROUP INC	513120	265,169	15	-8,992	15
RAYCOM MEDIA INC	513120				
RTL GROUP SA	513120	7,440,900	5	1,465,700	4
SAGA COMMUNICATIONS INC	513120	142,946	18	12,448	11
SHANGHAI MEDIA GROUP (SMG)	513120				
SINCLAIR BROADCAST GROUP	513120	715,138	11	53,977	9
TV AZTECA SA DE CV	513120				
UNIVISION COMMUNICATIONS	513120	2,166,652	9	349,174	6
YOUNG BROADCASTING INC	513120	225,153	17	-56,641	16
Television Broadcasting via the Internet or Wireless					
BRIGHTCOVE INC	513120A				
JOOST	513120A				
JUMPTV INC	513120A	2,061	1	-25,597	1
MOBITV INC	513120A				
Theme Parks/Rides/Game Centers					
CEDAR FAIR LP	713110	831,389	3	87,477	1
EURO DISNEY SCA	713110	1,441,190	1	-117,390	2
PALACE ENTERTAINMENT	713110				
SIX FLAGS INC	713110	945,665	2	-327,588	3
Toys/Hobbies/Games Stores					
GAMESTOP CORP	451120	3,091,783	1	100,784	1

Company	Industry Code	2006 Sales (U.S. $ thousands)	Sales Rank	2006 Profits (U.S. $ thousands)	Profits Rank
TV Shopping					
IAC/INTERACTIVECORP	454110B	6,277,638	1	192,635	1
SHOP AT HOME NETWORK LLC	454110B				
VALUEVISION MEDIA INC	454110B	691,851	2	-16,040	2
TV/Video/Theatrical, Production					
2929 ENTERTAINMENT	512110				
ALLIANCE ATLANTIS COMMUNICATIONS INC	512110	979,948	3	50,059	2
CENTRAL EUROPEAN MEDIA ENTERPRISES LTD	512110	603,115	6	20,424	3
CIRQUE DU SOLEIL INC	512110	620,000	5		
COLUMBIA TRISTAR MOTION PICTURE GROUP	512110				
DICK CLARK PRODUCTIONS INC	512110				
DREAMWORKS ANIMATION SKG	512110	394,842	8	15,125	4
DREAMWORKS SKG	512110				
FIRST LOOK STUDIOS INC	512110				
FOX FILMED ENTERTAINMENT	512110				
HARPO INC	512110	325,000	9		
LIBERTY MEDIA CORP	512110	8,613,000	1	1,021,000	1
LIONS GATE ENTERTAINMENT	512110	951,228	4	6,096	5
LUCASFILM LTD	512110				
METRO-GOLDWYN-MAYER INC (MGM)	512110	1,460,000	2		
MGM PICTURES	512110				
MIRAMAX FILM CORP	512110				
NEW LINE CINEMA	512110				
ON STAGE ENTERTAINMENT	512110				
PARAMOUNT PICTURES CORP	512110				
PIXAR ANIMATION STUDIOS	512110				
RENTRAK CORP	512110	93,394	10	4,466	6
SONY PICTURES ENTERTAINMENT	512110				
UNITED ARTISTS CORP	512110				
UNIVERSAL PICTURES	512110				
WALT DISNEY STUDIOS	512110				
WARNER BROS ENTERTAINMENT INC	512110				
WESTWOOD ONE INC	512110	493,995	7	-469,453	7
Video Rental					
BLOCKBUSTER INC	532230	5,523,500	1	54,700	1
HASTINGS ENTERTAINMENT	532230	537,931	4	5,695	4
HOLLYWOOD ENTERTAINMENT	532230				
MOVIE GALLERY INC	532230	2,540,000	2	49,488	2
NETFLIX INC	532230	996,700	3	49,100	3
REDBOX AUTOMATED RETAIL	532230				
Videos/Games/Software/Recorded Music Distribution					
ALLIANCE ENTERTAINMENT	422921				
INGRAM ENTERTAINMENT HOLDINGS INC	422921	764,000	1		

ALPHABETICAL INDEX

DREAMWORKS ANIMATION SKG INC
DREAMWORKS SKG
DTS INC
E W SCRIPPS CO
EBSCO INDUSTRIES INC
ECHOSTAR COMMUNICATIONS CORP
EDUCATIONAL DEVELOPMENT CORP
ELECTRONIC ARTS INC
EMAP PLC
EMI GROUP PLC
EMMIS COMMUNICATIONS CORP
ENDEAVOR AGENCY (THE)
ENTERCOM COMMUNICATIONS CORP
ENTERTAINMENT PROPERTIES TRUST
ENTRAVISION COMMUNICATIONS CORPORATION
ESPN INC
EURO DISNEY SCA
FIRST LOOK STUDIOS INC
FISHER COMMUNICATIONS INC
FORBES INC
FORD MODELS INC
FOX BROADCASTING COMPANY
FOX ENTERTAINMENT GROUP INC
FOX FILMED ENTERTAINMENT
FOX SPORTS NET INC
FREEDOM COMMUNICATIONS INC
GAMESTOP CORP
GAMETECH INTERNATIONAL INC
GAMING PARTNERS INTERNATIONAL CORP
GANNETT CO INC
GATEHOUSE MEDIA INC
GAYLORD ENTERTAINMENT CO
GEMSTAR-TV GUIDE INTERNATIONAL INC
GENERAL ELECTRIC CO (GE)
GLAM MEDIA INC
GLU MOBILE INC
GOLD'S GYM INTERNATIONAL
GOOGLE INC
GRANITE BROADCASTING CORP
GRAY TELEVISION INC
GRUPO RADIO CENTRO SA DE CV
GRUPO TELEVISA SA
GTECH HOLDINGS CORP
HALLMARK CARDS INC
HANDS-ON MOBILE
HARPERCOLLINS PUBLISHERS INC
HARPO INC
HARRAH'S ENTERTAINMENT INC
HARRIS INTERACTIVE INC
HARTE-HANKS INC
HARVEY ELECTRONICS INC
HASTINGS ENTERTAINMENT INC
HEARST CORPORATION (THE)
HEARST-ARGYLE TELEVISION INC
HERBST GAMING INC
HERSHEY CO
HOLLINGER INC
HOLLYWOOD ENTERTAINMENT CORP

HOLLYWOOD MEDIA CORP
HOOVER'S INC
HOT CABLE SYSTEMS MEDIA LTD
HOUGHTON MIFFLIN CO
IAC/INTERACTIVECORP
I-CABLE COMMUNICATIONS
IGN ENTERTAINMENT
IMAX CORPORATION
IMG WORLDWIDE INC
INGRAM ENTERTAINMENT HOLDINGS INC
INSIGHT COMMUNICATIONS COMPANY INC
INTEGRITY MEDIA INC
INTERACTIVE DATA CORPORATION
INTERNATIONAL CREATIVE MANAGEMENT (ICM)
INTERNATIONAL DATA GROUP INC
INTERNATIONAL GAME TECHNOLOGY
INTERNATIONAL LOTTERY & TOTALIZATOR
SYSTEMS
INTERPUBLIC GROUP OF COMPANIES INC
INTERTAN CANADA LTD
ION MEDIA NETWORKS
ISLE OF CAPRI CASINOS INC
ITV PLC
IVILLAGE INC
JOHN WILEY & SONS INC
JOHNSON PUBLISHING COMPANY INC
JOOST
JOURNAL COMMUNICATIONS INC
JOURNAL REGISTER CO
JUMPTV INC
JUPITERMEDIA CORP
KERZNER INTERNATIONAL LIMITED
KNOLOGY INC
LAGARDERE ACTIVE MEDIA
LAKES ENTERTAINMENT INC
LAMAR ADVERTISING CO
LANDMARK COMMUNICATIONS INC
LANDRY'S RESTAURANTS INC
LAS VEGAS SANDS CORP (THE VENETIAN)
LASERPACIFIC MEDIA CORP
LEE ENTERPRISES INC
LERNER PUBLISHING GROUP
LIBERTY GLOBAL INC
LIBERTY MEDIA CORP
LIFE TIME FITNESS INC
LIN TV CORP
LIONS GATE ENTERTAINMENT CORP
LIQUID DIGITAL MEDIA
LIVE NATION INC
LODGENET ENTERTAINMENT CORP
LOUD TECHNOLOGIES INC
LUCASARTS ENTERTAINMENT COMPANY LLC
LUCASFILM LTD
MACROVISION CORP
MAGNA ENTERTAINMENT CORP
MARKETWATCH INC
MARTHA STEWART LIVING OMNIMEDIA INC
MARVEL ENTERTAINMENT INC

MATSUSHITA ELECTRIC INDUSTRIAL CO LTD
MCCLATCHY COMPANY (THE)
MCGRAW HILL COS INC
MDI ENTERTAINMENT LLC
MEDIA GENERAL INC
MEDIACOM COMMUNICATIONS CORP
MEDIANEWS GROUP INC
MELCO PBL ENTERTAINMENT LIMITED
MEREDITH CORP
METRO INTERNATIONAL SA
METRO-GOLDWYN-MAYER INC (MGM)
MGM MIRAGE
MGM PICTURES
MICROSOFT CORP
MIDWAY GAMES INC
MIRAMAX FILM CORP
MOBITV INC
MODERN TIMES GROUP MTG AB
MORRIS COMMUNICATIONS COMPANY LLC
MOVIE GALLERY INC
MP3.COM INC
MTR GAMING GROUP INC
MTV NETWORKS
MULTIMEDIA GAMES INC
NAPSTER INC
NASPERS LIMITED
NATIONAL AMUSEMENTS INC
NBC UNIVERSAL
NETFLIX INC
NETRATINGS INC
NEW LINE CINEMA
NEW YORK TIMES CO (THE)
NEWS CORP
NEWS WORLD COMMUNICATIONS INC
NEXSTAR BROADCASTING GROUP INC
NIELSEN COMPANY BV (THE)
NINTENDO CO LTD
NTL: TELEWEST BUSINESS
NTN BUZZTIME INC
OMNICOM GROUP INC
ON COMMAND CORP
ON STAGE ENTERTAINMENT
PALACE ENTERTAINMENT
PARAMOUNT PICTURES CORP
PEARSON PLC
PENN NATIONAL GAMING INC
PENTON MEDIA INC
PINNACLE ENTERTAINMENT INC
PIONEER CORPORATION
PIXAR ANIMATION STUDIOS INC
PLAYBOY ENTERPRISES INC
PRIMACOM AG
PRIMEDIA INC
PROGRESSIVE GAMING INTERNATIONAL CORP
R R DONNELLEY & SONS CO
RADIO ONE
RADIOSHACK CORPORATION
RAINBOW MEDIA HOLDINGS LLC

RANDOM HOUSE INC
RANK GROUP PLC (THE)
RAYCOM MEDIA INC
RCN CORP
READER'S DIGEST ASSOCIATION INC
REALNETWORKS INC
REDBOX AUTOMATED RETAIL LLC
REED ELSEVIER GROUP PLC
REGAL ENTERTAINMENT GROUP
REGENT COMMUNICATIONS INC
RENAISSANCE ENTERTAINMENT CORP
RENTRAK CORP
REUTERS GROUP PLC
REX STORES CORP
RIVIERA HOLDINGS CORP
RODALE INC
ROGERS COMMUNICATIONS INC
RTL GROUP SA
SAGA COMMUNICATIONS INC
SALEM COMMUNICATIONS CORP
SALON MEDIA GROUP INC
SAMSUNG ELECTRONICS CO LTD
SANDS REGENT
SANYO ELECTRIC COMPANY LTD
SCHOLASTIC CORP
SCIENTIFIC GAMES CORPORATION
SEGA SAMMY HOLDINGS INC
SHANDA INTERACTIVE ENTERTAINMENT
LIMITED
SHANGHAI MEDIA GROUP (SMG)
SHARP CORPORATION
SHAW COMMUNICATIONS INC
SHOP AT HOME NETWORK LLC
SHUFFLE MASTER INC
SHUN TAK HOLDINGS LIMITED
SIMEX-IWERKS
SIMON & SCHUSTER INC
SINCLAIR BROADCAST GROUP INC
SIRIUS SATELLITE RADIO
SIX FLAGS INC
SKY NETWORK TELEVISION LIMITED
SONY BMG MUSIC ENTERTAINMENT
SONY CORPORATION
SONY PICTURES ENTERTAINMENT
SPANISH BROADCASTING SYSTEM INC
SRS LABS INC
STATION CASINOS INC
SUDDENLINK COMMUNICATIONS
TAKE-TWO INTERACTIVE SOFTWARE INC
TAYLOR NELSON SOFRES PLC (TNS)
THOMAS NELSON INC
THOMSON CORP (THE)
THQ INC
TICKETMASTER
TIME INC
TIME WARNER CABLE INC
TIME WARNER INC
TIVO INC

TRADER CLASSIFIED MEDIA NV
TRAFFIX INC
TRANS WORLD CORP
TRANS WORLD ENTERTAINMENT CORP
TRANS-LUX CORPORATION
TRIBUNE CO
TRUMP ENTERTAINMENT RESORTS INC
TURNER BROADCASTING SYSTEM
TV AZTECA SA DE CV
TWEETER HOME ENTERTAINMENT GROUP INC
UNITED ARTISTS CORPORATION
UNITED BUSINESS MEDIA PLC
UNITED ONLINE INC
UNITED TALENT AGENCY INC
UNIVERSAL MUSIC GROUP
UNIVERSAL PICTURES
UNIVISION COMMUNICATIONS INC
US NEWS AND WORLD REPORT LP
VAIL RESORTS INC
VALUE LINE INC
VALUEVISION MEDIA INC
VERIZON COMMUNICATIONS
VIACOM INC
VINDIGO INC
VIVENDI SA
VULCAN INC
WALT DISNEY COMPANY (THE)
WALT DISNEY STUDIOS (THE)
WARNER BROS ENTERTAINMENT INC
WARNER MUSIC GROUP
WASHINGTON POST CO
WASSERMAN MEDIA GROUP LLC
WENNER MEDIA LLC
WESTWOOD ONE INC
WHEREHOUSE ENTERTAINMENT (RECORD TOWN INC)
WILLIAM MORRIS AGENCY INC
WMS INDUSTRIES INC
WPP GROUP PLC
WYNN RESORTS LIMITED
XINHUA FINANCE LIMITED
XINHUA FINANCE MEDIA LIMITED
XM SATELLITE RADIO HOLDINGS INC
YAHOO! INC
YAHOO! SEARCH MARKETING GROUP
YOUBET.COM INC
YOUNG BROADCASTING INC
ZIFF DAVIS MEDIA INC

INDEX OF HEADQUARTERS LOCATION BY U.S. STATE

To help you locate firms geographically, the city and state of the headquarters of each company are in the following index.

ALABAMA
BOOKS A MILLION INC; Birmingham
COMMUNITY NEWSPAPER HOLDINGS INC; Birmingham
EBSCO INDUSTRIES INC; Birmingham
INTEGRITY MEDIA INC; Mobile
MOVIE GALLERY INC; Dothan
RAYCOM MEDIA INC; Montgomery

ARIZONA
AZTAR CORP; Phoenix
CLEAR CHANNEL OUTDOOR; Phoenix

CALIFORNIA
24 HOUR FITNESS USA; San Ramon
2929 ENTERTAINMENT; Santa Monica
ACME COMMUNICATIONS INC; Santa Ana
ACTIVISION INC; Santa Monica
AMERICAN GOLF CORP; Santa Monica
ANSCHUTZ ENTERTAINMENT GROUP; Los Angeles
APPLE INC; Cupertino
ASCENT MEDIA GROUP INC; Santa Monica
BOOTH CREEK SKI HOLDINGS INC; Truckee
BRASH ENTERTAINMENT LLC; Hollywood
BUY.COM INC; Aliso Viejo
CINEMASTAR LUXURY THEATERS INC; Oceanside
CNET NETWORKS INC; San Francisco
COLUMBIA TRISTAR MOTION PICTURE GROUP; Culver City
CREATIVE ARTISTS AGENCY INC; Los Angeles
CROWN MEDIA HOLDINGS INC; Studio City
CW NETWORK (THE); Burbank
DAILY JOURNAL CORP; Los Angeles
DICK CLARK PRODUCTIONS INC; Santa Monica
DIGITAL VIDEO SYSTEMS INC; Mountain View
DIRECTV GROUP INC (THE); El Segundo
DREAMWORKS ANIMATION SKG INC; Glendale
DREAMWORKS SKG; Glendale
DTS INC; Agoura Hills
ELECTRONIC ARTS INC; Redwood City
ENDEAVOR AGENCY (THE); Beverly Hills
ENTRAVISION COMMUNICATIONS CORPORATION; Santa Monica
FIRST LOOK STUDIOS INC; Century City
FOX BROADCASTING COMPANY; Los Angeles
FOX FILMED ENTERTAINMENT; Los Angeles
FOX SPORTS NET INC; Los Angeles
FREEDOM COMMUNICATIONS INC; Irvine
GEMSTAR-TV GUIDE INTERNATIONAL INC; Los Angeles

GLAM MEDIA INC; Brisbane
GLU MOBILE INC; San Mateo
GOOGLE INC; Mountain View
HANDS-ON MOBILE; San Francisco
IGN ENTERTAINMENT; Brisbane
INTERNATIONAL CREATIVE MANAGEMENT
(ICM); Los Angeles
INTERNATIONAL LOTTERY & TOTALIZATOR
SYSTEMS; Vista
LASERPACIFIC MEDIA CORP; Hollywood
LIONS GATE ENTERTAINMENT CORP; Santa Monica
LIQUID DIGITAL MEDIA; Redwood City
LIVE NATION INC; Beverly Hills
LUCASARTS ENTERTAINMENT COMPANY LLC;
San Francisco
LUCASFILM LTD; San Francisco
MACROVISION CORP; Santa Clara
MARKETWATCH INC; San Francisco
MCCLATCHY COMPANY (THE); Sacramento
METRO-GOLDWYN-MAYER INC (MGM); Los
Angeles
MGM PICTURES; Los Angeles
MOBITV INC; Emeryville
MP3.COM INC; San Francisco
NAPSTER INC; Los Angeles
NETFLIX INC; Los Gatos
NTN BUZZTIME INC; Carlsbad
PALACE ENTERTAINMENT; Newport Beach
PARAMOUNT PICTURES CORP; Hollywood
PIXAR ANIMATION STUDIOS INC; Emeryville
SALEM COMMUNICATIONS CORP; Camarillo
SALON MEDIA GROUP INC; San Francisco
SIMEX-IWERKS; Burbank
SONY PICTURES ENTERTAINMENT; Culver City
SRS LABS INC; Santa Ana
THQ INC; Aguora Hills
TICKETMASTER; Los Angeles
TIVO INC; Alviso
UNITED ARTISTS CORPORATION; Los Angeles
UNITED ONLINE INC; Woodland Hills
UNITED TALENT AGENCY INC; Beverly Hills
UNIVERSAL PICTURES; Universal City
WALT DISNEY COMPANY (THE); Burbank
WALT DISNEY STUDIOS (THE); Burbank
WARNER BROS ENTERTAINMENT INC; Burbank
WASSERMAN MEDIA GROUP LLC; Los Angeles
WILLIAM MORRIS AGENCY INC; Beverly Hills
YAHOO! INC; Sunnyvale
YAHOO! SEARCH MARKETING GROUP; Burbank
YOUBET.COM INC; Woodland Hills

COLORADO
AMERICAN COIN MERCHANDISING INC; Louisville
AMERICAN EDUCATIONAL PRODUCTS LLC; Fort
Collins
CENTURY CASINOS INC; Colorado Springs
ECHOSTAR COMMUNICATIONS CORP; Englewood
LIBERTY GLOBAL INC; Englewood

LIBERTY MEDIA CORP; Englewood
MEDIANEWS GROUP INC; Denver
ON COMMAND CORP; Denver
RENAISSANCE ENTERTAINMENT CORP; Louisville
VAIL RESORTS INC; Broomfield

CONNECTICUT
ESPN INC; Bristol
GENERAL ELECTRIC CO (GE); Fairfield
JUPITERMEDIA CORP; Darien
THOMSON CORP (THE); Stamford
TIME WARNER CABLE INC; Stamford
TRANS-LUX CORPORATION; Norwalk

DELAWARE
DOVER DOWNS GAMING & ENTERTAINMENT INC;
Dover

DISTRICT OF COLUMBIA
NEWS WORLD COMMUNICATIONS INC; Washington
WASHINGTON POST CO; Washington
XM SATELLITE RADIO HOLDINGS INC; Washington

FLORIDA
ALLIANCE ENTERTAINMENT CORP; Coral Springs
BEASLEY BROADCAST GROUP INC; Naples
DIAMONDHEAD CASINO CORPORATION; Madeira
Beach
HOLLYWOOD MEDIA CORP; Boca Raton
ION MEDIA NETWORKS; West Palm Beach
SPANISH BROADCASTING SYSTEM INC; Coconut
Grove

GEORGIA
CABLE NEWS NETWORK LP LLLP; Atlanta
CARMIKE CINEMAS INC; Columbus
CONCURRENT COMPUTER CORP; Duluth
COX COMMUNICATIONS INC; Atlanta
COX ENTERPRISES INC; Atlanta
COX RADIO INC; Atlanta
CUMULUS MEDIA INC; Atlanta
GRAY TELEVISION INC; Atlanta
KNOLOGY INC; West Point
MDI ENTERTAINMENT LLC; Alpharetta
MORRIS COMMUNICATIONS COMPANY LLC;
Augusta
PRIMEDIA INC; Norcross
TURNER BROADCASTING SYSTEM; Atlanta

ILLINOIS
BALLY TOTAL FITNESS HOLDING CORPORATION;
Chicago
HARPO INC; Chicago
JOHNSON PUBLISHING COMPANY INC; Chicago
MIDWAY GAMES INC; Chicago
PLAYBOY ENTERPRISES INC; Chicago
R R DONNELLEY & SONS CO; Chicago

REDBOX AUTOMATED RETAIL LLC; Oak Brook
Terrace
TRIBUNE CO; Chicago
WMS INDUSTRIES INC; Waukegan

INDIANA
EMMIS COMMUNICATIONS CORP; Indianapolis

IOWA
LEE ENTERPRISES INC; Davenport
MEREDITH CORP; Des Moines

KENTUCKY
CHURCHILL DOWNS INC; Louisville

LOUISIANA
LAMAR ADVERTISING CO; Baton Rouge

MARYLAND
DISCOVERY COMMUNICATIONS INC; Silver Spring
RADIO ONE; Lanham
SINCLAIR BROADCAST GROUP INC; Hunt Valley

MASSACHUSETTS
AVID TECHNOLOGY INC; Tewksbury
BOSE CORPORATION; Framingham
BRIGHTCOVE INC; Cambridge
COURIER CORP; North Chelmsford
HOUGHTON MIFFLIN CO; Boston
INTERACTIVE DATA CORPORATION; Bedford
INTERNATIONAL DATA GROUP INC; Boston
NATIONAL AMUSEMENTS INC; Dedham
TWEETER HOME ENTERTAINMENT GROUP INC;
Canton

MICHIGAN
BORDERS GROUP INC; Ann Arbor
BOYNE USA RESORTS; Boyne Falls
SAGA COMMUNICATIONS INC; Grosse Pointe Farms

MINNESOTA
BEST BUY CO INC; Richfield
CANTERBURY PARK HOLDING CORP; Shakopee
CONCRETE SOFTWARE INC; Eden Prairie
LAKES ENTERTAINMENT INC; Minnetonka
LERNER PUBLISHING GROUP; Minneapolis
LIFE TIME FITNESS INC; Eden Prairie
VALUEVISION MEDIA INC; Eden Prairie

MISSOURI
AMC ENTERTAINMENT INC; Kansas City
ANHEUSER BUSCH COS INC; St. Louis
CHARTER COMMUNICATIONS INC; St. Louis
ENTERTAINMENT PROPERTIES TRUST; Kansas City
HALLMARK CARDS INC; Kansas City
ISLE OF CAPRI CASINOS INC; St. Louis
SUDDENLINK COMMUNICATIONS; St. Louis

NEBRASKA
BERKSHIRE HATHAWAY INC; Omaha

NEVADA
AMERICAN WAGERING INC; Las Vegas
AMERISTAR CASINOS INC; Las Vegas
BALLY TECHNOLOGIES INC; Las Vegas
BOYD GAMING CORP; Las Vegas
CITADEL BROADCASTING CORP; Las Vegas
GAMETECH INTERNATIONAL INC; Reno
GAMING PARTNERS INTERNATIONAL CORP; Las
Vegas
HARRAH'S ENTERTAINMENT INC; Las Vegas
HERBST GAMING INC; Las Vegas
INTERNATIONAL GAME TECHNOLOGY; Reno
LAS VEGAS SANDS CORP (THE VENETIAN); Las
Vegas
MGM MIRAGE; Las Vegas
ON STAGE ENTERTAINMENT; Las Vegas
PINNACLE ENTERTAINMENT INC; Las Vegas
PROGRESSIVE GAMING INTERNATIONAL CORP;
Las Vegas
RIVIERA HOLDINGS CORP; Las Vegas
SANDS REGENT; Reno
SHUFFLE MASTER INC; Las Vegas
STATION CASINOS INC; Las Vegas
WYNN RESORTS LIMITED; Las Vegas

NEW JERSEY
AUDIBLE INC; Newark
HARVEY ELECTRONICS INC; Lyndhurst
JOHN WILEY & SONS INC; Hoboken
TRUMP ENTERTAINMENT RESORTS INC; Atlantic
City

NEW YORK
24/7 REAL MEDIA INC; New York
A&E TELEVISION NETWORKS; New York
ABC INC; New York
ADVANCE PUBLICATIONS INC; New York
AMERICAN EXPRESS CO; New York
ARBITRON INC; New York
ATARI INC; New York
BARNES & NOBLE INC; New York
BARNESANDNOBLE.COM INC; New York
BLOOMBERG LP; New York
CABLEVISION SYSTEMS CORP; Bethpage
CBS CORP; New York
CBS RADIO; New York
CONDE NAST PUBLICATIONS INC; New York
DAG MEDIA INC; New York
DELAWARE NORTH COMPANIES; Buffalo
DOUBLECLICK INC; New York
DOW JONES & CO INC; New York
FORBES INC; New York
FORD MODELS INC; New York
FOX ENTERTAINMENT GROUP INC; New York
GATEHOUSE MEDIA INC; Fairport

GRANITE BROADCASTING CORP; New York
HARPERCOLLINS PUBLISHERS INC; New York
HARRIS INTERACTIVE INC; Rochester
HEARST CORPORATION (THE); New York
HEARST-ARGYLE TELEVISION INC; New York
IAC/INTERACTIVECORP; New York
INSIGHT COMMUNICATIONS COMPANY INC; New York
INTERPUBLIC GROUP OF COMPANIES INC; New York
IVILLAGE INC; New York
KERZNER INTERNATIONAL LIMITED; New York
MARTHA STEWART LIVING OMNIMEDIA INC; New York
MARVEL ENTERTAINMENT INC; New York
MCGRAW HILL COS INC; New York
MEDIACOM COMMUNICATIONS CORP; Middletown
MIRAMAX FILM CORP; New York
MTV NETWORKS; New York
NBC UNIVERSAL; New York
NETRATINGS INC; New York
NEW LINE CINEMA; New York
NEW YORK TIMES CO (THE); New York
NEWS CORP; New York
OMNICOM GROUP INC; New York
RAINBOW MEDIA HOLDINGS LLC; Jericho
RANDOM HOUSE INC; New York
READER'S DIGEST ASSOCIATION INC; Pleasantville
SCHOLASTIC CORP; New York
SCIENTIFIC GAMES CORPORATION; New York
SIMON & SCHUSTER INC; New York
SIRIUS SATELLITE RADIO; New York
SIX FLAGS INC; New York
SONY BMG MUSIC ENTERTAINMENT; New York
TAKE-TWO INTERACTIVE SOFTWARE INC; New York
TIME INC; New York
TIME WARNER INC; New York
TRAFFIX INC; Pearl River
TRANS WORLD CORP; New York
TRANS WORLD ENTERTAINMENT CORP; Albany
UNIVERSAL MUSIC GROUP; New York
UNIVISION COMMUNICATIONS INC; New York
US NEWS AND WORLD REPORT LP; New York
VALUE LINE INC; New York
VERIZON COMMUNICATIONS; New York
VIACOM INC; New York
VINDIGO INC; New York
WARNER MUSIC GROUP; New York
WENNER MEDIA LLC; New York
WESTWOOD ONE INC; New York
WHEREHOUSE ENTERTAINMENT (RECORD TOWN INC); Albany
YOUNG BROADCASTING INC; New York
ZIFF DAVIS MEDIA INC; New York

NORTH CAROLINA
DIALOG; Cary

OHIO
AMERICAN GREETINGS CORP; Cleveland
BERRY COMPANY (THE); Dayton
CEDAR FAIR LP; Sandusky
E W SCRIPPS CO; Cincinnati
IMG WORLDWIDE INC; Cleveland
PENTON MEDIA INC; Cleveland
REGENT COMMUNICATIONS INC; Cincinnati
REX STORES CORP; Dayton

OKLAHOMA
CD WAREHOUSE INC; Oklahoma City
EDUCATIONAL DEVELOPMENT CORP; Tulsa

OREGON
HOLLYWOOD ENTERTAINMENT CORP; Wilsonville
RENTRAK CORP; Portland

PENNSYLVANIA
COMCAST CORP; Philadelphia
ENTERCOM COMMUNICATIONS CORP; Bala Cynwyd
HERSHEY CO; Hershey
JOURNAL REGISTER CO; Yardley
PENN NATIONAL GAMING INC; Wyomissing
RODALE INC; Emmaus

RHODE ISLAND
GTECH HOLDINGS CORP; Providence
LIN TV CORP; Providence

SOUTH DAKOTA
LODGENET ENTERTAINMENT CORP; Sioux Falls

TENNESSEE
ANDERSON COS; Knoxville
GAYLORD ENTERTAINMENT CO; Nashville
INGRAM ENTERTAINMENT HOLDINGS INC; La Vergne
REGAL ENTERTAINMENT GROUP; Knoxville
SHOP AT HOME NETWORK LLC; Nashville
THOMAS NELSON INC; Nashville

TEXAS
AT&T INC; San Antonio
BELO CORP; Dallas
BLOCKBUSTER INC; Dallas
CINEMARK INC; Plano
CLEAR CHANNEL COMMUNICATIONS INC; San Antonio
CLUBCORP INC; Dallas
CURVES INTERNATIONAL INC; Waco
DG FASTCHANNEL; Irving
GAMESTOP CORP; Grapevine
GOLD'S GYM INTERNATIONAL; Irving
HARTE-HANKS INC; San Antonio
HASTINGS ENTERTAINMENT INC; Amarillo

HOOVER'S INC; Austin
LANDRY'S RESTAURANTS INC; Houston
MULTIMEDIA GAMES INC; Austin
NEXSTAR BROADCASTING GROUP INC; Irving
RADIOSHACK CORPORATION; Fort Worth

UTAH
AMERICAN SKIING COMPANY; Park City

VIRGINIA
AMF BOWLING WORLDWIDE INC; Mechanicsville
AOL LLC; Dulles
CIRCUIT CITY STORES INC; Richmond
GANNETT CO INC; McLean
LANDMARK COMMUNICATIONS INC; Norfolk
MEDIA GENERAL INC; Richmond
RCN CORP; Herndon

WASHINGTON
AMAZON.COM INC; Seattle
DIGEO INC; Kirkland
FISHER COMMUNICATIONS INC; Seattle
LOUD TECHNOLOGIES INC; Woodinville
MICROSOFT CORP; Redmond
REALNETWORKS INC; Seattle
VULCAN INC; Seattle

WEST VIRGINIA
MTR GAMING GROUP INC; Chester

WISCONSIN
JOURNAL COMMUNICATIONS INC; Milwaukee

INDEX OF NON-U.S. HEADQUARTERS LOCATION BY COUNTRY

AUSTRALIA
ARISTOCRAT LEISURE LTD; Lane Cove

BERMUDA
CENTRAL EUROPEAN MEDIA ENTERPRISES LTD; Hamilton

CANADA
ALLIANCE ATLANTIS COMMUNICATIONS INC; Toronto
BIOWARE CORP; Edmonton
CANWEST GLOBAL COMMUNICATIONS; Winnipeg
CIRQUE DU SOLEIL INC; Montreal
CORUS ENTERTAINMENT INC; Toronto
HOLLINGER INC; Toronto
IMAX CORPORATION; Mississauga
INTERTAN CANADA LTD; Barrie
JUMPTV INC; Toronto
MAGNA ENTERTAINMENT CORP; Aurora
ROGERS COMMUNICATIONS INC; Toronto
SHAW COMMUNICATIONS INC; Calgary

CHINA
I-CABLE COMMUNICATIONS; Hong Kong
MELCO PBL ENTERTAINMENT LIMITED; Central
SHANDA INTERACTIVE ENTERTAINMENT LIMITED; Shanghai
SHANGHAI MEDIA GROUP (SMG); Shanghai
SHUN TAK HOLDINGS LIMITED; Hong Kong
XINHUA FINANCE LIMITED; Hong Kong
XINHUA FINANCE MEDIA LIMITED; Beijing

FRANCE
EURO DISNEY SCA; Chessy
LAGARDERE ACTIVE MEDIA; Levallois-Perret
VIVENDI SA; Paris

GERMANY
BERTELSMANN AG; Gutersloh
PRIMACOM AG; Mainz

ISRAEL
HOT CABLE SYSTEMS MEDIA LTD; Netanya

JAPAN
CLARION CO LTD; Toda
COLUMBIA MUSIC ENTERTAINMENT INC; Minato-ku
MATSUSHITA ELECTRIC INDUSTRIAL CO LTD; Osaka
NINTENDO CO LTD; Kyoto
PIONEER CORPORATION; Tokyo
SANYO ELECTRIC COMPANY LTD; Moriguchi

SEGA SAMMY HOLDINGS INC; 1-9-2 Higashi
Shimbashi, Minato-ku
SHARP CORPORATION; Osaka
SONY CORPORATION; Tokyo

KOREA
SAMSUNG ELECTRONICS CO LTD; Seoul

LUXEMBOURG
RTL GROUP SA; Luxembourg

MEXICO
GRUPO RADIO CENTRO SA DE CV; Mexico City
GRUPO TELEVISA SA; Colonia Santa Fe
TV AZTECA SA DE CV; Mexico City

NEW ZEALAND
SKY NETWORK TELEVISION LIMITED; Auckland

SOUTH AFRICA
NASPERS LIMITED; Cape Town

SWEDEN
MODERN TIMES GROUP MTG AB; Stockholm

THE NETHERLANDS
JOOST; Leiden
NIELSEN COMPANY BV (THE); Haarlem
TRADER CLASSIFIED MEDIA NV; Amsterdam

UNITED KINGDOM
BRITISH BROADCASTING CORPORATION (BBC);
London
BRITISH SKY BROADCASTING GROUP PLC;
Isleworth
DENNIS PUBLISHING LTD; London
DIGITAL BRIDGES LIMITED; London
EMAP PLC; Peterborough
EMI GROUP PLC; London
ITV PLC; London
METRO INTERNATIONAL SA; London
NTL: TELEWEST BUSINESS; Hook
PEARSON PLC; London
RANK GROUP PLC (THE); London
REED ELSEVIER GROUP PLC; London
REUTERS GROUP PLC; London
TAYLOR NELSON SOFRES PLC (TNS); London
UNITED BUSINESS MEDIA PLC; London
WPP GROUP PLC; London

**INDEX BY REGIONS OF THE U.S.
WHERE THE ENTERTAINMENT 400
FIRMS HAVE LOCATIONS**

WEST
24 HOUR FITNESS USA
24/7 REAL MEDIA INC
2929 ENTERTAINMENT
A&E TELEVISION NETWORKS
ABC INC
ACME COMMUNICATIONS INC
ACTIVISION INC
ADVANCE PUBLICATIONS INC
ALLIANCE ATLANTIS COMMUNICATIONS INC
ALLIANCE ENTERTAINMENT CORP
AMAZON.COM INC
AMC ENTERTAINMENT INC
AMERICAN COIN MERCHANDISING INC
AMERICAN EDUCATIONAL PRODUCTS LLC
AMERICAN EXPRESS CO
AMERICAN GOLF CORP
AMERICAN GREETINGS CORP
AMERICAN SKIING COMPANY
AMERICAN WAGERING INC
AMERISTAR CASINOS INC
AMF BOWLING WORLDWIDE INC
ANHEUSER BUSCH COS INC
ANSCHUTZ ENTERTAINMENT GROUP
APPLE INC
ARBITRON INC
ARISTOCRAT LEISURE LTD
ASCENT MEDIA GROUP INC
AT&T INC
ATARI INC
AVID TECHNOLOGY INC
AZTAR CORP
BALLY TECHNOLOGIES INC
BALLY TOTAL FITNESS HOLDING CORPORATION
BARNES & NOBLE INC
BEASLEY BROADCAST GROUP INC
BELO CORP
BERKSHIRE HATHAWAY INC
BERRY COMPANY (THE)
BERTELSMANN AG
BEST BUY CO INC
BLOCKBUSTER INC
BLOOMBERG LP
BOOTH CREEK SKI HOLDINGS INC
BORDERS GROUP INC
BOSE CORPORATION
BOYD GAMING CORP
BOYNE USA RESORTS
BRASH ENTERTAINMENT LLC
BRIGHTCOVE INC
BRITISH BROADCASTING CORPORATION (BBC)
BUY.COM INC
CABLE NEWS NETWORK LP LLLP

CARMIKE CINEMAS INC
CBS CORP
CBS RADIO
CD WAREHOUSE INC
CEDAR FAIR LP
CENTURY CASINOS INC
CHARTER COMMUNICATIONS INC
CINEMARK INC
CINEMASTAR LUXURY THEATERS INC
CIRCUIT CITY STORES INC
CIRQUE DU SOLEIL INC
CITADEL BROADCASTING CORP
CLARION CO LTD
CLEAR CHANNEL COMMUNICATIONS INC
CLEAR CHANNEL OUTDOOR
CLUBCORP INC
CNET NETWORKS INC
COLUMBIA TRISTAR MOTION PICTURE GROUP
COMCAST CORP
COMMUNITY NEWSPAPER HOLDINGS INC
CONDE NAST PUBLICATIONS INC
COURIER CORP
COX COMMUNICATIONS INC
COX ENTERPRISES INC
COX RADIO INC
CREATIVE ARTISTS AGENCY INC
CROWN MEDIA HOLDINGS INC
CUMULUS MEDIA INC
CURVES INTERNATIONAL INC
CW NETWORK (THE)
DAILY JOURNAL CORP
DELAWARE NORTH COMPANIES
DG FASTCHANNEL
DIALOG
DICK CLARK PRODUCTIONS INC
DIGEO INC
DIGITAL BRIDGES LIMITED
DIGITAL VIDEO SYSTEMS INC
DIRECTV GROUP INC (THE)
DISCOVERY COMMUNICATIONS INC
DOUBLECLICK INC
DOW JONES & CO INC
DREAMWORKS ANIMATION SKG INC
DREAMWORKS SKG
DTS INC
E W SCRIPPS CO
ECHOSTAR COMMUNICATIONS CORP
ELECTRONIC ARTS INC
EMAP PLC
EMMIS COMMUNICATIONS CORP
ENDEAVOR AGENCY (THE)
ENTERCOM COMMUNICATIONS CORP
ENTERTAINMENT PROPERTIES TRUST
ENTRAVISION COMMUNICATIONS CORPORATION
FIRST LOOK STUDIOS INC
FISHER COMMUNICATIONS INC
FORD MODELS INC
FOX BROADCASTING COMPANY

FOX ENTERTAINMENT GROUP INC
FOX FILMED ENTERTAINMENT
FOX SPORTS NET INC
FREEDOM COMMUNICATIONS INC
GAMESTOP CORP
GAMETECH INTERNATIONAL INC
GAMING PARTNERS INTERNATIONAL CORP
GANNETT CO INC
GATEHOUSE MEDIA INC
GAYLORD ENTERTAINMENT CO
GEMSTAR-TV GUIDE INTERNATIONAL INC
GENERAL ELECTRIC CO (GE)
GLAM MEDIA INC
GLU MOBILE INC
GOLD'S GYM INTERNATIONAL
GOOGLE INC
GRANITE BROADCASTING CORP
GRAY TELEVISION INC
HALLMARK CARDS INC
HANDS-ON MOBILE
HARRAH'S ENTERTAINMENT INC
HARRIS INTERACTIVE INC
HARTE-HANKS INC
HASTINGS ENTERTAINMENT INC
HEARST CORPORATION (THE)
HEARST-ARGYLE TELEVISION INC
HERBST GAMING INC
HERSHEY CO
HOLLYWOOD ENTERTAINMENT CORP
HOLLYWOOD MEDIA CORP
HOUGHTON MIFFLIN CO
IAC/INTERACTIVECORP
IGN ENTERTAINMENT
IMAX CORPORATION
IMG WORLDWIDE INC
INGRAM ENTERTAINMENT HOLDINGS INC
INTERACTIVE DATA CORPORATION
INTERNATIONAL CREATIVE MANAGEMENT (ICM)
INTERNATIONAL DATA GROUP INC
INTERNATIONAL GAME TECHNOLOGY
INTERNATIONAL LOTTERY & TOTALIZATOR
SYSTEMS
INTERPUBLIC GROUP OF COMPANIES INC
ION MEDIA NETWORKS
ISLE OF CAPRI CASINOS INC
JOHN WILEY & SONS INC
JOHNSON PUBLISHING COMPANY INC
JOURNAL COMMUNICATIONS INC
JUPITERMEDIA CORP
LAKES ENTERTAINMENT INC
LAMAR ADVERTISING CO
LANDMARK COMMUNICATIONS INC
LANDRY'S RESTAURANTS INC
LAS VEGAS SANDS CORP (THE VENETIAN)
LASERPACIFIC MEDIA CORP
LEE ENTERPRISES INC
LIBERTY GLOBAL INC
LIBERTY MEDIA CORP

LIFE TIME FITNESS INC
LIN TV CORP
LIONS GATE ENTERTAINMENT CORP
LIQUID DIGITAL MEDIA
LIVE NATION INC
LODGENET ENTERTAINMENT CORP
LOUD TECHNOLOGIES INC
LUCASARTS ENTERTAINMENT COMPANY LLC
LUCASFILM LTD
MACROVISION CORP
MAGNA ENTERTAINMENT CORP
MARKETWATCH INC
MARVEL ENTERTAINMENT INC
MATSUSHITA ELECTRIC INDUSTRIAL CO LTD
MCCLATCHY COMPANY (THE)
MCGRAW HILL COS INC
MEDIACOM COMMUNICATIONS CORP
MEDIANEWS GROUP INC
MEREDITH CORP
METRO-GOLDWYN-MAYER INC (MGM)
MGM MIRAGE
MGM PICTURES
MICROSOFT CORP
MIDWAY GAMES INC
MOBITV INC
MORRIS COMMUNICATIONS COMPANY LLC
MOVIE GALLERY INC
MP3.COM INC
MTR GAMING GROUP INC
MTV NETWORKS
MULTIMEDIA GAMES INC
NAPSTER INC
NATIONAL AMUSEMENTS INC
NBC UNIVERSAL
NETFLIX INC
NETRATINGS INC
NEW YORK TIMES CO (THE)
NEWS CORP
NEXSTAR BROADCASTING GROUP INC
NIELSEN COMPANY BV (THE)
NINTENDO CO LTD
NTN BUZZTIME INC
OMNICOM GROUP INC
ON COMMAND CORP
ON STAGE ENTERTAINMENT
PALACE ENTERTAINMENT
PARAMOUNT PICTURES CORP
PEARSON PLC
PENN NATIONAL GAMING INC
PENTON MEDIA INC
PINNACLE ENTERTAINMENT INC
PIONEER CORPORATION
PIXAR ANIMATION STUDIOS INC
PLAYBOY ENTERPRISES INC
PROGRESSIVE GAMING INTERNATIONAL CORP
R R DONNELLEY & SONS CO
RADIO ONE
RADIOSHACK CORPORATION

RAINBOW MEDIA HOLDINGS LLC
RAYCOM MEDIA INC
READER'S DIGEST ASSOCIATION INC
REALNETWORKS INC
REDBOX AUTOMATED RETAIL LLC
REGAL ENTERTAINMENT GROUP
REGENT COMMUNICATIONS INC
RENAISSANCE ENTERTAINMENT CORP
RENTRAK CORP
REX STORES CORP
RIVIERA HOLDINGS CORP
SAGA COMMUNICATIONS INC
SALEM COMMUNICATIONS CORP
SALON MEDIA GROUP INC
SAMSUNG ELECTRONICS CO LTD
SANDS REGENT
SANYO ELECTRIC COMPANY LTD
SCHOLASTIC CORP
SCIENTIFIC GAMES CORPORATION
SEGA SAMMY HOLDINGS INC
SHARP CORPORATION
SHOP AT HOME NETWORK LLC
SHUFFLE MASTER INC
SIMEX-IWERKS
SINCLAIR BROADCAST GROUP INC
SIX FLAGS INC
SONY BMG MUSIC ENTERTAINMENT
SONY CORPORATION
SONY PICTURES ENTERTAINMENT
SPANISH BROADCASTING SYSTEM INC
SRS LABS INC
STATION CASINOS INC
SUDDENLINK COMMUNICATIONS
THOMAS NELSON INC
THOMSON CORP (THE)
THQ INC
TICKETMASTER
TIME INC
TIME WARNER CABLE INC
TIME WARNER INC
TIVO INC
TRANS WORLD ENTERTAINMENT CORP
TRANS-LUX CORPORATION
TRIBUNE CO
TWEETER HOME ENTERTAINMENT GROUP INC
UNITED ARTISTS CORPORATION
UNITED BUSINESS MEDIA PLC
UNITED ONLINE INC
UNITED TALENT AGENCY INC
UNIVERSAL MUSIC GROUP
UNIVERSAL PICTURES
UNIVISION COMMUNICATIONS INC
VAIL RESORTS INC
VERIZON COMMUNICATIONS
VIACOM INC
VIVENDI SA
VULCAN INC
WALT DISNEY COMPANY (THE)

WALT DISNEY STUDIOS (THE)
WARNER BROS ENTERTAINMENT INC
WARNER MUSIC GROUP
WASHINGTON POST CO
WASSERMAN MEDIA GROUP LLC
WENNER MEDIA LLC
WESTWOOD ONE INC
WHEREHOUSE ENTERTAINMENT (RECORD TOWN INC)
WILLIAM MORRIS AGENCY INC
WMS INDUSTRIES INC
WPP GROUP PLC
WYNN RESORTS LIMITED
YAHOO! INC
YAHOO! SEARCH MARKETING GROUP
YOUBET.COM INC
YOUNG BROADCASTING INC
ZIFF DAVIS MEDIA INC

SOUTHWEST

24 HOUR FITNESS USA
2929 ENTERTAINMENT
ABC INC
ACME COMMUNICATIONS INC
ADVANCE PUBLICATIONS INC
AMAZON.COM INC
AMC ENTERTAINMENT INC
AMERICAN EXPRESS CO
AMERICAN GOLF CORP
AMERICAN GREETINGS CORP
AMF BOWLING WORLDWIDE INC
ANDERSON COS
ANHEUSER BUSCH COS INC
ANSCHUTZ ENTERTAINMENT GROUP
APPLE INC
ARBITRON INC
AT&T INC
AVID TECHNOLOGY INC
BALLY TECHNOLOGIES INC
BALLY TOTAL FITNESS HOLDING CORPORATION
BARNES & NOBLE INC
BELO CORP
BERKSHIRE HATHAWAY INC
BEST BUY CO INC
BIOWARE CORP
BLOCKBUSTER INC
BLOOMBERG LP
BOOKS A MILLION INC
BOOTH CREEK SKI HOLDINGS INC
BORDERS GROUP INC
BOSE CORPORATION
CABLE NEWS NETWORK LP LLLP
CARMIKE CINEMAS INC
CBS CORP
CBS RADIO
CD WAREHOUSE INC
CHARTER COMMUNICATIONS INC
CINEMARK INC

CIRCUIT CITY STORES INC
CITADEL BROADCASTING CORP
CLEAR CHANNEL COMMUNICATIONS INC
CLEAR CHANNEL OUTDOOR
CLUBCORP INC
CNET NETWORKS INC
COMCAST CORP
COMMUNITY NEWSPAPER HOLDINGS INC
COX COMMUNICATIONS INC
COX ENTERPRISES INC
COX RADIO INC
CUMULUS MEDIA INC
CURVES INTERNATIONAL INC
DAILY JOURNAL CORP
DELAWARE NORTH COMPANIES
DG FASTCHANNEL
DIALOG
DICK CLARK PRODUCTIONS INC
DIRECTV GROUP INC (THE)
E W SCRIPPS CO
ECHOSTAR COMMUNICATIONS CORP
EDUCATIONAL DEVELOPMENT CORP
ELECTRONIC ARTS INC
EMMIS COMMUNICATIONS CORP
ENTERCOM COMMUNICATIONS CORP
ENTERTAINMENT PROPERTIES TRUST
ENTRAVISION COMMUNICATIONS CORPORATION
FORD MODELS INC
FOX ENTERTAINMENT GROUP INC
FOX SPORTS NET INC
FREEDOM COMMUNICATIONS INC
GAMESTOP CORP
GAMETECH INTERNATIONAL INC
GANNETT CO INC
GATEHOUSE MEDIA INC
GAYLORD ENTERTAINMENT CO
GENERAL ELECTRIC CO (GE)
GOLD'S GYM INTERNATIONAL
GOOGLE INC
GRAY TELEVISION INC
HALLMARK CARDS INC
HARRAH'S ENTERTAINMENT INC
HARTE-HANKS INC
HASTINGS ENTERTAINMENT INC
HEARST CORPORATION (THE)
HEARST-ARGYLE TELEVISION INC
HERSHEY CO
HOLLYWOOD ENTERTAINMENT CORP
HOOVER'S INC
HOUGHTON MIFFLIN CO
IAC/INTERACTIVECORP
IMAX CORPORATION
INGRAM ENTERTAINMENT HOLDINGS INC
INSIGHT COMMUNICATIONS COMPANY INC
INTERPUBLIC GROUP OF COMPANIES INC
ION MEDIA NETWORKS
JOURNAL COMMUNICATIONS INC
LAKES ENTERTAINMENT INC

LAMAR ADVERTISING CO
LANDMARK COMMUNICATIONS INC
LANDRY'S RESTAURANTS INC
LEE ENTERPRISES INC
LIBERTY MEDIA CORP
LIFE TIME FITNESS INC
LIN TV CORP
LIVE NATION INC
LODGENET ENTERTAINMENT CORP
MAGNA ENTERTAINMENT CORP
MATSUSHITA ELECTRIC INDUSTRIAL CO LTD
MCGRAW HILL COS INC
MEDIANEWS GROUP INC
MEREDITH CORP
MICROSOFT CORP
MIDWAY GAMES INC
MORRIS COMMUNICATIONS COMPANY LLC
MOVIE GALLERY INC
MULTIMEDIA GAMES INC
NEW YORK TIMES CO (THE)
NEWS CORP
NEXSTAR BROADCASTING GROUP INC
NIELSEN COMPANY BV (THE)
NTN BUZZTIME INC
OMNICOM GROUP INC
PALACE ENTERTAINMENT
PEARSON PLC
PROGRESSIVE GAMING INTERNATIONAL CORP
R R DONNELLEY & SONS CO
RADIO ONE
RADIOSHACK CORPORATION
RAYCOM MEDIA INC
READER'S DIGEST ASSOCIATION INC
REDBOX AUTOMATED RETAIL LLC
REGAL ENTERTAINMENT GROUP
REGENT COMMUNICATIONS INC
REX STORES CORP
SAGA COMMUNICATIONS INC
SALEM COMMUNICATIONS CORP
SAMSUNG ELECTRONICS CO LTD
SCHOLASTIC CORP
SCIENTIFIC GAMES CORPORATION
SEGA SAMMY HOLDINGS INC
SINCLAIR BROADCAST GROUP INC
SIX FLAGS INC
SONY CORPORATION
SPANISH BROADCASTING SYSTEM INC
STATION CASINOS INC
SUDDENLINK COMMUNICATIONS
THOMAS NELSON INC
THOMSON CORP (THE)
THQ INC
TICKETMASTER
TIME INC
TIME WARNER CABLE INC
TIME WARNER INC
TRANS WORLD ENTERTAINMENT CORP
TRANS-LUX CORPORATION

TRIBUNE CO
TWEETER HOME ENTERTAINMENT GROUP INC
UNIVERSAL MUSIC GROUP
UNIVISION COMMUNICATIONS INC
VAIL RESORTS INC
VERIZON COMMUNICATIONS
VIVENDI SA
WALT DISNEY COMPANY (THE)
WASHINGTON POST CO
WENNER MEDIA LLC
WESTWOOD ONE INC
WHEREHOUSE ENTERTAINMENT (RECORD TOWN INC)
WPP GROUP PLC
YAHOO! INC

MIDWEST
24 HOUR FITNESS USA
24/7 REAL MEDIA INC
A&E TELEVISION NETWORKS
ABC INC
ACME COMMUNICATIONS INC
ACTIVISION INC
ADVANCE PUBLICATIONS INC
ALLIANCE ENTERTAINMENT CORP
AMAZON.COM INC
AMC ENTERTAINMENT INC
AMERICAN EXPRESS CO
AMERICAN GOLF CORP
AMERICAN GREETINGS CORP
AMERISTAR CASINOS INC
AMF BOWLING WORLDWIDE INC
ANHEUSER BUSCH COS INC
ANSCHUTZ ENTERTAINMENT GROUP
APPLE INC
ARBITRON INC
ARISTOCRAT LEISURE LTD
ASCENT MEDIA GROUP INC
AT&T INC
AVID TECHNOLOGY INC
AZTAR CORP
BALLY TOTAL FITNESS HOLDING CORPORATION
BARNES & NOBLE INC
BELO CORP
BERKSHIRE HATHAWAY INC
BERRY COMPANY (THE)
BERTELSMANN AG
BEST BUY CO INC
BLOCKBUSTER INC
BLOOMBERG LP
BOOKS A MILLION INC
BORDERS GROUP INC
BOSE CORPORATION
BOYD GAMING CORP
BOYNE USA RESORTS
CABLE NEWS NETWORK LP LLLP
CANTERBURY PARK HOLDING CORP
CANWEST GLOBAL COMMUNICATIONS

CARMIKE CINEMAS INC
CBS CORP
CBS RADIO
CD WAREHOUSE INC
CEDAR FAIR LP
CHARTER COMMUNICATIONS INC
CHURCHILL DOWNS INC
CINEMARK INC
CIRCUIT CITY STORES INC
CITADEL BROADCASTING CORP
CLEAR CHANNEL COMMUNICATIONS INC
CLEAR CHANNEL OUTDOOR
CLUBCORP INC
CNET NETWORKS INC
COMCAST CORP
COMMUNITY NEWSPAPER HOLDINGS INC
CONCRETE SOFTWARE INC
CONCURRENT COMPUTER CORP
CONDE NAST PUBLICATIONS INC
COURIER CORP
COX COMMUNICATIONS INC
COX ENTERPRISES INC
COX RADIO INC
CUMULUS MEDIA INC
CURVES INTERNATIONAL INC
DELAWARE NORTH COMPANIES
DG FASTCHANNEL
DIALOG
DICK CLARK PRODUCTIONS INC
DIRECTV GROUP INC (THE)
DISCOVERY COMMUNICATIONS INC
DOUBLECLICK INC
E W SCRIPPS CO
ECHOSTAR COMMUNICATIONS CORP
ELECTRONIC ARTS INC
EMMIS COMMUNICATIONS CORP
ENTERCOM COMMUNICATIONS CORP
ENTERTAINMENT PROPERTIES TRUST
FORD MODELS INC
FOX ENTERTAINMENT GROUP INC
FOX SPORTS NET INC
FREEDOM COMMUNICATIONS INC
GAMESTOP CORP
GAMETECH INTERNATIONAL INC
GANNETT CO INC
GATEHOUSE MEDIA INC
GENERAL ELECTRIC CO (GE)
GOLD'S GYM INTERNATIONAL
GOOGLE INC
GRANITE BROADCASTING CORP
GRAY TELEVISION INC
HALLMARK CARDS INC
HARPO INC
HARRAH'S ENTERTAINMENT INC
HARRIS INTERACTIVE INC
HARTE-HANKS INC
HASTINGS ENTERTAINMENT INC
HEARST CORPORATION (THE)

HEARST-ARGYLE TELEVISION INC
HERBST GAMING INC
HERSHEY CO
HOLLINGER INC
HOLLYWOOD ENTERTAINMENT CORP
HOUGHTON MIFFLIN CO
IAC/INTERACTIVECORP
IGN ENTERTAINMENT
IMAX CORPORATION
IMG WORLDWIDE INC
INGRAM ENTERTAINMENT HOLDINGS INC
INSIGHT COMMUNICATIONS COMPANY INC
INTERACTIVE DATA CORPORATION
INTERNATIONAL GAME TECHNOLOGY
INTERPUBLIC GROUP OF COMPANIES INC
ION MEDIA NETWORKS
ISLE OF CAPRI CASINOS INC
JOHN WILEY & SONS INC
JOHNSON PUBLISHING COMPANY INC
JOURNAL COMMUNICATIONS INC
JOURNAL REGISTER CO
KNOLOGY INC
LAKES ENTERTAINMENT INC
LAMAR ADVERTISING CO
LANDMARK COMMUNICATIONS INC
LANDRY'S RESTAURANTS INC
LEE ENTERPRISES INC
LERNER PUBLISHING GROUP
LIBERTY MEDIA CORP
LIFE TIME FITNESS INC
LIN TV CORP
LIVE NATION INC
LODGENET ENTERTAINMENT CORP
LOUD TECHNOLOGIES INC
MACROVISION CORP
MAGNA ENTERTAINMENT CORP
MATSUSHITA ELECTRIC INDUSTRIAL CO LTD
MCCLATCHY COMPANY (THE)
MCGRAW HILL COS INC
MEDIA GENERAL INC
MEDIACOM COMMUNICATIONS CORP
MEDIANEWS GROUP INC
MEREDITH CORP
MGM MIRAGE
MICROSOFT CORP
MIDWAY GAMES INC
MORRIS COMMUNICATIONS COMPANY LLC
MOVIE GALLERY INC
MTR GAMING GROUP INC
MULTIMEDIA GAMES INC
NATIONAL AMUSEMENTS INC
NBC UNIVERSAL
NEW YORK TIMES CO (THE)
NEWS CORP
NEXSTAR BROADCASTING GROUP INC
NIELSEN COMPANY BV (THE)
OMNICOM GROUP INC
ON STAGE ENTERTAINMENT

PALACE ENTERTAINMENT
PEARSON PLC
PENN NATIONAL GAMING INC
PENTON MEDIA INC
PINNACLE ENTERTAINMENT INC
PLAYBOY ENTERPRISES INC
PROGRESSIVE GAMING INTERNATIONAL CORP
R R DONNELLEY & SONS CO
RADIO ONE
RADIOSHACK CORPORATION
RAINBOW MEDIA HOLDINGS LLC
RAYCOM MEDIA INC
RCN CORP
READER'S DIGEST ASSOCIATION INC
REDBOX AUTOMATED RETAIL LLC
REGAL ENTERTAINMENT GROUP
REGENT COMMUNICATIONS INC
RENAISSANCE ENTERTAINMENT CORP
REX STORES CORP
SAGA COMMUNICATIONS INC
SALEM COMMUNICATIONS CORP
SAMSUNG ELECTRONICS CO LTD
SCHOLASTIC CORP
SCIENTIFIC GAMES CORPORATION
SEGA SAMMY HOLDINGS INC
SHARP CORPORATION
SHOP AT HOME NETWORK LLC
SHUFFLE MASTER INC
SINCLAIR BROADCAST GROUP INC
SIX FLAGS INC
SONY BMG MUSIC ENTERTAINMENT
SONY CORPORATION
SPANISH BROADCASTING SYSTEM INC
SUDDENLINK COMMUNICATIONS
THOMAS NELSON INC
THOMSON CORP (THE)
THQ INC
TICKETMASTER
TIME INC
TIME WARNER CABLE INC
TIME WARNER INC
TRANS WORLD ENTERTAINMENT CORP
TRANS-LUX CORPORATION
TRIBUNE CO
TRUMP ENTERTAINMENT RESORTS INC
TWEETER HOME ENTERTAINMENT GROUP INC
UNITED BUSINESS MEDIA PLC
UNITED ONLINE INC
UNIVERSAL MUSIC GROUP
UNIVISION COMMUNICATIONS INC
VALUEVISION MEDIA INC
VERIZON COMMUNICATIONS
VIACOM INC
VIVENDI SA
WALT DISNEY COMPANY (THE)
WASHINGTON POST CO
WENNER MEDIA LLC
WESTWOOD ONE INC

WHEREHOUSE ENTERTAINMENT (RECORD TOWN INC)
WMS INDUSTRIES INC
WPP GROUP PLC
XM SATELLITE RADIO HOLDINGS INC
YAHOO! INC
YAHOO! SEARCH MARKETING GROUP
YOUNG BROADCASTING INC

SOUTHEAST
24 HOUR FITNESS USA
A&E TELEVISION NETWORKS
ABC INC
ACME COMMUNICATIONS INC
ACTIVISION INC
ADVANCE PUBLICATIONS INC
ALLIANCE ENTERTAINMENT CORP
AMAZON.COM INC
AMC ENTERTAINMENT INC
AMERICAN EXPRESS CO
AMERICAN GOLF CORP
AMERICAN GREETINGS CORP
AMERISTAR CASINOS INC
AMF BOWLING WORLDWIDE INC
ANDERSON COS
ANHEUSER BUSCH COS INC
ANSCHUTZ ENTERTAINMENT GROUP
APPLE INC
ARBITRON INC
ARISTOCRAT LEISURE LTD
ASCENT MEDIA GROUP INC
AT&T INC
AVID TECHNOLOGY INC
BALLY TECHNOLOGIES INC
BALLY TOTAL FITNESS HOLDING CORPORATION
BARNES & NOBLE INC
BARNESANDNOBLE.COM INC
BEASLEY BROADCAST GROUP INC
BELO CORP
BERKSHIRE HATHAWAY INC
BERRY COMPANY (THE)
BERTELSMANN AG
BEST BUY CO INC
BLOCKBUSTER INC
BLOOMBERG LP
BOOKS A MILLION INC
BORDERS GROUP INC
BOSE CORPORATION
BOYD GAMING CORP
BOYNE USA RESORTS
CABLE NEWS NETWORK LP LLLP
CARMIKE CINEMAS INC
CBS CORP
CBS RADIO
CD WAREHOUSE INC
CHARTER COMMUNICATIONS INC
CHURCHILL DOWNS INC
CINEMARK INC

CIRCUIT CITY STORES INC
CITADEL BROADCASTING CORP
CLEAR CHANNEL COMMUNICATIONS INC
CLEAR CHANNEL OUTDOOR
CLUBCORP INC
CNET NETWORKS INC
COMCAST CORP
COMMUNITY NEWSPAPER HOLDINGS INC
CONCURRENT COMPUTER CORP
COX COMMUNICATIONS INC
COX ENTERPRISES INC
COX RADIO INC
CREATIVE ARTISTS AGENCY INC
CUMULUS MEDIA INC
CURVES INTERNATIONAL INC
DELAWARE NORTH COMPANIES
DG FASTCHANNEL
DIAMONDHEAD CASINO CORPORATION
DIRECTV GROUP INC (THE)
DISCOVERY COMMUNICATIONS INC
DREAMWORKS SKG
E W SCRIPPS CO
EBSCO INDUSTRIES INC
ECHOSTAR COMMUNICATIONS CORP
ELECTRONIC ARTS INC
EMMIS COMMUNICATIONS CORP
ENTERCOM COMMUNICATIONS CORP
ENTERTAINMENT PROPERTIES TRUST
ENTRAVISION COMMUNICATIONS CORPORATION
FIRST LOOK STUDIOS INC
FORD MODELS INC
FOX ENTERTAINMENT GROUP INC
FOX SPORTS NET INC
FREEDOM COMMUNICATIONS INC
GAMESTOP CORP
GANNETT CO INC
GATEHOUSE MEDIA INC
GAYLORD ENTERTAINMENT CO
GENERAL ELECTRIC CO (GE)
GOLD'S GYM INTERNATIONAL
GOOGLE INC
GRAY TELEVISION INC
HALLMARK CARDS INC
HARRAH'S ENTERTAINMENT INC
HARTE-HANKS INC
HASTINGS ENTERTAINMENT INC
HEARST CORPORATION (THE)
HEARST-ARGYLE TELEVISION INC
HERSHEY CO
HOLLYWOOD ENTERTAINMENT CORP
HOLLYWOOD MEDIA CORP
HOUGHTON MIFFLIN CO
IAC/INTERACTIVECORP
IMAX CORPORATION
IMG WORLDWIDE INC
INGRAM ENTERTAINMENT HOLDINGS INC
INTEGRITY MEDIA INC
INTERNATIONAL DATA GROUP INC

INTERPUBLIC GROUP OF COMPANIES INC
ION MEDIA NETWORKS
ISLE OF CAPRI CASINOS INC
JOURNAL COMMUNICATIONS INC
KNOLOGY INC
LAKES ENTERTAINMENT INC
LAMAR ADVERTISING CO
LANDMARK COMMUNICATIONS INC
LANDRY'S RESTAURANTS INC
LEE ENTERPRISES INC
LIBERTY MEDIA CORP
LIFE TIME FITNESS INC
LIN TV CORP
LIVE NATION INC
LODGENET ENTERTAINMENT CORP
MAGNA ENTERTAINMENT CORP
MATSUSHITA ELECTRIC INDUSTRIAL CO LTD
MCCLATCHY COMPANY (THE)
MDI ENTERTAINMENT LLC
MEDIA GENERAL INC
MEDIACOM COMMUNICATIONS CORP
MEREDITH CORP
MGM MIRAGE
MICROSOFT CORP
MORRIS COMMUNICATIONS COMPANY LLC
MOVIE GALLERY INC
NEW YORK TIMES CO (THE)
NEWS CORP
NEXSTAR BROADCASTING GROUP INC
NIELSEN COMPANY BV (THE)
NTN BUZZTIME INC
OMNICOM GROUP INC
ON STAGE ENTERTAINMENT
PALACE ENTERTAINMENT
PENN NATIONAL GAMING INC
PINNACLE ENTERTAINMENT INC
PRIMEDIA INC
PROGRESSIVE GAMING INTERNATIONAL CORP
R R DONNELLEY & SONS CO
RADIO ONE
RADIOSHACK CORPORATION
RAYCOM MEDIA INC
READER'S DIGEST ASSOCIATION INC
REDBOX AUTOMATED RETAIL LLC
REGAL ENTERTAINMENT GROUP
REGENT COMMUNICATIONS INC
REX STORES CORP
SAGA COMMUNICATIONS INC
SALEM COMMUNICATIONS CORP
SAMSUNG ELECTRONICS CO LTD
SCHOLASTIC CORP
SCIENTIFIC GAMES CORPORATION
SEGA SAMMY HOLDINGS INC
SHARP CORPORATION
SHOP AT HOME NETWORK LLC
SIMEX-IWERKS
SINCLAIR BROADCAST GROUP INC
SIX FLAGS INC

SONY CORPORATION
SPANISH BROADCASTING SYSTEM INC
SUDDENLINK COMMUNICATIONS
THOMAS NELSON INC
THOMSON CORP (THE)
TICKETMASTER
TIME INC
TIME WARNER CABLE INC
TIME WARNER INC
TRANS WORLD ENTERTAINMENT CORP
TRIBUNE CO
TURNER BROADCASTING SYSTEM
TWEETER HOME ENTERTAINMENT GROUP INC
UNIVERSAL MUSIC GROUP
UNIVISION COMMUNICATIONS INC
VERIZON COMMUNICATIONS
VIVENDI SA
WALT DISNEY COMPANY (THE)
WARNER MUSIC GROUP
WASHINGTON POST CO
WASSERMAN MEDIA GROUP LLC
WENNER MEDIA LLC
WESTWOOD ONE INC
WHEREHOUSE ENTERTAINMENT (RECORD TOWN INC)
WILLIAM MORRIS AGENCY INC
WMS INDUSTRIES INC
WPP GROUP PLC
XM SATELLITE RADIO HOLDINGS INC
YAHOO! INC
YOUNG BROADCASTING INC

NORTHEAST
24/7 REAL MEDIA INC
A&E TELEVISION NETWORKS
ABC INC
ACTIVISION INC
ADVANCE PUBLICATIONS INC
ALLIANCE ATLANTIS COMMUNICATIONS INC
ALLIANCE ENTERTAINMENT CORP
AMAZON.COM INC
AMC ENTERTAINMENT INC
AMERICAN COIN MERCHANDISING INC
AMERICAN EXPRESS CO
AMERICAN GOLF CORP
AMERICAN GREETINGS CORP
AMERICAN SKIING COMPANY
AMF BOWLING WORLDWIDE INC
ANHEUSER BUSCH COS INC
ANSCHUTZ ENTERTAINMENT GROUP
AOL LLC
APPLE INC
ARBITRON INC
ARISTOCRAT LEISURE LTD
ASCENT MEDIA GROUP INC
AT&T INC
ATARI INC
AUDIBLE INC

AVID TECHNOLOGY INC
AZTAR CORP
BALLY TECHNOLOGIES INC
BALLY TOTAL FITNESS HOLDING CORPORATION
BARNES & NOBLE INC
BARNESANDNOBLE.COM INC
BEASLEY BROADCAST GROUP INC
BELO CORP
BERKSHIRE HATHAWAY INC
BERRY COMPANY (THE)
BERTELSMANN AG
BEST BUY CO INC
BLOCKBUSTER INC
BLOOMBERG LP
BOOKS A MILLION INC
BOOTH CREEK SKI HOLDINGS INC
BORDERS GROUP INC
BOSE CORPORATION
BRIGHTCOVE INC
BRITISH BROADCASTING CORPORATION (BBC)
CABLE NEWS NETWORK LP LLLP
CABLEVISION SYSTEMS CORP
CARMIKE CINEMAS INC
CBS CORP
CBS RADIO
CD WAREHOUSE INC
CEDAR FAIR LP
CHARTER COMMUNICATIONS INC
CINEMARK INC
CIRCUIT CITY STORES INC
CIRQUE DU SOLEIL INC
CITADEL BROADCASTING CORP
CLEAR CHANNEL COMMUNICATIONS INC
CLEAR CHANNEL OUTDOOR
CLUBCORP INC
CNET NETWORKS INC
COMCAST CORP
COMMUNITY NEWSPAPER HOLDINGS INC
CONCURRENT COMPUTER CORP
CONDE NAST PUBLICATIONS INC
COURIER CORP
COX COMMUNICATIONS INC
COX ENTERPRISES INC
COX RADIO INC
CREATIVE ARTISTS AGENCY INC
CUMULUS MEDIA INC
CURVES INTERNATIONAL INC
DAG MEDIA INC
DAILY JOURNAL CORP
DELAWARE NORTH COMPANIES
DENNIS PUBLISHING LTD
DG FASTCHANNEL
DIALOG
DICK CLARK PRODUCTIONS INC
DIGITAL BRIDGES LIMITED
DIRECTV GROUP INC (THE)
DISCOVERY COMMUNICATIONS INC
DOUBLECLICK INC

DOVER DOWNS GAMING & ENTERTAINMENT INC
DOW JONES & CO INC
DREAMWORKS SKG
E W SCRIPPS CO
ECHOSTAR COMMUNICATIONS CORP
ELECTRONIC ARTS INC
EMAP PLC
EMI GROUP PLC
EMMIS COMMUNICATIONS CORP
ENDEAVOR AGENCY (THE)
ENTERCOM COMMUNICATIONS CORP
ENTERTAINMENT PROPERTIES TRUST
ENTRAVISION COMMUNICATIONS CORPORATION
ESPN INC
FIRST LOOK STUDIOS INC
FORBES INC
FORD MODELS INC
FOX ENTERTAINMENT GROUP INC
FOX SPORTS NET INC
FREEDOM COMMUNICATIONS INC
GAMESTOP CORP
GANNETT CO INC
GATEHOUSE MEDIA INC
GAYLORD ENTERTAINMENT CO
GENERAL ELECTRIC CO (GE)
GLAM MEDIA INC
GOLD'S GYM INTERNATIONAL
GOOGLE INC
GRANITE BROADCASTING CORP
GRAY TELEVISION INC
GTECH HOLDINGS CORP
HALLMARK CARDS INC
HARPERCOLLINS PUBLISHERS INC
HARRAH'S ENTERTAINMENT INC
HARRIS INTERACTIVE INC
HARTE-HANKS INC
HARVEY ELECTRONICS INC
HEARST CORPORATION (THE)
HEARST-ARGYLE TELEVISION INC
HERSHEY CO
HOLLINGER INC
HOLLYWOOD ENTERTAINMENT CORP
HOLLYWOOD MEDIA CORP
HOUGHTON MIFFLIN CO
IAC/INTERACTIVECORP
IGN ENTERTAINMENT
IMAX CORPORATION
IMG WORLDWIDE INC
INGRAM ENTERTAINMENT HOLDINGS INC
INSIGHT COMMUNICATIONS COMPANY INC
INTERACTIVE DATA CORPORATION
INTERNATIONAL CREATIVE MANAGEMENT (ICM)
INTERNATIONAL DATA GROUP INC
INTERPUBLIC GROUP OF COMPANIES INC
ION MEDIA NETWORKS
IVILLAGE INC
JOHN WILEY & SONS INC
JOHNSON PUBLISHING COMPANY INC

JOOST
JOURNAL COMMUNICATIONS INC
JOURNAL REGISTER CO
JUMPTV INC
JUPITERMEDIA CORP
KERZNER INTERNATIONAL LIMITED
LAGARDERE ACTIVE MEDIA
LAMAR ADVERTISING CO
LANDMARK COMMUNICATIONS INC
LANDRY'S RESTAURANTS INC
LAS VEGAS SANDS CORP (THE VENETIAN)
LEE ENTERPRISES INC
LIBERTY MEDIA CORP
LIFE TIME FITNESS INC
LIN TV CORP
LIONS GATE ENTERTAINMENT CORP
LIVE NATION INC
LODGENET ENTERTAINMENT CORP
LOUD TECHNOLOGIES INC
MACROVISION CORP
MAGNA ENTERTAINMENT CORP
MARTHA STEWART LIVING OMNIMEDIA INC
MARVEL ENTERTAINMENT INC
MATSUSHITA ELECTRIC INDUSTRIAL CO LTD
MCCLATCHY COMPANY (THE)
MCGRAW HILL COS INC
MEDIA GENERAL INC
MEDIACOM COMMUNICATIONS CORP
MEDIANEWS GROUP INC
MEREDITH CORP
METRO INTERNATIONAL SA
MGM MIRAGE
MICROSOFT CORP
MIRAMAX FILM CORP
MORRIS COMMUNICATIONS COMPANY LLC
MOVIE GALLERY INC
MTR GAMING GROUP INC
MTV NETWORKS
MULTIMEDIA GAMES INC
NAPSTER INC
NATIONAL AMUSEMENTS INC
NBC UNIVERSAL
NETRATINGS INC
NEW LINE CINEMA
NEW YORK TIMES CO (THE)
NEWS CORP
NEWS WORLD COMMUNICATIONS INC
NEXSTAR BROADCASTING GROUP INC
NIELSEN COMPANY BV (THE)
OMNICOM GROUP INC
ON STAGE ENTERTAINMENT
PALACE ENTERTAINMENT
PEARSON PLC
PENN NATIONAL GAMING INC
PENTON MEDIA INC
PINNACLE ENTERTAINMENT INC
PLAYBOY ENTERPRISES INC
PRIMEDIA INC

PROGRESSIVE GAMING INTERNATIONAL CORP
R R DONNELLEY & SONS CO
RADIO ONE
RADIOSHACK CORPORATION
RAINBOW MEDIA HOLDINGS LLC
RANDOM HOUSE INC
RAYCOM MEDIA INC
RCN CORP
READER'S DIGEST ASSOCIATION INC
REDBOX AUTOMATED RETAIL LLC
REED ELSEVIER GROUP PLC
REGAL ENTERTAINMENT GROUP
REGENT COMMUNICATIONS INC
RENAISSANCE ENTERTAINMENT CORP
REUTERS GROUP PLC
REX STORES CORP
RODALE INC
SAGA COMMUNICATIONS INC
SALEM COMMUNICATIONS CORP
SALON MEDIA GROUP INC
SAMSUNG ELECTRONICS CO LTD
SCHOLASTIC CORP
SCIENTIFIC GAMES CORPORATION
SEGA SAMMY HOLDINGS INC
SHARP CORPORATION
SHOP AT HOME NETWORK LLC
SIMON & SCHUSTER INC
SINCLAIR BROADCAST GROUP INC
SIRIUS SATELLITE RADIO
SIX FLAGS INC
SONY BMG MUSIC ENTERTAINMENT
SONY CORPORATION
SPANISH BROADCASTING SYSTEM INC
SUDDENLINK COMMUNICATIONS
TAKE-TWO INTERACTIVE SOFTWARE INC
TAYLOR NELSON SOFRES PLC (TNS)
THOMAS NELSON INC
THOMSON CORP (THE)
THQ INC
TICKETMASTER
TIME INC
TIME WARNER CABLE INC
TIME WARNER INC
TRAFFIX INC
TRANS WORLD CORP
TRANS WORLD ENTERTAINMENT CORP
TRANS-LUX CORPORATION
TRIBUNE CO
TRUMP ENTERTAINMENT RESORTS INC
TURNER BROADCASTING SYSTEM
TWEETER HOME ENTERTAINMENT GROUP INC
UNITED BUSINESS MEDIA PLC
UNITED ONLINE INC
UNITED TALENT AGENCY INC
UNIVERSAL MUSIC GROUP
UNIVISION COMMUNICATIONS INC
US NEWS AND WORLD REPORT LP
VAIL RESORTS INC

VALUE LINE INC
VALUEVISION MEDIA INC
VERIZON COMMUNICATIONS
VIACOM INC
VINDIGO INC
VIVENDI SA
WALT DISNEY COMPANY (THE)
WARNER MUSIC GROUP
WASHINGTON POST CO
WASSERMAN MEDIA GROUP LLC
WENNER MEDIA LLC
WESTWOOD ONE INC
WHEREHOUSE ENTERTAINMENT (RECORD TOWN INC)
WILLIAM MORRIS AGENCY INC
WMS INDUSTRIES INC
WPP GROUP PLC
XM SATELLITE RADIO HOLDINGS INC
YAHOO! INC
YAHOO! SEARCH MARKETING GROUP
YOUNG BROADCASTING INC
ZIFF DAVIS MEDIA INC

INDEX OF FIRMS WITH OPERATIONS
OUTSIDE THE U.S.

24 HOUR FITNESS USA
24/7 REAL MEDIA INC
A&E TELEVISION NETWORKS
ACTIVISION INC
ALLIANCE ATLANTIS COMMUNICATIONS INC
AMAZON.COM INC
AMC ENTERTAINMENT INC
AMERICAN EXPRESS CO
AMERICAN GREETINGS CORP
AMF BOWLING WORLDWIDE INC
ANHEUSER BUSCH COS INC
ANSCHUTZ ENTERTAINMENT GROUP
AOL LLC
APPLE INC
ARBITRON INC
ARISTOCRAT LEISURE LTD
ASCENT MEDIA GROUP INC
AT&T INC
ATARI INC
AUDIBLE INC
AVID TECHNOLOGY INC
BALLY TECHNOLOGIES INC
BALLY TOTAL FITNESS HOLDING CORPORATION
BERKSHIRE HATHAWAY INC
BERRY COMPANY (THE)
BERTELSMANN AG
BEST BUY CO INC
BIOWARE CORP
BLOCKBUSTER INC
BLOOMBERG LP
BORDERS GROUP INC
BOSE CORPORATION
BOYNE USA RESORTS
BRIGHTCOVE INC
BRITISH BROADCASTING CORPORATION (BBC)
BRITISH SKY BROADCASTING GROUP PLC
BUY.COM INC
CABLE NEWS NETWORK LP LLLP
CANWEST GLOBAL COMMUNICATIONS
CBS CORP
CD WAREHOUSE INC
CENTRAL EUROPEAN MEDIA ENTERPRISES LTD
CENTURY CASINOS INC
CINEMARK INC
CINEMASTAR LUXURY THEATERS INC
CIRCUIT CITY STORES INC
CIRQUE DU SOLEIL INC
CLARION CO LTD
CLEAR CHANNEL COMMUNICATIONS INC
CLEAR CHANNEL OUTDOOR
CLUBCORP INC
CNET NETWORKS INC
COLUMBIA MUSIC ENTERTAINMENT INC
COLUMBIA TRISTAR MOTION PICTURE GROUP
COMCAST CORP

CONCURRENT COMPUTER CORP
CONDE NAST PUBLICATIONS INC
CORUS ENTERTAINMENT INC
COX ENTERPRISES INC
CREATIVE ARTISTS AGENCY INC
CUMULUS MEDIA INC
CURVES INTERNATIONAL INC
DELAWARE NORTH COMPANIES
DENNIS PUBLISHING LTD
DG FASTCHANNEL
DIALOG
DIGITAL BRIDGES LIMITED
DIGITAL VIDEO SYSTEMS INC
DIRECTV GROUP INC (THE)
DISCOVERY COMMUNICATIONS INC
DOUBLECLICK INC
DOW JONES & CO INC
DREAMWORKS SKG
DTS INC
E W SCRIPPS CO
ECHOSTAR COMMUNICATIONS CORP
ELECTRONIC ARTS INC
EMAP PLC
EMI GROUP PLC
EMMIS COMMUNICATIONS CORP
ENTERTAINMENT PROPERTIES TRUST
EURO DISNEY SCA
FORBES INC
FORD MODELS INC
FOX ENTERTAINMENT GROUP INC
GAMESTOP CORP
GAMING PARTNERS INTERNATIONAL CORP
GANNETT CO INC
GEMSTAR-TV GUIDE INTERNATIONAL INC
GENERAL ELECTRIC CO (GE)
GLAM MEDIA INC
GLU MOBILE INC
GOLD'S GYM INTERNATIONAL
GOOGLE INC
GRUPO RADIO CENTRO SA DE CV
GRUPO TELEVISA SA
GTECH HOLDINGS CORP
HALLMARK CARDS INC
HANDS-ON MOBILE
HARPERCOLLINS PUBLISHERS INC
HARRAH'S ENTERTAINMENT INC
HARRIS INTERACTIVE INC
HARTE-HANKS INC
HEARST CORPORATION (THE)
HERSHEY CO
HOLLINGER INC
HOT CABLE SYSTEMS MEDIA LTD
HOUGHTON MIFFLIN CO
IAC/INTERACTIVECORP
I-CABLE COMMUNICATIONS
IGN ENTERTAINMENT
IMAX CORPORATION
IMG WORLDWIDE INC

INTEGRITY MEDIA INC
INTERACTIVE DATA CORPORATION
INTERNATIONAL CREATIVE MANAGEMENT (ICM)
INTERNATIONAL DATA GROUP INC
INTERNATIONAL GAME TECHNOLOGY
INTERNATIONAL LOTTERY & TOTALIZATOR
SYSTEMS
INTERPUBLIC GROUP OF COMPANIES INC
INTERTAN CANADA LTD
ISLE OF CAPRI CASINOS INC
ITV PLC
JOHN WILEY & SONS INC
JOHNSON PUBLISHING COMPANY INC
JOOST
JUMPTV INC
JUPITERMEDIA CORP
KERZNER INTERNATIONAL LIMITED
LAGARDERE ACTIVE MEDIA
LAMAR ADVERTISING CO
LANDMARK COMMUNICATIONS INC
LAS VEGAS SANDS CORP (THE VENETIAN)
LIBERTY GLOBAL INC
LIBERTY MEDIA CORP
LIONS GATE ENTERTAINMENT CORP
LIVE NATION INC
LODGENET ENTERTAINMENT CORP
LOUD TECHNOLOGIES INC
MACROVISION CORP
MAGNA ENTERTAINMENT CORP
MARVEL ENTERTAINMENT INC
MATSUSHITA ELECTRIC INDUSTRIAL CO LTD
MCGRAW HILL COS INC
MELCO PBL ENTERTAINMENT LIMITED
MEREDITH CORP
METRO INTERNATIONAL SA
MGM MIRAGE
MICROSOFT CORP
MIDWAY GAMES INC
MOBITV INC
MODERN TIMES GROUP MTG AB
MORRIS COMMUNICATIONS COMPANY LLC
MOVIE GALLERY INC
MP3.COM INC
MTV NETWORKS
MULTIMEDIA GAMES INC
NAPSTER INC
NASPERS LIMITED
NATIONAL AMUSEMENTS INC
NBC UNIVERSAL
NETRATINGS INC
NEW YORK TIMES CO (THE)
NEWS CORP
NEWS WORLD COMMUNICATIONS INC
NIELSEN COMPANY BV (THE)
NINTENDO CO LTD
NTL: TELEWEST BUSINESS
OMNICOM GROUP INC
PARAMOUNT PICTURES CORP

PEARSON PLC
PENN NATIONAL GAMING INC
PENTON MEDIA INC
PINNACLE ENTERTAINMENT INC
PIONEER CORPORATION
PLAYBOY ENTERPRISES INC
PRIMACOM AG
PROGRESSIVE GAMING INTERNATIONAL CORP
R R DONNELLEY & SONS CO
RADIOSHACK CORPORATION
RANDOM HOUSE INC
RANK GROUP PLC (THE)
READER'S DIGEST ASSOCIATION INC
REALNETWORKS INC
REDBOX AUTOMATED RETAIL LLC
REED ELSEVIER GROUP PLC
REGAL ENTERTAINMENT GROUP
RENTRAK CORP
REUTERS GROUP PLC
RODALE INC
ROGERS COMMUNICATIONS INC
RTL GROUP SA
SAGA COMMUNICATIONS INC
SAMSUNG ELECTRONICS CO LTD
SANYO ELECTRIC COMPANY LTD
SCHOLASTIC CORP
SCIENTIFIC GAMES CORPORATION
SEGA SAMMY HOLDINGS INC
SHANDA INTERACTIVE ENTERTAINMENT
LIMITED
SHANGHAI MEDIA GROUP (SMG)
SHARP CORPORATION
SHAW COMMUNICATIONS INC
SHUFFLE MASTER INC
SHUN TAK HOLDINGS LIMITED
SIMEX-IWERKS
SIMON & SCHUSTER INC
SIRIUS SATELLITE RADIO
SIX FLAGS INC
SKY NETWORK TELEVISION LIMITED
SONY BMG MUSIC ENTERTAINMENT
SONY CORPORATION
SONY PICTURES ENTERTAINMENT
SPANISH BROADCASTING SYSTEM INC
SRS LABS INC
TAKE-TWO INTERACTIVE SOFTWARE INC
TAYLOR NELSON SOFRES PLC (TNS)
THOMSON CORP (THE)
THQ INC
TICKETMASTER
TIME INC
TIME WARNER INC
TIVO INC
TRADER CLASSIFIED MEDIA NV
TRAFFIX INC
TRANS WORLD CORP
TRANS WORLD ENTERTAINMENT CORP
TRANS-LUX CORPORATION

TRIBUNE CO
TV AZTECA SA DE CV
UNITED BUSINESS MEDIA PLC
UNITED ONLINE INC
UNIVERSAL MUSIC GROUP
UNIVISION COMMUNICATIONS INC
VERIZON COMMUNICATIONS
VIACOM INC
VIVENDI SA
WALT DISNEY COMPANY (THE)
WARNER MUSIC GROUP
WASHINGTON POST CO
WASSERMAN MEDIA GROUP LLC
WILLIAM MORRIS AGENCY INC
WMS INDUSTRIES INC
WPP GROUP PLC
WYNN RESORTS LIMITED
XINHUA FINANCE LIMITED
XINHUA FINANCE MEDIA LIMITED
XM SATELLITE RADIO HOLDINGS INC
YAHOO! INC
YAHOO! SEARCH MARKETING GROUP
ZIFF DAVIS MEDIA INC

Individual Profiles
On Each Of
THE ENTERTAINMENT 400

24 HOUR FITNESS USA   www.24hourfitness.com

Industry Group Code: 713940 Ranks within this company's industry group: Sales: Profits:

Print Media/Publishing:	Movies:	Equipment/Supplies:	Broadcast/Cable:	Music/Audio:	Sports/Games/Gambling:
Newspapers:	Movie Theaters:	Equipment/Supplies:	Broadcast TV:	Music Production:	Games/Sports: Y
Magazines:	Movie Production:	Gambling Equipment:	Cable TV:	Retail Music:	Retail Games Stores:
Books:	TV/Video Prod.:	Special Services:	Satellite Broadcast:	Retail Audio Equip.:	Stadiums/Teams:
Book Stores:	Video Rental:	Advertising Services:	Radio:	Music Print./Dist.:	Gambling/Casinos:
Distribution/Printing:	Video Distribution:	Info. Sys. Software:	Online Information:	Multimedia:	Rides/Theme Parks:

TYPES OF BUSINESS:
Fitness Centers
Online Nutrition Information
Day Spa

BRANDS/DIVISIONS/AFFILIATES:
Forstmann Little & Company
California Fitness
24 Hour Fitness Active
24 Hour Fitness Sports
24 Hour Fitness Super-Sport
24 Hour Fitness Ultra-Sport
Re:fresh
Fit:perks

CONTACTS: *Note: Officers with more than one job title may be intentionally listed here more than once.*
Carl C. Liebert III, CEO
Colin Heggie, CFO/Exec. VP
Kevin D. Steele, VP-Sports Mktg.
Mark S. Mastrov, Chmn.

Phone: 925-543-3100	Fax: 925-543-3200
Toll-Free: 800-432-6348	
Address: 12647 Alcosta Blvd., 5th Fl., San Ramon, CA 94583 US	

GROWTH PLANS/SPECIAL FEATURES:

24 Hour Fitness USA is one of the world's largest privately owned and operated fitness center chains. The firm, owned by private equity company Forstmann Little and Co., has more than 3 million members and over 400 clubs across the globe. The company operates several types of clubs, including the 24 Hour Fitness Active club, Fitness EXPRESS, the Sports club, the Super-Sport club and the Ultra-Sport club. The 24 Hour Fitness Active clubs are approximately 25,000 square feet and may include free weights, cardio equipment, group exercise, personal training, locker rooms, sauna, steam room and a children' play area. 24 Hour Fitness EXPRESS clubs are anywhere from 6,000 to 10,000 square feet and offer only limited strength and cardio equipment and some exercise classes. The company's Sports clubs range from 35,000 to 50,000 square feet and include all of the Active clubs' amenities as well as basketball courts and pools. The Super-Sport clubs, generally over 50,000 square feet, have all of the Sports club offerings as well as tanning beds and massage therapy. The Ultra-Sport clubs are generally over 100,000 square feet and may also include a volleyball court, racquetball, squash, rock climbing, an indoor running track and executive locker rooms. The company has international locations in Malaysia, Singapore, Hong Kong and Taiwan, all under the name California Fitness. Re:fresh is the company's free-standing day spa located in San Francisco. The Fit:perks program offers discounts and benefits to all 24 Hour Fitness members. The company is the exclusive official fitness center of the U.S. Olympic Team through the 2008 Olympic Games in Beijing.

24 Hour Fitness sponsors several charitable events and organizations, including the American Cancer Society, the Magic Johnson Foundation, the Lance Armstrong Foundation and the Andre Agassi Charitable Foundation.

FINANCIALS: Sales and profits are in thousands of dollars—add 000 to get the full amount. 2007 Note: Financial information for 2007 was not available for all companies at press time.

2007 Sales: $	2007 Profits: $	U.S. Stock Ticker: Private
2006 Sales: $	2006 Profits: $	Int'l Ticker: Int'l Exchange:
2005 Sales: $	2005 Profits: $	Employees: 16,000
2004 Sales: $1,004,000	2004 Profits: $	Fiscal Year Ends: 12/31
2003 Sales: $1,000,000	2003 Profits: $	Parent Company: FORSTMANN LITTLE & CO

SALARIES/BENEFITS:

Pension Plan:	ESOP Stock Plan:	Profit Sharing:	Top Exec. Salary: $	Bonus: $
Savings Plan:	Stock Purch. Plan:		Second Exec. Salary: $	Bonus: $

OTHER THOUGHTS:
Apparent Women Officers or Directors:
Hot Spot for Advancement for Women/Minorities:

LOCATIONS: ("Y" = Yes)

West:	Southwest:	Midwest:	Southeast:	Northeast:	International:
Y	Y	Y	Y		Y

Note: Financial information, benefits and other data can change quickly and may vary from those stated here.

24/7 REAL MEDIA INC
www.247realmedia.com

Industry Group Code: 541810A Ranks within this company's industry group: Sales: 1 Profits: 2

Print Media/Publishing:	Movies:	Equipment/Supplies:		Broadcast/Cable:	Music/Audio:	Sports/Games/Gambling:
Newspapers:	Movie Theaters:	Equipment/Supplies:		Broadcast TV:	Music Production:	Games/Sports:
Magazines:	Movie Production:	Gambling Equipment:		Cable TV:	Retail Music:	Retail Games Stores:
Books:	TV/Video Prod.:	Special Services:	Y	Satellite Broadcast:	Retail Audio Equip.:	Stadiums/Teams:
Book Stores:	Video Rental:	Advertising Services:	Y	Radio:	Music Print./Dist.:	Gambling/Casinos:
Distribution/Printing:	Video Distribution:	Info. Sys. Software:		Online Information:	Multimedia:	Rides/Theme Parks:

TYPES OF BUSINESS:
Internet Advertising
Web Design
Software
Direct Marketing
Promotions
Data Analysis

BRANDS/DIVISIONS/AFFILIATES:
24/7 Web Alliance
24/7 Web Results
24/7 Search
Open AdStream 6 Network Edition
Decide DNA 6
Dentsu 24/7 Search Holdings
Rich Media Foundry
K.K. 24-7 Search

CONTACTS: Note: Officers with more than one job title may be intentionally listed here more than once.
David J. Moore, CEO
Jonathan K. Hsu, COO
Jonathan Hsu, CFO/Exec. VP
Ari Bluman, Sr. VP-US Sales
Oleg Vishnepolsky, CTO
Mark E. Moran, General Counsel/Sr. VP
Ari Bluman, Sr. VP-US Oper.
Matt Kain, VP-Corp. Dev.
Sushene Leitch, Dir.-Investor Rel.
Rob Wilson, Dir.-Europe
Douglas C. Wagner, Pres., 24/7 Search
Jack Smith, Sr.VP-Product Strategy
David J. Moore, Chmn.
Jae Woo Chung, Pres., TFSM Asia

Phone: 212-231-7100	Fax: 212-760-1774
Toll-Free: 877-247-2477	
Address: 132 W. 31st St., New York, NY 10001 US	

GROWTH PLANS/SPECIAL FEATURES:

24/7 Real Media, Inc. is a global provider of interactive technology and marketing solutions for web publishers, online advertisers, advertising agencies and e-marketers. The firm's services include advertising and direct marketing sales, search engine marketing services, online advertisement serving, web advertising, site representation and web analytics. The company sells its products and services from 20 locations in 12 countries in North America, Europe and Asia and the Pacific Rim. 24/7 Real Media is organized into three solution divisions: Technology, Media and Search. The Technology segment, through its Open AdSystem platform, is composed of service and software solutions designed for three customer segments: advertisers and agencies, web publishers and e-commerce merchants. Open AdStream 6 Network Edition (its newest version) manages over 850 billion web sites with over 12 billion impressions per month and over 117 million users. The Media division consists of 24/7 Web Alliance, an alliance of web sites that allow client advertisers to place targeted ad campaigns; and 24/7 Web Results, a subsidiary that provides performance-based marketing services for the Internet. The Search division, with its flagship product 24/7 Search, provides performance-based search marketing services for the Internet. Dentsu 24/7 Search, its Japanese subsidiary, targets markets in Asia and the Pacific Rim. The firm's Rich Media Foundry creates and traffics rich media advertising. In 2007, 24/7 Real Media launched Open AdStream Mobile Edition, a new solution that helps agencies integrate mobile and internet ad campaigns. Additionally in 2007, the firm launched Decide DNA 6.1, an upgraded version of its existing search engine, marketing platform that has an added mobile component. 24/7 recently integrated with China's largest search engine, Baidu.com, to expand its search capacity to reach Baidu's 162 million internet users. In 2007, the firm was acquired by WPP Group PLC for roughly $649 million.

FINANCIALS: Sales and profits are in thousands of dollars—add 000 to get the full amount. 2007 Note: Financial information for 2007 was not available for all companies at press time.

2007 Sales: $	2007 Profits: $	U.S. Stock Ticker: TFSM
2006 Sales: $200,243	2006 Profits: $-8,622	Int'l Ticker: Int'l Exchange:
2005 Sales: $139,794	2005 Profits: $ 38	Employees: 368
2004 Sales: $85,255	2004 Profits: $-3,155	Fiscal Year Ends: 12/31
2003 Sales: $49,181	2003 Profits: $-12,016	Parent Company:

SALARIES/BENEFITS:
Pension Plan:	ESOP Stock Plan: Y	Profit Sharing:	Top Exec. Salary: $270,450	Bonus: $436,025
Savings Plan:	Stock Purch. Plan:		Second Exec. Salary: $200,000	Bonus: $167,702

OTHER THOUGHTS:
Apparent Women Officers or Directors:
Hot Spot for Advancement for Women/Minorities:

LOCATIONS: ("Y" = Yes)
West:	Southwest:	Midwest:	Southeast:	Northeast:	International:
Y		Y		Y	Y

Note: Financial information, benefits and other data can change quickly and may vary from those stated here.

2929 ENTERTAINMENT   www.2929entertainment.com

Industry Group Code: 512110 Ranks within this company's industry group: Sales: Profits:

Print Media/Publishing:	Movies:		Equipment/Supplies:	Broadcast/Cable:		Music/Audio:	Sports/Games/Gambling:
Newspapers:	Movie Theaters:	Y	Equipment/Supplies:	Broadcast TV:		Music Production:	Games/Sports:
Magazines:	Movie Production:	Y	Gambling Equipment:	Cable TV:	Y	Retail Music:	Retail Games Stores:
Books:	TV/Video Prod.:	Y	Special Services:	Satellite Broadcast:		Retail Audio Equip.:	Stadiums/Teams:
Book Stores:	Video Rental:		Advertising Services:	Radio:		Music Print./Dist.:	Gambling/Casinos:
Distribution/Printing:	Video Distribution:	Y	Info. Sys. Software:	Online Information:		Multimedia:	Rides/Theme Parks:

TYPES OF BUSINESS:
Movie & TV Production & Distribution
Movie Theaters
Cable Television Networks

BRANDS/DIVISIONS/AFFILIATES:
Rysher Entertainment
Magnolia Pictures Distribution
Magnolia Home Entertainment
Landmark Theatre Corp.
2929 Productions
HDNet Films
HDNet Movies
Magnet

CONTACTS: *Note: Officers with more than one job title may be intentionally listed here more than once.*
Todd R. Wagner, CEO/Co-Owner
Sherry Yeaman, Press Contact
Marc Cuban, Co-Owner
Kevin Parke, Pres., Landmark Theaters/Exec. VP
Marc Butan, Pres., 2929 Productions
Shebnem Askin, Pres., 2929 Int'l

Phone: 310-309-5701	Fax: 310-309-5716
Toll-Free:	
Address: 2425 Olympic Blvd., Ste. 6040W, Santa Monica, CA 90404 US	

GROWTH PLANS/SPECIAL FEATURES:

2929 Entertainment has ownership stakes in movie and TV distribution and exhibition companies. Through subsidiary Rysher Entertainment, 2929 owns syndication rights to television shows such as Lifestyles of the Rich and Famous, Hogan's Heroes and Star Search; while Magnolia Pictures Distribution is an independent distribution company. Magnolia Home Entertainment, a division of Magnolia Pictures, has released a number of HD-DVD titles, including Bubble; Ong Bak: The Thai Warrior; Jesus Camp; and Color Me Kubrick. Landmark is one of the nation's largest art-house theater chains, with 59 theaters in 23 markets across the U.S. 2929 produces and finances movies through two production companies: 2929 Productions, which produces films in the $10- to $40-million budget range and HDNet Films, which produces smaller-budget movies shot exclusively in high definition, and considered for simultaneous release on DVD, TV and in theaters. 2929 Productions strives to produce films in one of three, often overlapping categories: Those that are rooted in actual historical events; are inspiring and provocative; or filmmaker-driven. Past releases of 2929 include Good Night and Good Luck; Akeelah and the Bee; Turistas; and Black Christmas. Its most recent films include We Own The Night; In Bloom; and What Just Happened? Another subsidiary, 2929 International, handles the worldwide distribution rights of theatrical feature films produced by the company's production subsidiaries. The firm also owns an interest in Lions Gate Entertainment. 2929 is owned by partners Mark Cuban (owner of the Dallas Mavericks) and Todd Wagner. Wagner and Cuban are also partnered in two general entertainment high-definition television show networks, HDNet and HDNet Movies, available through most major cable and satellite providers. In September 2007, Magnolia Pictures launched Magnet, responsible for releasing risk-taking, unconventional films. Some of its first releases will include Murder Party, a horror-comedy, and Not Quite Hollywood, a documentary about 1970s and '80s Australian filmmakers.

FINANCIALS: Sales and profits are in thousands of dollars—add 000 to get the full amount. 2007 Note: Financial information for 2007 was not available for all companies at press time.

2007 Sales: $	2007 Profits: $	U.S. Stock Ticker: Private
2006 Sales: $	2006 Profits: $	Int'l Ticker: Int'l Exchange:
2005 Sales: $	2005 Profits: $	Employees:
2004 Sales: $	2004 Profits: $	Fiscal Year Ends:
2003 Sales: $	2003 Profits: $	Parent Company:

SALARIES/BENEFITS:

Pension Plan:	ESOP Stock Plan:	Profit Sharing:	Top Exec. Salary: $	Bonus: $
Savings Plan:	Stock Purch. Plan:		Second Exec. Salary: $	Bonus: $

OTHER THOUGHTS:
Apparent Women Officers or Directors: 3
Hot Spot for Advancement for Women/Minorities: Y

LOCATIONS: ("Y" = Yes)

West:	Southwest:	Midwest:	Southeast:	Northeast:	International:
Y	Y				

A&E TELEVISION NETWORKS www.aetn.com

Industry Group Code: 513210 Ranks within this company's industry group: Sales: Profits:

Print Media/Publishing:		Movies:		Equipment/Supplies:		Broadcast/Cable:		Music/Audio:		Sports/Games/Gambling:	
Newspapers:		Movie Theaters:		Equipment/Supplies:		Broadcast TV:		Music Production:	Y	Games/Sports:	
Magazines:	Y	Movie Production:		Gambling Equipment:		Cable TV:	Y	Retail Music:		Retail Games Stores:	
Books:		TV/Video Prod.:	Y	Special Services:		Satellite Broadcast:		Retail Audio Equip.:		Stadiums/Teams:	
Book Stores:		Video Rental:		Advertising Services:		Radio:		Music Print./Dist.:		Gambling/Casinos:	
Distribution/Printing:		Video Distribution:		Info. Sys. Software:		Online Information:		Multimedia:		Rides/Theme Parks:	

TYPES OF BUSINESS:

Television Production
Cable Television
Magazine Publishing
Web Sites
CDs, DVDs & Videos

BRANDS/DIVISIONS/AFFILIATES:

Hearst Corporation
ABC, Inc.
NBC Universal
A&E Network (The)
Biography Channel (The)
History Channel (The)
History Channel en Espanol (The)
History International

CONTACTS: Note: Officers with more than one job title may be intentionally listed here more than once.

Abbe Raven, CEO
Abbe Raven, Pres.
Gerard Gruosso, CFO/Exec. VP
Whitney Goit, II, Exec. VP-Mktg. & Sales

Phone: 212-210-1400	**Fax:** 212-850-9370
Toll-Free:	
Address: 235 E. 45th St., New York, NY 10017 US	

GROWTH PLANS/SPECIAL FEATURES:

A&E Television Networks is an international media company with operations in television programming, magazine publishing, web sites, soundtrack CDs, and home videos and DVDs of its television programs. The company is a joint venture of The Hearst Corporation, ABC, Inc. and NBC Universal. A&E is primarily a cable television group that focuses its programming in history, the arts, current events, popular culture, reality and nature. The firm works through the following networks: A&E Network; The History Channel; The Biography Channel; History International; The History Channel en Espanol; Crime & Investigation Network; and the Military History Channel. The A&E Network reaches more than 92 million homes, and offers a variety of programming that includes a signature Real-Life Series. The History Channel, with more than 91 million subscribers, offers historical dramas and documentaries. The Biography Channel offers biographical programming in more than 40 million homes. The History Channel International looks at international culture and history with 24-hour English broadcasting and limited broadcasting in French and Italian. The History Channel en Espanol provides 24-hour continual broadcasting in Spanish with features that focus on Latino heritage and achievements. The Crime & Investigation Network offers crime, investigation and mystery programming. The Military History Channel offers 24-hour/seven-days-a-week programming that is dedicated to a wide array of military history features. The AETN International division markets A&E Network programming overseas, making A&E channels and programs available in over 125 countries. The AETN Consumer Products division distributes DVDs, oversees a variety of extension programs, operates a travel website and maintains an online store that offers over 6,000 products.

A&E offers an employee benefits package that includes an employee assistance program, a 401(k) tax deferred savings plan, a non-contributory pension plan, tuition assistance, flexible spending accounts and adoption assistance.

FINANCIALS: Sales and profits are in thousands of dollars—add 000 to get the full amount. 2007 Note: Financial information for 2007 was not available for all companies at press time.

2007 Sales: $	2007 Profits: $	**U.S. Stock Ticker:** Joint Venture
2006 Sales: $	2006 Profits: $	**Int'l Ticker:** Int'l Exchange:
2005 Sales: $625,000	2005 Profits: $	Employees: 600
2004 Sales: $	2004 Profits: $	Fiscal Year Ends: 12/31
2003 Sales: $885,800	2003 Profits: $	Parent Company:

SALARIES/BENEFITS:

Pension Plan: Y	ESOP Stock Plan:	Profit Sharing:	Top Exec. Salary: $	Bonus: $
Savings Plan: Y	Stock Purch. Plan:		Second Exec. Salary: $	Bonus: $

OTHER THOUGHTS:

Apparent Women Officers or Directors:
Hot Spot for Advancement for Women/Minorities:

LOCATIONS: ("Y" = Yes)

West:	Southwest:	Midwest:	Southeast:	Northeast:	International:
Y		Y	Y	Y	Y

ABC INC

abc.go.com

Industry Group Code: 513120 **Ranks within this company's industry group:** Sales: 3   Profits:

Print Media/Publishing:	Movies:		Equipment/Supplies:	Broadcast/Cable:		Music/Audio:	Sports/Games/Gambling:
Newspapers:	Movie Theaters:		Equipment/Supplies:	Broadcast TV:	Y	Music Production:	Games/Sports:
Magazines:	Movie Production:		Gambling Equipment:	Cable TV:	Y	Retail Music:	Retail Games Stores:
Books:	TV/Video Prod.:	Y	Special Services:	Satellite Broadcast:		Retail Audio Equip.:	Stadiums/Teams:
Book Stores:	Video Rental:		Advertising Services:	Radio:		Music Print./Dist.:	Gambling/Casinos:
Distribution/Printing:	Video Distribution:		Info. Sys. Software:	Online Information:		Multimedia:	Rides/Theme Parks:

TYPES OF BUSINESS:

Broadcast TV
Cable Networks
Television Production
Online Television

BRANDS/DIVISIONS/AFFILIATES:

Walt Disney Company (The)
Touchstone Television
Buena Vista Television
ABC Television Networks
Lost
Desperate Housewives
Ugly Betty
Grey's Anatomy

CONTACTS: *Note: Officers with more than one job title may be intentionally listed here more than once.*

Anne M. Sweeney, Pres., Disney-ABC Television Group
James L. Hedges, CFO/Exec. VP-ABC Television Network & Studios
Jeffrey S. Rosen, Sr. VP-Human Resources

Phone: 212-456-7777	Fax: 212-456-1424
Toll-Free:	
Address: 77 W. 66th St., 3rd Fl., New York, NY 10023 US	

GROWTH PLANS/SPECIAL FEATURES:

ABC, Inc., a subsidiary of The Walt Disney Co., operates the ABC Television Network. The network includes 10 owned stations that supplement roughly 231 affiliated stations operating under long-term agreements, reaching 99% of all U.S. households. The ABC Television Network broadcasts programs in the following 'dayparts': early morning, daytime, primetime, late night, news, children and sports. The network produces its own programs or acquires broadcast rights from other third-party producers, as well as production entities that are owned by the firm, and rights holders for network programming and pays varying amounts of compensation to affiliated stations for broadcasting the programs and commercial announcements included therein. It derives substantially all of its revenues from the sale to advertisers of time in network programs for commercial announcements. The ability to sell time for commercial announcements and the rates received are primarily dependent on the size and nature of the audience that the network can deliver to the advertiser as well as overall advertiser demand for time on network broadcasts. ABC produces many of the programs it broadcasts through its Touchstone Television subsidiary. In addition, the Buena Vista Television unit syndicates and distributes Disney products (both films and television shows) for broadcast. The company's Monday Night Football program is a long-standing leader in the prime-time lineup and the network also carries the NBA finals. ABC's web site makes full-length episodes of its most popular shows (Lost, Grey's Anatomy, Desperate Housewives, Ugly Betty, Six Degrees and Daybreak) available on the Internet for a small fee.

FINANCIALS: Sales and profits are in thousands of dollars—add 000 to get the full amount. 2007 Note: Financial information for 2007 was not available for all companies at press time.

2007 Sales: $	2007 Profits: $	**U.S. Stock Ticker: Subsidiary**
2006 Sales: $14,638,000	2006 Profits: $	**Int'l Ticker:** Int'l Exchange:
2005 Sales: $13,207,000	2005 Profits: $	Employees:
2004 Sales: $11,780,000	2004 Profits: $	Fiscal Year Ends: 9/30
2003 Sales: $10,941,000	2003 Profits: $	Parent Company: WALT DISNEY COMPANY (THE)

SALARIES/BENEFITS:

Pension Plan:	ESOP Stock Plan:	Profit Sharing:	Top Exec. Salary: $	Bonus: $
Savings Plan:	Stock Purch. Plan:		Second Exec. Salary: $	Bonus: $

OTHER THOUGHTS:

Apparent Women Officers or Directors: 1
Hot Spot for Advancement for Women/Minorities: Y

LOCATIONS: ("Y" = Yes)

West:	Southwest:	Midwest:	Southeast:	Northeast:	International:
Y	Y	Y	Y	Y	

ACME COMMUNICATIONS INC www.acmecommunications.com

Industry Group Code: 513120 Ranks within this company's industry group: Sales: 20 Profits: 14

Print Media/Publishing:	Movies:		Equipment/Supplies:	Broadcast/Cable:		Music/Audio:	Sports/Games/Gambling:
Newspapers:	Movie Theaters:		Equipment/Supplies:	Broadcast TV:	Y	Music Production:	Games/Sports:
Magazines:	Movie Production:		Gambling Equipment:	Cable TV:		Retail Music:	Retail Games Stores:
Books:	TV/Video Prod.:	Y	Special Services:	Satellite Broadcast:		Retail Audio Equip.:	Stadiums/Teams:
Book Stores:	Video Rental:		Advertising Services:	Radio:		Music Print./Dist.:	Gambling/Casinos:
Distribution/Printing:	Video Distribution:		Info. Sys. Software:	Online Information:		Multimedia:	Rides/Theme Parks:

TYPES OF BUSINESS:

Broadcast Television
Television Production

BRANDS/DIVISIONS/AFFILIATES:

ACME Televisions, LLC
Daily Buzz (The)
MyNetworkTV
CW (The)

CONTACTS: *Note: Officers with more than one job title may be intentionally listed here more than once.*

Jamie Kellner, CEO
Doug Gealy, COO
Doug Gealy, Pres.
Tom Allen, CFO/Exec. VP
Sharon Weiler, VP-Sales
Brent Stephenson, VP-Eng.
Ed Danduran, Controller/VP
Steve Bailey, VP-Promotion
Bob Shaw, VP-Programming
Mike Mingroni, VP-Graphics
Brent Stephenson, VP-FCC Compliance
Jamie Kellner, Chmn.

Phone: 714-245-9499	**Fax:** 714-245-9494
Toll-Free:	
Address: 2101 E. 4th St., Ste. 202, Santa Ana, CA 92705 US	

GROWTH PLANS/SPECIAL FEATURES:

ACME Communications, Inc. is a holding company with no independent operations other than through its indirect wholly-owned subsidiary, ACME Television, LLC. ACME Television, through its subsidiaries, owns and operates eight commercially licensed, full-power, broadcast television stations located throughout the U.S.: KWBQ-TV and KASY-TV, Albuquerque-Santa Fe, New Mexico; WBDT-TV, Dayton, Ohio; WBXX-TV, Knoxville, Tennessee; WIWB-TV, Green Bay-Appleton, Wisconsin; and WBUW-TV, Madison, Wisconsin. All but one of these stations are affiliates of The CW, a joint venture between CBS and Warner Brothers. The CW combines programming from the former UPN and WB networks. The remaining station, KASY-TV in Albuquerque-Santa Fe is an affiliate of MyNetworkTV, a Fox subsidiary. ACME broadcasts in markets that cover approximately 3% of all U.S. television households. ACME operates in medium sized markets due to lower operating costs and less competition than in larger markets. Its programming is targeted at young adults, teens and kids. In addition, the company provides local and regional sports programming as well as local news and weather updates. The firm also owns The Daily Buzz, a three hour morning news show that is produced jointly with Emmis Communications. In February 2007, the firm sold WTVK-TV in Fort Myers-Naples, FL, to Sun Broadcasting, Inc. for $45 million in cash. In October 2007, the company sold WBUI-TV in Decatur, IL to GOCOM Media of Illinois, LLC for $4 million in cash.

FINANCIALS: Sales and profits are in thousands of dollars—add 000 to get the full amount. 2007 Note: Financial information for 2007 was not available for all companies at press time.

2007 Sales: $	2007 Profits: $	**U.S. Stock Ticker:** ACME
2006 Sales: $34,789	2006 Profits: $-4,179	**Int'l Ticker:** Int'l Exchange:
2005 Sales: $34,203	2005 Profits: $-15,945	**Employees:** 186
2004 Sales: $39,257	2004 Profits: $-17,547	**Fiscal Year Ends:** 12/31
2003 Sales: $35,722	2003 Profits: $74,968	**Parent Company:**

SALARIES/BENEFITS:

Pension Plan:	ESOP Stock Plan:	Profit Sharing:	Top Exec. Salary: $387,750	Bonus: $
Savings Plan:	Stock Purch. Plan:		Second Exec. Salary: $387,750	Bonus: $

OTHER THOUGHTS:

Apparent Women Officers or Directors: 1
Hot Spot for Advancement for Women/Minorities:

LOCATIONS: ("Y" = Yes)

West:	Southwest:	Midwest:	Southeast:	Northeast:	International:
Y	Y	Y	Y		

ACTIVISION INC
www.activision.com

Industry Group Code: 511208 Ranks within this company's industry group: Sales: 3 Profits: 4

Print Media/Publishing:	Movies:	Equipment/Supplies:		Broadcast/Cable:	Music/Audio:	Sports/Games/Gambling:	
Newspapers:	Movie Theaters:	Equipment/Supplies:		Broadcast TV:	Music Production:	Games/Sports:	Y
Magazines:	Movie Production:	Gambling Equipment:		Cable TV:	Retail Music:	Retail Games Stores:	
Books:	TV/Video Prod.:	Special Services:	Y	Satellite Broadcast:	Retail Audio Equip.:	Stadiums/Teams:	
Book Stores:	Video Rental:	Advertising Services:		Radio:	Music Print./Dist.:	Gambling/Casinos:	
Distribution/Printing:	Video Distribution:	Info. Sys. Software:		Online Information:	Multimedia:	Rides/Theme Parks:	

TYPES OF BUSINESS:
Video Games
Logistics Services

BRANDS/DIVISIONS/AFFILIATES:
Activision Publishing, Inc.
Vicarious Visions
Tony Hawk's Pro Skater
Marvel: Ultimate Alliance
Quake
Doom
Bizarre Creations Ltd.
Vivendi Games

CONTACTS: *Note: Officers with more than one job title may be intentionally listed here more than once.*
Robert A. Kotick, CEO
William Chardavoyne, CFO/Exec. VP
Brian Hodous, Chief Customer Officer-Activision Publishing
Michael Rowe, Exec. VP-Human Resources
George Rose, General Counsel/Sr. VP/Corp. Sec.
Robert A. Kotick, Chmn.

Phone: 310-255-2000	**Fax:** 310-255-2100
Toll-Free:	
Address: 3100 Ocean Park Blvd., Santa Monica, CA 90405 US	

GROWTH PLANS/SPECIAL FEATURES:
Activision, Inc., which operates solely through its subsidiary Activision Publishing, is a leading international publisher and distributor of interactive entertainment software for the action, adventure, action-sports, racing, role-playing, simulation and strategy game genres. The company maintains a number of strategic relationships with intellectual property owners and has acquired the rights to publish products based on properties such as Hasbro's Transformers and Pro-skater Tony Hawk. The company has a distribution agreement with MTV Networks Kids and Family Group's Nickelodeon under which Activision will be the exclusive distributor of three new Nick Jr. PC CD-ROM titles, based on Dora The Explorer, The Backyardigans, and Go, Diego, Go! Activision develops products for the Sony PlayStation 2, Nintendo GameCube, Microsoft Xbox, Nintendo Game Boy and PC. The firm released four titles concurrently with the launches of the Sony Playstation 3, the Nintendo Wii, and Microsoft's Xbox360 including game title Call of Duty 3 for all three platforms. In addition, Activision published titles Marvel: Ultimate Alliance and new games in the Tony Hawk franchise for the Playstation 3 and Nintendo Wii consoles. Accompanying its publishing, the company maintains distribution operations in Europe that provide logistics and sales services to third-party publishers of interactive entertainment software, its own publishing operations and manufacturers of interactive entertainment hardware. In September 2007, the company acquired video game developer Bizarre Creations Ltd. In December 2007, the company announced a merger with Vivendi Games. The new company, Activision Blizzard, will incorporate Activision's current portfolio and will include Vivendi's Blizzard Entertainment Company as well as the game World of Warcraft.

FINANCIALS: Sales and profits are in thousands of dollars—add 000 to get the full amount. 2007 Note: Financial information for 2007 was not available for all companies at press time.

2007 Sales: $1,513,012	2007 Profits: $85,787	**U.S. Stock Ticker: ATVI**
2006 Sales: $1,468,000	2006 Profits: $40,251	**Int'l Ticker:** Int'l Exchange:
2005 Sales: $1,405,857	2005 Profits: $135,057	Employees: 2,125
2004 Sales: $947,656	2004 Profits: $77,715	Fiscal Year Ends: 3/31
2003 Sales: $864,100	2003 Profits: $66,200	Parent Company:

SALARIES/BENEFITS:

Pension Plan:	ESOP Stock Plan:	Profit Sharing:	Top Exec. Salary: $724,730	Bonus: $
Savings Plan: Y	Stock Purch. Plan: Y		Second Exec. Salary: $724,730	Bonus: $

OTHER THOUGHTS:
Apparent Women Officers or Directors: 2
Hot Spot for Advancement for Women/Minorities:

LOCATIONS: ("Y" = Yes)

West:	Southwest:	Midwest:	Southeast:	Northeast:	International:
Y		Y	Y	Y	Y

ADVANCE PUBLICATIONS INC   www.advance.net

Industry Group Code: 511120 Ranks within this company's industry group: Sales: 1   Profits:

Print Media/Publishing:		Movies:		Equipment/Supplies:		Broadcast/Cable:		Music/Audio:		Sports/Games/Gambling:	
Newspapers:	Y	Movie Theaters:		Equipment/Supplies:		Broadcast TV:	Y	Music Production:		Games/Sports:	
Magazines:	Y	Movie Production:		Gambling Equipment:		Cable TV:		Retail Music:		Retail Games Stores:	
Books:		TV/Video Prod.:		Special Services:	Y	Satellite Broadcast:		Retail Audio Equip.:		Stadiums/Teams:	
Book Stores:		Video Rental:		Advertising Services:		Radio:		Music Print./Dist.:		Gambling/Casinos:	
Distribution/Printing:		Video Distribution:		Info. Sys. Software:		Online Information:		Multimedia:		Rides/Theme Parks:	

TYPES OF BUSINESS:

Magazine Publishing
Online Publications
Newspaper Publishing
Newspaper Industry Consulting & Technology
Internet Service Provider
Broadcast Television

BRANDS/DIVISIONS/AFFILIATES:

Conde Nast Publications Inc
American City Business Journals
Parade Publications
Fairchild Publications
Glamour
Vogue
GQ
The New Yorker

CONTACTS: Note: Officers with more than one job title may be intentionally listed here more than once.

Samuel I. Newhouse, Jr., CEO
Charles H. Townsend, COO
Donald E. Newhouse, Pres.
Arthur Silverstein, CFO
Arthur Silverstein, VP-Human Resources
Peter Weinberger, Pres., Advance.net
Arthur Silverstein, VP-Finance
Charles H. Townsend, CEO-Conde Nast
Steve Newhouse, Chmn.-Advance.net
Samuel I. Newhouse, Jr., Chmn.

Phone: 212-286-2860	Fax: 718-981-1456
Toll-Free:	
Address: 4 Times Square, New York, NY 10036 US	

GROWTH PLANS/SPECIAL FEATURES:

Advance Publications, Inc. publishes a variety of magazines, newspapers and business weeklies. Its publishing subsidiaries include Conde Nast Publications, Parade Publications, Fairchild Publications, American City Business Journals and the Golf Digest Companies. Advance daily newspapers, including the Cleveland Plain Dealer and the New Orleans Times-Picayune, cover over 20 local markets, with more than 28 newspapers. Conde Nast publishes a well-known portfolio of magazines, including Glamour, Vogue, GQ, The New Yorker, Wired and Vanity Fair. The company's advance.net media unit maintains an Internet presence through subsidiaries CondeNet and Advance Internet. Advance Internet deals in sites that cater to the local needs and interests of various municipalities and states, as well as web sites for local newspapers. Affiliated local sites include: concierge.com, epicurious.com, otylo.oom, MaooLivo.com, NOLA.com, PennLive.com, NJ.com, SILive.com, Cleveland.com, Syracuse.com and OregonLive.com. Advance Internet has affiliated newspapers in nine states: Alabama (3 affiliates), Massachusetts (1), Michigan (11), New Jersey (14), Oregon (2), Pennsylvania (2) and New York (2). The subsidiary also maintains special-interest web sites dealing with careers, online car buying and selling and weather information. In February 2007, CondeNet launched flip.com, a website focusing on teen girls' creativity.

FINANCIALS: Sales and profits are in thousands of dollars—add 000 to get the full amount. 2007 Note: Financial information for 2007 was not available for all companies at press time.

2007 Sales: $	2007 Profits: $	U.S. Stock Ticker: Private
2006 Sales: $7,700,000	2006 Profits: $	Int'l Ticker: Int'l Exchange:
2005 Sales: $7,315,000	2005 Profits: $	Employees: 28,000
2004 Sales: $	2004 Profits: $	Fiscal Year Ends: 12/31
2003 Sales: $5,909,000	2003 Profits: $	Parent Company:

SALARIES/BENEFITS:

Pension Plan:	ESOP Stock Plan:	Profit Sharing:	Top Exec. Salary: $	Bonus: $
Savings Plan:	Stock Purch. Plan:		Second Exec. Salary: $	Bonus: $

OTHER THOUGHTS:

Apparent Women Officers or Directors:
Hot Spot for Advancement for Women/Minorities:

LOCATIONS: ("Y" = Yes)

West:	Southwest:	Midwest:	Southeast:	Northeast:	International:
Y	Y	Y	Y	Y	

Note: Financial information, benefits and other data can change quickly and may vary from those stated here.

ALLIANCE ATLANTIS COMMUNICATIONS INC
www.allianceatlantis.com

Industry Group Code: 512110 Ranks within this company's industry group: Sales: 3 Profits: 2

Print Media/Publishing:	Movies:		Equipment/Supplies:	Broadcast/Cable:		Music/Audio:	Sports/Games/Gambling:
Newspapers:	Movie Theaters:	Y	Equipment/Supplies:	Broadcast TV:	Y	Music Production:	Games/Sports:
Magazines:	Movie Production:	Y	Gambling Equipment:	Cable TV:	Y	Retail Music:	Retail Games Stores:
Books:	TV/Video Prod.:	Y	Special Services:	Satellite Broadcast:		Retail Audio Equip.:	Stadiums/Teams:
Book Stores:	Video Rental:		Advertising Services:	Radio:		Music Print./Dist.:	Gambling/Casinos:
Distribution/Printing:	Video Distribution:	Y	Info. Sys. Software:	Online Information:		Multimedia:	Rides/Theme Parks:

TYPES OF BUSINESS:
Television Production
Motion Picture Production & Distribution
Cable Television Networks
Movie Theaters

BRANDS/DIVISIONS/AFFILIATES:
CBS Productions
CSI: Crime Scene Investigation
CSI: Miami
CSI: NY
Distribution LP
Momentum Pictures
Aurom Producciones S.A.
Alliance Atlantis Cinemas

CONTACTS: *Note: Officers with more than one job title may be intentionally listed here more than once.*
Phyllis N. Yaffe, CEO
David Lazzarato, CFO/Exec. VP
Errol Da-Re, Exec. VP-Sales
Jacquelyn Saad, Sr. VP-Human Resources
Andrea Wood, General Counsel/Exec. VP
Andrew Callum, Sr. VP-Strategy
Heather Conway, Exec. VP-Public Affairs & Creative Svcs.
Andrew Akman, Sr. VP-Investor Rel.
Andrew Akman, Sr. VP-Finance & Corp. Dev.
Norm Bolen, Exec. VP-Content Group
Ted Riley, Exec. VP-Special Projects
Heather Conway, Exec. VP-Mktg.
Michael I. M. MacMillan, Exec. Chmn.

Phone: 416-967-1174	Fax: 416-960-0971
Toll-Free:	
Address: 121 Bloor St. E., Ste. 1500, Toronto, ON M4W 3M5 Canada	

GROWTH PLANS/SPECIAL FEATURES:
Alliance Atlantis Communications, Inc. has three principal business activities: Broadcasting, which generated 26.9% of the firm's revenues; entertainment, 34.5%; and motion picture distribution, 38.6%. The broadcasting division owns a controlling interest in 13 specialty channels in Canada; has a non-controlling interest in three more English-language specialty channels; and a 50% interest in two French-language specialty channels. The channels, which focus on the lifestyle and fact & fiction genres, are available through third-party providers, such as cable and satellite companies. Its channels have over 43.7 million subscribers which accounted for 39% of the division's revenue, with advertising generating 60% and other sources 1%. The entertainment division co-produces, co-owns and distributes the popular CSI franchise in all areas outside the U.S.; CBS Productions is the other co-producer and co-owner. The franchise includes CSI: Crime Scene Investigation, CSI: Miami and CSI: NY. Additionally, the division internationally licenses a library of approximately 1,000 titles representing 5,500 hours of programming. The motion picture distribution division holds an indirect, 51% limited partnership interest in Distribution LP, a leading distributor of motion pictures in Canada. It supplies theaters and TV stations, offering film, DVDs, made-for-TV movies and Video On Demand (VOD), with a presence the U.K. through subsidiary Momentum Pictures, and in Spain through subsidiary Aurom Producciones S.A. Distribution LP has film distribution agreements in Canada with New Line Cinema, Focus Features, IFC, Miramax Films, the Weinstein Company, Picturehouse, Newmarket Films and Remstar. It also exhibits movies through Alliance Atlantis Cinemas. On average, the division releases 196 DVD and 84 movie theater titles annually. It has licenses to 4,700 titles. The company was recently delisted from the NASDAQ, and filed with the SEC to terminate its registration in the U.S. Southhill Strategy, Inc. owns a 66.7% controlling interest in Alliance Atlantis.

FINANCIALS: Sales and profits are in thousands of dollars—add 000 to get the full amount. 2007 Note: Financial information for 2007 was not available for all companies at press time.

2007 Sales: $	2007 Profits: $	U.S. Stock Ticker:
2006 Sales: $979,948	2006 Profits: $50,059	Int'l Ticker: AAC Int'l Exchange: Toronto-TSX
2005 Sales: $893,970	2005 Profits: $60,725	Employees: 788
2004 Sales: $848,000	2004 Profits: $24,800	Fiscal Year Ends: 12/31
2003 Sales: $605,600	2003 Profits: $-12,800	Parent Company:

SALARIES/BENEFITS:
Pension Plan:	ESOP Stock Plan:	Profit Sharing:	Top Exec. Salary: $564,583	Bonus: $739,583
Savings Plan: Y	Stock Purch. Plan:		Second Exec. Salary: $500,000	Bonus: $250,000

OTHER THOUGHTS:
Apparent Women Officers or Directors: 5
Hot Spot for Advancement for Women/Minorities: Y

LOCATIONS: ("Y" = Yes)
West:	Southwest:	Midwest:	Southeast:	Northeast:	International:
Y				Y	Y

Note: Financial information, benefits and other data can change quickly and may vary from those stated here.

ALLIANCE ENTERTAINMENT CORP
www.aent.com

Industry Group Code: 422921 Ranks within this company's industry group: Sales: Profits:

Print Media/Publishing:	Movies:	Equipment/Supplies:	Broadcast/Cable:	Music/Audio:	Sports/Games/Gambling:
Newspapers:	Movie Theaters:	Equipment/Supplies:	Broadcast TV:	Music Production:	Games/Sports: Y
Magazines:	Movie Production:	Gambling Equipment:	Cable TV:	Retail Music:	Retail Games Stores:
Books:	TV/Video Prod.:	Special Services:	Satellite Broadcast:	Retail Audio Equip.:	Stadiums/Teams:
Book Stores:	Video Rental:	Advertising Services:	Radio:	Music Print./Dist.: Y	Gambling/Casinos:
Distribution/Printing:	Video Distribution: Y	Info. Sys. Software:	Online Information:	Multimedia:	Rides/Theme Parks:

TYPES OF BUSINESS:

Entertainment Products Distribution
E-Commerce Software
Online Entertainment Portal

BRANDS/DIVISIONS/AFFILIATES:

Yucaipa Companies
Source Interlink
Innovation Distribution Network (IDN)
Matrix Software
NCircle Entertainment
AEC Direct
Distribution & Fullfillment Services Group (DFS)
Information Services Group (IS)

CONTACTS: Note: Officers with more than one job title may be intentionally listed here more than once.

Alan Tuchman, CEO
Alan Tuchman, COO
Alan Tuchman, Pres.

Phone: 954-255-4000	Fax: 954-255-4078
Toll-Free: 800-329-7664	
Address: 4250 Coral Ridge Dr., Coral Springs, FL 33065 US	

GROWTH PLANS/SPECIAL FEATURES:

Alliance Entertainment Corp. (AEC) provides 30,000 storefronts and more than 3 million individual customers with entertainment products such as music, video games, DVDs and related home entertainment products. The company is divided into two branches: the distribution and fulfillment services group (DFS) and the information services group (IS). Through DFS, AEC operates two distribution centers totaling over 400,000 square feet with state-of-the-art material handling automation, located in Coral Springs, Florida and Louisville, Kentucky. Firm sales offices are based in California, Georgia, Pennsylvania and Vermont. The IS group, operated under AEC Direct, develops and provides support services, including e-commerce software, real-time inventory query, advanced checkout technology and flexible merchandising, which the company provides to its retailers. Other companies operating under AEC include Innovation Distribution Network (IDN), which brings retailers products from independent manufactures of music and games; Matrix Software, a developer and publisher of specialty astrological software; and NCircle Entertainment, which specializes in the sales, marketing and distribution of children's and family entertainment content. The firm's clients include Barnes and Noble, Blockbuster, Walgreens, Toys R' Us, Sears, Kmart, Meijer, Trans World Music, Circuit City, Best Buy, AOL, BJ's Wholesale Club, Borders and Hastings Entertainment. Source Interlink controls 50% of the company, with the rest held by Yucaipa Companies, a private investment firm and the largest shareholder of Source Interlink.

FINANCIALS: Sales and profits are in thousands of dollars—add 000 to get the full amount. 2007 Note: Financial information for 2007 was not available for all companies at press time.

2007 Sales: $	2007 Profits: $	U.S. Stock Ticker: Subsidiary
2006 Sales: $	2006 Profits: $	Int'l Ticker: Int'l Exchange:
2005 Sales: $	2005 Profits: $	Employees: 1,400
2004 Sales: $	2004 Profits: $	Fiscal Year Ends: 12/31
2003 Sales: $870,000	2003 Profits: $	Parent Company: SOURCE INTERLINK COMPANIES INC

SALARIES/BENEFITS:

Pension Plan:	ESOP Stock Plan:	Profit Sharing:	Top Exec. Salary: $	Bonus: $
Savings Plan:	Stock Purch. Plan:		Second Exec. Salary: $	Bonus: $

OTHER THOUGHTS:

Apparent Women Officers or Directors:
Hot Spot for Advancement for Women/Minorities:

LOCATIONS: ("Y" = Yes)

West:	Southwest:	Midwest:	Southeast:	Northeast:	International:
Y		Y	Y	Y	

AMAZON.COM INC

www.amazon.com

Industry Group Code: 451211E Ranks within this company's industry group: Sales: 1 Profits: 1

Print Media/Publishing:		Movies:		Equipment/Supplies:		Broadcast/Cable:		Music/Audio:		Sports/Games/Gambling:	
Newspapers:		Movie Theaters:		Equipment/Supplies:		Broadcast TV:		Music Production:		Games/Sports:	
Magazines:		Movie Production:		Gambling Equipment:		Cable TV:		Retail Music:	Y	Retail Games Stores:	
Books:	Y	TV/Video Prod.:		Special Services:		Satellite Broadcast:		Retail Audio Equip.:	Y	Stadiums/Teams:	
Book Stores:		Video Rental:		Advertising Services:		Radio:		Music Print./Dist.:		Gambling/Casinos:	
Distribution/Printing:		Video Distribution:	Y	Info. Sys. Software:		Online Information:		Multimedia:		Rides/Theme Parks:	

TYPES OF BUSINESS:

Online Retail
Online Books & Music Retail
Online Videos/DVDs Retail
Online Electronics Retail
Online Auctions
Online Household Goods Retail
E-Commerce Support & Hosting
Search Engine Technology

BRANDS/DIVISIONS/AFFILIATES:

Amazon Marketplace
Merchants@
A9.com, Inc.
alexa.com
Shopbop.com
imdb.com
CreateSpace

CONTACTS: *Note: Officers with more than one job title may be intentionally listed here more than once.*

Jeffrey P. Bezos, CEO
Jeffrey P. Bezos, Pres.
Thomas J. Szkutak, CFO/Sr. VP
Richard (Rick) Dalzell, CIO/Sr. VP
L. Michelle Wilson, General Counsel/Sr. VP/Sec.
Marc Onetto, Sr. VP-Worldwide Oper.
Jeffrey Blackburn, Sr. VP-Bus. Dev.
Brian Valentine, Sr. VP-e-commerce Platform
Shelley Reynolds, VP-Finance/Controller/Principal Acct. Officer
Sebastian J. Gunningham, Sr. VP-Merchant Svcs.
Andrew Jassy, Sr. VP-Web Svcs.
Steven Kessel, Sr. VP-Worldwide Digital Media
Jeff Wilke, Sr. VP-North American Retail
Jeffrey P. Bezos, Chmn.
Diego Piacentini, Sr. VP-Int'l Retail

Phone: 206-266-1000	Fax: 206-266-1821
Toll-Free:	
Address: 1200 12th Ave. S., Ste. 1200, Seattle, WA 98144-2734 US	

GROWTH PLANS/SPECIAL FEATURES:

Amazon.com, Inc., one of the leading Internet consumer-shopping sites, offers millions of new, used, refurbished and collectible items in categories such as apparel, software, consumer electronics, automotive, music, DVDs, pet supplies, office products, tools and books. The company operates several international web sites such as amazon.co.uk and amazon.de, serving the U.K. and Germany respectively, as well as sites for Canada, Japan, China and France. A large part of the firm's revenue comes from enabling e-commerce for others. For example, Amazon manages online sales for Office Depot and Target. The Amazon Marketplace and Merchants@ programs allow third parties to integrate their products on Amazon web sites; allow customers to shop for products owned by third parties using Amazon's features and technologies; and allow customers to complete transactions that include multiple sellers in a single checkout process. Amazon Marketplace serves individuals and small businesses, while the Merchants@ program serves larger companies, primarily concentrating on expanding the selection of new products available on Amazon's web sites. Amazon also provides technology services and other marketing and promotional services, especially through subsidiaries, a9.com and alexa.com. These sites focus on cutting-edge open search technology, scouring the web for image search results in addition to .html findings. It also operates imdb.com, an international movie database, offering film reviews and other information. Recently acquired Shopbop.com is a women's fashion, shoes, apparel and accessories retailer. In July 2006, Amazon launched its grocery store, offering over 14,000 dry grocery products. In August 2007, subsidiary CreateSpace began offering an online Books on Demand service for authors who would like to self-publish and sell their books on Amazon.com or on a self-designed eStore; CreateSpace offers similar services for musicians and filmmakers.

Amazon.com offers employees flexible spending accounts, relocation assistance and discount programs. Full-time employees also receive units of restricted stock.

FINANCIALS: Sales and profits are in thousands of dollars—add 000 to get the full amount. 2007 Note: Financial information for 2007 was not available for all companies at press time.

2007 Sales: $	2007 Profits: $	**U.S. Stock Ticker: AMZN**
2006 Sales: $10,711,000	2006 Profits: $190,000	**Int'l Ticker:** Int'l Exchange:
2005 Sales: $8,490,000	2005 Profits: $359,000	Employees: 13,900
2004 Sales: $6,921,124	2004 Profits: $588,000	Fiscal Year Ends: 12/31
2003 Sales: $5,263,699	2003 Profits: $35,282	Parent Company:

SALARIES/BENEFITS:

Pension Plan:	ESOP Stock Plan:	Profit Sharing:	Top Exec. Salary: $211,502	Bonus: $
Savings Plan: Y	Stock Purch. Plan: Y		Second Exec. Salary: $175,000	Bonus: $

OTHER THOUGHTS:

Apparent Women Officers or Directors: 2
Hot Spot for Advancement for Women/Minorities: Y

LOCATIONS: ("Y" = Yes)

West:	Southwest:	Midwest:	Southeast:	Northeast:	International:
Y	Y	Y	Y	Y	Y

Note: Financial information, benefits and other data can change quickly and may vary from those stated here.

AMC ENTERTAINMENT INC

www.amctheatres.com

Industry Group Code: 512131 **Ranks within this company's industry group:** Sales: 2 Profits: 4

Print Media/Publishing:	Movies:		Equipment/Supplies:	Broadcast/Cable:	Music/Audio:	Sports/Games/Gambling:
Newspapers:	Movie Theaters:	Y	Equipment/Supplies:	Broadcast TV:	Music Production:	Games/Sports:
Magazines:	Movie Production:		Gambling Equipment:	Cable TV:	Retail Music:	Retail Games Stores:
Books:	TV/Video Prod.:		Special Services:	Satellite Broadcast:	Retail Audio Equip.:	Stadiums/Teams:
Book Stores:	Video Rental:		Advertising Services:	Radio:	Music Print./Dist.:	Gambling/Casinos:
Distribution/Printing:	Video Distribution:		Info. Sys. Software:	Online Information:	Multimedia:	Rides/Theme Parks:

TYPES OF BUSINESS:

Movie Theaters
Online Movie Ticket Sales

BRANDS/DIVISIONS/AFFILIATES:

Digital Cinema Implementation Partners, LLC
Fandango
movietickets.com
Marquee Holdings, Inc.

CONTACTS: *Note: Officers with more than one job title may be intentionally listed here more than once.*

Peter C. Brown, CEO
Peter C. Brown, Pres.
Craig R. Ramsey, CFO/Exec. VP
Alice M. Rogers, Sr. VP-Mktg.
Keith P. Wiedenkeller, Sr. VP-Human Resources
Kevin M. Connor, General Counsel/Sec./Sr. VP
John D. McDonald, Exec. VP-US & Canada Oper.
Frank W. Rash, III, Sr. VP-Strategic Dev.
Alice M. Rogers, Sr. VP-Comm.
Terry W. Crawford, VP/Treas.
Samuel D. Gourley, Pres., AMC Film Programming
Scott Wall, VP-National Sales
Peter C. Brown, Chmn.
Mark A. McDonald, Exec. VP-Int'l Oper.

Phone: 816-221-4000	Fax: 816-480-4617
Toll-Free:	
Address: 920 Main St., Kansas City, MO 64105 US	

GROWTH PLANS/SPECIAL FEATURES:

AMC Entertainment, Inc. is one of the leading operators of movie theaters in North America. It currently operates 413 movie theaters with 5,603 screens located in the U.S., Canada, France, Japan, Portugal, Spain, Mexico, South America and the U.K. The firm is an industry leader in the development and operation of megaplex theaters, which have 14 screens or more, primarily in large metropolitan markets. AMC's megaplexes have consistently ranked among its top grossing facilities on a per-screen basis and are among the top grossing theaters in North America. The megaplex theater format, now adopted by many of AMC's competitors, has led to consolidation in the industry. New AMC theaters often include amenities such as digital sound, advanced curved screens, AMC LoveSeat-style seating, restaurants, and refreshment and merchandise kiosks. The movietickets.com web site, operated in conjunction with several partners, is dedicated to the sale of movie tickets and additional content that assists users with their movie-going plans. The website represents over 9,800 screens. AMC also owns approximately 9% of Fandango, an on-line movie ticketing company that represents approximately 13,000 screens. Through the course of 2007, the firm opened or announced the impending opening of roughly eight new theater locations. In March 2007, AMC Entertainment Inc., Cinemark USA, Inc. and Regal Entertainment Group formed an equal partnership to create Digital Cinema Implementation Partners, LLC. The company will plan and implement the deployment of digital cinema in theatres. In 2007, Marquee Holdings, Inc., the firm's parent company, made an initial public offering of common stock. In May, that initial offering was suspended, citing adverse market conditions. In December 2007, AMC entered a deal with IMAX Corporation to install 100 IMAX digital projection systems at AMC locations in 33 major U.S. markets.

FINANCIALS: Sales and profits are in thousands of dollars—add 000 to get the full amount. 2007 Note: Financial information for 2007 was not available for all companies at press time.

2007 Sales: $	2007 Profits: $	**U.S. Stock Ticker:** Private
2006 Sales: $1,730,450	2006 Profits: $-188,762	**Int'l Ticker:** **Int'l Exchange:**
2005 Sales: $1,806,600	2005 Profits: $-70,600	Employees: 21,400
2004 Sales: $1,782,820	2004 Profits: $-16,623	Fiscal Year Ends: 3/02
2003 Sales: $1,791,600	2003 Profits: $-20,300	Parent Company:

SALARIES/BENEFITS:

Pension Plan: Y	ESOP Stock Plan:	Profit Sharing:	Top Exec. Salary: $750,000	Bonus: $25,550
Savings Plan: Y	Stock Purch. Plan:		Second Exec. Salary: $482,000	Bonus: $16,250

OTHER THOUGHTS:

Apparent Women Officers or Directors: 1
Hot Spot for Advancement for Women/Minorities:

LOCATIONS: ("Y" = Yes)

West:	Southwest:	Midwest:	Southeast:	Northeast:	International:
Y	Y	Y	Y	Y	Y

Note: Financial information, benefits and other data can change quickly and may vary from those stated here.

AMERICAN COIN MERCHANDISING INC   www.sugarloaf-usa.com

Industry Group Code: 713990 **Ranks within this company's industry group:** Sales: Profits:

Print Media/Publishing:	Movies:	Equipment/Supplies:		Broadcast/Cable:	Music/Audio:	Sports/Games/Gambling:	
Newspapers:	Movie Theaters:	Equipment/Supplies:	Y	Broadcast TV:	Music Production:	Games/Sports:	Y
Magazines:	Movie Production:	Gambling Equipment:		Cable TV:	Retail Music:	Retail Games Stores:	
Books:	TV/Video Prod.:	Special Services:		Satellite Broadcast:	Retail Audio Equip.:	Stadiums/Teams:	
Book Stores:	Video Rental:	Advertising Services:		Radio:	Music Print./Dist.:	Gambling/Casinos:	
Distribution/Printing:	Video Distribution:	Info. Sys. Software:		Online Information:	Multimedia:	Rides/Theme Parks:	

TYPES OF BUSINESS:

Skill-Crane Game Machines
Simulators, Video Games & Rides
Plush Toy Manufacturing
Vending Machines

BRANDS/DIVISIONS/AFFILIATES:

Coinstar Inc
SugarLoaf Creations, Inc.
Folz Vending Company
Kiddie World
Rainbow Crane
SugarLoaf Toy Shoppe
SugarLoaf Bean Bag Shoppe
SugarLoaf Stop Shoppe

CONTACTS: *Note: Officers with more than one job title may be intentionally listed here more than once.*

Randall J. Fagundo, Pres.

Phone: 303-444-2559	**Fax:** 303-247-0480
Toll-Free: 800-735-2559	
Address: 397 S. Taylor Ave., Louisville, CO 80027 US	

GROWTH PLANS/SPECIAL FEATURES:

American Coin Merchandising, Inc. (ACMI), and its franchises own and manage more than 227,000 coin-operated pieces of equipment including over 18,000 skill-crane machines that dispense stuffed animals, plush toys, watches, jewelry and other items; 200,000 bulk vending machines; 6,000 children's ride machines; and 3,000 video game machines. These are installed in more than 33,000 retail locations. The firm operates under the names SugarLoaf Creations, Inc. and Folz Vending Company, and is a subsidiary of Coinstar, Inc., which operates 44,000 automated coin sorters primarily in supermarkets. ACMI/SugarLoaf manufactures all of the plush toys that are placed inside the skill crane machines. These machines are manufactured by subsidiary Rainbow Crane and are placed in supermarkets, mass merchandisers, bowling centers, bingo halls, bars, restaurants, warehouse clubs and similar locations, including Wal-Mart, Denny's and Kmart. Wal-Mart locations account for the largest share, 25.3%, of ACMI's total revenue. The machines come in a variety of shapes and sizes and offer different vending methods. Examples of machine names include the SugarLoaf Toy Shoppe, SugarLoaf Treasure Shoppe, SugarLoaf Bean Bag Shoppe and the SugarLoaf Stop Shoppe. The cranes stock products from Sesame Street and Harley Davidson. The company gives about one-third of machine revenue to host retailers for space rental, and estimates a typical 60-inch crane generates $300 per square foot per year to the host business which invests nothing in the machine. The Folz Vending subsidiary is responsible for the bulk vending business, which primarily offers gum, candy and small novelties. Through its subsidiary, Kiddie World, the company is the only U.S. supplier of Disney licensed rides. In 2007, Disney branded kiddie rides will be expanded to include characters from the movies Aladdin, Pirates of the Caribbean and Lilo & Stitch.

ACMI's employees receive a full range of health benefits, which include a prescription plan, life and accident insurance and paid vacations.

FINANCIALS: Sales and profits are in thousands of dollars—add 000 to get the full amount. 2007 Note: Financial information for 2007 was not available for all companies at press time.

2007 Sales: $	2007 Profits: $	**U.S. Stock Ticker: Subsidiary**
2006 Sales: $	2006 Profits: $	**Int'l Ticker:** Int'l Exchange:
2005 Sales: $	2005 Profits: $	Employees: 800
2004 Sales: $	2004 Profits: $	Fiscal Year Ends: 12/31
2003 Sales: $201,400	2003 Profits: $-2,000	Parent Company: COINSTAR INC

SALARIES/BENEFITS:

Pension Plan:	ESOP Stock Plan:	Profit Sharing:	Top Exec. Salary: $325,000	Bonus: $
Savings Plan: Y	Stock Purch. Plan:		Second Exec. Salary: $145,222	Bonus: $

OTHER THOUGHTS:

Apparent Women Officers or Directors:
Hot Spot for Advancement for Women/Minorities:

LOCATIONS: ("Y" = Yes)

West:	Southwest:	Midwest:	Southeast:	Northeast:	International:
Y				Y	

Note: Financial information, benefits and other data can change quickly and may vary from those stated here.

AMERICAN EDUCATIONAL PRODUCTS LLC   www.amep.com

Industry Group Code: 339000 Ranks within this company's industry group: Sales: Profits:

Print Media/Publishing:	Movies:	Equipment/Supplies:		Broadcast/Cable:	Music/Audio:	Sports/Games/Gambling:
Newspapers:	Movie Theaters:	Equipment/Supplies:	Y	Broadcast TV:	Music Production:	Games/Sports:
Magazines:	Movie Production:	Gambling Equipment:		Cable TV:	Retail Music:	Retail Games Stores:
Books: Y	TV/Video Prod.: Y	Special Services:		Satellite Broadcast:	Retail Audio Equip.:	Stadiums/Teams:
Book Stores:	Video Rental:	Advertising Services:		Radio:	Music Print./Dist.:	Gambling/Casinos:
Distribution/Printing:	Video Distribution:	Info. Sys. Software:		Online Information:	Multimedia:	Rides/Theme Parks:

TYPES OF BUSINESS:

Manufacturing-Educational Products
Educational Video Production
Map Manufacturing

BRANDS/DIVISIONS/AFFILIATES:

Aristotle Corporation
Scott Resources
Hubbard Scientific
National Teaching Aids
Ginsberg Scientific Inc
Gonge USA
Orbit USA
Tuzzles USA

CONTACTS: Note: Officers with more than one job title may be intentionally listed here more than once.

Michael Anderson, Pres.
Dean Johnson, CFO/VP
Crystal Salas, Head-Sales
Tom Halblieb, Head-Product Dev.

Phone: 970-484-7445	Fax: 970-484-1198
Toll-Free: 800-289-9299	
Address: 401 W. Hickory St., Fort Collins, CO 80522 US	

GROWTH PLANS/SPECIAL FEATURES:

American Educational Products, LLC (AEP) develops, manufactures and distributes educational products to parents, teachers, and public and private schools throughout the U.S. and in some international locations. The firm is an indirect subsidiary of The Aristotle Corporation, which manufactures medical teaching aids such as CPR mannequins and computer-based teaching aids. AEP's products are supplemental instructional aids for elementary to high school mathematics and science courses. The products attempt to present educational content in a format different than traditional textbooks. AEP serves as an original equipment manufacturer through four divisions. Scott Resources produces math manipulatives, math videos and teacher guides, exclusively manufacturing such math products as Fraction Bars, Decimal Squares, Clever Catch balls and the Math Chase series. Hubbard Scientific manufactures science educational materials in such areas as earth science, geology, astronomy, meteorology, oceanography, biology, zoology, botany, ecology, anatomy, physiology, chemistry, physical science, the environment, geography and health. National Teaching Aids (NTA) produces the Microslide Viewer and over 100 titles of Microslide Slide Lesson Sets. Finally, Ginsberg Scientific, Inc. provides lab equipment, glassware and measurement devices. Scott Resources additionally provides earth science educational materials, including bulk rock, minerals, fossil specimens and the Earth Science Videolabs series. The Hubbard subsidiary is also one of the world's largest manufacturers of raised relief maps, with a library of roughly 200 titles and custom map production capabilities. AEP additionally markets products from Gonge USA, a manufacturer of active play equipment for children such as trampolines; Orbit USA, a children's toy manufacturer; Tuzzles USA, a manufacturer of puzzles; and Yellowtails USA, a manufacturer of motor skill development equipment including jump ropes and juggling equipment.

FINANCIALS: Sales and profits are in thousands of dollars—add 000 to get the full amount. 2007 Note: Financial information for 2007 was not available for all companies at press time.

2007 Sales: $	2007 Profits: $	U.S. Stock Ticker: Subsidiary
2006 Sales: $	2006 Profits: $	Int'l Ticker: Int'l Exchange:
2005 Sales: $	2005 Profits: $	Employees: 95
2004 Sales: $	2004 Profits: $	Fiscal Year Ends: 12/31
2003 Sales: $	2003 Profits: $	Parent Company: ARISTOTLE CORPORATION

SALARIES/BENEFITS:

Pension Plan:	ESOP Stock Plan:	Profit Sharing:	Top Exec. Salary: $	Bonus: $
Savings Plan:	Stock Purch. Plan:		Second Exec. Salary: $	Bonus: $

OTHER THOUGHTS:

Apparent Women Officers or Directors: 1
Hot Spot for Advancement for Women/Minorities:

LOCATIONS: ("Y" = Yes)

West:	Southwest:	Midwest:	Southeast:	Northeast:	International:
Y					

AMERICAN EXPRESS CO   www.americanexpress.com

Industry Group Code: 522210 Ranks within this company's industry group: Sales: 1 Profits: 1

Print Media/Publishing:	Movies:	Equipment/Supplies:	Broadcast/Cable:	Music/Audio:	Sports/Games/Gambling:
Newspapers:	Movie Theaters:	Equipment/Supplies:	Broadcast TV:	Music Production:	Games/Sports:
Magazines: Y	Movie Production:	Gambling Equipment:	Cable TV:	Retail Music:	Retail Games Stores:
Books:	TV/Video Prod.:	Special Services: Y	Satellite Broadcast:	Retail Audio Equip.:	Stadiums/Teams:
Book Stores:	Video Rental:	Advertising Services: Y	Radio:	Music Print./Dist.:	Gambling/Casinos:
Distribution/Printing:	Video Distribution:	Info. Sys. Software:	Online Information:	Multimedia:	Rides/Theme Parks:

TYPES OF BUSINESS:

Credit Card Issuing
Travel-Related Services
Lending & Financing
Transaction Services
Point-of-Sale Systems
International Banking Services
Expense Management
Magazine Publishing

BRANDS/DIVISIONS/AFFILIATES:

American Express Travel Related Services Company
American Express Publishing Corporation
Food & Wine
Travel+Leisure
OPEN: The Small Business Network
Ameriprise Financial, Inc.
American Express Business Travel
Farrington American Express Travel Services Ltd.

CONTACTS: *Note: Officers with more than one job title may be intentionally listed here more than once.*

Kenneth I. Chenault, CEO
Alfred F. Kelly, Jr., Pres.
Daniel Henry, CFO/Exec. VP
John D. Hayes, Chief Mktg. Officer/Exec. VP-Global Advertising
L. Kevin Cox, Exec. VP-Human Resources & Quality
Stephen Squeri, CIO/Exec. VP
Louise M. Parent, General Counsel/Exec. VP
Thomas Schick, Exec. VP-Corp. Affairs & Comm.
Edward P. Gilligan, Group CEO-Business-to-Business
Ahswini Gupta, Pres., Risk, Info. Mgmt. & Banking Group
Judson C. Linville, CEO/Pres., Consumer Services
William H. Glenn, Pres., Global Establishment Svcs./Global Merchant
Kenneth I. Chenault, Chmn.
Douglas E. Buckminster, Pres., International Consumer

Phone: 212-640-2000	**Fax:** 212-619-9802
Toll-Free:	
Address: 200 Vesey St., World Financial Ctr., New York, NY 10285 US	

GROWTH PLANS/SPECIAL FEATURES:

American Express Co. (AmEx), founded in 1850, provides travel-related services, credit cards and international banking services. The company has three operating segments: Global Network & Merchant Services; U.S. Card Services and International & Global Commercial Services; and a corporate and other segment. Amex generates revenue from credit cards, traveler's checks and banking as well as airline, hotel and rental car reservations. Some other significant services include consumer and small business lending, merchant acquiring and transaction processing, point-of-sale systems, international banking and expense management. American Express cards, the firm's most notable product, are issued in over 40 currencies and enable card members to purchase goods and services worldwide. American Express Travel Related Services includes in-depth travel arrangement and reservations services. The company also has a wholesale travel business in the U.S. through subsidiary Travel Impressions. Another division, American Express Publishing, operates several leading magazines for affluent readers, including Food & Wine and Travel+Leisure. Amex has noted expertise in selling to the small business market and to the corporate travel and purchasing market. Recently, the firm introduced OPEN: The Small Business Network from American Express, which provides products, services, online account management tools and partnerships for small businesses. American Express Financial Advisors (AEFA), a $400 billion financial planning company that included more than 10,000 financial advisors, has been spun off as a free-standing company called Ameriprise Financial, Inc. In the first part of 2006, business was initiated, enhanced or resumed in Brazil, Cambodia and Bosnia. In July 2007, American Express Business Travel completed the acquisition of Farrington American Express Travel Services Limited in Hong Kong. In September 2007, the firm agreed to sell its international banking operations to Standard Chartered plc for $1.1 billion.

For its U.S. employees, AmEx provides health care plans; a life and disability insurance plan; travel discounts; and assistance programs covering legal advice, adoption, education and personal issues.

FINANCIALS: Sales and profits are in thousands of dollars—add 000 to get the full amount. 2007 Note: Financial information for 2007 was not available for all companies at press time.

2007 Sales: $	2007 Profits: $	**U.S. Stock Ticker: AXP**
2006 Sales: $27,136,000	2006 Profits: $3,707,000	**Int'l Ticker:** Int'l Exchange:
2005 Sales: $24,300,000	2005 Profits: $3,734,000	Employees: 65,400
2004 Sales: $22,000,000	2004 Profits: $3,445,000	Fiscal Year Ends: 12/31
2003 Sales: $25,866,000	2003 Profits: $2,987,000	Parent Company:

SALARIES/BENEFITS:

Pension Plan:	ESOP Stock Plan:	Profit Sharing:	Top Exec. Salary: $1,100,000	Bonus: $6,000,000
Savings Plan: Y	Stock Purch. Plan:		Second Exec. Salary: $575,000	Bonus: $1,850,000

OTHER THOUGHTS:

Apparent Women Officers or Directors: 1
Hot Spot for Advancement for Women/Minorities: Y

LOCATIONS: ("Y" = Yes)

West:	Southwest:	Midwest:	Southeast:	Northeast:	International:
Y	Y	Y	Y	Y	Y

Note: Financial information, benefits and other data can change quickly and may vary from those stated here.

AMERICAN GOLF CORP

www.americangolf.com

Industry Group Code: 713910 **Ranks within this company's industry group:** Sales: Profits:

Print Media/Publishing:	Movies:	Equipment/Supplies:		Broadcast/Cable:	Music/Audio:	Sports/Games/Gambling:	
Newspapers:	Movie Theaters:	Equipment/Supplies:		Broadcast TV:	Music Production:	Games/Sports:	Y
Magazines:	Movie Production:	Gambling Equipment:		Cable TV:	Retail Music:	Retail Games Stores:	
Books:	TV/Video Prod.:	Special Services:	Y	Satellite Broadcast:	Retail Audio Equip.:	Stadiums/Teams:	
Book Stores:	Video Rental:	Advertising Services:		Radio:	Music Print./Dist.:	Gambling/Casinos:	
Distribution/Printing:	Video Distribution:	Info. Sys. Software:		Online Information:	Multimedia:	Rides/Theme Parks:	

TYPES OF BUSINESS:

Golf Courses
Resorts
Golf Promotion
Real Estate

BRANDS/DIVISIONS/AFFILIATES:

American Golf Foundation
Platinum Club

CONTACTS: Note: Officers with more than one job title may be intentionally listed here more than once.

Tom Ferguson, CEO
Paul Major, Pres.
Mike Moecker, CFO/Sr. VP
Mark Friedman, General Counsel/Sec./Sr. VP
Keith Brown, Sr. VP/COO-West
Steve Paris, Sr. VP/COO-East
Craig Kniffen, Sr. VP-Maintenance

Phone: 310-664-4000	Fax: 310-664-4386
Toll-Free:	
Address: 2951 28th St., Santa Monica, CA 90405 US	

GROWTH PLANS/SPECIAL FEATURES:

American Golf Corporation is a premier manager of golf courses and resorts, owning and operating more than 160 private, resort and daily fee golf courses in the U.S. The company also sells real estate connected with its golf resorts and communities. Its ownerships are combined with a stated philosophy of developing the quality of life within these communities. American Golf's portfolio includes courses in 22 states, with its largest holdings in Arizona and California. The firm offers regional golfers clubs throughout the country that offer discount green fees, early twilight access and merchandise discounts. The company also offers the Platinum Club, which enables members to golf at participating American Golf private clubs and public courses all over the country for only a cart fee. Membership also allows golfers to reserve tee times up to 60 days in advance, and bring guests to private clubs for the prevailing guest rate. American Golf established the American Golf Foundation, a nonprofit organization devoted to promoting golf. The foundation utilizes a team of volunteer ambassadors to conduct fundraising activities, participate in community outreach programs, educate guests on proper golf course etiquette, rules and safety and help make the game of golf accessible to people of all ages and backgrounds.

FINANCIALS: Sales and profits are in thousands of dollars—add 000 to get the full amount. 2007 Note: Financial information for 2007 was not available for all companies at press time.

2007 Sales: $	2007 Profits: $	U.S. Stock Ticker: Private
2006 Sales: $	2006 Profits: $	Int'l Ticker: Int'l Exchange:
2005 Sales: $	2005 Profits: $	Employees: 10,000
2004 Sales: $	2004 Profits: $	Fiscal Year Ends: 12/31
2003 Sales: $700,000	2003 Profits: $	Parent Company:

SALARIES/BENEFITS:

Pension Plan:	ESOP Stock Plan:	Profit Sharing:	Top Exec. Salary: $	Bonus: $
Savings Plan:	Stock Purch. Plan:		Second Exec. Salary: $	Bonus: $

OTHER THOUGHTS:

Apparent Women Officers or Directors:
Hot Spot for Advancement for Women/Minorities:

LOCATIONS: ("Y" = Yes)

West:	Southwest:	Midwest:	Southeast:	Northeast:	International:
Y	Y	Y	Y	Y	

AMERICAN GREETINGS CORP

www.corporate.americangreetings.com

Industry Group Code: 511191 Ranks within this company's industry group: Sales: 2 Profits: 1

Print Media/Publishing:		Movies:		Equipment/Supplies:		Broadcast/Cable:		Music/Audio:		Sports/Games/Gambling:	
Newspapers:		Movie Theaters:		Equipment/Supplies:	Y	Broadcast TV:		Music Production:		Games/Sports:	
Magazines:		Movie Production:		Gambling Equipment:		Cable TV:		Retail Music:		Retail Games Stores:	
Books:		TV/Video Prod.:		Special Services:	Y	Satellite Broadcast:		Retail Audio Equip.:		Stadiums/Teams:	
Book Stores:		Video Rental:		Advertising Services:		Radio:		Music Print./Dist.:		Gambling/Casinos:	
Distribution/Printing:		Video Distribution:		Info. Sys. Software:		Online Information:		Multimedia:		Rides/Theme Parks:	

TYPES OF BUSINESS:

Greeting Cards
Gift Wrap
Party Supplies
Candles
Stationery
Digital Media
Online Greetings Services
Educational Products

BRANDS/DIVISIONS/AFFILIATES:

Carlton Cards
Guildhouse
DateWorks
DesignWare
AGI Shutz Merchandising
Learning Horizons
AG Interactive
bluemountain.com

CONTACTS: Note: Officers with more than one job title may be intentionally listed here more than once.

Zev Weiss, CEO
Jeffery M. Weiss, COO
Jeffery M. Weiss, Pres.
Stephen J. Smith, CFO/Sr. VP
Steven S. Willensky, Sr. VP/Exec. Sales & Mktg. Officer
Brian T. McGrath, Sr. VP-Human Resources
Rajiv Jain, CTO
George A. Wenz, VP-Mass Merch. Channel
Catherine M. Kilbane, General Counsel/Sr. VP/Sec.
Paul J. Conley, VP-Digital Media
Stephen J. Smith, VP-Investor Rel.
Stephen J. Smith, Treas.
Thomas H. Johnson, Sr. VP-Creative
William R. Mason, Sr. VP-Wal-Mart Team
Tamra Seldin, Sr. VP-Consumer Products
Morry Weiss, Chmn.
John S.N. Charlton, Sr. VP-Int'l Oper.
Michael L. Goulder, Sr. VP/Exec. Supply Chain Officer

Phone: 216-252-7300	Fax: 216-252-6778
Toll-Free:	
Address: 1 American Rd., Cleveland, OH 44144-3298 US	

GROWTH PLANS/SPECIAL FEATURES:

American Greetings Corp. is engaged in the design, manufacture and sale of everyday and seasonal greeting cards and other social expression products. The firm's products are sold across the U.S. and in countries around the world, including Canada, the U.K., Australia and China, under a variety of names, including AG Interactive, a subsidiary focusing on the digital media market. Besides greeting cards, the company's product lines also include gift wrap, party goods, candles, stationery, calendars, ornaments, ringtones, wallpapers, avatars and emoticons. The firm owns intellectual properties including Strawberry Shortcake, Care Bears, Holly Hobbie and Twisted Whiskers. The company also owns 92% of AmericanGreetings.com, which markets e-mail greetings, personalized printable greeting cards and other products through its web sites, including BlueMountain.com and egreetings.com. This subsidiary also offers design and verse content services for use in CD-ROM software products. American Greetings' largest customers include mass merchandisers and major drug stores. Early in 2007, the company sold its candle line and its Learning Horizons division as part of an effort to refocus its resources on its core social expression business. Also in 2007, American Greetings Properties and DIC Entertainment partnered to launch children's Saturday morning programming on CBS. Recently, AGI Interactive launched a new mobile e-card service with Image Semantics that allows consumers to send e-cards from the web to mobile phones. This partnership adds to AIG's list of digital technology partnerships, which include ventures with Concord Music Group and SI Mobile.

FINANCIALS: Sales and profits are in thousands of dollars—add 000 to get the full amount. 2007 Note: Financial information for 2007 was not available for all companies at press time.

2007 Sales: $	2007 Profits: $	**U.S. Stock Ticker: AM**
2006 Sales: $1,885,701	2006 Profits: $84,376	**Int'l Ticker:** Int'l Exchange:
2005 Sales: $1,883,367	2005 Profits: $95,279	Employees: 29,500
2004 Sales: $1,937,540	2004 Profits: $104,670	Fiscal Year Ends: 2/28
2003 Sales: $1,995,900	2003 Profits: $121,100	Parent Company:

SALARIES/BENEFITS:

Pension Plan: Y	ESOP Stock Plan:	Profit Sharing: Y	Top Exec. Salary: $790,000	Bonus: $518,082
Savings Plan: Y	Stock Purch. Plan:		Second Exec. Salary: $638,075	Bonus: $377,003

OTHER THOUGHTS:

Apparent Women Officers or Directors: 2
Hot Spot for Advancement for Women/Minorities: Y

LOCATIONS: ("Y" = Yes)

West:	Southwest:	Midwest:	Southeast:	Northeast:	International:
Y	Y	Y	Y	Y	Y

AMERICAN SKIING COMPANY

www.peaks.com

Industry Group Code: 713920 Ranks within this company's industry group: Sales: 2 Profits: 2

Print Media/Publishing:	Movies:	Equipment/Supplies:	Broadcast/Cable:	Music/Audio:	Sports/Games/Gambling:	
Newspapers:	Movie Theaters:	Equipment/Supplies:	Broadcast TV:	Music Production:	Games/Sports:	Y
Magazines:	Movie Production:	Gambling Equipment:	Cable TV:	Retail Music:	Retail Games Stores:	
Books:	TV/Video Prod.:	Special Services:	Satellite Broadcast:	Retail Audio Equip.:	Stadiums/Teams:	
Book Stores:	Video Rental:	Advertising Services:	Radio:	Music Print./Dist.:	Gambling/Casinos:	
Distribution/Printing:	Video Distribution:	Info. Sys. Software:	Online Information:	Multimedia:	Rides/Theme Parks:	

TYPES OF BUSINESS:

Ski Resorts
Real Estate Development
Alpine Resort Villages

BRANDS/DIVISIONS/AFFILIATES:

Canyons (The)
Steamboat
Sugarloaf/USA
Killington
Attitash Bear Peak
Mount Snow
Grand Summit Resort Properties, Inc.
Steamboat Grand Resort Hotel & Condominiums

CONTACTS: Note: Officers with more than one job title may be intentionally listed here more than once.

William J. Fair, CEO
Hernan R. Martinez, COO
William J. Fair, Pres.
Betsy Wallace, CFO/Sr. VP
Franklin Carey, Jr., Sr. VP-Mktg. & Sales
Foster A. Stewart, Jr., General Counsel/Corp. Sec./Sr. VP
Helen E. Wallace, Treas.
Stan Hansen, Sr. VP-Real Estate & Planning
Christopher Diamond, Pres., Steamboat Resort

Phone: 435-615-0340	**Fax:** 435-615-4780	
Toll-Free:		
Address: 136 Heber Ave., Ste. 303, Park City, UT 84060 US		

GROWTH PLANS/SPECIAL FEATURES:

American Skiing Company (ASC) owns and operates eight major ski resorts in New England and the Rockies. The resorts include Pico Mountain, Mount Snow and Killington in Vermont; Sugarloaf/USA and Sunday River in Maine; Attitash Bear Peak in New Hampshire; Steamboat in Steamboat Springs, Colorado; and the Canyons in Park City, Utah. The Canyons and Steamboat are rated among the best ski resorts in North America, and three of ASC's other resorts are ranked in the top 10 eastern resorts. As well as operating alpine resorts, the company develops mountainside condominiums and vacation timeshares. ASC operates alpine villages at prime locations within Sunday River, Mount Snow, Steamboat and Sugarloaf/USA, with new buildings currently under construction at Sugarloaf/USA. Recently, Mount Snow agreed to sell its separately operated Haystack Ski Resort in Wilmington, Vermont. Additionally, the company's Grand Summit Resort Properties, Inc. subsidiary completed an auction of units in its Steamboat Grand Resort Hotel & Condominiums complex in March 2006.

FINANCIALS: Sales and profits are in thousands of dollars—add 000 to get the full amount. 2007 Note: Financial information for 2007 was not available for all companies at press time.

2007 Sales: $	2007 Profits: $	**U.S. Stock Ticker: AESK**
2006 Sales: $307,810	2006 Profits: $-65,653	**Int'l Ticker:** Int'l Exchange:
2005 Sales: $276,477	2005 Profits: $-73,315	Employees: 1,300
2004 Sales: $284,111	2004 Profits: $-28,502	Fiscal Year Ends: 7/31
2003 Sales: $264,500	2003 Profits: $-44,374	Parent Company:

SALARIES/BENEFITS:

Pension Plan:	ESOP Stock Plan:	Profit Sharing:	Top Exec. Salary: $407,692	Bonus: $28,800
Savings Plan: Y	Stock Purch. Plan:		Second Exec. Salary: $269,300	Bonus: $

OTHER THOUGHTS:

Apparent Women Officers or Directors: 1
Hot Spot for Advancement for Women/Minorities:

LOCATIONS: ("Y" = Yes)

West:	Southwest:	Midwest:	Southeast:	Northeast:	International:
Y				Y	

Note: Financial information, benefits and other data can change quickly and may vary from those stated here.

AMERICAN WAGERING INC   www.americanwagering.com

Industry Group Code: 713290 Ranks within this company's industry group: Sales: 12   Profits: 9

Print Media/Publishing:	Movies:	Equipment/Supplies:		Broadcast/Cable:	Music/Audio:	Sports/Games/Gambling:	
Newspapers:	Movie Theaters:	Equipment/Supplies:		Broadcast TV:	Music Production:	Games/Sports:	
Magazines:	Movie Production:	Gambling Equipment:	Y	Cable TV:	Retail Music:	Retail Games Stores:	
Books:	TV/Video Prod.:	Special Services:	Y	Satellite Broadcast:	Retail Audio Equip.:	Stadiums/Teams:	
Book Stores:	Video Rental:	Advertising Services:		Radio:	Music Print./Dist.:	Gambling/Casinos:	Y
Distribution/Printing:	Video Distribution:	Info. Sys. Software:		Online Information:	Multimedia:	Rides/Theme Parks:	

TYPES OF BUSINESS:

Gambling Equipment
Sports Book Facilities
Race Book Computer Systems
Casino-Hotel

BRANDS/DIVISIONS/AFFILIATES:

Leroy's Horse and Sports Place, Inc.
AWI Manufacturing, Inc.
AWI Gaming, Inc.
Sturgeon's, LLC
Sturgeon's Inn & Casino
Computerized Bookmaking Systems, Inc.

CONTACTS: *Note: Officers with more than one job title may be intentionally listed here more than once.*

Victor J. Salerno, CEO
Victor J. Salerno, COO
Victor J. Salerno, Pres.
Melody Sulllivan, CFO
John Salerno, Sec.
Melody Sulllivan, Treas.
Bruce Dewing, Pres., AWIG
Victor J. Salerno, Chmn.

Phone: 702-735-5529	Fax: 702-735-0142
Toll-Free:	
Address: 675 Grier Dr., Las Vegas, NV 89119 US	

GROWTH PLANS/SPECIAL FEATURES:

American Wagering, Inc. was originally formed in 1995 as a holding company for Leroy's Horse and Sports Place. The company operates through three segments: wagering, systems and hotel/casino. The wagering segment is comprised of Leroy's Horse & Sports Place, Inc. and AWI International, Inc. Leroy's owns and operates 59 satellite race and sports books in the state of Nevada. AWI International provides services to gaming suppliers and gaming operators in foreign jurisdictions. Services include remote oddsmaking and posting of odds for regional sporting events (Australian-Rules Football, cricket, polo, etc.); remote operation and management of the gaming supplier's or operator's race and sports book system in the foreign jurisdiction; and the providing of wagering content to the gaming supplier or operator that is offered to the patron with the resulting wagers having been processed by the gaming supplier's or operator's race and sports system. In the systems segment, Computerized Bookmaking Systems, Inc. (CBS) designs, sells, installs and maintains computerized race and sports book systems for the Nevada gaming industry. CBS is used to process all wagers placed through Leroy's race and sports books satellites. AWI Manufacturing, Inc. (AWIM) leases self-service race and sports wagering kiosks to CBS customers. The hotel/casino segment is comprised of Sturgeon's, LLC and AWI Gaming, Inc. (AWIG). Sturgeon's, LLC owns and operates Sturgeon's Inn & Casino in Lovelock, Nevada. AWIG is the sole member of Sturgeon's, LLC; its purpose is to acquire other hotel/casino properties.

FINANCIALS: Sales and profits are in thousands of dollars—add 000 to get the full amount. 2007 Note: Financial information for 2007 was not available for all companies at press time.

2007 Sales: $19,370	2007 Profits: $1,831	**U.S. Stock Ticker: BETM**
2006 Sales: $12,524	2006 Profits: $ 419	**Int'l Ticker:** Int'l Exchange:
2005 Sales: $11,108	2005 Profits: $-1,128	Employees: 224
2004 Sales: $10,891	2004 Profits: $- 487	Fiscal Year Ends: 1/31
2003 Sales: $11,600	2003 Profits: $ 400	Parent Company:

SALARIES/BENEFITS:

Pension Plan:	ESOP Stock Plan:	Profit Sharing:	Top Exec. Salary: $240,000	Bonus: $21,791
Savings Plan: Y	Stock Purch. Plan:		Second Exec. Salary: $180,000	Bonus: $8,717

OTHER THOUGHTS:

Apparent Women Officers or Directors:
Hot Spot for Advancement for Women/Minorities:

LOCATIONS: ("Y" = Yes)

West:	Southwest:	Midwest:	Southeast:	Northeast:	International:
Y					

AMERISTAR CASINOS INC

www.ameristarcasinos.com

Industry Group Code: 721120 Ranks within this company's industry group: Sales: 8 Profits: 8

Print Media/Publishing:	Movies:	Equipment/Supplies:	Broadcast/Cable:	Music/Audio:	Sports/Games/Gambling:	
Newspapers:	Movie Theaters:	Equipment/Supplies:	Broadcast TV:	Music Production:	Games/Sports:	
Magazines:	Movie Production:	Gambling Equipment:	Cable TV:	Retail Music:	Retail Games Stores:	
Books:	TV/Video Prod.:	Special Services:	Satellite Broadcast:	Retail Audio Equip.:	Stadiums/Teams:	Y
Book Stores:	Video Rental:	Advertising Services:	Radio:	Music Print./Dist.:	Gambling/Casinos:	
Distribution/Printing:	Video Distribution:	Info. Sys. Software:	Online Information:	Multimedia:	Rides/Theme Parks:	

TYPES OF BUSINESS:

Casino Resorts
Casino Management

BRANDS/DIVISIONS/AFFILIATES:

Cactus Pete's Resort Casino
Ameristar Casino Hotel Kansas City
Ameristar Casino St. Charles
Ameristar Casino Hotel Council Bluffs
Ameristar Casino Hotel Vicksburg
Horseshu Hotel & Casino
Mountain High Casino
Kids Quest

CONTACTS: *Note: Officers with more than one job title may be intentionally listed here more than once.*

John M. Boushy, CEO
John M. Boushy, Pres.
Thomas M. Steinbauer, CFO/Exec. VP-Finance
Paul Eagleton, Chief Mktg. Officer
Ursula Conway, CIO
Mary Siero, VP-IT
Peter C. Walsh, General Counsel/Sr. VP
Angela R. Frost, Sr. VP-Oper.
Gordon R. Kanofsky, Exec. VP-Corp. Dev., Gov't & Legal Affairs
Karen J. Lynn, VP-Comm.
Thomas Malone, VP-Finance/Controller
Jack Mohn., VP-Design
Alan Rose, Sr. VP-Construction
Matthew A. Miele, Jr., VP-Procurement
Adrian Caldwell, Sr. VP/General Mgr.-Ameristar Vicksburg
Ray H. Neilsen, Chmn.

Phone: 702-567-7000	Fax: 702-369-8860
Toll-Free:	
Address: 3773 Howard Hughes Pkwy., Ste. 490 S., Las Vegas, NV 89169 US	

GROWTH PLANS/SPECIAL FEATURES:

Ameristar Casinos, Inc. (ASCA) is a gaming and entertainment company that develops, owns and operates casino facilities in six states: Colorado, Nevada, Nebraska, Missouri, Mississippi and Iowa. The company's subsidiaries include ASCA St. Charles; ASCA Kansas City; ASCA Council Bluffs in Omaha, Nebraska and southwestern Iowa; ASCA Vicksburg in Jackson, Mississippi and Monroe, Louisiana; ASCA Black Hawk in Denver, Colorado; and Cactus Pete's and the Horseshu in Jackpot, Nevada. The firm also offers a variety of casual dining and upscale restaurants as well as sports bars and private clubs for Star Awards members. ASCA St. Charles additionally offers two ballrooms for its guests, five meeting rooms and an executive board room. ASCA Kansas City includes a casino along with an 18-screen movie theater and amusements for children, which include arcades and an activity center named Kids Quest. ASCA Vicksburg is a permanently docked riverboat casino located on the Mississippi River while ASCA Council Bluffs offers a cruising riverboat casino that travels down the Missouri River. The Jackpot properties hold an outdoor entertainment facility that seats 3,550 people, arcades and tennis courts. The firm offers slot machines as well as a variety of table games such as blackjack, craps, roulette and live poker. In addition, ASCA St. Charles, ASCA Kansas City and Cactus Pete's offer poker, keno and sports book wagering. Ameristar leads the casino industry in the implementation of cashless slot technology and new-generation multi-coin (nickel and penny denomination) slot machines. In 2007, the company formed a partnership with Food Bank of the Rockies to provide meals for individuals and families in Colorado. ASCA also recently hosted a charity golf tournament that raised over a million dollars for paralysis research.

ASCA offers its employees life insurance, disability insurance, tuition reimbursement and employee assistance programs.

FINANCIALS: Sales and profits are in thousands of dollars—add 000 to get the full amount. 2007 Note: Financial information for 2007 was not available for all companies at press time.

2007 Sales: $	2007 Profits: $	**U.S. Stock Ticker: ASCA**
2006 Sales: $1,000,298	2006 Profits: $59,565	**Int'l Ticker:** Int'l Exchange:
2005 Sales: $961,358	2005 Profits: $66,285	Employees: 7,200
2004 Sales: $854,700	2004 Profits: $61,979	Fiscal Year Ends: 12/31
2003 Sales: $782,000	2003 Profits: $47,600	Parent Company:

SALARIES/BENEFITS:

Pension Plan:	ESOP Stock Plan:	Profit Sharing:	Top Exec. Salary: $850,000	Bonus: $703,568
Savings Plan: Y	Stock Purch. Plan:		Second Exec. Salary: $448,943	Bonus: $316,606

OTHER THOUGHTS:

Apparent Women Officers or Directors: 5
Hot Spot for Advancement for Women/Minorities: Y

LOCATIONS: ("Y" = Yes)

West:	Southwest:	Midwest:	Southeast:	Northeast:	International:
Y		Y	Y		

AMF BOWLING WORLDWIDE INC   www.amf.com

Industry Group Code: 713950 Ranks within this company's industry group: Sales: 1   Profits: 1

Print Media/Publishing:	Movies:	Equipment/Supplies:		Broadcast/Cable:	Music/Audio:	Sports/Games/Gambling:	
Newspapers:	Movie Theaters:	Equipment/Supplies:	Y	Broadcast TV:	Music Production:	Games/Sports:	Y
Magazines:	Movie Production:	Gambling Equipment:		Cable TV:	Retail Music:	Retail Games Stores:	
Books:	TV/Video Prod.:	Special Services:		Satellite Broadcast:	Retail Audio Equip.:	Stadiums/Teams:	
Book Stores:	Video Rental:	Advertising Services:		Radio:	Music Print./Dist.:	Gambling/Casinos:	
Distribution/Printing:	Video Distribution:	Info. Sys. Software:		Online Information:	Multimedia:	Rides/Theme Parks:	

TYPES OF BUSINESS:

Bowling Equipment
Bowling Centers
Billiards Tables
Bowling Software

BRANDS/DIVISIONS/AFFILIATES:

QubicaAMF
Highway 66
300 Centers
Code Hennessy & Simmons, LLC
QubicaAMF Worldwide
Skiller
300 Grill
Thunder Bowl

CONTACTS: *Note: Officers with more than one job title may be intentionally listed here more than once.*

Frederick R. Hipp, CEO
Frederick R. Hipp, Pres.
William McDonnell, CFO/VP
Merrell C. Wreden, VP-Mktg.
Anthony J. Ponsiglione, VP-Human Resources
J. Simon Shearer, Sr. VP-Facilities & Design
Joseph F. Scarnaty, VP-Food & Beverage

Phone: 804-730-4000	Fax: 804-559-6276
Toll-Free: 800-342-5263	
Address: 7313 Bell Creek Rd., Mechanicsville, VA 23111 US	

GROWTH PLANS/SPECIAL FEATURES:

AMF Bowling Worldwide, Inc., owned by private investment firm Code Hennessy & Simmons, LLC, is one of the largest owners and operators of commercial bowling centers in the U.S., with 361 bowling centers nationwide and 13 internationally. In fiscal 2006, bowling centers contributed roughly 93% of consolidated revenue AMF operates through three business segments: products, bowling centers and Holdings. The product segment includes its joint venture QubicaAMF. Through QubicaAMF, the company is one of the world's leading manufacturers of bowling center equipment, such as automatic pinspotters (which it introduced in 1946), scoring equipment, bowling center furniture, bowling pins, high-performance lanes, ball returns and spare parts, as well as bowling products such as shoes, shirts, balls and ball bags. The firm's bowling center segment recently developed new concept bowling centers featuring billiards, darts, video games, glow in the dark miniature golf and Xtreme Bowling with music and lights. In addition, the 300 brand includes fully stocked bars, lane side service and restaurants (called 300 Grill) which feature pizza, burgers and salads. These new centers, called 300 Centers, are located in Austin, Atlanta, Dallas, San Jose, Long Island and New York City. AMF owns 50% of QubicaAMF Worldwide, a joint venture with Italian manufacturer Qubica Worldwide. QubicaAMF manufactures bowling and amusement products including Bowland X and BES scoring systems; Conqueror Pro bowling management software, Thunder Bowl, Skiller, Pin Bowl and Highway 66 miniature bowling.

The company offers its employees benefits including flexible spending accounts, incentive programs, a 401(k) plan, tuition assistance, scholarships and education programs, and employee discounts on bowling, food and bowling products. AMF also sponsors the Dick Weber Scholarship League, which awards $350,000 worth of scholarship funds to young bowlers annually.

FINANCIALS: Sales and profits are in thousands of dollars—add 000 to get the full amount. 2007 Note: Financial information for 2007 was not available for all companies at press time.

2007 Sales: $	2007 Profits: $	U.S. Stock Ticker: Private
2006 Sales: $499,149	2006 Profits: $-15,885	Int'l Ticker: Int'l Exchange:
2005 Sales: $569,578	2005 Profits: $-10,698	Employees: 9,362
2004 Sales: $678,800	2004 Profits: $-66,800	Fiscal Year Ends: 6/30
2003 Sales: $667,600	2003 Profits: $3,400	Parent Company:

SALARIES/BENEFITS:

Pension Plan:	ESOP Stock Plan:	Profit Sharing:	Top Exec. Salary: $600,000	Bonus: $
Savings Plan: Y	Stock Purch. Plan:		Second Exec. Salary: $288,555	Bonus: $28,800

OTHER THOUGHTS:

Apparent Women Officers or Directors:
Hot Spot for Advancement for Women/Minorities:

LOCATIONS: ("Y" = Yes)

West:	Southwest:	Midwest:	Southeast:	Northeast:	International:
Y	Y	Y	Y	Y	Y

Note: Financial information, benefits and other data can change quickly and may vary from those stated here.

ANDERSON COS

www.andersonnews.com

Industry Group Code: 422920 Ranks within this company's industry group: Sales: Profits:

Print Media/Publishing:	Movies:	Equipment/Supplies:		Broadcast/Cable:	Music/Audio:		Sports/Games/Gambling:
Newspapers:	Movie Theaters:	Equipment/Supplies:		Broadcast TV:	Music Production:		Games/Sports:
Magazines:	Movie Production:	Gambling Equipment:		Cable TV:	Retail Music:		Retail Games Stores:
Books:	TV/Video Prod.:	Special Services:	Y	Satellite Broadcast:	Retail Audio Equip.:		Stadiums/Teams:
Book Stores:	Video Rental:	Advertising Services:		Radio:	Music Print./Dist.:	Y	Gambling/Casinos:
Distribution/Printing:	Video Distribution:	Info. Sys. Software:		Online Information:	Multimedia:		Rides/Theme Parks:

TYPES OF BUSINESS:

Book & Magazine Distributor
Music Distribution
Online Music Distribution

BRANDS/DIVISIONS/AFFILIATES:

Anderson Merchandisers LP
Geneva Media LLC
Liquid Digital Media

CONTACTS: Note: Officers with more than one job title may be intentionally listed here more than once.

Charles Anderson, CEO
Charles Anderson, Pres.
John Campbell, Sr. VP-Finance
Joel R. Anderson, Chmn.

Phone: 865-584-9765	Fax: 865-584-3498
Toll-Free:	
Address: 6016 Brookvale Ln., Ste. 151, Knoxville, TN 37919 US	

GROWTH PLANS/SPECIAL FEATURES:

Anderson News, LLC is a book and magazine distributor. It manages the shipping, distribution, merchandising and promotion of products produced by outside publishers and manufacturers. Anderson News markets thousands of books and magazines to retailers. Currently, approximately 40,000 retailers in the U.S in 45 states are serviced by the company. The firm serves retailers including bookstores, mass merchants, discount retailers and grocery stores. Its product lines include books, magazines, maps, comics and collectibles. Anderson News employs Mosaic Category Management, a proprietary software program, to increase store sales and efficiencies. The company also offers an online data-analysis tool for Anderson News clients. Magazines Anderson News distributes include Meredith Wedding Series, Better Homes and Gardens Creative Collection Series and All Recipes.com. The books that Anderson News distributes include such titles as The House by Danielle Steel; Irish Dreams by Nora Roberts; Angels All Over Town by Luanne Rice; The Templar Legacy by Steve Berry; McKettrick's Luck by Linda Lael Miller; and All Night Long by Jayne Ann Krentz. The company also runs Point-of-Purchase display promotions. Anderson News, LLC is the parent company of Geneva Media LLC through which it owns Liquid Digital Media. Liquid Digital Media is the online music distributor for Wal-Mart. Anderson Merchandisers, LP is an affiliate of the company based in Amarillo, Texas that distributes CDs to Wal-Mart.

FINANCIALS: Sales and profits are in thousands of dollars—add 000 to get the full amount. 2007 Note: Financial information for 2007 was not available for all companies at press time.

2007 Sales: $	2007 Profits: $	U.S. Stock Ticker: Private
2006 Sales: $	2006 Profits: $	Int'l Ticker: Int'l Exchange:
2005 Sales: $2,696,000	2005 Profits: $	Employees: 12,100
2004 Sales: $	2004 Profits: $	Fiscal Year Ends: 12/31
2003 Sales: $	2003 Profits: $	Parent Company:

SALARIES/BENEFITS:

Pension Plan:	ESOP Stock Plan:	Profit Sharing:	Top Exec. Salary: $	Bonus: $
Savings Plan:	Stock Purch. Plan:		Second Exec. Salary: $	Bonus: $

OTHER THOUGHTS:

Apparent Women Officers or Directors:
Hot Spot for Advancement for Women/Minorities:

LOCATIONS: ("Y" = Yes)

West:	Southwest:	Midwest:	Southeast:	Northeast:	International:
	Y		Y		

ANHEUSER BUSCH COS INC   www.anheuser-busch.com

Industry Group Code: 312120 Ranks within this company's industry group: Sales: 1 Profits: 1

Print Media/Publishing:	Movies:	Equipment/Supplies:		Broadcast/Cable:	Music/Audio:	Sports/Games/Gambling:
Newspapers:	Movie Theaters:	Equipment/Supplies:		Broadcast TV:	Music Production:	Games/Sports:
Magazines:	Movie Production:	Gambling Equipment:		Cable TV:	Retail Music:	Retail Games Stores:
Books:	TV/Video Prod.:	Special Services:	Y	Satellite Broadcast:	Retail Audio Equip.:	Stadiums/Teams:
Book Stores:	Video Rental:	Advertising Services:		Radio:	Music Print./Dist.:	Gambling/Casinos:
Distribution/Printing:	Video Distribution:	Info. Sys. Software:		Online Information:	Multimedia:	Rides/Theme Parks:

TYPES OF BUSINESS:

Breweries
Agriculture-Grain Processing
Packaging
Recycling
Rail Shipping
Transportation
Theme Parks
Resort & Spa

BRANDS/DIVISIONS/AFFILIATES:

Anheuser-Busch, Inc. (ABI)
Budweiser
Michelob
Busch Agricultural Resources, Inc.
Metal Container Corp.
Busch Gardens
SeaWorld
Rolling Rock

CONTACTS: Note: Officers with more than one job title may be intentionally listed here more than once.

August A. Busch, IV, CEO
August A. Busch, IV, Pres.
W. Randolph Baker, CFO/VP
David A. Peacock, VP-Mktg., AB Inc.
John T. Farrell, VP-Human Resources
Joseph P/ Castellano, CIO/VP
Douglas J. Muhleman, VP-Brewing Oper. & Tech.
Mark T. Bobak, Chief Legal Officer/VP
Michael J. Owens, VP-Bus. Oper., AB Inc.
Robert C. Lachky, Exec. VP-Global Industry Dev., AB Inc.
Francine I. Katz, VP-Comm. & Consumer Affairs
John F. Kelly, VP/Controller
Thomas W. Santel, Pres., AB Int'l Inc.
Michael S. Harding, CEO/Pres., AB Packaging Group, Inc.
Keith M. Kasen, Chmn./Pres., Busch Entertainment
Anthony T. Ponturo, VP-Global Media & Sports Mktg., AB, Inc.
August A. Busch, III, Chmn.
Stephen J. Burrows, CEO/Pres., APAC Oper., AB Int'l Inc.

Phone: 314-577-2000	Fax: 314-577-2900
Toll-Free: 800-342-5283	
Address: 1 Busch Pl., St. Louis, MO 63118 US	

GROWTH PLANS/SPECIAL FEATURES:

Anheuser-Busch Companies, Inc. (ABC) runs Anheuser-Busch, Inc. (ABI), the world's largest brewer of beer. ABC is also the parent company of Busch Entertainment Corporation, as well as several packaging and real estate companies. ABI produces beer through its 12 breweries, marketing it under brand names including Budweiser, Michelob, Busch, Natural Ice, Bare Knuckle and ZiegenBock, among others. ABI also brews Kirin beer in cooperation with Japan's Kirin Brewing Company and owns interest in Seattle-based Redhook Ale Brewery and Portland's Widmer Brothers Brewing Co. ABC's Busch Agricultural Resources, Inc. operates rice-milling facilities, grain elevators, barley processing plants and research facilities. The company's packaging business operates through Metal Container Corp.; Anheuser-Busch Recycling Corp.; Precision Printing and Packaging; and Eagle Packaging. ABC also owns and operates Manufacturers Railway Co., a transportation service business. Busch Entertainment Corp. owns and operates nine theme parks. Busch Gardens in Tampa Bay, Florida is an African-themed park featuring an 80-acre setting of the Serengeti Plain, thrill-rides and live entertainment. Busch Gardens in Williamsburg, Virginia, features European themed attractions, rides and shows. Water Country USA in Williamsburg is the mid-Atlantic's largest water park. SeaWorld parks in Orlando, Florida; San Diego, California; and San Antonio, Texas and Discovery Cove in Orlando offer marine-life entertainment and education. Sesame Place, outside of Philadelphia is a Sesame Street-themed park with water attractions and live shows. Busch Properties, Inc. operates the Kingsmill resort and spa in Williamsburg. The firm has recently been investing in Chinese beer, and it increased its interest in Tsingtao Brewing Co. to 27%. In May 2006, Anheuser-Busch agreed to buy the Rolling Rock brand from InBev $82 million.

Anheuser-Busch offers employees tuition reimbursement and employee assistance. Anheuser-Busch Entertainment also offers adoption benefits, free admission and family passes to Anheuser-Busch parks, complimentary event tickets and complimentary beer for employees over age 21.

FINANCIALS: Sales and profits are in thousands of dollars—add 000 to get the full amount. 2007 Note: Financial information for 2007 was not available for all companies at press time.

2007 Sales: $	2007 Profits: $	U.S. Stock Ticker: BUD
2006 Sales: $15,717,000	2006 Profits: $1,965,200	Int'l Ticker: Int'l Exchange:
2005 Sales: $15,035,700	2005 Profits: $1,744,400	Employees: 30,183
2004 Sales: $14,934,200	2004 Profits: $2,118,700	Fiscal Year Ends: 12/31
2003 Sales: $14,147,000	2003 Profits: $2,076,000	Parent Company:

SALARIES/BENEFITS:

Pension Plan: Y	ESOP Stock Plan:	Profit Sharing:	Top Exec. Salary: $1,399,516	Bonus: $3,000,000
Savings Plan: Y	Stock Purch. Plan: Y		Second Exec. Salary: $972,917	Bonus: $1,200,000

OTHER THOUGHTS:

Apparent Women Officers or Directors: 2
Hot Spot for Advancement for Women/Minorities: Y

LOCATIONS: ("Y" = Yes)

West:	Southwest:	Midwest:	Southeast:	Northeast:	International:
Y	Y	Y	Y	Y	Y

Note: Financial information, benefits and other data can change quickly and may vary from those stated here.

ANSCHUTZ ENTERTAINMENT GROUP www.aegworldwide.com

Industry Group Code: 711211 Ranks within this company's industry group: Sales: Profits:

Print Media/Publishing:	Movies:		Equipment/Supplies:		Broadcast/Cable:	Music/Audio:	Sports/Games/Gambling:	
Newspapers:	Movie Theaters:	Y	Equipment/Supplies:		Broadcast TV:	Music Production:	Games/Sports:	Y
Magazines:	Movie Production:	Y	Gambling Equipment:		Cable TV:	Retail Music:	Retail Games Stores:	
Books:	TV/Video Prod.:	Y	Special Services:	Y	Satellite Broadcast:	Retail Audio Equip.:	Stadiums/Teams:	Y
Book Stores:	Video Rental:		Advertising Services:	Y	Radio:	Music Print./Dist.:	Gambling/Casinos:	
Distribution/Printing:	Video Distribution:		Info. Sys. Software:		Online Information:	Multimedia:	Rides/Theme Parks:	

TYPES OF BUSINESS:

Stadiums & Sports Teams
Sports Team Franchises
Sports Facilities Management & Development
Entertainment Complexes
Entertainment Investments
Concerts & Live Entertainment Events
Filmed Entertainment
Marketing & Consulting Services

BRANDS/DIVISIONS/AFFILIATES:

Anschutz Company (The)
STAPLES Center
Regal Entertainment Group
Los Angeles Kings
O2 (The)
L.A. Live
Home Depot Center
Walden Media

CONTACTS: *Note: Officers with more than one job title may be intentionally listed here more than once.*

Timothy J. Leiweke, CEO
Timothy J. Leiweke, Pres.
Randy Phillips, CEO/Pres., AEG Live
Philip Anschutz, Chmn./CEO-The Anschutz Company
David Weil, CEO-Anschutz Film Group
Cary Granat, CEO-Walden Media

Phone: 213-763-7700	Fax: 303-298-8881
Toll-Free:	
Address: 1100 S. Flower St., Los Angeles, CA 90015 US	

GROWTH PLANS/SPECIAL FEATURES:

Anschutz Entertainment Group, Inc. (AEG) is a subsidiary of Anschutz Corporation and a leading sports and entertainment investment, development and management company. The firm owns the STAPLES Center, Toyota Sports Center, Toyota Park, NOKIA Theatre Times Square, The Forum and the Nokia Theater at Grand Prairie. Furthermore, the company cooperated with Home Depot to build the Home Depot National Training Center in Carson, California, an official U.S. Olympic training site. The company recently designed The O2, a 28 acre development located in the eastern part of London along the Thames River which includes a 20,000 seat arena. AEG also controls a number of domestic sports franchises, including the Los Angeles Kings, Los Angeles Riptide, Chicago Fire, Reading Royals, Houston Dynamo and the Manchester Monarchs. The firm's subsidiary AEG Marketing is a sponsorship, consulting and sales company. AEG Creative is a full service marketing and advertising agency. Parent firm Anschutz Corporation is an investment company that also has a 79% stake in the Regal Entertainment Group. Other interests of Anschutz Corp. include stakes in film and television production companies Crusader Entertainment and Walden Media. AEG Live is one of the world's leading concert promotion and touring companies comprised of stand-alone affiliate divisions, including AEG Live Events, AEG-TV and national entertainment promotion and touring divisions AEG LIVE Tours & Special Events, Concerts West, Goldenvoice, The Messina Group and AEG Exhibitions. AEG is currently overseeing the development of L.A. LIVE, a four million square foot, $2.5 billion downtown Los Angeles sports, residential and entertainment district featuring NOKIA Theatre Los Angeles, a 7,100 seat live theatre; a 54 story, 1,001 room convention headquarters hotel; Club NOKIA, a 2,200 capacity live music venue; a 14 screen Regal Cineplex; broadcast facilities for ESPN; and entertainment, restaurant and office space.

FINANCIALS: Sales and profits are in thousands of dollars—add 000 to get the full amount. 2007 Note: Financial information for 2007 was not available for all companies at press time.

2007 Sales: $	2007 Profits: $	**U.S. Stock Ticker: Subsidiary**
2006 Sales: $	2006 Profits: $	**Int'l Ticker:** Int'l Exchange:
2005 Sales: $	2005 Profits: $	Employees:
2004 Sales: $	2004 Profits: $	Fiscal Year Ends: 12/31
2003 Sales: $	2003 Profits: $	Parent Company: ANSCHUTZ COMPANY (THE)

SALARIES/BENEFITS:

Pension Plan:	ESOP Stock Plan:	Profit Sharing:	Top Exec. Salary: $	Bonus: $
Savings Plan:	Stock Purch. Plan:		Second Exec. Salary: $	Bonus: $

OTHER THOUGHTS:

Apparent Women Officers or Directors:
Hot Spot for Advancement for Women/Minorities:

LOCATIONS: ("Y" = Yes)

West:	Southwest:	Midwest:	Southeast:	Northeast:	International:
Y	Y	Y	Y	Y	Y

Note: Financial information, benefits and other data can change quickly and may vary from those stated here.

AOL LLC

www.aol.com

Industry Group Code: 514191 Ranks within this company's industry group: Sales: 2 Profits:

Print Media/Publishing:	Movies:	Equipment/Supplies:		Broadcast/Cable:	Music/Audio:	Sports/Games/Gambling:
Newspapers:	Movie Theaters:	Equipment/Supplies:		Broadcast TV:	Music Production:	Games/Sports:
Magazines:	Movie Production:	Gambling Equipment:		Cable TV:	Retail Music:	Retail Games Stores:
Books:	TV/Video Prod.:	Special Services:	Y	Satellite Broadcast:	Retail Audio Equip.:	Stadiums/Teams:
Book Stores:	Video Rental:	Advertising Services:	Y	Radio:	Music Print./Dist.:	Gambling/Casinos:
Distribution/Printing:	Video Distribution:	Info. Sys. Software:		Online Information:	Multimedia:	Rides/Theme Parks:

TYPES OF BUSINESS:

Online Content Provider
Online Music Services
Online Communities
Entertainment & Information Offerings
Instant Messaging
E-Mail
VoIP Telephony
Internet Service Provider

BRANDS/DIVISIONS/AFFILIATES:

Time Warner Inc
America Online, Inc.
Netscape
MapQuest
ICQ
Winamp
Questions and Answer Service Yedda, Inc.
ADTECH AG

CONTACTS: *Note: Officers with more than one job title may be intentionally listed here more than once.*

Randy Falco, CEO
Ron Grant, COO
Ron Grant, Pres.
Nisha Kumar, CFO/Exec. VP
John Burbank, Chief Mktg. Officer
Dave Harmon, Acting Exec. VP-Human Resources
Ted Cahall, Exec. VP-Platforms & Technologies
Kevin Conroy, Exec. VP-Prod.
Ira Parker, General Counsel/Exec. VP
Jon Werther, Exec. VP-Bus. Dev.
Tricia P. Wallace, Exec. VP-Corp. Comm.
Tiane M. Gordon, Sr. VP-Diversity & Inclusion
Bill Wilson, Exec. VP-Programming
Dave Morgan, Exec. VP-Global Advertising Strategy
Kimberly Partoll, Exec. VP-Customer Mgmt. & Paid Svcs.
Randy Falco, Chmn.
Maneesh Dhir, Exec. VP-Int'l

Phone: 703-265-1000	**Fax:** 703-433-7283
Toll-Free:	
Address: 22000 AOL Way, Dulles, VA 20166 US	

GROWTH PLANS/SPECIAL FEATURES:

AOL LLC, formerly America Online, Inc., a subsidiary of Time Warner, Inc., is a provider of online content including streaming video, voice over Internet protocol (VoIP) phone service, anti-virus software and parental controls. Though AOL had traditionally acquired revenue as a subscription Internet Service Provider (ISP), the company underwent a massive corporate restructuring in 2006 which de-emphasized the ISP aspects of the business and began offering services free to the general public that had formerly only been available to subscribers. As part of this restructuring, the company officially changed its name from America Online, Inc. to AOL LLC. Additionally, it began offering its suites of anti-virus software and Internet parental controls under the names Active Virus Shield and AOL Parental Controls, respectively. AOL has launched several new services including: My eAddress, which allows users to create their own custom e-mail address for free; In2TV, a broadband television network offering streaming and downloadable television shows from Time Warner's library; Gold Rush, an interactive treasure hunt game; and True Stories, a website that offers documentary films in both free streaming and low cost downloadable formats. The company owns several highly recognized brands such as Mapquest, an online map and directions provider; Winamp, a music player program; instant messaging programs ICQ and AOL Instant Messenger, which became an open source program in 2006; and the Netscape search engine. In 2007, AOL acquired TACODA, which focuses on behavioral solutions for advertisers and publishers; Questions and Answer Service Yedda, Inc., an Israeli semantic social search; ADTECH AG, an international online ad-serving company; and Third Screen Media, a mobile advertising network and mobile ad-serving and management platform provider. In November 2007, the company agreed to acquire Quigo, a site and content-targeted advertising company.

FINANCIALS: Sales and profits are in thousands of dollars—add 000 to get the full amount. 2007 Note: Financial information for 2007 was not available for all companies at press time.

2007 Sales: $	2007 Profits: $	**U.S. Stock Ticker:** Subsidiary
2006 Sales: $	2006 Profits: $	**Int'l Ticker:** **Int'l Exchange:**
2005 Sales: $8,300,000	2005 Profits: $	**Employees:** 19,000
2004 Sales: $8,692,000	2004 Profits: $	**Fiscal Year Ends:** 12/31
2003 Sales: $6,428,000	2003 Profits: $	**Parent Company:** TIME WARNER INC

SALARIES/BENEFITS:

Pension Plan:	ESOP Stock Plan:	Profit Sharing:	Top Exec. Salary: $	Bonus: $
Savings Plan:	Stock Purch. Plan:		Second Exec. Salary: $	Bonus: $

OTHER THOUGHTS:

Apparent Women Officers or Directors: 4
Hot Spot for Advancement for Women/Minorities: Y

LOCATIONS: ("Y" = Yes)

West:	Southwest:	Midwest:	Southeast:	Northeast:	International:
				Y	Y

APPLE INC

www.apple.com

Industry Group Code: 334111 Ranks within this company's industry group: Sales: 1   Profits: 1

Print Media/Publishing:	Movies:	Equipment/Supplies:		Broadcast/Cable:		Music/Audio:		Sports/Games/Gambling:
Newspapers:	Movie Theaters:	Equipment/Supplies:	Y	Broadcast TV:	Y	Music Production:		Games/Sports:
Magazines:	Movie Production:	Gambling Equipment:		Cable TV:		Retail Music:	Y	Retail Games Stores:
Books:	TV/Video Prod.:	Special Services:		Satellite Broadcast:		Retail Audio Equip.:		Stadiums/Teams:
Book Stores:	Video Rental:	Advertising Services:	Y	Radio:		Music Print./Dist.:	Y	Gambling/Casinos:
Distribution/Printing:	Video Distribution:	Info. Sys. Software:		Online Information:		Multimedia:		Rides/Theme Parks:

TYPES OF BUSINESS:

Computer Hardware-PCs
Software
Computer Accessories
Retail Stores
Portable Music Players
Online Music Sales
Cellular Phones
Home Entertainment Software & Systems

BRANDS/DIVISIONS/AFFILIATES:

Apple Computer Inc
MacBook Pro
Xserve
Mac OS X
Intel
iPod
iPhone
Safari

CONTACTS: *Note: Officers with more than one job title may be intentionally listed here more than once.*

Steve P. Jobs, CEO
Timothy D. Cook, COO
Peter Oppenheimer, CFO/Sr. VP
Philip W. Schiller, Sr. VP-Worldwide Prod. Mktg.
Bertrand Serlet, Sr. VP-Software Eng.
Daniel Cooperman, General Counsel
Ronald B. Johnson, Sr. VP-Retail
Jonathan Ive, Sr. VP-Industrial Design
Sina Tamaddon, Sr. VP-Applications
Tony Fadell, Sr. VP-iPod Div.
Bill Campbell, Chmn.

Phone: 408-996-1010	Fax: 408-974-2113
Toll-Free: 800-275-2273	
Address: 1 Infinite Loop, Cupertino, CA 95014 US	

GROWTH PLANS/SPECIAL FEATURES:

Apple, Inc. designs, manufactures and markets personal computers, portable digital music players and mobile communication devices; and sells a variety of related software, services, peripherals and networking solutions. The company's hardware products include the MacBook and MacBook Pro notebook computers; Mac Pro desktop computers; iMac desktop computers; Mac minis; and Xserve servers and Xserve RAID Storage Systems. The firm's Mac desktop and portable systems feature Intel microprocessors, the company's Mac OS X Version 10.5 Leopard operating system and iLife suite of software. Software products include Mac OS X, its proprietary operating system; iLife '08; iWork '08; Final Cut Studio 2; Logic Studio; and FileMaker Pro. Additional products include the iSight digital video cameras; various LCD flat-panel displays; the iPod line of portable digital music players and related accessories; Final Cut Studio, a high-definition video production suite of applications; and the iTunes digital music management software, which allows users to access MP3s to purchase, preview, download, share, organize and transfer to the iPod. Peripheral products include printers, storage devices, memory, digital videos, still cameras, a family of widescreen flat panel displays and Apple TV, which plays iTunes content wirelessly on a widescreen television. The firm operated 200 retail stores by the end of 2007, including stores in Canada, Japan, the U.K. and Italy. Apple's retail stores average an amazing $4,000 in sales per square foot per year. The company is expanding the chain with a new boutique format in high traffic spots like airports. The iPod accounts for a significant portion of the company's revenues, with over 100 million units sold and over 2 billion songs sold via iTunes. In June 2007, Apple released iPhone, which combines a mobile phone, a widescreen iPod with touch controls and wireless internet. In October 2007, Mac OS X Leopard was released and sold over 2 million copies in the first weekend.

FINANCIALS: Sales and profits are in thousands of dollars—add 000 to get the full amount. 2007 Note: Financial information for 2007 was not available for all companies at press time.

2007 Sales: $24,006,000	2007 Profits: $3,496,000	**U.S. Stock Ticker:** AAPL
2006 Sales: $19,315,000	2006 Profits: $1,989,000	**Int'l Ticker:** Int'l Exchange:
2005 Sales: $13,931,000	2005 Profits: $1,328,000	Employees: 23,700
2004 Sales: $8,279,000	2004 Profits: $266,000	Fiscal Year Ends: 9/30
2003 Sales: $6,207,000	2003 Profits: $69,000	Parent Company:

SALARIES/BENEFITS:

Pension Plan:	ESOP Stock Plan:	Profit Sharing:	Top Exec. Salary: $700,014	Bonus: $700,000
Savings Plan: Y	Stock Purch. Plan: Y		Second Exec. Salary: $600,012	Bonus: $600,000

OTHER THOUGHTS:

Apparent Women Officers or Directors:
Hot Spot for Advancement for Women/Minorities:

LOCATIONS: ("Y" = Yes)

West:	Southwest:	Midwest:	Southeast:	Northeast:	International:
Y	Y	Y	Y	Y	Y

ARBITRON INC

www.arbitron.com

Industry Group Code: 541910 **Ranks within this company's industry group:** Sales: 2 Profits: 2

Print Media/Publishing:	Movies:	Equipment/Supplies:		Broadcast/Cable:	Music/Audio:	Sports/Games/Gambling:
Newspapers:	Movie Theaters:	Equipment/Supplies:		Broadcast TV:	Music Production:	Games/Sports:
Magazines:	Movie Production:	Gambling Equipment:		Cable TV:	Retail Music:	Retail Games Stores:
Books:	TV/Video Prod.:	Special Services:	Y	Satellite Broadcast:	Retail Audio Equip.:	Stadiums/Teams:
Book Stores:	Video Rental:	Advertising Services:	Y	Radio:	Music Print./Dist.:	Gambling/Casinos:
Distribution/Printing:	Video Distribution:	Info. Sys. Software:		Online Information:	Multimedia:	Rides/Theme Parks:

TYPES OF BUSINESS:

Radio Audience Ratings
Market Research
Market Research Software & Technology

BRANDS/DIVISIONS/AFFILIATES:

Portable People Meter
Continental Research
Scarborough Research
Nielsen Company (The)

CONTACTS: *Note: Officers with more than one job title may be intentionally listed here more than once.*

Stephen B. Morris, CEO
Stephen B. Morris, Pres.
Sean Creamer, CFO
Pierre C. Bouvard, Pres., Sales & Mktg.
Owen Charlebois, Pres., R&D
V. Scott Henry, CIO/Exec. VP
Owen Charlebois, Pres., Tech.
Linda Dupree, Exec. VP-New Prod. Dev.
Claire L. Kummer, Exec. VP-Oper., Integration & Mfg.
Kathleen T. Ross, Chief Admin. Officer/Exec. VP
Tim Smith, Chief Legal Officer/Exec. VP
Owen Charlebois, Pres., Oper.
Sean Creamer, Exec. VP-Planning
Thom Mocarsky, Sr. VP-Press
Thom Mocarsky, Sr. VP-Investor Rel.
Sean Creamer, Exec. VP-Finance
Scott Musgrave, Sr. VP-Client Software Bus.
Bill Rose, Sr. VP-Mktg.
Carol Edwards, Sr. VP-Sales, Advertiser, Agency & Television
Jay Guyther, Sr. VP-Ratings Svcs.
Stephen B. Morris, Chmn.
Brad Bedford, VP-Int'l Sales

Phone: 212-887-1300	Fax: 212-887-1390
Toll-Free:	
Address: 142 W. 57th St., New York, NY 10019-3300 US	

GROWTH PLANS/SPECIAL FEATURES:

Arbitron, Inc., founded in 1912, is an international media and marketing research firm serving radio broadcasters, cable companies, advertisers, advertising agencies, out-of-home media and online media in the U.S., Mexico and Europe. Through its Scarborough Research joint venture with The Nielsen Company, Arbitron also serves television broadcasters and print media. Arbitron's core businesses are measuring network and local market radio audiences; measuring national radio audiences; providing application software for accessing and analyzing media audience data; and providing consumer, shopping and media usage information. The company utilizes two main methods for data acquisition: using diary methodology and the Portable People Meter. In the former case, willing participants are sent a small diary and asked to keep track of what kind of media they use and when for seven days. A typical survey period is 12 weeks and the firm processes more than 1.4 million diaries a year. The Portable People Meter is a small device carried or worn by the participants, which picks up on code signals embedded into the audio portion of a client company's broadcast using encoders provided by Arbitron. The Portable People Meter can detect codes in radio, television, Internet and cable broadcasts, as well as satellite radio and satellite television. The Portable People Meter automatically sends all of its recorded codes to Arbitron for tabulation. In addition to quantitative data, Arbitron provides qualitative information about media usage, retail and shopping habits, demographics and lifestyles in 75 U.S. markets. Arbitron also owns Continental Research, located in London. Continental conducts market research in the media, advertising, financial and telecommunications arenas in the U.K. and Europe.

Arbitron offers its employees flexible spending accounts, a Computer Ownership Assistance Program, employee discounts, credit union membership, tuition assistance, adoption subsidies, fitness discounts and medical, dental, vision and disability insurance.

FINANCIALS: Sales and profits are in thousands of dollars—add 000 to get the full amount. 2007 Note: Financial information for 2007 was not available for all companies at press time.

2007 Sales: $	2007 Profits: $	U.S. Stock Ticker: ARB
2006 Sales: $329,250	2006 Profits: $50,658	Int'l Ticker: Int'l Exchange:
2005 Sales: $309,995	2005 Profits: $67,308	Employees: 1,908
2004 Sales: $296,553	2004 Profits: $60,565	Fiscal Year Ends: 12/31
2003 Sales: $273,550	2003 Profits: $49,873	Parent Company:

SALARIES/BENEFITS:

Pension Plan:	ESOP Stock Plan:	Profit Sharing:	Top Exec. Salary: $593,208	Bonus: $642,889
Savings Plan: Y	Stock Purch. Plan: Y		Second Exec. Salary: $350,633	Bonus: $274,242

OTHER THOUGHTS:

Apparent Women Officers or Directors: 6
Hot Spot for Advancement for Women/Minorities: Y

LOCATIONS: ("Y" = Yes)

West:	Southwest:	Midwest:	Southeast:	Northeast:	International:
Y	Y	Y	Y	Y	Y

Note: Financial information, benefits and other data can change quickly and may vary from those stated here.

ARISTOCRAT LEISURE LTD

www.aristocrat.com.au

Industry Group Code: 713290 Ranks within this company's industry group: Sales: 3 Profits: 11

Print Media/Publishing:	Movies:	Equipment/Supplies:		Broadcast/Cable:	Music/Audio:	Sports/Games/Gambling:
Newspapers:	Movie Theaters:	Equipment/Supplies:		Broadcast TV:	Music Production:	Games/Sports:
Magazines:	Movie Production:	Gambling Equipment:	Y	Cable TV:	Retail Music:	Retail Games Stores:
Books:	TV/Video Prod.:	Special Services:	Y	Satellite Broadcast:	Retail Audio Equip.:	Stadiums/Teams:
Book Stores:	Video Rental:	Advertising Services:		Radio:	Music Print./Dist.:	Gambling/Casinos:
Distribution/Printing:	Video Distribution:	Info. Sys. Software:		Online Information:	Multimedia:	Rides/Theme Parks:

TYPES OF BUSINESS:

Gaming Machines Manufacturing
Gaming Consulting & Services
Gaming Management Systems & Software
Gaming Accessories

BRANDS/DIVISIONS/AFFILIATES:

Aristocrat Technologies, Inc.
Casino Data Systems
ReelPower
Bonus Bank
Lucky Devil
System Account Play
Hyperlink
ACE Interactive

CONTACTS: *Note: Officers with more than one job title may be intentionally listed here more than once.*

Paul Oneile, CEO/Managing Dir.
Simon Kelly, CFO
Steve Parker, Group General Mgr.-Sales & Mktg.
Paul Cavanagh-Downs, CIO
Gareth Phillips, CTO
Bruce Yahl, Group Mgr.-Legal & Commercial/Corp. Sec.
Ian Timmis, Group General Mgr.-Bus. & Strategic Dev.
Warren Jowett, Exec. General Mgr.-Australasia & Asia Pacific
Tim Parrott, CEO/Pres., Aristocrat Technologies, Americas
Julian Stanford, General Mgr.-Europe
Robert McLoughlin, Exec. Chmn.
David J. Simpson, Chmn.

Phone: 61-2-9413-6300	Fax: 61-2-9420-1352
Toll-Free:	
Address: 71 Longueville Rd., Lane Cove, New South Wales 2066 Australia	

GROWTH PLANS/SPECIAL FEATURES:

Aristocrat Leisure, Ltd. is a major manufacturer of gaming machines and their components, including games, systems and accessories. The firm supplies clubs, hotels, casinos and bars in more than 55 countries with its gaming machines and systems. Aristocrat operates in the U.S. through Casino Data Systems. In addition to its gaming products, the firm provides gaming services, including technical support, training and documentation, sales support and gaming analysis. Aristocrat also offers consulting services that include venue analysis, commercialized project management and specialized gaming training. The company produces three types of gaming machines: line games, the most traditional form of video reel games; ReelPower games, which allow players to purchase reels rather than lines; and specialty games, which consist of the Bonus Bank product Line (Mr. Cashman, Aristocrat Technologies, Inc., Lucky Devil, Lady Luok and Zorro). The firm's gaming systems include System 5000 (a slot machine management and promotion system for the club industry), System 6000 (a casino slot machine management solution), System Account Play (which allows members to set up a player account that they can transfer money directly to gaming machines by using a member card), Cashless Gaming (which allows players to move around the gaming area at a venue and play machines using their membership cards), System Analyst (a slot machine management reporting solution), Ticket Out Auto Redemption (which allows gaming machines to issue a barcoded payout ticket) and System Xpress (a systems upgrade that offers easy navigation and touch screen capabilities). Aristocrat's accessories include stools, signage and LCD displays. Hyperlink is the company's patented bonusing product, which links all electronic gaming machines to its progressive gaming platform.

Aristocrat offers its employees health insurance, educational assistance, online training programs and membership in a social club.

FINANCIALS: Sales and profits are in thousands of dollars—add 000 to get the full amount. 2007 Note: Financial information for 2007 was not available for all companies at press time.

2007 Sales: $	2007 Profits: $	U.S. Stock Ticker: ARLUF
2006 Sales: $862,500	2006 Profits: $-32,200	Int'l Ticker: ALL Int'l Exchange: Sydney-ASX
2005 Sales: $920,683	2005 Profits: $173,523	Employees: 2,282
2004 Sales: $804,583	2004 Profits: $100,974	Fiscal Year Ends: 12/31
2003 Sales: $735,000	2003 Profits: $-79,400	Parent Company:

SALARIES/BENEFITS:

Pension Plan:	ESOP Stock Plan:	Profit Sharing:	Top Exec. Salary: $	Bonus: $
Savings Plan: Y	Stock Purch. Plan: Y		Second Exec. Salary: $	Bonus: $

OTHER THOUGHTS:

Apparent Women Officers or Directors: 3
Hot Spot for Advancement for Women/Minorities: Y

LOCATIONS: ("Y" = Yes)

West:	Southwest:	Midwest:	Southeast:	Northeast:	International:
Y		Y	Y	Y	Y

ASCENT MEDIA GROUP INC

www.ascentmedia.com

Industry Group Code: 512191 Ranks within this company's industry group: Sales: Profits:

Print Media/Publishing:	Movies:		Equipment/Supplies:		Broadcast/Cable:	Music/Audio:	Sports/Games/Gambling:
Newspapers:	Movie Theaters:		Equipment/Supplies:		Broadcast TV:	Music Production:	Games/Sports:
Magazines:	Movie Production:	Y	Gambling Equipment:		Cable TV:	Retail Music:	Retail Games Stores:
Books:	TV/Video Prod.:	Y	Special Services:	Y	Satellite Broadcast:	Retail Audio Equip.:	Stadiums/Teams:
Book Stores:	Video Rental:		Advertising Services:		Radio:	Music Print./Dist.:	Gambling/Casinos:
Distribution/Printing:	Video Distribution:	Y	Info. Sys. Software:		Online Information:	Multimedia:	Rides/Theme Parks:

TYPES OF BUSINESS:

Motion Picture Post-Production & Distribution
Audio Post-Production Services
Creative Services
Network Services
Engineering & Consulting Services
Movie Restoration & Preservation

BRANDS/DIVISIONS/AFFILIATES:

Discovery Holding Company
Creative Services
Creative Sound Services
Management Services
Network Services
Company 3
Ascent Media Systems & Technology Services
Cinetech, Inc.

CONTACTS: *Note: Officers with more than one job title may be intentionally listed here more than once.*

George C. Platisa, CFO/Exec. VP
Jose Royo, CTO
William E. Niles, General Counsel/Sec./Exec. VP
Robert Solomon, Pres., Creative Svcs.
Margret Craig, COO-Network Svcs.
Richard Andrews, COO-Media Svcs.
Robert C. Rosenthal, COO-Creative Sound Svcs.
William (Bill) Fitzgerald, Chmn.

Phone: 310-434-7000	Fax: 310-434-7001
Toll-Free:	
Address: 520 Broadway, 5th Fl., Santa Monica, CA 90401 US	

GROWTH PLANS/SPECIAL FEATURES:

Ascent Media Group, Inc., a wholly-owned subsidiary of the Discovery Holding Company, provides creative and technical services to the media and entertainment industries. The company was recently organized into two global operating divisions: Creative services and network services. Its former management services group, which optimizes, archives, manages and repurposes media assets for global distribution, has been folded into the two main divisions. The creative services group develops content for films, television series, miniseries, commercials, music videos, advertising campaigns and corporate communications programming. The creative sound services division provides audio post-production services for feature films; TV series and movies; commercials; documentaries; independent films; and interactive games. Company 3, part of the group, produced 80 of the digital visual effects shots for the Transformers movie as well as scanning, coloring and conforming the entire film. Company 3 also worked extensively on the three Pirates of the Caribbean movies, most recently performing final post production, visual effects integration and color grading services for the third installment. The network services group provides outsourced solutions for media management, content distribution, and connectivity. Systems integration and consulting capabilities round out the division's comprehensive service offering. Ascent Media Systems and Technology Services, a subsidiary of the network services group, provides engineering, consultation and turnkey systems solutions for the broadcast, cable, entertainment, satellite, production/post-production and corporate video industries. Its customers include major motion picture studios, independent producers, broadcast networks, cable channels, advertising agencies and other companies that produce, own and distribute entertainment, news, sports, corporate, educational, industrial and advertising content. In recent years, Ascent has acquired the assets of Sony's System Integration Center and Cinetech, Inc., a leader in the motion picture restoration, protection and preservation services market.

Employees of Ascent Media receive medical, dental and vision coverage; vacation and sick leave; and company health screenings.

FINANCIALS: Sales and profits are in thousands of dollars—add 000 to get the full amount. 2007 Note: Financial information for 2007 was not available for all companies at press time.

2007 Sales: $	2007 Profits: $	U.S. Stock Ticker: Subsidiary
2006 Sales: $	2006 Profits: $	Int'l Ticker: Int'l Exchange:
2005 Sales: $697,700	2005 Profits: $	Employees: 4,000
2004 Sales: $631,200	2004 Profits: $	Fiscal Year Ends: 12/31
2003 Sales: $506,100	2003 Profits: $	Parent Company: DISCOVERY HOLDING COMPANY

SALARIES/BENEFITS:

Pension Plan:	ESOP Stock Plan:	Profit Sharing:	Top Exec. Salary: $753,846	Bonus: $
Savings Plan: Y	Stock Purch. Plan:		Second Exec. Salary: $451,620	Bonus: $

OTHER THOUGHTS:

Apparent Women Officers or Directors: 1
Hot Spot for Advancement for Women/Minorities:

LOCATIONS: ("Y" = Yes)

West:	Southwest:	Midwest:	Southeast:	Northeast:	International:
Y		Y	Y	Y	Y

AT&T INC
www.att.com

Industry Group Code: 513300A Ranks within this company's industry group: Sales: 2 Profits: 1

Print Media/Publishing:	Movies:	Equipment/Supplies:	Broadcast/Cable:	Music/Audio:	Sports/Games/Gambling:
Newspapers:	Movie Theaters:	Equipment/Supplies:	Broadcast TV:	Music Production:	Games/Sports:
Magazines:	Movie Production:	Gambling Equipment:	Cable TV: Y	Retail Music:	Retail Games Stores:
Books: Y	TV/Video Prod.:	Special Services: Y	Satellite Broadcast:	Retail Audio Equip.:	Stadiums/Teams:
Book Stores:	Video Rental:	Advertising Services:	Radio:	Music Print./Dist.:	Gambling/Casinos:
Distribution/Printing:	Video Distribution:	Info. Sys. Software:	Online Information:	Multimedia:	Rides/Theme Parks:

TYPES OF BUSINESS:

Local Telephone Service
Wireless Telecommunications
Long-Distance Telephone Service
Corporate Telecom, Backbone & Wholesale Services
Directory Publishing
Entertainment & Television via Internet
International Telephone Services
Internet Access via DSL

BRANDS/DIVISIONS/AFFILIATES:

Cingular Wireless
SBC Communications
Southwestern Bell
BellSouth
AT&T Corp.
Pacific Bell
yellowpages.com
SBC Yahoo! DSL

CONTACTS: Note: Officers with more than one job title may be intentionally listed here more than once.

Randall L. Stephenson, CEO
Randall L. Stephenson, Pres.
Richard G. Lindner, CFO/Sr. Exec. VP
Catherine M. Coughlin, Global Mktg. Officer/Sr. Exec. VP
William A. Blase Jr., Sr. Exec. VP-Human Resources
John Stankey, CTO/Sr. Exec. VP
Wayne Watts, General Counsel/Sr. Exec. VP
James W. Callaway, Sr. Exec. VP-Exec. Oper.
Forest Miller, Group Pres., Corp. Strategy & Dev.
James W. Cicconi, Sr. Exec. VP-External & Legislative Affairs
Ralph de la Vega, Group Pres., Regional Telecom. & Entertainment
Ralph de la Vega, Pres./CEO-AT&T Mobility
Rayford Wilkins, Jr., Group Pres., Diversified Bus.
Randall L. Stephenson, Chmn.

Phone: 210-821-4105	Fax: 314-331-9896
Toll-Free:	
Address: 175 E. Houston, San Antonio, TX 78205 US	

GROWTH PLANS/SPECIAL FEATURES:

AT&T, Inc., the result of the November 2005 merger between SBC Communications and AT&T Corp., is one of the world's largest providers of diversified telecommunications services. The company and its subsidiaries deliver an extensive portfolio of traditional and IP-based voice; broadband Internet; data transport; entertainment; networking; wireless; video services; advertising; and transport and termination of wholesale traffic services. AT&T offers Virtual Private Network (VPN), Voice over IP (VoIP), security and support services and provides interoperability with the world's five leading IP PBX vendors as well as being a top provider of broadband DSL and Wi-Fi. AT&T is positioning itself for the future as an aggressive provider of bundled telephone, wireless, Internet service and entertainment services. Entertainment offerings focus on video-on-demand and television via Internet. It is investing in a massive, multi billion dollar network improvement, which will offer Internet connection speeds of up to 25 Mbps to 18 million homes by the end of 2008. In January 2007, AT&T completed its acquisition of BellSouth for $86 billion. The merger created a company with 67.5 million local lines in 22 states, 100% ownership of Cingular Wireless (which now uses the AT&T brand) with 63.7 million subscribers, and 13 million broadband subscribers. In addition, the firm has 50,000 Wi-Fi hotspots in 80 nations; is America's largest directory publisher, delivering 178 million phone directories yearly; and is one of the world's largest providers of telecom backbone services, wholesale services and corporate services to Global 1000 corporations. Growth over the mid term will be focused on wireless subscriptions, the sale of advertising on its cell phone, TV and Internet services, Internet-based TV subscriptions and global corporate telecom services. In June 2007, the firm agreed to acquire Dobson Communications Corp. for $2.8 billion.

AT&T employees have access to adoption assistance, tuition aid and a service discount program.

FINANCIALS: Sales and profits are in thousands of dollars—add 000 to get the full amount. 2007 Note: Financial information for 2007 was not available for all companies at press time.

2007 Sales: $	2007 Profits: $	U.S. Stock Ticker: T
2006 Sales: $63,055,000	2006 Profits: $7,356,000	Int'l Ticker: Int'l Exchange:
2005 Sales: $43,764,000	2005 Profits: $4,786,000	Employees: 302,770
2004 Sales: $40,733,000	2004 Profits: $5,887,000	Fiscal Year Ends: 12/31
2003 Sales: $40,498,000	2003 Profits: $8,505,000	Parent Company:

SALARIES/BENEFITS:

Pension Plan: Y	ESOP Stock Plan:	Profit Sharing:	Top Exec. Salary: $2,100,000	Bonus: $6,783,000
Savings Plan: Y	Stock Purch. Plan:		Second Exec. Salary: $1,152,500	Bonus: $5,445,000

OTHER THOUGHTS:

Apparent Women Officers or Directors: 1
Hot Spot for Advancement for Women/Minorities:

LOCATIONS: ("Y" = Yes)

West:	Southwest:	Midwest:	Southeast:	Northeast:	International:
Y	Y	Y	Y	Y	Y

ATARI INC   www.atari.com

Industry Group Code: 511208 Ranks within this company's industry group: Sales: 7   Profits: 8

Print Media/Publishing:	Movies:	Equipment/Supplies:	Broadcast/Cable:	Music/Audio:	Sports/Games/Gambling:	
Newspapers:	Movie Theaters:	Equipment/Supplies:	Broadcast TV:	Music Production:	Games/Sports:	Y
Magazines:	Movie Production:	Gambling Equipment:	Cable TV:	Retail Music:	Retail Games Stores:	
Books:	TV/Video Prod.:	Special Services:	Satellite Broadcast:	Retail Audio Equip.:	Stadiums/Teams:	
Book Stores:	Video Rental:	Advertising Services:	Radio:	Music Print./Dist.:	Gambling/Casinos:	
Distribution/Printing:	Video Distribution:	Info. Sys. Software:	Online Information:	Multimedia:	Rides/Theme Parks:	

TYPES OF BUSINESS:

Computer Software-Video Games
Educational Software

BRANDS/DIVISIONS/AFFILIATES:

Infogrames Entertainment S.A.
V-Rally
Test Drive
Alone in the Dark
Roller Coaster Tycoon
Unreal
Dungeons & Dragons
Hasbro, Inc.

CONTACTS: *Note: Officers with more than one job title may be intentionally listed here more than once.*

Curtis G. Solsvig, III, Interim CEO
Arthuro Rodriguez, Acting CFO
Nique Fajors, VP-Mktg. & Sales
Jean-Marcel Nicolai, CTO
Jean-Marcel Nicolai, Sr. VP-Worldwide Prod. Dev.
Kristina Pappa, General Counsel/VP
Curtis G. Solsvig, III, Chief Restructuring Officer
Arthuro Rodriguez, Controller/VP
Eugene Davis, Chmn.

Phone: 212-726-6500	Fax: 212-679-3424
Toll-Free:	
Address: 417 5th Ave., New York, NY 10016 US	

GROWTH PLANS/SPECIAL FEATURES:

Atari, Inc., 51%-owned subsidiary of French software publisher Infogrames Entertainment S.A. (IESA), is a third-party publisher of interactive entertainment in the U.S. The firm represented approximately 30% of IESA's revenue. It publishes and distributes interactive entertainment software for gaming consoles such as the Sony PlayStation 2 and PlayStation 3; Microsoft Xbox and Xbox 360; Nintendo GameCube, Game Boy Advance, Wii and DS. It also publishes CD-ROM games for the PC platform and publishes and sublicenses games for wireless Internet and other evolving platforms. Until recently, it also developed games in-house, however, in the last few years it has sold off its remaining development studios. Atari still has games developed for it through external resources. Formerly known as GT Interactive Software Corp. and then Infogrames, Inc., the firm began its rebranding process as Atari in 2001 when IESA acquired, Hasbro Interactive, the interactive games division of Hasbro, Inc., selling only a few products under the Atari name before it completed the process in 2003 when IESA began using the Atari name for all its commercial operations worldwide. The corporation has built an extensive library of licensed properties that include some of the most recognizable names in popular entertainment. Atari's entertainment properties include popular franchises such as Driver, Unreal, V-Rally, Roller Backyard, Roller Coaster Tycoon, Alone in the Dark and Test Drive. It also publishes software based on key theme licenses, including The Matrix, Terminator, Mission: Impossible, Dragon Ball Z, Men In Black, Superman, Godzilla, Arthur & the Minimoys and Dungeons & Dragons. In addition, Atari holds an exclusive worldwide license on 10 Hasbro intellectual properties including Dungeons & Dragons, Monopoly, Scrabble, Risk, Game of Life, Clue, Yatzhee, Battleship, Boggle and Simon. During 2007, the firm sold the rights to the Driver games and other intellectual property, as well as two development studios, Reflections and Shiny, for $35 million.

FINANCIALS: Sales and profits are in thousands of dollars—add 000 to get the full amount. 2007 Note: Financial information for 2007 was not available for all companies at press time.

2007 Sales: $122,285	2007 Profits: $-69,711	U.S. Stock Ticker: ATAR
2006 Sales: $206,796	2006 Profits: $-68,986	Int'l Ticker: Int'l Exchange:
2005 Sales: $343,837	2005 Profits: $5,692	Employees: 143
2004 Sales: $468,944	2004 Profits: $ 766	Fiscal Year Ends: 3/31
2003 Sales: $404,600	2003 Profits: $-18,100	Parent Company:

SALARIES/BENEFITS:

Pension Plan:	ESOP Stock Plan:	Profit Sharing:	Top Exec. Salary: $640,951	Bonus: $
Savings Plan: Y	Stock Purch. Plan: Y		Second Exec. Salary: $345,455	Bonus: $

OTHER THOUGHTS:

Apparent Women Officers or Directors: 1
Hot Spot for Advancement for Women/Minorities: Y

LOCATIONS: ("Y" = Yes)

West:	Southwest:	Midwest:	Southeast:	Northeast:	International:
Y				Y	Y

AUDIBLE INC

www.audible.com

Industry Group Code: 451220E Ranks within this company's industry group: Sales: 2   Profits: 1

Print Media/Publishing:	Movies:	Equipment/Supplies:		Broadcast/Cable:	Music/Audio:		Sports/Games/Gambling:
Newspapers:	Movie Theaters:	Equipment/Supplies:		Broadcast TV:	Music Production:		Games/Sports:
Magazines:	Movie Production:	Gambling Equipment:		Cable TV:	Retail Music:		Retail Games Stores:
Books:	TV/Video Prod.:	Special Services:	Y	Satellite Broadcast:	Retail Audio Equip.:		Stadiums/Teams:
Book Stores:	Video Rental:	Advertising Services:		Radio:	Music Print./Dist.:	Y	Gambling/Casinos:
Distribution/Printing:	Video Distribution:	Info. Sys. Software:		Online Information:	Multimedia:		Rides/Theme Parks:

TYPES OF BUSINESS:

Audio Books-Online Sales
Audio Programming Software
Time-Shifted Radio Programming
Digital Audio Players
Educational Audio Materials

BRANDS/DIVISIONS/AFFILIATES:

audible.com
AudibleListener
Wall Street Journal (The)
New York Times Co (The)
Fast Company
Forbes Inc
Laugh Factory (The)
8001 Sunset Strip

CONTACTS: *Note: Officers with more than one job title may be intentionally listed here more than once.*

Donald R. Katz, CEO
Glenn M. Rogers, COO
William H. Mitchell, CFO
Guy Story, Jr., Chief Scientist
Brian M. Fielding, Exec. VP-Content & Legal Affairs
Guy Story, Jr., Sr. VP-Bus. Dev.
Beth Anderson, Sr. VP/Publisher
Will Lopes, VP-Customer Experience
Foy C. Sperring, Jr., VP-Customer Acquisition
Helene Godin, Corp. Counsel
Donald R. Katz, Chmn.

Phone: 973-820-0400	Fax:
Toll-Free:	
Address: 1 Washington Pk., 16th Fl., Newark, NJ 07102 US	

GROWTH PLANS/SPECIAL FEATURES:

Audible, Inc. provides Internet-delivered premium spoken audio content for playback on personal computers and mobile devices. The company offers a variety of software systems and audio programming software designed to download, store and play between two and 28 hours of content from its online store, audible.com. Audible sells a wide array of audio content, including educational materials, humor, periodicals, fiction, nonfiction and time-shifted radio programming making up more than 127,000 hours of audio content, comprised of 37,000 different programs. The company has several AudibleListener membership plans which provide discounts of individual content purchases, exposure to periodic sales and member-only free content offerings for an annual membership fee. The company also has partnerships with leading audiobook, magazine and newspaper publishers, as well as broadcasters, business information providers and educational and cultural institutions. Audible.com features daily selected audio content from The Wall Street Journal and The New York Times, both available on a subscription basis in time for the morning drive to work each day. Other publications offered include Fast Company, Forbes, Harvard Business Review and Scientific American. In addition, the site offers a large collection of audiobook bestsellers and classics by authors such as Stephen King, James Patterson, William Shakespeare and Jane Austen, as well as speeches, lectures and on-demand radio programs. In March 2007, Audible and The Laugh Factory announced a multi-year agreement for the production, marketing and distribution of a weekly one-hour original comedy show, 8001 Sunset Strip, which features performances from stand-up comedians and interviews with comedians, club patrons and employees.

FINANCIALS: Sales and profits are in thousands of dollars—add 000 to get the full amount. 2007 Note: Financial information for 2007 was not available for all companies at press time.

2007 Sales: $	2007 Profits: $	U.S. Stock Ticker: ADBL
2006 Sales: $82,178	2006 Profits: $-8,447	Int'l Ticker: Int'l Exchange:
2005 Sales: $63,237	2005 Profits: $- 653	Employees: 193
2004 Sales: $34,319	2004 Profits: $2,077	Fiscal Year Ends: 12/31
2003 Sales: $19,324	2003 Profits: $-3,560	Parent Company:

SALARIES/BENEFITS:

Pension Plan:	ESOP Stock Plan:	Profit Sharing:	Top Exec. Salary: $245,404	Bonus: $
Savings Plan:	Stock Purch. Plan:		Second Exec. Salary: $225,000	Bonus: $

OTHER THOUGHTS:

Apparent Women Officers or Directors: 2
Hot Spot for Advancement for Women/Minorities:

LOCATIONS: ("Y" = Yes)

West:	Southwest:	Midwest:	Southeast:	Northeast:	International:
				Y	Y

AVID TECHNOLOGY INC

www.avid.com

Industry Group Code: 511209 Ranks within this company's industry group: Sales: 1   Profits: 2

Print Media/Publishing:	Movies:	Equipment/Supplies:		Broadcast/Cable:	Music/Audio:	Sports/Games/Gambling:
Newspapers:	Movie Theaters:	Equipment/Supplies:	Y	Broadcast TV:	Music Production:	Games/Sports:
Magazines:	Movie Production:	Gambling Equipment:		Cable TV:	Retail Music:	Retail Games Stores:
Books:	TV/Video Prod.:	Special Services:		Satellite Broadcast:	Retail Audio Equip.:	Stadiums/Teams:
Book Stores:	Video Rental:	Advertising Services:		Radio:	Music Print./Dist.:	Gambling/Casinos:
Distribution/Printing:	Video Distribution:	Info. Sys. Software:		Online Information:	Multimedia:	Rides/Theme Parks:

TYPES OF BUSINESS:

Film Editing Systems
Digital Audio Equipment
Image Manipulation Products
Network & Storage Products
Special Effects Software

BRANDS/DIVISIONS/AFFILIATES:

Avid Xpress
Avid DS
Nitris
Softimage Face Robot
Alienbrain Studio

CONTACTS: *Note: Officers with more than one job title may be intentionally listed here more than once.*

Nancy Hawthorne, Interim CEO
Joel Legon, CFO/VP
Greg Estes, Chief Mktg. Officer/VP
Lynne D. Richter, Interim VP-Human Resources
Greg Munster, CIO/VP-Bus. Transformation
Paige Parsi, General Counsel/Corp. Sec./VP
Sharad Rastogi, VP-Corp. Dev./Gen. Mgr.-Pinnacle Systems
David M. Lebolt, VP/Gen. Mgr.-Digidesign
Graham Sharp, VP/Gen. Mgr.-Avid Video
Robert M. Halperin, Chmn.

Phone: 978-640-6789	Fax: 978-640-1366
Toll-Free:	
Address: Metropolitan Technology Park, 1 Park W., Tewksbury, MA 01876 US	

GROWTH PLANS/SPECIAL FEATURES:

Avid Technology, Inc. develops, markets, sells and supports a range of software and hardware products for the production, management and distribution of digital media content. Avid's products are designed for every class of user, from the home hobbyist to the feature film professional. The company's operations are organized into three business units: professional video, audio and consumer video. The professional video segment offers video and film editing systems, as well as 3D and special effects software, which are marketed to professional users; broadcast and cable companies; and corporate, government and educational users. Products offered within this segment include the Avid Xpress family, consisting of portable software-based editing systems; the Avid DS and Nitris family, consisting of real-time, uncompressed HD and SD solutions for high-quality finishing and mastering, including effects and color correction; Softimage Face Robot, a production toolset that simplifies the process of facial animation by creating organic skin movement; and Alienbrain Studio, multi-user file and asset management software for 3D professionals. Avid's audio segment offers solutions for audio creation, mixing, post production, collaboration, distribution and scoring to professional music studios; project studios; film and television production and post production facilities; television and radio broadcasters; new media production studios (creators of DVD and web content); performance venues; corporate, government and educational facilities; and home hobbyists and enthusiasts. The consumer video segment markets video editing and digital lifestyle products to the home consumer who wishes to create, edit, share, publish and view video content.

Avid offers its employees flexible spending accounts, an on-site fitness center, an employee assistance program, domestic partner benefits, tuition reimbursement, credit union membership, discount computer equipment, Children's World Centers, a service award program, cellular phone service, a virtual concierge, discount movie passes and medical, dental, vision and life insurance.

FINANCIALS: Sales and profits are in thousands of dollars—add 000 to get the full amount. 2007 Note: Financial information for 2007 was not available for all companies at press time.

2007 Sales: $	2007 Profits: $	**U.S. Stock Ticker: AVID**
2006 Sales: $910,578	2006 Profits: $-42,927	**Int'l Ticker:** Int'l Exchange:
2005 Sales: $775,443	2005 Profits: $33,980	Employees: 2,792
2004 Sales: $589,600	2004 Profits: $71,700	Fiscal Year Ends: 12/31
2003 Sales: $471,912	2003 Profits: $40,889	Parent Company:

SALARIES/BENEFITS:

Pension Plan:	ESOP Stock Plan:	Profit Sharing:	Top Exec. Salary: $551,000	Bonus: $
Savings Plan: Y	Stock Purch. Plan: Y		Second Exec. Salary: $333,000	Bonus: $

OTHER THOUGHTS:

Apparent Women Officers or Directors: 3
Hot Spot for Advancement for Women/Minorities: Y

LOCATIONS: ("Y" = Yes)

West:	Southwest:	Midwest:	Southeast:	Northeast:	International:
Y	Y	Y	Y	Y	Y

Note: Financial information, benefits and other data can change quickly and may vary from those stated here.

AZTAR CORP

www.aztar.com

Industry Group Code: 721120 Ranks within this company's industry group: Sales: Profits:

Print Media/Publishing:	Movies:	Equipment/Supplies:	Broadcast/Cable:	Music/Audio:	Sports/Games/Gambling:
Newspapers:	Movie Theaters:	Equipment/Supplies:	Broadcast TV:	Music Production:	Games/Sports:
Magazines:	Movie Production:	Gambling Equipment:	Cable TV:	Retail Music:	Retail Games Stores:
Books:	TV/Video Prod.:	Special Services:	Satellite Broadcast:	Retail Audio Equip.:	Stadiums/Teams: Y
Book Stores:	Video Rental:	Advertising Services:	Radio:	Music Print./Dist.:	Gambling/Casinos:
Distribution/Printing:	Video Distribution:	Info. Sys. Software:	Online Information:	Multimedia:	Rides/Theme Parks:

TYPES OF BUSINESS:

Casino Hotel
Riverboat Casinos

BRANDS/DIVISIONS/AFFILIATES:

Tropicana Atlantic City
Tropicana Las Vegas
Casino Aztar Evansville
Casino Aztar Caruthersville
Ramada Express Hotel and Casino
Folies Bergere
Tropicana Lehigh Valley
Columbia Entertainment

CONTACTS:
Note: Officers with more than one job title may be intentionally listed here more than once.

Robert M. Haddock, CEO
Robert M. Haddock, Pres.
Neil A. Ciarfalia, CFO
Nelson W. Armstrong, Jr., VP-Admin./Corp. Sec.
Joe C. Cole, VP-Corp. Comm.
Neil A. Ciarfalia, VP/Treas.
Meredith P. Sipek, VP/Controller
Robert M. Haddock, Chmn.

Phone: 602-381-4100	**Fax:** 602-381-4108
Toll-Free:	
Address: 2390 E. Camelback Rd., Ste. 400, Phoenix, AZ 85016-3452 US	

GROWTH PLANS/SPECIAL FEATURES:

Aztar Corporation operates casino hotels in Atlantic City, New Jersey; Las Vegas, Nevada; and Laughlin, Nevada and riverboat casinos in Caruthersville, Missouri; and Evansville, Indiana. Aztar operates five major casinos: the Tropicana Atlantic City, Tropicana Las Vegas, Ramada Express, Casino Aztar Evansville and Casino Aztar Caruthersville. The 14-acre Tropicana Atlantic City has a 220 yard ocean frontage and a 151,000-square-foot casino that contains 4,318 slot machines and 198 table games. Aztar recently added a new expansion called the Quarter at Tropicana, which consists of a 200,000-square-foot dining, entertainment and retail center. Tropicana Las Vegas boasts a 34 acre complex of 1,880 hotels and 61,000 square feet of casino space with 1,316 slot machines and 39 table games on the Las Vegas Strip. This location also holds one of the world's largest indoor/outdoor swimming pools, as well as a five-acre water park and the Folies Bergere, the longest-running show in Las Vegas. The Ramada Express Hotel and Casino on the Colorado River in Laughlin, Nevada features a Victorian-era railroad theme within its 1,498 hotel rooms and 54,000 square feet of casino space. Casino Aztar Evansville operates on the Ohio River and includes a 38,000 square foot casino and a riverboat designed to carry 2,700 passengers. The firm's first riverboat casino, the Casino Aztar Caruthersville, operates on the Mississippi River in Missouri and holds a capacity of 800 passengers, 701 slot machines and 19 table games. In January 2007, Columbia Entertainment completed its acquisition of Aztar for $2.1 billion.

Employees of Aztar receive benefits that vary by location. They may include pharmaceutical assistance, educational assistance, credit union services, local discounts and multiple employee events such as picnics and parties during the year.

FINANCIALS: Sales and profits are in thousands of dollars—add 000 to get the full amount. 2007 Note: Financial information for 2007 was not available for all companies at press time.

2007 Sales: $	2007 Profits: $	**U.S. Stock Ticker: Subsidiary**
2006 Sales: $	2006 Profits: $	**Int'l Ticker:** Int'l Exchange:
2005 Sales: $915,442	2005 Profits: $55,960	Employees: 9,800
2004 Sales: $789,993	2004 Profits: $28,500	Fiscal Year Ends: 12/31
2003 Sales: $789,024	2003 Profits: $60,930	Parent Company: COLUMBIA ENTERTAINMENT

SALARIES/BENEFITS:

Pension Plan:	ESOP Stock Plan:	Profit Sharing:	Top Exec. Salary: $868,400	Bonus: $1,075,000
Savings Plan: Y	Stock Purch. Plan:		Second Exec. Salary: $308,162	Bonus: $180,577

OTHER THOUGHTS:

Apparent Women Officers or Directors: 1
Hot Spot for Advancement for Women/Minorities:

LOCATIONS: ("Y" = Yes)

West:	Southwest:	Midwest:	Southeast:	Northeast:	International:
Y		Y		Y	

BALLY TECHNOLOGIES INC   www.ballytech.com

Industry Group Code: 713290 Ranks within this company's industry group: Sales: 5   Profits: 13

Print Media/Publishing:	Movies:	Equipment/Supplies:		Broadcast/Cable:	Music/Audio:	Sports/Games/Gambling:	
Newspapers:	Movie Theaters:	Equipment/Supplies:		Broadcast TV:	Music Production:	Games/Sports:	
Magazines:	Movie Production:	Gambling Equipment:	Y	Cable TV:	Retail Music:	Retail Games Stores:	
Books:	TV/Video Prod.:	Special Services:	Y	Satellite Broadcast:	Retail Audio Equip.:	Stadiums/Teams:	
Book Stores:	Video Rental:	Advertising Services:		Radio:	Music Print./Dist.:	Gambling/Casinos:	Y
Distribution/Printing:	Video Distribution:	Info. Sys. Software:		Online Information:	Multimedia:	Rides/Theme Parks:	

TYPES OF BUSINESS:

Gaming Machines
Electronic Slot & Video Gaming Machines
Gaming Software
Slot Monitoring & Casino Management Systems
Casino Hotel
Progressive Gaming Operations

BRANDS/DIVISIONS/AFFILIATES:

Alliance Gaming Corporation
Bally Gaming and Systems
Alpha Game Engine
Blazing 7s
Blues Brothers
Rainbow Hotel Casino

CONTACTS: Note: Officers with more than one job title may be intentionally listed here more than once.

Richard Haddrill, CEO
Gavin Isaacs, COO/Exec. VP
Richard Haddrill, Pres.
Robert C. Caller, CFO/Exec. VP
Robert Luciano, CTO
Mark Lerner, General Counsel/Sr. VP-Law & Govt./Sec.
Robert C. Caller, Treas.
Ramesh Srinivasan, Exec. VP-Bally Systems Division

Phone: 702-584-7600	Fax:
Toll-Free: 877-462-2559	
Address: 6601 S. Bermuda Rd., Las Vegas, NV 89119 US	

GROWTH PLANS/SPECIAL FEATURES:

Bally Technologies, Inc., formerly Alliance Gaming Corporation, is a leading global designer, manufacturer, operator and distributor of traditional and nontraditional gaming machines. Operating under the name Bally Gaming and Systems, the firm has marketed over 100,000 gaming machines in the last five years, and also sells used gaming machines and spare parts. The company's gaming equipment includes electronic slot and video gaming machines. Bally operates in two units (Bally Gaming & Systems and Rainbow), the first unit consists of three divisions: Gaming Equipment, which in 2006 accounted for 42% of the company's revenue, Systems, which accounted for 22% and Gaming Operations, which accounted for 26%. (The final 10% of revenues is generated by Rainbow Casino.) The Linux-based Alpha Game Engine operating system is approved in all major jurisdictions, including Nevada and various Native American jurisdictions. The firm has launched game themes such as Blazing 7s and Blues Brothers on the Alpha Game Engine, as well as titles developed by other companies. The systems division designs, integrates and sells specialized computer monitoring systems that provide casinos with networked accounting and security services, including slot monitoring systems, casino management systems and systems facilitating cashless play. The company owns and operates the Rainbow Hotel Casino, a dockside casino in Vicksburg, Mississippi with approximately 12 table games and 890 gaming devices. The firm's Gaming Operations division operates Wide- and Near-Area Progressive gaming systems, such as Thrillions, which allow players to compete for shared progressive jackpots via separate machines; as well as non-linked daily fee games. In April 2007, Bally contracted with Las Vegas Sands, Corp. to provide casino management, slot accounting and bonusing solutions for nine casinos in Las Vegas, Macau and Singapore.

The company offers employees comprehensive medical, life and disability insurance; travel accident benefits; credit union membership; a CollegeBound fund; and educational reimbursement.

FINANCIALS: Sales and profits are in thousands of dollars—add 000 to get the full amount. 2007 Note: Financial information for 2007 was not available for all companies at press time.

2007 Sales: $	2007 Profits: $	U.S. Stock Ticker: BYI
2006 Sales: $547,144	2006 Profits: $-46,071	Int'l Ticker: Int'l Exchange:
2005 Sales: $483,107	2005 Profits: $-22,563	Employees: 2,020
2004 Sales: $476,607	2004 Profits: $79,888	Fiscal Year Ends: 6/30
2003 Sales: $407,600	2003 Profits: $19,500	Parent Company:

SALARIES/BENEFITS:

Pension Plan:	ESOP Stock Plan:	Profit Sharing:	Top Exec. Salary: $980,000	Bonus: $
Savings Plan: Y	Stock Purch. Plan:		Second Exec. Salary: $370,000	Bonus: $

OTHER THOUGHTS:

Apparent Women Officers or Directors:
Hot Spot for Advancement for Women/Minorities:

LOCATIONS: ("Y" = Yes)

West:	Southwest:	Midwest:	Southeast:	Northeast:	International:
Y	Y		Y	Y	Y

Note: Financial information, benefits and other data can change quickly and may vary from those stated here.

BALLY TOTAL FITNESS HOLDING CORPORATION
www.ballyfitness.com

Industry Group Code: 713940 Ranks within this company's industry group: Sales: 1 Profits: 2

Print Media/Publishing:	Movies:	Equipment/Supplies:		Broadcast/Cable:	Music/Audio:	Sports/Games/Gambling:	
Newspapers:	Movie Theaters:	Equipment/Supplies:	Y	Broadcast TV:	Music Production:	Games/Sports:	Y
Magazines:	Movie Production:	Gambling Equipment:		Cable TV:	Retail Music:	Retail Games Stores:	
Books:	TV/Video Prod.:	Special Services:	Y	Satellite Broadcast:	Retail Audio Equip.:	Stadiums/Teams:	
Book Stores:	Video Rental:	Advertising Services:		Radio:	Music Print./Dist.:	Gambling/Casinos:	
Distribution/Printing:	Video Distribution:	Info. Sys. Software:		Online Information:	Multimedia:	Rides/Theme Parks:	

TYPES OF BUSINESS:

Fitness Clubs
Nutritional Supplements
Personal Training Services
Fitness Classes
Fitness Equipment
Martial Arts Training

BRANDS/DIVISIONS/AFFILIATES:

Bally Sports Clubs
Sports Clubs of Canada (The)
Build Your Own Membership (BYOM)
ballystore.com
Bally Total Martial Arts
Pinnacle Fitness

CONTACTS: *Note: Officers with more than one job title may be intentionally listed here more than once.*

Michael Feder, COO
William G. Fanelli, CFO
John Wildman, Interim Chief Mktg. Officer/Sr. VP-Sales
Gail Holmberg, CIO/Sr. VP
Harold Morgan, Chief Admin. Officer/Sr. VP
Marc D. Bassewitz, General Counsel/Sr. VP/Corp. Sec.
Thomas Massimino, Sr. VP-Oper.
William G. Fanelli, Sr. VP-Corp. Dev.
William G. Fanelli, Sr. VP-Finance
Teresa R. Willows, Sr. VP-Customer Care & Member Svcs.
Julie Adams, Sr. VP-Membership Svcs.
Don R. Kornstein, Chief Reconstructing Officer
Don R. Kornstein, Interim Chmn.

Phone: 773-380-3000	Fax: 773-693-2982
Toll-Free: 800-515-2582	
Address: 8700 W. Bryn Mawr Ave., Chicago, IL 60631 US	

GROWTH PLANS/SPECIAL FEATURES:

Bally Total Fitness Holding Corp. is one of North America's largest commercial operators of fitness centers. The firm operates nearly 400 fitness centers and over 30 franchises with approximately 3.5 million members. The firm's clubs are concentrated in major metropolitan areas through the U.S., but are also located in the Caribbean, Mexico, South Korea and China. The majority of the centers use the Bally Total Fitness or Bally Sports Clubs brands, with other facilities operating under brands such as The Sports Clubs of Canada. Bally provides state-of-the-art gyms featuring a broad selection of cardiovascular, conditioning and strength equipment, with extensive aerobic and group training programs. Many locations also include pools, racquet courts and other athletic facilities. Bally targets customers aged 18-54 with mid-level income. The firm offers various membership options and payment plans (such as the Build Your Own Membership program), ranging from single-club memberships to premium plans, which provide access to all centers nationwide. Other products and services include personal training and private-label nutritional products, such as meal replacement shakes and drinks, energy and snack bars and multi-vitamins, which are sold in 7,000 retail outlets. Bally's licensed portable exercise equipment is sold in more than 90,000 retail outlets. The firm's martial arts program includes on-on-one instruction with master teachers and opened its fourth franchise in Seoul, South Korea. In April 2007, the firm's stock was delisted. In June 2007, the firm sold its fitness clubs in Toronto, Canada to Extreme Fitness Inc. and GoodLife Fitness Centres inc. for $18 million. In October 2007, Bally announced that it had emerged from Chapter 11 Bankruptcy, for which the firm filed in July 2007.

Bally Total Fitness offers its employees a 401(k) plan; training programs; tuition reimbursement; and medical and dental insurance.

FINANCIALS: Sales and profits are in thousands of dollars—add 000 to get the full amount. 2007 Note: Financial information for 2007 was not available for all companies at press time.

2007 Sales: $	2007 Profits: $	**U.S. Stock Ticker:** BFTH.PK
2006 Sales: $1,059,051	2006 Profits: $43,067	**Int'l Ticker:** Int'l Exchange:
2005 Sales: $1,071,033	2005 Profits: $-9,614	Employees: 8,800
2004 Sales: $1,047,988	2004 Profits: $-30,256	Fiscal Year Ends: 12/31
2003 Sales: $953,500	2003 Profits: $-646,000	Parent Company:

SALARIES/BENEFITS:

Pension Plan:	ESOP Stock Plan:	Profit Sharing:	Top Exec. Salary: $575,000	Bonus: $900,000
Savings Plan: Y	Stock Purch. Plan:		Second Exec. Salary: $350,000	Bonus: $225,000

OTHER THOUGHTS:

Apparent Women Officers or Directors: 3
Hot Spot for Advancement for Women/Minorities: Y

LOCATIONS: ("Y" = Yes)

West:	Southwest:	Midwest:	Southeast:	Northeast:	International:
Y	Y	Y	Y	Y	Y

Note: Financial information, benefits and other data can change quickly and may vary from those stated here.

BARNES & NOBLE INC   www.barnesandnobleinc.com

Industry Group Code: 451211 Ranks within this company's industry group: Sales: 1 Profits: 1

Print Media/Publishing:		Movies:		Equipment/Supplies:		Broadcast/Cable:		Music/Audio:		Sports/Games/Gambling:	
Newspapers:		Movie Theaters:		Equipment/Supplies:		Broadcast TV:		Music Production:		Games/Sports:	
Magazines:		Movie Production:		Gambling Equipment:		Cable TV:		Retail Music:	Y	Retail Games Stores:	Y
Books:	Y	TV/Video Prod.:		Special Services:		Satellite Broadcast:		Retail Audio Equip.:		Stadiums/Teams:	
Book Stores:		Video Rental:		Advertising Services:		Radio:		Music Print./Dist.:		Gambling/Casinos:	
Distribution/Printing:		Video Distribution:		Info. Sys. Software:		Online Information:		Multimedia:		Rides/Theme Parks:	

TYPES OF BUSINESS:

Book Stores
Music & Software Sales
In-Store Cafes
Online Sales
Book Publishing
Book Distribution

BRANDS/DIVISIONS/AFFILIATES:

B. Dalton Bookseller
Barnes & Noble Bookseller
Sterling Publishing Co., Inc.
barnesandnoble.com

CONTACTS: *Note: Officers with more than one job title may be intentionally listed here more than once.*

Stephen Riggio, CEO
Mitchell S. Klipper, COO
Joseph Lombardi, CFO
Michelle Smith, VP-Human Resources
Chris Troia, CIO
Jennifer Daniels, General Counsel/VP/Sec.
David Deason, VP-Dev.
Marie J. Toulantis, CEO-Barnes & Noble.com
Mary Ellen Keating, Sr. VP-Corp. Comm. & Public Affairs
Andy Milevoj, Mgr.-Investor Rel.
Mark Bottini, VP/Dir.-Stores
J. Alan Kahn, Pres., Publishing Group
Leonard Riggio, Chmn.
William F. Duffy, Exec. VP-Logistics & Dist.

Phone: 212-633-3300	Fax: 212-352-3660
Toll-Free: 800-422-7717	
Address: 122 5th Ave., New York, NY 10011 US	

GROWTH PLANS/SPECIAL FEATURES:

Barnes & Noble, Inc. (B&N) is the nation's largest bookseller, operating 801 book stores in all 50 states. Approximately 700 stores operate under the Barnes & Noble Bookseller trade name, and roughly 100 stores operate under the B. Dalton Bookseller trade name. The company conducts the online part of its business through Barnesandnoble.com. The firm is also a general trade book publisher, offering many series of books with the label Barnes and Noble Classics. This is enabled in part through the firm's acquisition of Sterling Publishing, a non-fiction trade publisher. Sterling is now a subsidiary of the firm. B&N's principal business is the sale of trade books (generally hardcover and paperback consumer titles, excluding educational textbooks and specialized religious titles), mass market paperbacks (such as mystery, romance, science fiction and other popular fiction), children's books, bargain books, magazines, music and movies direct to customers. B&N stores are designed to be reminiscent of old-world libraries, with wood fixtures; antique-style chairs and tables; ample public space; a cafe serving sandwiches and Starbucks coffee; a children's area; music, DVD, books, video and game sections; and public restrooms. In-store music departments provides over 40,000 titles in classical music, opera, jazz, blues and pop rock. While stores average 25,000 square feet each, the largest are 60,000-square-foot giants stocking up to 200,000 titles. Typical stores stock approximately 60,000 core titles within a variety of popular subject categories reflecting local interests, which are supplemented by new releases and bestsellers. In total, B&N has publishing or distribution rights to nearly 10,000 titles.

The company offers its employees medical, vision and dental insurance; life insurance; business travel insurance; short- and long-term disability; a 401(k) plan; tuition assistance; a book loan program; and merchandise discounts.

FINANCIALS: Sales and profits are in thousands of dollars—add 000 to get the full amount. 2007 Note: Financial information for 2007 was not available for all companies at press time.

2007 Sales: $	2007 Profits: $	**U.S. Stock Ticker: BKS**
2006 Sales: $5,103,004	2006 Profits: $146,681	**Int'l Ticker:** Int'l Exchange:
2005 Sales: $4,873,595	2005 Profits: $143,376	Employees: 39,000
2004 Sales: $4,372,177	2004 Profits: $151,775	Fiscal Year Ends: 1/31
2003 Sales: $	2003 Profits: $	Parent Company:

SALARIES/BENEFITS:

Pension Plan:	ESOP Stock Plan:	Profit Sharing:	Top Exec. Salary: $786,538	Bonus: $
Savings Plan: Y	Stock Purch. Plan:		Second Exec. Salary: $636,538	Bonus: $1,000,000

OTHER THOUGHTS:

Apparent Women Officers or Directors: 4
Hot Spot for Advancement for Women/Minorities: Y

LOCATIONS: ("Y" = Yes)

West:	Southwest:	Midwest:	Southeast:	Northeast:	International:
Y	Y	Y	Y	Y	

Note: Financial information, benefits and other data can change quickly and may vary from those stated here.

BARNESANDNOBLE.COM INC

www.bn.com

Industry Group Code: 451211E **Ranks within this company's industry group:** Sales: Profits:

Print Media/Publishing:	Movies:	Equipment/Supplies:		Broadcast/Cable:	Music/Audio:	Sports/Games/Gambling:
Newspapers:	Movie Theaters:	Equipment/Supplies:		Broadcast TV:	Music Production:	Games/Sports:
Magazines:	Movie Production:	Gambling Equipment:		Cable TV:	Retail Music:	Retail Games Stores:
Books:	TV/Video Prod.:	Special Services:	Y	Satellite Broadcast:	Retail Audio Equip.:	Stadiums/Teams:
Book Stores:	Video Rental:	Advertising Services:		Radio:	Music Print./Dist.:	Gambling/Casinos:
Distribution/Printing:	Video Distribution:	Info. Sys. Software:		Online Information:	Multimedia:	Rides/Theme Parks:

TYPES OF BUSINESS:

Books, Online Retail
Online Publishing
Distance Learning
Music Sales
Affiliate Purchase Program

BRANDS/DIVISIONS/AFFILIATES:

Barnes & Noble Inc
Barnes & Noble University
B&N Screening Room
Meet the Writers
Barnes & Noble, Jr.

CONTACTS: Note: Officers with more than one job title may be intentionally listed here more than once.

Marie J. Toulantis, CEO
Kevin M. Frain, CFO
Kevin M. Frain, VP-Oper.
Leonard S. Riggio, Chmn.

Phone: 212-414-6000	Fax: 212-414-6140
Toll-Free:	
Address: 76 9th Ave., 9th Fl., New York, NY 10011-4962 US	

GROWTH PLANS/SPECIAL FEATURES:

BarnesAndNoble.com is an online retailer of books, magazines, software, DVDs, videos, music and other items, as well as a provider of online courses through Barnes and Noble University, serving customers in 230 countries. The firm is a wholly-owned subsidiary of Barnes and Noble, Inc. The online store's database of more than 1 million titles offers bestsellers; diverse books from small presses and university publishers; and access to approximately 30 million listings for out-of-print, used and rare books. The web site contains book descriptions, reviews and excerpts, as well as a section that features recommendations from other readers, based on bestsellers of the hour. Viewers can visit the Meet the Writers section, which offers audio and video interviews with a variety of writers. In addition, the web site has a feature which allows customers to sell used textbooks to BarnesAndNoble.com. The online music store sells classical, jazz, rock and world music, and offers exclusive interviews, free downloads, over 1 million sample audio clips, nearly 100,000 music reviews and a roster of 40,000 artist biographies. The company's PC Games and Video Store carries thousands of new and used titles, consoles, accessories and strategy guides. The web site also sells toys, games and office supplies. Barnes & Noble, Jr. is an online section devoted to children. B&N Screening Room is a web page where browsers can view and order more than 10,000 full length previews. There are a variety of book clubs which customers can register for online. Barnes and Noble owns and operates two facilities, in New Jersey and Tennessee, dedicated to distribution, fulfillment operations and customer service for the company's web site. Shipping costs are free if purchases are $25 or more.

FINANCIALS: Sales and profits are in thousands of dollars—add 000 to get the full amount. 2007 Note: Financial information for 2007 was not available for all companies at press time.

2007 Sales: $	2007 Profits: $	U.S. Stock Ticker: Subsidiary
2006 Sales: $	2006 Profits: $	Int'l Ticker: Int'l Exchange:
2005 Sales: $419,800	2005 Profits: $	Employees: 1,001
2004 Sales: $420,000	2004 Profits: $	Fiscal Year Ends: 1/31
2003 Sales: $424,800	2003 Profits: $-11,300	Parent Company: BARNES & NOBLE INC

SALARIES/BENEFITS:

Pension Plan:	ESOP Stock Plan:	Profit Sharing:	Top Exec. Salary: $	Bonus: $273,000
Savings Plan:	Stock Purch. Plan:		Second Exec. Salary: $293,269	Bonus: $293,269

OTHER THOUGHTS:

Apparent Women Officers or Directors: 1
Hot Spot for Advancement for Women/Minorities:

LOCATIONS: ("Y" = Yes)

West:	Southwest:	Midwest:	Southeast:	Northeast:	International:
			Y	Y	

Note: Financial information, benefits and other data can change quickly and may vary from those stated here.

BEASLEY BROADCAST GROUP INC
www.beasleybroadcasting.com
Industry Group Code: 513111 Ranks within this company's industry group: Sales: 11   Profits: 8

Print Media/Publishing:	Movies:	Equipment/Supplies:		Broadcast/Cable:	Music/Audio:	Sports/Games/Gambling:
Newspapers:	Movie Theaters:	Equipment/Supplies:		Broadcast TV:	Music Production:	Games/Sports:
Magazines:	Movie Production:	Gambling Equipment:		Cable TV:	Retail Music:	Retail Games Stores:
Books:	TV/Video Prod.:	Special Services:		Satellite Broadcast:	Retail Audio Equip.:	Stadiums/Teams:
Book Stores:	Video Rental:	Advertising Services:	Y	Radio:	Music Print./Dist.:	Gambling/Casinos:
Distribution/Printing:	Video Distribution:	Info. Sys. Software:		Online Information:	Multimedia:	Rides/Theme Parks:

TYPES OF BUSINESS:
Radio Station Owner/Operator
Radio Broadcasting
Online Media
Web Development

BRANDS/DIVISIONS/AFFILIATES:
Beasley Interactive
iBiquity
HD Radio Technology

CONTACTS: *Note: Officers with more than one job title may be intentionally listed here more than once.*
George G. Beasley, CEO
Bruce G. Beasley, COO
Bruce G. Beasley, Pres.
B. Caroline Beasley, CFO/Exec. VP
Patricia Russell, Dir.-Human Resources
Robert L. Demuth, CTO/VP
Joyce N. Fitch, General Counsel
Brian E. Beasley, VP-Oper.
Kathleen MacCarten-Bricketto, VP-Interactive Div.
Denyse S. Mesnik, Dir.-Corp. Comm.
Marie Tedesco, VP-Finance
Allen B. Shaw, Vice Chmn.
Shaun P. Greening, VP-Financial Reporting
George G. Beasley, Chmn.

Phone: 239-263-5000	Fax: 239-263-8191
Toll-Free:	
Address: 3033 Riviera Dr., Ste. 200, Naples, FL 34103 US	

GROWTH PLANS/SPECIAL FEATURES:
Beasley Broadcasting Group (BBG) is a U.S. radio broadcasting company. The company owns and operates 44 stations (27 FM and 17 AM) which broadcast to over 3.5 million listeners. Of these stations, 19 are located in seven of the top 50 U.S. radio markets: Atlanta, Philadelphia, Boston, Miami-Ft. Lauderdale, Las Vegas, and West Palm Beach. BBG seeks to acquire clusters of stations in high-growth large and mid-sized markets located primarily in the eastern U.S., with a special focus on markets including Atlanta, Las Vegas, Philadelphia, Miami and Jacksonville. The company's radio stations program a variety of formats, including rock, country, contemporary hit radio and talk. The firm also has an Internet presence through its Beasley Interactive division and is working to generate sales from advertising, e-commerce and web development. The company's CEO, George Beasley, controls nearly 80% of the firm. BBG is one of the largest radio broadcasters in the nation, transmitting simultaneous digital and analog broadcasts using HD Radio. The firm holds interest in iBiquity, the developer of HD Radio Technology, and is a member of the HD Digital Radio Alliance Association. In February 2007, the company acquired the assets of WJBR-FM in Wilmington, Delaware from NextMedia Group, Inc.

The firm's community initiatives include participation in the National Moment of Remembrance, holiday food and clothing bank drives and co-sponsoring Special Olympic awareness races.

FINANCIALS: Sales and profits are in thousands of dollars—add 000 to get the full amount. 2007 Note: Financial information for 2007 was not available for all companies at press time.
2007 Sales: $	2007 Profits: $	U.S. Stock Ticker: BBGI
2006 Sales: $125,190	2006 Profits: $10,134	Int'l Ticker: Int'l Exchange:
2005 Sales: $124,294	2005 Profits: $10,705	Employees: 662
2004 Sales: $122,205	2004 Profits: $12,031	Fiscal Year Ends: 12/31
2003 Sales: $114,482	2003 Profits: $12,771	Parent Company:

SALARIES/BENEFITS:
Pension Plan:	ESOP Stock Plan:	Profit Sharing:	Top Exec. Salary: $664,936	Bonus: $150,000
Savings Plan: Y	Stock Purch. Plan:		Second Exec. Salary: $432,490	Bonus: $75,000

OTHER THOUGHTS:
Apparent Women Officers or Directors: 6
Hot Spot for Advancement for Women/Minorities: Y

LOCATIONS: ("Y" = Yes)
West:	Southwest:	Midwest:	Southeast:	Northeast:	International:
Y			Y	Y	

Note: Financial information, benefits and other data can change quickly and may vary from those stated here.

BELO CORP

www.belo.com

Industry Group Code: 511110 Ranks within this company's industry group: Sales: 11 Profits: 6

Print Media/Publishing:		Movies:		Equipment/Supplies:		Broadcast/Cable:		Music/Audio:		Sports/Games/Gambling:	
Newspapers:	Y	Movie Theaters:		Equipment/Supplies:		Broadcast TV:	Y	Music Production:		Games/Sports:	
Magazines:		Movie Production:		Gambling Equipment:		Cable TV:	Y	Retail Music:		Retail Games Stores:	
Books:		TV/Video Prod.:	Y	Special Services:		Satellite Broadcast:		Retail Audio Equip.:		Stadiums/Teams:	
Book Stores:		Video Rental:		Advertising Services:		Radio:		Music Print./Dist.:		Gambling/Casinos:	
Distribution/Printing:		Video Distribution:		Info. Sys. Software:		Online Information:		Multimedia:		Rides/Theme Parks:	

TYPES OF BUSINESS:

Newspaper Publishing
Broadcast Television
Cable News Channels
Online Media

BRANDS/DIVISIONS/AFFILIATES:

Dallas Morning News (The)
Providence Journal (The)
Press-Enterprise (The)
Denton Record-Chronicle
Northwest Cable News
Texas Cable News
Belo Interactive, Inc.

CONTACTS: *Note: Officers with more than one job title may be intentionally listed here more than once.*

Robert W. Decherd, CEO
Dunia A. Shive, COO
Dunia A. Shive, Pres.
Dennis A. Williamson, CFO/Exec. VP
Marian Spitzberg, Sr. VP-Human Resources
W. Craig Harper, VP-Tech.
Guy H. Kerr, Sr. VP-Law & Gov't/Sec.
Paul Fry, VP-Investor Rel.
Carey P. Hendrickson, Chief Accounting Officer/Sr. VP
James M. Moroney III, Publisher/CEO-The Dallas Morning News
Donald F. Cass, Exec. VP-Media Oper.
Robert W. Decherd, Chmn.

Phone: 214-977-6606	**Fax:** 214-977-6603
Toll-Free:	
Address: 400 S. Record St., Ste. 600, Dallas, TX 75202-4841 US	

GROWTH PLANS/SPECIAL FEATURES:

Belo Corp., one of the largest media companies in the U.S., operates a diversified group of broadcast television stations, newspapers, cable news networks and web sites. Founded as a Texas newspaper company in 1842, the company publishes four daily newspapers, including The Dallas Morning News, which has earned eight Pulitzer Prizes since 1986 for its news reporting and photography. Belo also publishes The Providence Journal; The Press-Enterprise in Riverside, California; and the Denton Record-Chronicle in Denton, Texas. The firm's group of 19 television stations reaches 14% of U.S. television-watching households in. Six of Belo's television stations operate in the top 15 television markets. It owns four ABC affiliates, five CBS affiliates, four NBC affiliates, one FOX affiliate and two independent stations, as well as seven 24-hour cable news channels including Texas Cable News and Northwest Cable News. Four of its cable news channels are operated in partnership with Cox Communications. The firm also manages over 30 web sites, several interactive alliances and a broad range of Internet-based products and services.

Employee benefits include health, dental and vision coverage; life insurance; flexible spending accounts; 401(k) savings plan; tuition assistance; and employee assistance program.

FINANCIALS: Sales and profits are in thousands of dollars—add 000 to get the full amount. 2007 Note: Financial information for 2007 was not available for all companies at press time.

2007 Sales: $	2007 Profits: $	**U.S. Stock Ticker:** BLC
2006 Sales: $1,588,272	2006 Profits: $130,526	**Int'l Ticker:** **Int'l Exchange:**
2005 Sales: $1,525,770	2005 Profits: $127,688	Employees: 7,100
2004 Sales: $1,520,296	2004 Profits: $132,496	Fiscal Year Ends: 12/31
2003 Sales: $1,436,011	2003 Profits: $128,525	Parent Company:

SALARIES/BENEFITS:

Pension Plan:	ESOP Stock Plan:	Profit Sharing:	Top Exec. Salary: $925,000	Bonus: $1,100,000
Savings Plan: Y	Stock Purch. Plan:		Second Exec. Salary: $700,000	Bonus: $685,000

OTHER THOUGHTS:

Apparent Women Officers or Directors: 5
Hot Spot for Advancement for Women/Minorities: Y

LOCATIONS: ("Y" = Yes)

West:	Southwest:	Midwest:	Southeast:	Northeast:	International:
Y	Y	Y	Y	Y	

BERKSHIRE HATHAWAY INC   www.berkshirehathaway.com

Industry Group Code: 551110   Ranks within this company's industry group: Sales: 1   Profits: 1

Print Media/Publishing:	Movies:	Equipment/Supplies:	Broadcast/Cable:	Music/Audio:	Sports/Games/Gambling:
Newspapers: Y	Movie Theaters:	Equipment/Supplies:	Broadcast TV:	Music Production:	Games/Sports:
Magazines:	Movie Production:	Gambling Equipment:	Cable TV:	Retail Music:	Retail Games Stores:
Books: Y	TV/Video Prod.:	Special Services:	Satellite Broadcast:	Retail Audio Equip.:	Stadiums/Teams:
Book Stores:	Video Rental:	Advertising Services:	Radio:	Music Print./Dist.:	Gambling/Casinos:
Distribution/Printing:	Video Distribution:	Info. Sys. Software:	Online Information:	Multimedia:	Rides/Theme Parks:

TYPES OF BUSINESS:

Direct Property & Casualty Insurance & Reinsurance
Retail Operations
Foodservice Operations
Building Products & Services
Apparel & Footwear
Technology Training
Manufactured Housing & RVs
Business Jet Flexible Ownership Services

BRANDS/DIVISIONS/AFFILIATES:

General Re
GEICO
International Dairy Queen
Benjamin Moore & Co.
FlightSafety International, Inc.
Dexter Shoe Company
Borsheim's Jewelry Corp.
Acme Brick Company

CONTACTS: Note: Officers with more than one job title may be intentionally listed here more than once.

Warren E. Buffet, CEO
Marc D. Hamburg, CFO/VP
Forrest N. Krutter, Sec.
Marc D. Hamburg, Treas./VP
Charles T. Munger, Vice Chmn.
Jo Ellen Rieck, Dir.-Taxes
Mark D. Millard, Dir.-Financial Assets
Daniel J. Jakisch, Controller
Warren E. Buffet, Chmn.

Phone: 402-346-1400	Fax: 402-346-3375
Toll-Free:	
Address: 1440 Kiewit Plz., Omaha, NE 68131 US	

GROWTH PLANS/SPECIAL FEATURES:

Berkshire Hathaway, Inc. is a holding company that owns subsidiaries engaged in diverse business activities, most importantly insurance and reinsurance. Berkshire provides property and casualty insurance and reinsurance, and life accident and health reinsurance through approximately 60 U.S. and foreign businesses. General Re Corp., through its subsidiaries, conducts global reinsurance business in 61 cities and provides reinsurance worldwide. GEICO mainly provides private passenger auto insurance to individuals in 49 states in the U.S. and Washington, D.C. The company's financial subsidiaries include Clayton Homes, a manufactured housing company; XTRA Corporation, a provider of transportation equipment leases; furniture rental company CORT Business Services Corp.; and General Re Securities. Berkshire's apparel and footwear businesses include Fruit of the Loom, Garan, Fechheimer Brothers, H.H. Brown Shoe Group and Justin Brands. The firm manufactures and distributes building products through Acme Brick Company, Benjamin Moore & Co., Johns Manville and MiTek. Subsidiary FlightSafety provides training to aircraft and ship pilots; while NetJets, Inc. offers fractional ownership programs for aircraft. In addition, subsidiary International Dairy Queen services approximately 5,700 Dairy Queen, Orange Julius and Karmelkorn stores. Other non-insurance operations include grocery and foodservice distribution, furniture retail, jewelry retail, carpet manufacturing, utilities and energy, newspapers, cleaning products, confectioneries, agricultural equipment, kitchen tools and recreational vehicles. The firm acquired TTI, Inc., a privately-held electronic component distributor and its subsidiary, Mouser Electronics, in late 2006. In May 2007, Berkshire agreed to acquire jewelry manufacturers Bel-Oro International and Aurafin LLC. Upon completion of the acquisition, the two companies will be combined to form Richline Group.

Berkshire Hathaway's CEO, Warren Buffett, is world-famous for his business and investment expertise.

FINANCIALS: Sales and profits are in thousands of dollars—add 000 to get the full amount. 2007 Note: Financial information for 2007 was not available for all companies at press time.

2007 Sales: $	2007 Profits: $	**U.S. Stock Ticker: BRK**
2006 Sales: $98,539,000	2006 Profits: $1,015,000	**Int'l Ticker:** Int'l Exchange:
2005 Sales: $81,663,000	2005 Profits: $8,528,000	Employees: 217,000
2004 Sales: $74,382,000	2004 Profits: $7,308,000	Fiscal Year Ends: 12/31
2003 Sales: $64,288,000	2003 Profits: $8,151,000	Parent Company:

SALARIES/BENEFITS:

Pension Plan: Y	ESOP Stock Plan: Y	Profit Sharing:	Top Exec. Salary: $662,500	Bonus: $
Savings Plan:	Stock Purch. Plan:		Second Exec. Salary: $100,000	Bonus: $

OTHER THOUGHTS:

Apparent Women Officers or Directors: 2
Hot Spot for Advancement for Women/Minorities:

LOCATIONS: ("Y" = Yes)

West:	Southwest:	Midwest:	Southeast:	Northeast:	International:
Y	Y	Y	Y	Y	Y

Note: Financial information, benefits and other data can change quickly and may vary from those stated here.

BERRY COMPANY (THE)

www.lmberry.com

Industry Group Code: 511000 **Ranks within this company's industry group:** Sales: Profits:

Print Media/Publishing:	Movies:	Equipment/Supplies:	Broadcast/Cable:	Music/Audio:	Sports/Games/Gambling:
Newspapers:	Movie Theaters:	Equipment/Supplies:	Broadcast TV:	Music Production:	Games/Sports:
Magazines:	Movie Production:	Gambling Equipment:	Cable TV:	Retail Music:	Retail Games Stores:
Books: Y	TV/Video Prod.:	Special Services: Y	Satellite Broadcast:	Retail Audio Equip.:	Stadiums/Teams:
Book Stores:	Video Rental:	Advertising Services: Y	Radio:	Music Print./Dist.:	Gambling/Casinos:
Distribution/Printing:	Video Distribution:	Info. Sys. Software: Y	Online Information:	Multimedia:	Rides/Theme Parks:

TYPES OF BUSINESS:

Yellow Pages Advertising
Marketing
Sales
Management Training
Publishing
Strategic Planning
Investment Research

BRANDS/DIVISIONS/AFFILIATES:

AT&T Inc
Independent Line of Business
South Central Area
Berry Network, Inc.
Berry Sales & Marketing Solutions
Real Yellow Pages (The)
Berry Real Returns

CONTACTS: *Note: Officers with more than one job title may be intentionally listed here more than once.*

Dan Graham, CEO
Dan Graham, Pres.
Anita Moore, VP-Human Resources
Barb Bertrams, VP-IT & Publishing
Langley Kitchings, Asst. General Counsel/General Attorney
Carol Warner, VP-Finance
Kathy Geiger-Schwab, Exec. VP/Pres., Berry Network, Inc.
Kevin Payne, Group VP-Berry Network, Inc.
Greg Meineke, Group VP-South Central Area
John Snyder, Group VP-Independents

Phone: 937-296-2121	**Fax:** 937-296-2011
Toll-Free: 800-366-2379	
Address: 3170 Kettering Blvd., Dayton, OH 45439 US	

GROWTH PLANS/SPECIAL FEATURES:

The Berry Company (Berry), a wholly owned subsidiary of AT&T, Inc., is one of the largest yellow pages advertising sales agencies in the U.S. It has 41 offices located in 38 states; in total, the company covers over 700 markets. Berry provides yellow page directory services including electronic ad design; sales; marketing and sales support; and composition pagination, compilation, printing, billing and delivery. The company is organized into four operating units: Independent Line of Business (ILOB); South Central Area (SCA); Berry Network, Inc. (BNI); and Berry Sales & Marketing Solutions. ILOB consists of nine divisions that serve independent yellow page publishers in over 500 markets for over 80 telephone companies. SCA operates in nine divisions across five states and is dedicated to publishing print and Internet yellow pages for AT&T and also publishes AT&T's The Real Yellow Pages. BNI provides domestic clients with full-service marketing, research and strategic planning for investments for over 400 clients. The unit was recently selected as Kawasaki Motors Corp., U.S.A.'s national yellow pages advertising agency. As such, BNI will conduct a full-service ad campaign for more than 1,500 Kawasaki dealers, which will include directory selection, advertising placement, and billing and research services. Berry Sales & Marketing is a domestic and international consulting service that helps clients reach their growth potential through sales, marketing and management training and solutions. The company recently launched Berry Real Results, an interactive tool sales representatives can use to help demonstrate to prospective customers what sort of return on investment they can expect, reasons to buy Berry services and former advertising success stories.

Employees of Berry receive paid holidays; medical and dental plans; tuition reimbursement; a scholarship program; personal time; short- and long-term disability; life insurance; floating holidays; and child care discounts.

FINANCIALS: Sales and profits are in thousands of dollars—add 000 to get the full amount. 2007 Note: Financial information for 2007 was not available for all companies at press time.

2007 Sales: $	2007 Profits: $	**U.S. Stock Ticker: Subsidiary**
2006 Sales: $	2006 Profits: $	**Int'l Ticker:** Int'l Exchange:
2005 Sales: $	2005 Profits: $	Employees:
2004 Sales: $	2004 Profits: $	Fiscal Year Ends: 12/31
2003 Sales: $	2003 Profits: $	Parent Company: AT&T INC

SALARIES/BENEFITS:

Pension Plan: Y	ESOP Stock Plan:	Profit Sharing:	Top Exec. Salary: $	Bonus: $
Savings Plan: Y	Stock Purch. Plan:		Second Exec. Salary: $	Bonus: $

OTHER THOUGHTS:

Apparent Women Officers or Directors: 4
Hot Spot for Advancement for Women/Minorities: Y

LOCATIONS: ("Y" = Yes)

West:	Southwest:	Midwest:	Southeast:	Northeast:	International:
Y		Y	Y	Y	Y

BERTELSMANN AG
www.bertelsmann.com

Industry Group Code: 513120 Ranks within this company's industry group: Sales: 1 Profits: 1

Print Media/Publishing:		Movies:		Equipment/Supplies:		Broadcast/Cable:		Music/Audio:		Sports/Games/Gambling:	
Newspapers:	Y	Movie Theaters:		Equipment/Supplies:		Broadcast TV:	Y	Music Production:	Y	Games/Sports:	
Magazines:	Y	Movie Production:		Gambling Equipment:		Cable TV:	Y	Retail Music:	Y	Retail Games Stores:	
Books:	Y	TV/Video Prod.:	Y	Special Services:		Satellite Broadcast:		Retail Audio Equip.:		Stadiums/Teams:	
Book Stores:		Video Rental:		Advertising Services:	Y	Radio:		Music Print./Dist.:	Y	Gambling/Casinos:	
Distribution/Printing:		Video Distribution:		Info. Sys. Software:		Online Information:		Multimedia:		Rides/Theme Parks:	

TYPES OF BUSINESS:
Television Broadcasting
Radio Broadcasting
Magazine & Newspaper Publishing
Book Publishing
e-Commerce
Music Publishing
Print & Media Services
Book & Music Clubs

BRANDS/DIVISIONS/AFFILIATES:
RTL Group
Arvato AG
Gruner + Jahr AG
Direct Group
Random House
Bertelsmann Music Group (BMG)
Sony BMG Music Entertainment
Bertelsmann Digital Media Investments

CONTACTS: Note: Officers with more than one job title may be intentionally listed here more than once.
Gunter Thielen, CEO
Thomas Rabe, CFO
Immanuel Hermreck, Dir.-Human Resources
Johannes Mohn, Dir.-Media Tech.
Ulrich Koch, Dir.-Legal Dept.
Guenter Grueger, Dir.-Strategy & Controlling
Andreas Grafemeyer, Sr. VP-Media Rel.
Roger Schweitzer, Dir.-Finance & Treasury
Hartmut Ostrowski, Chmn.-Arvato AG
Gerhard Zeiler, CEO-RTL Group
Bernd Kundrun, Chmn./CEO-Gruner + Jahr AG
Fernando Carro, CEO-Direct Group
Gunter Thielen, Chmn.

Phone: 49-5241-80-0	Fax: 49-5241-80-9662
Toll-Free:	
Address: Carl-Bertelsmann-Strasse 270, Gutersloh, D-33311 Germany	

GROWTH PLANS/SPECIAL FEATURES:

Bertelsmann AG is a leading private media company operating in 63 countries worldwide. Its global reach encompasses television and radio; magazines and newspapers; music labels; book publishers; professional information; print and media services; book and music clubs; and e-commerce media. Each of the firm's primary subsidiaries handles a different aspect of media. Subsidiaries include RTL Group, which generated approximately 29% of Bertelsmann's 2006 revenue; Arvato AG, 22%; Gruner + Jahr AG, 15%; Direct Group, 14%; Random House, 10%; and Bertelsmann Music Group (BMG), 10%. RTL Group, one of the largest broadcasting and production companies in Europe, operates approximately 38 television stations and more than 29 radio stations in 10 countries reaching 200 million people daily. Arvato provides various media services in 37 countries worldwide through four divisions: Arvato Services supplies communications and logistics services; Arvato Print offers conventional printing services; Arvato Digital Services provides integrated services for audio, video, IT, games and other technology sectors; and Arvato Systems offers data centers and other IT services. Gruner + Jahr has more than 285 magazine and newspaper titles and accompanying web sites in 20 countries; professional web sites; and printing operations in the U.S. and Germany. Direct Group sells books, music and DVDs through the Internet and an assortment of book and music clubs. Random House, one of the world's largest book publishing groups, publishes authors such as Dan Brown, John Grisham and Danielle Steel. BMG is mainly composed of joint-venture Sony BMG Music Entertainment, with more than 200 labels including Columbia Records, RCA Records and Epic Record. Bertelsmann recently signed an agreement to sell BMG Music Publishing Group, a subsidiary of BMG, to Vivendi Universal for $2.09 billion. The firm also recently established a venture capital fund called Bertelsmann Digital Media Investments.

Bertelsmann offers recent graduates and undergraduates international internships in the media business.

FINANCIALS: Sales and profits are in thousands of dollars—add 000 to get the full amount. 2007 Note: Financial information for 2007 was not available for all companies at press time.

2007 Sales: $	2007 Profits: $	**U.S. Stock Ticker:**
2006 Sales: $25,458,500	2006 Profits: $3,198,000	**Int'l Ticker: BTG4** Int'l Exchange: Frankfurt-Euronext
2005 Sales: $21,415,000	2005 Profits: $1,246,090	Employees: 97,132
2004 Sales: $20,368,400	2004 Profits: $1,402,980	Fiscal Year Ends: 12/31
2003 Sales: $	2003 Profits: $	Parent Company:

SALARIES/BENEFITS:

Pension Plan:	ESOP Stock Plan:	Profit Sharing:	Top Exec. Salary: $	Bonus: $
Savings Plan: Y	Stock Purch. Plan:		Second Exec. Salary: $	Bonus: $

OTHER THOUGHTS:
Apparent Women Officers or Directors: 4
Hot Spot for Advancement for Women/Minorities: Y

LOCATIONS: ("Y" = Yes)

West:	Southwest:	Midwest:	Southeast:	Northeast:	International:
Y		Y	Y	Y	Y

Note: Financial information, benefits and other data can change quickly and may vary from those stated here.

BEST BUY CO INC

www.bestbuy.com

Industry Group Code: 443110 Ranks within this company's industry group: Sales: 1 Profits: 1

Print Media/Publishing:	Movies:	Equipment/Supplies:	Broadcast/Cable:	Music/Audio:	Sports/Games/Gambling:
Newspapers:	Movie Theaters:	Equipment/Supplies:	Broadcast TV:	Music Production:	Games/Sports:
Magazines:	Movie Production:	Gambling Equipment:	Cable TV:	Retail Music: Y	Retail Games Stores:
Books:	TV/Video Prod.:	Special Services:	Satellite Broadcast:	Retail Audio Equip.:	Stadiums/Teams:
Book Stores:	Video Rental:	Advertising Services: Y	Radio:	Music Print./Dist.:	Gambling/Casinos:
Distribution/Printing:	Video Distribution: Y	Info. Sys. Software: Y	Online Information:	Multimedia:	Rides/Theme Parks:

TYPES OF BUSINESS:

Consumer Electronics Stores
Retail Music & Video Sales
Personal Computers
Office Supplies
Furniture
Appliances
Cameras
Consumer Electronics Installation & Service

BRANDS/DIVISIONS/AFFILIATES:

Geek Squad
Future Shop, Ltd.
Magnolia Audio Video
Studio D
Pacific Sales
Jiangsu Five Star Appliance Co., Ltd.
Speakeasy, Inc.

CONTACTS: Note: Officers with more than one job title may be intentionally listed here more than once.

Bradbury H. Anderson, CEO/Vice Chmn.
Brian Dunn, COO
Brian Dunn, Pres.
James L. Muehlbauer, Interim CFO
Michael Linton, Chief Mktg. Officer/Exec. VP
Robert A. Willett, CIO
Joe Joyce, General Counsel/Sr. VP
Kalendu (Kal) Patel, Exec. VP-Strategy & Int'l
Susan Hoff, Sr. VP/Chief Comm. Officer
Sue Grafton, Chief Acct. Officer/Controller/VP
Robert A. Willett, COO/Pres., Best Buy Canada
Timothy D. McGeehan, Exec. VP-Retail Sales
David Hemler, Pres., Best Buy For Businesses
James L. Muehlbauer, Sr. VP/CFO-Best Buy US
Richard M. Schulze, Chmn.
Robert A. Willett, CEO-Best Buy Int'l
Michael London, Exec. VP-Global Sourcing

Phone: 612-291-1000	Fax: 612-292-4001
Toll-Free: 888-237-8289	
Address: 7601 Penn Ave. S., Richfield, MN 55423 US	

GROWTH PLANS/SPECIAL FEATURES:

Best Buy Co., Inc. is one of the nation's largest retailers of name-brand consumer electronics, entertainment software and appliances. Its products include home office equipment; cameras; computer and audio/video equipment furniture; computer upgrades; and car audio and security system installation. It offers product service and repair through 10,000 Geek Squad agents, available in all U.S. and Canadian Best Buy stores and 12 stand-alone Geek Squad stores. Best Buy operates 822 retail stores in 49 states and the Washington, D.C. and 121 Future Shop and 47 Best Buy stores in Canada. Sales per square foot per year average $940. The firm plans to open about 75 new Best Buy stores yearly, 60 in the U.S. and 15 in Canada. Much of its future growth will be in smaller cities, using the 20,000 square foot format. The eventual goal is roughly 1,000 Best Buy stores in the U.S. and 200 Best Buy and Future Shop stores in Canada. In addition, the Geek Squad will open about 50 free-standing stores in urban areas over the mid term, and Best Buy will open several consumer electronics stores in China. The firm is experimenting with a boutique store format called Studio D in Naperville, Illinois. The firm's 20 Magnolia Audio Video stores serve the upscale home electronics market. In March 2006, the company acquired Pacific Sales, which operates 14 kitchen and bath centers in California. In 2006, Best Buy acquired 75% of Chinese appliance and consumer electronics company Five Star, for $184 million, and it opened its first Chinese Best Buy store in Shanghai, with plans to open two to three more in the next year. In May 2007, Best Buy acquired Speakeasy, Inc., which provides small businesses with VoIP services, for $97 million.

Qualified employees enjoy savings and stock purchase plans, insurance coverage, employee discounts and tuition assistance.

FINANCIALS: Sales and profits are in thousands of dollars—add 000 to get the full amount. 2007 Note: Financial information for 2007 was not available for all companies at press time.

2007 Sales: $35,934,000	2007 Profits: $1,377,000	**U.S. Stock Ticker: BBY**
2006 Sales: $30,848,000	2006 Profits: $1,140,000	**Int'l Ticker:** Int'l Exchange:
2005 Sales: $27,433,000	2005 Profits: $984,000	Employees: 140,000
2004 Sales: $24,547,000	2004 Profits: $704,000	Fiscal Year Ends: 2/28
2003 Sales: $20,946,000	2003 Profits: $99,000	Parent Company:

SALARIES/BENEFITS:

Pension Plan:	ESOP Stock Plan:	Profit Sharing:	Top Exec. Salary: $1,172,995	Bonus: $2,650,969
Savings Plan: Y	Stock Purch. Plan: Y		Second Exec. Salary: $746,309	Bonus: $1,271,250

OTHER THOUGHTS:

Apparent Women Officers or Directors: 5
Hot Spot for Advancement for Women/Minorities: Y

LOCATIONS: ("Y" = Yes)

West:	Southwest:	Midwest:	Southeast:	Northeast:	International:
Y	Y	Y	Y	Y	Y

Note: Financial information, benefits and other data can change quickly and may vary from those stated here.

BIOWARE CORP   www.bioware.com

Industry Group Code: 511208 Ranks within this company's industry group: Sales: Profits:

Print Media/Publishing:	Movies:	Equipment/Supplies:	Broadcast/Cable:	Music/Audio:	Sports/Games/Gambling:	
Newspapers:	Movie Theaters:	Equipment/Supplies:	Broadcast TV:	Music Production:	Games/Sports:	Y
Magazines:	Movie Production:	Gambling Equipment:	Cable TV:	Retail Music:	Retail Games Stores:	
Books:	TV/Video Prod.:	Special Services:	Satellite Broadcast:	Retail Audio Equip.:	Stadiums/Teams:	
Book Stores:	Video Rental:	Advertising Services:	Radio:	Music Print./Dist.:	Gambling/Casinos:	
Distribution/Printing:	Video Distribution:	Info. Sys. Software:	Online Information:	Multimedia:	Rides/Theme Parks:	

TYPES OF BUSINESS:

Computer Software/Games
E-commerce

BRANDS/DIVISIONS/AFFILIATES:

Baldur's Gate
Mass Effect
BioWare Odyssey Engine
Star Wars: Knights of the Old Republic
Neverwinter Nights
Pandemic Studios, LLC
Elevation Partners
VG Holdings

CONTACTS: *Note: Officers with more than one job title may be intentionally listed here more than once.*

Ray Muzyka, CEO
Greg Zeschuk, Pres.
Richard Iwaniuk, Dir.-Finance
Greg Richardson, CEO-VG Holdings
Jillian Goldberg, VP-Mktg., VG Holdings

Phone: 780-430-0164	Fax: 780-439-6374
Toll-Free:	
Address: 200, 4445 Calgary Trail, Edmonton, AB T6H 5R7 Canada	

GROWTH PLANS/SPECIAL FEATURES:

BioWare Corp. is an electronic entertainment company specializing in creating computer and console video games, mainly in the role playing game (RPG) format, and is one of the most successful game developers in the world, selling hundreds of thousands, sometimes millions of units per title. Its first title, Shattered Steel, sold nearly 200,000 units. BioWare's best-selling game, Baldur's Gate, has sold over 2 million units for the PC. This title was followed by Baldur's Gate: Tales of the Sword Coast, Baldur's Gate II: Shadows of Amn and Baldur's Gate II: Throne of Bhaal. Together, the Baldur's Gate series of titles have sold almost 5 million copies. Other titles the company has released include Neverwinter Nights and Star Wars: Knights of the Old Republic. The company began a new handheld game development group in 2006, producing games for the Nintendo DS system. Its newest games are Dragon Age, a RPG still in development which is set in proprietary fantasy setting and Mass Effect, released in November 2007. BioWare also licenses its game engine technology. A number of games, including Planescape: Torment and the Icewind Dale series have been developed using BioWare's Infinity Engine; the Bioware Aurora Engine was used to power Neverwinter Nights 2 from Obsidian Entertainment and Atari; and the BioWare Odyssey Engine was used to make Star Wars: Knights of the Old Republic 2: The Sith Lords. It operates its own e-commerce site for its products at Store.bioware.com. Elevation Partners, a private equity firm, recently bought a majority ownership interest in BioWare and another major game developer, Pandemic Studios, LLC. Bioware and Pandemic have been brought together in a joint venture under the name VG Holdings, and will have separate creative operations, but will engage in some business operations together. In October 2007, EA Games agreed to acquire VG Holdings for approximately $775 million.

FINANCIALS: Sales and profits are in thousands of dollars—add 000 to get the full amount. 2007 Note: Financial information for 2007 was not available for all companies at press time.

2007 Sales: $	2007 Profits: $	**U.S. Stock Ticker: Private**	
2006 Sales: $	2006 Profits: $	**Int'l Ticker:** Int'l Exchange:	
2005 Sales: $	2005 Profits: $	Employees:	
2004 Sales: $18,400	2004 Profits: $	Fiscal Year Ends: 12/31	
2003 Sales: $	2003 Profits: $	Parent Company:	

SALARIES/BENEFITS:

Pension Plan:	ESOP Stock Plan:	Profit Sharing:	Top Exec. Salary: $	Bonus: $
Savings Plan:	Stock Purch. Plan:		Second Exec. Salary: $	Bonus: $

OTHER THOUGHTS:

Apparent Women Officers or Directors: 1
Hot Spot for Advancement for Women/Minorities:

LOCATIONS: ("Y" = Yes)

West:	Southwest:	Midwest:	Southeast:	Northeast:	International:
	Y				Y

BLOCKBUSTER INC

www.blockbuster.com

Industry Group Code: 532230 Ranks within this company's industry group: Sales: 1   Profits: 1

Print Media/Publishing:	Movies:		Equipment/Supplies:	Broadcast/Cable:	Music/Audio:	Sports/Games/Gambling:	
Newspapers:	Movie Theaters:		Equipment/Supplies:	Broadcast TV:	Music Production:	Games/Sports:	Y
Magazines:	Movie Production:		Gambling Equipment:	Cable TV:	Retail Music:	Retail Games Stores:	Y
Books:	TV/Video Prod.:		Special Services:	Satellite Broadcast:	Retail Audio Equip.:	Stadiums/Teams:	
Book Stores:	Video Rental:	Y	Advertising Services:	Radio:	Music Print./Dist.:	Gambling/Casinos:	
Distribution/Printing:	Video Distribution:		Info. Sys. Software:	Online Information:	Multimedia:	Rides/Theme Parks:	

TYPES OF BUSINESS:

Videocassette Rental Stores
DVD Rentals
Video Game Rentals & Sales
DVD & VHS Sales
Consumer Electronics Sales
Online Video Rental Service

BRANDS/DIVISIONS/AFFILIATES:

Xtra-Vision
Game Rush
Gamestation
Rent it! Like it! Buy it!
Blockbuster Total Access

CONTACTS: Note: Officers with more than one job title may be intentionally listed here more than once.

James W. Keyes, CEO
Thomas M. Casey, CFO/Exec. VP
Keith Morrow, CIO
David Podeschi, Sr. VP-Merch.
Eric H. Peterson, General Counsel/Exec. VP/Sec.
Frank G. Paci, Exec. VP-Strategic Planning & Dev.
Karen Raskopf, Sr. VP-Corp. Comm.
Angelika Torres, Dir.-Investor Rel.
James W. Keyes, Chmn.
David Podeschi, Sr. VP-Logistics & Distribution

Phone: 214-854-3000	Fax: 214-854-4848
Toll-Free:	
Address: 1201 Elm St., Dallas, TX 75270 US	

GROWTH PLANS/SPECIAL FEATURES:

Blockbuster, Inc. is a leading provider of rentable home movies and video games. The firm also rents DVD players, VCRs and video game consoles. It operates approximately 8,360 owned and franchised stores, including over 3,166 locations in 22 other countries and stores operating under different names. In Ireland, the company operates under the Xtra-Vision brand name; in Canada, Italy, Mexico and Denmark, the firm operates a chain called Game Rush; and operates in the U.K. as Gamestation. The U.S. generates approximately 65.6% of revenues; the U.K., 15.2%; Canada, 7.9%; and all other international operations, 11.3%. Blockbuster stores feature Rent it! Like it! Buy it!, a program designed to increase customer satisfaction with their purchases by offering a low-cost alternative to view a movie prior to making a purchasing decision. Blockbuster is engaged in an ongoing price war with Netflix, which offers unlimited online DVD rentals for a flat monthly fee with no late charges. In an effort to compete, the company launched Blockbuster Total Access in November 2006, with a similar operating model to that of Netflix, with 40,000 titles to choose from, no late fees and free shipping. However, the program also offers customers the opportunity to trade rentals in at participating Blockbuster stores and offers monthly coupons for movie or video game rentals. It currently has over 2 million paying subscribers. Blockbuster hopes to expand its in-store video game boutiques, giving customers new reasons to come to stores. During 2006, the firm divested itself of Movie Brands, Inc. and Movie Trading Co. In January 2007, it completed the sale of Rhino Video Games, a specialty game store.

Blockbuster offers its eligible employees tuition reimbursement; free video rentals and discounts on store merchandise; flexible schedules; credit union affiliation; auto and homeowners insurance programs; pet insurance; and an employee assistance program.

FINANCIALS: Sales and profits are in thousands of dollars—add 000 to get the full amount. 2007 Note: Financial information for 2007 was not available for all companies at press time.

2007 Sales: $	2007 Profits: $	**U.S. Stock Ticker:** BBI
2006 Sales: $5,523,500	2006 Profits: $54,700	**Int'l Ticker:** Int'l Exchange:
2005 Sales: $5,721,300	2005 Profits: $-588,100	Employees: 67,300
2004 Sales: $6,053,200	2004 Profits: $-1,248,800	Fiscal Year Ends: 12/31
2003 Sales: $5,911,700	2003 Profits: $-983,900	Parent Company:

SALARIES/BENEFITS:

Pension Plan:	ESOP Stock Plan:	Profit Sharing:	Top Exec. Salary: $2,550,000	Bonus: $3,052,500
Savings Plan: Y	Stock Purch. Plan:		Second Exec. Salary: $640,000	Bonus: $768,000

OTHER THOUGHTS:

Apparent Women Officers or Directors: 1
Hot Spot for Advancement for Women/Minorities:

LOCATIONS: ("Y" = Yes)

West:	Southwest:	Midwest:	Southeast:	Northeast:	International:
Y	Y	Y	Y	Y	Y

BLOOMBERG LP
www.bloomberg.com

Industry Group Code: 514100 Ranks within this company's industry group: Sales: 2   Profits: 1

Print Media/Publishing:		Movies:		Equipment/Supplies:		Broadcast/Cable:		Music/Audio:		Sports/Games/Gambling:	
Newspapers:		Movie Theaters:		Equipment/Supplies:		Broadcast TV:	Y	Music Production:		Games/Sports:	
Magazines:	Y	Movie Production:		Gambling Equipment:		Cable TV:		Retail Music:		Retail Games Stores:	
Books:		TV/Video Prod.:		Special Services:		Satellite Broadcast:		Retail Audio Equip.:		Stadiums/Teams:	
Book Stores:		Video Rental:		Advertising Services:	Y	Radio:		Music Print./Dist.:	Y	Gambling/Casinos:	
Distribution/Printing:		Video Distribution:		Info. Sys. Software:		Online Information:		Multimedia:		Rides/Theme Parks:	

TYPES OF BUSINESS:

Financial Data Publishing-Print & Online
Magazine Publishing
Management Software
Multimedia Presentation Services
Broadcast Television
Radio Broadcasting
Electronic Exchange Systems
Software

BRANDS/DIVISIONS/AFFILIATES:

Bloomberg Professional
Bloomberg Terminals
Bloomberg Tradebook
Bloomberg Electronic Trading Systems
Bloomberg Roadshows
Bloomberg Television
Bloomberg Magazine
Bloomberg News

CONTACTS: *Note: Officers with more than one job title may be intentionally listed here more than once.*

Lex Fenwick, CEO
Tom Secunda, Dir.-Worldwide Sales
Peter T. Grauer, Chmn.

Phone: 212-318-2000	Fax: 917-369-5000
Toll-Free:	
Address: 731 Lexington Ave., New York, NY 10022 US	

GROWTH PLANS/SPECIAL FEATURES:

Bloomberg LP is one of the world's largest information services, news and media companies, serving the financial services industry as well as government offices and agencies, corporations and news organizations in 126 countries. The firm's core business, the Bloomberg Professional service, is delivered online to Bloomberg Terminals that are rented by subscribers. The terminals provide traders and asset managers a combination of real-time, around-the-clock financial news, market data, analysis, electronic trading, multimedia report capabilities and e-mail on a single platform at an average monthly fee of about $1,500 per month per terminal. There are four primary services included with Bloomberg Professional. Bloomberg Tradebook is an electronic global agency trader offering customers the ability to trade on 65 markets in 54 countries. The Bloomberg Electronic Trading Systems allows the firm's professional services to work in conjunction with outside infrastructure and includes a global risk-management software solution and a portfolio management system. Bloomberg Data License provides access to the Bloomberg financial database and to more than 4 million financial instruments. Finally, Bloomberg Roadshows is a multimedia presentation service featuring synchronized slides, audio, streaming video and live video technology. Issuers and underwriters use it to target buy-side clients directly through distribution of presentations on all types of debt, equity, structured finance issues and research. The company also offers Bloomberg Television, broadcasting in seven languages across 10 networks into 200 million homes; Bloomberg Radio, providing business news to 750 affiliates worldwide; Bloomberg.com, offering financial news and information; and Bloomberg Magazine, specially edited for Bloomberg Professional subscribers. Bloomberg Law provides legal research tools. Finally, Bloomberg News, staffed with 1,600 reporters and editors in 94 bureaus worldwide, files more than 5,000 news stories daily. Michael Bloomberg, Mayor of New York City, is the firm's founder and owner of about 68% of its stock.

FINANCIALS: Sales and profits are in thousands of dollars—add 000 to get the full amount. 2007 Note: Financial information for 2007 was not available for all companies at press time.

2007 Sales: $	2007 Profits: $	U.S. Stock Ticker: Private
2006 Sales: $4,700,000	2006 Profits: $1,500,000	Int'l Ticker: Int'l Exchange:
2005 Sales: $4,100,000	2005 Profits: $	Employees: 9,800
2004 Sales: $3,100,000	2004 Profits: $	Fiscal Year Ends: 12/31
2003 Sales: $3,000,000	2003 Profits: $	Parent Company:

SALARIES/BENEFITS:

Pension Plan:	ESOP Stock Plan:	Profit Sharing:	Top Exec. Salary: $	Bonus: $
Savings Plan: Y	Stock Purch. Plan:		Second Exec. Salary: $	Bonus: $

OTHER THOUGHTS:

Apparent Women Officers or Directors:						

LOCATIONS: ("Y" = Yes)

	West:	Southwest:	Midwest:	Southeast:	Northeast:	International:
Hot Spot for Advancement for Women/Minorities:	Y	Y	Y	Y	Y	Y

BOOKS A MILLION INC
www.booksamillion.com

Industry Group Code: 451211 Ranks within this company's industry group: Sales: 3 Profits: 3

Print Media/Publishing:	Movies:	Equipment/Supplies:	Broadcast/Cable:	Music/Audio:	Sports/Games/Gambling:
Newspapers:	Movie Theaters:	Equipment/Supplies:	Broadcast TV:	Music Production:	Games/Sports:
Magazines:	Movie Production:	Gambling Equipment:	Cable TV:	Retail Music:	Retail Games Stores:
Books:	TV/Video Prod.:	Special Services:	Satellite Broadcast:	Retail Audio Equip.:	Stadiums/Teams:
Book Stores:	Video Rental:	Advertising Services:	Radio:	Music Print./Dist.:	Gambling/Casinos:
Distribution/Printing:	Video Distribution:	Info. Sys. Software:	Online Information:	Multimedia:	Rides/Theme Parks:

TYPES OF BUSINESS:
Book Stores
Newsstands
Coffee Bars
Wholesale Distribution
Online Sales
Internet Development & Services

BRANDS/DIVISIONS/AFFILIATES:
Books & Co.
Bookland
Joe Muggs
American Internet Services, Inc.
bamm.com
American Wholesale Book Company
Book$mart, Inc.
NetCentral

CONTACTS: Note: Officers with more than one job title may be intentionally listed here more than once.
Sandra B. Cochran, CEO
Sandra B. Cochran, Pres.
Douglas G. Markham, CFO
Sandra B. Cochran, Corp. Sec.
Terrance G. Finley, Pres., Merch. Group
Clyde B. Anderson, Chmn.

Phone: 205-942-3737	**Fax:** 205-942-6601
Toll-Free:	
Address: 402 Industrial Ln., Birmingham, AL 35211 US	

GROWTH PLANS/SPECIAL FEATURES:

Books-A-Million, Inc. is one of the leading book retailers in the southeastern United States. Books-A-Million currently operates more than 200 stores in 22 states and Washington D.C. The company has two business operating segments: Retail trade, which consists of its retail stores and distribution centers, and electronic commerce, which handles its online business. The company has developed three distinct store formats to address the various market areas it serves. The Books-A-Million Superstores average approximately 20,000 square feet and operate under the names Books-A-Million and Books & Co. The firm also operates Bookland and Books-A-Million stores, primarily mall-based stores located in small markets and averaging 4,000 square feet. Joe Muggs newsstands are concentrated in business and entertainment districts and are tailored to the demographics of the particular market area. Each newsstand carries an extensive collection of magazines and newspapers, along with hardcover and paperback books and also offers an espresso and coffee bar. All store formats offer a variety of bestsellers and other hardcover and paperback books, magazines, newspapers, cards and gifts. Many of the stores feature a coffee shop and a selection of merchandise under the Joe Muggs brand name. In addition to retail store formats, Books-A-Million, through its subsidiary American Internet Services, Inc. (AIS), offers its products over the Internet on its Booksamillion.com and Joemuggs.com web sites. The company also owns a book wholesale distribution subsidiary, American Wholesale Book Company, which markets primarily to other book stores, wholesale clubs, supermarkets, department stores and mass merchandisers, as well as Book$mart, Inc., a bargain book distributor. In addition, through AIS, Books-A-Million owns an Internet development and services company called NetCentral, based in Nashville, Tennessee.

FINANCIALS: Sales and profits are in thousands of dollars—add 000 to get the full amount. 2007 Note: Financial information for 2007 was not available for all companies at press time.

2007 Sales: $520,416	2007 Profits: $18,887	**U.S. Stock Ticker: BAMM**
2006 Sales: $503,751	2006 Profits: $13,067	**Int'l Ticker:** Int'l Exchange:
2005 Sales: $474,099	2005 Profits: $10,199	Employees: 5,000
2004 Sales: $457,234	2004 Profits: $7,201	Fiscal Year Ends: 1/31
2003 Sales: $442,700	2003 Profits: $1,400	Parent Company:

SALARIES/BENEFITS:

Pension Plan:	ESOP Stock Plan:	Profit Sharing:	Top Exec. Salary: $430,000	Bonus: $385,000
Savings Plan:	Stock Purch. Plan:		Second Exec. Salary: $330,000	Bonus: $253,855

OTHER THOUGHTS:
Apparent Women Officers or Directors: 1
Hot Spot for Advancement for Women/Minorities:

LOCATIONS: ("Y" = Yes)

West:	Southwest:	Midwest:	Southeast:	Northeast:	International:
	Y	Y	Y	Y	

BOOTH CREEK SKI HOLDINGS INC   www.boothcreek.com

Industry Group Code: 713920 Ranks within this company's industry group: Sales: Profits:

Print Media/Publishing:	Movies:	Equipment/Supplies:	Broadcast/Cable:	Music/Audio:	Sports/Games/Gambling:	
Newspapers:	Movie Theaters:	Equipment/Supplies:	Broadcast TV:	Music Production:	Games/Sports:	Y
Magazines:	Movie Production:	Gambling Equipment:	Cable TV:	Retail Music:	Retail Games Stores:	
Books:	TV/Video Prod.:	Special Services:	Satellite Broadcast:	Retail Audio Equip.:	Stadiums/Teams:	
Book Stores:	Video Rental:	Advertising Services:	Radio:	Music Print./Dist.:	Gambling/Casinos:	
Distribution/Printing:	Video Distribution:	Info. Sys. Software:	Online Information:	Multimedia:	Rides/Theme Parks:	

TYPES OF BUSINESS:

Ski Resorts
Golf Courses
Event Hosting
Summer Recreation

BRANDS/DIVISIONS/AFFILIATES:

Northstar-at-Tahoe
Sierra-at-Tahoe
Summit at Snoqualmie (The)
Waterville Valley
Cranmore Mountain Resort
Loon Mountain
Booth Creek Resorts

CONTACTS: Note: Officers with more than one job title may be intentionally listed here more than once.

Chris Ryman, COO
Chris Ryman, Pres.
Elizabeth Johnston Cole, CFO/Exec. VP/Treas.
Julie Maurer, VP-Mktg. & Sales
Laura Moriarty, VP-Human Resources
Jim Mandel, Legal Affairs, Real Estate & Commercial Properties
Heath Nielsen, VP-Oper./Commercial Properties
Tim Beck, Exec. VP-Planning
Brian J. Pope, VP-Finance & Acct.
Mark Petrozzi, VP-Risk Mgmt.

Phone: 530-550-7112	Fax: 530-550-5116
Toll-Free:	
Address: 11025 Pioneer Trail, Ste. 100, Truckee, CA 96161 US	

GROWTH PLANS/SPECIAL FEATURES:

Booth Creek Ski Holdings, operating as Booth Creek Resorts, is one of the largest ski resort operators in North America, with over 2 million visitors per year. The company's six resorts are located in California, New Hampshire and Washington, and are each within 200 miles of major skiing markets such as Boston, Seattle and the San Francisco Bay Area. Booth Creek's resorts feature over 6,500 acres of skiable terrain, 353 trails and 87 lifts, including 14 high-speed lifts and two gondolas. The firm's resorts are Northstar-at-Tahoe, Sierra-at-Tahoe, Waterville Valley, Cranmore Mountain Resort, Loon Mountain and The Summit at Snoqualmie. These resorts provide a full range of services, such as equipment rentals, skiing lessons and restaurants. In addition to alpine skiing and snowboarding, Booth Creek's resorts offer opportunities for cross-country skiing, telemarking, tubing, snowmobiling, snowshoeing and snowbiking. In the summer months, several Booth Creek properties are open for events and activities including golf, mountain biking, fly fishing, horseback riding, ATV tours and hiking and also have event facilities. At its California resorts, the company offers the Vertical Plus program. Through this program, frequent skiers and snowboarders can track the number of vertical feet that they ski via a personal wristband, which is scanned at participating lifts. These guests also receive discounts and gain access to special lift lines. Booth Creek recently finished a project to build a beginners' snowboard park at Loon Mountain and is extensively developing Northstar-at-Tahoe, adding condominiums, shopping facilities, a spa and other developments, including a Ritz-Carlton five star hotel; the Village at Northstar ski-in/ski-out community; and the Retreat at Northstar homesites.

Booth Creek's various resorts offer their employees perks such as skiing privileges, including reciprocal privileges at other resorts; guest vouchers; free lessons; food, gift shop and equipment rental discounts; ride sharing programs; housing assistance; and employee assistance.

FINANCIALS: Sales and profits are in thousands of dollars—add 000 to get the full amount. 2007 Note: Financial information for 2007 was not available for all companies at press time.

2007 Sales: $	2007 Profits: $	U.S. Stock Ticker: Private
2006 Sales: $	2006 Profits: $	Int'l Ticker: Int'l Exchange:
2005 Sales: $	2005 Profits: $	Employees: 4,109
2004 Sales: $115,400	2004 Profits: $-1,800	Fiscal Year Ends: 10/31
2003 Sales: $115,047	2003 Profits: $-5,361	Parent Company:

SALARIES/BENEFITS:

Pension Plan:	ESOP Stock Plan:	Profit Sharing:	Top Exec. Salary: $335,000	Bonus: $175,000
Savings Plan:	Stock Purch. Plan:		Second Exec. Salary: $275,000	Bonus: $175,000

OTHER THOUGHTS:

Apparent Women Officers or Directors: 4
Hot Spot for Advancement for Women/Minorities: Y

LOCATIONS: ("Y" = Yes)

West:	Southwest:	Midwest:	Southeast:	Northeast:	International:
Y	Y			Y	

Note: Financial information, benefits and other data can change quickly and may vary from those stated here.

BORDERS GROUP INC
www.bordersgroupinc.com

Industry Group Code: 451211 Ranks within this company's industry group: Sales: 2 Profits: 2

Print Media/Publishing:	Movies:	Equipment/Supplies:		Broadcast/Cable:	Music/Audio:		Sports/Games/Gambling:
Newspapers:	Movie Theaters:	Equipment/Supplies:		Broadcast TV:	Music Production:		Games/Sports:
Magazines:	Movie Production:	Gambling Equipment:		Cable TV:	Retail Music:	Y	Retail Games Stores:
Books:	TV/Video Prod.:	Special Services:	Y	Satellite Broadcast:	Retail Audio Equip.:		Stadiums/Teams:
Book Stores:	Video Rental:	Advertising Services:		Radio:	Music Print./Dist.:		Gambling/Casinos:
Distribution/Printing:	Video Distribution:	Info. Sys. Software:		Online Information:	Multimedia:		Rides/Theme Parks:

TYPES OF BUSINESS:
Book Stores
Music & Movie Retailing
Specialty Coffee
Online Sales

BRANDS/DIVISIONS/AFFILIATES:
Books, Inc.
Walden Book Co, Inc.
Borders UK Limited
Borders Australia Pty Limited
Waldenbooks
Books etc.
Paperchase Products Limited
Borders Express

CONTACTS: Note: Officers with more than one job title may be intentionally listed here more than once.
George L. Jones, CEO
George L. Jones, Pres.
Edward W. Wilheim, CFO/Exec. VP
Michael Tam, Chief Mktg. Officer
Daniel T. Smith, Sr. VP-Human Resources
Cedric J. Vanzura, Pres., Tech.
Susan Harwood, CIO
Cedric J. Vanzura, Exec. VP-Tech.
Robert P. Gruen, Exec. VP-Merch. & Mktg.
Thomas D. Carney, General Counsel/Sr. VP/Sec.
Kenneth H. Armstrong, Sr. VP-Store Oper.
Cedric J. Vanzura, Chief Strategy Officer
David Roche, Managing Dir./CEO-Borders U.K.
Cedric J. Vanzura, Exec. VP-Emerging Bus.
Jessica J. Harley, VP-Acquisition & Retention Mktg.
Gregory Josefowicz, Chmn.
John Campradt, Managing Dir.-Borders Asia Pacific

Phone: 734-477-1100	Fax: 734-477-1965
Toll-Free:	
Address: 100 Phoenix Dr., Ann Arbor, MI 48108 US	

GROWTH PLANS/SPECIAL FEATURES:
Borders Group, Inc. is the second-largest operator of book, music and movie superstores, and one of the largest operators of mall-based bookstores, in the world, based on both sales and number of stores. Borders Group's retail operations are carried out by its subsidiaries including, among others, Borders, Inc.; Walden Book Company, Inc.; Borders U.K. Limited; and Borders Australia Pty Limited. Borders group operates 567 superstores under the Borders name: 499 in the U.S., 41 in the U.K., 20 in Australia, three in Puerto Rico, two in New Zealand and one each in Singapore and Ireland. The company also operates 564 mall-based and other bookstores primarily under the Waldenbooks name in the U.S. and 30 bookstores under the Books etc. name in the U.K. Borders Group also owns and operates U.K.-based Paperchase Products Limited, a designer and retailer of stationery, cards and gifts. Paperchase operates 99 free-standing stores, primarily in the U.K. Paperchase shops are present in nearly 250 domestic Borders superstores. Borders superstores carry an average of 94,500 book titles; approximately 97.6% of domestic Borders superstores are in a book, music and movie format. A typical Borders superstore carries approximately 14,000 music titles and over 10,000 movie titles. The small format Waldenbooks Specialty Retail stores typically operate under the Waldenbooks, Borders Express and Borders Outlet names, carry on average 19,000 books, and in 2006, averaged $1.1 million in sales per store. The firm plans to revive its own branded e-commerce site in 2008, ending a deal with Amazon.com. Concurrently, the firm will franchise or sell nearly all of its 73 international stores and close nearly half of its domestic Waldenbooks stores.

Borders offers employees flexible spending accounts, adoption assistance, flexible schedules, domestic partner benefits, emergency assistance, scholarships, training and development opportunities and discounts on insurance, tickets and merchandise.

FINANCIALS: Sales and profits are in thousands of dollars—add 000 to get the full amount. 2007 Note: Financial information for 2007 was not available for all companies at press time.

2007 Sales: $4,063,900	2007 Profits: $-151,300	U.S. Stock Ticker: BGP
2006 Sales: $4,030,700	2006 Profits: $101,000	Int'l Ticker: Int'l Exchange:
2005 Sales: $3,879,500	2005 Profits: $131,900	Employees: 33,600
2004 Sales: $3,698,600	2004 Profits: $115,200	Fiscal Year Ends: 1/31
2003 Sales: $3,486,100	2003 Profits: $115,200	Parent Company:

SALARIES/BENEFITS:

Pension Plan:	ESOP Stock Plan:	Profit Sharing:	Top Exec. Salary: $432,212	Bonus: $
Savings Plan: Y	Stock Purch. Plan:		Second Exec. Salary: $374,519	Bonus: $

OTHER THOUGHTS:
Apparent Women Officers or Directors: 2
Hot Spot for Advancement for Women/Minorities:

LOCATIONS: ("Y" = Yes)

West:	Southwest:	Midwest:	Southeast:	Northeast:	International:
Y	Y	Y	Y	Y	Y

Note: Financial information, benefits and other data can change quickly and may vary from those stated here.

BOSE CORPORATION

www.bose.com

Industry Group Code: 334310 Ranks within this company's industry group: Sales: 7   Profits:

Print Media/Publishing:	Movies:	Equipment/Supplies:		Broadcast/Cable:	Music/Audio:		Sports/Games/Gambling:
Newspapers:	Movie Theaters:	Equipment/Supplies:	Y	Broadcast TV:	Music Production:		Games/Sports:
Magazines:	Movie Production:	Gambling Equipment:		Cable TV:	Retail Music:		Retail Games Stores:
Books:	TV/Video Prod.:	Special Services:		Satellite Broadcast:	Retail Audio Equip.:	Y	Stadiums/Teams:
Book Stores:	Video Rental:	Advertising Services:		Radio:	Music Print./Dist.:		Gambling/Casinos:
Distribution/Printing:	Video Distribution:	Info. Sys. Software:		Online Information:	Multimedia:		Rides/Theme Parks:

TYPES OF BUSINESS:

Audio Equipment-Manufacturing & Retailing
Speaker Technology
Home & Automobile Sound Systems
Professional Sound Systems
Noise Reduction Headsets
Materials Testing Equipment

BRANDS/DIVISIONS/AFFILIATES:

Wave
Acoustimass
Lifestyle
3-2-1 DVD
Acoustic Noise Canceling
Aviation Headset X
Triport Tactical
Auditioner

CONTACTS: Note: Officers with more than one job title may be intentionally listed here more than once.

Amar G. Bose, CEO
Bob Maresca, Pres.
Daniel A. Grady, CFO
Thomas Froschle, Dir.-Research
Joanne Berthiume, Spokeswoman
Amar G. Bose, Chmn.

Phone: 508-879-7330	Fax: 508-766-7543
Toll-Free: 800-278-8029	
Address: The Mountain, Framingham, MA 01701 US	

GROWTH PLANS/SPECIAL FEATURES:

Bose Corporation is a leading global manufacturer of audio products, with over 100 stores nationwide. It is best known for the development of its acoustic waveguide speaker technology found in Wave radio, Wave radio/CD and Acoustic Wave music systems. Acoustimass, another speaker technology, allows Bose to create speakers small enough to fit in the palm of a person's hand that produce sound quality previously thought impossible from small speakers. Nearly 60% of Bose`s annual sales are generated by its professional system division. The remaining 40% is generated by the company's home and personal audio segment. Bose manufactures sound systems for homes and automobiles, as well as professional audio products for large venues and stage performers. Its home product brands include Wave systems, Lifestyle home entertainment systems, 3-2-1 DVD systems, Acoustic Noise Canceling headphones/headsets, Acoustimass speaker systems and Direct/Reflecting speakers. Bose's automotive systems division designs customized systems for the manufacturers of certain makes and models of luxury cars. The company's professional products include custom-designed Bose professional sound systems for auditoriums, hotels, performance centers, places of worship, restaurants, retail locations, schools and stadiums. Each system includes a variety of professional component parts (speaker systems, loudspeakers, amplifiers, controllers, cards and accessories). Bose's Auditioner, an audio demonstration technology, allows builders, architects and facility managers to hear what a Bose system will sound like in their building, before any equipment is installed. In addition, Bose produces professional noise reduction headsets, such as the Aviation Headset X for commercial pilots, and Combat Vehicle Crewman and Triport Tactical headsets for the military. Bose's ElectroForce Systems Group, formerly EnduraTEC, provides materials testing equipment to research institutions, universities, medical device companies and engineering companies worldwide. In late 2006, the firm announced that Bose Corporation India (BCIPL) plans to open 12 new stores by mid-2008.

FINANCIALS: Sales and profits are in thousands of dollars—add 000 to get the full amount. 2007 Note: Financial information for 2007 was not available for all companies at press time.

2007 Sales: $	2007 Profits: $	U.S. Stock Ticker: Private
2006 Sales: $2,000,000	2006 Profits: $	Int'l Ticker: Int'l Exchange:
2005 Sales: $1,800,000	2005 Profits: $	Employees: 8,000
2004 Sales: $1,700,000	2004 Profits: $	Fiscal Year Ends: 3/31
2003 Sales: $1,600,000	2003 Profits: $	Parent Company:

SALARIES/BENEFITS:

Pension Plan:	ESOP Stock Plan:	Profit Sharing:	Top Exec. Salary: $	Bonus: $
Savings Plan: Y	Stock Purch. Plan:		Second Exec. Salary: $	Bonus: $

OTHER THOUGHTS:

Apparent Women Officers or Directors: 1
Hot Spot for Advancement for Women/Minorities:

LOCATIONS: ("Y" = Yes)

West:	Southwest:	Midwest:	Southeast:	Northeast:	International:
Y	Y	Y	Y	Y	Y

BOYD GAMING CORP

www.boydgaming.com

Industry Group Code: 721120 Ranks within this company's industry group: Sales: 4 Profits: 5

Print Media/Publishing:	Movies:	Equipment/Supplies:	Broadcast/Cable:	Music/Audio:	Sports/Games/Gambling:	
Newspapers:	Movie Theaters:	Equipment/Supplies:	Broadcast TV:	Music Production:	Games/Sports:	
Magazines:	Movie Production:	Gambling Equipment:	Cable TV:	Retail Music:	Retail Games Stores:	
Books:	TV/Video Prod.:	Special Services:	Satellite Broadcast:	Retail Audio Equip.:	Stadiums/Teams:	Y
Book Stores:	Video Rental:	Advertising Services:	Radio:	Music Print./Dist.:	Gambling/Casinos:	
Distribution/Printing:	Video Distribution:	Info. Sys. Software:	Online Information:	Multimedia:	Rides/Theme Parks:	

TYPES OF BUSINESS:

Casinos & Hotels
Casino Management

BRANDS/DIVISIONS/AFFILIATES:

California Hotel & Casino
Borgata Hotel & Casino
Blue Chip Hotel & Casino
Delta Downs Racetrack & Casino
Stardust Resort & Casino
Par-A-Dice Gaming Corp.
Sam's Town Hotel & Casino
Echalon Place

CONTACTS: Note: Officers with more than one job title may be intentionally listed here more than once.

William S. Boyd, CEO
Keith E. Smith, COO
Keith E. Smith, Pres.
Paul J. Chakmak, CFO/Exec. VP
William J. Noonan, Sr. VP-Admin.
Brian A. Larson, General Counsel/Sr. VP/Corp. Sec.
Christopher R. Gibase, Sr. VP-Oper.
Ellis Landau, Treas.
Marianne Boyd Johnson, Sr. VP
William R. Boyd, VP
Robert Boughner, CEO/Pres., Echelon Resorts
Hector Mon, Sr. VP-Oper. Central Regions
William S. Boyd, Chmn.

Phone: 702-792-7200	Fax: 702-792-7313
Toll-Free:	
Address: 2950 Industrial Rd., Las Vegas, NV 89109 US	

GROWTH PLANS/SPECIAL FEATURES:

Boyd Gaming Corp. is a multi-jurisdictional gaming company and one of the country's leading casino operators. Boyd is committed to providing high-quality entertainment to its primarily middle-income customers at an affordable price, focusing on slot machines and traditional gaming tables. The company currently owns and operates 18 casinos. In Nevada, these include the Stardust Resort and Casino, Sam's Town Hotel & Gambling Hall, El Dorado Casino, Joker's Wild Casino, California Hotel and Casino, Main Street Station Casino, Brewery and Hotel and the Fremont Hotel and Casino. In Mississippi, Boyd owns and operates a second Sam's Town Hotel & Gambling Hall in Tunica. In Louisiana, Boyd owns the Delta Downs Racetrack & Casino and the Treasure Chest Casino. In Illinois, the company owns the Par-a-Dice Hotel and Casino. In Indiana, its holdings consist of the Blue Chip Hotel and Casino. In conjunction with MGM Mirage, and as part of string of recent expansion moves, Boyd opened Borgata, a billion-dollar, 2,000-room resort in Atlantic City, New Jersey. More recently, the company also acquired Harrah's Shreveport Hotel and Casino, now known as Sam's Town Hotel and Casino; as well as Coast Casinos, Inc. for $1.3 billion. The latter merger brings with it Coast Casinos' Gold Coast, Suncoast, Orleans and Barbary Coast casinos. In February 2006, the company purchased a 40-acre plot of land in the northwest part of Las Vegas for about $35 million, with the intention of constructing another casino in the near future.

FINANCIALS: Sales and profits are in thousands of dollars—add 000 to get the full amount. 2007 Note: Financial information for 2007 was not available for all companies at press time.

2007 Sales: $	2007 Profits: $	U.S. Stock Ticker: BYD
2006 Sales: $2,192,634	2006 Profits: $116,778	Int'l Ticker: Int'l Exchange:
2005 Sales: $2,161,085	2005 Profits: $144,610	Employees: 18,300
2004 Sales: $1,707,207	2004 Profits: $111,454	Fiscal Year Ends: 12/31
2003 Sales: $1,394,529	2003 Profits: $40,933	Parent Company:

SALARIES/BENEFITS:

Pension Plan:	ESOP Stock Plan:	Profit Sharing: Y	Top Exec. Salary: $1,500,000	Bonus: $2,250,000
Savings Plan: Y	Stock Purch. Plan:		Second Exec. Salary: $825,000	Bonus: $446,534

OTHER THOUGHTS:

Apparent Women Officers or Directors: 1
Hot Spot for Advancement for Women/Minorities:

LOCATIONS: ("Y" = Yes)

West:	Southwest:	Midwest:	Southeast:	Northeast:	International:
Y		Y	Y		

Note: Financial information, benefits and other data can change quickly and may vary from those stated here.

BOYNE USA RESORTS

www.boyne.com

Industry Group Code: 713920 Ranks within this company's industry group: Sales: Profits:

Print Media/Publishing:	Movies:	Equipment/Supplies:	Broadcast/Cable:	Music/Audio:	Sports/Games/Gambling:	
Newspapers:	Movie Theaters:	Equipment/Supplies:	Broadcast TV:	Music Production:	Games/Sports:	Y
Magazines:	Movie Production:	Gambling Equipment:	Cable TV:	Retail Music:	Retail Games Stores:	
Books:	TV/Video Prod.:	Special Services:	Satellite Broadcast:	Retail Audio Equip.:	Stadiums/Teams:	
Book Stores:	Video Rental:	Advertising Services:	Radio:	Music Print./Dist.:	Gambling/Casinos:	
Distribution/Printing:	Video Distribution:	Info. Sys. Software:	Online Information:	Multimedia:	Rides/Theme Parks:	

TYPES OF BUSINESS:

Ski Resorts
Golf Courses
Real Estate Development
Retail Operations
Indoor Waterpark
Spas
Restaurants

BRANDS/DIVISIONS/AFFILIATES:

Big Sky Resort
Brighton Resort
Crystal Mountain
Cypress Mountain
Boyne Mountain
Boyne Highlands
Boyne Realty
Boyne Country Sports

CONTACTS: Note: Officers with more than one job title may be intentionally listed here more than once.

Stephen Kircher, Pres.
Julie Ard, Mgr.-Public Rel.
Ed Dembek, Controller
Stephen Kircher, Pres., Eastern Oper.

Phone: 231-549-6000	**Fax:** 231-549-6896
Toll-Free:	
Address: 1 Boyne Mountain Rd., Boyne Falls, MI 49713 US	

GROWTH PLANS/SPECIAL FEATURES:

Boyne USA Resorts, one of America's largest privately owned resort companies, owns and operates ski and golf resorts located in the western and midwestern U.S. The company's resorts include Big Sky Resort, Montana; Brighton, Utah; Crystal Mountain, Washington; Cypress Mountain, British Columbia; and Bay Harbor, Boyne Highlands and Boyne Mountain in Michigan. Boyne also operates the Gatlinburg Sky Lift in Gatlinburg, Tennessee, a scenic, year-round chairlift offering views of Great Smoky Mountain National Park. The resorts in Montana and Michigan run golf courses during the summer, as do Michigan's Country Club of Boyne, Crooked Tree Golf Club and the Inn at Bay Harbor. The company operates most of its resorts year-round, with winter snow sports and golf complemented by other activities, such as tennis, swimming, fly fishing, mountain biking, hiking, kayaking and water parks. Boyne Resorts also feature a number of restaurants and spas. Through subsidiary Boyne Realty, Boyne also markets and sells condominiums, cottages, homes and acreage on its own resort property, including locations Boyne Highlands Harbor Springs, Bay Harbor Petoskey, Boyne Mountain, Boyne City and Big Sky Resorts. The company has retail operations under the name Boyne Country Sports and offers online ski, golf and travel shopping. Boyne's web site allows customers to book lodging, purchase gift cards, arrange tee times and purchase apparel from Boyne Country Sports. In September 2007, Boyne Resorts will host the first annual Boyne 2 Boyne Marathon; the race package includes lodging at either the Boyne Highlands or Boyne Mountain, race fee, breakfast, dinner and add-on spa services.

Boyne offers its employees partial tuition reimbursement and discounts on meals, skiing, golfing and pro shop purchases.

FINANCIALS: Sales and profits are in thousands of dollars—add 000 to get the full amount. 2007 Note: Financial information for 2007 was not available for all companies at press time.

2007 Sales: $	2007 Profits: $	**U.S. Stock Ticker: Private**
2006 Sales: $	2006 Profits: $	**Int'l Ticker:** Int'l Exchange:
2005 Sales: $	2005 Profits: $	Employees:
2004 Sales: $	2004 Profits: $	Fiscal Year Ends: 12/31
2003 Sales: $	2003 Profits: $	Parent Company:

SALARIES/BENEFITS:

Pension Plan:	ESOP Stock Plan:	Profit Sharing:	Top Exec. Salary: $	Bonus: $
Savings Plan: Y	Stock Purch. Plan:		Second Exec. Salary: $	Bonus: $

OTHER THOUGHTS:

Apparent Women Officers or Directors: 1
Hot Spot for Advancement for Women/Minorities:

LOCATIONS: ("Y" = Yes)

West:	Southwest:	Midwest:	Southeast:	Northeast:	International:
Y		Y	Y		Y

Note: Financial information, benefits and other data can change quickly and may vary from those stated here.

BRASH ENTERTAINMENT LLC   www.brashent.com

Industry Group Code: 511208 Ranks within this company's industry group: Sales: Profits:

Print Media/Publishing:	Movies:	Equipment/Supplies:	Broadcast/Cable:	Music/Audio:	Sports/Games/Gambling:	
Newspapers:	Movie Theaters:	Equipment/Supplies:	Broadcast TV:	Music Production:	Games/Sports:	Y
Magazines:	Movie Production:	Gambling Equipment:	Cable TV:	Retail Music:	Retail Games Stores:	
Books:	TV/Video Prod.:	Special Services:	Satellite Broadcast:	Retail Audio Equip.:	Stadiums/Teams:	
Book Stores:	Video Rental:	Advertising Services:	Radio:	Music Print./Dist.:	Gambling/Casinos:	
Distribution/Printing:	Video Distribution:	Info. Sys. Software:	Online Information:	Multimedia:	Rides/Theme Parks:	

TYPES OF BUSINESS:
Video Game Production

BRANDS/DIVISIONS/AFFILIATES:
Alvin & The Chipmunks
Jumper
Saw
Lions Gate Films
Universal Studios Licensing
Twentieth Century Fox Licensing & Merchandising
Warner Bros. Interactive Entertainment
Vanguard Animation

CONTACTS: Note: Officers with more than one job title may be intentionally listed here more than once.
Mitch Davis, CEO
Nicholas Longano, COO
Nicholas Longano, Pres.
Bill Chardavoyne, CFO
Yasmin Naboa, Exec. VP-Mktg. & Sales
Patrick Sweeney, General Counsel/Sr. VP-Bus. Affairs
Tiffany Spencer, VP-Comm.
Larry Shapiro, Chief Creative Officer
Mitch Davis, Chmn.

Phone: 323-330-8500	Fax:
Toll-Free:	
Address: 6353 W. Sunset Blvd., 6th Fl., Hollywood, CA 90028 US	

GROWTH PLANS/SPECIAL FEATURES:
Brash Entertainment LLC, founded in June 2007, focuses exclusively on developing video games based on licensed film, music and television properties. It has 12 games in development and licenses for 40 titles. It is developing several games based on the Saw movies, by Lions Gate Films. The other studios Brash has licensed titles from include Universal Studios Licensing, Twentieth Century Fox Licensing and Merchandising, Warner Bros. Interactive Entertainment and Vanguard Animation. The firm's strategy involves harnessing the creative talent of some of the top independent video game developers. Further, it plans to focus on producing games; Warner Bros. Home Entertainment will function as the distribution arm for the firm's games. The primary investors in the firm are ABRY Partners, LLC; New York Life Capital Partners III, LP; Northwestern Mutual Life Insurance; and PPM America Private Equity Fund II, LLP. In August 2007, the company announced it would release its first video game, Alvin and the Chipmunks, alongside the movie release. The game will be available on the Sony PlayStation 2; Nintendo DS and Wii; and PC. In November 2007, Brash announced it was developing a game based on the upcoming sci-fi thriller, Jumper, to be released alongside the movie.

FINANCIALS: Sales and profits are in thousands of dollars—add 000 to get the full amount. 2007 Note: Financial information for 2007 was not available for all companies at press time.

2007 Sales: $	2007 Profits: $	U.S. Stock Ticker: Private
2006 Sales: $	2006 Profits: $	Int'l Ticker: Int'l Exchange:
2005 Sales: $	2005 Profits: $	Employees:
2004 Sales: $	2004 Profits: $	Fiscal Year Ends:
2003 Sales: $	2003 Profits: $	Parent Company:

SALARIES/BENEFITS:
Pension Plan:	ESOP Stock Plan:	Profit Sharing:	Top Exec. Salary: $	Bonus: $
Savings Plan:	Stock Purch. Plan:		Second Exec. Salary: $	Bonus: $

OTHER THOUGHTS:
Apparent Women Officers or Directors: 2
Hot Spot for Advancement for Women/Minorities:

LOCATIONS: ("Y" = Yes)
West:	Southwest:	Midwest:	Southeast:	Northeast:	International:
Y					

BRIGHTCOVE INC

www.brightcove.com

Industry Group Code: 513120A Ranks within this company's industry group: Sales: Profits:

Print Media/Publishing:	Movies:	Equipment/Supplies:	Broadcast/Cable:	Music/Audio:	Sports/Games/Gambling:
Newspapers:	Movie Theaters:	Equipment/Supplies:	Broadcast TV:	Music Production:	Games/Sports:
Magazines:	Movie Production:	Gambling Equipment:	Cable TV:	Retail Music:	Retail Games Stores:
Books:	TV/Video Prod.:	Special Services:	Satellite Broadcast:	Retail Audio Equip.:	Stadiums/Teams:
Book Stores:	Video Rental:	Advertising Services:	Radio:	Music Print./Dist.:	Gambling/Casinos:
Distribution/Printing:	Video Distribution:	Info. Sys. Software:	Online Information:	Multimedia:	Rides/Theme Parks:

TYPES OF BUSINESS:

Internet TV Broadcasting

BRANDS/DIVISIONS/AFFILIATES:

Brightcove Network
Brigtcove Platform
Brightcove AdNet
Pay-Media Service
Syndication Marketplace
AOL Video Distribution
Consumer Destination
MetaStories

CONTACTS: *Note: Officers with more than one job title may be intentionally listed here more than once.*

Jeremy Allaire, CEO
Jeremy Allaire, Pres.
Scot Rosenblum, CFO
Adam Berrey, VP-Mktg. & Strategy
Ed Godin, VP-Human Resources
Bob Mason, CTO
Tareef Kawaf, Sr. VP-Eng.
Andrew W. Feinberg, General Counsel/Sr. VP-Corp. Dev.
Tareef Kawaf, Sr. VP-Oper.
Elisabeth B. Carpenter, Sr. VP-Bus. Dev.
Eric Elia, VP-Creative Svcs.
Brian Monnin, VP-Publishing Products
Randy Fisher, VP-Svcs. & Support
Elisabeth B. Carpenter, Sr. VP-Worldwide Sales

Phone: 617-500-4947	Fax: 617-395-8352
Toll-Free:	
Address: 1 Cambridge Ctr., Cambridge, MA 02142 US	

GROWTH PLANS/SPECIAL FEATURES:

Brightcove, Inc. is an Internet television company that allows emerging media companies and independent producers to launch commercial broadband channels. Brightcove caters to content owners, allowing them to create, distribute and monetize Internet TV channels. This is done through two offerings: Brightcove Network, which publishes content for free and grants content owners half of ad revenues; and Brightcove Platform, in which publishers pay a usage fee but keep all ad revenues. In support of the Brightcove Network, the company's offerings include: Brightcove AdNet, which aggregates online video audiences, reaches consumers through niche channels and allows online video programmers the ability to more easily create advertising revenue; Pay-Media Service, which allows sale or rental of high-quality video downloads at prices determined by content owners; Syndication Marketplace, a place to discover Internet TV channels available for syndication to third party web sites; AOL Video Distribution; and Consumer Destination, where content is made available to consumers. Although the company was founded in 2004, Brightcove Network, its publicly accessible web site, didn't launch until October 2006 following its March 2006 commercial preview. Also in March 2006, the company acquired MetaStories, which allows users to weave together narrated photo galleries, video and other rich media offerings in a template driven manner. Brightcove has partnerships with major media companies including: Warner Music Group, which makes music videos, interviews and live performances available through the site; Time Life, which, among other things, broadcasts the TV series Get Smart (Brightcove also supports Time Life's fan sites and blogs); and Dow Jones Online, which features original reporting by reporters, columnists and bloggers. The company is backed by several major investors, including ACCEL, General Catalyst Partners, AOL, InterActiveCorp (IAC), The Hearst Corporation and Allen & Company, LLC. In December 2007, the company eliminated all user-submitted content.

FINANCIALS: Sales and profits are in thousands of dollars—add 000 to get the full amount. 2007 Note: Financial information for 2007 was not available for all companies at press time.

2007 Sales: $	2007 Profits: $	U.S. Stock Ticker: Private
2006 Sales: $	2006 Profits: $	Int'l Ticker: Int'l Exchange:
2005 Sales: $	2005 Profits: $	Employees:
2004 Sales: $	2004 Profits: $	Fiscal Year Ends:
2003 Sales: $	2003 Profits: $	Parent Company:

SALARIES/BENEFITS:

Pension Plan:	ESOP Stock Plan:	Profit Sharing:	Top Exec. Salary: $	Bonus: $
Savings Plan:	Stock Purch. Plan:		Second Exec. Salary: $	Bonus: $

OTHER THOUGHTS:

Apparent Women Officers or Directors: 1
Hot Spot for Advancement for Women/Minorities:

LOCATIONS: ("Y" = Yes)

West:	Southwest:	Midwest:	Southeast:	Northeast:	International:
Y				Y	Y

BRITISH BROADCASTING CORPORATION (BBC)
www.bbc.co.uk
Industry Group Code: 513120 Ranks within this company's industry group: Sales: 6 Profits: 13

Print Media/Publishing:	Movies:		Equipment/Supplies:		Broadcast/Cable:		Music/Audio:	Sports/Games/Gambling:
Newspapers:	Movie Theaters:		Equipment/Supplies:		Broadcast TV:	Y	Music Production:	Games/Sports:
Magazines:	Movie Production:		Gambling Equipment:		Cable TV:	Y	Retail Music:	Retail Games Stores:
Books:	TV/Video Prod.:	Y	Special Services:	Y	Satellite Broadcast:		Retail Audio Equip.:	Stadiums/Teams:
Book Stores:	Video Rental:		Advertising Services:		Radio:		Music Print./Dist.:	Gambling/Casinos:
Distribution/Printing:	Video Distribution:		Info. Sys. Software:		Online Information:		Multimedia:	Rides/Theme Parks:

TYPES OF BUSINESS:
Television Broadcasting
Television Production
News Agency
Radio Broadcasting
Online Publishing
Media Distribution & Services

BRANDS/DIVISIONS/AFFILIATES:
BBC
BBC One
BBC Two
CBBC Channel
Cbeebies
BBC Online
BBC World Service
BBC Trust

CONTACTS: Note: Officers with more than one job title may be intentionally listed here more than once.
Mark Thompson, Dir. General
Caroline Thomson, COO
Tim Davie, Dir.-Mktg.
Stephen Kelly, Dir.-BBC People
Ashley Highfield, Dir.-Future Media & Tech.
Caroline Thompson, Dir.-Strategy & Dist.
Tim Davie, Dir.-Comm. & Audiences
Zarin Patel, Dir.-Group Finance
Jenny Abramsky, Dir.-Radio & Music
Jana Bennett, Dir.-Vision/Television
Mark Byford, Deputy Dir. General
John Smith, CEO-BBC Worldwide, Ltd.

Phone: 44-20-7580-4468	Fax: 44-20-7765-1181

Toll-Free:
Address: Broadcasting House, Portland Pl., London, W1A 1AA UK

GROWTH PLANS/SPECIAL FEATURES:
British Broadcasting Corporation (BBC) is one of the most far-reaching news sources in the world. BBC One offers the broadest range of programming of any U.K. mainstream network, covering national and international sports events and issues. BBC Two is a mixed-genre channel that combines factual and specialist subjects with comedy and drama in an attempt to bring intelligent television to a wide audience. BBC One and Two are the company's two main public television stations. BBC Three, aimed primarily at younger viewers, combines news, current affairs, education, music, arts, science and coverage of international issues, as well as offering drama, comedy and entertainment. BBC Four strives to offer intellectually stimulating and culturally enriching programming then the typical mainstream line-up. BBC Worldwide One, of the company's major subsidiaries, offers international television programming such as BBC Prime and BBC America. Other television services include: CBBC and CBeebies for kids; BBC News; BBC Parliament; and BBC Sport. BBCi allows programmers to maximize coverage by providing viewers with increasing interactivity. BBC Online provides millions of users with a web portal operational in 33 languages, and BBC Radio offers listeners over 10 channels of programming. Other ventures include business and media services, such as media distribution and management, production and technology solutions. The BBC's Royal Charter expired at the end of 2006, a development that led to the replacement of the former Board of Governors with a unit called the BBC Trust. The transition is designed to make BBC administrators more accountable to its patrons, which support the company through television fees. In October 2007, the firm announced that it is laying off 1,800 employees, about 8% of its total work force.

Employees of BBC receive maternity and paternity leave; subsidized child care; and flexible working arrangements, including a job-share scheme.

FINANCIALS: Sales and profits are in thousands of dollars—add 000 to get the full amount. 2007 Note: Financial information for 2007 was not available for all companies at press time.

2007 Sales: $8,615,700	2007 Profits: $125,200	U.S. Stock Ticker: Government-Owned
2006 Sales: $6,966,700	2006 Profits: $6,300	Int'l Ticker: Int'l Exchange:
2005 Sales: $7,205,400	2005 Profits: $-353,600	Employees: 23,037
2004 Sales: $6,766,200	2004 Profits: $-454,400	Fiscal Year Ends: 3/31
2003 Sales: $5,559,000	2003 Profits: $-495,100	Parent Company:

SALARIES/BENEFITS:
Pension Plan: Y	ESOP Stock Plan:	Profit Sharing:	Top Exec. Salary: $1,258,471	Bonus: $
Savings Plan:	Stock Purch. Plan:		Second Exec. Salary: $857,131	Bonus: $

OTHER THOUGHTS:
Apparent Women Officers or Directors: 4
Hot Spot for Advancement for Women/Minorities: Y

LOCATIONS: ("Y" = Yes)
West:	Southwest:	Midwest:	Southeast:	Northeast:	International:
Y				Y	Y

Note: Financial information, benefits and other data can change quickly and may vary from those stated here.

BRITISH SKY BROADCASTING GROUP PLC   www.sky.com

Industry Group Code: 513220 Ranks within this company's industry group: Sales: 7   Profits: 5

Print Media/Publishing:	Movies:	Equipment/Supplies:	Broadcast/Cable:		Music/Audio:	Sports/Games/Gambling:	
Newspapers:	Movie Theaters:	Equipment/Supplies:	Broadcast TV:	Y	Music Production:	Games/Sports:	
Magazines:	Movie Production:	Gambling Equipment:	Cable TV:	Y	Retail Music:	Retail Games Stores:	
Books:	TV/Video Prod.:	Special Services:	Satellite Broadcast:		Retail Audio Equip.:	Stadiums/Teams:	
Book Stores:	Video Rental:	Advertising Services:	Radio:		Music Print./Dist.:	Gambling/Casinos:	Y
Distribution/Printing:	Video Distribution:	Info. Sys. Software:	Online Information:		Multimedia:	Rides/Theme Parks:	

TYPES OF BUSINESS:
Satellite TV Broadcasting
Digital TV
Broadcast TV
Mobile Phone TV
Interactive Television
Broadband Service
HD TV

BRANDS/DIVISIONS/AFFILIATES:
Sky One
Sky Travel
Sky News
Sky Sports
Sky Movies
Sky Broadband
Sky Active
News Corporation

CONTACTS: *Note: Officers with more than one job title may be intentionally listed here more than once.*
Jeremy Darroch, CEO
Mike Darcey, COO
Matthew Anderson, Group Dir.-Brand Mktg.
Beryl Cook, Dir.-People & Organizational Dev.
Didier Lebrat, CTO
James Conyers, General Counsel
Alun Webber, Group Dir.-Strategic Project Delivery
Matthew Anderson, Group Dir.-Comm.
Vic Wakeling, Managing Dir.-Sky Sports & Sky News
Jeff Hughes, Exec. VP
Brian Sullivan, Managing Dir.-Customer Group
Sophie T. Laing, Managing Dir.-Entertainment
K. Rupert Murdoch, Chmn.

Phone: 44-20-7705-3000	Fax: 44-20-7705-3453
Toll-Free:	
Address: Grant Way, Isleworth, Middlesex TW7 5QD UK	

GROWTH PLANS/SPECIAL FEATURES:
British Sky Broadcasting plc (BSkyB) is the U.K.'s premier pay television service. It distributes entertainment, news and sports programming to more than 8.6 million subscribers through cable and satellite. The firm offers over 100 channels and operates 28 on its own, including Sky One, Sky Travel, Sky News, Sky Sports and Sky Movies. Sky High Definition TV offers 12 HD channels. BSkyB owns the broadcast rights to England's professional soccer league and domestic cricket matches, as well as certain other sports events in the U.K. and Ireland, including rugby, motorsports, golf and boxing. In addition, the firm is marketing a digital video recorder similar to TiVo, called Sky+, offering 40 hours of recording time. Over 2 million Sky+ boxes have been installed as of January 2007. BSkyB has also developed an interactive television network, called Sky Active, allowing viewers to interact through contests, quizzes, voting events, or shopping, all through an electronic fixture connected to the television set and a modem. Sky Bet, Sky Poker and Sky Vegas offer a range of interactive betting and gambling services. The company recently began offering broadband service to many of its customers via Sky Broadband. In October 2007, the firm announced Sky Broadband broke the 1 million customer mark. The service, which now reaches 86% of regions in the U.K. receiving cable, offers a free wireless router, optional professional installation and a free 12 month subscription to McAfee security. Sky Broadband Base is a free service, offering 2 megabyte (Mb) download speeds, while Sky Broadband Max, available for $19 a month, offers 16 Mb download speeds. International media mogul Rupert Murdoch, the current chairman of the firm, is the owner of News Corporation, which owns a 36% controlling interest in BSkyB.

FINANCIALS: Sales and profits are in thousands of dollars—add 000 to get the full amount. 2007 Note: Financial information for 2007 was not available for all companies at press time.

2007 Sales: $9,119,749	2007 Profits: $959,868	U.S. Stock Ticker: BSY
2006 Sales: $7,534,012	2006 Profits: $1,000,781	Int'l Ticker: BSY Int'l Exchange: London-LSE
2005 Sales: $7,426,752	2005 Profits: $1,041,370	Employees: 12,642
2004 Sales: $6,607,900	2004 Profits: $784,400	Fiscal Year Ends: 6/30
2003 Sales: $5,252,800	2003 Profits: $313,700	Parent Company:

SALARIES/BENEFITS:

Pension Plan:	ESOP Stock Plan:	Profit Sharing:	Top Exec. Salary: $1,884,285	Bonus: $3,768,570
Savings Plan: Y	Stock Purch. Plan:		Second Exec. Salary: $1,041,315	Bonus: $1,666,105

OTHER THOUGHTS:
Apparent Women Officers or Directors: 4
Hot Spot for Advancement for Women/Minorities: Y

LOCATIONS: ("Y" = Yes)

West:	Southwest:	Midwest:	Southeast:	Northeast:	International:
					Y

Note: Financial information, benefits and other data can change quickly and may vary from those stated here.

BUY.COM INC

www.buy.com

Industry Group Code: 443110E Ranks within this company's industry group: Sales: Profits:

Print Media/Publishing:	Movies:		Equipment/Supplies:		Broadcast/Cable:	Music/Audio:		Sports/Games/Gambling:	
Newspapers:	Movie Theaters:		Equipment/Supplies:	Y	Broadcast TV:	Music Production:		Games/Sports:	
Magazines: Y	Movie Production:		Gambling Equipment:		Cable TV:	Retail Music:	Y	Retail Games Stores:	Y
Books: Y	TV/Video Prod.:		Special Services:	Y	Satellite Broadcast:	Retail Audio Equip.:	Y	Stadiums/Teams:	
Book Stores:	Video Rental:		Advertising Services:		Radio:	Music Print./Dist.:		Gambling/Casinos:	
Distribution/Printing:	Video Distribution:	Y	Info. Sys. Software:		Online Information:	Multimedia:		Rides/Theme Parks:	

TYPES OF BUSINESS:

Consumer Electronics, Online Retail
Book, Game, DVD, VHS & Music Sales
Software & Accessories Sales
Music Downloads
Social Networking Web Site
jewelry and watches

BRANDS/DIVISIONS/AFFILIATES:

Internet Superstore (The)
BuyMagazine
metails.com
buymusic.com
BuyTV.com
Yub.com

CONTACTS: Note: Officers with more than one job title may be intentionally listed here more than once.

Neel Grover, CEO
Greg Giraudi, COO/Exec. VP
Neel Grover, Pres.
Roger Andelin, CIO
Robb Brock, CTO
Greg Giraudi, General Counsel
Eoin Matthews, VP-Bus. Dev.
Lauren DeVries, Exec. VP-Finance
Scott Blum, Chmn.

Phone: 949-389-2000	Fax: 949-389-2800
Toll-Free: 888-880-1030	
Address: 85 Enterprise, Ste. 100, Aliso Viejo, CA 92656 US	

GROWTH PLANS/SPECIAL FEATURES:

Buy.com, Inc. is an online retailer that sells a wide variety of items, including computer hardware, computer accessories and software, electronics, cellular products and services, books, bags, games, toys, DVDs, CDs and music downloads. Under its trademarked moniker The Internet Superstore, the company offers more than 2 million products to over 10 million customers through the various online channels on the buy.com web site. Buy.com's computer products include computers, printers, monitors, modems and peripherals, and computer software titles from leading manufacturers including Microsoft, Adobe and Corel. The firm also stocks hardback, paperback and audio book titles, enabling customers to read the first chapter of many books, submit their own book reviews and read professional and customer reviews. In addition, the company retails DVD and VHS titles from a range of categories. Buy.com distributes BuyMagazine, a monthly digital publication that lists products for sale and contains editorial columns that help customers understand the features of the products offered. The company also owns metails.com, a social networking web site that allows users to create pages that outline specific interests, favorite products and other facts about themselves. Users can then search the Metails database for other individuals with common interests. They can also share specific product information and reviews with other users. Metails enables the purchasing of these products through partner e-retail sites, whereby the users themselves are rewarded for becoming referrers of products. BuyTV.com is another company site that focuses on entertainment-based retailing. Recently, the firm took its popular online platform, BuyTV, to broadcast television in the southern California market, reaching over five million households. In December 2007, the online store launched a new jewelry and watch store.

FINANCIALS: Sales and profits are in thousands of dollars—add 000 to get the full amount. 2007 Note: Financial information for 2007 was not available for all companies at press time.

2007 Sales: $	2007 Profits: $	U.S. Stock Ticker: BUYY
2006 Sales: $	2006 Profits: $	Int'l Ticker: Int'l Exchange:
2005 Sales: $	2005 Profits: $	Employees: 121
2004 Sales: $290,800	2004 Profits: $-15,400	Fiscal Year Ends: 12/31
2003 Sales: $238,200	2003 Profits: $-25,600	Parent Company:

SALARIES/BENEFITS:

Pension Plan:	ESOP Stock Plan:	Profit Sharing:	Top Exec. Salary: $	Bonus: $
Savings Plan:	Stock Purch. Plan:		Second Exec. Salary: $184,462	Bonus: $184,462

OTHER THOUGHTS:

Apparent Women Officers or Directors: 1
Hot Spot for Advancement for Women/Minorities:

LOCATIONS: ("Y" = Yes)

West:	Southwest:	Midwest:	Southeast:	Northeast:	International:
Y					Y

CABLE NEWS NETWORK LP LLLP   www.cnn.com

Industry Group Code: 513210 Ranks within this company's industry group: Sales: Profits:

Print Media/Publishing:	Movies:	Equipment/Supplies:	Broadcast/Cable:	Music/Audio:	Sports/Games/Gambling:
Newspapers:	Movie Theaters:	Equipment/Supplies:	Broadcast TV:	Music Production:	Games/Sports:
Magazines:	Movie Production:	Gambling Equipment:	Cable TV: Y	Retail Music:	Retail Games Stores:
Books:	TV/Video Prod.: Y	Special Services: Y	Satellite Broadcast:	Retail Audio Equip.:	Stadiums/Teams:
Book Stores:	Video Rental:	Advertising Services:	Radio:	Music Print./Dist.:	Gambling/Casinos:
Distribution/Printing:	Video Distribution:	Info. Sys. Software:	Online Information:	Multimedia:	Rides/Theme Parks:

TYPES OF BUSINESS:

TV News Production
News Radio Broadcasting
Satellite Networks
Online News Information
Syndicated News Service

BRANDS/DIVISIONS/AFFILIATES:

Turner Broadcasting
Time Warner
CNN Money
CNN Headline News
CNN International
CNN Radio
CNN Mobile
CNN Newsource

CONTACTS: *Note: Officers with more than one job title may be intentionally listed here more than once.*

Jim Walton, Pres., CNN Worldwide
Greg D'Alba, Exec. VP/COO-Advertising Sales & Mktg.
Jack Womack, Exec. VP-Admin., CNN/U.S.
David Payne, Sr. VP/General Mgr.-CNN.com
Susan Bunda, Sr. VP-News, CNN
Jonathan Klein, Pres., CNN/U.S.
Mitch Gelman, Sr. VP/Exec. Producer-CNN.com
Chris Cramer, Managing Dir.-CNN Int'l

Phone: 404-827-1700	Fax: 404-827-1099
Toll-Free:	
Address: 1 CNN Center, Atlanta, GA 30303 US	

GROWTH PLANS/SPECIAL FEATURES:

Cable News Network LP, LLLP, more commonly known as CNN, is a unit of Turner Broadcasting, which is owned by Time Warner. It operates 42 news bureaus around the world, including 11 in the U.S. The company operates 15 cable and satellite television networks, including CNN Money, CNN Airport Network and CNN en Espanol; two private, place-based networks (CNN Headline News and CNN International); two radio networks (CNN Radio and CNN en Espanol Radio); 12 network-affiliated web sites; CNN Mobile, which sends news reports and other information to members' wireless devices; and CNN Newsource, one of the world's most extensively syndicated news services. The firm's TV news programs include American Morning, House Call, Anderson Cooper 360, Paula Zahn Now, Lou Dobbs Tonight, CNN Presents, CNN Live Forum, CNN Live Today and The Situation Room. It also features the popular interview program, Larry King Live. CNN News Services, the administration business unit of CNN News Group, consists of six divisions: CNN Business Operations, cnn.com, CNN Content Sales/Business Development, CNN Newsource Sales, CNNRadio and Turner Learning. CNN recently launched CNN Pipeline, an on-demand broadband video service which gives subscribers access to over 50,000 videos. Recently, CNN introduced I-Report, which allows individual viewers to send their original content to CNN.com. Content is vetted before being released on the air or Internet. In 2007, CNN signed a deal with Second Life through which it operates an online virtual version of its real-world presence.

FINANCIALS: Sales and profits are in thousands of dollars—add 000 to get the full amount. 2007 Note: Financial information for 2007 was not available for all companies at press time.

2007 Sales: $	2007 Profits: $	**U.S. Stock Ticker: Subsidiary**
2006 Sales: $	2006 Profits: $	**Int'l Ticker:** Int'l Exchange:
2005 Sales: $794,000	2005 Profits: $	Employees: 4,000
2004 Sales: $	2004 Profits: $	Fiscal Year Ends: 12/31
2003 Sales: $	2003 Profits: $	Parent Company: TURNER BROADCASTING SYSTEM

SALARIES/BENEFITS:

Pension Plan:	ESOP Stock Plan:	Profit Sharing:	Top Exec. Salary: $	Bonus: $
Savings Plan:	Stock Purch. Plan:		Second Exec. Salary: $	Bonus: $

OTHER THOUGHTS:

Apparent Women Officers or Directors: 1
Hot Spot for Advancement for Women/Minorities:

LOCATIONS: ("Y" = Yes)

West:	Southwest:	Midwest:	Southeast:	Northeast:	International:
Y	Y	Y	Y	Y	Y

CABLEVISION SYSTEMS CORP   www.cablevision.com

Industry Group Code: 513220 Ranks within this company's industry group: Sales: 9 Profits: 19

Print Media/Publishing:	Movies:		Equipment/Supplies:		Broadcast/Cable:		Music/Audio:		Sports/Games/Gambling:	
Newspapers:	Movie Theaters:	Y	Equipment/Supplies:		Broadcast TV:	Y	Music Production:		Games/Sports:	
Magazines:	Movie Production:		Gambling Equipment:	Y	Cable TV:	Y	Retail Music:		Retail Games Stores:	
Books:	TV/Video Prod.:		Special Services:	Y	Satellite Broadcast:		Retail Audio Equip.:		Stadiums/Teams:	
Book Stores:	Video Rental:		Advertising Services:		Radio:		Music Print./Dist.:	Y	Gambling/Casinos:	
Distribution/Printing:	Video Distribution:		Info. Sys. Software:		Online Information:		Multimedia:		Rides/Theme Parks:	

TYPES OF BUSINESS:

Cable Television Service
Professional Sports Teams
Television Programming
Communications Services
Sports & Music Venues
Voice-Over-Cable Service
Movie Theaters
High-Speed Internet Service

BRANDS/DIVISIONS/AFFILIATES:

Rainbow Media Holdings, Inc.
Clearview Cinemas
Radio City Entertainment
New York Knicks
Madison Square Garden
Optimum Voice
Optimum Online
Lightpath

CONTACTS: Note: Officers with more than one job title may be intentionally listed here more than once.

James L. Dolan, CEO
Tom Rutledge, COO
James L. Dolan, Pres.
Michael Huseby, CFO/Exec. VP
Wilt Hildenbrand, Exec. VP-Tech.
Wilt Hildenbrand, Exec. VP-Eng.
Jonathan D. Schwartz, General Counsel/Exec. VP
Patricia Armstrong, Sr. VP-Investor Rel.
Kevin F. Watson, Sr. VP/Treas.
Hank J. Ratner, Vice Chmn.
John Bickham, Pres., Cable & Comm.
Joshua Sapan, CEO/Pres., Rainbow Media Holdings LLC
Dave Pistacchio, Exec. VP/General Mgr.-Lightpath
Charles F. Dolan, Chmn.

Phone: 516-803-2300	Fax: 516-803-3134
Toll-Free:	
Address: 1111 Stewart Ave., Bethpage, NY 11714 US	

GROWTH PLANS/SPECIAL FEATURES:

Cablevision Systems Corp. is a leading cable operator in the U.S. The company also has investments in cable programming networks, entertainment businesses and telecommunications companies. Cablevision serves nearly 4.5 million households and 600,000 businesses, primarily in and around the New York City metropolitan area. The firm owns the American Movie Classics channel, the Independent Film Channel, the WE: Women's Entertainment Channel, Fox Sports Net for multiple states and Radio City Entertainment (which operates Radio City Music Hall in New York City under a long-term lease). Through its wholly-owned subsidiary, Rainbow Media Holdings, Inc., Cablevision owns 60% of Madison Square Garden and the adjoining Theater at Madison Square Garden, several professional sports teams, and the Madison Square Garden Network. Telecommunications offerings include its iO: Interactive Optimum digital television offering, Optimum Online high-speed Internet service, Optimum Voice digital voice-over-cable service and Lightpath integrated business communication services, which provide switched telephone services and high-speed Internet access to the business market. Optimum Voice, Cablevision's new telephone service offering, is a voice-over-cable system enabled by installing a special adapter in the home. In 2006, the service served 1.2 million customers. The company also owns Clearview Cinemas, a chain of 52 movie theaters, and Northcoast Communications, LLC, a wireless personal communications services business. In May 2007, the firm agreed to be taken private by the Dolan family for roughly $10.6 billion. In July 2007, Comcast bought out Cablevision's 60% stake in Fox Sports Net (FSN) Bay Area, the cable broadcaster that airs the San Francisco Giants, Oakland A's, San Jose Sharks, Golden State Warriors and other local teams. 40% of the channel is still owned by a unit of News Corp. In a companion deal, Comcast bought out Cablevision's stake in FSN New England.

FINANCIALS: Sales and profits are in thousands of dollars—add 000 to get the full amount. 2007 Note: Financial information for 2007 was not available for all companies at press time.

2007 Sales: $	2007 Profits: $	U.S. Stock Ticker: Private
2006 Sales: $5,927,462	2006 Profits: $-126,465	Int'l Ticker: Int'l Exchange:
2005 Sales: $5,172,478	2005 Profits: $89,320	Employees: 22,075
2004 Sales: $4,750,037	2004 Profits: $-676,092	Fiscal Year Ends: 12/31
2003 Sales: $4,177,148	2003 Profits: $-297,311	Parent Company:

SALARIES/BENEFITS:

Pension Plan:	ESOP Stock Plan:	Profit Sharing:	Top Exec. Salary: $684,765	Bonus: $
Savings Plan:	Stock Purch. Plan:		Second Exec. Salary: $342,208	Bonus: $

OTHER THOUGHTS:

Apparent Women Officers or Directors: 1
Hot Spot for Advancement for Women/Minorities:

LOCATIONS: ("Y" = Yes)

West:	Southwest:	Midwest:	Southeast:	Northeast:	International:
				Y	

Note: Financial information, benefits and other data can change quickly and may vary from those stated here.

CANTERBURY PARK HOLDING CORP

www.canterburypark.com

Industry Group Code: 713210 Ranks within this company's industry group: Sales: 10   Profits: 7

Print Media/Publishing:	Movies:	Equipment/Supplies:	Broadcast/Cable:	Music/Audio:	Sports/Games/Gambling:	
Newspapers:	Movie Theaters:	Equipment/Supplies:	Broadcast TV:	Music Production:	Games/Sports:	Y
Magazines:	Movie Production:	Gambling Equipment:	Cable TV:	Retail Music:	Retail Games Stores:	
Books:	TV/Video Prod.:	Special Services:	Satellite Broadcast:	Retail Audio Equip.:	Stadiums/Teams:	
Book Stores:	Video Rental:	Advertising Services:	Radio:	Music Print./Dist.:	Gambling/Casinos:	Y
Distribution/Printing:	Video Distribution:	Info. Sys. Software:	Online Information:	Multimedia:	Rides/Theme Parks:	

TYPES OF BUSINESS:

Gambling-Horse Races
Simulcasting
Card Club
Event Hosting

BRANDS/DIVISIONS/AFFILIATES:

Canterbury Card Club
The Racino at Canterbury Park

CONTACTS: *Note: Officers with more than one job title may be intentionally listed here more than once.*

Randall D. Sampson, CEO/Gen. Mgr.
Randall D. Sampson, Pres.
David C. Hansen, CFO
John R. Harty, VP-Mktg.
Jerry Fuller, VP-Club Card Oper.
Kip Rakos, Mgr.-Corp. Comm.
Judy Dahlke, VP-Investor Rel.
David C. Hansen, VP-Finance/Sec.
Mark E. Erickson, VP-Facilities
Michael J. Garin, VP-Hospitality/Asst. Sec.
Eric Halstrom, VP-Racing & Simulcasting
Dale H. Schenian, Vice Chmn.
Curtis A. Sampson, Chmn.

Phone: 952-445-7223	Fax: 952-496-6400
Toll-Free: 800-340-6361	
Address: 1100 Canterbury Rd., Shakopee, MN 55379 US	

GROWTH PLANS/SPECIAL FEATURES:

Canterbury Park Holding Corp. hosts seasonal pari-mutuel wagering on live thoroughbred and quarter horse racing at its facilities in Shakopee, Minnesota from May through September. In addition, the firm offers simulcast racing from 20 different racetracks per day, seven days a week, 364 days per year. The firm's revenues are principally derived from pari-mutuel wagering and card club operations. In 2007, Card Club operations generated 53.8% of total revenues, wagering on horse races made up 29.3% and concessions accounted for 10%. Canterbury Park derives further revenues from related services and activities such as parking, admissions and programs and from other entertainment events held at the racetrack. When not conducting horse races, the firm hosts events such as snowmobile racing, arts and crafts shows, fundraisers, automobile shows and competitions and private parties. Canterbury Park also runs the Canterbury Card Club, in which patrons compete against each other in various unbanked card games, wagering against each other instead of the house. The card club is open 24 hours a day, seven days a week and offers poker and table games on up to 50 authorized tables. The firm continues to explore potential development opportunities for its 380-acre site in Shakopee. Over the next five years it looks to advance development plans for a unique commercial and entertainment complex.

Canterbury Park offers its employees a referral bonus program and employee discounts. The firm gives 5% of pre-tax profits to charity annually.

FINANCIALS: Sales and profits are in thousands of dollars—add 000 to get the full amount. 2007 Note: Financial information for 2007 was not available for all companies at press time.

2007 Sales: $	2007 Profits: $	**U.S. Stock Ticker: ECP**
2006 Sales: $55,840	2006 Profits: $3,125	**Int'l Ticker:** Int'l Exchange:
2005 Sales: $54,920	2005 Profits: $3,053	Employees: 690
2004 Sales: $54,899	2004 Profits: $3,862	Fiscal Year Ends: 12/31
2003 Sales: $47,846	2003 Profits: $2,870	Parent Company:

SALARIES/BENEFITS:

Pension Plan:	ESOP Stock Plan: Y	Profit Sharing:	Top Exec. Salary: $200,000	Bonus: $40,094
Savings Plan: Y	Stock Purch. Plan: Y		Second Exec. Salary: $141,539	Bonus: $29,155

OTHER THOUGHTS:

Apparent Women Officers or Directors: 1
Hot Spot for Advancement for Women/Minorities:

LOCATIONS: ("Y" = Yes)

West:	Southwest:	Midwest:	Southeast:	Northeast:	International:
		Y			

CANWEST GLOBAL COMMUNICATIONS

www.canwestglobal.com

Industry Group Code: 513120 Ranks within this company's industry group: Sales: 8 Profits: 7

Print Media/Publishing:		Movies:		Equipment/Supplies:		Broadcast/Cable:		Music/Audio:	Sports/Games/Gambling:
Newspapers:	Y	Movie Theaters:		Equipment/Supplies:		Broadcast TV:	Y	Music Production:	Games/Sports:
Magazines:		Movie Production:		Gambling Equipment:		Cable TV:	Y	Retail Music:	Retail Games Stores:
Books:		TV/Video Prod.:	Y	Special Services:	Y	Satellite Broadcast:		Retail Audio Equip.:	Stadiums/Teams:
Book Stores:		Video Rental:		Advertising Services:		Radio:		Music Print./Dist.:	Gambling/Casinos:
Distribution/Printing:		Video Distribution:		Info. Sys. Software:		Online Information:		Multimedia:	Rides/Theme Parks:

TYPES OF BUSINESS:

Television Broadcasting
Newspaper Publishing
Cable Broadcasting
Television Production & Distribution
Specialty TV Channels
Online Information
Web Site Development

BRANDS/DIVISIONS/AFFILIATES:

Global Television Network
E! Entertainment Television, Inc.
CanWest Entertainment
Tvtropolis
Mentv
Mystery
Alliance Atlantis Communications Inc
Cornerstone Publications, Inc

CONTACTS: Note: Officers with more than one job title may be intentionally listed here more than once.

Leonard J. Asper, CEO
Leonard J. Asper, Pres.
John E. Maguire, CFO
Grace M. Palombo, Sr. VP-Human Resources
Richard M. Leipsic, General Counsel/VP
John P. Culligan, Sr. VP-Corp. Dev.
Debbie Hutton, Sr. VP-Corp. Comm.
David A. Asper, Exec. VP/Chmn.-National Post
Gail S. Asper, Corp. Sec.
Kathleen A. Dore, Pres., Television CanWest Media Works
Dennis Skulsky, CEO/Pres., CanWest MediaWorks Publishing
Derek H. Burney, Chmn.
Rick Hetherington, Pres., European Oper.

Phone: 204-956-2025	Fax: 204-947-9841
Toll-Free:	
Address: 3100 TD Ctr., 201 Portage Ave., 31st Fl., Winnipeg, MB R3B 3L7 Canada	

GROWTH PLANS/SPECIAL FEATURES:

CanWest Global Communications is an international media company with interests in broadcast television, publications, specialty cable channels, out-of-home advertising and interactive operations in Canada, the U.K., the U.S., Australia, New Zealand, Indonesia, Singapore and Turkey. CanWest owns and operates the Global Television Network, which covers roughly 97% of Canada's English-language market, as well as five E! channels (formerly CH channels) which provide second signal coverage in six major markets. CanWest owns and operates 16 television stations licensed to provide over-the-air television broadcasting services in eight provinces. The Global Television Network consists of 11 stations broadcasting to all major metropolitan areas in Canada, including Toronto/Hamilton, Montreal, Vancouver/Victoria, Ottawa, Calgary, Edmonton, Quebec City, Halifax, Regina, Saskatoon and Winnipeg, which covers an estimated 23.6 million people. Five of the company's stations operate under a strategic alliance with E! Entertainment Television, Inc., and target a younger female audience than its Global Television Network. The company owns interests in a number of specialty cable channels including TVtropolis, Mentv, Mystery, Lonestar, Dejaview, Fox Sports World Canada, Xtreme Sports and CoolTV. CanWest is also one of the largest publishers of English-language newspapers in Canada with aggregate daily paid circulation of 1.3 million copies representing approximately 35% of Canada's average English-language daily newspaper total weekly paid circulation, and an estimated average weekly readership of 4.8 million people. In May 2007, CanWest delisted from the NYSE. In June 2007, the company sold its interest in MediaWorks Limited to HT Media Limited. In August 2007, CanWest and Goldman Sachs acquired Alliance Atlantis Communications, Inc. and subsequently reorganized Alliance's broadcasting, entertainment and motion picture distribution businesses into separate groups which will each be operated on a stand-alone basis. In November 2007, CanWest acquired three publication groups, Phoenix Media Group, Inc.; Cornerstone Publications, Inc.; and Sims Publications, Inc., all located in Windsor-Essex County.

FINANCIALS: Sales and profits are in thousands of dollars—add 000 to get the full amount. 2007 Note: Financial information for 2007 was not available for all companies at press time.

2007 Sales: $	2007 Profits: $	**U.S. Stock Ticker: CGS**
2006 Sales: $2,484,570	2006 Profits: $154,210	**Int'l Ticker: CGS.A** Int'l Exchange: Toronto-TSX
2005 Sales: $2,588,600	2005 Profits: $8,700	Employees: 10,656
2004 Sales: $1,611,000	2004 Profits: $-10,300	Fiscal Year Ends: 8/31
2003 Sales: $1,643,300	2003 Profits: $33,200	Parent Company:

SALARIES/BENEFITS:

Pension Plan:	ESOP Stock Plan:	Profit Sharing:	Top Exec. Salary: $503,954	Bonus: $526,365
Savings Plan:	Stock Purch. Plan:		Second Exec. Salary: $465,188	Bonus: $279,113

OTHER THOUGHTS:

Apparent Women Officers or Directors: 4
Hot Spot for Advancement for Women/Minorities: Y

LOCATIONS: ("Y" = Yes)

West:	Southwest:	Midwest:	Southeast:	Northeast:	International:
		Y			Y

Note: Financial information, benefits and other data can change quickly and may vary from those stated here.

CARMIKE CINEMAS INC
www.carmike.com

Industry Group Code: 512131 Ranks within this company's industry group: Sales: 3   Profits: 3

Print Media/Publishing:	Movies:		Equipment/Supplies:	Broadcast/Cable:	Music/Audio:	Sports/Games/Gambling:
Newspapers:	Movie Theaters:	Y	Equipment/Supplies:	Broadcast TV:	Music Production:	Games/Sports:
Magazines:	Movie Production:		Gambling Equipment:	Cable TV:	Retail Music:	Retail Games Stores:
Books:	TV/Video Prod.:		Special Services:	Satellite Broadcast:	Retail Audio Equip.:	Stadiums/Teams:
Book Stores:	Video Rental:		Advertising Services:	Radio:	Music Print./Dist.:	Gambling/Casinos:
Distribution/Printing:	Video Distribution:		Info. Sys. Software:	Online Information:	Multimedia:	Rides/Theme Parks:

TYPES OF BUSINESS:
Movie Theaters

BRANDS/DIVISIONS/AFFILIATES:
Hollywood Connection
Eastwynn Theatres, Inc.
Wooden Nickel Pub, Inc.
Military Services, Inc.
IQ 2000
IQ Zero
George G. Kerasotes Corporation

CONTACTS: *Note: Officers with more than one job title may be intentionally listed here more than once.*
Michael W. Patrick, CEO
Fred W. Van Noy, COO/Sr. VP
Michael W. Patrick, Pres.
Richard B. Hare, CFO
Lee Champion, General Counsel/Sr. VP/Corp. Sec.
Gary F. Krannacker, VP-Oper.
Richard B. Hare, Sr. VP-Finance/Treas.
Anthony J. Rhead, Sr. VP-Entertainment/Digital Cinema
H. Madison Shirley, Sr. VP-Concessions/Asst. Sec.
Larry B. Collins, VP-Film
Jeffery A. Cole, Asst. VP/Controller/Chief Acc. Officer
Michael W. Patrick, Chmn.

Phone: 706-576-3400	Fax: 706-576-2812
Toll-Free:	
Address: 1301 First Ave., Columbus, GA 31901 US	

GROWTH PLANS/SPECIAL FEATURES:
Carmike Cinemas, Inc. is a major chain of movie theaters in the U.S. The company operates 287 theatres and 2,427 screens in 37 states, primarily in the southeastern, northeastern and midwestern regions of the U.S. In addition, the company operates two family entertainment centers under the name Hollywood Connection. Carmike targets small to mid-sized communities; more than 80% of the company's theaters are located in towns with fewer than 100,000 residents. A Carmike theater typically includes a smaller number of screens than is usual in modern construction. These theaters, known as econoplexes, are intended for markets that are too small to host a megaplex (defined as a theater with more than 12 screens). Carmike Cinemas maintain low operating costs due to I.Q. 2000 and I.Q. Zero, information technology systems that instantly transmit all information to the corporate headquarters where executive management coordinates the administrative functions. Carmike's growth strategy centers on the development of new theaters and the addition of screens and other improvements to existing theaters, as well as selective acquisitions of theaters as available.

FINANCIALS: Sales and profits are in thousands of dollars—add 000 to get the full amount. 2007 Note: Financial information for 2007 was not available for all companies at press time.

2007 Sales: $	2007 Profits: $	U.S. Stock Ticker: CKEC
2006 Sales: $495,499	2006 Profits: $-19,389	Int'l Ticker: Int'l Exchange:
2005 Sales: $468,894	2005 Profits: $ 177	Employees: 7,383
2004 Sales: $495,337	2004 Profits: $27,941	Fiscal Year Ends: 12/31
2003 Sales: $493,085	2003 Profits: $107,378	Parent Company:

SALARIES/BENEFITS:

Pension Plan:	ESOP Stock Plan:	Profit Sharing:	Top Exec. Salary: $850,000	Bonus: $363,000
Savings Plan: Y	Stock Purch. Plan:		Second Exec. Salary: $325,000	Bonus: $82,915

OTHER THOUGHTS:
Apparent Women Officers or Directors: 1
Hot Spot for Advancement for Women/Minorities:

LOCATIONS: ("Y" = Yes)

West:	Southwest:	Midwest:	Southeast:	Northeast:	International:
Y	Y	Y	Y	Y	

Note: Financial information, benefits and other data can change quickly and may vary from those stated here.

CBS CORP

www.cbscorporation.com

Industry Group Code: 513120 Ranks within this company's industry group: Sales: 4 Profits: 3

Print Media/Publishing:		Movies:		Equipment/Supplies:		Broadcast/Cable:		Music/Audio:		Sports/Games/Gambling:	
Newspapers:		Movie Theaters:		Equipment/Supplies:		Broadcast TV:	Y	Music Production:		Games/Sports:	
Magazines:		Movie Production:		Gambling Equipment:		Cable TV:	Y	Retail Music:		Retail Games Stores:	
Books:	Y	TV/Video Prod.:	Y	Special Services:	Y	Satellite Broadcast:		Retail Audio Equip.:		Stadiums/Teams:	
Book Stores:		Video Rental:		Advertising Services:	Y	Radio:		Music Print./Dist.:		Gambling/Casinos:	
Distribution/Printing:		Video Distribution:		Info. Sys. Software:		Online Information:		Multimedia:		Rides/Theme Parks:	

TYPES OF BUSINESS:

Broadcast Television
News Organization
Outdoor Advertising
Radio Networks & Programming
Television Production
Cable TV Networks
Book Publishing

BRANDS/DIVISIONS/AFFILIATES:

Viacom Inc
CBS Television
Showtime Networks
CSTV: College Sports Television
60 Minutes
The NFL Today
Simon & Schuster Inc
Last.fm

CONTACTS: *Note: Officers with more than one job title may be intentionally listed here more than once.*

Leslie Moonves, CEO
Leslie Moonves, Pres.
Fredric G. Reynolds, CFO
Anthony G. Ambrosio, Exec. VP-Human Resources
David F. Poltrack, Chief Research Officer/Pres., CBS Vision
Amy Berkowitz, CIO/Sr. VP
Anthony G. Ambrosio, Exec. VP-Admin.
Louis J. Briskman, General Counsel/Exec. VP
Martin D. Franks, Exec. VP-Planning, Policy, Gov't. Rel.
Gil Schwartz, Chief Comm. Officer/Exec. VP
Martin M. Shea, Exec. VP-Investor Rel.
Susan C. Gordon, Chief Acct. Officer/Controller/Sr. VP
John Orlando, Sr. VP-Gov't Affairs
Angeline C. Straka, Sr. VP/Corp. Sec./Deputy Counsel
Richard M. Jones, Sr. VP/Gen. Tax Counsel
Joseph R. Ianniello, Sr. VP-Finance/Treas.
Sumner M. Redstone, Chmn.

Phone: 212-975-4321	Fax: 212-975-4516
Toll-Free:	
Address: 51 W. 52nd St., 35th Fl., New York, NY 10019 US	

GROWTH PLANS/SPECIAL FEATURES:

CBS Corp., spun-off from Viacom in January 2006, is one of the largest radio and television broadcasters in the U.S. CBS has four segments: television, radio, outdoor advertising and publishing. The company's television segment consists of CBS Television, Showtime Networks and CSTV: College Sports Television. CBS Television is comprised of the CBS Network, the company's 40 owned broadcast television stations; and CBS Paramount Network Television and CBS Television Distribution, the company's television production and syndication operations. The CBS Network, through CBS Entertainment, CBS News and CBS Sports, distributes news and public affairs broadcasts; sports and entertainment programming; and feature films to more than 200 domestic affiliates, including 21 of the company's television stations. CBS News provides regularly schedule news programs, including 60 Minutes, CBS Evening News with Katie Couric and The Early Show. CBS Sports broadcasts include The NFL Today; certain NCAA championships; the U.S. Open Tennis Championships; and the AFC championship game. Showtime Networks is the company's premium subscription television program services operation. CSTV is the company's cable network and online digital media business devoted to college athletics. The radio segment owns and operates 144 radio stations in 31 states markets through CBS Radio. Through CBS Outdoor, the company displays advertising on media, including billboards, transit shelters, buses, rail systems, mall kiosks, masts and stadium signage. The publishing segment consists of Simon & Schuster, which publishes and distributes consumer books under imprints such as Simon & Schuster, Pocket Books, Scribner and Free Press. In May 2007, CBS acquired Wallstrip, an online syndicator and producer of a daily webshow focused on financial news. Also in May 2007, the company acquired Last.fm, a global community-based music network, for $280 million. In October 2007, CBS acquired SignStorey, Inc., a leading distributor of video programming and advertising content to retail stores, for $71.5 million.

FINANCIALS: Sales and profits are in thousands of dollars—add 000 to get the full amount. 2007 Note: Financial information for 2007 was not available for all companies at press time.

2007 Sales: $	2007 Profits: $	U.S. Stock Ticker: CBS
2006 Sales: $14,320,200	2006 Profits: $1,660,500	Int'l Ticker: Int'l Exchange:
2005 Sales: $14,113,000	2005 Profits: $-7,089,100	Employees: 23,654
2004 Sales: $14,138,300	2004 Profits: $-17,462,200	Fiscal Year Ends: 12/31
2003 Sales: $26,585,300	2003 Profits: $1,416,900	Parent Company:

SALARIES/BENEFITS:

Pension Plan:	ESOP Stock Plan:	Profit Sharing:	Top Exec. Salary: $5,613,200	Bonus: $15,000,000
Savings Plan:	Stock Purch. Plan:		Second Exec. Salary: $3,050,000	Bonus: $7,320,000

OTHER THOUGHTS:

Apparent Women Officers or Directors: 4
Hot Spot for Advancement for Women/Minorities: Y

LOCATIONS: ("Y" = Yes)

West:	Southwest:	Midwest:	Southeast:	Northeast:	International:
Y	Y	Y	Y	Y	Y

Note: Financial information, benefits and other data can change quickly and may vary from those stated here.

CBS RADIO   www.cbsradio.com

Industry Group Code: 513111 Ranks within this company's industry group: Sales: Profits:

Print Media/Publishing:	Movies:	Equipment/Supplies:		Broadcast/Cable:	Music/Audio:	Sports/Games/Gambling:
Newspapers:	Movie Theaters:	Equipment/Supplies:		Broadcast TV:	Music Production:	Games/Sports:
Magazines:	Movie Production:	Gambling Equipment:		Cable TV:	Retail Music:	Retail Games Stores:
Books:	TV/Video Prod.:	Special Services:		Satellite Broadcast:	Retail Audio Equip.:	Stadiums/Teams:
Book Stores:	Video Rental:	Advertising Services:	Y	Radio:	Music Print./Dist.:	Gambling/Casinos:
Distribution/Printing:	Video Distribution:	Info. Sys. Software:		Online Information:	Multimedia:	Rides/Theme Parks:

TYPES OF BUSINESS:

Radio Broadcasting
Online Streaming Music
HD Digital Radio
Sports Broadcasting

BRANDS/DIVISIONS/AFFILIATES:

CBS Corporation .
CBS Radio Network
Globe (The)

CONTACTS: *Note: Officers with more than one job title may be intentionally listed here more than once.*

Dan Mason, CEO
Dan Mason, Pres.
Anton Guitano, CFO
David Goodman, Pres., Mktg.
Mark Zulli, Sr. VP-Human Resources
Lucy Hughes, Sr. VP-Research
Oli Stephensen, CTO/VP
Glynn Walden, Sr. VP-Eng.
Anton Guitano, Sr. Exec. VP-Oper.
Karen L. Mateo, VP- Comm.
Anton Guitano, Sr. Exec. VP-Finance
Michael Weiss, Pres., Sales
Chris Oliviero, VP-Programming
Sue McNamara, Sr. VP-Sales
Rich Lobel, Exec. VP-CBS Radio Altitude Group

Phone: 212-846-3939	Fax: 212-314-9228
Toll-Free:	
Address: 1515 Broadway, 46th Fl., New York, NY 10036 US	

GROWTH PLANS/SPECIAL FEATURES:

CBS Radio, a subsidiary of CBS Corporation, is a large radio broadcasting firm operating out of New York City. The company was formerly known as Infinity Broadcasting, but the name changed after CBS's split from Viacom. CBS Radio's network consists of 140 stations, all of which are located in the top 50 radio markets in the country. The firm offers a variety of programming ranging from adult contemporary music to news broadcasts and personality shows. The company operates over 100 stations broadcasting in HD, and more than 66 operating an HD2 channel. CBS Radio is home to the live broadcasts of 27 professional sports franchises, including the MLB, NFL, NBA, NHL and WNBA. The company has an alliance with Westwood One, a firm that provides stations with news, sports, weather and music content. Additionally, the company owns CBS Radio Network, which provides hourly newscasts to over 1,500 news and news/talk formatted stations. CBS Radio streams more than 100 of its music, talk, sports and news radio stations live online. In addition, the company streams several of its HD2 channels, and has created a number of customized stations exclusively for the Internet. In February 2007, the firm launched 94.7 The Globe, its first environmentally focused radio station, based in Washington, D.C. The Globe will purchase energy resources generated by wind and replace company vehicles with hybrid models.

FINANCIALS: Sales and profits are in thousands of dollars—add 000 to get the full amount. 2007 Note: Financial information for 2007 was not available for all companies at press time.

2007 Sales: $	2007 Profits: $	**U.S. Stock Ticker: Subsidiary**
2006 Sales: $	2006 Profits: $	Int'l Ticker: Int'l Exchange:
2005 Sales: $2,114,800	2005 Profits: $	Employees: 8,287
2004 Sales: $2,096,100	2004 Profits: $	Fiscal Year Ends: 12/31
2003 Sales: $	2003 Profits: $	Parent Company: CBS CORP

SALARIES/BENEFITS:

Pension Plan:	ESOP Stock Plan:	Profit Sharing:	Top Exec. Salary: $	Bonus: $
Savings Plan:	Stock Purch. Plan:		Second Exec. Salary: $	Bonus: $

OTHER THOUGHTS:

Apparent Women Officers or Directors: 3
Hot Spot for Advancement for Women/Minorities: Y

LOCATIONS: ("Y" = Yes)

West:	Southwest:	Midwest:	Southeast:	Northeast:	International:
Y	Y	Y	Y	Y	

CD WAREHOUSE INC   www.cdwarehouse.com

Industry Group Code: 451220 Ranks within this company's industry group: Sales: Profits:

Print Media/Publishing:	Movies:	Equipment/Supplies:	Broadcast/Cable:	Music/Audio:		Sports/Games/Gambling:
Newspapers:	Movie Theaters:	Equipment/Supplies:	Broadcast TV:	Music Production:		Games/Sports:
Magazines:	Movie Production:	Gambling Equipment:	Cable TV:	Retail Music:	Y	Retail Games Stores:
Books:	TV/Video Prod.:	Special Services:	Satellite Broadcast:	Retail Audio Equip.:		Stadiums/Teams:
Book Stores:	Video Rental:	Advertising Services:	Radio:	Music Print./Dist.:		Gambling/Casinos:
Distribution/Printing:	Video Distribution:	Info. Sys. Software:	Online Information:	Multimedia:		Rides/Theme Parks:

TYPES OF BUSINESS:

Music Stores
Pre-Owned CD & DVD Sales
Franchising

BRANDS/DIVISIONS/AFFILIATES:

Magnolia Entertainment, LLC
Disc Go Round
CD Exchange
CD Warehouse
Movie Exchange
Music Trader

CONTACTS: Note: Officers with more than one job title may be intentionally listed here more than once.

Christopher M. Salyer, CEO
Christopher M. Salyer, Pres.

Phone: 405-236-8742	Fax: 405-949-2566
Toll-Free: 800-641-2566	
Address: 900 N. Broadway, Oklahoma City, OK 73102 US	

GROWTH PLANS/SPECIAL FEATURES:

CD Warehouse, Inc. operates and franchises music stores specializing in used CDs. The company also sells new and used DVDs, t-shirts, video games, records and related music memorabilia. The company does business through two stores in Canada and 128 U.S. stores in 24 states and Washington, D.C., with stores typically offering between 10,000 and 16,000 CDs. The firm's stores operate under the names CD Warehouse, Music Trader, Disc Go Round, Movie Exchange and CD Exchange and are generally located in strip shopping centers. Typically, each store carries the majority of Billboard Top 100 music hits, in addition to a selection of pre-owned CDs, which are purchased for $1 to $5 and remarketed for $6 to $9. The stores generate the majority of their revenues from used CD sales, with customers able to trade CDs or sell them for cash or store credit. Franchise managers are given the company's proprietary software that helps decide whether the customer's used CDs should be accepted or rejected. The software indicates how much money the CD is worth and how many units the store should have in its inventory. Increasingly, CD Warehouse's stores are engaged in the buying, selling and trading of DVDs, as the company sees this as a huge growth market. CD Warehouse is owned by Magnolia Entertainment, LLC.

All CD Warehouse franchisees attend a corporate training program and are provided with comprehensive information packets. Support staff, assisting in everything from site selection to equipment and inventory ordering, can be provided to franchisees if requested.

FINANCIALS: Sales and profits are in thousands of dollars—add 000 to get the full amount. 2007 Note: Financial information for 2007 was not available for all companies at press time.

2007 Sales: $	2007 Profits: $	U.S. Stock Ticker: CDWR
2006 Sales: $	2006 Profits: $	Int'l Ticker: Int'l Exchange:
2005 Sales: $	2005 Profits: $	Employees: 293
2004 Sales: $	2004 Profits: $	Fiscal Year Ends: 12/31
2003 Sales: $	2003 Profits: $	Parent Company: MAGNOLIA ENTERTAINMENT LLC

SALARIES/BENEFITS:

Pension Plan:	ESOP Stock Plan:	Profit Sharing:	Top Exec. Salary: $200,000	Bonus: $25,000
Savings Plan: Y	Stock Purch. Plan:		Second Exec. Salary: $120,000	Bonus: $25,000

OTHER THOUGHTS:

Apparent Women Officers or Directors:
Hot Spot for Advancement for Women/Minorities:

LOCATIONS: ("Y" = Yes)

West:	Southwest:	Midwest:	Southeast:	Northeast:	International:
Y	Y	Y	Y	Y	Y

Note: Financial information, benefits and other data can change quickly and may vary from those stated here.

CEDAR FAIR LP   www.cedarfair.com

Industry Group Code: 713110 Ranks within this company's industry group: Sales: 3   Profits: 1

Print Media/Publishing:	Movies:	Equipment/Supplies:	Broadcast/Cable:	Music/Audio:	Sports/Games/Gambling:	
Newspapers:	Movie Theaters:	Equipment/Supplies:	Broadcast TV:	Music Production:	Games/Sports:	
Magazines:	Movie Production:	Gambling Equipment:	Cable TV:	Retail Music:	Retail Games Stores:	
Books:	TV/Video Prod.:	Special Services:	Satellite Broadcast:	Retail Audio Equip.:	Stadiums/Teams:	
Book Stores:	Video Rental:	Advertising Services:	Radio:	Music Print./Dist.:	Gambling/Casinos:	Y
Distribution/Printing:	Video Distribution:	Info. Sys. Software:	Online Information:	Multimedia:	Rides/Theme Parks:	

TYPES OF BUSINESS:

Amusement Parks
Water Parks
Hotels

BRANDS/DIVISIONS/AFFILIATES:

Castaway Bay
Valleyfair
Dorney Park
Wildwater Kingdom
Worlds of Fun
Knott's Berry Farm
Michigan's Adventure
Paramount Parks

CONTACTS: *Note: Officers with more than one job title may be intentionally listed here more than once.*

Richard L. Kinzel, CEO
Jacob T. Falfas, COO
Richard L. Kinzel, Pres.
Peter J. Crage, CFO
Craig J. Freeman, VP-Admin.
Robert A. Decker, Corp. VP-Planning & Design
Stacy Frole, Dir.-Investor Rel.
Peter J. Crage, Corp. VP-Finance
H. Philip Bender, Regional VP
Brian C. Witherow, VP/Corp. Controller
Richard L. Kinzel, Chmn.

Phone: 419-627-2233	Fax: 419-627-2260
Toll-Free:	
Address: 1 Cedar Point Dr., Sandusky, OH 44870-5259 US	

GROWTH PLANS/SPECIAL FEATURES:

Cedar Fair, L.P., and its affiliates own and operate 12 amusement parks, including Cedar Point, located on Lake Erie in Sandusky, Ohio; Knott's Berry Farm, located near Los Angeles, California; Dorney Park & Wildwater Kingdom, in South Whitehall Township, Pennsylvania; Valleyfair, in Shakopee, Minnesota; Worlds of Fun, in Kansas City, Missouri; Geauga Lake & Wildwater Kingdom, in Aurora, Ohio; and Michigan's Adventure, near Muskegon, Michigan. The company also owns and operates the Castaway Bay Indoor Waterpark Resort in Sandusky, Ohio, and five separate-gated outdoor water parks. Three of the outdoor water parks are located adjacent to Cedar Point, Knott's Berry Farm and Worlds of Fun, the fourth is located near San Diego, and the fifth is in Palm Springs, California. In addition to parks, Cedar Point owns and operates six hotel facilities. The park's only year-round hotel is Castaway Bay, an indoor water park resort. Castaway Bay features a tropical Caribbean theme with 237 hotel rooms centered around a 38,000-square-foot indoor water park. The park's largest hotel, the Hotel Breakers, has more than 600 guest rooms, including 230 in the 10-story Breakers Tower. Breakers Tower has 18 tower suites with spectacular views, an indoor pool and a TGI Friday's restaurant. Located near the Causeway entrance to the park is Breakers Express, a 350-room, limited-service seasonal hotel. Cedar Point also features the Sandcastle Suites Hotel, which features 187 suites, a courtyard pool, tennis courts and the Breakwater Cafe, a contemporary waterfront restaurant. In June 2006, Cedar Fair acquired Paramount Parks, a wholly owned subsidiary of CBS Corp., for a cash purchase of $1.24 billion. The acquisition includes Canada's Wonderland near Toronto, Canada; Kings Island near Cincinnati, Ohio; Kings Dominion near Richmond, Virginia; Carowinds in Charlotte, North Carolina; and Great America located in Santa Clara, California.

FINANCIALS: Sales and profits are in thousands of dollars—add 000 to get the full amount. 2007 Note: Financial information for 2007 was not available for all companies at press time.

2007 Sales: $	2007 Profits: $	**U.S. Stock Ticker: FUN**
2006 Sales: $831,389	2006 Profits: $87,477	**Int'l Ticker:** Int'l Exchange:
2005 Sales: $568,707	2005 Profits: $160,852	Employees: 31,850
2004 Sales: $541,972	2004 Profits: $78,315	Fiscal Year Ends: 12/31
2003 Sales: $509,976	2003 Profits: $85,888	Parent Company:

SALARIES/BENEFITS:

Pension Plan: Y	ESOP Stock Plan:	Profit Sharing:	Top Exec. Salary: $1,092,693	Bonus: $1,200,000
Savings Plan:	Stock Purch. Plan:		Second Exec. Salary: $521,731	Bonus: $420,000

OTHER THOUGHTS:

Apparent Women Officers or Directors: 1
Hot Spot for Advancement for Women/Minorities:

LOCATIONS: ("Y" = Yes)

West:	Southwest:	Midwest:	Southeast:	Northeast:	International:
Y		Y		Y	

CENTRAL EUROPEAN MEDIA ENTERPRISES LTD www.cetv-net.com

Industry Group Code: 512110 Ranks within this company's industry group: Sales: 6 Profits: 3

Print Media/Publishing:	Movies:	Equipment/Supplies:	Broadcast/Cable:	Music/Audio:	Sports/Games/Gambling:
Newspapers:	Movie Theaters:	Equipment/Supplies:	Broadcast TV: Y	Music Production:	Games/Sports:
Magazines:	Movie Production:	Gambling Equipment:	Cable TV:	Retail Music:	Retail Games Stores:
Books:	TV/Video Prod.: Y	Special Services:	Satellite Broadcast:	Retail Audio Equip.:	Stadiums/Teams:
Book Stores:	Video Rental:	Advertising Services:	Radio:	Music Print./Dist.:	Gambling/Casinos:
Distribution/Printing:	Video Distribution:	Info. Sys. Software:	Online Information:	Multimedia:	Rides/Theme Parks:

TYPES OF BUSINESS:

Television Broadcasting
Television Production

BRANDS/DIVISIONS/AFFILIATES:

Apax Partners
TV Markiza
Pro TV
Acasa
TV Nova
Galaxie Sport
Studio 1+1
Sport.ro

CONTACTS: *Note: Officers with more than one job title may be intentionally listed here more than once.*

Michael N. Garin, CEO
Adrian Sarbu, COO
Wallace MacMillan, CFO
Daniel Penn, General Counsel/Sec.
Romana Tomasova, Dir.-Corp. Comm.
Mark Wyllie, VP-Corp. Finance
Marina Williams, Exec. VP
Ronald S. Lauder, Chmn.
Marijan Jurenec, Regional Dir.-Adriatic

Phone: 441-296-1431	Fax:
Toll-Free:	
Address: P.O. Box HM66, Clarendon House 2, Church St., Hamilton, HM CX Bermuda	

GROWTH PLANS/SPECIAL FEATURES:

Central European Media Enterprises, Ltd. (CEME) is an international television broadcasting company with administrative offices in Bermuda, the Netherlands and the U.K. The firm's operations in Croatia generated 4% of 2006 segment revenues; the Czech Republic, 34%; Romania, 25%; the Slovak Republic, 12%; Slovenia, 9%; and Ukraine, 16%. Founded on the idea that the newly democratized nations of the former Soviet Bloc could support independent television broadcasting, CEME began operating in 1994 and quickly grew into a large and successful enterprise. The group invests in, develops and operates a collection of national and regional commercial television stations and networks across Central and Eastern Europe, reaching about 91 million viewers. Operating 14 stations in its six target countries, with market leadership in each of them, the company annually produces thousands of hours of original programming to support its broadcasting operations. Station names include Pro TV, Acasa, TV Nova, Pop TV, Galaxie Sport and Studio 1+1. Most of the stations affiliated with CEME air a variety of programs designed to appeal to a wide audience, including sporting events, news, game shows and locally produced programs. CEME has a number of exclusive broadcast rights granted by American and Western European corporations to air foreign news programs and popular films from abroad. Advertising accounted for 90% of the firm's segment revenue for 2006, with Procter & Gamble, Wrigley, Unilever, Nestle and Coca-Cola among the largest advertisers. In 2006, Apax Partners purchased a 49.7% stake in the company for approximately $190 million, following CEME's acquisition of TV Markiza, a television broadcaster in the Slovak Republic, earlier in the year. In March 2007, the firm acquired Sport.ro, a sports TV station in Romania, offering a variety of locally produced and global sports programming, including broadcast rights to major sporting events in soccer, rugby, handball, boxing and World Wrestling Entertainment (WWE).

FINANCIALS: Sales and profits are in thousands of dollars—add 000 to get the full amount. 2007 Note: Financial information for 2007 was not available for all companies at press time.

2007 Sales: $	2007 Profits: $	U.S. Stock Ticker: CETV
2006 Sales: $603,115	2006 Profits: $20,424	Int'l Ticker: CETV Int'l Exchange: Prague-PX
2005 Sales: $400,978	2005 Profits: $42,495	Employees: 3,300
2004 Sales: $182,339	2004 Profits: $18,531	Fiscal Year Ends: 12/31
2003 Sales: $118,526	2003 Profits: $346,012	Parent Company:

SALARIES/BENEFITS:

Pension Plan:	ESOP Stock Plan:	Profit Sharing:	Top Exec. Salary: $924,887	Bonus: $426,887
Savings Plan:	Stock Purch. Plan:		Second Exec. Salary: $625,000	Bonus: $1,400,000

OTHER THOUGHTS:

Apparent Women Officers or Directors: 3
Hot Spot for Advancement for Women/Minorities: Y

LOCATIONS: ("Y" = Yes)

West:	Southwest:	Midwest:	Southeast:	Northeast:	International: Y

Note: Financial information, benefits and other data can change quickly and may vary from those stated here.

CENTURY CASINOS INC

www.cnty.com

Industry Group Code: 713210 Ranks within this company's industry group: Sales: 9   Profits: 6

Print Media/Publishing:	Movies:	Equipment/Supplies:	Broadcast/Cable:	Music/Audio:	Sports/Games/Gambling:	
Newspapers:	Movie Theaters:	Equipment/Supplies:	Broadcast TV:	Music Production:	Games/Sports:	
Magazines:	Movie Production:	Gambling Equipment:	Cable TV:	Retail Music:	Retail Games Stores:	
Books:	TV/Video Prod.:	Special Services:	Satellite Broadcast:	Retail Audio Equip.:	Stadiums/Teams:	
Book Stores:	Video Rental:	Advertising Services:	Radio:	Music Print./Dist.:	Gambling/Casinos:	Y
Distribution/Printing:	Video Distribution:	Info. Sys. Software:	Online Information:	Multimedia:	Rides/Theme Parks:	

TYPES OF BUSINESS:

Casinos
Cruise Ship Casinos
Hotels & Restaurants

BRANDS/DIVISIONS/AFFILIATES:

Womacks Casino & Hotel
Century Casino Newcastle
Oceania Cruises, Inc.
Century Casino & Hotel
Century Casino Millennium
Century Casinos Africa (Pty) Limited
Caledon Casino, Hotel & Spa
Century Casinos Europe GmbH

CONTACTS: *Note: Officers with more than one job title may be intentionally listed here more than once.*

Erwin Haitzmann, Co-CEO
Larry J. Hannappel, COO
Peter Hoetzinger, Pres./Co-CEO
Andreas Terler, CIO
Niclas Schmiedmaier, Sr. Legal Counsel
Ray Sienko, Chief Acct. Officer
Larry J. Hannappel, Treas./Corp. Sec./Sr. VP
Michael Snider, SEC & Reporting Manager
Erwin Haitzmann, Chmn.

Phone: 719-527-8300	Fax: 719-527-8301
Toll-Free:	
Address: 1263 Lake Plaza Dr., Ste. A, Colorado Springs, CO 80906 US	

GROWTH PLANS/SPECIAL FEATURES:

Century Casinos, Inc. (CCI) is an international casino entertainment company involved in developing and operating gaming establishments and related lodging and restaurant facilities. The Company currently owns and operates the Womacks Casino and Hotel in Cripple Creek, Colorado; the Century Casino & Hotel in Edmonton, Alberta, Canada; and the Century Casino Millennium in the Marriott Hotel in Prague, Czech Republic. The firm also operates the casinos aboard the Silver Wind, Silver Cloud, The World of ResidenSea, and the vessels of Oceania Cruises; and owns a 65% interest in, and has a management contract for, Century Casino & Hotel in Central City, Colorado. Through its subsidiary Century Casinos Africa (Pty) Limited, the company owns and operates The Caledon Hotel, Spa & Casino near Cape Town, South Africa; and has a 60% interest in Century Casino Newcastle, in Newcastle, South Africa. Century also operates casinos aboard the Silver Wind, Silver Cloud and World of ResidenSea cruise ships, and aboard three of the vessels of Oceania Cruises. The company continues to pursue other international projects in various stages of development. In July 2007, the firm extended its casino concession agreement with Oceania Cruises, Inc. for five additional years. In March 2007, CCI's Austrian subsidiary, Century Casinos Europe GmbH, acquired a 33.3% ownership interest in Casinos Poland Ltd.

FINANCIALS: Sales and profits are in thousands of dollars—add 000 to get the full amount. 2007 Note: Financial information for 2007 was not available for all companies at press time.

2007 Sales: $	2007 Profits: $	U.S. Stock Ticker: CNTY
2006 Sales: $56,285	2006 Profits: $7,629	Int'l Ticker: Int'l Exchange:
2005 Sales: $37,445	2005 Profits: $4,481	Employees: 1,000
2004 Sales: $35,765	2004 Profits: $4,738	Fiscal Year Ends: 12/31
2003 Sales: $31,430	2003 Profits: $3,246	Parent Company:

SALARIES/BENEFITS:

Pension Plan:	ESOP Stock Plan:	Profit Sharing:	Top Exec. Salary: $341,331	Bonus: $247,500
Savings Plan: Y	Stock Purch. Plan:		Second Exec. Salary: $158,403	Bonus: $

OTHER THOUGHTS:

Apparent Women Officers or Directors: 1
Hot Spot for Advancement for Women/Minorities:

LOCATIONS: ("Y" = Yes)

West:	Southwest:	Midwest:	Southeast:	Northeast:	International:
Y					Y

CHARTER COMMUNICATIONS INC   www.charter.com

Industry Group Code: 513220 **Ranks within this company's industry group:** Sales: 10   Profits: 20

Print Media/Publishing:	Movies:	Equipment/Supplies:		Broadcast/Cable:		Music/Audio:	Sports/Games/Gambling:
Newspapers:	Movie Theaters:	Equipment/Supplies:		Broadcast TV:		Music Production:	Games/Sports:
Magazines:	Movie Production:	Gambling Equipment:	Y	Cable TV:	Y	Retail Music:	Retail Games Stores:
Books:	TV/Video Prod.:	Special Services:	Y	Satellite Broadcast:		Retail Audio Equip.:	Stadiums/Teams:
Book Stores:	Video Rental:	Advertising Services:		Radio:		Music Print./Dist.:	Gambling/Casinos:
Distribution/Printing:	Video Distribution:	Info. Sys. Software:		Online Information:		Multimedia:	Rides/Theme Parks:

TYPES OF BUSINESS:

Cable TV Service
Internet Access
Advanced Broadband Cable Services
Telephony Services
Voice Over Internet Protocol

BRANDS/DIVISIONS/AFFILIATES:

Charter Digital Cable
Charter OnDemand
Charter Cable TV
Charter HDTV
Charter Business
Charter Media

CONTACTS: Note: Officers with more than one job title may be intentionally listed here more than once.

Neil Smit, CEO
Michael J. Lovett, COO/Exec. VP
Neil Smit, Pres.
Jeffrey T. Fisher, CFO/Exec. VP
Robert A. Quigley, Chief Mktg. Officer/Exec. VP
Lynne F. Ramsey, Sr. VP-Human Resources
Marwan Fawaz, CTO
Grier C. Raclin, General Counsel/Exec. VP/Sec.
Eloise E. Schmitz, Sr. VP-Strategic Planning
Kevin D. Howard, Chief Acct. Officer/VP
Paul G. Allen, Chmn.

Phone: 314-965-0555	Fax: 314-965-9745
Toll-Free:	
Address: 12405 Powerscourt Dr., Ste. 100, St. Louis, MO 63131 US	

GROWTH PLANS/SPECIAL FEATURES:

Charter Communications Inc. is a broadband communications company. The company is the third-largest publicly traded cable operator in the U.S. The firm operates a broadband network consisting of coaxial and hybrid fiber cable, through which it offers traditional cable video programming (both analog and digital); high-speed Internet access; advanced broadband cable services such as Charter OnDemand video services, high definition television service and digital video recorder service; and telephone service. Telephone services are primarily provided using Voice over Internet Protocol (VoIP) to transmit digital voice signals over our systems. Charter's cable service package, Charter Cable TV, includes over 70 standard channels. Charter's advanced broadband services include Charter DVR (digital video recording); Charter HDTV (high-definition TV); Charter Digital Cable, with over 100 channels and over 45 all-digital music channels; Charter OnDemand; and pay-per-view. The company also provides business-to-business Internet access; data networking; video and music entertainment services; and business telephone through Charter Business. Advertising sales and production services are sold under the Charter Media brand. The company has roughly 5.7 million analog video customers in 29 states, of which 2.8 million were also video consumers; 2.4 million high-speed Internet customers, including roughly 268,900 who received only high-speed Internet access; and 445,800 telephone service customers, of which 27,200 received only telephone service. In 2006, video services accounted for 61% of total revenue.

The company offers its employees medical, dental and vision insurance; an employee assistance program; short- and long-term disability; AD&D and dependent life insurance; and a 401(k) plan.

FINANCIALS: Sales and profits are in thousands of dollars—add 000 to get the full amount. 2007 Note: Financial information for 2007 was not available for all companies at press time.

2007 Sales: $	2007 Profits: $	U.S. Stock Ticker: CHTR
2006 Sales: $5,504,000	2006 Profits: $-1,370,000	Int'l Ticker: Int'l Exchange:
2005 Sales: $5,033,000	2005 Profits: $-967,000	Employees: 15,500
2004 Sales: $4,760,000	2004 Profits: $-4,341,000	Fiscal Year Ends: 12/31
2003 Sales: $4,819,000	2003 Profits: $-238,000	Parent Company:

SALARIES/BENEFITS:

Pension Plan:	ESOP Stock Plan:	Profit Sharing:	Top Exec. Salary: $1,200,000	Bonus: $1,725,000
Savings Plan: Y	Stock Purch. Plan:		Second Exec. Salary: $680,768	Bonus: $805,000

OTHER THOUGHTS:

Apparent Women Officers or Directors: 3
Hot Spot for Advancement for Women/Minorities: Y

LOCATIONS: ("Y" = Yes)

West:	Southwest:	Midwest:	Southeast:	Northeast:	International:
Y	Y	Y	Y	Y	

Note: Financial information, benefits and other data can change quickly and may vary from those stated here.

CHURCHILL DOWNS INC

www.churchilldownsincorporated.com

Industry Group Code: 713210 Ranks within this company's industry group: Sales: 5 Profits: 3

Print Media/Publishing:	Movies:	Equipment/Supplies:		Broadcast/Cable:	Music/Audio:	Sports/Games/Gambling:	
Newspapers:	Movie Theaters:	Equipment/Supplies:		Broadcast TV:	Music Production:	Games/Sports:	Y
Magazines:	Movie Production:	Gambling Equipment:		Cable TV:	Retail Music:	Retail Games Stores:	
Books:	TV/Video Prod.:	Special Services:	Y	Satellite Broadcast:	Retail Audio Equip.:	Stadiums/Teams:	Y
Book Stores:	Video Rental:	Advertising Services:		Radio:	Music Print./Dist.:	Gambling/Casinos:	Y
Distribution/Printing:	Video Distribution:	Info. Sys. Software:		Online Information:	Multimedia:	Rides/Theme Parks:	

TYPES OF BUSINESS:

Horse Racing
Pari-mutuel Wagering
Simulcasting
Video Poker
Computer Graphics & Gambling Software
Online Retail

BRANDS/DIVISIONS/AFFILIATES:

Churchill Downs Management Company
Arlington Park Racecourse, LLC
Churchill Downs Investment Company
Calder Race Course
Fair Grounds Race Course
Hoosier Park, LP
Video Services, Inc.
Churchill Downs Simulcast Productions

CONTACTS: *Note: Officers with more than one job title may be intentionally listed here more than once.*

Robert L. Evans, CEO
Robert L. Evans, Pres.
William E. Mudd, CFO/Exec. VP
Vernon Niven, Exec. VP-Tech. Initiatives
Rebecca Reed, Sr. VP-Legal Affairs/Corp. Compliance Officer/Sec.
William C. Carstanjen, Exec. VP/Chief Dev. Officer
Donald R. Richardson, Sr. VP-Racing
Steven Sexton, Exec.VP./Pres., Churchill Downs Racetrack
C. Kenneth Dunn, Sr. VP-Fla. Operations/Calder Race Course, Inc.

Phone: 502-636-4400	Fax: 502-636-4430
Toll-Free:	
Address: 700 Central Ave., Louisville, KY 40208 US	

GROWTH PLANS/SPECIAL FEATURES:

Churchill Downs, Inc. (CDI) is principally a racing company that conducts pari-mutuel wagering on live Thoroughbred, Quarter Horse and Standard bred horse racing and simulcasts signals of races. Additionally, they offer racing services and video poker operations. All operations are managed by Churchill Downs Management Company. CDI owns five racing tracks: Churchill Downs, Arlington Park, Calder Race Course, Fair Grounds Race Course and Hoosier Park. Additionally, the company operates off-track betting facilities. Churchill Downs Management Company manages the firm's racing operations and Video Services, Inc., a video poker machine operator associated with Fair Grounds in Louisiana. The company also owns Churchill Downs Investment Company and has a 100% interest in Churchill Downs Simulcast Productions which provides computer graphics software for the display of betting statistics and other racing related information to the racing industry. In addition to traditional racing and betting, the company conducts simulcast wagering on horse racing year-round through the Churchill Downs Simulcast Network to both proprietary and external betting facilities. Sources of income include gambling, admissions and seating, concession commissions and license, rights, broadcast and sponsorship fees and the sale of Kentucky Derby merchandise through its web site. In addition, the firm has a 50% interest in Kentucky Off-Track Betting, Inc., an alliance between Churchill Downs, Ellis Park Race Course and Kentucky's other thoroughbred racetracks, which operates off-track betting facilities in the Kentucky cities of Maysville, Jamestown, Pineville and Corbin. In March 2007, CDI announced the anticipated launch of an advance deposit wagering platform called, TwinSpires.com. The service will offer racing fans the opportunity to wager on racing content owned primarily by CDI and Magna Entertainment Corporation. The company also acquired a 50% interest in a venture that will own and operate a horse racing television channel currently owned by MEC and HRTV.

FINANCIALS: Sales and profits are in thousands of dollars—add 000 to get the full amount. 2007 Note: Financial information for 2007 was not available for all companies at press time.

2007 Sales: $	2007 Profits: $	U.S. Stock Ticker: CHDN
2006 Sales: $376,671	2006 Profits: $29,811	Int'l Ticker: Int'l Exchange:
2005 Sales: $356,342	2005 Profits: $78,908	Employees: 2,500
2004 Sales: $304,888	2004 Profits: $8,915	Fiscal Year Ends: 12/31
2003 Sales: $348,505	2003 Profits: $23,379	Parent Company:

SALARIES/BENEFITS:

Pension Plan:	ESOP Stock Plan:	Profit Sharing: Y	Top Exec. Salary: $500,580	Bonus: $500,580
Savings Plan: Y	Stock Purch. Plan: Y		Second Exec. Salary: $320,000	Bonus: $247,680

OTHER THOUGHTS:

Apparent Women Officers or Directors: 1
Hot Spot for Advancement for Women/Minorities: Y

LOCATIONS: ("Y" = Yes)

West:	Southwest:	Midwest:	Southeast:	Northeast:	International:
		Y	Y		

Note: Financial information, benefits and other data can change quickly and may vary from those stated here.

CINEMARK INC
www.cinemark.com

Industry Group Code: 512131 Ranks within this company's industry group: Sales: Profits:

Print Media/Publishing:	Movies:		Equipment/Supplies:	Broadcast/Cable:	Music/Audio:	Sports/Games/Gambling:
Newspapers:	Movie Theaters:	Y	Equipment/Supplies:	Broadcast TV:	Music Production:	Games/Sports:
Magazines:	Movie Production:		Gambling Equipment:	Cable TV:	Retail Music:	Retail Games Stores:
Books:	TV/Video Prod.:		Special Services:	Satellite Broadcast:	Retail Audio Equip.:	Stadiums/Teams:
Book Stores:	Video Rental:		Advertising Services:	Radio:	Music Print./Dist.:	Gambling/Casinos:
Distribution/Printing:	Video Distribution:		Info. Sys. Software:	Online Information:	Multimedia:	Rides/Theme Parks:

TYPES OF BUSINESS:
Movie Theaters

BRANDS/DIVISIONS/AFFILIATES:
Cinemark Holdings, Inc.
Cinemark USA, Inc.
Cinemark Properties, Inc.
CNMK Investments, Inc.
Cinemark Investments Corporation
Brasil Holdings, LLC
Cinemark Mexico (USA), Inc.
Century Theaters, Inc.

CONTACTS: Note: Officers with more than one job title may be intentionally listed here more than once.
Alan W. Stock, CEO
Tim Warner, COO
Tim Warner, Pres.
Robert Copple, CFO
Terrell Falk, VP-Mktg.
Michael D. Cavalier, General Counsel/Sec./Sr. VP
Terrell Falk, VP-Comm.
Robert Copple, Treas./Exec. VP
Tandy Mitchell, Exec. VP/Asst. Sec.
Robert Copple, Asst. Sec.
Lee Roy Mitchell, Chmn.
Valmir Fernandes, Pres., Cinemark Int'l

Phone: 972-665-1000	Fax: 972-665-1004

Toll-Free: 800-246-3627
Address: 3900 Dallas Pkwy., Ste. 500, Plano, TX 75093-7865 US

GROWTH PLANS/SPECIAL FEATURES:
Cinemark, Inc., a subsidiary of newly formed Cinemark Holdings, Inc., is a multinational theater corporation that conducts all of its business through Cinemark USA, Inc. and its subsidiaries. The company operates over 395 theatres and over 4,479 screens in 37 states in the U.S. and internationally in 13 countries, primarily in Mexico and South and Central America. Cinemark International, a subsidiary, operates over 956 screens. Most of the company's domestic theaters are first run, while roughly 40 operate as discount theaters. The company's largest market in terms of revenue after the U.S. is Brazil, with Mexico a close second. It also has operations in Argentina, Chile, Ecuador, Peru, Honduras, El Salvador, Costa Rica, Panama, Columbia and Nicaragua. Each region has its own management office. Cinemark opened ten new domestic theaters with 121 screens and acquired one theatre with 12 screens in the first nine months of 2006. In October 2006, the company acquired Century Theaters, Inc., a national theater chain with 77 theaters in 12 states for approximately $681 million and assumption of $360 million in debt. Approximately $150 million of the purchase price was issued as stock in Cinemark Holdings, Inc. NationalCineMedia, which Cinemark jointly holds with Regal Crown Entertainment Group and AMC Entertainment, Inc., filed for a proposed IPO in late 2006. NationalCineMedia is focused on marketing, sale and distribution of cinema advertising and promotional products; it is one of the world's largest digital distribution networks.

FINANCIALS: Sales and profits are in thousands of dollars—add 000 to get the full amount. 2007 Note: Financial information for 2007 was not available for all companies at press time.

2007 Sales: $	2007 Profits: $	U.S. Stock Ticker: Subsidiary
2006 Sales: $	2006 Profits: $	Int'l Ticker: Int'l Exchange:
2005 Sales: $1,020,600	2005 Profits: $22,400	Employees: 8,100
2004 Sales: $	2004 Profits: $	Fiscal Year Ends: 12/31
2003 Sales: $	2003 Profits: $	Parent Company: CINEMARK HOLDINGS INC

SALARIES/BENEFITS:
Pension Plan:	ESOP Stock Plan:	Profit Sharing:	Top Exec. Salary: $	Bonus: $
Savings Plan: Y	Stock Purch. Plan:		Second Exec. Salary: $	Bonus: $

OTHER THOUGHTS:
Apparent Women Officers or Directors:
Hot Spot for Advancement for Women/Minorities:

LOCATIONS: ("Y" = Yes)
West:	Southwest:	Midwest:	Southeast:	Northeast:	International:
Y	Y	Y	Y	Y	Y

Note: Financial information, benefits and other data can change quickly and may vary from those stated here.

CINEMASTAR LUXURY THEATERS INC www.cinemastar.com

Industry Group Code: 512131 Ranks within this company's industry group: Sales: Profits:

Print Media/Publishing:	Movies:		Equipment/Supplies:	Broadcast/Cable:	Music/Audio:	Sports/Games/Gambling:
Newspapers:	Movie Theaters:	Y	Equipment/Supplies:	Broadcast TV:	Music Production:	Games/Sports:
Magazines:	Movie Production:		Gambling Equipment:	Cable TV:	Retail Music:	Retail Games Stores:
Books:	TV/Video Prod.:		Special Services:	Satellite Broadcast:	Retail Audio Equip.:	Stadiums/Teams:
Book Stores:	Video Rental:		Advertising Services:	Radio:	Music Print./Dist.:	Gambling/Casinos:
Distribution/Printing:	Video Distribution:		Info. Sys. Software:	Online Information:	Multimedia:	Rides/Theme Parks:

TYPES OF BUSINESS:
Movie Theaters

BRANDS/DIVISIONS/AFFILIATES:
CinemaStar Luxury Theaters, S.A. de C.V.
SCP Private Equity Partners, LP
Reel Rewards

CONTACTS: *Note: Officers with more than one job title may be intentionally listed here more than once.*
Jack R. Crosby, CEO
Kim Zolna, COO
Kim Zolna, Pres.
John Becker, CFO
Wayne Weisman, Chmn.
John D. Prock, Pres., CinemaStar Luxury Theaters S.A. de C.V.

Phone: 760-945-2500	Fax: 760-945-2510
Toll-Free:	
Address: 1949 Avenida Del Oro, Ste. 100, Oceanside, CA 92056 US	

GROWTH PLANS/SPECIAL FEATURES:

CinemaStar Luxury Theaters, Inc. develops, leases and operates multi-screen, first-run movie theater locations in southern California and northern Mexico. The company currently operates 40 screens in four theater complexes in San Bernardino, Oceanside, Riverside and Perris, California. It also operates in Mexico as CinemaStar Luxury Theaters S.A. de C.V., with a total of 41 screens in Tijuana, Ensenada and Ciudad Obregon. The company's theater complexes typically contain multiple auditoriums, each having 120 to 500 seats, allowing the company flexibility to adjust screening schedules by shifting films among the larger and smaller auditoriums within the same complex in response to audience demand. All theaters feature digital THX sound systems, top-quality projection and screen systems, high-quality seats and premium concession selections. CinemaStar emphasizes a high standard of customer service and experience. Promotional offerings include discounted group tickets, gift certificates and the Reel Rewards program, which awards repeat customers with free popcorn and movie tickets. The majority of the firm is owned by SCP Private Equity Partners.

FINANCIALS: Sales and profits are in thousands of dollars—add 000 to get the full amount. 2007 Note: Financial information for 2007 was not available for all companies at press time.

2007 Sales: $	2007 Profits: $	**U.S. Stock Ticker: Private**
2006 Sales: $	2006 Profits: $	**Int'l Ticker:** Int'l Exchange:
2005 Sales: $	2005 Profits: $	Employees: 400
2004 Sales: $	2004 Profits: $	Fiscal Year Ends: 3/31
2003 Sales: $	2003 Profits: $	Parent Company:

SALARIES/BENEFITS:

Pension Plan:	ESOP Stock Plan:	Profit Sharing:	Top Exec. Salary: $254,806	Bonus: $20,000
Savings Plan:	Stock Purch. Plan:		Second Exec. Salary: $161,538	Bonus: $

OTHER THOUGHTS:
Apparent Women Officers or Directors: 1
Hot Spot for Advancement for Women/Minorities:

LOCATIONS: ("Y" = Yes)

West:	Southwest:	Midwest:	Southeast:	Northeast:	International:
Y					Y

CIRCUIT CITY STORES INC
www.circuitcity.com

Industry Group Code: 443110 Ranks within this company's industry group: Sales: 2 Profits: 2

Print Media/Publishing:	Movies:	Equipment/Supplies:	Broadcast/Cable:	Music/Audio:		Sports/Games/Gambling:
Newspapers:	Movie Theaters:	Equipment/Supplies:	Broadcast TV:	Music Production:		Games/Sports:
Magazines:	Movie Production:	Gambling Equipment:	Cable TV:	Retail Music:		Retail Games Stores:
Books:	TV/Video Prod.:	Special Services:	Satellite Broadcast:	Retail Audio Equip.:	Y	Stadiums/Teams:
Book Stores:	Video Rental:	Advertising Services:	Radio:	Music Print./Dist.:		Gambling/Casinos:
Distribution/Printing:	Video Distribution:	Info. Sys. Software:	Online Information:	Multimedia:		Rides/Theme Parks:

TYPES OF BUSINESS:
Consumer Electronics Stores
Computers & Accessories
Home Office Products
Entertainment Software
Online Sales
Technical Services

BRANDS/DIVISIONS/AFFILIATES:
Circuit City Superstores
Source By Circuit City (The)
Battery Plus
InterTAN, Inc.
firedog
firedog.com

CONTACTS: *Note: Officers with more than one job title may be intentionally listed here more than once.*
Philip J. Schoonover, CEO
Philip J. Schoonover, Pres.
Bruce H. Besanko, CFO/Exec. VP
Eric A. Jonas, Jr., Sr. VP-Human Resources
William E. McCorey, Jr., CIO/Sr. VP
Philip J. Schoonover, Interim Exec. VP-Merch., Mktg. & Svcs.
Reginald D. Hedgebeth, General Counsel/Sr. VP/Sec.
Bill Cimino, Dir.-Corp. Comm.
Jessica Clarke, Investor Rel.
Philip J. Dunn, Treas./Controller/Sr. VP
George D. Clark, Jr., Exec. VP-Multi-Channel Sales
Steven P. Pappas, Sr. VP/Pres., Small Stores
Irynne V. MacKay, Sr. VP/General Merch. Manager
Marshall J. Whaling, Sr. VP-Retail Oper.
Philip J. Schoonover, Chmn.
Kelly E. Breitenbecher, Sr. VP-Supply Chain & Space Planning

Phone: 804-486-4000	Fax: 804-527-4164
Toll-Free: 800-843-2489	
Address: 9950 Mayland Dr., Richmond, VA 23233 US	

GROWTH PLANS/SPECIAL FEATURES:
Circuit City Stores, Inc. is a specialty retailer of consumer electronics, home office products, entertainment software and related services. The company operates in two segments: domestic and international. The domestic segment is engaged in the business of selling brand name consumer electronics, personal computers, entertainment software and related services in Circuit City stores in the U.S. and via its web site and firedog.com. The division operates 642 Superstores and 12 other stores in 158 U.S. media markets. The international segment, which is comprised of the operations of InterTAN, Inc., is engaged in the business of selling private label and brand name consumer electronics in Canada. The segment conducted business through 806 retail stores and dealer outlets, which consisted of 509 company-owned stores, 296 outlets and one Battery Plus store. The division re-branded most of its company owned stores and dealer outlets to The Source By Circuit City during fiscal year 2006. The international segment operates a web site at thesource.ca. Circuit City's web site provides shoppers with extensive product information, direct shipment of purchases, real-time inventory status of products in stores and the ability to order online and pick up at a store. During 2007, Circuit City's domestic segment launched the firedog brand to provide home theater installation and PC services in-store, at home and remotely. In early 2007, the firm announced plans to close 69 domestic and international stores and one distribution center in Kentucky. Additionally, 92 Rogers Plus stores will be returned to Rogers Wireless, Inc.

The company offers its employees dental, vision, life, short- and long-term disability insurance; a 401(k) plan; an employee assistance program; a stock purchase plan; a matching gifts program; and business travel accident insurance.

FINANCIALS: Sales and profits are in thousands of dollars—add 000 to get the full amount. 2007 Note: Financial information for 2007 was not available for all companies at press time.

2007 Sales: $12,430,000	2007 Profits: $-10,000	**U.S. Stock Ticker: CC**
2006 Sales: $11,514,000	2006 Profits: $147,000	**Int'l Ticker:** Int'l Exchange:
2005 Sales: $10,414,000	2005 Profits: $61,000	Employees: 43,011
2004 Sales: $9,745,400	2004 Profits: $-89,300	Fiscal Year Ends: 2/28
2003 Sales: $9,953,500	2003 Profits: $106,100	Parent Company:

SALARIES/BENEFITS:
Pension Plan:	ESOP Stock Plan:	Profit Sharing:	Top Exec. Salary: $894,615	Bonus: $
Savings Plan: Y	Stock Purch. Plan: Y		Second Exec. Salary: $570,192	Bonus: $

OTHER THOUGHTS:
Apparent Women Officers or Directors: 6
Hot Spot for Advancement for Women/Minorities: Y

LOCATIONS: ("Y" = Yes)
West:	Southwest:	Midwest:	Southeast:	Northeast:	International:
Y	Y	Y	Y	Y	Y

Note: Financial information, benefits and other data can change quickly and may vary from those stated here.

CIRQUE DU SOLEIL INC

www.cirquedusoleil.com

Industry Group Code: 512110 Ranks within this company's industry group: Sales: 5 Profits:

Print Media/Publishing:	Movies:	Equipment/Supplies:	Broadcast/Cable:	Music/Audio:	Sports/Games/Gambling:
Newspapers:	Movie Theaters:	Equipment/Supplies:	Broadcast TV:	Music Production:	Games/Sports:
Magazines:	Movie Production:	Gambling Equipment:	Cable TV:	Retail Music:	Retail Games Stores:
Books:	TV/Video Prod.:	Special Services:	Satellite Broadcast:	Retail Audio Equip.:	Stadiums/Teams:
Book Stores:	Video Rental:	Advertising Services:	Radio:	Music Print./Dist.:	Gambling/Casinos:
Distribution/Printing:	Video Distribution:	Info. Sys. Software:	Online Information:	Multimedia:	Rides/Theme Parks:

TYPES OF BUSINESS:

Theatrical Entertainment
Hotels & Restaurants
Merchandising

BRANDS/DIVISIONS/AFFILIATES:

La Nouba
O
Mystere
Zumanity
Ka
LOVE
Club Cirque
Varekai

CONTACTS: *Note: Officers with more than one job title may be intentionally listed here more than once.*

Guy Laliberte, CEO
Daniel Lamarre, COO
Daniel Lamarre, Pres.
Marc Gagnon, Exec. VP-Bus. Dev. & Services

Phone: 514-722-2324	Fax: 514-722-3692
Toll-Free: 800-678-2119	
Address: 8400 2nd Ave., Montreal, QC H1Z 4M6 Canada	

GROWTH PLANS/SPECIAL FEATURES:

Cirque du Soleil, Inc. is a circus production company that blends street entertainment, exotic costumes and cabaret. The firm has preformed for more than 50 million spectators in more than 100 cities on four continents. In 2007, Cirque had 14 shows touring around the world. The company has six permanent productions including: La Nouba in Walt Disney World; O, an aquatic show at the Bellagio; Mystere at Treasure Island; Zumanity, an adult-focused show at New York-New York; Ka, at the MGM Grand hotel in Las Vegas; LOVE, a Beatles tribute show presented in a custom theater at the Mirage Hotel; and Cirque's newest show, which features Chriss Angel and will open at Luxor Resort and Casino in summer 2008. The troupe's touring shows include Quidam, KOOZA, Corteo, Alegria, Dralion, Varekai, as well as its arena shows Saltimbanco and DELIRIUM. Cirque sells merchandise including music, DVDs, books, apparel, collectables and souvenirs, through the company's web site and at shows. The company also plans to enter into hotels and restaurants, with a nightclub called Club Cirque and a Cirque Resort in Las Vegas currently in development. In 2007, Cirque du Soleil opened its show Quidam in Dubai, United Arab Emirates. The company began a new ten-week holiday show in November 2007 at the Theater at Madison Square Garden. The show is contracted with Cablevision Systems Corp. for a minimum of four years. Cirque is in the planning stages of a new permanent Elvis-themed show in Las Vegas. It's expected to open at the MGM Mirage CityCenter in November 2009. The firm plans to grow to 22 shows by 2010.

Cirque du Soleil helps young people in difficult situations by allocating 1% of revenues each year to outreach programs. The firm operates a massive, 100,000 square foot training center in Canada.

FINANCIALS: Sales and profits are in thousands of dollars—add 000 to get the full amount. 2007 Note: Financial information for 2007 was not available for all companies at press time.

2007 Sales: $	2007 Profits: $	**U.S. Stock Ticker: Private**	
2006 Sales: $620,000	2006 Profits: $	**Int'l Ticker:** Int'l Exchange:	
2005 Sales: $	2005 Profits: $	Employees: 2,400	
2004 Sales: $	2004 Profits: $	Fiscal Year Ends: 12/31	
2003 Sales: $	2003 Profits: $	Parent Company:	

SALARIES/BENEFITS:

Pension Plan:	ESOP Stock Plan:	Profit Sharing:	Top Exec. Salary: $	Bonus: $
Savings Plan:	Stock Purch. Plan:		Second Exec. Salary: $	Bonus: $

OTHER THOUGHTS:

Apparent Women Officers or Directors:
Hot Spot for Advancement for Women/Minorities:

LOCATIONS: ("Y" = Yes)

West:	Southwest:	Midwest:	Southeast:	Northeast:	International:
Y				Y	Y

CITADEL BROADCASTING CORP

www.citadelcommunications.com

Industry Group Code: 513111 Ranks within this company's industry group: Sales: 5 Profits: 13

Print Media/Publishing:	Movies:	Equipment/Supplies:	Broadcast/Cable:	Music/Audio:	Sports/Games/Gambling:
Newspapers:	Movie Theaters:	Equipment/Supplies:	Broadcast TV:	Music Production:	Games/Sports:
Magazines:	Movie Production:	Gambling Equipment:	Cable TV:	Retail Music:	Retail Games Stores:
Books:	TV/Video Prod.:	Special Services:	Satellite Broadcast:	Retail Audio Equip.:	Stadiums/Teams:
Book Stores:	Video Rental:	Advertising Services:	Radio:	Music Print./Dist.:	Gambling/Casinos:
Distribution/Printing:	Video Distribution:	Info. Sys. Software:	Online Information:	Multimedia:	Rides/Theme Parks:

TYPES OF BUSINESS:
Radio Station Owner/Operator

BRANDS/DIVISIONS/AFFILIATES:
Forstmann, Little and Co.
Citadel License, Inc.
Citadel Broadcasting Company
FLCC Holdings, Inc.
ABC Radio Networks

CONTACTS: *Note: Officers with more than one job title may be intentionally listed here more than once.*
Farid Suleman, CEO
Judy Ellis, COO
Robert Freedline, CFO
Mike Pallad, VP-Sales
Dave Marchette, VP-Tech.
Jacquelyn J. Orr, General Counsel/VP/Sec.
TJ Lambert, Sr. VP-Affiliate Affairs
Randy L. Taylor, VP-Finance
Wayne Leland, Regional Pres.
Matt Hanlon, Regional Pres.
John Rossoto, Sr. VP-Citadel Interactive
Farid Suleman, Chmn.

Phone: 702-804-5200	Fax: 702-804-5936
Toll-Free:	
Address: 7201 W. Lake Mead Blvd., Ste. 400, Las Vegas, NV 89128 US	

GROWTH PLANS/SPECIAL FEATURES:
Citadel Broadcasting Corp. acquires, develops and operates radio stations in mid-sized markets across the U.S. The company currently owns and operates 169 FM and 61AM radio stations in 50 markets located in 24 states across the country. Citadel targets mid-sized markets due to less direct format competition and lower purchase prices. The company also considers mid-sized markets (defined as those ranked 30 to 150 by market revenue) attractive because they derive a significant portion of their revenue from local advertisers and there are more opportunities for consolidation in mid-sized markets than in larger markets. The company seeks to build station clusters through acquisitions in its existing and additional markets. Programming formats, geographic regions, audience demographics and advertising clients diversify the company's radio station portfolio. Citadel currently owns stations in cities including Providence, Rhode Island; Albuquerque, New Mexico; Baton Rouge, Louisiana; Salt Lake City, Utah; Little Rock, Arkansas; and Colorado Springs, Colorado. The firm's top 25 markets account for approximately 76% of its revenue. Citadel is 70% owned by Forstmann, Little and Co.

As a result of its recent acquisition of Walt Disney's ABC Radio Network, the company plans to earn an additional $100 to $200 million in sales proceeds over the next two years from the sale of radio stations that may need to be divested as a result of the merger.

FINANCIALS: Sales and profits are in thousands of dollars—add 000 to get the full amount. 2007 Note: Financial information for 2007 was not available for all companies at press time.

2007 Sales: $	2007 Profits: $	U.S. Stock Ticker: CDL
2006 Sales: $432,930	2006 Profits: $-48,014	Int'l Ticker: Int'l Exchange:
2005 Sales: $419,907	2005 Profits: $69,757	Employees: 3,428
2004 Sales: $411,495	2004 Profits: $74,568	Fiscal Year Ends: 12/31
2003 Sales: $371,500	2003 Profits: $-89,600	Parent Company:

SALARIES/BENEFITS:

Pension Plan:	ESOP Stock Plan:	Profit Sharing:	Top Exec. Salary: $1,200,000	Bonus: $
Savings Plan: Y	Stock Purch. Plan:		Second Exec. Salary: $500,000	Bonus: $200,000

OTHER THOUGHTS:
Apparent Women Officers or Directors: 2
Hot Spot for Advancement for Women/Minorities:

LOCATIONS: ("Y" = Yes)

West:	Southwest:	Midwest:	Southeast:	Northeast:	International:
Y	Y	Y	Y	Y	

CLARION CO LTD

www.clarion.com

Industry Group Code: 334310 **Ranks within this company's industry group:** Sales: 8   Profits: 5

Print Media/Publishing:	Movies:	Equipment/Supplies:	Broadcast/Cable:	Music/Audio:		Sports/Games/Gambling:
Newspapers:	Movie Theaters:	Equipment/Supplies:	Broadcast TV:	Music Production:		Games/Sports:
Magazines:	Movie Production:	Gambling Equipment:	Cable TV:	Retail Music:		Retail Games Stores:
Books:	TV/Video Prod.:	Special Services:	Satellite Broadcast:	Retail Audio Equip.:	Y	Stadiums/Teams:
Book Stores:	Video Rental:	Advertising Services:	Radio:	Music Print./Dist.:		Gambling/Casinos:
Distribution/Printing:	Video Distribution:	Info. Sys. Software:	Online Information:	Multimedia:		Rides/Theme Parks:

TYPES OF BUSINESS:

Audio & Video Equipment, Manufacturing
Navigation Systems
Security Systems
Satellite Radios

BRANDS/DIVISIONS/AFFILIATES:

Clarion Corp. of America
Clarion Sales Co., Ltd.
Clarion Devices Co., Ltd.
Nissan Motor
HCX
Joyride
N.I.C.E. (Navigation In-Car Entertainment)
Sirius

CONTACTS: *Note: Officers with more than one job title may be intentionally listed here more than once.*

Tatsuhiko Izumi, Pres.
Tetsuro Yoshimine, Chief Dir.-Sales & Mktg.
Yasuhiko Wada, Chief Dir.-Bus. Promotion
Matt Matsuda, Pres., Clarion Corp. of America

Phone: 81-48-443-1111	Fax: 81-48-445-3810
Toll-Free: 800-462-5274	
Address: 50 Kami-Toda, Toda, Saitama 335-8511 Japan	

GROWTH PLANS/SPECIAL FEATURES:

Clarion Co., Ltd., headquartered in Japan, develops cutting-edge audio technology for automobiles and recreational vehicles. The company has three operating segments: automobile equipment, special equipment and other equipment. Clarion's automobile equipment segment manufactures and sells car audio, navigation and multimedia equipment; it also sells peripheral devices, such as cassettes, compact discs, mini discs, DVDs, radio tuners, monitors, audio speakers, audiovisual car navigation systems and car computing systems. The special equipment segment provides audiovisual products, driving control systems and others, such as auto-guide systems, multimedia, navigation systems, as well as cameras and television checking systems for buses and other vehicles. The other equipment segment offers communications equipment such as spread spectrum wireless equipment and cellular phones. The company is a producer of Sirius satellite radios. The firm's most successful product, the Joyride multimedia system, combines many of its other products and contains an AM/FM tuner, a DVD player, a CD player, an MP3 decoder, built-in Dolby Digital and DTS audio decoders, an address book function, an optional navigation package powered by an Intel Pentium MMX processor and a satellite radio connection. Clarion's largest customers are carmakers who integrate the products into the vehicles during manufacturing, including Nissan Motor, which is also its largest shareholder, with an approximate 10% interest in the firm.

FINANCIALS: Sales and profits are in thousands of dollars—add 000 to get the full amount. 2007 Note: Financial information for 2007 was not available for all companies at press time.

2007 Sales: $	2007 Profits: $	**U.S. Stock Ticker:**
2006 Sales: $1,567,896	2006 Profits: $49,910	**Int'l Ticker: 6796** Int'l Exchange: Tokyo-TSE
2005 Sales: $1,660,537	2005 Profits: $47,597	Employees: 9,211
2004 Sales: $1,599,300	2004 Profits: $59,700	Fiscal Year Ends: 3/31
2003 Sales: $1,548,100	2003 Profits: $13,000	Parent Company:

SALARIES/BENEFITS:

Pension Plan:	ESOP Stock Plan:	Profit Sharing:	Top Exec. Salary: $	Bonus: $
Savings Plan:	Stock Purch. Plan:		Second Exec. Salary: $	Bonus: $

OTHER THOUGHTS:

Apparent Women Officers or Directors:
Hot Spot for Advancement for Women/Minorities:

LOCATIONS: ("Y" = Yes)

West:	Southwest:	Midwest:	Southeast:	Northeast:	International:
Y					Y

CLEAR CHANNEL COMMUNICATIONS INC
www.clearchannel.com

Industry Group Code: 513111 Ranks within this company's industry group: Sales: 1 Profits: 1

Print Media/Publishing:	Movies:	Equipment/Supplies:		Broadcast/Cable:	Music/Audio:	Sports/Games/Gambling:
Newspapers:	Movie Theaters:	Equipment/Supplies:		Broadcast TV:	Music Production:	Games/Sports:
Magazines:	Movie Production:	Gambling Equipment:		Cable TV:	Retail Music:	Retail Games Stores:
Books:	TV/Video Prod.:	Special Services:		Satellite Broadcast:	Retail Audio Equip.:	Stadiums/Teams:
Book Stores:	Video Rental:	Advertising Services:	Y	Radio:	Music Print./Dist.:	Gambling/Casinos:
Distribution/Printing:	Video Distribution:	Info. Sys. Software:		Online Information:	Multimedia:	Rides/Theme Parks:

TYPES OF BUSINESS:
Radio Station Owner/Operator
Outdoor Advertising

BRANDS/DIVISIONS/AFFILIATES:
Clear Channel Entertainment
Clear Channel Outdoor Holdings
Clear Channel Satellite Services

CONTACTS: *Note: Officers with more than one job title may be intentionally listed here more than once.*
Mark P. Mays, CEO
Randall T. Mays, Pres.
Randall T. Mays, CFO/Exec. VP
Bill Hamersly, Sr. VP-Human Resources
David Wilson, CIO/Sr. VP
Joe Shannon, CTO/VP
Andrew W. Levin, Chief Legal Officer/Exec. VP
Mike McGee, VP-Oper.
John T. Tippit, Sr. VP-Strategic Dev.
Lisa Dollinger, Chief Comm. Officer
Randy Palmer, Sr. VP-Investor Rel.
Julie Hill, Sr. VP-Finance
Jessica Marventano, Sr. VP-Gov't Affairs
Brian Coleman, VP/Treas.
Kathryn Johnson, Sr. VP-Corp. Rel.
Herb Hill, Sr. VP/Chief Acct. Officer
L. Lowry Mays, Chmn.

Phone: 210-822-2828	Fax: 210-822-2299
Toll-Free:	
Address: 200 E. Basse Rd., San Antonio, TX 78209 US	

GROWTH PLANS/SPECIAL FEATURES:
Clear Channel Communications, Inc. is a diversified media company with operations in radio broadcasting, domestic outdoor advertising and international outdoor advertising. In December 2006, Clear Channel announced it was selling all of its 42 television stations and 448 of its radio stations, which had previously made up approximately 52% of the company's revenue. The company now owns, programs and sells airtime for 700 domestic radio stations. Clear Channel also has interests in various domestic and international radio broadcasting companies. The firm recently launched its Less-is-More initiative, an effort to enhance the value of its radio advertising by lowering the amount of commercial minutes by 15-20% across its stations. Clear Channel owns Katz Media Group, a full-service media representation firm that sells national spot advertising time for clients in the radio and television industries throughout the U.S., representing over 2,800 radio stations and 390 television stations. Clear Channel is also the majority shareholder of Clear Channel Outdoor Holdings (CCO), the world's largest outdoor media company, which has annual sales of about $2.5 billion and over 823,500 advertising display faces in 49 domestic markets and 63 foreign countries. The display faces include billboards of various sizes, wallscapes, transit displays, taxi media and street furniture displays. In November 2006, Clear Channel announced that it had agreed to be acquired by a group of private equity firms led by Thomas H. Lee Partners and Bain Capital for about $18.7 billion and $8 billion in acquired debt. In April 2007, the firm sold 56 TV and 161 radio stations to Providence Equity Partners and other parties for a combined value of $1.5 billion.

Clear Channel's employees receive benefits including flex spending, a 401(k) savings plan and a stock purchase plan.

FINANCIALS: Sales and profits are in thousands of dollars—add 000 to get the full amount. 2007 Note: Financial information for 2007 was not available for all companies at press time.

2007 Sales: $	2007 Profits: $	**U.S. Stock Ticker: Private**
2006 Sales: $7,066,957	2006 Profits: $691,517	**Int'l Ticker:** Int'l Exchange:
2005 Sales: $6,578,805	2005 Profits: $935,662	Employees: 30,900
2004 Sales: $6,600,954	2004 Profits: $-4,038,169	Fiscal Year Ends: 12/31
2003 Sales: $8,930,899	2003 Profits: $1,145,591	Parent Company:

SALARIES/BENEFITS:

Pension Plan:	ESOP Stock Plan:	Profit Sharing:	Top Exec. Salary: $695,000	Bonus: $3,312,500
Savings Plan: Y	Stock Purch. Plan: Y		Second Exec. Salary: $622,917	Bonus: $987,552

OTHER THOUGHTS:
Apparent Women Officers or Directors: 9
Hot Spot for Advancement for Women/Minorities: Y

LOCATIONS: ("Y" = Yes)

West:	Southwest:	Midwest:	Southeast:	Northeast:	International:
Y	Y	Y	Y	Y	Y

Note: Financial information, benefits and other data can change quickly and may vary from those stated here.

CLEAR CHANNEL OUTDOOR www.clearchanneloutdoor.com

Industry Group Code: 541850 Ranks within this company's industry group: Sales: 1 Profits: 1

Print Media/Publishing:	Movies:	Equipment/Supplies:		Broadcast/Cable:	Music/Audio:	Sports/Games/Gambling:
Newspapers:	Movie Theaters:	Equipment/Supplies:		Broadcast TV:	Music Production:	Games/Sports:
Magazines:	Movie Production:	Gambling Equipment:		Cable TV:	Retail Music:	Retail Games Stores:
Books:	TV/Video Prod.:	Special Services:	Y	Satellite Broadcast:	Retail Audio Equip.:	Stadiums/Teams:
Book Stores:	Video Rental:	Advertising Services:	Y	Radio:	Music Print./Dist.:	Gambling/Casinos:
Distribution/Printing:	Video Distribution:	Info. Sys. Software:		Online Information:	Multimedia:	Rides/Theme Parks:

TYPES OF BUSINESS:

Outdoor Advertising
Mall & Airline Advertising
Outdoor Furniture Advertising
Live Event Advertising
Large Format Imaging & Printing
Electronic Billboard Technologies

BRANDS/DIVISIONS/AFFILIATES:

Clear Channel Adshel
Clear Channel Airports
Clear Channel Imaging
Clear Channel Malls
Clear Channel Spectacolor
Clear Channel Taxi Media

CONTACTS: *Note: Officers with more than one job title may be intentionally listed here more than once.*

Mark Mays, CEO
Paul Meyer, COO
Paul Meyer, Pres.
Randall Mays, CFO
Rocky Sisson, Global Dir.-Sales & Mktg.
Tony Jarvis, Exec. VP-Global Research
Michael Hudes, Global Dir.-Digital Media
Laura Toncheff, Exec. VP-Legal, Real Estate & Public Affairs
Mike Deeds, Exec. VP-Oper., Americas
Jonathan Bevan, Dir.-Corp. Dev
Randy Palmer, Dir.-Investor Rel.
Kurt Tingey, CFO/Exec. VP-Americas
Augusto Claux, Regional Pres., Latin America
Tim Stauning, Regional Pres., Eastern U.S.
Gene Leehan, Regional Pres., Western U.S.
Mark Thewlis, Regional Pres., Asia Pacific
Jonathan Bevan, CFO-Int'l.

Phone: 602-381-5700	Fax:
Toll-Free:	
Address: 2850 E. Camelback Rd., Ste. 300, Phoenix, AZ 85016 US	

GROWTH PLANS/SPECIAL FEATURES:

Clear Channel Outdoor (CCO), a subsidiary of Clear Channel Communications, is an outdoor advertising company with more than 973,000 out-of-home displays in over 60 countries around the globe. The company is organized into six divisions: Clear Channel Adshel, Clear Channel Airports, Clear Channel Imaging, Clear Channel Malls, Clear Channel Spectacolor and Clear Channel Taxi Media. CCO's Adshel division advertises through street furniture and operates over 6,000 municipal and transit contracts in 45 countries. The company's next division, airports, provides airport advertising services and annually places approximately 1 billion targeted advertising messages to airline passengers. In imaging, CCO offers large format UV digital printing for both indoor and outdoor advertising. Specialties include transit shelters, mobile panels, bus vinyls, mall kiosks, car cards, illuminated street displays and airport dioramas. Clear Channel Malls organizes marketing and advertising campaigns focused on the environment, demographics and the mindset of mall shoppers. The Spectacolor division works with clients to create advertising events such as living billboards, live events and wallscapes using the latest screens, fiber optics and lighting technologies. Finally, the Taxi Media division provides advertising services in 28 U.S. cities through its operation of more than 23,000 taxi panels. CCO's six divisions operate in two business segments: the Americas segment (AS), which accounts for approximately 45% ($1.2 billion) of the firm's revenues and includes the U.S., Canada and Latin America; and the international segment (IS), which accounts for about 55% ($1.5 billion) of the company's total revenues and consists of operations in Europe, Asia, Africa and Australia. About 94% of total revenues in the AS are the result of U.S. business/sales, while approximately 51% of the IS's revenues are generated through sales in France and the U.K. Recently, CCO launched its first indoor digital billboard network at Chicago's O'Hare International Airport.

FINANCIALS: Sales and profits are in thousands of dollars—add 000 to get the full amount. 2007 Note: Financial information for 2007 was not available for all companies at press time.

2007 Sales: $	2007 Profits: $	U.S. Stock Ticker: CCO
2006 Sales: $2,897,721	2006 Profits: $153,072	Int'l Ticker: Int'l Exchange:
2005 Sales: $2,666,078	2005 Profits: $61,573	Employees: 7,700
2004 Sales: $2,447,040	2004 Profits: $-155,380	Fiscal Year Ends: 12/31
2003 Sales: $2,174,597	2003 Profits: $-34,993	Parent Company:

SALARIES/BENEFITS:

Pension Plan:	ESOP Stock Plan:	Profit Sharing:	Top Exec. Salary: $	Bonus: $
Savings Plan:	Stock Purch. Plan:		Second Exec. Salary: $	Bonus: $

OTHER THOUGHTS:

Apparent Women Officers or Directors: 1
Hot Spot for Advancement for Women/Minorities:

LOCATIONS: ("Y" = Yes)

West:	Southwest:	Midwest:	Southeast:	Northeast:	International:
Y	Y	Y	Y	Y	Y

CLUBCORP INC

www.clubcorp.com

Industry Group Code: 713910 Ranks within this company's industry group: Sales: 1 Profits:

Print Media/Publishing:	Movies:	Equipment/Supplies:	Broadcast/Cable:	Music/Audio:	Sports/Games/Gambling:	
Newspapers:	Movie Theaters:	Equipment/Supplies:	Broadcast TV:	Music Production:	Games/Sports:	Y
Magazines:	Movie Production:	Gambling Equipment:	Cable TV:	Retail Music:	Retail Games Stores:	
Books:	TV/Video Prod.:	Special Services:	Satellite Broadcast:	Retail Audio Equip.:	Stadiums/Teams:	
Book Stores:	Video Rental:	Advertising Services:	Radio:	Music Print./Dist.:	Gambling/Casinos:	
Distribution/Printing:	Video Distribution:	Info. Sys. Software:	Online Information:	Multimedia:	Rides/Theme Parks:	

TYPES OF BUSINESS:

Golf Courses & Country Clubs
Business/Sports Clubs
Resorts

BRANDS/DIVISIONS/AFFILIATES:

Mission Hills Country Club
Firestone Country Club
Indian Wells Country Club
Homestead (The)
Boston College Club
Metropolitan Club

CONTACTS: Note: Officers with more than one job title may be intentionally listed here more than once.

Eric L. Affeldt, CEO
Eric L. Affeldt, Pres.
Jeffrey P. Mayer, CFO
Frank C. Gore, Exec. VP-Sales
John H. Longstreet, Sr. VP-People Strategy
Douglas T. Howe, Exec. VP-New Bus. Dev.
Angela A. Stephens, Exec. VP-Finance
Mark Burnett, Exec. VP-Golf & Country Club Div.
David B. Woodyard, Sr. VP-Bus. & Sports Div.
Douglas Miller, VP-Golf Course Mgmt.
Robert H. Dedman, Jr., Chmn.

Phone: 972-243-6191	Fax: 972-888-7700
Toll-Free:	
Address: 3030 LBJ Fwy., Ste. 600, Dallas, TX 75234 US	

GROWTH PLANS/SPECIAL FEATURES:

ClubCorp, Inc. is a leading owner and operator of nearly 170 golf courses, country clubs, private clubs and golf resorts in the U.S., with additional operations in Australia, Europe and Asia. The company has approximately 200,000 memberships and 170 operations in 29 states and 3 foreign countries (Australia, China and Mexico), including 73 private country clubs, 12 semi-private golf clubs, 9 public golf facilities, 3 destination golf resorts (Firestone Country Club, the Homestead and Barton Creek Resort and Spa) and 69 business/sports clubs (including 42 business clubs, 14 business/sports clubs and 3 sports clubs). The firm's operations include nationally recognized golf courses and country clubs such as the Firestone Country Club in Akron, Ohio; the Indian Wells Country Club in Indian Wells, California; The Homestead in Hot Springs, Virginia, the oldest resort in America; and the Mission Hills Country Club in Rancho Mirage, California. Additionally, the company's business and sports clubs can be found in major metropolitan areas, including the City Club on Bunker Hill in Los Angeles; the Citrus Club in Orlando, Florida; the Columbia Tower Club in Seattle; the Metropolitan Club in Chicago; the Tower Club in Dallas; the Boston College Club; and the City Club in Washington, D.C. In early 2006, the company added a fourth resort to its portfolio. The Ocean Edge Resort & Golf Club in Cape Cod, Massachusetts is located on 400 acres of property and features a romantic beach and boardwalk as well as 336 guest accommodations. Also in 2006, the firm sold nearly 170 clubs to KSL Capital Partners and the Pinehurst Resort in North Carolina to the Dedman family for a combined value of $1.8 billion.

The company offers internship programs for training in the areas of kitchen and catering; golf course operations and maintenance; accounting; and member relations.

FINANCIALS: Sales and profits are in thousands of dollars—add 000 to get the full amount. 2007 Note: Financial information for 2007 was not available for all companies at press time.

2007 Sales: $	2007 Profits: $	**U.S. Stock Ticker: Private**
2006 Sales: $1,020,000	2006 Profits: $	Int'l Ticker: Int'l Exchange:
2005 Sales: $1,028,088	2005 Profits: $70,754	Employees: 18,000
2004 Sales: $938,802	2004 Profits: $-6,242	Fiscal Year Ends: 12/31
2003 Sales: $892,709	2003 Profits: $-105,246	Parent Company:

SALARIES/BENEFITS:

Pension Plan:	ESOP Stock Plan:	Profit Sharing:	Top Exec. Salary: $500,000	Bonus: $281,250
Savings Plan:	Stock Purch. Plan:		Second Exec. Salary: $500,000	Bonus: $235,000

OTHER THOUGHTS:

Apparent Women Officers or Directors: 2
Hot Spot for Advancement for Women/Minorities: Y

LOCATIONS: ("Y" = Yes)

West:	Southwest:	Midwest:	Southeast:	Northeast:	International:
Y	Y	Y	Y	Y	Y

Note: Financial information, benefits and other data can change quickly and may vary from those stated here.

CNET NETWORKS INC

www.cnet.com

Industry Group Code: 514199 Ranks within this company's industry group: Sales: 2   Profits: 4

Print Media/Publishing:		Movies:	Equipment/Supplies:	Broadcast/Cable:	Music/Audio:	Sports/Games/Gambling:
Newspapers:		Movie Theaters:	Equipment/Supplies:	Broadcast TV:	Music Production:	Games/Sports:
Magazines:	Y	Movie Production:	Gambling Equipment:	Cable TV:	Retail Music:	Retail Games Stores:
Books:		TV/Video Prod.:	Special Services:	Satellite Broadcast:	Retail Audio Equip.:	Stadiums/Teams:
Book Stores:		Video Rental:	Advertising Services:	Radio:	Music Print./Dist.:	Gambling/Casinos:
Distribution/Printing:		Video Distribution:	Info. Sys. Software:	Online Information:	Multimedia:	Rides/Theme Parks:

TYPES OF BUSINESS:

Online Publishing
Technology Web Sites
Internet Search & Navigation Services
Online News
Music
Information Collection & Delivery

BRANDS/DIVISIONS/AFFILIATES:

ZDNet
CNET TV
Webshots
MP3.com
CNET Download.com
CNET News.com
mySimon
GameSpot

CONTACTS: *Note: Officers with more than one job title may be intentionally listed here more than once.*

Neil M. Ashe, CEO
George E. Mazzotta, CFO
Joseph Gillispie, Chief Mktg. Officer
Martha Papalia, VP-Corp. Comm.
Gloria Lee, Investor Rel.
David Bernstein, Sr. VP-Finance/Chief Acct. Officer
Sam Parker, Sr. VP-Network
Greg Mason, Sr. VP-Bus. Media & Channel
Martin Green, Sr. VP-Community
Jarl Mohn, Chmn.
Adam Power, Pres., Int'l Media

Phone: 415-344-2000	Fax: 415-395-9207
Toll-Free:	
Address: 235 2nd St., San Francisco, CA 94105 US	

GROWTH PLANS/SPECIAL FEATURES:

CNET Networks is a major global media company specializing in branding and operating web sites. The company distributes information to 13 countries via the Internet. Its online brands consist of four content categories: Business (ZDNet, Tech Republic and News.com); games and entertainment (TV.com, GameSpot, Chow.com); technology (CNET, CNET News.com, Download.com); and community (Webshots, MP3.com). ZDNet provides technology customers with information about computers and high-tech products. TechRepublic serves professionals representing the IT industry by providing information and tools for IT decision support and professional advice by job function. News.com focuses on the latest breaking news and in-depth coverage of industries such as technology, games and entertainment. CNET's games and entertainment brands consist mainly of GameSpot, an online downloadable music store. Complemented by GameFaqs and gamerankings.com, it gives users access to game reviews, previews, downloads, guides and hints. The firm's CNET.com site provides advice on technology and consumer electronics products and services through detailed reviews and recommendations. Download.com provides information to buyers and sellers of try-before-you-buy software, which allows customers to evaluate a software product before purchase. In 2006, the firm had an average of 116 million unique users per month, generating almost 104 million web pages per day. Recently, the firm sold its only magazine, Computer Shopper, to SX2 Media Labs, LLC. The firm also partnered with Cox Communications, TiVo, Inc. and TVN Entertainment to launch CNET TV, which distributes video footage on television and online. It launched CNET Podcast Central, featuring the following free podcasts: Gadget Girls, Studio C, MP3 Insider and The Real Deal. In addition, CNET's subsidiary, Webshots, launched AllYouCanUpload.com, a free photo uploading and hosting service. Also in 2006, the firm unveiled Chow.com, an online forum for food enthusiasts.

CNET provides employees with medical, dental and vision coverage; tuition reimbursement; on-site massage therapy; and tai chi/yoga classes.

FINANCIALS: Sales and profits are in thousands of dollars—add 000 to get the full amount. 2007 Note: Financial information for 2007 was not available for all companies at press time.

2007 Sales: $	2007 Profits: $	**U.S. Stock Ticker: CNET**
2006 Sales: $387,376	2006 Profits: $6,836	Int'l Ticker: Int'l Exchange:
2005 Sales: $338,047	2005 Profits: $19,583	Employees: 2,620
2004 Sales: $272,181	2004 Profits: $1,839	Fiscal Year Ends: 12/31
2003 Sales: $246,200	2003 Profits: $-26,300	Parent Company:

SALARIES/BENEFITS:

Pension Plan:	ESOP Stock Plan:	Profit Sharing:	Top Exec. Salary: $383,750	Bonus: $466,500
Savings Plan: Y	Stock Purch. Plan: Y		Second Exec. Salary: $357,962	Bonus: $375,533

OTHER THOUGHTS:

Apparent Women Officers or Directors: 2
Hot Spot for Advancement for Women/Minorities:

LOCATIONS: ("Y" = Yes)

West:	Southwest:	Midwest:	Southeast:	Northeast:	International:
Y	Y	Y	Y	Y	Y

COLUMBIA MUSIC ENTERTAINMENT INC columbia.jp

Industry Group Code: 512230 Ranks within this company's industry group: Sales: Profits:

Print Media/Publishing:	Movies:	Equipment/Supplies:	Broadcast/Cable:	Music/Audio:	Sports/Games/Gambling:
Newspapers:	Movie Theaters:	Equipment/Supplies:	Broadcast TV:	Music Production: Y	Games/Sports:
Magazines: Y	Movie Production:	Gambling Equipment:	Cable TV:	Retail Music:	Retail Games Stores:
Books: Y	TV/Video Prod.:	Special Services:	Satellite Broadcast:	Retail Audio Equip.:	Stadiums/Teams:
Book Stores:	Video Rental:	Advertising Services:	Radio:	Music Print./Dist.:	Gambling/Casinos:
Distribution/Printing:	Video Distribution:	Info. Sys. Software:	Online Information:	Multimedia:	Rides/Theme Parks:

TYPES OF BUSINESS:

Music Production
Software Manufacturing
Software Sales
Software Advertising
Musician Management

BRANDS/DIVISIONS/AFFILIATES:

Columbia Artist Management, Inc.
Columbia Songs, Inc.
C2 Design
CME, Inc.
Denon Digital, LLC
SLG, LLC
JAZZ Master Holdings, LLC
TDK Corp.

CONTACTS: Note: Officers with more than one job title may be intentionally listed here more than once.

Sadahiko Hirose, CEO/Representative Exec. Officer
Sadahiko Hirose, Pres.
Jiro Saeki, CFO/Sr. Managing Exec. Officer
Masashi Utsugi, Chief Dir.-Sales/Managing Exec. Officer
Masao Nakajima, Exec. Officer/CEO/Pres., Columbia Artists Mgmt.
Tadashi Yukawa, Chief Dir.-Intellectual Property Strategies
Masazumi Takuma, Sr. Managing Exec. Officer
Teiichi Takenaka, Dir.-Digital Bus./Managing Exec. Officer
Strauss Zelnick, Chmn./Representative Exec. Officer

Phone: 03-3588-2200	Fax:
Toll-Free:	
Address: 1-4-33 Roppongi 21 Mori Bldg., Roppongi, Minato-ku, Tokyo 106-8565 Japan	

GROWTH PLANS/SPECIAL FEATURES:

Columbia Music Entertainment, Inc. (CME), founded in 1910 as Nippon Phonograph Co., is a Japanese music production company, with additional operations in manufacturing, advertising and sales of audio and video software. Subsidiary Columbia Artist Management, Inc. provides music and training management services to musicians. Subsidiary Columbia Songs, Inc. is a copyright management company for music and TV programs, with approximately 30,000 songs under management. Subsidiary C2 Design designs and develops audio-visual software, posters, flyers and other promotional materials; provides editing and planning services for the publication of books, magazines and other publications; and provides merchandising, trademark and design rights and distribution management services. Subsidiary CME, Inc. is a holding company of production, manufacturing and sales companies of audio and multimedia products. Denon Digital, LLC, another subsidiary, is engaged in the manufacture and sales of such products as CDs and DVDs. Subsidiary SLG, LLC is engaged in the production and sales of audio and multimedia products. Subsidiary JAZZ Master Holdings, LLC manages original records in the jazz genre. In September 2007, CME acquired TDK Corp.'s music and video software unit for $13 million as part of a plan to expand into the games and educational software markets.

FINANCIALS: Sales and profits are in thousands of dollars—add 000 to get the full amount. 2007 Note: Financial information for 2007 was not available for all companies at press time.

2007 Sales: $	2007 Profits: $	**U.S. Stock Ticker:**
2006 Sales: $	2006 Profits: $	**Int'l Ticker: 6791** Int'l Exchange: Tokyo-TSE
2005 Sales: $	2005 Profits: $	Employees:
2004 Sales: $	2004 Profits: $	Fiscal Year Ends:
2003 Sales: $	2003 Profits: $	Parent Company:

SALARIES/BENEFITS:

Pension Plan:	ESOP Stock Plan:	Profit Sharing:	Top Exec. Salary: $	Bonus: $
Savings Plan:	Stock Purch. Plan:		Second Exec. Salary: $	Bonus: $

OTHER THOUGHTS:

Apparent Women Officers or Directors:
Hot Spot for Advancement for Women/Minorities:

LOCATIONS: ("Y" = Yes)

West:	Southwest:	Midwest:	Southeast:	Northeast:	International: Y

COLUMBIA TRISTAR MOTION PICTURE GROUP
www.sonypictures.com/movies

Industry Group Code: 512110 Ranks within this company's industry group: Sales: Profits:

Print Media/Publishing:	Movies:		Equipment/Supplies:	Broadcast/Cable:	Music/Audio:	Sports/Games/Gambling:
Newspapers:	Movie Theaters:		Equipment/Supplies:	Broadcast TV:	Music Production:	Games/Sports:
Magazines:	Movie Production:	Y	Gambling Equipment:	Cable TV:	Retail Music:	Retail Games Stores:
Books:	TV/Video Prod.:		Special Services:	Satellite Broadcast:	Retail Audio Equip.:	Stadiums/Teams:
Book Stores:	Video Rental:		Advertising Services:	Radio:	Music Print./Dist.:	Gambling/Casinos:
Distribution/Printing:	Video Distribution:	Y	Info. Sys. Software:	Online Information:	Multimedia:	Rides/Theme Parks:

TYPES OF BUSINESS:
Film Production & Distribution

BRANDS/DIVISIONS/AFFILIATES:
Sony Pictures Entertainment
Sony Corporation of America
Columbia Pictures
Sony Pictures Classics
Screen Gems
TriStar Pictures
Sony Pictures Releasing
Columbia Pictures Film Production Asia

CONTACTS: *Note: Officers with more than one job title may be intentionally listed here more than once.*
Steve Elzer, Sr. VP-Media Rel.
Andre Caraco, Exec. VP-Publicity
Gigi Semone, Exec. VP-Publicity
Amy Pascal, Chmn.-Sony Motion Picture Group
Jeff Blake, Chmn.-Worldwide Mktg. & Distribution

Phone: 310-244-4000	Fax: 310-244-2626
Toll-Free:	
Address: 10202 W. Washington Blvd., Culver City, CA 90232 US	

GROWTH PLANS/SPECIAL FEATURES:

Columbia TriStar Motion Picture Group (CTMPG) is the movie production, marketing, distribution and promotion subsidiary of Sony Pictures Entertainment, which is a subsidiary of Sony Corporation of America. The company releases roughly 25 films per year in the U.S. CTMPG produces and distributes its movies under four labels: Columbia Pictures, which produces wide-release movies including recent films such as Superbad and upcoming releases like Walk Hard: The Dewey Cox Story and The Water Horse: Legend of the Deep; Sony Pictures Classics, which acquires, markets and distributes foreign and American independent films such as the recently released Jane Austen Book Club and upcoming films like Youth Without Youth; Screen Gems, which produces lower-budget films, including Resident Evil: Extinction and forthcoming This Christmas; and TriStar Pictures, a marketing and acquisition unit focused on genre films, with recent releases including Feel the Noise. Columbia Pictures frequently partners with Revolution Studios to produce films, as well as with Sony/BMG. TriStar oversees a library of more than 3,500 films, including 12 Best Picture Academy Award winners. CTMPG releases its films through two subsidiaries: Sony Pictures Releasing (U.S.) and Sony Pictures Releasing International. Combined, they are responsible for the sale, distribution and marketing of all TriStar films in 67 countries. In December 2007, in anticipation of the release of producer Judd Apatow's comedy, Walk Hard, the company partnered with three high-traffic websites (MySpace, Rotten Tomatoes, IGN and movie related Walkhard-movie.com) to release an exclusive preview of the first ten minutes of the film.

Sony Pictures Entertainment offers its employees paid vacation, school credit, summer and academic year internships, and offers tuition reimbursement, a variety of insurance plans, a 401(k) plan, flexible spending accounts and an employee stock purchase plan. Benefits are extended to same-sex partners.

FINANCIALS: Sales and profits are in thousands of dollars—add 000 to get the full amount. 2007 Note: Financial information for 2007 was not available for all companies at press time.

2007 Sales: $	2007 Profits: $	**U.S. Stock Ticker: Subsidiary**
2006 Sales: $	2006 Profits: $	**Int'l Ticker:** Int'l Exchange:
2005 Sales: $	2005 Profits: $	Employees:
2004 Sales: $	2004 Profits: $	Fiscal Year Ends: 3/31
2003 Sales: $	2003 Profits: $	Parent Company: SONY CORPORATION

SALARIES/BENEFITS:

Pension Plan:	ESOP Stock Plan:	Profit Sharing:	Top Exec. Salary: $	Bonus: $
Savings Plan: Y	Stock Purch. Plan: Y		Second Exec. Salary: $	Bonus: $

OTHER THOUGHTS:
Apparent Women Officers or Directors: 1
Hot Spot for Advancement for Women/Minorities: Y

LOCATIONS: ("Y" = Yes)

West:	Southwest:	Midwest:	Southeast:	Northeast:	International:
Y					Y

COMCAST CORP

www.comcast.com

Industry Group Code: 513220 Ranks within this company's industry group: Sales: 2 Profits: 2

Print Media/Publishing:	Movies:	Equipment/Supplies:	Broadcast/Cable:	Music/Audio:	Sports/Games/Gambling:
Newspapers:	Movie Theaters:	Equipment/Supplies:	Broadcast TV:	Music Production:	Games/Sports:
Magazines:	Movie Production:	Gambling Equipment:	Cable TV: Y	Retail Music:	Retail Games Stores:
Books:	TV/Video Prod.: Y	Special Services: Y	Satellite Broadcast:	Retail Audio Equip.:	Stadiums/Teams:
Book Stores:	Video Rental:	Advertising Services: Y	Radio:	Music Print./Dist.:	Gambling/Casinos:
Distribution/Printing:	Video Distribution:	Info. Sys. Software: Y	Online Information:	Multimedia:	Rides/Theme Parks:

TYPES OF BUSINESS:

Cable Television
VoIP Service
Cable Network Programming
High-Speed Internet Service
Video-on-Demand
Advertising Services
Interactive Program Schedules
Wireless Services

BRANDS/DIVISIONS/AFFILIATES:

G4 Media
Comcast Interactive Media
Philadelphia 76ers
E! Entertainment
Golf Channel (The)
AZN Television
Yahoo!, Inc.
Fancast

CONTACTS: *Note: Officers with more than one job title may be intentionally listed here more than once.*

Brian L. Roberts, CEO
Stephen B. Burke, COO
John R. Alchin, Co-CFO/Exec. VP
Charisse Lillie, VP-Human Resources
Karen D. Buchholz, VP-Admin.
Marc A. Rockford, General Counsel/VP
Mark A. Coblitz, Sr. VP-Strategic Planning
D'Arcy F. Rudnay, Sr. VP-Corp. Comm.
Marlene S. Dooner, Sr. VP-Investor Rel.
William E. Dordelman, VP-Finance
Stephen B. Burke, Pres., Comcast Cable Comm.
Michael J. Angelakis, Co-CFO/Exec. VP
Robert S. Pick, Sr. VP-Corp. Dev.
Lawrence J. Salva, Chief Acct. Officer/Sr. VP/Controller
Brian L. Roberts, Chmn.

Phone: 215-665-1700	**Fax:** 215-981-7790
Toll-Free: 800-266-2278	
Address: 1500 Market St., Philadelphia, PA 19102-2148 US	

GROWTH PLANS/SPECIAL FEATURES:

Comcast Corp. is principally engaged in developing and operating hybrid fiber-coaxial broadband cable communications networks and providing programming content. Comcast is one of the largest cable operators in the U.S., with 24.2 million subscribers in 39 states. Comcast offers enhanced digital video, high-speed Internet, cable telephone services, video-on-demand, and cable telephone service (VoIP). The other significant portion of the company's business is cable network content. Comcast companies include E! Entertainment Television, Philadelphia 76ers, AZN Television and G4 Media. With over 12.1 million customers signed up for high speed Internet access, Comcast is one of America's largest providers of broadband access services, offering speeds of up to 16 Mbps. A major source of revenue is advertising, generating about $1.5 billion yearly. In 2007, Comcast also announced its Fancast.com online entertainment site. Fancast has made a deal with CBS Interactive to provide CBS programming via the Fancast site, which will allow users to search for programming that is then downloaded to a DVR for viewing. In April 2007, Comcast agreed to acquire Fandango. Both Fancast and Fandango will be managed by Comcast Interactive Media (CIM), which develops and operates Internet businesses. In April 2007, Comcast agreed with Insight Communications to split up their shared midsize cable operator, Insight, with 1.3 million subscribers in the Midwest and about $6.2 billion in assets. Also in 2007, Comcast Interactive Media and Yahoo! entered into a multi-year strategic partnership for online display and video advertising services on Comcast.net. Comcast.net has over 2.5 billion page views, more than 80 million videos viewed and 15 million unique visitors per month.

Comcast offers employees medical, dental, and vision coverage; life insurance; short- and long-term disability; educational reimbursement; an employee assistance program; a 401(k); an employee stock purchase plan; pre-paid legal services; pet insurance; and courtesy internet and cable services.

FINANCIALS: Sales and profits are in thousands of dollars—add 000 to get the full amount. 2007 Note: Financial information for 2007 was not available for all companies at press time.

2007 Sales: $	2007 Profits: $	**U.S. Stock Ticker: CMCSA**
2006 Sales: $26,339,000	2006 Profits: $2,533,000	**Int'l Ticker:** Int'l Exchange:
2005 Sales: $23,556,000	2005 Profits: $928,000	Employees: 90,000
2004 Sales: $20,307,000	2004 Profits: $970,000	Fiscal Year Ends: 12/31
2003 Sales: $18,348,000	2003 Profits: $3,240,000	Parent Company:

SALARIES/BENEFITS:

Pension Plan:	ESOP Stock Plan:	Profit Sharing:	Top Exec. Salary: $2,501,000	Bonus: $3,002,454
Savings Plan: Y	Stock Purch. Plan: Y		Second Exec. Salary: $2,001,000	Bonus: $

OTHER THOUGHTS:

Apparent Women Officers or Directors: 4
Hot Spot for Advancement for Women/Minorities: Y

LOCATIONS: ("Y" = Yes)

West:	Southwest:	Midwest:	Southeast:	Northeast:	International:
Y	Y	Y	Y	Y	Y

COMMUNITY NEWSPAPER HOLDINGS INC   www.cnhi.com

Industry Group Code: 511110 Ranks within this company's industry group: Sales: Profits:

Print Media/Publishing:		Movies:	Equipment/Supplies:		Broadcast/Cable:	Music/Audio:	Sports/Games/Gambling:
Newspapers:	Y	Movie Theaters:	Equipment/Supplies:		Broadcast TV:	Music Production:	Games/Sports:
Magazines:		Movie Production:	Gambling Equipment:		Cable TV:	Retail Music:	Retail Games Stores:
Books:		TV/Video Prod.:	Special Services:		Satellite Broadcast:	Retail Audio Equip.:	Stadiums/Teams:
Book Stores:		Video Rental:	Advertising Services:	Y	Radio:	Music Print./Dist.:	Gambling/Casinos:
Distribution/Printing:		Video Distribution:	Info. Sys. Software:		Online Information:	Multimedia:	Rides/Theme Parks:

TYPES OF BUSINESS:

Newspaper Publishing
Marketing Agencies
Online Publishing

BRANDS/DIVISIONS/AFFILIATES:

Eagle-Tribune Publishing Company
Eagle Marketing
XL Marketing

CONTACTS: *Note: Officers with more than one job title may be intentionally listed here more than once.*

Donna Barrett, CEO
Donna Barrett, Pres.
Lynn Pearson, CFO
George Wakefield, Chmn.

Phone: 205-298-7100	Fax: 205-298-7108
Toll-Free:	
Address: 3500 Colonnade Pkwy., Ste. 600, Birmingham, AL 35243 US	

GROWTH PLANS/SPECIAL FEATURES:

Community Newspaper Holdings, Inc. (CNHI) was founded to acquire community newspapers. The company seeks out newspapers in small markets with growth potential. For operational efficiency and in order to provide additional services to its readers, the firm attempts to buy newspapers in geographic proximity to each other. CNHI also has interests in a variety of ancillary publications and services that complement its newspapers. The company currently owns more than 100 daily, semiweekly and weekly publications in 25 states, with a combined circulation of more than 1 million. Oklahoma- and Texas-based newspapers make up approximately 30% of the firm's publications. Most of CNHI's papers have circulation ranging from 13,000 to 25,000. CNHI owns the Eagle-Tribune Publishing Company, a newspaper company serving over 340,000 readers in Massachusetts and New Hampshire. The company also runs two marketing agencies: Eagle Marketing, a full-service advertising agency which offers its clients high quality printed materials, design services, web site design and multimedia development, special event marketing, sales and targeted marketing options; and XL Marketing which focuses on brand development. Each of the firm's properties has an associated web site, plus a web site dedicated to employees of the company at cnhiReadership.com. In early 2007, the company sold the Santa Cruz Sentinel newspaper published in Santa Cruz, CA to MediaNews Group, Inc.

FINANCIALS: Sales and profits are in thousands of dollars—add 000 to get the full amount. 2007 Note: Financial information for 2007 was not available for all companies at press time.

2007 Sales: $	2007 Profits: $	U.S. Stock Ticker: Private
2006 Sales: $	2006 Profits: $	Int'l Ticker: Int'l Exchange:
2005 Sales: $	2005 Profits: $	Employees:
2004 Sales: $	2004 Profits: $	Fiscal Year Ends: 12/31
2003 Sales: $410,000	2003 Profits: $	Parent Company:

SALARIES/BENEFITS:

Pension Plan:	ESOP Stock Plan:	Profit Sharing:	Top Exec. Salary: $	Bonus: $
Savings Plan:	Stock Purch. Plan:		Second Exec. Salary: $	Bonus: $

OTHER THOUGHTS:

Apparent Women Officers or Directors: 2
Hot Spot for Advancement for Women/Minorities:

LOCATIONS: ("Y" = Yes)

West:	Southwest:	Midwest:	Southeast:	Northeast:	International:
Y	Y	Y	Y	Y	

CONCRETE SOFTWARE INC   www.concretesoftware.com

Industry Group Code: 511208 Ranks within this company's industry group: Sales: Profits:

Print Media/Publishing:	Movies:	Equipment/Supplies:	Broadcast/Cable:	Music/Audio:	Sports/Games/Gambling:	
Newspapers:	Movie Theaters:	Equipment/Supplies:	Broadcast TV:	Music Production:	Games/Sports:	Y
Magazines:	Movie Production:	Gambling Equipment:	Cable TV:	Retail Music:	Retail Games Stores:	
Books:	TV/Video Prod.:	Special Services:	Satellite Broadcast:	Retail Audio Equip.:	Stadiums/Teams:	
Book Stores:	Video Rental:	Advertising Services:	Radio:	Music Print./Dist.:	Gambling/Casinos:	
Distribution/Printing:	Video Distribution:	Info. Sys. Software:	Online Information:	Multimedia:	Rides/Theme Parks:	

TYPES OF BUSINESS:

Mobile Gaming Software

BRANDS/DIVISIONS/AFFILIATES:

Aces Omaha
Aces Texas Hold'em
Shoot Stuff
2020 Special Ops
Driving Log
Links Scorecard
3D Constructo Combat

CONTACTS: Note: Officers with more than one job title may be intentionally listed here more than once.

Keith Pichelman, CEO

Phone:	Fax: 952-556-8734
Toll-Free:	
Address: 6600 City W. Pkwy., Ste. 215, Eden Prairie, MN 55344 US	

GROWTH PLANS/SPECIAL FEATURES:

Concrete Software designs and produces software for mobile devices. The company provides software for mobile telephones manufactured by Nokia, Motorola, Sony Ericsson, Samsung, Siemens, NEC and LG; in addition, it produces software for other types of mobile devices made by BlackBerry, Palm, Pocket PC, TREO, and Microsoft. Concrete's product line includes games such as Aces Texas Hold'em-No Limit, Aces Blackjack, Aces Omaha-No Limit, Shoot Stuff and 2020 Special Ops. The company also offers non-gaming applications such as Links Scorecard and Driving Log, a program that keeps track of the distance one has driven with the help of a secure online synchronized database and GPS support. The company offers a paid update service for all of its software. In June 2006, it announced 3D Constructo Combat, the newest addition to its line of games.

FINANCIALS: Sales and profits are in thousands of dollars—add 000 to get the full amount. 2007 Note: Financial information for 2007 was not available for all companies at press time.

2007 Sales: $	2007 Profits: $	**U.S. Stock Ticker: Private**
2006 Sales: $	2006 Profits: $	**Int'l Ticker:** Int'l Exchange:
2005 Sales: $	2005 Profits: $	Employees:
2004 Sales: $	2004 Profits: $	Fiscal Year Ends:
2003 Sales: $	2003 Profits: $	Parent Company:

SALARIES/BENEFITS:

Pension Plan:	ESOP Stock Plan:	Profit Sharing:	Top Exec. Salary: $	Bonus: $
Savings Plan:	Stock Purch. Plan:		Second Exec. Salary: $	Bonus: $

OTHER THOUGHTS:

Apparent Women Officers or Directors:
Hot Spot for Advancement for Women/Minorities:

LOCATIONS: ("Y" = Yes)

West:	Southwest:	Midwest:	Southeast:	Northeast:	International:
		Y			

Note: Financial information, benefits and other data can change quickly and may vary from those stated here.

CONCURRENT COMPUTER CORP   www.ccur.com

Industry Group Code: 334111   Ranks within this company's industry group: Sales: 3   Profits: 3

Print Media/Publishing:	Movies:	Equipment/Supplies:		Broadcast/Cable:	Music/Audio:	Sports/Games/Gambling:
Newspapers:	Movie Theaters:	Equipment/Supplies:	Y	Broadcast TV:	Music Production:	Games/Sports:
Magazines:	Movie Production:	Gambling Equipment:		Cable TV:	Retail Music:	Retail Games Stores:
Books:	TV/Video Prod.:	Special Services:	Y	Satellite Broadcast:	Retail Audio Equip.:	Stadiums/Teams:
Book Stores:	Video Rental:	Advertising Services:		Radio:	Music Print./Dist.:	Gambling/Casinos:
Distribution/Printing:	Video Distribution:	Info. Sys. Software:		Online Information:	Multimedia:	Rides/Theme Parks:

TYPES OF BUSINESS:

Software-Real-Time & Video-on-Demand
Networking Systems Architecture
Operating Systems Software
Government Technology Services

BRANDS/DIVISIONS/AFFILIATES:

Everstream Holdings, Inc.
SUSE Linux Enterprise-Real Time
iHawk
ImaGen
PowerMAX Operating System
RedHawk Linux

CONTACTS: *Note: Officers with more than one job title may be intentionally listed here more than once.*

T. Gary Trimm, CEO
Warren K. Neuburger, COO
T. Gary Trimm, Pres.
Emory Berry, CFO
Gary Brust, VP-Worldwide Sales & Mktg. On-Demand
Suzanne Smith, VP-Worldwide Human Resources
Robert E. Chism, CTO
Michael Pasquinilli, VP-Eng.
Fred R. Langston, VP-Mfg.
Suzanne Smith, VP- Admin. Svcs.
Kirk L. Somers, General Counsel
Kirk L. Somers, VP-Investor Rel.
Scott Stroh, VP-Worldwide Sales & Mktg. Real-Time
Kenrick R. Jackson, VP-Concurrent Special Systems
Dave Mooney, VP-Quality Assurance
Steve G. Nussrallah, Chmn.
Del Kunert, VP-Int'l On-Demand

Phone: 678-258-4000	**Fax:** 678-258-4300
Toll-Free: 877-978-7363	
Address: 4375 River Green Pkwy., Ste. 100, Duluth, GA 30096 US	

GROWTH PLANS/SPECIAL FEATURES:

Concurrent Computer Corp. (CCC) provides computer systems for the video-on-demand market and real-time applications. The on-demand products consist of servers and related software, and are sold primarily to residential cable television operators that have upgraded their networks to support interactive digital services and are operated through subsidiary company Everstream Holdings, Inc. The firm's on-demand systems enable broadband telecommunication providers to streamline networks to customers. The customers are then able to control the video stream with familiar operations like pause, fast-forward and rewind. The company's real-time products consist of operating systems and diagnostic software tools combined with off-the-shelf hardware and services. These products provide a wide variety of companies with real-time computer systems for use in applications that require low latency response times such as simulation, image generation and data acquisition. These products are specifically designed for use with applications that acquire, process, store, analyze and display large amounts of rapidly changing data with microsecond response times. The company's real-time products include SUSE Linux Enterprise-Real Time, a version of the Novell open source Linux operating system, provided in partnership with Novell; iHawk servers; ImaGen imaging platform; PowerMAX, a UNIX based operating system; and RedHawk Linux, an operating system compatible with the popular Red Hat Linux. The company derived 13% of its 2006 revenues from the supply of products to U.S. government prime contractors and agencies of the U.S. government. This included selling computer systems, equipment, spare parts, and consulting services to government contractors such as Boeing, Lockheed-Martin and Raytheon.

FINANCIALS: Sales and profits are in thousands of dollars—add 000 to get the full amount. 2007 Note: Financial information for 2007 was not available for all companies at press time.

2007 Sales: $69,149	2007 Profits: $-12,171	**U.S. Stock Ticker: CCUR**
2006 Sales: $71,612	2006 Profits: $-9,345	**Int'l Ticker:** Int'l Exchange:
2005 Sales: $78,685	2005 Profits: $-7,729	Employees: 347
2004 Sales: $79,235	2004 Profits: $-5,725	Fiscal Year Ends: 6/30
2003 Sales: $75,453	2003 Profits: $-24,552	Parent Company:

SALARIES/BENEFITS:

Pension Plan:	ESOP Stock Plan:	Profit Sharing:	Top Exec. Salary: $360,837	Bonus: $43,470
Savings Plan: Y	Stock Purch. Plan:		Second Exec. Salary: $235,038	Bonus: $22,751

OTHER THOUGHTS:

Apparent Women Officers or Directors: 1
Hot Spot for Advancement for Women/Minorities:

LOCATIONS: ("Y" = Yes)

West:	Southwest:	Midwest:	Southeast:	Northeast:	International:
		Y	Y	Y	Y

CONDE NAST PUBLICATIONS INC www.condenast.com

Industry Group Code: 511120 Ranks within this company's industry group: Sales: Profits:

Print Media/Publishing:		Movies:	Equipment/Supplies:	Broadcast/Cable:	Music/Audio:	Sports/Games/Gambling:
Newspapers:		Movie Theaters:	Equipment/Supplies:	Broadcast TV:	Music Production:	Games/Sports:
Magazines:	Y	Movie Production:	Gambling Equipment:	Cable TV:	Retail Music:	Retail Games Stores:
Books:	Y	TV/Video Prod.:	Special Services:	Satellite Broadcast:	Retail Audio Equip.:	Stadiums/Teams:
Book Stores:		Video Rental:	Advertising Services:	Radio:	Music Print./Dist.:	Gambling/Casinos:
Distribution/Printing:		Video Distribution:	Info. Sys. Software:	Online Information:	Multimedia:	Rides/Theme Parks:

TYPES OF BUSINESS:

Magazine Publishing
Internet Publishing

BRANDS/DIVISIONS/AFFILIATES:

Advance Publications Inc
Vogue
Wired
Epicurious.com
New Yorker (The)
W
Vanity Fair
CondeNet

CONTACTS: Note: Officers with more than one job title may be intentionally listed here more than once.

Charles H. Townsend, CEO
John Bellando, COO
Charles H. Townsend, Pres.
Samuel I. Newhouse, Jr., Chmn.

Phone: 212-286-2860	Fax: 212-286-5960
Toll-Free:	
Address: 4 Times Sq., 17th Fl., New York, NY 10036 US	

GROWTH PLANS/SPECIAL FEATURES:

Conde Nast Publications, Inc., a subsidiary of Advance Publications, Inc., is a publisher of magazines and affiliated websites. Since a recent reorganization, it has four major business areas: editorial, advertising, corporate and online. The editorial segment handles the company's well known magazine portfolio, including Vogue, W, Glamour, Allure, Self, GQ, Details, Architectural Digest, Brides, Modern Bride, Elegant Bride, Domino, Golf Digest, Golf World, Conde Nast Traveler, Wired, The New Yorker, Vanity Fair, Gourmet, Bon Appetit and Conde Nast Portfolio, a monthly magazine focused on business. Cartoonbank.com is home of The Cartoon Bank, a New Yorker company, which is one of the largest stock houses of single-panel cartoons in the world, with over 85,000. The web site also offers matted and framed prints of individual cartoons. Fairchild Publications operates Women's Wear Daily, a publication that covers the beauty, fashion and retail industries; and Fairchild Books, an education publisher of books in fashion. The advertising segment sells, merchandises and promotes the firm's premium brands. Each magazine or web site has an advertising department comprised of promotions, sales, marketing and merchandising. The corporate division creates, markets, promotes and sells Conde Nast brands. The online segment operates through CondeNet, a creator and developer of upscale lifestyle brands online. CondeNet publishes online properties in categories such as travel (concierge.com), teen (flip.com), fashion (style.com), food (Epicurious.com) and men's lifestyle (men.style.com). Other web sites include NutritionData.com and WiredDigital.com. CondeNet owns Reddit.com, a social book marking site. In late 2006, Fairchild Publications sold Home Furnishings News to Macfadden Communications Group. In 2007, the company launched Stylefinder.com, a women's fashion web site targeting 15- to 45-year olds in the U.K. In December 2007, Conde Nast ceased publishing House & Garden.

The company offers employees medical and dental insurance; a 401(k) plan; short- and long-term disability insurance; tuition reimbursement; and an employee assistance program.

FINANCIALS: Sales and profits are in thousands of dollars—add 000 to get the full amount. 2007 Note: Financial information for 2007 was not available for all companies at press time.

2007 Sales: $	2007 Profits: $	**U.S. Stock Ticker: Subsidiary**
2006 Sales: $	2006 Profits: $	**Int'l Ticker:** Int'l Exchange:
2005 Sales: $	2005 Profits: $	Employees:
2004 Sales: $	2004 Profits: $	Fiscal Year Ends: 12/31
2003 Sales: $	2003 Profits: $	Parent Company: ADVANCE PUBLICATIONS INC

SALARIES/BENEFITS:

Pension Plan: Y	ESOP Stock Plan:	Profit Sharing:	Top Exec. Salary: $	Bonus: $
Savings Plan: Y	Stock Purch. Plan:		Second Exec. Salary: $	Bonus: $

OTHER THOUGHTS:

Apparent Women Officers or Directors:
Hot Spot for Advancement for Women/Minorities: Y

LOCATIONS: ("Y" = Yes)

West:	Southwest:	Midwest:	Southeast:	Northeast:	International:
Y		Y		Y	Y

Note: Financial information, benefits and other data can change quickly and may vary from those stated here.

CORUS ENTERTAINMENT INC   www.corusent.com

Industry Group Code: 513111 Ranks within this company's industry group: Sales: 2   Profits: 6

Print Media/Publishing:		Movies:		Equipment/Supplies:		Broadcast/Cable:		Music/Audio:		Sports/Games/Gambling:	
Newspapers:		Movie Theaters:		Equipment/Supplies:		Broadcast TV:	Y	Music Production:		Games/Sports:	
Magazines:		Movie Production:		Gambling Equipment:		Cable TV:	Y	Retail Music:		Retail Games Stores:	
Books:	Y	TV/Video Prod.:	Y	Special Services:	Y	Satellite Broadcast:		Retail Audio Equip.:		Stadiums/Teams:	
Book Stores:		Video Rental:		Advertising Services:	Y	Radio:		Music Print./Dist.:		Gambling/Casinos:	
Distribution/Printing:		Video Distribution:		Info. Sys. Software:		Online Information:		Multimedia:		Rides/Theme Parks:	

TYPES OF BUSINESS:

Radio Broadcasting
Television Broadcast & Cable
Animated Children's Programming
Children's Book Publishing
Digital Music Services
Radio Marketing Services
Online Media
Advertising Services

BRANDS/DIVISIONS/AFFILIATES:

YTV
Treehouse TV
W
Movie Central
Max Trax
Deep Sky
Nelvana
Kids Can Press

CONTACTS: *Note: Officers with more than one job title may be intentionally listed here more than once.*

John M. Cassaday, CEO
John M. Cassaday, Pres.
Thomas C. Peddie, CFO/Sr. VP
Hal Blackadar, VP-Human Resources
Gary Maavara, General Counsel/VP
Sally Tindall, Dir.-Media Rel./Publicity
David Spence, Controller/VP
Doug Murphy, Pres., Nelvana Enterprises
John P. Hayes, Pres., Corus Radio
Paul W. Robertson, Pres., Corus Television
John R. Perraton, Corp. Sec.
Heather A. Shaw, Exec. Chmn.

Phone: 416-642-3770	Fax: 416-642-3779
Toll-Free:	
Address: 181 Bay St., Ste. 1630, Toronto, ON M5J 2T3 Canada	

GROWTH PLANS/SPECIAL FEATURES:

Corus Entertainment, Inc. is a leading content producer and distributor working within Canada's entertainment industry. The company runs Canada's largest private radio operation and operates a variety of pay and specialty television networks and conventional broadcast channels in Canadian markets. The company's brands include YTV (Canada's leading youth network reaching more than 8.2 million households), Treehouse TV (designed for preschool children), W (designed for women ages 25-54) and Movie Central (a pay-per-view network with six channels). The company's Max Trax unit offers music content through digital cable providers in Canada. Corus operates Deep Sky, a radio marketing services division. The company's Nelvana subsidiary is a leading developer, producer and distributor of media content (mostly animation) for children worldwide. It airs on over 360 broadcast outlets internationally, in over 50 different languages. Corus also operates Kids Can Press, a publisher of children's literature. The company runs ytv.com, formerly Yabber.net, an online community designed for 8-15 year-olds, and owns 50% of TELETOON. Pending regulatory approval, the firm and CBC/Radio Canada have reached an agreement to have CBC/Radio Canada purchase Corus' 53% ownership stake in the digital service The Documentary Channel. Recently, Nelvana announced it would begin offering video-on-demand in the U.K. through an agreement with British Telecommunications. The firm announced the launch of its Digital Signage Division (TV screens featuring information and advertising in public places) through its subsidiary, Corus Custom Networks. The firm will also offer TV content from its W Network and CMT to retail clients.

FINANCIALS: Sales and profits are in thousands of dollars—add 000 to get the full amount. 2007 Note: Financial information for 2007 was not available for all companies at press time.

		U.S. Stock Ticker: CJR
2007 Sales: $	2007 Profits: $	Int'l Ticker: CJR.B Int'l Exchange: Toronto-TSX
2006 Sales: $630,060	2006 Profits: $30,770	Employees: 3,000
2005 Sales: $575,500	2005 Profits: $59,900	Fiscal Year Ends: 8/31
2004 Sales: $508,400	2004 Profits: $-17,600	Parent Company:
2003 Sales: $464,500	2003 Profits: $28,900	

SALARIES/BENEFITS:

Pension Plan: Y	ESOP Stock Plan:	Profit Sharing:	Top Exec. Salary: $	Bonus: $
Savings Plan:	Stock Purch. Plan: Y		Second Exec. Salary: $	Bonus: $

OTHER THOUGHTS:

Apparent Women Officers or Directors: 5
Hot Spot for Advancement for Women/Minorities: Y

LOCATIONS: ("Y" = Yes)

West:	Southwest:	Midwest:	Southeast:	Northeast:	International:
					Y

COURIER CORP
www.courier.com

Industry Group Code: 323000 Ranks within this company's industry group: Sales: 2 Profits: 2

Print Media/Publishing:		Movies:	Equipment/Supplies:		Broadcast/Cable:	Music/Audio:		Sports/Games/Gambling:
Newspapers:		Movie Theaters:	Equipment/Supplies:		Broadcast TV:	Music Production:		Games/Sports:
Magazines:		Movie Production:	Gambling Equipment:		Cable TV:	Retail Music:		Retail Games Stores:
Books:	Y	TV/Video Prod.:	Special Services:	Y	Satellite Broadcast:	Retail Audio Equip.:		Stadiums/Teams:
Book Stores:		Video Rental:	Advertising Services:	Y	Radio:	Music Print./Dist.:	Y	Gambling/Casinos:
Distribution/Printing:		Video Distribution:	Info. Sys. Software:		Online Information:	Multimedia:		Rides/Theme Parks:

TYPES OF BUSINESS:

Book Printing
Software Services
Intellectual Property Management
Multimedia Development
Commercial Printing
Prepress Services
Niche Book Publishing
Fulfillment Services

BRANDS/DIVISIONS/AFFILIATES:

Dover Publications, Inc.
Research & Education Association, Inc.
Federal Marketing Corporation
Creative Homeowner
DoverPublications.com
DoverDirect.com
REA.com
CreativeHomeowner.com

CONTACTS: Note: Officers with more than one job title may be intentionally listed here more than once.

James F. Conway, III, CEO
Robert P. Story, Jr., COO/Exec. VP
James F. Conway, III, Pres.
Peter M. Folger, CFO/Sr. VP
Rajeev Balakrishna, General Counsel/VP
Christopher Kuppig, VP-Bus. Dev.
Lee E. Cochrane, Treas./VP
Peter D. Tobin, VP
Eric J. Zimmerman, VP-Publishing
Gary S. Gluckow, VP
Diana L. Sawyer, VP
James F. Conway, III, Chmn.

Phone: 978-251-6000	Fax: 978-251-8228
Toll-Free:	
Address: 15 Wellman Ave., North Chelmsford, MA 01863 US	

GROWTH PLANS/SPECIAL FEATURES:

Courier Corporation, founded in 1824, is a leading domestic book manufacturer and specialty publisher. Courier also manufactures manuals, diskettes and CD-ROMs for publishers, software developers and other information providers. The company's principal book manufacturing markets are religious, educational and specialty trade books with products including Bibles, educational textbooks and consumer books. Courier's book manufacturing operations consist of electronic and conventional film processing, platemaking, printing and binding for both soft- and hard-bound books. Through its seven printing facilities, Courier serves the needs of certain market niches, such as short-run book manufacturing, printing on lightweight paper and four-color book manufacturing. Courier's specialty publishing operations consist of Dover Publications, Inc.; Research & Education Association, Inc. (REA); and Federal Marketing Corporation, which does business as Creative Homeowner. Dover publishes over 9,000 titles in more than 30 specialty categories, and sells its products through bookstores; children's stores; craft stores; gift shops; its retail website, DoverPublications.com; its business-to-business website, DoverDirect.com; and through its proprietary catalog, which it mails to nearly 400,000 consumers. REA publishes more than 900 test preparation and study-guide books for high school, college and graduate students, as well as professionals. REA sells its products globally through major bookseller chains, college bookstores, teachers' supply stores and its website, REA.com. Creative Homeowner is a New Jersey-based publisher and distributor of 120 titles, including books on home decoration, design and improvement; gardening and landscaping; home arts; and hunting and fishing. Its products are sold primarily through home and garden centers, as well as bookstores and direct to consumers over the Internet at creativehomeowner.com. Courier's major customers include The Gideons International, which generates approximately 20% of its sales, and Pearson plc, which generates approximately 16%.

The Printing Industry of America has named Courier a Best Workplace in the Americas for the eighth consecutive year.

FINANCIALS: Sales and profits are in thousands of dollars—add 000 to get the full amount. 2007 Note: Financial information for 2007 was not available for all companies at press time.

2007 Sales: $294,592	2007 Profits: $25,745	**U.S. Stock Ticker: CRRC**
2006 Sales: $269,051	2006 Profits: $28,380	**Int'l Ticker:** Int'l Exchange:
2005 Sales: $227,039	2005 Profits: $22,134	Employees: 1,830
2004 Sales: $211,179	2004 Profits: $20,540	Fiscal Year Ends: 9/30
2003 Sales: $202,000	2003 Profits: $20,100	Parent Company:

SALARIES/BENEFITS:

Pension Plan: Y	ESOP Stock Plan: Y	Profit Sharing: Y	Top Exec. Salary: $499,202	Bonus: $135,000
Savings Plan: Y	Stock Purch. Plan: Y		Second Exec. Salary: $399,011	Bonus: $120,000

OTHER THOUGHTS:

Apparent Women Officers or Directors: 3
Hot Spot for Advancement for Women/Minorities: Y

LOCATIONS: ("Y" = Yes)

West:	Southwest:	Midwest:	Southeast:	Northeast:	International:
Y		Y		Y	

COX COMMUNICATIONS INC   www.cox.com

Industry Group Code: 513220 Ranks within this company's industry group: Sales: Profits:

Print Media/Publishing:	Movies:	Equipment/Supplies:	Broadcast/Cable:	Music/Audio:	Sports/Games/Gambling:
Newspapers:	Movie Theaters:	Equipment/Supplies:	Broadcast TV:	Music Production:	Games/Sports:
Magazines:	Movie Production:	Gambling Equipment:	Cable TV: Y	Retail Music:	Retail Games Stores:
Books:	TV/Video Prod.: Y	Special Services:	Satellite Broadcast:	Retail Audio Equip.:	Stadiums/Teams:
Book Stores:	Video Rental:	Advertising Services:	Radio:	Music Print./Dist.:	Gambling/Casinos:
Distribution/Printing:	Video Distribution:	Info. Sys. Software:	Online Information:	Multimedia:	Rides/Theme Parks:

TYPES OF BUSINESS:

Cable TV Service
Digital Cable TV Service
Cable-Based Internet Access
Local & Long-Distance Phone Service
Video-On-Demand
VOIP Service
Commercial Telecommunications Services

BRANDS/DIVISIONS/AFFILIATES:

Cox Enterprises, Inc.
Cox Cable
Cox Digital Cable
Cox High Speed
Cox Digital Telephone
Cox Business Services
Phone Tools

CONTACTS: Note: Officers with more than one job title may be intentionally listed here more than once.

Patrick J. Esser, Pres.
John M. Dyer, CFO/Sr. VP
Joseph J. Rooney, Chief Mktg. Officer/Sr. VP
Mae A. Douglas, Chief People Officer/Sr. VP
Scott A. Hatfield, CIO/Sr. VP
Christopher J. Bowick, CTO
Christopher J. Bowick, Sr. VP-Eng.
James A. Hatcher, Sr. VP-Legal & Regulatory Affairs
Jill Campbell, Sr. VP-Oper.
Dallas S. Clement, Sr. VP-Strategy & Dev.
J. Lacey Lewis, VP-Investor Rel.
Susan W. Coker, Treas./VP
F. William Farina, Sr. VP-Advertising Sales
Robert C. Wilson, Sr. VP-Programming
Mark Bowser, VP-Bus. Svcs.
William J. Fitzsimmons, Chief Acct. Officer/VP-Acct. & Financial Planning
James Cox Kennedy, Chmn.
Sherryl D. Love, VP-Supply Chain Mgmt.

Phone: 404-843-5000	Fax: 404-843-5975
Toll-Free:	
Address: 1400 Lake Hearn Dr. NE, Atlanta, GA 30319 US	

GROWTH PLANS/SPECIAL FEATURES:

Cox Communications, Inc., owned by Cox Enterprises, Inc. is the U.S.'s third-largest cable broadband communications company, with cable systems in 20 states serving over 6 million customers nationwide. Cox offers a variety of residential services through its subsidiaries, including cable television under the Cox Cable brand; advanced digital video programming services under the Cox Digital Cable brand; high-speed Internet access via Cox High Speed; local and long-distance telephone services under the Cox Digital Telephone brand; and commercial voice, video and data services via Cox Business Services. The firm invests in telecommunications companies such as Sprint PCS, as well as programming networks, including the Discovery Channel and TV Works, a provider of software for digital cable systems. Cable television services include basic cable, expanded cable, pay-per-view and entertainment-on-demand packages. In December 2006, Cox introduced Phone Tools, its VoIP service. Unlike traditional VoIP services, it does not require a broadband Internet connection; instead signals travel over a private, managed IP-based data network. At the end of 2006, over 2 million households and 150,000 businesses were using the service. Cox has a joint venture with Sprint, Time Warner, Comcast, Nextel and Andvance/Newhouse that offers a combined package of cable TV, high-speed Internet access, VOIP and cellular service for a single price. In 2006, the company acquired Cable America's properties in Arizona, which represented roughly 35,000 subscribers. Also in 2006, Cox sold a number of properties representing over 900,000 subscribers to Cebridge Connections.

Cox employees receive discounted cable television, health club discounts and free tickets to cultural and sporting events. The firm also offers tuition reimbursement, 150 free online courses and discounts through Dell, Sprint, GM, Ford and Phillips Electronics. Other benefits include adoption assistance, an employee assistance program, a pension plan, a 401(k) savings plan and an employee stock purchase plan.

FINANCIALS: Sales and profits are in thousands of dollars—add 000 to get the full amount. 2007 Note: Financial information for 2007 was not available for all companies at press time.

2007 Sales: $	2007 Profits: $	U.S. Stock Ticker: Subsidiary
2006 Sales: $	2006 Profits: $	Int'l Ticker: Int'l Exchange:
2005 Sales: $6,722,300	2005 Profits: $-230,700	Employees:
2004 Sales: $6,106,100	2004 Profits: $-2,375,300	Fiscal Year Ends: 12/31
2003 Sales: $5,458,800	2003 Profits: $-137,801	Parent Company: COX ENTERPRISES INC

SALARIES/BENEFITS:

Pension Plan: Y	ESOP Stock Plan:	Profit Sharing:	Top Exec. Salary: $1,322,900	Bonus: $1,166,798
Savings Plan: Y	Stock Purch. Plan: Y		Second Exec. Salary: $760,000	Bonus: $574,560

OTHER THOUGHTS:

Apparent Women Officers or Directors: 4
Hot Spot for Advancement for Women/Minorities: Y

LOCATIONS: ("Y" = Yes)

West:	Southwest:	Midwest:	Southeast:	Northeast:	International:
Y	Y	Y	Y	Y	

COX ENTERPRISES INC

www.coxenterprises.com

Industry Group Code: 511110 Ranks within this company's industry group: Sales: 1 Profits:

Print Media/Publishing:		Movies:	Equipment/Supplies:		Broadcast/Cable:		Music/Audio:	Sports/Games/Gambling:	
Newspapers:	Y	Movie Theaters:	Equipment/Supplies:		Broadcast TV:	Y	Music Production:	Games/Sports:	
Magazines:		Movie Production:	Gambling Equipment:		Cable TV:	Y	Retail Music:	Retail Games Stores:	
Books:		TV/Video Prod.:	Special Services:	Y	Satellite Broadcast:		Retail Audio Equip.:	Stadiums/Teams:	
Book Stores:		Video Rental:	Advertising Services:	Y	Radio:		Music Print./Dist.:	Gambling/Casinos:	
Distribution/Printing:		Video Distribution:	Info. Sys. Software:		Online Information:		Multimedia:	Rides/Theme Parks:	

TYPES OF BUSINESS:

Newspaper Publishing
Television Broadcasting
Cable Television
Radio Stations
Online Information
Vehicle Auctions
Automotive E-Commerce
Technology Products

BRANDS/DIVISIONS/AFFILIATES:

Cox Television, Inc.
Manheim Auctions, Inc.
Cox Communications, Inc.
Cox Radio, Inc.
AutoTrader.com
Atlanta Journal-Constitution (The)
Austin American Statesman (The)
accessatlanta.com

CONTACTS:
Note: Officers with more than one job title may be intentionally listed here more than once.

James Cox Kennedy, CEO
Jimmy W. Hayes, COO
Jimmy W. Hayes, Pres.
Robert C. O'Leary, CFO/Exec. VP
Marybeth H. Leamer, VP-Human Resources
Timothy W. Hughes, Sr. VP-Admin.
Richard J. Jacobson, Sr. VP-Finance/Treas.
Dennis Berry, Vice Chmn.
John G. Boyette, Sr. VP-Investments & Admin.
Alexander V. Netchvolodoff, Sr. VP-Public Policy
John M. Dyer, Exec. VP
James Cox Kennedy, Chmn.

Phone: 404-843-5000	Fax:
Toll-Free:	
Address: 1400 Lake Hearn Drive 1400 Lake Hearn Dr., Atlanta, GA 30309 US	

GROWTH PLANS/SPECIAL FEATURES:

Cox Enterprises, Inc. maintains a diverse array of operations, ranging from television to automobile sales. Its major subsidiaries include: Cox Communications; Cox Newspapers; Cox Television; Cox Radio; Manheim Auctions, Inc.; and AutoTrader.com. Cox Communication, a broadband communications company, delivers cable TV, high-speed Internet and telecommunications services to 6.7 million customers in 22 states. Cox Television operates 15 network affiliated stations and two local cable channels in 11 markets, reaching roughly 30 million viewers. It owns three advertising sales rep firms (TeleRep, Harrinton, MMT Sales and Righter & Parson). Cox Newspapers publishes 17 daily papers and 25 non-dailies. The division also operates a direct mail business; and Cox Custom Media, a commercial newsletter publishing company. The firm's newspapers include The Atlanta Journal-Constitution and The Austin American Statesman. Through these newspaper subsidiaries Cox also operates approximately 20 online U.S. city guides, including AccessAtlanta.com, AccessLasVegas.com, RealPittsburgh.com and SanAntonio360.com, which are among the highest-ranked web sites of their kind in the country. Cox Radio, Inc., a majority owned subsidiary, is publicly traded. It operates 80 stations, 67 FM and 13 AM, in 18 markets to over 13 million listeners each week; and operates Internet venture CoxRadio Interactive. Through Manheim Auctions, the firm is a global remarketing organization that registers 10 million vehicles for sales events at its 135 locations worldwide and online annually. The division announced the opening of offices and business initiatives in China in 2006. It is the leader in automotive Internet commerce through AutoTrader.com, which aggregates in a single location an average of 2.8 million vehicle listings from approximately 37,000 dealers and 200,000 private owners, averaging 10 million shoppers each week. In 2007, Cox claimed PC Magazine's Reader's Choice award for its Internet service.

FINANCIALS:
Sales and profits are in thousands of dollars—add 000 to get the full amount. 2007 Note: Financial information for 2007 was not available for all companies at press time.

2007 Sales: $	2007 Profits: $	U.S. Stock Ticker: Private
2006 Sales: $13,200,000	2006 Profits: $	Int'l Ticker: Int'l Exchange:
2005 Sales: $12,000,000	2005 Profits: $	Employees: 80,000
2004 Sales: $15,522,000	2004 Profits: $	Fiscal Year Ends: 12/31
2003 Sales: $10,700,000	2003 Profits: $	Parent Company:

SALARIES/BENEFITS:

Pension Plan: Y	ESOP Stock Plan:	Profit Sharing:	Top Exec. Salary: $	Bonus: $
Savings Plan: Y	Stock Purch. Plan:		Second Exec. Salary: $	Bonus: $

OTHER THOUGHTS:

Apparent Women Officers or Directors: 1
Hot Spot for Advancement for Women/Minorities: Y

LOCATIONS: ("Y" = Yes)

West:	Southwest:	Midwest:	Southeast:	Northeast:	International:
Y	Y	Y	Y	Y	Y

Note: Financial information, benefits and other data can change quickly and may vary from those stated here.

COX RADIO INC

www.coxradio.com

Industry Group Code: 513111 Ranks within this company's industry group: Sales: 4 Profits: 10

Print Media/Publishing:	Movies:	Equipment/Supplies:		Broadcast/Cable:	Music/Audio:	Sports/Games/Gambling:
Newspapers:	Movie Theaters:	Equipment/Supplies:		Broadcast TV:	Music Production:	Games/Sports:
Magazines:	Movie Production:	Gambling Equipment:		Cable TV:	Retail Music:	Retail Games Stores:
Books:	TV/Video Prod.:	Special Services:		Satellite Broadcast:	Retail Audio Equip.:	Stadiums/Teams:
Book Stores:	Video Rental:	Advertising Services:	Y	Radio:	Music Print./Dist.:	Gambling/Casinos:
Distribution/Printing:	Video Distribution:	Info. Sys. Software:		Online Information:	Multimedia:	Rides/Theme Parks:

TYPES OF BUSINESS:

Radio Broadcasting
Radio Station Web Sites
Sales & Marketing Services

BRANDS/DIVISIONS/AFFILIATES:

Cox Enterprises, Inc.
Cox Radio Interactive
Cox Broadcasting, Inc.

CONTACTS: Note: Officers with more than one job title may be intentionally listed here more than once.

Robert F. Neil, CEO
Marc W. Morgan, COO/Exec. VP
Robert F. Neil, Pres.
Neil O. Johnston, CFO/VP
Roxann L. Miller, VP-Research
Richard Reis, Group VP
Gregg A. Lindahl, VP-Interactive & New Tech.
Jarett O'Connor, Regional VP
Caroline J. Devine, Regional VP
James C. Kennedy, Chmn.

Phone: 678-645-0000	Fax: 404-645-5294
Toll-Free:	
Address: 6205 Peachtree Dunwoody Rd., Atlanta, GA 30328 US	

GROWTH PLANS/SPECIAL FEATURES:

Cox Radio, Inc. is one of the largest radio broadcasting companies in the U.S., as well as one of the largest pure-play radio station groups. Cox Radio, Inc. is majority-owned by Cox Broadcasting, Inc., itself a subsidiary of Cox Enterprises, Inc. Cox Radio owns, operates or provides sales and marketing services for 80 radio stations (67 FM and 13 AM) in 18 markets. The firm operates three or more stations in 15 of its 18 markets. Moreover, it operates a wide range of programming formats in geographically diverse markets nationwide. The company is an indirect majority-owned subsidiary of Cox Enterprises, Inc., a newspaper and cable company headquartered in Atlanta, Georgia. Cox Enterprises is one of the largest media companies in the U.S. The business was operated as part of Cox Enterprises prior to its initial public offering, when Cox Enterprises transferred all of its U.S. radio operations to Cox Radio. Cox Radio, as part of Cox Enterprises, was a pioneer in radio broadcasting, building its first station in 1934. Cox Radio's business strategy seeks to maximize the revenues and broadcast cash flow of its radio stations by operating and developing clusters of stations in demographically attractive and rapidly growing markets, including Atlanta, Birmingham, Houston, Jacksonville, Miami, Orlando, San Antonio and Tampa. The company has a history of acquiring, repositioning and improving the performance of under-performing stations. Cox Radio's program formats span genres such as alternative, adult contemporary, oldies, news/talk, country, soul and gospel. The firm's newest division is Cox Radio Interactive (CXRi), whose purpose is to design, develop and assist Cox Radio's stations with their station web sites. CXRi also conducts research to determine what station listeners want from radio web sites.

Cox Radio offers its employees tax-sheltered spending accounts, an employee assistance program, paid vacation time and a 401(k).

FINANCIALS: Sales and profits are in thousands of dollars—add 000 to get the full amount. 2007 Note: Financial information for 2007 was not available for all companies at press time.

2007 Sales: $	2007 Profits: $	U.S. Stock Ticker: CXR
2006 Sales: $440,468	2006 Profits: $-24,447	Int'l Ticker: Int'l Exchange:
2005 Sales: $437,930	2005 Profits: $61,273	Employees: 2,119
2004 Sales: $438,213	2004 Profits: $67,966	Fiscal Year Ends: 12/31
2003 Sales: $425,873	2003 Profits: $66,625	Parent Company:

SALARIES/BENEFITS:

Pension Plan:	ESOP Stock Plan:	Profit Sharing:	Top Exec. Salary: $624,000	Bonus: $354,432
Savings Plan: Y	Stock Purch. Plan: Y		Second Exec. Salary: $456,287	Bonus: $194,378

OTHER THOUGHTS:

Apparent Women Officers or Directors: 3
Hot Spot for Advancement for Women/Minorities: Y

LOCATIONS: ("Y" = Yes)

West:	Southwest:	Midwest:	Southeast:	Northeast:	International:
Y	Y	Y	Y	Y	

Note: Financial information, benefits and other data can change quickly and may vary from those stated here.

CREATIVE ARTISTS AGENCY INC   www.caa.com

Industry Group Code: 711410 Ranks within this company's industry group: Sales: Profits:

Print Media/Publishing:	Movies:	Equipment/Supplies:		Broadcast/Cable:	Music/Audio:	Sports/Games/Gambling:
Newspapers:	Movie Theaters:	Equipment/Supplies:		Broadcast TV:	Music Production:	Games/Sports:
Magazines:	Movie Production:	Gambling Equipment:		Cable TV:	Retail Music:	Retail Games Stores:
Books:	TV/Video Prod.:	Special Services:	Y	Satellite Broadcast:	Retail Audio Equip.:	Stadiums/Teams:
Book Stores:	Video Rental:	Advertising Services:	Y	Radio:	Music Print./Dist.:	Gambling/Casinos:
Distribution/Printing:	Video Distribution:	Info. Sys. Software:		Online Information:	Multimedia:	Rides/Theme Parks:

TYPES OF BUSINESS:

Talent Agency
Market Research

BRANDS/DIVISIONS/AFFILIATES:

Intelligence Group (The)
Creative Artists Agency Contemporary Christian

CONTACTS: Note: Officers with more than one job title may be intentionally listed here more than once.

Richard Lovett, Pres.
Michael Mand, Head-Corp. Comm.
Rick Nicita, Chmn.

Phone: 424-288-2000	Fax: 310-288-2900
Toll-Free:	
Address: 2000 Avenue of the Stars, Los Angeles, CA 90067 US	

GROWTH PLANS/SPECIAL FEATURES:

Creative Artists Agency, Inc. (CAA) is one of the most prestigious talent agencies in the U.S. The firm represents talent of all kinds, including actors, athletes, writers, directors, and companies and their products. CAA maintains a division called The Intelligence Group, a market research and trend forecasting company. This division assists the firm in its mission to represent artists and sell entertainment properties. CAA also has a division dedicated to contemporary Christian music. Some of the artists represented by the division include Amy Grant, Jars of Clay, Michael W. Smith, Relient K, Third Day, Steven Curtis Chapman and TobyMac. This division also has a website (ccm.caa.com) with similar content to the college events website. CAA's most famous division is the one working with Hollywood talent. Hilary Swank, Christian Slater, Tom Cruise, Angelina Jolie and Julia Roberts are on the firm's roster. CAA's final division is dedicated to corporate clients, including Coca-Cola and Proctor & Gamble. The firm recently moved out of its Beverly Hills headquarters into a new location in Los Angeles. The firm also has offices in New York, New York; Nashville, Tennessee; St. Louis, Missouri; Calgary, Alabama; London, England; Beijing, China; and Stockholm, Sweden. In December 2007, the firm partnered with AVP, Inc., a lifestyle sports entertainment company, to work on projects in entertainment media and alternative media.

FINANCIALS: Sales and profits are in thousands of dollars—add 000 to get the full amount. 2007 Note: Financial information for 2007 was not available for all companies at press time.

2007 Sales: $	2007 Profits: $	U.S. Stock Ticker: Private
2006 Sales: $	2006 Profits: $	Int'l Ticker: Int'l Exchange:
2005 Sales: $	2005 Profits: $	Employees:
2004 Sales: $	2004 Profits: $	Fiscal Year Ends: 12/31
2003 Sales: $	2003 Profits: $	Parent Company:

SALARIES/BENEFITS:

Pension Plan:	ESOP Stock Plan:	Profit Sharing:	Top Exec. Salary: $	Bonus: $
Savings Plan:	Stock Purch. Plan:		Second Exec. Salary: $	Bonus: $

OTHER THOUGHTS:

Apparent Women Officers or Directors:
Hot Spot for Advancement for Women/Minorities:

LOCATIONS: ("Y" = Yes)

West:	Southwest:	Midwest:	Southeast:	Northeast:	International:
Y			Y	Y	Y

CROWN MEDIA HOLDINGS INC   www.crownmedia.net

Industry Group Code: 513210 Ranks within this company's industry group: Sales: 4 Profits: 4

Print Media/Publishing:	Movies:		Equipment/Supplies:	Broadcast/Cable:		Music/Audio:		Sports/Games/Gambling:
Newspapers:	Movie Theaters:		Equipment/Supplies:	Broadcast TV:		Music Production:		Games/Sports:
Magazines:	Movie Production:		Gambling Equipment:	Cable TV:	Y	Retail Music:		Retail Games Stores:
Books:	TV/Video Prod.:	Y	Special Services:	Satellite Broadcast:		Retail Audio Equip.:		Stadiums/Teams:
Book Stores:	Video Rental:		Advertising Services:	Radio:		Music Print./Dist.:		Gambling/Casinos:
Distribution/Printing:	Video Distribution:	Y	Info. Sys. Software:	Online Information:		Multimedia:		Rides/Theme Parks:

TYPES OF BUSINESS:
Cable Television
Film Distribution
Television Production

BRANDS/DIVISIONS/AFFILIATES:
Hallmark Channel (The)
Hallmark Movie Channel (The)
Hallmark Entertainment, Inc.
Crown Media Distribution

CONTACTS: *Note: Officers with more than one job title may be intentionally listed here more than once.*
Henry Schleiff, CEO
Henry Schleiff, Pres.
Brian Stewart, CFO
William Abbott, VP-Advertising Sales
Charles L. Stanford, VP-Legal Bus. Affairs/General Counsel
David Kenin, Exec. VP-Programming
Donald J. Hall, Jr., Co-Chmn.
Herbert A. Granath, Co-Chmn.

Phone: 818-755-2400	Fax: 303-220-7660
Toll-Free:	
Address: 12700 Ventura Blvd., Studio City, CA 91604 US	

GROWTH PLANS/SPECIAL FEATURES:
Crown Media Holdings, Inc. owns and operates two television channels, The Hallmark Channel and The Hallmark movie channel. These channels are available in the U.S. and over 110 international markets, reaching 85 million subscribers through more than 5,300 cable systems. Hallmark Entertainment, Inc. holds approximately 91% of the voting power for Crown Media Holdings. The firm focuses on family-friendly television; its primary target demographic is women aged 25-54. Crown Media also has approximately 600 television and movie programs in its library, which it distributes through Crown Media Distribution. Crown Media's program library includes Larry McMurtry's Lonesome Dove, 10th Kingdom, Sabrina the Teenage Witch, Dog of the Yukon: Call of the Wild, William Faulkner's Old Man, Rose Hill, Sarah Plain and Tall and What the Deaf Man Heard. Examples of third-party programming shown on the company's domestic channel include the popular series M*A*S*H, Magnum P.I., Matlock, Touched By An Angel, Rawhide, Bonanza and Perry Mason. Other examples of its third-party programming include acquired movies and miniseries such as Roots, North and South, The Thorn Birds and Shogun. Crown Media Holdings has a number of distribution agreements with leading cable television distributors, including AOL Time Warner, DirecTV, Adelphia, EchoStar and Sky Network. The company announced that it would begin broadcasting in high definition by 2008.

FINANCIALS: Sales and profits are in thousands of dollars—add 000 to get the full amount. 2007 Note: Financial information for 2007 was not available for all companies at press time.

2007 Sales: $	2007 Profits: $	U.S. Stock Ticker: CRWN	
2006 Sales: $201,179	2006 Profits: $-388,972	Int'l Ticker:	Int'l Exchange:
2005 Sales: $197,384	2005 Profits: $-232,758	Employees: 158	
2004 Sales: $138,236	2004 Profits: $-316,806	Fiscal Year Ends: 12/31	
2003 Sales: $99,433	2003 Profits: $-205,153	Parent Company:	

SALARIES/BENEFITS:

Pension Plan:	ESOP Stock Plan:	Profit Sharing:	Top Exec. Salary: $749,580	Bonus: $176,250
Savings Plan: Y	Stock Purch. Plan:		Second Exec. Salary: $682,998	Bonus: $152,862

OTHER THOUGHTS:
Apparent Women Officers or Directors: 1
Hot Spot for Advancement for Women/Minorities:

LOCATIONS: ("Y" = Yes)

West:	Southwest:	Midwest:	Southeast:	Northeast:	International:
Y					

CUMULUS MEDIA INC

www.cumulus.com

Industry Group Code: 513111 Ranks within this company's industry group: Sales: 8 Profits: 12

Print Media/Publishing:	Movies:	Equipment/Supplies:		Broadcast/Cable:	Music/Audio:	Sports/Games/Gambling:
Newspapers:	Movie Theaters:	Equipment/Supplies:		Broadcast TV:	Music Production:	Games/Sports:
Magazines:	Movie Production:	Gambling Equipment:		Cable TV:	Retail Music:	Retail Games Stores:
Books:	TV/Video Prod.:	Special Services:		Satellite Broadcast:	Retail Audio Equip.:	Stadiums/Teams:
Book Stores:	Video Rental:	Advertising Services:	Y	Radio:	Music Print./Dist.:	Gambling/Casinos:
Distribution/Printing:	Video Distribution:	Info. Sys. Software:		Online Information:	Multimedia:	Rides/Theme Parks:

TYPES OF BUSINESS:

Radio Station Operator
Sales & Marketing Services
Media Operations Software

BRANDS/DIVISIONS/AFFILIATES:

Aurora Communications, LLC
DBBC, LLC
Broadcast Software International, Inc.
Cumulus Broadcasting
AdVisory Board, Inc.
Cumulus Media Partners
Susquehanna Pfaltzgraff Radio

CONTACTS: *Note: Officers with more than one job title may be intentionally listed here more than once.*

Lewis W. Dickey, Jr., CEO
Jonathan Pinch, COO/Exec. VP
Lewis W. Dickey, Jr., Pres.
Martin R. Gausvik, CFO/Exec. VP
John W. Dickey, VP-Mktg. & Promotion
Richard Denning, General Counsel/VP
Martin R. Gausvik, Treas.
John W. Dickey, Exec. VP
Lewis W. Dickey, Jr., Chmn.

Phone: 404-949-0700	**Fax:** 404-443-0743
Toll-Free:	
Address: 14 Piedmont Ctr., Ste. 1400, Atlanta, GA 30305 US	

GROWTH PLANS/SPECIAL FEATURES:

Cumulus Media, Inc., the country's second-largest operator of FM and AM radio broadcasters, acquires and develops radio stations and clusters in regional mid-size markets. Cumulus owns over 344 stations in 67 U.S. markets. These stations are located in the U.S. with an additional network of five radio stations serving the English-language Caribbean market, including Barbados. Through Cumulus Media Partners, LLC, the company also operates in Tortola. The firm also provides sales and marketing services under local marketing, management and consulting agreements. Cumulus has diversified radio formats and target audiences within each market to attract larger and broader listener audiences and thereby interest a wider range of advertisers. The company owns DBBC, LLC, a broadcasting company operating 18 stations in Connecticut and New York and Aurora Communications, LLC, which owns and operates three stations in Nashville, Tennessee. It also owns Broadcast Software International, Inc., a media operations software and systems company. Cumulus uses Internet-based software applications to monitor daily sales performance by station and market compared with each station's respective budget. This system also allows stations to exchange ideas and views regarding station operations and ways to increase advertising revenues. Stations within each market share infrastructure in terms of office space, support personnel and certain senior management. However, each station is developed and marketed as an individual brand with its own identity, programming, programming personnel, inventory of time slots and sales force. Company revenues are generated from the sale of local, regional and national advertising time. Local sales represent, on average, four-fifths of the company's advertising revenues. In 2006, the firm joined with a private equity consortium to form Cumulus Media Partners, LLC and acquire Susquehanna Pfaltzgraff Radio for $1.2 billion. In July 2007, Cumulus agreed to be taken private by its CEO and Merrill Lynch Global Private Equity in a deal valued at $1.3 billion.

FINANCIALS: Sales and profits are in thousands of dollars—add 000 to get the full amount. 2007 Note: Financial information for 2007 was not available for all companies at press time.

2007 Sales: $	2007 Profits: $	**U.S. Stock Ticker: CMLS**
2006 Sales: $334,321	2006 Profits: $-44,588	**Int'l Ticker:** Int'l Exchange:
2005 Sales: $327,756	2005 Profits: $-213,367	Employees: 3,392
2004 Sales: $320,132	2004 Profits: $30,369	Fiscal Year Ends: 12/31
2003 Sales: $309,459	2003 Profits: $5,041	Parent Company:

SALARIES/BENEFITS:

Pension Plan: Y	ESOP Stock Plan:	Profit Sharing:	Top Exec. Salary: $825,000	Bonus: $800,000
Savings Plan: Y	Stock Purch. Plan: Y		Second Exec. Salary: $486,675	Bonus: $200,000

OTHER THOUGHTS:

Apparent Women Officers or Directors:
Hot Spot for Advancement for Women/Minorities:

LOCATIONS: ("Y" = Yes)

West:	Southwest:	Midwest:	Southeast:	Northeast:	International:
Y	Y	Y	Y	Y	Y

CURVES INTERNATIONAL INC   www.curvesinternational.com

Industry Group Code: 713940 Ranks within this company's industry group: Sales: Profits:

Print Media/Publishing:	Movies:	Equipment/Supplies:	Broadcast/Cable:	Music/Audio:	Sports/Games/Gambling:
Newspapers:	Movie Theaters:	Equipment/Supplies:	Broadcast TV:	Music Production:	Games/Sports: Y
Magazines: Y	Movie Production:	Gambling Equipment:	Cable TV:	Retail Music:	Retail Games Stores:
Books:	TV/Video Prod.:	Special Services: Y	Satellite Broadcast:	Retail Audio Equip.:	Stadiums/Teams:
Book Stores:	Video Rental:	Advertising Services:	Radio:	Music Print./Dist.:	Gambling/Casinos:
Distribution/Printing:	Video Distribution:	Info. Sys. Software:	Online Information:	Multimedia:	Rides/Theme Parks:

TYPES OF BUSINESS:

Fitness Centers
Magazine Publishing
Health Products
Travel Services
Online Information

BRANDS/DIVISIONS/AFFILIATES:

diane Magazine
CurvesTravel.com
Curves Travel
GlobalFit

CONTACTS: *Note: Officers with more than one job title may be intentionally listed here more than once.*

Gary Heavin, CEO/Founder
Michael Raymond, Pres.
Becky Frusher, Comm. Specialist
Diane Heavin, Founder

Phone: 254-399-9285	Fax: 254-399-9731
Toll-Free: 800-848-1096	
Address: 100 Ritchie Rd., Waco, TX 76712 US	

GROWTH PLANS/SPECIAL FEATURES:

Curves International is one of the largest fitness franchises in the world, with approximately 10,000 franchised locations in 55 countries including the U.S., Canada, Mexico, Central America, The Caribbean, Australia, New Zealand and the U.K. The company provides fitness and weight-loss facilities specifically designed for women. Curves currently provides over 4 million women with exercise and nutritional guidance. Its program provides a 30-minute circuit training workout session where all of the machines are arranged in a circle and clients can talk to each other as they move through the circuit. In addition to 30-minute workout sessions at Curves fitness facilities, the company provides a comprehensive program to educate and train women in healthy eating patterns. This program includes books, meal planners, tracking charts, weekly progress reports and other information geared toward helping women eat healthily. Through its web site, Curves provides links to other sites dedicated to educating women about the dangers of obesity and other serious diseases related to unhealthy living. The web site also features customizable online accounts, where members can access weight loss tips and meal plans. The company is also the creator of diane magazine, a quarterly magazine which features diet success stories, celebrity interviews, fitness tips and healthy recipes. Curves also recently launched its first franchise in Japan, with 2,000 more planned to open by 2010. Subsidiary Curves Travel operates mainly from CurvesTravel.com and offers deals and free booking and planning services to Curves members. In September 2007, Curves partnered with GlobalFit, a provider of healthy living benefits, to offer millions of American women a chance to enter the Curves program at a discounted rate.

FINANCIALS: Sales and profits are in thousands of dollars—add 000 to get the full amount. 2007 Note: Financial information for 2007 was not available for all companies at press time.

2007 Sales: $	2007 Profits: $	**U.S. Stock Ticker: Private**
2006 Sales: $	2006 Profits: $	**Int'l Ticker:** Int'l Exchange:
2005 Sales: $	2005 Profits: $	Employees:
2004 Sales: $	2004 Profits: $	Fiscal Year Ends: 12/31
2003 Sales: $	2003 Profits: $	Parent Company:

SALARIES/BENEFITS:

Pension Plan:	ESOP Stock Plan:	Profit Sharing:	Top Exec. Salary: $	Bonus: $
Savings Plan:	Stock Purch. Plan:		Second Exec. Salary: $	Bonus: $

OTHER THOUGHTS:

Apparent Women Officers or Directors: 2
Hot Spot for Advancement for Women/Minorities: Y

LOCATIONS: ("Y" = Yes)

West:	Southwest:	Midwest:	Southeast:	Northeast:	International:
Y	Y	Y	Y	Y	Y

CW NETWORK (THE)

www.cwtv.com

Industry Group Code: 513210 Ranks within this company's industry group: Sales: Profits:

Print Media/Publishing:	Movies:		Equipment/Supplies:		Broadcast/Cable:		Music/Audio:		Sports/Games/Gambling:	
Newspapers:	Movie Theaters:		Equipment/Supplies:		Broadcast TV:	Y	Music Production:	Y	Games/Sports:	
Magazines:	Movie Production:		Gambling Equipment:		Cable TV:		Retail Music:		Retail Games Stores:	
Books:	TV/Video Prod.:	Y	Special Services:		Satellite Broadcast:		Retail Audio Equip.:		Stadiums/Teams:	
Book Stores:	Video Rental:		Advertising Services:		Radio:		Music Print./Dist.:	Y	Gambling/Casinos:	
Distribution/Printing:	Video Distribution:	Y	Info. Sys. Software:		Online Information:		Multimedia:		Rides/Theme Parks:	

TYPES OF BUSINESS:
Television Broadcasting
Television Production
Soundtrack Recordings
DVD Distribution

BRANDS/DIVISIONS/AFFILIATES:
CBS Corp.
Time Warner, Inc.
WB
UPN
America's Next Top Model
Beauty and the Geek
Everybody Hates Chris
Smallville

CONTACTS: Note: Officers with more than one job title may be intentionally listed here more than once.
John Maatta, COO
Dawn Ostroff, Pres.
Mitch Nedick, CFO/Exec. VP
Rick Haskins, Exec. VP-Mktg. & Brand Strategy
Eric Cardinal, Sr. VP-Research
Elizabeth Tumulty, Sr. VP-Network Dist.
Michael Ross, Exec. VP-Bus. Affairs
Paul McGuire, Sr. VP-Comm.
Dawn Ostroff, Pres., Entertainment
Betsy Mc Gowen, Sr. VP/Gen. Mgr.-Kids WB! on The CW
Jennifer Bresnan, Sr. VP-Alternative Programming
Kim Fleary, Exec. VP-Comedy Dev.

Phone: 818-977-5000	**Fax:** 818-954-7667
Toll-Free:	
Address: 4000 Warner Blvd., Burbank, CA 91522 US	

GROWTH PLANS/SPECIAL FEATURES:
The CW Network is a joint venture between CBS Corp. and Warner Bros. Entertainment (subsidiary of Time Warner), formed by the merger of the fledgling WB (owned by Time Warner) and UPN (owned by CBS) networks in 2006. The company provides proprietary television programming during prime-time hours six nights a week; a five-day-a-week afternoon lineup; and a five-hour Saturday morning animation block. The CW's television shows include Smallville and Charmed and for teenagers and college students; family-oriented shows such as 7th Heaven, Beauty and the Geek, and Supernatural; and other popular programming, including America's Next Top Model, Everybody Hates Chris, One Tree Hill and Friday Night Smackdown. The firm also offers show soundtracks, DVD sets and related merchandise. During Saturday mornings, the CW provides children's programming, including the Pokomon cartoon series, Xiaolin Showdown, The Batman and Jackie Chan Adventure. The network is also introducing several new series, including Gossip Girl, Aliens in America, Reaper and Life is Wild. The CW is the U.S.'s fifth broadcast network, and the only network that specifically targets young adults age 18-34.

FINANCIALS: Sales and profits are in thousands of dollars—add 000 to get the full amount. 2007 Note: Financial information for 2007 was not available for all companies at press time.
2007 Sales: $	2007 Profits: $	**U.S. Stock Ticker: Joint Venture**
2006 Sales: $	2006 Profits: $	**Int'l Ticker:** Int'l Exchange:
2005 Sales: $	2005 Profits: $	Employees:
2004 Sales: $700,000	2004 Profits: $	Fiscal Year Ends: 12/31
2003 Sales: $660,000	2003 Profits: $	Parent Company:

SALARIES/BENEFITS:
Pension Plan:	ESOP Stock Plan:	Profit Sharing:	Top Exec. Salary: $	Bonus: $
Savings Plan:	Stock Purch. Plan:		Second Exec. Salary: $	Bonus: $

OTHER THOUGHTS:
Apparent Women Officers or Directors: 6
Hot Spot for Advancement for Women/Minorities: Y

LOCATIONS: ("Y" = Yes)
West:	Southwest:	Midwest:	Southeast:	Northeast:	International:
Y					

DAG MEDIA INC

www.newyellow.com

Industry Group Code: 511140 Ranks within this company's industry group: Sales: 3   Profits: 3

Print Media/Publishing:	Movies:	Equipment/Supplies:		Broadcast/Cable:	Music/Audio:	Sports/Games/Gambling:
Newspapers:	Movie Theaters:	Equipment/Supplies:		Broadcast TV:	Music Production:	Games/Sports:
Magazines:	Movie Production:	Gambling Equipment:		Cable TV:	Retail Music:	Retail Games Stores:
Books:	TV/Video Prod.:	Special Services:	Y	Satellite Broadcast:	Retail Audio Equip.:	Stadiums/Teams:
Book Stores:	Video Rental:	Advertising Services:	Y	Radio:	Music Print./Dist.:	Gambling/Casinos:
Distribution/Printing:	Video Distribution:	Info. Sys. Software:		Online Information:	Multimedia:	Rides/Theme Parks:

TYPES OF BUSINESS:

Directory Publishing
Yellow Pages Publications
Internet Portals
Hebrew-Language Publishing

BRANDS/DIVISIONS/AFFILIATES:

Jewish Israeli Yellow Pages (The)
Jewish Master Guide (The)
Kosher Yellow Pages
JewishYellow.com
JewishMasterguide.com
theonlykosherdirectory.com
Next Yellow (The)
Shopila Corporation

CONTACTS: *Note: Officers with more than one job title may be intentionally listed here more than once.*

Assaf N. Ran, CEO
Assaf N. Ran, Pres.
Inbar Evron-Yogev, CFO/Sec.
Mark Alhadeff, CTO
Hagit Evenhaim, General Counsel
Inbar Evron-Yogev, Treas.
Assaf N. Ran, Chmn.

Phone: 212-489-6800	Fax: 212-779-2947
Toll-Free: 800-261-2799	
Address: 192 Lexington Ave., New York, NY 10016 US	

GROWTH PLANS/SPECIAL FEATURES:

DAG Media, Inc. is a publisher and distributor of business directories, both online and in print, for niche markets, particularly aimed at the Jewish communities in the U.S. The firm's primary source of revenue is derived from the sales of advertising space in these directories. Its primary directories are the Jewish Israeli Yellow Pages and the Jewish Master Guide. The Jewish Israeli Yellow Pages is a bilingual directory using both English and Hebrew. All advertisements are published in both languages, unless the advertiser specifically requests English-only. Quebecor World, Inc. prints the book in the U.S. and transports the finished product to DAG Media's New York office for distribution. The Jewish Master Guide, also known as the Kosher Yellow Pages, is a yellow page directory targeting the specific needs of the Hasidic and Orthodox Jewish communities in the greater New York City area. Unlike the Jewish Israeli book, the Jewish Master Guide is printed in English only and does not include any advertisements for services or products that might be offensive to the Orthodox Jewish and Hasidic communities. This directory is distributed by placing copies in synagogues and businesses located in Orthodox Jewish and Hasidic neighborhoods. In addition to printed publications, DAG also operates Internet portals including JewishYellow.com, JewishMasterGuide.com, theonlykosherdirectory.com and its most recent nextyellow.com, a directory site that gives businesses leads when consumers use the site to search for services. The company's subsidiaries include DAG Interactive, Inc., through which it operates nextyellow.com, and the Shopila Corporation, which is 80% owned by DAG. The firm's e-commerce site, Sopila.com, acts as a mediator between wholesale suppliers and online shoppers by selling merchandise at low prices to consumers. In 2007, DAG launched its newest subsidiary, DAG Funding Solutions, Inc., centered on lending money to businesses.

FINANCIALS: Sales and profits are in thousands of dollars—add 000 to get the full amount. 2007 Note: Financial information for 2007 was not available for all companies at press time.

2007 Sales: $	2007 Profits: $	U.S. Stock Ticker: DAGM
2006 Sales: $ 232	2006 Profits: $- 174	Int'l Ticker: Int'l Exchange:
2005 Sales: $4,447	2005 Profits: $- 511	Employees: 6
2004 Sales: $5,949	2004 Profits: $1,035	Fiscal Year Ends: 12/31
2003 Sales: $9,086	2003 Profits: $1,599	Parent Company:

SALARIES/BENEFITS:

Pension Plan:	ESOP Stock Plan:	Profit Sharing:	Top Exec. Salary: $147,615	Bonus: $
Savings Plan:	Stock Purch. Plan:		Second Exec. Salary: $62,019	Bonus: $

OTHER THOUGHTS:

Apparent Women Officers or Directors: 1
Hot Spot for Advancement for Women/Minorities:

LOCATIONS: ("Y" = Yes)

West:	Southwest:	Midwest:	Southeast:	Northeast:	International:
				Y	

DAILY JOURNAL CORP

www.dailyjournal.com

Industry Group Code: 511110 Ranks within this company's industry group: Sales: 20   Profits: 12

Print Media/Publishing:		Movies:	Equipment/Supplies:		Broadcast/Cable:	Music/Audio:	Sports/Games/Gambling:
Newspapers:	Y	Movie Theaters:	Equipment/Supplies:		Broadcast TV:	Music Production:	Games/Sports:
Magazines:	Y	Movie Production:	Gambling Equipment:		Cable TV:	Retail Music:	Retail Games Stores:
Books:		TV/Video Prod.:	Special Services:	Y	Satellite Broadcast:	Retail Audio Equip.:	Stadiums/Teams:
Book Stores:		Video Rental:	Advertising Services:	Y	Radio:	Music Print./Dist.:	Gambling/Casinos:
Distribution/Printing:		Video Distribution:	Info. Sys. Software:		Online Information:	Multimedia:	Rides/Theme Parks:

TYPES OF BUSINESS:

Newspaper Publishing
Online Publishing
Information Services
Judicial Publishing Technology

BRANDS/DIVISIONS/AFFILIATES:

Los Angeles Daily Journal
San Francisco Daily Journal
Nevada Journal (The)
California Real Estate Journal
Daily Recorder (The)
San Jose Post (The)
Business Journal
SUSTAIN Technologies, Inc.

CONTACTS: *Note: Officers with more than one job title may be intentionally listed here more than once.*

Gerald L. Salzman, CEO
Gerald L. Salzman, Pres.
Gerald L. Salzman, CFO
Jeanette Decker, Dir.-Human Resources
Peter Daum, CTO
Ira A. Marshall, Corp. Sec.
Gerald L. Salzman, Treas.
Stephen Maitland-Lewis, Mktg Dir.-Los Angeles Daily Journal
Charles Munger, Chmn.

Phone: 213-229-5300	Fax: 213-680-3682
Toll-Free:	
Address: 915 E. First St., Los Angeles, CA 90012 US	

GROWTH PLANS/SPECIAL FEATURES:

Daily Journal Corporation operates web sites and publishes newspapers in California, Arizona and Nevada. The company also serves as a newspaper representative, specializing in public notice advertising. Its 15 publications in general circulation include the Los Angeles Daily Journal, San Francisco Daily Journal, The Daily Recorder, The San Jose Post, Business Journal, The Nevada Journal and California Real Estate Journal among others. These publications operate predominately on a subscription basis, and many of them cover issues concerning business, legal and real estate matters. Additionally, the company produces various information services, in print and online, including court rules, judicial profiles, bankruptcy notices and real estate services. Daily Journal's subsidiary SUSTAIN Technologies, Inc. provides technologies and applications to enable justice agencies to automate their operations, to allow users to file cases electronically and to allow courts to publish information online. Specialized information services include Judicial Profiles services, which contain biographical and professional information concerning nearly all judges in California; several court rules services, which reproduce court rules for certain state and federal courts in California; and online foreclosure information. Daily Journal supplements service to subscribers and advertisers with an increasing Internet-based online information service. Some of this online service comes as part of a newspaper subscription or advertising placement, and some can only be obtained when customers pay additional charges. The company also provides computer online foreclosure information to about 550 customers.

FINANCIALS: Sales and profits are in thousands of dollars—add 000 to get the full amount. 2007 Note: Financial information for 2007 was not available for all companies at press time.

2007 Sales: $	2007 Profits: $	U.S. Stock Ticker: DJCO
2006 Sales: $32,369	2006 Profits: $2,438	Int'l Ticker: Int'l Exchange:
2005 Sales: $33,272	2005 Profits: $4,287	Employees: 275
2004 Sales: $33,862	2004 Profits: $3,731	Fiscal Year Ends: 9/30
2003 Sales: $34,229	2003 Profits: $2,403	Parent Company:

SALARIES/BENEFITS:

Pension Plan:	ESOP Stock Plan:	Profit Sharing:	Top Exec. Salary: $250,000	Bonus: $300,000
Savings Plan: Y	Stock Purch. Plan:		Second Exec. Salary: $	Bonus: $

OTHER THOUGHTS:

Apparent Women Officers or Directors: 1
Hot Spot for Advancement for Women/Minorities:

LOCATIONS: ("Y" = Yes)

West:	Southwest:	Midwest:	Southeast:	Northeast:	International:
Y	Y			Y	

DELAWARE NORTH COMPANIES   www.delawarenorth.com

Industry Group Code: 453220 Ranks within this company's industry group: Sales: 1 Profits:

Print Media/Publishing:	Movies:	Equipment/Supplies:		Broadcast/Cable:	Music/Audio:	Sports/Games/Gambling:	
Newspapers:	Movie Theaters:	Equipment/Supplies:		Broadcast TV:	Music Production:	Games/Sports:	
Magazines:	Movie Production:	Gambling Equipment:	Y	Cable TV:	Retail Music:	Retail Games Stores:	
Books:	TV/Video Prod.:	Special Services:	Y	Satellite Broadcast:	Retail Audio Equip.:	Stadiums/Teams:	Y
Book Stores:	Video Rental:	Advertising Services:		Radio:	Music Print./Dist.:	Gambling/Casinos:	
Distribution/Printing:	Video Distribution:	Info. Sys. Software:		Online Information:	Multimedia:	Rides/Theme Parks:	

TYPES OF BUSINESS:

Concession Stands
Catering & Food Services
Park & Resort Visitor Services
Professional Hockey Team
Event Centers
Pari-Mutuel Wagering

BRANDS/DIVISIONS/AFFILIATES:

Sportservice Corp.
DNC Travel Hospitality Services
DNC Parks & Resorts
Boston Bruins
American Park 'n Swap
DNC International
TD BankNorth Garden

CONTACTS: *Note: Officers with more than one job title may be intentionally listed here more than once.*

Jeremy M. Jacobs, Sr., CEO
Charles Moran, Jr., COO
Charles Moran, Jr., Pres.
Karen L. Kemp, CFO
Eileen Morgan, VP-Human Resources
Gregory J. Lesperance, VP-Tech. & Bus. Process Solutions
Bryan J. Keller, General Counsel/VP
Stephen Nowaczyk, VP-Financial Planning & Analysis
Wendy A. Watkins, VP-Corp. Comm. & Public Rel.
Daniel J. Zimmer, Treas./VP
William J. Bissett, VP-External Affairs
Ronald A. Sultemeier, Pres., Gaming & Entertainment Corp.
John A. Wentzell, Pres., Boston & TD BankNorth Garden
Dennis J. Szefel, Pres., Hospitality Group
Jeremy M. Jacobs, Sr., Chmn.
Johnathan Tribe, Mgr.-Delaware North Int'l

Phone: 716-858-5000	Fax: 716-858-5479
Toll-Free:	
Address: 40 Fountain Plaza, Buffalo, NY 14202-2200 US	

GROWTH PLANS/SPECIAL FEATURES:

Delaware North Companies, Inc. (DNC), one of the largest private companies in America, is a holding company for seven subsidiaries that operate in food service, hospitality and recreation: DNC Gaming and Entertainment; Sportservice Corp.; DNC Parks and Resorts; DNC Travel Hospitality Services; American Park 'n Swap; DNC International; and TD BankNorth Garden. DNC Gaming and Entertainment is one of the largest and most successful operators of pari-mutuel facilities in the U.S., with gaming and racing properties in Arizona, Arkansas, Florida, New York and West Virginia, featuring wagering on greyhound and horse racing, video slot gaming and fine dining. Sportservice Corp., the oldest of the firm's subsidiaries, is one of the largest food service companies in the country, providing food, beverage and retail services at high-profile events and over 50 ballparks, arenas and stadiums in the U.S. and Canada. DNC Parks and Resorts provides recreational visitor services at national attractions including Yosemite, Grand Canyon, Niagara Falls and Kennedy Space Center. DNC Travel Hospitality Services operates food service and retail facilities in 30 airports across the country. Another subsidiary, American Park 'n Swap, turns idle buildings and empty parking lots into destination events with musical entertainment, an array of foods and flea-market-style retail merchandise ranging from jewelry to tools and furniture. DNC International brings the company's food and hospitality services to Australia. In addition, DNC owns the Boston Bruins professional hockey team and operates the TD BankNorth Garden, a $160-million facility that houses the Bruins, the Boston Celtics and other entertainment events.

FINANCIALS: Sales and profits are in thousands of dollars—add 000 to get the full amount. 2007 Note: Financial information for 2007 was not available for all companies at press time.

2007 Sales: $	2007 Profits: $	U.S. Stock Ticker: Private
2006 Sales: $2,040,000	2006 Profits: $	Int'l Ticker: Int'l Exchange:
2005 Sales: $2,000,000	2005 Profits: $	Employees: 50,000
2004 Sales: $1,700,000	2004 Profits: $	Fiscal Year Ends: 12/31
2003 Sales: $1,600,000	2003 Profits: $	Parent Company:

SALARIES/BENEFITS:

Pension Plan:	ESOP Stock Plan:	Profit Sharing:	Top Exec. Salary: $	Bonus: $
Savings Plan:	Stock Purch. Plan:		Second Exec. Salary: $	Bonus: $

OTHER THOUGHTS:

Apparent Women Officers or Directors: 3
Hot Spot for Advancement for Women/Minorities: Y

LOCATIONS: ("Y" = Yes)

West:	Southwest:	Midwest:	Southeast:	Northeast:	International:
Y	Y	Y	Y	Y	Y

Note: Financial information, benefits and other data can change quickly and may vary from those stated here.

DENNIS PUBLISHING LTD

www.dennis.co.uk

Industry Group Code: 511120 Ranks within this company's industry group: Sales: Profits:

Print Media/Publishing:		Movies:		Equipment/Supplies:		Broadcast/Cable:		Music/Audio:		Sports/Games/Gambling:	
Newspapers:		Movie Theaters:		Equipment/Supplies:		Broadcast TV:		Music Production:		Games/Sports:	
Magazines:	Y	Movie Production:		Gambling Equipment:		Cable TV:		Retail Music:		Retail Games Stores:	
Books:		TV/Video Prod.:		Special Services:	Y	Satellite Broadcast:		Retail Audio Equip.:		Stadiums/Teams:	
Book Stores:		Video Rental:		Advertising Services:	Y	Radio:		Music Print./Dist.:		Gambling/Casinos:	
Distribution/Printing:		Video Distribution:		Info. Sys. Software:		Online Information:		Multimedia:		Rides/Theme Parks:	

TYPES OF BUSINESS:

Magazine Publishing
Mailing Lists
Interactive Media
Mail Order & Fulfillment Services

BRANDS/DIVISIONS/AFFILIATES:

Maxim
Men's Fitness
Mac User
PC Pro
Week (The)
Fortean Times
Seymour Distribution Ltd.
Dennis Direct

CONTACTS: Note: Officers with more than one job title may be intentionally listed here more than once.

James Tye, CEO
Brett Reynolds, COO
Ian Leggett, Group Dir.-Finance
Ian Westwood, Managing Dir.-Monitoring & Tech. Div.
Kerin O'Connor, Exec. Dir./Managing Dir.-The Week
Bruce Sandell, Managing Dir.-Lifestyle Div.
Pete Wootton, Managing Dir.-Dennis Interactive
Julian Lloyd-Evans, Managing Dir.-Advertising
Felix Dennis, Chmn.

Phone: 44-207-907-6000	Fax: 44-207-907-6020
Toll-Free:	
Address: 30 Cleveland St., London, W1T 4JD UK	

GROWTH PLANS/SPECIAL FEATURES:

Dennis Publishing, Ltd. is an independent publisher of periodicals based in London. Operating through multiple subsidiaries in the U.K. and the U.S., it is one of the world's fastest-growing independently owned media companies. Dennis publishes over 50 magazines, web sites, digital magazines and mobile sites in the U.K and one publication in the U.S. These include: Maxim, a popular men's magazine aimed at men in their 20s, with a circulation of over 3.8 million copies a month in 35 editions in 45 countries; Men's Fitness; Evo; Computer Shopper; MacUser; PC Pro; The Week, the company's most profitable U.K. magazine; Custom PC; Stuff; Bizarre; Fortean Times; and Viz. Some of the firm's magazines are made available online through Dennis Interactive (DI), the company's media division. The web sites for these magazines attract over 1.75 million unique users per month, with over 40 million page views. Moreover, through Dennis List Solutions, the company offers direct mailing lists to advertisers. American subsidiary Dennis Publishing, Inc. handles the U.S. versions of its magazines out of its New York offices. Dennis Direct, another subsidiary, offers mail order and fulfillment services for the group's magazines, as well as for third party clients. In recent news, DI launched a full-service games portal, covering all game formats, including online multiplayer games. Recently, Dennis launched a new mobile version of Maxim (mobile.maxim.com), which is designed to work with all types of web-enabled mobile phones. Recently, the firm launched Monkey, a weekly digital men's magazine with no print counterpart. The company jointly owns Seymour Distribution Ltd., a major independent distributor of magazine titles, with Frontline. In December 2007, Dennis announced the launch of the Facebook bookazine, a magazine-book hybrid, about the social networking web site.

Dennis offers benefits including four weeks paid vacation, transportation reimbursement, 26 weeks paid maternity leave, private healthcare insurance and a retirement plan.

FINANCIALS: Sales and profits are in thousands of dollars—add 000 to get the full amount. 2007 Note: Financial information for 2007 was not available for all companies at press time.

2007 Sales: $	2007 Profits: $	U.S. Stock Ticker: Private
2006 Sales: $	2006 Profits: $	Int'l Ticker: Int'l Exchange:
2005 Sales: $106,100	2005 Profits: $- 300	Employees: 640
2004 Sales: $	2004 Profits: $	Fiscal Year Ends: 12/31
2003 Sales: $358,987	2003 Profits: $- 300	Parent Company:

SALARIES/BENEFITS:

Pension Plan: Y	ESOP Stock Plan:	Profit Sharing:	Top Exec. Salary: $	Bonus: $
Savings Plan:	Stock Purch. Plan:		Second Exec. Salary: $	Bonus: $

OTHER THOUGHTS:

Apparent Women Officers or Directors:
Hot Spot for Advancement for Women/Minorities:

LOCATIONS: ("Y" = Yes)

West:	Southwest:	Midwest:	Southeast:	Northeast:	International:
				Y	Y

Note: Financial information, benefits and other data can change quickly and may vary from those stated here.

DG FASTCHANNEL   www.dgsystems.com

Industry Group Code: 541870 Ranks within this company's industry group: Sales: 1   Profits: 1

Print Media/Publishing:	Movies:	Equipment/Supplies:		Broadcast/Cable:	Music/Audio:	Sports/Games/Gambling:
Newspapers:	Movie Theaters:	Equipment/Supplies:	Y	Broadcast TV:	Music Production:	Games/Sports:
Magazines:	Movie Production:	Gambling Equipment:		Cable TV:	Retail Music:	Retail Games Stores:
Books:	TV/Video Prod.:	Special Services:	Y	Satellite Broadcast:	Retail Audio Equip.:	Stadiums/Teams:
Book Stores:	Video Rental:	Advertising Services:	Y	Radio:	Music Print./Dist.:	Gambling/Casinos:
Distribution/Printing:	Video Distribution:	Info. Sys. Software:		Online Information:	Multimedia:	Rides/Theme Parks:

TYPES OF BUSINESS:

Advertising Distribution Services
Digital Content Distribution
Online Database-TV Commercials
Digital Transmission Equipment
Editing & Media Production Services

BRANDS/DIVISIONS/AFFILIATES:

Digital Generation Systems
FastChannel Network
SourceEcreative
AdGallery
Pathfire, Inc.

CONTACTS: *Note: Officers with more than one job title may be intentionally listed here more than once.*

Scott K. Ginsberg, CEO
Omar A. Choucair, CFO
Neil Nguyen, Exec. VP-Sales
Omar A. Choucair, Sec.
Neil Nguyen, Exec. VP-Oper.
Pamela Maythenyi, Sr. VP-Creative
Scott K. Ginsberg, Chmn.

Phone: 972-581-2000	**Fax:** 972-581-2001
Toll-Free: 800-324-5672	
Address: 750 W. John Carpenter Fwy., Ste. 700, Irving, TX 75039 US	

GROWTH PLANS/SPECIAL FEATURES:

DG FastChannel, formerly Digital Generation Systems, operates a nationwide digital network linking more than 5,000 advertisers and advertising agencies to diverse media destinations across the U.S. and Canada. The company was formed when Digital Generation Systems merged with FastChannel Network. The firm's services include online creative research; media production and duplication; distribution; media asset management; and broadcast business intelligence products. Online creative research is provided through the SourceEcreative, formerly Source TV, searchable database, containing content and credits for over 400,000 U.S. television commercials, 80,000 professionals and 16,000 companies, allowing advertisers to contact directors, composers and other talent for new commercials. Media production consists of editing, duplication, subtitling and captioning services as well as storage of client masters or storyboards. The firm's digital distribution services connect its advertisers with 4,500 TV, cable and network broadcast destinations 10,000 radio stations and 6,500 print publishing destinations, allowing advertisers to have content distributed to radio and television stations in as little as one hour and at times when physical delivery services are not available. Media asset management, through AdGallery, offers customers archival, analytical and creative tools for their advertisements. Lastly, broadcast business intelligence allows customers to monitor and confirm accurate airplay of their broadcast commercials. The firm is seeking the sale of subsidiary StarGuide Digital Networks, Inc., which offers engineering consulting services and designs and sells high-speed digital information transmission and distribution systems. In December 2007, the firm agreed to acquire the Vyvx advertising services business from Level 3 Communications, Inc. for $129 million. In June 2007, the company acquired Pathfire, Inc. for $30 million. Pathfire is a distributor of third-party programming, including syndicated programming and news such as Jeopardy, Wheel of Fortune and Friends, over Internet and satellite channels.

FINANCIALS: Sales and profits are in thousands of dollars—add 000 to get the full amount. 2007 Note: Financial information for 2007 was not available for all companies at press time.

2007 Sales: $	2007 Profits: $	**U.S. Stock Ticker: DGIT**
2006 Sales: $68,667	2006 Profits: $- 649	**Int'l Ticker:** Int'l Exchange:
2005 Sales: $51,824	2005 Profits: $-1,090	Employees: 376
2004 Sales: $62,366	2004 Profits: $3,204	Fiscal Year Ends: 12/31
2003 Sales: $57,687	2003 Profits: $4,199	Parent Company:

SALARIES/BENEFITS:

Pension Plan:	ESOP Stock Plan:	Profit Sharing:	Top Exec. Salary: $323,077	Bonus: $175,000
Savings Plan: Y	Stock Purch. Plan:		Second Exec. Salary: $229,230	Bonus: $105,000

OTHER THOUGHTS:

Apparent Women Officers or Directors: 1
Hot Spot for Advancement for Women/Minorities:

LOCATIONS: ("Y" = Yes)

West:	Southwest:	Midwest:	Southeast:	Northeast:	International:
Y	Y	Y	Y	Y	Y

DIALOG

www.dialog.com

Industry Group Code: 514199 Ranks within this company's industry group: Sales: Profits:

Print Media/Publishing:	Movies:	Equipment/Supplies:		Broadcast/Cable:	Music/Audio:	Sports/Games/Gambling:
Newspapers:	Movie Theaters:	Equipment/Supplies:		Broadcast TV:	Music Production:	Games/Sports:
Magazines:	Movie Production:	Gambling Equipment:		Cable TV:	Retail Music:	Retail Games Stores:
Books:	TV/Video Prod.:	Special Services:	Y	Satellite Broadcast:	Retail Audio Equip.:	Stadiums/Teams:
Book Stores:	Video Rental:	Advertising Services:		Radio:	Music Print./Dist.:	Gambling/Casinos:
Distribution/Printing:	Video Distribution:	Info. Sys. Software:		Online Information:	Multimedia:	Rides/Theme Parks:

TYPES OF BUSINESS:

Syndicated Online News Content
Business News & Information
Online Publishing Technologies

BRANDS/DIVISIONS/AFFILIATES:

Thomson Corporation
Dialog
Dialog DataStar

CONTACTS: *Note: Officers with more than one job title may be intentionally listed here more than once.*

Kevin Bonsor, Manager-Mktg. Comm.
David Brown, Gen. Manager-Dialog DataStar
Roger K. Summit, Chmn. Emeritus

Phone: 919-462-8600	**Fax:** 919-468-9890
Toll-Free: 800-334-2564	
Address: 11000 Regency Pkwy., Ste. 10, Cary, NC 0180327518 US	

GROWTH PLANS/SPECIAL FEATURES:

Dialog, a subsidiary of The Thomson Corporation, is a leading supplier of syndicated content services and electronic business publishing technologies. Its services allow customers to create content for millions of users through a variety of high-technology media, such as intranets, web sites, extranets, desktop applications and distribution channels. The company's over 1,400 customers can be split into two groups: employees of large organizations that depend on news for competitive advantage and visitors to web sites that content providers compete to retain. Working side by side with its corporate clientele, the company's services and content are designed to appeal to specialized audiences, encourage return visits and result in increased purchases and business traffic. Its products consist of Dialog and DataStar, which offer 900 Deep Web databases with 1.4 billion unique records. These products assist customers researching the fields of business; intellectual property; science and technology; and news and trade journals. In business, Dialog offers detailed information on 500,000 companies, as well as financial information for 14 million companies worldwide. In intellectual properties, the firm offers copyright and trademark information for 14 countries as well as the World Intellectual Property Organization (WIPO) and European Community; 15 million patents in 60 countries; 4 million trademark images; and English versions of Japanese trademarks and Korean patent application abstracts. Science and technology covers all manner of research, including breakthroughs, drug interactions, review abstracts, full text articles, numerical data and other information. News and trade journals include the full text from more than 200 newspapers including The New York Times and Le Monde; and newswire services from all the major providers, such as Reuters and AP. Dialog operates in 27 countries worldwide. The firm formerly offered NewsEdge, which Thomson sold to Acquire Media, and Profound, which was sold to MarketResearch.com. Both sales were completed in 2007.

FINANCIALS: Sales and profits are in thousands of dollars—add 000 to get the full amount. 2007 Note: Financial information for 2007 was not available for all companies at press time.

2007 Sales: $	2007 Profits: $	**U.S. Stock Ticker: Subsidiary**
2006 Sales: $	2006 Profits: $	**Int'l Ticker:** Int'l Exchange:
2005 Sales: $	2005 Profits: $	Employees: 309
2004 Sales: $	2004 Profits: $	Fiscal Year Ends: 12/31
2003 Sales: $	2003 Profits: $	Parent Company: THOMSON CORPORATION (THE)

SALARIES/BENEFITS:

Pension Plan:	ESOP Stock Plan:	Profit Sharing:	Top Exec. Salary: $	Bonus: $89,780
Savings Plan:	Stock Purch. Plan:		Second Exec. Salary: $182,313	Bonus: $182,313

OTHER THOUGHTS:

Apparent Women Officers or Directors: 4
Hot Spot for Advancement for Women/Minorities: Y

LOCATIONS: ("Y" = Yes)

West:	Southwest:	Midwest:	Southeast:	Northeast:	International:
Y	Y	Y		Y	Y

Note: Financial information, benefits and other data can change quickly and may vary from those stated here.

DIAMONDHEAD CASINO CORPORATION

Industry Group Code: 721120 Ranks within this company's industry group: Sales: Profits:

Print Media/Publishing:	Movies:	Equipment/Supplies:	Broadcast/Cable:	Music/Audio:	Sports/Games/Gambling:	
Newspapers:	Movie Theaters:	Equipment/Supplies:	Broadcast TV:	Music Production:	Games/Sports:	
Magazines:	Movie Production:	Gambling Equipment:	Cable TV:	Retail Music:	Retail Games Stores:	
Books:	TV/Video Prod.:	Special Services:	Satellite Broadcast:	Retail Audio Equip.:	Stadiums/Teams:	
Book Stores:	Video Rental:	Advertising Services:	Radio:	Music Print./Dist.:	Gambling/Casinos:	Y
Distribution/Printing:	Video Distribution:	Info. Sys. Software:	Online Information:	Multimedia:	Rides/Theme Parks:	

TYPES OF BUSINESS:

Casino

BRANDS/DIVISIONS/AFFILIATES:

GROWTH PLANS/SPECIAL FEATURES:

Diamondhead Casino Corporation intends to develop a themed, destination casino resort and hotel at its 404-acre site on the Bay of St. Louis in Diamondhead, Mississippi. The firm previously operated four casino gambling cruise ships in Florida; these were sold in 2000 so that the company could focus on the development of its Diamondhead property. That development is dependent upon the company obtaining the necessary capital, whether through equity and/or debt financing, to master plan, obtain permits for, and construct a casino resort. The firm is currently in discussions or negotiations with various parties interested in funding and/or developing all or part of the Diamondhead property. As of September 2007, the company did not have the financial resources to develop its proposed casino resort.

CONTACTS: *Note: Officers with more than one job title may be intentionally listed here more than once.*

Deborah A. Vitale, CEO
Deborah A. Vitale, Pres.
Robert A. Zimmerman, CFO
Gregory A. Harrison, Sec./VP
Deborah A. Vitale, Treas.
Deborah A. Vitale, Chmn.

Phone: 727-674-0055	**Fax:** 727-319-9125
Toll-Free:	
Address: 150 153rd Ave., Ste. 202, Madeira Beach, FL 33708 US	

FINANCIALS: Sales and profits are in thousands of dollars—add 000 to get the full amount. 2007 Note: Financial information for 2007 was not available for all companies at press time.

2007 Sales: $	2007 Profits: $	**U.S. Stock Ticker: DHCC.OB**
2006 Sales: $	2006 Profits: $	**Int'l Ticker:** Int'l Exchange:
2005 Sales: $	2005 Profits: $- 642	Employees: 4
2004 Sales: $ 168	2004 Profits: $- 640	Fiscal Year Ends: 12/31
2003 Sales: $ 357	2003 Profits: $- 421	Parent Company:

SALARIES/BENEFITS:

Pension Plan:	ESOP Stock Plan: Y	Profit Sharing:	Top Exec. Salary: $300,000	Bonus: $450,000
Savings Plan:	Stock Purch. Plan:		Second Exec. Salary: $	Bonus: $

OTHER THOUGHTS:

Apparent Women Officers or Directors: 1
Hot Spot for Advancement for Women/Minorities:

LOCATIONS: ("Y" = Yes)

West:	Southwest:	Midwest:	Southeast:	Northeast:	International:
			Y		

DICK CLARK PRODUCTIONS INC
www.dickclarkproductions.com
Industry Group Code: 512110 Ranks within this company's industry group: Sales: Profits:

Print Media/Publishing:	Movies:		Equipment/Supplies:		Broadcast/Cable:	Music/Audio:	Sports/Games/Gambling:	
Newspapers:	Movie Theaters:		Equipment/Supplies:		Broadcast TV:	Music Production:	Games/Sports:	
Magazines:	Movie Production:	Y	Gambling Equipment:		Cable TV:	Retail Music:	Retail Games Stores:	
Books:	TV/Video Prod.:	Y	Special Services:	Y	Satellite Broadcast:	Retail Audio Equip.:	Stadiums/Teams:	
Book Stores:	Video Rental:		Advertising Services:	Y	Radio:	Music Print./Dist.:	Gambling/Casinos:	
Distribution/Printing:	Video Distribution:		Info. Sys. Software:		Online Information:	Multimedia:	Rides/Theme Parks:	

TYPES OF BUSINESS:
Television Production
Film Production
Restaurants
Publicity Services

BRANDS/DIVISIONS/AFFILIATES:
Dick Clark Restaurants
Dick Clark Corporate Productions
Dick Clark Communications
Dick Clark's American Bandstand Grill
Dick Clark's American Bandstand Theater
Dick Clark's AB Grill
Dick Clark's AB Diner
Dick Clark's Bandstand-Food, Spirits & Fun

CONTACTS: Note: Officers with more than one job title may be intentionally listed here more than once.
Richard W. Clark, CEO
Francis C. La Maina, COO
Francis C. La Maina, Pres.
Brian Pope, General Counsel/VP-Bus. & Legal Affairs
Michael Mahan, Sr. VP-Corp. Dev.
Richard W. Clark, Chmn.

Phone: 310-255-4600	Fax:
Toll-Free:	
Address: 2900 Olympic Blvd., Santa Monica, CA 90404 US	

GROWTH PLANS/SPECIAL FEATURES:
Dick Clark Productions, Inc. (DCPI) is a diversified entertainment company with a variety of television, communications and restaurant businesses. The company develops and produces a wide range of television programming for television networks, first-run domestic syndicators, cable networks and advertisers. DCPI has been a significant supplier of television programming for over 50 years and has produced shows such as American Dreams, the Golden Globe Awards, the American Music Awards, the Academy of Country Music Awards, the Family Television Awards, the Daytime Emmy Awards, Bloopers and Beyond Belief: Fact or Fiction. Programming includes awards shows, comedy specials, children's programming, talk and game show series and dramatic series. The market for this programming is mainly composed of ABC, CBS, NBC, Fox and the new CW network. The company also licenses the rebroadcast rights to some of its programs, licenses certain segments of its programming to third parties, produces home videos and develops and produces theatrical motion pictures, generally in conjunction with third parties who provide the financing. DCPI operates a chain of five entertainment-themed restaurants named Dick Clark's American Bandstand Grill, located in Indianapolis, Newark, Kansas City, Phoenix and Salt Lake City. In addition, the firm offers television and entertainment-related publicity consulting services through Dick Clark Communications.

FINANCIALS: Sales and profits are in thousands of dollars—add 000 to get the full amount. 2007 Note: Financial information for 2007 was not available for all companies at press time.

2007 Sales: $	2007 Profits: $	U.S. Stock Ticker: Private
2006 Sales: $	2006 Profits: $	Int'l Ticker: Int'l Exchange:
2005 Sales: $	2005 Profits: $	Employees: 710
2004 Sales: $	2004 Profits: $	Fiscal Year Ends: 6/30
2003 Sales: $	2003 Profits: $	Parent Company:

SALARIES/BENEFITS:

Pension Plan:	ESOP Stock Plan:	Profit Sharing:	Top Exec. Salary: $975,000	Bonus: $444,740
Savings Plan:	Stock Purch. Plan:		Second Exec. Salary: $577,059	Bonus: $308,546

OTHER THOUGHTS:
Apparent Women Officers or Directors:
Hot Spot for Advancement for Women/Minorities: Y

LOCATIONS: ("Y" = Yes)

West:	Southwest:	Midwest:	Southeast:	Northeast:	International:
Y	Y	Y		Y	

Note: Financial information, benefits and other data can change quickly and may vary from those stated here.

DIGEO INC

www.digeo.com

Industry Group Code: 334310 Ranks within this company's industry group: Sales:　　Profits:

Print Media/Publishing:	Movies:	Equipment/Supplies:		Broadcast/Cable:		Music/Audio:	Sports/Games/Gambling:
Newspapers:	Movie Theaters:	Equipment/Supplies:	Y	Broadcast TV:		Music Production:	Games/Sports:
Magazines:	Movie Production:	Gambling Equipment:		Cable TV:	Y	Retail Music:	Retail Games Stores:
Books:	TV/Video Prod.:	Special Services:		Satellite Broadcast:		Retail Audio Equip.:	Stadiums/Teams:
Book Stores:	Video Rental:	Advertising Services:		Radio:		Music Print./Dist.:	Gambling/Casinos:
Distribution/Printing:	Video Distribution:	Info. Sys. Software:		Online Information:		Multimedia:	Rides/Theme Parks:

TYPES OF BUSINESS:

Cable TV Services
Interactive TV Services
Set-Top Boxes

BRANDS/DIVISIONS/AFFILIATES:

Moxi Digital, Inc
Moxi Media Center
Charter Communications Inc
Motorola Inc
Scientific Atlanta Inc
Sony Corporation
Moxi TV for PC
Windows XP

CONTACTS: *Note: Officers with more than one job title may be intentionally listed here more than once.*

Mike Fidler, CEO
Greg Gudorf, COO
Greg Gudorf, Pres.
Allison Cornia, VP-Mktg.
Chauncey Gammage, VP-Human Resources
Chuck Broadus, VP-Eng.
Byron Springer, Jr., General Counsel/VP
Allison Cornia, VP-Comm.
Bert Kolde, Sr. VP
Paul G. Allen, Chmn.

Phone: 425-896-6000	Fax: 425-896-6062
Toll-Free:	
Address: 8815 122nd Ave. NE, Kirkland, WA 98033 US	

GROWTH PLANS/SPECIAL FEATURES:

Digeo, Inc. is a cable television services company that focuses on interactive TV (iTV). The firm's merger with Moxi Digital, Inc. made it the industry's leading provider of advanced media center platforms and iTV services. Through its Emmy award-winning Moxi Media Center service, deployed in conjunction with several cable service providers, the company offers such popular features as high-definition TV and interactive viewing systems, in addition to music, photos and games. The service requires a specially designed set-top cable box that often includes a DVD player. Digeo's basic iTV service provides cable subscribers with eight information and commerce channels, including weather, local movie listings, news, sports, money, shopping and games. Also offered is a series of advanced services for the various needs of Moxi subscribers, including enhanced TV, digital video recording, telephone monitoring, advanced communication services, photos, music, games and wireless home networking. Digeo has designed its advanced platforms to work with partners including Charter, Motorola, Scientific Atlanta and Sony. In January 2007, Digeo announced plans to begin selling its Moxi digital media recorder (DMR) directly to consumers in 2008. In September 2007, the company announced that it is exploring joint venture development opportunities with Monster, a leading manufacturer of high-end cables. In December 2007, Digeo launched Moxi TV for PC, a software application enabling PC users with a TV tuner card and Windows XP to use their personal computer as a DMR.

FINANCIALS: Sales and profits are in thousands of dollars—add 000 to get the full amount. 2007 Note: Financial information for 2007 was not available for all companies at press time.

2007 Sales: $	2007 Profits: $	U.S. Stock Ticker: Private
2006 Sales: $	2006 Profits: $	Int'l Ticker:　Int'l Exchange:
2005 Sales: $	2005 Profits: $	Employees: 250
2004 Sales: $	2004 Profits: $	Fiscal Year Ends: 12/31
2003 Sales: $	2003 Profits: $	Parent Company:

SALARIES/BENEFITS:

Pension Plan:	ESOP Stock Plan: Y	Profit Sharing:	Top Exec. Salary: $	Bonus: $
Savings Plan: Y	Stock Purch. Plan:		Second Exec. Salary: $	Bonus: $

OTHER THOUGHTS:

Apparent Women Officers or Directors: 2
Hot Spot for Advancement for Women/Minorities:

LOCATIONS: ("Y" = Yes)

West:	Southwest:	Midwest:	Southeast:	Northeast:	International:
Y					

DIGITAL BRIDGES LIMITED

www.iplay.com

Industry Group Code: 511208 Ranks within this company's industry group: Sales: Profits:

Print Media/Publishing:	Movies:	Equipment/Supplies:	Broadcast/Cable:	Music/Audio:	Sports/Games/Gambling:	
Newspapers:	Movie Theaters:	Equipment/Supplies:	Broadcast TV:	Music Production:	Games/Sports:	Y
Magazines:	Movie Production:	Gambling Equipment:	Cable TV:	Retail Music:	Retail Games Stores:	
Books:	TV/Video Prod.:	Special Services:	Satellite Broadcast:	Retail Audio Equip.:	Stadiums/Teams:	
Book Stores:	Video Rental:	Advertising Services:	Radio:	Music Print./Dist.:	Gambling/Casinos:	
Distribution/Printing:	Video Distribution:	Info. Sys. Software:	Online Information:	Multimedia:	Rides/Theme Parks:	

TYPES OF BUSINESS:

Mobile Entertainment Software

BRANDS/DIVISIONS/AFFILIATES:

I-Play
Jewel Quest
24: Agent Down
Maria Sharapovna Tennis
2Fast 2Furious
3D Constructo Combat
I-Player
Ditto Studios

CONTACTS: *Note: Officers with more than one job title may be intentionally listed here more than once.*

Brian Greasely, CEO
David Gosen, COO
Colin Grant, CFO
Phil Cooke, CTO
Chris Wright, Head-Game Dev.
Krishna Gidwani, VP-Corp. Dev.
Andres Evju, General Mgr.-Americas
Stephane Labrunie, VP-Sales, Europe
Euan Stillie, Head-Quality Assurance & Deployment
Daniel Gan, VP-Asia Pacific

Phone: 44-207-901-1760	Fax: 44-207-901-1761
Toll-Free:	
Address: 1C Greencoat House, Francis St., London, SW1P 1DH UK	

GROWTH PLANS/SPECIAL FEATURES:

Digital Bridges, Ltd. develops and publishes downloadable and built-in entertainment software for cellular phones and other mobile devices. The company does business under the brand I-Play and markets its products to mobile networks, such as Orange, O2 and Vodafone, as well as through mobile retailers and distribution partners. The firm partners with entertainment companies and developers, network carriers, online portals and retailers. In return for its partners' services, Digital Bridges provides them with access to more than half a billion cell phone users worldwide. Financial backing for Digital Bridges comes from leading investment and venture capital firms Apax Partners and Argo Global Capital. The games offered by the company include Jewel Quest, 2Fast 2Furious, 3D Pool Urban Hustle, Maria Sharapovna Tennis, Boulder Dash, Moto-X II and 2005 SI Football Trivia. Some of its new releases include Pillowfight; Fast & Furious: Fugitive; Fast & Furious: Tokyo; GoodFellas; 24: Agent Down; My Dog; and Big Kahuna Reef: Hawaii Quest. The company has integrated Ditto Studios, a mobile game porting specialist and developer, into its I-Play operations, greatly accelerating delivery time through the use of Ditto's proprietary technology designed to provide mobile games to hundreds of different handsets simultaneously. In April 2006, the company entered into a licensing agreement with iWin, a San Francisco-based developer and publisher of online games. The agreement will allow the company to provide three new puzzle games to its customers. In May 2007, I-Play announced a partnership with Universal Studios which will make available streaming video service of Universal's archive of movies through the I-Player. In May 2007, Oberon Media announced its intention to acquire I-Play, though it intends to run to company under its existing name and brand.

FINANCIALS: Sales and profits are in thousands of dollars—add 000 to get the full amount. 2007 Note: Financial information for 2007 was not available for all companies at press time.

2007 Sales: $	2007 Profits: $	U.S. Stock Ticker: Private
2006 Sales: $	2006 Profits: $	Int'l Ticker: Int'l Exchange:
2005 Sales: $	2005 Profits: $	Employees:
2004 Sales: $	2004 Profits: $	Fiscal Year Ends: 12/31
2003 Sales: $	2003 Profits: $	Parent Company:

SALARIES/BENEFITS:

Pension Plan:	ESOP Stock Plan:	Profit Sharing:	Top Exec. Salary: $	Bonus: $
Savings Plan:	Stock Purch. Plan:		Second Exec. Salary: $	Bonus: $

OTHER THOUGHTS:

Apparent Women Officers or Directors:
Hot Spot for Advancement for Women/Minorities:

LOCATIONS: ("Y" = Yes)

West:	Southwest:	Midwest:	Southeast:	Northeast:	International:
Y				Y	Y

DIGITAL VIDEO SYSTEMS INC

www.dvsystems.com

Industry Group Code: 334310 Ranks within this company's industry group: Sales: Profits:

Print Media/Publishing:	Movies:	Equipment/Supplies:		Broadcast/Cable:	Music/Audio:		Sports/Games/Gambling:
Newspapers:	Movie Theaters:	Equipment/Supplies:	Y	Broadcast TV:	Music Production:		Games/Sports:
Magazines:	Movie Production:	Gambling Equipment:		Cable TV:	Retail Music:		Retail Games Stores:
Books:	TV/Video Prod.:	Special Services:		Satellite Broadcast:	Retail Audio Equip.:	Y	Stadiums/Teams:
Book Stores:	Video Rental:	Advertising Services:		Radio:	Music Print./Dist.:		Gambling/Casinos:
Distribution/Printing:	Video Distribution:	Info. Sys. Software:		Online Information:	Multimedia:		Rides/Theme Parks:

TYPES OF BUSINESS:

Electronic Equipment-DVD Products

BRANDS/DIVISIONS/AFFILIATES:

DVS Electronics (India) Ltd.

GROWTH PLANS/SPECIAL FEATURES:

Digital Video Systems, Inc. (DVS) specializes in developing digital video and optical disc technologies. The company has developed or acquired technologies for applications including automatic ad-insertion systems, network video servers, video CD players and commercial video kiosks. With operations in the U.S., China and India, the firm develops and markets primarily DVD-ROM drives and DVD loaders for consumer, commercial and computer peripherals markets, including home and portable DVD players, home theater systems, DVD recorders and automotive DVD players. The company also owns the DVD operations, patents and licenses to the DVD-related intellectual properties of Hyundai Electronics. In response to declining revenues due to the commoditization of the home DVD market, DVS has narrowed its focus to automotive and recordable DVD products and consumer digital entertainment products in India. DVS Electronics (India) Ltd., the firm's division in India, is pursuing exclusive digital content distribution agreements with Bollywood producers.

CONTACTS: Note: Officers with more than one job title may be intentionally listed here more than once.

Mali Kuo, CEO
Douglas T. Watson, COO
Shaun Kang, Pres.
Dean C. Seniff, CFO
Mali Kuo, Chmn./Co-CEO-DVS Korea
Mali Kuo, Chmn.
Shaun Kang, Co-CEO-DVS Korea

Phone: 650-938-8815	Fax: 650-938-8829
Toll-Free:	
Address: 357 Castro St., Ste. 5, Mountain View, CA 94041 US	

FINANCIALS: Sales and profits are in thousands of dollars—add 000 to get the full amount. 2007 Note: Financial information for 2007 was not available for all companies at press time.

2007 Sales: $	2007 Profits: $	**U.S. Stock Ticker: DVID**
2006 Sales: $	2006 Profits: $	**Int'l Ticker:** Int'l Exchange:
2005 Sales: $	2005 Profits: $	**Employees:** 225
2004 Sales: $87,200	2004 Profits: $-13,070	**Fiscal Year Ends:** 12/31
2003 Sales: $89,133	2003 Profits: $-8,345	**Parent Company:**

SALARIES/BENEFITS:

Pension Plan:	ESOP Stock Plan:	Profit Sharing:	Top Exec. Salary: $139,231	Bonus: $
Savings Plan:	Stock Purch. Plan:		Second Exec. Salary: $125,813	Bonus: $14,710

OTHER THOUGHTS:

Apparent Women Officers or Directors: 1
Hot Spot for Advancement for Women/Minorities:

LOCATIONS: ("Y" = Yes)

West:	Southwest:	Midwest:	Southeast:	Northeast:	International:
Y					Y

DIRECTV GROUP INC (THE)

www.directv.com

Industry Group Code: 513220   Ranks within this company's industry group: Sales: 3   Profits: 4

Print Media/Publishing:	Movies:	Equipment/Supplies:		Broadcast/Cable:	Music/Audio:	Sports/Games/Gambling:
Newspapers:	Movie Theaters:	Equipment/Supplies:	Y	Broadcast TV:	Music Production:	Games/Sports:
Magazines:	Movie Production:	Gambling Equipment:		Cable TV:	Retail Music:	Retail Games Stores:
Books:	TV/Video Prod.:	Special Services:		Satellite Broadcast:	Retail Audio Equip.:	Stadiums/Teams:
Book Stores:	Video Rental:	Advertising Services:		Radio:	Music Print./Dist.:	Gambling/Casinos:
Distribution/Printing:	Video Distribution:	Info. Sys. Software:		Online Information:	Multimedia:	Rides/Theme Parks:

TYPES OF BUSINESS:

Satellite Broadcasting
Commercial Satellite Fleet
Satellite-Based Internet Services
Digital Television

BRANDS/DIVISIONS/AFFILIATES:

DIRECTV Holdings, LLC
Hughes Electronics Corporation
Liberty Media Corp.
DIRECTV U.S.
DIRECTV Latin America
PanAmericana
Sky Brasil Servicos Ltda.
DIRECTV Sat-Go

CONTACTS: Note: Officers with more than one job title may be intentionally listed here more than once.

Chase Carey, CEO
Chase Carey, Pres.
Michael W. Palkovic, CFO
Romulo G. Pontual, CTO/Exec. VP
Larry D. Hunter, General Counsel/Exec. VP/Corp. Sec.
Michael W. Palkovic, Exec. VP-Oper.
Robert Mercer, Press Contact
Patrick T. Doyle, Chief Acct. Officer/Sr. VP/Treas./Controller
Rupert Murdoch, Chmn.
Bruce B. Churchill, CEO/Pres., Latin America & New Enterprises

Phone: 310-964-5000	Fax: 310-535-5225
Toll-Free:	
Address: 2230 E. Imperial Hwy., El Segundo, CA 90245-0956 US	

GROWTH PLANS/SPECIAL FEATURES:

The DIRECTV Group, Inc. is one of the world's top providers of digital television entertainment and wireless systems. The company's two business segments, DIRECTV U.S. and DIRECTV Latin America, are engaged in acquiring, promoting, selling and distributing digital entertainment programming via satellite to residential and commercial subscribers. DIRECTV U.S. is the one of the largest providers of direct-to-home digital television services, as well as in the multi-channel video programming distribution industry, with over 16 million subscribers and about 1,700 digital video and audio channels, including satellite radio and specialty networks. DIRECTV U.S. currently broadcasts its service from 11 geosynchronous satellites, ten owned and one leased, and has plans to launch one more in early 2008. DIRECTV Latin America comprises PanAmericana, a group of companies that primarily includes the wholly-owned subsidiary DIRECTV Latin America, LLC and its local operating companies that provide services in countries other than Brazil and Mexico. DIRECTV Latin America also includes 74% of Sky Brasil Servicos Ltda. (Sky Brazil) and 41% of Innova, S. de R.L. de C.V. (Sky Mexico). PanAmericana has approximately 1.4 million subscribers; Sky Brazil, 1.3 million; and Sky Mexico, 1.4 million. In August 2006, the company completed the merger of Galaxy Brasil Ltda. into Sky Brazil, and purchased News Corporation's and Liberty's interests in Sky Brazil. The firm is considering the launch of a massive, wireless voice and data network, probably based on WiMax, which would offer bundled services including TV, phone and Internet access. In December 2006, Liberty Media Corp. acquired sufficient DIRECTV stock from News Corp. to give Liberty Media a controlling stake in DIRECTV. In May 2007, the firm announced the launch of its Sat-Go portable satellite system, the world's first.

DIRECTV's employees receive medical and dental insurance; educational assistance; free products; and many other benefits.

FINANCIALS: Sales and profits are in thousands of dollars—add 000 to get the full amount. 2007 Note: Financial information for 2007 was not available for all companies at press time.

2007 Sales: $	2007 Profits: $	U.S. Stock Ticker: DTV
2006 Sales: $14,755,500	2006 Profits: $1,420,100	Int'l Ticker: Int'l Exchange:
2005 Sales: $13,164,500	2005 Profits: $335,900	Employees: 11,200
2004 Sales: $11,360,000	2004 Profits: $-1,944,000	Fiscal Year Ends: 12/31
2003 Sales: $10,121,200	2003 Profits: $-361,800	Parent Company:

SALARIES/BENEFITS:

Pension Plan: Y	ESOP Stock Plan:	Profit Sharing:	Top Exec. Salary: $2,151,000	Bonus: $4,000,000
Savings Plan: Y	Stock Purch. Plan:		Second Exec. Salary: $1,024,000	Bonus: $1,200,000

OTHER THOUGHTS:

Apparent Women Officers or Directors:
Hot Spot for Advancement for Women/Minorities:

LOCATIONS: ("Y" = Yes)

West:	Southwest:	Midwest:	Southeast:	Northeast:	International:
Y	Y	Y	Y	Y	Y

Note: Financial information, benefits and other data can change quickly and may vary from those stated here.

DISCOVERY COMMUNICATIONS INC   www.discovery.com

Industry Group Code: 513210 Ranks within this company's industry group: Sales: Profits:

Print Media/Publishing:	Movies:		Equipment/Supplies:	Broadcast/Cable:		Music/Audio:		Sports/Games/Gambling:
Newspapers:	Movie Theaters:		Equipment/Supplies:	Broadcast TV:		Music Production:		Games/Sports:
Magazines:	Movie Production:		Gambling Equipment:	Cable TV:	Y	Retail Music:		Retail Games Stores:
Books:	TV/Video Prod.:	Y	Special Services:	Satellite Broadcast:		Retail Audio Equip.:		Stadiums/Teams:
Book Stores:	Video Rental:		Advertising Services:	Radio:		Music Print./Dist.:		Gambling/Casinos:
Distribution/Printing:	Video Distribution:		Info. Sys. Software:	Online Information:		Multimedia:		Rides/Theme Parks:

TYPES OF BUSINESS:
Cable TV Networks
Digital Media
Catalog & Online Sales
Educational Products

BRANDS/DIVISIONS/AFFILIATES:
Discovery Channel
TLC
Animal Planet
Travel Channel
Discovery Kids
BBC America
Discovery HD
Discovery Channel Catalog (The)

CONTACTS: *Note: Officers with more than one job title may be intentionally listed here more than once.*
David Zaslav, CEO
David Zaslav, Pres.
Roger F. Millay, CFO/Sr. Exec. VP
Adria Alpert-Romm, Sr. Exec. VP-Human Resources
Mark Hollinger, General Counsel
Mark Hollinger, Sr. Exec. VP-Corp. Oper.
Bruce Campbell, Pres.-Bus. Dev., Digital Media & Emerging Networks
Bill Goodwyn, Pres., Domestic Dist. & Enterprises
William M. Campbell, III, Pres., U.S. Networks
W. Clark Bunting, Pres., Discovery Studios
Joe Abruzzese, Advertising Sales
John S. Hendricks, Chmn.
Greg Ricca, Pres./CEO-Int'l

Phone: 240-662-2000	Fax: 240-662-1868
Toll-Free:	
Address: 1 Discovery Pl., Silver Spring, MD 20910 US	

GROWTH PLANS/SPECIAL FEATURES:
Discovery Communications, Inc. is a leading global media and entertainment company headquartered in Silver Spring, Maryland. The firm operates through five main divisions: U.S. networks; international networks; commerce; education; and digital media. Its U.S. networks division is a provider of real-world media and entertainment through several TV channels, including the Discovery Channel; TLC; Animal Planet; Discovery Health; FitTV; Travel Channel; Discovery Times; Discovery Kids; BBC America; Discovery en Espanol; and Discovery HD Theater. With 28 offices outside of the U.S., the firm's international networks division serves over 170 countries and territories in 35 languages. International programming offers viewers both global perspectives and local stories. Examples of programming include DMAX, the first mainstream factual entertainment channel for men in Germany; Discovery HD, which provides high definition programming to 14 international markets; and Discovery Lifestyle Network, a global portfolio of three lifestyle brands that reaches 196 million households in 90 countries. The firm's commerce division extends the company's television brands to consumers through an array of educational products and services. The division encompasses Discovery's retail operations, including an e-commerce site that logs over 12 million unique visitors annually; The Discovery Channel Store Catalog, which is distributed to nearly 10 million consumers annually; and domestic licensing partnerships with manufacturers and retailers. The company's education division is a leading provider of video-based broadband educational content in the U.S., with web sites, school services and products that reach 35 million students across the country. The firm's digital media division includes broadband channels; Google Earth content offerings; a daily webcast called Discovery News; Discovery OnDemand, a video-on-demand service available in seven countries including the U.S.; and HD Theater, a 24-hour-a-day/7-day-a-week high definition network. In May 2007 Discovery Networks Asia launched three new channels in Malaysia: Discovery Science; Discovery Home & Health; and Discovery Real Time.

FINANCIALS: Sales and profits are in thousands of dollars—add 000 to get the full amount. 2007 Note: Financial information for 2007 was not available for all companies at press time.

2007 Sales: $	2007 Profits: $	**U.S. Stock Ticker: Joint Venture**
2006 Sales: $	2006 Profits: $	**Int'l Ticker:** Int'l Exchange:
2005 Sales: $2,700,000	2005 Profits: $	Employees: 6,000
2004 Sales: $2,365,000	2004 Profits: $	Fiscal Year Ends: 12/31
2003 Sales: $1,717,000	2003 Profits: $	Parent Company:

SALARIES/BENEFITS:

Pension Plan:	ESOP Stock Plan:	Profit Sharing:	Top Exec. Salary: $	Bonus: $
Savings Plan: Y	Stock Purch. Plan:		Second Exec. Salary: $	Bonus: $

OTHER THOUGHTS:
Apparent Women Officers or Directors: 1
Hot Spot for Advancement for Women/Minorities: Y

LOCATIONS: ("Y" = Yes)

West:	Southwest:	Midwest:	Southeast:	Northeast:	International:
Y		Y	Y	Y	Y

DOUBLECLICK INC

www.doubleclick.com

Industry Group Code: 541810A Ranks within this company's industry group: Sales: Profits:

Print Media/Publishing:	Movies:	Equipment/Supplies:		Broadcast/Cable:	Music/Audio:	Sports/Games/Gambling:
Newspapers:	Movie Theaters:	Equipment/Supplies:		Broadcast TV:	Music Production:	Games/Sports:
Magazines:	Movie Production:	Gambling Equipment:		Cable TV:	Retail Music:	Retail Games Stores:
Books:	TV/Video Prod.:	Special Services:		Satellite Broadcast:	Retail Audio Equip.:	Stadiums/Teams:
Book Stores:	Video Rental:	Advertising Services:	Y	Radio:	Music Print./Dist.:	Gambling/Casinos:
Distribution/Printing:	Video Distribution:	Info. Sys. Software:		Online Information:	Multimedia:	Rides/Theme Parks:

TYPES OF BUSINESS:

Online Advertising Services
Outsourcing Services
Advertising Software
Consumer Database Analysis

BRANDS/DIVISIONS/AFFILIATES:

Hellman & Friedman LLC
DART for Advertisers
DART for Publishers
DART Enterprise
DoubleClick Rich Media & Video
DoubleClick Ad Kit
Audience Interaction Metrics
Google Inc

CONTACTS: Note: Officers with more than one job title may be intentionally listed here more than once.

David S. Rosenblatt, CEO
Charlie Dickson, CFO
Marianne Caponnetto, Chief Sales & Mktg. Officer
Debbie Josephs, VP-Human Resources
Greg Tagaris, CIO
John M. Rehl, Sr. VP-Global Tech. Svcs.
Neal Mohan, Sr. VP-Prod. Dev.
Stephanie Abramson, General Counsel/Exec. VP
Neal Mohan, Sr. VP-Strategy
Stuart Frankel, Sr. VP/Gen. Mgr.-Performics
Chris Young, Exec. VP-Rich Media
Michael Rubenstein, VP/Gen. Mgr.-DoubleClick Advertising Exchange
Ben Regensburger, Pres., DoubleClick Int'l

Phone: 212-683-0001	Fax: 212-287-1203
Toll-Free: 866-459-7606	
Address: 111 8th Ave., 10th Fl., New York, NY 10011 US	

GROWTH PLANS/SPECIAL FEATURES:

DoubleClick, Inc., a subsidiary of Hellman & Friedman LLC, is a leading provider of products and services that enable direct marketers, publishers and advertisers to market to consumers on the Internet. The company has 17 offices and development hubs and 14 data centers worldwide. DoubleClick's products are offered in six categories: ad serving, rich media & video, search solutions, marketplace, optimization and workflow automation. In the ad serving category, the company's products include DART for Advertisers, a web-based ad management tool; DART for Publishers, a web-based tool for monetizing a publisher's advertising inventory; and DART Enterprise, an ad management tool offering relatively detailed business management features, such as inventory management, traffic pattern analysis and real-time campaign result reporting. In the rich media & video category, the company offers DoubleClick Rich Media & Video, which includes a service team of production, creative, trafficking and research experts; the DoubleClick Ad Kit; a range of rich media formats; an Audience Interaction Metrics package; and DoubleClick's Innovation Lab. In the search solutions category, the company offers DART Search and DoubleClick Performics Search. DoubleClick Advertising Exchange is the company's marketplace offering, offering immediate access to inventory for buyers and DoubleClick's proprietary Dynamic Allocation system for sellers. DART Adapt is the company's optimization product, capable of addressing the optimization needs of multiple campaign types. In the workflow automation category, DoubleClick's products include MediaVisor, a software application for advertising campaign management; and DART Sales Manager, a proposal and finance management tool. DoubleClick manages online advertising for companies such as MySpace, Ford Motors, MTV, and CBS Sports. In April 2007, DoubleClick agreed to be acquired by Google for $3.1 billion. The deal received U.S. antitrust clearance in December 2007.

FINANCIALS: Sales and profits are in thousands of dollars—add 000 to get the full amount. 2007 Note: Financial information for 2007 was not available for all companies at press time.

2007 Sales: $	2007 Profits: $	U.S. Stock Ticker: Subsidiary
2006 Sales: $	2006 Profits: $	Int'l Ticker: Int'l Exchange:
2005 Sales: $	2005 Profits: $	Employees: 1,223
2004 Sales: $301,600	2004 Profits: $37,500	Fiscal Year Ends: 12/31
2003 Sales: $271,337	2003 Profits: $16,918	Parent Company: HELLMAN & FRIEDMAN LLC

SALARIES/BENEFITS:

Pension Plan:	ESOP Stock Plan:	Profit Sharing:	Top Exec. Salary: $	Bonus: $444,600
Savings Plan:	Stock Purch. Plan:		Second Exec. Salary: $300,000	Bonus: $300,000

OTHER THOUGHTS:

Apparent Women Officers or Directors: 3
Hot Spot for Advancement for Women/Minorities: Y

LOCATIONS: ("Y" = Yes)

West:	Southwest:	Midwest:	Southeast:	Northeast:	International:
Y		Y		Y	Y

Note: Financial information, benefits and other data can change quickly and may vary from those stated here.

DOVER DOWNS GAMING & ENTERTAINMENT INC
www.doverdowns.com
Industry Group Code: 713210 Ranks within this company's industry group: Sales: 6   Profits: 4

Print Media/Publishing:	Movies:	Equipment/Supplies:	Broadcast/Cable:	Music/Audio:	Sports/Games/Gambling:	
Newspapers:	Movie Theaters:	Equipment/Supplies:	Broadcast TV:	Music Production:	Games/Sports:	Y
Magazines:	Movie Production:	Gambling Equipment:	Cable TV:	Retail Music:	Retail Games Stores:	
Books:	TV/Video Prod.:	Special Services:	Satellite Broadcast:	Retail Audio Equip.:	Stadiums/Teams:	
Book Stores:	Video Rental:	Advertising Services:	Radio:	Music Print./Dist.:	Gambling/Casinos:	Y
Distribution/Printing:	Video Distribution:	Info. Sys. Software:	Online Information:	Multimedia:	Rides/Theme Parks:	

TYPES OF BUSINESS:
Casinos & Gaming Facilities
Slot Machine Casino
Hotel & Conference Center
Horse Racing
Live Events

BRANDS/DIVISIONS/AFFILIATES:
Dover Downs Slots
Dover Downs Hotel & Conference Center
Dover Downs Raceway
Dover Downs, Inc.
Dover Downs Management Corp.

CONTACTS: *Note: Officers with more than one job title may be intentionally listed here more than once.*
Denis McGlynn, CEO
Edward J. Sutor, COO/Exec. VP
Denis McGlynn, Pres.
Timothy R. Horne, CFO
Klaus M. Belohoubek, General Counsel/Corp. Sec./Sr. VP
Timothy R. Horne, Treas./Sr. VP-Finance
Henry B. Tippie, Chmn.

Phone: 302-674-4600	Fax: 302-857-3253
Toll-Free: 800-711-5882	
Address: 1131 N. DuPont Hwy., Dover, DE 19901 US	

GROWTH PLANS/SPECIAL FEATURES:
Dover Downs Gaming & Entertainment, Inc. is a gaming and entertainment company with operations in Delaware, consisting of Dover Downs Slots, a 97,000-square-foot slot machine casino complex; the Dover Downs Hotel & Conference Center, sporting conference, banquet, dining, ballroom and concert hall facilities; and the Dover Downs Raceway, a harness racing track that includes pari-mutuel wagering on live and simulcast horse races on numerous tracks across North America. The casino operates 2,724 slot machines ranging from a penny to $100 to play. The hotel and conference center includes 232 rooms, a multi-purpose ballroom/concert hall, five dining areas, a swimming pool and a health spa. The hotel also offers entertainment to its guests, such as music concerts and live boxing. Dover Downs Raceway conducts live harness races between November and April, and all are simulcast to tracks and other off-track betting locations across North America on each of the company's more than 130 live race dates. The track is adjacent to the casino and hotel. Dover Downs Gaming & Entertainment is a public holding company, and has two wholly-owned subsidiaries: Dover Downs, Inc. and Dover Downs Management Corp.

Employee benefits include medical, dental and vision coverage; 401(k) savings plan; retirement pension plan; flexible spending accounts; employee assistance program; educational assistance; and a bonus program.

FINANCIALS: Sales and profits are in thousands of dollars—add 000 to get the full amount. 2007 Note: Financial information for 2007 was not available for all companies at press time.

2007 Sales: $	2007 Profits: $	U.S. Stock Ticker: DDE
2006 Sales: $236,451	2006 Profits: $25,328	Int'l Ticker: Int'l Exchange:
2005 Sales: $216,852	2005 Profits: $26,040	Employees: 888
2004 Sales: $207,300	2004 Profits: $16,400	Fiscal Year Ends: 12/31
2003 Sales: $207,499	2003 Profits: $17,237	Parent Company:

SALARIES/BENEFITS:

Pension Plan: Y	ESOP Stock Plan:	Profit Sharing:	Top Exec. Salary: $250,000	Bonus: $159,650
Savings Plan: Y	Stock Purch. Plan:		Second Exec. Salary: $240,000	Bonus: $71,278

OTHER THOUGHTS:
Apparent Women Officers or Directors:
Hot Spot for Advancement for Women/Minorities:

LOCATIONS: ("Y" = Yes)

West:	Southwest:	Midwest:	Southeast:	Northeast:	International:
				Y	

DOW JONES & CO INC

www.dj.com

Industry Group Code: 511110 Ranks within this company's industry group: Sales: 8 Profits: 3

Print Media/Publishing:		Movies:	Equipment/Supplies:		Broadcast/Cable:	Music/Audio:	Sports/Games/Gambling:
Newspapers:	Y	Movie Theaters:	Equipment/Supplies:		Broadcast TV:	Music Production:	Games/Sports:
Magazines:	Y	Movie Production:	Gambling Equipment:		Cable TV:	Retail Music:	Retail Games Stores:
Books:		TV/Video Prod.:	Special Services:		Satellite Broadcast:	Retail Audio Equip.:	Stadiums/Teams:
Book Stores:		Video Rental:	Advertising Services:	Y	Radio:	Music Print./Dist.:	Gambling/Casinos:
Distribution/Printing:		Video Distribution:	Info. Sys. Software:		Online Information:	Multimedia:	Rides/Theme Parks:

TYPES OF BUSINESS:

Newspaper Publishing-Financial News
Business Publishing
Community Newspapers
Electronic & Online Publishing
Financial Indices
Financial Information Services

BRANDS/DIVISIONS/AFFILIATES:

Wall Street Journal (The)
Marketwatch Inc
Dow Jones Newswires
News Corporation Limited (The)
MarketWatch
eFinancialNews Holdings, Ltd.
Dow Jones Industrial Averages
Ottaway Newspapers, Inc.

CONTACTS: Note: Officers with more than one job title may be intentionally listed here more than once.

Richard F. Zannino, CEO
Todd H. Larsen, COO
William B. Plummer, CFO/Exec. VP
Ann Marks, Chief Mktg. Officer
Jorge L. Figueredo, VP-Human Resources
William A. Godfrey, III, CIO/VP
Joseph A. Stern, General Counsel/Exec. VP/Corp. Sec.
Linda E. Dunbar, VP-Corp. Comm.
Thomas W. McGuirl, VP-Tax
Clare Hart, Pres., Enterprise Media Group/Exec. VP
John N. Wilcox, Pres., Local Media Group/ Sr. VP
Ann M. Sarnoff, Pres., Dow Jones Ventures
L. Gordon Crovitz, Pres., Consumer Media Group/Exec. VP
Peter McPherson, Chmn.

Phone: 212-416-2000	Fax: 212-416-4348
Toll-Free:	
Address: 1 World Financial Ctr., 200 Liberty St., New York, NY 10281 US	

GROWTH PLANS/SPECIAL FEATURES:

Dow Jones & Co., Inc. (DJ) is a global provider of business and financial news and information through newspapers, newswires, magazines, the Internet, television and radio stations. In addition, the firm owns certain general-interest community newspapers throughout the U.S. DJ operates through three business segments: consumer media, enterprise media and local media. Consumer media, which offers business and financial information content, comprises primarily The Wall Street Journal, one of the largest daily U.S. newspapers; Barron's, a weekly magazine that caters to professionals and investors (including print, online and conferences); and MarketWatch (including online, newsletters, television and radio). Enterprise media comprises product offerings under the Dow Jones brand and consists of Dow Jones Newswires, Dow Jones Financial Information Services, Dow Jones Indexes, Dow Jones Reprints/Permissions, Dow Jones Licensing Services and Factiva. Dow Jones Newswires is a provider of real-time business and financial news displayed on almost 300,000 terminals around the world. Through Dow Jones Indexes, the company licenses the Dow Jones Industrial Averages and other indexes as the basis for trading options, futures, annuities and other products. Local media includes the wholly-owned Ottaway Newspapers, Inc. subsidiary. Its community newspapers serve relatively small, isolated communities. In 2006, DJ purchased Reuter's 50% share in Factiva, making DJ the sole owner and agreed to sell six Ottaway community newspapers to Community Newspaper Holdings, Inc. for $282.5 million. In May 2007, DJ acquired eFinancialNews Holdings, Ltd., a private U.K. media company providing services in the financial services industry. In late 2007, the firm was acquired by Rupert Murdoch's News Corp. for $5 billion.

The company offers its employees medical and dental insurance; disability and life insurance; a 401(k) plan; a retirement program; an employee stock purchase plan; and education benefits.

FINANCIALS: Sales and profits are in thousands of dollars—add 000 to get the full amount. 2007 Note: Financial information for 2007 was not available for all companies at press time.

2007 Sales: $	2007 Profits: $	U.S. Stock Ticker: Subsidiary
2006 Sales: $1,783,870	2006 Profits: $386,564	Int'l Ticker: Int'l Exchange:
2005 Sales: $1,672,947	2005 Profits: $60,395	Employees: 7,400
2004 Sales: $1,574,307	2004 Profits: $99,548	Fiscal Year Ends: 12/31
2003 Sales: $1,548,500	2003 Profits: $170,600	Parent Company: NEWS CORP

SALARIES/BENEFITS:

Pension Plan: Y	ESOP Stock Plan:	Profit Sharing:	Top Exec. Salary: $588,099	Bonus: $412,000
Savings Plan: Y	Stock Purch. Plan: Y		Second Exec. Salary: $547,692	Bonus: $299,250

OTHER THOUGHTS:

Apparent Women Officers or Directors: 6
Hot Spot for Advancement for Women/Minorities: Y

LOCATIONS: ("Y" = Yes)

West:	Southwest:	Midwest:	Southeast:	Northeast:	International:
Y				Y	Y

Note: Financial information, benefits and other data can change quickly and may vary from those stated here.

DREAMWORKS ANIMATION SKG INC
www.dreamworksanimation.com
Industry Group Code: 512110 Ranks within this company's industry group: Sales: 8   Profits: 4

Print Media/Publishing:	Movies:		Equipment/Supplies:	Broadcast/Cable:	Music/Audio:	Sports/Games/Gambling:
Newspapers:	Movie Theaters:		Equipment/Supplies:	Broadcast TV:	Music Production:	Games/Sports:
Magazines:	Movie Production:	Y	Gambling Equipment:	Cable TV:	Retail Music:	Retail Games Stores:
Books:	TV/Video Prod.:		Special Services:	Satellite Broadcast:	Retail Audio Equip.:	Stadiums/Teams:
Book Stores:	Video Rental:		Advertising Services:	Radio:	Music Print./Dist.:	Gambling/Casinos:
Distribution/Printing:	Video Distribution:		Info. Sys. Software:	Online Information:	Multimedia:	Rides/Theme Parks:

TYPES OF BUSINESS:
Animated Film Production
Animation Software

BRANDS/DIVISIONS/AFFILIATES:
DreamWorks Studios
EMOtion
Nile
Virtual Studio Collaboration
Wallace & Gromit: Curse of the Were-Rabbit
Shrek
Over the Hedge
Paramount Pictures Corp

CONTACTS: Note: Officers with more than one job title may be intentionally listed here more than once.
Jeffrey Katzenberg, CEO
Ann Daly, COO
Lew Coleman, Pres.
Lew Coleman, Acting CFO
Katherine Kendrick, General Counsel/Sec.
Roger A. Enrico, Chmn.

Phone: 818-695-5000	Fax: 818-695-9944
Toll-Free:	
Address: 1000 Flower St., Glendale, CA 91201 US	

GROWTH PLANS/SPECIAL FEATURES:
DreamWorks Animation SKG, Inc. develops and produces computer-generated (CG) animated feature films that are distributed and marketed by Paramount. The firm uses proprietary software to produce its films, such as EMOtion, Nile and Virtual Studio Collaboration. Operations take place at two facilities in Glendale and Redwood City, California. The company has released a total of 13 animated films, including seven that were CG-only and one direct-to-video title. Films include such box office hits as Antz, Shrek and Shrek 2 (the third highest grossing film of all time, as of 2007). DreamWorks Animation has also collaborated with Aardman Animations to release Chicken Run and Wallace & Gromit: Curse of the Were-Rabbit. The company's recent films include Shark Tale (its second highest-grossing film), Madagascar, Shrek the Third (the best opening weekend ever for an animated film as of 2007) and Bee Movie. Over the Hedge, released in May 2006, was a modest hit grossing approximately $155 million domestically. Flushed Away, a film about sewer rats produced in conjunction with Aardman Animations, was released in November 2006. The firm has several films in production, including, Kung Fu Panda, scheduled for release in 2008; Madagascar 2, 2008; Monsters vs. Aliens, 2009; and How to Train Your Dragon, 2009. In addition, DreamWorks Animation has rights to Punk Farm and Mr. Peabody & Sherman. The company has a multi-picture, multi-year promotional alliance with Kellogg Company that began with the release of Flushed Away. The firm's distribution agreement with Paramount runs through 2012. In November 2006, DreamWorks Animation announced that it was developing Shrek the Halls, a television Christmas special. The movie premiered on ABC in December 2007.

DreamWorks Animation offers paid 10-12 week animation and engineering internships in the spring, summer and fall, as well as an entry-level outreach program for recent graduates.

FINANCIALS: Sales and profits are in thousands of dollars—add 000 to get the full amount. 2007 Note: Financial information for 2007 was not available for all companies at press time.

2007 Sales: $	2007 Profits: $	U.S. Stock Ticker: DWA
2006 Sales: $394,842	2006 Profits: $15,125	Int'l Ticker: Int'l Exchange:
2005 Sales: $462,316	2005 Profits: $104,585	Employees: 1,300
2004 Sales: $1,078,160	2004 Profits: $333,000	Fiscal Year Ends: 12/31
2003 Sales: $301,000	2003 Profits: $-187,100	Parent Company:

SALARIES/BENEFITS:

Pension Plan:	ESOP Stock Plan:	Profit Sharing:	Top Exec. Salary: $1,250,000	Bonus: $
Savings Plan:	Stock Purch. Plan:		Second Exec. Salary: $1,000,000	Bonus: $

OTHER THOUGHTS:
Apparent Women Officers or Directors: 4
Hot Spot for Advancement for Women/Minorities: Y

LOCATIONS: ("Y" = Yes)

West:	Southwest:	Midwest:	Southeast:	Northeast:	International:
Y					

Note: Financial information, benefits and other data can change quickly and may vary from those stated here.

DREAMWORKS SKG

www.dreamworks.com

Industry Group Code: 512110 Ranks within this company's industry group: Sales: Profits:

Print Media/Publishing:	Movies:		Equipment/Supplies:	Broadcast/Cable:	Music/Audio:	Sports/Games/Gambling:
Newspapers:	Movie Theaters:	Y	Equipment/Supplies:	Broadcast TV:	Music Production:	Games/Sports:
Magazines:	Movie Production:	Y	Gambling Equipment:	Cable TV:	Retail Music:	Retail Games Stores:
Books:	TV/Video Prod.:	Y	Special Services:	Satellite Broadcast:	Retail Audio Equip.:	Stadiums/Teams:
Book Stores:	Video Rental:		Advertising Services:	Radio:	Music Print./Dist.:	Gambling/Casinos:
Distribution/Printing:	Video Distribution:	Y	Info. Sys. Software:	Online Information:	Multimedia:	Rides/Theme Parks:

TYPES OF BUSINESS:

Film Production & Distribution
Television Production
Foreign Film Distribution

BRANDS/DIVISIONS/AFFILIATES:

DreamWorks Movies
DreamWorks TV
Paramount
Viacom
Dreamworks SKG

CONTACTS: Note: Officers with more than one job title may be intentionally listed here more than once.

Stacey Snider, CEO
Steven Spielberg, Principal/Co-founder
Christine Birch, Pres., Mktg.
Adam Goodman, Dir.-Production
David Geffen, Principal/Co-founder
Jeffrey Katzenberg, Principal/Co-founder
Stacey Snider, Co-Chmn.

Phone: 818-733-7000	Fax: 818-695-7574
Toll-Free:	
Address: 1000 Flower St., Glendale, CA 91201 US	

GROWTH PLANS/SPECIAL FEATURES:

DreamWorks, SKG, also known as DreamWorks Studios, is a subsidiary of Viacom. DreamWorks, SKG was formerly affiliated with DreamWorks Animation, SKG, the latter of which is now a separate entity which trades publicly. DreamWorks SKG is a leading producer of live-action motion pictures; network and cable television programming; home video and DVD entertainment; and consumer products. It was formed with the intention to create an artist-friendly studio to develop, produce and distribute film and music entertainment. DreamWorks was founded by Steven Spielberg, film director and producer; Jeffrey Katzenberg, a former Disney film executive and animation guru; and David Geffen, a recording industry executive. The firm has major offices in Glendale, Beverly Hills and Universal City, California; New York, New York; Nashville, Tennessee; London, England; and Toronto, Canada. The firm's most celebrated films include Oscar-winners American Beauty and Gladiator. DreamWorks TV produces network and cable television programs including Las Vegas and Into the West. Go Fish Pictures is the new distribution arm of DreamWorks, focusing largely on releasing foreign films, especially Japanese anime, in the U.S. In January 2006, DreamWorks separated itself from DreamWorks Animation SKG, which produces all of the company's animated works, including such hits as Shrek and Bee Movie. The company is further streamlining operations, having sold its record label and video game business and dramatically reducing television production.

DreamWorks offers both paid and unpaid internships for college students, with opportunities in almost all divisions of the film production business.

FINANCIALS: Sales and profits are in thousands of dollars—add 000 to get the full amount. 2007 Note: Financial information for 2007 was not available for all companies at press time.

2007 Sales: $	2007 Profits: $	U.S. Stock Ticker: Subsidiary
2006 Sales: $	2006 Profits: $	Int'l Ticker: Int'l Exchange:
2005 Sales: $	2005 Profits: $	Employees: 1,100
2004 Sales: $1,110,000	2004 Profits: $	Fiscal Year Ends: 12/31
2003 Sales: $1,250,000	2003 Profits: $	Parent Company: VIACOM INC

SALARIES/BENEFITS:

Pension Plan:	ESOP Stock Plan:	Profit Sharing:	Top Exec. Salary: $	Bonus: $
Savings Plan:	Stock Purch. Plan:		Second Exec. Salary: $	Bonus: $

OTHER THOUGHTS:

Apparent Women Officers or Directors:
Hot Spot for Advancement for Women/Minorities: Y

LOCATIONS: ("Y" = Yes)

West:	Southwest:	Midwest:	Southeast:	Northeast:	International:
Y			Y	Y	Y

DTS INC

www.dtsonline.com

Industry Group Code: 334310 Ranks within this company's industry group: Sales: 11   Profits: 7

Print Media/Publishing:	Movies:	Equipment/Supplies:		Broadcast/Cable:	Music/Audio:	Sports/Games/Gambling:
Newspapers:	Movie Theaters:	Equipment/Supplies:	Y	Broadcast TV:	Music Production:	Games/Sports:
Magazines:	Movie Production:	Gambling Equipment:		Cable TV:	Retail Music:	Retail Games Stores:
Books:	TV/Video Prod.:	Special Services:	Y	Satellite Broadcast:	Retail Audio Equip.:	Stadiums/Teams:
Book Stores:	Video Rental:	Advertising Services:		Radio:	Music Print./Dist.:	Gambling/Casinos:
Distribution/Printing:	Video Distribution:	Info. Sys. Software:		Online Information:	Multimedia:	Rides/Theme Parks:

TYPES OF BUSINESS:

Audio & Video Equipment, Manufacturing
Digital Multi-Channel (Surround Sound) Audio Technology
Digital Remastering
Video Restoration & Enhancement

BRANDS/DIVISIONS/AFFILIATES:

Digital Theater Systems
Jurassic Park
20th Century Fox
Buena Vista Pictures
Warner Bros Entertainment Inc
Pioneer Corporation
Sony Corporation
Yamaha Corporation

CONTACTS: Note: Officers with more than one job title may be intentionally listed here more than once.

Jon E. Kirchner, CEO
Jon E. Kirchner, Pres.
Melvin L. (Mel) Flanigan, CFO
Sharon Kong Faltemier, Sr. VP-Human Resources
Richard J. (Rick) Beaton, Sr. VP-R&D
Nicholas Clay, Sr. VP-Tech. & Strategy
Jan Wissmuller, Sr. VP-Prod. Dev.
Jan Wissmuller, Sr. VP-Eng.
Blake A. Welcher, General Counsel/Corp. Sec./Exec. VP
Andrea Nee, Exec. VP-Oper.
Patrick J. Watson, Sr. VP-Strategy & Bus. Dev.
Melvin L. (Mel) Flanigan, Exec. VP-Finance
Donald M. Bird, Sr. VP-Cinema Div.
Brian D. Towne, Sr. VP/Gen. Mgr.-Consumer Div.
William Neighbors, Pres., DTS Digital Cinema
John Lowry, Chief Technologist
Daniel E. Slusser, Chmn.
Kin Chan, Managing Dir.-Greater China

Phone: 818-735-4287	Fax:
Toll-Free:	
Address: 5171 Clareton Dr., Agoura Hills, CA 91301 US	

GROWTH PLANS/SPECIAL FEATURES:

DTS, Inc., formerly Digital Theater Systems, is a leading provider of high-quality digital multi-channel audio technology, products and services for entertainment markets worldwide. The company provides products and services to film studios, production companies and movie theaters to produce and play back digital surround-sound soundtracks for films. The first movie to use the firm's technology was Steven Spielberg's Jurassic Park in 1993. The company licenses its sound technology to all major film distributors in the U.S., including 20th Century Fox, Buena Vista Pictures, Warner Bros. Pictures and many international distributors. The firm's playback systems for DTS-formatted soundtracks have been installed in over 28,000 movie theaters worldwide. DTS also licenses its technology to consumer electronics manufacturers for inclusion in products such as audio/video receivers, DVD players and home theater systems. Its technology enables consumers to enjoy movies, video games and music in DTS multi-channel format. The company's consumer business has grown to become its largest business segment. To date, DTS has entered into licensing agreements with substantially all of the major consumer audio electronics manufacturers, including Pioneer, Sony and Yamaha. The company's technology is also found in over 115 music titles in various genres and DVDs for the consumer retail market. DTS licenses titles by well-known recording artists, then re-mixes and releases these titles in its digital multi-channel format. The company's subsidiary, DTS Digital Images, provides restoration and enhancement services on film and digital movies. These services allow archive material to be presented in high quality, high definition formats. In February 2007, DTS announced plans to sell its DTS Digital Cinema business.

DTS offers its employees a flexible spending account, an employee assistance program, discounted health club membership, a cafeteria plan and medical, dental, vision, disability, long term care and life insurance.

FINANCIALS: Sales and profits are in thousands of dollars—add 000 to get the full amount. 2007 Note: Financial information for 2007 was not available for all companies at press time.

2007 Sales: $	2007 Profits: $	**U.S. Stock Ticker:** DTSI
2006 Sales: $78,314	2006 Profits: $3,024	**Int'l Ticker:** Int'l Exchange:
2005 Sales: $75,252	2005 Profits: $7,908	Employees: 325
2004 Sales: $61,431	2004 Profits: $9,976	Fiscal Year Ends: 12/31
2003 Sales: $51,700	2003 Profits: $8,700	Parent Company:

SALARIES/BENEFITS:

Pension Plan:	ESOP Stock Plan:	Profit Sharing:	Top Exec. Salary: $359,338	Bonus: $
Savings Plan: Y	Stock Purch. Plan:		Second Exec. Salary: $250,962	Bonus: $42,000

OTHER THOUGHTS:

Apparent Women Officers or Directors: 1
Hot Spot for Advancement for Women/Minorities:

LOCATIONS: ("Y" = Yes)

West:	Southwest:	Midwest:	Southeast:	Northeast:	International:
Y					Y

E W SCRIPPS CO

www.scripps.com

Industry Group Code: 511110 Ranks within this company's industry group: Sales: 7   Profits: 4

Print Media/Publishing:		Movies:		Equipment/Supplies:		Broadcast/Cable:		Music/Audio:	Sports/Games/Gambling:
Newspapers:	Y	Movie Theaters:		Equipment/Supplies:		Broadcast TV:	Y	Music Production:	Games/Sports:
Magazines:	Y	Movie Production:		Gambling Equipment:		Cable TV:	Y	Retail Music:	Retail Games Stores:
Books:		TV/Video Prod.:	Y	Special Services:	Y	Satellite Broadcast:		Retail Audio Equip.:	Stadiums/Teams:
Book Stores:		Video Rental:		Advertising Services:		Radio:		Music Print./Dist.:	Gambling/Casinos:
Distribution/Printing:		Video Distribution:		Info. Sys. Software:		Online Information:		Multimedia:	Rides/Theme Parks:

TYPES OF BUSINESS:

Newspaper Publishing
Broadcast Television Stations
Television & Online Retail
Online Media
Newswire Service
Venture Capital
Newspapers

BRANDS/DIVISIONS/AFFILIATES:

Scripps Howard News Service
Home & Garden Television
Do It Yourself Network
Food Network
Fine Living
Fum Machineworks, Inc.
Recipezaar.com
uSwitch.com

CONTACTS: Note: Officers with more than one job title may be intentionally listed here more than once.

Kenneth W. Lowe, CEO
Richard A. Boehne, COO
Kenneth W. Lowe, Pres.
Joseph G. NeCastro, CFO
Jennifer L. Weber, Sr. VP-Human Resources
Mark Hale, Sr. VP-Tech. Oper.
B. Jeff Craig, CTO/VP
Joseph G. NeCastro, Sr. VP-Finance & Admin.
A. B. Cruz, III, General Counsel/Sr. VP
Richard A. Boehne, Exec. VP-Oper.
Kenneth W. Lowe, Exec. VP-Corp. Dev.
Timothy E. Strautberg, VP-Comm.
Timothy E. Strautberg, VP-Investor Rel.
Lori A. Hickock, VP/Controller
Tim Peterman, Sr. VP-Interactive Media
William B. Peterson, Sr. VP-Television
Douglas F. Lyons, VP-Finance & Admin.-Interactive Media
Mark G. Contreras, Sr. VP-Newspapers
William R. Burleigh, Chmn.

Phone: 513-977-3000	Fax: 513-977-3721
Toll-Free:	
Address: 312 Walnut St., 2800 Scripps Ctr., Cincinnati, OH 45202 US	

GROWTH PLANS/SPECIAL FEATURES:

The E.W. Scripps Company (Scripps) operates in five segments: newspapers, broadcast television, national television networks, interactive media and television retailing. The company operates 18 daily newspapers in the U.S. with a combined circulation of approximately 1.4 million daily subscribers. The firm also publishes several weekly and semiweekly community newspapers and operates the Scripps Howard News Service, the second-largest supplemental wire service in the U.S., covering stories in Washington, D.C., the U.S. and abroad. The company's newspapers each operate Internet sites featuring content included in their publications. Scripps Networks includes five national TV networks distributed by cable and satellite systems, including Home & Garden Television (HGTV); the Do It Yourself Network (DIY); the Food Network; and Fine Living and Great American Country (GAC). The Scripps Network stations also operate three web sites: FoodTV.com, HGTV.com and DIYnet.com. The broadcast television group includes 10 TV stations, nine of which are affiliated with national networks. The segment's stations derive revenue from local and national advertising. Additionally, Scripps syndicates over 150 comic strips, including Peanuts (which provides 95% of the firm's licensing revenues) and Dilbert through United Media and news features through United Feature Syndicate. Through Scripps Ventures, the company invests in new businesses, centered on early-stage Internet companies. The Scripps family owns approximately 87% of the company. In July 2007, Scripps Networks acquired Fum Machineworks, Inc., dba Recipezaar.com, a user-generated recipe and community site featuring more than 230,000 recipes. In October 2007, the firm announced plans to split into two companies: one comprising its cable networks and shopping sites, and the other with its local television stations and newspapers.

FINANCIALS: Sales and profits are in thousands of dollars—add 000 to get the full amount. 2007 Note: Financial information for 2007 was not available for all companies at press time.

2007 Sales: $	2007 Profits: $	U.S. Stock Ticker: SSP
2006 Sales: $2,498,077	2006 Profits: $353,220	Int'l Ticker: Int'l Exchange:
2005 Sales: $2,154,634	2005 Profits: $249,153	Employees: 9,000
2004 Sales: $1,874,351	2004 Profits: $303,800	Fiscal Year Ends: 12/31
2003 Sales: $1,874,845	2003 Profits: $270,815	Parent Company:

SALARIES/BENEFITS:

Pension Plan: Y	ESOP Stock Plan: Y	Profit Sharing:	Top Exec. Salary: $1,050,000	Bonus: $1,260,000
Savings Plan:	Stock Purch. Plan:		Second Exec. Salary: $650,000	Bonus: $455,000

OTHER THOUGHTS:

Apparent Women Officers or Directors: 5
Hot Spot for Advancement for Women/Minorities: Y

LOCATIONS: ("Y" = Yes)

West:	Southwest:	Midwest:	Southeast:	Northeast:	International:
Y	Y	Y	Y	Y	Y

Note: Financial information, benefits and other data can change quickly and may vary from those stated here.

EBSCO INDUSTRIES INC

www.ebscoind.com

Industry Group Code: 422920 Ranks within this company's industry group: Sales: 1 Profits:

Print Media/Publishing:		Movies:		Equipment/Supplies:		Broadcast/Cable:	Music/Audio:	Sports/Games/Gambling:
Newspapers:		Movie Theaters:		Equipment/Supplies:		Broadcast TV:	Music Production:	Games/Sports:
Magazines:	Y	Movie Production:		Gambling Equipment:		Cable TV:	Retail Music:	Retail Games Stores:
Books:	Y	TV/Video Prod.:	Y	Special Services:	Y	Satellite Broadcast:	Retail Audio Equip.:	Stadiums/Teams:
Book Stores:		Video Rental:		Advertising Services:		Radio:	Music Print./Dist.:	Gambling/Casinos:
Distribution/Printing:		Video Distribution:		Info. Sys. Software:		Online Information:	Multimedia:	Rides/Theme Parks:

TYPES OF BUSINESS:

Online Information Publishing
Publishing & Printing Services
Subscription Services
Online Bookstores
Information Services & Databases
Manufacturing-Sporting Goods & Firearms
Manufacturing-Furniture
Marketing Services

BRANDS/DIVISIONS/AFFILIATES:

EBSCO Information Services
EBSCO Magazine Express
Grand View Media Group
EBSCO Reception Room Subscription Services
Vulcan Service
EBSCO Subscription Services
EBSCO Publishing
ANB Insurance Services, Inc.

CONTACTS: *Note: Officers with more than one job title may be intentionally listed here more than once.*

F. Dixon Brooke, Jr., CEO
F. Dixon Brooke, Jr., Pres.
Richard L. Bozzelli, CFO/VP
John C. Thompson, VP/General Mgr.-Human Resources
John Fitts, VP/General Mgr.-Info. Systems & Svcs.
Becky Caldarello, VP/General Mgr.-Admin Svcs.
Joe K. Weed, VP/General Mgr.-Corp. Com.
Carol M. Johnson, Chief Accounting Officer/VP
Matt Carrington, Dir.-Acquisitions
Brooks Knapp, VP/General Mgr.-EBSCO Realty
James T. Stephens, Chmn.

Phone: 205-991-6600	Fax: 205-995-1636
Toll-Free:	
Address: 5724 Hwy. 280 E., Birmingham, AL 35242 US	

GROWTH PLANS/SPECIAL FEATURES:

EBSCO Industries, Inc. competes in a wide variety of markets including furniture and gun manufacturing, commercial insurance, publishing, fishing lures, online bookstores, and nursing and allied health databases. However, publishing is EBSCO's main focus. The firm operates through eight divisions: information services, manufacturing, general services, publishing services, outdoor products, real estate, business to business and corporate services. The information services segment provides books, databases, subscriptions and e-resource management to libraries and other organizations through EBSCO Information Services, EBSCO Subscription Services and EBSCO Publishing. The Publishing Services division provides publishing and related services as well as specialty marketing services. It offers magazine publishing services though Grand View Media Group and magazine subscription services through EBSCO Magazine Express, EBSCO Reception Room Subscription Services and Vulcan Service. Publications tend to focus on outdoors and hunting topics. Among other offerings, the General Services division provides insurance, military products and services, textbook distribution and promotional merchandise. The Real Estate division has interests in two planned communities, Mt. Laurel and Alys Beach. The firm's Manufacturing Division includes companies that develop a variety of products including wild game decoys, cameras and accessories, steel joists and specialty furniture. The Outdoor Products division manufactures a variety of sporting goods including rifle barrels, fishing lures and treestands. Commonwealth Productions, a television production company falls under Outdoor Products division. The Corporate Services division is responsible for all corporate functions within EBSCO Industries as a whole. The Business to Business segment provides office furniture and products via B2B Essentials; printing, binding and laminating equipment through subsidiary NSC International; specialty furniture through subsidiaries H. Wilson and Luxor; and trade show and literature displays through Siegel Display Products. The company recently acquired ANB Insurance Services, Inc.

EBSCO provides its employees with benefits including profit sharing; medical, dental, vision and life insurance; credit union membership; and tuition reimbursement.

FINANCIALS: Sales and profits are in thousands of dollars—add 000 to get the full amount. 2007 Note: Financial information for 2007 was not available for all companies at press time.

2007 Sales: $	2007 Profits: $	U.S. Stock Ticker: Private
2006 Sales: $2,300,000	2006 Profits: $	Int'l Ticker: Int'l Exchange:
2005 Sales: $2,000,000	2005 Profits: $	Employees: 5,000
2004 Sales: $1,800,000	2004 Profits: $	Fiscal Year Ends: 6/30
2003 Sales: $1,400,000	2003 Profits: $	Parent Company:

SALARIES/BENEFITS:

Pension Plan:	ESOP Stock Plan:	Profit Sharing: Y	Top Exec. Salary: $	Bonus: $
Savings Plan:	Stock Purch. Plan:		Second Exec. Salary: $	Bonus: $

OTHER THOUGHTS:

Apparent Women Officers or Directors: 2
Hot Spot for Advancement for Women/Minorities:

LOCATIONS: ("Y" = Yes)

West:	Southwest:	Midwest:	Southeast:	Northeast:	International:
			Y		

ECHOSTAR COMMUNICATIONS CORP www.dishnetwork.com

Industry Group Code: 513220 Ranks within this company's industry group: Sales: 5 Profits: 8

Print Media/Publishing:	Movies:	Equipment/Supplies:		Broadcast/Cable:	Music/Audio:	Sports/Games/Gambling:
Newspapers:	Movie Theaters:	Equipment/Supplies:	Y	Broadcast TV:	Music Production:	Games/Sports:
Magazines:	Movie Production:	Gambling Equipment:		Cable TV:	Retail Music:	Retail Games Stores:
Books:	TV/Video Prod.:	Special Services:		Satellite Broadcast:	Retail Audio Equip.:	Stadiums/Teams:
Book Stores:	Video Rental:	Advertising Services:		Radio:	Music Print./Dist.:	Gambling/Casinos:
Distribution/Printing:	Video Distribution:	Info. Sys. Software:		Online Information:	Multimedia:	Rides/Theme Parks:

TYPES OF BUSINESS:

Satellite Broadcasting
Satellite Receivers
DSL Internet
Satellite-Based Internet

BRANDS/DIVISIONS/AFFILIATES:

DISH Network Services Corp.
EchoStar Technologies Corp.
EchoStar Direct Broadcast Satellite System
TU Media Corp.
MobileDISH
RaySat

CONTACTS: *Note: Officers with more than one job title may be intentionally listed here more than once.*

Charles W. Ergen, CEO
Carl Vogel, Pres.
Bernie Han, CFO
James DeFranco, Exec. VP-Sales
Stephen Wood, Exec. VP-Human Resources
R. Stanton Dodge, General Counsel/Exec. VP/Sec.
Carol Kline, Exec. VP-Oper.
Tom Cullen, Exec. VP-Corp. Dev.
Kathie Gonzalez, Media Contact
Michael Kelly, Exec. VP-Commercial & Bus. Svcs.
Mark Jackson, Pres., EchoStar Technologies Corporation
David J. Rayner, Exec. VP-Installation & Svcs. Network
James DeFranco, Exec. VP-Dist.
Charles W. Ergen, Chmn.
Steven B. Schaver, Pres., EchoStar Int'l Corporation

Phone: 303-723-1000	Fax: 303-723-1399
Toll-Free: 800-333-3474	
Address: 9601 S. Meridian Blvd., Englewood, CO 80112 US	

GROWTH PLANS/SPECIAL FEATURES:

EchoStar Communications Corporation and its subsidiaries deliver satellite television products and services to over 13.4 million subscribers. The company refers to its entire line of services as the EchoStar Direct Broadcast Satellite System, which operates out of two units: DISH Network Services Corp. and EchoStar Technologies Corp. DISH Network offers direct broadcast satellite (DBS) subscription television service throughout the U.S. DBS employs frequency allocation and wide spacing between satellites, which permits higher-powered transmissions than other satellite services and allows for reception with a small dish. DISH Network's 14 owned or leased satellites, with plans to construct or lease six more by 2008, enable it to provide over 2,500 channels of video and audio services to subscribers throughout the U.S. and worldwide, including extensive Spanish-language programming and over 130 channels in foreign languages. EchoStar Technologies, the firm's engineering division, focuses on the design of satellite receivers, which are necessary for consumers to receive DISH Network programming, and the sale of set-top boxes to international satellite operators in the consumer market. Satellite services provide video, audio and data services to business television customers and other satellite users. In 2007, EchoStar invested $40 million in TU Media Corp., South Korea's only satellite digital multimedia broadcasting provider, to become the firm's second largest shareholder. In April 2007, EchoStar partnered with Google to establish the first automated system to buy, sell, deliver and measure television ads for EchoStar's satellite programming networks. In May 2007, EchoStar and DISH Network launched MobileDISH, an in-car satellite system that uses RaySat to work even when the vehicle is in motion.

EchoStar employees receive benefits such as a free satellite TV system and programming; medical, dental, and vision insurance; flexible spending options; employee assistance plans; and training and development through DISH University.

FINANCIALS: Sales and profits are in thousands of dollars—add 000 to get the full amount. 2007 Note: Financial information for 2007 was not available for all companies at press time.

2007 Sales: $	2007 Profits: $	**U.S. Stock Ticker: DISH**
2006 Sales: $9,818,486	2006 Profits: $608,272	Int'l Ticker: Int'l Exchange:
2005 Sales: $8,447,175	2005 Profits: $1,514,540	Employees: 21,000
2004 Sales: $7,158,471	2004 Profits: $214,769	Fiscal Year Ends: 12/31
2003 Sales: $5,739,296	2003 Profits: $707,548	Parent Company:

SALARIES/BENEFITS:

Pension Plan:	ESOP Stock Plan:	Profit Sharing: Y	Top Exec. Salary: $550,000	Bonus: $
Savings Plan: Y	Stock Purch. Plan: Y		Second Exec. Salary: $383,079	Bonus: $133,000

OTHER THOUGHTS:

Apparent Women Officers or Directors: 1
Hot Spot for Advancement for Women/Minorities:

LOCATIONS: ("Y" = Yes)

West:	Southwest:	Midwest:	Southeast:	Northeast:	International:
Y	Y	Y	Y	Y	Y

EDUCATIONAL DEVELOPMENT CORP   www.edcpub.com

Industry Group Code: 511130 Ranks within this company's industry group: Sales: 7 Profits: 7

Print Media/Publishing:		Movies:	Equipment/Supplies:	Broadcast/Cable:	Music/Audio:	Sports/Games/Gambling:
Newspapers:		Movie Theaters:	Equipment/Supplies:	Broadcast TV:	Music Production:	Games/Sports:
Magazines:		Movie Production:	Gambling Equipment:	Cable TV:	Retail Music:	Retail Games Stores:
Books:	Y	TV/Video Prod.:	Special Services:	Satellite Broadcast:	Retail Audio Equip.:	Stadiums/Teams:
Book Stores:		Video Rental:	Advertising Services:	Radio:	Music Print./Dist.:	Gambling/Casinos:
Distribution/Printing:		Video Distribution:	Info. Sys. Software:	Online Information:	Multimedia:	Rides/Theme Parks:

TYPES OF BUSINESS:

Children's Book Publishing
Book Distribution

BRANDS/DIVISIONS/AFFILIATES:

Usborne Publishing Limited
Usborne Kid Kits

CONTACTS: *Note: Officers with more than one job title may be intentionally listed here more than once.*

Randall W. White, CEO
Randall W. White, Pres.
Marilyn Welborn, Principal Financial Officer/Controller
Marilyn Welborn, Sec.
Randall W. White, Treas.
Ronald T. McDaniel, VP-Publishing Div.
Randall W. White, Chmn.

Phone: 918-622-4522	Fax: 918-665-7919
Toll-Free: 800-475-4522	
Address: 10302 E. 55th Pl., Tulsa, OK 74146-6515 US	

GROWTH PLANS/SPECIAL FEATURES:

Educational Development Corp. (EDC) is the sole U.S. trade publisher and distributor of a line of children's books produced in the U.K. by Usborne Publishing Limited. The company operates two divisions, the home business division and the publishing division. The home business division distributes books through independent consultants who hold book showings in individual homes, as well as through book fairs, direct sales and Internet sales. The division also distributes these titles to schools and public libraries. The division has approximately 9,800 consultants in all 50 states. The publishing division markets books to approximately 12,000 bookstores, toy stores, specialty stores and other retail outlets including museums and schools. EDC currently carries over 2,000 different book titles. EDC also distributes a product called Usborne Kid Kits. These Kid Kits take an Usborne book and combine it with specially selected items and/or toys that complement the information contained in the book. The kits are packaged in a reusable vinyl bag, with some kits also available in a box package. Currently, 60 different Kid Kits are available. The company operates out of its 105,000-square-foot office and warehouse facilities in Tulsa, Oklahoma.

FINANCIALS: Sales and profits are in thousands of dollars—add 000 to get the full amount. 2007 Note: Financial information for 2007 was not available for all companies at press time.

2007 Sales: $31,404	2007 Profits: $2,407	**U.S. Stock Ticker: EDUC**
2006 Sales: $31,789	2006 Profits: $2,398	**Int'l Ticker:** Int'l Exchange:
2005 Sales: $31,651	2005 Profits: $2,406	**Employees:** 82
2004 Sales: $30,362	2004 Profits: $2,373	**Fiscal Year Ends: 2/28**
2003 Sales: $24,880	2003 Profits: $2,038	**Parent Company:**

SALARIES/BENEFITS:

Pension Plan:	ESOP Stock Plan:	Profit Sharing:	Top Exec. Salary: $150,000	Bonus: $22,000
Savings Plan: Y	Stock Purch. Plan:		Second Exec. Salary: $	Bonus: $

OTHER THOUGHTS:

Apparent Women Officers or Directors: 1
Hot Spot for Advancement for Women/Minorities:

LOCATIONS: ("Y" = Yes)

West:	Southwest:	Midwest:	Southeast:	Northeast:	International:
	Y				

ELECTRONIC ARTS INC

www.ea.com

Industry Group Code: 511208 Ranks within this company's industry group: Sales: 2 Profits: 2

Print Media/Publishing:	Movies:	Equipment/Supplies:	Broadcast/Cable:	Music/Audio:	Sports/Games/Gambling:	
Newspapers:	Movie Theaters:	Equipment/Supplies:	Broadcast TV:	Music Production:	Games/Sports:	Y
Magazines:	Movie Production:	Gambling Equipment:	Cable TV:	Retail Music:	Retail Games Stores:	
Books:	TV/Video Prod.:	Special Services:	Satellite Broadcast:	Retail Audio Equip.:	Stadiums/Teams:	
Book Stores:	Video Rental:	Advertising Services:	Radio:	Music Print./Dist.:	Gambling/Casinos:	
Distribution/Printing:	Video Distribution:	Info. Sys. Software:	Online Information:	Multimedia:	Rides/Theme Parks:	

TYPES OF BUSINESS:

Computer Software-Video Games
Online Interactive Games
E-Commerce Sales
Mobile Games

BRANDS/DIVISIONS/AFFILIATES:

EA GAMES
EA SPORTS
EA SPORTS BIG
SIMS (The)
ea.com
Pogo
Phenomic Game Development
Singshot Media

CONTACTS: *Note: Officers with more than one job title may be intentionally listed here more than once.*

Lawrence F. Probst, III, CEO
Lawrence F. Probst, III, Pres.
Warren Jenson, CFO/Exec. VP
Gabrielle Toledano, Exec. VP-Human Resources
Warren Jenson, Chief Admin. Officer
Steve Bene, Acting General Counsel/VP
Joel Linzner, Sr. VP-Bus.
Peter Moore, Pres., EA Sports
V. Paul Lee, Pres., Worldwide Studios
Nancy Smith, Exec. VP-The Sims Franchise
Gerhard Florin, Exec. VP-International Publishing
Lawrence Probst, Chmn.
Hubert Larenaudie, Pres., Online-Asia

Phone: 650-628-1500	Fax: 650-628-1415
Toll-Free:	
Address: 209 Redwood Shores Pkwy., Redwood City, CA 94065 US	

GROWTH PLANS/SPECIAL FEATURES:

Electronic Arts, Inc. (EA) creates, markets and distributes entertainment software. The company currently develops software for 12 different hardware platforms: Sony PlayStation, PlayStation 2, PlayStation 3; PSP (Playstation Portable); Nintendo Wii, GameCube, DS and Game Boy; Microsoft Xbox and Xbox 360; Nokia N-Gage; and the PC. EA Studios' products fall under the EA GAMES, EA SPORTS and EA SPORTS BIG categories. EA GAMES produces the Medal of Honor, the Need for Speed and The SIMS series. Recent EA SPORTS tittles are Madden NFL 2007, NCAA Football 07 and Tiger Woods PGA Tour 07; and recent EA SPORTS BIG games include SSX Blur and NBA Street Homecourt. EA also distributes a number of co-published titles and titles developed by affiliated labels. The company's designers regularly work with celebrities and sports organizations to develop gaming products. EA has contracts with FIFA, NASCAR, PGA TOUR, Tiger Woods, Warner Bros. and the NFL, among others. The firm's second business segment, ea.com, conducts online and e-commerce activities, developing, publishing and distributing online interactive games, such as Pogo. In August 2006, EA acquired Phenomic Game Development, makers of the strategy game franchises The Settlers and SpellForce; and in February 2007, the company acquired Singshot Media, a San Francisco-based online karaoke community. In September 2006, the company announced plans to bring The SIMS 2 and Pogo.com games to in-flight entertainment worldwide. Also, in March 2007, AE began an online mobile phone service called EA SPORTS Link, which allows U.S. Cingular customers to trade sports game information and challenge one another to live, networked games.

EA offers its employees on-site fitness facilities and performance bonuses. In addition, the company offers extensive training programs, discounts on game systems, education reimbursement and a company store. Full-time employees receive a paid week off at Christmas.

FINANCIALS: Sales and profits are in thousands of dollars—add 000 to get the full amount. 2007 Note: Financial information for 2007 was not available for all companies at press time.

2007 Sales: $3,091,000	2007 Profits: $76,000	**U.S. Stock Ticker: ERTS**
2006 Sales: $2,951,000	2006 Profits: $236,000	**Int'l Ticker:** Int'l Exchange:
2005 Sales: $3,129,000	2005 Profits: $504,000	Employees: 7,900
2004 Sales: $2,957,141	2004 Profits: $577,292	Fiscal Year Ends: 3/31
2003 Sales: $2,482,200	2003 Profits: $317,100	Parent Company:

SALARIES/BENEFITS:

Pension Plan:	ESOP Stock Plan:	Profit Sharing:	Top Exec. Salary: $743,926	Bonus: $
Savings Plan: Y	Stock Purch. Plan: Y		Second Exec. Salary: $704,146	Bonus: $

OTHER THOUGHTS:

Apparent Women Officers or Directors: 2
Hot Spot for Advancement for Women/Minorities: Y

LOCATIONS: ("Y" = Yes)

West:	Southwest:	Midwest:	Southeast:	Northeast:	International:
Y	Y	Y	Y	Y	Y

EMAP PLC

www.emap.com

Industry Group Code: 511120 **Ranks within this company's industry group:** Sales: 5   Profits: 2

Print Media/Publishing:		Movies:	Equipment/Supplies:		Broadcast/Cable:		Music/Audio:		Sports/Games/Gambling:
Newspapers:		Movie Theaters:	Equipment/Supplies:		Broadcast TV:		Music Production:		Games/Sports:
Magazines:	Y	Movie Production:	Gambling Equipment:		Cable TV:	Y	Retail Music:		Retail Games Stores:
Books:		TV/Video Prod.:	Special Services:	Y	Satellite Broadcast:		Retail Audio Equip.:		Stadiums/Teams:
Book Stores:		Video Rental:	Advertising Services:	Y	Radio:		Music Print./Dist.:		Gambling/Casinos:
Distribution/Printing:		Video Distribution:	Info. Sys. Software:		Online Information:		Multimedia:		Rides/Theme Parks:

TYPES OF BUSINESS:

Magazine Publishing
Digital Television Channels
Radio Broadcasting
Exhibitions, Trade Shows & Conventions

BRANDS/DIVISIONS/AFFILIATES:

Kerrang
Empire
Classic Bike
Grazia
Arena
Heat
Retail Week
FHM

CONTACTS: *Note: Officers with more than one job title may be intentionally listed here more than once.*

Tom Moloney, CEO
Joanna Copestake, Investor Rel.
Derek Carter, CEO-Emap Comm.
Paul Keenan, CEO-Consumer Media
Alun Cathcart, Chmn.

Phone: 44-1733-213-700	**Fax:** 44-1733-213-701
Toll-Free:	
Address: Wentworth House, Wentworth St., Peterborough, PE1 1DS UK	

GROWTH PLANS/SPECIAL FEATURES:

Emap plc is a leading media conglomerate in the U.K. with over 200 brands, 50 lifestyle and specialist consumer magazines, 42 local and eight national commercial radio stations, and seven digital TV channels. The firm also organizes over 400 business-to-business events internationally each year. Emap's consumer media segment publishes 50 titles, including publications in the automotive, young women, entertainment, lifestyle and celebrity gossip categories. Titles include Kerrang, Arena, Classic Bike, Empire, Heat, FHM and Grazia. FHM, one of the world's top-selling men's magazines, has 30 international editions and over 1 million subscribers in the U.S. This segment also includes Emap Advertising, a full service marketing communications business. The company's communication division publishes business-to-business magazines covering international business, retail business, broadcasting and media, construction, health care and government. Titles include Broadcast, Construction News and Retail Week. This segment also produces exhibitions and events for each business segment. In December 2007, Emap's board of directors approved a recommended cash acquisition in which Eden Bidco will acquire all issued and to be issued share capital of Emap. Under the terms of the agreement, the firm will dispose of its consumer media division, and its radio division. Eden Bidco will then acquire the businesses that currently comprise the company's communication division.

FINANCIALS: Sales and profits are in thousands of dollars—add 000 to get the full amount. 2007 Note: Financial information for 2007 was not available for all companies at press time.

2007 Sales: $	2007 Profits: $	**U.S. Stock Ticker:** EMAPF
2006 Sales: $1,485,500	2006 Profits: $219,200	**Int'l Ticker:** EMA Int'l Exchange: London-LSE
2005 Sales: $2,006,500	2005 Profits: $103,300	Employees: 6,277
2004 Sales: $1,917,100	2004 Profits: $169,800	Fiscal Year Ends: 3/31
2003 Sales: $1,522,000	2003 Profits: $135,400	Parent Company:

SALARIES/BENEFITS:

Pension Plan:	ESOP Stock Plan:	Profit Sharing:	Top Exec. Salary: $921,518	Bonus: $153,013
Savings Plan:	Stock Purch. Plan:		Second Exec. Salary: $584,548	Bonus: $63,612

OTHER THOUGHTS:

Apparent Women Officers or Directors: 2
Hot Spot for Advancement for Women/Minorities: Y

LOCATIONS: ("Y" = Yes)

West:	Southwest:	Midwest:	Southeast:	Northeast:	International:
Y				Y	Y

EMI GROUP PLC

www.emigroup.com

Industry Group Code: 512230 Ranks within this company's industry group: Sales: 2 Profits: 2

Print Media/Publishing:	Movies:	Equipment/Supplies:	Broadcast/Cable:	Music/Audio:		Sports/Games/Gambling:
Newspapers:	Movie Theaters:	Equipment/Supplies:	Broadcast TV:	Music Production:	Y	Games/Sports:
Magazines:	Movie Production:	Gambling Equipment:	Cable TV:	Retail Music:		Retail Games Stores:
Books:	TV/Video Prod.:	Special Services:	Satellite Broadcast:	Retail Audio Equip.:		Stadiums/Teams:
Book Stores:	Video Rental:	Advertising Services:	Radio:	Music Print./Dist.:	Y	Gambling/Casinos:
Distribution/Printing:	Video Distribution:	Info. Sys. Software:	Online Information:	Multimedia:		Rides/Theme Parks:

TYPES OF BUSINESS:

Music Production
Music Publishing
Recording Studios
Licensing
Digital Music Licensing

BRANDS/DIVISIONS/AFFILIATES:

EMI Music
EMI Music Publshing
Terra Firma Capital Partners
Blue Note Records
Capitol
EMI Classics
Virgin
Abbey Road Studios

CONTACTS: Note: Officers with more than one job title may be intentionally listed here more than once.

Chris Roling, COO
Chris Roling, CFO-EMI Group & EMI Music
Roger Ames, Head-EMI Music N. America
Tony Wadsworth, Chmn./CEO-EMI Music UK & Ireland
Roger Faxon, CEO-EMI Music Publishing
Ashley Unwin, Dir.-Bus. Transformation-EMI Group & EMI Music
Jean-Francois (JF) Cecillon, Chmn.
Jean-Francois (JF) Cecillon, CEO-EMI Music Int'l

Phone: 44-20-7795-7000	Fax: 44-20-7795-7001
Toll-Free:	
Address: 27 Wrights Ln., London, W8 5SW UK	

GROWTH PLANS/SPECIAL FEATURES:

EMI Group is one of the largest global popular music publishers. EMI Group operates through two divisions, EMI Music and EMI Music Publishing (EMP). EMI Music represents over 1,300 recording artists and owns a catalog of over 3 million recorded tracks. The firm's artists include: Classic stars such as The Beatles and Pink Floyd; contemporary performers such as Norah Jones and The Beastie Boys; Emerging stars in countries around the world; and Classical and jazz performers including Itzak Perlman and Cassandra Wilson. The subsidiary's record labels include: Angel, Astralwerks, Blue Note, Capitol, Capitol Nashville, EMI, EMI Classics, EMI CMG, EMI Televisa Music, Mute, Parlophone and Virgin. EMI Music operates the renowned Abbey Road Studios in London and Capitol Studios in Los Angeles. EMP owns a catalog consisting of over 1 million songs. Best-selling songs include: Bohemian Rhapsody; Over the Rainbow; Singin' in the Rain; and Santa Claus is Coming to Town. EMP's signed writers and performers include Eminem, Jewel and Sting. EMI has been an innovator in digital music: it released the first ever digital album and was the first label to offer a video single online. The firm has license agreements with over 400 partners for digital distribution of its content. In early 2007, in cost-cutting efforts, EMI merged Capitol Records and the U.S. operations of Virgin Records into the new Capitol Music Group. Capitol and Virgin remain separate imprints. In August 2007, EMI was acquired by Terra Firma Capital Partners, a private equity investment firm, for $4.74 billion.

FINANCIALS: Sales and profits are in thousands of dollars—add 000 to get the full amount. 2007 Note: Financial information for 2007 was not available for all companies at press time.

2007 Sales: $	2007 Profits: $	**U.S. Stock Ticker: EMIPY**
2006 Sales: $4,092,680	2006 Profits: $232,390	**Int'l Ticker: EMI** Int'l Exchange: London-LSE
2005 Sales: $3,937,820	2005 Profits: $194,400	Employees:
2004 Sales: $	2004 Profits: $	Fiscal Year Ends: 3/31
2003 Sales: $	2003 Profits: $	Parent Company:

SALARIES/BENEFITS:

Pension Plan:	ESOP Stock Plan:	Profit Sharing:	Top Exec. Salary: $	Bonus: $
Savings Plan:	Stock Purch. Plan:		Second Exec. Salary: $	Bonus: $

OTHER THOUGHTS:

Apparent Women Officers or Directors: 1
Hot Spot for Advancement for Women/Minorities:

LOCATIONS: ("Y" = Yes)

West:	Southwest:	Midwest:	Southeast:	Northeast:	International:
				Y	Y

EMMIS COMMUNICATIONS CORP   www.emmis.com

Industry Group Code: 513111 Ranks within this company's industry group: Sales: 6   Profits: 2

Print Media/Publishing:		Movies:		Equipment/Supplies:		Broadcast/Cable:		Music/Audio:		Sports/Games/Gambling:	
Newspapers:		Movie Theaters:		Equipment/Supplies:		Broadcast TV:		Music Production:		Games/Sports:	
Magazines:	Y	Movie Production:		Gambling Equipment:		Cable TV:		Retail Music:		Retail Games Stores:	
Books:	Y	TV/Video Prod.:		Special Services:		Satellite Broadcast:		Retail Audio Equip.:		Stadiums/Teams:	
Book Stores:		Video Rental:		Advertising Services:	Y	Radio:		Music Print./Dist.:		Gambling/Casinos:	
Distribution/Printing:		Video Distribution:		Info. Sys. Software:		Online Information:		Multimedia:		Rides/Theme Parks:	

TYPES OF BUSINESS:

Radio Broadcasting
Television Broadcasting
Magazine Publishing
Book Publishing

BRANDS/DIVISIONS/AFFILIATES:

Texas Monthly Magazine
Los Angeles Magazine
Atlanta Magazine
Indianapolis Monthly Magazine
Cincinnati Magazine
Tu Ciudad
Country Sampler Magazine
WIBC

CONTACTS: *Note: Officers with more than one job title may be intentionally listed here more than once.*

Jeffrey H. (Jeff) Smulyan, CEO
Jeffrey H. (Jeff) Smulyan, Pres.
Patrick Walsh, CFO
Michael (Mickey) Levitan, Chief Human Resource Officer
Gary L. Kaseff, General Counsel/Exec. VP
Patrick Walsh, Treas.
Richard F. (Rick) Cummings, Pres., Radio
Gary Thoe, Pres., Publishing
Jeffrey H. (Jeff) Smulyan, Chmn.
Paul W. Fiddick, Pres., Int'l

Phone: 317-266-0100	Fax: 317-631-3750
Toll-Free:	

Address: 1 Emmis Plz., 40 Monument Cir., Ste. 700, Indianapolis, IN 46204 US

GROWTH PLANS/SPECIAL FEATURES:

Emmis Communications Corporation is a diversified media company, principally focused on radio broadcasting. Emmis owns and operates seven FM radio stations in New York, Los Angeles and Chicago, as well as fourteen FM and two AM radio stations in St. Louis, Austin (it has a 50.1% interest in its radio stations there) and Indianapolis and Terre Haute, Indiana. In addition to its domestic radio properties, Emmis operates an international radio business; publishes several city and regional magazines; and operates television stations that are held for sale. Internationally, Emmis owns and operates a network of radio stations in the Flanders region of Belgium, owns a national radio network in Slovakia, has a 59.5% interest in a national radio station in Hungary and has a roughly 60% interest in two national radio networks in Bulgaria. The company's publishing operations include Texas Monthly, Los Angeles, Atlanta, Indianapolis Monthly, Cincinnati, Tu Ciudad and Country Sampler. Emmis also owns and operates two television stations located in New Orleans and Honolulu, both of which it intends to sell in the next year. In October 2007, Emmis' radio station WIBC in Indianapolis announced plans to split into two stations, one broadcasting a news/talk format, and the other broadcasting an all sports format.

Emmis offers its employees tuition reimbursement, an employee assistance program, adoption assistance and medical, dental, vision and life insurance.

FINANCIALS: Sales and profits are in thousands of dollars—add 000 to get the full amount. 2007 Note: Financial information for 2007 was not available for all companies at press time.

2007 Sales: $	2007 Profits: $	**U.S. Stock Ticker: EMMS**
2006 Sales: $387,381	2006 Profits: $357,771	**Int'l Ticker:** Int'l Exchange:
2005 Sales: $351,820	2005 Profits: $-304,368	Employees: 1,940
2004 Sales: $326,618	2004 Profits: $2,256	Fiscal Year Ends: 12/31
2003 Sales: $562,400	2003 Profits: $-164,500	Parent Company:

SALARIES/BENEFITS:

Pension Plan:	ESOP Stock Plan:	Profit Sharing: Y	Top Exec. Salary: $880,000	Bonus: $369,600
Savings Plan: Y	Stock Purch. Plan: Y		Second Exec. Salary: $495,000	Bonus: $110,134

OTHER THOUGHTS:

Apparent Women Officers or Directors: 1
Hot Spot for Advancement for Women/Minorities:

LOCATIONS: ("Y" = Yes)

West:	Southwest:	Midwest:	Southeast:	Northeast:	International:
Y	Y	Y	Y	Y	Y

ENDEAVOR AGENCY (THE)

Industry Group Code: 711410 Ranks within this company's industry group: Sales: Profits:

Print Media/Publishing:	Movies:	Equipment/Supplies:		Broadcast/Cable:	Music/Audio:	Sports/Games/Gambling:
Newspapers:	Movie Theaters:	Equipment/Supplies:		Broadcast TV:	Music Production:	Games/Sports:
Magazines:	Movie Production:	Gambling Equipment:		Cable TV:	Retail Music:	Retail Games Stores:
Books:	TV/Video Prod.:	Special Services:	Y	Satellite Broadcast:	Retail Audio Equip.:	Stadiums/Teams:
Book Stores:	Video Rental:	Advertising Services:		Radio:	Music Print./Dist.:	Gambling/Casinos:
Distribution/Printing:	Video Distribution:	Info. Sys. Software:		Online Information:	Multimedia:	Rides/Theme Parks:

TYPES OF BUSINESS:

Talent Agency

BRANDS/DIVISIONS/AFFILIATES:

GROWTH PLANS/SPECIAL FEATURES:

The Endeavor Agency was formed when a group of agents left International Creative Management, Inc. in 1995. It is a talent and literary agency based in Beverly Hills, California. It represents writers, directors and actors such as Reese Witherspoon, Jude Law, Martin Scorsese, Matt Damon and Adam Sandler among others. In addition, its marketing division, partially owned by Interpublic, readies third party content for distribution. The firm does not maintain a web site. Endeavor uses a flat management structure and an incentive-based compensation plan, which has helped it lure top talent recruiters from other agencies. The company operates two offices, its headquarters in Beverly Hills and one in New York. In early 2007, Robert Newman, formerly of International Creative Management, left to join Endeavor, bringing with him directors Baz Luhrmann (Moulin Rouge) and Guillerom del Toro (Pan's Labyrinth).

CONTACTS: Note: Officers with more than one job title may be intentionally listed here more than once.

Ari Emanuel, Founding Partner
Sean Perry, Partner
Matt Solo, Partner
Robert Newman, Partner
Tom Strickler, Partner

Phone: 310-248-2000	**Fax:** 310-248-2020
Toll-Free:	
Address: 9601 Wilshire Blvd. Fl. 10, Beverly Hills, CA 90212 US	

FINANCIALS: Sales and profits are in thousands of dollars—add 000 to get the full amount. 2007 Note: Financial information for 2007 was not available for all companies at press time.

2007 Sales: $	2007 Profits: $	**U.S. Stock Ticker: Private**
2006 Sales: $	2006 Profits: $	**Int'l Ticker:** Int'l Exchange:
2005 Sales: $	2005 Profits: $	Employees:
2004 Sales: $	2004 Profits: $	Fiscal Year Ends:
2003 Sales: $	2003 Profits: $	Parent Company:

SALARIES/BENEFITS:

Pension Plan:	ESOP Stock Plan:	Profit Sharing:	Top Exec. Salary: $	Bonus: $
Savings Plan:	Stock Purch. Plan:		Second Exec. Salary: $	Bonus: $

OTHER THOUGHTS:

Apparent Women Officers or Directors:
Hot Spot for Advancement for Women/Minorities:

LOCATIONS: ("Y" = Yes)

West:	Southwest:	Midwest:	Southeast:	Northeast:	International:
Y				Y	

Note: Financial information, benefits and other data can change quickly and may vary from those stated here.

ENTERCOM COMMUNICATIONS CORP   www.entercom.com

Industry Group Code: 513111 Ranks within this company's industry group: Sales: 3 Profits: 4

Print Media/Publishing:	Movies:	Equipment/Supplies:		Broadcast/Cable:	Music/Audio:	Sports/Games/Gambling:
Newspapers:	Movie Theaters:	Equipment/Supplies:		Broadcast TV:	Music Production:	Games/Sports:
Magazines:	Movie Production:	Gambling Equipment:		Cable TV:	Retail Music:	Retail Games Stores:
Books:	TV/Video Prod.:	Special Services:		Satellite Broadcast:	Retail Audio Equip.:	Stadiums/Teams:
Book Stores:	Video Rental:	Advertising Services:	Y	Radio:	Music Print./Dist.:	Gambling/Casinos:
Distribution/Printing:	Video Distribution:	Info. Sys. Software:		Online Information:	Multimedia:	Rides/Theme Parks:

TYPES OF BUSINESS:

Radio Broadcasting
Radio Advertising
Digital Radio

BRANDS/DIVISIONS/AFFILIATES:

iBiquity Digital Corporation

CONTACTS: *Note: Officers with more than one job title may be intentionally listed here more than once.*

David J. Field, CEO
David J. Field, Pres.
Stephen F. Fisher, CFO/Exec. VP
Noreen McCormack, VP-Human Resources
John Graefe, Dir.-IT
Martin D. Hadfield, VP-Eng.
John C. Donlevie, General Counsel/Exec. VP/Corp. Sec.
Marijane Milton, VP-Training & Dev.
Sandy Smallens, Sr. VP-Digital
Eugene D. Levin, Treas./Controller
Melissa Forrest, VP/Market Mgr.-Austin
Steve Oshin, VP/General Mgr.-Seattle
Ken Beck, VP-News & Talk Programming
Pat Paxton, Sr. VP-Programming

Phone: 610-660-5610	**Fax:** 610-660-5620
Toll-Free:	
Address: 401 City Ave., Ste. 809, Bala Cynwyd, PA 19004 US	

GROWTH PLANS/SPECIAL FEATURES:

Entercom Communications Corp. is one of the nation's largest radio broadcasting companies. It owns and runs multi-station operations in 23 markets: Boston, Seattle, Denver, Sacramento, Cincinnati, Portland, Kansas City, Indianapolis, Milwaukee, Austin, Norfolk, Buffalo, New Orleans, Providence, Memphis, Greensboro, Rochester, Greenville/Spartanburg, Madison, Wichita, Wilkes-Barre/Scranton, Springfield and Gainesville/Ocala. The majority of each station's local and regional advertising sales are generated through direct solicitations of local advertising agencies and businesses. Entercom retains a national representative firm to sell national spot commercial airtime on its stations to advertisers outside of its local markets. This advertising accounts for almost 20% of each radio station's revenues on average. Entercom builds station clusters in large growth markets and acquires underdeveloped properties that offer potential for significant improvements in revenues, with a principal focus on the top 50 markets. Entercom's stations feature oldies, rock, news and talk, country, smooth jazz and sports. In addition, the company is the exclusive radio broadcaster of the Boston Celtics, Seattle Mariners, Buffalo Sabres, Seattle Seahawks, Kansas City Chiefs and a number of major college sports teams. The firm also broadcasts HD Radio (digital radio), owns a stake in iBiquity Digital Corporation, and is a founding member of the HD Digital Radio Alliance Association. In 2007, Entercom exchanged four radio stations in Cincinnati and three of its seven radio stations in Seattle for Bonneville International Corporation's three FM radio stations in San Francisco.

FINANCIALS: Sales and profits are in thousands of dollars—add 000 to get the full amount. 2007 Note: Financial information for 2007 was not available for all companies at press time.

2007 Sales: $	2007 Profits: $	**U.S. Stock Ticker: ETM**
2006 Sales: $440,485	2006 Profits: $47,981	**Int'l Ticker:** Int'l Exchange:
2005 Sales: $432,520	2005 Profits: $78,361	Employees: 2,812
2004 Sales: $423,455	2004 Profits: $75,634	Fiscal Year Ends: 12/31
2003 Sales: $401,056	2003 Profits: $71,780	Parent Company:

SALARIES/BENEFITS:

Pension Plan: Y	ESOP Stock Plan:	Profit Sharing:	Top Exec. Salary: $717,423	Bonus: $600,000
Savings Plan: Y	Stock Purch. Plan: Y		Second Exec. Salary: $551,864	Bonus: $

OTHER THOUGHTS:

Apparent Women Officers or Directors: 6
Hot Spot for Advancement for Women/Minorities: Y

LOCATIONS: ("Y" = Yes)

West:	Southwest:	Midwest:	Southeast:	Northeast:	International:
Y	Y	Y	Y	Y	

ENTERTAINMENT PROPERTIES TRUST   www.eprkc.com

Industry Group Code: 525930 Ranks within this company's industry group: Sales: 1 Profits: 1

Print Media/Publishing:	Movies:		Equipment/Supplies:	Broadcast/Cable:	Music/Audio:	Sports/Games/Gambling:
Newspapers:	Movie Theaters:	Y	Equipment/Supplies:	Broadcast TV:	Music Production:	Games/Sports:
Magazines:	Movie Production:		Gambling Equipment:	Cable TV:	Retail Music:	Retail Games Stores:
Books:	TV/Video Prod.:		Special Services:	Satellite Broadcast:	Retail Audio Equip.:	Stadiums/Teams:
Book Stores:	Video Rental:		Advertising Services:	Radio:	Music Print./Dist.:	Gambling/Casinos:
Distribution/Printing:	Video Distribution:		Info. Sys. Software:	Online Information:	Multimedia:	Rides/Theme Parks:

TYPES OF BUSINESS:

REIT-Entertainment Properties
Megaplex Movie Theaters
Entertainment Retail Centers
Ski Resorts

BRANDS/DIVISIONS/AFFILIATES:

Mad River Ski Resort
Crotched Mountain Ski Facility

CONTACTS: Note: Officers with more than one job title may be intentionally listed here more than once.

David M. Brain, CEO
Gregory K. Silvers, COO
David M. Brain, Pres.
Mark A. Peterson, CFO/VP/Treas.
Mark A. Peterson, VP-Admin.
Gregory K. Silvers, General Counsel/VP/Corp. Sec.
Jonathan B. Weis, Dir.-Corp. Comm.
Michael Hirons, VP-Finance
Robert J. Druten, Chmn.

Phone: 816-472-1700	Fax: 816-472-5794
Toll-Free: 888-377-7348	
Address: 30 Pershing Rd., Ste. 201, Kansas City, MO 64108 US	

GROWTH PLANS/SPECIAL FEATURES:

Entertainment Properties Trust (EPR) is a self-administered real estate investment trust (REIT) with 75 megaplex movie theaters, seven entertainment retail centers and other destination recreational and specialty properties. EPR's collection of properties totals a combined area of 7.8 million square feet, with 6.3 million square feet of megaplex theatres and 1.5 million square feet of retail, restaurant and other miscellaneous properties. EPR operates in 22 states in the U.S. and Canada and leases to theatre operators such as American Multi-Cinema, Inc. (AMC); Muvico Entertainment, LLC; Regal Entertainment Group; Consolidated Theatres; Rave Motion Pictures; AmStar Cinemas, LLC; Wallace Theatres; Cobb Theatres; Southern Theatres; and Kerasotes Theatres. Megaplex theatres usually have at least 10 screens with elevated, stadium style seating and amenities such as digital cinema, which allow greater enhancement to audio and visual experiences for theatre patrons. The firm's seven entertainment retail centers are located in Westminster, Colorado; New Rochelle, New York; and Ontario, Canada. Land parcels are often leased to restaurant and retail operators adjacent to its theater properties. Tenants of EPR's restaurant properties include Bennigan's, Texas Roadhouse, Cherrydale Shops, Stir Crazy, Sizzler, Mad River Mountain, Johnny Carino's and Asahi Sushi Bar. In March 2006, EPR acquired AMC Firewheel 18 in Garland Texas and AMC Columbia 14 in Coumbia Maryland for a combined total of $35 million. Also in March 2006, the firm acquired Crotched Mountain Ski Facility in Bennington, New Hampshire for $8 million. In early 2007, the firm acquired several theater properties: the Bayou 15 screen megaplex in Pensacola, Florida for roughly $14.9 million; and City Place 15 screen megaplex in Kalamazoo, Michigan for $17.1 million.

FINANCIALS: Sales and profits are in thousands of dollars—add 000 to get the full amount. 2007 Note: Financial information for 2007 was not available for all companies at press time.

2007 Sales: $	2007 Profits: $	U.S. Stock Ticker: EPR
2006 Sales: $195,500	2006 Profits: $70,432	Int'l Ticker: Int'l Exchange:
2005 Sales: $164,815	2005 Profits: $57,707	Employees: 13
2004 Sales: $133,315	2004 Profits: $48,250	Fiscal Year Ends: 12/31
2003 Sales: $91,160	2003 Profits: $32,131	Parent Company:

SALARIES/BENEFITS:

Pension Plan: Y	ESOP Stock Plan:	Profit Sharing: Y	Top Exec. Salary: $401,000	Bonus: $361,000
Savings Plan: Y	Stock Purch. Plan:		Second Exec. Salary: $253,000	Bonus: $190,000

OTHER THOUGHTS:

Apparent Women Officers or Directors:
Hot Spot for Advancement for Women/Minorities:

LOCATIONS: ("Y" = Yes)

West:	Southwest:	Midwest:	Southeast:	Northeast:	International:
Y	Y	Y	Y	Y	Y

Note: Financial information, benefits and other data can change quickly and may vary from those stated here.

ENTRAVISION COMMUNICATIONS CORPORATION
www.entravision.com

Industry Group Code: 513120 Ranks within this company's industry group: Sales: 14   Profits: 17

Print Media/Publishing:	Movies:	Equipment/Supplies:		Broadcast/Cable:		Music/Audio:	Sports/Games/Gambling:	
Newspapers:	Movie Theaters:	Equipment/Supplies:		Broadcast TV:	Y	Music Production:	Games/Sports:	
Magazines:	Movie Production:	Gambling Equipment:		Cable TV:		Retail Music:	Retail Games Stores:	
Books:	TV/Video Prod.:	Special Services:		Satellite Broadcast:		Retail Audio Equip.:	Stadiums/Teams:	
Book Stores:	Video Rental:	Advertising Services:	Y	Radio:		Music Print./Dist.:	Gambling/Casinos:	
Distribution/Printing:	Video Distribution:	Info. Sys. Software:		Online Information:		Multimedia:	Rides/Theme Parks:	

TYPES OF BUSINESS:

Television Broadcasting
Spanish-Language Broadcasting
Radio Broadcasting
Outdoor Advertising

BRANDS/DIVISIONS/AFFILIATES:

WNUE-FM
Mega Communications

CONTACTS: *Note: Officers with more than one job title may be intentionally listed here more than once.*

Walter F. Ulloa, CEO
Philip C. Wilkinson, COO
Philip C. Wilkinson, Pres.
John F. DeLorenzo, CFO/Exec. VP
Paul A. Zevnik, Corp. Sec.
John F. DeLorenzo, Treas.
Larry E. Safir, Exec. VP
Jeffery A. Liberman, Pres., Radio Div.
Christopher T. Young, Pres., Outdoor Div.
Walter F. Ulloa, Chmn.

Phone: 310-447-3870	Fax: 310-447-3899
Toll-Free:	
Address: 2425 Olympic Blvd., Ste. 6000 W., Santa Monica, CA 90404 US	

GROWTH PLANS/SPECIAL FEATURES:

Entravision Communications Corporation, along with its subsidiaries, is a diversified Spanish-language media company with a portfolio of television, radio and outdoor advertising assets, reaching approximately 65% of all Hispanics in the U.S, as well as the border markets of Mexico. The company owns and/or operates 51 primary television stations, the majority of which are located in the southwestern U.S., including the U.S./Mexico border markets. The television stations consist primarily of affiliates of Univision, serving 20 of the top 50 U.S. Hispanic markets. The company's television assets are primarily made up of the largest affiliate groups for Univision and TeleFutura, the two television networks of Univision Communications, Inc. The firm also owns and operates one of the largest groups of Spanish-language radio stations in the country, with 47 stations in 18 U.S. markets, including Spanish-language stations in Arizona, California, Colorado, Florida, Nevada, New Mexico and Texas. Entravision's outdoor advertising operations consist of approximately 10,400 advertising billboards located primarily in high-density Hispanic communities in Los Angeles and New York. The company generates its revenue from sales of national and local advertising time on television and radio stations as well as advertising on the firm's billboards. In November 2007, Entravision announced plans to explore strategic alternatives for its outdoor advertising operations. Also in November, the company agreed to acquire Spanish-language radio station WNUE-FM, serving the Orlando, Florida market, from Mega Communications for approximately $24 million.

FINANCIALS: Sales and profits are in thousands of dollars—add 000 to get the full amount. 2007 Note: Financial information for 2007 was not available for all companies at press time.

2007 Sales: $	2007 Profits: $	U.S. Stock Ticker: EVC
2006 Sales: $291,752	2006 Profits: $-134,599	Int'l Ticker: Int'l Exchange:
2005 Sales: $280,964	2005 Profits: $-9,657	Employees: 1,148
2004 Sales: $259,100	2004 Profits: $6,100	Fiscal Year Ends: 12/31
2003 Sales: $237,956	2003 Profits: $2,267	Parent Company:

SALARIES/BENEFITS:

Pension Plan:	ESOP Stock Plan:	Profit Sharing:	Top Exec. Salary: $810,000	Bonus: $618,000
Savings Plan:	Stock Purch. Plan:		Second Exec. Salary: $810,000	Bonus: $618,000

OTHER THOUGHTS:

Apparent Women Officers or Directors:
Hot Spot for Advancement for Women/Minorities:

LOCATIONS: ("Y" = Yes)

West:	Southwest:	Midwest:	Southeast:	Northeast:	International:
Y	Y		Y	Y	

ESPN INC

espn.go.com

Industry Group Code: 513210 Ranks within this company's industry group: Sales: Profits:

Print Media/Publishing:		Movies:		Equipment/Supplies:		Broadcast/Cable:		Music/Audio:		Sports/Games/Gambling:	
Newspapers:		Movie Theaters:		Equipment/Supplies:		Broadcast TV:		Music Production:		Games/Sports:	
Magazines:	Y	Movie Production:		Gambling Equipment:		Cable TV:	Y	Retail Music:		Retail Games Stores:	
Books:	Y	TV/Video Prod.:	Y	Special Services:		Satellite Broadcast:		Retail Audio Equip.:		Stadiums/Teams:	
Book Stores:		Video Rental:		Advertising Services:		Radio:		Music Print./Dist.:		Gambling/Casinos:	
Distribution/Printing:		Video Distribution:		Info. Sys. Software:		Online Information:		Multimedia:		Rides/Theme Parks:	

TYPES OF BUSINESS:

Sports Television-Cable
Sports Radio Broadcasting
Online Sports Information
Magazine & Book Publishing
Sports Websites

BRANDS/DIVISIONS/AFFILIATES:

ESPN
ESPN2
ESPNEWS
ESPN Deportes
ESPN Regional Television
ESPN Interactive
Walt Disney Company (The)
Hearst Corporation (The)

CONTACTS: *Note: Officers with more than one job title may be intentionally listed here more than once.*

George W. Bodenheimer, Pres.
Christine Driessen, CFO/Exec. VP
Sean H. R. Bratches, Exec. VP-Mktg. & Sales
George W. Bodenheimer, Pres., ABC Sports
George W. Bodenheimer, Chmn.

Phone: 860-766-2000	**Fax:** 860-766-2213
Toll-Free:	
Address: ESPN Plz., 935 Middle St., Bristol, CT 06010 US	

GROWTH PLANS/SPECIAL FEATURES:

ESPN, Inc. is 80%-owned by the Walt Disney Co. through Disney ABC Cable; the other 20% is owned by Hearst. It is a cable sports broadcaster that airs more than 5,100 live or original hours of sports programming for more than 65 sports yearly. It has seven domestic television networks: ESPN, ESPN 2, ESPN Classic (archived sports footage), ESPN Deportes (Spanish-language sports network), ESPNU (college sports network), ESPN Today (interactive sports channel) and ESPNEWS. It also operates ESPN HD and ESPN2 HD, which provide high-definition simulcast services. The company's other television subsidiaries include ESPN Regional Television, ESPN PPV, ESPN 360, ESPN On Demand, ESPN Interactive and ESPN International, which encompasses 30 international networks. The firm's radio subsidiaries include ESPN Radio in the U.S. and ESPN Deportes Radio, which is syndicated in 13 international countries. Its affiliated web sites include espn.com, espnDeportes.com, espnRadio.com, espnSoccerNet.com and expn.com. The company's publishing division includes ESPN The Magazine, Bassmaster Magazine, BASS Times, Fishing Tackle & Retailer and ESPN Books, publisher of the SportsCentury almanac. SportsTicker covers real-time sports news and statistics broadcasts. Through ESPN Enterprises, the firm has developed new products and businesses using the ESPN brand and assets, including the ESPN Zones sports-themed restaurant chain, a variety of consumer products (ESPN Videogames, DVDs, CDs, ESPN25, ESPN Golf Schools and ESPN Russell Racing Schools), the ESPN Sports Poll research polling service and the ESPN Club at Disney World Orlando. The firm also improves its brand awareness by hosting and managing various sporting events, including the X Games, ESPN Outdoors & BASS, the ESPY Awards, bowl games and Jimmy V Men's and Women's Basketball Classics. In Australia in early 2007, ESPN acquired a minority stake in a 19-team arena soccer league along with its broadcast rights. In late 2006, ESPN agreed to acquire American Sports Network from Setanta Sport Holdings Ltd. and Benchmark Capital Europe.

FINANCIALS: **Sales and profits are in thousands of dollars—add 000 to get the full amount. 2007 Note: Financial information for 2007 was not available for all companies at press time.**

2007 Sales: $	2007 Profits: $	**U.S. Stock Ticker: Subsidiary**
2006 Sales: $	2006 Profits: $	**Int'l Ticker:** Int'l Exchange:
2005 Sales: $4,031,000	2005 Profits: $	Employees: 3,400
2004 Sales: $3,223,000	2004 Profits: $	Fiscal Year Ends: 9/30
2003 Sales: $2,869,000	2003 Profits: $	Parent Company: WALT DISNEY COMPANY (THE)

SALARIES/BENEFITS:

Pension Plan:	ESOP Stock Plan:	Profit Sharing:	Top Exec. Salary: $	Bonus: $
Savings Plan:	Stock Purch. Plan:		Second Exec. Salary: $	Bonus: $

OTHER THOUGHTS:

Apparent Women Officers or Directors: 1
Hot Spot for Advancement for Women/Minorities:

LOCATIONS: ("Y" = Yes)

West:	Southwest:	Midwest:	Southeast:	Northeast:	International:
				Y	

Note: Financial information, benefits and other data can change quickly and may vary from those stated here.

EURO DISNEY SCA

www.eurodisney.com/en

Industry Group Code: 713110 Ranks within this company's industry group: Sales: 1 Profits: 2

Print Media/Publishing:	Movies:	Equipment/Supplies:	Broadcast/Cable:	Music/Audio:	Sports/Games/Gambling:
Newspapers:	Movie Theaters:	Equipment/Supplies:	Broadcast TV:	Music Production:	Games/Sports:
Magazines:	Movie Production:	Gambling Equipment:	Cable TV:	Retail Music:	Retail Games Stores:
Books:	TV/Video Prod.:	Special Services:	Satellite Broadcast:	Retail Audio Equip.:	Stadiums/Teams:
Book Stores:	Video Rental:	Advertising Services:	Radio:	Music Print./Dist.:	Gambling/Casinos:
Distribution/Printing:	Video Distribution:	Info. Sys. Software:	Online Information:	Multimedia:	Rides/Theme Parks:

TYPES OF BUSINESS:

Theme Park
Resorts
Hotels
Golf
Property Developments

BRANDS/DIVISIONS/AFFILIATES:

Disneyland Paris
Walt Disney Studios
Disney Village
Val d'Europe
EDL Hotels
Walt Disney Company (The)
Disney Wish Program
Buzz Lightyear Laser Blast

CONTACTS: *Note: Officers with more than one job title may be intentionally listed here more than once.*

Karl L. Holz, CEO
George Kalogridis, COO
Ignace Lahoud, CFO/Sr. VP
Federico J. Gonzalez, Sr. VP-Mktg.
Francois Pinon, General Counsel/VP-Legal Affairs
Dominique Cocquet, Sr. VP-Dev. & External Affairs
Jeff Archambault, VP-Comm. & Strategic Alliances
Andrew de Csillery, VP-Strategic Planning & Pricing
Norbert Stiekema, VP-Sale & Distribution
Neil Corbett, VP-Bus. Insight & Improvement
Patrick Avice, VP-Hotels & Convention Centers
Karl L. Holz, Chmn.

Phone: 33-1-64-74-4000	**Fax:** 33-1-64-74-5636
Toll-Free:	
Address: Route Nationale 34, Chessy, 77700 France	

GROWTH PLANS/SPECIAL FEATURES:

Euro Disney S.C.A. is a holding company that owns Euro Disney Associés (EDA), which in turn operates Disneyland Resort Paris, a top European vacation destination. EDA is 18%-owned by a subsidiary of The Walt Disney Company. The park receives over 12.8 million annual visits. Disneyland Resort Paris includes Disneyland Park, Walk Disney Studios Park, seven themed hotels, two convention centers, a 27-hole golf facility and Disney Village, a center for dining, shopping and entertainment. The subsidiary EDL Hotels is wholly owned by EDA, and operates five of the Disney themed hotels. These include: Disney's Newport Bay Club, Sequoia Lodge, Hotel Santa Fe, Hotel New York and Hotel Cheyenne. The Newport Bay Club offers one of the largest conference centers in France, and includes the Hotel New York convention center, amounts to about 10,500 square meters of space. Euro Disney has a large stake in Val d'Europe, an urban development project featuring a shopping center, an international business center, offices, apartments, homes and hotels. In 2006, the interactive ride Buzz Lightyear Laser Blast was opened in Discoveryland at the Disneyland Park. In June 2007, the company opened the Disney Wish Lounge, a place where children who are a part of the Disney Wish Program for children with life-threatening diseases, as well as their families, can rest without having to return to their hotel rooms.

Euro Disney offers Hote d'Acceuil Touristique, a training program resulting in a diploma recognized as preparing participants for various tourism-related fields, as well as many other training programs.

FINANCIALS: Sales and profits are in thousands of dollars—add 000 to get the full amount. 2007 Note: Financial information for 2007 was not available for all companies at press time.

2007 Sales: $	2007 Profits: $	**U.S. Stock Ticker: ERDBF.PK**
2006 Sales: $1,441,190	2006 Profits: $-117,390	**Int'l Ticker: EDL** Int'l Exchange: Paris-Euronext
2005 Sales: $1,295,800	2005 Profits: $-114,300	Employees: 12,162
2004 Sales: $1,291,700	2004 Profits: $-179,000	Fiscal Year Ends: 9/30
2003 Sales: $1,221,000	2003 Profits: $-64,900	Parent Company:

SALARIES/BENEFITS:

Pension Plan: Y	ESOP Stock Plan:	Profit Sharing:	Top Exec. Salary: $	Bonus: $
Savings Plan:	Stock Purch. Plan:		Second Exec. Salary: $	Bonus: $

OTHER THOUGHTS:

Apparent Women Officers or Directors:
Hot Spot for Advancement for Women/Minorities:

LOCATIONS: ("Y" = Yes)

West:	Southwest:	Midwest:	Southeast:	Northeast:	International:
					Y

FIRST LOOK STUDIOS INC

www.firstlookmedia.com

Industry Group Code: 512110 Ranks within this company's industry group: Sales: Profits:

Print Media/Publishing:	Movies:		Equipment/Supplies:		Broadcast/Cable:	Music/Audio:	Sports/Games/Gambling:
Newspapers:	Movie Theaters:		Equipment/Supplies:		Broadcast TV:	Music Production:	Games/Sports:
Magazines:	Movie Production:	Y	Gambling Equipment:		Cable TV:	Retail Music:	Retail Games Stores:
Books:	TV/Video Prod.:	Y	Special Services:		Satellite Broadcast:	Retail Audio Equip.:	Stadiums/Teams:
Book Stores:	Video Rental:		Advertising Services:	Y	Radio:	Music Print./Dist.:	Gambling/Casinos:
Distribution/Printing:	Video Distribution:	Y	Info. Sys. Software:	Y	Online Information:	Multimedia:	Rides/Theme Parks:

TYPES OF BUSINESS:

Independent Film Distribution
Film Production
Film Licensing
Television Production

BRANDS/DIVISIONS/AFFILIATES:

First Look International
First Look Pictures
First Look Home Entertainment
First Look Media
First Look Studios
First Look SPV LLC
Ventura Home Entertainment
DEJ Productions

CONTACTS: *Note: Officers with more than one job title may be intentionally listed here more than once.*

Trevor Short, CEO
Dean Wilson, COO
Reid Sullivan, CFO
Avi Lerner, Co-Chmn- First Look Holdings, LLC
Henry Winterstern, Co-Chmn-First Look Holdings, LLC

Phone: 424-202-5000	Fax:
Toll-Free:	
Address: 2000 Ave. of the Stars, Suite 410, Century City, CA 90067 US	

GROWTH PLANS/SPECIAL FEATURES:

First Look Studios, Inc. is owned by First Look Holdings, LLC, which was created in March 2007 to control and operate First Look Studios. First Look Studios serves as a producer and distributor for independently produced movies. The company is one of the founding members of the American Film Marketing Association (AFMA). The firm conducts its business through three operating segments: First Look International, the international sales division; First Look Pictures, the U.S. theatrical releasing division; and First Look Home Entertainment (FLHE), the U.S. video and DVD distribution operation. The firm produces independent and artistic films such as Paris, Je T'Aime; Welcome to Paradise; When Nietzsche Wept; and The Far Side of Jericho. Some of the best-known productions in its library of over 350 films include Antonia's Line, The Secret of Roan Inish, Waking Ned Devine and The Prophecy. The company also engages in licensing theatrical, video, pay television (HBO, Showtime and Encore), free television (USA, Sci-Fi and Lifetime), satellite and other distribution rights to foreign sub-distributors in major international territories and regions. In addition, the company distributes films domestically, licensing them for videocassette transference, DVD and pay-per-view through First Look Home Entertainment. The firm is currently expanding the FLHE division. First Look Studios owns and operates two studio facilities, one in New York and one in North Carolina, where the Dawson's Creek series was produced. The firm is currently restructuring management, as it is now operated by the newly-created First Look Holdings, LLC.

FINANCIALS: Sales and profits are in thousands of dollars—add 000 to get the full amount. 2007 Note: Financial information for 2007 was not available for all companies at press time.

2007 Sales: $	2007 Profits: $	**U.S. Stock Ticker: FRST.PK**
2006 Sales: $	2006 Profits: $	**Int'l Ticker:** Int'l Exchange:
2005 Sales: $	2005 Profits: $	Employees: 47
2004 Sales: $	2004 Profits: $	Fiscal Year Ends: 12/31
2003 Sales: $	2003 Profits: $	Parent Company: FIRST LOOK HOLDINGS LLC

SALARIES/BENEFITS:

Pension Plan:	ESOP Stock Plan:	Profit Sharing:	Top Exec. Salary: $295,200	Bonus: $212,500
Savings Plan:	Stock Purch. Plan:		Second Exec. Salary: $194,808	Bonus: $

OTHER THOUGHTS:

Apparent Women Officers or Directors:
Hot Spot for Advancement for Women/Minorities:

LOCATIONS: ("Y" = Yes)

West:	Southwest:	Midwest:	Southeast:	Northeast:	International:
Y			Y	Y	

Note: Financial information, benefits and other data can change quickly and may vary from those stated here.

FISHER COMMUNICATIONS INC   www.fsci.com

Industry Group Code: 513120 Ranks within this company's industry group: Sales: 19   Profits: 10

Print Media/Publishing:	Movies:	Equipment/Supplies:		Broadcast/Cable:		Music/Audio:		Sports/Games/Gambling:
Newspapers:	Movie Theaters:	Equipment/Supplies:		Broadcast TV:	Y	Music Production:		Games/Sports:
Magazines:	Movie Production:	Gambling Equipment:		Cable TV:		Retail Music:		Retail Games Stores:
Books:	TV/Video Prod.:	Special Services:	Y	Satellite Broadcast:		Retail Audio Equip.:		Stadiums/Teams:
Book Stores:	Video Rental:	Advertising Services:	Y	Radio:		Music Print./Dist.:		Gambling/Casinos:
Distribution/Printing:	Video Distribution:	Info. Sys. Software:		Online Information:		Multimedia:		Rides/Theme Parks:

TYPES OF BUSINESS:

Television Broadcasting
Radio Broadcasting
Media Content Distribution
Office Rental

BRANDS/DIVISIONS/AFFILIATES:

Fisher Broadcasting Company
Fisher Media Services Company
Fisher Plaza
African-American Broadcasting of Bellevue

CONTACTS: *Note: Officers with more than one job title may be intentionally listed here more than once.*

Colleen B. Brown, CEO
Warren J. Spector, COO
Colleen B. Brown, Pres.
S. Mae Fujita Numata, CFO/Sr. VP
John N. Tamerlano, VP-Sales
Karen L. Aliabadi, VP-Human Resources
Kelly D. Alford, CIO/VP
S. Mae Fujita Numata, Corp. Sec.
Joseph L. Lovejoy, Sr. VP-Media Oper.
Jodi A. Colligan, VP-Finance
Robert I. Dunlop, Sr. VP-Developing Media
Lawrence P. Roberts, VP-Special Projects
Troy A. McGuire, VP-News & Programming
Nancy J. Bruner, VP-Fisher Interactive Networks
Phelps K. Fisher, Chmn.

Phone: 206-404-7000	Fax: 206-404-7050
Toll-Free:	
Address: 100 4th Ave. N., Ste. 510, Seattle, WA 98109 US	

GROWTH PLANS/SPECIAL FEATURES:

Fisher Communications, Inc. is a communications and media company focused primarily on broadcasting. The company is divided into two subsidiaries: Fisher Broadcasting Company and Fisher Media Services Company.   Fisher Broadcasting operates the firm's television and radio stations, and Fisher Media handles Fisher Plaza. The firm's broadcasting operations provided approximately 94% of its 2006 revenue, with TV broadcasting accounting for approximately 75% of that revenue and radio broadcasting, 25%.   Fisher owns or operates 18 network-affiliated TV stations and owns a 50% interest in a company with another TV station, as well as owning or operating nine radio stations.   The TV and radio stations are located in Washington, Oregon, Idaho and Montana, with the television stations reaching an estimated 3.7 million households. The firm has a long history of affiliation with ABC and CBS, and recently formed an affiliate relationship with Univision, a Spanish-language network. In November 2006, it purchased two Univision-affiliated networks in Oregon for $19 million. The firm sells advertising for an FM station under a joint sales agreement.   Fisher Plaza, located in Seattle, Washington, is the company's communications center. The center is designed to enable the distribution of analog and digital media content through broadcast, satellite, cable, Internet, broadband and wireless distribution channels. The Plaza also rents office space, often to other median and communications companies.   The firm owns African-American Broadcasting of Bellevue. In August 2007, Fisher agreed to acquire two TV stations in Bakersfield, California, TV stations for $55 million. In December 2007, it sold 23.3% of Safeco Corp. for $40.6 million to help fund the planned Bakersfield acquisition.

FINANCIALS: Sales and profits are in thousands of dollars—add 000 to get the full amount. 2007 Note: Financial information for 2007 was not available for all companies at press time.

2007 Sales: $	2007 Profits: $	U.S. Stock Ticker: FSCI
2006 Sales: $135,691	2006 Profits: $16,836	Int'l Ticker: Int'l Exchange:
2005 Sales: $142,652	2005 Profits: $-5,072	Employees: 931
2004 Sales: $153,866	2004 Profits: $-11,953	Fiscal Year Ends: 12/31
2003 Sales: $138,387	2003 Profits: $8,228	Parent Company:

SALARIES/BENEFITS:

Pension Plan:	ESOP Stock Plan:	Profit Sharing:	Top Exec. Salary: $500,000	Bonus: $350,000
Savings Plan: Y	Stock Purch. Plan:		Second Exec. Salary: $230,000	Bonus: $128,800

OTHER THOUGHTS:

Apparent Women Officers or Directors: 6
Hot Spot for Advancement for Women/Minorities: Y

LOCATIONS: ("Y" = Yes)

West:	Southwest:	Midwest:	Southeast:	Northeast:	International:
Y					

FORBES INC

www.forbesinc.com

Industry Group Code: 511120 Ranks within this company's industry group: Sales: Profits:

Print Media/Publishing:		Movies:		Equipment/Supplies:		Broadcast/Cable:		Music/Audio:		Sports/Games/Gambling:	
Newspapers:		Movie Theaters:		Equipment/Supplies:		Broadcast TV:		Music Production:		Games/Sports:	
Magazines:	Y	Movie Production:		Gambling Equipment:		Cable TV:	Y	Retail Music:		Retail Games Stores:	
Books:	Y	TV/Video Prod.:	Y	Special Services:	Y	Satellite Broadcast:		Retail Audio Equip.:		Stadiums/Teams:	
Book Stores:		Video Rental:		Advertising Services:		Radio:		Music Print./Dist.:		Gambling/Casinos:	
Distribution/Printing:		Video Distribution:		Info. Sys. Software:		Online Information:		Multimedia:		Rides/Theme Parks:	

TYPES OF BUSINESS:

Magazine Publishing
Online Publishing & Forums
Television & Radio Production
Newsletters
Conferences

BRANDS/DIVISIONS/AFFILIATES:

Forbes Magazine
Forbes.com
Forbes Television
ForbesLife
Forbes Asia
American Heritage
ForbesAutos.com
Forbes Media LLC

CONTACTS: Note: Officers with more than one job title may be intentionally listed here more than once.

Steve Forbes Jr., CEO
Timothy C. Forbes, COO
Steve Forbes Jr., Pres.
Sean P. Hegarty, CFO/Exec. VP

Phone: 212-620-2200	Fax: 212-620-2245
Toll-Free: 800-295-0893	
Address: 60 5th Ave., New York, NY 10011 US	

GROWTH PLANS/SPECIAL FEATURES:

Forbes, Inc., a privately held publishing and new media company, is the publisher of Forbes Magazine, which celebrates its 91st anniversary in 2008. The company also includes: Forbes.com, a business web site with over 1,500 articles published daily; ForbesAutos.com; Forbes Conference Group, a producer of peer-driven forums for senior executives such as the Forbes CEO Forum; Forbes Newsletter Group, which publishes ten specialty newsletters and has marketing, content and distribution relationships with 35 outside newsletters; Forbes Investors Advisory Institute; Forbes Television, responsible for the co-branded show Forbes on Fox; Forbes Radio, which is responsible for a weekly three-hour radio show, Forbes on Radio; Forbes Custom Media, which provides clients with customized print and electronic publication services in areas such as financial services, business-to-business markets and technology; The Forbes Collection, a showcase of historical artifacts; ForbesLife (formerly Forbes FYI), a bi-monthly lifestyle magazine with a humorous bent; Forbes Asia, an English language bi-weekly with a circulation of 80,000 in the Asia/Pacific region; and American Heritage, a magazine which looks to the past to explain the present. The American Heritage division also publishes American Heritage of Invention & Technology, a quarterly magazine dedicated to the history of American innovations; American Legacy, a quarterly magazine dedicated to African-American history and culture; and AmericanHeritage.com, branded as History's Homepage. Forbes Magazine is published bi-weekly with over 60 concise articles. Including the magazine's eight local-language editions (Hebrew, Arabic, Russian, Polish, Japanese, Korean, Chinese and Turkish) and Forbes Asia, the magazine has a worldwide audience of over 5 million readers. Forbes, Inc. is also behind the Social Register Association which lists approximately 25,000 people in its twice yearly publication.

FINANCIALS: Sales and profits are in thousands of dollars—add 000 to get the full amount. 2007 Note: Financial information for 2007 was not available for all companies at press time.

2007 Sales: $	2007 Profits: $	U.S. Stock Ticker: Private
2006 Sales: $	2006 Profits: $	Int'l Ticker: Int'l Exchange:
2005 Sales: $450,000	2005 Profits: $	Employees:
2004 Sales: $	2004 Profits: $	Fiscal Year Ends: 12/31
2003 Sales: $	2003 Profits: $	Parent Company:

SALARIES/BENEFITS:

Pension Plan:	ESOP Stock Plan:	Profit Sharing:	Top Exec. Salary: $	Bonus: $
Savings Plan:	Stock Purch. Plan:		Second Exec. Salary: $	Bonus: $

OTHER THOUGHTS:

Apparent Women Officers or Directors:
Hot Spot for Advancement for Women/Minorities: Y

LOCATIONS: ("Y" = Yes)

West:	Southwest:	Midwest:	Southeast:	Northeast:	International:
				Y	Y

Note: Financial information, benefits and other data can change quickly and may vary from those stated here.

FORD MODELS INC   www.fordmodels.com

Industry Group Code: 711410 Ranks within this company's industry group: Sales: Profits:

Print Media/Publishing:	Movies:	Equipment/Supplies:		Broadcast/Cable:	Music/Audio:	Sports/Games/Gambling:
Newspapers:	Movie Theaters:	Equipment/Supplies:		Broadcast TV:	Music Production:	Games/Sports:
Magazines:	Movie Production:	Gambling Equipment:		Cable TV:	Retail Music:	Retail Games Stores:
Books:	TV/Video Prod.:	Special Services:	Y	Satellite Broadcast:	Retail Audio Equip.:	Stadiums/Teams:
Book Stores:	Video Rental:	Advertising Services:	Y	Radio:	Music Print./Dist.:	Gambling/Casinos:
Distribution/Printing:	Video Distribution:	Info. Sys. Software:		Online Information:	Multimedia:	Rides/Theme Parks:

TYPES OF BUSINESS:
Modeling Agency

BRANDS/DIVISIONS/AFFILIATES:

CONTACTS: *Note: Officers with more than one job title may be intentionally listed here more than once.*
Katie Ford, CEO
John Caplin, COO
John Caplin, Pres.
Mark Perlin, CFO

Phone: 212-219-6500	**Fax:** 212-966-5028
Toll-Free:	
Address: 111 5th Ave., New York, NY 10003 US	

GROWTH PLANS/SPECIAL FEATURES:

Ford Models, Inc. is one of the top fashion model representation agencies in the world. Based out of New York City, it also has offices in: Los Angeles and San Francisco, California; Miami; Chicago; Scottsdale, Arizona; Toronto; Paris; and Sao Paulo and Rio de Janeiro, Brazil. The company was founded in 1964 by Eileen and Jerry Ford and represents supermodels such as Vendela, Rachel Hunter, Christie Brinkley, Stephanie Seymour and Veronica Webb. The company operates through several divisions representing different categories of models. The children's division works with children aged six months and older that live within 100 miles of New York City, Chicago or Los Angeles. During the summer, the division also works with out-of-town models staying temporarily in the area. The men's division looks for men between the heights of 6 feet and 6-foot-2 and 18-25 years old. The plus-sized women's division works with women between the heights of 5-foot-8 and 5-foot-11, sizes 12-18 and between the ages of 15 and 30. The women's division works with women between the heights of 5-foot-8 and 5-foot-11, sizes 2-8 and between the ages of 18 and 21. Ford also has divisions specializing in mature models, classics and in models who display specific body parts, such as hands or feet. The company holds open casting at many of its locations throughout the year.

FINANCIALS: Sales and profits are in thousands of dollars—add 000 to get the full amount. 2007 Note: Financial information for 2007 was not available for all companies at press time.

2007 Sales: $	2007 Profits: $	**U.S. Stock Ticker: Private**
2006 Sales: $	2006 Profits: $	**Int'l Ticker:** Int'l Exchange:
2005 Sales: $	2005 Profits: $	Employees:
2004 Sales: $	2004 Profits: $	Fiscal Year Ends:
2003 Sales: $	2003 Profits: $	Parent Company:

SALARIES/BENEFITS:

Pension Plan:	ESOP Stock Plan:	Profit Sharing:	Top Exec. Salary: $	Bonus: $
Savings Plan:	Stock Purch. Plan:		Second Exec. Salary: $	Bonus: $

OTHER THOUGHTS:
Apparent Women Officers or Directors: 1
Hot Spot for Advancement for Women/Minorities:

LOCATIONS: ("Y" = Yes)

West:	Southwest:	Midwest:	Southeast:	Northeast:	International:
Y	Y	Y	Y	Y	Y

Note: Financial information, benefits and other data can change quickly and may vary from those stated here.

FOX BROADCASTING COMPANY

www.fox.com

Industry Group Code: 513210 Ranks within this company's industry group: Sales: Profits:

Print Media/Publishing:	Movies:	Equipment/Supplies:	Broadcast/Cable:		Music/Audio:	Sports/Games/Gambling:
Newspapers:	Movie Theaters:	Equipment/Supplies:	Broadcast TV:	Y	Music Production:	Games/Sports:
Magazines:	Movie Production:	Gambling Equipment:	Cable TV:		Retail Music:	Retail Games Stores:
Books:	TV/Video Prod.:	Special Services:	Satellite Broadcast:		Retail Audio Equip.:	Stadiums/Teams:
Book Stores:	Video Rental:	Advertising Services:	Radio:		Music Print./Dist.:	Gambling/Casinos:
Distribution/Printing:	Video Distribution:	Info. Sys. Software:	Online Information:		Multimedia:	Rides/Theme Parks:

TYPES OF BUSINESS:

Television Broadcasting
Television Stations

BRANDS/DIVISIONS/AFFILIATES:

Fox Entertainment Group, Inc.
News Corporation Limited (The)
FOX Television Network
Simpsons (The)
American Idol
House
24
COPS

CONTACTS: Note: Officers with more than one job title may be intentionally listed here more than once.

Kevin Reilly, Pres.
Jon Nesvig, Pres., Sales
Andrew Setos, Pres., Eng.
Del Mayberry, Exec. VP-Admin.
Del Mayberry, Exec. VP-Finance
Ed Wilson, Pres., FOX Television Network
Peter Liguori, Chmn.

Phone: 310-369-1000	Fax: 310-369-1283
Toll-Free:	
Address: 10201 W. Pico Blvd., Los Angeles, CA 90035 US	

GROWTH PLANS/SPECIAL FEATURES:

Fox Broadcasting Company (FOX), a subsidiary of Fox Entertainment Group, Inc., itself a subsidiary of News Corporation, operates the FOX Television Network. The company owns and operates 35 full-power stations located in 9 of the 10 largest designated market areas. Its television broadcast network consists of over 200 affiliated stations, including the full-power television stations that are owned by subsidiaries of FOX, which reach approximately 98% of all U.S. television households. The firm broadcasts approximately 15 hours of primetime, sports events and Sunday morning news television programming created by other Fox Entertainment subsidiaries, including Twentieth Century Fox Television, Fox Television Studios, Fox News Channel, Fox Sports Networks, FX Network and several foreign subsidiaries. The company principally derives its revenues from the sale of advertising time sold to national advertisers. FOX's most prominent primetime programs include The Simpsons, American Idol, House, 24, COPS, and America's Most Wanted. The firm licenses sports programming from organizations such as the NFL, MLB and NASCAR.

The company offers its employees benefits including flexible spending accounts, employee assistance, education reimbursement, credit union membership, company paid parking and discounts on local attractions and merchandise. FOX also offers both paid and academic credit internships.

FINANCIALS: Sales and profits are in thousands of dollars—add 000 to get the full amount. 2007 Note: Financial information for 2007 was not available for all companies at press time.

2007 Sales: $	2007 Profits: $	**U.S. Stock Ticker: Subsidiary**
2006 Sales: $	2006 Profits: $	**Int'l Ticker:** Int'l Exchange:
2005 Sales: $2,624,000	2005 Profits: $	Employees: 425
2004 Sales: $4,556,000	2004 Profits: $	Fiscal Year Ends: 6/30
2003 Sales: $4,359,000	2003 Profits: $	Parent Company: NEWS CORP

SALARIES/BENEFITS:

Pension Plan: Y	ESOP Stock Plan:	Profit Sharing:	Top Exec. Salary: $	Bonus: $
Savings Plan: Y	Stock Purch. Plan:		Second Exec. Salary: $	Bonus: $

OTHER THOUGHTS:

Apparent Women Officers or Directors:
Hot Spot for Advancement for Women/Minorities:

LOCATIONS: ("Y" = Yes)

West:	Southwest:	Midwest:	Southeast:	Northeast:	International:
Y					

FOX ENTERTAINMENT GROUP INC

www.fox.com

Industry Group Code: 513120 Ranks within this company's industry group: Sales: Profits:

Print Media/Publishing:	Movies:		Equipment/Supplies:		Broadcast/Cable:		Music/Audio:		Sports/Games/Gambling:	
Newspapers:	Movie Theaters:		Equipment/Supplies:		Broadcast TV:	Y	Music Production:	Y	Games/Sports:	Y
Magazines:	Movie Production:	Y	Gambling Equipment:		Cable TV:	Y	Retail Music:		Retail Games Stores:	
Books:	TV/Video Prod.:	Y	Special Services:		Satellite Broadcast:		Retail Audio Equip.:		Stadiums/Teams:	Y
Book Stores:	Video Rental:		Advertising Services:	Y	Radio:		Music Print./Dist.:		Gambling/Casinos:	
Distribution/Printing:	Video Distribution:	Y	Info. Sys. Software:		Online Information:		Multimedia:		Rides/Theme Parks:	

TYPES OF BUSINESS:

Broadcast Television
Film Distribution and Production
Television Programming
Online Communities and Game Sites
Professional Sports
Electronic Games
Cable TV Programming
Online Entertainment

BRANDS/DIVISIONS/AFFILIATES:

News Corporation
Fox Filmed Entertainment
Twentieth Century Fox Television
Fox Television Studios
Fox Interactive Media
MySpace.com
National Geographic Channel

CONTACTS: *Note: Officers with more than one job title may be intentionally listed here more than once.*

K. Rupert Murdoch, CEO
Peter F. Chernin, COO
Peter F. Chernin, Pres.
David F. DeVoe, CFO/Sr. Exec. VP
Lawrence A. Jacobs, General Counsel/Sr. Exec. VP
Ross Levinsohn, Pres., Fox Interactive Media
Lachlan K. Murdoch, Pres., Fox Television Stations
Anthony J. Vinciquerra, CEO/Pres., Fox Networks Group
Roger Ailes, Chmn./CEO-Fox News Channel
Mitsy Wilson, Sr. VP-Diversity Dev.
K. Rupert Murdoch, Chmn.

Phone: 212-852-7017	Fax: 212-852-7145
Toll-Free:	
Address: 1211 Ave. of the Americas, New York, NY 10036 US	

GROWTH PLANS/SPECIAL FEATURES:

Fox Entertainment Group, Inc. (FEG), a wholly-owned subsidiary of The News Corporation, is an entertainment conglomerate that operates through four business segments: filmed entertainment, television stations, television broadcast network and cable network programming. The company engages in feature film and television production and distribution principally through the following businesses: Fox Filmed Entertainment, a leading producer and distributor of feature films; Twentieth Century Fox Television, a producer of network television programming; Fox Television Studios, a leading producer of U.S. broadcast, cable and international programming; and Fox Interactive Media, a network of integrated Internet sites including Myspace.com, which has more than 60 million users worldwide. Twentieth Century Fox Home Entertainment, Inc. distributes motion pictures and other programming produced by units of Fox Entertainment and its affiliates in all home media formats, including digital media available for download from Apple's iTunes Music Store. The company's motion picture and television library consists of varying rights to well over 3,000 previously released motion pictures and many television programs. In television, Fox Television Stations owns and operates 35 full-power stations located in nine of the 10 largest designated market areas, reaching 98% of all U.S. television households. Its television broadcast network consists of approximately 200 affiliated stations, including the full-power stations that are owned by subsidiaries of Fox. The company produces television programs through Twentieth Century Fox Television, Fox Television Studios, Fox News Channel, Fox Sports Networks, FX Network, SPEED Channel, FUEL TV, Fox College Sports, Fox Movie Channel, Fox Sports International, National Geographic Channel, Fox Movie Channel and several foreign subsidiaries. The company also owns a 14.6% limited partnership interest in the Colorado Rockies, the baseball franchise in Denver, Colorado. In December 2006, Liberty Media Corp. acquired the firm's interest in DirecTV. During 2007, the firm began distributing movies in the Blu-ray high definition disk format.

FINANCIALS: Sales and profits are in thousands of dollars—add 000 to get the full amount. 2007 Note: Financial information for 2007 was not available for all companies at press time.

2007 Sales: $	2007 Profits: $	**U.S. Stock Ticker: Subsidiary**
2006 Sales: $	2006 Profits: $	**Int'l Ticker:** Int'l Exchange:
2005 Sales: $	2005 Profits: $	Employees:
2004 Sales: $12,175,000	2004 Profits: $1,353,000	Fiscal Year Ends: 6/30
2003 Sales: $11,002,000	2003 Profits: $1,031,000	Parent Company: NEWS CORP

SALARIES/BENEFITS:

Pension Plan: Y	ESOP Stock Plan:	Profit Sharing:	Top Exec. Salary: $4,508,694	Bonus: $21,175,000
Savings Plan: Y	Stock Purch. Plan:		Second Exec. Salary: $8,100,008	Bonus: $21,175,000

OTHER THOUGHTS:

Apparent Women Officers or Directors:
Hot Spot for Advancement for Women/Minorities:

LOCATIONS: ("Y" = Yes)

West:	Southwest:	Midwest:	Southeast:	Northeast:	International:
Y	Y	Y	Y	Y	Y

Note: Financial information, benefits and other data can change quickly and may vary from those stated here.

FOX FILMED ENTERTAINMENT
www.foxmovies.com

Industry Group Code: 512110 Ranks within this company's industry group: Sales: Profits:

Print Media/Publishing:	Movies:		Equipment/Supplies:	Broadcast/Cable:	Music/Audio:	Sports/Games/Gambling:
Newspapers:	Movie Theaters:	Y	Equipment/Supplies:	Broadcast TV:	Music Production:	Games/Sports:
Magazines:	Movie Production:	Y	Gambling Equipment:	Cable TV:	Retail Music:	Retail Games Stores:
Books:	TV/Video Prod.:	Y	Special Services:	Satellite Broadcast:	Retail Audio Equip.:	Stadiums/Teams:
Book Stores:	Video Rental:		Advertising Services:	Radio:	Music Print./Dist.:	Gambling/Casinos:
Distribution/Printing:	Video Distribution:	Y	Info. Sys. Software:	Online Information:	Multimedia:	Rides/Theme Parks:

TYPES OF BUSINESS:

Movie Production & Distribution
Animated Films
Television Production & Distribution
Video & DVD Distribution

BRANDS/DIVISIONS/AFFILIATES:

Fox Entertainment Group, Inc.
Twentieth Century Fox
Fox 2000
Fox Searchlight
Twentieth Century Fox Animation
Twentieth Century Fox Home Entertainment
Twentieth Century Fox Television
Fox Atomic

CONTACTS: Note: Officers with more than one job title may be intentionally listed here more than once.

Dean Hallett, CFO
Dean Hallett, VP-Oper. Strategy
David Lux, Sr. VP-Corp. Publicity
Thomas E. Rothman, Co-Chmn.
James N. Gianopulos, Co-Chmn.

Phone: 310-369-1000	Fax: 310-203-1558
Toll-Free:	
Address: 10201 W. Pico Blvd., Los Angeles, CA 90035 US	

GROWTH PLANS/SPECIAL FEATURES:

Fox Filmed Entertainment (FFE), a subsidiary of Fox Entertainment Group, Inc., is one of the world's major producers and distributors of feature films and a leader in U.S. television programming. FFE produces films through four studios: Twentieth Century Fox, Fox 2000, Fox Searchlight and Twentieth Century Fox Animation. The company's Twentieth Century Fox and Fox 2000 subsidiaries produce big-budget movies such as Titanic, Fight Club, Moulin Rouge, X-Men and the Star Wars series. Another subsidiary, Fox Searchlight, produces or funds smaller art-house film such as 2007's Juno. Twentieth Century Fox Animation produces animated films including Ice Age and The Simpsons Movie. Through Twentieth Century Fox Home Entertainment, the firm distributes motion pictures on video and DVD for sale and rental. Twentieth Century Fox Television produces and distributes programming for a variety of U.S. networks. Prominent shows have included Boston Legal, Judging Amy and The Simpsons. FFE newest theatrical movie studio, Fox Atomic targets 17-24 year olds with films, comics and digital content. In 2007, Fox Atomic released The Hills Have Eyes II, The Comebacks and 28 Weeks Later. In addition, FFE has certain distribution agreements with Regency Entertainment, Inc., a film company in which the firm holds a 20% interest. In 2007, the company released: Epic Movie, Reno 911: Miami, Pathfinder, Firehouse Dog, Fantastic Four: Rise of the Silver Surfer, Live Free or Die Hard and The Simpsons Movie, as well as Alvin and the Chipmunks, Alien Versus Predator: Requiem (AVP-R) and Hitman. Recently, Twentieth Century Fox Home Entertainment signed an exclusive deal with Zoke Culture Group to distribute DVDs in China.

FINANCIALS: Sales and profits are in thousands of dollars—add 000 to get the full amount. 2007 Note: Financial information for 2007 was not available for all companies at press time.

2007 Sales: $	2007 Profits: $	U.S. Stock Ticker: Subsidiary
2006 Sales: $	2006 Profits: $	Int'l Ticker: Int'l Exchange:
2005 Sales: $5,919,000	2005 Profits: $	Employees:
2004 Sales: $	2004 Profits: $	Fiscal Year Ends: 6/30
2003 Sales: $	2003 Profits: $	Parent Company: FOX ENTERTAINMENT GROUP INC

SALARIES/BENEFITS:

Pension Plan:	ESOP Stock Plan:	Profit Sharing:	Top Exec. Salary: $	Bonus: $
Savings Plan:	Stock Purch. Plan:		Second Exec. Salary: $	Bonus: $

OTHER THOUGHTS:

Apparent Women Officers or Directors:
Hot Spot for Advancement for Women/Minorities:

LOCATIONS: ("Y" = Yes)

West:	Southwest:	Midwest:	Southeast:	Northeast:	International:
Y					

Note: Financial information, benefits and other data can change quickly and may vary from those stated here.

FOX SPORTS NET INC

msn.foxsports.com

Industry Group Code: 513210 Ranks within this company's industry group: Sales: Profits:

Print Media/Publishing:	Movies:		Equipment/Supplies:		Broadcast/Cable:		Music/Audio:		Sports/Games/Gambling:	
Newspapers:	Movie Theaters:		Equipment/Supplies:		Broadcast TV:	Y	Music Production:		Games/Sports:	
Magazines:	Movie Production:	Y	Gambling Equipment:		Cable TV:	Y	Retail Music:		Retail Games Stores:	
Books:	TV/Video Prod.:	Y	Special Services:	Y	Satellite Broadcast:		Retail Audio Equip.:		Stadiums/Teams:	
Book Stores:	Video Rental:		Advertising Services:		Radio:		Music Print./Dist.:		Gambling/Casinos:	
Distribution/Printing:	Video Distribution:		Info. Sys. Software:		Online Information:		Multimedia:		Rides/Theme Parks:	

TYPES OF BUSINESS:

Sports Broadcasting
Film & TV Production & Distribution
Online Sports Broadcasting
Regional Sports Networks

BRANDS/DIVISIONS/AFFILIATES:

Fox Sports Net
Fox Entertainment Group, Inc.
News Corporation Limited (The)
National Sports Partners
National Advertising Partners

CONTACTS: *Note: Officers with more than one job title may be intentionally listed here more than once.*

Robert Thompson, Pres.
Lou D'Ermilio, Sr. VP-Media Rel.
David Rone, Exec. VP-Rights Acquisitions
Dan Bell, VP-Comm.
David Hill, Chmn.

Phone: 310-369-6000	**Fax:** 212-354-6902
Toll-Free:	

Address: 10201 W. Pico Blvd., Bldg. 101, 5th Fl., Los Angeles, CA 90035 US

GROWTH PLANS/SPECIAL FEATURES:

Fox Sports Net (FSN), Inc., owned by Fox Entertainment Group, itself a majority-owned subsidiary of The News Corporation Limited, produces and distributes films and television programs. The company provides professional and collegiate sports programming through interests in 15 regional sports networks (RSNs), as well as through Fox Sports Net, a national sports news program that operates through six additional RSNs. FSN's programming, which is received by 85 million households, combines the content of RSNs with national programming that is consistent throughout all regions. The company has the rights to broadcast the live events of 66 NBA, NHL, MLB teams, as well as several high school and collegiate teams. In addition, the firm hosts the ACC, Big 12 and Pac 10 conferences. Most of the company's revenue is culled through advertising time slots. The company has various partnerships with Rainbow Media Sports, with the result that the two companies have owned different stakes in various regional Fox Sports Net operations. The firm recently digitally distributed the five full-length NFL games from the 2007 Tostitos Bowl Bash (including preview shows and highlights), marking the first time FOX Sports has made downloadable content available for sports fans on the Internet.

Fox Sports Net offers its employees medical, dental, and vision plans; life insurance; child care on the studio lot; an employee assistance program; Credit union membership; advance movie screenings; and paid vacation.

FINANCIALS: Sales and profits are in thousands of dollars—add 000 to get the full amount. 2007 Note: Financial information for 2007 was not available for all companies at press time.

2007 Sales: $	2007 Profits: $	**U.S. Stock Ticker: Subsidiary**
2006 Sales: $	2006 Profits: $	**Int'l Ticker:** Int'l Exchange:
2005 Sales: $	2005 Profits: $	Employees:
2004 Sales: $	2004 Profits: $	Fiscal Year Ends: 6/30
2003 Sales: $	2003 Profits: $	Parent Company: NEWS CORP

SALARIES/BENEFITS:

Pension Plan: Y	ESOP Stock Plan:	Profit Sharing:	Top Exec. Salary: $	Bonus: $
Savings Plan: Y	Stock Purch. Plan:		Second Exec. Salary: $	Bonus: $

OTHER THOUGHTS:

Apparent Women Officers or Directors:
Hot Spot for Advancement for Women/Minorities:

LOCATIONS: ("Y" = Yes)

West:	Southwest:	Midwest:	Southeast:	Northeast:	International:
Y	Y	Y	Y	Y	

FREEDOM COMMUNICATIONS INC   www.freedom.com

Industry Group Code: 511110 Ranks within this company's industry group: Sales: Profits:

Print Media/Publishing:		Movies:	Equipment/Supplies:	Broadcast/Cable:		Music/Audio:	Sports/Games/Gambling:
Newspapers:	Y	Movie Theaters:	Equipment/Supplies:	Broadcast TV:	Y	Music Production:	Games/Sports:
Magazines:	Y	Movie Production:	Gambling Equipment:	Cable TV:		Retail Music:	Retail Games Stores:
Books:	Y	TV/Video Prod.:	Special Services:	Satellite Broadcast:		Retail Audio Equip.:	Stadiums/Teams:
Book Stores:		Video Rental:	Advertising Services:	Radio:		Music Print./Dist.:	Gambling/Casinos:
Distribution/Printing:		Video Distribution:	Info. Sys. Software:	Online Information:		Multimedia:	Rides/Theme Parks:

TYPES OF BUSINESS:

Newspaper Publishing
Magazine Publishing
Television Broadcasting
Online Publishing
Books & Calendars

BRANDS/DIVISIONS/AFFILIATES:

Community Newspapers, Inc.
Freedom Orange County Information
Orange County Register
EmeraldCoast.com
HighDesert.com
MyRGV.com
PanamaCity.com
Coloradosprings.com

CONTACTS: Note: Officers with more than one job title may be intentionally listed here more than once.

Scott N. Flanders, CEO
Scott N. Flanders, Pres.
Douglas S. Bennett, CFO
Marcy Bruskin, VP-Human Resources
Rachel Sagan, General Counsel/VP
Marcy Bruskin, VP-Organizational Dev.
Richard A. Wallace, VP-Corp. Affairs
JoAnne Norton, VP-Shareholder Rel.
Michael J. Mathieu, Pres., Freedom Interactive
Nancy Trillo, VP-Enterprise Finance
Jonathan Segal, Pres., Freedom Newspapers, Inc.
Doreen Wade, Pres., Freedom Broadcasting, Inc.
Thomas W. Bassett, Chmn.

Phone: 949-253-2300	Fax: 949-474-7675
Toll-Free:	
Address: 17666 Fitch Ave., Irvine, CA 92614-6022 US	

GROWTH PLANS/SPECIAL FEATURES:

Freedom Communications, Inc. is a media conglomerate that has interests in newspaper publishing, television broadcasting and Internet web sites. The company's newspaper division is divided into two parts: Community Newspapers, Inc. and Freedom Orange County Information (FOCI). Together, these divisions publish over 70 newspapers and nearly 240 niche publications. Community Newspapers is made up of 25 daily and 12 weekly publications in 10 states, including Arizona, California, Florida, New Mexico, North Carolina, Illinois, Indiana, Missouri, Texas and Ohio. The FOCI division is focused on the southern California market, and includes flagship publication, the Orange County Register. The combined circulation of Freedom's newspapers is more than 1.2 million. Recently, the company launched 239 niche products, including history books, pet calendars and worship guides. The company's television broadcasting segment consists of five CBS affiliates, three ABC affiliates and one CW affiliate acquired in December 2006. These stations are located in New York, Texas, Tennessee, Oregon, Rhode Island, Florida and Michigan. Using digital broadcast technology, three of the CBS affiliates and one ABC affiliate air the CW Network through a single digital signal. The company's Internet businesses, run by Freedom Interactive, are primarily community-oriented news and information sites including Coloradosprings.com, EmeraldCoast.com, HighDesert.com, MyRGV.com and PanamaCity.com. The interactive division has 33 websites and Internet portals, which have roughly 25 million page views monthly.

All of Freedom Communications' interests are run on a Libertarian philosophy stressing Integrity, Self-Responsibility, Respect for Individual Freedom, Community and Life-Long Learning.

FINANCIALS: Sales and profits are in thousands of dollars—add 000 to get the full amount. 2007 Note: Financial information for 2007 was not available for all companies at press time.

2007 Sales: $	2007 Profits: $	U.S. Stock Ticker: Private
2006 Sales: $	2006 Profits: $	Int'l Ticker: Int'l Exchange:
2005 Sales: $103,500	2005 Profits: $	Employees: 7,000
2004 Sales: $	2004 Profits: $	Fiscal Year Ends: 12/31
2003 Sales: $824,000	2003 Profits: $	Parent Company:

SALARIES/BENEFITS:

Pension Plan:	ESOP Stock Plan:	Profit Sharing:	Top Exec. Salary: $	Bonus: $
Savings Plan: Y	Stock Purch. Plan:		Second Exec. Salary: $	Bonus: $

OTHER THOUGHTS:

Apparent Women Officers or Directors: 8
Hot Spot for Advancement for Women/Minorities: Y

LOCATIONS: ("Y" = Yes)

West:	Southwest:	Midwest:	Southeast:	Northeast:	International:
Y	Y	Y	Y	Y	

Note: Financial information, benefits and other data can change quickly and may vary from those stated here.

GAMESTOP CORP   www.gamestop.com

Industry Group Code: 451120 Ranks within this company's industry group: Sales: 1   Profits: 1

Print Media/Publishing:		Movies:		Equipment/Supplies:		Broadcast/Cable:		Music/Audio:		Sports/Games/Gambling:	
Newspapers:		Movie Theaters:		Equipment/Supplies:		Broadcast TV:		Music Production:		Games/Sports:	
Magazines:	Y	Movie Production:		Gambling Equipment:		Cable TV:		Retail Music:		Retail Games Stores:	Y
Books:		TV/Video Prod.:		Special Services:		Satellite Broadcast:		Retail Audio Equip.:		Stadiums/Teams:	
Book Stores:		Video Rental:		Advertising Services:		Radio:		Music Print./Dist.:		Gambling/Casinos:	
Distribution/Printing:		Video Distribution:		Info. Sys. Software:		Online Information:		Multimedia:		Rides/Theme Parks:	

TYPES OF BUSINESS:

Video Games-Retail
PC Software Sales
Game Accessories
Online Sales
Magazine Publication

BRANDS/DIVISIONS/AFFILIATES:

EB Games
GameStop.com
ebgames.com
Game Informer Magazine

CONTACTS: *Note: Officers with more than one job title may be intentionally listed here more than once.*

R. Richard Fontaine, CEO
Daniel A. DeMatteo, COO
Steven R. Morgan, Pres.
David W. Carlson, CFO/Exec. VP
Michael N. Rosen, Sec.
Robert A. Lloyd, Chief Acct. Officer/Sr. VP
Daniel A. DeMatteo, Vice Chmn.
R. Richard Fontaine, Chmn.
Ronald Freeman, Exec. VP-Dist.

Phone: 817-424-2000	Fax: 817-424-2062
Toll-Free: 800-883-8895	
Address: 625 Westport Pkwy., Grapevine, TX 76051 US	

GROWTH PLANS/SPECIAL FEATURES:

GameStop Corp. is one of the world's largest retailers of video games and PC entertainment software. The company operates 4,778 retail stores throughout 50 U.S. states, eleven European countries, Australia and Canada. Approximately 3,800 of the company's stores are located in the U.S., operating primarily under the names GameStop and EB Games. In the next 12-18 months, the company plans to re-brand its EB stores to the GameStop brand, and it plans to open 500-550 new stores by February 2008. The stores offer both new and used video game hardware, software and accessories, as well as PC entertainment software; they are generally located in power strip centers or high-traffic shopping malls; and average approximately 1,500 square feet. The firm's used video game products provide a unique value proposition to the stores' customers and its purchasing of video game products provides its customers with an opportunity to trade in their used video game products for store credits and apply those credits towards other merchandise, which, in turn, drives more sales. Stores also typically feature several video game sampling areas, which provide our customers the opportunity to play games before purchase, as well as equipment to play video game clips. Additionally, GameStop operates two e-commerce web sites, gamestop.com and ebgames.com, as well as publishing Game Informer, one of the largest multi-platform video game magazines in the U.S., based on its 2.7 million subscribers. Paid Game Informer subscribers receive a GameStop loyalty card, which offers discounts on selected merchandise in the company's stores.

GameStop provides employees flexible spending accounts; 15% discounts at GameStop owned stores and 30% discounts at Barnes & Noble and B. Dalton Bookstores; paid vacation, holidays, sick days, jury duty and bereavement; tuition reimbursement; vision coverage; and dental and preferred provider organization (PPO) medical insurance.

FINANCIALS: Sales and profits are in thousands of dollars—add 000 to get the full amount. 2007 Note: Financial information for 2007 was not available for all companies at press time.

2007 Sales: $5,318,900	2007 Profits: $158,250	**U.S. Stock Ticker: GME**
2006 Sales: $3,091,783	2006 Profits: $100,784	**Int'l Ticker:** Int'l Exchange:
2005 Sales: $1,842,806	2005 Profits: $60,926	Employees: 32,000
2004 Sales: $1,578,838	2004 Profits: $63,467	Fiscal Year Ends: 1/31
2003 Sales: $1,352,800	2003 Profits: $52,400	Parent Company:

SALARIES/BENEFITS:

Pension Plan:	ESOP Stock Plan:	Profit Sharing:	Top Exec. Salary: $1,011,539	Bonus: $2,000,000
Savings Plan: Y	Stock Purch. Plan:		Second Exec. Salary: $810,385	Bonus: $1,600,000

OTHER THOUGHTS:

Apparent Women Officers or Directors:
Hot Spot for Advancement for Women/Minorities:

LOCATIONS: ("Y" = Yes)

West:	Southwest:	Midwest:	Southeast:	Northeast:	International:
Y	Y	Y	Y	Y	Y

Note: Financial information, benefits and other data can change quickly and may vary from those stated here.

GAMETECH INTERNATIONAL INC   www.gametech-inc.com

Industry Group Code: 713290 Ranks within this company's industry group: Sales: 11   Profits: 7

Print Media/Publishing:	Movies:	Equipment/Supplies:		Broadcast/Cable:	Music/Audio:	Sports/Games/Gambling:
Newspapers:	Movie Theaters:	Equipment/Supplies:		Broadcast TV:	Music Production:	Games/Sports:
Magazines:	Movie Production:	Gambling Equipment:	Y	Cable TV:	Retail Music:	Retail Games Stores:
Books:	TV/Video Prod.:	Special Services:	Y	Satellite Broadcast:	Retail Audio Equip.:	Stadiums/Teams:
Book Stores:	Video Rental:	Advertising Services:		Radio:	Music Print./Dist.:	Gambling/Casinos:
Distribution/Printing:	Video Distribution:	Info. Sys. Software:		Online Information:	Multimedia:	Rides/Theme Parks:

TYPES OF BUSINESS:

Electronic Bingo Game Systems
Bingo Software

BRANDS/DIVISIONS/AFFILIATES:

Traveler
Tracker
TED
Diamond Pro
AllTrack
AllTrack 2
Diamond VIP

CONTACTS: Note: Officers with more than one job title may be intentionally listed here more than once.

Jay M. Meilstrup, CEO
Jay M. Meilstrup, Pres.
Donald Tateishi, CFO
Nick Greenwood, VP-Sales & Prod. Mktg.
Justin K. Goodman, VP-R&D
Donald Tateishi, Corp. Sec.
Donald Tateishi, Treas.
Pat Crawford, VP-Bus. Affairs
Kevin Peterson, Gen. Manager-Summit Gaming
Richard T. Fedor, Chmn.

Phone: 775-850-6000	Fax: 775-850-6090
Toll-Free:	
Address: 900 Sandhill Rd., Reno, NV 89521 US	

GROWTH PLANS/SPECIAL FEATURES:

GameTech International, Inc. designs, develops and markets interactive electronic bingo terminals and systems for charitable, Native American and commercial bingo operators. The company installs both portable and fixed-base units in bingo halls in 41 out of the 47 states that allow electronic bingo and has international operations in six other countries. The firm installs the electronic bingo systems, typically at no cost to the operator, and charges either a fixed fee per use per session, a fixed weekly fee per unit or a percentage of the revenue generated by each unit. GameTech typically enters into 1-3 year contracts with bingo operators. The company's electronic bingo daubers enable players to play substantially more bingo cards than possible on paper cards, typically leading to more spending per player and higher profits per session for the operator. Daubers are sold under the Traveler, Tracker, TED and Diamond Pro brand names. The firm has exclusive licensing rights to bingo hall management software systems called AllTrack and AllTrack2, which provide bingo operators with a package of accounting and marketing information. In addition, GameTech offers its proprietary operating system known as the Diamond system. Diamond VIP allows bingo operators to verify when a player has legitimately won a game and whether the game was won on a card sold for the session being played. The Diamond and AllTrack systems can operate together, significantly enhancing management of a bingo hall. The company was recently granted a license to manufacture and distribute gaming devices by the Nevada Gaming Commission. In March 2007, the company acquired Summit Amusement & Distribuing, Ltd. for $38.9 million. Summit, which is now a division of GameTech, develops, manufactures and repairs entertainment driven gaming devices and associated software.

Employees of GameTech receive employee assistance plans; dependent care spending accounts; educational assistance; dental and life insurance; and vision and disability plans.

FINANCIALS: Sales and profits are in thousands of dollars—add 000 to get the full amount. 2007 Note: Financial information for 2007 was not available for all companies at press time.

2007 Sales: $	2007 Profits: $	U.S. Stock Ticker: GMTC
2006 Sales: $49,289	2006 Profits: $4,383	Int'l Ticker: Int'l Exchange:
2005 Sales: $49,651	2005 Profits: $1,336	Employees: 200
2004 Sales: $51,490	2004 Profits: $-9,906	Fiscal Year Ends: 10/31
2003 Sales: $52,329	2003 Profits: $1,191	Parent Company:

SALARIES/BENEFITS:

Pension Plan:	ESOP Stock Plan:	Profit Sharing:	Top Exec. Salary: $257,885	Bonus: $
Savings Plan: Y	Stock Purch. Plan:		Second Exec. Salary: $182,885	Bonus: $

OTHER THOUGHTS:

Apparent Women Officers or Directors:
Hot Spot for Advancement for Women/Minorities:

LOCATIONS: ("Y" = Yes)

West:	Southwest:	Midwest:	Southeast:	Northeast:	International:
Y	Y	Y			

Note: Financial information, benefits and other data can change quickly and may vary from those stated here.

GAMING PARTNERS INTERNATIONAL CORP
www.gpigaming.com

Industry Group Code: 713290 Ranks within this company's industry group: Sales: 9   Profits: 6

Print Media/Publishing:	Movies:	Equipment/Supplies:		Broadcast/Cable:	Music/Audio:	Sports/Games/Gambling:
Newspapers:	Movie Theaters:	Equipment/Supplies:		Broadcast TV:	Music Production:	Games/Sports:
Magazines:	Movie Production:	Gambling Equipment:	Y	Cable TV:	Retail Music:	Retail Games Stores:
Books:	TV/Video Prod.:	Special Services:	Y	Satellite Broadcast:	Retail Audio Equip.:	Stadiums/Teams:
Book Stores:	Video Rental:	Advertising Services:		Radio:	Music Print./Dist.:	Gambling/Casinos:
Distribution/Printing:	Video Distribution:	Info. Sys. Software:		Online Information:	Multimedia:	Rides/Theme Parks:

TYPES OF BUSINESS:
Casino Table Game Equipment
Gaming Furniture
Cards, Dice, Chips & Roulette Wheels
RFID-Equipped Devices
Gaming Table Accessories

BRANDS/DIVISIONS/AFFILIATES:
Paul-Son Gaming Supplies, Inc.
Bourgogne et Grasset
Bud Jones Company (The)
GPI USA
GPI SAS
GPI Mexicana
Air-Rail

CONTACTS: *Note: Officers with more than one job title may be intentionally listed here more than once.*
Gerard P. Charlier, CEO
Gerard P. Charlier, Pres.
David W. Grimes, CFO
Laura M. Cox, Chief Legal & Gaming Compliance Officer
Gay A. Nordfelt, Sec.

Phone: 702-384-2425	Fax: 702-384-1965
Toll-Free: 800-728-5766	
Address: 1700 Industrial Rd., Las Vegas, NV 89102 US	

GROWTH PLANS/SPECIAL FEATURES:
Gaming Partners International Corporation (GPI) manufactures gambling equipment, focusing on products such as dice, gaming chips, playing cards, layouts, plaques, roulette wheels and gaming furniture for casinos worldwide. GPI, with its headquarters in Las Vegas, was formed from the merger of Bourgogne et Grasset, The Bud Jones Company and Paul-Son Gaming Supplies, Inc. It is currently organized into three divisions, GPI USA, GPI SAS and GPI Mexicana. GPI SAS handles the company's European operations, while GPI Mexicana heads the firm's operations in Mexico. The firm is headquartered in Las Vegas, Nevada with manufacturing facilities located in Las Vegas, Nevada; San Luis Rio Colorado, Mexico; and Beaune, France. The company offers its products under the Paul-Son, Bud Jones and Bourgogne et Grasset name brands. The highest-security option the company offers is an anti-counterfeiting feature for casino gaming chips using radio frequency identification devices (RFIDs). An RFID microchip is embedded in a gaming chip, allowing casinos to efficiently and securely identify each chip, its location and denomination. Since a given casino will generally purchase all of its chips from one supplier, the company focuses on acquiring contracts with newly built casinos. In addition to tables and layouts, the firm also offers table accessories such as the Air-Rail system. The Air-Rail system provides a positive flow of air at the table blowing cigar and cigarette smoke away from the dealer and helps non-smokers to contend with second-hand smoke. Small air vent devices underneath the table draw the smoke in and disperse it wherever the casino's primary ventilation systems can distribute it.

FINANCIALS: Sales and profits are in thousands of dollars—add 000 to get the full amount. 2007 Note: Financial information for 2007 was not available for all companies at press time.

2007 Sales: $	2007 Profits: $	U.S. Stock Ticker: GPIC
2006 Sales: $73,954	2006 Profits: $5,129	Int'l Ticker: Int'l Exchange:
2005 Sales: $57,121	2005 Profits: $4,328	Employees: 760
2004 Sales: $44,585	2004 Profits: $2,614	Fiscal Year Ends: 5/31
2003 Sales: $36,171	2003 Profits: $1,233	Parent Company:

SALARIES/BENEFITS:
Pension Plan: Y	ESOP Stock Plan:	Profit Sharing:	Top Exec. Salary: $244,325	Bonus: $
Savings Plan: Y	Stock Purch. Plan:		Second Exec. Salary: $200,000	Bonus: $7,692

OTHER THOUGHTS:
Apparent Women Officers or Directors: 4
Hot Spot for Advancement for Women/Minorities: Y

LOCATIONS: ("Y" = Yes)
West:	Southwest:	Midwest:	Southeast:	Northeast:	International:
Y					Y

GANNETT CO INC

www.gannett.com

Industry Group Code: 511110 Ranks within this company's industry group: Sales: 2 Profits: 1

Print Media/Publishing:		Movies:		Equipment/Supplies:		Broadcast/Cable:		Music/Audio:		Sports/Games/Gambling:	
Newspapers:	Y	Movie Theaters:		Equipment/Supplies:		Broadcast TV:	Y	Music Production:		Games/Sports:	
Magazines:	Y	Movie Production:		Gambling Equipment:		Cable TV:	Y	Retail Music:		Retail Games Stores:	
Books:		TV/Video Prod.:		Special Services:	Y	Satellite Broadcast:		Retail Audio Equip.:		Stadiums/Teams:	
Book Stores:		Video Rental:		Advertising Services:	Y	Radio:		Music Print./Dist.:		Gambling/Casinos:	
Distribution/Printing:		Video Distribution:		Info. Sys. Software:		Online Information:		Multimedia:		Rides/Theme Parks:	

TYPES OF BUSINESS:

Newspaper Publishing
Broadcast & Cable Television
Radio Broadcasting
Electronic Information Services
Magazine Publishing
Online Publishing
Direct Marketing

BRANDS/DIVISIONS/AFFILIATES:

USA TODAY
USA WEEKEND
USATODAY.com
Gannett News Service
Captivate
Gannett Retail Advertising Group
Gannett Direct Marketing Services
Clipper

CONTACTS: Note: Officers with more than one job title may be intentionally listed here more than once.

Craig A. Dubow, CEO
Craig A. Dubow, Pres.
Gracia C. Martore, CFO/Exec. VP
Abigail Horrigan, VP-Mktg.
Roxanne V. Horning, VP-Human Resources
Thomas L. Chapple, Chief Admin. Officer/Sr. VP
Kurt Wimmer, General Counsel/Sr. VP
Daniel S. Ehrman, Jr., VP-Planning & Dev.
Tara J. Connell, VP-Corp. Comm.
George R. Gavagan, VP/Treas.
Dave Lougee, Pres., Gannett Broadcasting
Craig A. Moon, Publisher/Pres., USA TODAY
Paul Davidson, Chmn./CEO-Newsquest
Susan Clark-Johnson, Pres., Newspaper Div.
Craig A. Dubow, Chmn.
Karen R. Moreno, Pres., Gannett Supply

Phone: 703-854-6000	Fax: 703-364-0855
Toll-Free: 800-778-3299	
Address: 7950 Jones Branch Dr., McLean, VA 22107-0910 US	

GROWTH PLANS/SPECIAL FEATURES:

Gannett Co., Inc. is a diversified news and information company that serves audiences through publishing, television and the Internet. As one of the largest newspaper groups in the U.S., the company publishes 90 daily newspapers including USA TODAY, with a combined daily paid circulation of 7.2 million, and nearly 1,000 daily publications. Gannett also owns hundreds of non-daily and specialty U.S. publications, chief among them being USA WEEKEND, a weekly newspaper magazine with a circulation of 23 million delivered in nearly 600 Gannett and non-Gannett Sunday newspapers. Gannett additionally owns and operates 23 television stations, reaching more than 20.1 million households in the U.S., and operates over 130 web sites in the U.S. and U.K., including USATODAY.com. Other company operations include Gannett News Service and Captivate, which delivers advertising and program content via television screens installed in elevators in premier American office complexes. The company additionally utilizes its resources for extended services through divisions including Gannett Retail Advertising Group, Gannett Direct Marketing Services, Gannett Offset commercial printing, Gannett Media Technologies, Clipper direct-mail advertising and database marketing company Telematch. Specialty publications include coupon-filled shoppers, Spanish-language papers and free, weekly community tabloids. In March 2007, Gannett agreed to acquire newspaper assets from Southern Connecticut Newspapers for $73 million. In May 2007, the company sold four of its daily newspapers to GateHouseMedia, Inc. for $410 million. In June 2007, Gannett agreed to acquire the Central Ohio Advertiser Network from Journal Community Publishing Group. In October 2007, Gannett acquired a controlling interest in Schedule Star LLC, operator of HighSchoolSports.net and the Schedule Star solution.

Gannett offers its employees a flexible spending account, an employee home mortgage program, an adoption assistance plan, scholarships for dependents, a Wellness Works @ Gannett program, an employee assistance program and medical, prescription, dental, vision, mental health/substance abuse, life and accident insurance.

FINANCIALS: Sales and profits are in thousands of dollars—add 000 to get the full amount. 2007 Note: Financial information for 2007 was not available for all companies at press time.

2007 Sales: $	2007 Profits: $	U.S. Stock Ticker: GCI
2006 Sales: $8,033,354	2006 Profits: $1,160,782	Int'l Ticker: Int'l Exchange:
2005 Sales: $7,598,939	2005 Profits: $1,244,654	Employees: 49,675
2004 Sales: $7,283,662	2004 Profits: $1,317,186	Fiscal Year Ends: 12/31
2003 Sales: $6,711,115	2003 Profits: $1,211,213	Parent Company:

SALARIES/BENEFITS:

Pension Plan: Y	ESOP Stock Plan:	Profit Sharing:	Top Exec. Salary: $1,200,000	Bonus: $1,750,000
Savings Plan: Y	Stock Purch. Plan: Y		Second Exec. Salary: $876,923	Bonus: $1,250,000

OTHER THOUGHTS:

Apparent Women Officers or Directors: 12
Hot Spot for Advancement for Women/Minorities: Y

LOCATIONS: ("Y" = Yes)

West:	Southwest:	Midwest:	Southeast:	Northeast:	International:
Y	Y	Y	Y	Y	Y

Note: Financial information, benefits and other data can change quickly and may vary from those stated here.

GATEHOUSE MEDIA INC

www.gatehousemedia.com

Industry Group Code: 511110　Ranks within this company's industry group: Sales: 19　Profits: 14

Print Media/Publishing:		Movies:	Equipment/Supplies:	Broadcast/Cable:	Music/Audio:	Sports/Games/Gambling:
Newspapers:	Y	Movie Theaters:	Equipment/Supplies:	Broadcast TV:	Music Production:	Games/Sports:
Magazines:		Movie Production:	Gambling Equipment:	Cable TV:	Retail Music:	Retail Games Stores:
Books:		TV/Video Prod.:	Special Services:	Satellite Broadcast:	Retail Audio Equip.:	Stadiums/Teams:
Book Stores:		Video Rental:	Advertising Services:	Radio:	Music Print./Dist.:	Gambling/Casinos:
Distribution/Printing:		Video Distribution:	Info. Sys. Software:	Online Information:	Multimedia:	Rides/Theme Parks:

TYPES OF BUSINESS:

Newspaper Publishing
Community & Small Town Newspapers
Printing Services
Niche Publications

BRANDS/DIVISIONS/AFFILIATES:

CP Media, Inc.
Enterprise NewsMedia, LLC
SureWest Directories

CONTACTS: *Note: Officers with more than one job title may be intentionally listed here more than once.*

Michael E. Reed, CEO
Mark R. Thompson, CFO
Amy V. Kahn, Dir.-Human Resources
Paul Ameden, CIO
Polly G. Sack, General Counsel
Caroll Stacklin, Dir.-Strategic Oper.
Bill Blevins, VP-Online Oper.
Linda A. Hill, Corp. Controller
Brad Dennison, VP-Content/News Oper.
Kirk A. Davis, Pres./Publisher-GateHouse Media New England
Scott T. Champion, Co-Pres./Co-COO-Western Region
Randall W. Cope, Co-Pres./Co-COO-Southern Midwest Region

Phone: 585-598-0030	Fax:
Toll-Free:	
Address: 350 WillowBrook Office Park, Fairport, NY 14450 US	

GROWTH PLANS/SPECIAL FEATURES:

GateHouse Media, Inc. is America's largest publisher of community and small town newspapers. It owns over 445 community publications in 285 markets in 18 states. In addition, it operates 235 related websites. Publication formats include daily and weekly newspapers, shopping guides and business directories. These are broken down into 74 daily newspapers, 226 weekly newspapers (published up to three times a week) and 113 shoppers (advertising only publications). Additionally, GateHouse produces niche publications addressing specific local market interests such as recreation, sports, healthcare and real estate. In the last year, GateHouse produced 90 such publications. Functions such as ad composition, bookkeeping and production are centralized to provide GateHouse with operational efficiency. In 2006, 76% of revenues were generated by advertising broken down into local display (local retailers and local accounts), local classified (local employment, automotive, real estate and other advertisers) and national (national and major accounts such as wireless communications companies, airlines and hotels). In 2006, Circulation accounted for 17% of total revenue. Finally, commercial printing services provided to third parties contributed 7% of total revenue in 2006. GateHouse operates 53 print facilities, each of which produces an average of eight publications and is located within 60 miles of the communities it serves. In June 2006, GateHouse acquired the assets of CP Media, Inc. and the equity interests of Enterprise NewsMedia, LLC. In February 2007, acquired SureWest Directories from SureWest Communications for $110 million. SureWest publishes yellow page and white page directories in the Sacramento, California area.

FINANCIALS: Sales and profits are in thousands of dollars—add 000 to get the full amount. 2007 Note: Financial information for 2007 was not available for all companies at press time.

2007 Sales: $	2007 Profits: $	**U.S. Stock Ticker: GHS**
2006 Sales: $314,900	2006 Profits: $-1,600	**Int'l Ticker:**　Int'l Exchange:
2005 Sales: $205,000	2005 Profits: $-15,300	Employees: 4,000
2004 Sales: $200,100	2004 Profits: $-26,100	Fiscal Year Ends: 12/31
2003 Sales: $	2003 Profits: $	Parent Company:

SALARIES/BENEFITS:

Pension Plan:	ESOP Stock Plan:	Profit Sharing:	Top Exec. Salary: $230,769	Bonus: $
Savings Plan:	Stock Purch. Plan:		Second Exec. Salary: $202,769	Bonus: $100,000

OTHER THOUGHTS:

Apparent Women Officers or Directors: 4
Hot Spot for Advancement for Women/Minorities: Y

LOCATIONS: ("Y" = Yes)

West:	Southwest:	Midwest:	Southeast:	Northeast:	International:
Y	Y	Y	Y	Y	

GAYLORD ENTERTAINMENT CO
www.gaylordentertainment.com

Industry Group Code: 721110 Ranks within this company's industry group: Sales: 1 Profits: 1

Print Media/Publishing:	Movies:	Equipment/Supplies:		Broadcast/Cable:		Music/Audio:		Sports/Games/Gambling:	
Newspapers:	Movie Theaters:	Equipment/Supplies:		Broadcast TV:		Music Production:		Games/Sports:	
Magazines:	Movie Production:	Gambling Equipment:		Cable TV:		Retail Music:		Retail Games Stores:	
Books:	TV/Video Prod.:	Special Services:	Y	Satellite Broadcast:		Retail Audio Equip.:		Stadiums/Teams:	Y
Book Stores:	Video Rental:	Advertising Services:		Radio:		Music Print./Dist.:		Gambling/Casinos:	Y
Distribution/Printing:	Video Distribution:	Info. Sys. Software:		Online Information:		Multimedia:		Rides/Theme Parks:	

TYPES OF BUSINESS:

Hotels & Convention Centers
Vacation Property Management
Live Entertainment Venues
Online Vacation Rental Booking
Radio Station Operation
Golf Courses
Theme Parks

BRANDS/DIVISIONS/AFFILIATES:

ResortQuest International
Grand Ole Opry
Ryman Auditorium
General Jackson Showboat
Wildhorse Saloon
Gaylord Opryland Resort & Convention Center
Gaylord Palms Resort & Convention Center
Gaylord Texan Resort & Convention Center

CONTACTS: Note: Officers with more than one job title may be intentionally listed here more than once.

Colin V. Reed, CEO
Colin V. Reed, Pres.
David C. Kloeppel, CFO/Exec. VP
Melissa J. Buffington, Sr. VP-Human Resources
Rich Maradik, CIO/Sr. VP
Carter R. Todd, General Counsel/Sr. VP/Corp. Sec.
Melissa J. Buffington, Sr. VP-Comm.
Rob Tanner, Dir.-Investor Rel.
Mark Fioravanti, Treas/Sr. VP-Gaylord Entertainment
John Caparella, COO-Gaylord Hotels
John Imaizumi, Sr. VP/General Mgr.-Gaylord Texan Resort
Stephen Buchanan, Sr. VP-Media & Entertainment
Colin V. Reed, Chmn.

Phone: 615-316-6000	Fax: 615-316-6555
Toll-Free:	
Address: 1 Gaylord Dr., Nashville, TN 37214 US	

GROWTH PLANS/SPECIAL FEATURES:

Gaylord Entertainment Company owns and operates diversified hospitality businesses and attractions in four principal business segments: hospitality, with 68% of revenues; Opry and attractions, 8%; corporate; and ResortQuest, 24%. The hospitality segment manages the company's hotels including the Gaylord Opryland Resort in Nashville; the Gaylord Palms Resort in Kissimmee, Florida; the Gaylord Texan Resort in Grapevine, Texas; and the Gaylord National Resort in Prince George's County, Maryland. Each of the firm's resorts is designed to accommodate corporate meetings and events. The firm's Opry and attractions group operates country radio station WSM-AM radio; the General Jackson Showboat; the Gaylord Springs Golf Links, a championship golf course; and live music venues such as the Grand Ole Opry, the Ryman Auditorium and the Wildhorse Saloon. These attractions are located on the firm's Opry Complex property in Nashville, Tennessee. Gaylord's corporate segment includes investments in Viacom and the Nashville Predators hockey team. The ResortQuest division is the one of the U.S.'s leading vacation property management companies and a major online provider of reservations for vacation home rentals, providing management services to around 14,500 properties. The majority of these homes are second or vacation homes open to rental during off-seasons. In February 2007, the company announced a proposal for a $400 million expansion to Gaylord Opryland, including adding a new 400 room hotel and a 4,000 square foot convention center. In June 2007, Gaylord completed the sale of its ResortQuest mainland business to a subsidiary of Leucadia National Corporation for $35 million. Gaylord also completed the sale of the ResortQuest Hawaiian business to Interval Acquisition Corp. for approximately $109 million. Also in June 2007, Gaylord completed the sale of its interest in the Bass Pro Group, LLC back to the company for $222 million.

FINANCIALS: Sales and profits are in thousands of dollars—add 000 to get the full amount. 2007 Note: Financial information for 2007 was not available for all companies at press time.

2007 Sales: $	2007 Profits: $	**U.S. Stock Ticker: GET**
2006 Sales: $947,922	2006 Profits: $-79,435	**Int'l Ticker:** Int'l Exchange:
2005 Sales: $868,789	2005 Profits: $-33,950	Employees: 8,983
2004 Sales: $749,453	2004 Profits: $-53,638	Fiscal Year Ends: 12/31
2003 Sales: $448,800	2003 Profits: $ 900	Parent Company:

SALARIES/BENEFITS:

Pension Plan: Y	ESOP Stock Plan:	Profit Sharing:	Top Exec. Salary: $823,385	Bonus: $1,236,033
Savings Plan:	Stock Purch. Plan: Y		Second Exec. Salary: $488,885	Bonus: $550,421

OTHER THOUGHTS:

Apparent Women Officers or Directors: 1
Hot Spot for Advancement for Women/Minorities:

LOCATIONS: ("Y" = Yes)

West:	Southwest:	Midwest:	Southeast:	Northeast:	International:
Y	Y		Y	Y	

Note: Financial information, benefits and other data can change quickly and may vary from those stated here.

GEMSTAR-TV GUIDE INTERNATIONAL INC
www.gemstartvguide.com
Industry Group Code: 514199 Ranks within this company's industry group: Sales: 1   Profits: 1

Print Media/Publishing:		Movies:		Equipment/Supplies:		Broadcast/Cable:		Music/Audio:		Sports/Games/Gambling:	
Newspapers:		Movie Theaters:		Equipment/Supplies:		Broadcast TV:		Music Production:		Games/Sports:	
Magazines:	Y	Movie Production:		Gambling Equipment:		Cable TV:		Retail Music:		Retail Games Stores:	
Books:		TV/Video Prod.:		Special Services:	Y	Satellite Broadcast:		Retail Audio Equip.:		Stadiums/Teams:	
Book Stores:		Video Rental:		Advertising Services:	Y	Radio:		Music Print./Dist.:		Gambling/Casinos:	
Distribution/Printing:		Video Distribution:		Info. Sys. Software:		Online Information:		Multimedia:		Rides/Theme Parks:	

TYPES OF BUSINESS:
Online Information Service-TV Listings
Magazine & Catalog Publishing
Online Publishing
Program Promotion & Guide Services
Satellite Broadcast Services

BRANDS/DIVISIONS/AFFILIATES:
TV Guide
TV Guide SPOT
TV Guide Magazine
TV Guide Entertainment
TVG Network
TV Guide Online
TV Guide Data Solutions
TV Programming

CONTACTS: *Note: Officers with more than one job title may be intentionally listed here more than once.*
Richard Battista, CEO
Mike McKee, COO
Bedi A. Singh, CFO/Exec. VP
Alan Cohen, Chief Mktg. Officer
Dustin Finer, Sr. VP-Human Resources
Bob Foos, CIO/Sr. VP
Stephen H. Kay, General Counsel/Exec. VP
Sanjay Reddy, Sr. VP-Bus. Dev. & Strategic Planning
Eileen Murphy, Sr. VP-Corp. Comm.
Peter C. Halt, Chief Acct. Officer/Sr. VP
J. Scott Crystal, Pres., TV Guide Magazine
Richard Cusick, Sr. VP/General Mgr.-Digital Media
Steve Shannon, Exec. VP/General Mgr.-Prod. Dev.
Bob Shallow, VP/General Mgr.-Mobile Entertainment Group
Anthea Disney, Chmn.
Tonia O'Connor, Exec. VP-Distribution

Phone: 323-817-4600	**Fax:** 323-817-4623
Toll-Free:	
Address: 6922 Hollywood Blvd., 12th Fl., Los Angeles, CA 90028 US	

GROWTH PLANS/SPECIAL FEATURES:
Gemstar-TV Guide International, Inc. is a media, entertainment and technology company that develops, licenses, markets and distributes products and services targeted at the video guidance and entertainment needs of consumers worldwide. The company operates in four segments: cable and satellite; publishing; consumer electronics; and corporate. The cable and satellite segment includes the operations of TV Guide Channel, TV Guide Interactive, TVG Network, TV Guide SPOT and TV Guide Entertainment. TV Guide Channel offers television-related entertainment programming, program listings and descriptions primarily in the U.S. TV Guide Interactive licenses technologies and services related to television interactive program guide (IPG) to multiple system operator and digital broadcast satellite providers. TVG Network is a television network that combines live horse racing with the convenience of wagering from home via telephone, online, interactive set-top box and WAP enabled mobile wagering. TV Guide SPOT features advertiser supported on-demand short-form, originally-produced entertainment programs. TV Guide Entertainment focuses on distributing the firm's content and guidance products on mobile devices, including video-enabled cell phones and personal digital assistants. The publishing segment consists of TV Guide magazine, which provides access to Hollywood and its content; TV Guide online, a TV information, entertainment and guidance destination that provides consumers with a combination of entertainment news, TV programming, which provides celebrity information, localized channel listings, editorial guidance, community features and search features; and TV Guide Data Solutions, a data collection and distribution business that gathers and distributes program listings and channel lineups. The consumer electronics segment consists of CE IPG technology and patent licensing to third party guide developers. The corporate segment includes company-related functions. Gemstar-TV owns a 49% stake in a joint venture with Comcast, Guideworks LLC, which develops IPG for the cable industry. In December 2007, the company agreed to be acquired by Macrovision Corp. for roughly $2.8 billion.

FINANCIALS: Sales and profits are in thousands of dollars—add 000 to get the full amount. 2007 Note: Financial information for 2007 was not available for all companies at press time.

2007 Sales: $	2007 Profits: $	**U.S. Stock Ticker: GMST**
2006 Sales: $571,254	2006 Profits: $72,464	**Int'l Ticker:** Int'l Exchange:
2005 Sales: $604,192	2005 Profits: $54,815	Employees: 1,691
2004 Sales: $676,369	2004 Profits: $-94,461	Fiscal Year Ends: 12/31
2003 Sales: $878,700	2003 Profits: $-577,400	Parent Company:

SALARIES/BENEFITS:

Pension Plan:	ESOP Stock Plan:	Profit Sharing:	Top Exec. Salary: $915,815	Bonus: $624,863
Savings Plan:	Stock Purch. Plan:		Second Exec. Salary: $708,346	Bonus: $408,436

OTHER THOUGHTS:
Apparent Women Officers or Directors: 3
Hot Spot for Advancement for Women/Minorities: Y

LOCATIONS: ("Y" = Yes)

West:	Southwest:	Midwest:	Southeast:	Northeast:	International:
Y					Y

Note: Financial information, benefits and other data can change quickly and may vary from those stated here.

GENERAL ELECTRIC CO (GE)   www.ge.com

Industry Group Code: 522220A Ranks within this company's industry group: Sales: 1   Profits: 1

Print Media/Publishing:	Movies:		Equipment/Supplies:		Broadcast/Cable:		Music/Audio:		Sports/Games/Gambling:	
Newspapers:	Movie Theaters:		Equipment/Supplies:	Y	Broadcast TV:	Y	Music Production:		Games/Sports:	
Magazines:	Movie Production:	Y	Gambling Equipment:		Cable TV:	Y	Retail Music:		Retail Games Stores:	
Books:	TV/Video Prod.:	Y	Special Services:		Satellite Broadcast:		Retail Audio Equip.:		Stadiums/Teams:	
Book Stores:	Video Rental:		Advertising Services:		Radio:		Music Print./Dist.:	Y	Gambling/Casinos:	
Distribution/Printing:	Video Distribution:	Y	Info. Sys. Software:		Online Information:		Multimedia:		Rides/Theme Parks:	

TYPES OF BUSINESS:

Business Leasing & Finance
Energy Systems & Consulting
Insurance & Financial Services
Industrial & Electrical Equipment & Consumer Products
Television & Film Production & Distribution
Real Estate Investments & Finance
Medical Equipment
Transportation, Aircraft Engines, Rail Systems & Truck Fleet Management

BRANDS/DIVISIONS/AFFILIATES:

GE Commercial Finance
GE Consumer Finance
GE Healthcare
NBC Universal
GE Plastics
ZENON Evironmental, Inc.
GE Money

CONTACTS: Note: Officers with more than one job title may be intentionally listed here more than once.

Jeffrey R. Immelt, CEO
Keith S. Sherin, CFO
Dan Henson, Chief Mktg. Officer
John Lynch, Sr. VP-Corp. Human Resources
Mark M. Little, Sr. VP/Dir.-Global Research
Gary M. Reiner, CIO/Sr. VP
Brackett B. Denniston, III, General Counsel/Sr. VP
Wayne Hewett, VP-Oper.
Pamela Daley, Sr. VP-Corp. Bus. Dev.
Daniel Janki, Corp. Investor Comm.
Kathryn A. Cassidy, Treas./VP
Michael A. Neal, Vice Chmn./CEO/Pres., GE Commercial Finance
John G. Rice, Vice Chmn./CEO/Pres., GE Infrastructure
Lloyd G. Trotter, Vice Chmn./CEO/Pres., GE Industrial
Susan P. Peters, VP-Exec. Dev.
Jeffrey R. Immelt, Chmn.
Ferdinando (Nani) Beccalli-Falco, CEO/Pres., Int'l
Wayne Hewett, VP-Supply Chain

Phone: 203-373-2211	**Fax:** 203-373-3131
Toll-Free:	
Address: 3135 Easton Turnpike, Fairfield, CT 06828-0001 US	

GROWTH PLANS/SPECIAL FEATURES:

General Electric Co. (GE) is one of the world's largest and most diversified corporations, with six operating divisions: infrastructure, commercial finance, GE Money (formerly consumer finance), healthcare, NBC Universal and industrial. GE's infrastructure division, its largest operating segment, produces, sells, finances and services equipment for the air and rail transportation, water treatment and energy generation industries. GE's commercial finance segment offers financial services mainly to manufacturers, distributors and end-users, including loans and leases. GE Money offers credit and deposit products to consumers, retailers, banks and auto dealers in over 50 countries. The healthcare segment develops diagnostic and therapy equipment including MRI and CT scanners, x-ray, nuclear imaging and ultrasound equipment. NBC Universal, the company's network television affiliate, broadcasts to affiliated television stations within the U.S., produces live and recorded television programs, operates television broadcasting stations and produces and distributes films. GE's industrial segment produces and sells products including consumer appliances, industrial equipment, plastics and also provides asset management services for the transportation industry. In 2006, the company acquired ZENON Environmental, Inc., a leader in advanced membranes for water purification and wastewater treatment. Later in 2006, the company sold its silicone and quartz business for $3.4 billion to Apollo Management, LP. In January 2007, GE acquired the aerospace division of Smiths Group PLC for $4.8 billion; and agreed to acquire Abbott Laboratories for $8.13 billion. In March 2007, the firm agreed acquire PHH Corporation with the Blackstone Group for $1.69 billion. In April 2007, GE acquired Wave Biotech LLC, a disposable manufacturing technologies supplier to the biopharmaceutical industry. In August 2007, the firm sold GE Plastics to Saudi Basic Industries Corporation for $11.6 billion.

GE provides its employees with tuition, adoption, parenting and child care assistance; education and career counseling; and legal and financial information services.

FINANCIALS: Sales and profits are in thousands of dollars—add 000 to get the full amount. 2007 Note: Financial information for 2007 was not available for all companies at press time.

2007 Sales: $	2007 Profits: $	**U.S. Stock Ticker: GE**
2006 Sales: $163,391,000	2006 Profits: $20,829,000	**Int'l Ticker:** Int'l Exchange:
2005 Sales: $150,242,000	2005 Profits: $16,711,000	Employees: 319,000
2004 Sales: $134,481,000	2004 Profits: $16,285,000	Fiscal Year Ends: 12/31
2003 Sales: $134,187,000	2003 Profits: $15,002,000	Parent Company:

SALARIES/BENEFITS:

Pension Plan:	ESOP Stock Plan:	Profit Sharing:	Top Exec. Salary: $3,300,000	Bonus: $5,000,000
Savings Plan: Y	Stock Purch. Plan:		Second Exec. Salary: $2,500,000	Bonus: $6,900,000

OTHER THOUGHTS:

Apparent Women Officers or Directors: 10
Hot Spot for Advancement for Women/Minorities: Y

LOCATIONS: ("Y" = Yes)

West:	Southwest:	Midwest:	Southeast:	Northeast:	International:
Y	Y	Y	Y	Y	Y

Note: Financial information, benefits and other data can change quickly and may vary from those stated here.

GLAM MEDIA INC
www.glammedia.com

Industry Group Code: 514199 Ranks within this company's industry group: Sales: Profits:

Print Media/Publishing:	Movies:	Equipment/Supplies:		Broadcast/Cable:	Music/Audio:	Sports/Games/Gambling:
Newspapers:	Movie Theaters:	Equipment/Supplies:		Broadcast TV:	Music Production:	Games/Sports:
Magazines:	Movie Production:	Gambling Equipment:		Cable TV:	Retail Music:	Retail Games Stores:
Books:	TV/Video Prod.:	Special Services:	Y	Satellite Broadcast:	Retail Audio Equip.:	Stadiums/Teams:
Book Stores:	Video Rental:	Advertising Services:	Y	Radio:	Music Print./Dist.:	Gambling/Casinos:
Distribution/Printing:	Video Distribution:	Info. Sys. Software:		Online Information:	Multimedia:	Rides/Theme Parks:

TYPES OF BUSINESS:
Distributed Media Network
Online Portals
Niche Publishing

BRANDS/DIVISIONS/AFFILIATES:
Glam.com
Nylonmag
Fashiontribes
VideoJug
Popbytes
Smilebox
Teenfashionista
Glam Media Vertical Network

CONTACTS: *Note: Officers with more than one job title may be intentionally listed here more than once.*
Samir Arora, CEO
Ernie Cicogna, CFO
Scott Schiller, Exec. VP-Sales & Women's Markets
Fernando Ruarte, CTO
Fernando Ruarte, VP-Eng.
Dianna Mullins, VP-Glam Publisher Network Oper.
Jennifer Salant, VP-Bus. Dev.
Caroline Hacker, Manager-Corp. Comm.
John Trimble, Exec. VP-New Markets Sales
Carl Portale, VP/Dir.-Publishing
Joe Lagani, VP/Gen. Manager-GlamLiving
Scott Swanson, VP/Gen. Manager-Glam Media Publisher Network
Samir Arora, Chmn.
Ralf Hirt, VP-Int'l

Phone: 650-244-4000	Fax: 650-244-4004
Toll-Free:	
Address: 8000 Marina Blvd., Ste. 300, Brisbane, CA 94005 US	

GROWTH PLANS/SPECIAL FEATURES:

Glam Media, Inc. operates a distributed media network that reaches 43 million people through more than 530 lifestyle blogs and web sites, including its flagship, Glam.com. The firm focuses on women; its target user is 38 years old and has a household income of $72,000. Glam attempts to recreate the stylish feel of popular women's magazines on its web sites. Its original goal was to attract the advertising revenue being funneled into TV and print onto the web utilizing the idea of context driven advertising, or matching advertisements to the content. The company currently distributes content from more than 400 publishers, and its advertisers include Victoria's Secret, Target, ABC, Garnier, Crystal Light, Lacoste, Bergdorf Goodman, Maybelline, Neiman Marcus and Reebok. Some of its partners include the Lifetime television network, Oxygen, Cosmopolitan and AOL. Glam's web sites are divided between the following categories: Fashion, with 135 sites; Beauty, 62; Lifestyle, 108; Celebrity & Entertainment, 97; Health & Wellness, 16; Shopping, 85; Quizzes & Fun, 15; and Teens & GenY, 12. This planned diversity allows advertisers to target large groups such as fashion conscious women, or more selective groups, such as moms, food lovers or ethnic groups. Its web site names include Nylonmag, Fashiontribes, Ebeautydaily, Dogster/Catster, VideoJug, Popbytes, Nubella, ifit&healthy, Smilebox, Meez, Jargol, Teenfashionista and Girlsense. These web sites feature style tips, shopping guides, hair care advice, product reviews, recipes, celebrity photo galleries, movie reviews, exercise routines, games, virtual characters, gift guides and fashion blogs. The Glam Media Vertical Network (MVN) platform forms the heart of the firm's services. It offers advertising companies tools and infrastructure to create their own vertical networks. These offerings include training, consultation, pricing, publisher recruitment, ad serving, inventory management, billing systems, performance analysis, technical support, campaign optimization, reporting and custom content distribution applications.

FINANCIALS: Sales and profits are in thousands of dollars—add 000 to get the full amount. 2007 Note: Financial information for 2007 was not available for all companies at press time.

2007 Sales: $25,000	2007 Profits: $	U.S. Stock Ticker: Private
2006 Sales: $	2006 Profits: $	Int'l Ticker: Int'l Exchange:
2005 Sales: $	2005 Profits: $	Employees:
2004 Sales: $	2004 Profits: $	Fiscal Year Ends: 12/31
2003 Sales: $	2003 Profits: $	Parent Company:

SALARIES/BENEFITS:

Pension Plan:	ESOP Stock Plan:	Profit Sharing:	Top Exec. Salary: $	Bonus: $
Savings Plan:	Stock Purch. Plan:		Second Exec. Salary: $	Bonus: $

OTHER THOUGHTS:
Apparent Women Officers or Directors: 19
Hot Spot for Advancement for Women/Minorities: Y

LOCATIONS: ("Y" = Yes)

West:	Southwest:	Midwest:	Southeast:	Northeast:	International:
Y				Y	Y

GLU MOBILE INC

www.glu.com

Industry Group Code: 511208 Ranks within this company's industry group: Sales: 9   Profits: 7

Print Media/Publishing:	Movies:	Equipment/Supplies:	Broadcast/Cable:	Music/Audio:	Sports/Games/Gambling:	
Newspapers:	Movie Theaters:	Equipment/Supplies:	Broadcast TV:	Music Production:	Games/Sports:	Y
Magazines:	Movie Production:	Gambling Equipment:	Cable TV:	Retail Music:	Retail Games Stores:	
Books:	TV/Video Prod.:	Special Services: ·	Satellite Broadcast:	Retail Audio Equip.:	Stadiums/Teams:	
Book Stores:	Video Rental:	Advertising Services:	Radio:	Music Print./Dist.:	Gambling/Casinos:	
Distribution/Printing:	Video Distribution:	Info. Sys. Software:	Online Information:	Multimedia:	Rides/Theme Parks:	

TYPES OF BUSINESS:

Mobile Entertainment Applications
Mobile Phone Games

BRANDS/DIVISIONS/AFFILIATES:

iFone
Super K.O. Boxing!
Stranded
Ancient Empire

CONTACTS: Note: Officers with more than one job title may be intentionally listed here more than once.

Greg Ballard, CEO
Greg Ballard, Pres.
Rocky Pimentel, CFO/Exec. VP
Jill Braff, Sr. VP-Worldwide Mktg./General Mgr.-Americas
Rocky Francis, Mgr.-Global Human Resources
Ron Sha, CIO/VP
Alex Galvagni, CTO
Alex Galvani, Sr. VP-Prod. Dev.
Alex Galvagni, Sr. VP-Eng.
Kevin Chou, General Counsel/VP
Nate Jones, VP-Corp. Dev.
Eric Ludwig, VP-Finance
Sami Lababidi, CTO-EMEA
Greg Suarez, VP-Licensing
David Ward, Chmn.
Denis Guyennot, CEO-EMEA

Phone: 650-571-1550	Fax: 650-571-5698
Toll-Free:	
Address: 1800 Gateway Dr., 2nd Fl., San Mateo, CA 94404 US	

GROWTH PLANS/SPECIAL FEATURES:

Glu Mobile, Inc. is a global publisher of mobile games. The company has developed and published a portfolio of more than 100 casual and traditional games across a number of genres, including action, board game, card/casino, puzzle, sports, strategy/role playing games and TV/movie. The company has more than 1 billion subscribers worldwide served by its more than 150 wireless carriers and other distributors. The firm creates games and related applications based on third-party licensed brands and other intellectual property, as well as on its own original brands and intellectual property. Glu Mobile's business leverages the marketing resources and distribution infrastructure of wireless carriers and the brands and other intellectual property of third-party content owners, allowing it to focus its efforts on developing and publishing mobile games. For the first 9 months of 2006, the company's largest wireless carrier customers in each region by revenues were Verizon Wireless, Sprint Nextel, Cingular Wireless and T-Mobile in the U.S. In April 2006, GLU Mobile acquired iFone, a wireless entertainment publisher based in Manchester, U.K. In March 2007, Glu Mobile had its initial public offering of stock (IPO) and became a public company. In May 2007, Glu Mobile partnered with Warner Bros. Digital Distribution, which gives the company worldwide rights to develop, market and distribute mobile games and content based on select new film releases as well as games and content from Warner Bros. Entertainment's library.

FINANCIALS: Sales and profits are in thousands of dollars—add 000 to get the full amount. 2007 Note: Financial information for 2007 was not available for all companies at press time.

2007 Sales: $	2007 Profits: $	**U.S. Stock Ticker: GLUU**
2006 Sales: $46,166	2006 Profits: $-12,310	**Int'l Ticker:** Int'l Exchange:
2005 Sales: $25,651	2005 Profits: $-17,901	Employees: 243
2004 Sales: $7,022	2004 Profits: $-8,322	Fiscal Year Ends: 12/31
2003 Sales: $	2003 Profits: $	Parent Company:

SALARIES/BENEFITS:

Pension Plan:	ESOP Stock Plan:	Profit Sharing:	Top Exec. Salary: $	Bonus: $
Savings Plan:	Stock Purch. Plan:		Second Exec. Salary: $	Bonus: $

OTHER THOUGHTS:

Apparent Women Officers or Directors: 3
Hot Spot for Advancement for Women/Minorities: Y

LOCATIONS: ("Y" = Yes)

West:	Southwest:	Midwest:	Southeast:	Northeast:	International:
Y					Y

GOLD'S GYM INTERNATIONAL   www.goldsgym.com

Industry Group Code: 713940 Ranks within this company's industry group: Sales: Profits:

Print Media/Publishing:	Movies:	Equipment/Supplies:	Broadcast/Cable:	Music/Audio:	Sports/Games/Gambling:	
Newspapers:	Movie Theaters:	Equipment/Supplies:	Broadcast TV:	Music Production:	Games/Sports:	Y
Magazines:	Movie Production:	Gambling Equipment:	Cable TV:	Retail Music:	Retail Games Stores:	
Books:	TV/Video Prod.:	Special Services:	Satellite Broadcast:	Retail Audio Equip.:	Stadiums/Teams:	
Book Stores:	Video Rental:	Advertising Services:	Radio:	Music Print./Dist.:	Gambling/Casinos:	
Distribution/Printing:	Video Distribution:	Info. Sys. Software:	Online Information:	Multimedia:	Rides/Theme Parks:	

TYPES OF BUSINESS:
Fitness Centers

BRANDS/DIVISIONS/AFFILIATES:
GoldsGear.com

CONTACTS: *Note: Officers with more than one job title may be intentionally listed here more than once.*
David Schnabel, CEO
David Schnabel, Pres.
Randy Schultz, CFO
Lisa Zoellner, Chief Mktg. Officer
Bill Wade, CIO
Joel Tallman, VP-Oper.
Joel Tallman, VP-Franchising Oper.

Phone: 214-574-4653	Fax: 214-296-5000
Toll-Free: 866-465-3775	
Address: 125 E. John Carpenter Freeway, Ste. 1300, Irving, TX 75062 US	

GROWTH PLANS/SPECIAL FEATURES:

Gold's Gym International, Inc. is one of the largest co-ed gym chains in the world. With 3 million members, Gold's Gym has over 620 franchised gyms in 42 states and in 30 countries, including the U.K., Canada, Australia, Mexico, Peru, the Virgin Islands, Japan, India, Germany and Russia. Members of Gold's not only have access to what are recognized as the industry's leading gyms, but they can also work with personal trainers to devise meal plans and develop weight programs. Gold's Gym works with other companies in the health and fitness industry by offering flexible advertising campaigns, sponsorships and promotional opportunities within its gyms. Each gym offers all of the latest equipment and services, including group exercise classes, cardiovascular equipment, spinning, Pilates and yoga, while maintaining its core weight lifting tradition. In addition to managing its own web site, the firm operates GoldsGear.com, an online store that offers Gold's Gym branded merchandise.

The company offers its employees benefits that include medical, dental and vision insurance; a retirement savings plan; training in a team-oriented work environment; and a free gym membership.

FINANCIALS: Sales and profits are in thousands of dollars—add 000 to get the full amount. 2007 Note: Financial information for 2007 was not available for all companies at press time.

2007 Sales: $	2007 Profits: $	U.S. Stock Ticker: Private
2006 Sales: $	2006 Profits: $	Int'l Ticker: Int'l Exchange:
2005 Sales: $	2005 Profits: $	Employees:
2004 Sales: $	2004 Profits: $	Fiscal Year Ends: 2/28
2003 Sales: $	2003 Profits: $	Parent Company:

SALARIES/BENEFITS:

Pension Plan:	ESOP Stock Plan:	Profit Sharing:	Top Exec. Salary: $	Bonus: $
Savings Plan: Y	Stock Purch. Plan:		Second Exec. Salary: $	Bonus: $

OTHER THOUGHTS:
Apparent Women Officers or Directors:
Hot Spot for Advancement for Women/Minorities:

LOCATIONS: ("Y" = Yes)

West:	Southwest:	Midwest:	Southeast:	Northeast:	International:
Y	Y	Y	Y	Y	Y

GOOGLE INC

www.google.com

Industry Group Code: 514199B Ranks within this company's industry group: Sales: 1 Profits: 1

Print Media/Publishing:	Movies:	Equipment/Supplies:		Broadcast/Cable:	Music/Audio:	Sports/Games/Gambling:
Newspapers:	Movie Theaters:	Equipment/Supplies:		Broadcast TV:	Music Production:	Games/Sports:
Magazines:	Movie Production:	Gambling Equipment:		Cable TV:	Retail Music:	Retail Games Stores:
Books:	TV/Video Prod.:	Special Services:	Y	Satellite Broadcast:	Retail Audio Equip.:	Stadiums/Teams:
Book Stores:	Video Rental:	Advertising Services:	Y	Radio:	Music Print./Dist.:	Gambling/Casinos:
Distribution/Printing:	Video Distribution:	Info. Sys. Software:		Online Information:	Multimedia:	Rides/Theme Parks:

TYPES OF BUSINESS:

Search Engine-Internet
Paid Search Listing Advertising Services
News Site Search Service
Catalog Search Service
Shopping Site
Web Log Tool

BRANDS/DIVISIONS/AFFILIATES:

Google
Google AdWords
Google AdSense
MySpace
News Corps.
Adscape Media, Inc.

CONTACTS: Note: Officers with more than one job title may be intentionally listed here more than once.

Eric E. Schmidt, CEO
George Reyes, CFO/Sr. VP
Omid Kordestani, Sr. VP-Worldwide Sales & Bus. Dev.
Laszlo Bock, VP-People Oper.
Alan Eustace, Sr. VP-Research
Sergey Brin, Pres., Tech.
Larry Page, Pres., Products
Alan Eustace, Sr. VP-Eng.
Kent Walker, General Counsel/VP
Urs Holzle, Sr. VP-Oper./Google Fellow
David C. Drummond, VP-Corp. Dev./Chief Legal Officer
Sheryl Sandberg, VP-Global Online Sales & Oper.
Elliot Schrage, VP-Global Comm. & Public Affairs
Mark Fuchs, VP-Finance/Chief Acct. Officer
Marissa Mayer, VP-Search Products & User Experience
Vinton G. Cerf, VP/Chief Internet Evangelist
Kai-Fu Lee, VP/Pres., Greater China
Norio Murakami, VP/General Mgr./Pres., Google Japan
Eric E. Schmidt, Chmn.
Nikesh Arora, VP/Pres., EMEA

Phone: 650-250-0000	Fax: 650-253-0001
Toll-Free:	
Address: 1600 Amphitheatre Pkwy., Mountain View, CA 94043 US	

GROWTH PLANS/SPECIAL FEATURES:

Google, Inc. operates Google.com, one of the worlds largest and most used search engines, which indexes the content of over 8 billion Internet pages. While Google charges nothing for its search engine, it charges fees to other sites that use its search technology, and has a lucrative program that enables business clients to bid for ad space. Google provides its services in 116 different languages, with more than 50% of its searches coming from outside the U.S. The company's technology employs a unique, distributed-computing system utilizing thousands of low-end servers rather than a small number of high-powered computers. Google has teamed with the libraries of Harvard, Stanford, Oxford, the University of Michigan and The New York Public Library to digitally scan books in their collections and make them searchable online. The company offers Google AdWords, a global advertising program which presents ads to customers precisely when they are looking for what the advertiser has to offer. Google AdSense allows web sites in the Google Network to serve targeted ads from the AdWords advertisers. In August 2006, Google won the right to provide search technology to MySpace.com, owned by News Corp. Under the terms of the agreement, Google promises to pay News Corp. a minimum of $900 million in cash between 2007 and the second quarter of 2010. In March 2007, Google acquired Adscape Media, Inc., which delivers Internet videogame advertising placement. In April 2007, Google agreed to acquire marketing firm, DoubleClick Inc., for $3.1 billion. In July 2007, the firm agreed to acquire Postini, Inc., an e-mail security company, for $625 million.

Employee perks include adoption assistance; tuition reimbursement; flexible spending accounts; medical, dental, life and vision insurance; child care; and free on-site lunches and dinners. Google also provides recreation facilities, financial planning classes and on-site dry cleaning facilities.

FINANCIALS: Sales and profits are in thousands of dollars—add 000 to get the full amount. 2007 Note: Financial information for 2007 was not available for all companies at press time.

2007 Sales: $	2007 Profits: $	U.S. Stock Ticker: GOOG
2006 Sales: $10,604,917	2006 Profits: $3,077,446	Int'l Ticker: Int'l Exchange:
2005 Sales: $6,138,560	2005 Profits: $1,465,397	Employees: 10,674
2004 Sales: $3,189,223	2004 Profits: $399,119	Fiscal Year Ends: 12/31
2003 Sales: $1,465,934	2003 Profits: $105,648	Parent Company:

SALARIES/BENEFITS:

Pension Plan: Y	ESOP Stock Plan:	Profit Sharing:	Top Exec. Salary: $250,000	Bonus: $927,000
Savings Plan: Y	Stock Purch. Plan:		Second Exec. Salary: $250,000	Bonus: $764,367

OTHER THOUGHTS:

Apparent Women Officers or Directors: 5
Hot Spot for Advancement for Women/Minorities: Y

LOCATIONS: ("Y" = Yes)

West:	Southwest:	Midwest:	Southeast:	Northeast:	International:
Y	Y	Y	Y	Y	Y

Note: Financial information, benefits and other data can change quickly and may vary from those stated here.

GRANITE BROADCASTING CORP　　　www.granitetv.com

Industry Group Code: 513120　Ranks within this company's industry group: Sales:　Profits:

Print Media/Publishing:	Movies:	Equipment/Supplies:	Broadcast/Cable:		Music/Audio:	Sports/Games/Gambling:
Newspapers:	Movie Theaters:	Equipment/Supplies:	Broadcast TV:	Y	Music Production:	Games/Sports:
Magazines:	Movie Production:	Gambling Equipment:	Cable TV:		Retail Music:	Retail Games Stores:
Books:	TV/Video Prod.:	Special Services:	Satellite Broadcast:		Retail Audio Equip.:	Stadiums/Teams:
Book Stores:	Video Rental:	Advertising Services:	Radio:		Music Print./Dist.:	Gambling/Casinos:
Distribution/Printing:	Video Distribution:	Info. Sys. Software:	Online Information:		Multimedia:	Rides/Theme Parks:

TYPES OF BUSINESS:

Television Broadcasting

BRANDS/DIVISIONS/AFFILIATES:

CONTACTS: *Note: Officers with more than one job title may be intentionally listed here more than once.*

W. Don Cornwell, CEO
John Deushane, COO
Lawrence I Willis, CFO/Sr. VP
Ann Beemish, VP-Corp. Dev.
Ann Beemish, Treas.
W. Don Cornwell, Chmn.

Phone: 212-826-2530	Fax: 212-826-2858
Toll-Free:	
Address: 767 3rd Ave., 34th Fl., New York, NY 10017 US	

GROWTH PLANS/SPECIAL FEATURES:

Granite Broadcasting Corporation is a television broadcasting company specializing in developing and operating small to middle market television broadcast stations in the U.S. The company owns and operates or provides programming, sales and other services to 23 television channels in 11 markets: San Francisco, California; Detroit, Michigan; Buffalo, New York; Fresno, California; Syracuse, New York; Fort Wayne, Indiana; Peoria, Illinois; and Duluth, Minnesota-Superior, Wisconsin. All of these channels are affiliated with ABC, NBC, CBS, CW and MyNetworkTV broadcasting networks and reach approximately 6% of all U.S. television households. The company generates its revenue through its network affiliations, trading its advertising time for cash payments from the affiliated networks. Most of the television stations owned by the company are operated through separate wholly-owned subsidiaries. The company's business strategy is to provide high quality local news and sports for each of the markets it serves. Granite's goal is to become the leading provider of news, weather and sports information in these markets. In recent news, the company acquired WBNG-TV, a CBS affiliate in Binghamton and Elmira, New York for $45 million in cash. In addition, the firm's WDWB (Detroit, Michigan) and KBJR-DT (Duluth, Michigan) signed on as MyNetworkTV affiliates. Founder, chairman and CEO Don Cornwell owns 10% of Granite Broadcasting and controls all of the company's voting stock. The company has been operating under Chapter 11 bankruptcy since late 2006 and is in the midst of reorganization proceedings.

FINANCIALS: Sales and profits are in thousands of dollars—add 000 to get the full amount. 2007 Note: Financial information for 2007 was not available for all companies at press time.

2007 Sales: $	2007 Profits: $	U.S. Stock Ticker: GRRP.PK
2006 Sales: $	2006 Profits: $	Int'l Ticker:　Int'l Exchange:
2005 Sales: $86,160	2005 Profits: $-98,926	Employees: 749
2004 Sales: $80,500	2004 Profits: $-83,292	Fiscal Year Ends: 12/31
2003 Sales: $108,544	2003 Profits: $-46,948	Parent Company:

SALARIES/BENEFITS:

Pension Plan:	ESOP Stock Plan:	Profit Sharing:	Top Exec. Salary: $672,000	Bonus: $679,000
Savings Plan: Y	Stock Purch. Plan: Y		Second Exec. Salary: $672,000	Bonus: $480,000

OTHER THOUGHTS:

Apparent Women Officers or Directors: 1
Hot Spot for Advancement for Women/Minorities:

LOCATIONS: ("Y" = Yes)

West:	Southwest:	Midwest:	Southeast:	Northeast:	International:
Y		Y		Y	

GRAY TELEVISION INC

www.gray.tv

Industry Group Code: 513120 Ranks within this company's industry group: Sales: 13 Profits: 12

Print Media/Publishing:	Movies:	Equipment/Supplies:		Broadcast/Cable:		Music/Audio:	Sports/Games/Gambling:
Newspapers:	Movie Theaters:	Equipment/Supplies:		Broadcast TV:	Y	Music Production:	Games/Sports:
Magazines:	Movie Production:	Gambling Equipment:		Cable TV:		Retail Music:	Retail Games Stores:
Books:	TV/Video Prod.:	Special Services:	Y	Satellite Broadcast:		Retail Audio Equip.:	Stadiums/Teams:
Book Stores:	Video Rental:	Advertising Services:	Y	Radio:		Music Print./Dist.:	Gambling/Casinos:
Distribution/Printing:	Video Distribution:	Info. Sys. Software:		Online Information:		Multimedia:	Rides/Theme Parks:

TYPES OF BUSINESS:
Television Broadcasting

BRANDS/DIVISIONS/AFFILIATES:
Triple Crown Media

CONTACTS: Note: Officers with more than one job title may be intentionally listed here more than once.
J. Mack Robinson, CEO
Robert S. Prather, Jr., COO
Robert S. Prather, Jr., Pres.
James C. Ryan, CFO/Sr. VP
Robert A. Beizer, VP-Law/Sec.
Robert A. Beizer, VP-Dev.
Jason Effinger, Regional VP-Texas
Charlie Peterson, Regional VP-Midwest
Wayne M. Martin, Regional VP-Television
Tracey Jones, Regional VP/General Mgr.
J. Mack Robinson, Chmn.

Phone: 404-504-9828	Fax: 404-261-9607
Toll-Free:	
Address: 4370 Peachtree Rd. N.E., Atlanta, GA 30319 US	

GROWTH PLANS/SPECIAL FEATURES:

Gray Television, Inc. is a communications company that provides news and entertainment services to its television stations. The firm owns 36 primary television stations serving 30 television markets. These television stations are all affiliated with broadcast networks, including 17 stations affiliated with CBS, 10 affiliated with NBC, eight affiliated with ABC and one is affiliated with FOX. With 17 CBS affiliated stations, the company is the largest independent owner of CBS affiliates in the country. The combined TV station group reaches approximately 6.3% of total U.S. TV households. In addition, the firm operates 40 digital second channels including one affiliated with ABC, five affiliated with FOX, eight affiliated with CW and 16 affiliated with MyNetworkTV, plus eight local news/weather channels and two independent channels. The operating revenues of its television stations are derived primarily from broadcast advertising revenues, internet advertising revenues and, to a much lesser extent, from ancillary services such as production of commercials, tower rentals and compensation paid by the networks for broadcasting network programming. The firm recently spun-off Triple Crown Media. Prior to the spinoff, Gray Media contributed its Graylink Wireless Business and newspaper publishing (with a total of five newspapers) to Triple Crown Media. In connection with the spinoff, Triple Crown Media made a $40 million cash contribution to Gray. Following the spinoff, the company's business consists of one segment, television broadcasting. CEO Mack Robinson Jr. and his family own more than 30% of the firm.

FINANCIALS: Sales and profits are in thousands of dollars—add 000 to get the full amount. 2007 Note: Financial information for 2007 was not available for all companies at press time.

2007 Sales: $	2007 Profits: $	U.S. Stock Ticker: GTN
2006 Sales: $332,137	2006 Profits: $11,711	Int'l Ticker: Int'l Exchange:
2005 Sales: $261,553	2005 Profits: $3,362	Employees: 2,117
2004 Sales: $293,273	2004 Profits: $44,285	Fiscal Year Ends: 12/31
2003 Sales: $243,061	2003 Profits: $14,000	Parent Company:

SALARIES/BENEFITS:
Pension Plan: Y	ESOP Stock Plan:	Profit Sharing:	Top Exec. Salary: $768,000	Bonus: $750,000
Savings Plan: Y	Stock Purch. Plan: Y		Second Exec. Salary: $400,000	Bonus: $

OTHER THOUGHTS:
Apparent Women Officers or Directors: 1
Hot Spot for Advancement for Women/Minorities:

LOCATIONS: ("Y" = Yes)
West:	Southwest:	Midwest:	Southeast:	Northeast:	International:
Y	Y	Y	Y	Y	

GRUPO RADIO CENTRO SA DE CV   www.radiocentro.com.mx

Industry Group Code: 513111 Ranks within this company's industry group: Sales: 13   Profits: 5

Print Media/Publishing:	Movies:	Equipment/Supplies:		Broadcast/Cable:	Music/Audio:		Sports/Games/Gambling:
Newspapers:	Movie Theaters:	Equipment/Supplies:		Broadcast TV:	Music Production:	Y	Games/Sports:
Magazines:	Movie Production:	Gambling Equipment:		Cable TV:	Retail Music:		Retail Games Stores:
Books:	TV/Video Prod.:	Special Services:		Satellite Broadcast:	Retail Audio Equip.:		Stadiums/Teams:
Book Stores:	Video Rental:	Advertising Services:	Y	Radio:	Music Print./Dist.:		Gambling/Casinos:
Distribution/Printing:	Video Distribution:	Info. Sys. Software:		Online Information:	Multimedia:		Rides/Theme Parks:

TYPES OF BUSINESS:

Radio Broadcasting
Radio Programming

BRANDS/DIVISIONS/AFFILIATES:

Organizacion Impulsora de Radio
Red FM
Alfa Radio
Universal Stereo
Stereo Joya
Formato 21
Noticentro

CONTACTS: *Note: Officers with more than one job title may be intentionally listed here more than once.*

Carlos Aguirre, General Dir.
Pedro N. Beltran, CFO
Gonzalo Yanez, Dir.-Mktg.
Luis Cepero, Dir.-Audio Eng.
Pedro Beltran, Dir.-Admin.
Alvaro F. De la Mora, General Counsel
Sergio Gonzales, Dir.-Oper.
Alfredo Azpeitia, Dir.-Investor Rel.
Pedro N. Beltran, Dir.-Finance
Arturo Yanez, Sub-Dir.-Admin.
Eduardo Stevens, Dir.-Transmission Eng.
Luis M. Carrasco, Dir.-Commercial
Jose L. Ocampo, Dir.-Oper., Organization Implore de Radio
Francisco A. Gomez, Chmn.

Phone: 5254-063-690	Fax: 52-525-728-4875
Toll-Free:	
Address: Constituyentes 1154, 7 Piso, Colonia Lomas Altas, Mexico City, DF 11950 Mexico	

GROWTH PLANS/SPECIAL FEATURES:

Grupo Radio Centro S.A. de C.V. is Mexico's largest radio broadcaster, owning 14 radio stations. Of these, five AM and six FM stations are located in Mexico City. In addition to broadcasting, the company produces all the programming for the stations it own or operates, including musical programs, news, talk shows and special events programs. With an average audience share of 35.3% in Mexico City, Grupo Radio Centro is easily the most popular radio broadcasting company in the country's capital, which is the largest city on the continent. Its most popular stations include Red FM, Alfa Radio, Universal Stereo and Stereo Joya. Programming usually centers on contemporary music, classic rock and talk. The Noticentro news division, broadcast on the station Formato 21, broadcasts news 24 hours a day, with updates every 10 minutes. The company owns and operates 18 production studios, which produce the company's programming as well as advertisements, informational messages and promotional spots. Subsidiary Organizacion Impulsora de Radio provides sales and programming to affiliate stations; currently, it has 100 distributed transmitters in 71 important Mexican cities. Grupo Radio Centro's primary source of revenue is the sale of commercial airtime. About one third of the company's revenues are culled from its ten largest advertisers, the two most significant being Compañía Cervecera del Trópico, S.A. de C.V. and Tiendas Comercial Mexicana, S.A. de C.V. In election years, over 20% of broadcasting revenue is derived from political parties. In 2006, a presidential election year, political advertising accounted for 31% of total broadcasting revenue. Founded in 1946 by Don Francisco Aguirre, the company held its first public offering simultaneously on the Mexican Stock Exchange and the New York Stock Exchange in 1993. The Aguirre family holds approximately 50% of the company's voting shares through two Mexican trusts.

FINANCIALS: Sales and profits are in thousands of dollars—add 000 to get the full amount. 2007 Note: Financial information for 2007 was not available for all companies at press time.

2007 Sales: $	2007 Profits: $	U.S. Stock Ticker: RC
2006 Sales: $73,677	2006 Profits: $38,792	Int'l Ticker: RCENTROA Int'l Exchange: Mexico City-BMV
2005 Sales: $55,619	2005 Profits: $6,107	Employees: 457
2004 Sales: $49,500	2004 Profits: $1,808	Fiscal Year Ends: 12/31
2003 Sales: $73,400	2003 Profits: $5,400	Parent Company:

SALARIES/BENEFITS:

Pension Plan: Y	ESOP Stock Plan:	Profit Sharing: Y	Top Exec. Salary: $	Bonus: $
Savings Plan:	Stock Purch. Plan:		Second Exec. Salary: $	Bonus: $

OTHER THOUGHTS:

Apparent Women Officers or Directors: 3
Hot Spot for Advancement for Women/Minorities: Y

LOCATIONS: ("Y" = Yes)

West:	Southwest:	Midwest:	Southeast:	Northeast:	International:
					Y

GRUPO TELEVISA SA

www.televisa.com

Industry Group Code: 513120 Ranks within this company's industry group: Sales: 7 Profits: 5

Print Media/Publishing:		Movies:		Equipment/Supplies:		Broadcast/Cable:		Music/Audio:		Sports/Games/Gambling:	
Newspapers:		Movie Theaters:	Y	Equipment/Supplies:		Broadcast TV:	Y	Music Production:	Y	Games/Sports:	
Magazines:	Y	Movie Production:	Y	Gambling Equipment:		Cable TV:	Y	Retail Music:		Retail Games Stores:	
Books:		TV/Video Prod.:	Y	Special Services:	Y	Satellite Broadcast:		Retail Audio Equip.:		Stadiums/Teams:	Y
Book Stores:		Video Rental:		Advertising Services:	Y	Radio:		Music Print./Dist.:		Gambling/Casinos:	
Distribution/Printing:		Video Distribution:	Y	Info. Sys. Software:		Online Information:		Multimedia:		Rides/Theme Parks:	

TYPES OF BUSINESS:

Television Broadcasting
Cable Services
Satellite Services
Internet Services
Paging Services
Film & Music Production
Radio Broadcasting
Magazine Publishing

BRANDS/DIVISIONS/AFFILIATES:

Cablevision
SKY
Innova
Televisa Cinema
SkyTel
Editorial Televisa
Bestel
Editorial Atlantida S.A.

CONTACTS: Note: Officers with more than one job title may be intentionally listed here more than once.

Emilio A. Jean, CEO
Emilio A. Jean, Pres.
Salvi F. Viadero, CFO
Alejandro Quintero Iniguez, VP-Corp. Sales & Mktg.
Maximiliano A. Carlebach, VP-Tech. Svcs.
Jorge Eduardo Murguia Orozco, VP-Prod.
Maximiliano A. Carlebach, VP-Oper. & TV Prod.
Michel Boyance, Investor Rel. Officer
Salvi Folch Viadero, VP-Finance
Bernardo G. Martinez, Exec. VP
Alexandre M. Penna, CEO-Innova
Javier Merida Guzman, CEO-Radiopolis
Eduardo T. Michelsen, CEO-Editorial
Emilio A. Jean, Chmn.

Phone: 52-55-5261-2445	Fax: 52-55-5261-2494
Toll-Free:	
Address: Avenida Vasco De Quiroga No. 2000, Colonia Santa Fe, DF 01210 Mexico	

GROWTH PLANS/SPECIAL FEATURES:

Mexico's Grupo Televisa S.A. is one of the largest Spanish-speaking media companies in the world and a major participant in the international entertainment industry, with properties in television, cable, satellite services, Internet service, radio broadcasting, music recording, magazine publishing, professional sports, paging services and film production. The company broadcasts programs through its networks, cable system and its own satellite services. The firm typically holds over 70% of the television audience share in Mexico through its four television networks and approximately 260 affiliated stations, and distributes programming throughout Latin America, Europe, Asia and Africa. It also has a 51% interest in cable joint venture Cablevision, a cable services operator whose network consists of over 50 channels, as well as a 60% interest in Innova, the operator of the SKY direct-to-home satellite system. In addition, the company owns approximately 60% of SKY. Another subsidiary, Televisa Cinema, produces Mexican motion pictures and distributes national and international films. Televisa Video produces and distributes television programming on VHS and DVD for the home entertainment market. Through subsidiary SkyTel, Televisa provides Internet service, while esmas.com manages the company's web site and other related web sites. Editorial Televisa publishes magazines for the Spanish-speaking world, with 68 magazines distributed in more than 20 countries, including Spanish versions of magazines (Cosmopolitan, Maxim and Travel & Leisure) and original magazines (TVyNovelas and Vanidades). In addition, the company owns several soccer teams and sports and entertainment venues, as well as a 50% interest in Televisa Radio, which owns and operates 17 Mexican radio stations. Recent news includes the acquisition of the majority of the assets of Bestel by Cablestar, S.A. de C.V. and Editorial Atlantida, S.A., the leading magazine publishing company in Argentina.

FINANCIALS: Sales and profits are in thousands of dollars—add 000 to get the full amount. 2007 Note: Financial information for 2007 was not available for all companies at press time.

2007 Sales: $	2007 Profits: $	U.S. Stock Ticker: TV
2006 Sales: $3,406,340	2006 Profits: $771,055	Int'l Ticker: TLEVISAL Int'l Exchange: Mexico City-BMV
2005 Sales: $2,968,180	2005 Profits: $559,747	Employees: 14,100
2004 Sales: $2,768,072	2004 Profits: $407,635	Fiscal Year Ends: 12/31
2003 Sales: $2,098,800	2003 Profits: $320,400	Parent Company:

SALARIES/BENEFITS:

Pension Plan: Y	ESOP Stock Plan: Y	Profit Sharing:	Top Exec. Salary: $	Bonus: $
Savings Plan:	Stock Purch. Plan:		Second Exec. Salary: $	Bonus: $

OTHER THOUGHTS:

Apparent Women Officers or Directors:
Hot Spot for Advancement for Women/Minorities:

LOCATIONS: ("Y" = Yes)

West:	Southwest:	Midwest:	Southeast:	Northeast:	International:
					Y

Note: Financial information, benefits and other data can change quickly and may vary from those stated here.

GTECH HOLDINGS CORP

www.gtech.com

Industry Group Code: 713290 Ranks within this company's industry group: Sales: 2 Profits: 2

Print Media/Publishing:	Movies:	Equipment/Supplies:		Broadcast/Cable:	Music/Audio:	Sports/Games/Gambling:
Newspapers:	Movie Theaters:	Equipment/Supplies:		Broadcast TV:	Music Production:	Games/Sports:
Magazines:	Movie Production:	Gambling Equipment:	Y	Cable TV:	Retail Music:	Retail Games Stores:
Books:	TV/Video Prod.:	Special Services:	Y	Satellite Broadcast:	Retail Audio Equip.:	Stadiums/Teams:
Book Stores:	Video Rental:	Advertising Services:		Radio:	Music Print./Dist.:	Gambling/Casinos:
Distribution/Printing:	Video Distribution:	Info. Sys. Software:		Online Information:	Multimedia:	Rides/Theme Parks:

TYPES OF BUSINESS:

Lottery Systems
Lottery Technology Services
Online Game Products & Services

BRANDS/DIVISIONS/AFFILIATES:

Europrint
BillBird
Interlott
Finsoft
Innoka
Veikkaus Oy
Lottomatica S.p.A.
Creative Games International

CONTACTS: *Note: Officers with more than one job title may be intentionally listed here more than once.*

W. Bruce Turner, CEO
Jaymin B. Patel, COO
Jaymin B. Patel, Pres.
Stefano Bortoli, CFO/Sr. VP
Connie Laverty O'Connor, Chief Mktg. Officer/Sr. VP
John L. Pothin, Sr. VP-Human Resources
Charles Cautley, CTO/Sr. VP
Walter G. DeSocio, Chief Admin. Officer/Sr. VP
Atul Bali, Sr. VP-Corp. Dev. & Strategic Planning
Robert Vincent, VP-Corp. Comm.
Ross Dalton, Sr. VP-Printed Prod. & Licensed Content Markets
Alan Eland, Sr. VP-GTECH Americas
Donald R. Sweitzer, Sr. VP-Global Bus. Dev. & Public Affairs
Robert M. Dewey, Jr., Chmn.
Declan Harkin, Sr. VP-GTECH Int'l

Phone: 401-392-1000	Fax: 401-392-1234
Toll-Free:	
Address: GTECH Center, 10 Memorial Blvd., Providence, RI 02903 US	

GROWTH PLANS/SPECIAL FEATURES:

GTECH Holdings Corp., a subsidiary of Lottomatica S.p.A., is a global gaming technology and services company. The company's core business is the lottery industry, in which it does business in 45 countries. The company provides integrated online lottery solutions, services and products to governmental lottery authorities and governmental licensees worldwide. GTECH offers its customers a full range of lottery technology services, including the design, assembly, installation, operation, maintenance and marketing of online lottery systems and instant ticket support systems. The firm has introduced several new online products and services, including Aladdin, a credit-card-sized lottery ticket that can be reused up to 500 times; the Extra-Online game, an online lottery game that allows players to purchase an additional game with instant-ticket features; and e-scratch, a web-based interactive suite of scratch and reveal games. The company also owns IGI Europrint, a provider of promotional games, contests and sweepstakes; Leeward Islands Lottery Holding Company, which operates lotteries throughout the Caribbean; BillBird, an electronic bill payment service in Poland; Interlott, a leading ITVM technology company; Leeward Islands Lottery Holding Co., a lottery operator; Finsoft, a provider of real-time transaction and information management systems; and Innoka, jointly owned with Veikkaus Oy, the Finish National Lottery. In August 2006, GTECH was acquired by Lottomatica S.p.A. In February 2007, the company acquired Creative Games International, which specializes in the fast delivery of instant lottery tickets.

The company offers its employees medical, dental and vision plans; domestic partner benefits; business travel accident insurance; flexible spending accounts; a 401(k) plan; a college savings plan; education assistance; and employee assistance programs.

FINANCIALS: Sales and profits are in thousands of dollars—add 000 to get the full amount. 2007 Note: Financial information for 2007 was not available for all companies at press time.

2007 Sales: $	2007 Profits: $	**U.S. Stock Ticker: Subsidiary**
2006 Sales: $1,304,806	2006 Profits: $211,045	Int'l Ticker: Int'l Exchange:
2005 Sales: $1,257,235	2005 Profits: $196,394	Employees: 5,300
2004 Sales: $1,501,330	2004 Profits: $183,200	Fiscal Year Ends:
2003 Sales: $978,800	2003 Profits: $142,000	Parent Company: LOTTOMATICA SPA

SALARIES/BENEFITS:

Pension Plan:	ESOP Stock Plan:	Profit Sharing:	Top Exec. Salary: $746,154	Bonus: $
Savings Plan: Y	Stock Purch. Plan:		Second Exec. Salary: $488,077	Bonus: $

OTHER THOUGHTS:

Apparent Women Officers or Directors: 1
Hot Spot for Advancement for Women/Minorities:

LOCATIONS: ("Y" = Yes)

West:	Southwest:	Midwest:	Southeast:	Northeast:	International:
				Y	Y

HALLMARK CARDS INC   www.hallmark.com

Industry Group Code: 511191 Ranks within this company's industry group: Sales: 1   Profits:

Print Media/Publishing:		Movies:		Equipment/Supplies:		Broadcast/Cable:		Music/Audio:		Sports/Games/Gambling:	
Newspapers:		Movie Theaters:		Equipment/Supplies:		Broadcast TV:		Music Production:		Games/Sports:	
Magazines:		Movie Production:		Gambling Equipment:		Cable TV:	Y	Retail Music:		Retail Games Stores:	
Books:		TV/Video Prod.:	Y	Special Services:		Satellite Broadcast:		Retail Audio Equip.:		Stadiums/Teams:	
Book Stores:		Video Rental:		Advertising Services:		Radio:		Music Print./Dist.:		Gambling/Casinos:	
Distribution/Printing:		Video Distribution:	Y	Info. Sys. Software:		Online Information:		Multimedia:		Rides/Theme Parks:	

TYPES OF BUSINESS:
Greeting Cards Publishing
Cable Television Broadcasting
Crayons & Art Products
Portrait Studios
Stationery
Television Production & Distribution

BRANDS/DIVISIONS/AFFILIATES:
Hallmark Gold Crown
William Arthur, Inc.
Hallmark Channel
Crown Media Holdings
Hallmark Entertainment
Binney & Smith
Crayola
Picture People (The)

CONTACTS: Note: Officers with more than one job title may be intentionally listed here more than once.
Donald J. Hall, Jr., CEO
Donald J. Hall, Jr., Pres.
Tom Wright, Sr. VP-Human Resources
Donald J. Hall, Chmn.

Phone: 816-274-5111	Fax: 816-274-5061
Toll-Free: 800-425-5627	
Address: 2501 McGee St., Kansas City, MO 64108 US	

GROWTH PLANS/SPECIAL FEATURES:
Hallmark Cards, Inc. markets greeting cards and other products under its Gold Crown, Keepsake Ornaments, Maxine, Shoebox, Fresh Ink, Mahogany and Tree of Life brands. The company operates wholesale and retail businesses with over 50% share in the U.S. greeting card market. The wholesale business distributes products to over 43,000 U.S. retailers and more than 100 countries, with products in more than 30 languages. As a retailer, Hallmark distributes products in 3,700 Hallmark Gold Crown stores, with approximately 10% corporately owned and managed. The company's Crown Media Holdings subsidiary operates various cable television channels that are viewed by 73 million subscribers worldwide. The Hallmark Channel, Crown Media's most popular cable channel, licenses many programs from Hallmark Entertainment, which produces and distributes made-for-TV miniseries and movies. The firm's Binney & Smith subsidiary produces Crayola crayons, which are sold in over 80 countries. Binney & Smith also markets Liquitex fine art products, Revell-Monogram products and Silly Putty. The Picture People, another subsidiary, operates over 250 portrait studios in malls nationwide. Subsidiary William Arthur, Inc. specializes in customized holiday cards, general invitations and announcements, social and business stationery, wedding invitations and birth announcements.

The company offers its employees medical, dental and vision insurance; a 401(k) plan; a profit sharing ownership and savings plan; and tuition reimbursement.

FINANCIALS: Sales and profits are in thousands of dollars—add 000 to get the full amount. 2007 Note: Financial information for 2007 was not available for all companies at press time.

2007 Sales: $	2007 Profits: $	U.S. Stock Ticker: Private
2006 Sales: $4,100,000	2006 Profits: $	Int'l Ticker: Int'l Exchange:
2005 Sales: $4,200,000	2005 Profits: $	Employees: 16,000
2004 Sales: $4,400,000	2004 Profits: $	Fiscal Year Ends: 12/31
2003 Sales: $4,300,000	2003 Profits: $	Parent Company:

SALARIES/BENEFITS:
Pension Plan:	ESOP Stock Plan:	Profit Sharing: Y	Top Exec. Salary: $	Bonus: $88,501
Savings Plan: Y	Stock Purch. Plan:		Second Exec. Salary: $249,615	Bonus: $249,615

OTHER THOUGHTS:
Apparent Women Officers or Directors:
Hot Spot for Advancement for Women/Minorities:

LOCATIONS: ("Y" = Yes)
West:	Southwest:	Midwest:	Southeast:	Northeast:	International:
Y	Y	Y	Y	Y	Y

HANDS-ON MOBILE

www.mforma.com

Industry Group Code: 511208 Ranks within this company's industry group: Sales: Profits:

Print Media/Publishing:	Movies:	Equipment/Supplies:	Broadcast/Cable:	Music/Audio:	Sports/Games/Gambling:	
Newspapers:	Movie Theaters:	Equipment/Supplies:	Broadcast TV:	Music Production:	Games/Sports:	Y
Magazines:	Movie Production:	Gambling Equipment:	Cable TV:	Retail Music:	Retail Games Stores:	
Books:	TV/Video Prod.:	Special Services:	Satellite Broadcast:	Retail Audio Equip.:	Stadiums/Teams:	
Book Stores:	Video Rental:	Advertising Services:	Radio:	Music Print./Dist.:	Gambling/Casinos:	
Distribution/Printing:	Video Distribution:	Info. Sys. Software:	Online Information:	Multimedia:	Rides/Theme Parks:	

TYPES OF BUSINESS:

Mobile Media Content
Games
Information Subscription Services

BRANDS/DIVISIONS/AFFILIATES:

MFORMA Group, Inc.
Phame TV
ActionScreens 3D

CONTACTS: *Note: Officers with more than one job title may be intentionally listed here more than once.*

Jonathan Sacks, CEO
Keith McCurdy, COO
Lynne Crawford, Pres.
David White, CFO
John Rousseau, Pres., Media & Advertising Div.
Erik Pavelka, VP-Bus. Dev.
James Brelsford, Exec. VP-Corp. Affairs
Gilbert Kim, General Mgr.-Hands-On Mobile Korea
Grace Zhang, General Mgr.-Hands-On Mobile China
Daniel Kranzler, Chmn.
Eric Hobson, General Mgr.-Hands-On Mobile Europe

Phone: 415-848-0400	Fax: 415-399-1966
Toll-Free:	
Address: 580 California St., Ste. 600, San Francisco, CA 94104 US	

GROWTH PLANS/SPECIAL FEATURES:

Hands-On Mobile, formerly MFORMA Group, Inc., develops, publishes and distributes mobile content to more than 150 of the world's leading operators in 40 countries. Hands-On offers a range of games for Java, BREW, SMS, MMS, mophun and WAP systems. Its games fall into action, casino, classics, puzzle and sports categories. Action games include Blade: Trinity; Call of Duty; Fantastic Four; X-Men: The Last Stand; and others, mainly based on hit movies. Casino games include World Poker Tour (WPT) 7 Card Stud and WPT Texas Hold'em. Classic games include LEGO Bricks and Monopoly Tycoon 2007. Its puzzle games include IQ Academy and SuDoku Garden. Sports games include Ducati Extreme, Pro Bowling and Super Putt; the company also offers subscription services like Fantasy Football Companion and Baseball GameCenter, both by CBS SportsLine. It provides non-game services such as Flirting by Blind Date, Astrology Zone Mobile and Billboard Mobile Channel, a music service. Hands-On adapts games and applications from one handset standard and language into thousands of different product versions. The company has offices in London, Manchester, Beijing, Shanghai, Bangalore and Seoul. Hands-On's customers include AT&T, Sprint Nextel, T-Mobile, Verizon Wireless, Alltel, US Cellular and China Mobile. In April 2006, MFORMA Group, Inc. announced that it would change its name to Hands-On Mobile. Also in April 2006, Hands-On unveiled several new products, including Daily Devotions, a product that offers daily inspirations and prayers delivered by Pat Boone; and forthcoming games and products based on the notorious rock star Tommy Lee, with whom the company has partnered. In April 2007, it announced an agreement with Activision to offer Guitar Hero. In February 2007, it launched Phame TV, a user-generated video broadcast. Also in February 2007, partnering with Emdigo, it launched ActionScreens 3D, which allows customers to customize their phones with 3D characters.

FINANCIALS: Sales and profits are in thousands of dollars—add 000 to get the full amount. 2007 Note: Financial information for 2007 was not available for all companies at press time.

2007 Sales: $	2007 Profits: $	U.S. Stock Ticker: Private
2006 Sales: $	2006 Profits: $	Int'l Ticker: Int'l Exchange:
2005 Sales: $	2005 Profits: $	Employees:
2004 Sales: $	2004 Profits: $	Fiscal Year Ends:
2003 Sales: $	2003 Profits: $	Parent Company:

SALARIES/BENEFITS:

Pension Plan:	ESOP Stock Plan:	Profit Sharing:	Top Exec. Salary: $	Bonus: $
Savings Plan:	Stock Purch. Plan:		Second Exec. Salary: $	Bonus: $

OTHER THOUGHTS:

Apparent Women Officers or Directors: 2
Hot Spot for Advancement for Women/Minorities:

LOCATIONS: ("Y" = Yes)

West:	Southwest:	Midwest:	Southeast:	Northeast:	International:
Y					Y

HARPERCOLLINS PUBLISHERS INC   www.harpercollins.com

Industry Group Code: 511130 Ranks within this company's industry group: Sales: Profits:

Print Media/Publishing:	Movies:	Equipment/Supplies:	Broadcast/Cable:	Music/Audio:	Sports/Games/Gambling:
Newspapers:	Movie Theaters:	Equipment/Supplies:	Broadcast TV:	Music Production:	Games/Sports:
Magazines:	Movie Production:	Gambling Equipment:	Cable TV:	Retail Music:	Retail Games Stores:
Books: Y	TV/Video Prod.:	Special Services:	Satellite Broadcast:	Retail Audio Equip.:	Stadiums/Teams:
Book Stores:	Video Rental:	Advertising Services:	Radio:	Music Print./Dist.:	Gambling/Casinos:
Distribution/Printing:	Video Distribution:	Info. Sys. Software:	Online Information:	Multimedia:	Rides/Theme Parks:

TYPES OF BUSINESS:

Book Publishing
Online Publishing & E-Books
Audio Books

BRANDS/DIVISIONS/AFFILIATES:

News Corporation Limited (The)
ecco
Fourth Estate
Regan Books
PerfectBound
Amistad
Zondervan
Rayo

CONTACTS: Note: Officers with more than one job title may be intentionally listed here more than once.

Jane Friedman, CEO
Glenn D'Agnes, COO/Exec. VP
Jane Friedman, Pres.
Rick Schwartz, CIO/Exec. VP

Phone: 212-207-7000	Fax: 212-207-7145
Toll-Free:	
Address: 10 E. 53rd St., New York, NY 10022 US	

GROWTH PLANS/SPECIAL FEATURES:

HarperCollins Publishers, Inc., a subsidiary of The News Corporation, Ltd., publishes books that cover a wide range of interests. The company's worldwide publishing is divided into the following segments: U.S. general books, U.S. children's books, U.K., Canada, Australia and India. The firm focuses on literary and commercial fiction, business books, children's books, cookbooks, mystery, romance, reference and religious and spiritual books. The titles are released through imprints such as ecco, specializing in classic literature; Amistad, which focuses on authors of African descent; and Rayo, a publisher of books oriented towards the Latino community. Zondervan publishes Christian material, including the bestselling Purpose Driven Life series, and is the leading publisher of the Bible worldwide. The company's e-books are marketed and sold through the imprint PerfectBound in Adobe, Microsoft and Mobipocket formats. Harper Children's Audio offers bestselling children's literature on CD and cassette formats. HarperCollins has received substantial business from recent movie tie-ins, including Lord of the Rings, the Chronicles of Narnia, Charlie and the Chocolate Factory and Lemony Snicket's A Series of Unfortunate Events. The company's web site, HarperCollins.com, provides users with author interviews, forums to discuss political or social issues and literature and information on best-selling books and upcoming releases.

HarperCollins offers internship and rotational associate programs to students and recent graduates. Employee benefits include medical, dental, vision and prescription drug plans; retirement and savings plans; work/life opportunities; seminars; and various retail, fitness and entertainment discounts.

FINANCIALS: Sales and profits are in thousands of dollars—add 000 to get the full amount. 2007 Note: Financial information for 2007 was not available for all companies at press time.

2007 Sales: $	2007 Profits: $	U.S. Stock Ticker: Subsidiary
2006 Sales: $	2006 Profits: $	Int'l Ticker: Int'l Exchange:
2005 Sales: $	2005 Profits: $	Employees:
2004 Sales: $	2004 Profits: $	Fiscal Year Ends: 6/30
2003 Sales: $	2003 Profits: $	Parent Company: NEWS CORP

SALARIES/BENEFITS:

Pension Plan: Y	ESOP Stock Plan:	Profit Sharing:	Top Exec. Salary: $	Bonus: $
Savings Plan: Y	Stock Purch. Plan:		Second Exec. Salary: $	Bonus: $

OTHER THOUGHTS:

Apparent Women Officers or Directors: 1
Hot Spot for Advancement for Women/Minorities:

LOCATIONS: ("Y" = Yes)

West:	Southwest:	Midwest:	Southeast:	Northeast: Y	International: Y

Note: Financial information, benefits and other data can change quickly and may vary from those stated here.

HARPO INC

www.oprah.com

Industry Group Code: 512110 Ranks within this company's industry group: Sales: 9 Profits:

Print Media/Publishing:		Movies:		Equipment/Supplies:		Broadcast/Cable:		Music/Audio:		Sports/Games/Gambling:	
Newspapers:		Movie Theaters:		Equipment/Supplies:		Broadcast TV:	Y	Music Production:		Games/Sports:	
Magazines:	Y	Movie Production:	Y	Gambling Equipment:		Cable TV:		Retail Music:		Retail Games Stores:	
Books:		TV/Video Prod.:	Y	Special Services:		Satellite Broadcast:		Retail Audio Equip.:		Stadiums/Teams:	
Book Stores:		Video Rental:		Advertising Services:		Radio:		Music Print./Dist.:		Gambling/Casinos:	
Distribution/Printing:		Video Distribution:		Info. Sys. Software:		Online Information:		Multimedia:		Rides/Theme Parks:	

TYPES OF BUSINESS:

Movie & Television Production
Magazine Publishing
Online Retail
Radio Production

BRANDS/DIVISIONS/AFFILIATES:

Harpo Productions, Inc.
Harpo Studios, Inc.
Harpo Films, Inc.
Harpo Print, LLC
Oprah Winfrey Show (The)
O, The Oprah Magazine
Harpo Radio, Inc.
Oprah's Book Club

CONTACTS: *Note: Officers with more than one job title may be intentionally listed here more than once.*

Doug Pattison, CFO
Harriet Seitler, Exec. VP-Mktg. & Dev.
Harriet Seitler, Exec. VP-Dev.
Lisa Halliday, Dir.-Media & Corp. Rel.
Tim Bennett, Pres., Harpo Productions
Oprah Winfrey, Chmn.

Phone: 312-633-1000	Fax: 312-633-1976
Toll-Free:	
Address: 110 N. Carpenter St., Chicago, IL 60607 US	

GROWTH PLANS/SPECIAL FEATURES:

Harpo, Inc. (Oprah spelled backwards) is the creation of media star Oprah Winfrey, who is also the chairman of Harpo Productions, Harpo Studios, Harpo Films, Harpo Print, LLC and Harpo Video, Inc. Through these channels, the company markets The Oprah Winfrey Show, on the air since 1986, which is consistently the highest-rated talk show on television. The show is watched by an estimated 30 million viewers per week and is broadcast in 135 countries by CBS Paramount International Television and syndicated in 212 markets by King World. The company also makes feature-length movies, such as Beloved, and made-for-TV movies, such as Their Eyes Were Watching God. In addition, the company operates Oprah.com, an online extension of the TV show, and an online retailer, The Oprah Boutique. In cooperation with Hearst Corporation, the company publishes O, The Oprah Magazine, which has approximately 2.7 million subscribers. The magazine features Oprah on the cover each issue. The Oprah Book Club publicizes Winfrey's book recommendations online, through her television show and with Oprah's Book Club seals that are placed on certain editions of the book when they are sold through other retail outlets. It has been noted that Oprah's Book Club selections are consistently bestsellers during their time in the spotlight. Harpo Productions, in partnership with three other companies, produces the Rachel Ray show. Harpo Radio, Inc. also produces Oprah & Friends, a satellite radio channel on XM. In 2007, Harpo Productions, Inc. launched the Oprah Channel on YouTube.

FINANCIALS: Sales and profits are in thousands of dollars—add 000 to get the full amount. 2007 Note: Financial information for 2007 was not available for all companies at press time.

2007 Sales: $	2007 Profits: $	**U.S. Stock Ticker: Private**		
2006 Sales: $325,000	2006 Profits: $	**Int'l Ticker:** Int'l Exchange:		
2005 Sales: $290,000	2005 Profits: $	Employees: 341		
2004 Sales: $	2004 Profits: $	Fiscal Year Ends: 12/31		
2003 Sales: $275,000	2003 Profits: $	Parent Company:		

SALARIES/BENEFITS:

Pension Plan:	ESOP Stock Plan:	Profit Sharing:	Top Exec. Salary: $	Bonus: $
Savings Plan:	Stock Purch. Plan:		Second Exec. Salary: $	Bonus: $

OTHER THOUGHTS:

Apparent Women Officers or Directors: 3
Hot Spot for Advancement for Women/Minorities: Y

LOCATIONS: ("Y" = Yes)

West:	Southwest:	Midwest:	Southeast:	Northeast:	International:
		Y			

HARRAH'S ENTERTAINMENT INC   www.harrahs.com

Industry Group Code: 721120 Ranks within this company's industry group: Sales: 1   Profits: 3

Print Media/Publishing:	Movies:	Equipment/Supplies:	Broadcast/Cable:	Music/Audio:	Sports/Games/Gambling:	
Newspapers:	Movie Theaters:	Equipment/Supplies:	Broadcast TV:	Music Production:	Games/Sports:	
Magazines:	Movie Production:	Gambling Equipment:	Cable TV:	Retail Music:	Retail Games Stores:	
Books:	TV/Video Prod.:	Special Services:	Satellite Broadcast:	Retail Audio Equip.:	Stadiums/Teams:	Y
Book Stores:	Video Rental:	Advertising Services:	Radio:	Music Print./Dist.:	Gambling/Casinos:	
Distribution/Printing:	Video Distribution:	Info. Sys. Software:	Online Information:	Multimedia:	Rides/Theme Parks:	

TYPES OF BUSINESS:

Casino Hotels
Dockside & Riverboat Casinos
Racing Venues
Casino Management

BRANDS/DIVISIONS/AFFILIATES:

Harrah's Operating Company, Inc.
Horseshoe Entertainment
Total Rewards
Caesar's Entertainment, Inc.
Harrah's Phoenix Ak-Chin
Harrah's Rincon Casino and Resort
Harrah's Cherokee Casino and Hotel
Harrah's Prairie Brand Casino-Topeka

CONTACTS: *Note: Officers with more than one job title may be intentionally listed here more than once.*

Gary Loveman, CEO
Timothy J. Wilmott, COO
Gary Loveman, Pres.
Jonathan S. Halkyard, CFO
David Norton, Sr. VP-Relationship Mktg.
Mary Thomas, Sr. VP-Human Resources
Timothy S. Stanley, CIO/Sr. VP
Steve Brammell, General Counsel/Sr. VP
Anthony F. Santo, Sr. VP-Oper., Prod. & Svcs.
Richard E. Mirman, Sr. VP-Bus. Dev.
Janis L. Jones, Sr. VP-Comm. & Gov't Rel.
Jonathan S. Halkyard, Sr. VP/Treas.
Tom Jenkin, Pres., Western Div.
John Payne, Pres., Central Div.
Virginia E. Shanks, Sr. VP-Brand Mgmt.
Carlos Tolosa, Pres., Eastern Div.
Gary Loveman, Chmn.

Phone: 702-407-6000	Fax: 702-407-6037
Toll-Free:	
Address: 1 Harrahs Court, Las Vegas, NV 89119 US	

GROWTH PLANS/SPECIAL FEATURES:

Harrah's Entertainment, Inc. (HET) is one of the largest gaming companies in the world. The firm conducts business primarily through its subsidiary, Harrah's Operating Company, Inc. (HOC), and 48 other subsidiary casinos within the U.S., U.K., Canada, South Africa, Egypt and Uruguay. HET offers a variety of casino entertainment facilities under Harrah's, Caesars and Horseshoe brand names, which includes land-based, dockside and riverboat casinos, casino clubs, two cruise ship casinos and two racing venues. These facilities total approximately three million square feet of game space and 40,000 hotel rooms. In addition to the ownership of multiple casinos, HET also manages four casinos for Indian tribes: Harrah's Phoenix Ak-Chin, Harrah's Rincon Casino and Resort, Harrah's Cherokee Casino and Hotel and Harrah's Prairie Brand Casino-Topeka. HET offers reward incentives for returning customers under the Total Rewards card plan, which allows holders to earn reward credits for prizes such as vacations, event tickets and cars. HET also offers a variety of slot machines for its customers and hosts the World Series of Poker every year. In late 2006, HET acquired London Clubs International, which consists of four casinos in the greater London area and opened Harrah's Chester in Philadelphia for simulcasting and live harness racing. HET continues to expand and develop its facilities in Las Vegas, Atlantic City, Spain and the Bahamas. In 2007, HET entered into an agreement to be acquired within a year by an affiliate of Texas Pacific Group and Apollo Management, L.P. for $27.8 billion dollars.

HET offers its employees benefits such as educational assistance, store and room discounts and community outreach opportunities. HET also recently opened an employee health and wellness center for its Las Vegas employees.

FINANCIALS: Sales and profits are in thousands of dollars—add 000 to get the full amount. 2007 Note: Financial information for 2007 was not available for all companies at press time.

2007 Sales: $	2007 Profits: $	U.S. Stock Ticker: HET
2006 Sales: $9,673,900	2006 Profits: $535,800	Int'l Ticker: Int'l Exchange:
2005 Sales: $7,010,000	2005 Profits: $236,400	Employees: 85,000
2004 Sales: $4,396,800	2004 Profits: $367,709	Fiscal Year Ends: 12/31
2003 Sales: $4,126,200	2003 Profits: $292,700	Parent Company:

SALARIES/BENEFITS:

Pension Plan:	ESOP Stock Plan:	Profit Sharing:	Top Exec. Salary: $1,688,462	Bonus: $3,650,000
Savings Plan: Y	Stock Purch. Plan:		Second Exec. Salary: $1,096,154	Bonus: $1,973,075

OTHER THOUGHTS:

Apparent Women Officers or Directors: 3
Hot Spot for Advancement for Women/Minorities: Y

LOCATIONS: ("Y" = Yes)

West:	Southwest:	Midwest:	Southeast:	Northeast:	International:
Y	Y	Y	Y	Y	Y

Note: Financial information, benefits and other data can change quickly and may vary from those stated here.

HARRIS INTERACTIVE INC   www.harrisinteractive.com

Industry Group Code: 541910 Ranks within this company's industry group: Sales: 3 Profits: 3

Print Media/Publishing:	Movies:	Equipment/Supplies:		Broadcast/Cable:	Music/Audio:	Sports/Games/Gambling:
Newspapers:	Movie Theaters:	Equipment/Supplies:		Broadcast TV:	Music Production:	Games/Sports:
Magazines:	Movie Production:	Gambling Equipment:		Cable TV:	Retail Music:	Retail Games Stores:
Books:	TV/Video Prod.:	Special Services:	Y	Satellite Broadcast:	Retail Audio Equip.:	Stadiums/Teams:
Book Stores:	Video Rental:	Advertising Services:	Y	Radio:	Music Print./Dist.:	Gambling/Casinos:
Distribution/Printing:	Video Distribution:	Info. Sys. Software:		Online Information:	Multimedia:	Rides/Theme Parks:

TYPES OF BUSINESS:

Market Research
Internet-Based Research
Consulting Services

BRANDS/DIVISIONS/AFFILIATES:

Harris Poll
Harris Interactive Service Bureau
Wirthlin Report
Harris Interactive London
Harris Interactive Paris

CONTACTS: *Note: Officers with more than one job title may be intentionally listed here more than once.*

Gregory T. Novak, CEO
Gregory Novak, Pres.
Ronald E. Salluzzo, CFO
Dennis K. Bhame, Exec. VP-Human Resources
Leonard Bayer, Chief Scientist/Exec. VP
Leonard R. Bayer, CTO
Ronald E. Salluzzo, Corp. Sec.
David B. Vaden, Pres., North American & Global Oper.
Kyle R. Karnes, Exec. VP-Corp. Dev.
George H. Terhanian, Pres., Global Internet Research
Tracey McNerney, Comm.
Dee Allsop, Pres., US Solutions Research Groups
Katherine A. Binns, Pres., US Industry Research Groups
Jeff Stewart, Sr. VP/Head-Global Acct. Dev.
George Bell, Chmn.

Phone: 585-272-8400	Fax: 585-272-8680
Toll-Free: 800-866-7655	
Address: 60 Corporate Woods, Rochester, NY 14623 US	

GROWTH PLANS/SPECIAL FEATURES:

Harris Interactive, Inc. is a worldwide market research and consulting firm best known for the Harris Poll and for pioneering an accurate method for Internet market research. It has made significant expenditures to drive the transformation of the market research and polling industry to an Internet-based platform. The company is one of the largest Internet-based research and polling firms in the world, based on the size of its Internet panel, number of online surveys completed and the amount of revenue it derives from online research. Harris conducts research mainly for companies in the not-for-profit, public policy, advertising and public relations, automotive and transportation, consumer packaged goods, health care and pharmaceuticals, brand consulting, and technology and telecommunications industries. Harris also conducts international research through its various U.S. offices and foreign offices in London and Paris, as well as its global network of local market and opinion research firms. Harris has three main product and service categories: custom research, including Internet-based and traditional market research studies and polling conducted on specific issues for specific customers; multi-client research, including Internet-based studies conducted on general-interest issues and sold to numerous clients; and service bureau research, which consists of Internet-based data collection conducted for other market research firms by the company's Harris Interactive Service Bureau subsidiary. In 2007, the firm launched its Advanced Strategy Lab (ASL) in Europe, a lab utilizing the firm's qualitative research technology that has been used in the U.S. for a decade. Also in 2007, the company acquired three research firms outside the U.S., including Decima Research in Canada, MarketShare in Asian and MediaTransfer AG Netresearch & Consulting in Hamburg, Germany.

FINANCIALS: Sales and profits are in thousands of dollars—add 000 to get the full amount. 2007 Note: Financial information for 2007 was not available for all companies at press time.

2007 Sales: $211,803	2007 Profits: $9,076	U.S. Stock Ticker: HPOL
2006 Sales: $212,184	2006 Profits: $9,460	Int'l Ticker: Int'l Exchange:
2005 Sales: $193,635	2005 Profits: $1,583	Employees: 1,015
2004 Sales: $146,032	2004 Profits: $29,918	Fiscal Year Ends: 6/30
2003 Sales: $130,600	2003 Profits: $11,100	Parent Company:

SALARIES/BENEFITS:

Pension Plan:	ESOP Stock Plan:	Profit Sharing:	Top Exec. Salary: $493,269	Bonus: $96,048
Savings Plan: Y	Stock Purch. Plan: Y		Second Exec. Salary: $332,308	Bonus: $57,629

OTHER THOUGHTS:

Apparent Women Officers or Directors: 3
Hot Spot for Advancement for Women/Minorities: Y

LOCATIONS: ("Y" = Yes)

West:	Southwest:	Midwest:	Southeast:	Northeast:	International:
Y		Y		Y	Y

Note: Financial information, benefits and other data can change quickly and may vary from those stated here.

HARTE-HANKS INC

www.harte-hanks.com

Industry Group Code: 511110 Ranks within this company's industry group: Sales: 12   Profits: 7

Print Media/Publishing:		Movies:		Equipment/Supplies:		Broadcast/Cable:		Music/Audio:		Sports/Games/Gambling:	
Newspapers:	Y	Movie Theaters:		Equipment/Supplies:		Broadcast TV:		Music Production:		Games/Sports:	
Magazines:		Movie Production:		Gambling Equipment:		Cable TV:		Retail Music:		Retail Games Stores:	
Books:		TV/Video Prod.:		Special Services:	Y	Satellite Broadcast:		Retail Audio Equip.:		Stadiums/Teams:	
Book Stores:		Video Rental:		Advertising Services:	Y	Radio:		Music Print./Dist.:		Gambling/Casinos:	
Distribution/Printing:		Video Distribution:		Info. Sys. Software:		Online Information:		Multimedia:		Rides/Theme Parks:	

TYPES OF BUSINESS:

Shopper Newspaper Publishing
Direct Mail Services
Direct & Interactive Marketing Services
Customer Relationship Management Software
Marketing Material Printing

BRANDS/DIVISIONS/AFFILIATES:

Flyer (The)
PennySaver
Communique Direct
Global Address
Harte-Hanks Trillium Software-Germany GmbH
Aberdeen Group

CONTACTS: *Note: Officers with more than one job title may be intentionally listed here more than once.*

Richard M. Hochhauser, CEO
Dean H. Blythe, Pres.
Dean H. Blythe, CFO/Exec. VP
William A. Goldberg, Sr. VP-Mktg.
David Siesel, CTO
Bryan Pechersky, General Counsel/Sr. VP/Sec.
Jessica Huff, Chief Acct. Officer/VP-Finance
Gary J. Skidmore, Pres, Direct Mktg./Exec. VP
Peter E. Gorman, Exec. VP/Pres., Harte-Hanks Shoppers
Kathy Calta, Exec. VP-Direct Mktg, US
Larry Franklin, Chmn.
David Blythe, Sr. VP-Bus. Dev., Asia-Pacific

Phone: 210-829-9000	**Fax:** 210-829-9403
Toll-Free: 800-456-9748	
Address: 200 Concord Plaza Dr., Ste. 800, San Antonio, TX 78216 US	

GROWTH PLANS/SPECIAL FEATURES:

Harte-Hanks, Inc. is a worldwide direct and targeted marketing company that provides customer relationship management, marketing services and shopper publications to a wide range of local, regional, U.S. and international consumer and business-to-business marketers. The company operates two main businesses: shoppers and direct marketing. Harte-Hanks' shoppers division is one of North America's largest owners, operators and distributors of shopper publications. It prints 1,121 individual shopper editions each week with a circulation of approximately 12,000 each. The company's shopper business operates in selected local and regional markets in California with the PennySaver publication and in Florida with the Flyer. The shopper publications are produced at six production facilities (three in Southern California, one each in Northern California and Southern Florida and one in Tampa, Florida) and account for approximately 30 sales offices. In addition, the company operates as a service bureau, preparing list selections, maximizing deliverability and reducing clients' mailing costs. The direct marketing section (with 40 facilities worldwide and accounting for 60% of the company's revenue) gathers, analyzes and distributes customer and prospect data across all points of customer contact. The company helps clients to develop and execute targeted marketing communication programs through creative consultation and graphics design. Along with back-end services (printing and personalization of communication pieces) the firm uses laser printing, target mail and fulfillment, and transportation logistics to build customized marketing databases. This provides clients with easy-to-use tools to perform analysis in order to target their best customers and prospects. Late in 2007, the firm announced plans to acquire U.K.-based Information Arts Limited, a business-to-business insight and data services provider.

FINANCIALS: Sales and profits are in thousands of dollars—add 000 to get the full amount. 2007 Note: Financial information for 2007 was not available for all companies at press time.

2007 Sales: $	2007 Profits: $	**U.S. Stock Ticker: HHS**
2006 Sales: $1,184,688	2006 Profits: $111,792	**Int'l Ticker:** Int'l Exchange:
2005 Sales: $1,134,993	2005 Profits: $114,458	Employees: 6,843
2004 Sales: $1,030,461	2004 Profits: $97,568	Fiscal Year Ends: 12/31
2003 Sales: $944,576	2003 Profits: $87,362	Parent Company:

SALARIES/BENEFITS:

Pension Plan: Y	ESOP Stock Plan:	Profit Sharing:	Top Exec. Salary: $820,000	Bonus: $143,500
Savings Plan: Y	Stock Purch. Plan:		Second Exec. Salary: $394,000	Bonus: $17,730

OTHER THOUGHTS:

Apparent Women Officers or Directors: 2
Hot Spot for Advancement for Women/Minorities: Y

LOCATIONS: ("Y" = Yes)

West:	Southwest:	Midwest:	Southeast:	Northeast:	International:
Y	Y	Y	Y	Y	Y

HARVEY ELECTRONICS INC   www.harveyonline.com

Industry Group Code: 443110 Ranks within this company's industry group: Sales: 6 Profits: 5

Print Media/Publishing:	Movies:	Equipment/Supplies:		Broadcast/Cable:	Music/Audio:	Sports/Games/Gambling:
Newspapers:	Movie Theaters:	Equipment/Supplies:		Broadcast TV:	Music Production:	Games/Sports:
Magazines:	Movie Production:	Gambling Equipment:	Y	Cable TV:	Retail Music:	Retail Games Stores:
Books:	TV/Video Prod.:	Special Services:	Y	Satellite Broadcast:	Retail Audio Equip.:	Stadiums/Teams:
Book Stores:	Video Rental:	Advertising Services:		Radio:	Music Print./Dist.:	Gambling/Casinos:
Distribution/Printing:	Video Distribution:	Info. Sys. Software:		Online Information:	Multimedia:	Rides/Theme Parks:

TYPES OF BUSINESS:

Electronics Stores
High-End Electronics
Repair & Installation Services
Online Retail
Home Theatre Furniture

BRANDS/DIVISIONS/AFFILIATES:

Bang & Olufsen
Crestron
Lexicon
Linn
Marantz
McIntosh
NAD
Myer-Emco, Inc.

CONTACTS: *Note: Officers with more than one job title may be intentionally listed here more than once.*

Michael E. Recca, Interim CEO
Franklin C. Karp, Pres.
Joseph J. Calabrese, CFO/Exec. VP
Roland W. Hiemer, VP-Merch.
Joseph J. Calabrese, Corp. Sec.
Michael A. Beck, VP-Oper.
Joseph J. Calabrese, Treas.
D. Andrew Stackpole, Chmn.

Phone: 201-842-0078	Fax: 201-842-0317
Toll-Free:	
Address: 205 Chubb Ave., Lyndhurst, NJ 07071 US	

GROWTH PLANS/SPECIAL FEATURES:

Harvey Electronics, Inc. is engaged in the retail sale, service and custom installation of high-quality audio, video and home theater equipment. The equipment for sale includes high-fidelity components and systems, VCRs, DVD players, high-definition televisions, direct view projection televisions, plasma and LCD flat-panel televisions, audio/video furniture, digital satellite systems, conventional telephones, home theatre furniture, MP3 players, iPods, satellite radios, service contracts and related accessories. The company is one of the country's largest retailers of esoteric brands manufactured by Bang & Olufsen, Crestron, Lexicon, Linn, Marantz, McIntosh, NAD, Vienna Acoustics, Sonus Faber, Kef, Krell, Loewe, Martin Logan and Fujitsu. The firm currently owns eight Harvey specialty retail stores and one Bang & Olufsen stores. Most of the stores are located in the New York market, with additional stores in New Jersey and Connecticut. Audio products account for about 27% of total sales, while TV and projectors account for 36%. Harvey purchases its products from approximately 80 manufacturers, including Bang & Olufsen, Boston Acoustics, Fujitsu, Marantz, Monster Cable, Pioneer Elite, Runco, Samsung, Sharp and Sony. The company intends to maintain a strategic focus on custom installations, which account for more then half of Harvey's net sales. In mid-2006, Harvey received $4 million in growth capital from institutional investors led by Trinity Investment Partners LLC. In May 2007, the company agreed to acquire Myer-Emco, Inc., a Mid-Atlantic high-end retailer and custom installer of audio video systems. In November 2007, Harvey was delisted from the NASDAQ, but continues to trade over the counter.

FINANCIALS: Sales and profits are in thousands of dollars—add 000 to get the full amount. 2007 Note: Financial information for 2007 was not available for all companies at press time.

2007 Sales: $	2007 Profits: $	**U.S. Stock Ticker: HRVE**
2006 Sales: $36,028	2006 Profits: $-3,238	**Int'l Ticker:** Int'l Exchange:
2005 Sales: $40,444	2005 Profits: $- 830	Employees: 128
2004 Sales: $43,198	2004 Profits: $1,274	Fiscal Year Ends: 10/31
2003 Sales: $42,400	2003 Profits: $ 300	Parent Company:

SALARIES/BENEFITS:

Pension Plan: Y	ESOP Stock Plan:	Profit Sharing: Y	Top Exec. Salary: $165,000	Bonus: $9,000
Savings Plan: Y	Stock Purch. Plan:		Second Exec. Salary: $155,000	Bonus: $51,000

OTHER THOUGHTS:

Apparent Women Officers or Directors:
Hot Spot for Advancement for Women/Minorities:

LOCATIONS: ("Y" = Yes)

West:	Southwest:	Midwest:	Southeast:	Northeast:	International:
				Y	

HASTINGS ENTERTAINMENT INC   www.gohastings.com

Industry Group Code: 532230   Ranks within this company's industry group: Sales: 4   Profits: 4

Print Media/Publishing:	Movies:	Equipment/Supplies:	Broadcast/Cable:	Music/Audio:		Sports/Games/Gambling:	
Newspapers:	Movie Theaters:	Equipment/Supplies:	Broadcast TV:	Music Production:		Games/Sports:	
Magazines:	Movie Production:	Gambling Equipment:	Cable TV:	Retail Music:	Y	Retail Games Stores:	Y
Books:	TV/Video Prod.:	Special Services:	Satellite Broadcast:	Retail Audio Equip.:		Stadiums/Teams:	
Book Stores:	Video Rental: Y	Advertising Services:	Radio:	Music Print./Dist.:		Gambling/Casinos:	
Distribution/Printing:	Video Distribution:	Info. Sys. Software:	Online Information:	Multimedia:		Rides/Theme Parks:	

TYPES OF BUSINESS:
Video & DVD Rental Stores
Book Sales
Music Sales
Software Sales
Video Game Sales
Coffee Sales
Online Sales
Used Books, Music & DVDs

BRANDS/DIVISIONS/AFFILIATES:
Gohastings.com
Hard Back Cafe
Hastings Properties, Inc.
Hastings Internet, Inc.
goShip

CONTACTS: *Note: Officers with more than one job title may be intentionally listed here more than once.*
John H. Marmaduke, CEO
John H. Marmaduke, Pres.
Dan Crow, CFO
Kevin J. Ball, VP-Mktg.
David Moffatt, VP-Human Resources
John Hintz, VP-IT
Alan Van Ongevalle, Sr. VP-Merch.
Natalya A. Ballew, Corp. Sec.
Dan Crow, VP-Finance
Phil McConnell, VP-Product
John H. Marmaduke, Chmn.

Phone: 806-351-2300	**Fax:** 806-351-2424
Toll-Free: 877-427-8464	
Address: 3601 Plains Blvd., Amarillo, TX 79102 US	

GROWTH PLANS/SPECIAL FEATURES:

Hastings Entertainment, Inc. is a multimedia entertainment retailer that buys, sells and trades books, music, software, periodicals, videocassettes and DVDs and rents videocassettes, video games and DVDs. The firm has two wholly-owned subsidiaries: Hastings Properties, Inc. and Hastings Internet, Inc. Hastings targets mid-sized towns, those with populations less than 250,000 people, and currently operates approximately 154 superstores in 20 states, averaging 20,000 square feet each. Its superstores offer an extensive product assortment, with a product count ranging from 12,000 to 63,000 books titles; 5,000 to 25,000 music titles; 7,000 to 14,000 sale VHS, DVD and video game titles; 10,000 to 21,000 rental videos and video games; 3,000 to 29,000 used CDs, DVDs and video games; 1,000 to 20,000 used books; 2,000 to 4,000 boutique items, consumables and accessories; 1,000 to 4,000 periodicals; and up to 1,000 software titles. Music generates approximately 23% of revenues; books, 22%; video, 21%; rentals, 17%; video games, 9%; boutique, 4%; consumables, 3%; and other, 1%. Hastings typically operates a store-within-a-store format, dividing 92 of its superstores into some form of its three section format: Music, Books and Video. The firm operates Gohastings.com, which offers a broad selection of books, music, software, videocassettes, video games and DVDs over the Internet. It also sells its products via Amazon.com, utilizing its goShip program. Currently, 56 stores participate in the goShip program, which ships items sold on Amazon directly from store inventories. The company aims to achieve high levels of customer loyalty and repeat business. To this end, many of its stores offer such amenities as reading chairs and 66 stores offer Hard Back Cafe full-service coffee bars. Hastings buys used CDs, video games, DVDs and books from customers, offering used products as a low-cost alternative. It also provides budget-priced products in its major product categories.

FINANCIALS: Sales and profits are in thousands of dollars—add 000 to get the full amount. 2007 Note: Financial information for 2007 was not available for all companies at press time.

2007 Sales: $548,332	2007 Profits: $5,019	**U.S. Stock Ticker:** HAST
2006 Sales: $537,931	2006 Profits: $5,695	**Int'l Ticker:** **Int'l Exchange:**
2005 Sales: $542,016	2005 Profits: $5,809	Employees: 5,962
2004 Sales: $508,318	2004 Profits: $7,750	Fiscal Year Ends: 1/31
2003 Sales: $495,400	2003 Profits: $1,900	Parent Company:

SALARIES/BENEFITS:

Pension Plan:	ESOP Stock Plan:	Profit Sharing:	Top Exec. Salary: $318,654	Bonus: $397,188
Savings Plan:	Stock Purch. Plan:		Second Exec. Salary: $191,397	Bonus: $91,398

OTHER THOUGHTS:
Apparent Women Officers or Directors: 1
Hot Spot for Advancement for Women/Minorities:

LOCATIONS: ("Y" = Yes)

West:	Southwest:	Midwest:	Southeast:	Northeast:	International:
Y	Y	Y	Y		

HEARST CORPORATION (THE)   www.hearstcorp.com

Industry Group Code: 511110 Ranks within this company's industry group: Sales: 4   Profits:

Print Media/Publishing:		Movies:		Equipment/Supplies:		Broadcast/Cable:		Music/Audio:		Sports/Games/Gambling:	
Newspapers:	Y	Movie Theaters:		Equipment/Supplies:		Broadcast TV:	Y	Music Production:		Games/Sports:	
Magazines:	Y	Movie Production:		Gambling Equipment:		Cable TV:	Y	Retail Music:		Retail Games Stores:	
Books:		TV/Video Prod.:	Y	Special Services:	Y	Satellite Broadcast:		Retail Audio Equip.:		Stadiums/Teams:	
Book Stores:		Video Rental:		Advertising Services:	Y	Radio:		Music Print./Dist.:		Gambling/Casinos:	
Distribution/Printing:		Video Distribution:		Info. Sys. Software:		Online Information:		Multimedia:		Rides/Theme Parks:	

TYPES OF BUSINESS:

Newspaper Publishing
Magazine Publishing
Television Broadcasting & Production
Phone Directories
Internet Businesses
Syndicated Media Content
On-Demand Cable Television
Media Industry Services

BRANDS/DIVISIONS/AFFILIATES:

Associated Publishing Company (The)
Cosmopolitan
Esquire
Hearst-Argyle Television Inc
ESPN Inc
A&E Television Networks
Hearst Interactive Media
ZynexOrder

CONTACTS: Note: Officers with more than one job title may be intentionally listed here more than once.

Victor F. Ganzi, CEO
Victor F. Ganzi, Pres.
Ronald J. Doerfler, CFO/Sr. VP
James M. Asher, Chief Legal Officer
James M. Asher, Chief Dev. Officer/Sr. VP
Kendra Newton, Dir.-Public Rel.
Thomas W. Campo, Dir.-Investor Rel., Hearst-Argyle
Frank A. Bennack, Jr., Vice Chmn.
David J. Barrett, CEO/Pres., Hearst-Argyle Television
Richard P. Malloch, Pres., Hearst Business Media
George B. Irish, Pres., Hearst Newspapers/Sr. VP
George R. Hearst, Jr., Chmn.

Phone: 212-649-2000	Fax: 212-649-2108
Toll-Free:	
Address: 300 W. 57 St., New York, NY 10019-3791 US	

GROWTH PLANS/SPECIAL FEATURES:

The Hearst Corporation, the legacy of former media mogul William Randolph Hearst, operates newspapers, magazines, television and radio broadcasting, cable television, real estate, interactive media and business media. The company owns 20 weekly newspapers and 12 dailies, including the Houston Chronicle, San Francisco Chronicle and Seattle Post-Intelligencer. The newspaper segment also owns The Associated Publishing Company, which produces phone directories in Texas; White Directory Publishers, Inc., which produces phonebooks for areas in 11 states; and Hearst News Service, which syndicates Hearst newspaper stories. Hearst Magazines publishes 19 titles with more than 145 international editions. Its publications include Cosmopolitan; Country Living; Esquire; Good Housekeeping; Harpers BAZAAR; O, The Oprah Magazine; Popular Mechanics; Seventeen; SmartMoney; and Town & Country. Subsidiary Hearst-Argyle controls the broadcasting segment and owns 26 local television stations, which reach a combined 18% of U.S. viewers. The entertainment division comprises the A&E Television Networks, the ESPN networks, the History Channel and other cable channels; as well as King Features Syndicate, a major distributor of newspaper comics, puzzles, columns and editorials; and Reed Brennan Media Associates, a provider of pagination and editing services for more than 320 newspapers. Hearst Entertainment also owns an extensive movie library, exceeding 250 films. Hearst Interactive Media owns or has an interest in Internet-related companies including MetaTV, Circles, Mobility Technologies, Drugstore.com, Genealogy.com, Medscape, iVillage, Exodus Communications and XM Satellite Radio. The Business Media subsidiary provides information services to business and runs Zynex Health, which provides scientific research and best practice guidelines to health-care providers. Hearst Corporation also has interests in over 20 business-to-business companies, including Black Book Guides, MOTOR Information Systems, European Collision Database, Diversion, Electronic Engineers Master Catalog, Electronic Products Magazine, First DataBank, Floor Covering Weekly, IDG/Hearst, Stocknet and Used Car Pricing Guides. Recent acquisitions include Veretech, FleetCross and Kaango.

FINANCIALS: Sales and profits are in thousands of dollars—add 000 to get the full amount. 2007 Note: Financial information for 2007 was not available for all companies at press time.

2007 Sales: $	2007 Profits: $	U.S. Stock Ticker: Private
2006 Sales: $4,520,000	2006 Profits: $	Int'l Ticker: Int'l Exchange:
2005 Sales: $4,550,000	2005 Profits: $	Employees: 17,062
2004 Sales: $4,000,000	2004 Profits: $	Fiscal Year Ends: 12/31
2003 Sales: $4,100,000	2003 Profits: $	Parent Company:

SALARIES/BENEFITS:

Pension Plan:	ESOP Stock Plan:	Profit Sharing:	Top Exec. Salary: $	Bonus: $
Savings Plan:	Stock Purch. Plan:		Second Exec. Salary: $	Bonus: $

OTHER THOUGHTS:

Apparent Women Officers or Directors: 29
Hot Spot for Advancement for Women/Minorities: Y

LOCATIONS: ("Y" = Yes)

West:	Southwest:	Midwest:	Southeast:	Northeast:	International:
Y	Y	Y	Y	Y	Y

Note: Financial information, benefits and other data can change quickly and may vary from those stated here.

HEARST-ARGYLE TELEVISION INC   www.hearstargyle.com

Industry Group Code: 513120 Ranks within this company's industry group: Sales: 10   Profits: 8

Print Media/Publishing:	Movies:		Equipment/Supplies:	Broadcast/Cable:		Music/Audio:	Sports/Games/Gambling:
Newspapers:	Movie Theaters:		Equipment/Supplies:	Broadcast TV:	Y	Music Production:	Games/Sports:
Magazines:	Movie Production:		Gambling Equipment:	Cable TV:		Retail Music:	Retail Games Stores:
Books:	TV/Video Prod.:	Y	Special Services:	Satellite Broadcast:		Retail Audio Equip.:	Stadiums/Teams:
Book Stores:	Video Rental:		Advertising Services:	Radio:		Music Print./Dist.:	Gambling/Casinos:
Distribution/Printing:	Video Distribution:		Info. Sys. Software:	Online Information:		Multimedia:	Rides/Theme Parks:

TYPES OF BUSINESS:
Broadcast Television
Radio Stations
Web Sites
Television Production

BRANDS/DIVISIONS/AFFILIATES:
Hearst Corporation
Internet Broadcasting Systems

CONTACTS: *Note: Officers with more than one job title may be intentionally listed here more than once.*
David J. Barrett, CEO
David J. Barrett, Pres.
Harry T. Hawks, CFO/Exec. VP
Mary Danielski, VP-Mktg. & Creative Svcs.
Alvin Lustgarten, VP-IT
Martin Faubell, VP-Eng.
Alvin Lustgarten, VP-Admin
Jonathan Mintzer, General Counsel/VP/Corp. Sec.
Steven A. Hobbs, Exec. VP/Chief Dev. & Legal Officer
Ellen McClain, VP-Finance
Terry Mackin, Exec. VP
Kathleen Keefe, VP-Sales
Frederick I. Young, Sr. VP-News
Emerson Coleman, VP-Programming
Victor F. Ganzi, Chmn.

Phone: 212-887-6800	Fax: 212-887-6855
Toll-Free:	
Address: 300 West 57th St., New York, NY 10019 US	

GROWTH PLANS/SPECIAL FEATURES:
Hearst-Argyle Television, Inc. owns or manages 29 digital television stations that reach approximately 18% of U.S. television households. It is one of the country's largest independent TV station groups. Each one of Hearst-Argyle's owned or managed television stations are affiliated with one of the following major networks: ABC, NBC, CBS, CW or MyNetworkTV. The firm is the largest ABC-affiliate group, with 13 affiliated stations and the second-largest NBC affiliate group with 10 affiliated stations. Of the 25 markets where the company produces news, 19 are ranked either first or second in local morning and evening news programs. The programming for the television stations has three main components: programs produced by the affiliated networks (e.g. ABC's Grey's Anatomy, NBC's Law and Order and CBS' CSI: Crime Scene Investigation) and special events such as the Academy Awards, the Olympics and the Super Bowl; programs produced by the company such as local news, weather, sports and entertainment; and first-run syndicated programs acquired by the company such as The Oprah Winfrey Show and Entertainment Tonight. In addition, Hearst-Argyle is a leader in the convergence of local broadcast television and the internet through its investment in, and operating agreement with, Internet Broadcasting, which operates a nation-wide network of television websites. Its websites attracted a combined average of 3.9 million unique viewers and generated 106.9 million average page views per month during 2006. Hearst-Argyle's primary source of revenue is the sale of advertising to advertisers. It is an attractive carrier for advertisements because of its broad reach and compelling content on multiple media platforms. The firm is majority owned by publishing giant Hearst Corporation.

FINANCIALS: Sales and profits are in thousands of dollars—add 000 to get the full amount. 2007 Note: Financial information for 2007 was not available for all companies at press time.

2007 Sales: $	2007 Profits: $	U.S. Stock Ticker: HTV
2006 Sales: $785,402	2006 Profits: $98,723	Int'l Ticker: Int'l Exchange:
2005 Sales: $706,883	2005 Profits: $100,217	Employees: 3,312
2004 Sales: $779,879	2004 Profits: $123,942	Fiscal Year Ends: 12/31
2003 Sales: $686,775	2003 Profits: $94,221	Parent Company:

SALARIES/BENEFITS:
Pension Plan:	ESOP Stock Plan:	Profit Sharing:	Top Exec. Salary: $1,050,000	Bonus: $500,000
Savings Plan:	Stock Purch. Plan:		Second Exec. Salary: $705,000	Bonus: $250,000

OTHER THOUGHTS:
Apparent Women Officers or Directors: 5
Hot Spot for Advancement for Women/Minorities: Y

LOCATIONS: ("Y" = Yes)
West:	Southwest:	Midwest:	Southeast:	Northeast:	International:
Y	Y	Y	Y	Y	

Note: Financial information, benefits and other data can change quickly and may vary from those stated here.

HERBST GAMING INC

www.terribleherbst.com

Industry Group Code: 713210 Ranks within this company's industry group: Sales: Profits:

Print Media/Publishing:	Movies:	Equipment/Supplies:		Broadcast/Cable:	Music/Audio:	Sports/Games/Gambling:	
Newspapers:	Movie Theaters:	Equipment/Supplies:		Broadcast TV:	Music Production:	Games/Sports:	
Magazines:	Movie Production:	Gambling Equipment:	Y	Cable TV:	Retail Music:	Retail Games Stores:	
Books:	TV/Video Prod.:	Special Services:		Satellite Broadcast:	Retail Audio Equip.:	Stadiums/Teams:	
Book Stores:	Video Rental:	Advertising Services:		Radio:	Music Print./Dist.:	Gambling/Casinos:	Y
Distribution/Printing:	Video Distribution:	Info. Sys. Software:		Online Information:	Multimedia:	Rides/Theme Parks:	

TYPES OF BUSINESS:

Casino Operation
Slot Machine Operation
Slot Machhine Installation

BRANDS/DIVISIONS/AFFILIATES:

Terrible's Hotel & Casino
Rail City Casino
Sands Regency Casino Hotel
Gold Ranch Casino and RV Resort
Dayton Depot Casino and Red Hawk Sports Bar
Terrible's St. Jo Frontier Casino
Terrible's Mark Twain Casino
Terrible's Lakeside Casino Resort

CONTACTS: *Note: Officers with more than one job title may be intentionally listed here more than once.*

Edward J. Herbst, Pres.
Mary E. Higgins, CFO
Sean T. Higgins, General Counsel
Timothy P. Herbst, VP
Troy D. Herbst, VP
Edward J. Herbst, Chmn.

Phone: 702-889-7695	Fax: 702-889-7691
Toll-Free:	
Address: 3440 W. Russell Rd., Las Vegas, NV 89118 US	

GROWTH PLANS/SPECIAL FEATURES:

Herbst Gaming, Inc. is a diversified gaming company with slot route operations and casino operations. Herbst's slot route operations involve the exclusive installation and operation of slot machines in certain strategic, high traffic, non-casino locations, such as grocery stores, drug stores, convenience stores, bars and restaurants. The company owns and operates roughly 7,200 slot machines. Herbst's Nevada casino operations consist of Terrible's Hotel & Casino in Las Vegas, with 255 rooms, a buffet and a 24 hour cafe; Rail City Casino in Sparks, with roughly 16,600 square feet of gaming space, a 24 hour restaurant and a bar; Sands Regency Casino Hotel in Reno, with approximately 29,000 square feet of gaming space, 12,000 square feet of convention space, 833 rooms, three cocktail lounges, a comedy club, a health spa, Cabana Café, The Buffet at the Sands and Fuzio's, an Italian restaurant; Gold Ranch Casino and RV Resort in Verdl, with a 105 space RV park; and Dayton Depot Casino and Red Hawk Sports Bar in Dayton, with 16,000 square feet of casino space, a restaurant and two bars. Together, these casinos contain approximately 2,016 slot machines and 18 table games. Outside of Nevada, Herbst owns and operates Terrible's St. Jo Frontier Casino in St. Joseph, Missouri; Terrible's Mark Twain Casino in LaGrange, Missouri; Terrible's Lakeside Casino Resort in Osceola, Iowa. Together, these properties contain approximately 2,265 slot machines and 44 table games. In January 2007, Herbst acquired the Sands Regent for $119 million, including the Rail City Casino; the Sands Regency Casino Hotel; the Gold Ranch Casino and RV Resort; and Depot Casino and Red Hawk Sports Bar. In April 2007, the company acquired Buffalo Bill's, Primm Valley and Whiskey Pete's hotel casinos located in Primm, Nevada from MGM MIRAGE for $400 million.

FINANCIALS: Sales and profits are in thousands of dollars—add 000 to get the full amount. 2007 Note: Financial information for 2007 was not available for all companies at press time.

2007 Sales: $	2007 Profits: $	U.S. Stock Ticker: Private
2006 Sales: $	2006 Profits: $	Int'l Ticker: Int'l Exchange:
2005 Sales: $	2005 Profits: $	Employees:
2004 Sales: $	2004 Profits: $	Fiscal Year Ends: 12/31
2003 Sales: $	2003 Profits: $	Parent Company:

SALARIES/BENEFITS:

Pension Plan:	ESOP Stock Plan:	Profit Sharing:	Top Exec. Salary: $572,505	Bonus: $
Savings Plan:	Stock Purch. Plan:		Second Exec. Salary: $354,281	Bonus: $

OTHER THOUGHTS:

Apparent Women Officers or Directors: 1
Hot Spot for Advancement for Women/Minorities:

LOCATIONS: ("Y" = Yes)

West:	Southwest:	Midwest:	Southeast:	Northeast:	International:
Y		Y			

HERSHEY CO
www.hersheys.com

Industry Group Code: 311330 Ranks within this company's industry group: Sales: 1 Profits: 1

Print Media/Publishing:	Movies:	Equipment/Supplies:	Broadcast/Cable:	Music/Audio:	Sports/Games/Gambling:
Newspapers:	Movie Theaters:	Equipment/Supplies:	Broadcast TV:	Music Production:	Games/Sports:
Magazines:	Movie Production:	Gambling Equipment:	Cable TV:	Retail Music:	Retail Games Stores:
Books:	TV/Video Prod.:	Special Services:	Satellite Broadcast:	Retail Audio Equip.:	Stadiums/Teams:
Book Stores:	Video Rental:	Advertising Services:	Radio:	Music Print./Dist.:	Gambling/Casinos:
Distribution/Printing:	Video Distribution:	Info. Sys. Software:	Online Information:	Multimedia:	Rides/Theme Parks:

TYPES OF BUSINESS:
Candy Manufacturing
Baking Supplies
Chocolate Products
Confectionaries & Snacks
Amusement Park
Resorts/Hotels

BRANDS/DIVISIONS/AFFILIATES:
Kit Kat
Reese's
Hershey International
Pelon Pelo Rico
HERSHEYPARK
Hershey Entertainment and Resorts, Co.
Dagoba Organic Chocolate, LLC
Cacao Reserve

CONTACTS: Note: Officers with more than one job title may be intentionally listed here more than once.
David J. West, CEO
David J. West, COO/Exec. VP
David J. West, Pres.
Humberto P. Alfonso, CFO/Sr. VP
Michele G. Buck, Sr. VP-Chief Mktg. Officer, U.S.
Marcella K. Arline, Chief People Officer/Sr. VP
Daniel Azzara, VP-Global Innovation & Quality
George F. Davis, CIO/VP
Daniel T. Darcy, VP-Manufacturing
Burton H. Snyder, General Counsel/Sr. VP/Corp. Sec.
Gregg Tanner, Sr. VP-Global Oper.
Bryan C. Crittenden, VP-Bus. Dev.
Kirk Saville, Public Relations
Mark K. Pogharian, Dir.-Investor Rel.
Rosa C. Stroh, Treas.
Jay A. Cooper, VP-U.S. Chocolate
D. Michael Wege, VP-US Portfolio Brands & Mktg. Excellence
Bruce A. Brown, VP/Bus. Process Optimization
Richard H. Lenny, Chmn.
John P. Bilbrey, Sr. VP/Pres., Hershey Int'l

Phone: 717-534-4200	Fax: 717-534-6760
Toll-Free: 800-539-0261	
Address: 100 Crystal A Dr., Hershey, PA 17033-0810 US	

GROWTH PLANS/SPECIAL FEATURES:

Hershey Co. (formerly Hershey Foods Corp.) is one of the largest candy makers in the U.S., manufacturing over 50 brands, including five of the top ten chocolate brands in the country. The firm operates through three main divisions: the U.S. Confectionary group; the U.S. Snacks group; and Hershey International, which oversees the corporation's international interests and exports to over 60 countries worldwide. The company generates 80% of revenues from chocolate sales. Hershey's principal product groups include chocolate and non-chocolate confectionery products sold in the form of bar goods; packaged items; and grocery products such as baking ingredients, chocolate drink mixes, peanut butter, dessert toppings and beverages. Its products are sold primarily to grocery wholesalers and distributors, candy distributors, mass merchandisers, drug stores, vending companies, convenience stores, and concessionaries by full-time sales representatives, food brokers and part-time retail sales merchandisers throughout the U.S., Canada, Mexico and Brazil. Recently, it joined with Lotte Confectionery Co., LTD., Korea's leading confectionery and ice cream manufacturer, to produce and sell Hershey products in China. Additionally, the chocolate giant partnered with Godrej Beverages and Foods, Ltd. to develop and market Hershey chocolate in India under the company name Godrej Hershey Foods & Beverages Ltd. (with 51% Hershey ownership.) Most company operations occur in Hershey, Pennsylvania where the company runs HERSHEYPARK, an amusement park operated by subsidiary Hershey Entertainment and Resorts Company. In 2007, the company introduced Hershey's Bliss, a complement to its Hershey's dark chocolate line. This follows the earlier debut of Hershey's Antioxidant Milk Chocolate and Whole Bean Chocolate, additions to its Goodness Chocolate portfolio. In 2008, the chocolate company plans to continue to build on the market's existing demand for pure chocolate, and will reinvest in its core brands, global expansion, and its retail sales force.

Hershey's headquarters provides employees with a swimming pool and a gym. Other employee benefits include a counseling service, a casual dress code, health insurance, a 401(k) savings plan and free chocolate.

FINANCIALS: Sales and profits are in thousands of dollars—add 000 to get the full amount. 2007 Note: Financial information for 2007 was not available for all companies at press time.

2007 Sales: $	2007 Profits: $	U.S. Stock Ticker: HSY
2006 Sales: $4,944,230	2006 Profits: $559,061	Int'l Ticker: Int'l Exchange:
2005 Sales: $4,819,827	2005 Profits: $488,547	Employees: 13,750
2004 Sales: $4,429,200	2004 Profits: $590,900	Fiscal Year Ends: 12/31
2003 Sales: $4,172,551	2003 Profits: $457,584	Parent Company:

SALARIES/BENEFITS:

Pension Plan: Y	ESOP Stock Plan: Y	Profit Sharing:	Top Exec. Salary: $1,100,000	Bonus: $
Savings Plan: Y	Stock Purch. Plan: Y		Second Exec. Salary: $485,000	Bonus: $

OTHER THOUGHTS:
Apparent Women Officers or Directors: 3
Hot Spot for Advancement for Women/Minorities: Y

LOCATIONS: ("Y" = Yes)

West:	Southwest:	Midwest:	Southeast:	Northeast:	International:
Y	Y	Y	Y	Y	Y

Note: Financial information, benefits and other data can change quickly and may vary from those stated here.

HOLLINGER INC   www.hollinger.com

Industry Group Code: 511110 Ranks within this company's industry group: Sales: 21   Profits: 16

Print Media/Publishing:		Movies:	Equipment/Supplies:	Broadcast/Cable:	Music/Audio:	Sports/Games/Gambling:
Newspapers:	Y	Movie Theaters:	Equipment/Supplies:	Broadcast TV:	Music Production:	Games/Sports:
Magazines:	Y	Movie Production:	Gambling Equipment:	Cable TV:	Retail Music:	Retail Games Stores:
Books:		TV/Video Prod.:	Special Services:	Satellite Broadcast:	Retail Audio Equip.:	Stadiums/Teams:
Book Stores:		Video Rental:	Advertising Services:	Radio:	Music Print./Dist.:	Gambling/Casinos:
Distribution/Printing:		Video Distribution:	Info. Sys. Software:	Online Information:	Multimedia:	Rides/Theme Parks:

TYPES OF BUSINESS:

Newspaper Publishing
Online Publishing
Magazine Publishing

BRANDS/DIVISIONS/AFFILIATES:

Chicago Sun-Times
Digital Chicago
Digital New York
Post Tribune
Daily Southtown
Hollinger, Inc.
Hollinger Canadian Publishing Holdings Co.

CONTACTS: *Note: Officers with more than one job title may be intentionally listed here more than once.*

G. Wesley Voorheis, CEO
William E. Aziz, CFO/VP
Stanley Beck, Chmn.

Phone: 212-586-5666	Fax: 212-586-0010
Toll-Free:	
Address: 10 Toronto St., Toronto, ON M5C2B7 Canada	

GROWTH PLANS/SPECIAL FEATURES:

Hollinger, Inc., through subsidiaries and affiliated companies, is one of the leading publishers of English-language newspapers in the U.S. and U.K. It maintains web sites supporting each of its major newspapers and continues to develop a strategic online media presence. The 23 paid daily newspapers the firm owns or has an interest in have a worldwide daily combined circulation of about 2 million. Hollinger also owns or has an interest in over 250 non-daily newspapers, as well as magazines and other publications. The company's Chicago group consists of more than 100 papers including the Chicago Sun-Times, the fifth most read daily newspaper in the U.S.; the Post Tribune in Gary, Indiana; and the Daily Southtown. The group also publishes Digital Chicago magazine and Digital New York, which appear both on newsstands and online. Hollinger owns approximately 70% voting stock and 19.7% equity interest in the Sun-Times Media Group, Inc. (formerly Hollinger International, Inc.) which owns the Chicago Sun-Times and other community newspapers in and around Chicago. In 2007 the company commenced a bankruptcy-related restructuring that saw Hollinger sell off Cayman Free Press Limited and its Costa Rican subsidiary, which controls the La Republica newspaper.

FINANCIALS: Sales and profits are in thousands of dollars—add 000 to get the full amount. 2007 Note: Financial information for 2007 was not available for all companies at press time.

2007 Sales: $	2007 Profits: $	U.S. Stock Ticker: HLG
2006 Sales: $2,447	2006 Profits: $-16,590	Int'l Ticker: HLG.C Int'l Exchange: Toronto-TSX
2005 Sales: $457,889	2005 Profits: $-11,969	Employees: 3,082
2004 Sales: $464,439	2004 Profits: $234,668	Fiscal Year Ends: 12/31
2003 Sales: $1,061,200	2003 Profits: $-68,900	Parent Company:

SALARIES/BENEFITS:

Pension Plan:	ESOP Stock Plan:	Profit Sharing:	Top Exec. Salary: $1,714,087	Bonus: $1,100,000
Savings Plan: Y	Stock Purch. Plan:		Second Exec. Salary: $373,304	Bonus: $200,603

OTHER THOUGHTS:

Apparent Women Officers or Directors: 1
Hot Spot for Advancement for Women/Minorities:

LOCATIONS: ("Y" = Yes)

West:	Southwest:	Midwest:	Southeast:	Northeast:	International:
		Y		Y	Y

HOLLYWOOD ENTERTAINMENT CORP
www.hollywoodvideo.com

Industry Group Code: 532230 Ranks within this company's industry group: Sales: Profits:

Print Media/Publishing:	Movies:		Equipment/Supplies:		Broadcast/Cable:	Music/Audio:	Sports/Games/Gambling:
Newspapers:	Movie Theaters:		Equipment/Supplies:		Broadcast TV:	Music Production:	Games/Sports:
Magazines:	Movie Production:		Gambling Equipment:		Cable TV:	Retail Music:	Retail Games Stores:
Books:	TV/Video Prod.:		Special Services:		Satellite Broadcast:	Retail Audio Equip.:	Stadiums/Teams:
Book Stores:	Video Rental:	Y	Advertising Services:		Radio:	Music Print./Dist.:	Gambling/Casinos:
Distribution/Printing:	Video Distribution:		Info. Sys. Software:		Online Information:	Multimedia:	Rides/Theme Parks:

TYPES OF BUSINESS:
Video Rental Stores
Video Game Rentals & Sales

BRANDS/DIVISIONS/AFFILIATES:
Hollywood Video
Game Crazy
Movie Gallery, Inc.

CONTACTS: Note: Officers with more than one job title may be intentionally listed here more than once.
Timothy A. Winner, COO/Exec. VP
Joe T. Malugen, Chmn./Pres./CEO-Movie Gallery, Inc.

Phone: 503-570-1600	Fax: 503-570-1680
Toll-Free: 877-325-8687	
Address: 9275 SW Peyton Ln., Wilsonville, OR 97070 US	

GROWTH PLANS/SPECIAL FEATURES:
Hollywood Entertainment Corp., a subsidiary of Movie Gallery, Inc., is one of the largest retailers of rental videocassettes, DVDs and video games in the U.S., owning and operating more than 2,000 Hollywood Video retail superstores in 47 states and Washington, D.C. In part because of the firm's revenue sharing arrangements with studios, Hollywood has increased the availability of most new releases, typically acquiring 100-250 copies of hit movies for each Hollywood Video store, with the goal of offering more copies of popular new video releases and more titles than its competitors. The company's superstores typically carry over 10,000 movie and game titles on more than 25,000 videocassettes, DVDs and video games; and are typically located in high-traffic, high visibility, urban and suburban locations with convenient access and parking. The firm's Hollywoodvideo.com site offers reviews and advertises store promotions, and its Reel.com site offers reviews for movies still in theaters, as well as providing options to buy DVDs through Amazon.com. Hollywood operates Game Crazy, a store-within-a store concept through which customers sell, buy and trade new and used video games from a stock of more than 9,000 units. Hollywood currently has approximately 595 Game Crazy locations nationwide, including 14 free-standing locations. It also operates Gamecrazy.com, which offers brief game descriptions, a store locator and updates on soon-to-be released games. Following a recent unsolicited takeover attempt by Blockbuster, Hollywood Entertainment Corp. merged with Movie Gallery in a deal valued at $1.2 billion, forming a chain of over 4,500 stores. In September 2007, Movie Gallery announced its intention to close 520 Movie Gallery and Hollywood Video stores; and in October 2007, Movie Gallery filed for voluntary Chapter 11 bankruptcy protection.

Employees of the company receive flexible spending accounts; medical, dental and vision plans; and discounts on rentals and product purchases from company stores and selected retail partners.

FINANCIALS: Sales and profits are in thousands of dollars—add 000 to get the full amount. 2007 Note: Financial information for 2007 was not available for all companies at press time.

2007 Sales: $	2007 Profits: $	U.S. Stock Ticker: Subsidiary
2006 Sales: $	2006 Profits: $	Int'l Ticker: Int'l Exchange:
2005 Sales: $933,100	2005 Profits: $	Employees: 27,900
2004 Sales: $1,782,400	2004 Profits: $71,300	Fiscal Year Ends: 12/31
2003 Sales: $1,682,548	2003 Profits: $82,272	Parent Company: MOVIE GALLERY INC

SALARIES/BENEFITS:

Pension Plan:	ESOP Stock Plan:	Profit Sharing:	Top Exec. Salary: $1,269,231	Bonus: $
Savings Plan: Y	Stock Purch. Plan:		Second Exec. Salary: $342,461	Bonus: $

OTHER THOUGHTS:
Apparent Women Officers or Directors:
Hot Spot for Advancement for Women/Minorities:

LOCATIONS: ("Y" = Yes)

West:	Southwest:	Midwest:	Southeast:	Northeast:	International:
Y	Y	Y	Y	Y	

HOLLYWOOD MEDIA CORP

www.hollywood.com

Industry Group Code: 514199 Ranks within this company's industry group: Sales: 4 Profits: 3

Print Media/Publishing:		Movies:		Equipment/Supplies:		Broadcast/Cable:		Music/Audio:		Sports/Games/Gambling:	
Newspapers:		Movie Theaters:		Equipment/Supplies:		Broadcast TV:		Music Production:		Games/Sports:	
Magazines:		Movie Production:		Gambling Equipment:		Cable TV:	Y	Retail Music:		Retail Games Stores:	
Books:	Y	TV/Video Prod.:		Special Services:	Y	Satellite Broadcast:		Retail Audio Equip.:		Stadiums/Teams:	
Book Stores:		Video Rental:		Advertising Services:	Y	Radio:		Music Print./Dist.:		Gambling/Casinos:	
Distribution/Printing:		Video Distribution:		Info. Sys. Software:		Online Information:		Multimedia:		Rides/Theme Parks:	

TYPES OF BUSINESS:
Movie-Related Merchandise, Online Retail
Book Publishing
Entertainment-Related Web Sites
Entertainment Research Services
Online Ticket Sales
Advertising Services
Theater Marketing & Sales
Cable Television Networks

BRANDS/DIVISIONS/AFFILIATES:
CinemaSource
EventSource
ExhibitorAds
Broadway.com
1-800-BROADWAY
Theater Direct International
Theatre.com
Hollywood.com

CONTACTS: *Note: Officers with more than one job title may be intentionally listed here more than once.*
Mitchell Rubenstein, CEO
Laurie S. Silvers, Pres./Vice Chmn.
Laurie S. Silvers, Corp. Sec.
Scott A. Gomez, Chief Acct. Officer
Jerome Kane, Exec. VP-Broadway Ticketing
Mitchell Rubenstein, Chmn.

Phone: 561-998-8000	Fax: 561-998-2974
Toll-Free:	
Address: 2255 Glades Rd., Ste. 237 W, Boca Raton, FL 33431 US	

GROWTH PLANS/SPECIAL FEATURES:

Hollywood Media Corp. provides data, news and ticketing to consumers and businesses covering the entertainment, Internet and media industries. The firm operates an entertainment-related web site that includes movie descriptions and reviews, movie trailers, photos, movie showtime listings and entertainment news. Hollywood Media operates several divisions including Data Syndication, Broadway Ticketing, Ad Sales and Cable TV. The Data Syndication division is a provider of integrated database information and complementary data services to the entertainment, Internet and media industries, and is comprised of the Source business, which includes CinemaSource, EventSource and ExhibitorAds. CinemaSource is a leading supplier of movie showtimes, with movie showtime data for approximately 44,000 movie screens in the U.S., the U.K. and Canada. EventSource compiles and syndicates information on community events in cities throughout the U.S. and the U.K., including concerts, sporting events, festivals, fairs and shows. ExhibitorAds provides movie exhibitors with directory newspaper advertising services. Hollywood Media's Broadway Ticketing division is comprised of Broadway.com, 1-800-BROADWAY, Theater Direct International and U.K.-based Theatre.com, which provide access to theater tickets and service for shows on Broadway, off-Broadway and in London's West End theatre district. The company's Ad Sales division includes Hollywood.com, Broadway.com and CinemasOnline. Hollywood Media's Cable TV division includes Hollywood.com Television (HTV) and Broadway.com Television (BTV) which offer interactive entertainment and information with on-demand video content, previews, reviews, behind the scenes footage, interviews and coverage of entertainment industry events to cable company subscribers. Additionally, Hollywood Media owns 51% of the book publishing and packaging company Tekno Books and 50% of NetCo Partners, which owns Tom Clancy's Net Force. In February 2007, the company acquired the Broadway ticketing business of Showtix LLC for $2.6 million. In August 2007, Hollywood Media sold its Source business to West World Media LLC for $23 million.

FINANCIALS: Sales and profits are in thousands of dollars—add 000 to get the full amount. 2007 Note: Financial information for 2007 was not available for all companies at press time.

2007 Sales: $	2007 Profits: $	U.S. Stock Ticker: HOLL
2006 Sales: $115,895	2006 Profits: $9,523	Int'l Ticker: Int'l Exchange:
2005 Sales: $90,355	2005 Profits: $-8,913	Employees: 230
2004 Sales: $72,979	2004 Profits: $-11,598	Fiscal Year Ends: 12/31
2003 Sales: $64,859	2003 Profits: $-7,442	Parent Company:

SALARIES/BENEFITS:

Pension Plan:	ESOP Stock Plan:	Profit Sharing:	Top Exec. Salary: $424,356	Bonus: $250,000
Savings Plan:	Stock Purch. Plan:		Second Exec. Salary: $371,312	Bonus: $150,000

OTHER THOUGHTS:
Apparent Women Officers or Directors: 1
Hot Spot for Advancement for Women/Minorities: Y

LOCATIONS: ("Y" = Yes)

West	Southwest:	Midwest:	Southeast:	Northeast:	International:
Y			Y	Y	

HOOVER'S INC

www.hoovers.com

Industry Group Code: 514199 Ranks within this company's industry group: Sales: Profits:

Print Media/Publishing:		Movies:	Equipment/Supplies:	Broadcast/Cable:	Music/Audio:	Sports/Games/Gambling:
Newspapers:		Movie Theaters:	Equipment/Supplies:	Broadcast TV:	Music Production:	Games/Sports:
Magazines:		Movie Production:	Gambling Equipment:	Cable TV:	Retail Music:	Retail Games Stores:
Books:	Y	TV/Video Prod.:	Special Services:	Satellite Broadcast:	Retail Audio Equip.:	Stadiums/Teams:
Book Stores:		Video Rental:	Advertising Services:	Radio:	Music Print./Dist.:	Gambling/Casinos:
Distribution/Printing:		Video Distribution:	Info. Sys. Software:	Online Information:	Multimedia:	Rides/Theme Parks:

TYPES OF BUSINESS:
Online Corporate Intelligence
Reference Books
E-Commerce
Advertising Services
Sales & Marketing Lists

BRANDS/DIVISIONS/AFFILIATES:
Dun & Bradstreet Corp (The, D&B)
IPO Scorecard
Hoover's Handbooks

CONTACTS: Note: Officers with more than one job title may be intentionally listed here more than once.
David Mather, Pres.
Jim Currie, VP-Sales
Jeff Guillot, Leader-Tech. & Prod.
Chris Warwick, VP-Prod. Dev. & Mgmt.
Jim Currie, VP-Oper.
Russell Secker, Exec. VP-Customer Experience
Paul Rostkowski, VP-Advertising Sales

Phone: 512-374-4500	Fax: 512-374-4501
Toll-Free:	
Address: 5800 Airport Blvd., Austin, TX 78752 US	

GROWTH PLANS/SPECIAL FEATURES:
Hoover's, Inc., a subsidiary of Dun & Bradstreet (D&B), is an online provider of company and industry information, designed to meet the diverse needs of business organizations, sales executives, investors and researchers of many types. Hoover's customers can access information for their professional endeavors, including financial and competitive research as well as marketing and job search activities, through the company's web site. Hoover's core asset is its proprietary editorial content, which includes a database of 23 million companies, with coverage written and edited in-house on approximately 44,000 public and private enterprises. Hoover's also provides data on initial public offerings (through the IPO Scorecard pages), corporate news, executive biographical information, corporate financial data and access to such items as credit reports by D&B. While the firm's primary focus is the delivery of company intelligence via the Internet, it also publishes reference books including the Hoover's Handbooks. The company partners with Air2Web, a wireless technology firm, to provide customers with the ability to tap into key content and service offerings via wireless devices. The company generates about 80% of revenue from the sale of annual subscriptions to its premium-level data services, which include Lite, Pro, Pro Plus and Pro Premium. Significant revenue is also generated from licensing fees, e-commerce and the sale of advertising.

FINANCIALS: Sales and profits are in thousands of dollars—add 000 to get the full amount. 2007 Note: Financial information for 2007 was not available for all companies at press time.

2007 Sales: $	2007 Profits: $	**U.S. Stock Ticker: Subsidiary**
2006 Sales: $	2006 Profits: $	**Int'l Ticker:** Int'l Exchange:
2005 Sales: $70,000	2005 Profits: $	Employees: 231
2004 Sales: $50,000	2004 Profits: $	Fiscal Year Ends: 12/31
2003 Sales: $38,000	2003 Profits: $	Parent Company: DUN & BRADSTREET CORP (THE, D&B)

SALARIES/BENEFITS:
Pension Plan:	ESOP Stock Plan:	Profit Sharing:	Top Exec. Salary: $	Bonus: $75,000
Savings Plan: Y	Stock Purch. Plan:		Second Exec. Salary: $226,813	Bonus: $226,813

OTHER THOUGHTS:
Apparent Women Officers or Directors:
Hot Spot for Advancement for Women/Minorities:

LOCATIONS: ("Y" = Yes)
West:	Southwest:	Midwest:	Southeast:	Northeast:	International:
	Y				

HOT CABLE SYSTEMS MEDIA LTD   www.hot.net.il

Industry Group Code: 513220 Ranks within this company's industry group: Sales: Profits:

Print Media/Publishing:	Movies:	Equipment/Supplies:		Broadcast/Cable:		Music/Audio:	Sports/Games/Gambling:
Newspapers:	Movie Theaters:	Equipment/Supplies:		Broadcast TV:		Music Production:	Games/Sports:
Magazines:	Movie Production:	Gambling Equipment:		Cable TV:	Y	Retail Music:	Retail Games Stores:
Books:	TV/Video Prod.:	Special Services:	Y	Satellite Broadcast:		Retail Audio Equip.:	Stadiums/Teams:
Book Stores:	Video Rental:	Advertising Services:		Radio:		Music Print./Dist.:	Gambling/Casinos:
Distribution/Printing:	Video Distribution:	Info. Sys. Software:		Online Information:		Multimedia:	Rides/Theme Parks:

TYPES OF BUSINESS:

Cable Television Service
Broadband Internet Services
Mobile & International Phone Service

BRANDS/DIVISIONS/AFFILIATES:

Partner Communications
Barak, I.T.C.
HOT
Delek Investments Properties
Hot Telecom
MATAV-Cable Systems Media Ltd
Golden Channels & Co. Group
Tevel Israel International Communications Ltd.

CONTACTS: *Note: Officers with more than one job title may be intentionally listed here more than once.*

Meir Srebernik, CEO
Tal Peres, CFO
Ron Sharon, VP-Info. Systems
Ori Gur Arieh, General Counsel
Ayelet Shiloni, Integrated Investor Rel.
Meir Srebernik, Chmn.

Phone: 972-9-860-2160	Fax: 972-9-860-2282
Toll-Free:	
Address: 42 Pinkas St., North Industrial Area, PO Box 13600, Netanya, 42134 Israel	

GROWTH PLANS/SPECIAL FEATURES:

HOT Cable Systems Media Ltd. is one of three cable television operators in Israel. The firm operates digital and analog cable television systems and provides approximately 120 channels to 265,000 subscribers. In addition, the company provides cable-based high-speed Internet services with more than 126,500 subscribers. The company also holds a minority interest in Partner Communications, a company providing mobile phone service to 29% of Israeli citizens; and 10% of Barak, Ltd., a provider of international phone service. Approximately 25% of Israeli households are connected to subsidiary MATAV-Cable Systems Media Ltd.'s network, including the metropolitan areas of Bat Yam/Holon, Haifa and Netanya/Hadera and the rural areas of Kiryat Shmona, Safed, Tiberias, part of Galilee and the Golan Heights. MATAV, together with two additional Cable television operators, Golden Channels & Co. Group and Tevel Israel International Communications Ltd., formed the brand HOT, a nationwide cable television provider. HOT has approximately 1 million television subscribers and 450,000 Internet subscribers. The joint venture is part of an operational merger of the three cable companies that involves marketing, sales, engineering, customer service, operations and information systems, forming a monopoly of cable TV services in Israel. In addition, the company's joint venture owns Hot Telecom, a cable network fixed-line telephony service. In 2006, the firm announced plans to purchase all shares, assets and liabilities of Golden Channels & Co. Group and Tevel Israel International Communications Ltd. pending regulatory approval.

FINANCIALS: Sales and profits are in thousands of dollars—add 000 to get the full amount. 2007 Note: Financial information for 2007 was not available for all companies at press time.

2007 Sales: $	2007 Profits: $	U.S. Stock Ticker:
2006 Sales: $	2006 Profits: $	Int'l Ticker: MATV Int'l Exchange: Tel Aviv-TASE
2005 Sales: $	2005 Profits: $	Employees: 826
2004 Sales: $135,700	2004 Profits: $-19,300	Fiscal Year Ends: 12/31
2003 Sales: $125,100	2003 Profits: $-1,300	Parent Company:

SALARIES/BENEFITS:

Pension Plan:	ESOP Stock Plan:	Profit Sharing:	Top Exec. Salary: $	Bonus: $
Savings Plan:	Stock Purch. Plan:		Second Exec. Salary: $	Bonus: $

OTHER THOUGHTS:

Apparent Women Officers or Directors:
Hot Spot for Advancement for Women/Minorities:

LOCATIONS: ("Y" = Yes)

West:	Southwest:	Midwest:	Southeast:	Northeast:	International:
					Y

Note: Financial information, benefits and other data can change quickly and may vary from those stated here.

HOUGHTON MIFFLIN CO

www.hmco.com

Industry Group Code: 511130 Ranks within this company's industry group: Sales: Profits:

Print Media/Publishing:		Movies:	Equipment/Supplies:		Broadcast/Cable:	Music/Audio:	Sports/Games/Gambling:
Newspapers:		Movie Theaters:	Equipment/Supplies:		Broadcast TV:	Music Production:	Games/Sports:
Magazines:		Movie Production:	Gambling Equipment:		Cable TV:	Retail Music:	Retail Games Stores:
Books:	Y	TV/Video Prod.:	Special Services:	Y	Satellite Broadcast:	Retail Audio Equip.:	Stadiums/Teams:
Book Stores:		Video Rental:	Advertising Services:		Radio:	Music Print./Dist.:	Gambling/Casinos:
Distribution/Printing:		Video Distribution:	Info. Sys. Software:		Online Information:	Multimedia:	Rides/Theme Parks:

TYPES OF BUSINESS:

Book Publishing
Educational Materials
Software, CD-ROMs & Mixed Media
Textbooks
Electronic & Multimedia Publishing
Test Design & Consulting
Reference Materials

BRANDS/DIVISIONS/AFFILIATES:

McDougal Littell, Inc.
Great Source Education Group, Inc.
Cognitive Concepts, Inc.
Riverside Publishing Company
Edusoft
American Heritage Dictionary
Peterson Field Guides
Harcourt Education

CONTACTS: Note: Officers with more than one job title may be intentionally listed here more than once.

Anthony Lucki, CEO
Stephen Richards, COO/Exec. VP
Anthony Lucki, Pres.
Stephen Richards, CFO
Gerald Hughes, Sr. VP-Human Resources
Mike Quinn, CIO/VP
Clarence Thacker, VP-Mfg. & Corp. Fulfillment Svcs.
Paul Weaver, General Counsel/Sr. VP/Corp. Sec.
Collin Earnst, VP-Corp. Comm.
Cheryl Cramer, VP-Investor Rel.
Donna Lucki, Pres., School Div.
Rita H. Schaefer, Pres., McDougal Littell
June Smith, Pres., College Div.
Theresa Kelly, Pres., Trade & Reference Div.
Anthony Lucki, Chmn.

Phone: 617-351-5000	Fax: 617-351-1105
Toll-Free:	
Address: 222 Berkeley St., Fl. 5, Boston, MA 02116 US	

GROWTH PLANS/SPECIAL FEATURES:

Houghton Mifflin Co. and its subsidiaries publish textbooks and other educational materials and provide educational services, as well as publishing fiction, nonfiction, children's books, dictionaries and reference materials. The K-12 publishing segment operates through four divisions: School Division, which focuses on kindergarten through sixth grade; McDougal Littell, Inc., which publishes educational materials for grades 6-12; Great Source Education Group, Inc., which publishes curriculum-based supplementary and alternative instructional material for the K-12 and home school markets through Cognitive Concepts, Inc., Earobics and Write Source; and the Assessment Division, which develops and markets testing technology for K-12 through the Riverside Publishing Company. Houghton Mifflin's college division publishes textbooks, study guides and technology tools for introductory level college classes. Edusoft, now operating in conjunction with Riverside Publishing, is an online assessment tool that assists school districts in tracking test results. Houghton Mifflin's trade and reference division publishes adult and children's literature and nonfiction, poetry and cookbooks, as well as reference books including American Heritage dictionaries and Peterson Field Guides. While the firm has traditionally published printed materials, it has begun to publish in other formats, including computer software, laser discs, CD-ROM and other electronic and multimedia products. In late 2006, Houghton Mifflin agreed to be acquired by HM Rivergroup plc for approximately $3.4 billion in cash and debt assumption. In July 2007, Houghton Mifflin agreed to acquire Harcourt Education, Harcourt Trade and Greenwood-Heinemann from Reed Elsevier PLC for $4 billion.

Houghton Mifflin offers employees health, life and disability insurance; a 401(k); retirement plans; flexible spending accounts; scholarships; tuition reimbursement; employee assistance; banking and credit union services; and discounts on Houghton Mifflin books. The firm offers internships and temporary summer positions.

FINANCIALS: Sales and profits are in thousands of dollars—add 000 to get the full amount. 2007 Note: Financial information for 2007 was not available for all companies at press time.

2007 Sales: $	2007 Profits: $	U.S. Stock Ticker: Private
2006 Sales: $	2006 Profits: $	Int'l Ticker: Int'l Exchange:
2005 Sales: $1,282,100	2005 Profits: $-56,300	Employees: 3,554
2004 Sales: $1,218,900	2004 Profits: $-67,200	Fiscal Year Ends: 12/31
2003 Sales: $1,263,500	2003 Profits: $-71,600	Parent Company:

SALARIES/BENEFITS:

Pension Plan: Y	ESOP Stock Plan:	Profit Sharing:	Top Exec. Salary: $398,284	Bonus: $363,428
Savings Plan: Y	Stock Purch. Plan:		Second Exec. Salary: $355,054	Bonus: $331,955

OTHER THOUGHTS:

Apparent Women Officers or Directors: 5
Hot Spot for Advancement for Women/Minorities: Y

LOCATIONS: ("Y" = Yes)

West:	Southwest:	Midwest:	Southeast:	Northeast:	International:
Y	Y	Y	Y	Y	Y

Note: Financial information, benefits and other data can change quickly and may vary from those stated here.

IAC/INTERACTIVECORP

www.iac.com

Industry Group Code: 454110B Ranks within this company's industry group: Sales: 1 Profits: 1

Print Media/Publishing:	Movies:		Equipment/Supplies:		Broadcast/Cable:		Music/Audio:	Sports/Games/Gambling:
Newspapers:	Movie Theaters:		Equipment/Supplies:		Broadcast TV:	Y	Music Production:	Games/Sports:
Magazines:	Movie Production:		Gambling Equipment:		Cable TV:	Y	Retail Music:	Retail Games Stores:
Books:	TV/Video Prod.:	Y	Special Services:		Satellite Broadcast:		Retail Audio Equip.:	Stadiums/Teams:
Book Stores:	Video Rental:		Advertising Services:	Y	Radio:		Music Print./Dist.:	Gambling/Casinos:
Distribution/Printing:	Video Distribution:		Info. Sys. Software:		Online Information:		Multimedia:	Rides/Theme Parks:

TYPES OF BUSINESS:

Cable Television Shopping Programs
Entertainment & Event Ticket Sales
Catalog & Online Home Products & Apparel Retailing
e-Commerce, Online Advertising & Search Engines
Online Real Estate Services, Mortgages & Loans
Online Entertainment & Shopping Directories
Online Personals & Dating Services

BRANDS/DIVISIONS/AFFILIATES:

HSN
Cornerstone Brands
Ticketmaster
LendingTree.com
iNest Realty, Inc.
IAC Search & Media
Match.com
Expedia, Inc.

CONTACTS: Note: Officers with more than one job title may be intentionally listed here more than once.

Barry Diller, CEO
Doug Lebda, COO
Doug Lebda, Pres.
Thomas J. McInerney, CFO/Exec. VP
Johnny C. Taylor, Jr., Sr. VP-Human Resources
Michael Jackson, Pres., Programming
Jason Stewart, Chief Admin. Officer
Greg Blatt, General Counsel/Sec./Exec. VP
Kimberly Gorsuch-Bradbury, Sr. VP-Bus. Strategy
Jonathan L. Sanchez, Chief Comm. Officer/Sr. VP
Michael Schwerdtman, Sr. VP/Controller
Sean Moriarty, Pres./CEO-Ticketmaster
C.D. Davies, CEO-LendingTree, LLC
Jim Lanzone, CEO-Ask.com
Thomas Enraght-Moony, CEO-Match.com
Barry Diller, Chmn.

Phone: 212-314-7300	Fax: 212-314-7309
Toll-Free:	
Address: 555 W. 18th St., New York, NY 10011 US	

GROWTH PLANS/SPECIAL FEATURES:

IAC/InterActiveCorp operates approximately 60 brands. The company's Retailing U.S. operations controls HSN (formerly Home Shopping Network) television broadcasting; Cornerstone Brands published catalogs; and e-commerce sites principally consisting of HSN.com, Shoebuy.com and the web sites operated by Cornerstone Brands. HSN markets over 25,000 consumer products, including jewelry, computers, cookware and beauty products; and in 2006, its television programming reached 89 million homes. Cornerstone offerings include home furnishings and apparel, and it circulated 426 million catalogs in 2006. Retailing International operations include home shopping television broadcaster HSE-Germany, as well as minority interests in some Japanese and Chinese home shopping businesses. IAC's ticketing business primarily consists of Ticketmaster which primarily offers online services in the U.S. and abroad, selling tickets for live events such as sports and music, including the 2008 Beijing Olympic Games. IAC's lending services principally operate through LendingTree.com, offering home, automobile or personal loans and credit cards. RealEstate.com and iNest Realty, Inc., connect realtors with consumers online and provide other services. ServiceMagic offers consumers pre-screened, customer-rated home service professional referrals. The company's media and advertising services consist of Citysearch, a network of websites providing local city guides; Evite, a social planning website; and IAC Search & Media, formerly Ask Jeeves, Inc., which offers Internet search services though Ask.com. This segment also operates Zwinky, a social networking site; iWon.com, an entertainment portal; and other web sites. IAC's membership and subscriptions business consists of vacation services run by Interval International; personals services offered by Match.com, uDate.com, Chemistry.com and related brands; and discount services offered by Entertainment Publications, Inc., which offers coupon books and other products. The company also operates Expedia, Inc., the owner of Expedia.com and other web sites.

The company provides employees with medical, dental and vision care plans; life insurance; paid vacations; pet insurance; and flexible spending accounts.

FINANCIALS: Sales and profits are in thousands of dollars—add 000 to get the full amount. 2007 Note: Financial information for 2007 was not available for all companies at press time.

2007 Sales: $	2007 Profits: $	U.S. Stock Ticker: IACI
2006 Sales: $6,277,638	2006 Profits: $192,635	Int'l Ticker: Int'l Exchange:
2005 Sales: $5,416,506	2005 Profits: $868,212	Employees: 20,000
2004 Sales: $3,911,050	2004 Profits: $151,808	Fiscal Year Ends: 12/31
2003 Sales: $6,328,100	2003 Profits: $167,400	Parent Company:

SALARIES/BENEFITS:

Pension Plan:	ESOP Stock Plan:	Profit Sharing:	Top Exec. Salary: $750,000	Bonus: $1,300,000
Savings Plan: Y	Stock Purch. Plan: Y		Second Exec. Salary: $650,000	Bonus: $1,600,000

OTHER THOUGHTS:

Apparent Women Officers or Directors: 7
Hot Spot for Advancement for Women/Minorities: Y

LOCATIONS: ("Y" = Yes)

West:	Southwest:	Midwest:	Southeast:	Northeast:	International:
Y	Y	Y	Y	Y	Y

Note: Financial information, benefits and other data can change quickly and may vary from those stated here.

I-CABLE COMMUNICATIONS

www.i-cablecomm.com

Industry Group Code: 513220 Ranks within this company's industry group: Sales: 17 Profits: 13

Print Media/Publishing:	Movies:		Equipment/Supplies:		Broadcast/Cable:		Music/Audio:	Sports/Games/Gambling:
Newspapers:	Movie Theaters:	Y	Equipment/Supplies:		Broadcast TV:		Music Production:	Games/Sports:
Magazines:	Movie Production:	Y	Gambling Equipment:		Cable TV:	Y	Retail Music:	Retail Games Stores:
Books:	TV/Video Prod.:		Special Services:	Y	Satellite Broadcast:		Retail Audio Equip.:	Stadiums/Teams:
Book Stores:	Video Rental:		Advertising Services:	Y	Radio:		Music Print./Dist.:	Gambling/Casinos:
Distribution/Printing:	Video Distribution:		Info. Sys. Software:		Online Information:		Multimedia:	Rides/Theme Parks:

TYPES OF BUSINESS:

Cable TV Service
Internet Service Provider
VoIP Telephony Services
Film Production
Advertising-Mass Transit

BRANDS/DIVISIONS/AFFILIATES:

Hong Kong Cable Television, Ltd.
CABLE TV
Hong Kong Cable Enterprises
Global Media In Force Limited
Cable Guide Monthly
21126888.com
CABLE TV e-Programme Listing

CONTACTS: *Note: Officers with more than one job title may be intentionally listed here more than once.*

Stephen Tin Hoi Ng, CEO
Stephen Tin Hoi Ng, Pres.
William J. H. Kwan, CFO/Exec. Dir.
Felix W. K. Yip, VP-Human Resources
Felix W. K. Yip, VP-Admin. & Audit
Garmen K. Y. Chan, VP-External Affairs
Siuming Y. M. Tsui, COO, i-CABLE Satellite Television/Pres., Sundream
Vincent T. Y. Lam, Exec. Dir., i-CABLE Network
Benjamin W. S. Tong, Exec. Dir.-Hong Kong Cable Television
Ronald Y. C. Chiu, Exec. Dir., i-CABLE News & i-CABLE Sports
Stephen Tin Hoi Ng, Chmn.
Simon K. K. Yu, VP-Procurement

Phone: 852-2112-6868	Fax: 852-2112-7878
Toll-Free:	
Address: Cable TV Tower, 9 Hoi Shing Rd., Tsuen Wan, Hong Kong, China	

GROWTH PLANS/SPECIAL FEATURES:

I-Cable Communications is the leading cable systems operator in Hong Kong, with more than 700,000 subscribers to its pay-TV services. The Hong Kong Cable Television, or CABLE TV, subsidiary produces the majority of the company's content and currently operates 97 separate cable channels and produces over 10,000 hours of programming per year. I-Cable also offers dial-up and high speed Broadband Internet services. The company owns and operates one of Hong Kong's two telecommunications networks, covering over 2 million households with its hybrid fiber coaxial cable network, built to be two-way interactive, allowing high speed transmission of data and voice as well as video. Subsidiary Hong Kong Cable Enterprises (HKCE), formerly Global Media In Force Limited, is CABLE TV's exclusive sales distributor of commercial airtime and international program licensing. HKCE also acts as advertising sales distributor for Cable Guide Monthly magazine and other media. HKCE provides value added services through its 21126888.com online promotion platform and its CABLE TV e-Programme Listing.

FINANCIALS: Sales and profits are in thousands of dollars—add 000 to get the full amount. 2007 Note: Financial information for 2007 was not available for all companies at press time.

2007 Sales: $	2007 Profits: $	**U.S. Stock Ticker: ICABY**
2006 Sales: $327,600	2006 Profits: $24,500	**Int'l Ticker: 1097** Int'l Exchange: Hong Kong-HKEX
2005 Sales: $314,799	2005 Profits: $67,988	Employees: 3,275
2004 Sales: $305,200	2004 Profits: $43,700	Fiscal Year Ends: 12/31
2003 Sales: $276,000	2003 Profits: $28,400	Parent Company:

SALARIES/BENEFITS:

Pension Plan:	ESOP Stock Plan:	Profit Sharing:	Top Exec. Salary: $	Bonus: $
Savings Plan:	Stock Purch. Plan:		Second Exec. Salary: $	Bonus: $

OTHER THOUGHTS:

Apparent Women Officers or Directors:
Hot Spot for Advancement for Women/Minorities:

LOCATIONS: ("Y" = Yes)

West:	Southwest:	Midwest:	Southeast:	Northeast:	International:
					Y

IGN ENTERTAINMENT   corp.ign.com

Industry Group Code: 514199 Ranks within this company's industry group: Sales: Profits:

Print Media/Publishing:	Movies:	Equipment/Supplies:		Broadcast/Cable:	Music/Audio:	Sports/Games/Gambling:	
Newspapers:	Movie Theaters:	Equipment/Supplies:		Broadcast TV:	Music Production:	Games/Sports:	Y
Magazines:	Movie Production:	Gambling Equipment:		Cable TV:	Retail Music:	Retail Games Stores:	Y
Books:	TV/Video Prod.:	Special Services:	Y	Satellite Broadcast:	Retail Audio Equip.:	Stadiums/Teams:	
Book Stores:	Video Rental:	Advertising Services:		Radio:	Music Print./Dist.:	Gambling/Casinos:	
Distribution/Printing:	Video Distribution:	Info. Sys. Software:		Online Information:	Multimedia:	Rides/Theme Parks:	

TYPES OF BUSINESS:

Online Video Game Information
Online Software Retail & Distribution
Video Game Development Services
Online Movie Reviews
Video Game Market Statistics
Lifestyle Web Site

BRANDS/DIVISIONS/AFFILIATES:

Fox Interactive Media
IGN.com
GameSpy.com
TeemXbox.com
Voodoo Extreme
FilePlanet.com
AskMen.com
RottenTomatoes.com

CONTACTS: *Note: Officers with more than one job title may be intentionally listed here more than once.*

Mark Jung, CEO
Michael Sheridan, CFO
Ken Keller, CTO
Ken Keller, Exec. VP-Eng.
David Phillips, General Counsel/VP-Corp. Strategy
Richard Jalichandra, VP-Bus. Dev.
Dale Strang, Exec. VP-Media & Publishing
Jamie Berger, VP-Consumer Products
Mark Stieglitz, VP-Publisher Services
Peer Schneider, VP-Publishing

Phone: 415-508-2000	Fax: 415-508-2001
Toll-Free:	
Address: 8000 Marina Boulevard, 4th Fl., Brisbane, CA 94005 US	

GROWTH PLANS/SPECIAL FEATURES:

IGN Entertainment, a division of Fox Interactive Media, is a highly-trafficked provider of web-based video game information, software and services. Hosting a diverse network with a large variety of content, the company's online property receives over 35 million unique visits per month. IGN.com and GameSpy.com feature general information and resources, with the former boasting one of the highest visitation rates on the Internet from the 18-24-year-old male demographic. Other IGN web sites have more specialized content: TeemXbox.com, providing information on the Microsoft Xbox; The Vault Network, which serves players of role-playing (RPG) and massively multiplayer online (MMO) games; Planet Network, which links over 1,500 video game fan sites; and Voodoo Extreme, a frequently updated video game news source. IGN also provides software through three digital distribution sites: FilePlanet.com, featuring demos and trials of upcoming games; 3Dgamers.com, which offers a variety of files relating to 3D games; and Direct2Drive.com, an online store where customers can download PC games onto their hard drives. Further video game services include: Powered by GameSpy, offering technological services to game developers; GameStats.com, a resource for video game popularity statistics and other information; and GamerMetrics, which analyzes the traffic and buying patterns of IGN's visitors. Non-video game sites include AskMen.com, one of the leading male lifestyle web sites; and RottenTomatoes.com, a movie review and information site. Collectively, the company's sites have 35 million unique visitors per month, including 250,000 active paying subscribers. Recently, IGN launched Club.IGN.com, a community hub featuring blogs, interactive lists, reader reviews and FAQ submissions. The pages are fully customizable by users.

FINANCIALS: Sales and profits are in thousands of dollars—add 000 to get the full amount. 2007 Note: Financial information for 2007 was not available for all companies at press time.

2007 Sales: $	2007 Profits: $	U.S. Stock Ticker: Subsidiary
2006 Sales: $	2006 Profits: $	Int'l Ticker: Int'l Exchange:
2005 Sales: $	2005 Profits: $	Employees: 313
2004 Sales: $42,900	2004 Profits: $-14,100	Fiscal Year Ends: 6/30
2003 Sales: $17,500	2003 Profits: $-3,100	Parent Company: NEWS CORP

SALARIES/BENEFITS:

Pension Plan:	ESOP Stock Plan:	Profit Sharing:	Top Exec. Salary: $	Bonus: $
Savings Plan:	Stock Purch. Plan:		Second Exec. Salary: $	Bonus: $

OTHER THOUGHTS:

Apparent Women Officers or Directors:
Hot Spot for Advancement for Women/Minorities:

LOCATIONS: ("Y" = Yes)

West:	Southwest:	Midwest:	Southeast:	Northeast:	International:
Y		Y		Y	Y

IMAX CORPORATION

www.imax.com

Industry Group Code: 512131 **Ranks within this company's industry group:** Sales: 4 Profits: 2

Print Media/Publishing:	Movies:		Equipment/Supplies:		Broadcast/Cable:	Music/Audio:	Sports/Games/Gambling:
Newspapers:	Movie Theaters:	Y	Equipment/Supplies:	Y	Broadcast TV:	Music Production:	Games/Sports:
Magazines:	Movie Production:	Y	Gambling Equipment:		Cable TV:	Retail Music:	Retail Games Stores:
Books:	TV/Video Prod.:		Special Services:	Y	Satellite Broadcast:	Retail Audio Equip.:	Stadiums/Teams:
Book Stores:	Video Rental:		Advertising Services:		Radio:	Music Print./Dist.:	Gambling/Casinos:
Distribution/Printing:	Video Distribution:		Info. Sys. Software:		Online Information:	Multimedia:	Rides/Theme Parks:

TYPES OF BUSINESS:

Movie Theaters-Giant Screen Format
Giant-Screen Film Production & Distribution
Feature Film Reformatting
Audio & Video Technology

BRANDS/DIVISIONS/AFFILIATES:

IMAX 3D
IMAX Dome
AMC Entertainment Inc

CONTACTS: Note: Officers with more than one job title may be intentionally listed here more than once.

Bradley J. Wechsler, Co-CEO/Co-Chmn.
Edward MacNeil, CFO
G. Mary Ruby, Sr. VP-Human Resources
Brian Bonnick, Exec. VP-Tech.
Larry O'Reilly, Sr. VP-Theater Dev.
G. Mary Ruby, Sr. VP-Admin. & Legal Affairs/Corp. Sec.
Robert D. Lister, Exec. VP-Bus. & Legal Affairs/General Counsel
Mark Welton, Exec. VP-Theatre Oper.
Robert D. Lister, Exec. VP-Corp. Comm.
Joseph Sparacio, Exec. VP-Finance
Greg Foster, Chmn./Pres., Filmed Entertainment
Vigna Vivekanand, Co-Controller
David B. Keighley, Exec. VP
Mark Welton, Exec. VP-Corp. & Digital Dev.
Richard L. Gelfond, Co-Chmn./Co-CEO

Phone: 905-403-6500	Fax: 905-403-6450
Toll-Free:	
Address: 2525 Speakman Dr., Mississauga, ON L5K 1B1 Canada	

GROWTH PLANS/SPECIAL FEATURES:

IMAX Corporation is a leading global entertainment technology company, specializing in digital and film-based motion picture technologies and large-format 2D and 3D film presentations. IMAX's principal business is the design, manufacture, sale and lease of its proprietary large-format theaters, including its 166 commercial theaters and 118 theaters located in museums and science centers, with operations in 40 countries. The company is also engaged in the production, digital re-mastering, post-production and distribution of large-format films. Imax theater systems combine advanced, high-resolution projectors with film handling equipment and automated theater control systems; sound system components; and screen components as large as eight stories high to create immersive audio-visual experiences. The standard IMAX theater has stadium seating and a screen that is pitched between 19 and 25 degrees to allow for the full range of peripheral vision. More than 100 theaters are equipped with IMAX 3D. IMAX Dome theaters feature seats that are reclined 30 degrees and a 180-degree screen projected on the domed ceiling. To increase the demand for its theater systems, the company has positioned its theater network as a new distribution platform for Hollywood blockbuster films. To this end, IMAX has developed a technology that allows conventional 35 millimeter movies to be digitally converted to its large format; has introduced lower cost theater systems designed for multiplex owners; is continuing to build strong relationships with Hollywood studios and commercial exhibition companies; and is developing a new digital projector which it believes will result in even more Hollywood features being released to its network. In addition, the company produces adventure, science and nature films specifically for IMAX theaters. In December 2007, IMAX announced a joint-venture agreement with AMC Entertainment for the development of 100 IMAX theaters in 33 AMC locations over the next three years.

FINANCIALS: Sales and profits are in thousands of dollars—add 000 to get the full amount. 2007 Note: Financial information for 2007 was not available for all companies at press time.

2007 Sales: $	2007 Profits: $	**U.S. Stock Ticker: IMAX**
2006 Sales: $20,730	2006 Profits: $-11,990	**Int'l Ticker: IMX** Int'l Exchange: Toronto-TSX
2005 Sales: $144,930	2005 Profits: $16,598	Employees: 376
2004 Sales: $135,980	2004 Profits: $10,244	Fiscal Year Ends: 12/31
2003 Sales: $119,260	2003 Profits: $ 231	Parent Company:

SALARIES/BENEFITS:

Pension Plan: Y	ESOP Stock Plan:	Profit Sharing:	Top Exec. Salary: $658,846	Bonus: $375,000
Savings Plan:	Stock Purch. Plan:		Second Exec. Salary: $500,000	Bonus: $150,000

OTHER THOUGHTS:

Apparent Women Officers or Directors: 1
Hot Spot for Advancement for Women/Minorities: Y

LOCATIONS: ("Y" = Yes)

West:	Southwest:	Midwest:	Southeast:	Northeast:	International:
Y	Y	Y	Y	Y	Y

Note: Financial information, benefits and other data can change quickly and may vary from those stated here.

IMG WORLDWIDE INC

www.imgworld.com

Industry Group Code: 711410 Ranks within this company's industry group: Sales: Profits:

Print Media/Publishing:	Movies:		Equipment/Supplies:		Broadcast/Cable:	Music/Audio:	Sports/Games/Gambling:	
Newspapers:	Movie Theaters:		Equipment/Supplies:		Broadcast TV:	Music Production:	Games/Sports:	Y
Magazines:	Movie Production:		Gambling Equipment:		Cable TV:	Retail Music:	Retail Games Stores:	
Books:	TV/Video Prod.:	Y	Special Services:	Y	Satellite Broadcast:	Retail Audio Equip.:	Stadiums/Teams:	
Book Stores:	Video Rental:		Advertising Services:	Y	Radio:	Music Print./Dist.:	Gambling/Casinos:	
Distribution/Printing:	Video Distribution:		Info. Sys. Software:		Online Information:	Multimedia:	Rides/Theme Parks:	

TYPES OF BUSINESS:

Agents-Athletes
Agents-Models
Agents-Writers, Artists & Musicians
Event Marketing
Corporate Marketing Consulting Services
Sports Television Programming
Sports Schools & Training

BRANDS/DIVISIONS/AFFILIATES:

IMG Coaches
IMG Models
IMG Artists
IMG Consulting
Darlow Smithson Productions
Tiger Aspect Productions
Forstmann Little & Co.
Tennis Week Magazine

CONTACTS: Note: Officers with more than one job title may be intentionally listed here more than once.

Theodore J. Forstmann, CEO
Chris Albrecht, Pres., IMG Global Media
Michel Masquelier, Exec. VP/Head-Acquisition & Sales Worldwide
George Pyne, Pres., IMG Sports & Entertainment
Theodore J. Forstmann, Chmn.
Ian Todd, Pres., IMG Int'l

Phone: 216-522-1200	Fax: 216-522-1145
Toll-Free:	
Address: 1360 E. 9th St., Ste. 100, Cleveland, OH 44114 US	

GROWTH PLANS/SPECIAL FEATURES:

IMG Worldwide, Inc. is one of largest sports and lifestyle marketing and management agencies in the world. The company represents some of the world's top athletes, broadcasters, models, classical musicians, authors and newsmakers through 70 offices in 30 countries. The firm's sports clients include golfers Tiger Woods and Annika Sorenstam; tennis player Venus Williams; baseball player Derek Jeter; basketball player Charles Barkley; professional racecar driver Jeff Gordon; football player Peyton Manning; and hockey player Jaromir Jagr. The company pulls about 25% of its revenue from the golf unit, including fees for representing top players and income from producing events. It also represents sportscaster John Madden and other top athletic coaches through IMG Coaches. Furthermore, IMG runs a group of sports academies providing training programs in tennis, golf, baseball, basketball and other sports. Through IMG Models, an international modeling agency, the company represents Gisele and Cindy Crawford; while IMG Artists represents classical musicians such as violinist Itzhak Perlman and operatic soprano Kiri Te Kanawa. IMG promotes, manages and represents hundreds of sporting events and classical music events worldwide, including events at Wimbledon and Nobel Prize functions. IMG's content production division, made up of TWI, Darlow Smithson Productions (DSP) and Tiger Aspect Productions (TAP), is one of the world's largest independent producers and distributors of televised sports programming, managing a library of over 150,000 hours. It annually produces and distributes 11,000 hours of original programming to over 220 countries covering 200 sports, as well as producing factual and entertainment programs. IMG is held by private-equity firm Forstmann Little & Co. Recent acquisitions include Tennis Week Magazine, tennisweek.com, CSI Sports, Nunet AG, BSI Speedway, Quintus, Collegiate Licensing Company and Partners International. In November 2007, IMG agreed to acquire Host Communications Inc., a national college sports marketing company.

FINANCIALS: Sales and profits are in thousands of dollars—add 000 to get the full amount. 2007 Note: Financial information for 2007 was not available for all companies at press time.

2007 Sales: $	2007 Profits: $	U.S. Stock Ticker: Private
2006 Sales: $	2006 Profits: $	Int'l Ticker: Int'l Exchange:
2005 Sales: $	2005 Profits: $	Employees: 2,300
2004 Sales: $	2004 Profits: $	Fiscal Year Ends: 12/31
2003 Sales: $1,200,000	2003 Profits: $	Parent Company: FORSTMANN LITTLE & CO

SALARIES/BENEFITS:

Pension Plan:	ESOP Stock Plan:	Profit Sharing:	Top Exec. Salary: $	Bonus: $
Savings Plan:	Stock Purch. Plan:		Second Exec. Salary: $	Bonus: $

OTHER THOUGHTS:

Apparent Women Officers or Directors:
Hot Spot for Advancement for Women/Minorities: Y

LOCATIONS: ("Y" = Yes)

West:	Southwest:	Midwest:	Southeast:	Northeast:	International:
Y		Y	Y	Y	Y

INGRAM ENTERTAINMENT HOLDINGS INC
www.ingramentertainment.com

Industry Group Code: 422921 Ranks within this company's industry group: Sales: 1 Profits:

Print Media/Publishing:		Movies:		Equipment/Supplies:		Broadcast/Cable:	Music/Audio:	Sports/Games/Gambling:
Newspapers:		Movie Theaters:		Equipment/Supplies:		Broadcast TV:	Music Production:	Games/Sports:
Magazines:	Y	Movie Production:		Gambling Equipment:		Cable TV:	Retail Music:	Retail Games Stores:
Books:		TV/Video Prod.:		Special Services:	Y	Satellite Broadcast:	Retail Audio Equip.:	Stadiums/Teams:
Book Stores:		Video Rental:		Advertising Services:	Y	Radio:	Music Print./Dist.:	Gambling/Casinos:
Distribution/Printing:		Video Distribution:	Y	Info. Sys. Software:		Online Information:	Multimedia:	Rides/Theme Parks:

TYPES OF BUSINESS:

Digital Publication Distribution
Entertainment Product Distribution
Internet Services
Business-to-Business Sales
Marketing Services
Magazine Publishing
Graphic Design

BRANDS/DIVISIONS/AFFILIATES:

AccessIngram.com
MyVideoStore.com
Monarch Home Video
Ingram Publications
Entertainment Preview
Ingram Creative Services

CONTACTS: Note: Officers with more than one job title may be intentionally listed here more than once.

David B. Ingram, Pres.
William D. Daniel, CFO/Exec. VP
Bob Geistman, Sr. VP-Mktg. & Sales
John J. Fletcher, General Counsel/Sec./VP
Robert W. Webb, Exec. VP-Oper.
David B. Ingram, Chmn.
Robert W. Webb, Exec. VP-Purchasing

Phone: 615-287-4000	Fax: 615-287-4982
Toll-Free:	
Address: 2 Ingram Blvd., La Vergne, TN 37089 US	

GROWTH PLANS/SPECIAL FEATURES:

Ingram Entertainment Holdings, Inc. (IEI) is a leading national distributor of home entertainment products including DVD and video hardware and software; video games; electronics and accessories; audiobooks. The company provides support services for Internet retailers, business-to-business sales through Accessingram.com and creation and maintenance of customer web sites under the myvideostore.com program. Services include sell-through promotion programs, poster pack advertising programs, monthly publications that promote new and recently released titles, audiobook rental packages, and payment plan options for buyers. Additionally, IEI owns and operates its own proprietary line of video titles under the Monarch Home Video label. Services provided by the company include marketing and merchandising programs, publishing and Internet retail and design services. Divisions of the company include Ingram Publications, which publishes Entertainment Preview, a weekly industry magazine that keeps clients abreast of major studio news; and Ingram Creative Services, which provides services that include print, illustration, editorial, PowerPoint presentations, photography, media buying, media placement and transparency creation. The firm offers its services to over 10,000 retail locations including video specialty stores, Internet retailers, video game stores and drugstores and supermarkets.

FINANCIALS: Sales and profits are in thousands of dollars—add 000 to get the full amount. 2007 Note: Financial information for 2007 was not available for all companies at press time.

2007 Sales: $	2007 Profits: $	U.S. Stock Ticker: Private
2006 Sales: $764,000	2006 Profits: $	Int'l Ticker: Int'l Exchange:
2005 Sales: $839,000	2005 Profits: $	Employees: 685
2004 Sales: $980,000	2004 Profits: $	Fiscal Year Ends: 12/31
2003 Sales: $1,030,000	2003 Profits: $	Parent Company:

SALARIES/BENEFITS:

Pension Plan:	ESOP Stock Plan:	Profit Sharing:	Top Exec. Salary: $	Bonus: $
Savings Plan: Y	Stock Purch. Plan:		Second Exec. Salary: $	Bonus: $

OTHER THOUGHTS:

Apparent Women Officers or Directors: 2
Hot Spot for Advancement for Women/Minorities:

LOCATIONS: ("Y" = Yes)

West:	Southwest:	Midwest:	Southeast:	Northeast:	International:
Y	Y	Y	Y	Y	

INSIGHT COMMUNICATIONS COMPANY INC　　www.insight-com.com

Industry Group Code: 513220　Ranks within this company's industry group: Sales: 14　Profits: 16

Print Media/Publishing:	Movies:	Equipment/Supplies:		Broadcast/Cable:		Music/Audio:	Sports/Games/Gambling:
Newspapers:	Movie Theaters:	Equipment/Supplies:		Broadcast TV:		Music Production:	Games/Sports:
Magazines:	Movie Production:	Gambling Equipment:		Cable TV:	Y	Retail Music:	Retail Games Stores:
Books:	TV/Video Prod.:	Special Services:	Y	Satellite Broadcast:		Retail Audio Equip.:	Stadiums/Teams:
Book Stores:	Video Rental:	Advertising Services:	Y	Radio:		Music Print./Dist.:	Gambling/Casinos:
Distribution/Printing:	Video Distribution:	Info. Sys. Software:		Online Information:		Multimedia:	Rides/Theme Parks:

TYPES OF BUSINESS:

Cable TV Service
Broadband Services Provider
High-Definition Television
Video-on-Demand
Digital Phone Plans
Cable Advertising
Business Services

BRANDS/DIVISIONS/AFFILIATES:

Carlyle Group (The)
InsightBroadband
InsightDigital
InsightPhone
Insight Business
Insight Media
Insight Midwest, LP

CONTACTS: Note: Officers with more than one job title may be intentionally listed here more than once.

Michael S. Willner, CEO
Dinesh C. Jain, COO
Dinesh C. Jain, Pres.
John Abbot, CFO/Exec. VP
Jim Morgan, Sr. VP-Human Resources
Charles E. Dietz, Sr. VP-R&D
Charles E. Dietz, CTO
Elliot Brecher, General Counsel/Sr. VP
Sandra D. Colony, Sr. VP-Corp. Comm.
Daniel Mannino, Controller/Sr. VP
John W. Hutton, Sr. VP-Oper. East Region
Scott Cooley, Sr. VP-Oper. West Region
Gregg Graff, Sr. VP-Field Operations
Doug Giesen, Sr. VP-Oper. South Region
Sidney R. Knafel, Chmn.

Phone: 917-286-2300	Fax: 917-286-2301
Toll-Free:	
Address: 810 7th Ave., New York, NY 10019 US	

GROWTH PLANS/SPECIAL FEATURES:

Insight Communications Company, Inc. is a leading provider of entertainment and communications services to 1.3 million customers in mid-sized communities in Indiana, Kentucky, Illinois and Ohio. Insight's lines of service include InsightDigital, a digital television provider; InsightBroadband; and InsightPhone, providing local digital telephony. Products include a variety of traditional television cable plans as well as pay-per-view movies and events and broadband Internet. In addition, Insight's broadband network also supports numerous advanced services such as high-definition television (HDTV), digital video recorders (DVR), video-on-demand (VOD), subscription video-on-demand (SVOD), digital cable programming and digital phone plans. The company's commercial services division, InsightBusiness, provides commercial customers with data, video and hosting plans and services. In addition, the company offers cable advertising and marketing assistance through Insight Media, its advertising sales division.

The company's Insight Midwest, LP subsidiary, half of which is owned by an indirect subsidiary of Comcast Cable Holdings, LLC, possesses and operates systems serving the majority of Insight's customers. Insight Midwest delivers local telephone service under the AT&T Digital Phone brand. The company is owned by The Carlyle Group. In April 2007, Insight agreed with Comcast Corp. to split up their shared midsize cable operator, Insight, with 1.3 million subscribers in the Midwest and about $6.2 billion in assets. With the joint venture liquidated, Comcast gained direct ownership over approximately $290 million worth in operating cash flow through new systems for 2007.

FINANCIALS: Sales and profits are in thousands of dollars—add 000 to get the full amount. 2007 Note: Financial information for 2007 was not available for all companies at press time.

2007 Sales: $	2007 Profits: $	U.S. Stock Ticker: Private
2006 Sales: $1,262,600	2006 Profits: $-36,600	Int'l Ticker:　Int'l Exchange:
2005 Sales: $1,117,681	2005 Profits: $-84,929	Employees: 4,035
2004 Sales: $1,002,456	2004 Profits: $-13,799	Fiscal Year Ends: 12/31
2003 Sales: $902,592	2003 Profits: $-24,544	Parent Company: CARLYLE GROUP (THE)

SALARIES/BENEFITS:

Pension Plan:	ESOP Stock Plan:	Profit Sharing:	Top Exec. Salary: $635,000	Bonus: $317,500
Savings Plan:	Stock Purch. Plan:		Second Exec. Salary: $500,000	Bonus: $250,000

OTHER THOUGHTS:

Apparent Women Officers or Directors: 3
Hot Spot for Advancement for Women/Minorities: Y

LOCATIONS: ("Y" = Yes)

West:	Southwest:	Midwest:	Southeast:	Northeast:	International:
	Y	Y		Y	

INTEGRITY MEDIA INC

www.integritymusic.com

Industry Group Code: 512230 Ranks within this company's industry group: Sales: Profits:

Print Media/Publishing:	Movies:		Equipment/Supplies:		Broadcast/Cable:	Music/Audio:		Sports/Games/Gambling:	
Newspapers:	Movie Theaters:		Equipment/Supplies:		Broadcast TV:	Music Production:	Y	Games/Sports:	
Magazines:	Movie Production:		Gambling Equipment:		Cable TV:	Retail Music:		Retail Games Stores:	
Books:	TV/Video Prod.:	Y	Special Services:		Satellite Broadcast:	Retail Audio Equip.:		Stadiums/Teams:	
Book Stores:	Video Rental:		Advertising Services:		Radio:	Music Print./Dist.:	Y	Gambling/Casinos:	
Distribution/Printing:	Video Distribution:	Y	Info. Sys. Software:		Online Information:	Multimedia:		Rides/Theme Parks:	

TYPES OF BUSINESS:

Christian Music Publishing
Mobile Phone Media
Music Production
Videos
Songbooks & Sheet Music
Music Club

BRANDS/DIVISIONS/AFFILIATES:

Integrity Music
INO Records
Hosanna! Music
Worship Leader
Mworship
Sony BMG Music Entertainment

CONTACTS: Note: Officers with more than one job title may be intentionally listed here more than once.

P. Michael (Mike) Coleman, CEO
Jerry W. Weimer, COO/Co-Pres.
P. Michael (Mike) Coleman, Pres.
Donald S. Ellington, Sr. VP-Admin.
Donald S. Ellington, Sr. VP-Finance

Phone: 251-633-9000	Fax: 251-776-5014
Toll-Free: 800-533-6912	
Address: 1000 Cody Rd., Mobile, AL 36695 US	

GROWTH PLANS/SPECIAL FEATURES:

Integrity Media, Inc. produces and publishes Christian music, books and related products developed to facilitate worship, entertainment and education.   The company currently operates through two subsidiaries: Integrity Music and INO Records.   Integrity Music's product formats include cassettes, compact discs, software, videos and songbooks. The division also produces songs recorded in indigenous languages, utilizing local artists and local songs to produce the recordings. Integrity produces products in a broad range of languages, including Russian, Spanish, Mandarin Chinese, French, German, Portuguese and Indonesian. Integrity Music also operates a music club, Hosanna! Music, which sends new recordings to members in the U.S., Europe and Australia six times a year. The company offers worship leaders new worship music, worship planning resources and networking on the Internet through its Worship Leader connection. Through INO Records the company produces Christian music ranging from praise and worship music, its largest category, to other styles of adult contemporary Christian music and children's music. Products are sold primarily online and directly to consumers throughout the U.S. and in over 160 other countries worldwide. The firm operates international offices in the U.K., Australia, Singapore, and has recently expanded to South Africa. Integrity plans to expand into various markets through importers, who will sell company-provided products, or through distributors licensed to produce Integrity products from a master recording. Most recently, Integrity launched MWorship, a mobile phone service offering text message devotions, ring tones, music news and other services, in partnership with Sony BMG Music.

FINANCIALS: Sales and profits are in thousands of dollars—add 000 to get the full amount. 2007 Note: Financial information for 2007 was not available for all companies at press time.

2007 Sales: $	2007 Profits: $	U.S. Stock Ticker: Private
2006 Sales: $	2006 Profits: $	Int'l Ticker: Int'l Exchange:
2005 Sales: $	2005 Profits: $	Employees: 218
2004 Sales: $	2004 Profits: $	Fiscal Year Ends: 12/31
2003 Sales: $74,264	2003 Profits: $1,882	Parent Company:

SALARIES/BENEFITS:

Pension Plan:	ESOP Stock Plan:	Profit Sharing:	Top Exec. Salary: $333,644	Bonus: $
Savings Plan:	Stock Purch. Plan:		Second Exec. Salary: $241,552	Bonus: $253,303

OTHER THOUGHTS:

Apparent Women Officers or Directors: 1
Hot Spot for Advancement for Women/Minorities:

LOCATIONS: ("Y" = Yes)

West:	Southwest:	Midwest:	Southeast:	Northeast:	International:
			Y		Y

INTERACTIVE DATA CORPORATION www.interactivedata.com

Industry Group Code: 514100 Ranks within this company's industry group: Sales: 3 Profits: 3

Print Media/Publishing:	Movies:	Equipment/Supplies:		Broadcast/Cable:	Music/Audio:	Sports/Games/Gambling:
Newspapers:	Movie Theaters:	Equipment/Supplies:		Broadcast TV:	Music Production:	Games/Sports:
Magazines:	Movie Production:	Gambling Equipment:	Y	Cable TV:	Retail Music:	Retail Games Stores:
Books:	TV/Video Prod.:	Special Services:	Y	Satellite Broadcast:	Retail Audio Equip.:	Stadiums/Teams:
Book Stores:	Video Rental:	Advertising Services:	Y	Radio:	Music Print./Dist.:	Gambling/Casinos:
Distribution/Printing:	Video Distribution:	Info. Sys. Software:		Online Information:	Multimedia:	Rides/Theme Parks:

TYPES OF BUSINESS:

Financial Information
Stock Market & Equities Information
Portfolio Management Software
Consulting & Valuation Services
Online Information Service

BRANDS/DIVISIONS/AFFILIATES:

Interactive Data Pricing and Reference Data
FT Interactive Data
Interactive Data Real-Time Services
ComStock
Interactive Data Fixed Income Analytics
CMS BondEdge
eSignal
Xcitek LLC

CONTACTS: *Note: Officers with more than one job title may be intentionally listed here more than once.*

Stuart J. Clark, CEO
John L. King, COO
Stuart J. Clark, Pres.
Andrew Hajducky, CFO/Exec. VP/Treas.
Raymond L. D'Arcy, Pres., Sales & Mktg.
Andrea H. Loew, General Counsel/Exec. VP
Chuck Thompson, Pres., eSignal
Roger Sargeant, Managing Dir.-Interactive Data Europe
John L. King, COO-FT Interactive Data
Mark Hepsworth, Pres., Interactive Data Pricing & Reference Data
Laurie Adami, Pres., Interactive Data Fixed Income Analytics
Rona Fairhead, Chmn.
James Farrer, Managing Dir.-Interactive Data Asia Pacific

Phone: 781-687-8800	Fax: 781-687-8005
Toll-Free:	
Address: 32 Crosby Dr., Bedford, MA 01730 US	

GROWTH PLANS/SPECIAL FEATURES:

Interactive Data Corporation provides financial market data, analytics and related services to financial institutions, active traders and individual investors. Interactive Data distributes real-time, end-of-day and historically archived data to customers through a variety of products featuring Internet, dedicated line, satellite and dialup delivery protocols. Through a range of strategic alliances, it also provides links to financial service and software companies offering trading, analysis, portfolio management and valuation services. Interactive Data has four businesses that comprise its two segments: Institutional Services and Active Trader Services. The company's Institutional Services segment primarily targets financial institutions such as banks, brokerage firms, mutual fund companies, hedge funds, insurance companies and money management firms through three subsidiaries, each of which was renamed in February 2007 as part of a global marketing initiative to emphasize the Interactive Data brand to institutional clients. Subsidiary Interactive Data Pricing and Reference Data (formerly FT Interactive Data) provides historical, intraday and end-of-day pricing, evaluations and reference data for a range of securities, commodities and derivative instruments. Subsidiary Interactive Data Real-Time Services (formerly ComStock) provides global real-time and delayed financial market information covering equities, derivative instruments, futures, fixed income securities and foreign exchange. Subsidiary Interactive Data Fixed Income Analytics (formerly CMS BondEdge) provides fixed income analytics. In addition, the Institutional Services segment markets it offerings to financial information providers, information media companies, third-party redistributors and outsourcing organizations. Interactive Data's Active Trader Services segment targets active traders, individual investors and investment community professionals and is comprised of eSignal, which provides real-time financial market information and access to decision-support tools to assist in the analysis of securities traded on all major markets in the U.S. and internationally. In May 2007, Interactive Data acquired the market data divisions of Xcitek LLC and its subsidiary Xcitax LLC, for $25.3 million.

FINANCIALS: Sales and profits are in thousands of dollars—add 000 to get the full amount. 2007 Note: Financial information for 2007 was not available for all companies at press time.

2007 Sales: $	2007 Profits: $	U.S. Stock Ticker: IDC
2006 Sales: $612,403	2006 Profits: $93,362	Int'l Ticker: Int'l Exchange:
2005 Sales: $542,867	2005 Profits: $93,864	Employees: 2,200
2004 Sales: $484,565	2004 Profits: $80,271	Fiscal Year Ends: 12/31
2003 Sales: $442,690	2003 Profits: $72,200	Parent Company:

SALARIES/BENEFITS:

Pension Plan: Y	ESOP Stock Plan:	Profit Sharing:	Top Exec. Salary: $540,000	Bonus: $476,385
Savings Plan: Y	Stock Purch. Plan:		Second Exec. Salary: $367,000	Bonus: $263,107

OTHER THOUGHTS:

Apparent Women Officers or Directors: 4
Hot Spot for Advancement for Women/Minorities: Y

LOCATIONS: ("Y" = Yes)

West:	Southwest:	Midwest:	Southeast:	Northeast:	International:
Y		Y		Y	Y

INTERNATIONAL CREATIVE MANAGEMENT (ICM)
www.icmtalent.com

Industry Group Code: 711410 **Ranks within this company's industry group:** Sales: Profits:

Print Media/Publishing:	Movies:	Equipment/Supplies:		Broadcast/Cable:	Music/Audio:	Sports/Games/Gambling:
Newspapers:	Movie Theaters:	Equipment/Supplies:		Broadcast TV:	Music Production:	Games/Sports:
Magazines:	Movie Production:	Gambling Equipment:		Cable TV:	Retail Music:	Retail Games Stores:
Books:	TV/Video Prod.:	Special Services:	Y	Satellite Broadcast:	Retail Audio Equip.:	Stadiums/Teams:
Book Stores:	Video Rental:	Advertising Services:	Y	Radio:	Music Print./Dist.:	Gambling/Casinos:
Distribution/Printing:	Video Distribution:	Info. Sys. Software:		Online Information:	Multimedia:	Rides/Theme Parks:

TYPES OF BUSINESS:
Agents-Actors & Directors
Agents-Writers & Musicians
Agents-Literary
Agents-Lecture

BRANDS/DIVISIONS/AFFILIATES:
ICM Artists
ICM Foreign Rights
Life Rights
Broder Webb Chervin Silbermann Agency

CONTACTS: *Note: Officers with more than one job title may be intentionally listed here more than once.*
Jeffrey Berg, CEO
Chris Silbermann, Pres.
Richard B. Levy, General Counsel
Richard B. Levy, Chief Bus. Dev. Officer
Esther Newberg, Sr. VP
Jeffrey Berg, Chmn.

Phone: 310-550-4000	Fax: 310-550-4100
Toll-Free:	
Address: 10250 Constellation Blvd., Los Angeles, CA 90067 US	

GROWTH PLANS/SPECIAL FEATURES:
International Creative Management, Inc. (ICM) is one of the world's largest talent and literary agencies, with offices in Los Angeles, New York and London. The company represents actors, directors, musicians and writers, as well as creative talent in theater, commercials, public speaking and new media. ICM's clients include actors Woody Allen, Christopher Walken, Charlton Heston, Ellen Degeneres, William Shatner, Chris Rock and Orlando Bloom; musicians Courtney Love, Beyonce Knowles and Nadia Turner; authors Tom Bodett and Violet Blue; and directors Roman Polanski, Danny Boyle, Doug Atchinson and Robert Rodriguez. The company's music and performance subsidary, ICM Artists, represents classical instrumentalists, vocalists and conductors, chamber ensembles, choirs and dance and opera companies, as well as other performing groups. ICM's Foreign Rights department, based in London, sells ICM book and magazine products in the U.K. and other foreign countries and the Life Rights division secures the rights to newspaper and magazine articles as well as personal life stories of people who might serve as the basis for a television production. In mid 2006, ICM acquired the Broder Webb Chervin Silbermann Agency, an agency focused on TV talent.

FINANCIALS: Sales and profits are in thousands of dollars—add 000 to get the full amount. 2007 Note: Financial information for 2007 was not available for all companies at press time.

2007 Sales: $	2007 Profits: $	**U.S. Stock Ticker:** Private
2006 Sales: $	2006 Profits: $	**Int'l Ticker:** Int'l Exchange:
2005 Sales: $140,000	2005 Profits: $	Employees: 393
2004 Sales: $100,000	2004 Profits: $	Fiscal Year Ends: 6/30
2003 Sales: $	2003 Profits: $	Parent Company:

SALARIES/BENEFITS:

Pension Plan:	ESOP Stock Plan:	Profit Sharing:	Top Exec. Salary: $	Bonus: $
Savings Plan:	Stock Purch. Plan:		Second Exec. Salary: $	Bonus: $

OTHER THOUGHTS:
Apparent Women Officers or Directors:
Hot Spot for Advancement for Women/Minorities:

LOCATIONS: ("Y" = Yes)

West:	Southwest:	Midwest:	Southeast:	Northeast:	International:
Y				Y	Y

INTERNATIONAL DATA GROUP INC

www.idg.com

Industry Group Code: 511120 Ranks within this company's industry group: Sales: 2 Profits:

Print Media/Publishing:	Movies:	Equipment/Supplies:	Broadcast/Cable:	Music/Audio:	Sports/Games/Gambling:
Newspapers:	Movie Theaters:	Equipment/Supplies:	Broadcast TV:	Music Production:	Games/Sports:
Magazines: Y	Movie Production:	Gambling Equipment:	Cable TV:	Retail Music:	Retail Games Stores:
Books:	TV/Video Prod.:	Special Services:	Satellite Broadcast:	Retail Audio Equip.:	Stadiums/Teams:
Book Stores:	Video Rental:	Advertising Services:	Radio:	Music Print./Dist.:	Gambling/Casinos:
Distribution/Printing:	Video Distribution:	Info. Sys. Software:	Online Information:	Multimedia:	Rides/Theme Parks:

TYPES OF BUSINESS:

Publishing-Magazines
Conferences & Events
IT Consulting
Recruitment Services
Web Sites
Market Research & Analysis

BRANDS/DIVISIONS/AFFILIATES:

IDG Ventures
PC World
Macworld
Computerworld
Network World
ITCareers.com
BioITWorld Conference
CXO Media, Inc.

CONTACTS: *Note: Officers with more than one job title may be intentionally listed here more than once.*

Pat Kenealy, CEO
Ted Bloom, CFO
Howard Sholkin, Dir.-Mktg. Programs
Howard Sholkin, Dir.-Corp. Comm.
Bob Carrigan, Pres., IDG Comm.
Patrick J. McGovern, Chmn.

Phone: 617-534-1200	Fax: 617-423-0240
Toll-Free:	
Address: 1 Exeter Plaza, Fl. 15, Boston, MA 02116 US	

GROWTH PLANS/SPECIAL FEATURES:

International Data Group, Inc. (IDG) is the largest publisher of computer magazines and newspapers in the world, with over 300 publications in 85 countries and a readership of more than 140 million people per month.   Its English-language titles for IT executives, IT professionals, technology and media consumers, business managers, network professionals and channel providers include PC World, Cable in the Classroom, Computerworld, InfoWorld, CIO, GamePro, and Macworld.   The company is a leading provider of IT conferences and webcasts.   The firm's IDC research division is a provider of technology intelligence, market data, industry analysis and strategic guidance to the IT industry with over 775 research analysts worldwide in 50 countries.   This division provides subscription services, custom consulting, events and reports.   Additionally, IDG operates a network of over 400 web sites featuring technology content.   The company provides IT recruitment services and produces more than 170 globally branded conferences and events in over 40 countries, including the LinuxWorld Conference & Expo, Macworld Conference & Expo, and BioITWorld Conference.   The company produces 13 annual conferences and events in China. IDG's subsidiary, IDG Ventures, is a global network of venture capital funds with approximately $1.4 billion under management and a portfolio of over 220 companies.   Each IDG Ventures fund seeks to help companies understand their markets better and penetrate them faster than their competition through a large combination of global publishing, market research, conferences and exhibition resources.

ICG provides employees benefits including: Flexible spending accounts; maternity and adoption leave; internal training and development; tuition reimbursement; on-site fitness facilities; flexible scheduling; healthy living programs; laundry services; and arts, entertainment and sporting event tickets.   For the last four consecutive years, IDG has been named one of Fortune's 100 Best Companies to Work For. In addition, the firm sponsors the McGovern Institute for Brain Research at MIT.

FINANCIALS: Sales and profits are in thousands of dollars—add 000 to get the full amount. 2007 Note: Financial information for 2007 was not available for all companies at press time.

2007 Sales: $	2007 Profits: $	**U.S. Stock Ticker:** Private
2006 Sales: $3,020,000	2006 Profits: $	**Int'l Ticker:** Int'l Exchange:
2005 Sales: $	2005 Profits: $	Employees: 13,640
2004 Sales: $2,500,000	2004 Profits: $	Fiscal Year Ends: 9/30
2003 Sales: $2,410,000	2003 Profits: $	Parent Company:

SALARIES/BENEFITS:

Pension Plan:	ESOP Stock Plan: Y	Profit Sharing:	Top Exec. Salary: $	Bonus: $
Savings Plan: Y	Stock Purch. Plan:		Second Exec. Salary: $	Bonus: $

OTHER THOUGHTS:

Apparent Women Officers or Directors: 1
Hot Spot for Advancement for Women/Minorities:

LOCATIONS: ("Y" = Yes)

West:	Southwest:	Midwest:	Southeast:	Northeast:	International:
Y			Y	Y	Y

INTERNATIONAL GAME TECHNOLOGY   www.igt.com

Industry Group Code: 713290   Ranks within this company's industry group: Sales: 1   Profits: 1

Print Media/Publishing:	Movies:	Equipment/Supplies:		Broadcast/Cable:	Music/Audio:	Sports/Games/Gambling:
Newspapers:	Movie Theaters:	Equipment/Supplies:		Broadcast TV:	Music Production:	Games/Sports:
Magazines:	Movie Production:	Gambling Equipment:	Y	Cable TV:	Retail Music:	Retail Games Stores:
Books:	TV/Video Prod.:	Special Services:	Y	Satellite Broadcast:	Retail Audio Equip.:	Stadiums/Teams:
Book Stores:	Video Rental:	Advertising Services:		Radio:	Music Print./Dist.:	Gambling/Casinos:
Distribution/Printing:	Video Distribution:	Info. Sys. Software:		Online Information:	Multimedia:	Rides/Theme Parks:

TYPES OF BUSINESS:

Gambling Equipment
Computerized Gambling Devices
Gaming Technology & Services
Gambling Software
Consulting

BRANDS/DIVISIONS/AFFILIATES:

IGT Gaming Systems
EZ-Pay
ITG Online Entertainment
Megajackpots
IGT Canada, Inc.
WagerWorks, Inc.
China LotSynergy Holdings Limited
Digideal Corporation

CONTACTS: Note: Officers with more than one job title may be intentionally listed here more than once.

Thomas J. Matthews, CEO
Thomas J. Matthews, COO
Thomas J. Matthews, Pres.
David D. Johnson, General Counsel/Exec. VP/Corp. Sec.
Anthony Ciorciari, Exec. VP-Oper.
Richard Pennington, Exec. VP-Corp. Strategy
Pat Cavanaugh, VP-Investor Rel.
Daniel R. Siciliano, Chief Acct. Officer/Treas.
Stephen W. Morro, COO
Thomas J. Matthews, Chmn.

Phone: 775-448-7777	Fax: 775-448-0777
Toll-Free: 866-296-4232	
Address: 9295 Prototype Dr., Reno, NV 89521 US	

GROWTH PLANS/SPECIAL FEATURES:

International Game Technology (IGT) is a world leader in the development and manufacture of computerized casino gaming products. Primarily serving the casino gaming industry, the company sells its products in legalized gaming markets in the U.S., U.K., Australia, Europe, Japan, Latin America, New Zealand and South Africa. Products include traditional spinning-reel slot machines, video gaming machines, government-sponsored terminals and other gaming devices. In addition to the machines themselves, the company offers casino management software, including IGT Gaming Systems, which keep track of machine use, and the EZ-Pay system, which allows patrons to use cards with the machines instead of coins. The company operates in two business segments: the gaming division and the international division. The gaming division consists of the company's North American operations and includes North American sales, the firm's proprietary games such as Megajackpots, IGT casino management systems and solutions, and the company's North American manufacturers and distributors. This segment comprised 77% of consolidated revenues in fiscal 2007. The international division manages the sales, servicing and distribution centers as well as the manufacturing plants overseas. This segment comprised 23% of consolidated revenues in fiscal 2007. Recent news includes a $103 million investment in China LotSynergy Holdings Limited, enabling the company to gain access to the Chinese lottery market. IGT also acquired Digideal Corporation, a gaming technology company based in Washington.

IGT offers its employees comprehensive benefits including a prescription drug plan, adoption assistance, an employee assistance program, an onsite daycare facility, tuition reimbursement, fitness centers and employee discounts.

FINANCIALS: Sales and profits are in thousands of dollars—add 000 to get the full amount. 2007 Note: Financial information for 2007 was not available for all companies at press time.

2007 Sales: $2,621,400	2007 Profits: $508,200	**U.S. Stock Ticker: IGT**
2006 Sales: $2,511,700	2006 Profits: $473,600	**Int'l Ticker:** Int'l Exchange:
2005 Sales: $2,379,400	2005 Profits: $436,500	Employees: 5,400
2004 Sales: $2,484,800	2004 Profits: $488,700	Fiscal Year Ends: 9/30
2003 Sales: $2,128,100	2003 Profits: $390,700	Parent Company:

SALARIES/BENEFITS:

Pension Plan:	ESOP Stock Plan:	Profit Sharing: Y	Top Exec. Salary: $735,962	Bonus: $4,886,188
Savings Plan: Y	Stock Purch. Plan: Y		Second Exec. Salary: $478,654	Bonus: $805,579

OTHER THOUGHTS:

Apparent Women Officers or Directors: 4
Hot Spot for Advancement for Women/Minorities: Y

LOCATIONS: ("Y" = Yes)

West:	Southwest:	Midwest:	Southeast:	Northeast:	International:
Y		Y			Y

Note: Financial information, benefits and other data can change quickly and may vary from those stated here.

INTERNATIONAL LOTTERY & TOTALIZATOR SYSTEMS
www.ilts.com

Industry Group Code: 713290 Ranks within this company's industry group: Sales: 13   Profits: 10

Print Media/Publishing:	Movies:	Equipment/Supplies:		Broadcast/Cable:	Music/Audio:	Sports/Games/Gambling:
Newspapers:	Movie Theaters:	Equipment/Supplies:	Y	Broadcast TV:	Music Production:	Games/Sports:
Magazines:	Movie Production:	Gambling Equipment:	Y	Cable TV:	Retail Music:	Retail Games Stores:
Books:	TV/Video Prod.:	Special Services:	Y	Satellite Broadcast:	Retail Audio Equip.:	Stadiums/Teams:
Book Stores:	Video Rental:	Advertising Services:		Radio:	Music Print./Dist.:	Gambling/Casinos:
Distribution/Printing:	Video Distribution:	Info. Sys. Software:		Online Information:	Multimedia:	Rides/Theme Parks:

TYPES OF BUSINESS:

Software-Lottery & Racetrack Wagering
Computerized Wagering Hardware
Facilities Management Services
Ballot Counting Systems

BRANDS/DIVISIONS/AFFILIATES:

Unisyn Voting Solutions
ILTS InterTote System
Intelimark
DATAMARK
DataTrak
InkaVote
Berjaya Lottery Management (H.K.) Ltd.

CONTACTS: *Note: Officers with more than one job title may be intentionally listed here more than once.*

Jeffrey M. Johnson, CEO
Jeffrey M. Johnson, Pres.
T. Linh Nguyen, CFO
T. Linh Nguyen, Corp. Sec.
Theodore A. Johnson, Chmn.

Phone: 760-598-1655	**Fax:** 760-598-0219
Toll-Free:	
Address: 2310 Cousteau Ct., Vista, CA 92081 US	

GROWTH PLANS/SPECIAL FEATURES:

International Lottery & Totalizator Systems (ILTS) designs and services computerized wagering systems and terminals for racing organizations and lotteries worldwide. ILTS provides facilities management services to organizations authorized to conduct online lotteries. The company's wagering systems include three components: the hardware and operating systems that make up a central computer (a product known as the ILTS InterTote System); the DATAMARK and Intelimark families of point-of-sale terminals; and the communication network that links all terminals to the central computer. DATAMARK technology is capable of issuing tickets both for standard betting and pool wagers used in pari-mutuel wagering. The terminals facilitate multiple bets on one ticket and multiple selections for each bet. Utilizing its DataTrak technology, the company sets up the network needed to connect the terminals. The firm's technology can also be used in other transaction processing systems, such as automated tollbooth systems for turnpikes and electronic voting. ILTS supplies government-sponsored lotteries in 11 countries and services more than 200 racetracks worldwide. Notable clients include Global Technologies, Ltd., Philippine Gaming Management and M.I. Montreal Informatica. Berjaya Lottery Management (H.K.) Ltd. owns 71.3% of the outstanding voting stock of ILTS.

FINANCIALS: Sales and profits are in thousands of dollars—add 000 to get the full amount. 2007 Note: Financial information for 2007 was not available for all companies at press time.

2007 Sales: $11,046	2007 Profits: $ 499	**U.S. Stock Ticker: ITSI**
2006 Sales: $3,445	2006 Profits: $-2,344	**Int'l Ticker:** Int'l Exchange:
2005 Sales: $9,666	2005 Profits: $-1,762	Employees: 35
2004 Sales: $10,777	2004 Profits: $-1,786	Fiscal Year Ends: 4/30
2003 Sales: $22,800	2003 Profits: $ 800	Parent Company:

SALARIES/BENEFITS:

Pension Plan:	ESOP Stock Plan:	Profit Sharing:	Top Exec. Salary: $183,390	Bonus: $
Savings Plan: Y	Stock Purch. Plan:		Second Exec. Salary: $110,000	Bonus: $

OTHER THOUGHTS:

Apparent Women Officers or Directors:
Hot Spot for Advancement for Women/Minorities:

LOCATIONS: ("Y" = Yes)

West:	Southwest:	Midwest:	Southeast:	Northeast:	International:
Y					Y

INTERPUBLIC GROUP OF COMPANIES INC
www.interpublic.com

Industry Group Code: 541810 Ranks within this company's industry group: Sales: 3 Profits: 3

Print Media/Publishing:	Movies:	Equipment/Supplies:		Broadcast/Cable:	Music/Audio:	Sports/Games/Gambling:
Newspapers:	Movie Theaters:	Equipment/Supplies:		Broadcast TV:	Music Production:	Games/Sports:
Magazines:	Movie Production:	Gambling Equipment:		Cable TV:	Retail Music:	Retail Games Stores:
Books:	TV/Video Prod.:	Special Services:		Satellite Broadcast:	Retail Audio Equip.:	Stadiums/Teams:
Book Stores:	Video Rental:	Advertising Services:	Y	Radio:	Music Print./Dist.:	Gambling/Casinos:
Distribution/Printing:	Video Distribution:	Info. Sys. Software:		Online Information:	Multimedia:	Rides/Theme Parks:

TYPES OF BUSINESS:

Advertising Services
Marketing & Branding
Market Research
Public Relations
Online Marketing
Direct Marketing
Promotions & Events
Sports & Entertainment Marketing

BRANDS/DIVISIONS/AFFILIATES:

Draftfcb
Lowe Worldwide
McCann Worldgroup
McCann Erickson Advertising
MRM Worldwide
Momentum Worldwide
McCann Healthcare Worldwide
FutureBrand

CONTACTS: Note: Officers with more than one job title may be intentionally listed here more than once.

Michael I. Roth, CEO
Frank Mergenthaler, CFO/Exec. VP
Bant Breen, Pres., Interpublic Futures Mktg. Group
Timothy A. Sompolski, Chief Human Resources Officer/Exec. VP
Joseph W. Farrelly, CIO/Sr. VP
Nicholas J. Camera, General Counsel/Sr. VP/Corp. Sec.
Stephen Gatfield, Exec. VP-Strategy & Network Oper.
Bant Breen, Sr. VP/Dir.-Strategic Dev. & Innovation
Philippe Krakowsky, Exec. VP-Strategy & Corp. Rel.
Jerome J. Leshne, Sr. VP-Investor Rel.
Christopher Carroll, Chief Acct. Officer/Sr. VP/Controller
Thomas A. Dowling, Chief Risk Officer/Sr. VP
Jonathan B. Burleigh, Sr. VP-Finance & Dev.
Heide Gardner, Sr. VP/Chief Diversity Officer
Michael I. Roth, Chmn.
Terry Peigh, Sr. VP-Procurement, Real Estate & Travel

Phone: 212-704-1200	Fax: 212-704-1201
Toll-Free:	
Address: 1114 Ave. of the Americas, New York, NY 10036 US	

GROWTH PLANS/SPECIAL FEATURES:

The Interpublic Group of Companies, Inc. (IPG), founded in 1930, is a group comprising hundreds of advertising and specialized marketing and communications services companies that together represent one of the largest resources of advertising and marketing expertise in the world, with offices and affiliations in over 100 countries. Globally, IPG offers three distinct options for clients seeking large-scale, integrated capabilities across all its disciplines: Draftfcb, Lowe Worldwide and McCann Worldgroup. Launched in 2006, Draftfcb provides consumer advertising and behavioral, data-driven direct marketing. Lowe Worldwide is focused on delivering and sustaining high-value ideas in such markets as the U.K., the U.S., India, Sweden and Latin America. McCann Worldgroup provides best-in-class communications tools and resources in all regions of the world, through its operating units McCann Erickson Advertising, with operations in over 100 countries; MRM Worldwide, providing relationship marketing and digital expertise; Momentum Worldwide, providing experiential marketing; and McCann Healthcare Worldwide, providing healthcare communications. IPG's domestic agency brands include Campbell-Ewald, Campbell Mithun, Deutsch, Hill Holliday, The Martin Agency and Mullen. The company also has two leading media specialists, Initiative and Universal McCann, both of which operate independently but were aligned with Draftfcb and McCann Erickson in late 2006. Other subsidiaries of IPG include FutureBrand, Jack Morton, Octagon, Regan Campbell Ward and WeberShandwick. In 2006, the company formed the Futures Marketing Group, which houses existing high-growth media offerings such as the Interpublic Emerging Media Lab. IPG's largest clients include General Motors Corporation, Johnson & Johnson, Microsoft, Unilever and Verizon. In April 2007, IPG acquired Reprise Media, Inc., a leading provider of search engine marketing solutions. In July 2007, the company launched a joint venture mobile marketing company, Ansible, with Velti, a leading mobile technology provider. In October 2007, IPG acquired Translation Consulting + Brand Imaging, a leading branded entertainment agency.

FINANCIALS: Sales and profits are in thousands of dollars—add 000 to get the full amount. 2007 Note: Financial information for 2007 was not available for all companies at press time.

2007 Sales: $	2007 Profits: $	U.S. Stock Ticker: IPG
2006 Sales: $6,190,800	2006 Profits: $-31,700	Int'l Ticker: Int'l Exchange:
2005 Sales: $6,274,300	2005 Profits: $-262,900	Employees: 43,700
2004 Sales: $6,387,000	2004 Profits: $-538,400	Fiscal Year Ends: 12/31
2003 Sales: $6,161,700	2003 Profits: $-539,100	Parent Company:

SALARIES/BENEFITS:

Pension Plan:	ESOP Stock Plan:	Profit Sharing:	Top Exec. Salary: $1,250,000	Bonus: $1,500,000
Savings Plan:	Stock Purch. Plan:		Second Exec. Salary: $1,100,000	Bonus: $2,062,500

OTHER THOUGHTS:

Apparent Women Officers or Directors: 4
Hot Spot for Advancement for Women/Minorities: Y

LOCATIONS: ("Y" = Yes)

West:	Southwest:	Midwest:	Southeast:	Northeast:	International:
Y	Y	Y	Y	Y	Y

Note: Financial information, benefits and other data can change quickly and may vary from those stated here.

INTERTAN CANADA LTD

www.intertan.com

Industry Group Code: 443110 Ranks within this company's industry group: Sales: Profits:

Print Media/Publishing:	Movies:	Equipment/Supplies:		Broadcast/Cable:	Music/Audio:	Sports/Games/Gambling:
Newspapers:	Movie Theaters:	Equipment/Supplies:	Y	Broadcast TV:	Music Production:	Games/Sports:
Magazines:	Movie Production:	Gambling Equipment:	Y	Cable TV:	Retail Music:	Retail Games Stores:
Books:	TV/Video Prod.:	Special Services:		Satellite Broadcast:	Retail Audio Equip.:	Stadiums/Teams:
Book Stores:	Video Rental:	Advertising Services:		Radio:	Music Print./Dist.:	Gambling/Casinos:
Distribution/Printing:	Video Distribution:	Info. Sys. Software:		Online Information:	Multimedia:	Rides/Theme Parks:

TYPES OF BUSINESS:

Electronics Stores
Online Sales
Repair Services

BRANDS/DIVISIONS/AFFILIATES:

Circuit City Stores, Inc.
Source by Circuit City (The)
Thesourcecc.com
Battery Plus

CONTACTS: *Note: Officers with more than one job title may be intentionally listed here more than once.*

Steven Pappas, CEO
Lyndsay Walter, Sr. VP-Mktg.
Nick Bobrow, Sr. VP-Finance

Phone: 705-728-1617	Fax: 705-728-7844
Toll-Free:	
Address: 279 Bayview Dr., Barrie, ON L4M 4W5 Canada	

GROWTH PLANS/SPECIAL FEATURES:

InterTAN Canada Ltd., the wholly-owned subsidiary and Canadian arm of Circuit City Stores, Inc., sells consumer electronics products and services through company-operated retail stores and dealer outlets throughout Canada. InterTAN was originally founded as a holding company for the international retail operations of the Tandy Corporation, which is now known as RadioShack; later, InterTAN was spun off. The company's U.K. and Australian businesses were sold, leaving only the Canadian operations, which were subsequently acquired by Circuit City. The firm operates approximately 509 company-owned stores, 296 dealer-operated retail stores and one Battery Plus store. During 2006, it rebranded most of its company stores under the brand name The Source by Circuit City, with its old names consisting of Rogers Wireless, THS Studio and Logitech Electronics. In January 2007, Rogers Wireless terminated its agreement that allowed InterTAN to operate 92 Rogers Plus stores, thereby returning the stores back to Rogers Wireless' control. The company's stores are typically located in malls and shopping centers in order to conveniently provide products and services that meet a wide range of consumer electronic needs. The Source by Circuit City sells a range of electronic equipment such as cameras, computers, cell phones, audio/visual equipment and accessories, and it operates Thesourcecc.com, an e-commerce site. In addition to its merchandise, InterTAN provides after-sale services for all the products it sells during warranty periods and beyond. The company also offers out-of-warranty repair services. In February 2007, Circuit City began exploring strategic alternatives for InterTAN, including possibly selling the firm.

FINANCIALS: Sales and profits are in thousands of dollars—add 000 to get the full amount. 2007 Note: Financial information for 2007 was not available for all companies at press time.

2007 Sales: $	2007 Profits: $	**U.S. Stock Ticker: Subsidiary**
2006 Sales: $	2006 Profits: $	**Int'l Ticker:** Int'l Exchange:
2005 Sales: $454,900	2005 Profits: $	Employees: 3,521
2004 Sales: $	2004 Profits: $	Fiscal Year Ends: 2/28
2003 Sales: $403,000	2003 Profits: $7,700	Parent Company: CIRCUIT CITY STORES INC

SALARIES/BENEFITS:

Pension Plan:	ESOP Stock Plan:	Profit Sharing:	Top Exec. Salary: $500,000	Bonus: $34,723
Savings Plan:	Stock Purch. Plan:		Second Exec. Salary: $141,085	Bonus: $86,556

OTHER THOUGHTS:

	LOCATIONS: ("Y" = Yes)					
	West:	Southwest:	Midwest:	Southeast:	Northeast:	International:
Apparent Women Officers or Directors:						Y
Hot Spot for Advancement for Women/Minorities:						

ION MEDIA NETWORKS

www.paxson.com

Industry Group Code: 513120 **Ranks within this company's industry group:** Sales: 16   Profits: 18

Print Media/Publishing:	Movies:		Equipment/Supplies:	Broadcast/Cable:		Music/Audio:	Sports/Games/Gambling:
Newspapers:	Movie Theaters:		Equipment/Supplies:	Broadcast TV:	Y	Music Production:	Games/Sports:
Magazines:	Movie Production:		Gambling Equipment:	Cable TV:		Retail Music:	Retail Games Stores:
Books:	TV/Video Prod.:	Y	Special Services:	Satellite Broadcast:		Retail Audio Equip.:	Stadiums/Teams:
Book Stores:	Video Rental:		Advertising Services:	Radio:		Music Print./Dist.:	Gambling/Casinos:
Distribution/Printing:	Video Distribution:		Info. Sys. Software:	Online Information:		Multimedia:	Rides/Theme Parks:

TYPES OF BUSINESS:

Television Broadcasting
Television Production

BRANDS/DIVISIONS/AFFILIATES:

America 51, LP
i-TV
Hope Island
Chicken Soup for the Soul
Twice in a Lifetime
i: Independent Television
i-Health
Qubo

CONTACTS: Note: Officers with more than one job title may be intentionally listed here more than once.

R. Brandon Burgess, CEO
R. Brandon Burgess, Pres.
Richard Garcia, CFO/Sr. VP
Stephen P. Appel, Pres., Sales & Mktg.
David A. Glenn, Pres., Eng.
Adam K. Weinstein, Chief Legal Officer/Sr. VP/Sec.
W. Lawrence Patrick, Chmn.

Phone: 561-659-4122	Fax: 561-659-4252
Toll-Free:	
Address: 601 Clearwater Park Rd., West Palm Beach, FL 33401 US	

GROWTH PLANS/SPECIAL FEATURES:

ION Media Networks, (formerly Paxson Communications Corp.) owns one of the largest broadcast television groups in the U.S. with over 60 stations. The company's flagship station i-TV promotes works by independent programmers and producers and features wholesome, traditional value-based entertainment. ION broadcasts its i-TV network to about 92 million homes, reaching 83% of U.S. primetime television sets in 39 of the top 50 U.S. markets. The company's revenue comes from selling network long form paid programming (i.e. infomercials, which generate 48.6% of revenue), network spot advertising (18.8% of revenue), and station advertising (32.6% of revenue). The firm's business strategy focuses on providing quality family-oriented programming free of excessive violence, explicit sexual themes and vulgarity. The company reaches approximately 21% of U.S. prime time television households through cable and satellite distribution. In February 2007, ION launched Open Mobile Ventures Corporation, a business unit focused on the research and development of portable, mobile and out-of-home transmission technology using over-the-air digital television spectrum. Additionally, the firm recently acquired the rights to broadcast CBS's news program 48 Hours.

FINANCIALS: Sales and profits are in thousands of dollars—add 000 to get the full amount. 2007 Note: Financial information for 2007 was not available for all companies at press time.

2007 Sales: $	2007 Profits: $	U.S. Stock Ticker: PAX
2006 Sales: $228,896	2006 Profits: $-173,744	Int'l Ticker: Int'l Exchange:
2005 Sales: $254,176	2005 Profits: $-235,670	Employees: 453
2004 Sales: $276,630	2004 Profits: $-187,972	Fiscal Year Ends: 12/31
2003 Sales: $270,939	2003 Profits: $-76,213	Parent Company:

SALARIES/BENEFITS:

Pension Plan:	ESOP Stock Plan:	Profit Sharing:	Top Exec. Salary: $1,000,000	Bonus: $1,000,000
Savings Plan: Y	Stock Purch. Plan:		Second Exec. Salary: $576,154	Bonus: $700,000

OTHER THOUGHTS:

Apparent Women Officers or Directors:
Hot Spot for Advancement for Women/Minorities:

LOCATIONS: ("Y" = Yes)

West:	Southwest:	Midwest:	Southeast:	Northeast:	International:
Y	Y	Y	Y	Y	

ISLE OF CAPRI CASINOS INC   www.isleofcapricasino.com

Industry Group Code: 713210 Ranks within this company's industry group: Sales: 3   Profits: 10

Print Media/Publishing:	Movies:	Equipment/Supplies:	Broadcast/Cable:	Music/Audio:	Sports/Games/Gambling:	
Newspapers:	Movie Theaters:	Equipment/Supplies:	Broadcast TV:	Music Production:	Games/Sports:	
Magazines:	Movie Production:	Gambling Equipment:	Cable TV:	Retail Music:	Retail Games Stores:	
Books:	TV/Video Prod.:	Special Services:	Satellite Broadcast:	Retail Audio Equip.:	Stadiums/Teams:	
Book Stores:	Video Rental:	Advertising Services:	Radio:	Music Print./Dist.:	Gambling/Casinos:	Y
Distribution/Printing:	Video Distribution:	Info. Sys. Software:	Online Information:	Multimedia:	Rides/Theme Parks:	

TYPES OF BUSINESS:

Casinos
Horse Racing

BRANDS/DIVISIONS/AFFILIATES:

Rhythm City
IsleOne Players Club
Colorado Central Station
Isle of Capri
Fan Club
Pompano Park Harness Racing Track
Isle (The)
Rail Pass Club

CONTACTS: *Note: Officers with more than one job title may be intentionally listed here more than once.*

Bernard Goldstein, CEO
Virginia McDowell, COO
Virginia McDowell, Pres.
Dale Black, CFO/Sr. VP
Doug Burkhalter, Sr. VP-Mktg.
Ron Burgess, Sr. VP-Human Resources
Allan B. Solomon, General Counsel/Asst. Sec./Exec. VP
Robert Griffin, Sr. VP-Oper.
Gregory D. Guida, Sr. VP-Bus. Dev. & Legal Affairs/Sec.
Jill Haynes, Sr. Dir.-Corp. Comm.
Dale Black, Treas.
Robert S. Goldstein, Exec. Vice Chmn.
Bernard Goldstein, Chmn.
Donn Mitchell, Sr. VP-UK Oper.

Phone: 228-396-7000	Fax: 228-396-2634
Toll-Free: 800-843-4753	
Address: 600 Emerson Rd., Ste. 300, St. Louis, MO 63141 US	

GROWTH PLANS/SPECIAL FEATURES:

Isle of Capri Casinos, Inc. is a leading developer, owner and operator of branded gaming facilities and related lodging and entertainment facilities. The firm wholly owns and operates 12 gaming facilities in the U.S. located in Lake Charles, Louisiana; Lula, Biloxi and Natchez, Mississippi; Kansas City, Caruthersville and Boonville, Missouri; Waterloo, Bettendorf, Davenport and Marquette, Iowa; and a casino and pari-mutuel harness racing facility in Pompano Beach, Florida. The company also owns a 57% interest in two gaming facilities in Black Hawk, Colorado. International gaming interests include a casino in Freeport, Grand Bahama; and a two-thirds ownership interest in casinos in Dudley, Wolverhampton and Coventry, England. The company's casinos are aggressively marketed with a Caribbean theme under the Isle of Capri name and focus on a pre-existing loyal customer base. The company offers the following customer membership rewards programs: the IsleOne Players Club, at the Isle of Capri and The Isle properties; the Fan Club at Rhythm City-Davenport; and the Rail Pass Club at the Colorado Central Station-Black Hawk. These programs offer loyal customers points, cash, and complimentaries that can be redeemed by using a player's club card. In November 2007, the company entered an agreement to purchase the remaining 43% interest in Isle of Capri-Black Hawk for $64.6 million. Completion of this transaction will make the firm sole owner of that property.

Employee benefits include medical, vision and dental coverage; life insurance; short and long term disability; and 401(k) savings plan.

FINANCIALS: Sales and profits are in thousands of dollars—add 000 to get the full amount. 2007 Note: Financial information for 2007 was not available for all companies at press time.

2007 Sales: $1,001,400	2007 Profits: $-4,600	**U.S. Stock Ticker: ISLE**	
2006 Sales: $987,400	2006 Profits: $-18,900	**Int'l Ticker:** Int'l Exchange:	
2005 Sales: $947,572	2005 Profits: $18,038	Employees: 9,162	
2004 Sales: $939,529	2004 Profits: $27,749	Fiscal Year Ends: 4/30	
2003 Sales: $1,265,458	2003 Profits: $-45,593	Parent Company:	

SALARIES/BENEFITS:

Pension Plan:	ESOP Stock Plan:	Profit Sharing:	Top Exec. Salary: $600,000	Bonus: $121,346
Savings Plan: Y	Stock Purch. Plan:		Second Exec. Salary: $550,000	Bonus: $

OTHER THOUGHTS:

Apparent Women Officers or Directors: 2
Hot Spot for Advancement for Women/Minorities:

LOCATIONS: ("Y" = Yes)

West:	Southwest:	Midwest:	Southeast:	Northeast:	International:
Y		Y	Y		Y

ITV PLC

www.itvplc.com

Industry Group Code: 513220 **Ranks within this company's industry group:** Sales: 11   Profits: 9

Print Media/Publishing:	Movies:		Equipment/Supplies:		Broadcast/Cable:		Music/Audio:	Sports/Games/Gambling:	
Newspapers:	Movie Theaters:		Equipment/Supplies:		Broadcast TV:	Y	Music Production:	Games/Sports:	
Magazines:	Movie Production:		Gambling Equipment:		Cable TV:	Y	Retail Music:	Retail Games Stores:	
Books:	TV/Video Prod.:	Y	Special Services:		Satellite Broadcast:		Retail Audio Equip.:	Stadiums/Teams:	Y
Book Stores:	Video Rental:		Advertising Services:	Y	Radio:		Music Print./Dist.:	Gambling/Casinos:	
Distribution/Printing:	Video Distribution:		Info. Sys. Software:		Online Information:		Multimedia:	Rides/Theme Parks:	

TYPES OF BUSINESS:

Cable TV Channel
Satellite Channels
Broadcast TV
TV Production
Cinema Advertising

BRANDS/DIVISIONS/AFFILIATES:

ITV1
ITV2
ITV3
ITV4
ITV Production
Granada
Granada International
Carlton Screen Advertising

CONTACTS: Note: Officers with more than one job title may be intentionally listed here more than once.

Michael Grade, CEO
John Cresswell, COO
Henry Staunton, CFO
Jim Godfrey, Dir.-Corp. Affairs
Christy Swords, Dir.-Investor Rel.
John Cresswell, Dir.-Finance
Tom Betts, Dir.-Commercial & Acquisitions
Ben McOwen Wilson, COO-Consumer Bus.
Peter Burt, Chmn.

Phone: 44-20-8528-2000	Fax: 44-20-7261-3520
Toll-Free:	
Address: 200 Grays Inn Rd., London, WC1V 8HX UK	

GROWTH PLANS/SPECIAL FEATURES:

ITV plc, the result of a merger between Carlton Communications and Granada, is a leading media company in the U.K. and the Republic of Ireland. ITV operates through ITV1, ITV2, ITV3 and ITV4. ITV1 is the largest commercial television channel in the U.K., reaching 80% of the U.K.'s viewing audience. ITV2 has been one of the U.K.'s fastest-growing channels for the last two years. ITV2 airs ITV1 show spin-off programs including the popular The X-Factor. The prime demographic for ITV 2 is a younger, mainly female audience. The station features a mix of drama, comedy, movies, events and extensions of ITV1 popular shows. ITV3 shows proprietary contemporary British dramas including Prime Suspect and Inspector Morse. ITV3 is broadcast to around 13 million homes. ITV4 showcases programming targeted for a male audience, with relevant shows, movies and sports content. The ITV Production division is one of the largest commercial TV producers in the U.K. It produces more than 3,000 hours of original programming each year. ITV2, ITV3 and ITV4 produced 38% of all year on year multi-channel advertising revenue growth for the first half of 2007. Subsidiary Granada International is responsible for distribution in Britain and beyond, with footholds in the U.K., U.S., Australian and German markets. Other subsidiaries and assets include Carlton Screen Advertising, a 50% interest in Screenvision Europe and Screenvision U.S., a 16.9% interest in SMG plc, 25% interest in independent producer Mammoth and a 40% interest in ITN. The company recently acquired a 51% stake in Jaffe/Braunstein Entertainment LLC and the independent producer, 12 Yard. Also in 2007, the firm sold its stake in Manchester United Television for $6.5 million. Additionally, it sold its shareholdings in both the The Liverpool Football Club and Athletic Grounds Plc, and Arsenal Holdings plc for $35 million and $129 million consecutively.

FINANCIALS: Sales and profits are in thousands of dollars—add 000 to get the full amount. 2007 Note: Financial information for 2007 was not available for all companies at press time.

2007 Sales: $	2007 Profits: $	U.S. Stock Ticker: ITVPF
2006 Sales: $4,270,800	2006 Profits: $434,700	Int'l Ticker: ITV Int'l Exchange: London-LSE
2005 Sales: $3,796,687	2005 Profits: $394,144	Employees: 5,957
2004 Sales: $3,580,431	2004 Profits: $249,392	Fiscal Year Ends: 12/31
2003 Sales: $5,244,800	2003 Profits: $-419,600	Parent Company:

SALARIES/BENEFITS:

Pension Plan: Y	ESOP Stock Plan:	Profit Sharing:	Top Exec. Salary: $1,767,258	Bonus: $64,998
Savings Plan:	Stock Purch. Plan:		Second Exec. Salary: $946,988	Bonus: $70,277

OTHER THOUGHTS:

Apparent Women Officers or Directors: 1
Hot Spot for Advancement for Women/Minorities: Y

LOCATIONS: ("Y" = Yes)

West:	Southwest:	Midwest:	Southeast:	Northeast:	International:
					Y

Note: Financial information, benefits and other data can change quickly and may vary from those stated here.

IVILLAGE INC

www.ivillage.com

Industry Group Code: 514199 Ranks within this company's industry group: Sales: Profits:

Print Media/Publishing:		Movies:		Equipment/Supplies:		Broadcast/Cable:		Music/Audio:		Sports/Games/Gambling:	
Newspapers:		Movie Theaters:		Equipment/Supplies:		Broadcast TV:		Music Production:		Games/Sports:	
Magazines:	Y	Movie Production:		Gambling Equipment:		Cable TV:		Retail Music:		Retail Games Stores:	
Books:	Y	TV/Video Prod.:		Special Services:	Y	Satellite Broadcast:		Retail Audio Equip.:		Stadiums/Teams:	
Book Stores:		Video Rental:		Advertising Services:	Y	Radio:		Music Print./Dist.:		Gambling/Casinos:	
Distribution/Printing:		Video Distribution:		Info. Sys. Software:		Online Information:		Multimedia:		Rides/Theme Parks:	

TYPES OF BUSINESS:

Online Women's Network
Educational Publishing
Online Promotions & Direct Marketing
Consulting Services

BRANDS/DIVISIONS/AFFILIATES:

NBC Universal
iVillage.com
iVillage UK
iVillage Total Health
Astrology.com
GardenWeb
gURL.com
Newborn Channel

CONTACTS: *Note: Officers with more than one job title may be intentionally listed here more than once.*

Michael Gutkowski, COO
Peter R. Naylor, Sr. VP-Sales
Linda Boff, Chief Mktg. Officer
Deborah I. (Debi) Fine, Pres., iVillage Properties

Phone: 212-600-6000	Fax: 212-604-9133
Toll-Free:	
Address: 500 7th Ave. 14th Fl., New York, NY 10018 US	

GROWTH PLANS/SPECIAL FEATURES:

iVillage, Inc., a subsidiary of NBC Universal, Inc., is a leading women's media company consisting of several online and offline properties offering unique content, community applications, tools and interactive features. The company's iVillage.com website, with 31.4 million unique visitors, provides information on such topics as health, parenting, pregnancy, beauty, style, fitness, relationships, food and entertainment, as well as thousands of message boards and a variety of social networking tools. iVillage's brand extensions include iVillage UK, its U.K.-oriented online information network for women; iVillage Total Health, providing information on women's health issues; owned sites Astrology.com, GardenWeb and gURL.com; and the Newborn Channel. In 2006, the company was acquired by NBC Universal, Inc. for approximately $600 million. In July 2007, iVillage launched iVillage Weddings, a website offering wedding-oriented information and support.

iVillage offers its employees subsidized child care, adoption reimbursement, back-up child care, dependent scholarships, employee discounts, an employee assistance program, leadership development programs, tuition reimbursement, educational loans, health club discounts, fitness programs, flexible spending accounts, domestic partner benefits and medical, dental, vision and prescription insurance.

FINANCIALS: Sales and profits are in thousands of dollars—add 000 to get the full amount. 2007 Note: Financial information for 2007 was not available for all companies at press time.

2007 Sales: $	2007 Profits: $	**U.S. Stock Ticker: Subsidiary**	
2006 Sales: $	2006 Profits: $	**Int'l Ticker:** Int'l Exchange:	
2005 Sales: $91,061	2005 Profits: $9,456	Employees: 278	
2004 Sales: $66,903	2004 Profits: $2,677	Fiscal Year Ends: 12/31	
2003 Sales: $55,221	2003 Profits: $-27,129	Parent Company: NBC UNIVERSAL	

SALARIES/BENEFITS:

Pension Plan: Y	ESOP Stock Plan:	Profit Sharing:	Top Exec. Salary: $	Bonus: $
Savings Plan: Y	Stock Purch. Plan:		Second Exec. Salary: $327,000	Bonus: $327,000

OTHER THOUGHTS:

Apparent Women Officers or Directors: 2
Hot Spot for Advancement for Women/Minorities: Y

LOCATIONS: ("Y" = Yes)

West:	Southwest:	Midwest:	Southeast:	Northeast:	International:
				Y	

JOHN WILEY & SONS INC   www.wiley.com

Industry Group Code: 511130 Ranks within this company's industry group: Sales: 4   Profits: 3

Print Media/Publishing:	Movies:	Equipment/Supplies:	Broadcast/Cable:	Music/Audio:	Sports/Games/Gambling:
Newspapers:	Movie Theaters:	Equipment/Supplies:	Broadcast TV:	Music Production:	Games/Sports:
Magazines: Y	Movie Production:	Gambling Equipment:	Cable TV:	Retail Music:	Retail Games Stores:
Books: Y	TV/Video Prod.:	Special Services:	Satellite Broadcast:	Retail Audio Equip.:	Stadiums/Teams:
Book Stores:	Video Rental:	Advertising Services:	Radio:	Music Print./Dist.:	Gambling/Casinos:
Distribution/Printing:	Video Distribution:	Info. Sys. Software:	Online Information:	Multimedia:	Rides/Theme Parks:

TYPES OF BUSINESS:

Reference Book Publishing
Trade Books
Business Books
Scientific & Technical Books
Textbooks & Educational Materials
Professional Journals
Consumer Guides
Online Information

BRANDS/DIVISIONS/AFFILIATES:

Wiley InterScience
Wiley InterScience OnlineBooks
Mount Sinai Journal of Medicine
Moody's Corporation
Blackwell Publishing (Holdings) Ltd.
HEED
Whatsonwhen
Microsoft Official Academic Curriculum

CONTACTS: *Note: Officers with more than one job title may be intentionally listed here more than once.*

William J. Pesce, CEO
Ellis E. Cousens, COO/Exec. VP
William J. Pesce, Pres.
Ellis E. Cousens, CFO
William J. Arlington, Sr. VP-Human Resources
Warren C. Fristensky, CIO/Sr. VP-IT
Gary M. Rinck, General Counsel/Sr. VP
Timothy B. King, Sr. VP-Planning & Dev.
Deborah E. Wiley, Sr. VP-Corp. Comm.
Edward J. Melando, Corp. Controller/Chief Acct. Officer/VP
Rene Olivieri, COO-Wiley-Blackwell
Stephen A. Kippur, Exec. VP/Pres., Professional & Trade Publishing
Peter C. Donoughue, Managing Dir.-John Wiley & Sons Australia, Ltd.
John Jarvis, Sr. VP-Europe/Managing Dir.-Wiley Europe, Ltd.
Peter B. Wiley, Chmn.
Steve Smith, Sr. VP-Int'l Dev./COO-UK Publishing
Clifford Kline, Sr. VP-Distribution & Customer Service

Phone: 201-748-6000	Fax: 201-748-6088
Toll-Free:	
Address: 111 River St., Hoboken, NJ 07030-5774 US	

GROWTH PLANS/SPECIAL FEATURES:

John Wiley & Sons, Inc. (Wiley) publishes books, journals and electronic products primarily for the scientific, technical and medical (STM) markets. Wiley operates publishing, marketing and distribution centers in the U.S., Canada, Europe, Asia and Australia. It produces STM journals, encyclopedias, books and online products; professional and consumer books and subscription services in print and electronic media; and textbooks and higher education materials. Its STM publications cover life and medical sciences, chemistry, statistics, mathematics, and electrical and electronics engineering; and recently assumed publication of Mount Sinai Journal of Medicine. Wiley's professional products serve customers in areas including business, accounting, nonprofit institution management, computers, psychology, architecture, engineering, hospitality and culinary arts. The company's educational materials are largely targeted to the science, engineering, mathematics and accounting fields, with growing positions in business, education and modern languages. Some of its products include the popular For Dummies reference books and CliffsNotes. Through licensing agreements, Wiley provides academic and corporate customers with online access to STM content through Wiley InterScience, its web-based services. Wiley InterScience offers searchable access to more than 500 of the firm's STM journals and more than 1,500 titles from Wiley InterScience OnlineBooks. The collection spans over 7.5 million pages, representing more than 1.5 million articles of scientific and scholarly research dating back to 1799. In February 2007, Wiley acquired Blackwell Publishing (Holdings) Ltd. for $1.1 billion, forming Wiley-Blackwell to publish STM products. In 2006, Wiley acquired HEED (Health Economic Evaluations Database), and Whatsonwhen (online travel content); and expanded its partnership with Skyscape, Inc. and Microsoft Learning to develop, publish and deliver Microsoft Official Academic Curriculum (MOAC) e-learning tools and textbooks to college markets.

Employees of Wiley receive bereavement leave, tuition reimbursement, a matching gift program, adoption assistance, medical benefits, life insurance and paid medical leave.

FINANCIALS: Sales and profits are in thousands of dollars—add 000 to get the full amount. 2007 Note: Financial information for 2007 was not available for all companies at press time.

2007 Sales: $1,234,936	2007 Profits: $99,619	**U.S. Stock Ticker: JWA**
2006 Sales: $1,044,185	2006 Profits: $110,328	**Int'l Ticker:** Int'l Exchange:
2005 Sales: $974,048	2005 Profits: $83,841	Employees: 4,800
2004 Sales: $923,000	2004 Profits: $88,800	Fiscal Year Ends: 4/30
2003 Sales: $854,000	2003 Profits: $87,300	Parent Company:

SALARIES/BENEFITS:

Pension Plan: Y	ESOP Stock Plan:	Profit Sharing:	Top Exec. Salary: $863,333	Bonus: $1,392,196
Savings Plan: Y	Stock Purch. Plan: Y		Second Exec. Salary: $466,667	Bonus: $683,733

OTHER THOUGHTS:

Apparent Women Officers or Directors: 2
Hot Spot for Advancement for Women/Minorities: Y

LOCATIONS: ("Y" = Yes)

West:	Southwest:	Midwest:	Southeast:	Northeast:	International:
Y		Y		Y	Y

Note: Financial information, benefits and other data can change quickly and may vary from those stated here.

JOHNSON PUBLISHING COMPANY INC
www.johnsonpublishing.com

Industry Group Code: 511120 **Ranks within this company's industry group:** Sales: 8 Profits:

Print Media/Publishing:		Movies:		Equipment/Supplies:		Broadcast/Cable:		Music/Audio:		Sports/Games/Gambling:	
Newspapers:		Movie Theaters:		Equipment/Supplies:		Broadcast TV:		Music Production:		Games/Sports:	
Magazines:	Y	Movie Production:		Gambling Equipment:		Cable TV:		Retail Music:		Retail Games Stores:	
Books:	Y	TV/Video Prod.:		Special Services:	Y	Satellite Broadcast:		Retail Audio Equip.:		Stadiums/Teams:	
Book Stores:		Video Rental:		Advertising Services:		Radio:		Music Print./Dist.:		Gambling/Casinos:	
Distribution/Printing:		Video Distribution:		Info. Sys. Software:		Online Information:		Multimedia:		Rides/Theme Parks:	

TYPES OF BUSINESS:

Magazine Publishing
Book Publishing
Cosmetics & Skin Care Products
Traveling Fashion Show
Greeting Cards

BRANDS/DIVISIONS/AFFILIATES:

EBONY Magazine
JET Magazine
Fashion Fair Cosmetics
EBONY Fashion Fair
JPC Book Division
Ebony Home
Ebony Collection (The)
Ebony Inspirations

CONTACTS: *Note: Officers with more than one job title may be intentionally listed here more than once.*

Linda J. Rice, CEO
Linda J. Rice, Pres.
Eunice W. Johnson, Corp. Sec.
Eunice W. Johnson, Treas.
Eunice W. Johnson, Producer/Dir.-EBONY Fashion Fair

Phone: 312-322-9200	Fax: 312-322-0918
Toll-Free:	
Address: 820 S. Michigan Ave., Chicago, IL 60605 US	

GROWTH PLANS/SPECIAL FEATURES:

Johnson Publishing Company, Inc. is a major African-American-owned and -operated publishing company with businesses in publishing, cosmetics, television production and fashion. The company owns and operates both EBONY and JET magazines. With a monthly circulation around 1.5 million and a monthly readership of over 12 million, EBONY provides a forum to discuss issues and provide encouragement for African-Americans. JET, with a weekly circulation of over 900,000 and a weekly readership of more than 9 million, specializes in covering worldwide news. Johnson Publishing's other divisions include Fashion Fair Cosmetics, a top line of makeup and skincare for women of color, sold in 2,500 stores in the U.S., Canada, Africa, England, France, Switzerland, the Bahamas, Bermuda and the Virgin Islands; as well as the EBONY Fashion Fair, a global traveling fashion show designed to raise money for scholarships and charities in cities; and a book division, which publishes books by African-American authors covering topics such as history, culture, cooking and children's books. In the past, the company has been involved in television production. In February 2007, in celebration of Black History Month, Johnson Publishing, in a partnership with American Greetings, launched the Ebony Inspirations greeting card brand. The deal was brokered by TurnerPatteron licensing agency in partnership with Johnson Publishing's new licensing division. The division plans to introduce new brands including: Ebony Home; The Ebony Collection, apparel for women and men; and Ebony Jr.! brand.

FINANCIALS: Sales and profits are in thousands of dollars—add 000 to get the full amount. 2007 Note: Financial information for 2007 was not available for all companies at press time.

2007 Sales: $		2007 Profits: $		**U.S. Stock Ticker:** Private	
2006 Sales: $458,000		2006 Profits: $		**Int'l Ticker:** Int'l Exchange:	
2005 Sales: $495,700		2005 Profits: $		Employees: 1,100	
2004 Sales: $498,200		2004 Profits: $		Fiscal Year Ends: 12/31	
2003 Sales: $488,500		2003 Profits: $		Parent Company:	

SALARIES/BENEFITS:

Pension Plan:	ESOP Stock Plan:	Profit Sharing:	Top Exec. Salary: $	Bonus: $
Savings Plan:	Stock Purch. Plan:		Second Exec. Salary: $	Bonus: $

OTHER THOUGHTS:

Apparent Women Officers or Directors: 2
Hot Spot for Advancement for Women/Minorities: Y

LOCATIONS: ("Y" = Yes)

West:	Southwest:	Midwest:	Southeast:	Northeast:	International:
Y		Y		Y	Y

JOOST

www.joost.com

Industry Group Code: 513120A **Ranks within this company's industry group:** Sales: Profits:

Print Media/Publishing:	Movies:	Equipment/Supplies:		Broadcast/Cable:	Music/Audio:	Sports/Games/Gambling:
Newspapers:	Movie Theaters:	Equipment/Supplies:		Broadcast TV:	Music Production:	Games/Sports:
Magazines:	Movie Production:	Gambling Equipment:		Cable TV:	Retail Music:	Retail Games Stores:
Books:	TV/Video Prod.:	Special Services:	Y	Satellite Broadcast:	Retail Audio Equip.:	Stadiums/Teams:
Book Stores:	Video Rental:	Advertising Services:	Y	Radio:	Music Print./Dist.:	Gambling/Casinos:
Distribution/Printing:	Video Distribution:	Info. Sys. Software:		Online Information:	Multimedia:	Rides/Theme Parks:

TYPES OF BUSINESS:

TV Over IP
Advertising Services

BRANDS/DIVISIONS/AFFILIATES:

National Basketball Association (NBA)
NBA Channel
Coca Cola Company
Coke Bubbles
Major League Baseball (MLB)

CONTACTS: Note: Officers with more than one job title may be intentionally listed here more than once.

Mike Volpi, CEO
Fredrik de Wahl, Chief Strategy Officer
Yvette Alberdingk Thijm, Exec. VP-Content Strategy & Acquisition
Niklas Zennstrom, Exec. Co-Chmn.
Janus Friis, Exec. Co-Chmn.

Phone: 31-71-523-0533	**Fax:** 31-71-523-0759
Toll-Free:	
Address: Schipholweg 101 T, Leiden, 2316 XC The Netherlands	

GROWTH PLANS/SPECIAL FEATURES:

Joost is one of the first providers of broadcast quality, full-screen online television content and associated advertising services. It offers over 250 free channels of programming, available through a standard broadband Internet connection. Users get to pick what to watch and when to watch it. Joost's genres include comedy, drama, documentary, entertainment, film, cartoons & animation, lifestyles, music, music entertainment, sports & games and news. Some of the firm's popular channels include Comedy Central, Adult Swim, CNN, Reuters, Onion News Network, Guinness World Records TV, Sports Illustrated Swimsuit On Demand, Stuff.tv, Showtime, Paramount Pictures, Movieola: The Short Film Channel, CBS, Brazilian Music Channel, National Lampoon and IndyCar Series. Joost offers a variety of tools, called widgets, which allow users to chat, rate and blog while they're watching shows. In December 2007, PBS announced it would begin offering select full-length programming on Joost, including Scientific American Frontiers and History Detectives. In December 2007, the National Basketball Association (NBA) partnered with Joost to launch the NBA Channel, featuring rebroadcasts of memorable games and Top 10 lists. In November 2007, the Coca Cola Company released a specialized messaging widget for the firm, allowing Joost users to send an email to a friend, alerting them the user has left a comment on a scene just for them. When the recipient watches the scene, the comment appears in a transparent bubble on screen. The widget, called Coke Bubbles, is designed to recreate the feeling of watching a show together, chatting with friends, but unlimited by time and space constraints. In September 2007, the interactive media and Internet arm of Major League Baseball (MLB), MLB Advanced Media, announced an exclusive partnership with Joost, allowing the firm to offer highlight clips and on-demand game broadcasts of the MLB postseason, including Daily Rewind, a daily highlight program.

FINANCIALS: Sales and profits are in thousands of dollars—add 000 to get the full amount. 2007 Note: Financial information for 2007 was not available for all companies at press time.

2007 Sales: $	2007 Profits: $	**U.S. Stock Ticker: Private**
2006 Sales: $	2006 Profits: $	**Int'l Ticker:** Int'l Exchange:
2005 Sales: $	2005 Profits: $	Employees:
2004 Sales: $	2004 Profits: $	Fiscal Year Ends: 12/31
2003 Sales: $	2003 Profits: $	Parent Company:

SALARIES/BENEFITS:

Pension Plan:	ESOP Stock Plan:	Profit Sharing:	Top Exec. Salary: $	Bonus: $
Savings Plan:	Stock Purch. Plan:		Second Exec. Salary: $	Bonus: $

OTHER THOUGHTS:

Apparent Women Officers or Directors: 1
Hot Spot for Advancement for Women/Minorities:

LOCATIONS: ("Y" = Yes)

West:	Southwest:	Midwest:	Southeast:	Northeast:	International:
				Y	Y

Note: Financial information, benefits and other data can change quickly and may vary from those stated here.

JOURNAL COMMUNICATIONS INC

www.jc.com

Industry Group Code: 511110 Ranks within this company's industry group: Sales: 16 Profits: 10

Print Media/Publishing:		Movies:	Equipment/Supplies:		Broadcast/Cable:		Music/Audio:	Sports/Games/Gambling:
Newspapers:	Y	Movie Theaters:	Equipment/Supplies:		Broadcast TV:	Y	Music Production:	Games/Sports:
Magazines:		Movie Production:	Gambling Equipment:		Cable TV:		Retail Music:	Retail Games Stores:
Books:		TV/Video Prod.:	Special Services:	Y	Satellite Broadcast:		Retail Audio Equip.:	Stadiums/Teams:
Book Stores:		Video Rental:	Advertising Services:	Y	Radio:		Music Print./Dist.:	Gambling/Casinos:
Distribution/Printing:		Video Distribution:	Info. Sys. Software:		Online Information:		Multimedia:	Rides/Theme Parks:

TYPES OF BUSINESS:

Newspaper Publishing
Publishing
Television Broadcasting
Radio Broadcasting
Printing Services
Direct Marketing Services
Corporate Intercompany Eliminations
Corporate Expenses

BRANDS/DIVISIONS/AFFILIATES:

Milwaukee Journal SentinalJournal Sentinel, Inc.
Journal Community Publishing Group, Inc.
Journal Broadcast Corporation
IPC Print Services, Inc.
PrimeNet

CONTACTS: Note: Officers with more than one job title may be intentionally listed here more than once.

Steven J. Smith, CEO
Douglas G. Kiel, Pres.
Paul M. Bonaiuto, CFO/Exec. VP
Daniel L. Harmsen, VP-Human Resources
Mary H. Leahy, General Counsel/Sr. VP
Sara L. Wilkins, VP-Corp. Comm.
Sara L. Wilkins, VP-Investor Rel.
Karen O. Trickle, Treas./VP
Steven H. Wexler, CEO-Journal Broadcasting Group
James P. Prather, VP/Pres., News-Journal Broadcasting Group
Elizabeth Brenner, Exec. VP/COO-Publishing Businesses
Carl D. Gardner, VP/Exec. VP-TV & Radio, Journal Broadcasting Group
Steven J. Smith, Chmn.

Phone: 414-224-2000	Fax: 414-224-2469
Toll-Free: 800-388-2291	
Address: 333 W. State St., Milwaukee, WI 53203 US	

GROWTH PLANS/SPECIAL FEATURES:

Journal Communications, Inc. is a media and communications company whose business is divided into four segments: publishing; broadcasting; printing services; and other. The publishing business is conducted through wholly-owned subsidiaries Journal Sentinel, Inc. and Journal Community Publishing Group, Inc. The company publishes the Milwaukee Journal Sentinel, which serves as the principal daily and Sunday newspaper for the greater Milwaukee area, as well as 37 community newspapers and 29 shoppers in seven states. The Milwaukee Journal Sentinel has a daily circulation of approximately 230,000, and about 400,000 on Sundays. This segment also publishes nine niche products, such as automotive and boating focused publications. The broadcasting business is conducted through wholly-owned subsidiary Journal Broadcast Corporation and its subsidiaries, which together operate nine television stations and 36 radio stations in 12 states. This segment also operates two additional television stations under local marketing agreements. The company's printing services are conducted through wholly-owned subsidiary IPC Print Services, Inc. Services include complete production of magazines, professional journals and documentation material, with particular emphasis on scientific, medical and technical journals. The firm's other business consists of a direct marketing services business conducted through wholly-owned subsidiary, PrimeNet, as well as corporate intercompany eliminations and corporate expenses.

Employee benefits include medical, dental and vision insurance; life insurance; employee assistance program; retirement benefits; 401(k) plan; educational support and tuition reimbursement; and employee stock purchase plan.

FINANCIALS: Sales and profits are in thousands of dollars—add 000 to get the full amount. 2007 Note: Financial information for 2007 was not available for all companies at press time.

2007 Sales: $	2007 Profits: $	U.S. Stock Ticker: JRN
2006 Sales: $671,853	2006 Profits: $64,373	Int'l Ticker: Int'l Exchange:
2005 Sales: $624,013	2005 Profits: $66,243	Employees: 350
2004 Sales: $773,372	2004 Profits: $78,480	Fiscal Year Ends: 12/31
2003 Sales: $798,289	2003 Profits: $66,793	Parent Company:

SALARIES/BENEFITS:

Pension Plan: Y	ESOP Stock Plan:	Profit Sharing:	Top Exec. Salary: $700,000	Bonus: $126,000
Savings Plan: Y	Stock Purch. Plan: Y		Second Exec. Salary: $493,000	Bonus: $42,444

OTHER THOUGHTS:

Apparent Women Officers or Directors: 7
Hot Spot for Advancement for Women/Minorities: Y

LOCATIONS: ("Y" = Yes)

West:	Southwest:	Midwest:	Southeast:	Northeast:	International:
Y	Y	Y	Y	Y	

Note: Financial information, benefits and other data can change quickly and may vary from those stated here.

JOURNAL REGISTER CO

www.journalregister.com

Industry Group Code: 511110 Ranks within this company's industry group: Sales: 17 Profits: 15

Print Media/Publishing:		Movies:	Equipment/Supplies:		Broadcast/Cable:	Music/Audio:	Sports/Games/Gambling:
Newspapers:	Y	Movie Theaters:	Equipment/Supplies:		Broadcast TV:	Music Production:	Games/Sports:
Magazines:	Y	Movie Production:	Gambling Equipment:		Cable TV:	Retail Music:	Retail Games Stores:
Books:		TV/Video Prod.:	Special Services:		Satellite Broadcast:	Retail Audio Equip.:	Stadiums/Teams:
Book Stores:		Video Rental:	Advertising Services:	Y	Radio:	Music Print./Dist.:	Gambling/Casinos:
Distribution/Printing:		Video Distribution:	Info. Sys. Software:		Online Information:	Multimedia:	Rides/Theme Parks:

TYPES OF BUSINESS:

Newspaper & Magazine Publishing
Commercial Printing
Online Publishing
Employment Websites

BRANDS/DIVISIONS/AFFILIATES:

New Haven Register
Litchfield County Times
Connecticut Vacation Guide
Westchester/Fairfield County Times
Connecticut Magazine
Freeman Online
Hudson Valley Guide
Suburban Lifestyles

CONTACTS: Note: Officers with more than one job title may be intentionally listed here more than once.

James W. Hall, CEO
Scott A. Wright, COO
Scott A. Wright, Pres.
Julie A. Beck, CFO/Exec. VP
Allen J. Mailman, Sr. VP-Tech.
Edward J. Yocum, Jr., General Counsel/Corp. Sec./Sr. VP
Edward S. Condra, Sr. VP-Oper.
Judy Brenna, Dir.-Investor Rel.
William J. Higginson, Sr. VP-Prod.
Michael Murray, Sr. VP-Circulation
Daryl Hively, VP-Interactive Media
Laurel Lane, Corp. Dir.-Interactive Sales
James W. Hall, Chmn.

Phone: 215-504-4200	Fax: 215-504-4201

Toll-Free:

Address: 790 Township Line Rd., Ste. 300, Yardley, PA 19067 US

GROWTH PLANS/SPECIAL FEATURES:

Journal Register Company is a leading U.S. newspaper publisher, with a total daily circulation of approximately 559,000. The company owns and operates 22 daily newspapers, including the New Haven Register, Connecticut's second-largest daily and Sunday newspaper. Journal Register also owns 346 non-daily publications, with a total distribution of more than 6 million, in addition to several commercial printing and software development companies. The company strategically clusters its operations in six geographic areas: Greater Philadelphia; Michigan; Connecticut; Greater Cleveland; and the Capital-Saratoga and Mid-Hudson regions of New York. Journal Register also owns 227 individual web sites featuring its newspapers. The company's newspapers are characterized by an intense focus on coverage of local news and local sports and offer compelling graphic design in colorful, reader-friendly packages. The majority of the company's daily newspapers have been published for more than 100 years and are established franchises with strong identities in the communities they serve. In many cases, Journal Register's daily newspapers are the only general-circulation daily newspapers published in their respective communities. While newspaper publishing accounts for substantially all of the company's revenues, it also owns 19 employment websites and three commercial printing operations that compliment and enhance its publishing operations. In February 2007, the firm sold three daily community newspapers and a weekly newspaper group in Rhode Island to R.I.S.N. Operations, Inc. for $8.3 million. In the same month, the company sold two daily community newspapers and five non-daily publications in Massachusetts to GateHouse Media, Inc. for approximately $72 million.

FINANCIALS: Sales and profits are in thousands of dollars—add 000 to get the full amount. 2007 Note: Financial information for 2007 was not available for all companies at press time.

2007 Sales: $	2007 Profits: $	**U.S. Stock Ticker:** JRC
2006 Sales: $506,065	2006 Profits: $-6,238	**Int'l Ticker:** Int'l Exchange:
2005 Sales: $516,588	2005 Profits: $46,868	Employees: 6,000
2004 Sales: $469,092	2004 Profits: $116,513	Fiscal Year Ends: 12/31
2003 Sales: $405,986	2003 Profits: $71,990	Parent Company:

SALARIES/BENEFITS:

Pension Plan: Y	ESOP Stock Plan:	Profit Sharing:	Top Exec. Salary: $969,000	Bonus: $375,000
Savings Plan: Y	Stock Purch. Plan:		Second Exec. Salary: $325,000	Bonus: $95,000

OTHER THOUGHTS:

Apparent Women Officers or Directors: 4
Hot Spot for Advancement for Women/Minorities: Y

LOCATIONS: ("Y" = Yes)

West:	Southwest:	Midwest:	Southeast:	Northeast:	International:
		Y		Y	

JUMPTV INC

www.jumptv.com

Industry Group Code: 513120A Ranks within this company's industry group: Sales: 1 Profits: 1

Print Media/Publishing:	Movies:	Equipment/Supplies:		Broadcast/Cable:		Music/Audio:		Sports/Games/Gambling:	
Newspapers:	Movie Theaters:	Equipment/Supplies:		Broadcast TV:		Music Production:		Games/Sports:	
Magazines:	Movie Production:	Gambling Equipment:		Cable TV:	Y	Retail Music:		Retail Games Stores:	
Books:	TV/Video Prod.:	Special Services:	Y	Satellite Broadcast:		Retail Audio Equip.:		Stadiums/Teams:	
Book Stores:	Video Rental:	Advertising Services:		Radio:		Music Print./Dist.:		Gambling/Casinos:	
Distribution/Printing:	Video Distribution:	Info. Sys. Software:		Online Information:		Multimedia:		Rides/Theme Parks:	

TYPES OF BUSINESS:

Internet Protocol Television

BRANDS/DIVISIONS/AFFILIATES:

JumpTV International
Sports International Group
SportsYa.com
JumpTV USA Inc.
JumpTV Limited
Sports International Group LLC
Deportes Ya S.A.

CONTACTS: *Note: Officers with more than one job title may be intentionally listed here more than once.*

Jordan Banks, CEO
Kaleil Isaza Tuzman, COO
Kaleil Isaza Tuzman, Pres.
Jason Reid, CFO
Michael Haffner, Head-Mktg.
Dan O'Hara, Tech. Fellow
Brad Rosenberg, Dir.-Prod. Dev.
Jason Reid, Head-Admin.
Sean Coutts, Head-Oper.
Jeff Maser, VP-Corp. Dev.
Jason Reid, Head-Finance
Kevin Foong, Gen. Mgr.-Asia
Jeremy Hope, VP-Network Oper.
Carlos Nakhle, Head-Customer Retention & Operational Reporting
G. Scott Paterson, Chmn.
Amir Hegazi, Gen. Mgr.-Middle East & North Africa
Mike John-Baptiste, Head-Distribution

Phone: 416-368-0305	**Fax:** 416-368-6414
Toll-Free:	
Address: 463 King St. W., 3rd Fl., Toronto, ON M5V 1K4 Canada	

GROWTH PLANS/SPECIAL FEATURES:

JumpTV, Inc. is a leader in Internet Protocol Television (IPTV), providing access to international television streaming over the Internet. The company has offices in Toronto; New York; London; Bogota, Colombia; Amman, Jordan; Bangkok, Thailand; and Dubai, United Arab Emirates. JumpTV is partnered with over 180 television broadcasters in over 60 countries to provide live Internet streaming of broadcasters' 24-hour feeds. Currently, the firm offers channels from Europe, Asia, the Middle East and Africa. These streams are available to subscribers over a high-speed Internet connection. The channels are offered either separately or as part of a multi-channel bundle. One of the company's major programming draws is sports, particularly soccer. Sports, along with a few other shows, are available through pay-per-view and video-on-demand options. In 2006, JumpTV had approximately 24,500 subscribers with 28,000 subscriptions and had signed over 300 channels; it holds exclusive Internet rights to over 220 of these channels. The majority of the firm's subscribers are located in the U.S. (53%); the next largest segment comes from Europe (23%), with Spain making up 8% of the overall subscriber base. JumpTV is available in over 80 countries. In August 2007, the company completed the acquisition of the Broadband Network business unit of XOS Technologies Inc.

FINANCIALS: Sales and profits are in thousands of dollars—add 000 to get the full amount. 2007 Note: Financial information for 2007 was not available for all companies at press time.

2007 Sales: $	2007 Profits: $	**U.S. Stock Ticker:**
2006 Sales: $2,061	2006 Profits: $-25,597	**Int'l Ticker:** JTV Int'l Exchange: Toronto-TSX
2005 Sales: $1,081	2005 Profits: $-4,631	**Employees:**
2004 Sales: $	2004 Profits: $	**Fiscal Year Ends:** 12/31
2003 Sales: $	2003 Profits: $	**Parent Company:**

SALARIES/BENEFITS:

Pension Plan:	ESOP Stock Plan:	Profit Sharing:	Top Exec. Salary: $	Bonus: $
Savings Plan:	Stock Purch. Plan:		Second Exec. Salary: $	Bonus: $

OTHER THOUGHTS:

Apparent Women Officers or Directors: 3
Hot Spot for Advancement for Women/Minorities: Y

LOCATIONS: ("Y" = Yes)

West:	Southwest:	Midwest:	Southeast:	Northeast:	International:
				Y	Y

Note: Financial information, benefits and other data can change quickly and may vary from those stated here.

JUPITERMEDIA CORP

www.jupitermedia.com

Industry Group Code: 514199 Ranks within this company's industry group: Sales: 3 Profits: 2

Print Media/Publishing:	Movies:	Equipment/Supplies:		Broadcast/Cable:	Music/Audio:	Sports/Games/Gambling:
Newspapers:	Movie Theaters:	Equipment/Supplies:		Broadcast TV:	Music Production:	Games/Sports:
Magazines:	Movie Production:	Gambling Equipment:		Cable TV:	Retail Music:	Retail Games Stores:
Books:	TV/Video Prod.:	Special Services:	Y	Satellite Broadcast:	Retail Audio Equip.:	Stadiums/Teams:
Book Stores:	Video Rental:	Advertising Services:	Y	Radio:	Music Print./Dist.:	Gambling/Casinos:
Distribution/Printing:	Video Distribution:	Info. Sys. Software:		Online Information:	Multimedia:	Rides/Theme Parks:

TYPES OF BUSINESS:

Business & Technology News Portal
Online Image Library
Market Research
Trade Shows

BRANDS/DIVISIONS/AFFILIATES:

JupiterImages
JupiterOnlineMedia
internet.com
EarthWeb.com
Mediabistro.com
Graphics.com
JustTechJobs
JupiterEvents

CONTACTS: Note: Officers with more than one job title may be intentionally listed here more than once.

Alan M. Meckler, CEO
Christopher S. Cardell, COO
Christopher S. Cardell, Pres.
Donald J. O'Neil, CFO
Alan M. Meckler, Chmn.

Phone: 203-662-2800	Fax: 203-655-4686
Toll-Free:	
Address: 23 Old Kings Hwy. S., Darien, CT 06820 US	

GROWTH PLANS/SPECIAL FEATURES:

Jupitermedia Corp. is a leading global provider of original online information, images, research and events for information technology, business, design and art professionals. Jupitermedia develops and disseminates original content and provides access to one of the largest online image libraries. The firm delivers its content through a number of proprietary channels, including its extensive online media networks, online image networks, proprietary research business and its various trade shows and conferences. As part of its ongoing international expansion, Jupitermedia has international business-to-business portals in Germany, Hong Kong, Japan, Korea, Singapore and Turkey. The company's JupiterImages division is one of the leading paid subscription-based image companies in the world, with over 7 million online images serving creative professionals. It owns and markets products that include Comstock Images, photos.com and clipart.com. The firm owns and operates JupiterOnlineMedia, which consists of five online networks for IT professionals (internet.com and EarthWeb.com), developers (DevX.com) and media and creative professionals (Mediabistro.com and Graphics.com). JupiterOnlineMedia properties include more than 150 web sites, nearly 150 e-mail newsletters that are viewed by 20 million users and generate over 400 million page views monthly. JupiterOnlineMedia also offers two print magazines for creative professionals, Dynamic Graphics Magazine and STEP Inside Design Magazine. Jupitermedia owns JustTechJobs, a jobsite allowing professionals and employers to post jobs, search resumes and manage that information with online tools. The firm also owns JupiterEvents, which produces conferences and trade shows focused on IT and business-specific topics, including Web Video, ISPCON and Semantic Web. In January 2007, Jupitermedia acquired two annual ISPCON trade shows and the INBOX trade show from The Golden Group. In June 2007, the company acquired AdsOfTheWorld.com and CreativeBits.org. In July 2007, Jupitermedia acquired Mediabistro.com Inc. for $20 million.

Jupitermedia offers its employees a flexible spending account, tuition reimbursement and medical, dental, life and AD&D insurance.

FINANCIALS: Sales and profits are in thousands of dollars—add 000 to get the full amount. 2007 Note: Financial information for 2007 was not available for all companies at press time.

2007 Sales: $	2007 Profits: $	U.S. Stock Ticker: JUPM	
2006 Sales: $137,530	2006 Profits: $13,124	Int'l Ticker:	Int'l Exchange:
2005 Sales: $113,754	2005 Profits: $78,399	Employees: 678	
2004 Sales: $52,636	2004 Profits: $15,737	Fiscal Year Ends: 12/31	
2003 Sales: $38,713	2003 Profits: $1,382	Parent Company:	

SALARIES/BENEFITS:

Pension Plan:	ESOP Stock Plan:	Profit Sharing:	Top Exec. Salary: $315,000	Bonus: $
Savings Plan: Y	Stock Purch. Plan:		Second Exec. Salary: $315,000	Bonus: $

OTHER THOUGHTS:

Apparent Women Officers or Directors:
Hot Spot for Advancement for Women/Minorities:

LOCATIONS: ("Y" = Yes)

West:	Southwest:	Midwest:	Southeast:	Northeast:	International:
Y				Y	Y

Note: Financial information, benefits and other data can change quickly and may vary from those stated here.

KERZNER INTERNATIONAL LIMITED
www.kerzner.com

Industry Group Code: 721120 Ranks within this company's industry group: Sales: Profits:

Print Media/Publishing:	Movies:	Equipment/Supplies:	Broadcast/Cable:	Music/Audio:	Sports/Games/Gambling:	
Newspapers:	Movie Theaters:	Equipment/Supplies:	Broadcast TV:	Music Production:	Games/Sports:	
Magazines:	Movie Production:	Gambling Equipment:	Cable TV:	Retail Music:	Retail Games Stores:	
Books:	TV/Video Prod.:	Special Services:	Satellite Broadcast:	Retail Audio Equip.:	Stadiums/Teams:	
Book Stores:	Video Rental:	Advertising Services:	Radio:	Music Print./Dist.:	Gambling/Casinos:	Y
Distribution/Printing:	Video Distribution:	Info. Sys. Software:	Online Information:	Multimedia:	Rides/Theme Parks:	

TYPES OF BUSINESS:

Casino Hotels
Luxury Resort Hotels
Resort Development

BRANDS/DIVISIONS/AFFILIATES:

Atlantis
Palm (The)
Dig (The)
One&Only
Related Companies L.P. (The)
Istithmar PJSC
Colony Capital LLC
Providence Equity Partners, Inc.

CONTACTS:
Note: Officers with more than one job title may be intentionally listed here more than once.

Paul O'Neil, CEO
John R. Allison, CFO/Exec. VP
Richard M. Levine, General Counsel/Exec. VP
Solomon Kerzner, Chmn.

Phone: 212-659-5184	Fax: 212-659-5201
Toll-Free:	
Address: 730 Fifth Ave., 5th Fl., New York, NY 10019 US	

GROWTH PLANS/SPECIAL FEATURES:

Kerzner International, Ltd. (formerly Sun International Hotels) is a resort and gaming company that develops, operates and manages premier resort and casino properties. The company's flagship property is its Atlantis resort on Paradise Island, near Nassau in the Bahamas, which features the world's largest open-air aquarium and the largest hotel and casino in the Caribbean market. The 2,317-room resort features three interconnected hotel towers built around a seven-acre lagoon and a 34-acre marine environment. Kerzner International is currently expanding its Atlantis resort by 1,500 rooms and adding an 18-hole golf course on a nearby island and a water park including an area where guests can swim with dolphins. Also under development is the Palm, a joint venture with an affiliate of Nakheel, LLC. Located on one of two man-made islands shaped like date palms, the Palm will include a 1,000-room luxury hotel, an extensive water theme park and the Dig, an Atlantis-themed archeological experience. Kerzner International manages or owns interests in 10 beach resorts, six of which operate under the company's One&Only brand. In development and planning are One&Only Reethi Rah, Maldives, as well as locations in Cape Town, South Africa and Havana, Cuba. Mid-term expansion plans include a 2,000-room Atlantis casino hotel in Dubai, valued at $1.1 billion; a $230-million casino in Morocco; and three new casinos, valued at $1 billion, in the U.K. The Dubai Government is a major backer of the firm. Eventually, the company hopes to open an Atlantis casino hotel in Asia and sponsor a Native American casino in the Catskill Mountains. In March 2006, Kerzner International was acquired by an investor group consisting of Istithmar PJSC, Colony Capital LLC, Providence Equity Partners, Inc. and The Related Companies L.P. in a transaction valued at $3.6 billion.

FINANCIALS:
Sales and profits are in thousands of dollars—add 000 to get the full amount. 2007 Note: Financial information for 2007 was not available for all companies at press time.

2007 Sales: $	2007 Profits: $	U.S. Stock Ticker: Private
2006 Sales: $	2006 Profits: $	Int'l Ticker: Int'l Exchange:
2005 Sales: $721,524	2005 Profits: $50,648	Employees: 11,870
2004 Sales: $621,085	2004 Profits: $68,132	Fiscal Year Ends: 12/31
2003 Sales: $525,292	2003 Profits: $71,572	Parent Company:

SALARIES/BENEFITS:

Pension Plan:	ESOP Stock Plan:	Profit Sharing:	Top Exec. Salary: $	Bonus: $
Savings Plan: Y	Stock Purch. Plan:		Second Exec. Salary: $	Bonus: $

OTHER THOUGHTS:

Apparent Women Officers or Directors:
Hot Spot for Advancement for Women/Minorities:

LOCATIONS: ("Y" = Yes)

West:	Southwest:	Midwest:	Southeast:	Northeast:	International:
				Y	Y

KNOLOGY INC

www.knology.com

Industry Group Code: 513220 Ranks within this company's industry group: Sales: 19 Profits: 17

Print Media/Publishing:	Movies:	Equipment/Supplies:		Broadcast/Cable:		Music/Audio:	Sports/Games/Gambling:
Newspapers:	Movie Theaters:	Equipment/Supplies:		Broadcast TV:		Music Production:	Games/Sports:
Magazines:	Movie Production:	Gambling Equipment:	Y	Cable TV:	Y	Retail Music:	Retail Games Stores:
Books:	TV/Video Prod.:	Special Services:	Y	Satellite Broadcast:		Retail Audio Equip.:	Stadiums/Teams:
Book Stores:	Video Rental:	Advertising Services:		Radio:		Music Print./Dist.:	Gambling/Casinos:
Distribution/Printing:	Video Distribution:	Info. Sys. Software:		Online Information:		Multimedia:	Rides/Theme Parks:

TYPES OF BUSINESS:

Cable TV Service
Internet Service Provider
Local & Long-Distance Telephone Service
Passive Optical Network
Managed Integrated Network Solutions

BRANDS/DIVISIONS/AFFILIATES:

Prarie Wave Communications

CONTACTS: Note: Officers with more than one job title may be intentionally listed here more than once.

Rodger L. Johnson, CEO
Rodger L. Johnson, Pres.
M. Todd Holt, CFO
Michael B. Roddy, VP-Mktg.
Brad M. Vanacore, VP-Human Resources
Rick Perkins, VP-IT/Billing
Richard Luke, CTO
Chad S. Wachter, General Counsel/VP/Sec.
Bret T. McCants, VP-Oper.
Felix L. Boccucci, VP-New Bus. Dev.
Andrew Sivell, VP-Network Oper.
Allan H. Goodson, VP-Regional Oper.

Phone: 706-645-8553	Fax:
Toll-Free:	
Address: 1241 O. G. Skinner Dr., West Point, GA 31833 US	

GROWTH PLANS/SPECIAL FEATURES:

Knology, Inc. is a provider of video, voice, data and advanced communications services in nine markets throughout the southeastern United States. Knology's video services, which include digital and analog cable television, accounted for 44% of its revenues in 2006, while it's local and long-distance telephone service accounted for 32%, its data services, such as high-speed internet, accounted for 23% and other services accounted for 1%. The nine markets in which Knology provides its services are Huntsville and Montgomery, Alabama; Panama City and Pinellas County Florida; Augusta, Columbus and West Point, Georgia; Charleston, South Carolina; and Knoxville, Tennessee. In addition to separate video, voice and data services, Knology provides a broad range of service bundles. The company owns all of the networks that it uses, so it does not have to pay rent for bandwidth or rely on another company's communications lines. The firm's interactive broadband network is designed using redundant fiber-optic cables, and its fiber rings provide for rapid, automatic redirection of network traffic. The self-correcting properties of the fiber rings allow service to continue even during single-point failures. Knology's fiber-based business voice and data services include Passive Optical Network (PON), which supplies IP architecture with segmented voice and data bandwidth; and Managed Integrated Network Solutions (MATRIX), an integrated IP-based technology, which combines data and voice. In April 2007, Knology announced its acquisition of PrairieWave Communications, a voice, video and high-speed internet broadband services provider for Rapid City and Sioux Falls, South Dakota as well as portions of Minnesota and Iowa.

Knology, Inc. offers its employees tuition reimbursement, free or discounted Knology Services, an employee assistance program and group insurance coverage for major medical, prescription, dental and vision benefits as well as supplemental cancer insurance.

FINANCIALS: Sales and profits are in thousands of dollars—add 000 to get the full amount. 2007 Note: Financial information for 2007 was not available for all companies at press time.

2007 Sales: $	2007 Profits: $	U.S. Stock Ticker: KNOL
2006 Sales: $258,991	2006 Profits: $-39,505	Int'l Ticker: Int'l Exchange:
2005 Sales: $230,857	2005 Profits: $-55,402	Employees: 1,365
2004 Sales: $211,458	2004 Profits: $-75,564	Fiscal Year Ends: 12/31
2003 Sales: $172,938	2003 Profits: $-87,788	Parent Company:

SALARIES/BENEFITS:

Pension Plan:	ESOP Stock Plan:	Profit Sharing:	Top Exec. Salary: $420,487	Bonus: $423,775
Savings Plan: Y	Stock Purch. Plan:		Second Exec. Salary: $207,308	Bonus: $117,768

OTHER THOUGHTS:

Apparent Women Officers or Directors:
Hot Spot for Advancement for Women/Minorities:

LOCATIONS: ("Y" = Yes)

West:	Southwest:	Midwest:	Southeast:	Northeast:	International:
		Y	Y		

Note: Financial information, benefits and other data can change quickly and may vary from those stated here.

LAGARDERE ACTIVE MEDIA
www.hfmus.com

Industry Group Code: 511120 Ranks within this company's industry group: Sales: Profits:

Print Media/Publishing:		Movies:		Equipment/Supplies:		Broadcast/Cable:		Music/Audio:		Sports/Games/Gambling:	
Newspapers:	Y	Movie Theaters:		Equipment/Supplies:		Broadcast TV:	Y	Music Production:		Games/Sports:	
Magazines:	Y	Movie Production:		Gambling Equipment:		Cable TV:		Retail Music:		Retail Games Stores:	
Books:		TV/Video Prod.:	Y	Special Services:	Y	Satellite Broadcast:		Retail Audio Equip.:		Stadiums/Teams:	
Book Stores:		Video Rental:		Advertising Services:	Y	Radio:		Music Print./Dist.:		Gambling/Casinos:	
Distribution/Printing:		Video Distribution:		Info. Sys. Software:		Online Information:		Multimedia:		Rides/Theme Parks:	

TYPES OF BUSINESS:

Magazine Publishing
Photography Services
Media Buying
Newspaper Publishing
Magazine Advertising Services
Television Broadcasting & Production
Radio Broadcasting

BRANDS/DIVISIONS/AFFILIATES:

Lagardere SCA
Elle
Marie Claire
Car & Driver
Hachette Rusconi
Hachette Filipacchi Photos
Lagardere Images
Lagardere Global Advertising

CONTACTS: Note: Officers with more than one job title may be intentionally listed here more than once.

Jack Kliger, Pres./CEO-Hachette Filipacchi Media U.S., Inc.
Didier Quillot, Chmn.

Phone: 33-1-41-34-60-00	Fax: 33-1-41-34-77-77
Toll-Free:	
Address: 149-151 rue Anatole France, Levallois-Perret, 92300 France	

GROWTH PLANS/SPECIAL FEATURES:

Lagardere Active Media (LAM) was formed when former Lagardere SCA subsidiary, Hachette Filipacchi Medias (HFM), began merging with the Lagardere Active division. Lagardere, a French media and high-technology conglomerate, expects the merger will not be complete until 2010. The company is one of the world's leading magazine publishers, producing approximately 260 magazines and newspapers in 41 countries on five continents. It publishes 60 magazines in France alone. The combined circulation of its publications is over 1 billion, with more than 202 million from subscriptions. Its publications include fashion magazine Elle; Marie Claire; the Parisian local journal Paris Match; Car and Driver; Premiere; American Photo; Home; Flying; Popular Photography & Imaging; Premiere; Cycle World; and Woman's Day. It is focusing on international expansion, operating out of 16 international offices. Some of the firm's international ventures include: Hachette Filipacchi Media U.S., Inc., which is one of the largest magazine publishers in the U.S.; Hachette Filipacchi S.A., a leading magazine publisher in Spain; Hachette Rusconi, one of the top Italian magazine publishers; and Hachette Fujingaho, which is one of the leading publishers of high-end women's magazines in Japan. The firm's international operations also extend to China, Russia and the U.K. LAM's images division, Hachette Filipacchi Photos, has the dual purpose of improving the quality of the pictures reproduced in magazines and of developing the photographic activity essential to its print media core business. As part of the HFM/Active merger, Interdeco and Lagardere Active Publicite joined to form Lagardere Global Advertising, which is now one of France's leading advertising agencies. Also as result of the merger, Lagardere Images oversees all of the group's TV production activities. The group's audiovisual arm, Lagardere Active, owns radio stations such as Europe 1, Europe 2 and RFM; and TV channels such as Canal J, Filles TV, Gulli and Tiji.

FINANCIALS: Sales and profits are in thousands of dollars—add 000 to get the full amount. 2007 Note: Financial information for 2007 was not available for all companies at press time.

2007 Sales: $	2007 Profits: $	**U.S. Stock Ticker: Subsidiary**	
2006 Sales: $	2006 Profits: $	**Int'l Ticker:** Int'l Exchange:	
2005 Sales: $	2005 Profits: $	Employees:	
2004 Sales: $2,819,584	2004 Profits: $	Fiscal Year Ends: 12/31	
2003 Sales: $	2003 Profits: $	Parent Company: LAGARDERE SCA	

SALARIES/BENEFITS:

Pension Plan:	ESOP Stock Plan:	Profit Sharing:	Top Exec. Salary: $	Bonus: $
Savings Plan:	Stock Purch. Plan:		Second Exec. Salary: $	Bonus: $

OTHER THOUGHTS:

Apparent Women Officers or Directors:
Hot Spot for Advancement for Women/Minorities:

LOCATIONS: ("Y" = Yes)

West:	Southwest:	Midwest:	Southeast:	Northeast:	International:
				Y	Y

LAKES ENTERTAINMENT INC   www.lakesgaming.com

Industry Group Code: 713210 Ranks within this company's industry group: Sales: 8   Profits: 5

Print Media/Publishing:	Movies:		Equipment/Supplies:		Broadcast/Cable:	Music/Audio:	Sports/Games/Gambling:	
Newspapers:	Movie Theaters:		Equipment/Supplies:		Broadcast TV:	Music Production:	Games/Sports:	
Magazines:	Movie Production:		Gambling Equipment:	Y	Cable TV:	Retail Music:	Retail Games Stores:	
Books:	TV/Video Prod.:	Y	Special Services:		Satellite Broadcast:	Retail Audio Equip.:	Stadiums/Teams:	
Book Stores:	Video Rental:		Advertising Services:		Radio:	Music Print./Dist.:	Gambling/Casinos:	Y
Distribution/Printing:	Video Distribution:		Info. Sys. Software:		Online Information:	Multimedia:	Rides/Theme Parks:	

TYPES OF BUSINESS:
Casino Management
Televised Poker Events
Gaming Systems & Technology

BRANDS/DIVISIONS/AFFILIATES:
WPT Enterprises
World Poker Tour
WPT Studios
WPT Consumer Products
US Playing Card
FourWinds Casino
WPTonline.com

CONTACTS: *Note: Officers with more than one job title may be intentionally listed here more than once.*
Lyle Berman, CEO
Timothy J. Cope, Pres.
Timothy J. Cope, CFO
Diane Stone, VP-Human Resources
Scott Just, VP-Gaming
Lyle Berman, Chmn.

Phone: 612-449-9092	**Fax:** 612-449-9353
Toll-Free: 800-946-9464	
Address: 130 Cheshire Ln., Ste. 101, Minnetonka, MN 55305 US	

GROWTH PLANS/SPECIAL FEATURES:
Lakes Entertainment, Inc. is a casino development and management company that focuses on Native American-owned properties with a potential for long term development of related entertainment facilities. The company has development and management contracts with five different tribes: the Miwok Indians, the Pokagon Band of Potawatomi Indians, the Jamul Indian Village, the Pawnee Nation and the Iowa Tribe of Oklahoma. The contracts include one new casino in Michigan, two in California and three new and two existing casinos in Oklahoma. The firm also has a division dedicated to buying, patenting and licensing the rights for new table game concepts to market and distribute to casinos. The division has developed such games as: World Poker Tour; All-In Hold'Em; Rainbow Poker; Pyramid Poker; and Bonus Craps. The firm owns approximately 62% of WPT Enterprises (WPTE), a separate, publicly held media and entertainment company engaged in the development; production and marketing of gaming themed televised programming. WPTE operates through four entities: WPT Studios (generates 76% of WPTE's total revenues); WPT Consumer Products; WPT Corporate Alliance; and WPT online gaming. WPTE is the creator of the World Poker Tour television show, which is based on a series of high-stakes poker tournaments, and airs on the Travel Channel in the U.S. and nearly 140 global markets. The firm's online gaming aspect generates revenue through an agreement with WagerWorks, Inc. Per the agreement, WPT online.com features an online casino with slot machines, table games, and an online poker room. In August 2007, the Four Winds Casino Resort in New Buffalo, Michigan, which is under a five-year management contract with Lakes Entertainment, opened to the public.

FINANCIALS: Sales and profits are in thousands of dollars—add 000 to get the full amount. 2007 Note: Financial information for 2007 was not available for all companies at press time.

2007 Sales: $	2007 Profits: $	**U.S. Stock Ticker: LACO**
2006 Sales: $81,600	2006 Profits: $19,800	**Int'l Ticker:** Int'l Exchange:
2005 Sales: $18,222	2005 Profits: $-11,870	Employees: 123
2004 Sales: $17,557	2004 Profits: $-4,041	Fiscal Year Ends: 12/31
2003 Sales: $4,268	2003 Profits: $-1,769	Parent Company:

SALARIES/BENEFITS:

Pension Plan:	ESOP Stock Plan:	Profit Sharing:	Top Exec. Salary: $507,200	Bonus: $200,000
Savings Plan: Y	Stock Purch. Plan: Y		Second Exec. Salary: $357,200	Bonus: $140,000

OTHER THOUGHTS:
Apparent Women Officers or Directors: 1
Hot Spot for Advancement for Women/Minorities:

LOCATIONS: ("Y" = Yes)

West:	Southwest:	Midwest:	Southeast:	Northeast:	International:
Y	Y	Y	Y		

Note: Financial information, benefits and other data can change quickly and may vary from those stated here.

LAMAR ADVERTISING CO

www.lamar.com

Industry Group Code: 541850 Ranks within this company's industry group: Sales: 2   Profits: 2

Print Media/Publishing:	Movies:	Equipment/Supplies:		Broadcast/Cable:	Music/Audio:	Sports/Games/Gambling:
Newspapers:	Movie Theaters:	Equipment/Supplies:		Broadcast TV:	Music Production:	Games/Sports:
Magazines:	Movie Production:	Gambling Equipment:		Cable TV:	Retail Music:	Retail Games Stores:
Books:	TV/Video Prod.:	Special Services:	Y	Satellite Broadcast:	Retail Audio Equip.:	Stadiums/Teams:
Book Stores:	Video Rental:	Advertising Services:	Y	Radio:	Music Print./Dist.:	Gambling/Casinos:
Distribution/Printing:	Video Distribution:	Info. Sys. Software:		Online Information:	Multimedia:	Rides/Theme Parks:

TYPES OF BUSINESS:

Billboards
Highway Logo Signs
Graphic Design Services
Transit Advertising

BRANDS/DIVISIONS/AFFILIATES:

Lamar Media Corp.
Obie Media Corp.

CONTACTS: *Note: Officers with more than one job title may be intentionally listed here more than once.*

Kevin P. Reilly, Jr., CEO
Sean Reilly, COO
Kevin P. Reilly, Jr., Pres.
Keith A. Istre, CFO
Thomas F. Teepell, Chief Mktg. Officer
Tammy Duncan, VP-Human Resources
James R. McIlwain, General Counsel
Robert B. Switzer, VP-Oper.
Keith A. Istre, Treas.
Sean Reilly, Pres., Outdoor Div.
Tom Sirmon, Regional Mgr.-Gulf Coast Region
Everett Stewart, Pres., Interstate Logos
John M. Miller, VP/Dir.-Nat'l Sales

Phone: 225-926-1000	Fax: 225-923-1005
Toll-Free: 1-800-235-2627	
Address: 5551 Corporate Blvd., Ste. 2-A, Baton Rouge, LA 70808 US	

GROWTH PLANS/SPECIAL FEATURES:

Lamar Advertising Co. is the holding company for Lamar Media Corporation, one of the largest and most experienced owners and operators of outdoor advertising structures in the U.S. The firm operates 150 outdoor advertising companies in more than 44 states and Puerto Rico. The company is one of the U.S. leaders in the highway logo sign business, with operations in 19 of the 25 states that have privatized their logo programs as well as in the province of Ontario, Canada. Logo signs are signs located near highway exits that display brand-name information on available gas, food, lodging and camping services. Operating more than 149,000 billboards and 97,500 logo sign displays, the company earns revenue by leasing display space and, through its graphics division, designing advertisements for its clients. Lamar also owns and operates approximately 300 digital billboard advertising displays in 34 states and Canada. The company also helps with the strategic placement of advertisements throughout an advertiser's market by using software that allows it to analyze the target audience and its demographics. This amounts to a fully integrated service for advertising customers, covering their billboard display requirements from ad copy production to placement and maintenance. Moreover, Lamar has over 70 transit advertising franchises that operate transit advertising displays on bus shelters, buses and bus benches in 18 states and Canada. Over the past decade, the firm has pursued an aggressive growth strategy through strategic acquisitions of outdoor advertising assets, including outdoor advertising businesses as well as isolated purchases of outdoor advertising displays. Local advertising accounted for 78% of the firm's net revenues in the last year. The company's recent efforts to increase its revenue and cash flow entail highly-targeted local marketing efforts to improve display occupancy rates and increasing advertising rates where and when demand can absorb rate increases.

FINANCIALS: Sales and profits are in thousands of dollars—add 000 to get the full amount. 2007 Note: Financial information for 2007 was not available for all companies at press time.

2007 Sales: $	2007 Profits: $	U.S. Stock Ticker: LAMR
2006 Sales: $1,120,091	2006 Profits: $43,899	Int'l Ticker: Int'l Exchange:
2005 Sales: $1,021,656	2005 Profits: $41,779	Employees: 3,300
2004 Sales: $883,510	2004 Profits: $13,155	Fiscal Year Ends: 12/31
2003 Sales: $810,139	2003 Profits: $-46,851	Parent Company:

SALARIES/BENEFITS:

Pension Plan: Y	ESOP Stock Plan:	Profit Sharing: Y	Top Exec. Salary: $700,000	Bonus: $700,000
Savings Plan: Y	Stock Purch. Plan: Y		Second Exec. Salary: $500,000	Bonus: $437,500

OTHER THOUGHTS:

Apparent Women Officers or Directors: 1
Hot Spot for Advancement for Women/Minorities:

LOCATIONS: ("Y" = Yes)

West:	Southwest:	Midwest:	Southeast:	Northeast:	International:
Y	Y	Y	Y	Y	Y

Note: Financial information, benefits and other data can change quickly and may vary from those stated here.

LANDMARK COMMUNICATIONS INC www.landmarkcom.com

Industry Group Code: 511110 Ranks within this company's industry group: Sales: 9   Profits:

Print Media/Publishing:	Movies:	Equipment/Supplies:	Broadcast/Cable:	Music/Audio:	Sports/Games/Gambling:
Newspapers: Y	Movie Theaters:	Equipment/Supplies:	Broadcast TV: Y	Music Production:	Games/Sports:
Magazines: Y	Movie Production:	Gambling Equipment:	Cable TV: Y	Retail Music:	Retail Games Stores:
Books:	TV/Video Prod.:	Special Services: Y	Satellite Broadcast:	Retail Audio Equip.:	Stadiums/Teams:
Book Stores:	Video Rental:	Advertising Services: Y	Radio:	Music Print./Dist.:	Gambling/Casinos:
Distribution/Printing:	Video Distribution:	Info. Sys. Software:	Online Information:	Multimedia:	Rides/Theme Parks:

TYPES OF BUSINESS:
Newspaper Publishing
Cable TV Programming
TV Broadcasting
Education Services
Tradeshows & Events
Database Marketing
Classified Magazines
Wireless Internet Services

BRANDS/DIVISIONS/AFFILIATES:
Weather Channel (The)
Weather.com
WSI Corporation
Virginia-Pilot (The)
News & Record
Roanoke Times (The)
Landmark Community Newspapers, Inc.
Capital Gazette Communications

CONTACTS:
Note: Officers with more than one job title may be intentionally listed here more than once.
Frank Batten, Jr., CEO
Decker Anstrom, COO
Decker Anstrom, Pres.
Teresa F. Blevins, CFO/Exec. VP
Charlie W. Hill, Exec. VP-Human Resources
Guy Friddell, III, Corp. Counsel/Exec. VP/Corp. Sec.
Richard F. Barry, III, Vice Chmn.
Colleen R. Pittman, VP-Tax, Audit & Analysis
Debora Wilson, Pres., The Weather Channel Companies
Emily Neilson, Gen. Mgr./Pres., KLAS-TV
Frank Batten, Jr., Chmn.

Phone: 757-446-2000	Fax: 757-446-2983
Toll-Free: 800-446-2004	
Address: 150 W. Brambleton Ave., Norfolk, VA 23510 US	

GROWTH PLANS/SPECIAL FEATURES:
Landmark Communications, Inc. is a privately held media company with interests in newspapers, television broadcasting, cable TV programming and electronic publishing companies. The firm also has holdings in database marketing, career education and tradeshows. The company owns the Weather Channel networks, including The Weather Channel, Inc., Weather.com and WSI Corporation. Landmark's publishing segment publishes three metro newspapers in North Carolina and Virginia: The Virginia-Pilot, News & Record and The Roanoke Times. Through Landmark Community Newspapers, Inc., the firm also publishes nearly 100 paid and free newspapers, shoppers and special-interest publications. Capital Gazette Communications is Landmark's Maryland-based news operation, publishing six newspapers and one magazine with a combined circulation of over 150,000: The Capital, The Maryland Gazette, The Bowie Blade News, The Crofton News Crier, The West County Gazette, The South County Gazette and Waterfront Living Magazine. The firm's broadcasting segment owns KLAS TV, a high-definition Las Vegas, Nevada TV channel; and the channels NewsChannel 5 and NewsChannel 5+ in Nashville, Tennessee. Subsidiary Landmark Interactive offers interactive advertising and marketing services to consumers, businesses and marketers through three divisions. The online marketing services division assists publishers and advertisers in attracting customers through such services as lead generation, ad targeting, geo-location, predictive modeling and email marketing. The technology services division provides online security services including online fraud prevention and website monitoring. Landmark Interactive's companies also provide a number of consumer marketplaces for entrepreneurs interested in franchises and business opportunities. Landmark's data and telecommunications services segment consists of Continental Broadband, which provides Internet access to business customers using fixed wireless technology. Landmark also owns Dominion Enterprises, a media and information services company serving employment, real estate, automotive, recreation and industrial markets.

Landmark offers its employees health and dependent care flexible spending accounts; a 401(k) plan; and medical, dental, vision and life insurance.

FINANCIALS: Sales and profits are in thousands of dollars—add 000 to get the full amount. 2007 Note: Financial information for 2007 was not available for all companies at press time.

2007 Sales: $	2007 Profits: $	U.S. Stock Ticker: Private
2006 Sales: $1,750,000	2006 Profits: $	Int'l Ticker: Int'l Exchange:
2005 Sales: $1,719,000	2005 Profits: $	Employees: 12,000
2004 Sales: $	2004 Profits: $	Fiscal Year Ends: 12/31
2003 Sales: $743,000	2003 Profits: $	Parent Company:

SALARIES/BENEFITS:
Pension Plan:	ESOP Stock Plan:	Profit Sharing:	Top Exec. Salary: $	Bonus: $
Savings Plan: Y	Stock Purch. Plan:		Second Exec. Salary: $	Bonus: $

OTHER THOUGHTS:
Apparent Women Officers or Directors: 7
Hot Spot for Advancement for Women/Minorities: Y

LOCATIONS: ("Y" = Yes)
West:	Southwest:	Midwest:	Southeast:	Northeast:	International:
Y	Y	Y	Y	Y	Y

Note: Financial information, benefits and other data can change quickly and may vary from those stated here.

LANDRY'S RESTAURANTS INC www.landrysrestaurants.com

Industry Group Code: 722110 Ranks within this company's industry group: Sales: 1 Profits: 1

Print Media/Publishing:	Movies:	Equipment/Supplies:	Broadcast/Cable:	Music/Audio:	Sports/Games/Gambling:	
Newspapers:	Movie Theaters:	Equipment/Supplies:	Broadcast TV:	Music Production:	Games/Sports:	
Magazines:	Movie Production:	Gambling Equipment:	Cable TV:	Retail Music:	Retail Games Stores:	
Books:	TV/Video Prod.:	Special Services:	Satellite Broadcast:	Retail Audio Equip.:	Stadiums/Teams:	
Book Stores:	Video Rental:	Advertising Services:	Radio:	Music Print./Dist.:	Gambling/Casinos:	Y
Distribution/Printing:	Video Distribution:	Info. Sys. Software:	Online Information:	Multimedia:	Rides/Theme Parks:	

TYPES OF BUSINESS:

Casual Dining Restaurants
Hotel & Casino Resorts

BRANDS/DIVISIONS/AFFILIATES:

Crab House (The)
Landry's Seafood House
Rainforest Cafe
Chart House (The)
Saltgrass Steak House
Golden Nugget Hotels & Casinos
T-Rex Café
Yak & Yeti

CONTACTS: *Note: Officers with more than one job title may be intentionally listed here more than once.*

Tilman J. Fertitta, CEO
Tilman J. Fertitta, Pres.
Richard H. Liem, CFO/Exec. VP
Steven L. Scheinthal, Exec. VP-Admin.
Steven L. Scheinthal, General Counsel/Corp. Sec.
Jeffrey L. Cantwell, Sr. VP- Dev.
K. Kelly Roberts, Chief Admin. Officer-Hospitality & Gaming Division
Richard E. Ervin, Exec. VP-Restaurant Oper.
Tilman J. Fertitta, Chmn.

Phone: 713-850-1010	Fax: 713-850-7205
Toll-Free: 800-552-6379	
Address: 1510 W. Loop S., Houston, TX 77027 US	

GROWTH PLANS/SPECIAL FEATURES:

Landry's Restaurants, Inc. is a restaurant, hospitality and entertainment company principally engaged in the ownership and operation of casual dining restaurants, primarily under the names of Rainforest Café, Saltgrass Steak House, Landry's Seafood House, The Crab House, Charley's Crab and The Chart House. The firm owns and operates over 179 full-service and certain limited-service restaurants in 29 states. Landry's Restaurants also owns and operates select hospitality businesses including hotel and casino resorts, such as the Golden Nugget Hotels and Casinos in downtown Las Vegas and Laughlin, Nevada. The firm operates its restaurants through three divisions: the Landry's Division, its seafood and signature restaurants; Rainforest Café, the rainforest-themed casual dining restaurants; and Saltgrass Steak House, the Texas-Western themed casual dining restaurants. The Landry's division is comprised of Landry's Seafood House, The Crab House, Chart House, C.A. Muer, Grotto, Pesce, Vic & Anthony's Steakhouse, Willie G's Seafood and Steak House, La Griglia and Brenner's Steakhouse. The Rainforest Café restaurants provide casual dining in a rainforest-themed environment, complete with thunderstorms, waterfalls and active wildlife. Each Café consists of a restaurant and a retail village. In 2006, retail sales and alcoholic beverage sales accounted for about 22% of the division's restaurant revenue. The Saltgrass Steak House offer casual dining in a Texas-Western theme. Prototype buildings welcome guests into a stone and wood beam ranch house complete with a fireplace and a saloon-style bar. In 2006, alcoholic beverages generated 12% of the segment's revenue. Landry's Restaurants also has a specialty growth division, which includes the Downtown Aquarium in Houston that features a restaurant; and Kemah Boardwalk in Texas, an amusement, entertainment and retail complex. In February 2006, the company acquired 80% of T-Rex Café, Inc. from Schussler Creative, Inc. and a majority in Yak&Yeti, an Asian-themed eatery.

FINANCIALS: Sales and profits are in thousands of dollars—add 000 to get the full amount. 2007 Note: Financial information for 2007 was not available for all companies at press time.

2007 Sales: $	2007 Profits: $	U.S. Stock Ticker: LNY
2006 Sales: $1,134,301	2006 Profits: $-21,770	Int'l Ticker: Int'l Exchange:
2005 Sales: $897,460	2005 Profits: $44,815	Employees: 20,055
2004 Sales: $804,903	2004 Profits: $66,522	Fiscal Year Ends: 12/31
2003 Sales: $1,105,755	2003 Profits: $44,914	Parent Company:

SALARIES/BENEFITS:

Pension Plan:	ESOP Stock Plan:	Profit Sharing:	Top Exec. Salary: $1,450,000	Bonus: $1,585,000
Savings Plan:	Stock Purch. Plan:		Second Exec. Salary: $350,000	Bonus: $385,000

OTHER THOUGHTS:

Apparent Women Officers or Directors:
Hot Spot for Advancement for Women/Minorities:

LOCATIONS: ("Y" = Yes)

West:	Southwest:	Midwest:	Southeast:	Northeast:	International:
Y	Y	Y	Y	Y	

LAS VEGAS SANDS CORP (THE VENETIAN)
www.lasvegassands.com
Industry Group Code: 721120 Ranks within this company's industry group: Sales: 3 Profits: 4

Print Media/Publishing:	Movies:	Equipment/Supplies:	Broadcast/Cable:	Music/Audio:	Sports/Games/Gambling:	
Newspapers:	Movie Theaters:	Equipment/Supplies:	Broadcast TV:	Music Production:	Games/Sports:	
Magazines:	Movie Production:	Gambling Equipment:	Cable TV:	Retail Music:	Retail Games Stores:	
Books:	TV/Video Prod.:	Special Services:	Satellite Broadcast:	Retail Audio Equip.:	Stadiums/Teams:	
Book Stores:	Video Rental:	Advertising Services:	Radio:	Music Print./Dist.:	Gambling/Casinos:	Y
Distribution/Printing:	Video Distribution:	Info. Sys. Software:	Online Information:	Multimedia:	Rides/Theme Parks:	

TYPES OF BUSINESS:
Hotel Casinos
Convention & Conference Centers
Shopping Center Development
Casino Property Development

BRANDS/DIVISIONS/AFFILIATES:
Venetian Resort Hotel Casino (The)
Sands Expo (The)
Palazzo Resort Hotel Casino (The)
Sands Macao Casino (The)
Venetian Macao Resort Hotel Casino (The)
Cotai Strip

CONTACTS: *Note: Officers with more than one job title may be intentionally listed here more than once.*
Sheldon G. Adelson, CEO
William P. Weidner, COO
William P. Weidner, Pres.
Robert P. Rozek, CFO/Chief Acct. Officer
Michael C. Schindler, Corp. VP-Dev. & Asset Mgmt.
Scott A. Henry, Sr. VP-Finance
Robert G. Goldstein, Sr. VP
Bradley H. Stone, Exec. VP
Sheldon G. Adelson, Chmn.
Mark A. Brown, Pres., Sands Macao

Phone: 702-414-1000	Fax: 702-414-4884
Toll-Free:	
Address: 3355 S. Las Vegas Blvd. S., Rm. 1A, Las Vegas, NV 89109 US	

GROWTH PLANS/SPECIAL FEATURES:
Las Vegas Sands, Corp. (LVSI) is a leading international developer of hotels, resorts and casinos. LVSI owns and operates The Venetian Resort Hotel Casino; The Sands Expo and Convention Center in Las Vegas, Nevada; and The Sands Macao Casino in Macao, China. The Venetian, one of the world's largest and most luxurious casino resorts, is a Renaissance Venice-themed resort on the Las Vegas Strip. The Venetian is the Strip's first and only all-suites hotel, with over 4,000 suites in addition to its gaming facility, spa services, wedding packages and entertainment packages (including shows and musical events). The Venetian also maintains 17 restaurants, two of which feature food personalities Wolfgang Puck and Thomas Keller. The Venetian is connected to The Sands Expo Center, a 1.15 million square foot convention and trade show facility. The Palazzo Casino Resort, scheduled to open adjacent to the Venetian in 2007, will feature a 50-floor tower with 3,025 suites. The Palazzo will also have six villas, up to 11,000 square feet each, which will have 3-4 bedrooms, media rooms, private pools, private salons, massage areas, heated spas and personal gyms. Also in 2007, the firm plans to open the Venetian Macao, a hotel, resort and convention complex that will feature 3,000 suites, 30 restaurants, 350 retail shops and a 15,000 seat event center. In August 2006, the company began construction on an integrated resort in Singapore, a project worth an estimated $3.6 billion. In December 2006, the firm received a state gaming license in Pennsylvania, which will allow the company to begin construction for a shopping, dining and entertainment complex in Bethlehem, Pennsylvania in the coming months. The firm is currently finishing the last two sites (not including the Venetian) that are part of the first phase of construction of the Cotai Strip in Macao.

FINANCIALS: Sales and profits are in thousands of dollars—add 000 to get the full amount. 2007 Note: Financial information for 2007 was not available for all companies at press time.

2007 Sales: $	2007 Profits: $	U.S. Stock Ticker: LVS
2006 Sales: $2,340,178	2006 Profits: $442,003	Int'l Ticker: Int'l Exchange:
2005 Sales: $1,824,225	2005 Profits: $283,686	Employees: 15,280
2004 Sales: $1,258,570	2004 Profits: $495,183	Fiscal Year Ends: 12/31
2003 Sales: $641,500	2003 Profits: $37,400	Parent Company:

SALARIES/BENEFITS:
Pension Plan:	ESOP Stock Plan:	Profit Sharing:	Top Exec. Salary: $1,009,615	Bonus: $2,576,697
Savings Plan: Y	Stock Purch. Plan:		Second Exec. Salary: $1,004,564	Bonus: $1,987,316

OTHER THOUGHTS:
Apparent Women Officers or Directors:
Hot Spot for Advancement for Women/Minorities:

LOCATIONS: ("Y" = Yes)
West:	Southwest:	Midwest:	Southeast:	Northeast:	International:
Y				Y	Y

Note: Financial information, benefits and other data can change quickly and may vary from those stated here.

LASERPACIFIC MEDIA CORP　　　www.laserpacific.com

Industry Group Code: 512191　Ranks within this company's industry group: Sales:　Profits:

Print Media/Publishing:	Movies:	Equipment/Supplies:		Broadcast/Cable:	Music/Audio:	Sports/Games/Gambling:
Newspapers:	Movie Theaters:	Equipment/Supplies:		Broadcast TV:	Music Production:	Games/Sports:
Magazines:	Movie Production:	Gambling Equipment:		Cable TV:	Retail Music:	Retail Games Stores:
Books:	TV/Video Prod.:	Special Services:	Y	Satellite Broadcast:	Retail Audio Equip.:	Stadiums/Teams:
Book Stores:	Video Rental:	Advertising Services:		Radio:	Music Print./Dist.:	Gambling/Casinos:
Distribution/Printing:	Video Distribution:	Info. Sys. Software:		Online Information:	Multimedia:	Rides/Theme Parks:

TYPES OF BUSINESS:

Post-Production Services-Film & Television
DVD Technology
Audio Processing Services

BRANDS/DIVISIONS/AFFILIATES:

Eastman Kodak Co
High Definition Laboratory
Electronic Laboratory
inDI

CONTACTS: *Note: Officers with more than one job title may be intentionally listed here more than once.*

Brian Burr, CEO
Leon D. Silverman, Pres.
Randolph D. Blim, CTO
Bill Roberts, Sr. VP-Finance

Phone: 323-462-6266	Fax: 323-464-3233
Toll-Free:	
Address: 809 N. Cahuenga Blvd., Hollywood, CA 90038 US	

GROWTH PLANS/SPECIAL FEATURES:

LaserPacific Media Corp., a subsidiary of Eastman Kodak Co., specializes in post-production services for films and television programs. The company offers services that include 16 and 35 mm film processing, digital intermediates (DI), telecine transfer, color timing, insertion of digital graphics and visual effects, sound editing and mixing, digital compression service and duplication. LaserPacific encoded the first DVD ROM title, designed the first animated menus seen on a DVD for a feature film and pioneered the use of dual layer technology. Through the development of the Electronic Laboratory, the company was a leading force in the television industry's transition from analog, film-based methods to new electronic and digital post-production techniques. It has worked on a variety of television shows, including Everwood, Touched By An Angel, Diagnosis Murder, Judging Amy and The Simpsons. LaserPacific has won six Emmy Awards for outstanding achievement in television engineering development. With the opening of its High Definition Laboratory in 1998, LaserPacific became a leader in the delivery of digital high-definition sound services and currently has 24-frame progressive high-definition capabilities. Moreover, the company opened Hollywood's first Motion Picture Experts Group (MPEG) compression facility, which created some of the first DVDs. The firm offers a complete range of audio services. These include sound editing, two mixing stages, and foley and automated dialogue replacement (ADR) recording rooms. LaserPacific also offers DI for independent filmmakers through inDI, a cost effective method that transfers dailies to high definition allowing filmmakers on a tight budget to circumvent a second scanning of the film after shooting has been completed. The inDI workflow yields results that are similar to a 2K DI scan.

FINANCIALS: Sales and profits are in thousands of dollars—add 000 to get the full amount. 2007 Note: Financial information for 2007 was not available for all companies at press time.

2007 Sales: $	2007 Profits: $	**U.S. Stock Ticker: Subsidiary**
2006 Sales: $	2006 Profits: $	**Int'l Ticker:**　Int'l Exchange:
2005 Sales: $	2005 Profits: $	Employees:　226
2004 Sales: $	2004 Profits: $	Fiscal Year Ends: 12/31
2003 Sales: $	2003 Profits: $	Parent Company: EASTMAN KODAK CO

SALARIES/BENEFITS:

Pension Plan:	ESOP Stock Plan:	Profit Sharing:	Top Exec. Salary: $350,000	Bonus: $30,000
Savings Plan:	Stock Purch. Plan:		Second Exec. Salary: $275,004	Bonus: $30,000

OTHER THOUGHTS:　　　　　　　　　　　　　LOCATIONS: ("Y" = Yes)

Apparent Women Officers or Directors:
Hot Spot for Advancement for Women/Minorities:

West:	Southwest:	Midwest:	Southeast:	Northeast:	International:
Y					

LEE ENTERPRISES INC

www.lee.net

Industry Group Code: 511110 Ranks within this company's industry group: Sales: 13   Profits: 9

Print Media/Publishing:		Movies:	Equipment/Supplies:		Broadcast/Cable:	Music/Audio:	Sports/Games/Gambling:
Newspapers:	Y	Movie Theaters:	Equipment/Supplies:		Broadcast TV:	Music Production:	Games/Sports:
Magazines:		Movie Production:	Gambling Equipment:		Cable TV:	Retail Music:	Retail Games Stores:
Books:		TV/Video Prod.:	Special Services:	Y	Satellite Broadcast:	Retail Audio Equip.:	Stadiums/Teams:
Book Stores:		Video Rental:	Advertising Services:	Y	Radio:	Music Print./Dist.:	Gambling/Casinos:
Distribution/Printing:		Video Distribution:	Info. Sys. Software:		Online Information:	Multimedia:	Rides/Theme Parks:

TYPES OF BUSINESS:

Newspaper Publishing
Specialty Publications
Advertising Services
Internet Publishing & Services
Commercial Printing

BRANDS/DIVISIONS/AFFILIATES:

Quad-Cities Group
William Street Press
TNI Partners
Pulitzer
Star Publishing Company
Citizen Star Publishing Company
Madison Newspapers
TownNews.com

CONTACTS: Note: Officers with more than one job title may be intentionally listed here more than once.

Mary E. Junck, CEO
Mary E. Junck, Pres.
Carl G. Schmidt, CFO/VP
Paul M. Farrell, VP-Mktg. & Sales
Vytenis P. Kuraitis, VP-Human Resources
Brian E. Kardell, CIO/VP-Prod.
Karen J. Guest, Chief Legal Officer/VP-Law
Gregory P. Schermer, VP-Interactive Media
Daniel K. Hayes, VP-Corp. Comm.
Carl G. Schmidt, Treas.
Joyce Dehli, VP-News
Greg R. Veon, VP-Publishing
Kevin D. Mowbray, VP-Publishing
Nancy L. Green, VP-Circulation
Mary E. Junck, Chmn.

Phone: 563-383-2100	Fax: 563-323-9608
Toll-Free: 800-468-9716	
Address: 201 N. Harrison St., Davenport, IA 52801 US	

GROWTH PLANS/SPECIAL FEATURES:

Lee Enterprises, Inc. publishes 55 daily newspapers in 23 states and nearly 300 weekly, classified and specialty publications, as well as associated online services. The company owns and operates its newspapers (with a combined circulation of 1.6 million daily and 1.9 million on Sunday) through eight publishing subsidiaries, including Madison Newspapers, Lincoln Group, Quad-Cities Group, Central Illinois Newspaper Group, River Valley Group, Missoula Group, Magic Valley Group and Mid-Valley News Group. Lee also offers commercial printing services through William Street Press; Hawkeye Printing and Trico Communications; Platen Press; Farcountry Press and Broadwater Printing; Journal Star Commercial Printing; Little Nickel Quik Print; Spokane Print and Mail; Triangle Press; and Wingra Printing. Approximately 77% of the firm's revenues come from retail, national, classified, niche publications and online advertising. Lee's Internet activities consist of web sites supporting its newspapers as well as its subsidiary, INN Partners, L.C (d.b.a TownNews.com), a provider of web infrastructure for more than 1,000 small daily and weekly newspapers and shoppers. The firm also owns a minority interest in PowerOne Media and CityXpress Corp., which provide integrated online classified solutions for the newspaper industry; integrated online editorial content; and transactional and promotional opportunities. Other holdings include online news sites ZWire and AdQuest. In November 2007, Lee Enterprises announced a strategic alliance with Zillow.com in which the publishing consortium will offer its classified real estate advertising customer base the opportunity to also post listings in Zillow.com's national platform. The firm also recently announced plans to acquire 10% interest in Kaango, LLC, the company that operates Kaango.com, an advanced online classified advertising site.

Lee Enterprises offers employees comprehensive health insurance, flexible healthcare spending accounts, vacation, time off, and company-paid short-term and long-term disability benefits. It also offers retirement account plans, tuition reimbursement, personal computer and gym membership discounts.

FINANCIALS: Sales and profits are in thousands of dollars—add 000 to get the full amount. 2007 Note: Financial information for 2007 was not available for all companies at press time.

2007 Sales: $1,127,661	2007 Profits: $80,999	U.S. Stock Ticker: LEE
2006 Sales: $1,128,648	2006 Profits: $70,832	Int'l Ticker: Int'l Exchange:
2005 Sales: $818,890	2005 Profits: $76,878	Employees: 9,250
2004 Sales: $643,277	2004 Profits: $86,071	Fiscal Year Ends: 9/30
2003 Sales: $656,741	2003 Profits: $78,041	Parent Company:

SALARIES/BENEFITS:

Pension Plan: Y	ESOP Stock Plan:	Profit Sharing:	Top Exec. Salary: $800,000	Bonus: $300,000
Savings Plan: Y	Stock Purch. Plan:		Second Exec. Salary: $450,000	Bonus: $70,000

OTHER THOUGHTS:

Apparent Women Officers or Directors: 4
Hot Spot for Advancement for Women/Minorities: Y

LOCATIONS: ("Y" = Yes)

West:	Southwest:	Midwest:	Southeast:	Northeast:	International:
Y	Y	Y	Y	Y	

LERNER PUBLISHING GROUP   www.lernerbooks.com

Industry Group Code: 511130 Ranks within this company's industry group: Sales: Profits:

Print Media/Publishing:		Movies:	Equipment/Supplies:	Broadcast/Cable:	Music/Audio:	Sports/Games/Gambling:
Newspapers:		Movie Theaters:	Equipment/Supplies:	Broadcast TV:	Music Production:	Games/Sports:
Magazines:		Movie Production:	Gambling Equipment:	Cable TV:	Retail Music:	Retail Games Stores:
Books:	Y	TV/Video Prod.:	Special Services:	Satellite Broadcast:	Retail Audio Equip.:	Stadiums/Teams:
Book Stores:		Video Rental:	Advertising Services:	Radio:	Music Print./Dist.:	Gambling/Casinos:
Distribution/Printing:		Video Distribution:	Info. Sys. Software:	Online Information:	Multimedia:	Rides/Theme Parks:

TYPES OF BUSINESS:

Book Publishing
Educational Books
Children's Books
Online Information

BRANDS/DIVISIONS/AFFILIATES:

Lerner Publications
Carolrhoda Books, Inc.
First Avenue Editions
ediciones Lerner
Millbrook Press
Twenty-First Century Books
Kar-Ben Publishing
Visual Geography Series Online

CONTACTS: *Note: Officers with more than one job title may be intentionally listed here more than once.*

Harry Lerner, CEO
Adam Lerner, Pres.
Margaret Wunderlich, CFO
Adam Lerner, Publisher

Phone: 612-332-3344	Fax: 800-332-1132
Toll-Free: 800-328-4929	
Address: 1251 Washington Ave. N, Minneapolis, MN 55401 US	

GROWTH PLANS/SPECIAL FEATURES:

Lerner Publishing Group is a publisher of both hardcover and paperback K-12 children's books for the retail, school and library markets. The company currently has more than 2,500 titles in print on a variety of subjects, most of which fall into the nonfiction category, including biographies, social studies, science, geography, sports, picture books, activity books and multicultural issues, as well as fiction. Books range from information-intensive school and library books to graphic, colorful general-interest titles. The firm publishes through eight divisions and imprints: Lerner Publications; Carolrhoda Books; First Avenue Editions; Millbrook Press; Twenty-First Century Books; ediciones Lerner; Kar-Ben Publishing; and LernerClassroom.com. The ediciones Lerner series offers Spanish language material. Lerner's new Kar-Ben Publishing group produces a library of Jewish children books. Lerner also publishes two free educational web sites: Visual Geography Series Online, which offers country-specific information, links and downloadable photos and maps at vgsbooks.com; and In America Books Online, which provides links and information on America's various immigrant populations at InAmericaBooks.com. In addition to libraries, schools and other educational organizations, the company's books are purchased by traditional book stores such as Barnes and Noble and Borders; educational stores such as the Discovery Store; and non-traditional channels such as direct sales, catalogs, book clubs and fairs and non-book retail stores, including museums, gift shops and toy stores. In 2007, the company announced its partnership with Global Turnkey Solutions (GTS), a publishing solutions provider. As a result of the new partnership, Lerner hopes to streamline its distribution center operations to more efficiently meet its fulfillment and distribution goals.

FINANCIALS: Sales and profits are in thousands of dollars—add 000 to get the full amount. 2007 Note: Financial information for 2007 was not available for all companies at press time.

2007 Sales: $	2007 Profits: $	**U.S. Stock Ticker: Private**
2006 Sales: $	2006 Profits: $	**Int'l Ticker:** Int'l Exchange:
2005 Sales: $	2005 Profits: $	Employees: 46
2004 Sales: $	2004 Profits: $	Fiscal Year Ends:
2003 Sales: $12,000	2003 Profits: $- 700	Parent Company:

SALARIES/BENEFITS:

Pension Plan:	ESOP Stock Plan:	Profit Sharing:	Top Exec. Salary: $153,000	Bonus: $30,000
Savings Plan:	Stock Purch. Plan:		Second Exec. Salary: $146,000	Bonus: $15,000

OTHER THOUGHTS:

Apparent Women Officers or Directors: 1
Hot Spot for Advancement for Women/Minorities:

LOCATIONS: ("Y" = Yes)

West:	Southwest:	Midwest:	Southeast:	Northeast:	International:
		Y			

LIBERTY GLOBAL INC

www.lgi.com

Industry Group Code: 513220 **Ranks within this company's industry group:** Sales: 8   Profits: 6

Print Media/Publishing:	Movies:	Equipment/Supplies:		Broadcast/Cable:		Music/Audio:	Sports/Games/Gambling:
Newspapers:	Movie Theaters:	Equipment/Supplies:		Broadcast TV:		Music Production:	Games/Sports:
Magazines:	Movie Production:	Gambling Equipment:	Y	Cable TV:	Y	Retail Music:	Retail Games Stores:
Books:	TV/Video Prod.:	Special Services:	Y	Satellite Broadcast:		Retail Audio Equip.:	Stadiums/Teams:
Book Stores:	Video Rental:	Advertising Services:		Radio:		Music Print./Dist.:	Gambling/Casinos:
Distribution/Printing:	Video Distribution:	Info. Sys. Software:		Online Information:		Multimedia:	Rides/Theme Parks:

TYPES OF BUSINESS:

Video, Voice & Broadband Internet Access Services
Telephony Services
Voice Over Internet Protocol
Mobile Telephony

BRANDS/DIVISIONS/AFFILIATES:

Austar United
Jupiter Telecommunications Co., Ltd.
VTR GlobalCom, S.A.
UPC Holding BV
Liberty Global Switzerland, Inc.
Chellomedia BV
INODE Telekommunikationsdienstleistungs GmbH

CONTACTS: Note: Officers with more than one job title may be intentionally listed here more than once.

Michael T. Fries, CEO
Michael T. Fries, Pres.
Charles H. R. Bracken, Co-CFO/Sr. VP/Principal Financial Officer
Amy M. Blair, Sr. VP-Global Human Resources
Balan Nair, CTO
Elizabeth M. Markowski, General Counsel/Sr. VP/Sec.
Shane O'Neill, Chief Strategy Officer/Sr. VP/Pres., Chellomedia
Frederick G Westerman III, Sr. VP-Corp. Comm.
Frederick G Westerman III, Sr. VP-Investor Rel.
Bernard C. Dvorak, Co-CFO/Sr. VP/Chief Acct. Officer
Mauricio Ramos, Pres., Liberty Global Latin America
W. Gene Musselman, Pres./COO-UPC Broadband
John C. Malone, Chmn.
Miranda Curtis, Pres., Liberty Global Japan

Phone: 303-220-6600	Fax: 303-220-6601
Toll-Free:	
Address: 12300 Liberty Blvd., Englewood, CO 80112 US	

GROWTH PLANS/SPECIAL FEATURES:

Liberty Global, Inc. (LGI) is an international broadband communications provider of video, voice and broadband Internet access services. In select markets, LGI also offers telephony services; voice over Internet protocol; and mobile telephony using third party network. The firm operates broadband operations companies in 17 countries, principally in Europe, Japan and Chile. Through indirect wholly-owned subsidiaries UPC Holding BV and Liberty Global Switzerland, Inc., LGI provides broadband communications services in ten European countries. Through its indirect controlling ownership interest in Jupiter Telecommunication Co., Ltd., LGI offers broadband communications services in Japan and through Austar United in Australia. Through 80% owned subsidiary VTR Global Com, S.A., the firm provides broadband communications services in Chile. LGI also has consolidated direct-to-home satellite operations in Australia; consolidated broadband communications operations in Puerto Rico, Brazil and Peru; non-controlling interests in broadband communications companies in Europe and Japan; consolidated interests in certain programming businesses in Europe and Argentina; and non-controlling interests in certain programming businesses in Europe, Japan, Australia and the Americas. The company's consolidated programming interests in Europe are held through indirect wholly-owned subsidiary Chellomedia BV, which also provides interactive digital services and owns or manages investments in various businesses in Europe. LGI has roughly 16 million customers and 23 million service subscribers including video, Internet, telephone and wireless. In January 2006, LGI sold UPC Norge AS, its Norwegian broadband communications operator, for roughly $536.7 million. In March 2006, subsidiary UPC Austria GmbH acquired INODE Telekommunikationsdienstleistungs GmbH for $111 million. In June 2006, the company sold NBC Nordic Broadband Services AB, its Swedish broadband communications operator, for $403.9 million. In July 2006, the firm sold UPC France SA, its French broadband communications provider, for $1.5 billion. In December 2006, LGI sold UPC Belgium NV/SA, its broadband communications systems operator in Belgium, for $243.3 million.

FINANCIALS: Sales and profits are in thousands of dollars—add 000 to get the full amount. 2007 Note: Financial information for 2007 was not available for all companies at press time.

2007 Sales: $	2007 Profits: $	**U.S. Stock Ticker: LBTYA**
2006 Sales: $6,487,500	2006 Profits: $706,200	**Int'l Ticker:** Int'l Exchange:
2005 Sales: $5,151,332	2005 Profits: $-80,097	Employees: 20,500
2004 Sales: $2,531,889	2004 Profits: $-21,481	Fiscal Year Ends: 12/31
2003 Sales: $108,390	2003 Profits: $20,889	Parent Company:

SALARIES/BENEFITS:

Pension Plan:	ESOP Stock Plan:	Profit Sharing:	Top Exec. Salary: $900,346	Bonus: $1,600,000
Savings Plan:	Stock Purch. Plan:		Second Exec. Salary: $649,271	Bonus: $1,000,000

OTHER THOUGHTS:

Apparent Women Officers or Directors: 3
Hot Spot for Advancement for Women/Minorities: Y

LOCATIONS: ("Y" = Yes)

West:	Southwest:	Midwest:	Southeast:	Northeast:	International:
Y					Y

Note: Financial information, benefits and other data can change quickly and may vary from those stated here.

LIBERTY MEDIA CORP   www.libertymedia.com

Industry Group Code: 512110 Ranks within this company's industry group: Sales: 1   Profits: 1

Print Media/Publishing:	Movies:		Equipment/Supplies:		Broadcast/Cable:		Music/Audio:		Sports/Games/Gambling:	
Newspapers:	Movie Theaters:		Equipment/Supplies:		Broadcast TV:		Music Production:		Games/Sports:	
Magazines:	Movie Production:		Gambling Equipment:		Cable TV:	Y	Retail Music:		Retail Games Stores:	
Books:	TV/Video Prod.:	Y	Special Services:	Y	Satellite Broadcast:		Retail Audio Equip.:		Stadiums/Teams:	Y
Book Stores:	Video Rental:		Advertising Services:		Radio:		Music Print./Dist.:		Gambling/Casinos:	
Distribution/Printing:	Video Distribution:	Y	Info. Sys. Software:		Online Information:		Multimedia:		Rides/Theme Parks:	

TYPES OF BUSINESS:

Television Shopping Network
Television Production
Video Distribution
Online Retail
Satellite Television

BRANDS/DIVISIONS/AFFILIATES:

QVC, Inc.
Starz Entertainment
Provide Commerce, Inc.
FUN Technologies, Inc.
TruePosition, Inc.
BuySeasons, Inc.
DirecTV
Leisure Arts, Inc.

CONTACTS: *Note: Officers with more than one job title may be intentionally listed here more than once.*

Gregory B. Maffei, CEO
Gregory B. Maffei, Pres.
Charles Y. Tanabe, General Counsel/Sec./Exec. VP
David J. A. Flowers, Treas./Sr. VP
Albert E. Rosenthaler, Sr. VP
Christopher W. Shean, Controller/Sr. VP
Meade Rudasill, COO-QVC, Inc.
Mike George, CEO/Pres., QVC, Inc.
John C. Malone, Chmn.

Phone: 720-875-5400	Fax: 720-875-7469
Toll-Free:	
Address: 12300 Liberty Blvd., Englewood, CO 80112 US	

GROWTH PLANS/SPECIAL FEATURES:

Liberty Media Corp. is a holding company that, through its ownership of interests in subsidiaries and other companies, is primarily engaged in the video and on-line commerce, media, communications and entertainment industries in the U.S., Europe and Asia. The company's more significant operating subsidiaries include QVC, Inc. and Starz Entertainment. QVC markets and sells a wide variety of consumer products in the U.S. and several foreign countries, primarily by means of televised shopping programs and via the Internet through its domestic and international websites. Starz Entertainment provides video programming distributed by cable operators, direct-to-home satellite providers, other distributors and via the Internet throughout the U.S. Other consolidated subsidiaries include Provide Commerce, Inc., FUN Technologies, Inc., TruePosition, Inc., Starz Media, LLC, and BuySeasons, Inc. Recent acquisitions include Provide Commerce, BuySeasons, Inc. The company recently completed a restructuring pursuant to which Liberty was organized as a holding company and entered into a stock purchase agreement to sell its controlling interest in OpenTV for approximately $113 million. In December 2006, the company sold its On Command subsidiary to LodgeNet Entertainment Corporation. In December 2006, Liberty Media Corp. completed a significant $11 billion asset swap with News Corp. Under the agreement, Liberty received News Corp.'s 38.5% stake in DirecTV, $550 million in cash and three regional sports networks. News Corp. received Liberty's $11.2 billion stake in News Corp. itself. This gives Liberty controlling interest in DirecTV. In May 2007, Liberty acquired Leisure Arts, Inc., a subsidiary of Time Warner, Inc. which holds the Atlanta Braves, for $960 million in cash plus other considerations. In August 2007, the firm made an investment in BORBA LLC, which sells nutraceutical skin care products, which has been successful retailing its products on QVC and elsewhere.

FINANCIALS: Sales and profits are in thousands of dollars—add 000 to get the full amount. 2007 Note: Financial information for 2007 was not available for all companies at press time.

2007 Sales: $	2007 Profits: $	**U.S. Stock Ticker:** LINTA	
2006 Sales: $8,613,000	2006 Profits: $1,021,000	**Int'l Ticker:**	**Int'l Exchange:**
2005 Sales: $7,646,000	2005 Profits: $944,000	Employees: 14,705	
2004 Sales: $7,682,000	2004 Profits: $46,000	Fiscal Year Ends: 12/31	
2003 Sales: $4,028,000	2003 Profits: $-1,222,000	Parent Company:	

SALARIES/BENEFITS:

Pension Plan:	ESOP Stock Plan:	Profit Sharing:	Top Exec. Salary: $1,000,000	Bonus: $1,625,000
Savings Plan: Y	Stock Purch. Plan:		Second Exec. Salary: $715,000	Bonus: $200,000

OTHER THOUGHTS:

Apparent Women Officers or Directors:
Hot Spot for Advancement for Women/Minorities:

LOCATIONS: ("Y" = Yes)

West:	Southwest:	Midwest:	Southeast:	Northeast:	International:
Y	Y	Y	Y	Y	Y

LIFE TIME FITNESS INC   www.lifetimefitness.com

Industry Group Code: 713940 Ranks within this company's industry group: Sales: 2 Profits: 1

Print Media/Publishing:	Movies:	Equipment/Supplies:	Broadcast/Cable:	Music/Audio:	Sports/Games/Gambling:	
Newspapers:	Movie Theaters:	Equipment/Supplies:	Broadcast TV:	Music Production:	Games/Sports:	Y
Magazines:	Movie Production:	Gambling Equipment:	Cable TV:	Retail Music:	Retail Games Stores:	
Books:	TV/Video Prod.:	Special Services:	Satellite Broadcast:	Retail Audio Equip.:	Stadiums/Teams:	
Book Stores:	Video Rental:	Advertising Services:	Radio:	Music Print./Dist.:	Gambling/Casinos:	
Distribution/Printing:	Video Distribution:	Info. Sys. Software:	Online Information:	Multimedia:	Rides/Theme Parks:	

TYPES OF BUSINESS:
Fitness Center
Cardiovascular Equipment
Free Weights
Individual Training
Fitness Classes
Magazine
Nutrition

BRANDS/DIVISIONS/AFFILIATES:
Life Time Fitness Triathlon
Experience Life Magazine
Ask The E-trainer

CONTACTS: *Note: Officers with more than one job title may be intentionally listed here more than once.*
Bahram Akradi, CEO
Michael J. Gerend, COO/Exec. VP
Bahram Akradi, Pres.
Michael R. Robinson, CFO/Exec. VP
Eric J. Buss, General Counsel/Sec./Exec. VP
Mark L. Zaebst, Exec. VP-Real Estate Dev.

Phone: 952-947-0000	Fax: 952-947-9137
Toll-Free:	
Address: 6442 City W. Pkwy., Eden Prairie, MN 55344 US	

GROWTH PLANS/SPECIAL FEATURES:
Life Time Fitness Center, headquartered in Eden Prairie, Minnesota, operates 61 fitness centers in 13 states throughout the U.S. Each fitness center contains hundreds of cardiovascular equipment and weight machines as well as fitness classes, rock climbing caverns, free lockers and 24-hour access. Additionally, the firm offers indoor and outdoor swimming pools; basketball and racquetball courts; personal training; group fitness programs; child care centers; cafes; and spas. In addition to offering regular and add-on package memberships, the firm also offers corporate memberships that can be customized according to company needs. Life Time Fitness Centers also publishes Experience Life, a magazine which offers health, fitness and quality-of-life topics. Many of these topics can be accessed on the firm's web site, which offers information concerning training, health tips, fitness facts and recipes. The firm's web site also features an Ask The E-trainer forum, allowing customers to post questions and receive answers from qualified professionals concerning fitness and medical issues. Life Time's online store offers apparel, nutrition bars, shakes, sports drinks, vitamins and weight management products. In 2006, the firm launched the Life Time Fitness Triathlon, held annually in Minneapolis. In 2007, Life Time opened a new fitness center in Dublin, Ohio.

FINANCIALS: Sales and profits are in thousands of dollars—add 000 to get the full amount. 2007 Note: Financial information for 2007 was not available for all companies at press time.

2007 Sales: $	2007 Profits: $	U.S. Stock Ticker: LTM
2006 Sales: $511,897	2006 Profits: $50,565	Int'l Ticker: Int'l Exchange:
2005 Sales: $390,116	2005 Profits: $41,213	Employees: 250
2004 Sales: $312,033	2004 Profits: $25,338	Fiscal Year Ends: 12/31
2003 Sales: $	2003 Profits: $	Parent Company:

SALARIES/BENEFITS:

Pension Plan:	ESOP Stock Plan:	Profit Sharing:	Top Exec. Salary: $	Bonus: $
Savings Plan:	Stock Purch. Plan:		Second Exec. Salary: $	Bonus: $

OTHER THOUGHTS:
Apparent Women Officers or Directors:
Hot Spot for Advancement for Women/Minorities:

LOCATIONS: ("Y" = Yes)

West:	Southwest:	Midwest:	Southeast:	Northeast:	International:
Y	Y	Y	Y	Y	

Note: Financial information, benefits and other data can change quickly and may vary from those stated here.

LIN TV CORP

www.lintv.com

Industry Group Code: 513120 Ranks within this company's industry group: Sales: 12   Profits: 19

Print Media/Publishing:	Movies:	Equipment/Supplies:	Broadcast/Cable:		Music/Audio:	Sports/Games/Gambling:
Newspapers:	Movie Theaters:	Equipment/Supplies:	Broadcast TV:	Y	Music Production:	Games/Sports:
Magazines:	Movie Production:	Gambling Equipment:	Cable TV:		Retail Music:	Retail Games Stores:
Books:	TV/Video Prod.:	Special Services:	Satellite Broadcast:		Retail Audio Equip.:	Stadiums/Teams:
Book Stores:	Video Rental:	Advertising Services:	Radio:		Music Print./Dist.:	Gambling/Casinos:
Distribution/Printing:	Video Distribution:	Info. Sys. Software:	Online Information:		Multimedia:	Rides/Theme Parks:

TYPES OF BUSINESS:
Television Broadcasting

BRANDS/DIVISIONS/AFFILIATES:
Banks Broadcasting, Inc.

CONTACTS: Note: Officers with more than one job title may be intentionally listed here more than once.
Vincent L. Sadusky, CEO
Vincent L. Sadusky, Pres./Treas.
Bart Catalane, CFO/Sr. VP
Edward L. Munson, Jr., VP-Station Sales
Dan Donohue, VP-Human Resources
Larry Oaks, VP-Tech.
Denise Parent, General Counsel/VP/Sec.
Robb Richter, VP-Internet
Courtney Guertin, PR Specialist
William A. Cunningham, VP/Controller
Scott Blumenthal, Exec. VP-Television
Gregory M. Schmidt, Exec. VP-Digital Media
Douglas McCormick, Chmn.
Rebecca Duke, VP-Dist.

Phone: 401-454-2880	Fax: 401-454-6990
Toll-Free:	
Address: 4 Richmond Sq., Ste. 230E, Providence, RI 02906 US	

GROWTH PLANS/SPECIAL FEATURES:

LIN TV Corp. owns and operates a network of approximately 29 television stations, primarily in the midwestern and northeastern regions of the U.S. These include two under local marketing agreements, three low-power networks, many low-power broadcast television stations and five other television stations. LIN's stations cover approximately 9% of U.S. television households. The company generally has more than one station in the markets where it operates, and this multi-channel strategy increases its share of the TV audience. The firm operates the number-one or number-two news stations in 72% of its markets. Local advertisers account for approximately 56% of the company's revenue. All of the company's stations are affiliated with one of the national broadcasting networks: NBC, ABC, CBS, FOX, CW, Telefutura or Univision. The company has a number of proprietary interests in other television stations. The largest of these include its 33.3% interest in WAND (TV) Partnership with Block Communications, Inc., which owns and operates WAND-TV in Illinois. LIN also has a 50% interest in Banks Broadcasting, Inc., which owns and operates CW affiliates KWCV-TV in Kansas and KNIN-TV in Idaho. Early in 2007 the firm announced the acquisition of KASA, the FOX affiliate in Albuquerque, New Mexico, from Raycom Media for $55 million. A month later, the company completed negations with InterMedia Partners a second time in the sale of its Puerto Rico operations to InterMedia for $130 million. Also in 2007, the LIN partnered with VMIX to broadcast user-generated videos and audio, among other media-related content, on LIN's station sites. The firm recently completed the sale its one-third interest in WAND(TV) for $6.75 million. In November 2007, the company launched LIN TV Channels on YouTube.

LIN offers a scholarship program for minorities interested in journalism and broadcasting.

FINANCIALS: Sales and profits are in thousands of dollars—add 000 to get the full amount. 2007 Note: Financial information for 2007 was not available for all companies at press time.

2007 Sales: $	2007 Profits: $	**U.S. Stock Ticker: TVL**
2006 Sales: $426,100	2006 Profits: $-234,500	**Int'l Ticker:** Int'l Exchange:
2005 Sales: $321,149	2005 Profits: $-26,141	Employees: 2,119
2004 Sales: $315,242	2004 Profits: $93,038	Fiscal Year Ends: 12/31
2003 Sales: $349,500	2003 Profits: $-90,400	Parent Company:

SALARIES/BENEFITS:

Pension Plan: Y	ESOP Stock Plan:	Profit Sharing:	Top Exec. Salary: $512,462	Bonus: $837,500
Savings Plan: Y	Stock Purch. Plan:		Second Exec. Salary: $492,308	Bonus: $

OTHER THOUGHTS:
Apparent Women Officers or Directors: 2
Hot Spot for Advancement for Women/Minorities:

LOCATIONS: ("Y" = Yes)

West:	Southwest:	Midwest:	Southeast:	Northeast:	International:
Y	Y	Y	Y	Y	

Note: Financial information, benefits and other data can change quickly and may vary from those stated here.

LIONS GATE ENTERTAINMENT CORP   www.lionsgate.com

Industry Group Code: 512110 Ranks within this company's industry group: Sales: 4   Profits: 5

Print Media/Publishing:	Movies:		Equipment/Supplies:		Broadcast/Cable:		Music/Audio:	Sports/Games/Gambling:
Newspapers:	Movie Theaters:		Equipment/Supplies:		Broadcast TV:	Y	Music Production:	Games/Sports:
Magazines:	Movie Production:	Y	Gambling Equipment:		Cable TV:	Y	Retail Music:	Retail Games Stores:
Books:	TV/Video Prod.:	Y	Special Services:	Y	Satellite Broadcast:		Retail Audio Equip.:	Stadiums/Teams:
Book Stores:	Video Rental:		Advertising Services:		Radio:		Music Print./Dist.:	Gambling/Casinos:
Distribution/Printing:	Video Distribution:	Y	Info. Sys. Software:		Online Information:		Multimedia:	Rides/Theme Parks:

TYPES OF BUSINESS:

Film Production
TV Production & Distribution
Film Distribution
Video-on-Demand Services

BRANDS/DIVISIONS/AFFILIATES:

Lions Gate Films Corp.
Lions Gate Television
Lions Gate Entertainment, Inc.
CinemaNow, Inc.
Trimark
Maple Pictures Corp.
Image Entertainment, Inc.
Debmar-Mercury LLC

CONTACTS: Note: Officers with more than one job title may be intentionally listed here more than once.

Jon Feltheimer, CEO
Steven Beeks, Co-COO
Steven Beeks, Pres.
Jim Keegan, CFO
Wayne Levin, General Counsel
Wayne Levin, Exec. VP-Corp. Oper.
Michael Burns, Co-Chmn.
Joe Drake, CEO-Mandate Pic./Co-COO
Joe Drake, Pres., Lionsgate Motion Picture Group
Jon Feltheimer, Co-Chmn.

Phone: 310-449-9200	**Fax:** 310-255-3870
Toll-Free:	
Address: 2700 Colorado Ave., Santa Monica, CA 90404 US	

GROWTH PLANS/SPECIAL FEATURES:

Lions Gate Entertainment Corp. is an independent producer and distributor of motion pictures, television programming, home entertainment, video-on-demand and music content. The firm releases approximately 15-18 motion pictures. In the last three years, it has released an average of 77 hours of television programming per year. Lions Gate acquires individual properties, including films and television programs, libraries, and entertainment studios and companies, to enhance its competitive position and generate revenue. Lions Gate currently distributes its library of approximately 8,100 motion picture titles and approximately 3,800 television episodes and programs directly to retailers, video rental stores, and pay and free television channels in the U.S., the U.K. and Ireland, and indirectly to other international markets through third parties. Subsidiary Lions Gate Television (LGTV) produces movies-of-the-week, television series and miniseries for cable networks, such as The Dead Zone, Weeds, Wildfire, Dresden Files and made-for-TV movies. The company owns a minority interest in CinemaNow, Inc., a provider of video-on-demand services for feature films that holds distribution rights to more than 3,000 film titles, and a minority interest in Maple Pictures Corp., a Canadian film and television distributor. In 2006, Lions Gate purchased 18% of Image Entertainment, Inc., which is a home video and television distribution company specializing in digital distribution of television programs, public domain and copyrighted feature films, and music concerts. Also in 2006, the company acquired Debmar-Mercury LLC, a top television distributor; additionally, the company sold its studio facilities in North Vancouver, British Columbia to Bosa Development Corporation for $36.1 million. Movies released in 2007 include Sicko, Bratz, Good Luck, Chuck, War, 3:10 to Yuma, The Eye and Saw 4.

FINANCIALS: Sales and profits are in thousands of dollars—add 000 to get the full amount. 2007 Note: Financial information for 2007 was not available for all companies at press time.

2007 Sales: $	2007 Profits: $	**U.S. Stock Ticker: LGF**
2006 Sales: $951,228	2006 Profits: $6,096	**Int'l Ticker: LGF** Int'l Exchange: Toronto-TSX
2005 Sales: $842,586	2005 Profits: $20,336	Employees: 354
2004 Sales: $375,910	2004 Profits: $-95,157	Fiscal Year Ends: 3/31
2003 Sales: $301,800	2003 Profits: $1,100	Parent Company:

SALARIES/BENEFITS:

Pension Plan:	ESOP Stock Plan:	Profit Sharing:	Top Exec. Salary: $850,000	Bonus: $800,000
Savings Plan:	Stock Purch. Plan:		Second Exec. Salary: $645,833	Bonus: $650,000

OTHER THOUGHTS:

Apparent Women Officers or Directors:
Hot Spot for Advancement for Women/Minorities:

LOCATIONS: ("Y" = Yes)

West:	Southwest:	Midwest:	Southeast:	Northeast:	International:
Y				Y	Y

Note: Financial information, benefits and other data can change quickly and may vary from those stated here.

LIQUID DIGITAL MEDIA   liquidaudio.com

Industry Group Code: 451220E Ranks within this company's industry group: Sales: Profits:

Print Media/Publishing:	Movies:	Equipment/Supplies:		Broadcast/Cable:	Music/Audio:		Sports/Games/Gambling:
Newspapers:	Movie Theaters:	Equipment/Supplies:		Broadcast TV:	Music Production:		Games/Sports:
Magazines:	Movie Production:	Gambling Equipment:		Cable TV:	Retail Music:		Retail Games Stores:
Books:	TV/Video Prod.:	Special Services:	Y	Satellite Broadcast:	Retail Audio Equip.:		Stadiums/Teams:
Book Stores:	Video Rental:	Advertising Services:		Radio:	Music Print./Dist.:	Y	Gambling/Casinos:
Distribution/Printing:	Video Distribution:	Info. Sys. Software:		Online Information:	Multimedia:		Rides/Theme Parks:

TYPES OF BUSINESS:

Internet-Based Music Retailing
Online Media Distribution Services

BRANDS/DIVISIONS/AFFILIATES:

Liquid Audio
Anderson Media Corporation
Geneva Media LLC

CONTACTS: *Note: Officers with more than one job title may be intentionally listed here more than once.*

Pat Scandalis, VP-Tech.

Phone: 650-549-2000	Fax: 650-549-2001
Toll-Free:	
Address: 999 Main St., Redwood City, CA 94063 US	

GROWTH PLANS/SPECIAL FEATURES:

Liquid Digital Media, formerly Liquid Audio, is an online digital music business that changed its name in late 2003 after being acquired by wholesaler Anderson Media Corporation through its subsidiary Geneva Media LLC. Liquid Digital offers a catalogue of over 2.5 million digital music tracks from all major labels, as well as from numerous independents. Liquid Digital's representatives are trained to custom-design music media solutions for clients interested in distributing music online. These services include video and audio encoding; Digital Rights Management (DRM) secure packaging; metadata management; image processing and conversion; content hosting; distribution and fulfillment; and marketing support and reporting. Clients can feature music through real-time streams, free downloads and time-limited downloads. Liquid Digital offers merchant services including catalog distribution, download management, windows media DRM licensing, customer service, technical support, fulfillment API, reporting/reconciliation, physical/digital tie-ins, front end design and development, merchandising, and application and tool development. Liquid Digital was the first company to offer secure music online.

FINANCIALS: Sales and profits are in thousands of dollars—add 000 to get the full amount. 2007 Note: Financial information for 2007 was not available for all companies at press time.

2007 Sales: $	2007 Profits: $	U.S. Stock Ticker: Subsidiary
2006 Sales: $	2006 Profits: $	Int'l Ticker: Int'l Exchange:
2005 Sales: $	2005 Profits: $	Employees:
2004 Sales: $	2004 Profits: $	Fiscal Year Ends: 12/31
2003 Sales: $	2003 Profits: $	Parent Company: ANDERSON MEDIA CORPORATION

SALARIES/BENEFITS:

Pension Plan:	ESOP Stock Plan:	Profit Sharing:	Top Exec. Salary: $310,198	Bonus: $
Savings Plan:	Stock Purch. Plan:		Second Exec. Salary: $235,220	Bonus: $

OTHER THOUGHTS:

Apparent Women Officers or Directors:
Hot Spot for Advancement for Women/Minorities:

LOCATIONS: ("Y" = Yes)

West:	Southwest:	Midwest:	Southeast:	Northeast:	International:
Y					

LIVE NATION INC

www.livenation.com

Industry Group Code: 711310 Ranks within this company's industry group: Sales: 1 Profits: 1

Print Media/Publishing:	Movies:	Equipment/Supplies:		Broadcast/Cable:	Music/Audio:		Sports/Games/Gambling:	
Newspapers:	Movie Theaters:	Equipment/Supplies:		Broadcast TV:	Music Production:	Y	Games/Sports:	Y
Magazines:	Movie Production:	Gambling Equipment:		Cable TV:	Retail Music:		Retail Games Stores:	
Books:	TV/Video Prod.:	Special Services:	Y	Satellite Broadcast:	Retail Audio Equip.:		Stadiums/Teams:	Y
Book Stores:	Video Rental: Y	Advertising Services:		Radio:	Music Print./Dist.:		Gambling/Casinos:	
Distribution/Printing:	Video Distribution: Y	Info. Sys. Software:		Online Information:	Multimedia:		Rides/Theme Parks:	

TYPES OF BUSINESS:

Concerts & Events Production
Theater Production
Sports Representation
DVD Production & Distribution

BRANDS/DIVISIONS/AFFILIATES:

House of Blues
Fillmore (The)
Live Nation Artists
Gibson Amphitheater
Murat Theater
Tweeter Center
Wembley Arena
Nikon

CONTACTS: Note: Officers with more than one job title may be intentionally listed here more than once.

Michael Rapino, CEO
Kathy Willard, CFO/Exec. VP
Michael G. Rowles, General Counsel/Exec. VP
Lee Ann Gliha, Exec. VP-Finance
Jason Garner, CEO-North American Music
Bryan Perez, Pres., Global Digital
Alan Ridgeway, CEO-Int'l Music
Michael Cohl, Chmn./CEO-Artist Nation
Randall T. Mays, Chmn.
Thomas Johansson, Chmn.-Int'l Music

Phone: 310-867-7000	Fax: 310-867-7001
Toll-Free:	
Address: 9348 Civic Center Dr., Beverly Hills, CA 90210 US	

GROWTH PLANS/SPECIAL FEATURES:

Live Nation, Inc. (LN) is one of the world's largest live entertainment companies. The company regularly promotes and/or produces tours for artists such The Rolling Stones, Barbra Streisand, Madonna, U2 and Coldplay. Globally, the firm owns, operates, has booking rights for and has an equity interest in over 160 venues. In addition, LN produces, promotes or hosts theatrical, specialized motor sports and other live entertainment events. The company operates in four segments: events; venues and sponsorship; digital distribution; and other. The events business, which generates 79% of revenue, promotes and/or produces live music shows, theatrical performances and specialized motor sports events in owned or operated venues and in rented third-party venues. The venues and sponsorship business, 17% of net sales, involves the management and operation of owned or operated venues and the sale of various types of sponsorship and advertising. The firm's owned or operated venues include Tweeter Center at the Waterfront, PNC Bank Arts Center, Gibson Amphitheater at Universal City Walk, Murat Theater, Nikon at Jones Beach Theater in New York, London's Wembley Arena, House of Blues clubs and The Fillmore venues. Through equity, booking or similar arrangements, LN also has the rights to book events at 34 additional venues. In addition, its national sponsorship programs include companies such as American Express, Anheuser Busch and Verizon. The digital distribution business involves the management of third-party relationships, in-house ticketing operations and online and wireless distribution activities. The other segment provides integrated sports marketing and management services, primarily for professional athletes. The marketing and management services generally involve the negotiation of player contracts with professional sports teams and endorsement contracts with major brands. It also provides ancillary services, such as financial advisory or management services to clients. In November 2007, division Live Nation Artists agree to acquire Signatures Network, Inc.

FINANCIALS: Sales and profits are in thousands of dollars—add 000 to get the full amount. 2007 Note: Financial information for 2007 was not available for all companies at press time.

2007 Sales: $	2007 Profits: $	U.S. Stock Ticker: LYV
2006 Sales: $3,691,559	2006 Profits: $-31,442	Int'l Ticker: Int'l Exchange:
2005 Sales: $2,936,845	2005 Profits: $-130,619	Employees: 4,400
2004 Sales: $2,806,128	2004 Profits: $16,260	Fiscal Year Ends: 12/31
2003 Sales: $	2003 Profits: $	Parent Company:

SALARIES/BENEFITS:

Pension Plan:	ESOP Stock Plan:	Profit Sharing:	Top Exec. Salary: $636,083	Bonus: $
Savings Plan:	Stock Purch. Plan:		Second Exec. Salary: $530,250	Bonus: $435,000

OTHER THOUGHTS:

Apparent Women Officers or Directors: 3
Hot Spot for Advancement for Women/Minorities: Y

LOCATIONS: ("Y" = Yes)

West:	Southwest:	Midwest:	Southeast:	Northeast:	International:
Y	Y	Y	Y	Y	Y

Note: Financial information, benefits and other data can change quickly and may vary from those stated here.

LODGENET ENTERTAINMENT CORP   www.lodgenet.com

Industry Group Code: 513220 Ranks within this company's industry group: Sales: 18 Profits: 14

Print Media/Publishing:	Movies:	Equipment/Supplies:		Broadcast/Cable:		Music/Audio:		Sports/Games/Gambling:
Newspapers:	Movie Theaters:	Equipment/Supplies:		Broadcast TV:		Music Production:		Games/Sports:
Magazines:	Movie Production:	Gambling Equipment:		Cable TV:	Y	Retail Music:		Retail Games Stores:
Books:	TV/Video Prod.:	Special Services:	Y	Satellite Broadcast:		Retail Audio Equip.:		Stadiums/Teams:
Book Stores:	Video Rental:	Advertising Services:	Y	Radio:		Music Print./Dist.:		Gambling/Casinos:
Distribution/Printing:	Video Distribution:	Info. Sys. Software:		Online Information:		Multimedia:		Rides/Theme Parks:

TYPES OF BUSINESS:

Cable TV Service-Hospitality Industry
Satellite TV Service
Broadband Internet Access
Network-Based Video Games
Video-on-Demand

BRANDS/DIVISIONS/AFFILIATES:

DIRECTV Group Inc (The)
StayOnline, Inc.
Ascent Media Group Inc
On Command Corp
Sheraton
Ritz-Carlton Hotel Company LLC (The)
La Quinta Inns
Marriott International Inc

CONTACTS: Note: Officers with more than one job title may be intentionally listed here more than once.

Scott C. Petersen, CEO
Scott C. Petersen, Pres.
Gary H. Ritondaro, CFO
Scott E. Young, Chief Mktg. Officer/Sr. VP
Gary H. Ritondaro, Sr. VP-Info.
Steven R. Pofahl, Sr. VP-Tech. Oper.
David M. Bankers, Sr. VP-Prod. & Tech. Dev.
Gary H. Ritondaro, Sr. VP-Admin.
James G. Naro, General Counsel/Sr. VP
Gary H. Ritondaro, Sr. VP-Finance
Steven D. Truckenmiller, Sr. VP-Programming & Content Mgmt.
Stephen D. McCarty, Sr. VP-Hotel Rel. & Sales
Scott C. Petersen, Chmn.

Phone: 605-988-1000	Fax: 605-988-1511
Toll-Free: 888-563-4363	
Address: 3900 W. Innovation St., Sioux Falls, SD 57107-7002 US	

GROWTH PLANS/SPECIAL FEATURES:

LodgeNet Entertainment Corporation is one of the world's largest providers of broadband interactive television services to the hospitality industry. It is a specialized communications company that provides on-demand digital movies, digital music and music videos, video games, high-speed Internet access and other interactive television services designed to serve the needs of the lodging industry and the traveling public. The company serves more than 6,000 hotels, resorts and casinos throughout the U.S., Canada and select international markets. LodgeNet provides both guest-pay and free-to-guest services to its clients. Guest-pay services are purchased by guests on a per-view, hourly or daily basis and include on-demand movies, network-based video games, Internet-enhanced television and high-speed Internet access. Complimentary guest services include satellite-delivered premium cable television programming and other interactive entertainment and information services that are paid for by the hotel. The company also has an agreement with DIRECTV that allows LodgeNet to provide the programming to its guests. LodgeNet's clients include hotel chains such as Sheraton, Ritz-Carlton, Harrah's Casino Hotels, La Quinta Inns, Red Roof Inns, Marriott, Holiday Inn, Hilton, Radisson, Westin, Doubletree and Embassy Suites. Recent acquisitions include StayOnline, Inc. for $15 million and Ascent Entertainment Group, Inc., the owner of On Command Corporation, for $380 million.

LodgeNet offers its employees a flexible spending account and medical, dental, vision, life and disability insurance.

FINANCIALS: Sales and profits are in thousands of dollars—add 000 to get the full amount. 2007 Note: Financial information for 2007 was not available for all companies at press time.

2007 Sales: $	2007 Profits: $	**U.S. Stock Ticker: LNET**
2006 Sales: $288,213	2006 Profits: $1,841	**Int'l Ticker:** Int'l Exchange:
2005 Sales: $275,771	2005 Profits: $-6,959	Employees: 803
2004 Sales: $266,441	2004 Profits: $-20,781	Fiscal Year Ends: 12/31
2003 Sales: $250,100	2003 Profits: $-35,100	Parent Company:

SALARIES/BENEFITS:

Pension Plan:	ESOP Stock Plan:	Profit Sharing:	Top Exec. Salary: $450,000	Bonus: $397,210
Savings Plan: Y	Stock Purch. Plan: Y		Second Exec. Salary: $350,000	Bonus: $208,810

OTHER THOUGHTS:

Apparent Women Officers or Directors:
Hot Spot for Advancement for Women/Minorities:

LOCATIONS: ("Y" = Yes)

West:	Southwest:	Midwest:	Southeast:	Northeast:	International:
Y	Y	Y	Y	Y	Y

Note: Financial information, benefits and other data can change quickly and may vary from those stated here.

LOUD TECHNOLOGIES INC   www.loud-technologies.com

Industry Group Code: 334310 Ranks within this company's industry group: Sales: 9   Profits: 8

Print Media/Publishing:	Movies:	Equipment/Supplies:		Broadcast/Cable:	Music/Audio:		Sports/Games/Gambling:
Newspapers:	Movie Theaters:	Equipment/Supplies:	Y	Broadcast TV:	Music Production:		Games/Sports:
Magazines:	Movie Production:	Gambling Equipment:		Cable TV:	Retail Music:		Retail Games Stores:
Books:	TV/Video Prod.:	Special Services:		Satellite Broadcast:	Retail Audio Equip.:	Y	Stadiums/Teams:
Book Stores:	Video Rental:	Advertising Services:		Radio:	Music Print./Dist.:		Gambling/Casinos:
Distribution/Printing:	Video Distribution:	Info. Sys. Software:		Online Information:	Multimedia:		Rides/Theme Parks:

TYPES OF BUSINESS:

Audio Equipment
Recording Equipment
Audio Software
Audio & Music Accessories

BRANDS/DIVISIONS/AFFILIATES:

Mackie Designs, Inc.
Alvarez
Ampeg
Crate
EAW
Knilling
SIA
TAPCO

CONTACTS: Note: Officers with more than one job title may be intentionally listed here more than once.

James T. (Jamie) Engen, CEO
James T. (Jamie) Engen, Pres.
Gerald Y. (Gerry) Ng, CFO
Ken Berger, Sr. VP-Mktg.
Gary M. Reilly, Sr. VP-Eng.
Shawn C. Powers, Sr. VP-Oper.
Mark E. Kuchenrither, VP
Jason H. Neimark, VP
Clarence E. Terry, VP
James T. (Jamie) Engen, Chmn.
Frank Loyko, Jr., Sr. VP-Int'l Sales

Phone: 425-487-4333	Fax: 425-487-4337
Toll-Free:	
Address: 16220 Wood-Red Rd. N.E., Woodinville, WA 98072 US	

GROWTH PLANS/SPECIAL FEATURES:

LOUD Technologies, Inc. (LOUD), formerly Mackie Designs, Inc., develops, manufactures, sells and supports professional audio and recording equipment under the Alvarez, Ampeg, Crate, EAW, Knilling, Mackie, SIA and TAPCO brand names. LOUD's primary product lines include sound reinforcement speakers; analog mixers; guitar and bass amplifiers; professional loudspeaker systems; and branded musical instruments. A mixer serves as the central component of any professional audio system by electronically blending, routing and enhancing sound sources, such as voices, musical instruments, sound effects and audio tape, video tape and other pre-recorded material. The firm's products can be found in professional and project recording studios; video and broadcast suites; post-production facilities; sound reinforcement applications including churches and nightclubs; retail locations; and on major musical concert tours. In the U.S., LOUD uses a network of independent representatives for the sale of its EAW and SIA products, which are sold in musical instrument stores, professional audio outlets and several mail order outlets. For Alvarez, Ampeg, Crate, Mackie, St. Louis Music Accessories, Tapco and Knilling products, the company uses a dedicated, domestic employee sales force that sells to musical instrument stores, retail locations, professional audio outlets and several mail order outlets. Internationally, LOUD's products are offered direct to dealers in the U.K., Canada, France, Germany, Belgium, the Netherlands and Luxembourg primarily through its subsidiaries in the U.K. and Canada. LOUD also sells direct to dealers in Japan. In March 2007, LOUD agreed to acquire U.K. company Martin Audio Limited.

FINANCIALS: Sales and profits are in thousands of dollars—add 000 to get the full amount. 2007 Note: Financial information for 2007 was not available for all companies at press time.

2007 Sales: $	2007 Profits: $	**U.S. Stock Ticker: LTEC**
2006 Sales: $215,033	2006 Profits: $ 625	**Int'l Ticker:** Int'l Exchange:
2005 Sales: $204,328	2005 Profits: $3,757	Employees: 658
2004 Sales: $123,276	2004 Profits: $-2,291	Fiscal Year Ends: 12/31
2003 Sales: $130,766	2003 Profits: $-21,795	Parent Company:

SALARIES/BENEFITS:

Pension Plan:	ESOP Stock Plan:	Profit Sharing:	Top Exec. Salary: $325,000	Bonus: $68,567
Savings Plan: Y	Stock Purch. Plan:		Second Exec. Salary: $190,000	Bonus: $49,867

OTHER THOUGHTS:

Apparent Women Officers or Directors:
Hot Spot for Advancement for Women/Minorities:

LOCATIONS: ("Y" = Yes)

West:	Southwest:	Midwest:	Southeast:	Northeast:	International:
Y		Y		Y	Y

Note: Financial information, benefits and other data can change quickly and may vary from those stated here.

LUCASARTS ENTERTAINMENT COMPANY LLC
www.lucasarts.com

Industry Group Code: 511208 Ranks within this company's industry group: Sales: Profits:

Print Media/Publishing:	Movies:	Equipment/Supplies:	Broadcast/Cable:	Music/Audio:	Sports/Games/Gambling:	
Newspapers:	Movie Theaters:	Equipment/Supplies:	Broadcast TV:	Music Production:	Games/Sports:	Y
Magazines:	Movie Production:	Gambling Equipment:	Cable TV:	Retail Music:	Retail Games Stores:	
Books:	TV/Video Prod.:	Special Services:	Satellite Broadcast:	Retail Audio Equip.:	Stadiums/Teams:	
Book Stores:	Video Rental:	Advertising Services:	Radio:	Music Print./Dist.:	Gambling/Casinos:	
Distribution/Printing:	Video Distribution:	Info. Sys. Software:	Online Information:	Multimedia:	Rides/Theme Parks:	

TYPES OF BUSINESS:
Computer Software-Games
Online Retail

BRANDS/DIVISIONS/AFFILIATES:
Lucasfilm, Ltd.
Star Wars: Knights of the Old Republic
Star Wars: Battlefront
Indiana Jones & the Emperor's Tomb
Armed and Dangerous
Thrillville
Secret Weapons Over Normandy
Star Wars: The Force Unleashed

CONTACTS: *Note: Officers with more than one job title may be intentionally listed here more than once.*
Jim Ward, Pres.
Kevin Kebodeaux, Dir.-Global Sales
Peter Hirschmann, VP-Prod. Dev.
Mike Nelson, VP-Admin.
Seth Steinberg, General Counsel
Seth Steinberg, Dir.-Bus. Affairs
Kevin Weston, VP-Finance
Atsuko Matsumoto, Sr. Dir.-Prod. Svcs.
Sean Denny, Dir.-Consumer Insights
Kevin Kurtz, Dir.-Global Mktg.
Ken Epstein, Dir.-Mktg. Svcs.
George Lucas, Chmn.
Mary Bihr, VP-Global Publishing

Phone: 415-507-4545	Fax: 415-507-0300
Toll-Free:	
Address: 1110 Gorgas Ave., San Francisco, CA 94129 US	

GROWTH PLANS/SPECIAL FEATURES:
LucasArts Entertainment Company LLC, a subsidiary of Lucasfilm, Ltd., produces games for PCs, Xbox, Xbox 360 and Playstation. The company was founded in 1982 by George Lucas to produce games with the Star Wars and Indiana Jones brand names. Today there are more than 50 game titles in these series. Current titles include Star Wars Knights of the Old Republic II: The Sith Lords, Star Wars: Battlefront II and Indiana Jones and the Emperor's Tomb. LucasArts' Star Wars franchise has been highly successful, particularly Star Wars: Knights of the Old Republic developed with Bioware Corp. Following its success, the company released a slew of new titles, including Republic Commando, Knights of the Old Republic II and Galaxies: Jump to Lightspeed, a multiplayer game. Some of its newest additions to the Star Wars franchise include the LEGO Star Wars games and Star Wars: Empire at War. The company has branched out into many other titles, including Thrillville, Armed and Dangerous and Secret Weapons Over Normandy. The company offers its games and game paraphernalia for direct sale on its web site, Store.lucasarts.com. In September 2007, the firm announced its newest game, Star Wars: The Force Unleashed, would be released in spring 2008 for the Wii, allowing players to use the Wii controllers to swing a lightsaber and direct force powers. In October 2007, LucasArts and Bioware again partnered to develop an as-yet unannounced interactive entertainment product.

LucasArts offers its employees medical, dental and life insurance, as well as fitness programs, tuition assistance, employee parties, child care, community activities, an observatory and access to the Sky Walker Ranch and company sailboat. The firm's new offices include a 350-seat theater, a 1,600-square-foot stage with 34 cameras including 3-D, a child care center, a fitness center, 15 editing suites and an ultra-fast 1-gigabyte network hookup at every desktop.

FINANCIALS: Sales and profits are in thousands of dollars—add 000 to get the full amount. 2007 Note: Financial information for 2007 was not available for all companies at press time.

2007 Sales: $	2007 Profits: $	**U.S. Stock Ticker: Subsidiary**
2006 Sales: $	2006 Profits: $	**Int'l Ticker:** Int'l Exchange:
2005 Sales: $	2005 Profits: $	Employees:
2004 Sales: $	2004 Profits: $	Fiscal Year Ends: 4/30
2003 Sales: $	2003 Profits: $	Parent Company: LUCASFILM LTD

SALARIES/BENEFITS:

Pension Plan:	ESOP Stock Plan:	Profit Sharing:	Top Exec. Salary: $	Bonus: $
Savings Plan: Y	Stock Purch. Plan:		Second Exec. Salary: $	Bonus: $

OTHER THOUGHTS:
Apparent Women Officers or Directors: 2
Hot Spot for Advancement for Women/Minorities:

LOCATIONS: ("Y" = Yes)

West:	Southwest:	Midwest:	Southeast:	Northeast:	International:
Y					

Note: Financial information, benefits and other data can change quickly and may vary from those stated here.

LUCASFILM LTD

www.lucasfilm.com

Industry Group Code: 512110 Ranks within this company's industry group: Sales: Profits:

Print Media/Publishing:	Movies:		Equipment/Supplies:		Broadcast/Cable:	Music/Audio:	Sports/Games/Gambling:	
Newspapers:	Movie Theaters:		Equipment/Supplies:		Broadcast TV:	Music Production:	Games/Sports:	Y
Magazines:	Movie Production:	Y	Gambling Equipment:		Cable TV:	Retail Music:	Retail Games Stores:	
Books: Y	TV/Video Prod.:	Y	Special Services:	Y	Satellite Broadcast:	Retail Audio Equip.:	Stadiums/Teams:	
Book Stores:	Video Rental:		Advertising Services:		Radio:	Music Print./Dist.:	Gambling/Casinos:	
Distribution/Printing:	Video Distribution:		Info. Sys. Software:		Online Information:	Multimedia:	Rides/Theme Parks:	

TYPES OF BUSINESS:

Film Production
Special Effects
Sound Effects
Digital Animation
Software & Video Games
Online Publishing
Merchandising

BRANDS/DIVISIONS/AFFILIATES:

Industrial Light & Magic
Skywalker Sound
Lucas Digital
LucasArts
Lucas Online
Indiana Jones
Star Wars
Lucasfilm Animation Singapore

CONTACTS: Note: Officers with more than one job title may be intentionally listed here more than once.

Micheline Chau, COO
Micheline Chau, Pres.
Jan van der Voort, Chief Admin. Officer
Chrissie England, Pres., Industrial Light & Magic
Glenn Kiser, VP/General Mgr.-Skywalker Sound
Howard Roffman, Pres., Lucas Licensing
Jim Ward, Sr. VP/Pres., LucasArts
George Lucas, Chmn.

Phone: 415-662-1800	Fax:
Toll-Free:	
Address: 1110 Gorgas Ave., San Francisco, CA 94129 US	

GROWTH PLANS/SPECIAL FEATURES:

Lucasfilm Ltd., created by filmmaker George Lucas in 1971, is one of the most successful independent production companies. It has produced some of the most popular films in history, including the original Star Wars trilogy and the more recent prequels, along with the Indiana Jones films. Star Wars Episode I: The Phantom Menace has earned approximately $920 million since its release in 1999 and claims the number five spot on the list of all-time highest grossing films. The company operates through seven divisions. Lucasfilm is responsible for production, promotion and strategic management of theatrical, television and entertainment properties. Industrial Light & Magic (ILM) creates digital and visual special effects for the entertainment industry and has received 31 Academy Award nominations and 14 awards. Skywalker Sound produces post-production digital sound effects, for which it has won 18 Academy Awards. LucasArts is a software company that develops computer games based on Lucas's movies. The firm's licensing division is responsible for licensing and merchandising Lucasfilm properties. Animation and Lucasfilm Animation Singapore are digital animation studios. Finally, Lucasfilm's online division produces entertainment, education, reference and e-commerce sites for Lucasfilm properties. Since 2005, the company has been operating out of the Letterman Digital Arts Center. This new center brings the entire organization together and enables units producing games and films to collaborate more closely and share technologies. In 2007, Lucasfilm celebrated the 30th anniversary of Star Wars. The company also announced a new Indiana Jones film, to be called Indiana Jones and the Kingdom of the Crystal Skull.

The Letterman Digital Arts Center contains a 300-seat theater, a childcare center, a fitness center and an ultra-fast 1-gigabyte network hookup at every desktop.

FINANCIALS: Sales and profits are in thousands of dollars—add 000 to get the full amount. 2007 Note: Financial information for 2007 was not available for all companies at press time.

2007 Sales: $	2007 Profits: $	U.S. Stock Ticker: Private
2006 Sales: $	2006 Profits: $	Int'l Ticker: Int'l Exchange:
2005 Sales: $1,483,000	2005 Profits: $	Employees: 1,500
2004 Sales: $	2004 Profits: $	Fiscal Year Ends: 3/31
2003 Sales: $1,200,000	2003 Profits: $	Parent Company:

SALARIES/BENEFITS:

Pension Plan:	ESOP Stock Plan:	Profit Sharing:	Top Exec. Salary: $	Bonus: $
Savings Plan: Y	Stock Purch. Plan:		Second Exec. Salary: $	Bonus: $

OTHER THOUGHTS:

Apparent Women Officers or Directors: 3
Hot Spot for Advancement for Women/Minorities: Y

LOCATIONS: ("Y" = Yes)

West:	Southwest:	Midwest:	Southeast:	Northeast:	International:
Y					

Note: Financial information, benefits and other data can change quickly and may vary from those stated here.

MACROVISION CORP

www.macrovision.com

Industry Group Code: 511202 Ranks within this company's industry group: Sales: 1 Profits: 1

Print Media/Publishing:	Movies:	Equipment/Supplies:		Broadcast/Cable:	Music/Audio:	Sports/Games/Gambling:
Newspapers:	Movie Theaters:	Equipment/Supplies:	Y	Broadcast TV:	Music Production:	Games/Sports:
Magazines:	Movie Production:	Gambling Equipment:		Cable TV:	Retail Music:	Retail Games Stores:
Books:	TV/Video Prod.:	Special Services:	Y	Satellite Broadcast:	Retail Audio Equip.:	Stadiums/Teams:
Book Stores:	Video Rental:	Advertising Services:		Radio:	Music Print./Dist.:	Gambling/Casinos:
Distribution/Printing:	Video Distribution:	Info. Sys. Software:		Online Information:	Multimedia:	Rides/Theme Parks:

TYPES OF BUSINESS:

Software-Video Copyright Protection
Digital Rights Management Technologies

BRANDS/DIVISIONS/AFFILIATES:

InstallShield
FLEXnet
FLEXnet Manager
FLEXnet Publisher
Mediabolic, Inc.
Blu-ray Disc Security Technology

CONTACTS: *Note: Officers with more than one job title may be intentionally listed here more than once.*

Alfred J. Amoroso, CEO
Alfred J. Amoroso, Pres.
James Budge, CFO/Exec. VP
Corey Ferengul, Exec. VP-Mktg. & Solutions
Eileen Schloss, Exec. VP-Human Resources
Robert Doyle, Sr. VP-Eng.
Stephen Yu, General Counsel/Exec. VP/Corp. Sec.
Jim Wickett, Exec. VP-Corp. Dev.
Mark Bishof, Exec. VP/General Mgr.-Software
Eric Free, Exec. VP/General Mgr-Embedded Solutions
Eric Rodli, Exec. VP/General Mgr.-Entertainment
David Rowley, Sr. VP/General Mgr.-Asia-Pacific
John O. Ryan, Chmn.
Jim Ryan, Sr. VP/General Mgr.-EMEA
Michael Buchheim, Exec. VP/General Mgr.-Distribution & Commerce

Phone: 408-562-8400	**Fax:** 408-567-1800
Toll-Free:	
Address: 2830 De La Cruz Blvd., Santa Clara, CA 95050 US	

GROWTH PLANS/SPECIAL FEATURES:

Macrovision Corp. enables businesses reliant on the development of software or content to protect, enhance or distribute their offering among digital distribution channels and destination services. These digital lifecycle management solutions include anti-piracy and content protection technologies and services; digital rights management products and technologies; embedded licensing technologies; usage monitoring for enterprises; access control and billing; and several other related technologies and services. The company markets the FLEXnet licensing platform and the InstallShield suite of software installation, repackaging and update solutions. It also operates a game network for digital distribution of downloadable personal computer games and markets its Rights products, which enable the sale and security of digital goods and services, such as text, audio, video, streaming media, games and applications. Macrovision develops and markets its commerce, protection and management solutions for software, entertainment and information publishing industries across three distinct customer groups: entertainment and content producers and distributors; software publishers; and enterprise end users. For the entertainment and content producers and distributors, the Macrovision solutions enable the delivery, protection and use of digital goods in the entertainment and content marketplaces. The company offers software publishers the FLEXnet Publisher product, as well as back-office products and a hosted update service that enables manufacturers to keep their deployed products up to date and automatically deliver updates over the Internet. FLEXnet Manager allows enterprise end users to capture and analyze software usage data to help determine where to allocate software purchases and related costs and help administer software access rights over global networks. In 2007, Macrovision acquired Mediabolic, Inc.; and Blu-ray Disc Security Technology from Cryptography Research, Inc. The company agreed to acquire All Media Guide Holdings, Inc. and Gemstar-TV Guide.

The company offers its employees medical, dental, life and disability insurance; an employee stock purchase plan; educational assistance; and a health club membership.

FINANCIALS: Sales and profits are in thousands of dollars—add 000 to get the full amount. 2007 Note: Financial information for 2007 was not available for all companies at press time.

2007 Sales: $	2007 Profits: $	**U.S. Stock Ticker: MVSN**
2006 Sales: $247,590	2006 Profits: $33,043	**Int'l Ticker:** Int'l Exchange:
2005 Sales: $203,230	2005 Profits: $22,115	Employees: 784
2004 Sales: $182,099	2004 Profits: $36,730	Fiscal Year Ends: 12/31
2003 Sales: $128,346	2003 Profits: $26,941	Parent Company:

SALARIES/BENEFITS:

Pension Plan:	ESOP Stock Plan:	Profit Sharing:	Top Exec. Salary: $500,000	Bonus: $555,000
Savings Plan: Y	Stock Purch. Plan: Y		Second Exec. Salary: $350,000	Bonus: $163,380

OTHER THOUGHTS:

Apparent Women Officers or Directors: 2
Hot Spot for Advancement for Women/Minorities:

LOCATIONS: ("Y" = Yes)

West:	Southwest:	Midwest:	Southeast:	Northeast:	International:
Y		Y		Y	Y

MAGNA ENTERTAINMENT CORP   www.magnaent.com

Industry Group Code: 713210 Ranks within this company's industry group: Sales: 4   Profits: 12

Print Media/Publishing:	Movies:	Equipment/Supplies:	Broadcast/Cable:		Music/Audio:	Sports/Games/Gambling:	
Newspapers:	Movie Theaters:	Equipment/Supplies:	Broadcast TV:		Music Production:	Games/Sports:	Y
Magazines:	Movie Production:	Gambling Equipment:	Cable TV:	Y	Retail Music:	Retail Games Stores:	
Books:	TV/Video Prod.:	Special Services:	Satellite Broadcast:		Retail Audio Equip.:	Stadiums/Teams:	Y
Book Stores:	Video Rental:	Advertising Services:	Radio:		Music Print./Dist.:	Gambling/Casinos:	Y
Distribution/Printing:	Video Distribution:	Info. Sys. Software:	Online Information:		Multimedia:	Rides/Theme Parks:	

TYPES OF BUSINESS:
Racetracks-Horse Racing
Cable Television Network
Simulcasting
Account Wagering
Horse Bedding Products
Pari-Mutuel Gambling Information Technology

BRANDS/DIVISIONS/AFFILIATES:
StreuFex
Gulfstream Park
XpressBet
HorseRacing TV
Racetrack Television Network

CONTACTS: Note: Officers with more than one job title may be intentionally listed here more than once.
Frank Stronach, Interim CEO
W. Thomas Hodgson, Pres.
Blake S. Tohana, CFO/Exec. VP
Stuart Morris, VP-Mktg.
William G. Ford, Sec.
James (Jim) Bromby, Sr. VP-Oper.
Mary L. Seymour, Controller/VP
Brant Latta, Sr. VP-Oper.
Corey Johnsen, Pres., MEC Operations in the Southwest
Joe A. De Francis, Exec. VP
Frank DeMarco, Jr., VP-Regulatory Affairs
Frank Stronach, Chmn.

Phone: 905-726-2462	Fax: 905-726-7448
Toll-Free:	
Address: 337 Magna Dr., Aurora, ON L4G 7K1 Canada	

GROWTH PLANS/SPECIAL FEATURES:
Magna Entertainment Corp. (MEC) is a leading North American owner and operator of thoroughbred racetracks and one of the world's leading simulcast broadcasters of live racing content to inter-track, off-track and account wagering gamers. The company currently operates or manages eight thoroughbred racetracks, one standardbred harness racing track, two racetracks that run both thoroughbred and quarterhorse meets and one track that runs both thoroughbred and standardbred meets. Supporting its racetracks, the firm owns and operates thoroughbred training centers near San Diego, California; in Palm Beach County, Florida; and in the Baltimore, Maryland area. The company also owns and operates production facilities in Austria and North Carolina for StreuFex, a straw-based horse bedding product, and owns a large real estate portfolio including two golf courses with related facilities. It will be adding to its real estate holdings with a residential and commercial development around the Gulfstream Park racetrack. MEC operates off-track betting facilities and a national account wagering business known as XpressBet, which permits customers to place wagers by telephone and over the Internet on horse races at more than 100 racetracks in North America and internationally and began slot operations at its Gulfstream Parks track. MEC owns 50% of HorseRacing TV, focused exclusively on horse racing, currently available to more than 13 million cable and satellite TV customers. The firm also has a minority interest in the Racetrack Television Network, which telecasts races from all of its racetracks. In June 2007, the firm agreed to sell its San Luis Rey Downs training center, near San Diego, to a subsidiary of MI Developments Inc. (MID) for $24 million. In March 2007, Magna sold 157 acres of land near its Palm Beach County training center to MID for $35 million. In March 2007, the firm added 705 slot machines to the Gulfstream Park location, bringing the total there to 1,221.

FINANCIALS: Sales and profits are in thousands of dollars—add 000 to get the full amount. 2007 Note: Financial information for 2007 was not available for all companies at press time.

2007 Sales: $	2007 Profits: $	U.S. Stock Ticker: MECA
2006 Sales: $702,139	2006 Profits: $-87,351	Int'l Ticker: MEC Int'l Exchange: Toronto-TSX
2005 Sales: $604,428	2005 Profits: $-105,293	Employees: 5,300
2004 Sales: $683,393	2004 Profits: $-95,636	Fiscal Year Ends: 12/31
2003 Sales: $686,598	2003 Profits: $-105,100	Parent Company:

SALARIES/BENEFITS:
Pension Plan:	ESOP Stock Plan:	Profit Sharing:	Top Exec. Salary: $615,000	Bonus: $
Savings Plan: Y	Stock Purch. Plan:		Second Exec. Salary: $305,660	Bonus: $268,688

OTHER THOUGHTS:
Apparent Women Officers or Directors: 1
Hot Spot for Advancement for Women/Minorities:

LOCATIONS: ("Y" = Yes)
West:	Southwest:	Midwest:	Southeast:	Northeast:	International:
Y	Y	Y	Y	Y	Y

Note: Financial information, benefits and other data can change quickly and may vary from those stated here.

MARKETWATCH INC   www.marketwatch.com

Industry Group Code: 514100 Ranks within this company's industry group: Sales: Profits:

Print Media/Publishing:	Movies:		Equipment/Supplies:		Broadcast/Cable:	Music/Audio:	Sports/Games/Gambling:
Newspapers:	Movie Theaters:		Equipment/Supplies:		Broadcast TV:	Music Production:	Games/Sports:
Magazines:	Movie Production:		Gambling Equipment:		Cable TV:	Retail Music:	Retail Games Stores:
Books:	TV/Video Prod.:	Y	Special Services:	Y	Satellite Broadcast:	Retail Audio Equip.:	Stadiums/Teams:
Book Stores:	Video Rental:		Advertising Services:		Radio:	Music Print./Dist.:	Gambling/Casinos:
Distribution/Printing:	Video Distribution:		Info. Sys. Software:		Online Information:	Multimedia:	Rides/Theme Parks:

TYPES OF BUSINESS:

Online Financial Information
Television & Radio Programming

BRANDS/DIVISIONS/AFFILIATES:

Dow Jones & Company Inc
bigcharts.com
virtualstockexchange.com
Hulbert Financial Digest
Retirement Weekly
ETF Trader
MarketWatch Weekend
MarketWatch.com Radio Network

CONTACTS: *Note: Officers with more than one job title may be intentionally listed here more than once.*

Maria Molland, General Mgr.
Brian Quinn, VP-Advertising Sales
Jamie Thingelstad, CTO

Phone: 415-439-6400	Fax: 415-439-6485
Toll-Free:	
Address: 201 California St., 13th Fl., San Francisco, CA 94111 US	

GROWTH PLANS/SPECIAL FEATURES:

MarketWatch, Inc., a wholly-owned subsidiary of Dow Jones & Company, Inc., is a financial media company providing web-based, real-time business news, financial programming and analytic tools. It operates two main web sites, marketwatch.com and bigcharts.com, as well as virtualstockexchange.com, a stock market simulation web site. In addition to business and financial news, the sites offer in-depth commentary on trends and events, personal finance commentary and data, community features and other services, designed to provide a one-stop-shop for audiences. Other features include a mutual fund center, a seasonal tax guide, market advisors and research columns. Customers create personal user settings including portfolio trackers, news and quotes, custom views, allocation analysis, financials and charting. MarketWatch also delivers relevant financial news to user e-mail accounts, hosts investment discussion communities, offers personalized automatic alerts and through portfolio creation provides customers with wireless capabilities.   The company's MarketWatch Licensing Services group is a leading licensor of market news, data, investment analysis tools and other online applications to financial services firms, media companies, wireless carriers and Internet service providers. The firm also sells subscription-based content for individual investors under the Hulbert Financial Digest, Retirement Weekly and ETF Trader brand names.   MarketWatch produces the syndicated MarketWatch Weekend television program and provides business and financial news updates every 30 minutes on the MarketWatch.com Radio Network.

The company offers its employees medical and dental insurance; life and disability insurance; a 401(k) plan; and education benefits.

FINANCIALS: Sales and profits are in thousands of dollars—add 000 to get the full amount. 2007 Note: Financial information for 2007 was not available for all companies at press time.

2007 Sales: $	2007 Profits: $	**U.S. Stock Ticker: Subsidiary**
2006 Sales: $	2006 Profits: $	**Int'l Ticker:** Int'l Exchange:
2005 Sales: $50,000	2005 Profits: $	Employees: 337
2004 Sales: $48,000	2004 Profits: $	Fiscal Year Ends: 12/31
2003 Sales: $47,173	2003 Profits: $2,655	Parent Company: DOW JONES & COMPANY INC

SALARIES/BENEFITS:

Pension Plan:	ESOP Stock Plan:	Profit Sharing:	Top Exec. Salary: $	Bonus: $226,686
Savings Plan: Y	Stock Purch. Plan:		Second Exec. Salary: $285,000	Bonus: $285,000

OTHER THOUGHTS:

Apparent Women Officers or Directors: 2
Hot Spot for Advancement for Women/Minorities:

LOCATIONS: ("Y" = Yes)

West:	Southwest:	Midwest:	Southeast:	Northeast:	International:
Y					

MARTHA STEWART LIVING OMNIMEDIA INC
www.marthastewart.com
Industry Group Code: 511120 Ranks within this company's industry group: Sales: 10   Profits: 6

Print Media/Publishing:		Movies:		Equipment/Supplies:		Broadcast/Cable:		Music/Audio:		Sports/Games/Gambling:	
Newspapers:		Movie Theaters:		Equipment/Supplies:		Broadcast TV:		Music Production:		Games/Sports:	
Magazines:	Y	Movie Production:		Gambling Equipment:		Cable TV:		Retail Music:		Retail Games Stores:	
Books:	Y	TV/Video Prod.:	Y	Special Services:		Satellite Broadcast:		Retail Audio Equip.:		Stadiums/Teams:	
Book Stores:		Video Rental:		Advertising Services:		Radio:		Music Print./Dist.:		Gambling/Casinos:	
Distribution/Printing:		Video Distribution:		Info. Sys. Software:		Online Information:		Multimedia:		Rides/Theme Parks:	

TYPES OF BUSINESS:
Magazine Publishing
Television & Video Production
Book Publishing
Home & Garden Products
Web Sites
Satellite Radio
Merchandising

BRANDS/DIVISIONS/AFFILIATES:
Martha Stewart Living
Martha Stewart Signature
Martha Stewart Weddings
Blueprint
Everyday Food
Martha Stewart: The Catalog For Living
Martha Stewart Radio
Body+Soul Magazine

CONTACTS: *Note: Officers with more than one job title may be intentionally listed here more than once.*
Susan Lyne, CEO
Susan Lyne, Pres.
Howard Hochhauser, CFO
Lee Heffernan, Sr. VP-Integrated Mktg.
Tom Barreca, Sr. VP-Digital & Emerging Media
Robin Marino, Pres., Merch.
Gregory Barton, General Counsel/Corp. Sec.
Holly Brown, Pres., Internet
Howard Hochhauser, VP-Investor Rel.
Sheraton Kalouria, Pres., Television
Gael Towey, Chief Creative Officer
Lauren Stanich, Pres., Publishing
Wenda Harris Millard, Pres., Media
Charles Koppelman, Chmn.

Phone: 212-827-8000	**Fax:** 212-827-8204
Toll-Free:	
Address: 11 West 42nd St., New York, NY 10036 US	

GROWTH PLANS/SPECIAL FEATURES:
Martha Stewart Living Omnimedia, Inc. (MSL) is an integrated content and commerce company that creates how-to content and merchandise for homemakers and other consumers. The company leverages the Martha Stewart brand name across media and retail outlets, focusing on domestic arts. Content and merchandise span eight core areas: home, cooking and entertaining, gardening, crafts, holidays, housekeeping and organizing, weddings, and baby/kids. MSL operates through four business segments: publishing, broadcasting, merchandising and Internet. The publishing segment (accounting for 54% yearly revenue) currently publishes five magazines (Martha Stewart Living, Everyday Food, Martha Stewart Weddings, Body + Soul, and Blueprint) and more than 50 special-interest books. In 2007, MSL secured a book deal with Clarkson-Potter Publishing to publish an additional 10 books over five years. The broadcasting segment develops television programming, featuring Everyday Food, MARTHA and the Martha Stewart Living program which airs on Style Network. The company widened its television presence in 2007 by acquiring two cable television licensing deals with The Fine Living TV Network and DIY Network to air syndicated and segments of past shows. The company also produces theme-based DVDs (distributed with Warner Home Video) and a satellite radio channel (Martha Stewart Living Radio). Merchandise is distributed under several labels, including Martha Stewart Everyday (the firm's mass-market brand label) and Martha Stewart Signature. MSL's Internet segment consists of Martha Stewart: The Catalog for Living, MarthaStewart.com and MarthasFlowers.com. In the spring of 2008, MSL and 1-800-FLOWERS.COM will launch a co-branded floral and gift basket program. Other partnerships in the last year include the introduction of two housing communities with KB Homes in North Carolina and Colorado; and a bridal and tabletop line with Wedgwood U.S.A., Inc. The company also recently invested $10 million with GTCR Golder Rauner, LLC towards ownership in Wilton Products Inc., a craft store conglomerate.

FINANCIALS: Sales and profits are in thousands of dollars—add 000 to get the full amount. 2007 Note: Financial information for 2007 was not available for all companies at press time.

2007 Sales: $	2007 Profits: $	**U.S. Stock Ticker: MSO**
2006 Sales: $288,341	2006 Profits: $-16,995	**Int'l Ticker:** Int'l Exchange:
2005 Sales: $212,433	2005 Profits: $-75,789	Employees: 755
2004 Sales: $187,438	2004 Profits: $-59,600	Fiscal Year Ends: 12/31
2003 Sales: $245,848	2003 Profits: $-2,771	Parent Company:

SALARIES/BENEFITS:
Pension Plan: Y	ESOP Stock Plan:	Profit Sharing:	Top Exec. Salary: $900,000	Bonus: $1,000,000
Savings Plan: Y	Stock Purch. Plan:		Second Exec. Salary: $495,000	Bonus: $425,000

OTHER THOUGHTS:
Apparent Women Officers or Directors: 7
Hot Spot for Advancement for Women/Minorities: Y

LOCATIONS: ("Y" = Yes)
West:	Southwest:	Midwest:	Southeast:	Northeast:	International:
				Y	

MARVEL ENTERTAINMENT INC   www.marvel.com

Industry Group Code: 511130 Ranks within this company's industry group: Sales: 5   Profits: 5

Print Media/Publishing:		Movies:		Equipment/Supplies:	Broadcast/Cable:	Music/Audio:	Sports/Games/Gambling:
Newspapers:		Movie Theaters:	Y	Equipment/Supplies:	Broadcast TV:	Music Production:	Games/Sports:
Magazines:	Y	Movie Production:	Y	Gambling Equipment:	Cable TV:	Retail Music:	Retail Games Stores:
Books:	Y	TV/Video Prod.:		Special Services:	Satellite Broadcast:	Retail Audio Equip.:	Stadiums/Teams:
Book Stores:		Video Rental:		Advertising Services:	Radio:	Music Print./Dist.:	Gambling/Casinos:
Distribution/Printing:		Video Distribution:		Info. Sys. Software:	Online Information:	Multimedia:	Rides/Theme Parks:

TYPES OF BUSINESS:

Comic Book Publishing
Toys
Licensing & Merchandising
Movie Production
Online Services

BRANDS/DIVISIONS/AFFILIATES:

Hasbro
Marvel Comics
Marvel Digital Comics Unlimited
X-Men
Incredible Hulk
Fantastic Four
Daredevil
Ghost Rider

CONTACTS: *Note: Officers with more than one job title may be intentionally listed here more than once.*

Isaac Perlmutter, CEO
Kenneth West, CFO/Exec. VP
JoAnn McLaughlin, Exec. VP-Merch.
Benjamin Dean, Sec.
Alan Fine, Chief Mktg. Officer-Marvel Characters, Inc.
Alan Fine, CEO-Publishing & Toy Divisions
David Maisel, Exec. VP-Office of the Chief Exec.
John Turitzin, Exec. VP-Office of the Chief Exec.
Morton E. Handel, Chmn.

Phone: 212-576-4000	Fax: 212-576-8517
Toll-Free:	
Address: 417 Fifth Ave., 11th Floor, New York, NY 10016 US	

GROWTH PLANS/SPECIAL FEATURES:

Marvel Entertainment, Inc. is one of the world's most prominent character-based entertainment companies, with a proprietary library of over 5,000 characters, mostly superheroes. The company operates in the licensing, comic book publishing and toy businesses in both domestic and international markets. Marvel's library of characters includes Spider-Man, X-Men, Fantastic Four and the Incredible Hulk. The company's business is divided into four divisions: licensing; publishing; toys; and film production. The licensing division licenses the company's characters for use in a wide variety of products, including toys, electronic games, apparel, accessories and collectibles. This division also receives fees from the sale of licenses to a variety of media, including television and video games. The publishing segment has been in business since 1939 and publishes in many foreign countries in a variety of languages. Comic books are distributed through three channels: comic book specialty stores, traditional retail outlets and subscription sales. The toy segment designs, develops, markets and distributes a limited line of toys worldwide. Toys are currently produced and sold exclusively by Hasbro, according to an agreement that began at the beginning of 2007 and will remain active until the end of 2011. The film production segment develops, produces and distributes films, which are financed by a company owned $525 million film facility. The first two films produced by the film production segment, Iron Man and The Incredible Hulk, are scheduled for release in 2008. In November 2007, the firm introduced Marvel Digital Comics Unlimited, an online subscription service that allows access to thousands of comic book titles from Marvel's historic comic book archive.

FINANCIALS: Sales and profits are in thousands of dollars—add 000 to get the full amount. 2007 Note: Financial information for 2007 was not available for all companies at press time.

2007 Sales: $	2007 Profits: $	U.S. Stock Ticker: MVL
2006 Sales: $351,798	2006 Profits: $58,704	Int'l Ticker: Int'l Exchange:
2005 Sales: $390,507	2005 Profits: $102,819	Employees: 255
2004 Sales: $513,468	2004 Profits: $124,877	Fiscal Year Ends: 12/31
2003 Sales: $347,626	2003 Profits: $151,648	Parent Company:

SALARIES/BENEFITS:

Pension Plan:	ESOP Stock Plan:	Profit Sharing:	Top Exec. Salary: $987,981	Bonus: $1,323,520
Savings Plan: Y	Stock Purch. Plan:		Second Exec. Salary: $500,000	Bonus: $1,125,000

OTHER THOUGHTS:

Apparent Women Officers or Directors: 2
Hot Spot for Advancement for Women/Minorities:

LOCATIONS: ("Y" = Yes)

West:	Southwest:	Midwest:	Southeast:	Northeast:	International:
Y				Y	Y

MATSUSHITA ELECTRIC INDUSTRIAL CO LTD

www.panasonic.net

Industry Group Code: 334310 **Ranks within this company's industry group:** Sales: 1 Profits: 2

Print Media/Publishing:	Movies:	Equipment/Supplies:	Broadcast/Cable:	Music/Audio:		Sports/Games/Gambling:
Newspapers:	Movie Theaters:	Equipment/Supplies:	Broadcast TV:	Music Production:		Games/Sports:
Magazines:	Movie Production:	Gambling Equipment:	Cable TV:	Retail Music:		Retail Games Stores:
Books:	TV/Video Prod.:	Special Services:	Satellite Broadcast:	Retail Audio Equip.:	Y	Stadiums/Teams:
Book Stores:	Video Rental:	Advertising Services:	Radio:	Music Print./Dist.:		Gambling/Casinos:
Distribution/Printing:	Video Distribution:	Info. Sys. Software:	Online Information:	Multimedia:		Rides/Theme Parks:

TYPES OF BUSINESS:

Audio & Video Equipment, Manufacturing
Industrial Equipment & Machinery
Home Appliances
Electronic Components
Cellular Phones
Medical Equipment
Photovoltaic Equipment
Batteries

BRANDS/DIVISIONS/AFFILIATES:

Panasonic
Quasar
Technics
JVC
National
Toray Industries, Inc.
Matsushita PDP Company Ltd.

CONTACTS: Note: Officers with more than one job title may be intentionally listed here more than once.

Koshi Kitadai, Sr. Managing Exec. Officer
Fumio Ohtsubo, Pres.
Shunzo Ushimaru, Sr. Managing Dir.-Mktg.
Shinichi Fukushima, Managing Dir.-Personnel & Gen. Affairs
Takae Makita, Exec. Officer-Info. Systems
Susumu Koike, Exec. VP-Tech. & Semiconductors
Ikusaburo Kashima, Dir.-Corp. Legal Affairs
Takahiro Mori, Managing Dir.-Planning
Yoichi Nagata, Dir.-Overseas Investor Rel.
Tetsuya Kawakami, Exec. VP-Acct.
Joachim Reinhart, COO-Panasonic Europe Ltd.
Koshi Kitadai, Pres., Panasonic Electronic Devices Co., Ltd.
Yoshiaki Kushiki, Pres., Panasonic Mobile Communications Co., Ltd.
Toru Ishida, Pres., Matsushita Battery Industrial Co., Ltd.
Kunio Nakamura, Chmn.
Nobutane Yamamoto, Exec. Officer-Corp. Procurement

Phone: 81-6-6908-1121	Fax: 81-6-6908-2351
Toll-Free:	
Address: 1006 Oaza Kadoma, Kadoma, Osaka, 571-8501 Japan	

GROWTH PLANS/SPECIAL FEATURES:

Matsushita Electric Industrial Co., Ltd. (MEI) produces primarily consumer electronics products marketed under brand names such as Panasonic, National, Quasar, Technics and JVC. The company's business areas are audio, visual and communications (AVC); home appliances; components and devices; MEW and PanaHome; JVC; and other business. MEI's AVC products, which accounted for 38% of 2006 sales, include computers; monitors; optical disk drives; cell phones; copying machines and printers; plasma, LCD and CRT TVs; VCRs; camcorders; DVD players and recorders; and audio equipment. Home appliance products, 12% of sales, include refrigerators, air conditioners, washing machines, dryers, vacuum cleaners, dishwashers, microwave ovens, cooking appliances, medical equipment, electric lamps, vending machines and electric and gas heating equipment. Components and devices, 13% of sales, include semiconductors, batteries, electric motors and general components such as circuit boards and speakers. The MEW and PanaHome segment, 17% of sales, supplies lighting fixtures, interior furnishing materials, automation controls, rental apartment housing, home remodeling, residential real estate and medical and nursing care facilities. The JVC segment, 7% of sales, produces business-use AV equipment; AV software for DVDs, video tapes and CDs; and other equipment similar to the AVC division's. The other business segment, 13% of sales, includes industrial robots, bicycles and electronic-components-mounting machines. In April 2007, the company discontinued and liquidated its operations at Panasonic Electronics Devices do Brasil Ltda. and its subsidiary Panasonic Componentes Electronicos da Amazonia Ltda. In January 2007, it announced plans to construct its fifth plasma display panel (PDP) plant through its joint venture with Toray Industries, Inc., a chemical group, called Matsushita PDP Company Ltd. Construct is slated to begin in November 2007, and production in 2009. The joint venture has already invested close to $2.3 billion in the plant, which should produce 1 million PDPs a month.

FINANCIALS: Sales and profits are in thousands of dollars—add 000 to get the full amount. 2007 Note: Financial information for 2007 was not available for all companies at press time.

2007 Sales: $81,831,200	2007 Profits: $1,949,650	**U.S. Stock Ticker: MC**
2006 Sales: $75,601,800	2006 Profits: $1,312,500	**Int'l Ticker: 6752** Int'l Exchange: Tokyo-TSE
2005 Sales: $81,298,000	2005 Profits: $546,000	Employees: 328,645
2004 Sales: $71,920,600	2004 Profits: $405,200	Fiscal Year Ends: 3/31
2003 Sales: $61,681,000	2003 Profits: $-162,000	Parent Company:

SALARIES/BENEFITS:

Pension Plan:	ESOP Stock Plan:	Profit Sharing:	Top Exec. Salary: $	Bonus: $
Savings Plan:	Stock Purch. Plan:		Second Exec. Salary: $	Bonus: $

OTHER THOUGHTS:

Apparent Women Officers or Directors:
Hot Spot for Advancement for Women/Minorities:

LOCATIONS: ("Y" = Yes)

West:	Southwest:	Midwest:	Southeast:	Northeast:	International:
Y	Y	Y	Y	Y	Y

Note: Financial information, benefits and other data can change quickly and may vary from those stated here.

MCCLATCHY COMPANY (THE)   www.mcclatchy.com

Industry Group Code: 511110   Ranks within this company's industry group: Sales: 10   Profits: 17

Print Media/Publishing:		Movies:		Equipment/Supplies:		Broadcast/Cable:		Music/Audio:		Sports/Games/Gambling:	
Newspapers:	Y	Movie Theaters:		Equipment/Supplies:		Broadcast TV:		Music Production:		Games/Sports:	
Magazines:		Movie Production:		Gambling Equipment:		Cable TV:		Retail Music:		Retail Games Stores:	
Books:		TV/Video Prod.:		Special Services:	Y	Satellite Broadcast:		Retail Audio Equip.:		Stadiums/Teams:	
Book Stores:		Video Rental:		Advertising Services:	Y	Radio:		Music Print./Dist.:		Gambling/Casinos:	
Distribution/Printing:		Video Distribution:		Info. Sys. Software:		Online Information:		Multimedia:		Rides/Theme Parks:	

TYPES OF BUSINESS:

Newspaper Publishing
Online Publishing
Direct Marketing
Paper Manufacturing

BRANDS/DIVISIONS/AFFILIATES:

Sacramento Bee (The)
Star Tribune (The)
Anchorage Daily News
News & Observer (The)
RealCities.com
McClatchy Interactive
Newsprint Ventures, Inc.
Knight Ridder, Inc.

CONTACTS: *Note: Officers with more than one job title may be intentionally listed here more than once.*

Gary B. Pruitt, CEO
Gary B. Pruitt, Pres.
Patrick J. Talamantes, CFO/VP-Finance
Heather L. Fagundes, VP-Human Resources
Karole Morgan-Prager, General Counsel/VP/Corp. Sec.
Frank Whittaker, VP-Oper
Christian A. Hendricks, VP-Interactive Media
Patrick J. Talamantes, VP-Finance
Maggie Wilderotter, Chmn./CEO-Citizens Communications
Robert J. Weill, VP-Oper.
Lynn Dickerson, VP-Oper.
Howard Weaver, VP-News
Gary B. Pruitt, Chmn.

Phone: 916-321-1855	Fax: 916-321-1869
Toll-Free:	
Address: 2100 Q St., Sacramento, CA 95816 US	

GROWTH PLANS/SPECIAL FEATURES:

The McClatchy Company is the second largest newspaper company in the U.S, with 31 daily newspapers and 50 non-dailies in 29 U.S. markets. The firm's portfolio of publications includes The Sacramento Bee, The News & Observer, The Fresno Bee, Anchorage Daily News, The News Tribune, Tri-City Herald, The Beaufort Gazette, The Modesto Bee, The Island Packet and The Herald. Advertising accounts for approximately 84% of the firm's total revenues, while circulation accounts for about 14%. Over the decades, McClatchy's newspapers have been awarded 13 Pulitzer Prizes, three of which were gold medals for public service. The firm's largest newspaper is The Star Tribune in Minneapolis-St. Paul, Minnesota. The company's oldest and second-largest daily newspaper is The Sacramento Bee, originally published in 1857. McClatchy's core newspaper business is supplemented by a growing array of niche products and direct marketing initiatives. The company operates RealCities.com, (the largest national network of regional and city websites); McClatchy Interactive (an online publishing business that provides newspapers with content publishing tools and software development); and is part owner of Career Builder.com, the largest online classified employment listing service. The firm also operates Newsprint Ventures, Inc., which in turn operates the Ponderay newsprint mill near Spokane, Washington. In July 2007, the company sold former subsidiary Newscom LLC to Mainstream Data. In March 2007, the firm sold the Star Tribune newspaper of Minneapolis, Minnesota to Avista Capital Partners for approximately $530 million.

FINANCIALS: Sales and profits are in thousands of dollars—add 000 to get the full amount. 2007 Note: Financial information for 2007 was not available for all companies at press time.

2007 Sales: $	2007 Profits: $	**U.S. Stock Ticker: MNI**
2006 Sales: $1,675,190	2006 Profits: $-155,577	**Int'l Ticker:** Int'l Exchange:
2005 Sales: $807,480	2005 Profits: $160,519	Employees: 16,791
2004 Sales: $783,273	2004 Profits: $155,900	Fiscal Year Ends: 12/31
2003 Sales: $1,099,391	2003 Profits: $150,222	Parent Company:

SALARIES/BENEFITS:

Pension Plan: Y	ESOP Stock Plan:	Profit Sharing:	Top Exec. Salary: $1,050,000	Bonus: $1,950,000
Savings Plan: Y	Stock Purch. Plan:		Second Exec. Salary: $532,000	Bonus: $300,000

OTHER THOUGHTS:

Apparent Women Officers or Directors: 8
Hot Spot for Advancement for Women/Minorities: Y

LOCATIONS: ("Y" = Yes)

West:	Southwest:	Midwest:	Southeast:	Northeast:	International:
Y		Y	Y	Y	

MCGRAW HILL COS INC

www.mcgraw-hill.com

Industry Group Code: 511130 Ranks within this company's industry group: Sales: 2 Profits: 2

Print Media/Publishing:		Movies:		Equipment/Supplies:		Broadcast/Cable:		Music/Audio:		Sports/Games/Gambling:	
Newspapers:		Movie Theaters:		Equipment/Supplies:		Broadcast TV:	Y	Music Production:		Games/Sports:	
Magazines:	Y	Movie Production:		Gambling Equipment:		Cable TV:		Retail Music:		Retail Games Stores:	
Books:	Y	TV/Video Prod.:		Special Services:	Y	Satellite Broadcast:		Retail Audio Equip.:		Stadiums/Teams:	
Book Stores:		Video Rental:		Advertising Services:	Y	Radio:		Music Print./Dist.:	Y	Gambling/Casinos:	
Distribution/Printing:		Video Distribution:		Info. Sys. Software:	Y	Online Information:		Multimedia:		Rides/Theme Parks:	

TYPES OF BUSINESS:

Book Publishing
Financial Information
Magazine Publishing
Online Data
Research Services
Television Broadcasting

BRANDS/DIVISIONS/AFFILIATES:

Standard & Poor's
S&P 500
McGraw-Hill Education
BuisinessWeek Magazine
McGraw-Hill Construction
Aviation Week
McGraw-Hill Broadcasting
JD Power & Associates

CONTACTS: Note: Officers with more than one job title may be intentionally listed here more than once.

Harold W. McGraw, III, CEO
Harold W. McGraw, III, Pres.
Robert J. Bahash, CFO/Exec. VP
David L. Murphy, Exec. VP-Human Resources
Bruce D. Marcus, CIO/Exec. VP
Kenneth M. Vittor, General Counsel/Exec. VP
Deven Sharma, Exec. VP-Global Strategy
Steven H. Weiss, VP-Corp. Comm.
Henry Hirschberg, Pres., McGraw-Hill Education
Glenn S. Goldberg, Pres., Info. & Media Svcs.
Deven Sharma, Pres., Standard & Poor's
Peter C. Davis, Exec. VP-Global Strategy
Harold W. McGraw, III, Chmn.

Phone: 212-512-2000	Fax: 212-512-4502
Toll-Free:	
Address: 1221 Ave. of the Americas, New York, NY 10020 US	

GROWTH PLANS/SPECIAL FEATURES:

McGraw-Hill Companies, Inc. is a leading global information services provider focused in the financial, education and media services markets.   Within the financial services segment, the company operates Standard & Poor's. Standard & Poor's plays an integral role in the global financial infrastructure, providing credit ratings, independent investment information, analytical services and corporate valuations, including the S&P 1200, a global equity performance benchmark, and the S&P 500, a U.S. portfolio index.   In education, McGraw-Hill Education is leading kindergarten through 12th grade publisher in the U.S., providing traditional textbooks as well as online multimedia tools and courses for students and educators.   In media services, the company operates BusinessWeek Magazine, Aviation Week and Platts, a leading provider of energy information and marketing services, delivered through newsletters, Internet-based news, magazines, databases, conferences and consulting services.   McGraw-Hill Broadcasting encompasses four local television stations, all ABC affiliates, in Denver, Colorado; Indianapolis, Indiana; and San Diego and Bakersfield, California.   The company has 280 offices in 40 countries.   In 2007, McGraw-Hill acquired Goldman Sachs Commodity Index and two equity index families from the Goldman Sachs Group, Inc.   Soon after, the firm sold its Standard & Poor's mutual fund data business to Morningstar, Inc. Following this sale, Standard & Poor's acquired ClariFl, a leading provider of software and services focused on quantitative portfolio management and research.   McGraw-Hill also sold its Benziger product line, which serves the Catholic school market, to CFM Religion Publishing Group, LLC.   Recently, the firm's Standard & Poors holding acquired IMAKE Consulting and ABSXchange to enhance the company's capacity to survey and analyze financial markets.

McGraw-Hill offers employee benefits including continuing development; adoption and tuition assistance; parental leave; flexible work arrangements; childcare, sickcare; before and after school care; and summer and holiday care.

FINANCIALS: Sales and profits are in thousands of dollars—add 000 to get the full amount. 2007 Note: Financial information for 2007 was not available for all companies at press time.

2007 Sales: $	2007 Profits: $	**U.S. Stock Ticker: MHP**
2006 Sales: $6,255,138	2006 Profits: $882,231	**Int'l Ticker:** Int'l Exchange:
2005 Sales: $6,003,642	2005 Profits: $844,306	Employees: 20,214
2004 Sales: $5,250,538	2004 Profits: $755,823	Fiscal Year Ends: 12/31
2003 Sales: $4,999,382	2003 Profits: $687,650	Parent Company:

SALARIES/BENEFITS:

Pension Plan:	ESOP Stock Plan:	Profit Sharing:	Top Exec. Salary: $1,242,000	Bonus: $1,938,000
Savings Plan: Y	Stock Purch. Plan:		Second Exec. Salary: $826,000	Bonus: $1,100,000

OTHER THOUGHTS:

Apparent Women Officers or Directors:
Hot Spot for Advancement for Women/Minorities:

LOCATIONS: ("Y" = Yes)

West:	Southwest:	Midwest:	Southeast:	Northeast:	International:
Y	Y	Y		Y	Y

Note: Financial information, benefits and other data can change quickly and may vary from those stated here.

MDI ENTERTAINMENT LLC   www.mdientertainment.com

Industry Group Code: 541800 Ranks within this company's industry group: Sales: Profits:

Print Media/Publishing:	Movies:	Equipment/Supplies:		Broadcast/Cable:	Music/Audio:	Sports/Games/Gambling:	
Newspapers:	Movie Theaters:	Equipment/Supplies:	Y	Broadcast TV:	Music Production:	Games/Sports:	
Magazines:	Movie Production:	Gambling Equipment:	Y	Cable TV:	Retail Music:	Retail Games Stores:	
Books:	TV/Video Prod.:	Special Services:	Y	Satellite Broadcast:	Retail Audio Equip.:	Stadiums/Teams:	
Book Stores:	Video Rental:	Advertising Services:	Y	Radio:	Music Print./Dist.:	Gambling/Casinos:	Y
Distribution/Printing:	Video Distribution:	Info. Sys. Software:		Online Information:	Multimedia:	Rides/Theme Parks:	

TYPES OF BUSINESS:

Lottery-Focused Marketing
Events & Promotions
Web Design
Electronic Lottery Cards
Advertising
Game Development
Research

BRANDS/DIVISIONS/AFFILIATES:

Scientific Games Corp

CONTACTS: *Note: Officers with more than one job title may be intentionally listed here more than once.*

Steven M. Saferin, Pres.
Bev Opie, Sr. VP-Mktg. & Sales
Don Walsh, Sr. VP-Merch. & Prod. Dev.
Anne Villa, VP-Oper.
Carla Schaefer, Sr. VP-Bus. Dev.
Bob Kowalczyk, VP-Internet Svcs.
Anne Villa, VP-Finance
Lami Adabonyan, Web Dev.
Charles Kline, Exec. VP
Kyle Rogers, Exec. VP

Phone: 770-664-3700	**Fax:** 770-343-8798
Toll-Free:	
Address: 1500 Bluegrass Lakes Pkwy., Alpharetta, GA 30004 US	

GROWTH PLANS/SPECIAL FEATURES:

MDI Entertainment, LLC, a subsidiary of Scientific Games Corp., specializes in creating, marketing and implementing entertainment-based promotions mainly in the U.S. and Canada. Its strategic focus is to develop and market lottery ticket games based on well-known entertainment and pop cultural icon licensed properties. MDI's basic selling proposition to lotteries is that a licensed lottery game will create appeal and interest among a segment of consumers much better than a generic lottery game, which will hold no value for many potential lottery customers. The company encourages lotteries to establish a constant stream of different licensed games, about one per quarter, as part of their overall product marketing program. Beginning with brands such as Star Trek, Wheel of Fortune and Twilight Zone, the firm's licensed games division now includes nearly 100 brands, such as Harley-Davidson; World Poker Tour; Betty Boop; and Elvis Presley. The company's revenue comes from two main sources: the sale of bonus prize products to lotteries using MDI-licensed games; and license/royalty fees paid by lotteries for the rights to market the games in their jurisdictions. MDI purchases prize products resold to lotteries from other licensees of a particular brand, often becoming one of the largest customers of the suppliers. Products are sold to lotteries in bulk, and then MDI fulfills prizes individually to lottery winners as designated by the lottery, which are packaged as elements of a full-service lottery promotion tied to licenses that the company acquires. The company also provides such services as website development; advertising support; game development; promotions; and research for its lottery customers. In May 2007, the company entered an exclusive 10-year agreement with Electronic Game Card, Inc. to distribute the Electronic GameCard, an electronic and interactive lottery ticket product that has been marketed successfully in Iowa and Kansas.

FINANCIALS: Sales and profits are in thousands of dollars—add 000 to get the full amount. 2007 Note: Financial information for 2007 was not available for all companies at press time.

2007 Sales: $	2007 Profits: $	**U.S. Stock Ticker: Subsidiary**
2006 Sales: $	2006 Profits: $	**Int'l Ticker:** Int'l Exchange:
2005 Sales: $	2005 Profits: $	Employees: 22
2004 Sales: $	2004 Profits: $	Fiscal Year Ends: 12/31
2003 Sales: $	2003 Profits: $	Parent Company: SCIENTIFIC GAMES CORPORATION

SALARIES/BENEFITS:

Pension Plan:	ESOP Stock Plan:	Profit Sharing:	Top Exec. Salary: $330,750	Bonus: $
Savings Plan:	Stock Purch. Plan:		Second Exec. Salary: $201,212	Bonus: $

OTHER THOUGHTS:

Apparent Women Officers or Directors: 23
Hot Spot for Advancement for Women/Minorities: Y

LOCATIONS: ("Y" = Yes)

West:	Southwest:	Midwest:	Southeast:	Northeast:	International:
			Y		

MEDIA GENERAL INC

www.media-general.com

Industry Group Code: 511110 Ranks within this company's industry group: Sales: 14 Profits: 8

Print Media/Publishing:		Movies:	Equipment/Supplies:		Broadcast/Cable:		Music/Audio:	Sports/Games/Gambling:	
Newspapers:	Y	Movie Theaters:	Equipment/Supplies:		Broadcast TV:	Y	Music Production:	Games/Sports:	Y
Magazines:		Movie Production:	Gambling Equipment:		Cable TV:		Retail Music:	Retail Games Stores:	
Books:		TV/Video Prod.:	Special Services:	Y	Satellite Broadcast:		Retail Audio Equip.:	Stadiums/Teams:	
Book Stores:		Video Rental:	Advertising Services:	Y	Radio:		Music Print./Dist.:	Gambling/Casinos:	
Distribution/Printing:		Video Distribution:	Info. Sys. Software:	Y	Online Information:		Multimedia:	Rides/Theme Parks:	

TYPES OF BUSINESS:

Newspaper Publishing
Broadcast Television
Interactive Media
Gaming & Advergaming

BRANDS/DIVISIONS/AFFILIATES:

Tampa Tribune (The)
Richmond Times-Dispatch
Blockdot.com
Central Virginia Gazette (The)
Winston-Salem Journal
Mechanicsville Local (The)

CONTACTS: Note: Officers with more than one job title may be intentionally listed here more than once.

Marshall N. Morton, CEO
O. Reid Ashe, Jr., COO/Exec. VP
Marshall N. Morton, Pres.
John A. Schauss, CFO/VP-Finance
James F. Woodward, VP-Human Resources
George L. Mahoney, General Counsel/VP/Corp. Sec.
Lou Anne J. Nabhan, VP-Corp. Comm.
John A. Schauss, VP-Finance
H. Graham Woodlief, Jr., VP/Pres., Publishing Div.
James A. Zimmerman, VP/Pres., Broadcasting Div.
C. Kirk Read, VP/Pres., Interactive Media Div.
J. Stewart Bryan, III, Chmn.

Phone: 804-649-6000	Fax: 804-649-6066
Toll-Free:	
Address: 333 E. Franklin St., Richmond, VA 23219 US	

GROWTH PLANS/SPECIAL FEATURES:

Media General, Inc. is an independent communications company, situated primarily in the Southeast with interests in newspapers, television stations and interactive media. The business incorporates three different divisions: publishing (50% of revenue), broadcasting (50%) and the interactive media division (integrated). Its publishing division includes three metropolitan newspapers, one each in Richmond, Tampa and Winston-Salem; 25 daily community newspapers in Virginia, North Carolina, Florida, Alabama and South Carolina; and over 150 weekly newspapers and other publications. Media General's broadcast division owns and operates 32 broadcast television stations affiliated with NBC, ABC, CBS and CW, and located primarily in the southeastern U.S. Media General's stations reach more than 32% of all television households in the Southeast and 9.5% nationwide. The interactive media division operates more than 75 online enterprises affiliated with the company's newspapers and television stations. The division also crosses over into the gaming and advergaming (the use of interactive games to deliver advertising) sectors. The company's corporate strategy emphasizes convergence, meaning integration of the three divisions to create a superior information base for the consumer. An example of these efforts is the Tampa market, where The Tampa Tribune, WFLA-TV and TBO.com share the company's news center facility and work side by side to provide comprehensive news, information and entertainment. Recently, Media General entered into a strategic alliance with Yahoo! Inc., joining a national consortium of over 200 newspapers to deliver classified advertising to consumers. The division is currently working with Yahoo! to transition the online career sections of its 25 daily newspapers to a Yahoo!HotJobs-driven platform. In 2007, the company announced it was considering the purchase of five television stations in mid-sized markets.

Media General offers its employees flexible benefits including various health and welfare programs, insurance programs, tuition reimbursement and counseling assistance.

FINANCIALS: Sales and profits are in thousands of dollars—add 000 to get the full amount. 2007 Note: Financial information for 2007 was not available for all companies at press time.

2007 Sales: $	2007 Profits: $	U.S. Stock Ticker: MEG
2006 Sales: $983,189	2006 Profits: $79,042	Int'l Ticker: Int'l Exchange:
2005 Sales: $876,377	2005 Profits: $-243,042	Employees: 7,200
2004 Sales: $900,400	2004 Profits: $80,200	Fiscal Year Ends: 12/31
2003 Sales: $837,423	2003 Profits: $58,685	Parent Company:

SALARIES/BENEFITS:

Pension Plan:	ESOP Stock Plan:	Profit Sharing:	Top Exec. Salary: $785,000	Bonus: $475,592
Savings Plan: Y	Stock Purch. Plan: Y		Second Exec. Salary: $730,000	Bonus: $324,332

OTHER THOUGHTS:

Apparent Women Officers or Directors: 1
Hot Spot for Advancement for Women/Minorities:

LOCATIONS: ("Y" = Yes)

West:	Southwest:	Midwest:	Southeast:	Northeast:	International:
		Y	Y	Y	

Note: Financial information, benefits and other data can change quickly and may vary from those stated here.

MEDIACOM COMMUNICATIONS CORP www.mediacomcc.com

Industry Group Code: 513220 Ranks within this company's industry group: Sales: 15   Profits: 18

Print Media/Publishing:	Movies:	Equipment/Supplies:		Broadcast/Cable:		Music/Audio:	Sports/Games/Gambling:
Newspapers:	Movie Theaters:	Equipment/Supplies:		Broadcast TV:	Y	Music Production:	Games/Sports:
Magazines:	Movie Production:	Gambling Equipment:	Y	Cable TV:	Y	Retail Music:	Retail Games Stores:
Books:	TV/Video Prod.:	Special Services:	Y	Satellite Broadcast:		Retail Audio Equip.:	Stadiums/Teams:
Book Stores:	Video Rental:	Advertising Services:		Radio:		Music Print./Dist.:	Gambling/Casinos:
Distribution/Printing:	Video Distribution:	Info. Sys. Software:		Online Information:		Multimedia:	Rides/Theme Parks:

TYPES OF BUSINESS:

Cable TV Service
Internet Service
Digital Cable
Telephone Service

BRANDS/DIVISIONS/AFFILIATES:

Mediacom Online
Mediacom OnlineMax
Mediacom Phone

CONTACTS: *Note: Officers with more than one job title may be intentionally listed here more than once.*

Rocco B. Commisso, CEO
Mark E. Stephan, CFO/Exec. VP/Treas.
Michael Rahimi, VP-Mktg.
Italia Commisso-Weinand, Sr. VP-Human Resources
Joseph E. Young, General Counsel/Sr. VP/Corp. Sec.
John G. Pascarelli, Exec. VP-Oper.
Calvin G. Craib, Sr. VP-Bus. Dev.
Brian M. Walsh, Controller
Charles J. Bartolotta, Sr. VP-Customer Oper.
Edward S. Pardini, Sr. VP-North Central Div.
Rocco B. Commisso, Chmn.

Phone: 845-695-2600	Fax: 845-695-2699
Toll-Free:	
Address: 100 Crystal Run Rd., Middletown, NY 10941 US	

GROWTH PLANS/SPECIAL FEATURES:

Mediacom Communications Corp provides customers with a wide array of broadband products and services to approximately 1.38 million basic subscribers, 528,000 digital customers, 578,000 high-speed data customers and 105,000 telephone customers to 2.5 million homes. The firm offers its customers a full array of traditional analog video services, which includes basic service, digital video service, pay-per-view service, high definition television, digital voice recorders and video-on-demand. In addition, the company offers Mediacom Online, which offers consumers packages of cable modem-based services with varied speeds and prices. Mediacom's premium Internet service, Mediacom OnlineMax, allows maximum downloads and upload speeds of 15Mbps and 1Mbps and includes content such as americangreetings.com, Britannica Online, Disney Connection, ESPN 360 and MLB Gameday. The firm's Mediacom Phone offers customers unlimited local, regional and long-distance calling within the U.S., Puerto Rico, U.S. Virgin Islands and Canada, which is delivered over VoIP that digitizes voice signals and routes them as data packets through Mediacom's controlled broadband cable systems. Mediacom also offers businesses high speed data services, customized Internet access and data transport solutions for industries that serve the healthcare, financial services and education market. The firm also generates additional revenues from the sale of advertising time on 44 of its satellite-delivered channels, which includes CNN, Lifetime, Discovery, ESPN, TBS and USA. In February 2007, Mediacom announced that it would increase the maximum download speed of its residential Internet service from 5Mbps to 8Mbps and double its maximum upload speed from 256 Kbps to 512Kbps.

Mediacom offers employees broadband service, an education enrichment program, flexible spending accounts, NCTI reimbursement, health insurance and an employee referral bonus program.

FINANCIALS: Sales and profits are in thousands of dollars—add 000 to get the full amount. 2007 Note: Financial information for 2007 was not available for all companies at press time.

2007 Sales: $	2007 Profits: $	**U.S. Stock Ticker: MCCC**
2006 Sales: $1,210,400	2006 Profits: $-124,922	**Int'l Ticker:** Int'l Exchange:
2005 Sales: $1,098,822	2005 Profits: $-222,228	Employees: 4,248
2004 Sales: $1,057,226	2004 Profits: $13,552	Fiscal Year Ends: 12/31
2003 Sales: $1,004,889	2003 Profits: $-62,475	Parent Company:

SALARIES/BENEFITS:

Pension Plan:	ESOP Stock Plan: Y	Profit Sharing:	Top Exec. Salary: $800,000	Bonus: $425,000
Savings Plan: Y	Stock Purch. Plan:		Second Exec. Salary: $280,000	Bonus: $60,000

OTHER THOUGHTS:

Apparent Women Officers or Directors: 1
Hot Spot for Advancement for Women/Minorities:

LOCATIONS: ("Y" = Yes)

West:	Southwest:	Midwest:	Southeast:	Northeast:	International:
Y		Y	Y	Y	

MEDIANEWS GROUP INC

www.medianewsgroup.com

Industry Group Code: 511110 **Ranks within this company's industry group:** Sales: 15 Profits: 13

Print Media/Publishing:		Movies:		Equipment/Supplies:		Broadcast/Cable:		Music/Audio:		Sports/Games/Gambling:	
Newspapers:	Y	Movie Theaters:		Equipment/Supplies:		Broadcast TV:	Y	Music Production:		Games/Sports:	
Magazines:		Movie Production:		Gambling Equipment:		Cable TV:		Retail Music:		Retail Games Stores:	
Books:		TV/Video Prod.:		Special Services:	Y	Satellite Broadcast:		Retail Audio Equip.:		Stadiums/Teams:	
Book Stores:		Video Rental:		Advertising Services:	Y	Radio:		Music Print./Dist.:		Gambling/Casinos:	
Distribution/Printing:		Video Distribution:		Info. Sys. Software:		Online Information:		Multimedia:		Rides/Theme Parks:	

TYPES OF BUSINESS:

Newspaper Publishing
Television Broadcasting
Radio Broadcasting
Commercial Printing
Electronic Advertising
Online Publishing
Website Development & Maintenance Services
Real Estate Marketing Services

BRANDS/DIVISIONS/AFFILIATES:

MediaNews Group Interactive (MNGi)
PowerOne Media
SeeitBuyit
Rate Watch
Santa Cruz Sentinel
Hearst Corporation (The)
Kaango Ventures, LLC
Connecticut Post

CONTACTS: Note: Officers with more than one job title may be intentionally listed here more than once.

William Dean Singleton, CEO/Vice Chmn.
Steven B. Rossi, COO/Exec. VP
Joseph J. Lodovic, IV, Pres.
Ronald A. Mayo, CFO/VP
Charles M. Kamen, VP-Human Resources
David M. Bessen, CIO/VP
Patricia Robinson, Corp. Sec.
Anthony F. Tierno, Sr. VP-Oper.
Elizabeth A. (Liz) Gaier, Sr. VP-New Bus. Dev.
James L. McDougald, Treas.
David J. Butler, VP-News
Linda K. Bradford, VP-Shared Svcs.
Steven M. (Steve) Barkmeier, VP-Tax
Stephen M. Hesse, Sr. VP-Circulation
Richard B. Scudder, Chmn.

Phone: 303-954-6360	Fax: 303-954-6320
Toll-Free:	
Address: 101 W. Colfax Ave., Ste. 1100, Denver, CO 80202 US	

GROWTH PLANS/SPECIAL FEATURES:

MediaNews Group, Inc. (MNG) is a leading private newspaper company in the U.S., publishing 57 daily and roughly 100 non-daily newspapers in 12 states, with a combined daily and Sunday paid circulation of approximately 2.6 million and 2.9 million, respectively. The company also owns metropolitan daily newspapers in San Jose, St. Paul, Denver, Salt Lake City and Detroit. MNG's principal sources of revenue are print advertising and circulation. Other sources of revenue include commercial printing and electronic advertising. In addition, the company owns a CBS affiliate television station in Anchorage, Alaska and four radio stations in Texas. The company also owns MediaNews Group Interactive (MNGi), which maintains 74 web sites, most affiliated with the company's newspapers. Services include providing the company's newspapers with the tools, technologies and services they require to maintain their presence as competitive web sites in each of the communities they serve. These services include hosting, online publishing/site delivery, maintenance, ongoing development, training, advertisement delivery, site analytics and business development support. 72% of the group's revenue is generated by automotive and real estate advertising. The company has investments in PowerOne Media, a provider of classified advertising technologies; and SeeitBuyit, incorporated as Rate Watch, a marketing and promotional services company that provides real estate industry listing and selling tools. MNG's new consolidated printing plant in Denver is expected to come online in January 2008. In February 2007, the company acquired the Santa Cruz Sentinel. In November 2007, MNG and Hearst Corporation acquired Kaango Ventures, LLC for approximately $20 million. In October 2007, the company expanded its Connecticut joint-venture with Hearst Corporation, which originally included the Connecticut Post and The News-Times, to include The Advocate and Greenwich Time.

FINANCIALS: Sales and profits are in thousands of dollars—add 000 to get the full amount. 2007 Note: Financial information for 2007 was not available for all companies at press time.

2007 Sales: $1,329,800	2007 Profits: $35,600	**U.S. Stock Ticker:** Private	
2006 Sales: $835,900	2006 Profits: $1,100	**Int'l Ticker:** Int'l Exchange:	
2005 Sales: $779,300	2005 Profits: $39,900	Employees: 12,700	
2004 Sales: $753,800	2004 Profits: $27,600	Fiscal Year Ends: 6/30	
2003 Sales: $738,598	2003 Profits: $40,828	Parent Company:	

SALARIES/BENEFITS:

Pension Plan:	ESOP Stock Plan:	Profit Sharing:	Top Exec. Salary: $962,475	Bonus: $450,000
Savings Plan:	Stock Purch. Plan:		Second Exec. Salary: $639,600	Bonus: $400,000

OTHER THOUGHTS:

Apparent Women Officers or Directors: 4
Hot Spot for Advancement for Women/Minorities: Y

LOCATIONS: ("Y" = Yes)

West:	Southwest:	Midwest:	Southeast:	Northeast:	International:
Y	Y	Y		Y	

MELCO PBL ENTERTAINMENT LIMITED   www.melco-pbl.com

Industry Group Code: 713210 Ranks within this company's industry group: Sales: 11   Profits: 11

Print Media/Publishing:	Movies:	Equipment/Supplies:	Broadcast/Cable:	Music/Audio:	Sports/Games/Gambling:	
Newspapers:	Movie Theaters:	Equipment/Supplies:	Broadcast TV:	Music Production:	Games/Sports:	
Magazines:	Movie Production:	Gambling Equipment:	Cable TV:	Retail Music:	Retail Games Stores:	
Books:	TV/Video Prod.:	Special Services:	Satellite Broadcast:	Retail Audio Equip.:	Stadiums/Teams:	
Book Stores:	Video Rental:	Advertising Services:	Radio:	Music Print./Dist.:	Gambling/Casinos:	Y
Distribution/Printing:	Video Distribution:	Info. Sys. Software:	Online Information:	Multimedia:	Rides/Theme Parks:	

TYPES OF BUSINESS:

Casino Resort Operations
Electronic Gaming
Casino Resort Development

BRANDS/DIVISIONS/AFFILIATES:

Melco International Development Limited
Publishing & Broadcasting Limited
Melco PBL Gaming
Crown Macau Hotel Casino
Tenmasa
Aurora
City of Dreams
Mocha Clubs

CONTACTS: *Note: Officers with more than one job title may be intentionally listed here more than once.*

Lawrence Ho, CEO/Co-Chmn.
Gary Saunders, COO/Exec. VP
Simon Dewhurst, CFO/Exec. VP
Akiko Takahashi, Dir.-Human Resources
Stephanie Cheung, General Counsel/Corp. Sec.
Richard Tsiang, Chief Dev. Officer/Exec. VP
Ted (Ying Tat) Chan, Head-Special Projects
Constance (Ching Hui) Hsu, COO-Mocha Clubs
Greg Hawkins, CEO-Crown Macau
Nigel Dean, Dir.-Internal Audit
James Packer, Co-Chmn.

Phone: 852-2598-3600	**Fax:** 852-2537-3618
Toll-Free:	
Address: Penthouse, 38th Fl., The Centrium, 60 Wyndham St., Central, Hong Kong China	

GROWTH PLANS/SPECIAL FEATURES:

Melco PBL Entertainment Limited (Melco PBL), a joint-venture between Melco International Development Limited and Publishing & Broadcasting Limited, develops, owns and, through its subsidiary Melco PBL Gaming, operates casino gaming and entertainment resort facilities in Macau. Melco PBL is one of only six companies granted concessions or sub-concessions to operate casino resort facilities in Macau. The company's Crown Macau Hotel Casino, opened in May 2007, is an exclusive hotel and casino primarily devoted to the high-end gaming market, with 36 stories, approximately 220 gaming tables, 550 gaming machines, exclusive private gaming salons, 216 rooms, a day spa, an outdoor garden podium and several high-end restaurants, including Tenmasa, a tempura restaurant; Aurora, a French restaurant; Ying, a Cantonese restaurant; and Kira, a Japanese restaurant. Melco PBL is currently planning its City of Dreams development located on Macau's Cotai Strip, which will be modeled on the Las Vegas Strip. Plans for the development include a central 420,000 square foot casino; the bubble, an architectural landmark which will constantly host surprise attractions; three hotels with a total of 1,600 rooms; and a 50,000 square foot mall. For the Macau peninsula shoreline, the company is currently developing plans for a hotel and casino complex. Melco PBL's seven Mocha Clubs provide electronic gaming in a café style setting, with a total of 1,100 machines, including jackpot products, electronic gaming tables and slot machines. Each Mocha Club features a unique theme.

Melco offers its employees an educational assistance program, an employee recognition program, career development opportunities, employee gathering activities and medical and dental insurance.

FINANCIALS: Sales and profits are in thousands of dollars—add 000 to get the full amount. 2007 Note: Financial information for 2007 was not available for all companies at press time.

2007 Sales: $	2007 Profits: $	**U.S. Stock Ticker: MPEL**
2006 Sales: $36,101	2006 Profits: $-73,479	**Int'l Ticker:** Int'l Exchange:
2005 Sales: $17,328	2005 Profits: $-3,259	Employees: 657
2004 Sales: $	2004 Profits: $	Fiscal Year Ends: 12/31
2003 Sales: $	2003 Profits: $	Parent Company:

SALARIES/BENEFITS:

Pension Plan: Y	ESOP Stock Plan:	Profit Sharing:	Top Exec. Salary: $	Bonus: $
Savings Plan:	Stock Purch. Plan:		Second Exec. Salary: $	Bonus: $

OTHER THOUGHTS:

Apparent Women Officers or Directors: 2
Hot Spot for Advancement for Women/Minorities:

LOCATIONS: ("Y" = Yes)

West:	Southwest:	Midwest:	Southeast:	Northeast:	International:
					Y

MEREDITH CORP

www.meredith.com

Industry Group Code: 511120 Ranks within this company's industry group: Sales: 4 Profits: 3

Print Media/Publishing:		Movies:		Equipment/Supplies:		Broadcast/Cable:		Music/Audio:		Sports/Games/Gambling:	
Newspapers:		Movie Theaters:		Equipment/Supplies:		Broadcast TV:	Y	Music Production:		Games/Sports:	
Magazines:	Y	Movie Production:		Gambling Equipment:		Cable TV:		Retail Music:		Retail Games Stores:	
Books:	Y	TV/Video Prod.:		Special Services:		Satellite Broadcast:		Retail Audio Equip.:		Stadiums/Teams:	
Book Stores:		Video Rental:		Advertising Services:	Y	Radio:		Music Print./Dist.:		Gambling/Casinos:	
Distribution/Printing:		Video Distribution:		Info. Sys. Software:	Y	Online Information:		Multimedia:		Rides/Theme Parks:	

TYPES OF BUSINESS:

Magazine Publishing
Television Broadcasting
Marketing Services
Book Publishing
Interactive Media
Advertising Agencies

BRANDS/DIVISIONS/AFFILIATES:

Better Homes and Gardens
American Baby
ReadyMade
Genex
New Media Strategies
Directive Corp.
Healia
Better.tv

CONTACTS: Note: Officers with more than one job title may be intentionally listed here more than once.

Stephen M. Lacy, CEO
Stephen M. Lacy, Pres.
Suku V. Radia, CFO/VP
John S. Zeiser, General Counsel/Corp. Sec.
John S. Zeiser, Chief Dev. Officer
Mike Lovell, VP-Investor Rel.
Suku V. Radia, Acting Treas.
Paul Karpowicz, Pres., Broadcasting Group
Jack Griffin, Pres., Publishing Group
Steven M. Cappaert, Corp. Controller
William T. Kerr, Chmn.

Phone: 515-284-3000	**Fax:** 515-284-2700
Toll-Free:	
Address: 1716 Locust St., Des Moines, IA 50309 US	

GROWTH PLANS/SPECIAL FEATURES:

Meredith Corp., a U.S. media and marketing company, engages in magazine and book publishing, television broadcasting, integrated marketing and interactive media. It operates in two segments: publishing and broadcasting. The publishing segment targets women and focuses on the home and family market. Over 25 subscription magazines, including Better Homes and Garden, Family Circle, Ladies' Home Journal, Parents, American Baby, Fitness and More and roughly 180 special interests publications were published in 2007. The division also includes book publishing, with over 400 books in print; integrated marketing; a large consumer database; an extensive Internet presence that consists of 25 web sites and strategic alliances other Internet sites; brand licensing activities; and other related operations. The broadcasting segment includes 13 network-affiliated television stations across the U.S. and one AM radio station. The television stations consists of six CBS affiliates, three FOX affiliates, two MyNetworkTV affiliates, one NBC affiliate and one CW affiliate. The division also includes 18 web sites. Meredith owns ReadyMade, a multimedia brand targeting adults in their 20s and 30s that includes a do-it-yourself lifestyle magazine, a web site, a branded book, branded products such as project plans and kits, and customer marketing operations. Recent acquisitions include Genex, an interactive marketing services firm that specializes in online customer relationship marketing; New Media Strategies, an interactive word-of-mouth marketing company; Healia, a consumer health search engine specializing in finding personalized health information online; and Directive Corp., a customer intelligence firm. In May 2007, the firm launched Better.tv, its first broadband network. Better.tv features over 20 channels of video information covering a range of topics that include food, family, home, style, remodeling, entertainment, relationships, fitness and health. In July 2007, the company stopped the production of Child magazine.

The company offers its employees medical and dental insurance, tuition reimbursement and an employee assistance program.

FINANCIALS: Sales and profits are in thousands of dollars—add 000 to get the full amount. 2007 Note: Financial information for 2007 was not available for all companies at press time.

2007 Sales: $1,615,985	2007 Profits: $162,346	**U.S. Stock Ticker: MDP**
2006 Sales: $1,561,465	2006 Profits: $144,792	**Int'l Ticker:** Int'l Exchange:
2005 Sales: $1,217,300	2005 Profits: $129,042	Employees: 3,160
2004 Sales: $1,161,652	2004 Profits: $110,716	Fiscal Year Ends: 6/30
2003 Sales: $1,080,100	2003 Profits: $5,400	Parent Company:

SALARIES/BENEFITS:

Pension Plan: Y	ESOP Stock Plan:	Profit Sharing:	Top Exec. Salary: $810,000	Bonus: $1,523,813
Savings Plan: Y	Stock Purch. Plan: Y		Second Exec. Salary: $625,000	Bonus: $700,000

OTHER THOUGHTS:

Apparent Women Officers or Directors: 1
Hot Spot for Advancement for Women/Minorities:

LOCATIONS: ("Y" = Yes)

West:	Southwest:	Midwest:	Southeast:	Northeast:	International:
Y	Y	Y	Y	Y	Y

METRO INTERNATIONAL SA   www.metro.lu

Industry Group Code: 511110 Ranks within this company's industry group: Sales: 18 Profits: 11

Print Media/Publishing:		Movies:		Equipment/Supplies:		Broadcast/Cable:		Music/Audio:		Sports/Games/Gambling:	
Newspapers:	Y	Movie Theaters:		Equipment/Supplies:		Broadcast TV:		Music Production:		Games/Sports:	
Magazines:		Movie Production:		Gambling Equipment:		Cable TV:		Retail Music:		Retail Games Stores:	
Books:		TV/Video Prod.:		Special Services:		Satellite Broadcast:		Retail Audio Equip.:		Stadiums/Teams:	
Book Stores:		Video Rental:		Advertising Services:	Y	Radio:		Music Print./Dist.:		Gambling/Casinos:	
Distribution/Printing:		Video Distribution:		Info. Sys. Software:		Online Information:		Multimedia:		Rides/Theme Parks:	

TYPES OF BUSINESS:

Newspaper Publishing
Free Daily Newspapers

BRANDS/DIVISIONS/AFFILIATES:

Metro Boston
Metro USA
Mempo

CONTACTS: *Note: Officers with more than one job title may be intentionally listed here more than once.*

Per Mikael Jensen, CEO
Per Mikael Jensen, Pres.
Frank Mooty, CFO/Sr. VP
Sidonie Kingsmill, Dir.-Global Mktg.
William Skerrett, VP-Human Resources
Steve Nylundh, Exec. VP-Corp. Dev.
Martin Alsander, Exec. VP
Robert Patterson, Exec. VP
Dennis Malamatinas, Chmn.

Phone: 44-20-7016-1300	Fax: 44-20-7016-1400
Toll-Free:	
Address: Interpark House, 7 Down St., 3rd Fl., London, W1J 7AJ UK	

GROWTH PLANS/SPECIAL FEATURES:

Metro International S.A., one of the largest and fastest growing international newspapers, publishes 60 editions of a free daily newspaper in 100 major cities across Europe, North and South America and Asia, attracting over 20 million daily readers in 21 countries and 19 languages. It publishes newspapers on weekday mornings for distribution in high-traffic commuter zones or on public transportation networks. Weekend editions are published in Sweden, Holland and Chile on Saturdays. All Metro editions carry headline local, national and international news in a standardized, accessible format and design. The newspapers are distributed through self-service racks or by hand distributors located in or around public transport networks (such as subways, trains, buses and trams), office buildings and retail outlets; at key distribution points on busy streets; or in other high-density population areas such as college campuses. The company derives revenue solely from selling space for display or classified advertisements in its newspapers. Its advertising revenue has grown at a compound annual rate of 41% since its first publication in 1995. The timing and method of Metro's distribution enables it to target a high proportion of young, professional readers who are not typically reading a daily newspaper. Metro daily readership averages 40% under the age of 30 and 70% under the age of 45, with an equal share of men and women readers. In U.S. operations, Metro distributes in New York City, Boston and Philadelphia. In 2007, Metro launched two new editions for distribution in Calgary and Edmonton, Canada's top six markets accounting for 45% of the country's population. Also in 2007 the company moved into Sao Paulo, Brazil with a new edition as part of a joint venture and franchise agreement with Grupo Bandeirantes, a leading Brazilian television broadcaster.

FINANCIALS: Sales and profits are in thousands of dollars—add 000 to get the full amount. 2007 Note: Financial information for 2007 was not available for all companies at press time.

2007 Sales: $	2007 Profits: $	U.S. Stock Ticker: MTOAF
2006 Sales: $416,534	2006 Profits: $12,975	Int'l Ticker: MTRO SDB A Int'l Exchange: Stockholm-SSE
2005 Sales: $359,650	2005 Profits: $-7,032	Employees: 1,200
2004 Sales: $302,400	2004 Profits: $-8,689	Fiscal Year Ends: 12/31
2003 Sales: $203,600	2003 Profits: $-6,900	Parent Company:

SALARIES/BENEFITS:

Pension Plan:	ESOP Stock Plan:	Profit Sharing:	Top Exec. Salary: $	Bonus: $
Savings Plan:	Stock Purch. Plan:		Second Exec. Salary: $	Bonus: $

OTHER THOUGHTS:

Apparent Women Officers or Directors:
Hot Spot for Advancement for Women/Minorities:

LOCATIONS: ("Y" = Yes)

West:	Southwest:	Midwest:	Southeast:	Northeast:	International:
				Y	Y

METRO-GOLDWYN-MAYER INC (MGM)   www.mgm.com

Industry Group Code: 512110 Ranks within this company's industry group: Sales: 2 Profits:

Print Media/Publishing:	Movies:		Equipment/Supplies:	Broadcast/Cable:	Music/Audio:	Sports/Games/Gambling:
Newspapers:	Movie Theaters:		Equipment/Supplies:	Broadcast TV:	Music Production:	Games/Sports:
Magazines:	Movie Production:	Y	Gambling Equipment:	Cable TV:	Retail Music:	Retail Games Stores:
Books:	TV/Video Prod.:	Y	Special Services:	Satellite Broadcast:	Retail Audio Equip.:	Stadiums/Teams:
Book Stores:	Video Rental:		Advertising Services:	Radio:	Music Print./Dist.:	Gambling/Casinos:
Distribution/Printing:	Video Distribution:	Y	Info. Sys. Software:	Online Information:	Multimedia:	Rides/Theme Parks:

TYPES OF BUSINESS:

Film Production & Distribution
Television, Video & Music Production & Distribution
Broadcast & Cable Television

BRANDS/DIVISIONS/AFFILIATES:

MGM Studios
United Artists Films
Orion Pictures
MGM Television Entertainment
MGM Networks
American Movie Classics
Independent Film Channel (The)
WE: Women's Entertainment

CONTACTS: *Note: Officers with more than one job title may be intentionally listed here more than once.*

Harry E. Sloan, CEO
Rick Sands, COO
Steve Hendry, CFO/Exec. VP
Scott Packman, General Counsel/Exec. VP/Sec.
Jeff Pryor, Exec. VP-Corp. Comm.
Douglas A. Lee, Exec. VP-Worldwide Digital Media
Gary Marenzi, Co-Pres., Worldwide Television
Bruce Tuchman, Exec. VP-MGM Networks
Clark Woods, Pres., Domestic Theatrical Distribution
Harry E. Sloan, Chmn.
Erik Lomis, Exec. VP-Int'l Theatrical & Home Entertainment

Phone: 310-449-3000	Fax: 310-449-8857
Toll-Free:	
Address: 10250 Constellation Blvd., Los Angeles, CA 90067 US	

GROWTH PLANS/SPECIAL FEATURES:

Metro-Goldwyn-Mayer, Inc. (MGM) produces and distributes entertainment products worldwide, including motion pictures, television programming, home video, interactive media, music and licensed merchandise. The firm's operating units include MGM Studios, United Artists Films, Orion Pictures, MGM Television Entertainment, MGM Networks, MGM Distribution Co., MGM Worldwide Television Distribution, MGM Home Entertainment, MGM On Stage, MGM Consumer Products, MGM Music, MGM Interactive and MGM Direct. The company has accumulated a library of more than 4,000 theatrically released films and a significant television library. Films in MGM's library have won over 208 Academy Awards. The company owns 22 James Bond films, five titles in the Rocky film franchise and nine titles in the Pink Panther franchise. The library also includes over 10,400 episodes from television series previously broadcast on prime-time network television, including episodes of The Addams Family, Pink Panther and In the Heat of the Night. Television programs in the firm's library have won 87 Emmy awards and 18 Golden Globe awards. Moreover, MGM has a 20% ownership interest in Rainbow Media's national cable networks, including American Movie Classics (AMC), The Independent Film Channel (IFC) and WE: Women's Entertainment. The company's television production studio produces the current shows Stargate SG-1, Stargate Atlantis, Dead Like Me and The Outer Limits. The firm also holds equity interests in a number of international television channels. MGM is owned by a consortium led by Sony Corp. of America, Providence Equity Partners, Comcast, Quadrangle Group and DLJ Merchant Banking Partners.

The company offers its employees medical, dental and vision insurance; life, disability and personal accident insurance; flexible spending accounts; domestic partners insurance; an employee assistance program; an education assistance program; and employee screenings.

FINANCIALS: Sales and profits are in thousands of dollars—add 000 to get the full amount. 2007 Note: Financial information for 2007 was not available for all companies at press time.

2007 Sales: $	2007 Profits: $	U.S. Stock Ticker: Private
2006 Sales: $1,460,000	2006 Profits: $	Int'l Ticker: Int'l Exchange:
2005 Sales: $1,430,000	2005 Profits: $	Employees: 400
2004 Sales: $1,724,800	2004 Profits: $-29,200	Fiscal Year Ends: 12/31
2003 Sales: $1,883,044	2003 Profits: $-161,714	Parent Company:

SALARIES/BENEFITS:

Pension Plan:	ESOP Stock Plan:	Profit Sharing:	Top Exec. Salary: $2,500,000	Bonus: $1,125,000
Savings Plan: Y	Stock Purch. Plan:		Second Exec. Salary: $2,300,000	Bonus: $1,035,000

OTHER THOUGHTS:

Apparent Women Officers or Directors:
Hot Spot for Advancement for Women/Minorities:

LOCATIONS: ("Y" = Yes)

West:	Southwest:	Midwest:	Southeast:	Northeast:	International:
Y					

MGM MIRAGE

www.mgmmirage.com

Industry Group Code: 721120 Ranks within this company's industry group: Sales: 2 Profits: 1

Print Media/Publishing:	Movies:	Equipment/Supplies:	Broadcast/Cable:	Music/Audio:	Sports/Games/Gambling:	
Newspapers:	Movie Theaters:	Equipment/Supplies:	Broadcast TV:	Music Production:	Games/Sports:	
Magazines:	Movie Production:	Gambling Equipment:	Cable TV:	Retail Music:	Retail Games Stores:	
Books:	TV/Video Prod.:	Special Services:	Satellite Broadcast:	Retail Audio Equip.:	Stadiums/Teams:	Y
Book Stores:	Video Rental:	Advertising Services:	Radio:	Music Print./Dist.:	Gambling/Casinos:	
Distribution/Printing:	Video Distribution:	Info. Sys. Software:	Online Information:	Multimedia:	Rides/Theme Parks:	

TYPES OF BUSINESS:

Casino Hotels & Resorts

BRANDS/DIVISIONS/AFFILIATES:

Bellagio
MGM Grand Las Vegas
Mandalay Bay
Mirage (The)
Luxor
Whiskey Pete's
Excalibur
Treasure Island

CONTACTS: *Note: Officers with more than one job title may be intentionally listed here more than once.*

J. Terrence Lanni, CEO
James J. Murren, Pres.
James J. Murren, CFO
Richard Vosburgh, Sr. VP-Human Resources
Tom Peck, CIO/Sr. VP
Aldo Manzini, Chief Admin. Officer/Exec. VP
Gary N. Jacobs, General Counsel/Exec. VP
James J. Murren, Treas.
John T. Redmond, CEO/Pres., MGM Grand Resorts, LLC
Robert H. Baldwin, CEO/Pres., Mirage Resorts, Inc.
Merlinda Gallegos, VP-Corp. Philanthropy
Mark Stolarczyk, Asst. VP-Corp. Purchasing
J. Terrence Lanni, Chmn.
Teresa Reynolds, Chief Procurement Officer

Phone: 702-693-7120	Fax: 702-693-8626
Toll-Free:	
Address: 3600 Las Vegas Blvd. S., Las Vegas, NV 89109 US	

GROWTH PLANS/SPECIAL FEATURES:

MGM Mirage (MGM) is one of the world's leading hotel and gaming companies, with 26 casino resorts located in Nevada, Mississippi, Michigan and Australia and investments in three casino resorts in Nevada, New Jersey and Illinois. MGM casinos on the Las Vegas strip include the Bellagio, MGM Grand Las Vegas, Mandalay Bay, The Mirage, Luxor, Treasure Island, New York-New York, Excalibur, Monte Carlo and Circus Circus Las Vegas. Subsidiary Primm Valley Resorts owns Whiskey Pete's, Buffalo Bill's, Primm Valley Resort. MGM also has two championship golf courses at the California/Nevada state line and sites in Reno, Laughlin and Jean. Major casinos outside of Nevada are the MGM Grand Detroit, the Beau Rivage in Biloxi, Mississippi, the Gold Strike in Tunica, Mississippi and a 50% part ownership of operations in Atlantic City, New Jersey and Elgin Illinois. The majority of locations offer slot machines, video poker machines and table games. MGM casinos also house a variety of restaurants, bars, pools, golf courses and lounges. Almost half of the company's current revenues are derived from properties gained through the monumental $7.9 billion acquisition of Mandalay Resort Group in mid-2005. MGM is currently developing Project CityCenter in Las Vegas: a $7 billion casino resort with 4,000-rooms; two 400-room non-casino hotels; 470,000 square feet of retail, restaurant and entertainment space; and 2.3 million square feet of residential space for 2,700 luxury condominiums. In 2007, MGM entered into a partnership agreement with Diamond Resorts and American Nevada Corp. to create a mixed-use development in Jean, Nevada. In 2006, MGM also agreed to sell Primm Valley Resorts to Herbst Gaming, Inc. for $400 million and Laughlin Properties to a group led by Anthony Marnell III for $200 million.

MGM offers its employees tuition reimbursement, flexible spending accounts and an on-site child care.

FINANCIALS: Sales and profits are in thousands of dollars—add 000 to get the full amount. 2007 Note: Financial information for 2007 was not available for all companies at press time.

2007 Sales: $	2007 Profits: $	**U.S. Stock Ticker: MGM**
2006 Sales: $7,175,956	2006 Profits: $648,264	**Int'l Ticker:** Int'l Exchange:
2005 Sales: $6,128,843	2005 Profits: $443,256	Employees: 70,000
2004 Sales: $4,001,804	2004 Profits: $412,332	Fiscal Year Ends: 12/31
2003 Sales: $3,908,800	2003 Profits: $243,700	Parent Company:

SALARIES/BENEFITS:

Pension Plan:	ESOP Stock Plan:	Profit Sharing:	Top Exec. Salary: $2,000,000	Bonus: $6,089,729
Savings Plan: Y	Stock Purch. Plan:		Second Exec. Salary: $1,500,000	Bonus: $4,562,205

OTHER THOUGHTS:

Apparent Women Officers or Directors: 2
Hot Spot for Advancement for Women/Minorities:

LOCATIONS: ("Y" = Yes)

West:	Southwest:	Midwest:	Southeast:	Northeast:	International:
Y		Y	Y	Y	Y

MGM PICTURES

www.mgm.com

Industry Group Code: 512110 **Ranks within this company's industry group:** Sales: Profits:

Print Media/Publishing:	Movies:		Equipment/Supplies:	Broadcast/Cable:	Music/Audio:	Sports/Games/Gambling:	
Newspapers:	Movie Theaters:	Y	Equipment/Supplies:	Broadcast TV:	Music Production:	Games/Sports:	Y
Magazines:	Movie Production:	Y	Gambling Equipment:	Cable TV:	Retail Music:	Retail Games Stores:	
Books:	TV/Video Prod.:	Y	Special Services:	Satellite Broadcast:	Retail Audio Equip.:	Stadiums/Teams:	
Book Stores:	Video Rental:		Advertising Services:	Radio:	Music Print./Dist.:	Gambling/Casinos:	
Distribution/Printing:	Video Distribution:	Y	Info. Sys. Software:	Online Information:	Multimedia:	Rides/Theme Parks:	

TYPES OF BUSINESS:

Movie Production
Movie Distribution
Television Programming

BRANDS/DIVISIONS/AFFILIATES:

Metro-Goldwyn-Mayer Inc (MGM)
Providence Equity Partners
Texas Pacific Group
Comcast Corporation
Sony Corporation of America
Stargate SG-1
James Bond: Casino Royale
Rocky Balboa

CONTACTS: Note: Officers with more than one job title may be intentionally listed here more than once.

Harry E. Sloan, Chmn./CEO-Metro-Goldwyn-Mayer, Inc.

Phone: 310-449-3000	Fax: 310-449-8750
Toll-Free:	
Address: 10250 Constellation Blvd., Los Angeles, CA 90067 US	

GROWTH PLANS/SPECIAL FEATURES:

MGM Pictures, one of the many operating units of Metro-Goldwyn-Mayer, Inc. (MGM), produces and distributes movies in a wide range of genres. Other MGM subsidiaries include MGM Television Entertainment, MGM Networks, MGM Distribution Co., MGM Worldwide Television Distribution and MGM Home Entertainment. MGM Pictures has a prodigious film library, including over 4,000 titles and 10,400 television episodes. It gained early recognition for musicals such as Fiddler on the Roof and West Side Story. MGM Pictures produces leading science fiction television show Stargate SG-1, its spin-off Stargate Atlantis, Chappelle's Show, Reno 911! and The Outer Limits. Recent film projects include Rocky Balboa, Mr. Brooks, Lions for Lambs, James Bond: Casino Royale, Rescue Dawn and Feast of Love. The firm has teamed up with third-party developers to turn some of its movie and television franchises into video games, including games based on Rocky Balboa, From Russia with Love and Stargate. Many of the firm's movies, including Rob Roy, The Usual Suspects and Ghost World, are now available for download on iTunes. MGM was recently acquired by a consortium composed of Providence Equity Partners, which owns 29% of the firm; TPG, 21%; Sony Corporation of America, 20%; Comcast Corporation, 20%; DLJ Merchant Banking Partners, 7%; and Quadrangle Group, 3%. Sony Pictures Entertainment will assume certain distribution responsibilities for MGM's film library, and the two companies expect to co-finance and co-produce certain pictures. MGM has shown support for the high definition Blu-ray Disc format, releasing Flyboys, its first Blu-ray title, in January 2007. In December 2007, MGM announced it would co-produce two new movies based on The Hobbit with New Line Cinema and Peter Jackson.

Employees of MGM receive dependent care plans, flexible spending accounts, domestic partner insurance, employee assistance, educational assistance, health club memberships and on-site amenities.

FINANCIALS: Sales and profits are in thousands of dollars—add 000 to get the full amount. 2007 Note: Financial information for 2007 was not available for all companies at press time.

2007 Sales: $	2007 Profits: $	**U.S. Stock Ticker: Subsidiary**
2006 Sales: $	2006 Profits: $	**Int'l Ticker:** Int'l Exchange:
2005 Sales: $	2005 Profits: $	Employees:
2004 Sales: $	2004 Profits: $	Fiscal Year Ends: 12/31
2003 Sales: $	2003 Profits: $	Parent Company: METRO-GOLDWYN-MAYER INC (MGM)

SALARIES/BENEFITS:

Pension Plan:	ESOP Stock Plan:	Profit Sharing:	Top Exec. Salary: $	Bonus: $
Savings Plan: Y	Stock Purch. Plan:		Second Exec. Salary: $	Bonus: $

OTHER THOUGHTS:

Apparent Women Officers or Directors:
Hot Spot for Advancement for Women/Minorities:

LOCATIONS: ("Y" = Yes)

West:	Southwest:	Midwest:	Southeast:	Northeast:	International:
Y					

MICROSOFT CORP

www.microsoft.com

Industry Group Code: 511204 Ranks within this company's industry group: Sales: 1   Profits: 1

Print Media/Publishing:	Movies:	Equipment/Supplies:		Broadcast/Cable:		Music/Audio:		Sports/Games/Gambling:	
Newspapers:	Movie Theaters:	Equipment/Supplies:	Y	Broadcast TV:		Music Production:		Games/Sports:	Y
Magazines: Y	Movie Production:	Gambling Equipment:		Cable TV:	Y	Retail Music:		Retail Games Stores:	
Books: Y	TV/Video Prod.:	Special Services:	Y	Satellite Broadcast:		Retail Audio Equip.:		Stadiums/Teams:	
Book Stores:	Video Rental:	Advertising Services:		Radio:		Music Print./Dist.:	Y	Gambling/Casinos:	
Distribution/Printing:	Video Distribution:	Info. Sys. Software:		Online Information:		Multimedia:		Rides/Theme Parks:	

TYPES OF BUSINESS:

Computer Software
Personal Communications Services
Video Games Systems
Directory Assistance
Voice-Enabled Mobile Search
Internet Search Engine
E-Mail Services
Instant Messaging

BRANDS/DIVISIONS/AFFILIATES:

Windows
Microsoft Office 12
Windows Vista
Xbox 360
MSN
Microsoft Dynamics
Microsoft Live
Tellme Networks, Inc.

CONTACTS: *Note: Officers with more than one job title may be intentionally listed here more than once.*

Steve Ballmer, CEO
Kevin Turner, COO
Christopher Liddell, CFO
Yusuf Mehdi, Sr. VP/Chief Advertising Strategist
Lisa Brummel, Sr. VP-Human Resources
Rick Rashid, Sr. VP-Research
Shahla Aly, Interim CIO
Frank H. Brod, VP-Admin.
Brad Smith, General Counsel/Sr. VP-Legal & Corp. Affairs/Sec.
Bruce Jaffe, VP-Corp. Dev.
Martha Bejar, VP-Comm. Sector
Frank H. Brod, VP-Finance/Chief Acct. Officer
Jeff Bell, VP-Global Mktg., Interactive Entertainment Bus.
Neil Holloway, Pres., Microsoft EMEA
Todd Holmdahl, VP-Gaming & Xbox Product Group
Maria Martinez, VP-Worldwide Svcs.
Bill Gates, Chmn.
Jean-Philippe Courtois, Pres., Microsoft Int'l

Phone: 425-882-8080	**Fax:** 425-936-7329
Toll-Free: 800-642-7676	
Address: 1 Microsoft Way, Redmond, WA 98052-6399 US	

GROWTH PLANS/SPECIAL FEATURES:

Microsoft Corp. develops, manufactures and supports software for businesses, government and consumers. The company offers online services; input devices; operating systems; server applications; business and consumer productivity applications; software development tools; and Internet and intranet software and technologies. Microsoft operates in seven segments. The client segment produces technical architecture, engineering and product delivery of the Windows product family. Products include Windows XP Professional and Home; Media Center Edition; and Tablet PC Edition. The server and tools segment develops and markets Windows server products and operating systems; builds standalone and software development lifecycle tools for software architects, developers, testers and project managers; and provides consulting and product support services. The information worker segment consists of the Microsoft Office system of programs, services and software solutions. The Microsoft business solution segment through the Microsoft Dynamics brand offers financial management, customer relationship management, supply chain management and analytics applications. The MSN segment provides services such as e-mail and instant messaging; online information offerings such as MSN Search, MapPoint and MSN portals and channels; and a variety of online paid offerings. The mobile and embedded devices segment develops and markets products that extend the Windows platform to mobile devices such as PDAs and phones and to embedded devices. The home and entertainment segment develops, produces and markets the Xbox video game system, PC software games, online games and other devices. In 2006, the firm partnered with DIRECTV to explore digital music, television and movies in portable devices. In early 2007, Microsoft released Windows Vista. In May 2007, the firm agreed to acquire aQuantive, Inc. for roughly $6 billion. In May 2007, the firm acquired Tellme Networks, Inc., a provider of nationwide directory assistance and voice-enabled mobile search.

Microsoft offers its employees a 401(k) plan; an employee stock purchase plan; medical, dental and vision care; and life insurance.

FINANCIALS: Sales and profits are in thousands of dollars—add 000 to get the full amount. 2007 Note: Financial information for 2007 was not available for all companies at press time.

2007 Sales: $51,122,000	2007 Profits: $14,065,000	**U.S. Stock Ticker: MSFT**
2006 Sales: $44,282,000	2006 Profits: $12,599,000	**Int'l Ticker:** Int'l Exchange:
2005 Sales: $39,788,000	2005 Profits: $12,254,000	Employees: 79,000
2004 Sales: $36,835,000	2004 Profits: $8,168,000	Fiscal Year Ends: 6/30
2003 Sales: $32,187,000	2003 Profits: $9,993,000	Parent Company:

SALARIES/BENEFITS:

Pension Plan:	ESOP Stock Plan:	Profit Sharing:	Top Exec. Salary: $616,667	Bonus: $350,000
Savings Plan: Y	Stock Purch. Plan: Y		Second Exec. Salary: $616,667	Bonus: $350,000

OTHER THOUGHTS:

Apparent Women Officers or Directors: 18
Hot Spot for Advancement for Women/Minorities: Y

LOCATIONS: ("Y" = Yes)

West:	Southwest:	Midwest:	Southeast:	Northeast:	International:
Y	Y	Y	Y	Y	Y

MIDWAY GAMES INC

www.midway.com

Industry Group Code: 511208 Ranks within this company's industry group: Sales: 8 Profits: 9

Print Media/Publishing:	Movies:	Equipment/Supplies:	Broadcast/Cable:	Music/Audio:	Sports/Games/Gambling:	
Newspapers:	Movie Theaters:	Equipment/Supplies:	Broadcast TV:	Music Production:	Games/Sports:	Y
Magazines:	Movie Production:	Gambling Equipment:	Cable TV:	Retail Music:	Retail Games Stores:	
Books:	TV/Video Prod.:	Special Services:	Satellite Broadcast:	Retail Audio Equip.:	Stadiums/Teams:	
Book Stores:	Video Rental:	Advertising Services:	Radio:	Music Print./Dist.:	Gambling/Casinos:	
Distribution/Printing:	Video Distribution:	Info. Sys. Software:	Online Information:	Multimedia:	Rides/Theme Parks:	

TYPES OF BUSINESS:

Computer Software, Games & Entertainment

BRANDS/DIVISIONS/AFFILIATES:

Pong
Spy Hunter
Blitz
Mortal Kombat
High Voltage Software, Inc.
Artificial Mind and Movement Inc.
Midway Games GmbH
Happy Feet

CONTACTS: *Note: Officers with more than one job title may be intentionally listed here more than once.*

David F. Zucker, CEO
David F. Zucker, Pres.
Thomas E. Powell, CFO
Steven M. Allison, Chief Mktg. Officer/Sr. VP-Mktg.
Deborah K. Fulton, General Counsel/Sec./Sr. VP
Thomas E. Powell, Exec. VP-Finance/Treas.
James Boyle, VP-Finance/Controller/Asst. Treas.
Miguel Iribarren, VP-Publishing
Kenneth D. Cron, Chmn.
Matthew V. Booty, Sr. VP-Worldwide Studios

Phone: 773-961-2222	Fax: 773-961-1099
Toll-Free:	
Address: 2704 W. Roscoe St., Chicago, IL 60618 US	

GROWTH PLANS/SPECIAL FEATURES:

Midway Games, Inc. is a leading developer and producer of gaming software for all major videogame systems, including Playstation 3 from Sony; Xbox 360 from Microsoft; Nintendo's Wii and Game Boy Advance systems; and personal computers. To date, the company has published over 400 titles. The firm's early games in the 1980s included Pong, Asteroids, Gauntlet, Defender and Spy Hunter, while its current offerings include Blitz, Rampage, Happy Feet, The Grim Adventures of Billy & Mandy, The Ant Bully, Unreal Anthology and the Mortal Kombat series. Mortal Kombat has been the company's most successful game, selling in excess of 20 million copies across seven different consoles as well as being licensed into other areas, such as film and television. The largest purchasers of Midway games are retailers Wal-Mart and Gamestop. Midway Games GmbH in Germany and Midway Games SAS in France are responsible for the company's German and French sales, marketing and distribution operations. Sumner Redstone, Chairman and majority shareholder of Viacom, Inc., owns 88% of Midway. As of 2007, the firm maintained 10 internal product development teams staffed with approximately 660 developers, and held game development agreements with third-party development groups, such as Artificial Mind and Movement Inc., and High Voltage Software, Inc.

FINANCIALS: Sales and profits are in thousands of dollars—add 000 to get the full amount. 2007 Note: Financial information for 2007 was not available for all companies at press time.

2007 Sales: $	2007 Profits: $	U.S. Stock Ticker: MWY
2006 Sales: $165,574	2006 Profits: $-77,783	Int'l Ticker: Int'l Exchange:
2005 Sales: $150,078	2005 Profits: $-112,487	Employees: 850
2004 Sales: $161,600	2004 Profits: $-19,945	Fiscal Year Ends: 12/31
2003 Sales: $92,524	2003 Profits: $-115,227	Parent Company:

SALARIES/BENEFITS:

Pension Plan:	ESOP Stock Plan:	Profit Sharing:	Top Exec. Salary: $600,193	Bonus: $
Savings Plan:	Stock Purch. Plan:		Second Exec. Salary: $342,121	Bonus: $

OTHER THOUGHTS:

Apparent Women Officers or Directors: 2
Hot Spot for Advancement for Women/Minorities: Y

LOCATIONS: ("Y" = Yes)

West:	Southwest:	Midwest:	Southeast:	Northeast:	International:
Y	Y	Y			Y

# MIRAMAX FILM CORP												www.miramax.com

Industry Group Code: 512110 Ranks within this company's industry group: Sales: Profits:

Print Media/Publishing:	Movies:		Equipment/Supplies:	Broadcast/Cable:	Music/Audio:	Sports/Games/Gambling:
Newspapers:	Movie Theaters:		Equipment/Supplies:	Broadcast TV:	Music Production:	Games/Sports:
Magazines:	Movie Production:	Y	Gambling Equipment:	Cable TV:	Retail Music:	Retail Games Stores:
Books:	TV/Video Prod.:		Special Services:	Satellite Broadcast:	Retail Audio Equip.:	Stadiums/Teams:
Book Stores:	Video Rental:		Advertising Services:	Radio:	Music Print./Dist.:	Gambling/Casinos:
Distribution/Printing:	Video Distribution:	Y	Info. Sys. Software:	Online Information:	Multimedia:	Rides/Theme Parks:

TYPES OF BUSINESS:

Movie Production & Distribution
Online Merchandise Retail

BRANDS/DIVISIONS/AFFILIATES:

Walt Disney Company (The)
Dimension Films
Buena Vista Home Entertainment

CONTACTS: *Note: Officers with more than one job title may be intentionally listed here more than once.*

Daniel Battsek, Pres.
Elliot Slutzky, Sr. VP/Mgr.-General Sales
Michael Luisi, Exec. VP-Bus. Affairs & Oper.

Phone: 917-606-5500	Fax: 917-606-5535
Toll-Free:	
Address: 161 Ave. of the Americas, New York, NY 10013 US	

GROWTH PLANS/SPECIAL FEATURES:

Miramax Film Corp., a subsidiary of The Walt Disney Co., is a producer and distributor of acclaimed and award-winning movies such as The Aviator, Gangs of New York, The Hours, Shakespeare In Love, The English Patient and Frida. Founded in 1979 by brothers Bob and Harvey Weinstein, the firm was originally known for producing small, quirky art-house pictures, but it has recently developed bigger-budget movies, such as Chicago. Miramax's Dimension Films division found success in the teen horror genre with the Scary Movie and Scream titles. It also produced the Spy Kids series. Miramax sells movie-related merchandise via its web site. Disney Studios purchased the company for $75 million in 1993. The Weinsteins recently left the company to start a new film production company called The Weinstein Company. Films under the Miramax name will continue to be released through Disney's Buena Vista Home Entertainment division. Miramax hits include Pulp Fiction, Good Will Hunting, Kill Bill 1 and 2, Garden State, Cold Mountain and Sin City.

FINANCIALS: Sales and profits are in thousands of dollars—add 000 to get the full amount. 2007 Note: Financial information for 2007 was not available for all companies at press time.

2007 Sales: $	2007 Profits: $	U.S. Stock Ticker: Subsidiary
2006 Sales: $	2006 Profits: $	Int'l Ticker: Int'l Exchange:
2005 Sales: $	2005 Profits: $	Employees:
2004 Sales: $	2004 Profits: $	Fiscal Year Ends: 9/30
2003 Sales: $	2003 Profits: $	Parent Company: WALT DISNEY COMPANY (THE)

SALARIES/BENEFITS:

Pension Plan:	ESOP Stock Plan:	Profit Sharing:	Top Exec. Salary: $	Bonus: $
Savings Plan:	Stock Purch. Plan:		Second Exec. Salary: $	Bonus: $

OTHER THOUGHTS:

Apparent Women Officers or Directors:
Hot Spot for Advancement for Women/Minorities:

LOCATIONS: ("Y" = Yes)

West:	Southwest:	Midwest:	Southeast:	Northeast:	International:
				Y	

MOBITV INC

www.mobitv.com

Industry Group Code: 513120A **Ranks within this company's industry group:** Sales: Profits:

Print Media/Publishing:	Movies:	Equipment/Supplies:		Broadcast/Cable:		Music/Audio:	Sports/Games/Gambling:
Newspapers:	Movie Theaters:	Equipment/Supplies:		Broadcast TV:	Y	Music Production:	Games/Sports:
Magazines:	Movie Production:	Gambling Equipment:		Cable TV:		Retail Music:	Retail Games Stores:
Books:	TV/Video Prod.:	Special Services:	Y	Satellite Broadcast:		Retail Audio Equip.:	Stadiums/Teams:
Book Stores:	Video Rental:	Advertising Services:		Radio:		Music Print./Dist.:	Gambling/Casinos:
Distribution/Printing:	Video Distribution:	Info. Sys. Software:		Online Information:		Multimedia:	Rides/Theme Parks:

TYPES OF BUSINESS:

Mobile Phone Media Service
Cellular Telephone Television Network
Cellular Telephone Radio Network
Cellular Telephone Satellite Radio Network

BRANDS/DIVISIONS/AFFILIATES:

MobiTV
MobiRadio
XM Radio Mobile

CONTACTS: *Note: Officers with more than one job title may be intentionally listed here more than once.*

Charlie Nooney, CEO
Bruce Gilpin, COO
Paul Scanlan, Pres.
Bill Losch, CFO
Kay Johansson, CTO
Charlie Nooney, Chmn.

Phone: 510-450-5000	**Fax:** 510-450-5001
Toll-Free:	
Address: 6425 Christie Ave, 5th Fl., Emeryville, CA 94608 US	

GROWTH PLANS/SPECIAL FEATURES:

MobiTV, Inc., formerly Idetic, Inc., is a private company that markets its mobile television and radio services to the world's mobile phone users. Launched in 1999, MobiTV delivers live television feeds in real time over existing cellular networks, requiring no additional equipment. The subscription service is available to a variety of cellular carriers, including Sprint, Cingular, Midwest Wireless and Alltel. Users in Canada receive services from Bell Mobility, Rogers Wireless and Telus Mobility. At this time, MobiTV is also available in Brazil, Mexico, the Dominican Republic, Nicaragua, Peru and Ecuador. In addition to cell phones, the service is available to handheld Treo or Palm devices. MobiTV viewers can expect to receive MSNBC, ABC News Now, CNN, Fox News, Fox Sports, ESPN 3GTV, MLB, NBC Mobile, CNBC, CSPAN, the Discovery Channel, TLC, the Weather Channel, and a large variety of networks offering music, comedy, cartoon and regional interest programming. The firm also offers MobiRadio, which gives access to over 50 channels of radio music, talk and news, as well as XM Radio Mobile, a satellite radio service.

FINANCIALS: Sales and profits are in thousands of dollars—add 000 to get the full amount. 2007 Note: Financial information for 2007 was not available for all companies at press time.

2007 Sales: $	2007 Profits: $	**U.S. Stock Ticker:** Private
2006 Sales: $	2006 Profits: $	**Int'l Ticker:** Int'l Exchange:
2005 Sales: $	2005 Profits: $	Employees:
2004 Sales: $	2004 Profits: $	Fiscal Year Ends:
2003 Sales: $	2003 Profits: $	Parent Company:

SALARIES/BENEFITS:

Pension Plan:	ESOP Stock Plan:	Profit Sharing:	Top Exec. Salary: $	Bonus: $
Savings Plan:	Stock Purch. Plan:		Second Exec. Salary: $	Bonus: $

OTHER THOUGHTS:

Apparent Women Officers or Directors:
Hot Spot for Advancement for Women/Minorities:

LOCATIONS: ("Y" = Yes)

West:	Southwest:	Midwest:	Southeast:	Northeast:	International:
Y					Y

MODERN TIMES GROUP MTG AB   www.mtg.se

Industry Group Code: 513120 **Ranks within this company's industry group:** Sales: Profits:

Print Media/Publishing:		Movies:		Equipment/Supplies:		Broadcast/Cable:		Music/Audio:		Sports/Games/Gambling:	
Newspapers:		Movie Theaters:		Equipment/Supplies:		Broadcast TV:	Y	Music Production:		Games/Sports:	Y
Magazines:	Y	Movie Production:	Y	Gambling Equipment:		Cable TV:	Y	Retail Music:		Retail Games Stores:	
Books:		TV/Video Prod.:	Y	Special Services:		Satellite Broadcast:		Retail Audio Equip.:		Stadiums/Teams:	
Book Stores:		Video Rental:		Advertising Services:		Radio:		Music Print./Dist.:		Gambling/Casinos:	Y
Distribution/Printing:		Video Distribution:		Info. Sys. Software:		Online Information:		Multimedia:		Rides/Theme Parks:	

TYPES OF BUSINESS:

Television Broadcasting & Cable
Radio Broadcasting
Television & Film Production
Internet Businesses
Home Shopping Network
Gambling Operations
Magazine Publishing
Video Games

BRANDS/DIVISIONS/AFFILIATES:

Viasat Broadcasting
Modern Studios
TV Shop24/7
RIX FM
BET24.com
Balkan Media Group Limited
Linus & Lotta Postorder AB
Helsingin Dataclub Oy

CONTACTS: *Note: Officers with more than one job title may be intentionally listed here more than once.*

Hans-Holger Albrecht, CEO
Andrew Barron, COO
Hans-Holger Albrecht, Pres.
Mathias Hermansson, CFO
Petra Colleen, Head-Admin.
Hasse Breitholtz, Exec. VP-MTG/Managing Dir.-Modern Studios
Anders Nilsson, Managing Dir.-Free-to-Air & Pay-TV & Radio, Sweden
Hein E. Hattestad, Managing Dir.-Free-to-Air & Pay-TV & Radio, Norway
Jorgen Madsen, Managing Dir.-Free-to-Air & Pay-TV & Radio, Denmar
David Chance, Chmn.

Phone: 46-8-562-000-50	**Fax:** 46-8-205-074
Toll-Free:	
Address: Skeppsbron 18, Box 2094, Stockholm, SE-103 13 Sweden	

GROWTH PLANS/SPECIAL FEATURES:

Modern Times Group MTG AB is a major player in European television, radio and media services. The company is organized into four divisions: Viasat Broadcasting, MTG radio, Modern Studios and Online. Viasat Broadcasting, reaching over 100 million people in 24 countries in the Nordic region and Central and Eastern Europe, is arranged into Free-TV and Pay-TV. Free-TV consists of TV3, ZTV, TV8, TV3+, 3+, Tango TV, DTV, TV Prima and Viasat 3, reaching viewers in Sweden, Norway, Denmark, Finland, Estonia, the Czech Republic, Russia, Latvia and Lithuania. The pay-TV division owns channels that are sold in Gold and Silver packages to viewers in Sweden, Norway, Denmark, Finland, Latvia and various Eastern European countries. In addition, the company distributes about 30 third-party channels, including Viasat Sport 2, Viasat Sport 3, Viasat Sport 24, TV1000 Action, TV1000 Classic, TV1000 Nordic, TV1000 Family, Viasat History, Viasat Explorer, Toon Disney, Cartoon Network and E!Entertainment Television. MTG Radio's flagship station brand, RIX FM operates 53 of the 86 commercial stations in Sweden, including Star FM, Power Hit FM, Lugna Favoriter, NRJ, Svenska Favoriter and Bandit. Modern Studio produces television programming, videos, movies, electronic games and magazines in 72 countries, through its seven subsidiaries: Strix (TV production house), Sonet Film (film distributor), Engine (music and video), Modern TV, Brombergs Bokforlag, Redaktorema and Zoommobile. The company's Online business operates a home shopping network (CDON.com), which features TV Shop24/7 and PIN 24 and operates in more than 50 countries. MTG also owns 90% of BET24.com, a betting and gaming company. In December 2007, the company acquired Linus & Lotta Postorder AB, an online retailer of children's´ clothing in the Nordic region. Also in December 2007, the company sold Sonet Film to Svensk Filmindustri.

FINANCIALS: Sales and profits are in thousands of dollars—add 000 to get the full amount. 2007 Note: Financial information for 2007 was not available for all companies at press time.

2007 Sales: $	2007 Profits: $	**U.S. Stock Ticker:**	
2006 Sales: $	2006 Profits: $	**Int'l Ticker:** MTG B	Int'l Exchange: Stockholm-SSE
2005 Sales: $1,036,941	2005 Profits: $160,099	Employees: 1,554	
2004 Sales: $880,727	2004 Profits: $87,627	Fiscal Year Ends: 12/31	
2003 Sales: $870,900	2003 Profits: $39,900	Parent Company:	

SALARIES/BENEFITS:

Pension Plan: Y	ESOP Stock Plan:	Profit Sharing:	Top Exec. Salary: $	Bonus: $
Savings Plan:	Stock Purch. Plan:		Second Exec. Salary: $	Bonus: $

OTHER THOUGHTS:

Apparent Women Officers or Directors: 2
Hot Spot for Advancement for Women/Minorities:

LOCATIONS: ("Y" = Yes)

West:	Southwest:	Midwest:	Southeast:	Northeast:	International:
					Y

MORRIS COMMUNICATIONS COMPANY LLC

www.morriscomm.com

Industry Group Code: 511110 Ranks within this company's industry group: Sales: Profits:

Print Media/Publishing:		Movies:	Equipment/Supplies:		Broadcast/Cable:	Music/Audio:	Sports/Games/Gambling:
Newspapers:	Y	Movie Theaters:	Equipment/Supplies:		Broadcast TV:	Music Production:	Games/Sports:
Magazines:	Y	Movie Production:	Gambling Equipment:		Cable TV:	Retail Music:	Retail Games Stores:
Books:	Y	TV/Video Prod.:	Special Services:		Satellite Broadcast:	Retail Audio Equip.:	Stadiums/Teams:
Book Stores:		Video Rental:	Advertising Services:	Y	Radio:	Music Print./Dist.:	Gambling/Casinos:
Distribution/Printing:		Video Distribution:	Info. Sys. Software:	Y	Online Information:	Multimedia:	Rides/Theme Parks:

TYPES OF BUSINESS:

Newspaper Publishing
Radio Broadcasting
Magazine Publishing
Book Publishing
Outdoor Advertising
Online Publishing
Printing Services

BRANDS/DIVISIONS/AFFILIATES:

Morris Publishing Group, LLC
Globe Pequot Press (The)
Falcon Guides
Morris Desert Radio Group
Anchorage Media Group
Fairway Outdoor Advertising
Morris DigitalWorks
Network Media

CONTACTS: *Note: Officers with more than one job title may be intentionally listed here more than once.*

William S. Morris, III, CEO
William S. Morris, IV, Pres.
Steve K. Stone, CFO/Sr. VP
Martha J. McHaney, VP-Human Resources
James E. Smith, VP-Market Research
Paul V. Buckley, CIO
Morris M. May, VP-Administrative Svcs.
Craig S. Mitchell, Sec.
Craig S. Mitchell, Sr. VP-Finance/Treas.
William S. Morris, IV, CEO-Morris Publishing Group
Scott Watrous, Pres., The Globe Pequot Press
Carl N. Cannon, Exec. VP-Newspapers
J. Tyler Morris, VP-The Cowboy Publishing Group
William S. Morris, III, Chmn.

Phone: 706-724-0851	Fax: 706-722-7125
Toll-Free: 800-622-6358	
Address: 725 Broad St., Augusta, GA 30901 US	

GROWTH PLANS/SPECIAL FEATURES:

Morris Communications Company LLC is one of the most widespread publishing groups in the U.S., with operations in 32 states and Washington, D.C., as well as in London, Paris, Asia and Monaco. Its publishing activities range from its core newspaper business to magazines, books, online publishing and specialty printing services, with additional business in radio broadcasting and outdoor advertising. Morris Publishing Group, LLC, the firm's newspaper subsidiary, publishes 13 daily, 13 non-daily and 14 free community newspapers as well as 17 city magazines in the U.S. Another company subsidiary, The Globe Pequot Press, one of the world's leading publishers and distributors of outdoor recreation and leisure titles, has more than 2,800 travel guides for every continent and books for anglers, equestrians and other outdoor enthusiasts, notably the well-know Falcon Guides. The company also has a commercial printing operation that produces the firm's local newspapers and shoppers, as well as business forms, business cards, letterheads, circulars, ad inserts, newsletters and catalogs. Morris's radio broadcasting operations include 33 stations and two networks operating through several radio station groups, most notably the Columbia River Media Group, the Grays Harbor Radio Group, the Morris Desert Media Radio Group and the Anchorage Media Group. Fairway Outdoor Advertising provides outdoor advertising services, including posters and bulletins in North Carolina, South Carolina, Minnesota, Alabama and Georgia. Subsidiary Morris DigitalWorks develops online publishing platforms and tools such as MDClassifieds and SiteWeaver. The company's recent acquisitions include Network Media, a Hawaii-based publishing and broadcast firm, and the assets of Chattanooga Outdoor Advertising. In December 2007, Morris Publishing sold 14 daily and three non-daily newspapers; one of its commercial printing operations, Flashes Publishing; and related free, non-daily publications, all to GateHouse Media, Inc., for $115 million, reducing Morris to one publishing company and 13 daily and 13 non-daily newspapers publications.

FINANCIALS: Sales and profits are in thousands of dollars—add 000 to get the full amount. 2007 Note: Financial information for 2007 was not available for all companies at press time.

2007 Sales: $	2007 Profits: $	**U.S. Stock Ticker: Private**
2006 Sales: $	2006 Profits: $	**Int'l Ticker:** Int'l Exchange:
2005 Sales: $465,100	2005 Profits: $31,300	Employees: 6,000
2004 Sales: $455,700	2004 Profits: $30,300	Fiscal Year Ends: 12/31
2003 Sales: $533,000	2003 Profits: $	Parent Company:

SALARIES/BENEFITS:

Pension Plan:	ESOP Stock Plan:	Profit Sharing:	Top Exec. Salary: $	Bonus: $
Savings Plan: Y	Stock Purch. Plan:		Second Exec. Salary: $	Bonus: $

OTHER THOUGHTS:

Apparent Women Officers or Directors: 3
Hot Spot for Advancement for Women/Minorities: Y

LOCATIONS: ("Y" = Yes)

West:	Southwest:	Midwest:	Southeast:	Northeast:	International:
Y	Y	Y	Y	Y	Y

Note: Financial information, benefits and other data can change quickly and may vary from those stated here.

MOVIE GALLERY INC

www.moviegallery.com

Industry Group Code: 532230 Ranks within this company's industry group: Sales: 2   Profits: 2

Print Media/Publishing:	Movies:		Equipment/Supplies:	Broadcast/Cable:	Music/Audio:	Sports/Games/Gambling:
Newspapers:	Movie Theaters:		Equipment/Supplies:	Broadcast TV:	Music Production:	Games/Sports:
Magazines:	Movie Production:		Gambling Equipment:	Cable TV:	Retail Music:	Retail Games Stores: Y
Books:	TV/Video Prod.:	Y	Special Services:	Satellite Broadcast:	Retail Audio Equip.:	Stadiums/Teams:
Book Stores:	Video Rental:	Y	Advertising Services:	Radio:	Music Print./Dist.:	Gambling/Casinos:
Distribution/Printing:	Video Distribution:		Info. Sys. Software:	Online Information:	Multimedia:	Rides/Theme Parks:

TYPES OF BUSINESS:

Video Rental Stores
Online Sales
Video Game Sales
DVD & VHS Sales
Game Stores

BRANDS/DIVISIONS/AFFILIATES:

Movie Gallery
Hollywood Video
Game Crazy
VHQ Entertainment

CONTACTS: *Note: Officers with more than one job title may be intentionally listed here more than once.*

Joe T. Malugen, CEO
Joe T. Malugen, Pres.
Thomas D. Johnson, Jr., CFO/Exec. VP
Mark S. Loyd, Chief Merch. Officer
S. Page Todd, General Counsel/Sec./Exec VP
Jeffrey S. Stubbs, Pres., Retail Oper.
H. Harrison Parrish, Vice Chmn./Sr. VP
S. Page Todd, Chief Compliance Officer
Joe T. Malugen, Chmn.

Phone: 334-677-2108	Fax: 334-794-4688
Toll-Free: 800-677-2106	
Address: 900 W. Main St., Dothan, AL 36301 US	

GROWTH PLANS/SPECIAL FEATURES:

Movie Gallery, Inc. owns and operates approximately 3,955 video stores located in 50 states and Canada, through its brands Movie Gallery and Hollywood Video. One of the largest North American home entertainment retailers, the company sells and rents videocassettes, DVDs and video games. Movie Gallery stores are primarily located in small towns and suburban areas and focus on rural and secondary markets, competing with independently owned stores and small regional chains. Hollywood Video stores are larger and primarily target urban centers and surrounding suburban neighborhoods. Approximately 595 Hollywood Video stores include a Game Crazy store-in-store concept where game enthusiasts can buy, sell and trade new and used video game hardware, software and accessories. Game Crazy, which typically carries 9,000 video game and hardware units, also has 14 stand alone stores. Movie Gallery maintains a flexible store format, tailoring the size, inventory and look of each store to local demographics. Movie Gallery also prepares a customized video program, MGTV, which plays on televisions in the stores. Stores offer 2,700 to 16,000 movie titles and 200 to 1,500 video games. The company's web sites, hollywoodvideo.com, gamecrazy.com, reel.com and moviegallery.com, sell new and used movies and used video games, as well as providing movie news, reviews and information on upcoming releases. The company recently acquired Canadian-based VHQ Entertainment, adding 61 stores in Canada. Movie Gallery is currently combining employment forces, closing some stores and restructuring its Alabama and Oregon offices. In 2006, the firm began to restructure and downsize the leases of approximately 3,300 stores, attempting to sublease an average of 2,500 square feet square feet of retail space at each location. To facilitate its debt restructuring, the firm filed for Chapter 11 bankruptcy in October 2007. It closed over 600 stores during 2006.

Employees of Movie Gallery receive product discounts and performance-based salary increases.

FINANCIALS: Sales and profits are in thousands of dollars—add 000 to get the full amount. 2007 Note: Financial information for 2007 was not available for all companies at press time.

2007 Sales: $	2007 Profits: $	U.S. Stock Ticker: MOVI
2006 Sales: $2,540,000	2006 Profits: $49,488	Int'l Ticker: Int'l Exchange:
2005 Sales: $1,987,327	2005 Profits: $-552,740	Employees: 41,400
2004 Sales: $791,177	2004 Profits: $49,488	Fiscal Year Ends: 12/31
2003 Sales: $528,988	2003 Profits: $20,934	Parent Company:

SALARIES/BENEFITS:

Pension Plan:	ESOP Stock Plan:	Profit Sharing:	Top Exec. Salary: $1,019,231	Bonus: $1,625,000
Savings Plan: Y	Stock Purch. Plan: Y		Second Exec. Salary: $400,000	Bonus: $260,000

OTHER THOUGHTS:

	LOCATIONS: ("Y" = Yes)					
Apparent Women Officers or Directors:	West:	Southwest:	Midwest:	Southeast:	Northeast:	International:
Hot Spot for Advancement for Women/Minorities:	Y	Y	Y	Y	Y	Y

Note: Financial information, benefits and other data can change quickly and may vary from those stated here.

MP3.COM INC

www.mp3.com

Industry Group Code: 451220E Ranks within this company's industry group: Sales: Profits:

Print Media/Publishing:	Movies:	Equipment/Supplies:		Broadcast/Cable:	Music/Audio:		Sports/Games/Gambling:
Newspapers:	Movie Theaters:	Equipment/Supplies:		Broadcast TV:	Music Production:		Games/Sports:
Magazines:	Movie Production:	Gambling Equipment:		Cable TV:	Retail Music:		Retail Games Stores:
Books:	TV/Video Prod.:	Special Services:	Y	Satellite Broadcast:	Retail Audio Equip.:	Y	Stadiums/Teams:
Book Stores:	Video Rental:	Advertising Services:		Radio:	Music Print./Dist.:	Y	Gambling/Casinos:
Distribution/Printing:	Video Distribution:	Info. Sys. Software:		Online Information:	Multimedia:		Rides/Theme Parks:

TYPES OF BUSINESS:

Online Digital Music Sales
Audio Hosting
Digital Music Information Portal

BRANDS/DIVISIONS/AFFILIATES:

CNET Netoworks Inc

CONTACTS: *Note: Officers with more than one job title may be intentionally listed here more than once.*

Vince Broady, Sr. VP-Games & Entertainment, CNET Networks
Shelby Bonnie, Chmn./CEO-CNET Networks

Phone: 415-344-2000	Fax:
Toll-Free:	
Address: 235 2nd St., San Francisco, CA 94105 US	

GROWTH PLANS/SPECIAL FEATURES:

MP3.com, Inc., a subsidiary of CNET Networks, Inc., operates a web site offering users a wide selection of articles, reviews, free streaming music, forums information on mp3 players and a collection of millions of digital music tracks from a wide range of genres that is its primary attraction for most users. Customers can purchase and listen to music media without leaving their homes, as MP3.com offers both tracks and albums to be played on computers and digital music players. After setting up a free account, consumers can build their MP3 collections, track favorite artists and chart their own musical tastes. Users can also participate in 18 separate forums ranging from music genre specific boards, MP3 player reviews, to a forum for promoting music and a musician's lounge. The company specializes in promoting lesser-known artists, numbering some 700,000, accessible through bios, discographies, reviews, videos, photos and news. Over 6 million 30-second song clips are available on the site with links to digital-music providers where legal downloads are available. MP3.com recently re-opened its servers to allow artists to upload audio files. The company now offers band profiles; 100 MB of audio storage (which will hold approximately 85 songs); unlimited space for videos; and software to upload and edit music, videos and photos. Bands have the ability to see which zip codes their music is being downloaded in. The site has also added the ability to create and save play lists through its new Flash audio player.

The company offers its employees medical, dental and vision insurance; wellness programs; an employee assistance plan; a 401(k) plan; a CNET employee stock purchase plan; short- and long-term disability insurance; and tuition reimbursement.

FINANCIALS: Sales and profits are in thousands of dollars—add 000 to get the full amount. 2007 Note: Financial information for 2007 was not available for all companies at press time.

2007 Sales: $	2007 Profits: $	**U.S. Stock Ticker: Subsidiary**
2006 Sales: $	2006 Profits: $	**Int'l Ticker:** Int'l Exchange:
2005 Sales: $	2005 Profits: $	Employees: 308
2004 Sales: $	2004 Profits: $	Fiscal Year Ends: 12/31
2003 Sales: $	2003 Profits: $	Parent Company: CNET NETWORKS INC

SALARIES/BENEFITS:

Pension Plan:	ESOP Stock Plan:	Profit Sharing:	Top Exec. Salary: $	Bonus: $302,250
Savings Plan:	Stock Purch. Plan:		Second Exec. Salary: $246,160	Bonus: $246,160

OTHER THOUGHTS:

Apparent Women Officers or Directors:
Hot Spot for Advancement for Women/Minorities:

LOCATIONS: ("Y" = Yes)

West:	Southwest:	Midwest:	Southeast:	Northeast:	International:
Y					Y

MTR GAMING GROUP INC   www.mtrgaming.com

Industry Group Code: 721120 Ranks within this company's industry group: Sales: 10   Profits: 9

Print Media/Publishing:	Movies:	Equipment/Supplies:	Broadcast/Cable:	Music/Audio:	Sports/Games/Gambling:	
Newspapers:	Movie Theaters:	Equipment/Supplies:	Broadcast TV:	Music Production:	Games/Sports:	Y
Magazines:	Movie Production:	Gambling Equipment:	Cable TV:	Retail Music:	Retail Games Stores:	
Books:	TV/Video Prod.:	Special Services:	Satellite Broadcast:	Retail Audio Equip.:	Stadiums/Teams:	Y
Book Stores:	Video Rental:	Advertising Services:	Radio:	Music Print./Dist.:	Gambling/Casinos:	
Distribution/Printing:	Video Distribution:	Info. Sys. Software:	Online Information:	Multimedia:	Rides/Theme Parks:	

TYPES OF BUSINESS:
Gaming Facilities
Horse Racing Venues
Casinos
Hotels

BRANDS/DIVISIONS/AFFILIATES:
Scioto Downs
Mountaineer Race Track and Gaming Resort
Binion's Horseshoe Hotel and Casino
Ramada Inn and Speedway Casino
Jackson Trotting Association
Jackson Harness Raceway
Speakeasy Gaming of Las Vegas, Inc.
Presque Isle Downs and Casino

CONTACTS: Note: Officers with more than one job title may be intentionally listed here more than once.
Edson R. Arneault, CEO
David Hughes, COO
Edson R. Arneault, Pres.
John W. Bittner, Jr., CFO
Robert A. Blatt, VP
Rose Mary Williams, Corp. Sec.
Patrick J. Arneault, VP-Dev., Mountaineer Park & Presque Isle Downs
Richard Knight, CEO/General Mgr./Pres., Presque Isle Downs, Inc.
Edson R. Arneault, Chmn.

Phone: 304-387-5712	Fax: 304-387-2167
Toll-Free: 800-804-0468	
Address: P.O. Box 356, State Rte. 2 S., Chester, WV 26034 US	

GROWTH PLANS/SPECIAL FEATURES:
MTR Gaming Group, Inc. owns and operates unique gaming facilities throughout the U.S. The company's flagship property, Mountaineer Race Track and Gaming Resort in Chester, West Virginia, encompasses 121,956 square feet of gaming space that houses 3,220 slot machines, a thoroughbred racetrack, 359 hotel rooms, a spa, a fitness center, a golf course, dining and entertainment, a theater and events center and a convention center. In February 2007, MTR opened the Presque Isle Downs and Casino, which consists of a 140,000 square foot clubhouse with 2000 slot machines and a horse racing facility with a one-mile track, grandstand, barns and a paddock. The company also operates the Ramada Inn and Speedway Casino in North Las Vegas, Nevada, which has more than 400 slots and a 95-room hotel; Scioto Downs, a harness horse racing facility in Columbus, Ohio; and Binion's Horseshoe Hotel and Casino in Las Vegas, which is operated jointly with an affiliate of Harrah's. The company's subsidiary, MTR-Harness, Inc. acquired a 50% interest in the North Metro Harness Initiative, LLC, which received a contract to construct and operate a harness racetrack and card room in Columbus Township in Minnesota. In early 2007, MTR's subsidiary, Speakeasy Gaming of Las Vegas, Inc., entered into a definitive agreement to sell its Speedway Casino in northern Las Vegas to Mandekic Companies, LLC for $18.175 million.

FINANCIALS: Sales and profits are in thousands of dollars—add 000 to get the full amount. 2007 Note: Financial information for 2007 was not available for all companies at press time.

2007 Sales: $	2007 Profits: $	U.S. Stock Ticker: MNTG
2006 Sales: $382,610	2006 Profits: $4,446	Int'l Ticker: Int'l Exchange:
2005 Sales: $358,295	2005 Profits: $7,769	Employees: 3,500
2004 Sales: $315,222	2004 Profits: $14,455	Fiscal Year Ends: 12/31
2003 Sales: $293,606	2003 Profits: $15,100	Parent Company:

SALARIES/BENEFITS:

Pension Plan: Y	ESOP Stock Plan:	Profit Sharing:	Top Exec. Salary: $957,206	Bonus: $100,000
Savings Plan: Y	Stock Purch. Plan:		Second Exec. Salary: $335,225	Bonus: $

OTHER THOUGHTS:
Apparent Women Officers or Directors: 1
Hot Spot for Advancement for Women/Minorities:

LOCATIONS: ("Y" = Yes)

West:	Southwest:	Midwest:	Southeast:	Northeast:	International:
Y		Y		Y	

MTV NETWORKS

www.mtv.com

Industry Group Code: 513210 Ranks within this company's industry group: Sales: Profits:

Print Media/Publishing:	Movies:		Equipment/Supplies:		Broadcast/Cable:		Music/Audio:		Sports/Games/Gambling:
Newspapers:	Movie Theaters:	Y	Equipment/Supplies:		Broadcast TV:		Music Production:	Y	Games/Sports:
Magazines:	Movie Production:	Y	Gambling Equipment:		Cable TV:	Y	Retail Music:		Retail Games Stores:
Books:	TV/Video Prod.:	Y	Special Services:		Satellite Broadcast:		Retail Audio Equip.:		Stadiums/Teams:
Book Stores:	Video Rental:		Advertising Services:	Y	Radio:		Music Print./Dist.:		Gambling/Casinos:
Distribution/Printing:	Video Distribution:		Info. Sys. Software:		Online Information:		Multimedia:		Rides/Theme Parks:

TYPES OF BUSINESS:

Television Programming
Film Production
Radio
Online Portal
Recorded Music
Merchandise Sales

BRANDS/DIVISIONS/AFFILIATES:

Viacom Inc
Nickelodeon
VH1
Punk'd
Real World (The)
Total Request Live
MTVU
Harmonix Music Systems, Inc.

CONTACTS: Note: Officers with more than one job title may be intentionally listed here more than once.

Judy McGrath, CEO
Colette Chestnut, CFO/Exec. VP
Alicin Reidy-Williamson, Sr. VP-Corp. Responsibility & Public Affairs
Judy McGrath, Chmn.

Phone: 212-258-8000	Fax: 212-258-6175
Toll-Free:	
Address: 1515 Broadway, New York, NY 10036 US	

GROWTH PLANS/SPECIAL FEATURES:

MTV Networks Co., a business segment of Viacom, Inc., is one of the world's largest television networks and one of the leading multimedia brands for the youth. It owns and operates the MTV, VH1, CMT (Country Music Television), Comedy Central and Nickelodeon television networks, as well as other locally programmed channels. Operating 135 television networks, MTV broadcasting alone reaches over 496 million households in 179 countries and 22 languages. The company's other holdings include 171 operated web sites, along with publishing, recorded music, radio, home video, licensing and merchandising and feature film divisions. The firm produces films through a close association with Paramount Pictures. On the small screen, MTV has seen success in the production of quirky shows such as The Real World, The Osbournes, Total Request Live, Cribs, Diary and Punk'd. MTVU, a channel owned by MTV Networks, is the only 24-hour network created for and by college students. The channel's flagship products are music videos from emerging artists not seen anywhere else and short-term series like Stand In, where celebrities such as Bill Gates, Elle Wiesel and Madonna surprise-teach a class for the day. The mtv.com site caters to an audience of music fans in their teens and 20's and provides information on show times, merchandise ordering for consumer products based on its brand names, music downloads and band information. Recent acquisitions include Atom Entertainment, Inc.; four web sites featuring casual games, short films and video; and Harmonix Music Systems, Inc., creator of the video game Guitar Hero.

FINANCIALS: Sales and profits are in thousands of dollars—add 000 to get the full amount. 2007 Note: Financial information for 2007 was not available for all companies at press time.

2007 Sales: $	2007 Profits: $	U.S. Stock Ticker: Subsidiary
2006 Sales: $	2006 Profits: $	Int'l Ticker: Int'l Exchange:
2005 Sales: $	2005 Profits: $	Employees:
2004 Sales: $5,471,000	2004 Profits: $	Fiscal Year Ends: 12/31
2003 Sales: $	2003 Profits: $	Parent Company: VIACOM INC

SALARIES/BENEFITS:

Pension Plan:	ESOP Stock Plan:	Profit Sharing:	Top Exec. Salary: $	Bonus: $
Savings Plan:	Stock Purch. Plan:		Second Exec. Salary: $	Bonus: $

OTHER THOUGHTS:

Apparent Women Officers or Directors: 3
Hot Spot for Advancement for Women/Minorities: Y

LOCATIONS: ("Y" = Yes)

West:	Southwest:	Midwest:	Southeast:	Northeast:	International:
Y				Y	Y

MULTIMEDIA GAMES INC   www.multimediagames.com

Industry Group Code: 713290   Ranks within this company's industry group: Sales: 8   Profits: 8

Print Media/Publishing:		Movies:		Equipment/Supplies:		Broadcast/Cable:		Music/Audio:		Sports/Games/Gambling:	
Newspapers:		Movie Theaters:		Equipment/Supplies:		Broadcast TV:		Music Production:		Games/Sports:	
Magazines:		Movie Production:		Gambling Equipment:	Y	Cable TV:		Retail Music:		Retail Games Stores:	
Books:		TV/Video Prod.:	Y	Special Services:	Y	Satellite Broadcast:		Retail Audio Equip.:		Stadiums/Teams:	
Book Stores:		Video Rental:		Advertising Services:		Radio:		Music Print./Dist.:		Gambling/Casinos:	
Distribution/Printing:		Video Distribution:		Info. Sys. Software:		Online Information:		Multimedia:		Rides/Theme Parks:	

TYPES OF BUSINESS:

Gambling Technology
Video Gaming Machines
Electronic Bingo Games
Bingo Television Shows

BRANDS/DIVISIONS/AFFILIATES:

BetNet
MegaMania
Flash 21
People's Choice
Meltdown
Fruit Stand
Bad Monkey
Jungle Juice

CONTACTS: *Note: Officers with more than one job title may be intentionally listed here more than once.*

Clifton E. Lind, CEO
Clifton E. Lind, Pres.
Randy S. Cieslewicz, CFO/VP-Tax, Budget & Corp. Compliance
Gary L. Loebig, Exec. VP-Sales
Scott A. Zinnecker, Sr. VP-Human Resources
Brendan M. O'Connor, CTO/Exec. VP
L. Danny White, VP-Mfg. & Field Svcs.
James A. Bannerot, Legal Coordinator
Scott A. Zinnecker, Sr. VP-Central Oper.
P. Howard Chalmers, Sr. VP-Planning
P. Howard Chalmers, Sr. VP-Corp. Comm.
Shannon C. Brooks, Controller/VP
Robert (Skip) Lannert, Exec. VP-Class II Gaming
Joseph R. Enzminger, Chief Software Architect/VP
Gordon T. Sjodin, Exec. VP-Special Projects & Sales
Troy W. Jungmann, VP-Database Dev.
Michael J. Maples, Sr., Chmn.

Phone: 512-334-7500	Fax: 512-334-7695
Toll-Free:	

Address: 206 Wild Basin Rd., Bldg. B, Ste. 400, Austin, TX 78746 US

GROWTH PLANS/SPECIAL FEATURES:

Multimedia Games, Inc. develops and distributes electronic gaming and paper bingo systems for Native American bingo operations, charitable bingo operations, casinos, sweepstakes, racetracks and video lottery systems. Products include interactive systems, server-based gaming systems, interactive electronic games, player terminals, stand-alone player terminals, video lottery terminals, electronic scratch ticket systems, electronic instant lottery systems, player tracking systems, casino cash management systems, slot accounting systems, slot management systems, unified currencies and electronic and paper bingo systems. The company also designs and develops network systems that allow electronic gaming terminals to be linked to one another within a single facility or across multiple facilities. Most of its revenue comes from installing gaming systems, such as player terminals and back-office systems and equipment. The gaming systems primarily operate across proprietary local-area and wide-area broadband networks. Multimedia Games operates its interactive bingo games on behalf of its tribal customers through a multi-channel telecommunications network called BetNet. Employing combinations of frame relay, intranets, satellite, telephone, Internet and local area networks, BetNet enables distant players to play the same game and compete for pooled prizes in a progressive jackpot game. The company also produces high-stakes TV bingo game shows that are televised live to multiple participating Native American bingo halls linked via closed-circuit satellite and broadband telephone communications networks. Its proprietary games include MegaMania, Big Cash Bingo, Flash 21, People's Choice, Meltdown, Fruit Stand, Bad Monkey and Jungle Juice. Multimedia Games was recently selected to provide traditional bingo gaming services, electronic bingo, technical support and related services to Apuestas Internacionales S.A. de C.V., a Mexican gaming company. Multimedia will provide these services in 65 locations throughout Mexico. In exchange for these services, Multimedia will receive a percentage of each gaming station's win.

FINANCIALS: Sales and profits are in thousands of dollars—add 000 to get the full amount. 2007 Note: Financial information for 2007 was not available for all companies at press time.

2007 Sales: $121,917	2007 Profits: $- 744	**U.S. Stock Ticker: MGAM**
2006 Sales: $145,112	2006 Profits: $3,532	Int'l Ticker: Int'l Exchange:
2005 Sales: $153,216	2005 Profits: $17,643	Employees: 427
2004 Sales: $153,675	2004 Profits: $32,772	Fiscal Year Ends: 9/30
2003 Sales: $368,766	2003 Profits: $31,655	Parent Company:

SALARIES/BENEFITS:

Pension Plan:	ESOP Stock Plan:	Profit Sharing:	Top Exec. Salary: $450,000	Bonus: $
Savings Plan: Y	Stock Purch. Plan:		Second Exec. Salary: $185,000	Bonus: $43,000

OTHER THOUGHTS:

Apparent Women Officers or Directors: 3
Hot Spot for Advancement for Women/Minorities: Y

LOCATIONS: ("Y" = Yes)

West:	Southwest:	Midwest:	Southeast:	Northeast:	International:
Y	Y	Y		Y	Y

NAPSTER INC

www.napster.com

Industry Group Code: 451220E Ranks within this company's industry group: Sales: 1   Profits: 2

Print Media/Publishing:	Movies:	Equipment/Supplies:		Broadcast/Cable:	Music/Audio:		Sports/Games/Gambling:
Newspapers:	Movie Theaters:	Equipment/Supplies:	Y	Broadcast TV:	Music Production:	Y	Games/Sports:
Magazines:	Movie Production:	Gambling Equipment:		Cable TV:	Retail Music:	Y	Retail Games Stores:
Books:	TV/Video Prod.:	Special Services:		Satellite Broadcast:	Retail Audio Equip.:	Y	Stadiums/Teams:
Book Stores:	Video Rental:	Advertising Services:	Y	Radio:	Music Print./Dist.:	Y	Gambling/Casinos:
Distribution/Printing:	Video Distribution:	Info. Sys. Software:		Online Information:	Multimedia:		Rides/Theme Parks:

TYPES OF BUSINESS:

Online Music Retailing
Digital Media Software
Online Radio
Online Retail-Media Hardware
Mobile Phone Media Sales

BRANDS/DIVISIONS/AFFILIATES:

Napster To Go
Napster Light
shop.napster.com
Napster Mobile
NapsterLinks
Narchive
Napster UK

CONTACTS: Note: Officers with more than one job title may be intentionally listed here more than once.

Chris Gorog, CEO
Christopher Allen, COO
Bradford D. Duea, Pres.
Nand Gangwani, CFO
Chris Gorog, Chmn.

Phone: 310-281-5000	Fax: 408-367-3101
Toll-Free: 866-280-7694	
Address: 9044 Melrose Ave., Los Angeles, CA 90069 US	

GROWTH PLANS/SPECIAL FEATURES:

Napster, Inc. operates an online music service with over 830,000 subscribers. The company serves markets in the North America, Japan and parts of Europe. Napster offers its customers a digital music subscription service with unlimited access to over 4 million tracks in a wide variety of music genres with both major and independent record labels. Members also have access to over 50 interactive radio stations and complete information about the music offered. The Napster To Go membership includes everything in a standard membership, plus the ability to transfer an unlimited amount of music from Napster to their MP3 players, PCs or music-enabled cell phones. The company's Napster Light allows customers to purchase songs and albums individually. On its e-commerce site shop, Napster offers music devices for personal use, automobiles and living rooms; computer audio equipment; accessories; and branded merchandise. A major growth strategy for the company is to continue to pursue and execute strategic partnerships. The firm expanded its mobile market in 2007 when it launched a wireless music service branded Napster Mobile. In conjunction with Ericsson, Napster offers ringtones, over-the-air (OTA) downloads with dual delivery and wallpapers via a variety of mobile carriers in the U.S. and Europe. Using Napster Mobile, customers are able to purchase music downloads from the full music catalog using their mobile phone handset and have the songs delivered OTA to handsets with an additional copy sent to their PC.

FINANCIALS: Sales and profits are in thousands of dollars—add 000 to get the full amount. 2007 Note: Financial information for 2007 was not available for all companies at press time.

2007 Sales: $111,081	2007 Profits: $-36,826	**U.S. Stock Ticker:** NAPS	
2006 Sales: $94,691	2006 Profits: $-54,945	**Int'l Ticker:** Int'l Exchange:	
2005 Sales: $46,729	2005 Profits: $-29,506	Employees: 138	
2004 Sales: $99,300	2004 Profits: $44,400	Fiscal Year Ends: 3/31	
2003 Sales: $120,400	2003 Profits: $-9,900	Parent Company:	

SALARIES/BENEFITS:

Pension Plan:	ESOP Stock Plan:	Profit Sharing:	Top Exec. Salary: $625,000	Bonus: $
Savings Plan:	Stock Purch. Plan:		Second Exec. Salary: $300,000	Bonus: $

OTHER THOUGHTS:

Apparent Women Officers or Directors:
Hot Spot for Advancement for Women/Minorities:

LOCATIONS: ("Y" = Yes)

West:	Southwest:	Midwest:	Southeast:	Northeast:	International:
Y				Y	Y

NASPERS LIMITED

www.naspers.co.za

Industry Group Code: 513220 Ranks within this company's industry group: Sales: 12   Profits: 11

Print Media/Publishing:		Movies:		Equipment/Supplies:		Broadcast/Cable:		Music/Audio:		Sports/Games/Gambling:	
Newspapers:	Y	Movie Theaters:		Equipment/Supplies:		Broadcast TV:		Music Production:		Games/Sports:	
Magazines:	Y	Movie Production:		Gambling Equipment:		Cable TV:	Y	Retail Music:		Retail Games Stores:	
Books:	Y	TV/Video Prod.:		Special Services:	Y	Satellite Broadcast:		Retail Audio Equip.:		Stadiums/Teams:	
Book Stores:		Video Rental:		Advertising Services:	Y	Radio:		Music Print./Dist.:		Gambling/Casinos:	
Distribution/Printing:		Video Distribution:		Info. Sys. Software:		Online Information:		Multimedia:		Rides/Theme Parks:	

TYPES OF BUSINESS:

Cable Television
Internet Subscriber Platforms
Printing & Distribution Services
Content Protection Technology
Magazine & Book Publishing
Private Education

BRANDS/DIVISIONS/AFFILIATES:

MIH Holdings
Irdeto Access
Entriq
Media 24
Via Afrika
Educor
Tiscali
MIH Limited

CONTACTS: *Note: Officers with more than one job title may be intentionally listed here more than once.*

Cobus Stofberg, CEO
Giancarlo Civita, COO
Steve Ward, Group CFO
Andre Coetzee, Group Counsel
Antonie Roux, CEO-Internet Oper.
Beverly Branford, Dir.-Investor Rel.
Mark Sorour, Chief Investment Officer
Cobus Stofberg, CEO-MIH Holdings
Jim Volkwyn, CEO-Pay TV Platforms
Graham Kill, CEO-Irdeto Access
Ton Vosloo, Chmn.

Phone: 27-21-406-2121	**Fax:** 27-21-406-3753
Toll-Free:	
Address: 40 Heerengrarcht, Cape Town, 8001 South Africa	

GROWTH PLANS/SPECIAL FEATURES:

Naspers is a multinational media company with operations in pay television, Internet subscriber platforms, print media, book publishing, private education and technology markets. Naspers is located in South Africa, where it generates 72% of its revenues, with other operations located elsewhere in sub-Saharan Africa, Greece, Cyprus, Brazil, the Netherlands, the U.S., Thailand and China. The company's operations are divided into two business segments: electronic media (68% of total revenues) and print media. The electronic media segment offers pay television through MIH Holdings. The firm also provides content protection technologies to more than 40 countries worldwide through Irdeto Access. Irdeto's products enable pay-media operators to encrypt and decrypt their broadcast or multicast signals, while Entriq, another subsidiary, operates a media authorization network that enables content and broadband service providers to protect, track, sell and syndicate online media. Media 24, Naspers' print media segment, consists of book publishing and private education operation with approximately 35 magazine titles and 50 newspaper titles. The company's book publishing activities are conducted through Via Afrika, a leading African publisher, with an extensive portfolio of fiction, nonfiction, reference, academic, religious and illustrated books. The firm's private education business is conducted through Educor, which offers programs ranging from adult basic education and training to higher education and corporate training.   In January 2007, the company acquired a 30% minority stake in Mail.ru, a Russian Internet company, and a 30% stake in MXit Lifestyle (Pty) Ltd.   In July 2007, Naspers acquired a 30% interest in ACL Wireless Ltd., an India-based mobile software developer. In October 2007, thet firm acquired a controlling stake in GADU GADU S.A., a Polish instant messenger company.

FINANCIALS: Sales and profits are in thousands of dollars—add 000 to get the full amount. 2007 Note: Financial information for 2007 was not available for all companies at press time.

2007 Sales: $	2007 Profits: $	**U.S. Stock Ticker:**
2006 Sales: $2,128,200	2006 Profits: $341,000	**Int'l Ticker: NPN** Int'l Exchange: Johannesburg-JSE
2005 Sales: $2,243,200	2005 Profits: $417,800	Employees: 15,710
2004 Sales: $2,025,673	2004 Profits: $78,356	Fiscal Year Ends: 3/31
2003 Sales: $1,396,100	2003 Profits: $40,700	Parent Company:

SALARIES/BENEFITS:

Pension Plan: Y	ESOP Stock Plan:	Profit Sharing:	Top Exec. Salary: $270,255	Bonus: $303,788
Savings Plan:	Stock Purch. Plan:		Second Exec. Salary: $	Bonus: $

OTHER THOUGHTS:

Apparent Women Officers or Directors: 4
Hot Spot for Advancement for Women/Minorities: Y

LOCATIONS: ("Y" = Yes)

West:	Southwest:	Midwest:	Southeast:	Northeast:	International:
					Y

Note: Financial information, benefits and other data can change quickly and may vary from those stated here.

NATIONAL AMUSEMENTS INCwww.national-amusements.com

Industry Group Code: 512131 Ranks within this company's industry group: Sales: Profits:

Print Media/Publishing:	Movies:		Equipment/Supplies:		Broadcast/Cable:	Music/Audio:	Sports/Games/Gambling:	
Newspapers:	Movie Theaters:	Y	Equipment/Supplies:		Broadcast TV:	Music Production:	Games/Sports:	Y
Magazines:	Movie Production:		Gambling Equipment:		Cable TV:	Retail Music:	Retail Games Stores:	
Books:	TV/Video Prod.:		Special Services:		Satellite Broadcast:	Retail Audio Equip.:	Stadiums/Teams:	
Book Stores:	Video Rental:		Advertising Services:	Y	Radio:	Music Print./Dist.:	Gambling/Casinos:	
Distribution/Printing:	Video Distribution:		Info. Sys. Software:	Y	Online Information:	Multimedia:	Rides/Theme Parks:	

TYPES OF BUSINESS:

Movie Theaters
Online Ticketing
Video Games
Slot Machines
Advertising Services

BRANDS/DIVISIONS/AFFILIATES:

Showcase Cinemas
Multiplex Cinemas
Cinema de Lux
Viacom
Midway Games
CyGamZ
CBS
Ritz 16 Theater

CONTACTS: *Note: Officers with more than one job title may be intentionally listed here more than once.*

Sumner M. Redstone, CEO
Shari E. Redstone, Pres.
Jerome Magner, Sr. VP-Finance/Treas.
Sumner M. Redstone, Chmn.

Phone: 781-461-1600	**Fax:** 781-407-0052
Toll-Free:	
Address: 200 Elm St., Dedham, MA 02026 US	

GROWTH PLANS/SPECIAL FEATURES:

National Amusements, Inc. (NAI) operates under the Showcase Cinemas, KinoStar, Multiplex Cinemas and Cinema de Lux brands, which together operate over 1,500 screens in 119 theaters across the U.S., Europe and Latin America. National Amusements is an equal partner in the online ticketing service, MovieTickets.com, and is the parent company of both Viacom and CBS Corporation. NAI has among the highest per-screen revenue totals of any theatre circuit in the U.S. Features include Descriptive Video Service, which provides descriptive narration to visually impaired moviegoers over headsets, and Rear Window Captioning, which superimposes captions on movie screen by a system of reflectors. The firm offers customized advertising opportunities including onscreen slide advertising, rolling stock commercials, lobby monitor placement and web site opportunities. The company has stakes in Midway Games, a video game publisher which it will promote in conjunction with CyGamZ, an interactive gaming venue. CyGamZ offers full-service dining, both PC and console-based games, high-tech audio and plasma screen displays. The franchise is being launched with Intel, Alienware and Pepsi. In 2007, CyGamZ hosted gaming tournaments, including Tom Clancy's Rainbow Six Vegas Tournament; the locations also feature rooms equipped for parties or business meetings. In 2006, NAI opened the first IMAX theater in Argentina. The firm's high-end Cinema De Lux (CDL) concept outfits theaters with martini bars, Starbucks coffee counters, concierge desks, private party rooms, theaters that boast luxurious leather reclining seats which are assigned (as opposed to open seating), live performances before showings and escorted seating service. In 2007, NAI acquired the Ritz 16 Theater business, building and property in Voorhees New Jersey from Posel Voorhees, L.L.C. of Philadelphia. The theater will be renamed the Showcase at the Ritz Center.

NAI's corporate employees receive benefits including pension and 401(k) plans and movie passes. Theater staff have access to free movies.

FINANCIALS: Sales and profits are in thousands of dollars—add 000 to get the full amount. 2007 Note: Financial information for 2007 was not available for all companies at press time.

2007 Sales: $	2007 Profits: $	**U.S. Stock Ticker: Private**
2006 Sales: $	2006 Profits: $	**Int'l Ticker:** Int'l Exchange:
2005 Sales: $	2005 Profits: $	Employees:
2004 Sales: $	2004 Profits: $	Fiscal Year Ends: 12/31
2003 Sales: $	2003 Profits: $	Parent Company:

SALARIES/BENEFITS:

Pension Plan: Y	ESOP Stock Plan:	Profit Sharing:	Top Exec. Salary: $	Bonus: $
Savings Plan: Y	Stock Purch. Plan:		Second Exec. Salary: $	Bonus: $

OTHER THOUGHTS:

Apparent Women Officers or Directors: 1
Hot Spot for Advancement for Women/Minorities:

LOCATIONS: ("Y" = Yes)

West:	Southwest:	Midwest:	Southeast:	Northeast:	International:
Y		Y		Y	Y

Note: Financial information, benefits and other data can change quickly and may vary from those stated here.

NBC UNIVERSAL

www.nbcuni.com

Industry Group Code: 513210 **Ranks within this company's industry group:** Sales: 2   Profits: 2

Print Media/Publishing:	Movies:		Equipment/Supplies:		Broadcast/Cable:		Music/Audio:		Sports/Games/Gambling:	
Newspapers:	Movie Theaters:		Equipment/Supplies:		Broadcast TV:	Y	Music Production:		Games/Sports:	
Magazines:	Movie Production:		Gambling Equipment:		Cable TV:	Y	Retail Music:		Retail Games Stores:	
Books:	TV/Video Prod.:	Y	Special Services:		Satellite Broadcast:		Retail Audio Equip.:		Stadiums/Teams:	
Book Stores:	Video Rental:		Advertising Services:		Radio:		Music Print./Dist.:		Gambling/Casinos:	
Distribution/Printing:	Video Distribution:	Y	Info. Sys. Software:		Online Information:		Multimedia:		Rides/Theme Parks:	

TYPES OF BUSINESS:

Television Broadcasting
Online News & Information
TV & Movie Production
Radio Broadcasting
Interactive Online Content
Cable Television Programming
Theme Parks
Film, TV & Home Video Distribution

BRANDS/DIVISIONS/AFFILIATES:

General Electric Company (GE)
Vivendi Universal Entertainment
NBC
Universal Pictures
Universal Studios
MSNBC
Universal Parks & Resorts
Telemundo

CONTACTS: *Note: Officers with more than one job title may be intentionally listed here more than once.*

Jeff Zucker, CEO
Jeff Zucker, Pres.
Lynn Calpeter, CFO/Exec. VP
Marc Chini, Exec. VP-Human Resources
John Eck, CIO/Pres., Media Works
Rick Cotton, General Counsel/Exec. VP
Cory Shields, Exec. VP-Comm.
Beth Comstock, Pres., Integrated Media
Jay Ireland, Pres., NBC Universal Television Stations
Paula Madison, Exec. VP-Diversity
Steve Capus, Pres., NBC News
Robert C. Wright, Chmn.
Peter Smith, Pres., NBC Universal Int'l
Jean-Briac Perrette, Pres., Digital Dist.

Phone: 212-664-4444	Fax: 212-664-4085
Toll-Free:	
Address: 30 Rockefeller Plaza, New York, NY 10112 US	

GROWTH PLANS/SPECIAL FEATURES:

NBC Universal is one of the world's leading media and entertainment companies in the development, production and marketing of entertainment, news and information to a global audience. The company is a subsidiary of General Electric (GE) and the product of a 2004 merger of Vivendi Universal Entertainment with NBC (National Broadcasting Company).   The company is 20%-owned by Vivendi Universal and 80%-owned by GE. Assets merged into the new organization include Universal Pictures, Universal Television and the Universal Studios theme parks.   In addition, the company oversees the NBC Television Network.   NBC Universal TV Stations operates 10 NBC affiliate stations and 16 Telemundo stations in major U.S. markets. The firm operates cable channels including Bravo, CNBC, MSNBC and USA Networks and holds a partial interest in A&E.   NBC Internet, Inc., a wholly-owned subsidiary of NBC, operates a network of web sites centered around nbci.com and msnbc.com, integrating access across all of its major media platforms, including Internet, broadcast and cable television and radio. International assets include sales and distribution positions for video and DVD titles, television programming and feature films in more than 200 countries around the world.   Universal Recreation Group brings together the operations of Universal Parks and Resorts, including wholly-owned Universal Studios Hollywood and Universal CityWalk Hollywood, and major interests in both Universal Orlando properties (including Islands of Adventure, CityWalk Orlando and Universal Studios Florida) and international locations including Universal Studios Japan and Universal Mediterranean in Spain. In 2007, NBC Universal launched Get On Board, a comprehensive, company-wide program to improve the environmental impact of its operations by reducing greenhouse gases, raising awareness about green issues and stimulating change in the media and entertainment industry.

NBC Universal offers a large number of internships to college students and graduates each year.

FINANCIALS: Sales and profits are in thousands of dollars—add 000 to get the full amount. 2007 Note: Financial information for 2007 was not available for all companies at press time.

2007 Sales: $	2007 Profits: $	**U.S. Stock Ticker:** Subsidiary
2006 Sales: $16,188,000	2006 Profits: $2,919,000	**Int'l Ticker:** Int'l Exchange:
2005 Sales: $14,689,000	2005 Profits: $3,092,000	Employees: 15,000
2004 Sales: $12,886,000	2004 Profits: $2,558,000	Fiscal Year Ends: 12/31
2003 Sales: $6,871,000	2003 Profits: $1,998,000	Parent Company: GENERAL ELECTRIC CO (GE)

SALARIES/BENEFITS:

Pension Plan:	ESOP Stock Plan:	Profit Sharing:	Top Exec. Salary: $	Bonus: $450,000
Savings Plan: Y	Stock Purch. Plan:		Second Exec. Salary: $336,549	Bonus: $336,549

OTHER THOUGHTS:

Apparent Women Officers or Directors: 3
Hot Spot for Advancement for Women/Minorities: Y

LOCATIONS: ("Y" = Yes)

West:	Southwest:	Midwest:	Southeast:	Northeast:	International:
Y		Y		Y	Y

NETFLIX INC

www.netflix.com

Industry Group Code: 532230 Ranks within this company's industry group: Sales: 3 Profits: 3

Print Media/Publishing:	Movies:		Equipment/Supplies:	Broadcast/Cable:	Music/Audio:	Sports/Games/Gambling:
Newspapers:	Movie Theaters:		Equipment/Supplies:	Broadcast TV:	Music Production:	Games/Sports:
Magazines:	Movie Production:		Gambling Equipment:	Cable TV:	Retail Music:	Retail Games Stores:
Books:	TV/Video Prod.:		Special Services:	Satellite Broadcast:	Retail Audio Equip.:	Stadiums/Teams:
Book Stores:	Video Rental:	Y	Advertising Services:	Radio:	Music Print./Dist.:	Gambling/Casinos:
Distribution/Printing:	Video Distribution:		Info. Sys. Software:	Online Information:	Multimedia:	Rides/Theme Parks:

TYPES OF BUSINESS:

Online DVD Rental

BRANDS/DIVISIONS/AFFILIATES:

Red Envelope Entertainment, LLC

CONTACTS: Note: Officers with more than one job title may be intentionally listed here more than once.

Reed Hastings, CEO
Barry McCarthy, CFO
Leslie Kilgore, Chief Mktg. Officer
Patty McCord, Chief Talent Officer
Neil Hunt, Chief Product Officer
Ted Sarandos, Chief Content Officer
Reed Hastings, Chmn.

Phone: 408-540-3700	Fax:
Toll-Free:	
Address: 100 Winchester Cir., Los Gatos, CA 95032 US	

GROWTH PLANS/SPECIAL FEATURES:

Netflix, Inc. is one of the largest online movie rental subscription services providing over 7 million subscribers access to a library of more than 90,000 movie, television and other filmed entertainment titles on DVD. In addition, it has more than 5,000 titles available on its web site for instant viewing. The company offers nine subscription plans, starting at $4.99 a month. There are no due dates, no late fees and no shipping fees. Subscribers select titles at the firm's web site, receive the movies on DVD by mail and return them at their convenience using prepaid mailers. After a DVD has been returned, Netflix mails the next available DVD in a subscriber's queue. The firm's proprietary recommendation service enables it to create a customized store for each subscriber and to generate personalized recommendations. The company focuses on improving its web site experience and functionality and seeks to create value-added feature for its subscribers, such as the social networking feature, Friends, and the queue management feature, Profiles. Netflix purchases titles directly from studios, distributors and independent producers. It also develops and acquires content through wholly-owned subsidiary, Red Envelope Entertainment, LLC, which is dedicated to developing and acquiring original content productions. Netflix operates more than 100 shipping centers nationwide, allowing it to provide fast delivery and return service to subscribers. The company promotes its service to consumers through various marketing programs, including online promotions, television and ration advertising, package inserts, direct mail and other promotions with third parties. These programs encourage consumers to subscribe to the firm's services and may include a free trial period. At the end of the free trial period, subscribers are automatically enrolled as paying subscribers, unless they cancel their subscription. All subscribers are billed monthly in advance. The firm is experiencing significant competitive from Blockbuster's relatively new online DVD ordering service.

FINANCIALS: Sales and profits are in thousands of dollars—add 000 to get the full amount. 2007 Note: Financial information for 2007 was not available for all companies at press time.

2007 Sales: $	2007 Profits: $	U.S. Stock Ticker: NFLX
2006 Sales: $996,700	2006 Profits: $49,100	Int'l Ticker: Int'l Exchange:
2005 Sales: $688,000	2005 Profits: $41,900	Employees: 1,300
2004 Sales: $506,228	2004 Profits: $20,838	Fiscal Year Ends: 12/31
2003 Sales: $272,243	2003 Profits: $6,512	Parent Company:

SALARIES/BENEFITS:

Pension Plan:	ESOP Stock Plan:	Profit Sharing:	Top Exec. Salary: $650,000	Bonus: $
Savings Plan: Y	Stock Purch. Plan:		Second Exec. Salary: $500,000	Bonus: $

OTHER THOUGHTS:

Apparent Women Officers or Directors: 2
Hot Spot for Advancement for Women/Minorities:

LOCATIONS: ("Y" = Yes)

West:	Southwest:	Midwest:	Southeast:	Northeast:	International:
Y					

Note: Financial information, benefits and other data can change quickly and may vary from those stated here.

NETRATINGS INC

www.nielsen-netratings.com

Industry Group Code: 541910 Ranks within this company's industry group: Sales: 4 Profits: 4

Print Media/Publishing:	Movies:	Equipment/Supplies:		Broadcast/Cable:	Music/Audio:	Sports/Games/Gambling:
Newspapers:	Movie Theaters:	Equipment/Supplies:		Broadcast TV:	Music Production:	Games/Sports:
Magazines:	Movie Production:	Gambling Equipment:		Cable TV:	Retail Music:	Retail Games Stores:
Books:	TV/Video Prod.:	Special Services:	Y	Satellite Broadcast:	Retail Audio Equip.:	Stadiums/Teams:
Book Stores:	Video Rental:	Advertising Services:	Y	Radio:	Music Print./Dist.:	Gambling/Casinos:
Distribution/Printing:	Video Distribution:	Info. Sys. Software:		Online Information:	Multimedia:	Rides/Theme Parks:

TYPES OF BUSINESS:

Internet Audience Information & Analysis
Marketing Services
Market Research

BRANDS/DIVISIONS/AFFILIATES:

Nielsen/NetRatings
Nielsen Company BV (The)
VNU NV
NetView
AdRelevance
@Plan
MegaPanel
SiteCensus

CONTACTS: *Note: Officers with more than one job title may be intentionally listed here more than once.*

Todd Sloan, CFO
Todd Sloan, Corp. Sec.
Manish Bhatia, Exec. VP-Global Oper.
Todd Sloan, Exec. VP-Corp. Dev.
John A. Dimling, Chmn.

Phone: 212-703-5900	Fax: 212-703-5901
Toll-Free: 888-634-1222	
Address: 120 W. 45th St., 35th Fl., New York, NY 10036 US	

GROWTH PLANS/SPECIAL FEATURES:

NetRatings, Inc., operating under the Nielsen/NetRatings brand, is a subsidiary of The Nielsen Company (formerly VNU Group) providing Internet audience measurement and analysis. NetRatings became a fully-owned subsidiary of Nielsen in June 2007. The company's products and services are designed to aid companies in making critical business decisions regarding Internet strategies and initiatives. The firm's primary products and services include NetView, AdRelevance, @Plan, MegaPanel, SiteCensus, WebRF, Web Intercept and Homescan Online. NetView, NetRatings' original product, provides in-depth measurement of audience behavior online and in the digital media universe, including instant messaging and media players. AdRelevance offers comprehensive and accurate information on online advertising. @Plan is a leading resource for demographic, lifestyle and product preferences that guide advertisers, agencies and web publishers in online marketing and media strategies. MegaPanel provides increased breadth and depth of Internet behavior and activity for the market research industry, including e-commerce transaction information. SiteCensus offers extensive web analytical services based on traffic flows and visitor behaviors. WebRF offers advertisers and web publishers the ability to plan and evaluate the impact of Internet advertising. WebIntercept allows clients to survey Internet users based on their real-time online behavior. Homescan Online improves the effectiveness of online marketing for the consumer packaged goods industry and web publishers.

FINANCIALS: Sales and profits are in thousands of dollars—add 000 to get the full amount. 2007 Note: Financial information for 2007 was not available for all companies at press time.

2007 Sales: $	2007 Profits: $	**U.S. Stock Ticker: Subsidiary**
2006 Sales: $81,769	2006 Profits: $2,829	**Int'l Ticker:** Int'l Exchange:
2005 Sales: $68,017	2005 Profits: $-8,395	Employees: 397
2004 Sales: $59,300	2004 Profits: $-17,419	Fiscal Year Ends: 12/31
2003 Sales: $41,432	2003 Profits: $-25,135	Parent Company: NIELSEN COMPANY BV (THE)

SALARIES/BENEFITS:

Pension Plan:	ESOP Stock Plan:	Profit Sharing:	Top Exec. Salary: $358,333	Bonus: $280,000
Savings Plan:	Stock Purch. Plan:		Second Exec. Salary: $256,250	Bonus: $128,750

OTHER THOUGHTS:

Apparent Women Officers or Directors:
Hot Spot for Advancement for Women/Minorities:

LOCATIONS: ("Y" = Yes)

West:	Southwest:	Midwest:	Southeast:	Northeast:	International:
Y				Y	Y

NEW LINE CINEMA
www.newline.com

Industry Group Code: 512110 Ranks within this company's industry group: Sales: Profits:

Print Media/Publishing:	Movies:		Equipment/Supplies:	Broadcast/Cable:	Music/Audio:	Sports/Games/Gambling:
Newspapers:	Movie Theaters:		Equipment/Supplies:	Broadcast TV:	Music Production:	Games/Sports:
Magazines:	Movie Production:	Y	Gambling Equipment:	Cable TV:	Retail Music:	Retail Games Stores:
Books:	TV/Video Prod.:	Y	Special Services:	Satellite Broadcast:	Retail Audio Equip.:	Stadiums/Teams:
Book Stores:	Video Rental:		Advertising Services:	Radio:	Music Print./Dist.:	Gambling/Casinos:
Distribution/Printing:	Video Distribution:	Y	Info. Sys. Software:	Online Information:	Multimedia:	Rides/Theme Parks:

TYPES OF BUSINESS:
Movie Production
Video & DVD Distribution
Online Retail
Merchandising & Licensing

BRANDS/DIVISIONS/AFFILIATES:
Time Warner Inc
Fine Line Features
New Line Home Video
New Line Television
New Line Theater Distribution
New Line International Releasing, Inc.
Material Entertainment
Picturehouse

CONTACTS: *Note: Officers with more than one job title may be intentionally listed here more than once.*
Robert K. Shaye, Co-CEO/Co-Chmn.
Stephen Abramson, CFO
Ben Zinkin, Sr. Exec. VP-Bus. & Legal Affairs
Stephen L. Einhorn, Pres./COO-New Line Home Entertainment
Camela Galano, Pres., New Line Int'l Releasing, Inc.
Jim Rosenthal, Pres., New LineTelevision
Chris Carlisle, Pres., New Line Domestic Mktg.
Michael Lynne, Co-Chmn./Co-CEO
Rolf Mittweg, Pres./COO-New Line Worldwide

Phone: 212-649-4900	Fax: 212-649-4966
Toll-Free:	
Address: 888 7th Ave., 19th Fl., New York, NY 10106 US	

GROWTH PLANS/SPECIAL FEATURES:
New Line Cinema Corp., a subsidiary of Time Warner, Inc., is a distributor and producer of motion pictures. The company operates through two main film divisions: New Line Cinema (NLC) and Fine Line Features (FLF). NLC produces, markets and distributes blockbuster films such as the Lord of the Rings trilogy and the Austin Powers series. FLF produces and acquires art-house films such as Vera Drake, Maria Full of Grace and The Sea Inside. Through its other subsidiaries, the company has operations in home entertainment, television, music, theater, licensing, merchandising and international marketing and distribution. New Line Home Video distributes the company's films on video and DVD, while New Line Television licenses its movies for pay-per-view and network and cable television. New Line Theater Distribution handles the distribution of the company's movies to theaters around the country, while New Line International Releasing, Inc. sells the international distribution rights to its films by country and region. The firm sells movie merchandising through its retail web site, shop.newline.com. New Line and U.K.-based Entertainment Film Distributors also operate a joint venture, Material Entertainment, a London-based production company scheduled to produce four films a year. New Line Cinema and HBO recently paired up to create Picturehouse, a specialized film company. Picturehouse released several films in 2006, including Tristram Shandy, The Notorious Bettie Page and Fur. In December 2007, New Line released The Golden Compass, based on the first book in the His Dark Materials trilogy by Philip Pullman.

FINANCIALS: Sales and profits are in thousands of dollars—add 000 to get the full amount. 2007 Note: Financial information for 2007 was not available for all companies at press time.

2007 Sales: $	2007 Profits: $	U.S. Stock Ticker: Subsidiary
2006 Sales: $	2006 Profits: $	Int'l Ticker: Int'l Exchange:
2005 Sales: $	2005 Profits: $	Employees:
2004 Sales: $	2004 Profits: $	Fiscal Year Ends: 12/31
2003 Sales: $	2003 Profits: $	Parent Company: TIME WARNER INC

SALARIES/BENEFITS:
Pension Plan:	ESOP Stock Plan:	Profit Sharing:	Top Exec. Salary: $	Bonus: $
Savings Plan:	Stock Purch. Plan:		Second Exec. Salary: $	Bonus: $

OTHER THOUGHTS:
Apparent Women Officers or Directors: 1
Hot Spot for Advancement for Women/Minorities:

LOCATIONS: ("Y" = Yes)
West:	Southwest:	Midwest:	Southeast:	Northeast:	International:
				Y	

NEW YORK TIMES CO (THE)

www.nytco.com

Industry Group Code: 511110 Ranks within this company's industry group: Sales: 6 Profits: 18

Print Media/Publishing:		Movies:		Equipment/Supplies:		Broadcast/Cable:		Music/Audio:		Sports/Games/Gambling:	
Newspapers:	Y	Movie Theaters:		Equipment/Supplies:		Broadcast TV:	Y	Music Production:		Games/Sports:	
Magazines:	Y	Movie Production:		Gambling Equipment:		Cable TV:		Retail Music:		Retail Games Stores:	
Books:	Y	TV/Video Prod.:		Special Services:	Y	Satellite Broadcast:		Retail Audio Equip.:		Stadiums/Teams:	
Book Stores:		Video Rental:		Advertising Services:	Y	Radio:		Music Print./Dist.:		Gambling/Casinos:	
Distribution/Printing:		Video Distribution:		Info. Sys. Software:		Online Information:		Multimedia:		Rides/Theme Parks:	

TYPES OF BUSINESS:

Newspaper Publishing
Broadcast TV
Broadcast Radio
Online Publishing
Newsprint & Paper Manufacturing
Newspaper Distribution

BRANDS/DIVISIONS/AFFILIATES:

New York Times (The)
Boston Globe (The)
WQXR-FM
About Inc
International Herald Tribune
Worcester Telegram & Gazette
ConsumerSearch.com
UCompareHealthCare.com

CONTACTS: Note: Officers with more than one job title may be intentionally listed here more than once.

Janet L. Robinson, CEO
Janet L. Robinson, Pres.
James M. Follo, CFO
David K. Norton, Sr. VP-Human Resources
Michael Zimbalist, VP-Research & Dev. Oper.
David A. Thurm, CIO/VP
Kenneth A. Richieri, General Counsel/Sr. VP
James C. Lessersohn, Sr. VP-Corp. Dev.
Catherine J. Mathis, Sr. VP-Corp. Comm.
George Barrios, Treas./VP
Martin A. Nisenholtz, Sr. VP-Digital Oper.
Stuart P. Stoller, Sr. VP-Process Eng.
R. Anthony Benten, Corp. Controller/VP
Rhonda L. Brauer, Sec./Corp. Governance Officer/Sr. Counsel
Arthur O. Sulzberger, Jr., Chmn.

Phone: 212-556-1234	Fax: 212-556-7389
Toll-Free:	
Address: 620 8th Ave., New York, NY 10018 US	

GROWTH PLANS/SPECIAL FEATURES:

The New York Times Co. is a global media company with operations in newspapers, television, radio and the Internet. It operates in two segments: news media and About.com. The news media group consists of the New York Times media group, which includes NYTimes.com, the International Herald Tribune, IHT.com, a newspaper distributor in the New York City metropolitan area, news, photos and graphics services, news and features syndication, and a New York City radio station, WQXR-FM; the New England media group, which includes The Boston Globe, Boston.com and the Worcester Telegram & Gazette and its web site; and the regional media group, which includes 14 daily newspapers in six states, and related print and digital businesses. About.com is an Internet consumer solutions source that provides users with information and advice on thousands of topics. New York Times owns equity interests in a Canadian newsprint company and a supercalendered paper manufacturing partnership in Maine; New England Sports Ventures, LLC, which owns the Boston Red Sox, Fenway Park and adjacent real estate, roughly 80% of New England Sports Network and 50% of Roush Fenway Racing, a NASCAR team; and Metro Boston LLC, which publishes a free daily newspaper catering to young professionals and students in the Boston metropolitan area. In 2007, About.com acquired UCompareHealthCare.com, a site that provides consumers with access to ratings and related information on hospitals, mammography centers, nursing homes, doctors and fertility clinics; and ConsumerSearch.com, an online publisher of meta-reviews. In May 2007, New York Times sold its broadcast media group to Oak Hill Capital Partners. In 2007, the firm sold its WQEW-AM radio station.

The company offers its employees medical, dental and vision insurance; short- and long-term disability insurance; life and AD&D insurance; a 401(k) plan; a pension plan; an employee stock purchase plan; tuition reimbursement; and an employee assistance program.

FINANCIALS: Sales and profits are in thousands of dollars—add 000 to get the full amount. 2007 Note: Financial information for 2007 was not available for all companies at press time.

2007 Sales: $	2007 Profits: $	U.S. Stock Ticker: NYT
2006 Sales: $3,289,903	2006 Profits: $-543,443	Int'l Ticker: Int'l Exchange:
2005 Sales: $3,231,128	2005 Profits: $253,473	Employees: 11,585
2004 Sales: $3,159,412	2004 Profits: $287,631	Fiscal Year Ends: 12/31
2003 Sales: $3,227,200	2003 Profits: $302,700	Parent Company:

SALARIES/BENEFITS:

Pension Plan: Y	ESOP Stock Plan:	Profit Sharing:	Top Exec. Salary: $1,087,000	Bonus: $560,521
Savings Plan: Y	Stock Purch. Plan: Y		Second Exec. Salary: $1,000,000	Bonus: $841,000

OTHER THOUGHTS:

Apparent Women Officers or Directors: 15
Hot Spot for Advancement for Women/Minorities: Y

LOCATIONS: ("Y" = Yes)

West:	Southwest:	Midwest:	Southeast:	Northeast:	International:
Y	Y	Y	Y	Y	Y

Note: Financial information, benefits and other data can change quickly and may vary from those stated here.

NEWS CORP

www.newscorp.com

Industry Group Code: 513120 Ranks within this company's industry group: Sales: 2 Profits: 2

Print Media/Publishing:		Movies:		Equipment/Supplies:		Broadcast/Cable:		Music/Audio:		Sports/Games/Gambling:	
Newspapers:	Y	Movie Theaters:		Equipment/Supplies:		Broadcast TV:	Y	Music Production:		Games/Sports:	Y
Magazines:	Y	Movie Production:	Y	Gambling Equipment:		Cable TV:	Y	Retail Music:		Retail Games Stores:	
Books:	Y	TV/Video Prod.:	Y	Special Services:	Y	Satellite Broadcast:		Retail Audio Equip.:		Stadiums/Teams:	
Book Stores:		Video Rental:		Advertising Services:	Y	Radio:		Music Print./Dist.:		Gambling/Casinos:	
Distribution/Printing:		Video Distribution:	Y	Info. Sys. Software:		Online Information:		Multimedia:		Rides/Theme Parks:	

TYPES OF BUSINESS:

Television Broadcasting & Distribution
Film & Television Production
Newspaper Publishing
Online Media
Advertising Services
Magazine & Book Publishing
Satellite Television

BRANDS/DIVISIONS/AFFILIATES:

MySpace
Intermix Media
Fox Entertainment Group Inc
Fox Broadcasting Company
HarperCollins Publishers Inc
New York Post
Liberty Media Corp
Dow Jones & Co Inc

CONTACTS: Note: Officers with more than one job title may be intentionally listed here more than once.

K. Rupert Murdoch, CEO
Peter Chernin, COO
Peter Chernin, Pres.
David F. DeVoe, CFO/Sr. Exec. VP
Gary Ginsberg, Exec. VP-Global Mktg.
Beryl Cook, Chief Human Resources Officer
Lawrence A. Jacobs, General Counsel/Sr. Exec. VP
Gary Ginsberg, Exec. VP-Corp. Affairs
Anthea Disney, Exec. VP-Content
Michael Regan, Exec. VP-Gov't Affairs
Genie Gavenchak, Chief Compliance & Ethics Officer/Sr. VP
Leon Hertz, Exec. VP
K Rupert Murdoch, Chmn.
James Murdoch, Chmn./CEO-Europe & Asia

Phone: 212-852-7000	Fax: 212-852-7147
Toll-Free:	
Address: 1211 Ave. of the Americas, 8th Fl., New York, NY 10036 US	

GROWTH PLANS/SPECIAL FEATURES:

News Corp. is an entertainment company with operations in eight industry segments: filmed entertainment; television; cable network programming; direct broadcast satellite television; magazines and inserts; newspapers; book publishing; and other. The filmed entertainment segment produces and acquires live-action and animated motion pictures for distribution and licensing in all formats in entertainment media; and the production and licensing of television programming worldwide. Subsidiaries include Fox Filmed Entertainment and Twentieth Century Fox Television. The television segment operates broadcast television stations; broadcasts network programming in the U.S.; and develops, produces and broadcasts television programming in Asia. The cable networking programming division produces and licenses news, sports, general entertainment and movie programming for distribution to distributors worldwide. The direct broadcast satellite television segment operates through SKY Italia, which currently distributes over 100 channels of basic and premium programming services via satellite and broadband to subscribers in Italy. The magazines and inserts group is engaged in marketing operations, primarily the publication of free standing inserts and the provision of in-store marketing products and services; and magazine publishing, such as The Weekly Standard. The newspapers segment publishes newspapers and magazines in the U.K., Ireland, Australia and the U.S., including The Sun, News of the World and the New York Post. The book publishing division operates through HarperCollins Publishers, which primarily publishes fiction and non-fiction for the general consumer. The other segment includes News' Internet businesses, including Myspace.com; interests in various companies; and other operations. In December 2006, Liberty Media Corp. completed a significant $11 billion asset swap with News. Under the agreement, Liberty received News' 38.5% stake in DIRECTV, $550 million in cash and three regional sports networks. News received Liberty's $11.2 billion stake in News itself. This gives Liberty controlling interest in DIRECTV. In December 2007, News Corp. acquired Dow Jones & Co., Inc. for roughly $5 billion.

FINANCIALS: Sales and profits are in thousands of dollars—add 000 to get the full amount. 2007 Note: Financial information for 2007 was not available for all companies at press time.

2007 Sales: $28,655,000	2007 Profits: $3,426,000	**U.S. Stock Ticker: NWS**
2006 Sales: $25,327,000	2006 Profits: $2,314,000	**Int'l Ticker:** Int'l Exchange:
2005 Sales: $23,859,000	2005 Profits: $2,128,000	Employees: 44,000
2004 Sales: $20,959,000	2004 Profits: $1,647,000	Fiscal Year Ends: 6/30
2003 Sales: $17,474,000	2003 Profits: $1,046,000	Parent Company:

SALARIES/BENEFITS:

Pension Plan:	ESOP Stock Plan:	Profit Sharing:	Top Exec. Salary: $8,100,000	Bonus: $15,795,000
Savings Plan: Y	Stock Purch. Plan:		Second Exec. Salary: $8,100,000	Bonus: $10,397,500

OTHER THOUGHTS:

Apparent Women Officers or Directors: 3
Hot Spot for Advancement for Women/Minorities: Y

LOCATIONS: ("Y" = Yes)

West:	Southwest:	Midwest:	Southeast:	Northeast:	International:
Y	Y	Y	Y	Y	Y

Note: Financial information, benefits and other data can change quickly and may vary from those stated here.

NEWS WORLD COMMUNICATIONS INC www.washtimes.com

Industry Group Code: 511110 Ranks within this company's industry group: Sales: Profits:

Print Media/Publishing:		Movies:	Equipment/Supplies:		Broadcast/Cable:	Music/Audio:	Sports/Games/Gambling:
Newspapers:	Y	Movie Theaters:	Equipment/Supplies:		Broadcast TV:	Music Production:	Games/Sports:
Magazines:	Y	Movie Production:	Gambling Equipment:		Cable TV:	Retail Music:	Retail Games Stores:
Books:		TV/Video Prod.:	Special Services:	Y	Satellite Broadcast:	Retail Audio Equip.:	Stadiums/Teams:
Book Stores:		Video Rental:	Advertising Services:		Radio:	Music Print./Dist.:	Gambling/Casinos:
Distribution/Printing:		Video Distribution:	Info. Sys. Software:		Online Information:	Multimedia:	Rides/Theme Parks:

TYPES OF BUSINESS:

Newspaper Publication
Magazine Publication
Online News & Information
News Agency

BRANDS/DIVISIONS/AFFILIATES:

Washington Times (The)
National Weekly
World & I (The)
Middle East Times
GolfStyles
World Peace Herald
Tiempos Del Mundo
United Press International

CONTACTS: Note: Officers with more than one job title may be intentionally listed here more than once.

Chung Hwan Kwak, Pres.
Keith Cooperrider, CFO/VP
Glenn Murphy, Mgr.-Sales & Mktg.
Goldie Butler, Dir.-Research
Art Crofoot, Mgr.-Internet Advertising
Brian Bauman, Mgr.-Corp. Comm. & Mktg.
Wesley Pruden, Editor in Chief-The Washington Times
Jeffrey T. Kuhner, Editor-Insight
Steve Osmond, Editor-The World & I
Joseph Weber, Editor-Metropolitan Times
Chung Hwan Kwak, Chmn.
Francisco Quintanilla, Dir.-Int'l Mktg.

Phone: 202-636-3000	Fax: 202-269-1245
Toll-Free:	
Address: 3600 New York Ave. NE, Washington, DC 20002-1947 US	

GROWTH PLANS/SPECIAL FEATURES:

News World Communications, Inc., founded in 1982 by Reverend Sun Myung Moon, is a media company owned by the Unification Church. The company's flagship publication, The Washington Times, is a well-known yet financially insolvent newspaper based in the U.S. capital, with a readership of over 100,000. In addition to its daily and weekly issues, the Times also offers online subscriptions from its web site, washtimes.com. Additional company newspapers include National Weekly, a weekly edition of The Washington times providing the week's biggest news and commentary; Insight Magazine, an online publication focusing on politics in Washington; The World & I, a monthly educational publication featuring articles on current events, the arts, natural science, culture and literature; Egypt-based Middle East Times; GolfStyles magazine; World Peace Herald, a global online general-interest news publication; and a group of internationally distributed papers, Tiempos Del Mundo, Segye Ilbo, Segye Times USA, Chongyohak Shinmun and Sekai Nippo. News World also owns the United Press International (UPI) news agency, with services in English, Spanish and Arabic.

FINANCIALS: Sales and profits are in thousands of dollars—add 000 to get the full amount. 2007 Note: Financial information for 2007 was not available for all companies at press time.

2007 Sales: $	2007 Profits: $	U.S. Stock Ticker: Private
2006 Sales: $	2006 Profits: $	Int'l Ticker: Int'l Exchange:
2005 Sales: $	2005 Profits: $	Employees:
2004 Sales: $	2004 Profits: $	Fiscal Year Ends: 3/31
2003 Sales: $	2003 Profits: $	Parent Company:

SALARIES/BENEFITS:

Pension Plan:	ESOP Stock Plan:	Profit Sharing:	Top Exec. Salary: $	Bonus: $
Savings Plan:	Stock Purch. Plan:		Second Exec. Salary: $	Bonus: $

OTHER THOUGHTS:

Apparent Women Officers or Directors: 2
Hot Spot for Advancement for Women/Minorities:

LOCATIONS: ("Y" = Yes)

West:	Southwest:	Midwest:	Southeast:	Northeast:	International:
				Y	Y

NEXSTAR BROADCASTING GROUP INC   www.nexstar.tv

Industry Group Code: 513120 Ranks within this company's industry group: Sales: 15   Profits: 15

Print Media/Publishing:	Movies:	Equipment/Supplies:	Broadcast/Cable:		Music/Audio:	Sports/Games/Gambling:
Newspapers:	Movie Theaters:	Equipment/Supplies:	Broadcast TV:	Y	Music Production:	Games/Sports:
Magazines:	Movie Production:	Gambling Equipment:	Cable TV:		Retail Music:	Retail Games Stores:
Books:	TV/Video Prod.:	Special Services:	Satellite Broadcast:		Retail Audio Equip.:	Stadiums/Teams:
Book Stores:	Video Rental:	Advertising Services:	Radio:		Music Print./Dist.:	Gambling/Casinos:
Distribution/Printing:	Video Distribution:	Info. Sys. Software:	Online Information:		Multimedia:	Rides/Theme Parks:

TYPES OF BUSINESS:
Television Broadcasting

BRANDS/DIVISIONS/AFFILIATES:
Mission

CONTACTS: *Note: Officers with more than one job title may be intentionally listed here more than once.*
Perry A. Sook, CEO
Duane A. Lammers, COO/Exec. VP
Perry A. Sook, Pres.
Matt Devine, CFO/Exec. VP
Blake Russell, VP-Mktg.
Phil Reyna, Dir.-Human Resources
Richard Stolpe, VP/Dir.-Eng.
Blake Russell, VP-Oper.
Shirley E. Green, VP-Finance
Rajiv Lulla, Sr. VP-New Media
Chris Manson, VP-News
Timothy Busch, Sr. VP/Regional Mgr.
Gabe Nill, Controller/VP
Perry A. Sook, Chmn.

Phone: 972-373-8800	Fax: 972-373-8888
Toll-Free:	
Address: 909 Lake Carolyn Pkwy., Ste. 1450, Irving, TX 75039 US	

GROWTH PLANS/SPECIAL FEATURES:
Nexstar Broadcasting Group, Inc. is a television broadcasting company focused exclusively on the acquisition, development and operation of television stations in medium-sized markets in the U.S. The company owns and operates 32 stations and provides sales or other services to an additional 17 stations that are owned by Mission and other entities. In the 17 of the 29 markets that it serves, the firm owns, operates, programs or provides sales and other services to more than one station. The stations Nexstar owns, operates, programs or provides sales and other services to are in markets located in New York, Pennsylvania, Illinois, Indiana, Missouri, Texas, Louisiana, Arkansas, Alabama, Montana and Maryland. These stations are diverse in their network affiliations: 44 have primary affiliation agreements with one of the four major networks, 12 with NBC, 14 with Fox, nine with ABC and nine with CBS. Four of the remaining five stations have agreements with MyNetworkTV and one station has an agreement with the CW. The stations belonging to the company provide free over-the-air programming to the firm's markets' television viewing audiences. This programming includes programs produced by networks with which the stations are affiliates; programs that the stations produce; and first-run and rerun syndicated programs that the stations acquire. The primary source of revenue is the sale of commercial air time to local and national advertisers. Nexstar has various local service agreements with Mission, owned by an independent third party, through which the company provides sales, programming and other services to 15 television stations owned and operated by Mission.

FINANCIALS: Sales and profits are in thousands of dollars—add 000 to get the full amount. 2007 Note: Financial information for 2007 was not available for all companies at press time.

2007 Sales: $	2007 Profits: $	U.S. Stock Ticker: NXST
2006 Sales: $265,169	2006 Profits: $-8,992	Int'l Ticker: Int'l Exchange:
2005 Sales: $228,939	2005 Profits: $-48,730	Employees: 2,214
2004 Sales: $249,531	2004 Profits: $-20,500	Fiscal Year Ends: 12/31
2003 Sales: $214,332	2003 Profits: $-71,799	Parent Company:

SALARIES/BENEFITS:
Pension Plan:	ESOP Stock Plan:	Profit Sharing:	Top Exec. Salary: $674,519	Bonus: $900,000
Savings Plan:	Stock Purch. Plan:		Second Exec. Salary: $324,808	Bonus: $165,000

OTHER THOUGHTS:
Apparent Women Officers or Directors: 1
Hot Spot for Advancement for Women/Minorities:

LOCATIONS: ("Y" = Yes)
West:	Southwest:	Midwest:	Southeast:	Northeast:	International:
Y	Y	Y	Y	Y	

Note: Financial information, benefits and other data can change quickly and may vary from those stated here.

NIELSEN COMPANY BV (THE)
www.nielsen.com

Industry Group Code: 541910 Ranks within this company's industry group: Sales: Profits:

Print Media/Publishing:		Movies:	Equipment/Supplies:		Broadcast/Cable:	Music/Audio:	Sports/Games/Gambling:
Newspapers:		Movie Theaters:	Equipment/Supplies:		Broadcast TV:	Music Production:	Games/Sports:
Magazines:	Y	Movie Production:	Gambling Equipment:		Cable TV:	Retail Music:	Retail Games Stores:
Books:		TV/Video Prod.:	Special Services:	Y	Satellite Broadcast:	Retail Audio Equip.:	Stadiums/Teams:
Book Stores:		Video Rental:	Advertising Services:	Y	Radio:	Music Print./Dist.:	Gambling/Casinos:
Distribution/Printing:		Video Distribution:	Info. Sys. Software:		Online Information:	Multimedia:	Rides/Theme Parks:

TYPES OF BUSINESS:

Market Research
Magazine Publishing
Media/Entertainment Audience Research
Trade Publications
Directories
Business Consulting

BRANDS/DIVISIONS/AFFILIATES:

VNU NV
ACNielsen
ACNielsen HCI
BASES
Claritas
Decisions Made Easy
IMS
Nielsen Media Research

CONTACTS: *Note: Officers with more than one job title may be intentionally listed here more than once.*

David L. Calhoun, CEO
Brian J. West, CFO
Roberto Llamas, Chief Human Resources Officer
Susan D. Whiting, Exec. VP/Chmn.-Nielsen Media Research
James W. Cuminale, Chief Legal Officer
Thomas A. (Thom) Mastrelli, Exec. VP-Corp. Dev.
Itzhak Fisher, Exec. Chmn.-Nielsen Online
John A. Loftus, Chief Comm. Officer/Sr. VP
Bienvenido C. (Nonoy) Niles, Jr., Pres., ACNielsen Asia Pacific
Lennart Bengtsson, Pres., ACNielsen EEMEA
Patrick Dodd, Dir.-ACNielsen Europe
Jon Mandel, CEO-NielsenConnect
David L. Calhoun, Chmn.
Mitchell J. Habib, Exec. VP-Global Bus. Svcs.

Phone: 31-23-546-34-63	**Fax:** 31-23-546-39-38
Toll-Free:	
Address: Ceylonpoort 5-25, Haarlem, 2037 AA The Netherlands	

GROWTH PLANS/SPECIAL FEATURES:

The Nielsen Company B.V., formerly VNU NV, is a leading global provider of marketing information, audience measurement and business media products and services with operations in over 100 countries. The company changed its name from VNU in January 2007. Subsidiary ACNielsen provides marketing information primarily to manufacturers and retailers of fast-moving consumer goods. ACNielsen HCI is Nielsen's global pharmaceutical promotion research organization. Nielsen's BASES subsidiary provides pre-market consumer insights for marketers of consumer packaged goods. Subsidiary Claritas provides marketing research demographic data, marketing software and market segmentation services. Decisions Made Easy (DME), another subsidiary, provides sales and supply chain data management services. IMS is Nielsen's provider of information systems and solutions for the media industry. Nielsen Entertainment provides market information, creative testing, marketing solutions and analytical tools focused on film, music, home entertainment, books and interactive entertainment. Subsidiary Nielsen Media Research provides television, radio and print audience measurement and advertising information services. Nielsen Online, formed by the combination of Nielsen/NetRatings and Nielsen BuzzMetrics, provides independent measurement and analysis of online audiences, advertising, video, blogs, consumer-generated media, word of mouth, commerce and consumer behavior. PERQ/HCI is Nielsen's U.S. healthcare journal advertising and expenditure reporter. Subsidiary Scarborough Research provides information regarding the shopping patterns, lifestyle and media habits of U.S. consumers. Subsidiary SRDS provides media rates and data. Additional subsidiaries include ACNielsen Analytic Consulting, ACNielsen Homescan & Spectra, Nielsen Outdoor, Nielsen Sports and Nielsen Mobile. In February 2007, Nielsen acquired Turkish advertising intelligence company Bilesim Medya. In April 2007, the company acquired the remaining 42% interest of BuzzMetrics it did not already own. In June 2007, Nielsen acquired NetRatings. In August 2007, Nielsen acquired Telephia, a leading provider of syndicated consumer research to the telecom and mobile media markets.

FINANCIALS: Sales and profits are in thousands of dollars—add 000 to get the full amount. 2007 Note: Financial information for 2007 was not available for all companies at press time.

2007 Sales: $	2007 Profits: $	**U.S. Stock Ticker: Private**
2006 Sales: $	2006 Profits: $	**Int'l Ticker:** Int'l Exchange:
2005 Sales: $4,180,121	2005 Profits: $307,738	Employees: 42,000
2004 Sales: $4,009,084	2004 Profits: $295,722	Fiscal Year Ends: 12/31
2003 Sales: $4,872,400	2003 Profits: $163,100	Parent Company:

SALARIES/BENEFITS:

Pension Plan:	ESOP Stock Plan:	Profit Sharing:	Top Exec. Salary: $	Bonus: $
Savings Plan:	Stock Purch. Plan:		Second Exec. Salary: $	Bonus: $

OTHER THOUGHTS:

Apparent Women Officers or Directors: 1
Hot Spot for Advancement for Women/Minorities:

LOCATIONS: ("Y" = Yes)

West:	Southwest:	Midwest:	Southeast:	Northeast:	International:
Y	Y	Y	Y	Y	Y

NINTENDO CO LTD

www.nintendo.com

Industry Group Code: 334111 Ranks within this company's industry group: Sales: 2 Profits: 2

Print Media/Publishing:	Movies:	Equipment/Supplies:		Broadcast/Cable:	Music/Audio:	Sports/Games/Gambling:	
Newspapers:	Movie Theaters:	Equipment/Supplies:	Y	Broadcast TV:	Music Production:	Games/Sports:	Y
Magazines:	Movie Production:	Gambling Equipment:		Cable TV:	Retail Music:	Retail Games Stores:	
Books:	TV/Video Prod.:	Special Services:		Satellite Broadcast:	Retail Audio Equip.:	Stadiums/Teams:	
Book Stores:	Video Rental:	Advertising Services:		Radio:	Music Print./Dist.:	Gambling/Casinos:	
Distribution/Printing:	Video Distribution:	Info. Sys. Software:		Online Information:	Multimedia:	Rides/Theme Parks:	

TYPES OF BUSINESS:

Video Games
Video Game Hardware & Software

BRANDS/DIVISIONS/AFFILIATES:

GameCube
Nintendo DS
Game Boy Advance
Wii
Mario Brothers
Legend of Zelda (The)
Donkey Kong
Pokemon

CONTACTS: *Note: Officers with more than one job title may be intentionally listed here more than once.*

Satoru Iwata, Pres.
Yoshihiro Mori, Sr. Managing Dir.
Shinji Hatano, Sr. Managing Dir.
Genyo Takeda, Sr. Managing Dir.
Shigeru Miyamoto, Sr. Managing Dir.
Reginald Fils-Aime, COO/Pres., Nintendo of America, Inc.

Phone: 81-75-662-9600	Fax: 81-75-662-9620
Toll-Free:	
Address: 11-1 Kamitoba, Hokotate-cho, Minami-ku, Kyoto, 601-8501 Japan	

GROWTH PLANS/SPECIAL FEATURES:

Nintendo Co., Ltd. makes video game hardware and software. Although based in Kyoto, Japan, the company owns subsidiaries in the U.S., Australia and several countries in Europe. Overseas sales accounted for 66.5% of the firm's 2007 sales. The company's main products are the video game systems and related software and merchandise for the Nintendo DS and DS Lite, which sold approximately 23.6 million units in 2007; Game Boy Advance, 4.3 million; GameCube, 73,000; and Wii, 5.8 million. Nintendo has recently focused on selling the Nintendo DS and the Game Boy Advance, its portable devices. Game Boy Advance is essentially a portable version of home-based video consoles, while the DS sports extra features, including a dual-screen format, an LCD touch screen, wireless connectivity and voice recognition capabilities. The GameCube video game console system, with a standard television hook-up, sells slightly behind Microsoft's Xbox and Sony's PlayStation. Nintendo's Wii, its newest console and successor to the GameCube, released in 2006, offers a unique remote resembling a TV remote. The Wii remote allows for point-and-click-style game play, and is motion-sensitive. The Wii offers a menu that provides users with a variety of entertainment, information and communication channels. The company's software covers a large number of well-known video games, including proprietary titles Mario Brothers, Donkey Kong, Pokemon and The Legend of Zelda. Nintendo has been aware that the currently constricting market for video games largely involves, first, an over-saturated market and, second, the traditional inability of brands to market outside of the young male demographic. Therefore current marketing campaigns have been attempting to offer unique approaches to hardware and branch out into the older adult and female markets. Examples include the Wii system and the new Touch! Generations software line, which includes Nintendo DS titles such as Nintendogs, a virtual pet program, and Brain Age.

FINANCIALS: Sales and profits are in thousands of dollars—add 000 to get the full amount. 2007 Note: Financial information for 2007 was not available for all companies at press time.

2007 Sales: $8,188,400	2007 Profits: $1,478,000	**U.S. Stock Ticker: NTDOY**
2006 Sales: $4,327,100	2006 Profits: $836,600	**Int'l Ticker: 7974** Int'l Exchange: Tokyo-TSE
2005 Sales: $4,788,400	2005 Profits: $812,800	Employees: 2,977
2004 Sales: $4,869,400	2004 Profits: $314,200	Fiscal Year Ends: 3/31
2003 Sales: $4,206,500	2003 Profits: $561,300	Parent Company:

SALARIES/BENEFITS:

Pension Plan:	ESOP Stock Plan:	Profit Sharing:	Top Exec. Salary: $	Bonus: $
Savings Plan:	Stock Purch. Plan:		Second Exec. Salary: $	Bonus: $

OTHER THOUGHTS:

Apparent Women Officers or Directors:
Hot Spot for Advancement for Women/Minorities:

LOCATIONS: ("Y" = Yes)

West:	Southwest:	Midwest:	Southeast:	Northeast:	International:
Y					Y

NTL: TELEWEST BUSINESS

www.ntl.com

Industry Group Code: 513220 Ranks within this company's industry group: Sales: Profits:

Print Media/Publishing:	Movies:	Equipment/Supplies:		Broadcast/Cable:		Music/Audio:	Sports/Games/Gambling:
Newspapers:	Movie Theaters:	Equipment/Supplies:	Y	Broadcast TV:		Music Production:	Games/Sports:
Magazines:	Movie Production:	Gambling Equipment:	Y	Cable TV:	Y	Retail Music:	Retail Games Stores:
Books:	TV/Video Prod.:	Special Services:	Y	Satellite Broadcast:		Retail Audio Equip.:	Stadiums/Teams:
Book Stores:	Video Rental:	Advertising Services:		Radio:		Music Print./Dist.:	Gambling/Casinos:
Distribution/Printing:	Video Distribution:	Info. Sys. Software:		Online Information:		Multimedia:	Rides/Theme Parks:

TYPES OF BUSINESS:

Fixed-line Telecommunications
High-Speed Internet Svcs.
Telephony Svcs.
Voice Svcs.
Business Telecommunications
Data Svcs.

BRANDS/DIVISIONS/AFFILIATES:

ntl Incorporated
Telewest Global, Inc.
Virgin Media Group

CONTACTS: *Note: Officers with more than one job title may be intentionally listed here more than once.*

Stephen Beynon, Managing Dir.
David Buckingham, Dir.-Finance
Andrew McGrath, Dir.-Mktg.
Hilary Grealis, Dir.-Human Resources
Joe McQueen, Dir.-Oper./Customer Svcs.
Andrew McGrath, Dir.-Strategy
Paul Rusby, Dir.-Svc. Providers
John Cunningham, Dir.-Bus. Svcs.
Christopher Small, Dir.-Public Sector

Phone:	Fax:
Toll-Free: 800-953-0180	
Address: Bartley Wood Bus. Pk., Bartley Way, Hook, RG27 9UP UK	

GROWTH PLANS/SPECIAL FEATURES:

ntl:Telewest Business, formerly NTL Incorporated, was formed through the merger of the business division of ntl Incorporated and Telewest Global, Inc. The merger, one of the largest in U.K. telecom's history, means the combined company is now part of the second largest fixed line telecommunications company in the U.K. The company is part of the Virgin Media group, the U.K.'s leading media provider. ntl:Telewest has over 15 years of experience in delivering communications solutions for government, public sector and commercial organizations. The company boasts a network that can provide services to any U.K. business, sales and support teams in more than 40 locations throughout the U.K. and $26.7 billion invested in a national next generation network. The company offers a national product portfolio of voice, data, Internet, and IP solutions for all U.K. businesses, form developing businesses right up to large companies; public sector organizations; and service providers. The company's network is built to the office, enabling the delivery of high bandwidth IP and voice services to U.K. businesses. ntl:Telewest's network includes: 162 voice telephony switches across the U.K.; approximately 116,000 miles of local and metro network (the second largest in the U.K.); 266 Ethernet nodes across the U.K.; three national digital head-ends; three public datacenters; 10 Gbps core IP network, supporting all its IP and Internet services; 45 Cisco BPX ATM switches; and 83 IP POPs for Internet and VPN services. In 2007, ntl:Telewest became the first U.K. provider with MEF 14 accreditation ensuring its Ethernet product portfolio continues to be industry leading in the U.K. Also in 2007, the company announced the completion of a major investment program, which resulted in it now having the U.K.'s fastest business communications network, with enhancements to 300 network points across the U.K.

FINANCIALS: Sales and profits are in thousands of dollars—add 000 to get the full amount. 2007 Note: Financial information for 2007 was not available for all companies at press time.

2007 Sales: $	2007 Profits: $	U.S. Stock Ticker: NTLI
2006 Sales: $	2006 Profits: $	Int'l Ticker: Int'l Exchange:
2005 Sales: $3,402,304	2005 Profits: $735,411	Employees: 12,480
2004 Sales: $3,494,332	2004 Profits: $-847,033	Fiscal Year Ends: 12/31
2003 Sales: $3,645,200	2003 Profits: $-954,200	Parent Company:

SALARIES/BENEFITS:

Pension Plan:	ESOP Stock Plan:	Profit Sharing:	Top Exec. Salary: $1,166,667	Bonus: $370,000
Savings Plan:	Stock Purch. Plan:		Second Exec. Salary: $1,020,359	Bonus: $1,061,411

OTHER THOUGHTS:

Apparent Women Officers or Directors: 1
Hot Spot for Advancement for Women/Minorities:

LOCATIONS: ("Y" = Yes)

West:	Southwest:	Midwest:	Southeast:	Northeast:	International:
					Y

NTN BUZZTIME INC

www.ntn.com

Industry Group Code: 511208 Ranks within this company's industry group: Sales: 10 Profits: 6

Print Media/Publishing:	Movies:	Equipment/Supplies:		Broadcast/Cable:		Music/Audio:	Sports/Games/Gambling:	
Newspapers:	Movie Theaters:	Equipment/Supplies:	Y	Broadcast TV:		Music Production:	Games/Sports:	Y
Magazines:	Movie Production:	Gambling Equipment:		Cable TV:	Y	Retail Music:	Retail Games Stores:	
Books:	TV/Video Prod.:	Y	Special Services:	Y	Satellite Broadcast:		Retail Audio Equip.:	Stadiums/Teams:	
Book Stores:	Video Rental:	Advertising Services:		Radio:		Music Print./Dist.:	Gambling/Casinos:	
Distribution/Printing:	Video Distribution:	Info. Sys. Software:		Online Information:		Multimedia:	Rides/Theme Parks:	

TYPES OF BUSINESS:

Interactive Sports & Trivia Games
On-Site Wireless Communications Products
Restaurant & Hospitality Software

BRANDS/DIVISIONS/AFFILIATES:

NTN Communications
Buzztime Play-Along TV
Buzztime Interactive Television Network
iTV Network
Buzztime Distribution
Buzztime Entertainment
iTV2
Playmaker

CONTACTS: *Note: Officers with more than one job title may be intentionally listed here more than once.*

Dario L. Santana, CEO
Dario L. Santana, Pres.
Kendra Berger, CFO
Steve Riccabona, VP-Mktg. & Sales, NTN iTV Network
Michele Richards, CTO
Mariana Danilovic, Exec. VP-Bus. Dev.
Jake Tauber, Exec. VP-Content & Programming
Michael K. Fleming, Chmn.

Phone: 760-438-7400	Fax:
Toll-Free:	
Address: 5966 La Place Ct., Ste. 100, Carlsbad, CA 92008 US	

GROWTH PLANS/SPECIAL FEATURES:

NTN Buzztime, Inc., formerly NTN Communications, develops and distributes multiplayer interactive television entertainment through the Buzztime Play-Along TV brand. NTN Buzztime operates principally through two divisions: Entertainment and Hospitality. The Entertainment division is comprised of the Buzztime Interactive Television Network (iTV Network) and Buzztime Distribution, formerly known as Buzztime Entertainment. The iTV Network distributes an interactive promotional television game network to over 4,000 restaurants, sports bars, taverns and pubs primarily in North America and the U.K. The iTV Network includes 3,629 U.S. subscribers, 355 Canadian subscribers and 55 U.K. subscribers. Approximately 28% of its Network subscribers come from leading national chains in the casual dining restaurant segment such as Buffalo Wild Wings, TGIFriday's, Bennigan's Irish Grill, Applebee's and Damon's Grill. The company also has a technology platform, iTV2, which allows two channels of Buzztime entertainment programming to be electronically delivered to each location, allowing channel one to remain as a primarily trivia-based offering to its long-time loyal players, while channel two is devoted to new content such as Texas Hold'em, Buzztime Billiards and Crazy Golf. The iTV2 system uses the Playmaker, a hand-held 900 MHz radio frequency device with a monochrome LCD display and sealed keypad. The company has also developed a more advanced 2.4 GHz Playmaker. Buzztime Distribution distributes the company's content and technology to other third-party consumer platforms, including cable television; satellite television; mobile phones; online; retail games and toys; airlines; and books. The Hospitality division is comprised of NTN Wireless Communications and Software Solutions, both of which the company intends to sell and considers to be discontinued operations. In March 2007, NTN Buzztime sold NTN Wireless Communications to HM Electronics. In October 2007, the company agreed to sell its NTN Software Solutions intellectual property assets for $215,000.

FINANCIALS: Sales and profits are in thousands of dollars—add 000 to get the full amount. 2007 Note: Financial information for 2007 was not available for all companies at press time.

2007 Sales: $	2007 Profits: $	**U.S. Stock Ticker: NTN**	
2006 Sales: $32,985	2006 Profits: $-4,773	**Int'l Ticker:** Int'l Exchange:	
2005 Sales: $30,749	2005 Profits: $-2,019	Employees: 217	
2004 Sales: $26,284	2004 Profits: $-4,979	Fiscal Year Ends: 12/31	
2003 Sales: $29,489	2003 Profits: $-2,711	Parent Company:	

SALARIES/BENEFITS:

Pension Plan:	ESOP Stock Plan:	Profit Sharing:	Top Exec. Salary: $285,000	Bonus: $
Savings Plan:	Stock Purch. Plan:		Second Exec. Salary: $227,789	Bonus: $

OTHER THOUGHTS:

Apparent Women Officers or Directors: 2
Hot Spot for Advancement for Women/Minorities: Y

LOCATIONS: ("Y" = Yes)

West:	Southwest:	Midwest:	Southeast:	Northeast:	International:
Y	Y		Y		

Note: Financial information, benefits and other data can change quickly and may vary from those stated here.

OMNICOM GROUP INC

www.omnicomgroup.com

Industry Group Code: 541810 Ranks within this company's industry group: Sales: 2 Profits: 2

Print Media/Publishing:	Movies:	Equipment/Supplies:		Broadcast/Cable:	Music/Audio:	Sports/Games/Gambling:
Newspapers:	Movie Theaters:	Equipment/Supplies:		Broadcast TV:	Music Production:	Games/Sports:
Magazines:	Movie Production:	Gambling Equipment:		Cable TV:	Retail Music:	Retail Games Stores:
Books:	TV/Video Prod.:	Special Services:	Y	Satellite Broadcast:	Retail Audio Equip.:	Stadiums/Teams:
Book Stores:	Video Rental:	Advertising Services:	Y	Radio:	Music Print./Dist.:	Gambling/Casinos:
Distribution/Printing:	Video Distribution:	Info. Sys. Software:		Online Information:	Multimedia:	Rides/Theme Parks:

TYPES OF BUSINESS:

Advertising Services
Public Relations
Market Research
Marketing & Brand Consulting
Interactive & Search Engine Marketing
Media Planning & Buying
Health Care Communications
Printing

BRANDS/DIVISIONS/AFFILIATES:

BBDO Worldwide Network
DDB Worldwide
TBWA Worldwide
Arnell Group
Goodby, Silverstein & Partners
OMD Worldwide
Ketchum
DAS

CONTACTS: *Note: Officers with more than one job title may be intentionally listed here more than once.*

John D. Wren, CEO
John D. Wren, Pres.
Randall J. Weisenburger, CFO/Exec. VP
Michael J. O'Brien, General Counsel/Sr. VP/Corp. Sec.
Philip J. Angelastro, VP-Finance/Controller
Michael Birkin, Vice Chmn.
Bruce Redditt, Exec. VP
Janet Riccio, Exec. VP
Philip J. George, Tax Counsel
Bruce Crawford, Chmn.

Phone: 212-415-3600	Fax: 212-415-3530
Toll-Free:	
Address: 437 Madison Ave., New York, NY 10022 US	

GROWTH PLANS/SPECIAL FEATURES:

Omnicom Group, Inc. is a holding company that, through its subsidiaries, is one of the largest advertising, marketing and corporate communications companies in the world. The firm owns more than 160 subsidiary agencies that operate in all major markets worldwide. Its agencies provide an extensive range of services, mainly focusing four fundamental disciplines, including traditional media advertising, customer relationship management, public relations and specialty communications. The company's holdings are managed by the Diversified Agency Services (DAS) division. Omnicom's traditional media advertising is based in three areas: global advertising brands, such as BBDO Worldwide, DDB Worldwide and TBWA Worldwide; national advertising agencies, including Arnell Group, Element 79 Partners, GSD&M, Martin/Williams, Merkley + Partners, Zimmerman Advertising and Goodby, Silverstein & Parners; and media services, which has two dull service media companies, OMD Worldwide and PHD Network, and several media specialist companies. Customer relationship management includes three of the top 10 promotional marketing agencies, and the segment focuses on marketing for sports and events, promotions, non-profit organizations and events, the entertainment industry, as well as field marketing and branding, consultants and design. Within the public relations segment, Omnicom's Diversified Agency Services includes Fleishman-Hillard, Ketchum and Porter Novelli, all of which are within the top seven public relationship firms in the world. The company also has a number of specialist agencies within the division. Specialty communications contains healthcare communications companies, as well as recruitment communications, multicultural marketing and financial and corporate advertising. Other group activities of note include experiential marketing, instore design, mobile marketing, package design, custom printing, reputation consulting and search engine marketing. Recent acquisitions include majority stakes in 180 Amsterdam, Gotocustomer Services India, EVB and Unisono Fieldmarketing International Limited. In 2006, the company acquired Rodgers Townsend, a St. Louis-based advertising agency.

FINANCIALS: Sales and profits are in thousands of dollars—add 000 to get the full amount. 2007 Note: Financial information for 2007 was not available for all companies at press time.

2007 Sales: $	2007 Profits: $	**U.S. Stock Ticker: OMC**
2006 Sales: $11,376,900	2006 Profits: $864,000	Int'l Ticker: Int'l Exchange:
2005 Sales: $10,481,100	2005 Profits: $790,700	Employees: 66,000
2004 Sales: $9,747,200	2004 Profits: $723,500	Fiscal Year Ends: 12/31
2003 Sales: $8,621,404	2003 Profits: $675,883	Parent Company:

SALARIES/BENEFITS:

Pension Plan: Y	ESOP Stock Plan:	Profit Sharing: Y	Top Exec. Salary: $1,007,560	Bonus: $2,400,000
Savings Plan:	Stock Purch. Plan: Y		Second Exec. Salary: $1,000,000	Bonus: $6,000,000

OTHER THOUGHTS:

Apparent Women Officers or Directors: 1
Hot Spot for Advancement for Women/Minorities: Y

LOCATIONS: ("Y" = Yes)

West:	Southwest:	Midwest:	Southeast:	Northeast:	International:
Y	Y	Y	Y	Y	Y

Note: Financial information, benefits and other data can change quickly and may vary from those stated here.

ON COMMAND CORP
www.oncommand.com

Industry Group Code: 513220 Ranks within this company's industry group: Sales: Profits:

Print Media/Publishing:	Movies:	Equipment/Supplies:		Broadcast/Cable:	Music/Audio:	Sports/Games/Gambling:
Newspapers:	Movie Theaters:	Equipment/Supplies:		Broadcast TV:	Music Production:	Games/Sports:
Magazines:	Movie Production:	Gambling Equipment:		Cable TV:	Retail Music:	Retail Games Stores:
Books:	TV/Video Prod.:	Special Services:	Y	Satellite Broadcast:	Retail Audio Equip.:	Stadiums/Teams:
Book Stores:	Video Rental:	Advertising Services:	Y	Radio:	Music Print./Dist.:	Gambling/Casinos:
Distribution/Printing:	Video Distribution: Y	Info. Sys. Software:		Online Information:	Multimedia:	Rides/Theme Parks:

TYPES OF BUSINESS:
Pay-Per-View Entertainment
High-Speed Internet Access
Advertising Sales

BRANDS/DIVISIONS/AFFILIATES:
LodgeNet Entertainment Corp.
OCX

CONTACTS: Note: Officers with more than one job title may be intentionally listed here more than once.
Christopher Sophinos, CEO
Christopher Sophinos, Pres.
Chris O'Toole, CFO/Sr. VP
Tad Walden, Sr. VP-Mktg. & Programming
Chris O'Toole, Treas.

Phone: 720-873-3200	**Fax:** 720-873-3397
Toll-Free: 800-797-7654	
Address: 4610 S. Ulster St., 6th Fl., Denver, CO 80237 US	

GROWTH PLANS/SPECIAL FEATURES:
On Command Corporation, a subsidiary of LodgeNet Entertainment Corp., is a leading provider of entertainment, Internet services, business information and guest services to the lodging industry. Its customers include more than 100 well-known hotel chains such as Four Seasons; Marriott; Hilton; Hyatt; and Embassy Suites. The firm and its distribution network serve more than 300 million guests annually through approximately 800,000 hotel guest rooms in more than 20 countries. The company's services include On-Demand Movies; Sony PlayStation video games; HDTV; Group Features; MotionControl; On-Demand TV; Events On Demand; and Internet access. In addition, the company offers a video concierge service, which allows a hotel to promote and communicate all of its services to its guests via the in-room television. The company aggressively promotes its OCX multimedia services platform, which features an improved graphical user interface for movies and games and TV-based Internet with a keyboard.

FINANCIALS: Sales and profits are in thousands of dollars—add 000 to get the full amount. 2007 Note: Financial information for 2007 was not available for all companies at press time.
2007 Sales: $ 2007 Profits: $
2006 Sales: $ 2006 Profits: $
2005 Sales: $ 2005 Profits: $
2004 Sales: $ 2004 Profits: $
2003 Sales: $ 2003 Profits: $

U.S. Stock Ticker: Subsidiary
Int'l Ticker: Int'l Exchange:
Employees: 620
Fiscal Year Ends: 12/31
Parent Company: LODGENET ENTERTAINMENT CORP

SALARIES/BENEFITS:
| Pension Plan: | ESOP Stock Plan: | Profit Sharing: | Top Exec. Salary: $324,989 | Bonus: $50,000 |
| Savings Plan: Y | Stock Purch. Plan: Y | | Second Exec. Salary: $299,063 | Bonus: $90,312 |

OTHER THOUGHTS:
Apparent Women Officers or Directors:
Hot Spot for Advancement for Women/Minorities:

LOCATIONS: ("Y" = Yes)
West:	Southwest:	Midwest:	Southeast:	Northeast:	International:
Y					

ON STAGE ENTERTAINMENT   www.legendsinconcert.com

Industry Group Code: 512110 Ranks within this company's industry group: Sales: Profits:

Print Media/Publishing:	Movies:	Equipment/Supplies:	Broadcast/Cable:	Music/Audio:	Sports/Games/Gambling:	
Newspapers:	Movie Theaters:	Equipment/Supplies:	Broadcast TV:	Music Production:	Games/Sports:	Y
Magazines:	Movie Production:	Gambling Equipment:	Cable TV:	Retail Music:	Retail Games Stores:	
Books:	TV/Video Prod.:	Special Services:	Satellite Broadcast:	Retail Audio Equip.:	Stadiums/Teams:	
Book Stores:	Video Rental:	Advertising Services:	Radio:	Music Print./Dist.:	Gambling/Casinos:	
Distribution/Printing:	Video Distribution:	Info. Sys. Software:	Online Information:	Multimedia:	Rides/Theme Parks:	

TYPES OF BUSINESS:

Theatrical Productions
Dinner Theaters

BRANDS/DIVISIONS/AFFILIATES:

Legends in Concert

GROWTH PLANS/SPECIAL FEATURES:

On Stage Entertainment produces and markets theatrical productions and operates live theaters and dinner theaters. The company's flagship production, Legends in Concert, features impersonators who perform as famous performance artists, for example, Elvis Presley, the Blues Brothers, Tina Turner, Michael Jackson and Marilyn Monroe. The company markets its productions directly to audiences at theaters in resort and urban tourist locations. Although the company started in Las Vegas, it owns permanent venues in Atlantic City, New Jersey; Myrtle Beach, South Carolina; Branson, Missouri; and Hollywood, Florida. On Stage also markets its productions to commercial clients, which include casinos, corporations, fairs and expositions, theme and amusement parks and cruise lines. In addition, the company sells souvenirs, such as clothing and videotapes. The firm has performed for major corporate clients such as McDonald's, Anheuser-Busch, Hewlett Packard, IBM, Pitney Bowes, Levi Strauss and Exxon.

CONTACTS: *Note: Officers with more than one job title may be intentionally listed here more than once.*

Jeffery Victor, COO
Jeffery Victor, Pres.
Tim Soldan, Mgr.-Marketing & Sales

Phone: 702-253-1333	Fax: 702-253-1122
Toll-Free:	
Address: 333 Orville Wright Ct., Las Vegas, NV 89119 US	

FINANCIALS: Sales and profits are in thousands of dollars—add 000 to get the full amount. 2007 Note: Financial information for 2007 was not available for all companies at press time.

2007 Sales: $	2007 Profits: $	U.S. Stock Ticker: Private
2006 Sales: $	2006 Profits: $	Int'l Ticker: Int'l Exchange:
2005 Sales: $	2005 Profits: $	Employees: 400
2004 Sales: $	2004 Profits: $	Fiscal Year Ends: 12/31
2003 Sales: $21,700	2003 Profits: $	Parent Company:

SALARIES/BENEFITS:

Pension Plan:	ESOP Stock Plan:	Profit Sharing:	Top Exec. Salary: $308,333	Bonus: $87,500
Savings Plan:	Stock Purch. Plan:		Second Exec. Salary: $114,400	Bonus: $

OTHER THOUGHTS:

Apparent Women Officers or Directors:
Hot Spot for Advancement for Women/Minorities:

LOCATIONS: ("Y" = Yes)

West:	Southwest:	Midwest:	Southeast:	Northeast:	International:
Y		Y	Y	Y	

PALACE ENTERTAINMENT   www.palaceentertainment.com

Industry Group Code: 713110 Ranks within this company's industry group: Sales: Profits:

Print Media/Publishing:	Movies:	Equipment/Supplies:	Broadcast/Cable:	Music/Audio:	Sports/Games/Gambling:	
Newspapers:	Movie Theaters:	Equipment/Supplies:	Broadcast TV:	Music Production:	Games/Sports:	Y
Magazines:	Movie Production:	Gambling Equipment:	Cable TV:	Retail Music:	Retail Games Stores:	
Books:	TV/Video Prod.:	Special Services:	Satellite Broadcast:	Retail Audio Equip.:	Stadiums/Teams:	
Book Stores:	Video Rental:	Advertising Services:	Radio:	Music Print./Dist.:	Gambling/Casinos:	
Distribution/Printing:	Video Distribution:	Info. Sys. Software:	Online Information:	Multimedia:	Rides/Theme Parks:	

TYPES OF BUSINESS:
Amusement Parks
Auto Racetracks
Water Parks

BRANDS/DIVISIONS/AFFILIATES:
Malibu Grand Prix
Mountasia
SpeedZone
Wet 'N Wild
Big Kahuna's
Mountasia
Raging Waters
MidOcean Partners

CONTACTS: Note: Officers with more than one job title may be intentionally listed here more than once.
John Cora, CEO
John Cora, Pres.
Cynthia P. Kellogg, CFO/Sr. VP

Phone: 949-261-0404	Fax: 949-261-1414
Toll-Free:	
Address: 4590 MacArthur Blvd., Ste. 400, Newport Beach, CA 92660 US	

GROWTH PLANS/SPECIAL FEATURES:

Palace Entertainment owns and operates multiple-attraction entertainment and amusement parks designed for families. The company operates a total of 35 parks and has well over 12 million visitors per year. Primarily, it operates facilities that feature water parks, miniature golf courses, go-karts, bumper boats, batting cages, arcades, souvenir concession stands and, in some parks, scaled grand-prix-style racetracks utilizing the company's proprietary Malibu Grand Prix race cars. Palace has also introduced a new type of entertainment center called SpeedZone, with locations in Los Angeles and Dallas. Designed for teens, these centers include the Malibu Grand Prix attraction and the new Top Eliminator high-speed racing venue along with other regular amusements. The Grand Prix and Top Eliminator attractions feature cars designed by professionals in the racing industry. The company also operates water parks, including Wet 'N Wild in Las Vegas, Nevada and Greensboro, North Carolina; Raging Waters in San Dimas and San Jose, California; Splish Splash in Riverhead, New York; Big Kahuna's in Destin, Florida; Water Country in Portsmouth, New Hampshire; Mountain Creek in Vernon, New Jersey; and Wild Waters in Ocala, Florida. Palace also owns Boomers, Castle Park, Silver Springs, Malibu Grand Prix, Mountasia and SpeedZone family entertainment parks in California, Texas, Florida, Georgia and New York. In February 2006, MidOcean Partners, a New York and London-based private investment firm, announced its acquisition of Palace Entertainment. Palace will continue all of its operations.

FINANCIALS: Sales and profits are in thousands of dollars—add 000 to get the full amount. 2007 Note: Financial information for 2007 was not available for all companies at press time.

2007 Sales: $	2007 Profits: $	**U.S. Stock Ticker: Private**
2006 Sales: $	2006 Profits: $	**Int'l Ticker:** Int'l Exchange:
2005 Sales: $	2005 Profits: $	Employees: 871
2004 Sales: $	2004 Profits: $	Fiscal Year Ends: 12/31
2003 Sales: $	2003 Profits: $	Parent Company:

SALARIES/BENEFITS:

Pension Plan:	ESOP Stock Plan:	Profit Sharing:	Top Exec. Salary: $310,577	Bonus: $317,779
Savings Plan: Y	Stock Purch. Plan:		Second Exec. Salary: $147,404	Bonus: $86,332

OTHER THOUGHTS:
Apparent Women Officers or Directors:
Hot Spot for Advancement for Women/Minorities:

LOCATIONS: ("Y" = Yes)

West:	Southwest:	Midwest:	Southeast:	Northeast:	International:
Y	Y	Y	Y	Y	

PARAMOUNT PICTURES CORP   www.paramount.com

Industry Group Code: 512110 **Ranks within this company's industry group:** Sales: Profits:

Print Media/Publishing:	Movies:		Equipment/Supplies:		Broadcast/Cable:	Music/Audio:	Sports/Games/Gambling:
Newspapers:	Movie Theaters:		Equipment/Supplies:		Broadcast TV:	Music Production:	Games/Sports:
Magazines:	Movie Production:	Y	Gambling Equipment:		Cable TV:	Retail Music:	Retail Games Stores:
Books:	TV/Video Prod.:	Y	Special Services:	Y	Satellite Broadcast:	Retail Audio Equip.:	Stadiums/Teams:
Book Stores:	Video Rental:		Advertising Services:		Radio:	Music Print./Dist.:	Gambling/Casinos:
Distribution/Printing:	Video Distribution:	Y	Info. Sys. Software:		Online Information:	Multimedia:	Rides/Theme Parks:

TYPES OF BUSINESS:

Film Production & Distribution
Television Production
Post-Production Services
Home Video & DVD Production & Distribution

BRANDS/DIVISIONS/AFFILIATES:

Viacom Inc
Paramount Pictures
Paramount Classics
Paramount Vantage
MTV Films
Nickelodeon Movies
DreamWorks LLC
Sweeney Todd: The Demon Barber of Fleet Street

CONTACTS: Note: Officers with more than one job title may be intentionally listed here more than once.

Brad Gray, CEO
Frederick D. Huntsberry, COO
Mark Badagliacca, CFO/Exec. VP
Scott Aversano, Pres., MTV Films & Nickelodeon Movies
Kelley Avery, Pres., Worldwide Home Entertainment
John Lesher, Pres., Paramount Vantage
Stacey Snider, Co-Chmn./CEO-DreamWorks
Brad Grey, Chmn.
Andrew Cripps, Pres., Paramount Pictures Int'l

Phone: 323-956-5000	Fax:
Toll-Free:	
Address: 5555 Melrose Ave., Ste. 121, Hollywood, CA 90038 US	

GROWTH PLANS/SPECIAL FEATURES:

Paramount Pictures Corp., a subsidiary of Viacom, Inc., is a producer and distributor of feature films that has a library consisting of roughly 3,500 motion pictures and programs. It produces and distributes feature films and television programs under brands such as Paramount Pictures, Paramount Classics, Paramount Vantage, DreamWorks, MTV Films and Nickelodeon Movies. The company has over 30 production service departments catering to the production community, 30 sound stages, nine exterior sets, production offices and built-in amenities. The studio's recent releases include Transformers and Sweeney Todd: The Demon Barber of Fleet Street. Paramount releases about a dozen films annually. The company also produces television shows, including J.A.G., Dr. Phil, Entertainment Tonight, the various Star Trek series and Judge Judy. Some of the studio's most successful productions include The Godfather, Grease, the Indiana Jones Trilogy, Titanic, Braveheart and Forrest Gump. Paramount maintains an active licensing department, as well as a center for post-production services. The firm distributes motion pictures and other entertainment content on DVD, video-on-demand, cable services and other platforms in the U.S. and internationally. In 2006, Paramount acquired DreamWorks Pictures. In May 2007, subsidiary Paramount Licensing, Inc. announced that it would open a theme park in Seoul, South Korea. The park will open in 2009, and is the first theme park in the country to be developed by an international firm. Daewoo Motor Sales Corp. is the firm's partner in the venture. In June 2007, Ruwaad Holdings and Paramount Licensing announced an agreement for an opening of a theme park in the United Arab Emirates.

The company offers its employees medical, dental and vision insurance; life, disability and accident insurance; a 401(k) plan; flexible spending accounts; same sex domestic partner benefits; an employee assistance program; and employee screenings.

FINANCIALS: Sales and profits are in thousands of dollars—add 000 to get the full amount. 2007 Note: Financial information for 2007 was not available for all companies at press time.

2007 Sales: $	2007 Profits: $	**U.S. Stock Ticker: Subsidiary**
2006 Sales: $	2006 Profits: $	**Int'l Ticker:** Int'l Exchange:
2005 Sales: $2,898,700	2005 Profits: $	Employees:
2004 Sales: $2,205,600	2004 Profits: $	Fiscal Year Ends: 12/31
2003 Sales: $	2003 Profits: $	Parent Company: VIACOM INC

SALARIES/BENEFITS:

Pension Plan:	ESOP Stock Plan:	Profit Sharing:	Top Exec. Salary: $	Bonus: $
Savings Plan: Y	Stock Purch. Plan:		Second Exec. Salary: $	Bonus: $

OTHER THOUGHTS:

Apparent Women Officers or Directors: 2
Hot Spot for Advancement for Women/Minorities:

LOCATIONS: ("Y" = Yes)

West:	Southwest:	Midwest:	Southeast:	Northeast:	International:
Y					Y

PEARSON PLC

www.pearson.com

Industry Group Code: 511130 Ranks within this company's industry group: Sales: 1   Profits: 1

Print Media/Publishing:		Movies:		Equipment/Supplies:		Broadcast/Cable:		Music/Audio:		Sports/Games/Gambling:	
Newspapers:	Y	Movie Theaters:		Equipment/Supplies:		Broadcast TV:		Music Production:		Games/Sports:	
Magazines:		Movie Production:		Gambling Equipment:		Cable TV:		Retail Music:		Retail Games Stores:	
Books:	Y	TV/Video Prod.:		Special Services:	Y	Satellite Broadcast:		Retail Audio Equip.:		Stadiums/Teams:	
Book Stores:		Video Rental:		Advertising Services:		Radio:		Music Print./Dist.:		Gambling/Casinos:	
Distribution/Printing:		Video Distribution:		Info. Sys. Software:		Online Information:		Multimedia:		Rides/Theme Parks:	

TYPES OF BUSINESS:

Book Publishing
Educational Products
Financial Newspaper
Online Publishing
Testing Services

BRANDS/DIVISIONS/AFFILIATES:

Penguin
Financial Times (The)
Pearson Education
Putnam
Viking
Pearson Prentice Hall
ft.com
Puffin

CONTACTS: *Note: Officers with more than one job title may be intentionally listed here more than once.*

Marjorie Scardino, CEO
Robin Freestone, CFO
David Bell, Dir.-People
Philip J. Hoffman, Sec.
Charles Goldsmith, Media-Pearson Plc.
John Makinson, Chmn./Chief Exec.-Penguin
Oliver Fleurot, CEO-The Financial Times
Rona Fairhead, Chief Exec.-Financial Times Group
Steve Dowling, Pres./CEO-Pearson School Companies
Glen Moreno, Chmn.
John Fallon, CEO-EAMEA

Phone: 44-20-7010-2000	**Fax:** 44-20-7010-6060
Toll-Free: 800-269-2977	
Address: 80 Strand, London, WC2R ORL UK	

GROWTH PLANS/SPECIAL FEATURES:

Pearson plc is one of the foremost publishers in the world. The Pearson group of companies comprises the Penguin group, The Financial Times and Pearson Education. Penguin publishes several different genres of books including classics, new authors, children's books and reference books. Penguin also publishes under the Allen Lane, Avery, Berkley Books, Dutton and Hamish Hamilton among others. In addition, Penguin is a leading illustrated reference publisher under the Dorling Kindersley (DK) imprint. The Financial Times Group (FT) provides financial and business information through The Financial Times Newspaper and ft.com, its online partner. FT Investor, a part of ft.com, provides free, up-to-date financial and market news to European private investors.   FT specializes in international and global issues; through a controlling interest in Interactive Data Corporation, it is a leading source of international securities pricing and specialist information to global institutional, professional and individual investors. In addition, the FT group owns a 50% stake in The Economist Group. Pearson Education (PE) offers textbooks, software and testing material for students in preschool through college, as well as web sites for online assessment tests and digital courseware. PE's imprints include Prentice Hall, Addison Wesley, Longman, Allyn & Bacon, Addison-Wesley Professional, Peachpit Press, Que and Cisco Press. In 2007, the company won a five year testing contract with the U.S. Department of Education, extending its existing partnership with the department. Also in 2007, the firm's subsidiary, Person VUE, joined into a partnership with the Federation of State Massage Therapy Boards to deliver certification testing for the organization.   Most recently, Pearson acquired eCollege, and Harcourt Assessment and Harcourt Education International.   In late 2007, the conglomerate announced plans to sell Groupe Les Echos SA to LVMH for $346 million.

FINANCIALS: Sales and profits are in thousands of dollars—add 000 to get the full amount. 2007 Note: Financial information for 2007 was not available for all companies at press time.

2007 Sales: $	2007 Profits: $	**U.S. Stock Ticker:** PSO
2006 Sales: $8,343,090	2006 Profits: $945,830	**Int'l Ticker:** PSON Int'l Exchange: London-LSE
2005 Sales: $7,045,000	2005 Profits: $	Employees: 33,389
2004 Sales: $6,357,000	2004 Profits: $169,000	Fiscal Year Ends: 12/31
2003 Sales: $7,219,000	2003 Profits: $98,000	Parent Company:

SALARIES/BENEFITS:

Pension Plan: Y	ESOP Stock Plan:	Profit Sharing: Y	Top Exec. Salary: $1,134,588	Bonus: $1,461,772
Savings Plan:	Stock Purch. Plan: Y		Second Exec. Salary: $832,031	Bonus: $1,004,415

OTHER THOUGHTS:

Apparent Women Officers or Directors: 3
Hot Spot for Advancement for Women/Minorities: Y

LOCATIONS: ("Y" = Yes)

West:	Southwest:	Midwest:	Southeast:	Northeast:	International:
Y	Y	Y		Y	Y

Note: Financial information, benefits and other data can change quickly and may vary from those stated here.

PENN NATIONAL GAMING INC

www.pngaming.com

Industry Group Code: 713210 Ranks within this company's industry group: Sales: 1   Profits: 1

Print Media/Publishing:	Movies:	Equipment/Supplies:	Broadcast/Cable:	Music/Audio:	Sports/Games/Gambling:	
Newspapers:	Movie Theaters:	Equipment/Supplies:	Broadcast TV:	Music Production:	Games/Sports:	
Magazines:	Movie Production:	Gambling Equipment:	Cable TV:	Retail Music:	Retail Games Stores:	
Books:	TV/Video Prod.:	Special Services:	Satellite Broadcast:	Retail Audio Equip.:	Stadiums/Teams:	Y
Book Stores:	Video Rental:	Advertising Services:	Radio:	Music Print./Dist.:	Gambling/Casinos:	
Distribution/Printing:	Video Distribution:	Info. Sys. Software:	Online Information:	Multimedia:	Rides/Theme Parks:	

TYPES OF BUSINESS:

Horse Racetracks
Casinos

BRANDS/DIVISIONS/AFFILIATES:

Charles Town Races & Slots
Freehold Racetrack
Argosy Gaming Company
Hollywood Casino
Penn National Race Course

CONTACTS:
Note: Officers with more than one job title may be intentionally listed here more than once.

Peter M. Carlino, CEO
William J. Clifford, CFO/Sr. VP-Finance
Gene Clark, Sr. VP-Human Resources
Jordan B. Savitch, General Counsel/Sr. VP
Leonard M. DeAngelo, Exec. VP-Oper.
Steven T. Snyder, Sr. VP-Corp. Dev.
Robert S. Ippolito, Treas./VP
Robert S. Ippolito, Corp. Sec.
John Finamore, Sr. VP-Regional Oper.
James Baum, Sr. VP-Project Dev.
Thomas Auriemma, Chief Compliance Officer/VP
Peter M. Carlino, Chmn.

Phone: 610-373-2400	Fax: 610-376-2842
Toll-Free:	
Address: 825 Berkshire Blvd., Ste. 200, Wyomissing, PA 19610 US	

GROWTH PLANS/SPECIAL FEATURES:

Penn National Gaming, Inc. is a multi-jurisdictional owner and operator of gaming properties and horse racetracks. The company owns or operates 18 gaming facilities, located in Canada, Colorado, Louisiana, Maine, Mississippi, Missouri, Illinois, Iowa, Indiana, New Jersey, Ohio, Pennsylvania and West Virginia. These facilities, which are focused on serving customers within driving distance, include two thoroughbred racetracks, three harness racetracks, five land-based casinos and nine dockside casinos (one facility combines a land-based casino and thoroughbred racing, but these have been listed separately here). The casinos total 753,560 gaming square footage and contain a combined 21,304 gaming machines, 397 table games and 1,474 hotel rooms. The largest of these by revenue, is the Charles Town Races & Slots in West Virginia. Penn's New Jersey track, Freehold Racetrack, is a 50%-owned joint venture. It also runs six off-track wagering facilities throughout Pennsylvania. The company intends to continue to expand its gaming operations through the implementation of a disciplined capital expenditure program at its existing properties, as well as the continued pursuit of strategic acquisitions of gaming properties in attractive regional markets. In recent news, the firm was granted a license for the placement of slot machines at the Hollywood Casino, currently under construction, at Penn National Race Course. The firm anticipates that this casino will be 365,000 square feet and will be sized for 3,000 slot machines. In 2006, Penn was able to re-open two of its dockside casinos that were damaged by Hurricane Katrina in 2005.

Penn National Gaming offers its employees flexible spending accounts; medical, dental and vision coverage; life, AD&D and disability insurance; a 401(k) plan; paid time off; and an employee assistance program.

FINANCIALS:
Sales and profits are in thousands of dollars—add 000 to get the full amount. 2007 Note: Financial information for 2007 was not available for all companies at press time.

2007 Sales: $	2007 Profits: $	U.S. Stock Ticker: PENN
2006 Sales: $2,244,547	2006 Profits: $327,088	Int'l Ticker: Int'l Exchange:
2005 Sales: $1,369,105	2005 Profits: $120,930	Employees: 14,874
2004 Sales: $1,105,290	2004 Profits: $71,484	Fiscal Year Ends: 12/31
2003 Sales: $1,012,681	2003 Profits: $51,471	Parent Company:

SALARIES/BENEFITS:

Pension Plan:	ESOP Stock Plan:	Profit Sharing:	Top Exec. Salary: $1,000,000	Bonus: $1,000,000
Savings Plan: Y	Stock Purch. Plan:		Second Exec. Salary: $850,000	Bonus: $850,000

OTHER THOUGHTS:

Apparent Women Officers or Directors: 1
Hot Spot for Advancement for Women/Minorities:

LOCATIONS: ("Y" = Yes)

West:	Southwest:	Midwest:	Southeast:	Northeast:	International:
Y		Y	Y	Y	Y

PENTON MEDIA INC

www.penton.com

Industry Group Code: 511120 Ranks within this company's industry group: Sales: Profits:

Print Media/Publishing:	Movies:	Equipment/Supplies:	Broadcast/Cable:	Music/Audio:	Sports/Games/Gambling:
Newspapers:	Movie Theaters:	Equipment/Supplies:	Broadcast TV:	Music Production:	Games/Sports:
Magazines: Y	Movie Production:	Gambling Equipment:	Cable TV:	Retail Music:	Retail Games Stores:
Books:	TV/Video Prod.:	Special Services: Y	Satellite Broadcast:	Retail Audio Equip.:	Stadiums/Teams:
Book Stores:	Video Rental:	Advertising Services:	Radio:	Music Print./Dist.:	Gambling/Casinos:
Distribution/Printing:	Video Distribution:	Info. Sys. Software:	Online Information:	Multimedia:	Rides/Theme Parks:

TYPES OF BUSINESS:

Trade Magazine Publishing
Trade Shows & Conferences
Online Media Products
Research & Marketing
E-Commerce

BRANDS/DIVISIONS/AFFILIATES:

MidOcean Partners
U.S. Equity Partners II
Wasserstein & Co. LP

CONTACTS: Note: Officers with more than one job title may be intentionally listed here more than once.

John French, CEO
Eric Lundberg, CFO/Exec. VP
Jerry Okabe, VP-Audience Mktg. & Circulation
Kurt Nelson, VP-Human Resources
Shawn Etheridge, Sr. VP-Info. Prod. Group
Cindi Reding, CTO
Lisa Parks, VP-Production
Eric Jacobson, Sr. VP-Admin.
Robert Feinberg, General Counsel/Corp. Sec./VP
Blair Johnson, VP-Bus. Dev.
Steve Martin, Corp. Controller
Darrell Denny, Exec. VP-Lifestyle Media Group
Bob MacArthur, Sr. VP-Industrial Media Group
Margaret Pederson, Pres., Penton Exhibitions Group
Warren Bimblick, Sr. VP-Financial Svcs. & Mktg. Media Group

Phone: 216-696-7000	Fax: 216-696-1752
Toll-Free:	
Address: 1300 E. 9th St., Cleveland, OH 44114 US	

GROWTH PLANS/SPECIAL FEATURES:

Penton Media, Inc., founded in 1886, is a leading business-to-business media company in the U.S., serving over 6 million business professionals every month. Penton is a private company, owned by MidOcean Partners and U.S. Equity Partners II, an investment fund sponsored by Wasserstein & Co. LP and its co-investors. MidOcean acquired a 50% interest in the company in 2007 shortly after it was acquired and taken private by Wasserstein. Penton's brands are focused on 30 industries and include 113 trade magazines; 145 websites; 200 e-newsletters; 96 industry trade shows and conferences; and over 500 information data products. It focuses on a broad range of markets including agriculture, aviation, logistics, marketing, design engineering, fitness, trucking, public services, mechanical systems and broadcasting. For advertisers, the company provides print and online ad rates; ad specifications; editorial information; circulation numbers; exhibitions; buyers guides; special advertising opportunities; and sales and editorial contact information. Penton provides market intelligence including demographic market profiles, purchasing practices, brand preference, state of the industry, salary surveys, advertising effectiveness, industry white papers and custom research, with a database of over 3 million business-to-business names.

Penton offers its employees a flexible spending account, flexible work schedules, a business casual dress code and medical, dental, disability and life insurance.

FINANCIALS: Sales and profits are in thousands of dollars—add 000 to get the full amount. 2007 Note: Financial information for 2007 was not available for all companies at press time.

2007 Sales: $	2007 Profits: $	U.S. Stock Ticker: Subsidiary
2006 Sales: $	2006 Profits: $	Int'l Ticker: Int'l Exchange:
2005 Sales: $192,847	2005 Profits: $-8,422	Employees: 703
2004 Sales: $194,833	2004 Profits: $-67,191	Fiscal Year Ends: 12/31
2003 Sales: $188,742	2003 Profits: $-93,131	Parent Company: MIDOCEAN PARTNERS

SALARIES/BENEFITS:

Pension Plan:	ESOP Stock Plan:	Profit Sharing:	Top Exec. Salary: $425,000	Bonus: $175,855
Savings Plan: Y	Stock Purch. Plan:		Second Exec. Salary: $341,250	Bonus: $133,852

OTHER THOUGHTS:

Apparent Women Officers or Directors: 3
Hot Spot for Advancement for Women/Minorities: Y

LOCATIONS: ("Y" = Yes)

West:	Southwest:	Midwest:	Southeast:	Northeast:	International:
Y		Y		Y	Y

PINNACLE ENTERTAINMENT INC   www.pnkinc.com

Industry Group Code: 721120 Ranks within this company's industry group: Sales: 9   Profits: 7

Print Media/Publishing:	Movies:	Equipment/Supplies:	Broadcast/Cable:	Music/Audio:	Sports/Games/Gambling:	
Newspapers:	Movie Theaters:	Equipment/Supplies:	Broadcast TV:	Music Production:	Games/Sports:	Y
Magazines:	Movie Production:	Gambling Equipment:	Cable TV:	Retail Music:	Retail Games Stores:	
Books:	TV/Video Prod.:	Special Services:	Satellite Broadcast:	Retail Audio Equip.:	Stadiums/Teams:	
Book Stores:	Video Rental:	Advertising Services:	Radio:	Music Print./Dist.:	Gambling/Casinos:	Y
Distribution/Printing:	Video Distribution:	Info. Sys. Software:	Online Information:	Multimedia:	Rides/Theme Parks:	

TYPES OF BUSINESS:

Casinos
Hospitality & Entertainment Facilities

BRANDS/DIVISIONS/AFFILIATES:

L'Auberge du Lac
Belterra Casino Resort
Boomtown Bossier
Boomtown Reno
Embassy Suites
President Riverboad Casino
Casino Magic Argentina
Casino at Emerald Bay

CONTACTS: *Note: Officers with more than one job title may be intentionally listed here more than once.*

Daniel R. Lee, CEO
Alain Uboldi, COO
Wade W. Hundley, Pres.
Stephen H. Capp, CFO/Exec. VP
Keith Henson, VP-Relationship Mktg.
Humberto Trueba Jr., Sr. VP-Human Resources
Carol Pride, CIO
R. Dale Dodd, VP-Admin.
John A. Godfrey, General Counsel/Exec. VP/Sec.
Sarah Lee Tucker, VP-Oper.
Donna Negrotto, VP-Construction & Bus. Dev.
James W. Barich, Sr. VP-Public Rel. & Gov't
Christopher K. Plant, VP-Investor Rel./Treas.
Dan Boudreaux, Chief Acct. Officer
Larry Buck, Pres., Atlantic City
Suzanne Chabre, VP-Brand Mgmt.
John Durham, VP-Hotel Oper.
Kimberly C. Townsend, Exec. VP-Atlantic City
Daniel R. Lee, Chmn.

Phone: 702-784-7777	Fax: 702-784-7778
Toll-Free:	
Address: 3800 Howard Hughes Pkwy., Las Vegas, NV 89109 US	

GROWTH PLANS/SPECIAL FEATURES:

Pinnacle Entertainment, Inc. is a developer, owner and operator of casinos and related hospitality and entertainment facilities. The company currently operates six domestic casinos, three of which are being expanded and enhanced. The firm has two additional casino facilities under construction. Pinnacle has also acquired three additional sites in new markets where it expects to build casino facilities in future years. The company's largest casino resort, L'Auberge du Lac in Louisiana, offers roughly 750 guestrooms and suites; several restaurants; about 28,000 square feet of meeting space; a championship gold course; retail shops; and a full-service spa. L'Auberge is the largest hotel in Louisiana outside of New Orleans. Pinnacle's Indiana property, Belterra Casino Resort, features a large casino and a 608-guestroom hotel; six restaurants; 33,000 square feet of meeting and conference space; a 1,750-sear entertainment showroom; a swimming pool; a spa; and a 180 hole championship gold course. The Boomtown Bossier property in Louisiana features a regional hotel built around a dockside riverboat casino and includes a 188-guestroom hotel with four master suites and 88 junior suite, four restaurants and roughly 1,860 parking spaces. The Boomtown Reno Nevada-based property offers 318 guestrooms; three restaurants; an 80-seat lounge; a 30,000-square-foot amusement center; and roughly 1,500 parking spaces. In addition, the property also has a full-service truck stop with a satellite casino; a gas station and mini-mart; and a 203-space recreational vehicle park. Pinnacle also owns the 297-suite Embassy Suites hotel in St. Louis; the President Riverboat Casino; Casino Magic Argentina; and the Casino at Emerald Bay boutique casino. In late 2006, Pinnacle began construction of an additional $45 million 250 guestrooms. When completed, L'Auberge will have roughly 1000 guestrooms.

The company offers its employees a 401(k) plan; health, vision, life, AD&D, short- and long-term disability insurance; and tuition reimbursement.

FINANCIALS: Sales and profits are in thousands of dollars—add 000 to get the full amount. 2007 Note: Financial information for 2007 was not available for all companies at press time.

2007 Sales: $	2007 Profits: $	**U.S. Stock Ticker:** PNK
2006 Sales: $912,357	2006 Profits: $76,886	**Int'l Ticker:** Int'l Exchange:
2005 Sales: $668,463	2005 Profits: $6,125	Employees: 7,186
2004 Sales: $466,543	2004 Profits: $9,161	Fiscal Year Ends: 12/31
2003 Sales: $524,162	2003 Profits: $-28,242	Parent Company:

SALARIES/BENEFITS:

Pension Plan:	ESOP Stock Plan:	Profit Sharing:	Top Exec. Salary: $875,000	Bonus: $1,812,500
Savings Plan: Y	Stock Purch. Plan:		Second Exec. Salary: $477,308	Bonus: $580,000

OTHER THOUGHTS:

Apparent Women Officers or Directors: 8
Hot Spot for Advancement for Women/Minorities: Y

LOCATIONS: ("Y" = Yes)

West:	Southwest:	Midwest:	Southeast:	Northeast:	International:
Y		Y	Y	Y	Y

Note: Financial information, benefits and other data can change quickly and may vary from those stated here.

PIONEER CORPORATION

www.pioneer.co.jp

Industry Group Code: 334310 Ranks within this company's industry group: Sales: 6 Profits: 11

Print Media/Publishing:	Movies:	Equipment/Supplies:		Broadcast/Cable:	Music/Audio:	Sports/Games/Gambling:
Newspapers:	Movie Theaters:	Equipment/Supplies:	Y	Broadcast TV:	Music Production:	Games/Sports:
Magazines:	Movie Production:	Gambling Equipment:		Cable TV:	Retail Music:	Retail Games Stores:
Books:	TV/Video Prod.:	Special Services:	Y	Satellite Broadcast:	Retail Audio Equip.:	Stadiums/Teams:
Book Stores:	Video Rental:	Advertising Services:		Radio:	Music Print./Dist.:	Gambling/Casinos:
Distribution/Printing:	Video Distribution:	Info. Sys. Software:		Online Information:	Multimedia:	Rides/Theme Parks:

TYPES OF BUSINESS:

Consumer Electronics
Audio/Video Equipment
CD/DVD Players
Automotive Electronics
Telecommunications Equipment
Research & Development
Software Development

BRANDS/DIVISIONS/AFFILIATES:

Pioneer Electronics (USA), Inc.
Discovision Associates
Pioneer Display Products Corp.
Pioneer Home Entertainment Co.
Tohoku Pioneer Corporation
Pioneer Europe
Pioneer China Holding Co., Ltd.

CONTACTS: Note: Officers with more than one job title may be intentionally listed here more than once.

Tamihiko Sudo, CEO
Tamihiko Sudo, Pres.
Hideki Okayasu, CFO
Toshiyuki Ito, Exec. Officer/General Mgr.-Personnel
Shinji Yasuda, General Mgr.-R&D
Masao Kawabata, Managing Exec. Officer/Dir.-Corp. Comm.
Hideki Okayasu, General Mgr.-Finance & Acct.
Akira Haeno, General Mgr.-Mobile Entertainment Business Group
Koki Aizawa, Exec. Officer-RW Coordination Center
Shinji Yasuda, Chief Dir.-Home Entertainment Bus. Group
Hajime Ishizuka, Sr. Managing Dir. & Representative Dir.
Toshiyuki Ito, Chmn.

Phone: 81-3-3495-6774	Fax: 81-3-3495-4301
Toll-Free:	
Address: 1-4-1, Meguro 1-chome, Meguro-ku, Tokyo, 153-8654 Japan	

GROWTH PLANS/SPECIAL FEATURES:

Pioneer Corporation is one of the leading manufacturers of consumer electronics in the world, operating mainly in four segments: home electronics, car electronics (earning 40% of its revenue), patent licensing and others. Headquartered in Japan and originally a speaker manufacturer, Pioneer now develops, designs, and manufactures (in its 30-plus facilities worldwide) amplifiers, hi-fi stereos, car electronics, cable-TV systems, audio and video equipment, CD players, and factory automation systems and parts. Pioneer was the first company to release global positioning systems (GPS) to the consumer market. The firm also makes DVD, CD-R/RW and DVD-R/RW drives, plasma-screen TVs and OLED displays. The company's primary markets are Japan, North America, Europe and Asia. Additionally, the company sells its products to customers in consumer and business markets through sales offices in Japan and through sales subsidiaries of Pioneer and independent distributors outside of Japan. In addition, on an OEM basis, Pioneer markets certain products, such as car electronics products, recordable DVD drives, plasma displays and OLED displays to other companies.

Pioneer is involved numerous community activities, including the sponsorship of a professional and amateur orchestras and other music groups, numerous music education programs, sports teams, international exchanges and environmental conservation efforts.

FINANCIALS: Sales and profits are in thousands of dollars—add 000 to get the full amount. 2007 Note: Financial information for 2007 was not available for all companies at press time.

2007 Sales: $	2007 Profits: $	U.S. Stock Ticker:
2006 Sales: $6,354,100	2006 Profits: $-715,270	Int'l Ticker: 6773 Int'l Exchange: Tokyo-TSE
2005 Sales: $6,906,476	2005 Profits: $-82,140	Employees: 38,826
2004 Sales: $6,612,100	2004 Profits: $234,300	Fiscal Year Ends: 3/31
2003 Sales: $5,935,600	2003 Profits: $134,000	Parent Company:

SALARIES/BENEFITS:

Pension Plan:	ESOP Stock Plan:	Profit Sharing:	Top Exec. Salary: $	Bonus: $
Savings Plan:	Stock Purch. Plan:		Second Exec. Salary: $	Bonus: $

OTHER THOUGHTS:

Apparent Women Officers or Directors:
Hot Spot for Advancement for Women/Minorities:

LOCATIONS: ("Y" = Yes)

West:	Southwest:	Midwest:	Southeast:	Northeast:	International:
Y					Y

PIXAR ANIMATION STUDIOS INC   www.pixar.com

Industry Group Code: 512110 Ranks within this company's industry group: Sales: Profits:

Print Media/Publishing:	Movies:		Equipment/Supplies:	Broadcast/Cable:	Music/Audio:	Sports/Games/Gambling:
Newspapers:	Movie Theaters:		Equipment/Supplies:	Broadcast TV:	Music Production:	Games/Sports:
Magazines:	Movie Production:	Y	Gambling Equipment:	Cable TV:	Retail Music:	Retail Games Stores:
Books:	TV/Video Prod.:		Special Services:	Satellite Broadcast:	Retail Audio Equip.:	Stadiums/Teams:
Book Stores:	Video Rental:		Advertising Services:	Radio:	Music Print./Dist.:	Gambling/Casinos:
Distribution/Printing:	Video Distribution:	Y	Info. Sys. Software:	Online Information:	Multimedia:	Rides/Theme Parks:

TYPES OF BUSINESS:

Computer-Animated Film Production
Special Effects Software
Video & Soundtrack Sales
Children's Merchandise

BRANDS/DIVISIONS/AFFILIATES:

Walt Disney Company (The)
Toy Story
Monsters, Inc.
Finding Nemo
Incredibles (The)
Cars
RenderMan
Ratatouille

CONTACTS: *Note: Officers with more than one job title may be intentionally listed here more than once.*

Steve Jobs, CEO
Edwin E. Catmull, Pres.
John Lasseter, Chief Creative Officer

Phone: 510-922-3000	Fax: 510-922-3151
Toll-Free:	
Address: 1200 Park Ave., Emeryville, CA 94608 US	

GROWTH PLANS/SPECIAL FEATURES:

Pixar Animation Studios, Inc., a subsidiary of The Walt Disney Co., is a pioneer in computer-animated feature films through its combination of creative, technical and production capabilities. Pixar began its productions with an agreement with the Walt Disney Company to develop up to three computer-animated feature films to be marketed and distributed by Disney. The first film produced was Toy Story, which met with wide success and established Pixar as the leader in computer-animated films. Pixar has released eight films to date: Toy Story, A Bug's Life, Toy Story 2, Monsters, Inc., Finding Nemo, The Incredibles, Cars and Ratatouille (released in June 2007), all of which have been successful at the box office. Toy Story won a Golden Globe award for Best Picture, Musical or Comedy in 1999 and Finding Nemo won an Academy Award for Best Animated Feature. The firm releases a new film about every 18 months, and the average film's production budget is $90 million. Along with box office revenues, Pixar generates revenue through the sale of home videos, children's merchandise and soundtracks. The company also makes short films, such as the Academy Award-winning For the Birds, that help it to develop new ideas and win acclaim, further establishing the Pixar brand. The firm's RenderMan software has helped create visual special effects for films including Star Wars Episode 1: The Phantom Menace, The Matrix and Gladiator. The software's creators won an Oscar for significant advancements to the field of motion picture rendering. In May 2006, Walt Disney acquired Pixar for $7.4 billion. In June 2007, Pixar released Ratatouille, a film about a rat who aspires to be a French chef.

Pixar offers paid technical and non-technical internships to college students. All employees are offered complete benefits, including stock options and three weeks vacation.

FINANCIALS: Sales and profits are in thousands of dollars—add 000 to get the full amount. 2007 Note: Financial information for 2007 was not available for all companies at press time.

2007 Sales: $	2007 Profits: $	**U.S. Stock Ticker: Subsidiary**
2006 Sales: $	2006 Profits: $	**Int'l Ticker:** Int'l Exchange:
2005 Sales: $289,116	2005 Profits: $152,938	Employees: 850
2004 Sales: $273,472	2004 Profits: $141,722	Fiscal Year Ends: 12/31
2003 Sales: $262,498	2003 Profits: $124,768	Parent Company: WALT DISNEY COMPANY (THE)

SALARIES/BENEFITS:

Pension Plan:	ESOP Stock Plan:	Profit Sharing:	Top Exec. Salary: $2,862,307	Bonus: $
Savings Plan: Y	Stock Purch. Plan:		Second Exec. Salary: $545,019	Bonus: $

OTHER THOUGHTS:

Apparent Women Officers or Directors:
Hot Spot for Advancement for Women/Minorities: Y

LOCATIONS: ("Y" = Yes)

West:	Southwest:	Midwest:	Southeast:	Northeast:	International:
Y					

PLAYBOY ENTERPRISES INC   www.playboyenterprises.com

Industry Group Code: 511120   Ranks within this company's industry group: Sales: 9   Profits: 5

Print Media/Publishing:		Movies:		Equipment/Supplies:		Broadcast/Cable:		Music/Audio:		Sports/Games/Gambling:	
Newspapers:		Movie Theaters:		Equipment/Supplies:		Broadcast TV:		Music Production:		Games/Sports:	
Magazines:	Y	Movie Production:		Gambling Equipment:		Cable TV:	Y	Retail Music:		Retail Games Stores:	
Books:	Y	TV/Video Prod.:	Y	Special Services:		Satellite Broadcast:		Retail Audio Equip.:		Stadiums/Teams:	
Book Stores:		Video Rental:		Advertising Services:		Radio:		Music Print./Dist.:		Gambling/Casinos:	Y
Distribution/Printing:		Video Distribution:	Y	Info. Sys. Software:		Online Information:		Multimedia:		Rides/Theme Parks:	

TYPES OF BUSINESS:
Magazine Publishing
Adult Entertainment
Movie, Video & Game Production
Internet Gaming
Online Sales & Subscriptions
Cable TV Networks

BRANDS/DIVISIONS/AFFILIATES:
Playboy Magazine
Playboy Channel (The)
Spice Entertainment
SIRIUS Satellite
Playboy Club
playboygaming.com
Playboy.com, Inc.
Club Jenna, Inc.

CONTACTS: Note: Officers with more than one job title may be intentionally listed here more than once.
Christie Hefner, CEO
Linda G. Havard, CFO
Carol A. Devine, Sr. VP-Human Resources
Howard Shapiro, Exec. VP-Admin.
Howard Shapiro, General Counsel/Sec./Exec. VP-Law
Linda G. Havard, Exec. VP-Oper.
Robert D. Campbell, Sr. VP-Strategic Planning/Treas.
Martha O. Lindeman, Sr. VP-Corp. Comm.
Martha O. Lindeman, Sr. VP-Investor Rel.
Linda G. Havard, Exec. VP-Finance
Hugh M. Hefner, Editor-in-Chief/Chief Creative Officer
Michael S. Dannhauser, Controller/Sr. VP
Bob Meyers, Exec. VP/Pres., Media
Alex L. Vaickus, Exec. VP/Pres., Global Licensing
Christie Hefner, Chmn.
Robert F. O'Donnel, Exec. VP-Int'l Publishing

Phone: 312-751-8000	Fax: 312-751-2818
Toll-Free:	
Address: 680 N. Lake Shore Dr., Chicago, IL 60611 US	

GROWTH PLANS/SPECIAL FEATURES:
Playboy Enterprises, Inc. (PEI) is a multimedia entertainment company that publishes Playboy Magazine worldwide; operates the Playboy and Spice television networks; and distributes programming via home video and DVD. The firm operates in three segments: entertainment, publishing and licensing. The entertainment group's operations include the production and marketing of television programming for the company's domestic and international TV businesses, web-based entertainment experiences, wireless content distribution, e-commerce, DVD products and satellite radio under the Playboy, Spice and other brand names. In addition to producing a number of shows for its own networks, the division also produces series to air on third party networks, including Girls Next Door on E!. The publishing segment's operations include the publication of Playboy magazine, special editions and other domestic publishing businesses, including books and calendars, as well as the licensing of international editions of Playboy magazine. Playboy magazine, the firm's flagship product, is one of the best-selling monthly men's magazines in the world. It is a general-interest magazine, targeted to men, which includes photography, entertainment, humor, cartoons and articles on current issues, interests and trends. The magazine consistently includes interviews with high-profile political, business, entertainment and sports figures; pictorials of famous women; and content by authors, such as Stephen King. Circulation of the U.S. edition is roughly 3 million copies monthly; the combined average circulation of the 22 licensed international editions is roughly 1.1 million copies monthly. The licensing division's operations include the licensing of consumer products, Playboy-branded retail stores, location-based entertainment and certain revenue-generating marketing activities. In 2006, the company acquired Club Jenna, Inc., a multimedia adult entertainment business, whose assets include film production, DVD, online and mobile businesses and a library of content. In 2006, PEI re-launched the Playboy Club in Las Vegas and Playboy Radio launched SIRIUS Satellite Radio. In 2007, PlayboyGaming.com, an online casino and poker site, was launched.

FINANCIALS: Sales and profits are in thousands of dollars—add 000 to get the full amount. 2007 Note: Financial information for 2007 was not available for all companies at press time.

2007 Sales: $	2007 Profits: $	U.S. Stock Ticker: PLA
2006 Sales: $331,142	2006 Profits: $2,285	Int'l Ticker: Int'l Exchange:
2005 Sales: $338,153	2005 Profits: $- 735	Employees: 782
2004 Sales: $329,376	2004 Profits: $9,989	Fiscal Year Ends: 12/31
2003 Sales: $315,844	2003 Profits: $-7,557	Parent Company:

SALARIES/BENEFITS:
Pension Plan:	ESOP Stock Plan:	Profit Sharing:	Top Exec. Salary: $1,000,000	Bonus: $
Savings Plan:	Stock Purch. Plan:		Second Exec. Salary: $700,000	Bonus: $

OTHER THOUGHTS:
Apparent Women Officers or Directors: 4
Hot Spot for Advancement for Women/Minorities: Y

LOCATIONS: ("Y" = Yes)
West:	Southwest:	Midwest:	Southeast:	Northeast:	International:
Y		Y		Y	Y

PRIMACOM AG
www.primacom.de

Industry Group Code: 513220 Ranks within this company's industry group: Sales: 20   Profits: 15

Print Media/Publishing:	Movies:	Equipment/Supplies:		Broadcast/Cable:		Music/Audio:		Sports/Games/Gambling:
Newspapers:	Movie Theaters:	Equipment/Supplies:		Broadcast TV:		Music Production:		Games/Sports:
Magazines:	Movie Production:	Gambling Equipment:		Cable TV:	Y	Retail Music:		Retail Games Stores:
Books:	TV/Video Prod.:	Special Services:	Y	Satellite Broadcast:		Retail Audio Equip.:		Stadiums/Teams:
Book Stores:	Video Rental:	Advertising Services:		Radio:		Music Print./Dist.:		Gambling/Casinos:
Distribution/Printing:	Video Distribution:	Info. Sys. Software:		Online Information:		Multimedia:		Rides/Theme Parks:

TYPES OF BUSINESS:

Cable TV Service
Video-on-Demand
Internet Services
Telephony Services
Online Radio Broadcasting

BRANDS/DIVISIONS/AFFILIATES:

prima Kabel TV
primatv
primaspeed
Liberty Media Corporation
Orion Cable GmbH

CONTACTS: *Note: Officers with more than one job title may be intentionally listed here more than once.*

Wolfgang Preuss, CEO
Thomas Eibeck, Regional Mgr.-Tech., Saxonia
Peter Hinkelmann, Managing Dir./Regional Mgr.-Saxonia
Gabriele Lindemann, Managing Dir./Regional Mgr.-Berlin

Phone: 49-0-6131-944-0	Fax: 49-0-6131-944-501
Toll-Free:	
Address: An der Ochsenwiese 3, Mainz, 55124 Germany	

GROWTH PLANS/SPECIAL FEATURES:

PrimaCom AG is a private cable network provider with operations in Germany and the Netherlands, offering analogue television, radio and digital television service (primatv) to approximately 1.3 million subscribers. Customers have access to more than 100 television and radio programs, interactive video-on-demand, high-speed Internet and telephony. PrimaCom currently has potential access to approximately 2 million homes and serves approximately 1.3 million customers in Germany and 300,000 in the Netherlands. The firm concentrates its operations on small and rural areas of Germany, and its largest consumer base is drawn from citizens of the formerly communist eastern section of Germany. PrimaCom's networks are located primarily in small to medium-sized cities in 10 German states and in the Netherlands. Its core regions are Saxony, Saxony-Anhalt, Thuringia, Rheinland-Pfalz and the Netherlands. In 2007, German cable operator Orion Cable acquired 91% of the company's stock.

FINANCIALS: Sales and profits are in thousands of dollars—add 000 to get the full amount. 2007 Note: Financial information for 2007 was not available for all companies at press time.

2007 Sales: $	2007 Profits: $	U.S. Stock Ticker:
2006 Sales: $167,160	2006 Profits: $-21,680	Int'l Ticker: PRC Int'l Exchange: Frankfurt
2005 Sales: $169,870	2005 Profits: $344,710	Employees: 496
2004 Sales: $287,400	2004 Profits: $-154,900	Fiscal Year Ends: 12/31
2003 Sales: $248,500	2003 Profits: $-148,200	Parent Company:

SALARIES/BENEFITS:

Pension Plan:	ESOP Stock Plan:	Profit Sharing:	Top Exec. Salary: $	Bonus: $
Savings Plan:	Stock Purch. Plan:		Second Exec. Salary: $	Bonus: $

OTHER THOUGHTS:

Apparent Women Officers or Directors: 2
Hot Spot for Advancement for Women/Minorities:

LOCATIONS: ("Y" = Yes)

West:	Southwest:	Midwest:	Southeast:	Northeast:	International: Y

PRIMEDIA INC

www.primediainc.com

Industry Group Code: 511120 Ranks within this company's industry group: Sales: 7 Profits: 4

Print Media/Publishing:	Movies:	Equipment/Supplies:	Broadcast/Cable:	Music/Audio:	Sports/Games/Gambling:
Newspapers:	Movie Theaters:	Equipment/Supplies:	Broadcast TV:	Music Production:	Games/Sports:
Magazines: Y	Movie Production:	Gambling Equipment:	Cable TV:	Retail Music:	Retail Games Stores:
Books:	TV/Video Prod.:	Special Services:	Satellite Broadcast:	Retail Audio Equip.:	Stadiums/Teams:
Book Stores:	Video Rental:	Advertising Services:	Radio:	Music Print./Dist.:	Gambling/Casinos:
Distribution/Printing:	Video Distribution:	Info. Sys. Software:	Online Information:	Multimedia:	Rides/Theme Parks:

TYPES OF BUSINESS:

Magazine Publishing
Housing Guides
Magazine Distribution
Online Media

BRANDS/DIVISIONS/AFFILIATES:

Motor Trend
Lowrider
4Wheel & Off Road
EQUUS
Power & Motoryacht
Apartment Guide
New Home Guide
KKR & CO LP (Kohlberg Kravis Roberts & Co)

CONTACTS: Note: Officers with more than one job title may be intentionally listed here more than once.

Robert Metz, CEO
Robert Metz, Pres.
Kim Payne, CFO/Sr. VP
Michaelanne C. Discepolo, Exec. VP-Human Resources
Keith Belknap, General Counsel/Sr. VP/Sec.
Robert J. Sforzo, Chief Acct. Officer/Sr. VP
Carl Salas, Treas./Sr. VP
Dean B. Nelson, Chmn.

Phone: 678-421-3000	Fax:
Toll-Free: 800-216-1423	
Address: 3585 Engineering Dr., Ste. 100, Norcross, GA 30092 US	

GROWTH PLANS/SPECIAL FEATURES:

Primedia, Inc. is a targeted media company whose properties comprise more than 100 brands that connect buyers and sellers through print publications, Internet sites, events, licensing, merchandising and video. The company operates in two segments: enthusiast media and consumer guides. The enthusiast media segment encompasses the firm's consumer magazines, Internet sites, events, licensing and merchandising and video. The division publishes 56 automotive magazines, including consumer automotive titles such as Automobile and Motor Trend, which cater to the high-end and new car automotive market, as well as highly specialized enthusiast titles such as Hot Rod, Truckin', Super Street, Lowrider, Motorcyclist, 4Wheel & Off-Road and Four Wheeler. Supplementing the automotive print publications, Primedia has a presence on the Internet with each of its related web sites to each publication. The division is a publisher of magazines for other enthusiast markets with such titles as Stereophile, Power & Motoryacht and EQUUS. It also publishes numerous magazines targeting action sports enthusiasts such as Surfing, Skateboarder and Snowboarder. Additionally, the company publishes two soap opera magazines, Soap Opera Digest and Soap Opera Weekly, as well as a number of smaller, privately-owned or regionally-based magazines. The consumer guide segment is a publisher and distributor of free guides in the U.S. with Apartment Guide, New Home Guide, Auto Guide and their respective web sites. The division's products are dedicated directories of category specific content that attract consumers who are actively in the market to rent an apartment or buy a new home or a pre-owned automobile. The Apartment Guide publication is distributed in 74 regional markets and has a monthly circulation of 1.5 million. ApartmentGuide.com attracts roughly 1.6 million unique visitors per month. In 2007, Primedia sold its Outdoors group for $170 million; and its Films Media Group to Facts on File, Inc. Private equity firm KKR & Co. owns about 60% of the company.

FINANCIALS: Sales and profits are in thousands of dollars—add 000 to get the full amount. 2007 Note: Financial information for 2007 was not available for all companies at press time.

2007 Sales: $	2007 Profits: $	U.S. Stock Ticker: PRM
2006 Sales: $849,309	2006 Profits: $38,252	Int'l Ticker: Int'l Exchange:
2005 Sales: $821,729	2005 Profits: $564,618	Employees: 2,800
2004 Sales: $1,307,100	2004 Profits: $35,500	Fiscal Year Ends: 12/31
2003 Sales: $1,345,600	2003 Profits: $38,900	Parent Company:

SALARIES/BENEFITS:

Pension Plan:	ESOP Stock Plan:	Profit Sharing:	Top Exec. Salary: $1,000,000	Bonus: $112,885
Savings Plan:	Stock Purch. Plan:		Second Exec. Salary: $556,442	Bonus: $312,721

OTHER THOUGHTS:

Apparent Women Officers or Directors: 3
Hot Spot for Advancement for Women/Minorities: Y

LOCATIONS: ("Y" = Yes)

West:	Southwest:	Midwest:	Southeast:	Northeast:	International:
			Y	Y	

Note: Financial information, benefits and other data can change quickly and may vary from those stated here.

PROGRESSIVE GAMING INTERNATIONAL CORP
www.progressivegaming.net

Industry Group Code: 713290 Ranks within this company's industry group: Sales: 10   Profits: 12

Print Media/Publishing:	Movies:	Equipment/Supplies:		Broadcast/Cable:	Music/Audio:	Sports/Games/Gambling:
Newspapers:	Movie Theaters:	Equipment/Supplies:		Broadcast TV:	Music Production:	Games/Sports:
Magazines:	Movie Production:	Gambling Equipment:	Y	Cable TV:	Retail Music:	Retail Games Stores:
Books:	TV/Video Prod.:	Special Services:	Y	Satellite Broadcast:	Retail Audio Equip.:	Stadiums/Teams:
Book Stores:	Video Rental:	Advertising Services:		Radio:	Music Print./Dist.:	Gambling/Casinos:
Distribution/Printing:	Video Distribution:	Info. Sys. Software:		Online Information:	Multimedia:	Rides/Theme Parks:

TYPES OF BUSINESS:
Gambling Equipment
Slot Machines
Jackpot Systems
Gaming Software
Tracking & Accounting Systems
Casino Networking Systems

BRANDS/DIVISIONS/AFFILIATES:
Intelligent Table System
Peer to Peer Texas Hold'Em
Rapid Bet Live Wireless
Tablelink
Caribbean Stud
TableMax
VirtGame Corp.
PitTrak

CONTACTS: *Note: Officers with more than one job title may be intentionally listed here more than once.*
Russel H. McMeekin, CEO
Russel H. McMeekin, Pres.
Heather A. Rollo, CFO/Exec. VP/Treasurer
Robert J. Parente, Exec. VP-Sales & Mktg.
Thomas Galanty, CTO/Exec.VP
Robert B. Ziems, General Counsel/Exec. VP/Sec.
Thomas M. Galanty, Exec. VP-Global Oper.
Robert B. Ziems, VP-Bus. Dev.
Heather A. Rollo, Treas.
Derek Harmer, Sr. VP-Sports & Wireless Oper.
Peter G. Boynton, Chmn.
Neil Crossan, Exec. VP-Int'l

Phone: 702-896-3890	Fax: 702-896-2461
Toll-Free: 800-336-8449	
Address: 920 Pilot Rd., Las Vegas, NV 89119 US	

GROWTH PLANS/SPECIAL FEATURES:

Progressive Gaming International Corporation manufactures, develops, acquires and markets branded slot machines and table games, progressive jackpot systems and player tracking and accounting systems for slot machines and table games. The company's customers include casinos, other gaming suppliers, operators of wide-area gaming networks and lottery authorities. The firm's operations occur in two main business sectors: slot and table games, and systems. Slot and table games include Progressive Black Jack, Texas Hold'Em Bonus, Caribbean Stud and licensed games Garfield and KISS. The systems segment designs and develops electronic player tracking and game monitoring and accounting systems for slot and table games. These systems are sold or leased to casino operators and governmental agencies. In 2007, Progressive Gaming and Cantor expanded its mobile gaming partnership as Progressive became the worldwide distributor of Cantor's mobile gaming systems; additionally, Cantor has licensed rights to Rapid Bet Live and PrimeLine for use with their mobile gaming system's sports wagering applications, allowing the companies to offer multiple wireless gaming applications worldwide. The company announced plans to expand its Rapid Bet Live wireless wagering technology to the Bahamas. Also in 2007, the firm sold its rights and contracts for all of Progressive's proprietary table game titles to Shuffle Master, a leading provider of specialty table games. The company recently announced a 10-year partnership with Elixir Group Limited that will extend Progressive's wireless gaming technology into the Asia pacific region. Other recent expansions for the company include the integration of Progressive's Casinolink technology in casinos located in the new San Juan-Luis Munoz Marin International Airport in Puerto Rico and the implementation of the firm's licensed RFID technology into the gaming tables at Foxwoods Resort Casino in Las Vegas, to be fully implemented throughout the casino by May 2008.

FINANCIALS: Sales and profits are in thousands of dollars—add 000 to get the full amount. 2007 Note: Financial information for 2007 was not available for all companies at press time.

2007 Sales: $	2007 Profits: $	U.S. Stock Ticker: PGIC
2006 Sales: $69,509	2006 Profits: $-36,624	Int'l Ticker: Int'l Exchange:
2005 Sales: $78,221	2005 Profits: $-5,983	Employees: 308
2004 Sales: $96,374	2004 Profits: $ 259	Fiscal Year Ends: 12/31
2003 Sales: $91,803	2003 Profits: $-34,216	Parent Company:

SALARIES/BENEFITS:

Pension Plan:	ESOP Stock Plan:	Profit Sharing:	Top Exec. Salary: $757,635	Bonus: $
Savings Plan: Y	Stock Purch. Plan:		Second Exec. Salary: $469,962	Bonus: $

OTHER THOUGHTS:
Apparent Women Officers or Directors: 1
Hot Spot for Advancement for Women/Minorities:

LOCATIONS: ("Y" = Yes)

West:	Southwest:	Midwest:	Southeast:	Northeast:	International:
Y	Y	Y	Y	Y	Y

R R DONNELLEY & SONS CO

www.rrdonelley.com

Industry Group Code: 323000 Ranks within this company's industry group: Sales: 1 Profits: 1

Print Media/Publishing:	Movies:	Equipment/Supplies:	Broadcast/Cable:	Music/Audio:	Sports/Games/Gambling:
Newspapers:	Movie Theaters:	Equipment/Supplies:	Broadcast TV:	Music Production:	Games/Sports:
Magazines: Y	Movie Production:	Gambling Equipment:	Cable TV:	Retail Music:	Retail Games Stores:
Books:	TV/Video Prod.:	Special Services:	Satellite Broadcast:	Retail Audio Equip.:	Stadiums/Teams:
Book Stores:	Video Rental:	Advertising Services:	Radio:	Music Print./Dist.:	Gambling/Casinos:
Distribution/Printing:	Video Distribution:	Info. Sys. Software:	Online Information:	Multimedia:	Rides/Theme Parks:

TYPES OF BUSINESS:

Commercial Printing
Distributors-Books, Magazines, Catalogs & Direct Mail
Digital Content Management
Creative Services
Logistics Services

BRANDS/DIVISIONS/AFFILIATES:

RR Donnelley Global Document Solutions
Office Tiger
Banta Corporation
Perry-Judd's Holdings, Inc.
Von Hoffmann

CONTACTS: Note: Officers with more than one job title may be intentionally listed here more than once.

Thomas J. Quinlan III, CEO
John R. Paloian, COO
Thomas J. Quinlan III, Pres.
Kenneth E. O'Brien, CIO
Suzanne S. Bettman, General Counsel/Corp. Sec/Chief Compliance Officer
Thomas J. Quinlan III, Exec. VP-Oper.
Miles W. McHugh, Controller/Chief Acct. Officer/Sr. VP
John R. Paloian, Group Pres., RR Donnelley Global Print Solutions
Stephen M. Wolf, Chmn.

Phone: 312-326-8000	Fax:
Toll-Free:	
Address: 111 S. Wacker Dr., Chicago, IL 60606 US	

GROWTH PLANS/SPECIAL FEATURES:

R. R. Donnelley & Sons Co., founded in 1864, provides print and related services, including business process outsourcing, to customers in the publishing, healthcare, advertising, retail, technology, financial services and other industries. R. R. Donnelley operates through two business segments: Global Print Solutions and Global Services. Global Print Solutions provides print services to consumer magazine and catalog publishers; retailers; yellow and white pages directory publishers; and religious, educational and specialty book publishers. The segment also consolidates and delivers company-printed products, as well as products printed by third parties; offers content creation, database management, printing, personalization, finishing and distribution services; and provides short-run commercial print services. Global Services provides digital solutions for conventional and digital photography; creative, color matching, page production and content management services; and information management, content assembly and print services for such products as annual reports, marketing brochures and marketing inserts. Within the Global Services segment, RR Donnelley Global Document Solutions provides business outsourcing services, transactional print and mail services, data and print management and document production, primarily in the U.K. Office Tiger provides integrated process outsourcing and transaction processing services throughout North America, Europe, India, the Philippines and Sri Lanka. In January 2007, R. R. Donnelley completed the purchase of two printing companies: Banta Corporation for $1.3 billion and Perry-Judd's Holdings, Inc. for $176 million. In May 2007, the company completed the purchase of Von Hoffmann, a printer of books and related products, for $412.5 million. In June the company unified its services under the R. R. Donnelley brand, including its Office Tiger brand.

R. R. Donnelley offers its employees a dependent care plan, a pension plan, a 401(k) plan, an employee stock purchase plan, an employee assistance program, an adoption assistance program, a health care flexible spending account and medical, dental and vision coverage programs.

FINANCIALS: Sales and profits are in thousands of dollars—add 000 to get the full amount. 2007 Note: Financial information for 2007 was not available for all companies at press time.

2007 Sales: $	2007 Profits: $	U.S. Stock Ticker: RRD
2006 Sales: $9,316,600	2006 Profits: $400,600	Int'l Ticker: Int'l Exchange:
2005 Sales: $8,430,200	2005 Profits: $137,100	Employees: 53,000
2004 Sales: $7,156,400	2004 Profits: $178,300	Fiscal Year Ends: 12/31
2003 Sales: $4,787,162	2003 Profits: $176,509	Parent Company:

SALARIES/BENEFITS:

Pension Plan: Y	ESOP Stock Plan:	Profit Sharing:	Top Exec. Salary: $1,000,000	Bonus: $4,250,000
Savings Plan: Y	Stock Purch. Plan: Y		Second Exec. Salary: $500,000	Bonus: $1,000,000

OTHER THOUGHTS:

Apparent Women Officers or Directors: 1
Hot Spot for Advancement for Women/Minorities: Y

LOCATIONS: ("Y" = Yes)

West:	Southwest:	Midwest:	Southeast:	Northeast:	International:
Y	Y	Y	Y	Y	Y

RADIO ONE
www.radio-one.com

Industry Group Code: 513111 Ranks within this company's industry group: Sales: 7   Profits: 9

Print Media/Publishing:	Movies:	Equipment/Supplies:	Broadcast/Cable:	Music/Audio:	Sports/Games/Gambling:
Newspapers:	Movie Theaters:	Equipment/Supplies:	Broadcast TV: Y	Music Production:	Games/Sports:
Magazines:	Movie Production:	Gambling Equipment:	Cable TV:	Retail Music:	Retail Games Stores:
Books:	TV/Video Prod.:	Special Services: Y	Satellite Broadcast:	Retail Audio Equip.:	Stadiums/Teams:
Book Stores:	Video Rental:	Advertising Services:	Radio:	Music Print./Dist.:	Gambling/Casinos:
Distribution/Printing:	Video Distribution:	Info. Sys. Software:	Online Information:	Multimedia:	Rides/Theme Parks:

TYPES OF BUSINESS:
Radio Broadcasting
Television Broadcasting
Digital Broadcasting Technology

BRANDS/DIVISIONS/AFFILIATES:
TV One
Reach Media, Inc.
iBiquity
Syndication One
BlackAmericaWeb.com

CONTACTS: Note: Officers with more than one job title may be intentionally listed here more than once.
Alfred C. Liggins, III, CEO
Mary C. Sneed, COO
Alfred C. Liggins, III, Pres.
Scott R. Royster, CFO/Exec. VP
Alejandro A. Clabiorne, VP-Mktg.
Jackie Kindall, VP-Human Resources
Amy E. Vokes, VP-Research
Leslie C. Bauer, CIO
John W. Mathews, VP-Eng.
Linda J. E. Vilardo, Chief Admin. Officer/VP
Mike Plantamura, General Counsel/VP
Zemira Z. Jones, VP-Oper.
Alfred C. Liggins, III, Treas.
Catherine L. Hughes, Corp. Sec.
Deborah A. Cowan, Sr. VP-Finance
Barry Mayo, Pres, Radio Division
Pamela B. Somers, Sr. VP-Corp. Sales
Catherine L. Hughes, Chmn.

Phone: 301-306-1111	Fax: 301-306-9426
Toll-Free:	
Address: 5900 Princess Garden Pkwy., 7th Fl., Lanham, MD 20706 US	

GROWTH PLANS/SPECIAL FEATURES:
Radio One, Inc. is one of the largest radio broadcasting corporations in the U.S., focusing primarily on African-American and urban audiences. The company, which mostly focuses on radio, owns 54 stations in 17 urban markets, several located in top African-American markets, including Atlanta, Houston, Los Angeles, Detroit and New York. In addition to broadcast radio, the company has expanded its portfolio to include XM Satellite Radio with its XM 169 The POWER subscription station. Approximately 13 million listeners tune in to Radio One's programming every week. As part of its corporate strategy, Radio One makes acquisitions of underperforming radio stations in new and existing markets that have a significant African-American presence. The firm owns 36% of TV One, a network it created with Comcast. In addition, Radio One owns 51% of Reach Media, Inc., with its popular Tom Joyner Morning Show. The company also owns a stake in iBiquity, a developer of digital broadcast technology (in-band-on-channel). The company's Syndication One programming consists of a lineup of programs that discuss, analyze and dissect ideas and issues targeted to the African-American audiences and appealing to the general market. In 2007, the firm sold off several radio stations including its WKAF-FM station in Boston for approximately $30 million and WTPS-AM in Miami for $12.25 million. It also agreed to sell its radio stations in the Dayton metropolitan area and five of its radio stations in the Louisville to Main Line Broadcasting, LLC. Additionally, it sold its radio station in the Minneapolis to Northern Lights Broadcasting, LLC and assets of its radio stations in the Augusta market to Perry Broadcasting Company for approximately $3.1 million. Recently, the firm acquired a stake in Giant Magazine, LLC and entered into an agreement to acquire the assets of WPRS-FM, in Washington, D.C.

FINANCIALS: Sales and profits are in thousands of dollars—add 000 to get the full amount. 2007 Note: Financial information for 2007 was not available for all companies at press time.

2007 Sales: $	2007 Profits: $	**U.S. Stock Ticker: ROIA**
2006 Sales: $367,017	2006 Profits: $-6,730	**Int'l Ticker:** Int'l Exchange:
2005 Sales: $368,658	2005 Profits: $45,874	Employees: 1,690
2004 Sales: $319,761	2004 Profits: $61,602	Fiscal Year Ends: 12/31
2003 Sales: $303,200	2003 Profits: $53,800	Parent Company:

SALARIES/BENEFITS:
Pension Plan:	ESOP Stock Plan:	Profit Sharing:	Top Exec. Salary: $417,700	Bonus: $190,000
Savings Plan: Y	Stock Purch. Plan:		Second Exec. Salary: $551,250	Bonus: $560,000

OTHER THOUGHTS:
Apparent Women Officers or Directors: 9
Hot Spot for Advancement for Women/Minorities: Y

LOCATIONS: ("Y" = Yes)
West:	Southwest:	Midwest:	Southeast:	Northeast:	International:
Y	Y	Y	Y	Y	

RADIOSHACK CORPORATION

www.radioshackcorporation.com

Industry Group Code: 443110 Ranks within this company's industry group: Sales: 3 Profits: 3

Print Media/Publishing:	Movies:	Equipment/Supplies:		Broadcast/Cable:	Music/Audio:	Sports/Games/Gambling:
Newspapers:	Movie Theaters:	Equipment/Supplies:	Y	Broadcast TV:	Music Production:	Games/Sports:
Magazines:	Movie Production:	Gambling Equipment:		Cable TV:	Retail Music:	Retail Games Stores:
Books:	TV/Video Prod.:	Special Services:		Satellite Broadcast:	Retail Audio Equip.:	Stadiums/Teams:
Book Stores:	Video Rental:	Advertising Services:		Radio:	Music Print./Dist.:	Gambling/Casinos:
Distribution/Printing:	Video Distribution:	Info. Sys. Software:		Online Information:	Multimedia:	Rides/Theme Parks:

TYPES OF BUSINESS:

Consumer Electronics Stores
Cellular Telephone Sales & Distribution
Internet Services Sales & Distribution
Audio & Video Equipment Distribution
Personal Computer Sales
Customer Support Services
Online Retail

BRANDS/DIVISIONS/AFFILIATES:

Radioshack.com
Axiom Telecom
Brightstar Corp.
Dangaard Telecom

CONTACTS: *Note: Officers with more than one job title may be intentionally listed here more than once.*

Julian C. Day, CEO
James F. Gooch, CFO/Exec. VP
Jim Hamilton, Exec. VP-Mktg. & Merch.
Cara D. Kinzey, Sr. VP-IT
Wesley V. Lowzinski, Sr. VP/General Merch. Mgr.
Jim Fredericks, Exec. VP-Admin.
David S. Goldberg, General Counsel/Sr. VP/Corp. Sec.
Kay Jackson, Sr. Dir.-Public Rel.
James M .Grant, Sr. Dir.-Investor Rel.
David P. Johnson, Controller/Sr. VP
Joe Formichelli, Exec. VP-Retail Oper.
Julian C. Day, Chmn.
John G. Ripperton, Sr. VP-Supply Chain

Phone: 817-415-3011	Fax: 817-415-2647
Toll-Free:	
Address: Riverfront Campus, 300 RadioShack Cir., Fort Worth, TX 76102-1964 US	

GROWTH PLANS/SPECIAL FEATURES:

RadioShack Corporation engages primarily in the retail sale of consumer electronics goods and services through its RadioShack store chain and non-RadioShack branded kiosk operations. The company operates roughly 4,400 stores under the RadioShack brand, located in Puerto Rico, the U.S. Virgin Islands and throughout the U.S. in major shopping malls, strip centers and individual storefronts; approximately 770 kiosks located throughout the U.S., primarily inside Sam's Club locations; and stand-alone Sprint Nextel kiosks in major shopping malls. In addition to this, RadioShack has a network of roughly 1,580 dealer outlets, 36 of which are located outside of North America. These outlets provide private label and third-party branded products and services to smaller communities. Products, services and information are also available through radioshack.com. The firm's product lines include wireless telephones and communication devices such as scanners and two-way radios; flat panel televisions; residential telephones; DVD players; computers and direct-to-home (DTH) satellite systems; home entertainment; wireless, imaging and computer accessories; general and special purpose batteries; wire, cable and connectivity products; satellite radios; memory players; radio-controlled cars; and digital cameras. RadioShack also offers access to third-party services such as wireless telephone and DTH satellite activation; satellite radio service; prepaid wireless airtime; and extended service plans. In 2006, RadioShack formed a distribution, supply chain and retail alliance with Axiom Telecom, Brightstar Corp. and Dangaard Telecom, which will serve the wireless telecommunications industry worldwide. In April 2007, RadioShack announced that its free standard ground shipping program for orders from its web site to a local RadioShack location is now available nationwide.

RadioShack offers its employees medical, dental, vision and life benefit plans; flexible spending accounts; a 401(k) plan; and access to a credit union.

FINANCIALS: Sales and profits are in thousands of dollars—add 000 to get the full amount. 2007 Note: Financial information for 2007 was not available for all companies at press time.

2007 Sales: $	2007 Profits: $	U.S. Stock Ticker: RSH
2006 Sales: $4,777,500	2006 Profits: $73,400	Int'l Ticker: Int'l Exchange:
2005 Sales: $5,081,700	2005 Profits: $267,000	Employees: 40,000
2004 Sales: $4,841,200	2004 Profits: $337,200	Fiscal Year Ends: 12/31
2003 Sales: $4,649,300	2003 Profits: $298,500	Parent Company:

SALARIES/BENEFITS:

Pension Plan:	ESOP Stock Plan:	Profit Sharing:	Top Exec. Salary: $488,462	Bonus: $490,412
Savings Plan: Y	Stock Purch. Plan:		Second Exec. Salary: $460,192	Bonus: $

OTHER THOUGHTS:

Apparent Women Officers or Directors: 2
Hot Spot for Advancement for Women/Minorities: Y

LOCATIONS: ("Y" = Yes)

West:	Southwest:	Midwest:	Southeast:	Northeast:	International:
Y	Y	Y	Y	Y	Y

Note: Financial information, benefits and other data can change quickly and may vary from those stated here.

RAINBOW MEDIA HOLDINGS LLC   www.rainbow-media.com

Industry Group Code: 513210 Ranks within this company's industry group: Sales: Profits:

Print Media/Publishing:		Movies:		Equipment/Supplies:		Broadcast/Cable:		Music/Audio:		Sports/Games/Gambling:	
Newspapers:		Movie Theaters:		Equipment/Supplies:		Broadcast TV:		Music Production:		Games/Sports:	
Magazines:		Movie Production:		Gambling Equipment:		Cable TV:	Y	Retail Music:		Retail Games Stores:	
Books:		TV/Video Prod.:	Y	Special Services:	Y	Satellite Broadcast:		Retail Audio Equip.:		Stadiums/Teams:	Y
Book Stores:		Video Rental:		Advertising Services:	Y	Radio:		Music Print./Dist.:		Gambling/Casinos:	
Distribution/Printing:		Video Distribution:		Info. Sys. Software:		Online Information:		Multimedia:		Rides/Theme Parks:	

TYPES OF BUSINESS:

Cable Television Broadcasting
Local News Network
Sports Teams
Sports & Performance Venues
Advertisement Sales
Network Services

BRANDS/DIVISIONS/AFFILIATES:

Cablevision Systems Corp
Rainbow Network Communications
Madison Square Garden LP
American Movie Classics (AMC)
fuse
Independent Film Channel (IFC)
WE
LIFESKOOL

CONTACTS: *Note: Officers with more than one job title may be intentionally listed here more than once.*

Joshua W. Sapan, CEO
Joshua W. Sapan, Pres.
Robert Broussard, Pres., Network Sales
Charlene Weisler, Sr. VP-Research
David R. Kline, Sr. VP-Info. Systems & Broadcasting
Steven Pontillo, Sr. VP-Tech.
David Deitch, General Counsel/Sr. VP/Pres., Bus. Affairs
Mike DiPasquale, Sr. VP-Oper.
Glenn Oakley, Sr. VP-Bus. Dev.
Ellen Kroner, Sr. VP-Corp. Comm. & Mktg.
John Huffman, Exec. VP-Finance
David L. Kline, COO/Pres., Rainbow Advertising Sales Corp.
Rob Battles, Sr. VP-Creative Svcs.
Ed Carroll, Pres., Entertainment Svcs.
Andrea Greenberg, Pres., Rainbow Media Ventures
Harold Gronenthal, Sr. VP-Int'l Dev. & Program Acquisitions

Phone: 516-803-3000	Fax: 516-803-3003
Toll-Free:	
Address: 200 Jericho Quadrangle, Jericho, NY 11753 US	

GROWTH PLANS/SPECIAL FEATURES:

Rainbow Media Holdings, LLC, a subsidiary of the Cablevision Systems Corporation, is a producer and distributor of cable television programming. Managing a broad swath of the TV business, the company owns 18 national networks, including 15 high definition stations, three regional sports networks (covering New England, Chicago and the San Francisco Bay Area and operated in conjunction with Fox Sports) and six on-demand channels. Rainbow also has seven independent ad sales divisions and a technical services department called Rainbow Network Communications.   This division both handles the technological issues of company businesses and is also hired out to work for other networks, such as Bravo. Additionally, Rainbow is the owner of Madison Square Garden, LP. Not limited to the famous sports venue in New York, this subsidiary also comprises Radio City Music Hall and its subsidiaries, the Hartford Civic Center and six local sports teams, which include the New York Knicks and New York Rangers.   Highlights from Rainbow's cable media portfolio include: American Movie Classics (AMC), the company's flagship, devoted solely to classic film; fuse, an interactive music channel sporting music videos, interviews and concerts; the Independent Film Channel (IFC) companies, which not only broadcast films from low-budget and emerging producers but also assist in their development; WE, the women's entertainment channel; and the VOOM group of high definition networks. The on-demand channels, which are available to hotel customers as well as home subscribers, offer magazine-like specialty programming (on LIFESKOOL), sports information (on SPORTSKOOL) and selections from the fuse, IFC and WE networks.

FINANCIALS: Sales and profits are in thousands of dollars—add 000 to get the full amount. 2007 Note: Financial information for 2007 was not available for all companies at press time.

2007 Sales: $	2007 Profits: $	U.S. Stock Ticker: Subsidiary
2006 Sales: $	2006 Profits: $	Int'l Ticker: Int'l Exchange:
2005 Sales: $	2005 Profits: $	Employees: 499
2004 Sales: $	2004 Profits: $	Fiscal Year Ends: 12/31
2003 Sales: $	2003 Profits: $	Parent Company: CABLEVISION SYSTEMS CORP

SALARIES/BENEFITS:

Pension Plan:	ESOP Stock Plan:	Profit Sharing:	Top Exec. Salary: $	Bonus: $
Savings Plan:	Stock Purch. Plan:		Second Exec. Salary: $	Bonus: $

OTHER THOUGHTS:

Apparent Women Officers or Directors: 5
Hot Spot for Advancement for Women/Minorities: Y

LOCATIONS: ("Y" = Yes)

West:	Southwest:	Midwest:	Southeast:	Northeast:	International:
Y		Y		Y	

RANDOM HOUSE INC
www.randomhouse.com

Industry Group Code: 511130 Ranks within this company's industry group: Sales: Profits:

Print Media/Publishing:		Movies:	Equipment/Supplies:	Broadcast/Cable:	Music/Audio:	Sports/Games/Gambling:
Newspapers:		Movie Theaters:	Equipment/Supplies:	Broadcast TV:	Music Production:	Games/Sports:
Magazines:		Movie Production:	Gambling Equipment:	Cable TV:	Retail Music:	Retail Games Stores:
Books:	Y	TV/Video Prod.:	Special Services:	Satellite Broadcast:	Retail Audio Equip.:	Stadiums/Teams:
Book Stores:		Video Rental:	Advertising Services:	Radio:	Music Print./Dist.:	Gambling/Casinos:
Distribution/Printing:		Video Distribution:	Info. Sys. Software:	Online Information:	Multimedia:	Rides/Theme Parks:

TYPES OF BUSINESS:
Book Publishing

BRANDS/DIVISIONS/AFFILIATES:
Bertelsmann AG
Bantam Dell Publishing Group
Doubleday Broadway Publishing Group
Random House Children's Books
RAndom House Audio Publishing Group
Random House Information Group
Random House Webster's College Dictionary
Multomah Publishers

CONTACTS: *Note: Officers with more than one job title may be intentionally listed here more than once.*
Peter Olson, CEO
Edward Volini, CFO
Edward Volini, Chief Admin. Officer
Richard Sarnoff, Exec. VP-Corp. Dev.
Richard Sarnoff, Pres., Random House Ventures
Peter Olson, Chmn.

Phone: 212-782-9000	**Fax:** 212-940-7381
Toll-Free:	
Address: 1745 Broadway, New York, NY 10019 US	

GROWTH PLANS/SPECIAL FEATURES:
Random House, Inc., a subsidiary of German media conglomerate Bertelsmann AG, is one of the world's largest English-language general trade book publishers. The company's publishing groups include the Bantam Dell Publishing Group, the Doubleday Broadway Publishing Group, the Crown Publishing Group, the Knopf Publishing Group, Random House Children's Books, the Random House Audio Publishing Group, the Random House Diversified Publishing Group, the Random House Publishing Group, the Random House Information Group and Random House Ventures. All of the firm's publishing houses have complete editorial freedom, and the whole company operates through a decentralized business structure, meaning that each house has the freedom to publish whatever it wants, without having to go through its parent company. Publishing under the Random House name, the company releases a broad variety of titles, including fiction, non-fiction and reference books, such as the widely popular Random House Webster's College Dictionary. Other divisions of the publishing house devote themselves to children's books, discount books, large print and audio books. Ballantine Books publishes some of the best-known writers in fiction, such as Anne Rice, John Irving and Stephen King, with other activities in the areas of health, history, psychology and biography. Bantam's author list also includes Dean Koontz, Tom Robbins and Tami Hoag. Doubleday specializes in some of the best-known authors in recent history, such as Rudyard Kipling, Aldous Huxley and Bram Stoker, as well as modern authors such as John Grisham and Margeret Atwood. Alfred A. Knopf's authors have collected more Nobel Prizes, National Book Awards, Pulitzer Prizes and National Book Critics Circle Awards than those of almost any other book publisher. In 2006, Random House acquired Multnomah Publishers, an evangelical Christian book publishing house.

The company offers its employees medical, dental and vision insurance; life insurance; a 401(k) plan; tuition reimbursement; and employee discounts.

FINANCIALS: Sales and profits are in thousands of dollars—add 000 to get the full amount. 2007 Note: Financial information for 2007 was not available for all companies at press time.

2007 Sales: $	2007 Profits: $	**U.S. Stock Ticker: Subsidiary**
2006 Sales: $	2006 Profits: $	**Int'l Ticker:** Int'l Exchange:
2005 Sales: $2,185,200	2005 Profits: $	Employees: 5,395
2004 Sales: $2,442,900	2004 Profits: $	Fiscal Year Ends: 12/31
2003 Sales: $2,229,200	2003 Profits: $	Parent Company: BERTELSMANN AG

SALARIES/BENEFITS:

Pension Plan:	ESOP Stock Plan:	Profit Sharing:	Top Exec. Salary: $	Bonus: $
Savings Plan: Y	Stock Purch. Plan:		Second Exec. Salary: $	Bonus: $

OTHER THOUGHTS:
Apparent Women Officers or Directors:
Hot Spot for Advancement for Women/Minorities:

LOCATIONS: ("Y" = Yes)

West:	Southwest:	Midwest:	Southeast:	Northeast:	International:
				Y	Y

Note: Financial information, benefits and other data can change quickly and may vary from those stated here.

RANK GROUP PLC (THE)　　　　www.rank.com

Industry Group Code: 713210　Ranks within this company's industry group: Sales: 2　Profits: 2

Print Media/Publishing:	Movies:	Equipment/Supplies:		Broadcast/Cable:	Music/Audio:	Sports/Games/Gambling:	
Newspapers:	Movie Theaters:	Equipment/Supplies:		Broadcast TV:	Music Production:	Games/Sports:	
Magazines:	Movie Production:	Gambling Equipment:	Y	Cable TV:	Retail Music:	Retail Games Stores:	
Books:	TV/Video Prod.:	Special Services:		Satellite Broadcast:	Retail Audio Equip.:	Stadiums/Teams:	
Book Stores:	Video Rental:	Advertising Services:		Radio:	Music Print./Dist.:	Gambling/Casinos:	Y
Distribution/Printing:	Video Distribution:	Info. Sys. Software:		Online Information:	Multimedia:	Rides/Theme Parks:	

TYPES OF BUSINESS:

Gambling Resorts & Casinos
Gambling Equipment

BRANDS/DIVISIONS/AFFILIATES:

Mecca Bingo
Grosvenor Casinos
Top Rank Espana
Blue Square
Hard Rock

GROWTH PLANS/SPECIAL FEATURES:

The Rank Group plc is a British holding company with interests in a variety of entertainment business. The company's main segments consist of an assortment of casinos and gaming facilities. The Rank Group owns and operates: Mecca Bingo, which is the second-largest bingo club operator in the U.K. with 114 facilities; Grosvenor Casinos, which is the second largest casino operator in the U.K., with 35 facilities including two in Belgium; Top Rank Espana, which operates 11 bingo clubs in major cities across Spain; and Blue Square, which provides on-line distribution for Rank's retail gaming businesses, and Blue Square branded poker, sports betting and casino products. In March 2007, the company completed the sale of its Hard Rock business to Seminole Hard Rock Entertainment Inc. for approximately $965 million.

CONTACTS: *Note: Officers with more than one job title may be intentionally listed here more than once.*

Ian Burke, CEO
Peter Gill, Dir.-Finance
Christine Ray, Dir.-Group Human Resources
Pamela Coles, Corp. Sec.
Lesly Hughes, Head-PR
Dan Waugh, Dir.-Investor Rel.
Simon Wykes, Managing Dir.-Mecca Bingo
Cyril Drabinsky, Pres., Deluxe Film
Peter Johnson, Chmn.

Phone: 020-7706-1111	**Fax:** 020-7262-9886
Toll-Free:	
Address: 6 Connaught Pl., London, W2 2EZ UK	

FINANCIALS: Sales and profits are in thousands of dollars—add 000 to get the full amount. 2007 Note: Financial information for 2007 was not available for all companies at press time.

2007 Sales: $	2007 Profits: $	**U.S. Stock Ticker:**
2006 Sales: $1,076,200	2006 Profits: $233,000	**Int'l Ticker:** RNK　Int'l Exchange: London-LSE
2005 Sales: $1,408,887	2005 Profits: $-362,519	Employees: 19,002
2004 Sales: $1,369,418	2004 Profits: $-24,863	Fiscal Year Ends: 12/31
2003 Sales: $3,434,700	2003 Profits: $181,400	Parent Company:

SALARIES/BENEFITS:

Pension Plan: Y	ESOP Stock Plan:	Profit Sharing:	Top Exec. Salary: $998,648	Bonus: $
Savings Plan:	Stock Purch. Plan:		Second Exec. Salary: $712,761	Bonus: $

OTHER THOUGHTS:

Apparent Women Officers or Directors: 4
Hot Spot for Advancement for Women/Minorities: Y

LOCATIONS: ("Y" = Yes)

West:	Southwest:	Midwest:	Southeast:	Northeast:	International:
					Y

RAYCOM MEDIA INC
www.raycommedia.com

Industry Group Code: 513120 Ranks within this company's industry group: Sales: Profits:

Print Media/Publishing:	Movies:	Equipment/Supplies:		Broadcast/Cable:		Music/Audio:	Sports/Games/Gambling:	
Newspapers:	Movie Theaters:	Equipment/Supplies:		Broadcast TV:	Y	Music Production:	Games/Sports:	
Magazines:	Movie Production:	Gambling Equipment:		Cable TV:		Retail Music:	Retail Games Stores:	
Books:	TV/Video Prod.:	Special Services:	Y	Satellite Broadcast:		Retail Audio Equip.:	Stadiums/Teams:	Y
Book Stores:	Video Rental:	Advertising Services:	Y	Radio:		Music Print./Dist.:	Gambling/Casinos:	
Distribution/Printing:	Video Distribution:	Info. Sys. Software:	Y	Online Information:		Multimedia:	Rides/Theme Parks:	

TYPES OF BUSINESS:
Television Broadcasting
Golf Courses
Event Management
Postproduction Services
Telecommunications

BRANDS/DIVISIONS/AFFILIATES:
Raycom Sports
Raycom Post
CableVantage
Broadview Media
Liberty Corporation

CONTACTS: Note: Officers with more than one job title may be intentionally listed here more than once.
Paul McTear, CEO
Wayne Daugherty, COO/Exec. VP
Paul McTear, Pres.
Mellisa Thurber, CFO/VP
Anne Adkins, VP-Mktg.
Clyde Baucom, VP-Human Resources
Billy McDowell, VP-Research
David Folsom, CTO/VP
Rebecca Bryan, General Counsel/VP
Marty Edelman, VP-Television
Leon Long, VP-Television
Susana Schuler, VP-News
Mary C. McDonnell, Exec. VP-Programming

Phone: 334-206-1400	Fax: 334-206-1555
Toll-Free:	
Address: RSA Tower, Fl. 20, 201 Monroa St., Montgomery, AL 36104 US	

GROWTH PLANS/SPECIAL FEATURES:

Raycom Media, Inc., an employee-owned company, is one of the largest broadcasters in the U.S. It owns and/or operates 42 television stations in 18 states. 16 of the firm's stations are affiliated with NBC, eight with CBS, five with ABC, five with FOX, three with MyNetwork TV and two stations are affiliated with the CW. In addition to broadcasting, Raycom Media, through its subsidiary Raycom Sports, is involved in event management, information systems support and design and syndicated television programming; the subsidiary also hosts Alabama's Robert Trent Jones Golf Trail web site. Through Raycom Sports, the company owns and operates two LPGA Golf tournaments and the Continental Tire Bowl; and produces pre-season NFL football games. Raycom's subsidiary Raycom Post is a post production facility in Burbank, California. Subsidiary CableVantage is a cable advertising sales group located in Columbia, South Carolina. Finally, the company's Broadview Media subsidiary is a postproduction and telecommunications company. Through a partnership with Lincoln Financial Media, Raycom owns all marketing and television rights to Atlantic Coast Conference basketball.

Raycom Media offers its employees a 401(k) plan; flexible spending accounts; disability benefits; and medical, vision and dental insurance.

FINANCIALS: Sales and profits are in thousands of dollars—add 000 to get the full amount. 2007 Note: Financial information for 2007 was not available for all companies at press time.

2007 Sales: $	2007 Profits: $	U.S. Stock Ticker: Private
2006 Sales: $	2006 Profits: $	Int'l Ticker: Int'l Exchange:
2005 Sales: $	2005 Profits: $	Employees:
2004 Sales: $	2004 Profits: $	Fiscal Year Ends: 12/31
2003 Sales: $	2003 Profits: $	Parent Company:

SALARIES/BENEFITS:

Pension Plan:	ESOP Stock Plan:	Profit Sharing:	Top Exec. Salary: $	Bonus: $
Savings Plan: Y	Stock Purch. Plan:		Second Exec. Salary: $	Bonus: $

OTHER THOUGHTS:
Apparent Women Officers or Directors: 5
Hot Spot for Advancement for Women/Minorities: Y

LOCATIONS: ("Y" = Yes)

West:	Southwest:	Midwest:	Southeast:	Northeast:	International:
Y	Y	Y	Y	Y	

RCN CORP

www.rcn.com

Industry Group Code: 513300A Ranks within this company's industry group: Sales: 3 Profits: 3

Print Media/Publishing:	Movies:	Equipment/Supplies:	Broadcast/Cable:		Music/Audio:	Sports/Games/Gambling:
Newspapers:	Movie Theaters:	Equipment/Supplies:	Broadcast TV:		Music Production:	Games/Sports:
Magazines:	Movie Production:	Gambling Equipment:	Cable TV:	Y	Retail Music:	Retail Games Stores:
Books:	TV/Video Prod.:	Special Services:	Satellite Broadcast:		Retail Audio Equip.:	Stadiums/Teams:
Book Stores:	Video Rental:	Advertising Services:	Radio:		Music Print./Dist.:	Gambling/Casinos:
Distribution/Printing:	Video Distribution:	Info. Sys. Software:	Online Information:		Multimedia:	Rides/Theme Parks:

TYPES OF BUSINESS:

Local & Long-Distance Telephone Service
High-Speed Internet Access
Cable Television Service
Home Surveillance

BRANDS/DIVISIONS/AFFILIATES:

RCN Business Solutions
MegaModem
MegaModem Mach 20
WebWatch
Consolidated Edison Communications

CONTACTS: *Note: Officers with more than one job title may be intentionally listed here more than once.*

Peter D. Aquino, CEO
Michael T. Sicoli, CFO/Exec. VP
Benjamin R. Preston, General Counsel/Sr. VP/Sec.
Richard Ramlall, Sr. VP-Strategic & External Affairs
Leslie Sears, Controller/Sr. VP
John D. Filipowicz, Sr. VP-Residential Markets
P. K. Ramani, Sr. VP/Chief Svcs. Officer
James F. Mooney, Chmn.

Phone: 703-434-8200	**Fax:** 609-734-6164
Toll-Free: 800-746-4726	
Address: 196 Van Buren St., Ste. 300, Herndon, VA 20170 US	

GROWTH PLANS/SPECIAL FEATURES:

RCN Corp. is a facilities-based competitive provider of bundled cable TV, phone and high-speed Internet services delivered over the company's own advanced fiber-optic network. RCN has approximately 406,000 residential and small business customers in and around Boston, New York, eastern Philadelphia, Chicago and Washington, D.C. Subsidiary RCN Business Solutions provides bulk video, high capacity data and voice services in the same markets as RCN Corporation, but to Fortune 1000 and medium-sized business customers. RCN offers both digital-only and analog cable television service. The company is a residentially focused competitive local exchange carrier (CLEC), meaning that it is has independent access to phone numbers, can initiate and terminate calls anywhere in the U.S. or internationally, and provide 911 access to all voice customers by means of a traditional circuit-switched communications network. RCN's Megaband network provides a sophisticated broadband fiber-optic platform capable of offering an array of communications services, including voice, television and high-speed Internet. The network employs SONET ring backbone architecture and localized nodes to ensure RCN's fiber optics travel to within 900 feet of its customers, thereby providing lower maintenance costs than local networks. MegaModem Mach 20 is a high-speed Internet service that delivers data at 20 Mbps downstream and 2Mbps upstream. The company also offers WebWatch, a wireless home surveillance system accessible via the Internet. In March 2006, the firm acquired Consolidated Edison Communications, for $32 million, which now does business as RCN Business Solutions. In March 2007, the company sold its San Francisco, CA properties to Astound Broadband, LLC, a subsidiary of Wave Broadband LLC, for $45 million, and has decided to exit the San Francisco market. In June 2007, RCN agreed to acquire Neon Communications Group, Inc., a facilities-based wholesale communications provider that operates in the12-state Northeast and mid-Atlantic region, for up to $260 million.

FINANCIALS: Sales and profits are in thousands of dollars—add 000 to get the full amount. 2007 Note: Financial information for 2007 was not available for all companies at press time.

2007 Sales: $	2007 Profits: $	**U.S. Stock Ticker:** RCNI
2006 Sales: $585,476	2006 Profits: $-11,856	**Int'l Ticker:** Int'l Exchange:
2005 Sales: $530,412	2005 Profits: $-136,112	Employees: 1,800
2004 Sales: $486,861	2004 Profits: $1,006,156	Fiscal Year Ends: 12/31
2003 Sales: $484,900	2003 Profits: $-499,093	Parent Company:

SALARIES/BENEFITS:

Pension Plan:	ESOP Stock Plan:	Profit Sharing:	Top Exec. Salary: $540,000	Bonus: $330,480
Savings Plan:	Stock Purch. Plan:		Second Exec. Salary: $540,000	Bonus: $330,480

OTHER THOUGHTS:

Apparent Women Officers or Directors: 1
Hot Spot for Advancement for Women/Minorities:

LOCATIONS: ("Y" = Yes)

West:	Southwest:	Midwest:	Southeast:	Northeast:	International:
		Y		Y	

READER'S DIGEST ASSOCIATION INC   www.rd.com

Industry Group Code: 511120 Ranks within this company's industry group: Sales: 3   Profits: 7

Print Media/Publishing:		Movies:		Equipment/Supplies:		Broadcast/Cable:		Music/Audio:		Sports/Games/Gambling:	
Newspapers:		Movie Theaters:		Equipment/Supplies:		Broadcast TV:		Music Production:		Games/Sports:	
Magazines:	Y	Movie Production:		Gambling Equipment:		Cable TV:		Retail Music:		Retail Games Stores:	
Books:	Y	TV/Video Prod.:	Y	Special Services:		Satellite Broadcast:		Retail Audio Equip.:		Stadiums/Teams:	
Book Stores:		Video Rental:		Advertising Services:	Y	Radio:		Music Print./Dist.:	Y	Gambling/Casinos:	
Distribution/Printing:		Video Distribution:		Info. Sys. Software:	Y	Online Information:		Multimedia:		Rides/Theme Parks:	

TYPES OF BUSINESS:

Magazine Publishing
Book Publishing
Television & Video Production
Music Collections
Electronic Media
Direct Marketing
Online Sales

BRANDS/DIVISIONS/AFFILIATES:

Reader's Digest Magazine
QSP, Inc.
Every Day with Rachael Ray
Country Woman
American Woodworker
Family Handyman
Reader's Digest Select Editions
Allrecipes.com

CONTACTS: Note: Officers with more than one job title may be intentionally listed here more than once.

Mary Berner, CEO
Jean Clifton, CFO/Sr. VP
Lisa Cribari, VP-Global Human Resources
Jeffery S. Spar, CIO/VP
Albert L. Perruzza, Sr. VP-Global Oper.
William Adler, VP-Global Comm.
Eva Dillon, Pres. & Group Publisher-RD Large Print
Emma Lawson, Sr. VP-Global Mktg. & Publishing
Alyce Alston, Pres., Home & Garden/Pres., Health & Wellness
Michael A. Brennan, Pres., RD Europe
Harvey Golub, Chmn.
Paul Heath, Pres., RD Asia-Pacific

Phone: 914-238-1000	Fax: 914-238-4559
Toll-Free:	
Address: Reader's Digest Rd., Pleasantville, NY 10570-7000 US	

GROWTH PLANS/SPECIAL FEATURES:

Reader's Digest Association, Inc. publishes and markets magazines, books, music collections and home videos. Reader's Digest Magazine (the company's flagship monthly) consists of original and previously published articles in condensed form and condensed versions of current full-length books. Reader's Digest's worldwide circulation is 18 million, with 50 editions in 21 different languages distributed in over 60 countries, reaching nearly 100 million readers worldwide. The company also publishes specialty magazines (Family Handyman, Taste of Home and Every Day with Rachael Ray). In addition, the firm produces and distributes Reader's Digest Select Editions (formerly Condensed Books), general books, recorded music collections and home video products. The company's general books include: reference books; cookbooks; how-to and do-it-yourself books; and children's books. Other books pertain to subjects such as history, travel, religion, health, nature, home, computers and puzzles. Reader's Digest's music collections include about 10,000 titles across a broad range of musical styles, released as compilations on CDs and cassettes internationally. The company also sells home video products featuring travel, natural history, history and children's animated programs. Reader's Digest conducts marketing via direct mail, direct response television, telemarketing, catalogs, retail, online, and through the Books Are Fun display marketing campaign. The company's subsidiary QSP, Inc. coordinates book sales and magazine drives as fundraisers for schools. The company recently acquired Allrecipes.com for $66 million. In March 2007, the firm was acquired by Ripplewood Holdings LLC for $2.6 billion, thus returning the firm to private ownership for the first time in 17 years. Also in 2007, the firm launched publication in Romania, Slovenia and Croatia.

Readers Digest's employees receive health insurance, 401(k) plans, flexible spending accounts, tuition reimbursement and adoption assistance.

FINANCIALS: Sales and profits are in thousands of dollars—add 000 to get the full amount. 2007 Note: Financial information for 2007 was not available for all companies at press time.

2007 Sales: $	2007 Profits: $	**U.S. Stock Ticker: Private**
2006 Sales: $2,386,200	2006 Profits: $-117,400	**Int'l Ticker:** Int'l Exchange:
2005 Sales: $2,389,700	2005 Profits: $-90,900	Employees: 4,200
2004 Sales: $2,388,500	2004 Profits: $49,500	Fiscal Year Ends: 6/30
2003 Sales: $2,474,900	2003 Profits: $61,300	Parent Company:

SALARIES/BENEFITS:

Pension Plan: Y	ESOP Stock Plan: Y	Profit Sharing:	Top Exec. Salary: $819,505	Bonus: $550,000
Savings Plan: Y	Stock Purch. Plan: Y		Second Exec. Salary: $611,951	Bonus: $450,000

OTHER THOUGHTS:

Apparent Women Officers or Directors: 11
Hot Spot for Advancement for Women/Minorities: Y

LOCATIONS: ("Y" = Yes)

West:	Southwest:	Midwest:	Southeast:	Northeast:	International:
Y	Y	Y	Y	Y	Y

REALNETWORKS INC

www.realnetworks.com

Industry Group Code: 511209 Ranks within this company's industry group: Sales: 2 Profits: 1

Print Media/Publishing:	Movies:	Equipment/Supplies:	Broadcast/Cable:	Music/Audio:	Sports/Games/Gambling:	
Newspapers:	Movie Theaters:	Equipment/Supplies:	Broadcast TV:	Music Production:	Games/Sports:	Y
Magazines:	Movie Production:	Gambling Equipment:	Cable TV:	Retail Music:	Retail Games Stores:	
Books:	TV/Video Prod.:	Special Services:	Satellite Broadcast:	Retail Audio Equip.:	Stadiums/Teams:	
Book Stores:	Video Rental:	Advertising Services:	Radio:	Music Print./Dist.: Y	Gambling/Casinos:	
Distribution/Printing:	Video Distribution:	Info. Sys. Software:	Online Information:	Multimedia:	Rides/Theme Parks:	

TYPES OF BUSINESS:

Digital Media Services
Computer Software-Streaming Audio & Video
Online Retail-Digital Media
Mobile Games
Mobile Music
Mobile Video

BRANDS/DIVISIONS/AFFILIATES:

RealPlayer
RadioPass
Rhapsody
RealMusic
RealPlayer Music Store
SuperPass
SonyNetservices
Atrativa

CONTACTS: *Note: Officers with more than one job title may be intentionally listed here more than once.*

Robert Glaser, CEO
Michael Eggers, CFO/Sr. VP
Savino R. Ferrales, Sr. VP-Human Resources
Robert Kimball, General Counsel/Sec./Sr. VP-Legal & Bus. Affairs
Dan Sheeran, Sr. VP-Bus. Dev. & Corp. Partnerships
John Giamatteo, Exec. VP-Worldwide Bus. Prod. & Svcs.
Carla Stratfold, Sr. VP-North America Sales
Harold Zeitz, Sr. VP-Media Software & Svcs., Games Div.
Robert Glaser, Chmn.

Phone: 206-674-2700	Fax: 206-674-2699
Toll-Free:	
Address: 2601 Elliott Ave., Seattle, WA 98121 US	

GROWTH PLANS/SPECIAL FEATURES:

RealNetworks, Inc. is a creator of digital media services and software. The company operates in two segments: consumer products and services; and technology products and solutions. The consumer products and services segment consists of music services; media software and services; and games. The music services subdivision owns and manages a set of digital music products and services designed to provide consumers with broad access to digital music. Music services include Rhapsody, a membership based music service offering unlimited access to a catalog of millions of tracks; RadioPass, an Internet radio subscription services; and RealMusic, an offering to consumers outside the U.S. of Internet radio, music downloads, music news and other music content. The media software and services subdivision provides technology that facilitates the delivery and consumption of digital media over the Internet. Products include RealPlayer, which enables consumers to discover, play and manage audio and video programming on the Internet; and SuperPass, a subscription service that offers video and digital music and games content, commercial-free Internet radio stations, advanced CD burning and expanded features for the RealPlayer. The games subdivision owns and operates a casual digital games service that includes downloadable and online games products and subscription services focused primarily on gamers for personal computers (PCs) and mobile wireless platforms. RealNetworks develops original content for these services through the game studios Gamehouse, Mr. Goodliving, Ltd. and Zylom. The technology products and solutions segment develops and markets software products and services that enable media and communications companies to distribute digital media content to PCs, mobile phones and other non-PC devices. Through WiderThan Co., Ltd., the firm develops digital entertainment services for wireless carriers, such as ringback tones, music-on-demand and video-on-demand services. In 2007, RealNetworks acquired SonyNetservices and Atrativa.

FINANCIALS: Sales and profits are in thousands of dollars—add 000 to get the full amount. 2007 Note: Financial information for 2007 was not available for all companies at press time.

2007 Sales: $	2007 Profits: $	U.S. Stock Ticker: RNWK
2006 Sales: $395,261	2006 Profits: $145,216	Int'l Ticker: Int'l Exchange:
2005 Sales: $325,059	2005 Profits: $312,345	Employees: 1,594
2004 Sales: $266,719	2004 Profits: $-23,000	Fiscal Year Ends: 12/31
2003 Sales: $202,377	2003 Profits: $-21,500	Parent Company:

SALARIES/BENEFITS:

Pension Plan:	ESOP Stock Plan:	Profit Sharing:	Top Exec. Salary: $400,000	Bonus: $2,500,000
Savings Plan: Y	Stock Purch. Plan:		Second Exec. Salary: $350,000	Bonus: $735,725

OTHER THOUGHTS:

Apparent Women Officers or Directors: 2
Hot Spot for Advancement for Women/Minorities:

LOCATIONS: ("Y" = Yes)

West:	Southwest:	Midwest:	Southeast:	Northeast:	International:
Y					Y

REDBOX AUTOMATED RETAIL LLC   www.redbox.com

Industry Group Code: 532230 Ranks within this company's industry group: Sales: Profits:

Print Media/Publishing:	Movies:		Equipment/Supplies:	Broadcast/Cable:	Music/Audio:	Sports/Games/Gambling:
Newspapers:	Movie Theaters:		Equipment/Supplies:	Broadcast TV:	Music Production:	Games/Sports:
Magazines:	Movie Production:		Gambling Equipment:	Cable TV:	Retail Music:	Retail Games Stores:
Books:	TV/Video Prod.:		Special Services:	Satellite Broadcast:	Retail Audio Equip.:	Stadiums/Teams:
Book Stores:	Video Rental:	Y	Advertising Services:	Radio:	Music Print./Dist.:	Gambling/Casinos:
Distribution/Printing:	Video Distribution:		Info. Sys. Software:	Online Information:	Multimedia:	Rides/Theme Parks:

TYPES OF BUSINESS:

DVD Rentals

BRANDS/DIVISIONS/AFFILIATES:

Redbox
Coinstar, Inc.
McDonald's Corp.

CONTACTS: Note: Officers with more than one job title may be intentionally listed here more than once.

Gregg Kaplan, CEO
Greg Waring, Dir.-Mktg.
Matt Sheehan, VP-Bus. Dev. & Sales
Brian Rady, VP-Finance

Phone: 630-756-8000	Fax:
Toll-Free:	
Address: 1 Tower Ln., Ste. 1200, Oak Brook Terrace, IL 60181 US	

GROWTH PLANS/SPECIAL FEATURES:

Redbox Automated Retail LLC, headquartered in Illinois, is one of the largest retailers of DVDs in the U.S. The company vends DVDs through kiosks in locations such as McDonald's, Albertsons grocery stores and Stop & Shops. Currently, there are over 1,400 kiosks in McDonald's locations and more than 2,600 in grocery stores. Counting all locations, there are over 5,000 kiosks deployed. Wal-Mart is testing the kiosks in ten cities and Puerto Rico. With movies priced at $1 a day, the Kiosks average over 50 rentals a day. The kiosks offer only new releases, with between 100 and 120 titles, and hold 500 DVDs. Movies can also be rented online and picked up at Redbox locations. Customers can return the movies to any Redbox location. Titles are held for only five to six months, after which they are sold back to distributors. McDonald's Corp. has a 47% stake in the company with Coinstar, Inc. holding 47.3%. Over the next five years, the company plans to expand from its current 5,000 kiosks to over 10,000. By the end of 2007, it plans to have more locations than Blockbuster (approximately 5,000). It costs the firm roughly $16,000 to install a kiosk. In 2006, the firm rented over 21 million DVDs. The firm nearly doubled its presence in 2007, and will have rented 40 million by year's end. In recent news, the firm placed kiosks in Walgreens locations in Chicago and Houston. In October 2007, it announced plans to place kiosks in 33 Walgreens locations in Columbus, Ohio and 160 throughout Phoenix, Arizona. In 2007, the firm put 300 Redbox locations in convenience stores nationwide.

FINANCIALS: Sales and profits are in thousands of dollars—add 000 to get the full amount. 2007 Note: Financial information for 2007 was not available for all companies at press time.

2007 Sales: $	2007 Profits: $	**U.S. Stock Ticker: Joint Venture**
2006 Sales: $	2006 Profits: $	**Int'l Ticker:** Int'l Exchange:
2005 Sales: $	2005 Profits: $	Employees:
2004 Sales: $	2004 Profits: $	Fiscal Year Ends:
2003 Sales: $	2003 Profits: $	Parent Company:

SALARIES/BENEFITS:

Pension Plan:	ESOP Stock Plan:	Profit Sharing:	Top Exec. Salary: $	Bonus: $
Savings Plan:	Stock Purch. Plan:		Second Exec. Salary: $	Bonus: $

OTHER THOUGHTS:

Apparent Women Officers or Directors:
Hot Spot for Advancement for Women/Minorities:

LOCATIONS: ("Y" = Yes)

West:	Southwest:	Midwest:	Southeast:	Northeast:	International:
Y	Y	Y	Y	Y	Y

REED ELSEVIER GROUP PLC   www.reed-elsevier.com

Industry Group Code: 511140 Ranks within this company's industry group: Sales: 1   Profits: 1

Print Media/Publishing:		Movies:		Equipment/Supplies:		Broadcast/Cable:	Music/Audio:		Sports/Games/Gambling:	
Newspapers:		Movie Theaters:		Equipment/Supplies:		Broadcast TV:	Music Production:		Games/Sports:	
Magazines:	Y	Movie Production:		Gambling Equipment:		Cable TV:	Retail Music:		Retail Games Stores:	
Books:	Y	TV/Video Prod.:		Special Services:	Y	Satellite Broadcast:	Retail Audio Equip.:		Stadiums/Teams:	
Book Stores:		Video Rental:		Advertising Services:		Radio:	Music Print./Dist.:		Gambling/Casinos:	
Distribution/Printing:		Video Distribution:		Info. Sys. Software:		Online Information:	Multimedia:		Rides/Theme Parks:	

TYPES OF BUSINESS:

Online Information Publishing
Textbooks
Scientific Journals
Business Magazines
Legal Databases
Online Databases

BRANDS/DIVISIONS/AFFILIATES:

Elsevier Science & Technology
Elsevier Health Sciences
LexisNexis
Harcourt Group
Reed Business
LexisNexis International
Reed Exhibitions
Harcourt Education International

CONTACTS: *Note: Officers with more than one job title may be intentionally listed here more than once.*

Crispin Davis, CEO
Mark Armour, CFO
Ian Fraser, Dir.-Human Resources
Mark Popolano, CTO
Nick Baker, Chief Strategy Officer
Erik Engstrom, CEO-Elsevier
Gerard van de Aast, CEO-Reed Business
Andrew Prozes, CEO-LexisNexis Group
Patrick Tierney, CEO-Harcourt Education
Jan Hommen, Chmn.

Phone: 44-20-7930-7077	Fax: 44-20-7166-5799
Toll-Free:	
Address: 1-3 Strand, London, WC2N 5JR UK	

GROWTH PLANS/SPECIAL FEATURES:

Reed Elsevier Group plc provides students and professionals with valuable information in the fields of science, medicine, law, education and business, publishing more than 15,000 different journals, books and reference works. The firm also produces over 500 online information services. Elsevier Science and Technology publishes scientific and technical information through journals and books, in print and electronic media, including ScienceDirect, MDL, Academic Press, BioMedNet and Solid State Communications. Imprints of this segment include Elsevier, Academic Press and Butterworth Heinemann. Elsevier Health Sciences offers a broad range of journals, in both print and electronic media, serving healthcare researchers and practitioners. The segment operates under the Mosby, Churchill Livingstone, Excerpta Medica, Masson, Doyma, Netter and Saunders imprints. The LexisNexis unit maintains one of the largest databases in the world and is a leading online source for legal matters and public records, with additional resources for news and business information. This information is marketed to legal professionals, law firms, schools, corporations and governments. The segment is comprised of LexisNexis United States and LexisNexis International. The education division of the company, known as the Harcourt Group, is comprised of the Harcourt Education U.S. Schools and Testing businesses, which provide print and multimedia teaching and assessment materials; and Harcourt Education International, which provides educational content to students and teachers, principally in the U.K., Australia, New Zealand and southern Africa. The Reed Business is comprised of Reed Business Information, the business magazine, website and information businesses operating principally in the U.S., the U.K., Europe and Asia; and Reed Exhibitions, an international exhibition organizing business. The Reed Elsevier Group plc is equally owned by Reed Elsevier plc and Reed Elsevier NV. In December 2007, the firm sold the Harcourt Education U.S. Schools business to Houghton Mifflin Riverdeep Group for $4 billion.

FINANCIALS: Sales and profits are in thousands of dollars—add 000 to get the full amount. 2007 Note: Financial information for 2007 was not available for all companies at press time.

2007 Sales: $	2007 Profits: $	**U.S. Stock Ticker: Joint Venture**
2006 Sales: $10,570,400	2006 Profits: $1,223,900	**Int'l Ticker:** Int'l Exchange:
2005 Sales: $8,982,132	2005 Profits: $806,719	Employees: 36,800
2004 Sales: $8,366,240	2004 Profits: $801,459	Fiscal Year Ends: 12/31
2003 Sales: $8,756,200	2003 Profits: $593,800	Parent Company:

SALARIES/BENEFITS:

Pension Plan: Y	ESOP Stock Plan:	Profit Sharing:	Top Exec. Salary: $	Bonus: $54,000
Savings Plan: Y	Stock Purch. Plan:		Second Exec. Salary: $1,100,000	Bonus: $1,100,000

OTHER THOUGHTS:

Apparent Women Officers or Directors: 2
Hot Spot for Advancement for Women/Minorities:

LOCATIONS: ("Y" = Yes)

West:	Southwest:	Midwest:	Southeast:	Northeast:	International:
				Y	Y

REGAL ENTERTAINMENT GROUP www.regalcinemas.com

Industry Group Code: 512131 Ranks within this company's industry group: Sales: 1 Profits: 1

Print Media/Publishing:	Movies:		Equipment/Supplies:		Broadcast/Cable:	Music/Audio:	Sports/Games/Gambling:
Newspapers:	Movie Theaters:	Y	Equipment/Supplies:		Broadcast TV:	Music Production:	Games/Sports:
Magazines:	Movie Production:		Gambling Equipment:		Cable TV:	Retail Music:	Retail Games Stores:
Books:	TV/Video Prod.:		Special Services:	Y	Satellite Broadcast:	Retail Audio Equip.:	Stadiums/Teams:
Book Stores:	Video Rental:		Advertising Services:	Y	Radio:	Music Print./Dist.:	Gambling/Casinos:
Distribution/Printing:	Video Distribution:		Info. Sys. Software:		Online Information:	Multimedia:	Rides/Theme Parks:

TYPES OF BUSINESS:

Movie Theaters
In-Theater Advertising
Theater Rental & Special Events

BRANDS/DIVISIONS/AFFILIATES:

Regal Cinemas
United Artists Theaters
Hoyts Cinema
Edwards Theaters
National CineMedia
American Multi-Cinema, Inc.
Cinemark Media, Inc.
Regal Guest Response System

CONTACTS: *Note: Officers with more than one job title may be intentionally listed here more than once.*

Michael L. Campbell, CEO
Gregory W. Dunn, COO
Gregory W. Dunn, Pres.
Amy E. Miles, CFO/Exec.VP
Dick Westerling, Sr. VP-Mktg. & Advertising
Peter B. Brandow, General Counsel/Sec./Exec.VP
Donald De Laria, VP-Investor Rel.
Kurt C. Hall, Chmn./Pres./CEO, Nat'l CineMedia
Clifford E. Marks, Chief Mktg. Officer/Pres., Sales, Nat'l CineMedia
Gary W. Ferrara, CFO/Exec.VP, Nat'l CineMedia
Tom Galley, CTO/COO/Exec. VP, Nat'l CineMedia

Phone: 865-922-1123	**Fax:** 865-922-3188
Toll-Free: 800-784-8477	
Address: 7132 Regal Ln., Knoxville, TN 37918 US	

GROWTH PLANS/SPECIAL FEATURES:

Regal Entertainment Group (REG), through its subsidiaries, is one of the largest motion picture exhibitors in the world. The firm's nationwide network of theaters, including Regal Cinemas, United Artists Theaters, Hoyts Cinemas and Edwards Theaters, operates 6,355 screens in 526 locations in 39 states and Washington, D.C. Many of REG's screens are located in film licensing zones in which it is the sole exhibitor, providing the firm with access to all films distributed by major distributors and eliminating its need to compete with other exhibitors for films in that zone. Furthermore, REG operates theaters in 43 of the top 50 demographic market areas, drawing over 247 million annual attendees. Joint venture National CineMedia (NCM), a partnership with American Multi-Cinema, Inc. and Cinemark Media, Inc., offers ancillary services such Advertising; CineMeetings and Events; and Alternative In-Theater Programming, such as Regal First-Look, behind the scenes movie featurettes. NCM represents 12,000 screens in 1,100 theaters, representing 30% of U.S. screens. Advertising on theater screens and NCM activities accounted for approximately 6.7% of the firm's 2006 revenues; concessions, 26.8%; and admissions, 66.5%. In May 2007, firm announced that one of the new products, Regal Guest Response System (RGRS) was being utilized in 114 theaters. RGRS is a pager system given to select customers that alerts management of disturbances in the auditorium such as sound, picture, piracy or other problems. The company offers Real D 3D screens in 132 locations. In September 2006, the firm acquired four theaters and 58 screens in New York, Massachusetts, Texas, and Washington from AMC Entertainment, Inc. for $34.1 million in cash and two Regal theaters with 32 screens in Oklahoma and Arkansas.

REG offers corporate employees paid vacations, free movies and dental and medical insurance. Movie theater salaries vary based on location, with medical and dental insurance available for full-time salaried managers.

FINANCIALS: Sales and profits are in thousands of dollars—add 000 to get the full amount. 2007 Note: Financial information for 2007 was not available for all companies at press time.

2007 Sales: $	2007 Profits: $	**U.S. Stock Ticker: RGC**
2006 Sales: $2,598,100	2006 Profits: $86,300	**Int'l Ticker:** Int'l Exchange:
2005 Sales: $2,516,700	2005 Profits: $91,800	Employees: 24,049
2004 Sales: $2,468,000	2004 Profits: $82,500	Fiscal Year Ends: 12/31
2003 Sales: $2,489,900	2003 Profits: $185,400	Parent Company:

SALARIES/BENEFITS:

Pension Plan:	ESOP Stock Plan:	Profit Sharing:	Top Exec. Salary: $593,632	Bonus: $634,100
Savings Plan: Y	Stock Purch. Plan:		Second Exec. Salary: $403,077	Bonus: $345,000

OTHER THOUGHTS:

Apparent Women Officers or Directors: 1
Hot Spot for Advancement for Women/Minorities:

LOCATIONS: ("Y" = Yes)

West:	Southwest:	Midwest:	Southeast:	Northeast:	International:
Y	Y	Y	Y	Y	Y

REGENT COMMUNICATIONS INC
www.regentcomm.com

Industry Group Code: 513111 Ranks within this company's industry group: Sales: 12 Profits: 11

Print Media/Publishing:	Movies:	Equipment/Supplies:		Broadcast/Cable:	Music/Audio:	Sports/Games/Gambling:
Newspapers:	Movie Theaters:	Equipment/Supplies:		Broadcast TV:	Music Production:	Games/Sports:
Magazines:	Movie Production:	Gambling Equipment:		Cable TV:	Retail Music:	Retail Games Stores:
Books:	TV/Video Prod.:	Special Services:		Satellite Broadcast:	Retail Audio Equip.:	Stadiums/Teams:
Book Stores:	Video Rental:	Advertising Services:	Y	Radio:	Music Print./Dist.:	Gambling/Casinos:
Distribution/Printing:	Video Distribution:	Info. Sys. Software:		Online Information:	Multimedia:	Rides/Theme Parks:

TYPES OF BUSINESS:
Radio Broadcasting

BRANDS/DIVISIONS/AFFILIATES:

CONTACTS: Note: Officers with more than one job title may be intentionally listed here more than once.
William L. Stakelin, CEO
William L. Stakelin, Pres.
Anthony Vasconcellos, CFO/Exec. VP
Larry Downes, VP-Tech. & Digital Media
David J. Remund, VP-Eng.
Fred L. Murr, Sr. VP-Oper.
Robert Allen, Jr., VP-Finance & Acct.
Robert J. Ausfeld, VP-Regional
Matthew A. Yeoman, VP-Oper.
Robert A. Moody, VP-Programming
Michael J. Grimsley, VP-Regional
William P. Sutter, Jr., Chmn.

Phone: 513-651-1190	Fax: 513-651-1195

Toll-Free:

Address: 2000 5th 3rd Ctr., 511 Walnut St., Cincinnati, OH 45202 US

GROWTH PLANS/SPECIAL FEATURES:
Regent Communications, Inc. is a radio broadcasting company focused on acquiring, developing and operating radio stations in mid-size markets. It currently owns 51 FM and 17 AM radio stations in 14 markets in Colorado, Illinois, Indiana, Kentucky, Louisiana, Michigan, Minnesota, New York and Texas. The company offers a variety of programming that ranges from adult contemporary music to news talk programs and country music. The firm depends almost solely on advertising revenues, which consisted of 85% of net sales in 2006. Regent's primary expansion strategy is to focus on the acquisition of radio stations in small and mid-sized markets, where reduced competition facilitates the purchase of stations for sale. Ownership of multiple stations in the same market places the company in a better position to grow steadily and encompass a broader range of demographic groups, a strategy aimed at raising advertising revenues. Furthermore, this makes the firm less susceptible to economic downturns due to advertising revenues being localized. In early 2007, Regent acquired WBZZ-FM (formerly WNYQ-FM) in Albany, New York from Vox New York, LLC for about $5 million. In October 2007, the company agreed to sells four radio stations serving the Watertown, New York market to KXOJ, Inc. for roughly $6.2 million. The cluster includes the WRFY-FM, WCIZ-FM, WTNY-AM and WNER-AM.

FINANCIALS: Sales and profits are in thousands of dollars—add 000 to get the full amount. 2007 Note: Financial information for 2007 was not available for all companies at press time.

2007 Sales: $	2007 Profits: $	U.S. Stock Ticker: RGCI
2006 Sales: $85,033	2006 Profits: $-26,597	Int'l Ticker: Int'l Exchange:
2005 Sales: $78,800	2005 Profits: $-6,639	Employees: 880
2004 Sales: $84,187	2004 Profits: $13,235	Fiscal Year Ends: 12/31
2003 Sales: $80,578	2003 Profits: $5,706	Parent Company:

SALARIES/BENEFITS:

Pension Plan:	ESOP Stock Plan:	Profit Sharing:	Top Exec. Salary: $341,397	Bonus: $218,494
Savings Plan:	Stock Purch. Plan:		Second Exec. Salary: $258,500	Bonus: $165,440

OTHER THOUGHTS:
Apparent Women Officers or Directors:
Hot Spot for Advancement for Women/Minorities:

LOCATIONS: ("Y" = Yes)

West:	Southwest:	Midwest:	Southeast:	Northeast:	International:
Y	Y	Y	Y	Y	

RENAISSANCE ENTERTAINMENT CORP   www.recfair.com

Industry Group Code: 711310 Ranks within this company's industry group: Sales: Profits:

Print Media/Publishing:	Movies:	Equipment/Supplies:		Broadcast/Cable:	Music/Audio:	Sports/Games/Gambling:	
Newspapers:	Movie Theaters:	Equipment/Supplies:		Broadcast TV:	Music Production:	Games/Sports:	Y
Magazines:	Movie Production:	Gambling Equipment:		Cable TV:	Retail Music:	Retail Games Stores:	
Books:	TV/Video Prod.:	Special Services:	Y	Satellite Broadcast:	Retail Audio Equip.:	Stadiums/Teams:	
Book Stores:	Video Rental:	Advertising Services:		Radio:	Music Print./Dist.:	Gambling/Casinos:	
Distribution/Printing:	Video Distribution:	Info. Sys. Software:		Online Information:	Multimedia:	Rides/Theme Parks:	

TYPES OF BUSINESS:

Renaissance Entertainment Parks
Food & Beverages
Halloween Events
Skiing Facilities

BRANDS/DIVISIONS/AFFILIATES:

Bristol Renaissance Faire
Southern California Renaissance Pleasure Faire
New York Renaissance Faire
Forest of Fear
Ski Sterling Forest

CONTACTS: *Note: Officers with more than one job title may be intentionally listed here more than once.*

Charles S. Leavell, CEO
J. Stanley Gilbert, COO
J. Stanley Gilbert, Pres.
Charles S. Leavell, CFO

Phone: 303-664-0300	Fax: 303-664-0303
Toll-Free:	
Address: 275 Century Cir., Ste. 102, Louisville, CO 80027 US	

GROWTH PLANS/SPECIAL FEATURES:

Renaissance Entertainment Corp. (REC) owns and operates Renaissance fairs in the U.S. The company's fairs include the New York Renaissance Faire; the Bristol Faire in Kenosha, Wisconsin; and the Southern California Renaissance Pleasure Faire in Irwindale, California. All of the company's Renaissance fairs are outdoor family entertainment events that romanticize the ambiance of a Renaissance-era marketplace. These marketplaces include craft shops, period food, dancers, jousters, musicians and historical characters from Elizabethan England. The fairs run from 6-8 weekends, all day long, with comedies and dramas enacted on multiple stages and minstrels and troubadors that walk about singing and dancing. More than 100 foods and desserts are offered, including shepherd's pie, roasted turkey legs, crepes and strawberries and cream. Each year, the fairs bring in approximately 700,000 people. During the winter months, the firm operates a ski resort in New York called Ski Sterling Forest. For Halloween, the New York fair site is turned into the Forest of Fear, a haunted house with various Halloween-inspired games, such as an axe toss, as well as various attractions such as Circus of the Damned and the Slaughter House. The firm's major sponsors have included Anheuser-Busch, Miller Brewing Co., Aquafina Water, Hard Core Cider, Red Hook Ale, Andis Systems, Pepsi Cola Co., Grand Pacific Resorts, Canandaigua Wines, Samuel Adams and Guinness Import Co.

Renaissance Entertainment offers its employees seasonal and weekend employment opportunities with flexible schedules and complimentary tickets. Most positions require some acting skills and the willingness to dress in period clothing.

FINANCIALS: Sales and profits are in thousands of dollars—add 000 to get the full amount. 2007 Note: Financial information for 2007 was not available for all companies at press time.

2007 Sales: $	2007 Profits: $	U.S. Stock Ticker: Private
2006 Sales: $	2006 Profits: $	Int'l Ticker: Int'l Exchange:
2005 Sales: $	2005 Profits: $	Employees: 36
2004 Sales: $	2004 Profits: $	Fiscal Year Ends: 12/31
2003 Sales: $	2003 Profits: $	Parent Company:

SALARIES/BENEFITS:

Pension Plan:	ESOP Stock Plan:	Profit Sharing:	Top Exec. Salary: $160,000	Bonus: $
Savings Plan:	Stock Purch. Plan:		Second Exec. Salary: $120,000	Bonus: $

OTHER THOUGHTS:

Apparent Women Officers or Directors: 2
Hot Spot for Advancement for Women/Minorities:

LOCATIONS: ("Y" = Yes)

West:	Southwest:	Midwest:	Southeast:	Northeast:	International:
Y		Y		Y	

RENTRAK CORP

www.rentrak.com

Industry Group Code: 512110 Ranks within this company's industry group: Sales: 10   Profits: 6

Print Media/Publishing:	Movies:		Equipment/Supplies:		Broadcast/Cable:	Music/Audio:	Sports/Games/Gambling:
Newspapers:	Movie Theaters:		Equipment/Supplies:		Broadcast TV:	Music Production:	Games/Sports:
Magazines:	Movie Production:		Gambling Equipment:		Cable TV:	Retail Music:	Retail Games Stores:
Books:	TV/Video Prod.:		Special Services:	Y	Satellite Broadcast:	Retail Audio Equip.:	Stadiums/Teams:
Book Stores:	Video Rental:		Advertising Services:	Y	Radio:	Music Print./Dist.:	Gambling/Casinos:
Distribution/Printing:	Video Distribution:	Y	Info. Sys. Software:		Online Information:	Multimedia:	Rides/Theme Parks:

TYPES OF BUSINESS:

Video Distribution
Online Services
Software Development

BRANDS/DIVISIONS/AFFILIATES:

formovies.com
Box Office Essentials
Supply Chain Essentials
Retail Essentials
Home Video Essentials
OnDemand Essentials
Essentials Suite

CONTACTS: *Note: Officers with more than one job title may be intentionally listed here more than once.*

Paul A. Rosenbaum, CEO
Kenneth Papagan, Pres.
Mark Thoenes, CFO/Exec. VP
Christopher Roberts, Sr. VP-Sales & Mktg.
Amir Yazdani, CIO/Exec. VP-IT
Kenneth Papagan, Chief Strategy Officer
Cathy Hetzel, Pres., AMI Div.
Marty Graham, Pres., PPT Div.
Rom Giambra, Sr. VP-Theatrical, AMI Div.
Timothy Erwin, VP-Sales & Customer Rel., PPT Div.
Paul A. Rosenbaum, Chmn.

Phone: 503-284-7581	Fax: 503-331-2734
Toll-Free:	
Address: 1 Airport Ctr., 7700 NE Ambassador Pl., Portland, OR 97220 US	

GROWTH PLANS/SPECIAL FEATURES:

Rentrak Corp. is a video distribution company that operates in two business divisions: pay-per-transaction (PPT) and advanced media and information (AMI). The PPT division focuses on managing business operations that facilitate the delivery of home entertainment content products and related rental and sales information for that content to home video specialty stores and other retailers throughout the U.S. and Canada. Through this division, the company tracks sales and rental information of DVDs, VHS tapes and videogames which have been subleased or sublicensed to retailers. In addition, the PPT division offers retailers Rentrak Profit Maker Software and Video Retailer Essentials Software which allows retailers to order new products through Point of Sale systems. This division also operates formovies.com, a web site that helps customers find local video stores and research the titles carried by those stores. The AMI segment concentrates on the management and growth of the Essentials Suite of business intelligence services as well as operating direct revenue sharing services and the Essentials Suite of software and services. As part of the Essentials Suite, the company offers Box Office Essentials, which reports domestic and international theatrical gross receipt ticket sales to motion picture studios and movie theater owners; Home Video Essentials, which measures rentals from both retailers and online channels; OnDemand Essentials, which measures viewership of on demand content in the cable and broadband industries; Retail Essentials, which reports DVD, VHS and video game sales; and Supply Chain Essentials, for managing the flow of products and funds at every point in the supply chain until the product reaches the consumer.

FINANCIALS: Sales and profits are in thousands of dollars—add 000 to get the full amount. 2007 Note: Financial information for 2007 was not available for all companies at press time.

2007 Sales: $105,998	2007 Profits: $6,048	U.S. Stock Ticker: RENT
2006 Sales: $93,394	2006 Profits: $4,466	Int'l Ticker: Int'l Exchange:
2005 Sales: $98,538	2005 Profits: $5,242	Employees: 245
2004 Sales: $78,132	2004 Profits: $1,310	Fiscal Year Ends: 3/31
2003 Sales: $86,200	2003 Profits: $- 500	Parent Company:

SALARIES/BENEFITS:

Pension Plan:	ESOP Stock Plan:	Profit Sharing:	Top Exec. Salary: $446,721	Bonus: $52,000
Savings Plan: Y	Stock Purch. Plan:		Second Exec. Salary: $300,000	Bonus: $45,518

OTHER THOUGHTS:

Apparent Women Officers or Directors: 2
Hot Spot for Advancement for Women/Minorities:

LOCATIONS: ("Y" = Yes)

West:	Southwest:	Midwest:	Southeast:	Northeast:	International:
Y					Y

REUTERS GROUP PLC

www.reuters.com

Industry Group Code: 514100 Ranks within this company's industry group: Sales: 1 Profits: 2

Print Media/Publishing:	Movies:	Equipment/Supplies:	Broadcast/Cable:	Music/Audio:	Sports/Games/Gambling:
Newspapers:	Movie Theaters:	Equipment/Supplies:	Broadcast TV:	Music Production:	Games/Sports:
Magazines: Y	Movie Production:	Gambling Equipment:	Cable TV:	Retail Music:	Retail Games Stores:
Books: Y	TV/Video Prod.:	Special Services:	Satellite Broadcast:	Retail Audio Equip.:	Stadiums/Teams:
Book Stores:	Video Rental:	Advertising Services: Y	Radio:	Music Print./Dist.:	Gambling/Casinos:
Distribution/Printing:	Video Distribution:	Info. Sys. Software: Y	Online Information:	Multimedia:	Rides/Theme Parks:

TYPES OF BUSINESS:

Financial Information
Online Information Publishing
Online Stock Trading
Market Research Distribution
Stock Market Data
Multimedia News Agency

BRANDS/DIVISIONS/AFFILIATES:

Reuters Investor
Reuters Trade Access
Bridge Information Systems
Reuters Foundation

CONTACTS: Note: Officers with more than one job title may be intentionally listed here more than once.

Thomas Glocer, CEO
Devin Wenig, COO
David J. Grigson, CFO
Lee Ann Daly, Chief Mktg. Officer
Stephen Dando, Group Dir.-Human Resources
David Lister, CIO
Roy Lowrance, CTO
Rosemary Martin, General Counsel/Company Sec.
John Alcantara, Global Head-Service Oper.
David Craig, Group Dir.-Strategy
Ed Williams, Dir.-Corp. Affairs
Miriam McKay, Global Head-Investor Rel.
Jon Robson, Pres., Americas
David Schlesinger, Editor-in-Chief
Alexander Hungate, Managing Dir.-Asia
Christopher Hagman, Managing Dir.-Global Sales & Svcs. Oper.
Niall FitzGerald, Chmn.
Joerg Floeck, Managing Dir.-EMEA

Phone: 44-20-7250-1122	**Fax:** 44-20-7542-4064
Toll-Free: 800-435-0101	
Address: 85 Fleet St., 77th Fl., London, EC4P 4AJ UK	

GROWTH PLANS/SPECIAL FEATURES:

Reuters Group plc provides news and business updates through a variety of media, including online forums, direct data feed, a magazine and books. It is one of the world's largest international multimedia news agencies, supplying news in the form of text, graphics, video and pictures to media organizations across the globe. The company's core product is an online trading, real-time market data and news system sold on subscription to professionals in corporate, financial and media offices. It competes against Bloomberg in this sector. These sales and trading subscriptions are sold worldwide at about $545 per month, with approximately 370,000 current subscribers. Reuters subscriptions include financial analysis tools that can assist traders and asset managers with investment decisions. Other financial products include Reuters Investor, previously known as Multex, which provides access to market research and stock analysis via online sales of individual reports. Reuters also has a hosted version of its Reuters Trade Access platform for North America, a cross-asset online portfolio valuation and interactive real-time position keeping system. The company will initially provide the platform to the hedge fund market. Its other information feeds and tools include enterprise products designed to help customers automate their business, including trading room and data software; research and asset management products, providing analysis and information to assist customers in making investment decisions; and media products, including its multimedia web sites and other news agencies. Sales and trading contributed 65.9% of Reuters' 2006 revenue; enterprise products, 15.9%; research and asset management, 11.6%; and media, 6.6%. In December 2006, Reuters sold the majority of its 50% stake in Factiva to joint-venture partner Dow Jones for roughly $178 million. In May 2007, Reuters began merger talks with Thomson Corporation. If the agreement is approved, Reuters will be acquired by Thomson for $17.5 billion, and the new company will be called Thomson-Reuters.

FINANCIALS: Sales and profits are in thousands of dollars—add 000 to get the full amount. 2007 Note: Financial information for 2007 was not available for all companies at press time.

2007 Sales: $	2007 Profits: $	**U.S. Stock Ticker: RTRSY**
2006 Sales: $5,027,000	2006 Profits: $597,500	**Int'l Ticker: RTR** Int'l Exchange: London-LSE
2005 Sales: $4,189,700	2005 Profits: $838,391	Employees: 16,302
2004 Sales: $4,068,480	2004 Profits: $652,215	Fiscal Year Ends: 12/31
2003 Sales: $5,683,400	2003 Profits: $87,844	Parent Company:

SALARIES/BENEFITS:

Pension Plan:	ESOP Stock Plan:	Profit Sharing:	Top Exec. Salary: $1,708,380	Bonus: $2,331,400
Savings Plan:	Stock Purch. Plan:		Second Exec. Salary: $951,580	Bonus: $1,083,523

OTHER THOUGHTS:

Apparent Women Officers or Directors: 4
Hot Spot for Advancement for Women/Minorities: Y

LOCATIONS: ("Y" = Yes)

West:	Southwest:	Midwest:	Southeast:	Northeast:	International:
				Y	Y

Note: Financial information, benefits and other data can change quickly and may vary from those stated here.

REX STORES CORP

www.rextv.com

Industry Group Code: 443110　Ranks within this company's industry group:　Sales: 5　Profits: 4

Print Media/Publishing:	Movies:	Equipment/Supplies:	Broadcast/Cable:	Music/Audio:		Sports/Games/Gambling:
Newspapers:	Movie Theaters:	Equipment/Supplies:	Broadcast TV:	Music Production:		Games/Sports:
Magazines:	Movie Production:	Gambling Equipment:	Cable TV:	Retail Music:		Retail Games Stores:
Books:	TV/Video Prod.:	Special Services:	Satellite Broadcast:	Retail Audio Equip.:	Y	Stadiums/Teams:
Book Stores:	Video Rental:	Advertising Services:	Radio:	Music Print./Dist.:		Gambling/Casinos:
Distribution/Printing:	Video Distribution:	Info. Sys. Software:	Online Information:	Multimedia:		Rides/Theme Parks:

TYPES OF BUSINESS:

Electronics Stores
Appliances
Furniture
Online Sales

BRANDS/DIVISIONS/AFFILIATES:

rexstores.com
Leyelland/Hockley County Ethanol LLC
Big River Resources LLC
Millennium Ethanol LLC
Patriot Renewable Fuels LLC
One Earth Energy LLC

CONTACTS: *Note: Officers with more than one job title may be intentionally listed here more than once.*

Stuart A. Rose, CEO
David L. Bearden, COO
David L. Bearden, Pres.
Douglas L. Bruggeman, CFO/VP-Finance
David Fuchs, VP-Mgmt. Info. Systems
Edward M. Kress, Corp. Sec.
Keith B. Magby, VP-Oper.
Douglas L. Bruggeman, Treas.
Philip J. Kellar, VP-Store Oper.
Zafar A. Rizvi, VP
Stuart A. Rose, Chmn.

Phone: 937-276-3931	Fax: 937-276-8643
Toll-Free:	
Address: 2875 Needmore Rd., Dayton, OH 45414 US	

GROWTH PLANS/SPECIAL FEATURES:

REX Stores Corp. is a specialty retailer in the consumer electronics and appliance industry. The firm operates 183 stores in 35 states, serving over 200 small- and medium-sized towns with populations between 20,000 and 300,000. REX stores offer a broad selection of brand-name products within selected major product categories, including big-screen and standard-sized televisions; audio and video equipment, such as VCRs, DVD players, stereos, camcorders and radios; ready-to-assemble furniture; and major household appliances, such as air conditioners, microwaves, washers, dryers and refrigerators. REX also provides extended service contracts. Leading brands sold by the firm include Frigidaire, Hitachi, JVC, Panasonic, Philips Magnavox, RCA, Sharp, Sony, Toshiba and Whirlpool. In total, the company sells approximately 1,200 products produced by nearly 60 manufacturers. Stores are supplied by three large regional distribution centers in Ohio, Wyoming and Florida. The company often offers customers special sales through its retail stores and e-commerce site, rexstores.com. Advertisements are primarily concentrated in newspapers, with additional television and radio marketing strategies in select markets with populations under 85,000. The firm's strategy involves continuing to open stores in small- to medium-sized markets. It plans to focus on markets with a newspaper circulation that can efficiently and cost-effectively utilize print advertising materials. In 2006, REX closed its Galesburg, Illinois store. Also in 2006, Rex made a move to invest heavily in the ethanol business to diversify its earnings. The company invested enough in Leyelland/Hockley County Ethanol LLC to gain a majority ownership interest. In addition, Rex has taken a minority ownership interest in Big River Resources LLC, Millennium Ethanol LLC, Patriot Renewable Fuels LLC and One Earth Energy LLC.

FINANCIALS: Sales and profits are in thousands of dollars—add 000 to get the full amount. 2007 Note: Financial information for 2007 was not available for all companies at press time.

2007 Sales: $347,334	2007 Profits: $11,351	U.S. Stock Ticker: RSC
2006 Sales: $374,451	2006 Profits: $28,269	Int'l Ticker:　　Int'l Exchange:
2005 Sales: $358,098	2005 Profits: $27,549	Employees:　818
2004 Sales: $392,476	2004 Profits: $27,440	Fiscal Year Ends: 1/31
2003 Sales: $428,600	2003 Profits: $22,900	Parent Company:

SALARIES/BENEFITS:

Pension Plan:	ESOP Stock Plan:	Profit Sharing:	Top Exec. Salary: $229,100	Bonus: $24,539
Savings Plan:	Stock Purch. Plan:		Second Exec. Salary: $200,000	Bonus: $54,920

OTHER THOUGHTS:

Apparent Women Officers or Directors:
Hot Spot for Advancement for Women/Minorities:

LOCATIONS: ("Y" = Yes)

West:	Southwest:	Midwest:	Southeast:	Northeast:	International:
Y	Y	Y	Y	Y	

RIVIERA HOLDINGS CORP

www.theriviera.com

Industry Group Code: 721120 Ranks within this company's industry group: Sales: 11 Profits: 11

Print Media/Publishing:	Movies:	Equipment/Supplies:	Broadcast/Cable:	Music/Audio:	Sports/Games/Gambling:	
Newspapers:	Movie Theaters:	Equipment/Supplies:	Broadcast TV:	Music Production:	Games/Sports:	
Magazines:	Movie Production:	Gambling Equipment:	Cable TV:	Retail Music:	Retail Games Stores:	
Books:	TV/Video Prod.:	Special Services:	Satellite Broadcast:	Retail Audio Equip.:	Stadiums/Teams:	Y
Book Stores:	Video Rental:	Advertising Services:	Radio:	Music Print./Dist.:	Gambling/Casinos:	
Distribution/Printing:	Video Distribution:	Info. Sys. Software:	Online Information:	Multimedia:	Rides/Theme Parks:	

TYPES OF BUSINESS:

Casino Hotel
Casino Management

BRANDS/DIVISIONS/AFFILIATES:

Riviera Hotel and Casino
Black Hawk Casino
Riviera Operating Corporation
An Evening at La Cage
Splash
Player's Club
Crazy Girls

CONTACTS: Note: Officers with more than one job title may be intentionally listed here more than once.

William L. Westerman, CEO
William L. Westerman, Pres.
Mark B. Lefever, CFO
Tullio J. Marchionne, General Counsel/Exec. VP
Duane R. Krohn, Exec. VP-Finance/Treas.
Ronald P. Johnson, Exec. VP-Gaming, Riviera Operating Corp.
Jerome P. Grippe, Exec. VP-Oper., Riviera Operating Corp.
Robert A. Vannucci, COO/Pres., Riviera Operating Corp.
William L. Westerman, Chmn.

Phone: 702-734-5110	**Fax:** 702-794-9663
Toll-Free: 800-634-3420	
Address: 2901 Las Vegas Blvd. S., Las Vegas, NV 89109 US	

GROWTH PLANS/SPECIAL FEATURES:

Riviera Holdings Corp., through its wholly owned subsidiary Riviera Operating Corporation, owns and operates the Riviera Hotel and Casino, located on Las Vegas Boulevard in Las Vegas, Nevada. It also owns and operates the Riviera Black Hawk Casino through its wholly owned subsidiary Riviera Black Hawk, Inc., a limited-stakes casino located in Black Hawk, Colorado. The Riviera opened in 1955 and has a reputation for delivering high-quality, traditional Las Vegas-style gaming, entertainment and other amenities. The casino has 110,000 square feet of gaming space with approximately 1,150 slot machines and 40 gaming tables, including blackjack, craps, roulette and poker. It also features 160,000 square feet of convention, meeting and banquet space. The Riviera offers live entertainment shows, such as An Evening at La Cage, a female impersonation show; Crazy Girls, an adult revue; and Splash, a variety show. Black Hawk Casino, located about 40 miles west of Denver, is one of the largest full-service casinos in Colorado. The Player's Club program, in addition to rewarding frequent players, collects data about its members, which the company uses to customize promotions to attract repeat visitors. Through the company's web site, travelers to Las Vegas can book rooms, buy souvenirs, check Player's Club point balances and make other reservations before their trip. The company continues to explore the possibility of development of an approximately 60,000-square-foot entertainment complex to be constructed directly over the casino, which could contain specialty themed entertainment that would appeal to the main target audience, adults age 45 to 65. The exit of this complex would deliver patrons directly to the casino. It is also exploring several options for the development of its existing 26-acre site, including a joint venture for the development of a condominium, time-share or an additional hotel tower and parking garage.

FINANCIALS: Sales and profits are in thousands of dollars—add 000 to get the full amount. 2007 Note: Financial information for 2007 was not available for all companies at press time.

2007 Sales: $	2007 Profits: $	**U.S. Stock Ticker:** RIV
2006 Sales: $200,944	2006 Profits: $- 335	**Int'l Ticker:** **Int'l Exchange:**
2005 Sales: $202,227	2005 Profits: $-3,999	Employees: 1,500
2004 Sales: $201,350	2004 Profits: $-2,086	Fiscal Year Ends: 6/30
2003 Sales: $190,200	2003 Profits: $-14,453	Parent Company:

SALARIES/BENEFITS:

Pension Plan:	ESOP Stock Plan: Y	Profit Sharing:	Top Exec. Salary: $1,000,000	Bonus: $
Savings Plan: Y	Stock Purch. Plan:		Second Exec. Salary: $300,000	Bonus: $114,000

OTHER THOUGHTS:

Apparent Women Officers or Directors:
Hot Spot for Advancement for Women/Minorities:

LOCATIONS: ("Y" = Yes)

West:	Southwest:	Midwest:	Southeast:	Northeast:	International:
Y					

RODALE INC

www.rodale.com

Industry Group Code: 511120 Ranks within this company's industry group: Sales: Profits:

Print Media/Publishing:		Movies:		Equipment/Supplies:		Broadcast/Cable:		Music/Audio:		Sports/Games/Gambling:	
Newspapers:		Movie Theaters:		Equipment/Supplies:		Broadcast TV:		Music Production:		Games/Sports:	
Magazines:	Y	Movie Production:		Gambling Equipment:		Cable TV:		Retail Music:		Retail Games Stores:	
Books:	Y	TV/Video Prod.:		Special Services:		Satellite Broadcast:		Retail Audio Equip.:		Stadiums/Teams:	
Book Stores:		Video Rental:		Advertising Services:		Radio:		Music Print./Dist.:		Gambling/Casinos:	
Distribution/Printing:		Video Distribution:		Info. Sys. Software:		Online Information:		Multimedia:		Rides/Theme Parks:	

TYPES OF BUSINESS:

Magazine Publishing
Book Publishing
Online Publishing

BRANDS/DIVISIONS/AFFILIATES:

Prevention
Women's Health
Runner's World
Organic Gardening
Mountain Bike
South Beach Diet
An Inconvenient Truth
FrenchWomenDontGetFat.com

CONTACTS: *Note: Officers with more than one job title may be intentionally listed here more than once.*

Steve Murphy, CEO
Steve Murphy, Pres.
Lester Rackoff, CFO/Sr. VP
Bill Ostroff, Chief Mktg. Officer
Paul McGinley, General Counsel
Mia Carbonell, Sr. VP-Corp. Comm.
Ardath Rodale, Chief Inspiration Officer
Bill Ostroff, Pres., Rodale Interactive
MaryAnn Bekkedahl, Exec. VP/Group Publisher-Rodale Magazines
Liz Perl, VP/Publisher-Rodale Trade Books
Maria Rodale, Chmn.

Phone: 610-967-5171	Fax: 610-967-8963
Toll-Free:	
Address: 33 E. Minor St., Emmaus, PA 18098 US	

GROWTH PLANS/SPECIAL FEATURES:

Rodale, Inc. publishes magazines and books related to health and lifestyles. It reaches more than 70 million people worldwide through its media properties, subscription online properties, trade books and integrated market solutions. The company is also active in direct-response marketing and has more than 26 million customers in its database. The firm's portfolio of magazines includes Prevention, Women's Health, Runner's World, Organic Gardening, Mountain Bike, Bicycling, Best Life, Runner's World and Running Times. Rodale maintains a web site for each magazine. As a major independent U.S. book publisher, the company also publishes about 100 books a year, including the popular South Beach Diet, Al Gore's An Inconvenient Truth and Martha Stewart's The Martha Rules. The firm's book publications include memoirs, biographies, narrative nonfiction, self-help, science and nature, psychology, current events and personal finance. Media products include BiggestLoserClub.com, Bob Greene's TheBestLife.com and FrenchWomenDontGetFat.com. Rodale's products reach costumers through retail and direct response channels, and its products span multiple media platforms and formats, including video, print and Internet. Rodale International has a presence in more than 40 countries with 76 editions. International magazine publications include Men's Health, Prevention, Best Life and Runner's World.

The company offers its employees medical, alternative medicine, dental and vision coverage; short- and long-term disability plans; life and AD&D insurance; a retirement and savings plan; flexible spending accounts; tuition reimbursement; an employee assistance program; a college savings plan; and critical illness insurance.

FINANCIALS: Sales and profits are in thousands of dollars—add 000 to get the full amount. 2007 Note: Financial information for 2007 was not available for all companies at press time.

2007 Sales: $	2007 Profits: $	U.S. Stock Ticker: Private
2006 Sales: $	2006 Profits: $	Int'l Ticker: Int'l Exchange:
2005 Sales: $500,000	2005 Profits: $	Employees: 950
2004 Sales: $	2004 Profits: $	Fiscal Year Ends: 12/31
2003 Sales: $	2003 Profits: $	Parent Company:

SALARIES/BENEFITS:

Pension Plan: Y	ESOP Stock Plan:	Profit Sharing:	Top Exec. Salary: $	Bonus: $
Savings Plan: Y	Stock Purch. Plan:		Second Exec. Salary: $	Bonus: $

OTHER THOUGHTS:

Apparent Women Officers or Directors: 7
Hot Spot for Advancement for Women/Minorities: Y

LOCATIONS: ("Y" = Yes)

West:	Southwest:	Midwest:	Southeast:	Northeast:	International:
				Y	Y

ROGERS COMMUNICATIONS INC

www.rogers.com

Industry Group Code: 513220 Ranks within this company's industry group: Sales: 6 Profits: 7

Print Media/Publishing:		Movies:		Equipment/Supplies:		Broadcast/Cable:		Music/Audio:		Sports/Games/Gambling:	
Newspapers:		Movie Theaters:		Equipment/Supplies:		Broadcast TV:	Y	Music Production:		Games/Sports:	
Magazines:	Y	Movie Production:		Gambling Equipment:		Cable TV:	Y	Retail Music:		Retail Games Stores:	
Books:		TV/Video Prod.:	Y	Special Services:	Y	Satellite Broadcast:		Retail Audio Equip.:		Stadiums/Teams:	Y
Book Stores:		Video Rental:	Y	Advertising Services:	Y	Radio:		Music Print./Dist.:		Gambling/Casinos:	
Distribution/Printing:		Video Distribution:		Info. Sys. Software:		Online Information:		Multimedia:		Rides/Theme Parks:	

TYPES OF BUSINESS:

Cable TV Service
Internet Service Provider
Cellular Phone Service
Video Stores
Television Broadcasting
Magazine Publishing
Radio Stations
Telephone Service

BRANDS/DIVISIONS/AFFILIATES:

Rogers Cable, Inc.
Rogers Wireless Communications, Inc.
Rogers Media, Inc.
Rogers Video
Rogers Retail
Rogers Sportsnet
ONMI.1
ONMI.2

CONTACTS: *Note: Officers with more than one job title may be intentionally listed here more than once.*

Edward S. Rogers, CEO
Edward S. Rogers, Pres.
William W. Linton, CFO/Sr. VP-Finance
Kevin P. Pennington, Chief Human Resources Officer/Sr. VP
Ronan D. McGrath, CIO/Pres., Rogers Shared Operations
David P. Miller, General Counsel/Sr. VP/Sec.
Melinda M. Rogers, Sr. VP-Strategy & Dev.
Jan L. Innes, VP-Comm.
Bruce Mann, VP-Investor Rel.
John G. Gossling, VP-Financial Oper.
Alan D. Horn, Pres./CEO-Rogers Telecommunications, Ltd.
Anthony P. Viner, Pres./CEO-Rogers Media, Inc.
M. Lorraine Daly, VP/Treas.
Nadir Mohamed, Pres./COO-Comm. Div.
Alan D. Horn, Chmn.

Phone: 416-935-7777	Fax: 416-935-3597
Toll-Free:	
Address: 333 Bloor St. E., 10th Fl., Toronto, ON A6 M4W 1G9 Canada	

GROWTH PLANS/SPECIAL FEATURES:

Rogers Communications, Inc. is a Canadian company engaged in a wide variety of television, broadband, cellular telephone and publishing businesses. Rogers conducts business via three subsidiaries: Rogers Cable, Inc.; Rogers Wireless Communications, Inc.; and Rogers Media, Inc. Rogers Cable is one of Canada's largest cable television service providers, serving approximately 1.13 million households in Ontario, New Brunswick and Newfoundland. Its services include cable television, digital cable, high-definition television, video-on-demand, high-speed Internet access through RogersYahoo! and interactive television. The cable division also operates Rogers Video, Canada's second largest chain of video stores. Rogers Wireless is one of Canada's largest wireless voice and data communications service providers serving 6.8 million customers, and is Canada's only carrier using the world standard GSM technology platform. Rogers Home Phone uses voice-over-cable and circuit switched technologies and has approximately 716,000 subscribers. Rogers Media is composed of Rogers Broadcasting and Rogers Publishing. Rogers Broadcasting operates 51 radio stations, 41 FM and ten AM, throughout Canada, as well as multiple television stations. In addition, the firm owns the Toronto Blue Jays baseball team, Rogers Centre (formerly SkyDome) and a 50% stake in Dome Productions, a high-definition television production and broadcasting venture. Rogers Publishing is one of Canada's largest magazine publishers, producing 70 consumer magazines and trade publications such as Maclean's, Canadian Business, Chatelaine, L'actualite, Flare, Today's Parent and MoneySense. In 2006, the firm began deploying a 3G wireless network. In January 2007, Rogers Video acquired about 170 stores from the wireless segment, bringing its total to 467. The new addition is called Rogers Retail and provides a direct retail channel for the company's products and services.

Rogers offers its employees a pension plan; medical and dental coverage; personal computer loans; education assistance; service recognition awards; employee and family assistance programs; and product discounts.

FINANCIALS: Sales and profits are in thousands of dollars—add 000 to get the full amount. 2007 Note: Financial information for 2007 was not available for all companies at press time.

2007 Sales: $	2007 Profits: $	U.S. Stock Ticker: RCI
2006 Sales: $7,583,888	2006 Profits: $669,318	Int'l Ticker: RCI.B Int'l Exchange: Toronto-TSX
2005 Sales: $6,419,688	2005 Profits: $-268,207	Employees: 22,500
2004 Sales: $4,656,529	2004 Profits: $-224,700	Fiscal Year Ends: 12/31
2003 Sales: $3,763,000	2003 Profits: $100,300	Parent Company:

SALARIES/BENEFITS:

Pension Plan: Y	ESOP Stock Plan:	Profit Sharing:	Top Exec. Salary: $	Bonus: $
Savings Plan:	Stock Purch. Plan: Y		Second Exec. Salary: $	Bonus: $

OTHER THOUGHTS:

Apparent Women Officers or Directors: 3
Hot Spot for Advancement for Women/Minorities: Y

LOCATIONS: ("Y" = Yes)

West:	Southwest:	Midwest:	Southeast:	Northeast:	International:
					Y

RTL GROUP SA

www.rtlgroup.com

Industry Group Code: 513120 Ranks within this company's industry group: Sales: 5 Profits: 4

Print Media/Publishing:	Movies:	Equipment/Supplies:	Broadcast/Cable:		Music/Audio:	Sports/Games/Gambling:
Newspapers:	Movie Theaters:	Equipment/Supplies:	Broadcast TV:	Y	Music Production:	Games/Sports:
Magazines:	Movie Production:	Gambling Equipment:	Cable TV:	Y	Retail Music:	Retail Games Stores:
Books:	TV/Video Prod.:	Special Services:	Satellite Broadcast:		Retail Audio Equip.:	Stadiums/Teams:
Book Stores:	Video Rental:	Advertising Services:	Radio:		Music Print./Dist.:	Gambling/Casinos:
Distribution/Printing:	Video Distribution:	Info. Sys. Software:	Online Information:		Multimedia:	Rides/Theme Parks:

TYPES OF BUSINESS:

Television Broadcasting
Television Production
Radio Broadcasting

BRANDS/DIVISIONS/AFFILIATES:

VOX
M6
RTL-TVI
Club RTL
RTL Klub
REN TV
Bertelsmann AG

CONTACTS: *Note: Officers with more than one job title may be intentionally listed here more than once.*

Gerhard Zeiler, CEO
Elmar Heggen, CFO/Head-Corp. Center
Oliver Herrgesell, Exec. VP-Mktg.
Romain Mannelli, Exec. VP-Corp. Human Resources
Vincent de Dorlodot, General Counsel
Andreas Walker, Exec. VP-Regional Oper.
Claire Davenport, Exec. VP-Corp. Strategy & Bus. Synergies
Oliver Herrgesell, Exec. VP-Comm.
Alain Berwick, CEO-RTL Radio
Gert Zimmer, Exec. VP-RTL Radio Deutschland
Fons van Westerloo, CEO-RTL Nederland
Anke Schaferkordt, CEO-RTL Television
Siegfried Luther, Chmn.

Phone: 352-2486-1	Fax: 352-2486-2760
Toll-Free:	
Address: 45 Blvd. Pierre Frieden, Luxembourg, L-1543 Luxembourg	

GROWTH PLANS/SPECIAL FEATURES:

RTL Group S.A., based in Luxembourg, is one of the largest television and radio broadcasters in Europe, with 42 television stations and 32 radio stations in 10 countries: Germany, France, Belgium, the Netherlands, the U.K., Luxembourg, Spain, Russia, Hungary and Croatia. The company's television segment, which reaches over 200 million viewers, includes VOX in Germany; M6 in France; RTL-TVI and Club RTL in Belgium; RTL Klub in Hungary; REN TV in Russia; and five stations in the U.K. RTL produces over 10,000 hours of programming per year, shown in 22 countries. RTL also owns the rights to approximately 19,000 hours of programming in 150 countries. RTL's long-term strategy is to increase the number of channels it offers so as to further target niche audiences; diversify into music, DVDs, magazines and other media-related businesses; and in general reduce its dependency on advertising for revenue. The company is also seeking to expand geographically into a greater number of countries. RTL Group is 89.8%-owned by Bertelsmann AG, which also owns BMG and Random House. In February 2007, the Luxembourg government, RTL Group, CLT-UFA (an RTL Group subsidiary) and Bertelsmann AG signed a new concession contract that will run until the end of 2020. Under the terms of the contract the Luxembourg Government will continue to make internationally awarded television and radio frequencies available to CLT-UFA, which in return will continue to produce and finance a public TV program for the government. In June 2007, RTL Group and John de Mol's Talpa Media Holding signed an asset deal in the Netherlands wherein radio station Radio 538 will be integrated with TV group, RTL Nederland, which will also acquire TV assets from Talpa Media. Talpa Media will receive a 26.3% stake in RTL Nederland.

FINANCIALS: Sales and profits are in thousands of dollars—add 000 to get the full amount. 2007 Note: Financial information for 2007 was not available for all companies at press time.

2007 Sales: $	2007 Profits: $	U.S. Stock Ticker:
2006 Sales: $7,440,900	2006 Profits: $1,465,700	Int'l Ticker: RTL Int'l Exchange: Luxembourg-LUX
2005 Sales: $6,207,333	2005 Profits: $747,621	Employees: 8,778
2004 Sales: $5,919,721	2004 Profits: $524,305	Fiscal Year Ends: 12/31
2003 Sales: $5,588,200	2003 Profits: $-58,700	Parent Company:

SALARIES/BENEFITS:

Pension Plan:	ESOP Stock Plan:	Profit Sharing:	Top Exec. Salary: $	Bonus: $
Savings Plan:	Stock Purch. Plan:		Second Exec. Salary: $	Bonus: $

OTHER THOUGHTS:

Apparent Women Officers or Directors: 4
Hot Spot for Advancement for Women/Minorities: Y

LOCATIONS: ("Y" = Yes)

West:	Southwest:	Midwest:	Southeast:	Northeast:	International:
					Y

SAGA COMMUNICATIONS INC www.sagacommunications.com

Industry Group Code: 513120 Ranks within this company's industry group: Sales: 18   Profits: 11

Print Media/Publishing:	Movies:		Equipment/Supplies:		Broadcast/Cable:		Music/Audio:	Sports/Games/Gambling:
Newspapers:	Movie Theaters:		Equipment/Supplies:		Broadcast TV:	Y	Music Production:	Games/Sports:
Magazines:	Movie Production:		Gambling Equipment:		Cable TV:		Retail Music:	Retail Games Stores:
Books:	TV/Video Prod.:	Y	Special Services:		Satellite Broadcast:		Retail Audio Equip.:	Stadiums/Teams:
Book Stores:	Video Rental:		Advertising Services:	Y	Radio:		Music Print./Dist.:	Gambling/Casinos:
Distribution/Printing:	Video Distribution:		Info. Sys. Software:		Online Information:		Multimedia:	Rides/Theme Parks:

TYPES OF BUSINESS:

Television Broadcasting
Radio Broadcasting
Local News Coverage
Television Broadcasting

BRANDS/DIVISIONS/AFFILIATES:

CONTACTS: Note: Officers with more than one job title may be intentionally listed here more than once.

Edward K. Christian, CEO
Edward K. Christian, Pres.
Samuel D. Bush, CFO/Sr. VP
Marcia Lobaito, Dir.-Human Resources
Tracy Cleeton, Dir.-IT
Marcia Lobaito, Corp. Sec.
Warren S. Lada, Sr. VP-Oper.
Marcia K. Lobaito, Dir.-Bus. Affairs/Sr. VP
Samuel D. Bush, Sr.VP/Treas.
Steven J. Goldstein, Exec. VP/Group Dir.-Program
Marcia Lobaito, Sr.VP/Dir.-Bus. Affairs
Michelle Novak, Programming Coordinator/ Research Dir.
Catherine A. Bobinski, Chief Acct. Officer/VP/Controller
Edward K. Christian, Chmn.

Phone: 313-886-7070	Fax: 313-886-7150
Toll-Free:	
Address: 73 Kercheval Ave., Ste. 201, Grosse Pointe Farms, MI 48236-3603 US	

GROWTH PLANS/SPECIAL FEATURES:

Saga Communications, Inc. operates radio and television stations and state radio networks in mid-sized markets. The company concentrates its broadcast operations in 26 markets across the United States, including Columbus, Ohio; Norfolk, Virginia; Milwaukee, Wisconsin; Manchester, New Hampshire; Des Moines, Iowa and Joplin, Missouri. A significant portion of its revenue depends on the sale of local advertising. Saga's portfolio currently consists of five television stations, four low-power television stations, three state radio networks, two farm radio networks, 30 AM radio stations and 59 FM stations. The firm's radio stations play a variety of music, ranging from classical to country, and the television stations maintain affiliations with CBS, ABC, FOX, Univision, NBC, UPN and Telemundo. Saga also produces the local news shown on its affiliate stations. Saga concentrates on developing strong decentralized local management at its stations responsible for the day-to-day station operations in their market areas. The firm recognizes mergers and acquisitions as an important factor in its growth. In 2007, the firm acquired WCNR-FM, an FM radio station serving the Charlottesville, Virginia market for $3.25 million. Recently, the company announced plans to buy two FM radio stations, one serving the Asheville, NC market and the other serving the Courtland, NY market.

FINANCIALS: Sales and profits are in thousands of dollars—add 000 to get the full amount. 2007 Note: Financial information for 2007 was not available for all companies at press time.

2007 Sales: $	2007 Profits: $	**U.S. Stock Ticker: SGA**
2006 Sales: $142,946	2006 Profits: $12,448	**Int'l Ticker:** Int'l Exchange:
2005 Sales: $140,790	2005 Profits: $10,566	Employees: 1,341
2004 Sales: $134,644	2004 Profits: $15,842	Fiscal Year Ends: 12/31
2003 Sales: $121,297	2003 Profits: $13,884	Parent Company:

SALARIES/BENEFITS:

Pension Plan:	ESOP Stock Plan:	Profit Sharing:	Top Exec. Salary: $549,003	Bonus: $281,976
Savings Plan: Y	Stock Purch. Plan:		Second Exec. Salary: $309,576	Bonus: $37,500

OTHER THOUGHTS:

Apparent Women Officers or Directors: 3
Hot Spot for Advancement for Women/Minorities: Y

LOCATIONS: ("Y" = Yes)

West:	Southwest:	Midwest:	Southeast:	Northeast:	International:
Y	Y	Y	Y	Y	Y

Note: Financial information, benefits and other data can change quickly and may vary from those stated here.

SALEM COMMUNICATIONS CORP
www.salemcommunications.com

Industry Group Code: 513111 Ranks within this company's industry group: Sales: 9   Profits: 7

Print Media/Publishing:	Movies:	Equipment/Supplies:	Broadcast/Cable:	Music/Audio:		Sports/Games/Gambling:
Newspapers:	Movie Theaters:	Equipment/Supplies:	Broadcast TV:	Music Production:	Y	Games/Sports:
Magazines: Y	Movie Production:	Gambling Equipment:	Cable TV:	Retail Music:		Retail Games Stores:
Books:	TV/Video Prod.:	Special Services:	Satellite Broadcast:	Retail Audio Equip.:		Stadiums/Teams:
Book Stores:	Video Rental:	Advertising Services:	Radio:	Music Print./Dist.:	Y	Gambling/Casinos:
Distribution/Printing:	Video Distribution:	Info. Sys. Software:	Online Information:	Multimedia:		Rides/Theme Parks:

TYPES OF BUSINESS:
Radio Broadcasting
Religious & Family Radio
Online Christian Content & Radio Streaming
Magazine Publishing
Internet Content Provider

BRANDS/DIVISIONS/AFFILIATES:
Salem Radio Network
Salem Radio Representatives
Salem Web Network
Salem Publishing
crosswalk.com
oneplace.com
CCM Magazine
christianjobs.com

CONTACTS: *Note: Officers with more than one job title may be intentionally listed here more than once.*
Edward G. Atsinger, III, CEO
Joe D. Davis, COO/Exec. VP
Edward G. Atsinger, III, Pres.
David A.R. Evans, CFO
Christopher J. Henderson, VP-Human Resources
Russell R. Hauth, Sr. VP-Admin.
Jonathan L. Block, General Counsel
Robert C. Adair, Sr. VP-Oper.
David A. R. Evans, Exec. VP-Bus. Dev.
Russell R. Hauth, Sr. VP-Public Affairs
Evan D. Masyr, VP-Acct. & Finance
Dennis Ciapura, Sr. VP-Broadcast Dev.
Michael Reichert, VP-Oper.
Stuart W. Epperson, Chmn.

Phone: 805-987-0400	Fax: 805-384-4520
Toll-Free:	
Address: 4880 Santa Rosa Rd., Ste. 300, Camarillo, CA 93012 US	

GROWTH PLANS/SPECIAL FEATURES:
Salem Communications Corp. is among the largest religious- and family-themed radio broadcasting companies in the U.S., operating 91 radio stations (32 FM and 72 AM), including 61 stations in 23 of the top 25 markets nationwide. The stations are mainly divided into three segments (reaching more than 4 million listeners weekly): Christian talk and teaching, conservative news/talk and contemporary Christian music. The firm owns Salem Radio Network, Salem Radio Representatives, Salem Web Network and Salem Publishing and is the exclusive provider of Christian radio content for XM Satellite Radio. Salem Radio Network syndicates talk, news and music programming for 2,000 affiliated radio stations. Salem Radio Representatives is the firm's national sales and advertising force. Salem Web Network is a leading Internet provider of Christian content and online radio streaming with 69 radio station web sites (including crosswalk.com, lightsource.com, oneplace.com, christianity.com, christianjobs.com and churchstaffing.com), which generate more than 2 million unique visitors per month and 400 million page views annually. Salem Publishing owns and operates a number of magazine titles published in the Christian Music Industry, such as its flagship publication Contemporary Christian Music (CCM) Magazine, Youthworker, Faith Talk, Singing News and Crosswalk. Recent acquisitions include WTPS-AM in Miami, Florida; CMCentral.com; and the ChristianMusicPlanet Brand.

FINANCIALS: Sales and profits are in thousands of dollars—add 000 to get the full amount. 2007 Note: Financial information for 2007 was not available for all companies at press time.

2007 Sales: $	2007 Profits: $	**U.S. Stock Ticker: SALM**
2006 Sales: $227,769	2006 Profits: $18,999	**Int'l Ticker:** Int'l Exchange:
2005 Sales: $209,642	2005 Profits: $12,662	Employees: 1,526
2004 Sales: $195,638	2004 Profits: $7,333	Fiscal Year Ends: 12/31
2003 Sales: $178,348	2003 Profits: $- 677	Parent Company:

SALARIES/BENEFITS:

Pension Plan:	ESOP Stock Plan:	Profit Sharing:	Top Exec. Salary: $850,000	Bonus: $501,750
Savings Plan: Y	Stock Purch. Plan:		Second Exec. Salary: $700,000	Bonus: $167,250

OTHER THOUGHTS:
Apparent Women Officers or Directors:
Hot Spot for Advancement for Women/Minorities:

LOCATIONS: ("Y" = Yes)

West:	Southwest:	Midwest:	Southeast:	Northeast:	International:
Y	Y	Y	Y	Y	

Note: Financial information, benefits and other data can change quickly and may vary from those stated here.

SALON MEDIA GROUP INC

www.salon.com

Industry Group Code: 514199 **Ranks within this company's industry group:** Sales: 5 Profits: 5

Print Media/Publishing:	Movies:	Equipment/Supplies:	Broadcast/Cable:	Music/Audio:	Sports/Games/Gambling:
Newspapers:	Movie Theaters:	Equipment/Supplies:	Broadcast TV:	Music Production:	Games/Sports:
Magazines:	Movie Production:	Gambling Equipment:	Cable TV:	Retail Music:	Retail Games Stores:
Books:	TV/Video Prod.:	Special Services:	Satellite Broadcast:	Retail Audio Equip.:	Stadiums/Teams:
Book Stores:	Video Rental:	Advertising Services:	Radio:	Music Print./Dist.:	Gambling/Casinos:
Distribution/Printing:	Video Distribution:	Info. Sys. Software:	Online Information:	Multimedia:	Rides/Theme Parks:

TYPES OF BUSINESS:

Online News & Media
Online Communities

BRANDS/DIVISIONS/AFFILIATES:

salon.com
Table Talk
Well (The)
Salon Premium
War Room
King Kaufman's Sports Daily
Daou Report (The)
Literary Guide to the World

CONTACTS:
Note: Officers with more than one job title may be
intentionally listed here more than once.
Christopher Neimeth, CEO
Conrad Lowry, CFO
Joan Walsh, Editor-In-Chief

Phone: 415-645-9200	Fax: 415-625-9204
Toll-Free:	
Address: 101 Spear St., Ste. 203, San Francisco, CA 94105 US	

GROWTH PLANS/SPECIAL FEATURES:

Salon Media Group, Inc. is an Internet media company providing online news and information. Salon's web site features ten content sections that offer news, interviews and regular columnists on topics including arts and entertainment, politics, technology and business, books, sports, parenting and health, and comics. Salon Media Group's other media offerings include Table Talk, an interactive forum, and The Well, a paid subscription community. The site's online communities allow users to interact and discuss Salon content with other users and with Salon's editorial staff. The company has created a front-page roadblock and splash page through which an advertiser owns all the advertising space on Salon's home page for a given period of time and the firm provides a rapidly updated array of news, features, interviews, columnists and blogs. The company's daily reports are built around nine features: War Room; the Fix; Audiophile (downloadable music); the Daou Report (opinionated blogsphere guide); King Kaufman's Sports Daily; Since you Asked; Broadsheet (women's news digest); How the World Works (editorial blog about globalization); and Video Dog (an archive of video clips). Salon Premium, a paid subscription service, offers subscribers access to exclusive new content; the option to view Salon content without advertising banners, pop-ups or other forms of advertising; access to select unabridged content; and the ability to easily download content in text format.

FINANCIALS:
Sales and profits are in thousands of dollars—add 000 to get the full amount. 2007 Note: Financial information for 2007 was not available for all companies at press time.

2007 Sales: $7,800	2007 Profits: $-1,600	**U.S. Stock Ticker: SALN.OB**	
2006 Sales: $6,500	2006 Profits: $-1,100	**Int'l Ticker:** Int'l Exchange:	
2005 Sales: $6,628	2005 Profits: $- 518	Employees: 64	
2004 Sales: $4,499	2004 Profits: $-6,046	Fiscal Year Ends: 3/31	
2003 Sales: $4,003	2003 Profits: $-5,597	Parent Company:	

SALARIES/BENEFITS:

Pension Plan: Y	ESOP Stock Plan:	Profit Sharing:	Top Exec. Salary: $170,000	Bonus: $
Savings Plan: Y	Stock Purch. Plan:		Second Exec. Salary: $170,000	Bonus: $

OTHER THOUGHTS:

Apparent Women Officers or Directors: 4
Hot Spot for Advancement for Women/Minorities: Y

LOCATIONS: ("Y" = Yes)

West:	Southwest:	Midwest:	Southeast:	Northeast:	International:
Y				Y	

SAMSUNG ELECTRONICS CO LTD   www.samsung.com

Industry Group Code: 334310 Ranks within this company's industry group: Sales: 3   Profits: 1

Print Media/Publishing:	Movies:	Equipment/Supplies:		Broadcast/Cable:	Music/Audio:		Sports/Games/Gambling: .
Newspapers:	Movie Theaters:	Equipment/Supplies:	Y	Broadcast TV:	Music Production:		Games/Sports:
Magazines:	Movie Production:	Gambling Equipment:		Cable TV:	Retail Music:		Retail Games Stores:
Books:	TV/Video Prod.:	Special Services:		Satellite Broadcast:	Retail Audio Equip.:	Y	Stadiums/Teams:
Book Stores:	Video Rental:	Advertising Services:		Radio:	Music Print./Dist.:		Gambling/Casinos:
Distribution/Printing:	Video Distribution:	Info. Sys. Software:		Online Information:	Multimedia:		Rides/Theme Parks:

TYPES OF BUSINESS:

Consumer Electronics
Semiconductors
Cellular Phones
Computers & Accessories
Digital Cameras
Fuel-Cell Technology
LCD Displays
Memory Products

BRANDS/DIVISIONS/AFFILIATES:

Samsung Group (The)
Samsung NEC Mobile Displays Co., Ltd.
Samsung Semiconductor
Women's Dream Plaza

CONTACTS: *Note: Officers with more than one job title may be intentionally listed here more than once.*

Jong-Yong Yun, Co-CEO/Vice Chmn.
In Joo Kim, Co-Pres.
Yoon-Woo Lee, Co-CEO
Jong Yong Yoon, Co-CEO
Doh-Seok Choi, Co-Pres./Co-CEO
Hak Soo Lee, Co-CEO
Gun Hee Lee, Chmn./Co-CEO

Phone: 82-2-727-7114	Fax: 82-2-727-7985
Toll-Free:	
Address: 250, 2-ga, Taepyung-ro, Jung-gu, Seoul, 100-742 Korea	

GROWTH PLANS/SPECIAL FEATURES:

Samsung Electronics Co., Ltd., part of The Samsung Group, is a global leader in semiconductor, telecommunications and digital convergence technology. The firm operates in five business segments: Digital Media, which generates 26.53% of revenues; Telecommunications, 25.89%; Digital Appliances, 7%; Semiconductors, 26.53%; and LCDs, 13.97%. The digital media segment produces color monitors, DVD and Blu-ray players, notebook PCS, printers, camcorders and mp3 players. The telecommunication networks segment has activities in both telecommunication systems and mobile telephones. The firm debuted the world's first 4G mobile telephone in August 2006. The digital appliance segment makes air conditioners, vacuum cleaners, refrigerators, washers, ovens and other appliances. The semiconductor segment consists of three divisions: memory, system LSI and storage. In the semiconductor segment, sales of high-capacity devices grew due to the application of 90nm and 80nm processing in the DRAM lineup and 60nm processing in the NAND flash memory products. The system LSI portion produces smart card ICs used in European mobile phones and CPUs used in automobile navigation systems. Finally, the LCDs segment makes products used in televisions, monitors and displays for mobile products. The company offers one of the largest plasma TVs in the world, a high-definition flat-screen measuring a full 80 inches across, and one of the largest LCD TVs with a 70-inch screen. The firm's Green Management initiative focuses on reducing the environmental impact of its products and processing techniques and eliminating workplace pollutants. Samsung has over 100 subsidiaries worldwide. Roughly 26% of Samsung's workforce is in engaged in research and development activities. In 2006, the firm registered 17,377 patents worldwide, with over 2,400 in the U.S. Currently, the firm is engaged in the development of new WiMAX, next-generation NAND flash drives and the commercialization of the world's first 1GB DRAM. The firm is looking to add twenty new product types by 2010.

FINANCIALS: Sales and profits are in thousands of dollars—add 000 to get the full amount. 2007 Note: Financial information for 2007 was not available for all companies at press time.

2007 Sales: $	2007 Profits: $	U.S. Stock Ticker: SSNLF.PK
2006 Sales: $63,495,000	2006 Profits: $8,535,460	Int'l Ticker: 000830 Int'l Exchange: Seoul-KRX
2005 Sales: $61,863,800	2005 Profits: $8,227,470	Employees: 64,000
2004 Sales: $56,892,753	2004 Profits: $10,648,314	Fiscal Year Ends: 12/31
2003 Sales: $36,740,000	2003 Profits: $4,990,400	Parent Company:

SALARIES/BENEFITS:

Pension Plan:	ESOP Stock Plan:	Profit Sharing:	Top Exec. Salary: $	Bonus: $
Savings Plan:	Stock Purch. Plan:		Second Exec. Salary: $	Bonus: $

OTHER THOUGHTS:

Apparent Women Officers or Directors:
Hot Spot for Advancement for Women/Minorities:

LOCATIONS: ("Y" = Yes)

West:	Southwest:	Midwest:	Southeast:	Northeast:	International:
Y	Y	Y	Y	Y	Y

Note: Financial information, benefits and other data can change quickly and may vary from those stated here.

SANDS REGENT

www.sandsregency.com

Industry Group Code: 721120 Ranks within this company's industry group: Sales: 12   Profits: 10

Print Media/Publishing:	Movies:	Equipment/Supplies:	Broadcast/Cable:	Music/Audio:		Sports/Games/Gambling:	
Newspapers:	Movie Theaters:	Equipment/Supplies:	Broadcast TV:	Music Production:	Y	Games/Sports:	
Magazines:	Movie Production:	Gambling Equipment:	Cable TV:	Retail Music:		Retail Games Stores:	
Books:	TV/Video Prod.:	Special Services:	Satellite Broadcast:	Retail Audio Equip.:		Stadiums/Teams:	Y
Book Stores:	Video Rental:	Advertising Services:	Radio:	Music Print./Dist.:		Gambling/Casinos:	
Distribution/Printing:	Video Distribution:	Info. Sys. Software:	Online Information:	Multimedia:		Rides/Theme Parks:	

TYPES OF BUSINESS:

Casino Hotel
Convention Center

BRANDS/DIVISIONS/AFFILIATES:

Zante, Inc.
Sands Regency Casino and Hotel
Gold Ranch Casino and RV Resort
Last Chance, Inc.
Rail City Casino
Plantation Investments
Red Hawk Sports Bar
Herbst Gaming, Inc.

CONTACTS: Note: Officers with more than one job title may be intentionally listed here more than once.

Ferenc Szony, CEO
Robert Medeiros, COO
Ferenc Szony, Pres.

Phone: 775-348-2200	Fax: 775-348-6241
Toll-Free: 800-648-3553	
Address: 345 N. Arlington Ave., Reno, NV 89501 US	

GROWTH PLANS/SPECIAL FEATURES:

Sands Regent, a subsidiary of Herbst Gaming, Inc., owns and operates casinos and related tourist amenities in Nevada within the Terrible Herbst family of properties. The company's marquee operation, the Sands Regency Casino and Hotel in downtown Reno, is held by subsidiary Zante, Inc. and features some 850 hotel rooms and 29,000 square feet of gaming space. While the company derives most of its revenue from its 17 gaming tables, 544 slot machines and sportsbook, it also operates a comedy club, cocktail lounges, a video arcade and a music lounge. Other services include beauty and gift shops; restaurants and fast-food eateries; and a 12,000-square-foot convention and meeting center that accommodates 1,000 people. Sands Regent subsidiary Last Chance, Inc. operates the Gold Ranch Casino and RV Resort in Verdi, 12 miles west of Reno. Gold Ranch is the first casino gaming attraction that travelers encounter on Interstate 80 when entering Nevada from California, and the last when leaving. Facilities include an 8,300-square-foot casino with 243 slot machines, two restaurants, two bars, a California lottery station, an ARCO gas station and a convenience store, as well as a 105-space RV park. The company subsidiary Plantation Investments is the operator of Rail City Casino in Sparks. Rail City Casino has approximately 16,600 square feet of gaming space and features more than 650 slots, six table games, keno and a sportsbook. The casino also has a family-style restaurant and a sports bar, with a convenient off-highway location. In Dayton, Nevada, Sands Regent owns and operates Depot Casino and Red Hawk Sports Bar. In January 2007, Sands Regent was acquired Herbst Gaming, Inc. for $119 million.

Sands' employees receive medical, dental and vision insurance; paid gaming registration; a 401(k) with employer match; tuition reimbursement; a free meal during shifts; and supplemental insurance.

FINANCIALS: Sales and profits are in thousands of dollars—add 000 to get the full amount. 2007 Note: Financial information for 2007 was not available for all companies at press time.

2007 Sales: $	2007 Profits: $	U.S. Stock Ticker: Subsidiary
2006 Sales: $92,574	2006 Profits: $2,431	Int'l Ticker: Int'l Exchange:
2005 Sales: $81,132	2005 Profits: $3,831	Employees: 1,239
2004 Sales: $62,349	2004 Profits: $6,910	Fiscal Year Ends: 6/30
2003 Sales: $55,700	2003 Profits: $1,900	Parent Company: HERBST GAMING INC

SALARIES/BENEFITS:

Pension Plan:	ESOP Stock Plan:	Profit Sharing:	Top Exec. Salary: $370,000	Bonus: $99,160
Savings Plan: Y	Stock Purch. Plan:		Second Exec. Salary: $190,000	Bonus: $50,920

OTHER THOUGHTS:

Apparent Women Officers or Directors:
Hot Spot for Advancement for Women/Minorities:

LOCATIONS: ("Y" = Yes)

West:	Southwest:	Midwest:	Southeast:	Northeast:	International:
Y					

Note: Financial information, benefits and other data can change quickly and may vary from those stated here.

SANYO ELECTRIC COMPANY LTD
www.sanyo.com

Industry Group Code: 334310 Ranks within this company's industry group: Sales: 5 Profits: 12

Print Media/Publishing:	Movies:	Equipment/Supplies:		Broadcast/Cable:	Music/Audio:	Sports/Games/Gambling:
Newspapers:	Movie Theaters:	Equipment/Supplies:	Y	Broadcast TV:	Music Production:	Games/Sports:
Magazines:	Movie Production:	Gambling Equipment:		Cable TV:	Retail Music:	Retail Games Stores:
Books:	TV/Video Prod.:	Special Services:		Satellite Broadcast:	Retail Audio Equip.:	Stadiums/Teams:
Book Stores:	Video Rental:	Advertising Services:		Radio:	Music Print./Dist.:	Gambling/Casinos:
Distribution/Printing:	Video Distribution:	Info. Sys. Software:		Online Information:	Multimedia:	Rides/Theme Parks:

TYPES OF BUSINESS:

Consumer Electronics
Fuel-Cell Technology
Communications Equipment
Industrial Equipment
Home Appliances
Batteries & Electronic Components
Photovoltaic Technology
Research & Development

BRANDS/DIVISIONS/AFFILIATES:

Solar Ark
Katana
SANYO North America Corporation
SANYO Solar USA, LLC
HIT Power 21

CONTACTS:
Note: Officers with more than one job title may be intentionally listed here more than once.
Seiichiro Sano, Pres.
Koichi Maeda, Exec. VP
Kazuhiko Suruta, Exec. VP
Kentaro Yamagishi, Exec. VP
Mitsuru Honma, Sr. VP

Phone: 81-6-6991-1181	**Fax:** 81-81-6991-5411
Toll-Free:	
Address: 5-5 Keihan-Hondori 2-Chome, Moriguchi, Osaka 570-8677 Japan	

GROWTH PLANS/SPECIAL FEATURES:

Sanyo Electric Co., Ltd. is a subsidiary of Sanyo Group, a worldwide conglomerate with 83 manufacturing companies, 37 sales companies and 38 companies in other business sectors. Sanyo offers electronics in categories including AV/information and communications equipment, home appliances, industrial and commercial equipment, electronic devices and batteries, and others. The AV/information segment manufactures and markets electronic devices such as optical pickups, TVs, PCs, mobile phones, MP3 players and digital cameras. The home appliances segment manufactures washing machines, microwaves, refrigerators and air conditioners, as well as other home appliances. The industrial and commercial equipment segment manufactures items such as heating and air conditioning systems, security cameras, micro motors and photovoltaic modules. The electronic device segment produces and markets liquid crystal displays (LCDs), semiconductors, batteries and electronic components. Sanyo also produces miscellaneous products that account for about 4% of revenues. In addition, the firm conducts research on batteries, flash memory, semiconductors, systems-on-a-chip and photonic devices using nanotechnology. Sanyo invests heavily in research and development and is focused on becoming a world technological leader in LCDs, electronic devices and environmental technology, including a joint venture with Samsung to develop fuel-cell technology. The company built the Solar Ark, an enormous solar power demonstration project that is expected to produce 630 kilowatts of power. Sanyo recently launched a multimedia phone called Katana with Sprint that offers music, live TV, high resolution digital imaging and web browsing.

Sanyo offers its employees a 401(k) retirement plan, educational assistance, an employee assistance program and company picnics, holiday parties, and community service activities.

FINANCIALS:
Sales and profits are in thousands of dollars—add 000 to get the full amount. 2007 Note: Financial information for 2007 was not available for all companies at press time.

2007 Sales: $	2007 Profits: $	**U.S. Stock Ticker:** SANYY
2006 Sales: $21,804,658	2006 Profits: $-1,757,786	**Int'l Ticker:** 6764 Int'l Exchange: Tokyo-TSE
2005 Sales: $24,173,700	2005 Profits: $-1,603,200	Employees: 106,389
2004 Sales: $24,527,700	2004 Profits: $126,400	Fiscal Year Ends: 3/31
2003 Sales: $18,949,000	2003 Profits: $-606,800	Parent Company:

SALARIES/BENEFITS:

Pension Plan:	ESOP Stock Plan:	Profit Sharing:	Top Exec. Salary: $	Bonus: $
Savings Plan: Y	Stock Purch. Plan:		Second Exec. Salary: $	Bonus: $

OTHER THOUGHTS:

Apparent Women Officers or Directors:
Hot Spot for Advancement for Women/Minorities:

LOCATIONS: ("Y" = Yes)

West:	Southwest:	Midwest:	Southeast:	Northeast:	International:
Y					Y

Note: Financial information, benefits and other data can change quickly and may vary from those stated here.

SCHOLASTIC CORP

www.scholastic.com

Industry Group Code: 511130 **Ranks within this company's industry group:** Sales: 3 Profits: 4

Print Media/Publishing:		Movies:		Equipment/Supplies:		Broadcast/Cable:		Music/Audio:		Sports/Games/Gambling:	
Newspapers:		Movie Theaters:		Equipment/Supplies:		Broadcast TV:		Music Production:		Games/Sports:	
Magazines:	Y	Movie Production:		Gambling Equipment:		Cable TV:		Retail Music:		Retail Games Stores:	
Books:	Y	TV/Video Prod.:	Y	Special Services:		Satellite Broadcast:		Retail Audio Equip.:		Stadiums/Teams:	
Book Stores:		Video Rental:		Advertising Services:		Radio:		Music Print./Dist.:	Y	Gambling/Casinos:	
Distribution/Printing:		Video Distribution:		Info. Sys. Software:		Online Information:		Multimedia:		Rides/Theme Parks:	

TYPES OF BUSINESS:

Children's Book Publishing
Children's TV Programming
Educational Software
Educational Magazines
Book Fairs & Clubs
Consumer Products
Movies

BRANDS/DIVISIONS/AFFILIATES:

Babysitters' Club (The)
Clifford the Big Red Dog
Goosebumps
Harry Potter
Magic School Bus (The)
READ 180
Wiggleworks
Scholastic Reading Counts

CONTACTS: *Note: Officers with more than one job title may be intentionally listed here more than once.*

Richard Robinson, CEO
Richard Robinson, Pres.
Maureen O'Connell, CFO
Richard Spaulding, Exec. VP-Mktg.
Peter Watts, Sr. VP-Corp. Human Resources/Employee Svcs.
Beth Ford, Sr. VP-IT
Maureen O'Connell, Chief Admin. Officer/Exec. VP
Devereux Chatillon, General Counsel/Sr. VP/Sec.
Beth Ford, Sr. VP-Global Oper.
Heather J. Myers, Sr. VP-Strategic Planning & Bus. Dev.
Kyle Good, VP-Corp. Comm. & Media Relations
Ernest B. Fleishman, Sr. VP-Corp. Rel.
Karen A. Maloney, Sr. VP-Finance/Chief Acct. Officer
Deborah A. Forte, Exec. VP/Pres., Scholastic Media
Lisa Holton, Exec. VP/Pres., Book Fairs & Trade
Margery W. Mayer, Exec. VP/Pres., Scholastic Education
Judith A. Newman, Exec. VP/Pres., Book Clubs
Richard Robinson, Chmn.
Hugh Roome, Exec. VP/Pres., Scholastic Int'l

Phone: 212-343-6100	Fax: 212-343-6934
Toll-Free: 800-724-6527	
Address: 557 Broadway, New York, NY 10012 US	

GROWTH PLANS/SPECIAL FEATURES:

Scholastic Corporation is a global children's publishing and media company. Scholastic creates educational and entertaining materials and products for use in school and at home. The company categorizes its businesses into four operating segments: Children's Book Publishing and Distribution; Educational Publishing; Media, Licensing and Advertising; and International. The firm's children's book publishing and distribution segment accounted for 53% of revenues in 2007; approximately 400 million books were sold worldwide and 50% were from internet sales. The international segment (accounting for 21% of sales in 2007) manufactures and distributes products and services in 135 countries and 35 languages. Through its Educational Publishing segment, the company specializes in materials that cover subjects such as English, math, science, social studies, current events and foreign languages. A major focus of this division is reading improvement materials and the effective use of technology to support learning. Scholastic's technology based products include READ 180, FASTT Math and Scholastic Reading Counts. Scholastic's Media, Licensing and Advertising segment focuses on the production and/or distribution of software, programming and consumer products and the development of advertising revenue. Through this division, the company produces children's television programming, DVD's, feature films and branded websites based on many of its successful titles. .In 2007, the company participated in the organization of a new children's programming network, which produces educational children's television programming under the name qubo. The network features bilingual content with a mission to promote literacy and values in children's television. Also in 2007, Scholastic partnered with Nintendo to develop two video games: I Spy Fun House and Scholastic Animal Genius. Recently, Scholastic Entertainment Inc. released The Golden Compass, a feature film based on the best-selling trilogy, His Dark Materials.

Scholastic offers employees tuition reimbursement, a work/life assistance program and leave programs including child care, military and compassionate leaves.

FINANCIALS: Sales and profits are in thousands of dollars—add 000 to get the full amount. 2007 Note: Financial information for 2007 was not available for all companies at press time.

2007 Sales: $	2007 Profits: $	U.S. Stock Ticker: SCHL
2006 Sales: $2,283,800	2006 Profits: $68,600	Int'l Ticker: Int'l Exchange:
2005 Sales: $2,079,900	2005 Profits: $64,300	Employees: 10,400
2004 Sales: $2,233,800	2004 Profits: $58,400	Fiscal Year Ends: 5/31
2003 Sales: $1,958,300	2003 Profits: $58,600	Parent Company:

SALARIES/BENEFITS:

Pension Plan: Y	ESOP Stock Plan:	Profit Sharing:	Top Exec. Salary: $861,194	Bonus: $
Savings Plan: Y	Stock Purch. Plan: Y		Second Exec. Salary: $610,056	Bonus: $65,000

OTHER THOUGHTS:

Apparent Women Officers or Directors: 8
Hot Spot for Advancement for Women/Minorities: Y

LOCATIONS: ("Y" = Yes)

West:	Southwest:	Midwest:	Southeast:	Northeast:	International:
Y	Y	Y	Y	Y	Y

Note: Financial information, benefits and other data can change quickly and may vary from those stated here.

SCIENTIFIC GAMES CORPORATIONwww.scientificgames.com

Industry Group Code: 713290 Ranks within this company's industry group: Sales: 4 Profits: 3

Print Media/Publishing:	Movies:	Equipment/Supplies:		Broadcast/Cable:	Music/Audio:	Sports/Games/Gambling:	
Newspapers:	Movie Theaters:	Equipment/Supplies:		Broadcast TV:	Music Production:	Games/Sports:	
Magazines:	Movie Production:	Gambling Equipment:	Y	Cable TV:	Retail Music:	Retail Games Stores:	
Books:	TV/Video Prod.:	Special Services:		Satellite Broadcast:	Retail Audio Equip.:	Stadiums/Teams:	Y
Book Stores:	Video Rental:	Advertising Services:		Radio:	Music Print./Dist.:	Gambling/Casinos:	
Distribution/Printing:	Video Distribution:	Info. Sys. Software:		Online Information:	Multimedia:	Rides/Theme Parks:	

TYPES OF BUSINESS:

Gambling Equipment-Computer-Based Lottery Systems
Pari-Mutuel Wagering Systems
Satellite Broadcasting Services
Telecommunications Products
Off-Track Betting Facilities Management
Lottery Services
Race Simulcasting
Prepaid Phone Cards

BRANDS/DIVISIONS/AFFILIATES:

The Global Draw Limited
Scientific Games Racing LLC
Games Media Limited
Games Media Ltd.
Guard Libang
Inspur

CONTACTS: *Note: Officers with more than one job title may be intentionally listed here more than once.*

A. Lorne Weil, CEO
Michael R. Chambrello, COO
Michael R. Chambrello, Pres.
DeWayne E. Laird, CFO/VP
Brooks Pierce, VP-Corp. Mktg.
Sally L. Conkright, Chief Human Resource Officer
Steven W. Beason, CTO/VP/Pres., Lottery Systems Group
Sally L. Conkright, VP-Admin.
Ira H. Raphaelson, General Counsel/Corp. Sec./VP
David Pye, VP-Corp. Dev.
Lisa D. Lettieri, Dir.-Corp. Comm.
Stephen L. Gibbs, Chief Acct. Officer/VP
Martin E. Schloss, Sr. VP
Larry A. Potts, VP/Chief Compliance Officer/Dir.-Security
William J. Huntley, VP/Pres., Racing, Sports & Gaming Tech.
Steven M. Saferin, VP/Pres., Properties
A. Lorne Weil, Chmn.

Phone: 212-754-2233	Fax: 212-754-2372
Toll-Free: 800-367-9345	
Address: 750 Lexington Ave., New York, NY 10022 US	

GROWTH PLANS/SPECIAL FEATURES:

Scientific Games Corp. is a leading supplier of technology-based products, systems and services to gaming markets worldwide, including 34 of the 42 U.S. jurisdictions that currently sell lottery tickets and over 50 countries. Scientific Games operates in three business segments: Printed Products Group, Lottery Systems Group and Diversified Gaming Group. The Printed Products Group is composed of its instant lottery ticket business and its prepaid phone card business, providing lotteries with some of the world's most popular entertainment brands, including Major League Baseball, NASCAR, National Basketball Association, Wheel-of-Fortune, Monopoly, World Poker Tour and The World Series of Poker. The Lottery Systems Group provides sophisticated, customized computer software, equipment and data communication services to government-sponsored and privately-operated lotteries in the U.S. and internationally. This business includes the provision of transaction processing software for the accounting and validation of both instant and online lottery games, point-of-sale terminals, central site computers, communications technology and ongoing support and maintenance for these products. The Diversified Gaming Group provides services and systems to private and public operators in the wide area gaming markets and in the pari-mutuel wagering industry, with products including fixed odds betting terminals; video lottery terminals; monitor games; wagering systems for the pari-mutuel racing industry; sports betting systems and services; and Amusement With Prize and Skill With Prize terminals. Business units within the Diversified Gaming Group include The Global Draw Limited, Scientific Games Racing LLC and Games Media Limited. In recent news, Scientific Games acquired Games Media Ltd., a U.K.-based company. In July 2007, the company acquired a 50% interest in Guard Libang, a Chinese lottery ticket services provider, and in May it formed a joint venture with another Chinese company, Inspur.

Scientific Games offers its employees tuition reimbursement, flexible spending accounts, service awards, free parking and credit union membership.

FINANCIALS: Sales and profits are in thousands of dollars—add 000 to get the full amount. 2007 Note: Financial information for 2007 was not available for all companies at press time.

2007 Sales: $	2007 Profits: $	**U.S. Stock Ticker:** SGMS
2006 Sales: $781,683	2006 Profits: $66,761	**Int'l Ticker:** Int'l Exchange:
2005 Sales: $781,683	2005 Profits: $75,319	Employees: 5,500
2004 Sales: $725,495	2004 Profits: $65,742	Fiscal Year Ends: 12/31
2003 Sales: $560,900	2003 Profits: $52,100	Parent Company:

SALARIES/BENEFITS:

Pension Plan:	ESOP Stock Plan:	Profit Sharing:	Top Exec. Salary: $870,000	Bonus: $
Savings Plan: Y	Stock Purch. Plan: Y		Second Exec. Salary: $616,270	Bonus: $

OTHER THOUGHTS:

Apparent Women Officers or Directors: 1
Hot Spot for Advancement for Women/Minorities: Y

LOCATIONS: ("Y" = Yes)

West:	Southwest:	Midwest:	Southeast:	Northeast:	International:
Y	Y	Y	Y	Y	Y

Note: Financial information, benefits and other data can change quickly and may vary from those stated here.

SEGA SAMMY HOLDINGS INC www.segasammy.co.jp/english

Industry Group Code: 511208 Ranks within this company's industry group: Sales: 1 Profits: 1

Print Media/Publishing:	Movies:		Equipment/Supplies:		Broadcast/Cable:	Music/Audio:	Sports/Games/Gambling:	
Newspapers:	Movie Theaters:		Equipment/Supplies:	Y	Broadcast TV:	Music Production:	Games/Sports:	Y
Magazines:	Movie Production:	Y	Gambling Equipment:	Y	Cable TV:	Retail Music:	Retail Games Stores:	Y
Books:	TV/Video Prod.:		Special Services:	Y	Satellite Broadcast:	Retail Audio Equip.:	Stadiums/Teams:	
Book Stores:	Video Rental:		Advertising Services:		Radio:	Music Print./Dist.:	Gambling/Casinos:	Y
Distribution/Printing:	Video Distribution:		Info. Sys. Software:		Online Information:	Multimedia:	Rides/Theme Parks:	

TYPES OF BUSINESS:

Computer Software-Games
Arcade Games
Amusement Centers
Toys
Ring Tones & Mobile Phone Media
Animation Production
Karaoke Machines
Display Design & Construction Services

BRANDS/DIVISIONS/AFFILIATES:

Sega Corporation
Sammy NetWorks Co., Ltd.
H-I System Corporation
Nissho Inter Life Co., Ltd.
SI Electronics, Ltd.
TMS Entertainment, Ltd.
SEGA Music Networks Co., Ltd.
Ginzahanbai (Ginza) Corporation

CONTACTS: Note: Officers with more than one job title may be intentionally listed here more than once.

Hajime Satomi, CEO
Hajime Satomi, Pres.
Akira Sugano, Exec. Officer/Manager-Admin. Div.
Koichi Fukazawa, Exec. Officer/Manager-Corp. Planning Div.
Shunichi Shimizu, Gen. Manager-Acct. & Financial Department
Seijin Tanno, Pres./CEO-Nissho Inter Life
Hisao Oguchi, Exec. VP, Sega Corporation/Vice Chmn.
Hajime Satomi, Pres./COO/CEO-Sega Corporation
Toru Katamoto, Pres./COO-Sammy Corporation
Hajime Satomi, Chmn.

Phone: 81-3-621-59955	Fax: 81-3-5736-7066
Toll-Free:	
Address: Shiodome Sumitomo Bldg. 21F, 1-9-2 Higashi Shimbashi, Minato-ku, Tokyo 105-0021 Japan	

GROWTH PLANS/SPECIAL FEATURES:

Sega Sammy Holdings, Inc. (SSH), the product of a merger between Sega Corporation and Sammy Corporation, operates amusement centers and produces game software and arcade games. The company is organized into five segments: Pachislot and Pachinko Machines (PPM), which generated 40% of 2007 sales; Amusement Machine Sales (AMS), 14.3%; Amusement Center Operations (ACO), 19.7%; Consumer Business, 22.6%; and Others, 3.4%. During 2007, the PPM segment installed 523,422 pachislot and 132,981 pachinko machines, down from previous years. In the AMS segment, the company uses the ALL.Net P-ras business model, wherein it sells game hardware and provides mother board and software at no cost. SSH is paid by content use. This model allows operators of amusement centers to introduce new machines with a small initial investment. The ACO segment owns and operates 449 amusement centers, including those operated by TMS entertainment, opening 18 and closing 31 stores in 2007. The consumer business segment manufactures software for home video game consoles, Internet game play, and mobile phones, as well as having operations in the traditional toy market. Entertainment software generated 64% of the division's sales, networks and other products, 36%. Some of the company's 61 subsidiaries and affiliates include Sega Corporation; Sammy NetWorks Co., LTD., developer of ring tones and games for mobile phones; TMS Entertainment, LTD., an animation planning and production firm; H-I System Corporation, which makes amusement hall computers and prize POS systems; Nissho Inter Life Co., Ltd., which engages in planning, design, management and construction of displays and commercial facilities; and Sega Music Networks Co., Ltd., involved in the production and sales of karaoke machines. SSH recently acquired three new subsidiaries: Sports Interactive Ltd.; Ginza Co., Ltd; and Secret Level, Inc. It also recently launched LB Style Square, official shops for its Love And Berry Dress Up and Dance! game.

FINANCIALS: Sales and profits are in thousands of dollars—add 000 to get the full amount. 2007 Note: Financial information for 2007 was not available for all companies at press time.

2007 Sales: $	2007 Profits: $	**U.S. Stock Ticker: SGAMY.PK**
2006 Sales: $4,656,310	2006 Profits: $557,350	**Int'l Ticker: 6460** Int'l Exchange: Tokyo-TSE
2005 Sales: $4,340,090	2005 Profits: $425,650	Employees: 6,416
2004 Sales: $1,810,400	2004 Profits: $82,900	Fiscal Year Ends: 3/31
2003 Sales: $1,645,600	2003 Profits: $25,500	Parent Company:

SALARIES/BENEFITS:

Pension Plan: Y	ESOP Stock Plan:	Profit Sharing:	Top Exec. Salary: $	Bonus: $
Savings Plan:	Stock Purch. Plan:		Second Exec. Salary: $	Bonus: $

OTHER THOUGHTS:

Apparent Women Officers or Directors:
Hot Spot for Advancement for Women/Minorities:

LOCATIONS: ("Y" = Yes)

West:	Southwest:	Midwest:	Southeast:	Northeast:	International:
Y	Y	Y	Y	Y	Y

Note: Financial information, benefits and other data can change quickly and may vary from those stated here.

SHANDA INTERACTIVE ENTERTAINMENT LIMITED
www.snda.com/en/index.jsp

Industry Group Code: 511208 Ranks within this company's industry group: Sales: 6 Profits: 3

Print Media/Publishing:		Movies:		Equipment/Supplies:		Broadcast/Cable:		Music/Audio:		Sports/Games/Gambling:	
Newspapers:		Movie Theaters:		Equipment/Supplies:		Broadcast TV:		Music Production:		Games/Sports:	Y
Magazines:	Y	Movie Production:		Gambling Equipment:		Cable TV:		Retail Music:		Retail Games Stores:	
Books:		TV/Video Prod.:		Special Services:		Satellite Broadcast:		Retail Audio Equip.:		Stadiums/Teams:	
Book Stores:		Video Rental:		Advertising Services:	Y	Radio:		Music Print./Dist.:		Gambling/Casinos:	
Distribution/Printing:		Video Distribution:		Info. Sys. Software:		Online Information:		Multimedia:		Rides/Theme Parks:	

TYPES OF BUSINESS:
Online Gaming

BRANDS/DIVISIONS/AFFILIATES:
EZ Pod
EZ Center
InterJoy Technology, Ltd.
Jisheng Technology
Fenglin Huoshan Technology
Actoz Soft Co., Ltd
Gametea
Shanda Networking

CONTACTS: *Note: Officers with more than one job title may be intentionally listed here more than once.*
Tianqiao Chen, CEO
Jun Tang, Pres.
Grace Wu, CFO/VP
Qunzhao Tan, Sr. VP/CTO
Lijun Li, Assoc. Dir-General Admin.
Gehui Zhu, Assoc. Dir.-Public Rel.
Frank Liang, Dir.-Investor Rel.
Danian Chen, Exec. VP
Haibin Qu, Exec. VP
Jingying Wang, Sr. VP
Hai Ling, Sr. VP
Tianqiao Chen, Chmn.

Phone: 021-50504740	Fax: 021-50504740-8088
Toll-Free:	
Address: No. 1 Office Bldg., No.690 Bibo Road, Shanghai, 201203 China	

GROWTH PLANS/SPECIAL FEATURES:
Shanda is one of the largest operators of online games in China, offering a portfolio of free and fee-based games including The Legend of Mir II and The World of Legend. The games fall into one of two categories: casual games (Internet based), and massively multiplayer online role-playing games (MMORPG) which allow users to connect games installed on their computers to the Internet in order to interact with other gamers. Shanda's casual games include BNB, Fortress 2 and GetAmped. The firm's fee-based MMORPG games include The Sign, The Age and The Tactical Commander. Shanda gains revenue from online advertising, staffs a research and development center to acquire game development companies and earns revenue from short messaging services (SMS) and sales of publications and other related products based on its games and characters. However, the firm's principal source of revenue consists of the fees paid by online game users. Its customers purchase pre-paid game cards (sold in both virtual and physical form) to add value to their accounts in order to play. In recent news, the firm acquired Aurora Technology, an online gaming company, and disposed of its stake in SINA Corp. In 2007, Shanda acquired the operating rights for several games, including AION, FreeJack, Company of Heroes Online and Dead or Alive Online. Additionally, the company licensed its in-house developed games World of Legend, Magical Land and Crazy Kart to several overseas distributors.

FINANCIALS: Sales and profits are in thousands of dollars—add 000 to get the full amount. 2007 Note: Financial information for 2007 was not available for all companies at press time.

2007 Sales: $	2007 Profits: $	U.S. Stock Ticker: SNDA	
2006 Sales: $211,900	2006 Profits: $67,800	Int'l Ticker:	Int'l Exchange:
2005 Sales: $235,014	2005 Profits: $20,480	Employees: 2,392	
2004 Sales: $156,900	2004 Profits: $73,600	Fiscal Year Ends: 12/31	
2003 Sales: $	2003 Profits: $	Parent Company:	

SALARIES/BENEFITS:
Pension Plan: Y	ESOP Stock Plan:	Profit Sharing:	Top Exec. Salary: $	Bonus: $
Savings Plan:	Stock Purch. Plan:		Second Exec. Salary: $	Bonus: $

OTHER THOUGHTS:
Apparent Women Officers or Directors: 2
Hot Spot for Advancement for Women/Minorities: Y

LOCATIONS: ("Y" = Yes)
West:	Southwest:	Midwest:	Southeast:	Northeast:	International:
					Y

SHANGHAI MEDIA GROUP (SMG)   www.smg.sh.cn

Industry Group Code: 513120 Ranks within this company's industry group: Sales: Profits:

Print Media/Publishing:		Movies:		Equipment/Supplies:		Broadcast/Cable:		Music/Audio:		Sports/Games/Gambling:	
Newspapers:	Y	Movie Theaters:		Equipment/Supplies:		Broadcast TV:	Y	Music Production:		Games/Sports:	
Magazines:	Y	Movie Production:		Gambling Equipment:		Cable TV:	Y	Retail Music:		Retail Games Stores:	
Books:		TV/Video Prod.:	Y	Special Services:		Satellite Broadcast:		Retail Audio Equip.:		Stadiums/Teams:	
Book Stores:		Video Rental:		Advertising Services:		Radio:		Music Print./Dist.:		Gambling/Casinos:	
Distribution/Printing:		Video Distribution:		Info. Sys. Software:		Online Information:		Multimedia:		Rides/Theme Parks:	

TYPES OF BUSINESS:

Television Broadcasting
TV Production
Radio Production
Radio Broadcasting
Online TV Broadcasting
Cable TV Network
Newspaper Publishing
Magazine Publishing

BRANDS/DIVISIONS/AFFILIATES:

Radio Shanghai
Eastern Radio Shanghai
Shanghai Television
Oriental Television Station
Shanghai Cable Television
Shanghai Dragon Mobile Media Company
Oriental CJ

CONTACTS: *Note: Officers with more than one job title may be intentionally listed here more than once.*

Li Ruigang, Pres.

Phone: 86-21-6256-5899	Fax: 86-21-6256-2752
Toll-Free:	
Address: 651 W. Nanjing Rd., Shanghai, 200041 China	

GROWTH PLANS/SPECIAL FEATURES:

Shanghai Media Group (SMG) is a Chinese-language producer and provider of radio and TV entertainment. In addition, it is engaged in the performing arts, sports and technical service sectors. SMG is the result of a 2001 merger of Radio Shanghai, Eastern Radio Shanghai, Shanghai Television, Oriental Television Station and Shanghai Cable Television. The company broadcasts 258 hours of TV and 214 hours of radio each day. TV and radio content produced by the firm includes news, entertainment, sports, finance, music, TV series, documentaries and animated features. SMG operates 13 analog TV channels, seven of which are cable channels that cover the Shanghai area; four are terrestrial channels for Shanghai and the surrounding areas and two are satellite channels for Chinese and overseas subscribers. Other TV interests include one broadband online TV channel, one mobile phone TV channel (through its Shanghai Dragon Mobile Media Company subsidiary) and one national IPTV service platform. The firm also operates 11 analog radio stations, 16 national digital pay channels, five newspapers and magazines and five sports clubs. Moreover, SMG partners with Korea's CJ Home Shopping to oversee Oriental CJ, a home shopping company. In early 2007, CJ Home Shopping took on another partner, Jiaxing TV, to launch the home shopping program in the province of Zhejiang. Also in 2007, the firm began providing ESPN's English League Premier soccer coverage via its IPTV platform. The company announced plans in 2007 to launch a 24-hour-a-day English-language television news channel in an attempt to internationalize its portfolio.

FINANCIALS: Sales and profits are in thousands of dollars—add 000 to get the full amount. 2007 Note: Financial information for 2007 was not available for all companies at press time.

2007 Sales: $	2007 Profits: $	**U.S. Stock Ticker: Private**	
2006 Sales: $	2006 Profits: $	**Int'l Ticker:** Int'l Exchange:	
2005 Sales: $	2005 Profits: $	Employees:	
2004 Sales: $	2004 Profits: $	Fiscal Year Ends:	
2003 Sales: $	2003 Profits: $	Parent Company:	

SALARIES/BENEFITS:

Pension Plan:	ESOP Stock Plan:	Profit Sharing:	Top Exec. Salary: $	Bonus: $
Savings Plan:	Stock Purch. Plan:		Second Exec. Salary: $	Bonus: $

OTHER THOUGHTS:

Apparent Women Officers or Directors:
Hot Spot for Advancement for Women/Minorities:

LOCATIONS: ("Y" = Yes)

West:	Southwest:	Midwest:	Southeast:	Northeast:	International:
					Y

Note: Financial information, benefits and other data can change quickly and may vary from those stated here.

SHARP CORPORATION

sharp-world.com

Industry Group Code: 334310 Ranks within this company's industry group: Sales: 4   Profits: 4

Print Media/Publishing:	Movies:	Equipment/Supplies:		Broadcast/Cable:	Music/Audio:	Sports/Games/Gambling:
Newspapers:	Movie Theaters:	Equipment/Supplies:	Y	Broadcast TV:	Music Production:	Games/Sports:
Magazines:	Movie Production:	Gambling Equipment:		Cable TV:	Retail Music:	Retail Games Stores:
Books:	TV/Video Prod.:	Special Services:		Satellite Broadcast:	Retail Audio Equip.: Y	Stadiums/Teams:
Book Stores:	Video Rental:	Advertising Services:		Radio:	Music Print./Dist.:	Gambling/Casinos:
Distribution/Printing:	Video Distribution:	Info. Sys. Software:		Online Information:	Multimedia:	Rides/Theme Parks:

TYPES OF BUSINESS:

Audiovisual & Communications Equipment
Electronic Components
Solar Cells & Modules
Home Appliances
Computers & Information Equipment
Consumer Electronics
LCD Flat Panel TVs, Monitors & Displays

BRANDS/DIVISIONS/AFFILIATES:

AQUOS
Kameyama Plant No. 2
Sharp Electronics Co. Ltd.

CONTACTS: *Note: Officers with more than one job title may be intentionally listed here more than once.*

Katsuhiko Machida, CEO
Mikio Katayama, COO
Mikio Katayama, Pres.
Masaaki Ohtsuka, Sr. Exec. Dir.-Domestic Sales & Mktg.
Nobuyuki Taniguchi, Gen. Mgr.-Human Resources
Toru Chiba, Gen. Mgr.-Corp. R&D
Kenji Ohta, CTO/Sr. Exec. Dir.
Takuji Okawara, Gen. Mgr.-One-of-a-Kind Prod. Planning
Hiroshi Saji, Sr. Exec. VP/Chief General Admin. Officer
Takashi Nakagawa, Exec. Dir.-Legal Affairs & Intellectual Property
Masafumi Matsumoto, Sr. Exec. VP-Bus. Oper.
Yoshisuke Hasegawa, Exec. Dir.-Comm. Systems/Gen. Mgr.
Tetsuo Onishi, Gen. Mgr.-Corp. Acct. & Control
Toshishige Hamano, Sr. Exec. Dir.-Solar Systems Group
Yoshiaki Ibuchi, Chief Environmental Protection Officer
Shigeaki Mizushima, Gen. Mgr.-Display Tech. Dev.
Masatsugu Teragawa, Gen. Mgr.-Audio Visual Systems & Large LCD Bus.
Katsuhiko Machida, Chmn.
Toshihiko Fujimoto, Gen. Mgr.-Int'l Bus. & Americas
Takashi Okuda, Gen. Mgr.-Corp. Procurement

Phone: 81-6-6621-1221	**Fax:** 81-6-6627-1759
Toll-Free:	
Address: 22-22 Nagaike-cho, Abeno-ku, Osaka, 545-8522 Japan	

GROWTH PLANS/SPECIAL FEATURES:

Sharp Corporation, with more than $27 billion in assets, designs, manufactures and distributes electronic products, information system products and home appliances. Its electronic products include LCD TVs, video projectors, 1-Bit digital audio systems and Blu-ray disc players. Sharp information system products include digital copier/printers, data projectors, fax machines, scientific calculators, electronic organizers, mobile phones, LCD monitors and wireless PDAs. The firm's home appliances include superheated steam ovens and plasmacluster products, such as air conditioners, air purifiers, laundry drying dehumidifiers, humidifiers and refrigerators/freezers. Sharp has 27 sales subsidiaries in 22 countries, 23 manufacturing bases in 13 countries and five research and development bases in four countries. The firm is also a leading manufacturer of solar cells. In March 2006, it was listed by PV News as the worldwide leader in total production of solar cells and modules. The company operates its own manufacturing plants for LCD TVs and makes large investments in research and development for LCD technology, recently introducing triple directional viewing technology, which allows one screen to produce three different images. Sharp recently began producing and marketing its new AQUOS line of LCD TVs, with an industry-best 2000:1 contrast ratio and available with as large as 65-inch screens. The firm's state-of-the-art Kameyama Plant No. 2 became operational in August 2006. The facility features an energy supply system based on integrating diverse power sources distributed within the plant into a single large-scale system independent of the utility power grid. These sources include the world's largest photovoltaic power system. In November 2007, subsidiary Sharp Electronics Co. Ltd. was dissolved.

FINANCIALS: Sales and profits are in thousands of dollars—add 000 to get the full amount. 2007 Note: Financial information for 2007 was not available for all companies at press time.

2007 Sales: $	2007 Profits: $	**U.S. Stock Ticker: SHCAY**
2006 Sales: $24,113,009	2006 Profits: $764,405	**Int'l Ticker: 6753** Int'l Exchange: Tokyo-TSE
2005 Sales: $23,960,934	2005 Profits: $724,953	Employees: 46,872
2004 Sales: $21,367,300	2004 Profits: $574,700	Fiscal Year Ends: 3/31
2003 Sales: $16,741,800	2003 Profits: $272,000	Parent Company:

SALARIES/BENEFITS:

Pension Plan:	ESOP Stock Plan:	Profit Sharing:	Top Exec. Salary: $	Bonus: $
Savings Plan:	Stock Purch. Plan:		Second Exec. Salary: $	Bonus: $

OTHER THOUGHTS:

Apparent Women Officers or Directors: 3
Hot Spot for Advancement for Women/Minorities: Y

LOCATIONS: ("Y" = Yes)

West:	Southwest:	Midwest:	Southeast:	Northeast:	International:
Y		Y	Y	Y	Y

SHAW COMMUNICATIONS INC

www.shaw.ca

Industry Group Code: 513220 Ranks within this company's industry group: Sales: 13 Profits: 10

Print Media/Publishing:	Movies:	Equipment/Supplies:		Broadcast/Cable:		Music/Audio:	Sports/Games/Gambling:
Newspapers:	Movie Theaters:	Equipment/Supplies:		Broadcast TV:		Music Production:	Games/Sports:
Magazines:	Movie Production:	Gambling Equipment:	Y	Cable TV:	Y	Retail Music:	Retail Games Stores:
Books:	TV/Video Prod.:	Special Services:	Y	Satellite Broadcast:		Retail Audio Equip.:	Stadiums/Teams:
Book Stores:	Video Rental:	Advertising Services:		Radio:		Music Print./Dist.:	Gambling/Casinos:
Distribution/Printing:	Video Distribution:	Info. Sys. Software:		Online Information:		Multimedia:	Rides/Theme Parks:

TYPES OF BUSINESS:

Cable TV Service
Internet Service Provider
Satellite Services
Digital Phone Services
Internet Infrastructure Services
Video-On-Demand

BRANDS/DIVISIONS/AFFILIATES:

High-Speed Xtreme
Video Cablesystems, Inc.
Shaw Business Solutions
Shaw Digital Phone
Canadian Satellite Communications, Inc.
Pemberton Cable
Whistler Cable Television Ltd.
Star Choice, a Shaw Company

CONTACTS: Note: Officers with more than one job title may be intentionally listed here more than once.

Jim Shaw, CEO
Peter J. Bissonette, Pres.
Steve Wilson, CFO/Sr. VP
David Taniguchi, Sr. Counsel/Asst. Corp. Sec.
Bradley S. Shaw, Sr. VP-Oper.
Michael D'Avella, Sr. VP-Planning
Ken Stein, Sr. VP-Corp. & Regulatory Affairs
Rhonda Bashnick, VP-Finance
Douglas J. Black, Corp. Sec.
J. R. Shaw, Exec. Chmn.

Phone: 403-750-4500	Fax: 403-750-4501
Toll-Free:	
Address: 630 3rd Ave. SW, Ste. 900, Calgary, AB T2P 4L4 Canada	

GROWTH PLANS/SPECIAL FEATURES:

Shaw Communications, Inc. is a diversified Canadian communications company whose core business is providing broadband cable television, high-speed Internet, digital phone, telecommunications services and satellite direct-to-home services. The company serves over 3 million customers. Shaw offers its services in two divisions: cable and satellite. The cable segment is the firm's core business. Offerings include basic cable, digital cable, pay-per-view and video-on-demand (VOD). Through this segment, the company also provides Internet access services to residential and small-business subscribers via a cable connection and cable modem. Shaw's High-Speed Xtreme service, offering significantly faster download and upload speeds than basic options, was extended to new geographic areas in 2006. The firm's Internet infrastructure services are offered through Shaw Business Solutions (formerly Big Pipe, Inc.) In addition, Shaw recently began offering the Shaw Digital Phone service employing PacketCable technology. The company's satellite segment operates through subsidiary Canadian Satellite Communications, Inc. In 2006, Shaw's VOD library expanded with new partnerships with Warner Bros. and Sony Pictures. In 2006 and 2007, Shaw agreed to acquire a number of cable and Internet companies and assets: Saltspring Cablevision's cable system on Saltspring Island; Pemberton Cable from Coast Mountain Communications; Sunshine Communication's systems in Grand Forks, British Columbia; Whistler Cable Television Ltd.; Norcom Telecommunications Limited; and six cable systems from Mascon Communications. In October 2006, Shaw re-branded all of its subsidiaries with the Shaw name: Cancom Tracking, a provider of on-board computing and communications for the trucking industry, is now called Shaw Tracking; Cancom Broadcast, a full service commercial signal distribution network, is now Shaw Broadcast Services; Star Choice Communications, Inc., a direct-to-home satellite television provider, is now Star Choice, a Shaw Company; and Big Pipe, Inc., a provider of fiber-optic networking and Internet services, is now Shaw Business Solutions.

FINANCIALS: Sales and profits are in thousands of dollars—add 000 to get the full amount. 2007 Note: Financial information for 2007 was not available for all companies at press time.

2007 Sales: $	2007 Profits: $	U.S. Stock Ticker: SJR
2006 Sales: $2,122,630	2006 Profits: $395,520	Int'l Ticker: SJR.B Int'l Exchange: Toronto-TSX
2005 Sales: $1,861,800	2005 Profits: $135,300	Employees: 6,000
2004 Sales: $1,585,600	2004 Profits: $69,300	Fiscal Year Ends: 8/31
2003 Sales: $1,605,120	2003 Profits: $-36,968	Parent Company:

SALARIES/BENEFITS:

Pension Plan:	ESOP Stock Plan:	Profit Sharing:	Top Exec. Salary: $721,787	Bonus: $4,958,252
Savings Plan: Y	Stock Purch. Plan:		Second Exec. Salary: $673,981	Bonus: $3,134,796

OTHER THOUGHTS:

Apparent Women Officers or Directors: 1
Hot Spot for Advancement for Women/Minorities:

LOCATIONS: ("Y" = Yes)

West:	Southwest:	Midwest:	Southeast:	Northeast:	International:
					Y

Note: Financial information, benefits and other data can change quickly and may vary from those stated here.

SHOP AT HOME NETWORK LLC   www.shopathometv.com

Industry Group Code: 454110B Ranks within this company's industry group: Sales: Profits:

Print Media/Publishing:	Movies:	Equipment/Supplies:	Broadcast/Cable:		Music/Audio:	Sports/Games/Gambling:
Newspapers:	Movie Theaters:	Equipment/Supplies:	Broadcast TV:	Y	Music Production:	Games/Sports:
Magazines:	Movie Production:	Gambling Equipment:	Cable TV:		Retail Music:	Retail Games Stores:
Books:	TV/Video Prod.:	Special Services: Y	Satellite Broadcast:		Retail Audio Equip.:	Stadiums/Teams:
Book Stores:	Video Rental:	Advertising Services:	Radio:		Music Print./Dist.:	Gambling/Casinos:
Distribution/Printing:	Video Distribution:	Info. Sys. Software:	Online Information:		Multimedia:	Rides/Theme Parks:

TYPES OF BUSINESS:

Television Shopping
Online Sales
Television Stations
Satellite Television

BRANDS/DIVISIONS/AFFILIATES:

ShopAtHomeTV.com
Jewelry Television

CONTACTS: Note: Officers with more than one job title may be intentionally listed here more than once.

Tim Engle, Pres.
Andy Caldwell, VP-Affiliate Mktg.
Kelly Fletcher, VP-Public Relations
Patsy Harris, Dir.-Distribution
Harris Bagley, Exec. VP-Affiliate Distribution
Burt Bagley, VP-Cable Distribution (Eastern Region)
Ray Pearson, VP-Cable Distribution (Western Region)
Tim Engle, Chmn.

Phone: 615-263-8000	Fax: 615-263-8084
Toll-Free: 866-366-4010	
Address: 5388 Hickory Hollow Parkway, Nashville, TN 37013 US	

GROWTH PLANS/SPECIAL FEATURES:

Shop at Home Network LLC, owned by Jewelry Television, operates Shop At Home Network, a nationally televised home shopping channel. Shop at Home Network sells merchandise 24-hours a day through interactive electronic media, including broadcast, cable, and satellite television. Shop At Home caters to men between the ages of 30 and 50, offering primarily jewelry, entertainment memorabilia, trading cards, knives and coins, emphasizing drop shipping as opposed to in-house stocking. The firm's sports and collectible products account for about 57% of sales. Shop at Home Network's television programming is available in over 80 million households through cable. In 2006, the firm sold five Shop At Home Broadcast Stations (WSAH 43 Bridgeport and Hartford, Connecticut; WMFP Boston, Massachusetts; KCNS San Francisco, California; WRAY Raleigh, North Carolina; and WOAC Cleveland, Ohio) to Multicultural Television Broadcasting, LLC for $170 million. Additional stations affiliated with Shop At Home are: WJJA (Milwaukee, Wisconsin), WYLE (Huntsville, Alabama), KSVM-LP (Santa Barbara, California), and WJYS (Chicago, Illinois). The company also operates a web site at ShopAtHomeTV.com. The company's advertisements and a show host convey information about the merchandise and demonstrate various uses for each product. Shop At Home seeks to differentiate itself from other televised shopping programmers by using an informal, personal style of presentation and by offering unique products. The firm has the studio and broadcasting capability to produce multiple live shows simultaneously, and it occasionally provides multiple broadcasts to differing viewer groups during peak viewing times. Some stations air Jewelry TV in the late morning and early afternoon. Jewelry Television acquired the company for $17 million from E.W Scripps Company in 2006.

The Shop at Home Network offers its employees a 401(k) plan, discounted stock purchase, flexible spending accounts, a pension plan and a credit union.

FINANCIALS: Sales and profits are in thousands of dollars—add 000 to get the full amount. 2007 Note: Financial information for 2007 was not available for all companies at press time.

2007 Sales: $	2007 Profits: $	U.S. Stock Ticker: Subsidiary
2006 Sales: $	2006 Profits: $	Int'l Ticker: Int'l Exchange:
2005 Sales: $	2005 Profits: $	Employees: 12
2004 Sales: $	2004 Profits: $	Fiscal Year Ends: 12/31
2003 Sales: $6,700	2003 Profits: $-2,500	Parent Company: JEWELRY TELEVISION

SALARIES/BENEFITS:

Pension Plan:	ESOP Stock Plan:	Profit Sharing:	Top Exec. Salary: $200,000	Bonus: $73,050
Savings Plan: Y	Stock Purch. Plan:		Second Exec. Salary: $176,923	Bonus: $75,000

OTHER THOUGHTS:

Apparent Women Officers or Directors: 4
Hot Spot for Advancement for Women/Minorities: Y

LOCATIONS: ("Y" = Yes)

West:	Southwest:	Midwest:	Southeast:	Northeast:	International:
Y		Y	Y	Y	

SHUFFLE MASTER INC

www.shufflemaster.com

Industry Group Code: 713290 Ranks within this company's industry group: Sales: 7 Profits: 5

Print Media/Publishing:	Movies:	Equipment/Supplies:		Broadcast/Cable:	Music/Audio:	Sports/Games/Gambling:
Newspapers:	Movie Theaters:	Equipment/Supplies:		Broadcast TV:	Music Production:	Games/Sports:
Magazines:	Movie Production:	Gambling Equipment:	Y	Cable TV:	Retail Music:	Retail Games Stores:
Books:	TV/Video Prod.:	Special Services:	Y	Satellite Broadcast:	Retail Audio Equip.:	Stadiums/Teams:
Book Stores:	Video Rental:	Advertising Services:		Radio:	Music Print./Dist.:	Gambling/Casinos:
Distribution/Printing:	Video Distribution:	Info. Sys. Software:		Online Information:	Multimedia:	Rides/Theme Parks:

TYPES OF BUSINESS:

Gaming Machines
Automated Card Shufflers
Table & Video Slot Games
Slot Machine Operating Systems

BRANDS/DIVISIONS/AFFILIATES:

Utility Products
Entertainment Products
Stargames
King
Deck Mate
MD2 Workstation
Vegas Star
Table Master

CONTACTS: *Note: Officers with more than one job title may be intentionally listed here more than once.*

Mark L. Yoseloff, CEO
Paul C. Meyer, COO
Paul C. Meyer, Pres.
Paul C. Meyer, Acting CFO
Jerome R. Smith, General Counsel/Sr. VP
Coreen Sawdon, Chief Acct. Officer/Sr. VP
R. Brooke Dunn, Sr. VP
Mark L. Yoseloff, Chmn.

Phone: 702-897-7150	Fax: 702-260-6691
Toll-Free:	
Address: 1106 Palms Airport Dr., Las Vegas, NV 89119 US	

GROWTH PLANS/SPECIAL FEATURES:

Shuffle Master, Inc. develops, manufactures and markets automatic card shuffling and chip counting equipment as well as table and video slot machine games for use in the gaming industry. The business is divided into two segments: utility products and entertainment products. The utility segment includes automatic shufflers, which are marketed under the trademarks Deck Mate; iDeal; King; one2six; MDI; and MD2. This segment also includes the Easy Chipper chip sorting machine and the MD2 Workstation, which combines proprietary software with a card batch shuffler to analyze the accuracy and composition of each deck. The firm is also jointly developing the Table iD system with outside companies IGT and PGIC. This system is intended to integrate sorting and shuffling hardware with player tracking, bet recognition and automated gaming chip tracking to create a comprehensive table management system. The entertainment products segment includes a line of proprietary table games that includes Let it Ride; Three Card Poker; Crazy 4 Poker; Mississippi Stud; and Casino War. This segment also produces electronic content delivery systems, including Table Master; Vegas Star; Rapid Table Games; and Casino on Demand. Additionally, the entertainment segment, through Australian subsidiary Stargames, offers a line of electronic gaming machines.

FINANCIALS: Sales and profits are in thousands of dollars—add 000 to get the full amount. 2007 Note: Financial information for 2007 was not available for all companies at press time.

2007 Sales: $	2007 Profits: $	**U.S. Stock Ticker:** SHFL
2006 Sales: $163,468	2006 Profits: $6,802	**Int'l Ticker:** Int'l Exchange:
2005 Sales: $112,860	2005 Profits: $29,180	Employees: 550
2004 Sales: $84,783	2004 Profits: $24,144	Fiscal Year Ends: 10/31
2003 Sales: $67,427	2003 Profits: $16,934	Parent Company:

SALARIES/BENEFITS:

Pension Plan:	ESOP Stock Plan:	Profit Sharing:	Top Exec. Salary: $402,000	Bonus: $50,000
Savings Plan: Y	Stock Purch. Plan:		Second Exec. Salary: $319,000	Bonus: $40,000

OTHER THOUGHTS:

Apparent Women Officers or Directors: 1
Hot Spot for Advancement for Women/Minorities:

LOCATIONS: ("Y" = Yes)

West:	Southwest:	Midwest:	Southeast:	Northeast:	International:
Y		Y			Y

Note: Financial information, benefits and other data can change quickly and may vary from those stated here.

SHUN TAK HOLDINGS LIMITED   www.shuntakgroup.com

Industry Group Code: 721110 Ranks within this company's industry group: Sales: Profits:

Print Media/Publishing:	Movies:	Equipment/Supplies:	Broadcast/Cable:	Music/Audio:	Sports/Games/Gambling:	
Newspapers:	Movie Theaters:	Equipment/Supplies:	Broadcast TV:	Music Production:	Games/Sports:	
Magazines:	Movie Production:	Gambling Equipment:	Cable TV:	Retail Music:	Retail Games Stores:	
Books:	TV/Video Prod.:	Special Services:	Satellite Broadcast:	Retail Audio Equip.:	Stadiums/Teams:	
Book Stores:	Video Rental:	Advertising Services:	Radio:	Music Print./Dist.:	Gambling/Casinos:	Y
Distribution/Printing:	Video Distribution:	Info. Sys. Software:	Online Information:	Multimedia:	Rides/Theme Parks:	

TYPES OF BUSINESS:

Investment Holding Company
High-Speed Ferry Services
Real Estate Investment
Hotel Management
Casino Management

BRANDS/DIVISIONS/AFFILIATES:

Far East Hydrofoil Co. Ltd.
Shun Tak-China Travel Shipping Investments Limited
TuboJET
The Belcher's
Sociedade de Turismo e Diversoes de Macau, S.A.
Cheung Sha Wan Shipyards
Jardine Shun Tak Insurance Brokers Ltd.

CONTACTS: Note: Officers with more than one job title may be intentionally listed here more than once.

Daisy Ho, CFO
Stanley Ho, Chmn.

Phone: 852-2859-3111	Fax: 852-2857-7181
Toll-Free:	
Address: Penthouse, 39 Fl. West Tower, 200 Connaught Rd., Hong Kong, Hong Kong China	

GROWTH PLANS/SPECIAL FEATURES:

Shun Tak Holdings Limited is a sprawling investment holding company. The company is a publicly traded Hong Kong-based conglomerate with core businesses in the shipping, property, investments and hospitality sectors. Shun Tak, though its subsidiary Far East Hydrofoil Co. Ltd., offers 24-hour passenger ferry service between Hong Kong and Macau. It also operates and manages Shun Tak-China Travel Shipping Investments Limited, a joint venture of which it owns 71% and China Travel International Investments owns the remainder. The company also owns TurboJET, a deluxe highs-speed ferry services company. Shun Tak's property division develops and invests in property in Hong Kong and Macau. Its major interests in residential and commercial properties include The Belcher's, a complex of six residential towers on a retail podium that covers 2.9 million square feet; Liberte, a complex of seven residential towers on a retail podium that covers 1.9 million square feet; the Cheung Sha Wan Shipyards; and Shun Tak Business Centre, an office and retail property that covers 521,467 square feet. The group's investments segment has interests in the Sociedade de Turismo e Diversoes de Macau, S.A. (SDTM) and the Jardine Shun Tak Insurance Brokers Ltd. SDTM has held a monopoly on gambling operations in Macau for over 40 years until 2002. It now possesses one of the three gambling licenses given by Macao. Of the 17 casinos in Macao, SDTM operates 14. Shun Tak's hospitality segment is engaged in hotel and casino management, with a 50% interest in Mandarin Oriental and a 34.9% interest in The Westin Resort. The group also manages Hotel Lisboa and Hotel Sintra in Macau.

FINANCIALS: Sales and profits are in thousands of dollars—add 000 to get the full amount. 2007 Note: Financial information for 2007 was not available for all companies at press time.

2007 Sales: $	2007 Profits: $	U.S. Stock Ticker:	
2006 Sales: $	2006 Profits: $	Int'l Ticker: 0242	Int'l Exchange: Hong Kong-HKEX
2005 Sales: $	2005 Profits: $	Employees:	
2004 Sales: $	2004 Profits: $	Fiscal Year Ends:	
2003 Sales: $	2003 Profits: $	Parent Company:	

SALARIES/BENEFITS:

Pension Plan:	ESOP Stock Plan:	Profit Sharing:	Top Exec. Salary: $	Bonus: $
Savings Plan:	Stock Purch. Plan:		Second Exec. Salary: $	Bonus: $

OTHER THOUGHTS:

Apparent Women Officers or Directors: 3
Hot Spot for Advancement for Women/Minorities: Y

LOCATIONS: ("Y" = Yes)

West:	Southwest:	Midwest:	Southeast:	Northeast:	International:
					Y

SIMEX-IWERKS

www.simex-iwerks.com

Industry Group Code: 512131 Ranks within this company's industry group: Sales: Profits:

Print Media/Publishing:	Movies:		Equipment/Supplies:		Broadcast/Cable:	Music/Audio:	Sports/Games/Gambling:
Newspapers:	Movie Theaters:	Y	Equipment/Supplies:	Y	Broadcast TV:	Music Production:	Games/Sports:
Magazines:	Movie Production:	Y	Gambling Equipment:		Cable TV:	Retail Music:	Retail Games Stores:
Books:	TV/Video Prod.:		Special Services:	Y	Satellite Broadcast:	Retail Audio Equip.:	Stadiums/Teams:
Book Stores:	Video Rental:		Advertising Services:		Radio:	Music Print./Dist.:	Gambling/Casinos:
Distribution/Printing:	Video Distribution:		Info. Sys. Software:		Online Information:	Multimedia:	Rides/Theme Parks:

TYPES OF BUSINESS:

Movie Theaters-3D
Ride Simulation Theaters
Equipment & Facility Leasing
Format Conversion Services

BRANDS/DIVISIONS/AFFILIATES:

Iwerks Entertainment, Inc.
Simex, Inc.
Extreme Screens

CONTACTS: Note: Officers with more than one job title may be intentionally listed here more than once.

Michael Needham, CEO
Michael Needham, Pres.
David Needham, Sr. VP-Sales
Brian Peebles, Sr. VP-Oper.
Shiori Sudo, Exec. VP/Head-Film Distrib.
Mike Frueh, VP/General Mgr.
Mark Cornell, Sr. Dir.-Attractions Dev.
Michael Needham, Chmn.

Phone: 818-841-7766	Fax: 818-840-6192
Toll-Free: 800-388-8628	
Address: 4520 Valerio St., Burbank, CA 91505-1046 US	

GROWTH PLANS/SPECIAL FEATURES:

SimEx-Iwerks, formed by the acquisition of Iwerks Entertainment, Inc. by SimEx, Inc., designs, engineers, manufactures, markets and services high-tech entertainment attractions that employ a variety of projection, show control, ride simulation and software technologies. The company sells and installs ride simulation attractions in specialty theaters, large-format theaters and theaters that include special 3-D effects. Its Extreme Screens brand of theatres feature 80 foot tall by 80 foot wide screens and can project 2-D and 3-D pictures. SimEx-Iwerks also licenses and distributes the films in its library to ride simulation and large-format theaters and specialty theater attractions. The company has a catalog of over 125 titles, many available in French, Spanish, Mandarin, Korean, Japanese, Portuguese and German. The firm produces and distributes films in the 8/70 and 15/70 film formats for third parties and also invests in joint ventures by contributing its ride simulation technology, design and equipment and by participating in theater profits. In addition, SimEx-Iwerks leases camera equipment and rents post-production facilities. The primary markets for the company's attractions are theme parks, museums, movie theaters and various types of location-based entertainment centers, destination centers and special event venues. The company produces six different motion-ride simulators ranging from open platforms to enclosed cabins and having seating capacities between six and 90. SimEx-Iwerks has installed more than 250 specialty-format theater attractions in 37 countries, including 119 ride simulation theaters that the company supports with a library of 50 ride simulation films, the industry's largest premium ride simulation film library.

FINANCIALS: Sales and profits are in thousands of dollars—add 000 to get the full amount. 2007 Note: Financial information for 2007 was not available for all companies at press time.

2007 Sales: $	2007 Profits: $	U.S. Stock Ticker: Private
2006 Sales: $	2006 Profits: $	Int'l Ticker: Int'l Exchange:
2005 Sales: $	2005 Profits: $	Employees: 89
2004 Sales: $	2004 Profits: $	Fiscal Year Ends: 6/30
2003 Sales: $	2003 Profits: $	Parent Company:

SALARIES/BENEFITS:

Pension Plan:	ESOP Stock Plan:	Profit Sharing:	Top Exec. Salary: $247,373	Bonus: $
Savings Plan:	Stock Purch. Plan:		Second Exec. Salary: $140,481	Bonus: $

OTHER THOUGHTS:

Apparent Women Officers or Directors: 1
Hot Spot for Advancement for Women/Minorities:

LOCATIONS: ("Y" = Yes)

West:	Southwest:	Midwest:	Southeast:	Northeast:	International:
Y			Y		Y

SIMON & SCHUSTER INC

www.simonsays.com

Industry Group Code: 511130 Ranks within this company's industry group: Sales: Profits:

Print Media/Publishing:	Movies:	Equipment/Supplies:	Broadcast/Cable:	Music/Audio:		Sports/Games/Gambling:
Newspapers:	Movie Theaters:	Equipment/Supplies:	Broadcast TV:	Music Production:	Y	Games/Sports:
Magazines:	Movie Production:	Gambling Equipment:	Cable TV:	Retail Music:		Retail Games Stores:
Books: Y	TV/Video Prod.:	Special Services:	Satellite Broadcast:	Retail Audio Equip.:		Stadiums/Teams:
Book Stores:	Video Rental:	Advertising Services:	Radio:	Music Print./Dist.:	Y	Gambling/Casinos:
Distribution/Printing:	Video Distribution:	Info. Sys. Software:	Online Information:	Multimedia:		Rides/Theme Parks:

TYPES OF BUSINESS:

Book Publishing & Distribution
Online Publishing
E-Books
CDs & CD-ROMs
Audio Books
Children's Publishing

BRANDS/DIVISIONS/AFFILIATES:

CBS Corporation
Fireside
Atria
Free Press (The)
Scribner
Pocket Books
Touchstone
Aladdin

CONTACTS: *Note: Officers with more than one job title may be intentionally listed here more than once.*

Carolyn K. Reidy, CEO
Carolyn K. Reidy, Pres.
David England, CFO/Sr. VP
Michael Selleck, Exec. VP-Mktg. & Sales
Carolyn Connolly, Sr. VP-Human Resources
Anne L. Davies, CIO/Sr. VP
Elisa Rivlin, General Counsel/Sr. VP
Dennis Eulau, Exec. VP-Oper.
Kate Tentler, Sr. VP-Digital Media
Adam Rothberg, VP/Dir.-Corp. Comm.
Rick Richter, Pres., Children's Publishing Division
Christopher Lynch, Exec. VP/Publisher-Simon & Schuster Audio
Farnscois McHardy, Managing Dir.-Simon & Schuster Australia
Ian S. Chapman, Managing Dir.-Simon & Schuster UK
Joe D'Onofrio, Sr. VP-Supply Chain Oper.

Phone: 212-698-7000	**Fax:** 212-698-7099
Toll-Free: 800-223-2336	
Address: 1230 Ave. of the Americas, New York, NY 10020 US	

GROWTH PLANS/SPECIAL FEATURES:

Simon & Schuster, Inc. (S&S), a subsidiary of CBS Corporation, publishes print titles in a wide variety of genres, as well as CDs, CD-ROMs, novelty format books and e-books. The company publishes under imprints such as Simon & Schuster, Pocket Books, Scribner, Free Press, Atria, Fireside, Touchstone, Atheneum Books for Young Readers, Little Simon, Simon Spotlight, and Simon Spotlight Entertainment. S&S distributes titles in 100 countries around the world through seven main divisions: the adult publishing group, children's publishing, audio, online, U.K., Canada and Australia. The company's web site, simonsays.com, which includes sites based in the U.K., Canada and Simon & Schuster, Inc. (S&S), a subsidiary of CBS Corporation, publishes print titles in a wide variety of genres, as well as CDs, CD-ROMs, novelty format books and e-books. The company publishes under imprints such as Simon & Schuster, Pocket Books, Scribner, The Free Press, Atria, Fireside, Touchstone, Atheneum Books for Young Readers, Little Simon, Simon Spotlight, and Simon Spotlight Entertainment. S&S distributes titles in 100 countries around the world through seven main divisions: the adult publishing group, children's publishing, audio, online, U.K., Canada and Australia. Stephen King, Dr. Phil McGraw, Stephen Ambrose and Bob Dylan have all signed contracts to have books published and marketed through S&S. The company's web site, simonsays.com, which includes sites based in the U.K., Canada and Australia, provides users with a forum to discuss books; newsletters with information on new releases; and an e-books section allowing customers to purchase books online. The Simon & Schuster Audio division publishes audio books including fiction, nonfiction and self-improvement titles, as well as Pimsleur Language Programs. The firm's children's publishing division offers acclaimed backlist titles, including famous characters such as Raggedy Ann, The Hardy Boys, Nancy Drew and Buffy the Vampire Slayer. In January 2007, Simon & Schuster began a local publishing program in India.

S&S offers an Associates Program for recent graduates. This one-year program rotates new employees through various departments, offering broad experience in the publishing business. The firm also offers internship positions.

FINANCIALS: Sales and profits are in thousands of dollars—add 000 to get the full amount. 2007 Note: Financial information for 2007 was not available for all companies at press time.

2007 Sales: $	2007 Profits: $	**U.S. Stock Ticker:** Subsidiary
2006 Sales: $	2006 Profits: $	**Int'l Ticker:** Int'l Exchange:
2005 Sales: $	2005 Profits: $	**Employees:**
2004 Sales: $796,000	2004 Profits: $	**Fiscal Year Ends:** 12/31
2003 Sales: $	2003 Profits: $	**Parent Company:** CBS CORP

SALARIES/BENEFITS:

Pension Plan:	ESOP Stock Plan:	Profit Sharing:	Top Exec. Salary: $	Bonus: $
Savings Plan:	Stock Purch. Plan:		Second Exec. Salary: $	Bonus: $

OTHER THOUGHTS:

Apparent Women Officers or Directors: 5
Hot Spot for Advancement for Women/Minorities: Y

LOCATIONS: ("Y" = Yes)

West:	Southwest:	Midwest:	Southeast:	Northeast:	International:
				Y	Y

Note: Financial information, benefits and other data can change quickly and may vary from those stated here.

SINCLAIR BROADCAST GROUP INC

www.sbgi.net

Industry Group Code: 513120 Ranks within this company's industry group: Sales: 11   Profits: 9

Print Media/Publishing:	Movies:	Equipment/Supplies:		Broadcast/Cable:		Music/Audio:	Sports/Games/Gambling:
Newspapers:	Movie Theaters:	Equipment/Supplies:		Broadcast TV:	Y	Music Production:	Games/Sports:
Magazines:	Movie Production:	Gambling Equipment:		Cable TV:		Retail Music:	Retail Games Stores:
Books:	TV/Video Prod.:	Special Services:	Y	Satellite Broadcast:		Retail Audio Equip.:	Stadiums/Teams:
Book Stores:	Video Rental:	Advertising Services:	Y	Radio:		Music Print./Dist.:	Gambling/Casinos:
Distribution/Printing:	Video Distribution:	Info. Sys. Software:		Online Information:		Multimedia:	Rides/Theme Parks:

TYPES OF BUSINESS:

Radio & TV Station Owner/Operator
Broadcasting & Programming Services

BRANDS/DIVISIONS/AFFILIATES:

Alarm Funding Associates

CONTACTS: *Note: Officers with more than one job title may be intentionally listed here more than once.*

David D. Smith, CEO
David D. Smith, Pres.
David B. Amy, CFO/Exec. VP
Donald H. Thompson, VP-Human Resources
Nat S. Ostroff, VP-New Tech.
Barry M. Faber, General Counsel/VP
David R. Bochenek, Chief Acct. Officer/VP
Lucy A. Rutishauser, VP-Corp. Finance/Treas.
J. Duncan Smith, Sec./VP
Frederick G. Smith, VP
Steven M. Marks, COO-Television Div.
David D. Smith, Chmn.
Thomas I. Water, III, VP-Purchasing

Phone: 410-568-1500	Fax: 410-568-1533
Toll-Free:	
Address: 10706 Beaver Dam Rd., Hunt Valley, MD 21030 US	

GROWTH PLANS/SPECIAL FEATURES:

Sinclair Broadcast Group, Inc., which reaches roughly 22% of U.S. television households, is a diversified broadcasting company that owns, provides programming and operating services and sales services to 57 television stations in 35 markets. The company has 11 duopoly markets where it owns and operates at least two stations within the same market. The firm has 11 local marketing agreements where it owns and operates one station in the market and provides programming and operating services to or by another station within that market. In the remaining 15 markets, the company has a single television station. Sinclair Broadcasting focuses on mid-size markets. The television station group is diverse in network affiliation: FOX (19 stations); MyNetworkTV (17 stations); ABC (10) stations; ABC (10 stations); The CW (nine Stations); CBS (two stations) and NBC (one station). The company broadcasts free over-the-air programming to television viewing audiences in the communities it serves through its local television stations. The programming provided consists of network provided programs, news produced locally, local sporting events and syndicated entertainment programs. The firm produces news through 19 stations in 13 markets including two stations that have a local news sharing agreement with a competitive station in that market. Sinclair Broadcast has 13 stations with local news sharing arrangements with a competitive station in that market, which produces the news aired on the company's station. The firm provides live local sporting events on many of its stations by acquiring the local television broadcast rights for these events. Additionally, it purchases and barters for popular syndicated programming for third parties. In November 2007, Sinclair Broadcasting purchased 95% of Alarm Funding Associates for $5.5 million.

The company offers its employees health, dental and vision insurance; life and AD&D insurance; short- and long-term disability insurance; a 401(k) plan; an employee stock purchase plan; and education reimbursement.

FINANCIALS: Sales and profits are in thousands of dollars—add 000 to get the full amount. 2007 Note: Financial information for 2007 was not available for all companies at press time.

2007 Sales: $	2007 Profits: $	U.S. Stock Ticker: SBGI
2006 Sales: $715,138	2006 Profits: $53,977	Int'l Ticker: Int'l Exchange:
2005 Sales: $692,067	2005 Profits: $185,932	Employees: 2,786
2004 Sales: $708,279	2004 Profits: $24,022	Fiscal Year Ends: 12/31
2003 Sales: $738,741	2003 Profits: $24,392	Parent Company:

SALARIES/BENEFITS:

Pension Plan:	ESOP Stock Plan:	Profit Sharing:	Top Exec. Salary: $1,000,000	Bonus: $
Savings Plan: Y	Stock Purch. Plan: Y		Second Exec. Salary: $658,320	Bonus: $410,000

OTHER THOUGHTS:

Apparent Women Officers or Directors: 1
Hot Spot for Advancement for Women/Minorities:

LOCATIONS: ("Y" = Yes)

West:	Southwest:	Midwest:	Southeast:	Northeast:	International:
Y	Y	Y	Y	Y	

Note: Financial information, benefits and other data can change quickly and may vary from those stated here.

SIRIUS SATELLITE RADIO   www.sirius.com

Industry Group Code: 513111A Ranks within this company's industry group: Sales: 2 Profits: 2

Print Media/Publishing:	Movies:	Equipment/Supplies:	Broadcast/Cable:	Music/Audio:	Sports/Games/Gambling:
Newspapers:	Movie Theaters:	Equipment/Supplies:	Broadcast TV:	Music Production:	Games/Sports:
Magazines:	Movie Production:	Gambling Equipment:	Cable TV:	Retail Music:	Retail Games Stores:
Books:	TV/Video Prod.:	Special Services:	Satellite Broadcast:	Retail Audio Equip.:	Stadiums/Teams:
Book Stores:	Video Rental:	Advertising Services:	Radio:	Music Print./Dist.:	Gambling/Casinos:
Distribution/Printing:	Video Distribution:	Info. Sys. Software:	Online Information:	Multimedia:	Rides/Theme Parks:

TYPES OF BUSINESS:

Satellite Radio Broadcasting

BRANDS/DIVISIONS/AFFILIATES:

CD Radio, Inc.
Martha Stewart Radio
Sirius Canada
Ford Motor Co.

CONTACTS: *Note: Officers with more than one job title may be intentionally listed here more than once.*

Mel Karmazin, CEO
David Frear, CFO/Exec. VP
John Schultz, Sr. VP-Human Resources
Patrick Donnelly, General Counsel/Exec. VP
James Meyer, Pres., Oper. & Sales
Andreas Lazar, Sr. VP-Bus. Dev.
Scott Greenstein, Pres., Entertainment & Sports
Joseph Clayton, Chmn.

Phone: 212-899-5100	**Fax:** 212-584-5200
Toll-Free: 888-539-7474	
Address: 1221 Ave. of the Americas, 36th Fl., New York, NY 10020 US	

GROWTH PLANS/SPECIAL FEATURES:

Sirius Satellite Radio, Inc. owns and operates a subscription-based satellite radio service featuring digital audio music and news. The company's three satellites broadcast 69 channels of commercial-free music and 65 channels of news, sports, weather, comedy, talk, public radio and children's programming. Sirius broadcasts content from other networks, such as CNN, NPR, BBC, FOX, The Weather Channel, E!, ESPN and The Discovery Channel, as well as its own original programming. As of the beginning of 2007, Sirius had over 6 million subscribers. The firm has entered into agreements with consumer electronics manufacturers, including Kenwood Corporation, Sony Electronics and Visteon Automotive Systems, to market Sirius receivers for use in cars, boats and homes. Its receivers are now available at over 25,000 national and regional retailers, including Best Buy and Circuit City. Sirius has partnerships with manufacturers and retailers to make its hardware available as an option for car buyers, and thus far, has factory-installed its systems in 132 vehicle models. Sirius Canada has launched service in Canada with 110 channels of commercial-free music, news, sports, talk and entertainment programming, including 10 channels of Canadian content. The company also offers, or is developing, ancillary services. In 2006, Sirius introduced a service that provides graphic information as to road closings, traffic flow and incident data to consumers with in-vehicle navigation systems and a marine weather service that provides a range of information, including sea surface temperatures, wave heights and extended forecasts, to recreational boaters. In 2007, the company plans to introduce a video service that will offer premium video content designed primarily for children in the backseat of vehicles. In February 2007, Sirius agreed to a merger of equals with XM Satellite Radio Holdings, Inc. The $11.4 billion merger is subject to massive regulatory oversight, which may derail the deal.

FINANCIALS: Sales and profits are in thousands of dollars—add 000 to get the full amount. 2007 Note: Financial information for 2007 was not available for all companies at press time.

2007 Sales: $	2007 Profits: $	**U.S. Stock Ticker:** SIRI
2006 Sales: $637,235	2006 Profits: $-1,104,867	**Int'l Ticker:** Int'l Exchange:
2005 Sales: $242,245	2005 Profits: $-862,997	Employees: 772
2004 Sales: $66,854	2004 Profits: $-712,162	Fiscal Year Ends: 12/31
2003 Sales: $12,872	2003 Profits: $-226,215	Parent Company:

SALARIES/BENEFITS:

Pension Plan:	ESOP Stock Plan:	Profit Sharing:	Top Exec. Salary: $1,250,000	Bonus: $3,000,000
Savings Plan: Y	Stock Purch. Plan: Y		Second Exec. Salary: $778,396	Bonus: $462,500

OTHER THOUGHTS:

Apparent Women Officers or Directors: 3
Hot Spot for Advancement for Women/Minorities: Y

LOCATIONS: ("Y" = Yes)

West:	Southwest:	Midwest:	Southeast:	Northeast:	International:
				Y	Y

SIX FLAGS INC

www.sixflags.com

Industry Group Code: 713110 Ranks within this company's industry group: Sales: 2   Profits: 3

Print Media/Publishing:	Movies:	Equipment/Supplies:	Broadcast/Cable:	Music/Audio:	Sports/Games/Gambling:	
Newspapers:	Movie Theaters:	Equipment/Supplies:	Broadcast TV:	Music Production:	Games/Sports:	
Magazines:	Movie Production:	Gambling Equipment:	Cable TV:	Retail Music:	Retail Games Stores:	
Books:	TV/Video Prod.:	Special Services:	Satellite Broadcast:	Retail Audio Equip.:	Stadiums/Teams:	
Book Stores:	Video Rental:	Advertising Services:	Radio:	Music Print./Dist.:	Gambling/Casinos:	Y
Distribution/Printing:	Video Distribution:	Info. Sys. Software:	Online Information:	Multimedia:	Rides/Theme Parks:	

TYPES OF BUSINESS:
Theme Parks

BRANDS/DIVISIONS/AFFILIATES:
Marine World
Six Flags Wild Safari
Six Flags Great Adventure
Kingda Ka
Six Flags Darien Lake
Waterworld USA
Splashtown
Wild Waves and Enchanted Village

CONTACTS: *Note: Officers with more than one job title may be intentionally listed here more than once.*
Mark Shapiro, CEO
Mark Shapiro, Pres.
Jeff Speed, CFO/Exec. VP
Mike Antinoro, Exec. VP-Entertainment & Mktg.
James M. Coughlin, General Counsel
Mark Quenzel, VP-Park Strategy & Mgmt.
Andrew Schleimer, Exec. VP-In-Park Svcs.
Lou Koskovolis, Exec. VP-Corp. Alliances
Daniel Snyder, Chmn.

Phone: 212-652-9403	Fax:
Toll-Free:	
Address: 1540 Broadway, 15th Fl., New York, NY 10036 US	

GROWTH PLANS/SPECIAL FEATURES:

Six Flags, Inc. is the largest regional theme park operator in the world, with 27 parks in operation in North America and a yearly attendance of about 28.5 million. Six Flags parks offer families a selection of state-of-the-art thrill rides, water attractions, themed areas, concerts and shows, restaurants, game venues and merchandise outlets. The company offers more than 900 rides, including over 130 roller coasters. The company's theme parks include Six Flags Marine World (in California), which features marine mammals and exotic land animals; Six Flags Wild Safari (New Jersey), a 350 acre drive-through safari; and Six Flags Great Adventure (New Jersey), the firm's largest park and the 21st largest theme park in North America. The company holds exclusive long-term licenses for theme park usage of Warner Bros. and DC Comics characters, including Bugs Bunny, Daffy Duck, Batman and Superman. In 2005, the company opened the Kingda Ka roller coaster in the Six Flags Great Adventure Park in Jackson, New Jersey. The ride currently holds the record for tallest and fastest roller coaster in the world, at 456 feet high and attaining 128 mph. In 2007, the company agreed to sell seven of its parks in a single transaction. The parks are: Six Flags Darien Lake, near Buffalo, New York; Waterworld USA in Concord, California; Six Flags Elitch Gardens in Denver, Colorado; Splashtown in Houston, Texas; Frontier City theme park and the White Water Bay water park in Oklahoma City, Oklahoma; and Wild Waves and Enchanted Village near Seattle, Washington.

Six Flags offers seasonal employment targeted especially to international student workers and provides accommodations and transportation (where necessary) at all of it parks. Additional employee benefits include free park tickets, discounts at park stores, site-seeing trips, employee parties and a flexible work schedule.

FINANCIALS: Sales and profits are in thousands of dollars—add 000 to get the full amount. 2007 Note: Financial information for 2007 was not available for all companies at press time.

2007 Sales: $	2007 Profits: $	U.S. Stock Ticker: SIX
2006 Sales: $945,665	2006 Profits: $-327,588	Int'l Ticker: Int'l Exchange:
2005 Sales: $956,757	2005 Profits: $-110,938	Employees: 35,500
2004 Sales: $879,586	2004 Profits: $-464,800	Fiscal Year Ends: 12/31
2003 Sales: $1,007,276	2003 Profits: $-61,700	Parent Company:

SALARIES/BENEFITS:

Pension Plan: Y	ESOP Stock Plan:	Profit Sharing:	Top Exec. Salary: $1,055,192	Bonus: $
Savings Plan: Y	Stock Purch. Plan:		Second Exec. Salary: $639,846	Bonus: $300,000

OTHER THOUGHTS:
Apparent Women Officers or Directors:
Hot Spot for Advancement for Women/Minorities:

LOCATIONS: ("Y" = Yes)

West:	Southwest:	Midwest:	Southeast:	Northeast:	International:
Y	Y	Y	Y	Y	Y

Note: Financial information, benefits and other data can change quickly and may vary from those stated here.

SKY NETWORK TELEVISION LIMITED

www.sky.co.nz

Industry Group Code: 513220 Ranks within this company's industry group: Sales: 16   Profits: 12

Print Media/Publishing:	Movies:	Equipment/Supplies:	Broadcast/Cable:	Music/Audio:	Sports/Games/Gambling:
Newspapers:	Movie Theaters:	Equipment/Supplies:	Broadcast TV: Y	Music Production:	Games/Sports:
Magazines:	Movie Production:	Gambling Equipment:	Cable TV: Y	Retail Music:	Retail Games Stores:
Books:	TV/Video Prod.:	Special Services: Y	Satellite Broadcast:	Retail Audio Equip.:	Stadiums/Teams:
Book Stores:	Video Rental:	Advertising Services:	Radio:	Music Print./Dist.:	Gambling/Casinos: Y
Distribution/Printing:	Video Distribution:	Info. Sys. Software:	Online Information:	Multimedia:	Rides/Theme Parks:

TYPES OF BUSINESS:

Satellite TV
Broadcast TV
Pay Per View TV
Rugby Team
Radio Stations
Online Movie Rentals
Gambling Services

BRANDS/DIVISIONS/AFFILIATES:

SkyBet Trackside
SkyBet Sport
Independent Newspapers Limited
News Corporation

CONTACTS: *Note: Officers with more than one job title may be intentionally listed here more than once.*

John Fellet, CEO
Jason Hollingworth, CFO
Mike Watson, Dir.-Mktg.
Charles Ingley, Dir.-Tech.
Brian Green, Dir.-Eng.
Martin Wrigley, Mgr.-Oper.
Tony O'Brien, Dir.-Comm.
John Simmons, General Mgr.
Kevin Cameron, Dir.-Sport
Travis Dunbar, Dir.-Movies & Entertainment
Richard Last, Dir.-Advertising
Peter Macourt, Chmn.

Phone: 64-9-579-9999	**Fax:** 64-9-525-8324
Toll-Free:	

Address: 10 Panorama Rd., Mt. Wellington, Auckland, New Zealand

GROWTH PLANS/SPECIAL FEATURES:

SKY Network Television Limited is the largest provider of pay-television services in New Zealand. SKY offers a range of sports, movies, music, on-demand and general content across more than 80 channels. SKY's channel line-up includes six sports channels, five movie channels, five general entertainment channels, four documentary channels, three news channels, three children's channels and other niche channels. In addition to television channels, SKY offers digital music channels and its SkyBet Trackside and SkyBet Sport services through which subscribers can place wagers on horse races and other sporting events through their cable receiver. SKY has a total subscriber base of over 711,000. The firm offers digital and UHF services. The UHF package includes four channels, which require a decoder rented from the company to view. The firm's digital services offer over 40 satellite channels available in a variety of packages. The company also owns the rights to broadcast international rugby in New Zealand, a lucrative market and a significant incentive for customers to subscribe.

FINANCIALS: Sales and profits are in thousands of dollars—add 000 to get the full amount. 2007 Note: Financial information for 2007 was not available for all companies at press time.

2007 Sales: $	2007 Profits: $	**U.S. Stock Ticker:**
2006 Sales: $383,840	2006 Profits: $42,090	**Int'l Ticker: SKT** Int'l Exchange: Wellington-NZX
2005 Sales: $347,306	2005 Profits: $56,002	Employees: 600
2004 Sales: $278,200	2004 Profits: $22,300	Fiscal Year Ends: 6/30
2003 Sales: $227,700	2003 Profits: $ 400	Parent Company:

SALARIES/BENEFITS:

Pension Plan:	ESOP Stock Plan:	Profit Sharing:	Top Exec. Salary: $	Bonus: $
Savings Plan:	Stock Purch. Plan:		Second Exec. Salary: $	Bonus: $

OTHER THOUGHTS:

Apparent Women Officers or Directors:
Hot Spot for Advancement for Women/Minorities:

LOCATIONS: ("Y" = Yes)

West:	Southwest:	Midwest:	Southeast:	Northeast:	International: Y

Note: Financial information, benefits and other data can change quickly and may vary from those stated here.

SONY BMG MUSIC ENTERTAINMENT   www.sonybmg.com

Industry Group Code: 512230 Ranks within this company's industry group: Sales: Profits:

Print Media/Publishing:	Movies:	Equipment/Supplies:	Broadcast/Cable:	Music/Audio:		Sports/Games/Gambling:
Newspapers:	Movie Theaters:	Equipment/Supplies:	Broadcast TV:	Music Production:	Y	Games/Sports:
Magazines:	Movie Production:	Gambling Equipment:	Cable TV:	Retail Music:		Retail Games Stores:
Books:	TV/Video Prod.:	Special Services:	Satellite Broadcast:	Retail Audio Equip.:		Stadiums/Teams:
Book Stores:	Video Rental:	Advertising Services:	Radio:	Music Print./Dist.:		Gambling/Casinos:
Distribution/Printing:	Video Distribution:	Info. Sys. Software:	Online Information:	Multimedia:		Rides/Theme Parks:

TYPES OF BUSINESS:
Recorded Music Production
Record Labels

BRANDS/DIVISIONS/AFFILIATES:
Sony Music Entertainment
BMG Entertainment
Sony Corporation of America
Bertelsmann
Arista Records
Columbia Records
RCA Victor Group
Jive Records

CONTACTS: Note: Officers with more than one job title may be intentionally listed here more than once.
Rolf Schmidt-Holtz, CEO
Tim Bowen, COO
Kevin Kelleher, CFO/Exec. VP
Andrew Lack, Chmn.

Phone: 212-833-7100	Fax: 212-833-7416
Toll-Free:	
Address: 550 Madison Ave., New York, NY 10022-3211 US	

GROWTH PLANS/SPECIAL FEATURES:
Sony BMG Music Entertainment, formed in 2004 through the merger of Sony Music Entertainment and Bertelsmann A.G., is an international record label owner and operator. Sony Corporation of America and Bertelsmann own equal shares of the company. Sony BMG has offices in Argentina, Australia, Austria, Belgium, Brazil, Canada, Chile, China, Columbia, Costa Rica, Czech Republic, Denmark, Ecuador, Finland, France, Germany, Greece, Hong Kong, Hungary, India, Indonesia, Ireland, Italy, Japan, Korea, Malaysia, Mexico, New Zealand, Norway, the Philippines, Poland, Portugal, Russia, Singapore, South Africa, Spain, Sweden, Switzerland, Taiwan, Thailand, Turkey, Uruguay, Venezuela, the U.K. and the U.S. Company record labels include Arista Records, Columbia Records, Epic Records, J Records, Jive Records, LaFace Records, Legacy Recordings, Provident Music Group, RCA Records, RCA Victor Group, SONY BMG Masterworks, and Verity Records. Artists that are featured under these labels include Avril Lavigne, Britney Spears, Sean Kingston, Chris Brown and Alicia Keys.

FINANCIALS: Sales and profits are in thousands of dollars—add 000 to get the full amount. 2007 Note: Financial information for 2007 was not available for all companies at press time.

2007 Sales: $	2007 Profits: $	U.S. Stock Ticker: Joint Venture
2006 Sales: $	2006 Profits: $	Int'l Ticker: Int'l Exchange:
2005 Sales: $5,000,000	2005 Profits: $	Employees: 10,000
2004 Sales: $	2004 Profits: $	Fiscal Year Ends: 3/31
2003 Sales: $	2003 Profits: $	Parent Company:

SALARIES/BENEFITS:
Pension Plan:	ESOP Stock Plan:	Profit Sharing:	Top Exec. Salary: $	Bonus: $
Savings Plan:	Stock Purch. Plan:		Second Exec. Salary: $	Bonus: $

OTHER THOUGHTS:
Apparent Women Officers or Directors:
Hot Spot for Advancement for Women/Minorities:

LOCATIONS: ("Y" = Yes)
West:	Southwest:	Midwest:	Southeast:	Northeast:	International:
Y		Y		Y	Y

Note: Financial information, benefits and other data can change quickly and may vary from those stated here.

SONY CORPORATION

www.sony.net

Industry Group Code: 334310 Ranks within this company's industry group: Sales: 2   Profits: 3

Print Media/Publishing:	Movies:		Equipment/Supplies:		Broadcast/Cable:	Music/Audio:		Sports/Games/Gambling:	
Newspapers:	Movie Theaters:	Y	Equipment/Supplies:	Y	Broadcast TV:	Music Production:	Y	Games/Sports:	Y
Magazines:	Movie Production:	Y	Gambling Equipment:		Cable TV:	Retail Music:		Retail Games Stores:	
Books:	TV/Video Prod.:	Y	Special Services:	Y	Satellite Broadcast:	Retail Audio Equip.:	Y	Stadiums/Teams:	
Book Stores:	Video Rental:		Advertising Services:	Y	Radio:	Music Print./Dist.:		Gambling/Casinos:	
Distribution/Printing:	Video Distribution:	Y	Info. Sys. Software:		Online Information:	Multimedia:		Rides/Theme Parks:	

TYPES OF BUSINESS:

Consumer Electronics Manufacturer
Film & Television Production
Music Production
Personal Computers
Semiconductors
Technology Research
Video Games
Financial Services, Banking & Insurance

BRANDS/DIVISIONS/AFFILIATES:

Sony Style
Sony Computer Entertainment, Inc.
PlayStation
Sony Pictures Entertainment
Columbia TriStar
Sony Financial Holdings
Sony BMG
Epic Records

CONTACTS: *Note: Officers with more than one job title may be intentionally listed here more than once.*

Howard Stringer, CEO
Ryoji Chubachi, Pres.
Nobuyuki Oneda, CFO/Exec. VP
Keiji Kimura, Exec. VP-Tech. Strategies & Intellectual Property
Nicole Seligman, General Counsel/Exec. VP
Keiji Kimura, Exec. VP-Electronics Bus. Strategies
Ryoji Chubachi, CEO-Electronics
Yutaka Nakagawa, Exec. Deputy Pres., Semiconductor & Component
Katsumi Ihara, Exec. Deputy Pres., Consumer Products Group
Howard Stringer, Chmn.

Phone: 81-3-6748-2111	Fax:
Toll-Free:	
Address: 7-1 Konan, 1-Chome, Minato-ku, Tokyo, 108-0075 Japan	

GROWTH PLANS/SPECIAL FEATURES:

Sony Corporation, a leading consumer electronics firm, produces consumer and industrial electronic products and entertainment. Sony's retail division, Sony Style, branded Maison Sony in Quebec, operates 80 Sony stores in Canada, as well as 16 Sony Outlet and 40 Sony Style stores in the U.S. Sony Corporation has five business segments: Electronics, generating 65.4% of the firm's 2007 revenues; Games, 11.7%; Pictures, 11.7%; Financial Services, 7.5%; and All Others, 3.7%. The Electronics segment divides its products between audio, including home audio systems and car navigation equipment; video, such as cameras and DVD players; televisions, including computer displays and rear-projection TVs; information and communications, including PCs, printers and broadcast- and professional-use audio equipment; semiconductors; components, such as batteries and recoding equipment; and others, such as manufacturing CDs, DVDs and Blu-ray discs. The Games section, through Sony Computer Entertainment, Inc., manufactures and markets hardware and related software for Sony's PlayStation products, including the PlayStation 3, released in November 2006. It also licenses third-party software designers and operates U.S. and European subsidiaries that market its products. The Pictures segment, through Sony Pictures Entertainment, produces and distributes movies and television programs worldwide; acquires and distributes home videos; and operates studio facilities. The division operates Columbia TriStar, Columbia Pictures, Sony Pictures Classics and Columbia TriStar Home Entertainment. Sony Financial Holdings owns companies involved in insurance, banking and brokerage. The All Others segment includes the company's music division, which produces and distributes music through Sony BMG, a joint venture with Bertelsmann AG, releasing music under the Columbia Records, Epic Records and RCA Records labels. Sony products released in 2006 include its latest Blu-ray recorder; BRAVIA flat TVs; HD camcorder HANDYCAM; and personal computer VAIO. In May 2007, Viacom, Inc. agreed to sell its music publishing business to Sony/ATV Music Publishing for about $370 million.

FINANCIALS: Sales and profits are in thousands of dollars—add 000 to get the full amount. 2007 Note: Financial information for 2007 was not available for all companies at press time.

2007 Sales: $70,513,400	2007 Profits: $1,073,800	U.S. Stock Ticker: SNE
2006 Sales: $64,021,000	2006 Profits: $1,047,270	Int'l Ticker: 6758 Int'l Exchange: Tokyo-TSE
2005 Sales: $66,912,000	2005 Profits: $1,531,000	Employees: 163,000
2004 Sales: $71,215,714	2004 Profits: $840,854	Fiscal Year Ends: 3/31
2003 Sales: $63,264,000	2003 Profits: $978,000	Parent Company:

SALARIES/BENEFITS:

Pension Plan: Y	ESOP Stock Plan:	Profit Sharing:	Top Exec. Salary: $	Bonus: $
Savings Plan:	Stock Purch. Plan:		Second Exec. Salary: $	Bonus: $

OTHER THOUGHTS:

Apparent Women Officers or Directors: 1
Hot Spot for Advancement for Women/Minorities: Y

LOCATIONS: ("Y" = Yes)

West:	Southwest:	Midwest:	Southeast:	Northeast:	International:
Y	Y	Y	Y	Y	Y

Note: Financial information, benefits and other data can change quickly and may vary from those stated here.

SONY PICTURES ENTERTAINMENT www.sonypictures.com

Industry Group Code: 512110 Ranks within this company's industry group: Sales: Profits:

Print Media/Publishing:	Movies:		Equipment/Supplies:		Broadcast/Cable:	Music/Audio:	Sports/Games/Gambling:	
Newspapers:	Movie Theaters:	Y	Equipment/Supplies:		Broadcast TV:	Music Production:	Games/Sports:	Y
Magazines:	Movie Production:	Y	Gambling Equipment:		Cable TV:	Retail Music:	Retail Games Stores:	
Books:	TV/Video Prod.:	Y	Special Services:	Y	Satellite Broadcast:	Retail Audio Equip.:	Stadiums/Teams:	
Book Stores:	Video Rental:		Advertising Services:	Y	Radio:	Music Print./Dist.:	Gambling/Casinos:	
Distribution/Printing:	Video Distribution:	Y	Info. Sys. Software:		Online Information:	Multimedia:	Rides/Theme Parks:	

TYPES OF BUSINESS:

Film Production & Distribution
Television Production & Distribution
Video Distribution
Film & TV Merchandising & Licensing
Digital Animation & Visual Effects
Online Games

BRANDS/DIVISIONS/AFFILIATES:

Sony Corporation
Sony Pictures Classics
Columbia TriStar Motion Picture Group
Columbia Pictures
Sony Pictures Home Entertainment
Sony Pictures Television
Sony Pictures Digital
Sony Pictures Studios

CONTACTS: Note: Officers with more than one job title may be intentionally listed here more than once.

Michael Lynton, CEO
Amy Pascal, Co-Chmn.
Yair Landau, Pres., Sony Pictures Digital
Jeff Blake, Chmn.-Worldwide Mktg., Columbia Tristar
Jeff Blake, Chmn.-Worldwide Distribution, Columbia Tristar
Michael Lynton, Co-Chmn.

Phone: 310-244-4000	Fax: 310-244-2626
Toll-Free:	
Address: 10202 W. Washington Blvd., Culver City, CA 90232 US	

GROWTH PLANS/SPECIAL FEATURES:

Sony Pictures Entertainment, Inc. (SPE) is the media and entertainment subsidiary of Sony Corp. U.S.A., the U.S. branch of Tokyo-based Sony Corp. The company produces motion pictures through Columbia TriStar Motion Picture Group, which releases approximately 22 films per year. Columbia TriStar produces and distributes movies under four labels: Columbia Pictures, which produces wide-release movies; Sony Pictures Classics, which acquires, markets and distributes prestigious foreign and American independent films; Screen Gems, which produces lower-budget films than Columbia Pictures; and TriStar Pictures, a marketing and acquisition unit focused on genre films. TriStar owns a library of more than 3,500 films. The company releases its films through two subsidiaries: Sony Pictures Releasing (U.S.) and Sony Pictures Releasing International. Combined, they are responsible for the sale, distribution and marketing of all SPE films in 67 countries. Sony Pictures Home Entertainment distributes over 2,500 of the firm's own and acquired third-party movies on DVD and VHS. Sony Pictures Television Group currently produces and distributes approximately 60 programs worldwide and grants licensing rights to its library of television programs and motion pictures to U.S. network affiliates and independent stations through Sony Pictures Television and internationally through Sony Pictures Television International. Sony Pictures Consumer Products manages the licensing and merchandising opportunities for the firm's films and television programs. Sony Pictures Digital oversees Sony Pictures Animation (a computer-generated film company), Sony Pictures Imageworks (a digital animation and visual effects company) and Sony Online Entertainment (an online game developer). Sony Pictures Studios features 22 sound stages and post-production facilities. SPE also owns Grouper, an online video sharing community. Additionally, in conjunction with the Patton Media Group it owns Monumental Pictures, which produces and distributes Russian language films in Russia, the Commonwealth of Independent States and Mongolia.

FINANCIALS: Sales and profits are in thousands of dollars—add 000 to get the full amount. 2007 Note: Financial information for 2007 was not available for all companies at press time.

2007 Sales: $	2007 Profits: $	**U.S. Stock Ticker: Subsidiary**
2006 Sales: $	2006 Profits: $	**Int'l Ticker:** Int'l Exchange:
2005 Sales: $6,857,000	2005 Profits: $	Employees: 5,700
2004 Sales: $	2004 Profits: $	Fiscal Year Ends: 3/31
2003 Sales: $6,700,000	2003 Profits: $	Parent Company: SONY CORPORATION

SALARIES/BENEFITS:

Pension Plan:	ESOP Stock Plan:	Profit Sharing:	Top Exec. Salary: $	Bonus: $
Savings Plan:	Stock Purch. Plan:		Second Exec. Salary: $	Bonus: $

OTHER THOUGHTS:

Apparent Women Officers or Directors: 1
Hot Spot for Advancement for Women/Minorities: Y

LOCATIONS: ("Y" = Yes)

West:	Southwest:	Midwest:	Southeast:	Northeast:	International:
Y					Y

Note: Financial information, benefits and other data can change quickly and may vary from those stated here.

SPANISH BROADCASTING SYSTEM INC
www.spanishbroadcasting.com
Industry Group Code: 513111 Ranks within this company's industry group: Sales: 10   Profits: 3

Print Media/Publishing:	Movies:	Equipment/Supplies:	Broadcast/Cable:		Music/Audio:	Sports/Games/Gambling:
Newspapers:	Movie Theaters:	Equipment/Supplies:	Broadcast TV:	Y	Music Production:	Games/Sports:
Magazines:	Movie Production:	Gambling Equipment:	Cable TV:		Retail Music:	Retail Games Stores:
Books:	TV/Video Prod.:	Special Services:	Satellite Broadcast:		Retail Audio Equip.:	Stadiums/Teams:
Book Stores:	Video Rental:	Advertising Services:	Radio:		Music Print./Dist.:	Gambling/Casinos:
Distribution/Printing:	Video Distribution:	Info. Sys. Software:	Online Information:		Multimedia:	Rides/Theme Parks:

TYPES OF BUSINESS:
Radio Broadcasting
Spanish-Language Radio
Television Broadcasting
Online News & Entertainment

BRANDS/DIVISIONS/AFFILIATES:
LaMusica.com
Mega TV
Mega Media Holdings, Inc.
WDLP Licensing, Inc.
SBS Miami Broadcast Center, Inc.

CONTACTS: *Note: Officers with more than one job title may be intentionally listed here more than once.*
Raul Alarcon, Jr., CEO
Marko Radlovic, COO/Exec. VP
Raul Alarcon, Jr., Pres.
Joseph A. Garcia, CFO/Exec. VP
Joseph A. Garcia, Corp. Sec.
Raul Alarcon, Jr., Chmn.

Phone: 305-441-6901	Fax: 305-446-5148
Toll-Free:	
Address: 2601 S. Bayshore Dr., PH2, Coconut Grove, FL 33133 US	

GROWTH PLANS/SPECIAL FEATURES:
Spanish Broadcasting System, Inc. (SBS) is one of the largest publicly traded Hispanic-controlled media and entertainment companies in the U.S. It owns and operates 20 radio stations in markets that reach roughly 51% of the U.S. Hispanic population; and two television stations, which reach about 1.5 million households in the South Florida market. The radio stations are located in six of the top-ten Hispanic markets of Los Angeles, New York, Puerto Rico, Chicago, Miami and San Francisco. They broadcast a variety of Hispanic programs from news to traditional and contemporary music. The two television stations operate as one television operation, branded MEGA TV, serving the South Florida market. As part of its operating business, the company also operates LaMusica.com, Mega.tv and its radio stations' web sites, bilingual web sites providing content related to Latin music, entertainment, news and culture. Occasionally, the firm produces live concerts and events throughout the U.S. and Puerto Rico. Due to the cultural diversity of the Hispanic population from region to region in the U.S., most decisions regarding day-to-day programming, sales and promotional efforts are made by local managers. This approach improves flexibility and responsiveness to changing conditions in each of the firm's markets. Subsidiaries include Mega Media Holdings, Inc. and WDLP Licensing, Inc. In early 2007, subsidiary SBS Miami Broadcast Center, Inc. acquired property located in Florida for roughly $9 million. SBS plans on building a new broadcasting facility there and consolidate the Miami radio and television operations when the construction is over.

FINANCIALS: Sales and profits are in thousands of dollars—add 000 to get the full amount. 2007 Note: Financial information for 2007 was not available for all companies at press time.

2007 Sales: $	2007 Profits: $	U.S. Stock Ticker: SBSA
2006 Sales: $176,931	2006 Profits: $49,870	Int'l Ticker: Int'l Exchange:
2005 Sales: $169,832	2005 Profits: $-35,270	Employees: 700
2004 Sales: $156,443	2004 Profits: $28,018	Fiscal Year Ends: 12/31
2003 Sales: $135,266	2003 Profits: $-8,750	Parent Company:

SALARIES/BENEFITS:

Pension Plan:	ESOP Stock Plan:	Profit Sharing:	Top Exec. Salary: $1,226,889	Bonus: $741,216
Savings Plan:	Stock Purch. Plan:		Second Exec. Salary: $500,000	Bonus: $100,000

OTHER THOUGHTS:
Apparent Women Officers or Directors:
Hot Spot for Advancement for Women/Minorities:

LOCATIONS: ("Y" = Yes)

West:	Southwest:	Midwest:	Southeast:	Northeast:	International:
Y	Y	Y	Y	Y	Y

SRS LABS INC

www.srslabs.com

Industry Group Code: 334310   Ranks within this company's industry group: Sales: 13   Profits: 6

Print Media/Publishing:	Movies:	Equipment/Supplies:		Broadcast/Cable:	Music/Audio:	Sports/Games/Gambling:
Newspapers:	Movie Theaters:	Equipment/Supplies:	Y	Broadcast TV:	Music Production:	Games/Sports:
Magazines:	Movie Production:	Gambling Equipment:		Cable TV:	Retail Music:	Retail Games Stores:
Books:	TV/Video Prod.:	Special Services:	Y	Satellite Broadcast:	Retail Audio Equip.:	Stadiums/Teams:
Book Stores:	Video Rental:	Advertising Services:		Radio:	Music Print./Dist.:	Gambling/Casinos:
Distribution/Printing:	Video Distribution:	Info. Sys. Software:		Online Information:	Multimedia:	Rides/Theme Parks:

TYPES OF BUSINESS:

Audio & Video Equipment Technology
Technology Licensing
Audio Processing Systems

BRANDS/DIVISIONS/AFFILIATES:

Circle Surround
TruSurround
TruBass
FOCUS
SRSWOWcast Technologies
SRSWOW HD

CONTACTS: Note: Officers with more than one job title may be intentionally listed here more than once.

Thomas C. K. Yuen, CEO
Thomas C. K. Yuen, Pres.
Ulrich Gottschling, CFO
David J. Frerichs, Exec. VP-Strategic Mktg.
Alan D. Kraemer, CTO/Exec. VP
Sarah Yang, Sr. Dir.-Software Eng.
Lionel Cheng, VP-Oper.
David J. Frerichs, Exec. VP-Corp. Dev.
Jennifer A. Drescher, VP-Corp. Comm.
Jennifer A. Drescher, Dir.-Investor Rel.
Ulrich Gottschling, Treas.
Michael J. Franzi, VP-Sales & Licensing
Thomas C. K. Yuen, Chmn.

Phone: 949-442-1070	Fax: 949-852-1099
Toll-Free: 800-243-2733	
Address: 2909 Daimler St., Santa Ana, CA 92705 US	

GROWTH PLANS/SPECIAL FEATURES:

SRS Labs, Inc. is a leading developer and provider of audio and voice technology solutions for the home theater, portable audio, wireless, computer, game, automotive, Internet and telecommunications markets. Through its wholly-owned subsidiary SRSWOWcast.com, Inc. the firm develops and licenses audio, voice and surround sound technology solutions to leading original equipment manufacturers, software providers and semiconductor companies worldwide. SRS Labs' WOW playback enhancement technology improves the dynamics and bass performance of mono or stereo audio when used with smaller speakers or headphones or when the audio has been digitally compressed into formats such as MP3 or Windows Media Audio. TruSurround, the company's virtual audio solution, plays 5.1 multi-channel content over two speakers. Circle Surround, the company's encoding and decoding format, enables the distribution of up to 6.1 channels of audio over two-channel carriers such as digital media files, standard and high definition television, radio, and CDs. The firm's Voice Processing brand works with wireless technologies to increase audio integrity. In 2007, the firm announced the sale of its CHS/SRS LLC joint venture to Coming Home Studios, LLC. To date, SRS lab technology has been used in approximately 600 million products. 91% of the firm's revenues are generated in Japan, Korea and China.

FINANCIALS: Sales and profits are in thousands of dollars—add 000 to get the full amount. 2007 Note: Financial information for 2007 was not available for all companies at press time.

2007 Sales: $	2007 Profits: $	U.S. Stock Ticker: SRSL
2006 Sales: $18,500	2006 Profits: $4,700	Int'l Ticker: Int'l Exchange:
2005 Sales: $23,228	2005 Profits: $-1,424	Employees: 113
2004 Sales: $21,602	2004 Profits: $1,579	Fiscal Year Ends: 12/31
2003 Sales: $19,814	2003 Profits: $ 459	Parent Company:

SALARIES/BENEFITS:

Pension Plan:	ESOP Stock Plan:	Profit Sharing: Y	Top Exec. Salary: $300,000	Bonus: $136,744
Savings Plan: Y	Stock Purch. Plan:		Second Exec. Salary: $264,507	Bonus: $9,907

OTHER THOUGHTS:

Apparent Women Officers or Directors: 4
Hot Spot for Advancement for Women/Minorities: Y

LOCATIONS: ("Y" = Yes)

West:	Southwest:	Midwest:	Southeast:	Northeast:	International:
Y					Y

STATION CASINOS INC   www.stationcasinos.com

Industry Group Code: 721120 Ranks within this company's industry group: Sales: 6 Profits: 6

Print Media/Publishing:	Movies:	Equipment/Supplies:		Broadcast/Cable:	Music/Audio:	Sports/Games/Gambling:	
Newspapers:	Movie Theaters:	Equipment/Supplies:		Broadcast TV:	Music Production:	Games/Sports:	
Magazines:	Movie Production:	Gambling Equipment:	Y	Cable TV:	Retail Music:	Retail Games Stores:	
Books:	TV/Video Prod.:	Special Services:	Y	Satellite Broadcast:	Retail Audio Equip.:	Stadiums/Teams:	Y
Book Stores:	Video Rental:	Advertising Services:		Radio:	Music Print./Dist.:	Gambling/Casinos:	Y
Distribution/Printing:	Video Distribution:	Info. Sys. Software:		Online Information:	Multimedia:	Rides/Theme Parks:	

TYPES OF BUSINESS:

Casino Hotel
Casino Management
Restaurants
Movie Theaters & Entertainment Venues

BRANDS/DIVISIONS/AFFILIATES:

Palace Station Hotel & Casino
Texas Station Gambling Hall & Hotel
Boulder Station Hotel & Casino
Santa Fe Station Hotel & Casino
Barley's Casino & Brewing Company
Sunset Station Hotel & Casino
Fiesta Rancho Casino Hotel
Thunder Valley Casino

CONTACTS: *Note: Officers with more than one job title may be intentionally listed here more than once.*

Frank J. Fertitta, III, CEO
William W. Warner, COO/Exec. VP
Lorenzo J. Fertitta, Pres.
Scott M. Nielson, Chief Dev. Officer/Exec. VP
Richard J. Haskins, General Counsel/Exec. VP
Lori Nelson, Dir.-Corp. Comm.
Frank J. Fertitta III, Chmn.

Phone: 702-367-2411	**Fax:** 702-367-2424
Toll-Free: 800-544-2411	
Address: 2411 W. Sahara Ave., Las Vegas, NV 89102 US	

GROWTH PLANS/SPECIAL FEATURES:

Station Casinos, Inc. is a gaming and entertainment company concentrated in the Las Vegas area. Station's properties include eight major casino and hotel properties; six smaller casino properties; 54 restaurants; entertainment venues; 50 movie theaters; 120 bowling lanes; convention banquet space; and gaming offerings such as video poker, slot machines, table games, bingo, race and sports wagering. The company owns and operates 2,200 hotel rooms within its casinos, including Palace Station, Boulder Station, Texas Station Gambling Hall & Hotel, Sunset Station, Santa Fe Station, Fiesta Rancho Casino Hotel, Fiesta Henderson Casino Hotel, Wild Wild West Gambling Hall & Hotel, Wildfire Casino, Magic Star Casino and Gold Rush Casino. The firm also owns a 50% interest in Green Valley Ranch Station Casino and Barley's Casino & Brewing Company. The casinos cater to Las Vegas residents and repeat visitors. Station's loyalty program, Boarding Pass, collects points through the company's locations and rewards members with free game play. The firm also purchased 50 acres near Las Vegas to build a regional gaming and entertainment facility. In February 2007, Station Casinos began the process of converting from a public company to a privately held business after the completion of a $5.4 billion acquisition by Fertitta Colony Partners LLC, a consortium made up of Colony Capital LLC and Station's founding family, the Fertittas.

Station Casinos offers its employees child care and on-site dentistry. The firm annually raffles off the general manager to work an employee's job for one day, and the money raised goes to various charities.

FINANCIALS: Sales and profits are in thousands of dollars—add 000 to get the full amount. 2007 Note: Financial information for 2007 was not available for all companies at press time.

2007 Sales: $	2007 Profits: $	**U.S. Stock Ticker:** STN
2006 Sales: $1,339,024	2006 Profits: $110,212	**Int'l Ticker:** Int'l Exchange:
2005 Sales: $1,108,833	2005 Profits: $161,886	**Employees:** 14,600
2004 Sales: $986,742	2004 Profits: $66,350	**Fiscal Year Ends:** 12/31
2003 Sales: $858,100	2003 Profits: $44,343	**Parent Company:**

SALARIES/BENEFITS:

Pension Plan:	ESOP Stock Plan:	Profit Sharing:	Top Exec. Salary: $1,839,230	Bonus: $3,750,000
Savings Plan: Y	Stock Purch. Plan:		Second Exec. Salary: $1,414,231	Bonus: $2,175,000

OTHER THOUGHTS:

Apparent Women Officers or Directors:
Hot Spot for Advancement for Women/Minorities:

LOCATIONS: ("Y" = Yes)

West:	Southwest:	Midwest:	Southeast:	Northeast:	International:
Y	Y				

SUDDENLINK COMMUNICATIONS   www.suddenlink.com

Industry Group Code: 513220 Ranks within this company's industry group: Sales: Profits:

Print Media/Publishing:	Movies:	Equipment/Supplies:		Broadcast/Cable:		Music/Audio:	Sports/Games/Gambling:
Newspapers:	Movie Theaters:	Equipment/Supplies:		Broadcast TV:		Music Production:	Games/Sports:
Magazines:	Movie Production:	Gambling Equipment:		Cable TV:	Y	Retail Music:	Retail Games Stores:
Books:	TV/Video Prod.:	Special Services:	Y	Satellite Broadcast:		Retail Audio Equip.:	Stadiums/Teams:
Book Stores:	Video Rental:	Advertising Services:	Y	Radio:		Music Print./Dist.:	Gambling/Casinos:
Distribution/Printing:	Video Distribution:	Info. Sys. Software:		Online Information:		Multimedia:	Rides/Theme Parks:

TYPES OF BUSINESS:
Cable TV Service
High-Speed Internet Services

BRANDS/DIVISIONS/AFFILIATES:
Cebridge Connections
Sprint Nextel Corp
Alliance Entertainment Corp
Tele-Media
Thompson
USA Media
Charter Communications Inc
Cox Communications Inc

CONTACTS: Note: Officers with more than one job title may be intentionally listed here more than once.
Jerald L. (Jerry) Kent, CEO
Thomas P. (Tom) McMillin, COO/Exec. VP
Mary E. Meduski, CFO/Exec. VP
Mary R. Meier, Sr. VP-Mktg.
Douglas G. (Doug) Wiley, Sr. VP-Human Resources
Robert L. (Bob) Putnam, CIO/Sr. VP
Terry M. Cordova, CTO/Sr. VP
Peggy Woodruff-Migas, VP-Contract Admin.
Craig Rosenthal, General Counsel/VP
Pete Abel, VP-Corp. Comm., Community & Gov't Relations
Douglas W. (Doug) Faust, Chief Acct. Officer/Sr. VP
John E. Fuhler, Sr. VP-Fiscal Oper.
Ralph G. Kelly, Sr. VP/Treas.
Patricia L. (Patty) McCaskill, Sr. VP-Programming
John R. McFerron, Sr. VP-Customer Care

Phone: 314-965-2020	Fax: 314-965-0500
Toll-Free:	
Address: 12444 Powerscourt Dr., Ste. 450, St. Louis, MO 63131 US	

GROWTH PLANS/SPECIAL FEATURES:
Suddenlink Communications, formerly Cebridge Connections, owns and operates cable television systems and provides high-speed Internet services, serving smaller, rural communities in the central U.S. The firm has approximately 1.4 million customers in over 15 states. Suddenlink offers a range of services to business and residential communities, including video, voice and Internet. The company's video offerings include basic, expanded basic and digital packages of TV programming, as well as high-definition television and video-on-demand. Suddenlink offers Internet and phone service in several communities, which it plans to expand to more communities in the near future. The company's phone service is provided in partnership with Sprint Nextel. Suddenlink is a member of a programming consortium of small to mid-sized cable system operators that creates efficiencies in the securing and administration of programming contracts. The company derives revenues from customer fees, the sale of local spot advertising time and affiliations with home shopping services. Suddenlink has assumed responsibility for cable systems previously owned by Alliance, Tele-Media, Thompson, USA Media, Cox and Charter. Following the acquisitions of cable systems from Charter Communications and Cox Communications in 2006, Cebridge Connections changed its name to Suddenlink Communications. The acquisitions brought their customer base from approximately 400,000 customers to 1.4 million.

FINANCIALS: Sales and profits are in thousands of dollars—add 000 to get the full amount. 2007 Note: Financial information for 2007 was not available for all companies at press time.

2007 Sales: $	2007 Profits: $	U.S. Stock Ticker: Private	
2006 Sales: $	2006 Profits: $	Int'l Ticker: Int'l Exchange:	
2005 Sales: $	2005 Profits: $	Employees: 885	
2004 Sales: $	2004 Profits: $	Fiscal Year Ends: 12/31	
2003 Sales: $	2003 Profits: $	Parent Company:	

SALARIES/BENEFITS:

Pension Plan:	ESOP Stock Plan:	Profit Sharing:	Top Exec. Salary: $350,000	Bonus: $150,000
Savings Plan:	Stock Purch. Plan:		Second Exec. Salary: $201,923	Bonus: $

OTHER THOUGHTS:
Apparent Women Officers or Directors: 7
Hot Spot for Advancement for Women/Minorities: Y

LOCATIONS: ("Y" = Yes)

West:	Southwest:	Midwest:	Southeast:	Northeast:	International:
Y	Y	Y	Y	Y	

TAKE-TWO INTERACTIVE SOFTWARE INC
www.take2games.com

Industry Group Code: 511208 Ranks within this company's industry group: Sales: 4   Profits: 10

Print Media/Publishing:	Movies:	Equipment/Supplies:	Broadcast/Cable:	Music/Audio:	Sports/Games/Gambling:	
Newspapers:	Movie Theaters:	Equipment/Supplies:	Broadcast TV:	Music Production:	Games/Sports:	Y
Magazines:	Movie Production:	Gambling Equipment:	Cable TV:	Retail Music:	Retail Games Stores:	
Books:	TV/Video Prod.:	Special Services:	Satellite Broadcast:	Retail Audio Equip.:	Stadiums/Teams:	
Book Stores:	Video Rental:	Advertising Services:	Radio:	Music Print./Dist.:	Gambling/Casinos:	
Distribution/Printing:	Video Distribution:	Info. Sys. Software:	Online Information:	Multimedia:	Rides/Theme Parks:	

TYPES OF BUSINESS:
Computer Software-Video Games
Software Distribution

BRANDS/DIVISIONS/AFFILIATES:
Rockstar Games
Global Star Software
2K Games
2K Sports
2K Play
Jack of All Games
Civilization
Grand Theft Auto

CONTACTS: *Note: Officers with more than one job title may be intentionally listed here more than once.*
Benjamin Feder, CEO
Paul Eibeler, Pres.
Lainie Goldstein, CFO
Seth Krauss, General Counsel/Exec. VP
Jim Ankner, Corp. Press
Jim Ankner, Investor Rel.
Lainie Goldstein, Chief Acct. Officer
Christoph Hartmann, Pres., 2K
Sam Houser, Exec. Producer-Rockstar Games
Steve Lux, VP-Publishing
Strauss Zelnick, Chmn.

Phone: 646-536-2842	Fax: 646-536-2926
Toll-Free:	
Address: 622 Broadway, New York, NY 10012 US	

GROWTH PLANS/SPECIAL FEATURES:

Take-Two Interactive Software, Inc. develops, publishes and distributes software games for PCs and video game consoles. The firm has license agreements with Sony, Microsoft and Nintendo and develops and publishes software in North America and Europe for the PlayStation 2, PlayStation 3, PSP (Play Station Portable), Xbox, Xbox 360, Game Boy Advance, Nintendo DS, Wii and GameCube. It publishes its products under its subsidiaries Rockstar Games, Global Star Software and 2K Games. Rockstar creates original content for mature audiences on video game console systems. Its game titles include The Warriors, Midnight Club, Manhunt and Grand Theft Auto. Global Star publishes racing, family, action and children's games, under such titles as Dora The Explorer, Family Feud and Deal or No Deal. 2K Games and its divisions, which include 2K Sports, mainly publishes sports games, such as NBA 2K7, College Hoops 2K8; games developed from popular entertainment properties, including Ghost Rider and Fantastic Four: Rise of the Silver Surfer; and other games, such as Bioshock (released in August 2007), The Elder Scrolls IV: Oblivion and the Civilization series. Jack of All Games distributes internally developed and third-party software, hardware, and accessories in the U.S. to Wal-Mart, GameStop, Best Buy, Circuit City and other retailers. Outside the U.S., Take-Two has development studios in the U.K., Canada, Australia, China and France; product testing studios in the U.K.; sales and marketing offices in Switzerland, the U.K., France, Germany, Spain, Italy, Australia, the Netherlands and New Zealand; and distribution centers in Canada. In September 2007, 2K Games formed 2K Play in partnership with Nickelodeon to publish games such as Dora the Explorer and Go, Diego, Go! 2K Play will absorb the Global Star Software label.

FINANCIALS: Sales and profits are in thousands of dollars—add 000 to get the full amount. 2007 Note: Financial information for 2007 was not available for all companies at press time.

2007 Sales: $	2007 Profits: $	U.S. Stock Ticker: TTWO
2006 Sales: $1,037,840	2006 Profits: $-184,889	Int'l Ticker: Int'l Exchange:
2005 Sales: $1,201,220	2005 Profits: $35,314	Employees: 2,020
2004 Sales: $1,127,751	2004 Profits: $62,119	Fiscal Year Ends: 10/31
2003 Sales: $793,976	2003 Profits: $71,565	Parent Company:

SALARIES/BENEFITS:

Pension Plan:	ESOP Stock Plan:	Profit Sharing:	Top Exec. Salary: $800,000	Bonus: $50,000
Savings Plan: Y	Stock Purch. Plan:		Second Exec. Salary: $385,000	Bonus: $50,000

OTHER THOUGHTS:
Apparent Women Officers or Directors: 1
Hot Spot for Advancement for Women/Minorities:

LOCATIONS: ("Y" = Yes)

West:	Southwest:	Midwest:	Southeast:	Northeast:	International:
				Y	Y

TAYLOR NELSON SOFRES PLC (TNS) www.tnsglobal.com

Industry Group Code: 541910 Ranks within this company's industry group: Sales: 1 Profits: 1

Print Media/Publishing:	Movies:	Equipment/Supplies:		Broadcast/Cable:	Music/Audio:	Sports/Games/Gambling:
Newspapers:	Movie Theaters:	Equipment/Supplies:		Broadcast TV:	Music Production:	Games/Sports:
Magazines:	Movie Production:	Gambling Equipment:		Cable TV:	Retail Music:	Retail Games Stores:
Books:	TV/Video Prod.:	Special Services:	Y	Satellite Broadcast:	Retail Audio Equip.:	Stadiums/Teams:
Book Stores:	Video Rental:	Advertising Services:	Y	Radio:	Music Print./Dist.:	Gambling/Casinos:
Distribution/Printing:	Video Distribution:	Info. Sys. Software:		Online Information:	Multimedia:	Rides/Theme Parks:

TYPES OF BUSINESS:

Market Research
Internet Market Research
Business & Advertising Software

BRANDS/DIVISIONS/AFFILIATES:

TNS
AdEval
MarketWhys
Conversion Model
NeedScope System
Optima
TNS Interactive
NFO World Group

CONTACTS: *Note: Officers with more than one job title may be intentionally listed here more than once.*

David Lowden, CEO
Andy Boland, Group Dir.-Finance
Rachel Argyle, Sr. Exec.-Public Rel.
Anthony Cowling, Chmn.

Phone: 44-20-8967-0007	Fax: 44-20-8967-4060
Toll-Free:	
Address: TNS House, Westgate, London, W5 1UA UK	

GROWTH PLANS/SPECIAL FEATURES:

Taylor Nelson Sofres plc (TNS) is one of the largest market research conglomerates in the world, with operations serving customers in 70 countries. The company provides research in several industry sectors, including automotive, consumer purchasing and behavior, political and social polling, health care, information technology, media intelligence, telecommunications and television audience measurement. The firm's business solutions include AdEval, an advertising pre-testing system that evaluates an advertisement's performance; Conversion Model, a psychological measure of customer commitment; MarketWhys, a brand and advertising tracking system; Miriad, a data integration, analysis and delivery platform; NeedScope System, a system for measuring consumer needs and motivations; Optima, a brand portfolio management tool that analyzes how and why consumers choose the brands they do; and TRI*M, a management information system that monitors a company's shareholder relationship. Through its TNS Interactive business unit, the company also provides Internet and new media research. Another division of TNS, NFO World Group, is a leading provider of panel-based market research in the U.S. Recent acquisitions include Retail Forward Inc., Conversa Global, PressWatch GmbH, ID Magasin and Landis Strategy & Innovation, LLC.

FINANCIALS: Sales and profits are in thousands of dollars—add 000 to get the full amount. 2007 Note: Financial information for 2007 was not available for all companies at press time.

2007 Sales: $	2007 Profits: $	U.S. Stock Ticker: TYNLY
2006 Sales: $2,000,120	2006 Profits: $79,470	Int'l Ticker: TNN Int'l Exchange: London-LSE
2005 Sales: $1,989,760	2005 Profits: $109,150	Employees: 12,731
2004 Sales: $1,788,700	2004 Profits: $38,900	Fiscal Year Ends: 12/31
2003 Sales: $1,403,700	2003 Profits: $22,900	Parent Company:

SALARIES/BENEFITS:

Pension Plan:	ESOP Stock Plan:	Profit Sharing:	Top Exec. Salary: $	Bonus: $
Savings Plan:	Stock Purch. Plan:		Second Exec. Salary: $	Bonus: $

OTHER THOUGHTS:

Apparent Women Officers or Directors: 1
Hot Spot for Advancement for Women/Minorities:

LOCATIONS: ("Y" = Yes)

West:	Southwest:	Midwest:	Southeast:	Northeast:	International:
				Y	Y

Note: Financial information, benefits and other data can change quickly and may vary from those stated here.

THOMAS NELSON INC
www.thomasnelson.com

Industry Group Code: 511130 **Ranks within this company's industry group:** Sales: 6 Profits: 6

Print Media/Publishing:	Movies:	Equipment/Supplies:	Broadcast/Cable:	Music/Audio:	Sports/Games/Gambling:
Newspapers:	Movie Theaters:	Equipment/Supplies:	Broadcast TV:	Music Production:	Games/Sports:
Magazines:	Movie Production:	Gambling Equipment:	Cable TV:	Retail Music:	Retail Games Stores:
Books: Y	TV/Video Prod.:	Special Services:	Satellite Broadcast:	Retail Audio Equip.:	Stadiums/Teams:
Book Stores:	Video Rental:	Advertising Services:	Radio:	Music Print./Dist.:	Gambling/Casinos:
Distribution/Printing:	Video Distribution:	Info. Sys. Software:	Online Information:	Multimedia:	Rides/Theme Parks:

TYPES OF BUSINESS:
Book Publishing
Religious Publications
Gifts & Stationery
CD-ROMs

BRANDS/DIVISIONS/AFFILIATES:
Nelson Electronic and Reference
Integrity Publishers

CONTACTS: *Note: Officers with more than one job title may be intentionally listed here more than once.*
Michael S. Hyatt, CEO
Michael S. Hyatt, Pres.
Stuart M. Bitting, CFO
Jerry Park, Chief Mktg. Officer
Joe L. Powers, Corp. Sec.
Vance Lawson, Sr. VP-Oper.
Byron Williamson, Exec. VP-Strategic Dev.
Joe L. Powers, Treas./Exec. VP
Vance Lawson, Sr. VP-Finance
Mark Schoenwald, Exec. VP/Chief Sales Officer
Mary Graham, Exec. VP/Chief Live Events Officer
Tamara L. Heim, Exec. VP/Chief Publishing Officer
Sam Moore, Chmn.
Ted Squires, Exec. VP-World Publishing

Phone: 615-889-9000	Fax: 615-391-5225
Toll-Free: 800-251-4000	
Address: 501 Nelson Pl., Nashville, TN 37214 US	

GROWTH PLANS/SPECIAL FEATURES:
Thomas Nelson, Inc is a leading publisher, producer and distributor of books (hardcover and paperback) emphasizing Christian, inspirational and family value themes. The firm is one of the largest publishers of Christian and inspirational books and Bibles in the U.S., distributing through Christian bookstores, mass merchandisers (Barnes & Noble, Target and Wal-Mart) and direct sales to consumers, churches and ministries. The company translates its English titles into foreign languages and distributes its products internationally in South America, Europe, Australia, New Zealand, Africa, Asia and Mexico. In addition, the company publishes speakers such as Lisa Bevere, Ted Dekker, John Eldredge and Billy Graham. The company sells previously published titles (earning 54% of the firm's publishing revenues in 2006), Bibles (2,500 copies sold in 2006), commentaries, study guides and other Bible help texts. Products range from paperbacks to deluxe leather-bound Bibles to CD-ROM to audio and video products. Authors and titles are supported through radio, television, cooperative advertising, author appearances and in-store promotions. Electronic Bibles, biblical reference books, and software for preparing Bible study lessons are published through the firm's subsidiary Nelson Electronic and Reference. Recently, after acquiring Integrity Publishers (the wholly-owned publishing subsidiary of Integrity Media), Thomas Nelson sold all of its subsidiaries in order to restructure its publishing units. Per this restructuring, the firm hopes to streamline its titles, thereby eliminating overlapping imprints. In the future, all titles will be printed with only the firm's name and logo on the jacket. In 2006, Thomas Nelson became a privately held firm.

FINANCIALS: Sales and profits are in thousands of dollars—add 000 to get the full amount. 2007 Note: Financial information for 2007 was not available for all companies at press time.
2007 Sales: $	2007 Profits: $	U.S. Stock Ticker: Private
2006 Sales: $253,057	2006 Profits: $20,977	Int'l Ticker: Int'l Exchange:
2005 Sales: $237,817	2005 Profits: $19,817	Employees: 650
2004 Sales: $222,619	2004 Profits: $16,165	Fiscal Year Ends: 3/31
2003 Sales: $217,200	2003 Profits: $10,200	Parent Company:

SALARIES/BENEFITS:
Pension Plan:	ESOP Stock Plan: Y	Profit Sharing: Y	Top Exec. Salary: $450,000	Bonus: $289,300
Savings Plan: Y	Stock Purch. Plan:		Second Exec. Salary: $300,000	Bonus: $161,000

OTHER THOUGHTS:
Apparent Women Officers or Directors: 2
Hot Spot for Advancement for Women/Minorities:

LOCATIONS: ("Y" = Yes)
West:	Southwest:	Midwest:	Southeast:	Northeast:	International:
Y	Y	Y	Y	Y	

THOMSON CORP (THE)
www.thomson.com

Industry Group Code: 511140 **Ranks within this company's industry group:** Sales: 2 Profits: 2

Print Media/Publishing:		Movies:		Equipment/Supplies:		Broadcast/Cable:		Music/Audio:		Sports/Games/Gambling:	
Newspapers:	Y	Movie Theaters:		Equipment/Supplies:		Broadcast TV:		Music Production:		Games/Sports:	
Magazines:		Movie Production:		Gambling Equipment:	Y	Cable TV:		Retail Music:		Retail Games Stores:	
Books:	Y	TV/Video Prod.:		Special Services:	Y	Satellite Broadcast:		Retail Audio Equip.:		Stadiums/Teams:	
Book Stores:		Video Rental:		Advertising Services:	Y	Radio:		Music Print./Dist.:		Gambling/Casinos:	
Distribution/Printing:		Video Distribution:		Info. Sys. Software:		Online Information:		Multimedia:		Rides/Theme Parks:	

TYPES OF BUSINESS:

Information Services & Software
Legal & Regulatory Information Services
Financial Information & Technology
Health Care Information Tools
Scientific Data Tools

BRANDS/DIVISIONS/AFFILIATES:

Westlaw
Thompson & Thompson
FindLaw
Solucient
Investext
CompuMark
Sweet & Maxwell
BAR/BRI

CONTACTS: Note: Officers with more than one job title may be intentionally listed here more than once.

Richard J. Harrington, CEO
James C. Smith, COO/Exec. VP
Richard J. Harrington, Pres.
Robert D. Daleo, CFO/Exec. VP
Gustav Carlson, Chief Mktg. Officer/Sr. VP
Robert B. Bogart, Exec. VP-Human Resources
Michael E. Wilens, CTO
Deidre Stanley, General Counsel/Sr. VP
Richard Benson-Armer, Chief Strategy Officer/Sr. VP
Gustav Carslon, Chief Comm. Officer
Frank Golden, VP-Investor Rel.
Robert C. Cullen, Pres./CEO-Healthcare
Sharon Rowlands, Pres./CEO-Financial
Roy M. Martin Jr., Pres./CEO-Acct. & Tax
Mike Boswood, Pres./CEO-Int'l Legal & Regulatory
David K. R. Thomson, Chmn.

Phone: 203-539-8000	Fax: 203-539-7734
Toll-Free:	
Address: Metro Ctr., 1 Station Place, Stamford, CT 06902 US	

GROWTH PLANS/SPECIAL FEATURES:

The Thomson Corp. provides specialized information in digital and print formats through operations in 46 countries. The company currently operates in five segments (legal, financial, tax and accounting, scientific and healthcare), serving over 20 million information users. The legal segment provides workflow solutions to legal, compliance, intellectual property, government and business professionals throughout the world. Major brands include Westlaw, Fee, Aranzadi, Thomson Elite, FindLaw, LIVEDGAR, Thomson & Thompson, BAR/BRI, CompuMark and Sweet & Maxwell. The financial segment offers products and integration services to financial and technology professionals in the investment banking, corporate, wealth management, institutional and fixed income sectors; its flagship brand is Thomson ONE. Other major businesses and brands include Baseline, First Call, Investext, SDC Platinum, AutEx, Datactroam, I/B/E/S, Street Events, TradeWeb and Thomson Transaction Services. The tax and account segment provides integrated information and workflow solutions for accounting and tax professionals in North America. Major brands include Checkpoint, RIA and Creative Solutions. The scientific segment offers information and services to researchers, scientists and information professionals in the academic, scientific, government and corporate marketplaces. Major information solutions and businesses include Derwent World Patents Index, Thomson Pharma, MicroPatent, Web of Knowledge and ISI Web of Science. The healthcare segment provides information and services to physicians and other professionals in the healthcare, government and corporate markets. Major information solutions and businesses include Medstat, PDR (Physicians' Desk Reference), Micromedex and Solucient. In May 2007, the firm agreed to sell Nelson Canada and the assets of the learning group to funds managed by Apax Partners and OMERS Capital Partners for $7.75 billion. This comes as Thomson is considering a $17.5 billion merger-acquisition of Reuters Group PLC. In October 2007, Thomson sold Thomson Prometric to Education Testing Services.

The company offers its employees health insurance, flex time, tuition reimbursement and a stock purchase plan.

FINANCIALS: Sales and profits are in thousands of dollars—add 000 to get the full amount. 2007 Note: Financial information for 2007 was not available for all companies at press time.

2007 Sales: $	2007 Profits: $	**U.S. Stock Ticker:** TOC
2006 Sales: $6,641,000	2006 Profits: $1,143,000	**Int'l Ticker:** TOC Int'l Exchange: Toronto-TSX
2005 Sales: $8,703,000	2005 Profits: $934,000	Employees: 32,375
2004 Sales: $8,098,000	2004 Profits: $1,011,000	Fiscal Year Ends: 12/31
2003 Sales: $7,606,000	2003 Profits: $846,000	Parent Company:

SALARIES/BENEFITS:

Pension Plan:	ESOP Stock Plan:	Profit Sharing:	Top Exec. Salary: $	Bonus: $1,840,800
Savings Plan: Y	Stock Purch. Plan: Y		Second Exec. Salary: $950,000	Bonus: $950,000

OTHER THOUGHTS:

Apparent Women Officers or Directors: 2
Hot Spot for Advancement for Women/Minorities: Y

LOCATIONS: ("Y" = Yes)

West:	Southwest:	Midwest:	Southeast:	Northeast:	International:
Y	Y	Y	Y	Y	Y

Note: Financial information, benefits and other data can change quickly and may vary from those stated here.

THQ INC   www.thq.com

Industry Group Code: 511208 Ranks within this company's industry group: Sales: 5   Profits: 5

Print Media/Publishing:	Movies:	Equipment/Supplies:	Broadcast/Cable:	Music/Audio:	Sports/Games/Gambling:	
Newspapers:	Movie Theaters:	Equipment/Supplies:	Broadcast TV:	Music Production:	Games/Sports:	Y
Magazines:	Movie Production:	Gambling Equipment:	Cable TV:	Retail Music:	Retail Games Stores:	
Books:	TV/Video Prod.:	Special Services:	Satellite Broadcast:	Retail Audio Equip.:	Stadiums/Teams:	
Book Stores:	Video Rental:	Advertising Services:	Radio:	Music Print./Dist.:	Gambling/Casinos:	
Distribution/Printing:	Video Distribution:	Info. Sys. Software:	Online Information:	Multimedia:	Rides/Theme Parks:	

TYPES OF BUSINESS:
Software-Video Games
Mobile Gaming Software

BRANDS/DIVISIONS/AFFILIATES:
Relic Entertainment
Vigil Games
Paradigm Entertainment
Kaos Studios
Company of Heroes
Destroy All Humans!
Saints Row
THQ Wireless

CONTACTS: Note: Officers with more than one job title may be intentionally listed here more than once.
Brian J. Farrell, CEO
Brian J. Farrell, Pres.
Rasmus van der Colff, Interim CFO
Scott Guthrie, Exec. VP-Sales & Dist., The Americas
Bill Goodmen, Exec. VP-Human Resources
Bill Goodmen, Exec. VP-Admin.
James M. Kennedy, Sec./Exec. VP-Bus. & Legal Affairs
Liz Pieri, VP-Mktg. Comm.
Julie MacMedan, VP-Investor Rel.
Rasmus van der Colff, Controller/VP
Jack Sorensen, Exec. VP-Worldwide Studios
Bob Aniello, Sr. VP-Worldwide Mktg.
Marko Hein, Gen. Manager-THQ Int'l GmbH
Doug Clemmer, Pres., THQ Wireless, Inc.
Brian J. Farrell, Chmn.
Ian Curran, Exec. VP-Int'l

Phone: 818-871-5000	Fax: 818-871-7590
Toll-Free:	
Address: 29903 Agoura Rd., Aguora Hills, CA 91301 US	

GROWTH PLANS/SPECIAL FEATURES:
THQ, Inc. is a worldwide publisher, marketer and developer of proprietary and licensed video game software for Sony PSP, PlayStation 2 and PlayStation 3; Microsoft Xbox and Xbox 360;, Nintendo GameCube, Game Boy Advance, DS and Wii; PCs; and mobile devices. It develops titles through 16 development studios under a new strategy called Studio located in the U.S., Australia, Canada and the U.K. The strategy is designed to leverage resources across the entire organization to benefit each of the separate studios. Its studios include Relic Entertainment; Sandblast Games; Locomotive Games; Mass Media; Heavy Iron Studios; Incinerator Studios; Concrete Games; Rainbow Studios; Vigil Games; Paradigm Entertainment; Volition, Inc.; Kaos Studios; Helixe; Juice Games; THQ Studio Australia; and Blue Tongue Entertainment. Games based on the company's own intellectual property include Company of Heroes, Destroy All Humans!, Juiced, MX vs. ATV, Red Faction and Saints Row. Additionally, the firm recently acquired the Stuntman franchise from Atari. Its games based on properties it licenses from third parties include Hot Wheels, Scooby-Doo, Sonic the Hedgehog, SpongeBob SquarePants, World Wrestling Entertainment, Bratz, Warhammer 40,000 and several Disney/Pixar properties, including Finding Nemo, Cars and Ratatouille. The firm also has software and artwork developed for it by third parties. Subsidiary THQ Wireless, Inc. produces ringtones and videogames for mobile phones, including products related to the Star Wars franchise, which the firm only develops for wireless applications. The company's corporate strategy focuses on improving its internal development capabilities and technology base, increasing its international presence and exploring the potential of the mobile interactive entertainment segment. In December 2007, THQ Wireless forged a new, expanded agreement with LucasFilm Ltd., which will allow the subsidiary to develop new wireless products based on the Indiana Jones franchise in addition to its current Star Wars license.

FINANCIALS: Sales and profits are in thousands of dollars—add 000 to get the full amount. 2007 Note: Financial information for 2007 was not available for all companies at press time.

2007 Sales: $	2007 Profits: $	U.S. Stock Ticker: THQI
2006 Sales: $806,560	2006 Profits: $34,269	Int'l Ticker: Int'l Exchange:
2005 Sales: $756,731	2005 Profits: $62,790	Employees: 1,600
2004 Sales: $640,846	2004 Profits: $35,839	Fiscal Year Ends: 3/31
2003 Sales: $66,800	2003 Profits: $-7,686	Parent Company:

SALARIES/BENEFITS:

Pension Plan:	ESOP Stock Plan:	Profit Sharing:	Top Exec. Salary: $626,045	Bonus: $913,713
Savings Plan: Y	Stock Purch. Plan:		Second Exec. Salary: $450,000	Bonus: $500,400

OTHER THOUGHTS:
Apparent Women Officers or Directors: 2
Hot Spot for Advancement for Women/Minorities:

LOCATIONS: ("Y" = Yes)

West:	Southwest:	Midwest:	Southeast:	Northeast:	International:
Y	Y	Y		Y	Y

Note: Financial information, benefits and other data can change quickly and may vary from those stated here.

TICKETMASTER

www.ticketmaster.com

Industry Group Code: 454110A Ranks within this company's industry group: Sales: Profits:

Print Media/Publishing:	Movies:	Equipment/Supplies:		Broadcast/Cable:	Music/Audio:	Sports/Games/Gambling:
Newspapers:	Movie Theaters:	Equipment/Supplies:		Broadcast TV:	Music Production:	Games/Sports:
Magazines:	Movie Production:	Gambling Equipment:		Cable TV:	Retail Music:	Retail Games Stores:
Books:	TV/Video Prod.:	Special Services:	Y	Satellite Broadcast:	Retail Audio Equip.:	Stadiums/Teams:
Book Stores:	Video Rental:	Advertising Services:		Radio:	Music Print./Dist.:	Gambling/Casinos:
Distribution/Printing:	Video Distribution:	Info. Sys. Software:		Online Information:	Multimedia:	Rides/Theme Parks:

TYPES OF BUSINESS:

Event Ticket Sales
Campsite Reservation
Web-Based Ticketing Software
Network Ticketing Services

BRANDS/DIVISIONS/AFFILIATES:

IAC/InterActiveCorp
ReserveAmerica
Admission.com
LiveDaily
Cottonblend
TicketWeb
Emma Entertainment Holdings HK Limited
Ticketmaster.com/affiliates

CONTACTS: Note: Officers with more than one job title may be intentionally listed here more than once.

Sean Moriarty, CEO
Sean Moriarty, Pres.
Susan Bracey, CFO/Exec. VP
Beverly K. Carmichael, Chief People Officer/Sr. VP-Human Resources
Brian Pike, CTO
Edward J. Weiss, General Counsel/Exec. VP
Mike McGee, Exec. VP-North American Bus. Oper.
Eric Korman, Exec. VP-Corp. & Bus. Dev.
David Goldberg, Exec. VP-Global Music Svcs.
Eric Korman, Exec. VP-TicketWeb & ReserveAmerica
Marla Hoicowitz, Exec. VP-Eastern Region
Michael Walthius, Exec. VP-Central Region
Terry Barnes, Chmn.
Tommy Higgins, Exec. VP-Ticketmaster Europe

Phone: 213-381-2000	Fax: 213-386-1244
Toll-Free:	
Address: 3701 Wilshire Blvd., Los Angeles, CA 90010 US	

GROWTH PLANS/SPECIAL FEATURES:

Ticketmaster, a subsidiary and operating division of IAC/InterActiveCorp, focuses on retail sales and resale of tickets to live music, sports, arts and family entertainment events, with operations in 20 global markets. It sold over 128 million tickets in 2006. Ticketmaster operates through numerous companies, including Ticketmaster, responsible for ticket sales through 6,500 retail locations, 20 call centers and Ticketmaster.com, which generates the main portion of the company's income. It also offers regional Ticketmaster web sites. ReserveAmerica is one of the leading providers of campsite reservation services and campsite reservation software in North America, serving more than 100,000 campsites in 48 states. It mainly works with U.S. state and federal agencies. Admission.com is a leading provider of computerized network ticketing services in Quebec and exclusive provider of tickets for 80% of the venues and four professional sports teams within Quebec. LiveDaily offers daily entertainment news updates, interviews, reviews and, of course, tickets. Cottonblend offers interactive web site development and design. Lastly, TicketWeb is a provider of Internet-based box-office ticketing software and services, offering TicketWeb 2.0 Software that allows clients to perform box office functions, such as ticket and seating reservation, through a standard web browser. Ticketmaster has formed a joint venture to sell tickets to the 2008 Beijing Olympics. In May 2007, the company acquired a majority interest in Chinese ticketing and event promotions company, Emma Entertainment Holdings HK Limited. In November 2007, the firm launched its first affiliate program for the U.S. The affiliates register at Ticketmaster.com/affiliates, earning commissions from Ticketmaster and TicketWeb sales generated through links on their web sites. The company plans to take the program worldwide soon.

Employees of Ticketmaster receive medical, dental, vision and prescription drug plans.

FINANCIALS: Sales and profits are in thousands of dollars—add 000 to get the full amount. 2007 Note: Financial information for 2007 was not available for all companies at press time.

2007 Sales: $	2007 Profits: $	U.S. Stock Ticker: Subsidiary
2006 Sales: $	2006 Profits: $	Int'l Ticker: Int'l Exchange:
2005 Sales: $950,200	2005 Profits: $	Employees: 4,600
2004 Sales: $	2004 Profits: $	Fiscal Year Ends: 12/31
2003 Sales: $743,000	2003 Profits: $	Parent Company: IAC/INTERACTIVECORP

SALARIES/BENEFITS:

Pension Plan:	ESOP Stock Plan:	Profit Sharing:	Top Exec. Salary: $	Bonus: $250,000
Savings Plan: Y	Stock Purch. Plan:		Second Exec. Salary: $387,500	Bonus: $387,500

OTHER THOUGHTS:

Apparent Women Officers or Directors: 1
Hot Spot for Advancement for Women/Minorities:

LOCATIONS: ("Y" = Yes)

West:	Southwest:	Midwest:	Southeast:	Northeast:	International:
Y	Y	Y	Y	Y	Y

Note: Financial information, benefits and other data can change quickly and may vary from those stated here.

TIME INC

www.time.com

Industry Group Code: 511120 **Ranks within this company's industry group:** Sales: Profits:

Print Media/Publishing:		Movies:		Equipment/Supplies:		Broadcast/Cable:		Music/Audio:		Sports/Games/Gambling:	
Newspapers:		Movie Theaters:		Equipment/Supplies:		Broadcast TV:		Music Production:		Games/Sports:	
Magazines:	Y	Movie Production:		Gambling Equipment:		Cable TV:		Retail Music:		Retail Games Stores:	
Books:	Y	TV/Video Prod.:	Y	Special Services:		Satellite Broadcast:		Retail Audio Equip.:		Stadiums/Teams:	
Book Stores:		Video Rental:		Advertising Services:		Radio:		Music Print./Dist.:		Gambling/Casinos:	
Distribution/Printing:		Video Distribution:		Info. Sys. Software:		Online Information:		Multimedia:		Rides/Theme Parks:	

TYPES OF BUSINESS:

Magazine Publishing
TV Production
Book Publishing

BRANDS/DIVISIONS/AFFILIATES:

Essence Communications Partners
People
Sports Illustrated
Grupo Editorial Expansion
Southern Living
Fortune
Southern Progress Corporation
IPC Group, Ltd.

CONTACTS: *Note: Officers with more than one job title may be intentionally listed here more than once.*

Ann S. Moore, CEO
John Squires, COO
Howard Averill, CFO
Kerry Bessey, VP-Human Resources
John Redpath, General Counsel
Jim Kelly, Managing Editor-Times Inc.
John Huey, Editor-In-Chief, Time, Inc.
Ann S. Moore, Chmn.
Richard Atkinson, CEO-Int'l

Phone: 212-522-1212	Fax: 212-522-0602
Toll-Free:	
Address: 1271 Ave. of the Americas, New York, NY 10020-1393 US	

GROWTH PLANS/SPECIAL FEATURES:

Time, Inc. operates the magazine publishing business unit of its parent company, Time Warner, Inc. The company publishes over 125 magazines worldwide, including: Time; People; Sports Illustrated; Entertainment Weekly; Southern Living; In Style; Fortune; Money; Real Simple; Cooking Light; and 80 magazines published by IPC Group, Ltd., a U.K. an Australia subsidiary of the company. Time magazine summarizes current news and weekly events and publishes Time for Kids, a current events magazine for children ages 5-13. People magazine reports on celebrities and other notable personalities and produces People en Espanol, teen People and Who Weekly in the U.K. Sports Illustrated covers sports (Sports Illustrated for Kids is geared at pre-teenagers) and Entertainment Weekly reviews and reports on entertainment. In Style magazine focuses on celebrities, beauty and fashion. Fortune reports on worldwide economic and business developments. Money reports primarily on personal finance. Real Simple focuses on lifestyle and provides solutions for simplifying various aspects of life. Through Southern Progress Corporation, Time, Inc. publishes seven magazines, including Southern Living, Sunset, Cooking Light and Health. IPC Group publishes What's on TV, TV Times, Woman, Marie Claire, Homes & Gardens, Horse & Hound and others. Time4 Media publishes 17 popular sport and outdoor magazines including Golf, Ski, Skiing, Outdoor Life, Transworld Skateboarding and Yachting. Time, Inc. also publishes This Old House magazine and produces several television series, including This Old House and Ask This Old House. In early 2007, Time agreed to sell Bonnier Magazine Group 18 of its smaller titles including: Popular Science; Parenting; and Field & Stream. Later in 2007, the company's Sports Illustrated Group acquired the website FanNation.com from Sports Technologies, Inc. and Time closed LIFE magazine.

FINANCIALS: Sales and profits are in thousands of dollars—add 000 to get the full amount. 2007 Note: Financial information for 2007 was not available for all companies at press time.

2007 Sales: $	2007 Profits: $	**U.S. Stock Ticker: Subsidiary**	
2006 Sales: $	2006 Profits: $	**Int'l Ticker:** Int'l Exchange:	
2005 Sales: $5,846,000	2005 Profits: $	Employees: 11,000	
2004 Sales: $5,700,000	2004 Profits: $	Fiscal Year Ends: 12/31	
2003 Sales: $5,533,000	2003 Profits: $	Parent Company: TIME WARNER INC	

SALARIES/BENEFITS:

Pension Plan:	ESOP Stock Plan:	Profit Sharing:	Top Exec. Salary: $	Bonus: $
Savings Plan:	Stock Purch. Plan:		Second Exec. Salary: $	Bonus: $

OTHER THOUGHTS:

Apparent Women Officers or Directors: 2
Hot Spot for Advancement for Women/Minorities:

LOCATIONS: ("Y" = Yes)

West:	Southwest:	Midwest:	Southeast:	Northeast:	International:
Y	Y	Y	Y	Y	Y

TIME WARNER CABLE INC www.timewarnercable.com

Industry Group Code: 513220 Ranks within this company's industry group: Sales: 4 Profits: 3

Print Media/Publishing:	Movies:	Equipment/Supplies:		Broadcast/Cable:		Music/Audio:	Sports/Games/Gambling:
Newspapers:	Movie Theaters:	Equipment/Supplies:		Broadcast TV:		Music Production:	Games/Sports:
Magazines:	Movie Production:	Gambling Equipment:		Cable TV:	Y	Retail Music:	Retail Games Stores:
Books:	TV/Video Prod.:	Special Services:	Y	Satellite Broadcast:		Retail Audio Equip.:	Stadiums/Teams:
Book Stores:	Video Rental:	Advertising Services:	Y	Radio:		Music Print./Dist.:	Gambling/Casinos:
Distribution/Printing:	Video Distribution:	Info. Sys. Software:	Y	Online Information:		Multimedia:	Rides/Theme Parks:

TYPES OF BUSINESS:

Cable Television
Internet Access
VoIP Service
Video-On-Demand Service

BRANDS/DIVISIONS/AFFILIATES:

Time Warner, Inc.
Road Runner
Digital Phone
Time Warner cable, LLC
Time Warner NY Cable Holding Inc.
Time Warner NY Cable LLC
Time Warner Entertainment Company, L.P.
Time Warner Entertainment-Advance/Newhouse Partner

CONTACTS: Note: Officers with more than one job title may be intentionally listed here more than once.

Glenn A. Britt, CEO
Landel C. Hobbs, COO
Glenn A. Britt, Pres.
Robert D. Marcus, CFO
Sam Howe, Exec. VP/Chief Mktg. Officer
Tomas Mathews, VP-Human Resources
Mike L. LaJoie, CTO/Exec. VP
Marc Lawrence-Apfelbaum, General Counsel/Exec. VP
William R. Goetz, Jr., Exec. VP-Oper.
Carl U. J. Rossetti, Exec. VP-Corp. Dev.
Ellen East, Exec. VP-Corp. Comm.
Barry S. Rosenblum, Exec. VP-Oper.
Terry O'Connell, Exec. VP-Oper.
Carol Hevey, Exec. VP-Oper.
Wayne D. Knighton, Exec. VP-Oper.
Don Logan, Chmn.

Phone: 203-328-0600	Fax: 203-328-0690
Toll-Free:	
Address: 290 Harbor Dr., Stamford, CT 06902-6732 US	

GROWTH PLANS/SPECIAL FEATURES:

Time Warner Cable owns and manages clustered cable television operations within the U.S. The firm is a subsidiary of Time Warner, Inc., a global media and entertainment company with operations in entertainment, cable networks, cable TV service and sports franchises, and publishing, including magazines, books and direct marketing. Time Warner Cable is a provider of new digital technology including digital phones (with 1.6 million subscribers), digital video recorders (DVRs), high definition television (HDTV), video-on-demand (VOD) and high-speed Internet with service to approximately 11 million cable subscribers, including 7 million (52%) digital video customers. The firm's subscribers are typically charged monthly subscription fees based on the level of service selected and, in some cases, equipment usage fees. Time Warner Cable's systems offer basic and standard analog video service, which together provide approximately 70 channels on average, including local broadcast signals, which are available for a fixed monthly fee. Subscribers to Time Warner Cable's analog video service may purchase premium channels for an additional monthly fee, with discounts for the packages including more than one premium service. Video service revenues account for approximately 75% of the company's revenues. Through the firm's cable-based ISP Road Runner and other providers, Time Warner Cable provides Internet access to more than 3.4 million customers. The company also offers Digital Phone, a VoIP telephony service, through a partnership with Sprint. In 2006, the company and Comcast Corporation acquired substantially all of the assets of Adelphia Communications Corporation. Additionally, Comcast redeemed its ownership interest in Time Warner Cable, with the result that the firm is now about 84% owned by Time Warner, Inc. and 16% owned by Adelphia.

FINANCIALS: Sales and profits are in thousands of dollars—add 000 to get the full amount. 2007 Note: Financial information for 2007 was not available for all companies at press time.

2007 Sales: $	2007 Profits: $	**U.S. Stock Ticker: Subsidiary**
2006 Sales: $11,767,000	2006 Profits: $1,976,000	**Int'l Ticker:** Int'l Exchange:
2005 Sales: $9,498,000	2005 Profits: $	Employees: 43,000
2004 Sales: $8,484,000	2004 Profits: $	Fiscal Year Ends: 12/31
2003 Sales: $	2003 Profits: $	Parent Company: TIME WARNER INC

SALARIES/BENEFITS:

Pension Plan: Y	ESOP Stock Plan:	Profit Sharing:	Top Exec. Salary: $1,000,000	Bonus: $4,300,000
Savings Plan: Y	Stock Purch. Plan: Y		Second Exec. Salary: $900,000	Bonus: $2,152,000

OTHER THOUGHTS:

Apparent Women Officers or Directors: 6
Hot Spot for Advancement for Women/Minorities: Y

LOCATIONS: ("Y" = Yes)

West:	Southwest:	Midwest:	Southeast:	Northeast:	International:
Y	Y	Y	Y	Y	

Note: Financial information, benefits and other data can change quickly and may vary from those stated here.

TIME WARNER INC   www.timewarner.com

Industry Group Code: 513220 Ranks within this company's industry group: Sales: 1   Profits: 1

Print Media/Publishing:		Movies:		Equipment/Supplies:		Broadcast/Cable:		Music/Audio:		Sports/Games/Gambling:	
Newspapers:		Movie Theaters:		Equipment/Supplies:		Broadcast TV:		Music Production:	Y	Games/Sports:	
Magazines:	Y	Movie Production:	Y	Gambling Equipment:		Cable TV:		Retail Music:		Retail Games Stores:	
Books:	Y	TV/Video Prod.:	Y	Special Services:	Y	Satellite Broadcast:		Retail Audio Equip.:	Y	Stadiums/Teams:	
Book Stores:		Video Rental:		Advertising Services:	Y	Radio:		Music Print./Dist.:		Gambling/Casinos:	Y
Distribution/Printing:		Video Distribution:		Info. Sys. Software:		Online Information:		Multimedia:		Rides/Theme Parks:	

TYPES OF BUSINESS:

Cable TV Networks
Television Production
Internet Service Provider
Magazine Publishing
Entertainment Investments
Film Production
e-Commerce
Cable TV Service

BRANDS/DIVISIONS/AFFILIATES:

AOL
Warner Bros.
Relegence Corporation
Userplane
Aldelphia Communications
Time, Inc.
Home Box Office, Inc.
Time Warner Cable, Inc.

CONTACTS: *Note: Officers with more than one job title may be intentionally listed here more than once.*

Jeffrey Bewkes, CEO
Jeffrey Bewkes, Pres.
John Martin, CFO/Exec. VP
Patricia Fili-Krushel, Exec. VP-Admin.
Paul Cappuccio, General Counsel/Exec. VP
Edward Adler, Exec. VP-Corp. Comm.
James Burtson, Sr. VP-Investor Rel.
Carol Melton, Exec. VP-Global Public Policy
Olaf Olafsson, Exec. VP
Sandra Dewey, Sr. VP-Original Programming, Turner Entertainment
Michael Lanzillotta, VP-Bus. Affairs, Court TV
Richard Parsons, Chmn.

Phone: 212-484-8000	**Fax:** 212-489-6183
Toll-Free:	
Address: One Time Warner Ctr., New York, NY 10019 US	

GROWTH PLANS/SPECIAL FEATURES:

Time Warner, Inc., the result of the merger of America Online (AOL) and Time Warner, is a leading global media and entertainment company. Its principal business objective is to create and distribute branded information and entertainment throughout the world. The firm operates in five segments, AOL, cable, filmed entertainment, networks and publishing. The company's AOL segment has traditionally been one of the world's largest Internet service providers; however, in 2006, AOL restructured to become an advertising supported global web services business. The company's cable business, Time Warner Cable, Inc. (TWC) and its subsidiaries together form the second-largest cable operator in the U.S. Additionally, this segment offers high speed data services and digital voice services to residential and business customers. The company's filmed entertainment segment, operated principally through subsidiary Warner Bros. Entertainment Group, produces and distributes theatrical motion pictures, television shows, animation and other programming, distributes home video product, and licenses rights to the company's feature films, television programming and characters. The company's networks segment consists principally of domestic and international basic cable networks and pay television programming services. This segment includes basic cable networks owned by subsidiary Turner Broadcasting System, Inc. (TBS) and pay television programming, including the HBO and Cinemax channels, operated by Home Box Office, Inc. Time Warner's publishing business publishes 145 magazines worldwide, offers direct book marketing and publishes a collection of niche books. In 2006, subsidiary AOL acquired Relegence Corporation and Userplane; and sold its English, French and German Internet access businesses to different companies. Also in 2006, subsidiary TWC acquired Aldelphia Communications in a cash and stock transaction. Due to Adelphia's Chapter 11 restructuring in January 2007, the TWC stock included in the acquisition was distributed to Adelphia's creditors, making TWC a publicly traded company.

FINANCIALS: Sales and profits are in thousands of dollars—add 000 to get the full amount. 2007 Note: Financial information for 2007 was not available for all companies at press time.

2007 Sales: $	2007 Profits: $	**U.S. Stock Ticker:** TWX
2006 Sales: $44,224,000	2006 Profits: $6,552,000	**Int'l Ticker:** Int'l Exchange:
2005 Sales: $42,401,000	2005 Profits: $2,671,000	Employees: 92,700
2004 Sales: $40,993,000	2004 Profits: $3,108,000	Fiscal Year Ends: 12/31
2003 Sales: $39,565,000	2003 Profits: $2,639,000	Parent Company:

SALARIES/BENEFITS:

Pension Plan:	ESOP Stock Plan:	Profit Sharing:	Top Exec. Salary: $1,500,000	Bonus: $7,500,000
Savings Plan: Y	Stock Purch. Plan:		Second Exec. Salary: $1,000,000	Bonus: $6,000,000

OTHER THOUGHTS:

Apparent Women Officers or Directors: 3
Hot Spot for Advancement for Women/Minorities: Y

LOCATIONS: ("Y" = Yes)

West:	Southwest:	Midwest:	Southeast:	Northeast:	International:
Y	Y	Y	Y	Y	Y

TIVO INC

www.tivo.com

Industry Group Code: 334310 **Ranks within this company's industry group:** Sales: 10 Profits: 10

Print Media/Publishing:	Movies:	Equipment/Supplies:		Broadcast/Cable:	Music/Audio:	Sports/Games/Gambling:
Newspapers:	Movie Theaters:	Equipment/Supplies:	Y	Broadcast TV:	Music Production:	Games/Sports:
Magazines:	Movie Production:	Gambling Equipment:		Cable TV:	Retail Music:	Retail Games Stores:
Books:	TV/Video Prod.:	Special Services:	Y	Satellite Broadcast:	Retail Audio Equip.:	Stadiums/Teams:
Book Stores:	Video Rental:	Advertising Services:	Y	Radio:	Music Print./Dist.:	Gambling/Casinos:
Distribution/Printing:	Video Distribution:	Info. Sys. Software:		Online Information:	Multimedia:	Rides/Theme Parks:

TYPES OF BUSINESS:

Television Home Recording Technology
Digital Video Recorders
Advertising Services

BRANDS/DIVISIONS/AFFILIATES:

TiVoToGo
TiVo KidZone
TiVoCast
Season Pass
WishList
TiVo Product Watch
TiVo Online

CONTACTS: Note: Officers with more than one job title may be intentionally listed here more than once.

Tom Rogers, CEO
Tom Rogers, Pres.
Cal Hoagland, Interim CFO
Clent Richardson, Chief Mktg. Officer
Nancy Kato, Sr. VP-Human Resources
James Barton, CTO/Sr. VP
Matthew Zinn, General Counsel/Sr. VP
Karen Bressner, Sr. VP-Advertising Sales
Joe Miller, Sr. VP-Consumer Sales & Distribution
Mark Roberts, Sr. VP-Consumer Prod. & Oper.
Matthew Zinn, Chief Privacy Officer

Phone: 408-519-9100	Fax: 408-519-5330
Toll-Free:	
Address: 2160 Gold St., PO Box 2160, Alviso, CA 95002 US	

GROWTH PLANS/SPECIAL FEATURES:

TiVo, Inc. is a provider of technology and services for digital video recorders. The subscription-based TiVo provides consumers with an easy way to record, watch and control television and receive videos, pictures and movies from cable, broadcast and broadband sources. TiVo offers such features as Season Pass recordings, WishList searches, TiVoToGo transfers, TiVoCast content (which includes premium content delivered from Amazon Unbox), TiVo KidZone (which offers parental controls), TiVo Online Scheduling and TiVo Product Watch. The company has roughly 4.4 million subscribers. It distributes the TiVo service through consumer electronics retailers and through its online store. Additionally, the firm provides the service through agreements with television service providers such as satellite television providers, including DIRECTV, and in the future cable television operators, such as Comcast and Cox, and digital subscriber line providers such as BellSouth and EarthLink. TiVo's technology portfolio for enabling the TiVo services includes the TiVo service client software platform, the TiVo service infrastructure and TiVo-enabled DVR hardware design. The TiVo service client software runs on TiVo-enabled DVRs and includes system components such as media-oriented file system, a high-performance transactional database, an integrated security system and application components such as media management and user interface. The TiVo service infrastructure enables the ongoing operation of the TiVo service, managing the distribution of propriety services and specialized content such as program guide data, showcases and TiVo client software upgrades. The DVR hardware design is a specification developed by TiVo for set-top boxes contained a hard disk drive, a CPU and memory, digital video chips, a modem and other components. TiVo also provides marketing solutions for the television industry, including a unique platform for advertisers and audience research measurement.

The company offers its employees a 401(k) plan; an employee stock purchase plan; health insurance; an employee assistance program; life and AD&D insurance; a college savings plan; and flexible spending accounts.

FINANCIALS: Sales and profits are in thousands of dollars—add 000 to get the full amount. 2007 Note: Financial information for 2007 was not available for all companies at press time.

2007 Sales: $258,589	2007 Profits: $-47,754	**U.S. Stock Ticker:** TIVO
2006 Sales: $195,925	2006 Profits: $-34,398	**Int'l Ticker:** Int'l Exchange:
2005 Sales: $172,055	2005 Profits: $-79,842	Employees: 451
2004 Sales: $141,080	2004 Profits: $-32,018	Fiscal Year Ends: 1/31
2003 Sales: $96,010	2003 Profits: $-80,596	Parent Company:

SALARIES/BENEFITS:

Pension Plan:	ESOP Stock Plan:	Profit Sharing:	Top Exec. Salary: $750,000	Bonus: $303,000
Savings Plan: Y	Stock Purch. Plan: Y		Second Exec. Salary: $285,000	Bonus: $141,768

OTHER THOUGHTS:

Apparent Women Officers or Directors: 2
Hot Spot for Advancement for Women/Minorities: Y

LOCATIONS: ("Y" = Yes)

West:	Southwest:	Midwest:	Southeast:	Northeast:	International:
Y					Y

TRADER CLASSIFIED MEDIA NV
www.trader.com

Industry Group Code: 511120 Ranks within this company's industry group: Sales: Profits:

Print Media/Publishing:		Movies:	Equipment/Supplies:		Broadcast/Cable:	Music/Audio:	Sports/Games/Gambling:
Newspapers:	Y	Movie Theaters:	Equipment/Supplies:		Broadcast TV:	Music Production:	Games/Sports:
Magazines:		Movie Production:	Gambling Equipment:		Cable TV:	Retail Music:	Retail Games Stores:
Books:		TV/Video Prod.:	Special Services:	Y	Satellite Broadcast:	Retail Audio Equip.:	Stadiums/Teams:
Book Stores:		Video Rental:	Advertising Services:	Y	Radio:	Music Print./Dist.:	Gambling/Casinos:
Distribution/Printing:		Video Distribution:	Info. Sys. Software:		Online Information:	Multimedia:	Rides/Theme Parks:

TYPES OF BUSINESS:
Classified Ad Publications
Web Sites
Periodical Publishing

BRANDS/DIVISIONS/AFFILIATES:
Trader.com
AutoTrader
Sports & Antiques
LaCentrale.fr
Infojobs.net
Hebdo.net
Commercial Property Guide
Homebase.ca

CONTACTS: *Note: Officers with more than one job title may be intentionally listed here more than once.*
John H. MacBain, CEO
Didier Breton, COO
John H. MacBain, Pres.
Francois Jallot, CFO
Peter Reese, VP-Mktg.
William Clark, VP-Human Resources
Zouhaire Sekkat, CIO
Elizabeth Pauchet, General Counsel
Paul Guest, VP-Oper.
Paul Guest, VP-Finance
Eric de Teyssonniere de Gramont, Chmn.

Phone: 212.815.2345	Fax:
Toll-Free:	
Address: Overschiestraat 61, Amsterdam, 1062 XD The Netherlands	

GROWTH PLANS/SPECIAL FEATURES:
Trader Classified Media N.V., formerly Trader.com, is a publishing company that sells classified advertising services. The firm offers content in multiple categories such as jobs, personal ads, computers, production equipment and leisure, but concentrates largely on its core categories, which include real estate, automotive and general merchandise. Trader operates in 19 countries around the world and owns approximately 400 publications and 50 web sites. The firm's printed publications have more than 9 million readers per week, while its web sites attract 7.3 million visitors per month. Trader's print publications range from the general to the specific and include titles such as Auto Trader, Sport & Antiques and Commercial Property Guide. The company's web sites include Autotrader.ca, BuySell.com, Hebdo.net, Homebase.ca and Occasion.ca. The firm also has a 60% stake in a major European Internet employment web site, Infojobs.net. In June 2007 the company ended its operations in Taiwan and sold its 55% stake in Car News to a minority shareholder.

FINANCIALS: Sales and profits are in thousands of dollars—add 000 to get the full amount. 2007 Note: Financial information for 2007 was not available for all companies at press time.

2007 Sales: $	2007 Profits: $	U.S. Stock Ticker: TRDFF
2006 Sales: $	2006 Profits: $	Int'l Ticker: TRD Int'l Exchange: Paris-Euronext
2005 Sales: $372,323	2005 Profits: $15,277	Employees: 3,400
2004 Sales: $319,533	2004 Profits: $299,803	Fiscal Year Ends: 12/31
2003 Sales: $494,530	2003 Profits: $302,964	Parent Company:

SALARIES/BENEFITS:
Pension Plan:	ESOP Stock Plan:	Profit Sharing:	Top Exec. Salary: $	Bonus: $
Savings Plan:	Stock Purch. Plan:		Second Exec. Salary: $	Bonus: $

OTHER THOUGHTS:
Apparent Women Officers or Directors: 1
Hot Spot for Advancement for Women/Minorities:

LOCATIONS: ("Y" = Yes)
West:	Southwest:	Midwest:	Southeast:	Northeast:	International:
					Y

TRAFFIX INC

www.traffixinc.com

Industry Group Code: 541810A **Ranks within this company's industry group:** Sales: 2 Profits: 1

Print Media/Publishing:	Movies:	Equipment/Supplies:		Broadcast/Cable:	Music/Audio:	Sports/Games/Gambling:
Newspapers:	Movie Theaters:	Equipment/Supplies:		Broadcast TV:	Music Production:	Games/Sports:
Magazines:	Movie Production:	Gambling Equipment:		Cable TV:	Retail Music:	Retail Games Stores:
Books:	TV/Video Prod.:	Special Services:	Y	Satellite Broadcast:	Retail Audio Equip.:	Stadiums/Teams:
Book Stores:	Video Rental:	Advertising Services:	Y	Radio:	Music Print./Dist.:	Gambling/Casinos:
Distribution/Printing:	Video Distribution:	Info. Sys. Software:		Online Information:	Multimedia:	Rides/Theme Parks:

TYPES OF BUSINESS:

Online Direct Marketing
Database Marketing
Online Dating Service
Online Tech Support

BRANDS/DIVISIONS/AFFILIATES:

Traffix Performance Marketing
SendTraffic
Hot Rocket Marketing
mxFocus
RocketProfit
iMatchup.com
Q121.com
LoveFreeGames.com

CONTACTS: *Note: Officers with more than one job title may be intentionally listed here more than once.*

Jeffrey L. Schwartz, CEO
Richard Wentworth, COO
Andrew Stollman, Pres.
Daniel Harvey, CFO
Andrew Stollman, Sec.
Jeffrey L. Schwartz, Chmn.

Phone: 845-620-1212	Fax: 845-620-1717
Toll-Free:	
Address: 1 Blue Hill Plz., Pearl River, NY 10965 US	

GROWTH PLANS/SPECIAL FEATURES:

Traffix, Inc. is a database marketing company that uses its online media network and proprietary ad-serving optimization technology to generate leads, customers and sales for itself and its corporate clients. The firm's marketing services for companies include the development of complete, creative promotions; broadcasting online promotions; creating and hosting customized web sites; and comprehensive results reporting for use in promotion analysis. Traffix generates revenues from direct marketing activities, as well as sales and rentals of its proprietary, profiled databases. The company operates through one segment, Online Advertising and Media services, with four business groups: SendTraffic, a search engine marketing firm; Hot Rocket Marketing, an online direct response media firm; recently launched mxFocus, which develops and distributes content for mobile phones and other wireless devices on every major wireless carrier; and Traffix Performance Marketing. Performance Marketing offers marketers advertising distribution through Traffix's network of web sites including EZ-Tracks.com, Reciperewards.com, PrizeDistributors, Inc, Musicoffaith.com, AtlasCreditGroup.com, TheBargainSpot.com, AltasAutomotiveGroup.com, EZGreets.com, GameFiesta.com, PrizeAmerica.com and LoveFreeGames.com. In addition, Traffix offers services in e-mail marketing, Results Analysis, and syndication of its advertising campaigns to third party media. Recently, the company has launched two new websites: iMatchup.com, an online dating program conducted over the Internet and Q121.com, a social networking site that gives users the ability to transfer content to and from their mobile phones as well as sending text messages to individuals or groups anonymously. In September 2007, Traffix and New Motion, Inc. signed merger agreement which would result in Traffix becoming a wholly-owned subsidiary of New Motion.

FINANCIALS: Sales and profits are in thousands of dollars—add 000 to get the full amount. 2007 Note: Financial information for 2007 was not available for all companies at press time.

2007 Sales: $	2007 Profits: $	U.S. Stock Ticker: TRFX	
2006 Sales: $72,844	2006 Profits: $1,903	Int'l Ticker:	Int'l Exchange:
2005 Sales: $62,856	2005 Profits: $2,428	Employees: 93	
2004 Sales: $37,281	2004 Profits: $1,014	Fiscal Year Ends: 11/30	
2003 Sales: $32,389	2003 Profits: $ 421	Parent Company:	

SALARIES/BENEFITS:

Pension Plan:	ESOP Stock Plan:	Profit Sharing:	Top Exec. Salary: $605,000	Bonus: $106,758
Savings Plan:	Stock Purch. Plan:		Second Exec. Salary: $544,500	Bonus: $136,758

OTHER THOUGHTS:

Apparent Women Officers or Directors:
Hot Spot for Advancement for Women/Minorities:

LOCATIONS: ("Y" = Yes)

West:	Southwest:	Midwest:	Southeast:	Northeast:	International:
				Y	Y

Note: Financial information, benefits and other data can change quickly and may vary from those stated here.

TRANS WORLD CORP

www.transwc.com

Industry Group Code: 713210 Ranks within this company's industry group: Sales: 12   Profits: 8

Print Media/Publishing:	Movies:	Equipment/Supplies:	Broadcast/Cable:	Music/Audio:	Sports/Games/Gambling:	
Newspapers:	Movie Theaters:	Equipment/Supplies:	Broadcast TV:	Music Production:	Games/Sports:	
Magazines:	Movie Production:	Gambling Equipment:	Cable TV:	Retail Music:	Retail Games Stores:	
Books:	TV/Video Prod.:	Special Services:	Satellite Broadcast:	Retail Audio Equip.:	Stadiums/Teams:	
Book Stores:	Video Rental:	Advertising Services:	Radio:	Music Print./Dist.:	Gambling/Casinos:	Y
Distribution/Printing:	Video Distribution:	Info. Sys. Software:	Online Information:	Multimedia:	Rides/Theme Parks:	

TYPES OF BUSINESS:

Casinos
Hotels & Restaurants

BRANDS/DIVISIONS/AFFILIATES:

Trans World Gaming Corp.
American Chance Casinos
Route 55
Route 59
Ceska Kubice
Dolni Dvoriste Hotel
Znojmo
Value Partners

CONTACTS: *Note: Officers with more than one job title may be intentionally listed here more than once.*

Rami S. Ramadan, CEO
Rami S. Ramadan, Pres.
Rami S. Ramadan, CFO
Roland Stamberger, Dir.-Regional Mktg.
Sarah Wagner, Dir.-Project Dev.
Jill Yarussi, Mgr-Admin.
Jill Yarussi, Mgr.-Corp. Comm.
Hung Le, Corp. Controller
Dieter Bettschar, Regional Casino Mgr.
Tomas Kment, Dir.-Admin.
Pavel Marsik, Regional Controller-Europe
Paul Benkley, Managing Dir-Europe Oper.

Phone: 212-983-3355	Fax: 212-983-8129
Toll-Free:	
Address: 545 5th Ave., Ste. 940, New York, NY 10017 US	

GROWTH PLANS/SPECIAL FEATURES:

TransWorld Corporation, formerly Trans World Gaming Corp., owns and operates small-to-medium casinos and hotels in the Czech Republic. The company's European partner (branded American Chance Casinos, or ACC) operates the casino division. Each casino focuses on a different American theme including: 1920s Chicago, 1950s Miami Beach, the Pacific South Seas and the Southern Antebellum era. Built on border towns, the casinos include: Ceska Kubice (located on the Czech-German border); Trans World (located on the Czech-German border); Route 59 (located on the Czech-Austrian border); Route 55 (located on the Czech-Austrian border); and Grand Casino and Nightclub Lav (the company's newest operation located on Croatia's Adriatic coast.) The casinos feature games including American roulette, blackjack, Red Dog, poker, automatic roulette and slot machines. Trans World plans on constructing three hotels by 2008, each located near an ACC casino. Dolni Dvoriste Hotel (near Route 55) and Folmava (near Ceska) will each feature a restaurant, spa and fitness center. Znojmo (near Route 59) will feature a restaurant, bar, night club, spa and fitness center. In addition, the firm plans on developing four-star hotels featuring 80-400 rooms in Europe. Trans World Director Timothy G. Ewing controls about 45% of the company's shares through Texas-based investment firm Value Partners.

FINANCIALS: Sales and profits are in thousands of dollars—add 000 to get the full amount. 2007 Note: Financial information for 2007 was not available for all companies at press time.

2007 Sales: $	2007 Profits: $	**U.S. Stock Ticker: TWOC**
2006 Sales: $26,216	2006 Profits: $2,027	**Int'l Ticker:** Int'l Exchange:
2005 Sales: $23,249	2005 Profits: $ 79	Employees: 564
2004 Sales: $18,938	2004 Profits: $1,247	Fiscal Year Ends: 12/31
2003 Sales: $17,600	2003 Profits: $ 200	Parent Company:

SALARIES/BENEFITS:

Pension Plan:	ESOP Stock Plan:	Profit Sharing:	Top Exec. Salary: $400,000	Bonus: $
Savings Plan:	Stock Purch. Plan: Y		Second Exec. Salary: $99,959	Bonus: $

OTHER THOUGHTS:

Apparent Women Officers or Directors: 2
Hot Spot for Advancement for Women/Minorities:

LOCATIONS: ("Y" = Yes)

West:	Southwest:	Midwest:	Southeast:	Northeast:	International:
				Y	Y

TRANS WORLD ENTERTAINMENT CORP   www.twec.com

Industry Group Code: 451220 Ranks within this company's industry group: Sales: 1 Profits: 1

Print Media/Publishing:	Movies:	Equipment/Supplies:	Broadcast/Cable:	Music/Audio:		Sports/Games/Gambling:
Newspapers:	Movie Theaters:	Equipment/Supplies:	Broadcast TV:	Music Production:		Games/Sports:
Magazines:	Movie Production:	Gambling Equipment:	Cable TV:	Retail Music:	Y	Retail Games Stores:
Books:	TV/Video Prod.:	Special Services:	Satellite Broadcast:	Retail Audio Equip.:		Stadiums/Teams:
Book Stores:	Video Rental:	Advertising Services:	Radio:	Music Print./Dist.:	Y	Gambling/Casinos:
Distribution/Printing:	Video Distribution: Y	Info. Sys. Software:	Online Information:	Multimedia:		Rides/Theme Parks:

TYPES OF BUSINESS:

Music Stores
CDs, DVDs, Videos & Video Games
Online Sales
Digital Music Content
Used Music & Video Retail

BRANDS/DIVISIONS/AFFILIATES:

Record Town, Inc.
f.Y.e. (For Your Entertainment)
Suncoast
Sam Goody
Wherehouse Music & Movies
Second Spin
Planet Music
Fye.com

CONTACTS: *Note: Officers with more than one job title may be intentionally listed here more than once.*

Robert J. Higgins, CEO
James A. Litwak, COO
James A. Litwak, Pres.
John J. Sullivan, CFO/Exec. VP
John J. Sullivan, Sec.
Bruce J. Eisenberg, Exec. VP-Real Estate
Robert J. Higgins, Chmn.

Phone: 518-452-1242	Fax: 518-452-3547
Toll-Free:	
Address: 38 Corporate Cir., Albany, NY 12203 US	

GROWTH PLANS/SPECIAL FEATURES:

Trans World Entertainment Corp. (TWE) is a specialty retailer of compact discs, prerecorded audiocassettes and videocassettes, DVDs, videogames and related products in the U.S. The firm operates approximately 992 mall-based and free-standing stores in all 50 U.S. states, Washington, D.C., Puerto Rico and the Virgin Islands. Trans World owns 100% of Record Town, Inc., through which it conducts most of its operations, and Second Spin, a used CD, video and DVD retailer. Stores are divided into mall based stores, predominately under the brand name f.Y.e. (For Your Entertainment), and freestanding stores under various names. Mall stores include traditional f.Y.e. stores, carrying a full complement of entertainment products; f.Y.e. Superstores, offering a broader and deeper product assortment; and video only stores under the names Saturday Matinee and Suncoast. The freestanding stores operate under the brand names f.Y.e., Sam Goody, Coconuts Music & Movies, Strawberries, Wherehouse Music & Movies, CD World, Spec's Music and Second Spin. The stores carry a full complement of entertainment software, music, home video, video games and related products; and are located in freestanding, strip mall and downtown locations. Freestanding stores also include the 31,400-square-foot Planet Music superstore in Virginia Beach, Virginia, which offers an extensive catalog of music, DVD and VHS video, games and related merchandise; and six freestanding f.Y.e. Superstores, averaging 53,000 square feet. TWE operates a number of e-commerce websites including Fye.com, Wherehouse.com and Secondspin.com. In 2006, the firm acquired Mix & Burn, LLC, a provider of digital content to retailers nationwide. In March 2006, TWE acquired substantially all of the assets of Musicland Holding Corp., which operates 335 retail stores, and associated web sites, under the names Sam Goody, Samgoody.com, Suncoast Motion Picture Company, Suncoast.com, On Cue and MediaPlay.com. The firm operates 210 of Musicland's stores.

FINANCIALS: Sales and profits are in thousands of dollars—add 000 to get the full amount. 2007 Note: Financial information for 2007 was not available for all companies at press time.

2007 Sales: $	2007 Profits: $	U.S. Stock Ticker: TWMC
2006 Sales: $1,238,486	2006 Profits: $ 609	Int'l Ticker: Int'l Exchange:
2005 Sales: $1,365,133	2005 Profits: $41,841	Employees: 8,100
2004 Sales: $1,330,626	2004 Profits: $23,067	Fiscal Year Ends: 1/31
2003 Sales: $1,281,900	2003 Profits: $-45,500	Parent Company:

SALARIES/BENEFITS:

Pension Plan:	ESOP Stock Plan:	Profit Sharing:	Top Exec. Salary: $1,274,038	Bonus: $
Savings Plan:	Stock Purch. Plan:		Second Exec. Salary: $458,654	Bonus: $

OTHER THOUGHTS:

Apparent Women Officers or Directors: 1
Hot Spot for Advancement for Women/Minorities:

LOCATIONS: ("Y" = Yes)

West:	Southwest:	Midwest:	Southeast:	Northeast:	International:
Y	Y	Y	Y	Y	Y

Note: Financial information, benefits and other data can change quickly and may vary from those stated here.

TRANS-LUX CORPORATION

www.trans-lux.com

Industry Group Code: 334310 Ranks within this company's industry group: Sales: 12   Profits: 9

Print Media/Publishing:	Movies:		Equipment/Supplies:		Broadcast/Cable:	Music/Audio:	Sports/Games/Gambling:
Newspapers:	Movie Theaters:	Y	Equipment/Supplies:	Y	Broadcast TV:	Music Production:	Games/Sports:
Magazines:	Movie Production:		Gambling Equipment:		Cable TV:	Retail Music:	Retail Games Stores:
Books:	TV/Video Prod.:		Special Services:		Satellite Broadcast:	Retail Audio Equip.:	Stadiums/Teams:
Book Stores:	Video Rental:		Advertising Services:		Radio:	Music Print./Dist.:	Gambling/Casinos:
Distribution/Printing:	Video Distribution:		Info. Sys. Software:		Online Information:	Multimedia:	Rides/Theme Parks:

TYPES OF BUSINESS:

Electronic Equipment-Information Displays
Movie Theaters
Data, Graphics & Picture Displays

BRANDS/DIVISIONS/AFFILIATES:

CaptiVision
CaptiVue
ProLine
GraphixWall
GraphixMax
Entertainment Division

CONTACTS: Note: Officers with more than one job title may be intentionally listed here more than once.

Thomas Brandt, Co-CEO
Michael R. Mulcahy, Pres./Co-CEO
Angela D. Toppi, CFO
Thomas F. Mahoney, Sr. VP-Sales
Angela D. Toppi, Exec. VP-Human Resources
Karl P. Hirschauer, Sr. VP-Eng.
Al L. Miller, Exec. VP-Electronic Display Mfg.
Angela D. Toppi, Corp. Sec./Treas.
Thomas Brandt, Exec. VP-Finance & Real Estate Oper.
Thomas Brandt, Exec. VP-Entertainment Div.
John A. Long, Sr. VP-Trans-Lux West & Trans-Lux Fair-Play
Gene Jankowski, Chmn.

Phone: 203-853-4321	Fax: 203-852-0836
Toll-Free: 800-243-5544	
Address: 110 Richards Ave., Norwalk, CT 06856-5090 US	

GROWTH PLANS/SPECIAL FEATURES:

Trans-Lux Corporation manufactures, distributes and services large-scale, multi-color, real-time electronic information displays utilizing LED, plasma and LCD screens; and bulb based technologies including graphics and video displays. Its indoor and outdoor displays are used in many international industries, including brokerage firms, banks, energy companies, insurance and mutual fund companies, sports stadiums, educational institutions and outdoor advertisers. Displays can be found in corporate and government communication centers, retail outlets, casinos, race tracks, train stations, bus terminals, airports, on highways and in movie theatres. Trans-Lux provides products tailored to customers, including hardware components and software; on-site installation; and maintenance coverage. The CaptiVue line of outdoor displays has the capacity to include full color and blue monochrome configurations in LED messages. Trans-Lux's Fuel Price Changer displays used CaptiVue technology. CaptiVision is a line of jumbo, 4.4 trillion-color monitors delivering video and animation for indoor markets. ProLine, the firm's proprietary controller software, is designed for screens that require fast-changing information and imagery, such as in sports and commercial markets, allowing the combination of text with live or recorded video, newswire feeds, cable TV and animations on a single display. GraphixWall and GraphixMax, the firm's indoor fixed size and tillable graphic display products allow for large custom displays such as flight information and baggage claim at airports; automatic call directories at contact centers; and promoting products in financial and retail environments. Trans-Lux's Entertainment Division owns and operates 64 theater screens in 12 locations in the western mountain states.

Employees of Trans-Lux receive flexible spending accounts; medical benefits; life, disability, auto and homeowners' insurance; flextime arrangements; credit union membership; tuition reimbursement; on-site training courses; recognition programs; and paid time off. The company also offers preventative health programs such as stress reduction seminars; blood pressure and cholesterol screenings; flu shots; and a summer walking program.

FINANCIALS: Sales and profits are in thousands of dollars—add 000 to get the full amount. 2007 Note: Financial information for 2007 was not available for all companies at press time.

2007 Sales: $	2007 Profits: $	U.S. Stock Ticker: TLX
2006 Sales: $53,911	2006 Profits: $-1,647	Int'l Ticker: Int'l Exchange:
2005 Sales: $54,368	2005 Profits: $-1,793	Employees: 431
2004 Sales: $52,579	2004 Profits: $ 539	Fiscal Year Ends: 12/31
2003 Sales: $56,022	2003 Profits: $1,054	Parent Company:

SALARIES/BENEFITS:

Pension Plan: Y	ESOP Stock Plan:	Profit Sharing:	Top Exec. Salary: $340,406	Bonus: $
Savings Plan: Y	Stock Purch. Plan:		Second Exec. Salary: $279,562	Bonus: $

OTHER THOUGHTS:

Apparent Women Officers or Directors: 1
Hot Spot for Advancement for Women/Minorities:

LOCATIONS: ("Y" = Yes)

West:	Southwest:	Midwest:	Southeast:	Northeast:	International:
Y	Y	Y		Y	Y

Note: Financial information, benefits and other data can change quickly and may vary from those stated here.

TRIBUNE CO

www.tribune.com

Industry Group Code: 511110 Ranks within this company's industry group: Sales: 3 Profits: 2

Print Media/Publishing:		Movies:		Equipment/Supplies:		Broadcast/Cable:		Music/Audio:		Sports/Games/Gambling:	
Newspapers:	Y	Movie Theaters:		Equipment/Supplies:		Broadcast TV:	Y	Music Production:		Games/Sports:	Y
Magazines:		Movie Production:		Gambling Equipment:		Cable TV:		Retail Music:		Retail Games Stores:	
Books:		TV/Video Prod.:	Y	Special Services:		Satellite Broadcast:		Retail Audio Equip.:		Stadiums/Teams:	
Book Stores:		Video Rental:		Advertising Services:		Radio:		Music Print./Dist.:		Gambling/Casinos:	
Distribution/Printing:		Video Distribution:		Info. Sys. Software:		Online Information:		Multimedia:		Rides/Theme Parks:	

TYPES OF BUSINESS:

Newspaper Publishing
Online News & Information
TV & Radio Broadcasting
TV Programming Development
Professional Sports Teams
Media Marketing

BRANDS/DIVISIONS/AFFILIATES:

Los Angeles Times
Chicago Tribune
Newsday
Superstation WGN
Chicago Cubs
Tribune Entertainment
Tribune Interactive, Inc.
Tribune Broadcasting Company

CONTACTS: Note: Officers with more than one job title may be intentionally listed here more than once.

Samuel Zell, CEO
Samuel Zell, Pres.
Luis E. Lewin, Sr. VP-Human Resources
Gerald Spector, Chief Admin. Officer
Crane H. Kenney, General Counsel/Sr. VP/Corp. Sec.
Thomas D. Leach, Sr. VP-Dev.
Donald C. Grenesko, Sr. VP-Finance & Admin.
Randy Michaels, Exec. VP/CEO-Interactive & Broadcasting
Gerald Spector, Exec. VP
Timothy J. Landon, Pres., Tribune Broadcasting
Scott Smith, Pres., Tribune Publishing
Samuel Zell, Chmn.

Phone: 312-222-9100	Fax: 312-222-1573
Toll-Free:	
Address: 435 N. Michigan Ave., Chicago, IL 60611 US	

GROWTH PLANS/SPECIAL FEATURES:

Tribune Company, through its subsidiaries, publishes newspapers, provides broadcast television and radio entertainment, and develops and distributes information and entertainment through the Internet. The company's primary newspapers include the Los Angeles Times, Chicago Tribune, Newsday, South Florida Sun-Sentinel, Orlando Sentinel and Baltimore Sun. Tribune also owns entertainment listings, a media marketing company and Superstation WGN on national cable, among other related businesses. The firm's broadcasting and entertainment segment includes affiliations in major U.S cities with The CW Television Network, the FOX Network, MyNetworkTV and ABC in addition to several radio stations, the Chicago Cubs baseball team and Tribune Entertainment, a television programming-development company. The interactive segment manages the web sites of the company's daily newspapers and television stations. In April 2007 the company announced plans to sell the Chicago Cubs. In December 2007, the company went private, merging with an acquisition subsidiary of the Tribune Employee Stock Ownership Plan. Chicago real-estate tycoon Sam Zell arranged the $8.2 billion deal with a personal investment of $315 million, effectively putting him in control of Tribune Co.

FINANCIALS: Sales and profits are in thousands of dollars—add 000 to get the full amount. 2007 Note: Financial information for 2007 was not available for all companies at press time.

2007 Sales: $	2007 Profits: $	U.S. Stock Ticker: Private
2006 Sales: $5,517,708	2006 Profits: $593,995	Int'l Ticker: Int'l Exchange:
2005 Sales: $5,511,283	2005 Profits: $534,689	Employees: 21,000
2004 Sales: $5,631,431	2004 Profits: $555,536	Fiscal Year Ends: 12/31
2003 Sales: $5,594,800	2003 Profits: $891,400	Parent Company:

SALARIES/BENEFITS:

Pension Plan:	ESOP Stock Plan:	Profit Sharing:	Top Exec. Salary: $999,327	Bonus: $1,400,000
Savings Plan:	Stock Purch. Plan:		Second Exec. Salary: $578,365	Bonus: $525,000

OTHER THOUGHTS:

Apparent Women Officers or Directors:
Hot Spot for Advancement for Women/Minorities:

LOCATIONS: ("Y" = Yes)

West:	Southwest:	Midwest:	Southeast:	Northeast:	International:
Y	Y	Y	Y	Y	Y

Note: Financial information, benefits and other data can change quickly and may vary from those stated here.

TRUMP ENTERTAINMENT RESORTS INC
www.trumpcasinos.com
Industry Group Code: 721120 Ranks within this company's industry group: Sales: 7   Profits: 12

Print Media/Publishing:	Movies:	Equipment/Supplies:	Broadcast/Cable:	Music/Audio:	Sports/Games/Gambling:
Newspapers:	Movie Theaters:	Equipment/Supplies:	Broadcast TV:	Music Production:	Games/Sports:
Magazines:	Movie Production:	Gambling Equipment:	Cable TV:	Retail Music:	Retail Games Stores:
Books:	TV/Video Prod.:	Special Services:	Satellite Broadcast:	Retail Audio Equip.:	Stadiums/Teams:
Book Stores:	Video Rental:	Advertising Services:	Radio:	Music Print./Dist.:	Gambling/Casinos: Y
Distribution/Printing:	Video Distribution:	Info. Sys. Software:	Online Information:	Multimedia:	Rides/Theme Parks:

TYPES OF BUSINESS:
Casino Hotels
Casino Management

BRANDS/DIVISIONS/AFFILIATES:
Trump Plaza Hotel & Casino
Trump Taj Mahal Casino Resort
Trump Marina Hotel Casino
Diamondhead Casino Corporation
Trump Hotels & Casino Resorts, Inc.
Xanadu Theater

CONTACTS: *Note: Officers with more than one job title may be intentionally listed here more than once.*
Mark Juliano, CEO
Mark Juliano, COO
Dale Black, CFO/Exec. VP
Gregg Caren, VP-Hotel Sales
Craig D. Keyser, Exec. VP-Human Resources
Virginia McDowell, CIO/Exec. VP
Craig D. Keyser, Exec. VP-Admin.
Robert M. Pickus, General Counsel/Exec. VP/Sec.
Eric Hausler, Sr. VP-Dev.
Joseph A. Fusco, Exec. VP-Gov't Rel. & Regulatory Affairs
John P. Burke, Exec. VP/Corp. Treas.
Richard M. Santoro, Exec. VP-Asset Protection & Risk Mgmt.
Paul B. Keller, Exec. VP-Design & Construction
Mark Sachais, VP-Mktg., Trump Plaza Hotel & Casino
Donald J. Trump, Chmn.

Phone: 609-449-6515	Fax: 609-449-6586
Toll-Free:	
Address: 1000 Boardwalk, Atlantic City, NJ 08401 US	

GROWTH PLANS/SPECIAL FEATURES:
Trump Entertainment Resorts (TRMP), formerly Trump Hotels & Casino Resorts, Inc., operates in Atlantic City with three casino properties: the Trump Plaza Hotel and Casino; the Trump Taj Mahal Casino Resort; and the Trump Marina Hotel and Casino. All TRMP casinos occupy about a 22% share of the gaming revenue and a 20% share of hotel space within the city. Together, these three properties comprise approximately 330,000 square feet of gaming space with over 9,300 slot machines, 370 gaming tables and 2,880 hotel rooms and suites. The Trump Taj Mahal is located on 39.4 acres of land with 1,250 hotel rooms and 13 dining locations. In addition, the casino features 158,500 square feet of gaming space with approximately 200 table games and Xanadu Theater, an entertainment complex with a seating capacity of 1,200 people. Trump Plaza Hotel and Casino features 900 hotel rooms with 96,000 square feet of casino space for 2, 280 slot machines and 90 table games. Additional amenities include 18,000 square feet of conference space, a cabaret theater, spa, arcade, and three cocktail lounges. Trump Marina Hotel Casino offers a 27-story hotel with 728 guest rooms and 79,000 square feet of gaming space for 2,020 slot machines, 70 table games and a simulcast racetrack facility. In 2006, the company dedicated $140 million to update and improve its three casinos, which included several food and retail outlets and renovation of its existing facilities. TRMP also broke ground on a new $250 million, 786-room hotel tower at Trump Taj Mahal. In June 2006, the company signed a joint-venture agreement with Diamondhead Casino Corporation to build and operate a destination casino resort in Diamondhead, Mississippi.

TRMP offers its employees a complete benefits package; paid vacation time; uniforms and cleaning; employee parties; and meals.

FINANCIALS: Sales and profits are in thousands of dollars—add 000 to get the full amount. 2007 Note: Financial information for 2007 was not available for all companies at press time.

2007 Sales: $	2007 Profits: $	**U.S. Stock Ticker: TRMP**
2006 Sales: $1,026,162	2006 Profits: $-18,507	**Int'l Ticker:** Int'l Exchange:
2005 Sales: $992,221	2005 Profits: $251,856	Employees: 7,300
2004 Sales: $1,002,938	2004 Profits: $-191,300	Fiscal Year Ends: 12/31
2003 Sales: $1,029,110	2003 Profits: $-87,300	Parent Company:

SALARIES/BENEFITS:

Pension Plan: Y	ESOP Stock Plan:	Profit Sharing:	Top Exec. Salary: $1,468,415	Bonus: $
Savings Plan: Y	Stock Purch. Plan:		Second Exec. Salary: $1,208,830	Bonus: $

OTHER THOUGHTS:
Apparent Women Officers or Directors: 2
Hot Spot for Advancement for Women/Minorities:

LOCATIONS: ("Y" = Yes)

West:	Southwest:	Midwest:	Southeast:	Northeast:	International:
		Y		Y	

TURNER BROADCASTING SYSTEM   www.turner.com

Industry Group Code: 513210 Ranks within this company's industry group: Sales: Profits:

Print Media/Publishing:	Movies:		Equipment/Supplies:		Broadcast/Cable:		Music/Audio:		Sports/Games/Gambling:	
Newspapers:	Movie Theaters:		Equipment/Supplies:		Broadcast TV:		Music Production:		Games/Sports:	
Magazines:	Movie Production:		Gambling Equipment:		Cable TV:	Y	Retail Music:		Retail Games Stores:	
Books:	TV/Video Prod.:	Y	Special Services:		Satellite Broadcast:		Retail Audio Equip.:		Stadiums/Teams:	Y
Book Stores:	Video Rental:		Advertising Services:		Radio:		Music Print./Dist.:		Gambling/Casinos:	
Distribution/Printing:	Video Distribution:		Info. Sys. Software:		Online Information:		Multimedia:		Rides/Theme Parks:	

TYPES OF BUSINESS:
Cable Programming
News Programs
Sports Teams

BRANDS/DIVISIONS/AFFILIATES:
CNN
TBS
TNT
CourtTV
Cartoon Network
Boomerang
TCM Latin America
Time Warner, Inc.

CONTACTS: Note: Officers with more than one job title may be intentionally listed here more than once.
Philip I. Kent, CEO
Greg D'Alba, COO
Steve Koonin, Pres.
John E. Kampfe, CFO/Exec. VP
Kelly Regal, VP-Human Resources
Scott Teissler, CTO/Exec. VP-Tech.
Louise Sams, General Counsel/Exec. VP
Jim McCaffrey, Exec. VP-Oper.
Jim McCaffrey, Exec. VP-Strategy
Kelly Regal, Exec. VP-Corp. Comm.
Andrew T. Heller, Pres., Domestic Distribution
Mark Lazarus, Pres., Turner Entertainment Group
Jim Walton, Pres., CNN Worldwide
Philip I. Kent, Chmn.
Louise Sams, Pres., TBS Int'l

Phone: 404-827-1700	Fax: 404-827-2437
Toll-Free: 866-463-6899	
Address: 1 CNN Center, 100 International Blvd., Atlanta, GA 30303 US	

GROWTH PLANS/SPECIAL FEATURES:

Turner Broadcasting System (TBS), a Time Warner subsidiary, produces news and entertainment programming internationally, as well as basic cable programming. The company's domestic program subsidiaries include news stations CNN, CNN Headline News and CNNfn (financial news); cable broadcasting networks TBS, TNT, TCM, TNT HD, Court TV and Game Tap; and animation networks Cartoon Network, Adult Swim and Boomerang. Internationally, the firm owns CNN International and CNN Espanol in news; TNT Brazil, TNT Mexico, TNT Argentina, TCM U.K., TCM France, TCM Spain and TCM Latin America in entertainment; and versions of the Cartoon Network in Mexico, Argentina, Brazil, Chile, Venezuela, Latin America, Europe, Taiwan, India, and Japan, as well as Pogo, Boomerang U.K. and Toonami U.K. in animation. TBS also owns the Atlanta Braves baseball team and the pga.com and nascar.com sports web sites. In October 2007, the company acquired seven of Latin American firm Claxson Interactive's pay television networks, including Fashion TV, HTV, Infinito, I.Sat, MuchMusic, Retro and Space.

TBS offers its employees domestic partner and dependent insurance, transportation reimbursement, a credit union, an on-site athletic facility, tuition reimbursement, company-wide advancement training and an employee assistance program. In addition, employees are entitled to infertility treatment benefits, adoption assistance, back-up child care reimbursement, veterinary pet insurance, free sports tickets, free admission to studio series performances, as well as discounts at the Turner Store and on Time Warner merchandise.

FINANCIALS: Sales and profits are in thousands of dollars—add 000 to get the full amount. 2007 Note: Financial information for 2007 was not available for all companies at press time.

2007 Sales: $	2007 Profits: $	**U.S. Stock Ticker: Subsidiary**
2006 Sales: $	2006 Profits: $	**Int'l Ticker:** Int'l Exchange:
2005 Sales: $9,611,000	2005 Profits: $	Employees:
2004 Sales: $9,054,000	2004 Profits: $	Fiscal Year Ends: 12/31
2003 Sales: $8,434,000	2003 Profits: $	Parent Company: TIME WARNER INC

SALARIES/BENEFITS:

Pension Plan:	ESOP Stock Plan:	Profit Sharing:	Top Exec. Salary: $	Bonus: $
Savings Plan:	Stock Purch. Plan:		Second Exec. Salary: $	Bonus: $

OTHER THOUGHTS:
Apparent Women Officers or Directors: 3
Hot Spot for Advancement for Women/Minorities: Y

LOCATIONS: ("Y" = Yes)

West:	Southwest:	Midwest:	Southeast:	Northeast:	International:
			Y	Y	

Note: Financial information, benefits and other data can change quickly and may vary from those stated here.

TV AZTECA SA DE CV

www.tvazteca.com

Industry Group Code: 513120 Ranks within this company's industry group: Sales: Profits:

Print Media/Publishing:	Movies:		Equipment/Supplies:	Broadcast/Cable:		Music/Audio:		Sports/Games/Gambling:	
Newspapers:	Movie Theaters:		Equipment/Supplies:	Broadcast TV:	Y	Music Production:	Y	Games/Sports:	
Magazines:	Movie Production:		Gambling Equipment:	Cable TV:		Retail Music:		Retail Games Stores:	
Books:	TV/Video Prod.:	Y	Special Services:	Satellite Broadcast:		Retail Audio Equip.:		Stadiums/Teams:	Y
Book Stores:	Video Rental:		Advertising Services:	Radio:		Music Print./Dist.:		Gambling/Casinos:	
Distribution/Printing:	Video Distribution:		Info. Sys. Software:	Online Information:		Multimedia:		Rides/Theme Parks:	

TYPES OF BUSINESS:

Spanish-Language Television Networks
Internet Services
Soccer Team
Music Production

BRANDS/DIVISIONS/AFFILIATES:

todito.com
Azteca Internet
Azteca America
TV Azteca 7
TV Azteca 13
Azteca Music
Monarcas Morelia
Fundacion Azteca

CONTACTS: *Note: Officers with more than one job title may be intentionally listed here more than once.*

Mario San Roman, CEO
Carlos Hesles, CFO
Ricardo B. Salinas, Chmn.

Phone: 52-55-1720-1313	Fax: 52-55-1720-1464
Toll-Free:	
Address: Periferico Sur 4121, Colonia Fuentes del Pedregal, Mexico City, DF 14141 Mexico	

GROWTH PLANS/SPECIAL FEATURES:

TV Azteca S.A. de C.V. is one of the largest producers of Spanish-language television programming in the world. It operates the TV Azteca 7 and TV Azteca 13 networks, and has a total of 555 owned and operated stations across Mexico. The firm's programming includes a broad selection of news, sports and entertainment programs. These include Spanish-language versions of programs from the U.S., such as the Spanish version of The Simpsons, Los Simpson, as well as original programming such as news programs that focus on the Latin American market. The company also broadcasts in the U.S. via wholly-owned subsidiary Azteca America network. In addition, TV Azteca owns Azteca Internet; soccer team Monarcas Morelia; and music company Azteca Music. A popular Internet feature is todito.com, a Spanish-language Internet portal. The company also underwrites Fundacion Azteca and Fundacion Azteca America, a non-profit organization dedicated to the improvement of education and social services, as well as promoting a campaign against drug abuse in Mexico.

FINANCIALS: Sales and profits are in thousands of dollars—add 000 to get the full amount. 2007 Note: Financial information for 2007 was not available for all companies at press time.

2007 Sales: $	2007 Profits: $	**U.S. Stock Ticker:**
2006 Sales: $	2006 Profits: $	**Int'l Ticker: TVAZTCACPO** Int'l Exchange: Mexico City-BMV
2005 Sales: $797,000	2005 Profits: $114,000	Employees: 4,228
2004 Sales: $803,000	2004 Profits: $149,000	Fiscal Year Ends: 12/31
2003 Sales: $648,000	2003 Profits: $140,000	Parent Company:

SALARIES/BENEFITS:

Pension Plan:	ESOP Stock Plan:	Profit Sharing:	Top Exec. Salary: $	Bonus: $
Savings Plan:	Stock Purch. Plan:		Second Exec. Salary: $	Bonus: $

OTHER THOUGHTS:

Apparent Women Officers or Directors:
Hot Spot for Advancement for Women/Minorities:

LOCATIONS: ("Y" = Yes)

West:	Southwest:	Midwest:	Southeast:	Northeast:	International:
					Y

TWEETER HOME ENTERTAINMENT GROUP INC
www.tweeter.com
Industry Group Code: 443110 Ranks within this company's industry group: Sales: 4   Profits: 6

Print Media/Publishing:	Movies:	Equipment/Supplies:		Broadcast/Cable:	Music/Audio:	Sports/Games/Gambling:
Newspapers:	Movie Theaters:	Equipment/Supplies:	Y	Broadcast TV:	Music Production:	Games/Sports:
Magazines:	Movie Production:	Gambling Equipment:	Y	Cable TV:	Retail Music:	Retail Games Stores:
Books:	TV/Video Prod.:	Special Services:	Y	Satellite Broadcast:	Retail Audio Equip.:	Stadiums/Teams:
Book Stores:	Video Rental:	Advertising Services:		Radio:	Music Print./Dist.:	Gambling/Casinos:
Distribution/Printing:	Video Distribution:	Info. Sys. Software:		Online Information:	Multimedia:	Rides/Theme Parks:

TYPES OF BUSINESS:
Audio & Video Equipment Stores
Installation Services
Consumer Electronics

BRANDS/DIVISIONS/AFFILIATES:
Tweeter
HiFi Buys
Showcase Home Entertainment
Sound Advice
Schultze Asset Management, LLC

CONTACTS: *Note: Officers with more than one job title may be intentionally listed here more than once.*
Joseph McGuire, CEO
Joseph McGuire, Pres.
Greg Hunt, CFO/Sr. VP
Bob Staples, Sr. VP-Sales
William Morrison, CIO/Sr. VP
Philo Pappas, Chief Merch. Officer/Sr. VP
Bob Staples, Sr. VP-Oper.
Jeff Duhamel, Dir.-Corp. Comm.
Patrick Reynolds, Chief Mktg. Officer/VP
Bob Staples, Sr. VP-Installation Svcs.
Samuel Bloomberg, Chmn.

Phone: 781-830-3000	**Fax:** 781-830-3223
Toll-Free: 877-893-3837	
Address: 40 Pequot Way, Canton, MA 02021 US	

GROWTH PLANS/SPECIAL FEATURES:
Tweeter Home Entertainment Group, Inc. is a specialty retailer of mid- to high-end audio and video electronics. It owns and operates over 100 stores in 18 states under the Tweeter, Sound Advice, HiFi buys and Showcase Home Entertainment names. The stores feature an extensive selection of home and car audio systems and components, portable audio equipment and home video products, including large-screen plasma and LCD televisions, global positioning satellite systems, DVD players, digital satellite systems, cell phones, automobile security systems, VCRs and camcorders. The firm stocks products from Alpine, B&K, Bose, Boston Acoustics, Clarion, Denon, Mirage, Martin Logan, Mitsubishi, Monster Cable, Panasonic, Philips, Pioneer, Polk, Samsung, Sharp, Sony and Yamaha. Tweeter's stores display products in sound rooms architecturally and acoustically designed to simulate the customer's home or car environment. Its Sound Advice stores in Florida and Arizona specialize in cutting-edge high-end products with custom installation in homes, businesses and cars, in addition to serving as consultants to customers. The company offers custom entertainment packages tailored to meet the needs of each customer; these include basic, bronze, silver, gold and platinum with free installation for each. Tweeter differentiates itself from other electronic retailers because it delivers service to its customers in five complete steps: Consultaion, Inspection, Selection, Installation and Follow-up. Nearly a third of Tweeter's revenue is generated during the winter holiday season. In March 2007, the firm closed 49 stores, two regional facilities and cut 20% of its workforce. In June 2007, the company filed for reorganization under Chapter. 11 U.S. bankruptcy code. In July, 2007, Schultze Asset Management, LLC acquired Tweeter.

The firm provides employees with tuition reimbursement, merchandise discounts and free concert tickets.

FINANCIALS: Sales and profits are in thousands of dollars—add 000 to get the full amount. 2007 Note: Financial information for 2007 was not available for all companies at press time.

2007 Sales: $	2007 Profits: $	**U.S. Stock Ticker: TWTR**
2006 Sales: $775,287	2006 Profits: $-16,483	**Int'l Ticker:** Int'l Exchange:
2005 Sales: $795,090	2005 Profits: $-74,353	**Employees:** 2,600
2004 Sales: $778,200	2004 Profits: $-18,100	Fiscal Year Ends: 9/30
2003 Sales: $786,996	2003 Profits: $-11,662	Parent Company:

SALARIES/BENEFITS:
Pension Plan:	ESOP Stock Plan:	Profit Sharing:	Top Exec. Salary: $445,000	Bonus: $
Savings Plan: Y	Stock Purch. Plan: Y		Second Exec. Salary: $405,000	Bonus: $

OTHER THOUGHTS:
Apparent Women Officers or Directors: 1
Hot Spot for Advancement for Women/Minorities:

LOCATIONS: ("Y" = Yes)
West:	Southwest:	Midwest:	Southeast:	Northeast:	International:
Y	Y	Y	Y	Y	

Note: Financial information, benefits and other data can change quickly and may vary from those stated here.

UNITED ARTISTS CORPORATION   www.unitedartists.com

Industry Group Code: 512110 Ranks within this company's industry group: Sales: Profits:

Print Media/Publishing:	Movies:		Equipment/Supplies:	Broadcast/Cable:	Music/Audio:	Sports/Games/Gambling:
Newspapers:	Movie Theaters:		Equipment/Supplies:	Broadcast TV:	Music Production:	Games/Sports:
Magazines:	Movie Production:	Y	Gambling Equipment:	Cable TV:	Retail Music:	Retail Games Stores:
Books:	TV/Video Prod.:	Y	Special Services:	Satellite Broadcast:	Retail Audio Equip.:	Stadiums/Teams:
Book Stores:	Video Rental:		Advertising Services:	Radio:	Music Print./Dist.:	Gambling/Casinos:
Distribution/Printing:	Video Distribution:		Info. Sys. Software:	Online Information:	Multimedia:	Rides/Theme Parks:

TYPES OF BUSINESS:
Film Production
Television Production
Film Distribution

BRANDS/DIVISIONS/AFFILIATES:
Metro-Goldwyn-Mayer Inc (MGM)

CONTACTS: Note: Officers with more than one job title may be intentionally listed here more than once.
Paula Wagner, CEO
Elliot Kleinberg, COO
Dennis Rice, Pres., Worldwide Mktg. & Publicity
Tom Cruise, Mng. Partner
Don Granger, Pres., Production

Phone: 310-449-3000	Fax: 310-449-8857
Toll-Free:	
Address: 10250 Constellation Blvd., Los Angeles, CA 90067 US	

GROWTH PLANS/SPECIAL FEATURES:
United Artists Corporation (UA), a subsidiary of Metro-Goldwyn-Mayer, Inc. (MGM), which is in turn owned by Comcast and Sony, was founded in 1919 by Hollywood legends Charlie Chaplin, Mary Pickford, Douglas Fairbanks and D.W. Griffith with the intent to allow artists and actors to control their own work. Reformed in 2006, the new UA is the result of a partnership between MGM and actor Tom Cruise, along with his long-time production partner Paula Wagner. The two acquired a small stake in the studio and will control production; Paula Wagner will act as CEO and Cruise will produce and act in films. UA produces, sells and acquires limited-release and foreign films and is branded as an art house film distributor. The firm has produced more than 1,200 films including Scarface; West Side Story; and the Pink Panther, Rocky and James Bond franchises. Recent films include Capote, Art School Confidential, Valkyrie and Lions for Lambs. UA has also produced more than 2,600 television shows, including thirtysomething, The Outer Limits and The Fugitive. In October 2007, the company announced that it would develop Die a Little, a crime thriller produced by Richard Gladstein.

FINANCIALS: Sales and profits are in thousands of dollars—add 000 to get the full amount. 2007 Note: Financial information for 2007 was not available for all companies at press time.

2007 Sales: $	2007 Profits: $	U.S. Stock Ticker: Subsidiary
2006 Sales: $	2006 Profits: $	Int'l Ticker: Int'l Exchange:
2005 Sales: $	2005 Profits: $	Employees:
2004 Sales: $	2004 Profits: $	Fiscal Year Ends: 12/31
2003 Sales: $	2003 Profits: $	Parent Company: METRO-GOLDWYN-MAYER INC (MGM)

SALARIES/BENEFITS:
Pension Plan:	ESOP Stock Plan:	Profit Sharing:	Top Exec. Salary: $	Bonus: $
Savings Plan:	Stock Purch. Plan:		Second Exec. Salary: $	Bonus: $

OTHER THOUGHTS:
Apparent Women Officers or Directors: 1
Hot Spot for Advancement for Women/Minorities:

LOCATIONS: ("Y" = Yes)
West:	Southwest:	Midwest:	Southeast:	Northeast:	International:
Y					

UNITED BUSINESS MEDIA PLCwww.unitedbusinessmedia.com

Industry Group Code: 511120 **Ranks within this company's industry group:** Sales: 6 Profits: 1

Print Media/Publishing:		Movies:	Equipment/Supplies:		Broadcast/Cable:	Music/Audio:	Sports/Games/Gambling:
Newspapers:	Y	Movie Theaters:	Equipment/Supplies:		Broadcast TV:	Music Production:	Games/Sports:
Magazines:	Y	Movie Production:	Gambling Equipment:		Cable TV:	Retail Music:	Retail Games Stores:
Books:		TV/Video Prod.:	Special Services:	Y	Satellite Broadcast:	Retail Audio Equip.:	Stadiums/Teams:
Book Stores:		Video Rental:	Advertising Services:	Y	Radio:	Music Print./Dist.:	Gambling/Casinos:
Distribution/Printing:		Video Distribution:	Info. Sys. Software:		Online Information:	Multimedia:	Rides/Theme Parks:

TYPES OF BUSINESS:

Diversified Publishing
Market Research
Press Release Distribution
Business-to-Business Publishing
Media Investments

BRANDS/DIVISIONS/AFFILIATES:

NOP World
PR Newswire
CMP Media
Roper ASW
Channel 5 Television Group
Independent Television News, Ltd.
SDN, Ltd.
Eurisko

CONTACTS: Note: Officers with more than one job title may be intentionally listed here more than once.

David Levin, CEO
Malcolm Wall, COO
Nigel Wilson, CFO
Anne Siddell, Corp. Sec.
Alix Raine, Sr. VP-Comm.
Catherine Southgate, Head-Investor Rel.
Charles Gregson, Exec. Dir.-Bus. Info.
Henry Elkington, CEO-CMPMedica
Jime Essink, CEO-CMP Asia
Charles Gregson, CEO-PR Newswire
Geoffrey Unwin, Chmn.

Phone: 44-20-7921-5000	**Fax:** 44-20-7928-2717
Toll-Free:	
Address: Ludgate House, 245 Blackfriars Rd., London, SE1 9UY UK	

GROWTH PLANS/SPECIAL FEATURES:

United Business Media plc (UBM) offers a range of market information services. It is a market research, news distribution and professional media company with operations primarily in the U.S. and U.K., as well as business interests in Europe, Asia Pacific and Latin America. UBM's primary business provides professional media and market information solutions to customers through NOP World, PR Newswire and CMP Media. The professional media division, which includes CMP Media, is the largest business-to-business publisher in the U.S. high-tech sector, with a market share approximately twice that of its nearest competitor. The news distribution division, which includes PR Newswire, is one of the world's leading electronic distributors of corporate news, with over 40,000 customers worldwide including over 50% of U.S. Fortune 500 companies. The market research division is the world's ninth-largest market research business, with strong positions in several key sectors of the market including media, health care, automotive, business-to-business and consumer sectors. UBM also has consumer and business-to-business publishing interests, including classified advertising periodicals. It retains a number of broadcast investments including a 35.37% stake in Channel 5 Television Group, a U.K. television broadcaster; a 20% stake in Independent Television News, Ltd.; a 33.3% stake in SDN, Ltd.; and a 20% stake in Satellite Information Systems. UBM also owns Eurisko, the largest independent market research firm in Italy. Recent acquisitions include Vintage Filings LLC, Physicians Practice LLC, How Machines Work Corporation, Ithaca Holdings, Decorex and Energy Events UK Ltd. In November 2007, UBM announced that it has acquired Portelligent, Inc.

FINANCIALS: Sales and profits are in thousands of dollars—add 000 to get the full amount. 2007 Note: Financial information for 2007 was not available for all companies at press time.

		U.S. Stock Ticker:
2007 Sales: $	2007 Profits: $	Int'l Ticker: UBM Int'l Exchange: London-LSE
2006 Sales: $1,447,300	2006 Profits: $286,700	Employees: 5,000
2005 Sales: $1,172,006	2005 Profits: $824,641	Fiscal Year Ends: 12/31
2004 Sales: $966,534	2004 Profits: $408,872	Parent Company:
2003 Sales: $1,241,600	2003 Profits: $-68,800	

SALARIES/BENEFITS:

Pension Plan:	ESOP Stock Plan:	Profit Sharing:	Top Exec. Salary: $1,220,000	Bonus: $
Savings Plan:	Stock Purch. Plan:		Second Exec. Salary: $585,000	Bonus: $117,000

OTHER THOUGHTS:

Apparent Women Officers or Directors: 1
Hot Spot for Advancement for Women/Minorities:

LOCATIONS: ("Y" = Yes)

West:	Southwest:	Midwest:	Southeast:	Northeast:	International:
Y		Y		Y	Y

Note: Financial information, benefits and other data can change quickly and may vary from those stated here.

UNITED ONLINE INC

www.unitedonline.net

Industry Group Code: 514191 Ranks within this company's industry group: Sales: 1 Profits: 1

Print Media/Publishing:	Movies:	Equipment/Supplies:		Broadcast/Cable:	Music/Audio:	Sports/Games/Gambling:
Newspapers:	Movie Theaters:	Equipment/Supplies:		Broadcast TV:	Music Production:	Games/Sports:
Magazines:	Movie Production:	Gambling Equipment:		Cable TV:	Retail Music:	Retail Games Stores:
Books:	TV/Video Prod.:	Special Services:	Y	Satellite Broadcast:	Retail Audio Equip.:	Stadiums/Teams:
Book Stores:	Video Rental:	Advertising Services:	Y	Radio:	Music Print./Dist.:	Gambling/Casinos:
Distribution/Printing:	Video Distribution:	Info. Sys. Software:		Online Information:	Multimedia:	Rides/Theme Parks:

TYPES OF BUSINESS:

Internet Service Provider
Market Research
VoIP Provider
Social Networking Web Sites
Online Loyalty Marketing

BRANDS/DIVISIONS/AFFILIATES:

Juno
NetZero
Classmates.com
MyPoints.com
PrivatePhone
Juno SpeedBand
CyberTarget
Names Database (The)

CONTACTS: *Note: Officers with more than one job title may be intentionally listed here more than once.*

Mark R. Goldston, CEO
Mark R. Goldston, Pres.
Scott H. Ray, CFO/Exec. VP
Jeremy Helfand, Chief Sales Officer/Exec. VP
Gerald J. Popek, CTO/Exec. VP
Frederic A. Randall, Jr., General Counsel/Exec. VP/Sec.
Robert Taragan, Exec. VP-Oper.
Scott Matulis, VP-Corp. Comm.
Erik Randerson, VP-Investor Rel.
Neil P. Edwards, Sr. VP-Finance/Treas./Chief Accounting Officer
Robert Taragan, General Mgr.-CyberTarget
Matt Wisk, Chief Marketing Officer/Exec. VP
Mark R. Goldston, Chmn.

Phone: 818-287-3000	Fax: 818-287-3001
Toll-Free:	
Address: 21301 Burbank Blvd., Woodland Hills, CA 91367 US	

GROWTH PLANS/SPECIAL FEATURES:

United Online, Inc. is a nationwide provider of consumer Internet and media services. Formed from the merger of NetZero, Inc. and Juno Online Services, Inc., the company offers two primary services. Its Content and Media services offer social networking through its website ClassMates.com and online loyalty marketing through MyPoints.com. Its communication services include monthly subscription-based Internet access through NetZero and Juno, often offering plans at less than half the cost of its major competitors; e-mail; and Voice over Internet Protocol (VoIP) through PrivatePhone and NetZero Voice, both sold on CDs at Best Buy stores. Each service works from any phone jack using a standard dial-up connection, does not require any new hardware and can be downloaded from the Internet. Its dial-up services are available in more than 9,500 cities in the U.S. and Canada. The company also offers NetZero HiSpeed and Juno SpeedBand next-generation dial-up Internet access which deliver web surfing up to five times faster than its standard services. Advertisers are provided with market research capabilities through United's CyberTarget division. With access to millions of NetZero and Juno Internet users, CyberTarget creates unique real-time market research in an Internet environment. In April 2006, United Online subsidiary Classmates Online, Inc., acquired Opobox, Inc., which operates The Names Database, a service that allows members to privately contact former acquaintances around the world, for approximately $10 million. Also in April 2006, United acquired MyPoints, Inc., a provider of member driven Internet direct marketing which offers customers reward incentives for online purchases and other ecommerce related activities through its website, from UAL Corp. for approximately $56 million. In November 2006, the company began offering NetZero DSL through an agreement with Verizon Internet Services. In May 2007, the company began offering Juno DSL in parts of 34 states as well as Washington D.C.

FINANCIALS: Sales and profits are in thousands of dollars—add 000 to get the full amount. 2007 Note: Financial information for 2007 was not available for all companies at press time.

2007 Sales: $	2007 Profits: $	U.S. Stock Ticker: UNTD
2006 Sales: $522,654	2006 Profits: $42,272	Int'l Ticker: Int'l Exchange:
2005 Sales: $525,061	2005 Profits: $47,127	Employees: 1,006
2004 Sales: $448,617	2004 Profits: $117,480	Fiscal Year Ends: 12/31
2003 Sales: $277,295	2003 Profits: $27,792	Parent Company:

SALARIES/BENEFITS:

Pension Plan:	ESOP Stock Plan:	Profit Sharing:	Top Exec. Salary: $880,000	Bonus: $1,398,714
Savings Plan: Y	Stock Purch. Plan: Y		Second Exec. Salary: $440,000	Bonus: $589,357

OTHER THOUGHTS:

Apparent Women Officers or Directors:
Hot Spot for Advancement for Women/Minorities:

LOCATIONS: ("Y" = Yes)

West:	Southwest:	Midwest:	Southeast:	Northeast:	International:
Y		Y		Y	Y

UNITED TALENT AGENCY INC

www.unitedtalent.com

Industry Group Code: 711410 Ranks within this company's industry group: Sales: Profits:

Print Media/Publishing:	Movies:	Equipment/Supplies:		Broadcast/Cable:	Music/Audio:	Sports/Games/Gambling:
Newspapers:	Movie Theaters:	Equipment/Supplies:		Broadcast TV:	Music Production:	Games/Sports:
Magazines:	Movie Production:	Gambling Equipment:		Cable TV:	Retail Music:	Retail Games Stores:
Books:	TV/Video Prod.:	Special Services:	Y	Satellite Broadcast:	Retail Audio Equip.:	Stadiums/Teams:
Book Stores:	Video Rental:	Advertising Services:	Y	Radio:	Music Print./Dist.:	Gambling/Casinos:
Distribution/Printing:	Video Distribution:	Info. Sys. Software:		Online Information:	Multimedia:	Rides/Theme Parks:

TYPES OF BUSINESS:

Talent Agency

BRANDS/DIVISIONS/AFFILIATES:

CONTACTS:
Note: Officers with more than one job title may be intentionally listed here more than once.

Adam Ware, Head-Bus. Dev.
Chris Day, Head- Corp. Comm.
Wayne Fitterman, Head-Production Dep.
Andrew Thau, Head-Corp. Affairs
Jim Berkus, Chmn.

Phone: 310-273-6700	Fax: 310-247-1111
Toll-Free:	
Address: 950 Wilshire Blvd., Ste. 500, Beverly Hills, CA 90212-2401 US	

GROWTH PLANS/SPECIAL FEATURES:

United Talent Agency, Inc., commonly known as UTA, is a broadly situated talent agency based out of California. It is one of the largest talent agencies in the U.S., generally counted as one of the big four. UTA represents talent in all areas of entertainment, including music, television, movies, books, commercials, licensing, live entertainment, video games and digital media. UTA also represents behind the scenes personnel such as gaffers, key grips, editors, directors of photography and art directors. The firm represents such luminaries as Johnny Depp, Harrison Ford, Ben Stiller, Sandra Oh, Kate Bosworth, the Olsen twins, Liv Tyler, Vince Vaughn and Jack Black. Recently, the firm began searching for Internet video talent through websites such as YouTube and finding work for individuals thus discovered. The firm operates an agent training program that trains individuals interested in becoming talent agents. After completion of the highly-competitive program, trainees may be promoted to agent status within the firm. As of December 2006, the firm had 19 full partners. UTA recently became carbon neutral, a feat that was accomplished by planting enough trees to outweigh the firm's CO2 emissions for the year.

FINANCIALS:
Sales and profits are in thousands of dollars—add 000 to get the full amount. 2007 Note: Financial information for 2007 was not available for all companies at press time.

2007 Sales: $	2007 Profits: $	**U.S. Stock Ticker:** Private
2006 Sales: $	2006 Profits: $	**Int'l Ticker:** Int'l Exchange:
2005 Sales: $	2005 Profits: $	Employees:
2004 Sales: $	2004 Profits: $	Fiscal Year Ends:
2003 Sales: $	2003 Profits: $	Parent Company:

SALARIES/BENEFITS:

Pension Plan:	ESOP Stock Plan:	Profit Sharing:	Top Exec. Salary: $	Bonus: $
Savings Plan:	Stock Purch. Plan:		Second Exec. Salary: $	Bonus: $

OTHER THOUGHTS:

Apparent Women Officers or Directors:
Hot Spot for Advancement for Women/Minorities: Y

LOCATIONS: ("Y" = Yes)

West:	Southwest:	Midwest:	Southeast:	Northeast:	International:
Y				Y	

UNIVERSAL MUSIC GROUP

www.umusic.com

Industry Group Code: 512230 **Ranks within this company's industry group:** Sales: Profits:

Print Media/Publishing:	Movies:	Equipment/Supplies:	Broadcast/Cable:	Music/Audio:		Sports/Games/Gambling:
Newspapers:	Movie Theaters:	Equipment/Supplies:	Broadcast TV:	Music Production:	Y	Games/Sports:
Magazines:	Movie Production:	Gambling Equipment:	Cable TV:	Retail Music:		Retail Games Stores:
Books:	TV/Video Prod.:	Special Services:	Satellite Broadcast:	Retail Audio Equip.:		Stadiums/Teams:
Book Stores:	Video Rental:	Advertising Services:	Radio:	Music Print./Dist.:	Y	Gambling/Casinos:
Distribution/Printing:	Video Distribution:	Info. Sys. Software:	Online Information:	Multimedia:		Rides/Theme Parks:

TYPES OF BUSINESS:

Music Production & Distribution
Recorded Music Sales
Music Publishing

BRANDS/DIVISIONS/AFFILIATES:

Vivendi SA
Interscope
Polydor Records
Mercury Records
Deutsche Grammophon
Decca Records
International Music Feed (The)
Verve Music Group (The)

CONTACTS: *Note: Officers with more than one job title may be intentionally listed here more than once.*

Douglas Morris, CEO
Zach Horowitz, COO
Zach Horowitz, Pres.
Marinus N. Henny, CFO
Douglas Morris, Chmn.

Phone: 212-841-8000	**Fax:** 212-331-2580
Toll-Free:	
Address: 1755 Broadway, New York, NY 10019 US	

GROWTH PLANS/SPECIAL FEATURES:

Universal Music Group (UMG), a subsidiary of Vivendi S.A., is a music recording company. The firm develops, markets, sells and distributes recorded music through a network of joint ventures, subsidiaries and licensees in 77 countries. UMG adult contemporary music labels include Interscope Geffen A&M Records, Island Def Jam Music, Barclay, Mercury Records and Polydor Records. Additionally, the company owns classical music record labels, such as Deutsche Grammophon; Decca Records, which has one of the greatest opera catalogs in the world; Philips; Emarcy; and ECM. The classical division also controls Broadway Catalog and contemporary and classical albums under the Decca Broadway label such as Wicked, Mamma Mia, Les Miserables, Man From La Mancha, Phantom of the Opera and Sunset Boulevard. The firm is also responsible for the success of original soundtracks such as The Aviator, King Kong, Braveheart and Frida. The Verve Music Group is UMG's jazz recording company. The label is comprised of Verve, which focuses on traditional jazz; adult music label Verve Forecast; GRP, a contemporary jazz label; and Impulse!, which focuses on reissues of its famed catalogue. The company's Universal Music Publishing Group, with 47 offices in 41 countries, is one of the largest global music publishing catalogs. In the U.S., UMG markets music under The Decca Label Group, which operates via Universal Music Classical and Decca Label Group; and distributes music through Universal Music Group Distribution, comprised of Universal Music Distribution, Fontana and Vivendi Visual Entertainment. UMG backs and funds The International Music Feed 24-hour music television network dedicated to delivering all-music programming featuring live concerts, music videos and artist interviews. UMG has an impressive artist repertoire across all music categories, including Andrea Bocelli, Luciano Pavarotti, Louis Armstrong, Billie Holiday, Bryan Adams, Mariah Carey, Eminem, Kanye West, U2, Sting, Enrique Iglesias and Metallica.

FINANCIALS: Sales and profits are in thousands of dollars—add 000 to get the full amount. 2007 Note: Financial information for 2007 was not available for all companies at press time.

2007 Sales: $	2007 Profits: $	**U.S. Stock Ticker: Subsidiary**
2006 Sales: $	2006 Profits: $	**Int'l Ticker:** Int'l Exchange:
2005 Sales: $5,794,800	2005 Profits: $	Employees: 9,661
2004 Sales: $6,810,500	2004 Profits: $	Fiscal Year Ends: 12/31
2003 Sales: $6,243,400	2003 Profits: $	Parent Company: VIVENDI SA

SALARIES/BENEFITS:

Pension Plan:	ESOP Stock Plan:	Profit Sharing:	Top Exec. Salary: $	Bonus: $
Savings Plan:	Stock Purch. Plan:		Second Exec. Salary: $	Bonus: $

OTHER THOUGHTS:

Apparent Women Officers or Directors:
Hot Spot for Advancement for Women/Minorities:

LOCATIONS: ("Y" = Yes)

West:	Southwest:	Midwest:	Southeast:	Northeast:	International:
Y	Y	Y	Y	Y	Y

Note: Financial information, benefits and other data can change quickly and may vary from those stated here.

UNIVERSAL PICTURES
www.universalpictures.com

Industry Group Code: 512110 Ranks within this company's industry group: Sales: Profits:

Print Media/Publishing:	Movies:		Equipment/Supplies:	Broadcast/Cable:	Music/Audio:	Sports/Games/Gambling:
Newspapers:	Movie Theaters:		Equipment/Supplies:	Broadcast TV:	Music Production:	Games/Sports:
Magazines:	Movie Production:	Y	Gambling Equipment:	Cable TV:	Retail Music:	Retail Games Stores:
Books:	TV/Video Prod.:		Special Services:	Satellite Broadcast:	Retail Audio Equip.:	Stadiums/Teams:
Book Stores:	Video Rental:		Advertising Services:	Radio:	Music Print./Dist.:	Gambling/Casinos:
Distribution/Printing:	Video Distribution:	Y	Info. Sys. Software:	Online Information:	Multimedia:	Rides/Theme Parks:

TYPES OF BUSINESS:
Film Production & Distribution
Online Video Distribution

BRANDS/DIVISIONS/AFFILIATES:
Universal Studios
NBC Universal
Focus Features

CONTACTS: Note: Officers with more than one job title may be intentionally listed here more than once.
Eddie Egan, Co-Pres., Mktg.
Adam Fogelson, Co-Pres., Mktg.
Marc Shmuger, Chmn.

Phone: 818-777-1000	Fax: 818-777-6431
Toll-Free:	
Address: 100 Universal City Plz., Universal City, CA 91608 US	

GROWTH PLANS/SPECIAL FEATURES:
Universal Pictures produces and distributes theatrical and non-theatrical films. The company is the main motion picture production and distribution arm of Universal Studios, a subsidiary of NBC Universal. Focus Features, the specialty film unit of Universal Pictures, produces, internationally distributes and finances motion pictures. Universal Pictures produces a variety of movies, including internally developed titles, co-productions, specialty motion pictures, direct-to-video titles, specialty video, classic titles and related consumer products. Previous films have included Academy Award-winning movies such as A Beautiful Mind, The Pianist and Lost in Translation, as well as Ray, The Producers and Bruce Almighty. Recently, the firm announced an agreement that will make its movies available to ITVN (Internet Protocol Television) subscribers through an IPTV set-top box. The company has a partnership with online rental firm Lovefilm for a new download feature in the U.K., download-to-own. The new product allows individuals to download movies in three formats: instant download on PC, instant download for laptop, or a DVD copy sent by mail. The download process takes 40 minutes, and costs between $17.50 and $35. Eventually, Universal Pictures will have all 6,500 movies in its catalogue available for downloading. Additionally, the firm has a partnership with Microsoft to release HD DVD titles using VC-1 (compression standard) and iHD.

FINANCIALS: Sales and profits are in thousands of dollars—add 000 to get the full amount. 2007 Note: Financial information for 2007 was not available for all companies at press time.

2007 Sales: $	2007 Profits: $	U.S. Stock Ticker: Subsidiary	
2006 Sales: $	2006 Profits: $	Int'l Ticker: Int'l Exchange:	
2005 Sales: $	2005 Profits: $	Employees:	
2004 Sales: $	2004 Profits: $	Fiscal Year Ends: 12/31	
2003 Sales: $6,622,000	2003 Profits: $	Parent Company: NBC UNIVERSAL	

SALARIES/BENEFITS:

Pension Plan:	ESOP Stock Plan:	Profit Sharing:	Top Exec. Salary: $	Bonus: $
Savings Plan:	Stock Purch. Plan:		Second Exec. Salary: $	Bonus: $

OTHER THOUGHTS:
Apparent Women Officers or Directors:
Hot Spot for Advancement for Women/Minorities:

LOCATIONS: ("Y" = Yes)

West:	Southwest:	Midwest:	Southeast:	Northeast:	International:
Y					

UNIVISION COMMUNICATIONS INC   www.univision.com

Industry Group Code: 513120   Ranks within this company's industry group: Sales: 9   Profits: 6

Print Media/Publishing:	Movies:		Equipment/Supplies:	Broadcast/Cable:		Music/Audio:	Sports/Games/Gambling:
Newspapers:	Movie Theaters:		Equipment/Supplies:	Broadcast TV:	Y	Music Production:	Games/Sports:
Magazines:	Movie Production:		Gambling Equipment:	Cable TV:		Retail Music:	Retail Games Stores:
Books:	TV/Video Prod.:	Y	Special Services:	Satellite Broadcast:		Retail Audio Equip.:	Stadiums/Teams:
Book Stores:	Video Rental:		Advertising Services:	Radio:		Music Print./Dist.:	Gambling/Casinos:
Distribution/Printing:	Video Distribution:		Info. Sys. Software:	Online Information:		Multimedia:	Rides/Theme Parks:

TYPES OF BUSINESS:

Spanish Television Broadcasting
Cable Television Programming
Online Portal
Radio Broadcasting

BRANDS/DIVISIONS/AFFILIATES:

Univision Television Group
Galavision
TeleFutura
Univision Online, Inc.
Univision Radio, Inc.
Broadcasting Media Partners, Inc.

CONTACTS: *Note: Officers with more than one job title may be intentionally listed here more than once.*

A. Jerrold Perenchio, CEO
Ray Rodriguez, COO
Ray Rodriguez, Pres.
Andrew W. Hobson, CFO/Sr. Exec. VP
C. Douglas Kranwinkle, General Counsel/Exec. VP
Andrew W. Hobson, Chief Strategic Officer
A. Jerrold Perenchio, Chmn.

Phone: 212-455-5200	Fax:
Toll-Free:	
Address: 605 3rd Ave., 12th Fl., New York, NY 10158 US	

GROWTH PLANS/SPECIAL FEATURES:

Univision Communications, Inc. is the leading Spanish-language media company in the U.S. The company believes that the breadth and diversity of its services provide it with a competitive advantage over both Spanish- and English-language broadcasters in appealing to the Hispanic market, which now represents 13% of the U.S. population and a potential audience of more than 35 million. Univision currently operates in three business segments: television, which is the company's principle business segment and consists of the Univision and TeleFutura national broadcast networks and the Galavisión cable television network; radio, which is operated through Univision Radio, Inc., and owns 69 radio stations in 16 of the top 25 U.S. Hispanic markets, in addition to four stations in Puerto Rico; and internet, which is run through Univision Online, Inc. and consists of univision.com, a web portal with an annual average of 3 billion hits. Each of these three segments represents the largest Spanish-language media application in their respective fields within the U.S. Following the completion of the March 2007 acquisition of Univision by Broadcasting Media Partners, Inc., a consortium of private-equity investors, the company sold the subsidiaries that made up its music and recording business segment, which included the Univision, Fonovisa, Disa and La Calle labels. The firm is able to reach 99% of all U.S. Hispanic households via its nationwide Univision broadcast and cable channels. TeleFutura is the company's 24-hour Spanish-language broadcast television network, reaching 87% of U.S. Hispanic households. The company's Galavision network is the leading Spanish-language cable television network, with more than 5.9 million Hispanic cable subscribers. Broadcast is supported by the Univision Television Group, which owns and operates 18 full-power and eight low-power Univision Network stations and one full-power UPN station.

FINANCIALS: Sales and profits are in thousands of dollars—add 000 to get the full amount. 2007 Note: Financial information for 2007 was not available for all companies at press time.

2007 Sales: $	2007 Profits: $	**U.S. Stock Ticker: Subsidiary**
2006 Sales: $2,166,652	2006 Profits: $349,174	**Int'l Ticker:** Int'l Exchange:
2005 Sales: $1,952,531	2005 Profits: $187,179	Employees: 4,233
2004 Sales: $1,786,935	2004 Profits: $255,883	Fiscal Year Ends: 12/31
2003 Sales: $1,311,015	2003 Profits: $155,427	Parent Company: BROADCASTING MEDIA PARTNERS, INC

SALARIES/BENEFITS:

Pension Plan:	ESOP Stock Plan:	Profit Sharing:	Top Exec. Salary: $800,000	Bonus: $1,000,000
Savings Plan:	Stock Purch. Plan:		Second Exec. Salary: $750,000	Bonus: $1,000,000

OTHER THOUGHTS:

Apparent Women Officers or Directors:
Hot Spot for Advancement for Women/Minorities:

LOCATIONS: ("Y" = Yes)

West:	Southwest:	Midwest:	Southeast:	Northeast:	International:
Y	Y	Y	Y	Y	Y

US NEWS AND WORLD REPORT LP www.usnews.com

Industry Group Code: 511120 Ranks within this company's industry group: Sales: Profits:

Print Media/Publishing:	Movies:	Equipment/Supplies:	Broadcast/Cable:	Music/Audio:	Sports/Games/Gambling:
Newspapers:	Movie Theaters:	Equipment/Supplies:	Broadcast TV:	Music Production:	Games/Sports:
Magazines: Y	Movie Production:	Gambling Equipment:	Cable TV:	Retail Music:	Retail Games Stores:
Books:	TV/Video Prod.:	Special Services:	Satellite Broadcast:	Retail Audio Equip.:	Stadiums/Teams:
Book Stores:	Video Rental:	Advertising Services:	Radio:	Music Print./Dist.:	Gambling/Casinos:
Distribution/Printing:	Video Distribution:	Info. Sys. Software:	Online Information:	Multimedia:	Rides/Theme Parks:

TYPES OF BUSINESS:

Magazine Publishing
Online Media

BRANDS/DIVISIONS/AFFILIATES:

usnews.com
America's Best Colleges
America's Best Leaders
America's Best Hospitals
America's Best Graduate Schools
America's Best Health Plans

CONTACTS: Note: Officers with more than one job title may be intentionally listed here more than once.

William D. Holiber, Pres./Publisher
Thomas H. Peck, CFO
Cynthia Powell, Dir.-Public Rel.
Mortimer Zuckerman, Chmn./Editor-in-Chief

Phone: 212-716-6800	Fax: 212-643-7842
Toll-Free:	
Address: 450 W. 33rd St., 11th Fl., New York, NY 10001 US	

GROWTH PLANS/SPECIAL FEATURES:

U.S. News and World Report L.P. is a publisher of periodicals and Internet content, including its flagship weekly U.S. News and World Report magazine with a circulation of over 2 million. The magazine offers news on money and business, education, health, science and technology, entertainment and politics, with well-known and widely respected contributors such as Lou Dobbs and David Gergen. U.S. News Chairman and Editor-in-Chief Mortimer Zuckerman has owned the company since 1984, and during his tenure has overseen the development of the company's interactive arm, usnews.com, and the continued expansion of the magazine's standalone special issues. U.S. News offers advertisers placement in demographically segmented editions of its weekly magazine organized by geographic region, as well as targeted editions for high income and business decision makers. The company also publishes annual reports and yearly rankings of graduate and undergraduate schools, hospitals and mutual funds. The prominence of these annual guides has greatly enhanced U.S. News' advertising profile, extending its global reach to some 11 million readers.

FINANCIALS: Sales and profits are in thousands of dollars—add 000 to get the full amount. 2007 Note: Financial information for 2007 was not available for all companies at press time.

2007 Sales: $	2007 Profits: $	U.S. Stock Ticker: Private
2006 Sales: $	2006 Profits: $	Int'l Ticker: Int'l Exchange:
2005 Sales: $	2005 Profits: $	Employees:
2004 Sales: $	2004 Profits: $	Fiscal Year Ends: 1/31
2003 Sales: $	2003 Profits: $	Parent Company:

SALARIES/BENEFITS:

Pension Plan:	ESOP Stock Plan:	Profit Sharing:	Top Exec. Salary: $	Bonus: $
Savings Plan:	Stock Purch. Plan:		Second Exec. Salary: $	Bonus: $

OTHER THOUGHTS:

Apparent Women Officers or Directors:
Hot Spot for Advancement for Women/Minorities:

LOCATIONS: ("Y" = Yes)

West:	Southwest:	Midwest:	Southeast:	Northeast:	International:
				Y	

Note: Financial information, benefits and other data can change quickly and may vary from those stated here.

VAIL RESORTS INC

www.vailresorts.com

Industry Group Code: 713920 Ranks within this company's industry group: Sales: 1 Profits: 1

Print Media/Publishing:	Movies:	Equipment/Supplies:		Broadcast/Cable:	Music/Audio:	Sports/Games/Gambling:	
Newspapers:	Movie Theaters:	Equipment/Supplies:		Broadcast TV:	Music Production:	Games/Sports:	Y
Magazines:	Movie Production:	Gambling Equipment:	Y	Cable TV:	Retail Music:	Retail Games Stores:	
Books:	TV/Video Prod.:	Special Services:	Y	Satellite Broadcast:	Retail Audio Equip.:	Stadiums/Teams:	
Book Stores:	Video Rental:	Advertising Services:		Radio:	Music Print./Dist.:	Gambling/Casinos:	
Distribution/Printing:	Video Distribution:	Info. Sys. Software:		Online Information:	Multimedia:	Rides/Theme Parks:	

TYPES OF BUSINESS:

Ski Resorts
Luxury Hotels & Lodging
Real Estate Development

BRANDS/DIVISIONS/AFFILIATES:

RockResorts
Grand Teton Lodge Company
Vail Resorts Development Company
Vail Resorts Management Company
Vail Resorts Lodging Company
Vail Village
Breckenridge
Keystone

CONTACTS: *Note: Officers with more than one job title may be intentionally listed here more than once.*

Robert A. Katz, CEO
Jeffrey W. Jones, CFO/Sr. Exec. VP
Christopher E. Jarnot, Sr. VP-Mktg & Sales.
Martha D. Rehm, General Counsel/Exec. VP
Kelly Ladyga, Dir.-Corp. Comm.
Mark Schoppet, VP/Controller
William A. Jensen, Co-Pres., Mountain Div.
Roger McCarthy, Co-Pres., Mountain Div.
William Hall, VP-Lodging Division
Keith Fernandez, Pres., Vail Resorts Development Company
Joe R. Micheletto, Chmn.

Phone: 970-845-2500	**Fax:** 970-479-3002
Toll-Free: 888-222-9324	
Address: 390 Interlocken Crescent, Ste. 1000, Broomfield, CO 80021 US	

GROWTH PLANS/SPECIAL FEATURES:

Vail Resorts, Inc. (VRI), one of the leading resort operators in North America, is organized as a holding company, operating through various subsidiaries. VRI and its subsidiaries currently operate in three business segments: Mountain, Lodging and Real Estate. In the mountain segment, the company owns and operates five world-class ski resorts and related ancillary businesses at Vail, Breckenridge, Keystone and Beaver Creek mountains in Colorado and the Heavenly Ski Resort in the Lake Tahoe area of California and Nevada. These resorts use federal land under the terms of Special Use Permits granted by the USDA Forest Service. The company also holds a 61.7% interest in SSI Venture, LLC, a retail and rental company. In the lodging segment, VRI owns and operates various hotels, as well as RockResorts International, LLC, a luxury hotel management company, and Grand Teton Lodge Company, which operates three resorts within Grand Teton National Park (under a National Park Service concessionaire contract), and the Jackson Hole Golf & Tennis Club in Wyoming. Vail Resorts Development Company, a wholly owned subsidiary, conducts the operations of the company's real estate segment. VRI's mountain business and its lodging properties at or around the company's ski resorts are seasonal in nature, with peak operating seasons from mid-November through mid-April. The company's operations at GTLC generally run from mid-May through mid-October. The company also has non-majority owned investments in various other entities. In recent news, VRI is undergoing a five-year, $500-million redevelopment project in Vail Village and the neighboring LionsHead area.

The firm offers its employees free and discounted ski passes and lessons; discounts on company food, lodging, gear rental, retail, child care, airfare, fitness clubs and bus passes. Vail offers health insurance for full-time employees.

FINANCIALS: Sales and profits are in thousands of dollars—add 000 to get the full amount. 2007 Note: Financial information for 2007 was not available for all companies at press time.

2007 Sales: $940,536	2007 Profits: $61,397	**U.S. Stock Ticker: MTN**
2006 Sales: $838,852	2006 Profits: $45,756	**Int'l Ticker:** Int'l Exchange:
2005 Sales: $809,987	2005 Profits: $23,138	Employees: 14,900
2004 Sales: $726,643	2004 Profits: $-5,959	Fiscal Year Ends: 7/31
2003 Sales: $710,398	2003 Profits: $-8,527	Parent Company:

SALARIES/BENEFITS:

Pension Plan:	ESOP Stock Plan:	Profit Sharing:	Top Exec. Salary: $484,417	Bonus: $
Savings Plan:	Stock Purch. Plan:		Second Exec. Salary: $405,320	Bonus: $407,500

OTHER THOUGHTS:

Apparent Women Officers or Directors: 3
Hot Spot for Advancement for Women/Minorities: Y

LOCATIONS: ("Y" = Yes)

West:	Southwest:	Midwest:	Southeast:	Northeast:	International:
Y	Y			Y	

VALUE LINE INC
www.valueline.com

Industry Group Code: 514100 Ranks within this company's industry group: Sales: 4 Profits: 4

Print Media/Publishing:		Movies:		Equipment/Supplies:		Broadcast/Cable:		Music/Audio:		Sports/Games/Gambling:	
Newspapers:		Movie Theaters:		Equipment/Supplies:		Broadcast TV:		Music Production:		Games/Sports:	
Magazines:		Movie Production:		Gambling Equipment:	Y	Cable TV:		Retail Music:		Retail Games Stores:	
Books:	Y	TV/Video Prod.:		Special Services:	Y	Satellite Broadcast:		Retail Audio Equip.:		Stadiums/Teams:	
Book Stores:		Video Rental:		Advertising Services:	Y	Radio:		Music Print./Dist.:		Gambling/Casinos:	
Distribution/Printing:		Video Distribution:		Info. Sys. Software:		Online Information:		Multimedia:		Rides/Theme Parks:	

TYPES OF BUSINESS:
Financial Data Publishing
Financial Periodicals
Investment Management/Fund Advising
Research Services
Electronic Financial Tools
Broker-Dealer
Advertising Agency

BRANDS/DIVISIONS/AFFILIATES:
Value Line Publishing, Inc.
Value Line Investment Survey (The)
Value Line 600
Value Line Securities, Inc.
Vanderbilt Advertising Agency, Inc.
Compupower Corporation
Value Line Distribution Center, Inc.
Arnold Bernhard & Company, Inc.

CONTACTS: Note: Officers with more than one job title may be intentionally listed here more than once.
Jean Bernhard Buttner, CEO
Jean Bernhard Buttner, Pres.
Mitchell E. Appel, CFO
Samuel Eisenstadt, Research Chmn./Sr. VP
Howard A. Brecher, Corp. Sec./VP
Steven R. Anastasio, Treas.
Jean Bernhard Buttner, Chmn.

Phone: 212-907-1500	Fax: 212-818-9747
Toll-Free:	
Address: 220 E. 42nd St., New York, NY 10017-5891 US	

GROWTH PLANS/SPECIAL FEATURES:
Value Line, Inc. publishes investment-related periodicals through its wholly-owned subsidiary, Value Line Publishing, Inc. (VLP), and provides investment advisory services to mutual funds, institutions and individual clients. VLP publishes The Value Line Investment Survey, one of the nation's major periodical investment services, as well as the Value Line Investment Survey – Small and Mid-Cap Edition, The Value Line Mutual Fund Survey (published once every three weeks), The Value Line No-Load Fund Advisor, The Value Line Special Situations Service (published semi-monthly), The Value Line Options Survey (published 24 times a year), The Value Line Convertibles Survey (published semi-monthly), Value Line Select and The Value Line 600 (published monthly). In addition, the company has five electronic tools: Value Line Investment Analyzer; Value Line Mutual Fund Survey for Windows; Value Line DataFile; and The Value Line Research Center. Value Line is the investment advisor for the Value Line Family of Mutual Funds, which, as of July 2007, include 14 open-end investment companies. In addition, the company manages investments for private and institutional clients and, through VLP, provides financial database information through computer media and computer time-sharing facilities. The company's other subsidiaries include a registered broker-dealer, Value Line Securities, Inc., and an advertising agency, Vanderbilt Advertising Agency, Inc. These subsidiaries primarily provide services used by the company in its publishing and investment management businesses. Subsidiary Compupower Corporation serves the subscription fulfillment needs of the company's publishing operations. Value Line Distribution Center, Inc. handles mailing of publications to the company's subscribers. The firm's web site offers intraday market commentary webcasts; educational programming offering video instruction on the company's products; and Value Line's Research Center, the firm's second-generation web site. Arnold Bernhard & Company, Inc. owns approximately 86.5% of Value Line's shares.

FINANCIALS: Sales and profits are in thousands of dollars—add 000 to get the full amount. 2007 Note: Financial information for 2007 was not available for all companies at press time.

2007 Sales: $83,635	2007 Profits: $24,607	**U.S. Stock Ticker: VALU**
2006 Sales: $85,186	2006 Profits: $23,439	**Int'l Ticker:** Int'l Exchange:
2005 Sales: $84,478	2005 Profits: $21,318	Employees: 206
2004 Sales: $85,270	2004 Profits: $20,350	Fiscal Year Ends: 4/30
2003 Sales: $82,100	2003 Profits: $19,987	Parent Company:

SALARIES/BENEFITS:

Pension Plan:	ESOP Stock Plan:	Profit Sharing:	Top Exec. Salary: $935,632	Bonus: $
Savings Plan: Y	Stock Purch. Plan:		Second Exec. Salary: $382,500	Bonus: $

OTHER THOUGHTS:
Apparent Women Officers or Directors: 1
Hot Spot for Advancement for Women/Minorities:

LOCATIONS: ("Y" = Yes)

West:	Southwest:	Midwest:	Southeast:	Northeast:	International:
				Y	

VALUEVISION MEDIA INC

www.shopnbc.com

Industry Group Code: 454110B Ranks within this company's industry group: Sales: 2 Profits: 2

Print Media/Publishing:	Movies:	Equipment/Supplies:	Broadcast/Cable:		Music/Audio:	Sports/Games/Gambling:
Newspapers:	Movie Theaters:	Equipment/Supplies:	Broadcast TV:		Music Production:	Games/Sports:
Magazines:	Movie Production:	Gambling Equipment:	Cable TV:	Y	Retail Music:	Retail Games Stores:
Books:	TV/Video Prod.:	Special Services:	Satellite Broadcast:		Retail Audio Equip.:	Stadiums/Teams:
Book Stores:	Video Rental:	Advertising Services:	Radio:		Music Print./Dist.:	Gambling/Casinos:
Distribution/Printing:	Video Distribution:	Info. Sys. Software:	Online Information:		Multimedia:	Rides/Theme Parks:

TYPES OF BUSINESS:

Television Shopping Programs
Online Sales
Fulfillment, Warehousing & Telemarketing Services
Credit Cards

BRANDS/DIVISIONS/AFFILIATES:

ValueVision Interactive, Inc.
Shop NBC
VVI Fulfillment Center, Inc.
shopnbc.com
General Electric

CONTACTS: *Note: Officers with more than one job title may be intentionally listed here more than once.*

John D. Buck, Interim CEO
John D. Buck, Interim Pres.
Frank P. Elsenbast, CFO/Sr. VP
Bryan Venberg, Sr. VP-Human Resources
Karen F. Johnston, Sr. VP-Merch.
Nathan E. Fagre, General Counsel/Sr. VP/Sec.
Brenda Boehler, Exec. VP-TV & Internet Sales
John D. Buck, Chmn.

Phone: 952-943-6000	Fax: 952-943-6711
Toll-Free:	
Address: 6740 Shady Oak Rd., Eden Prairie, MN 55344 US	

GROWTH PLANS/SPECIAL FEATURES:

ValueVision Media, Inc. is a direct marketing company that markets, sells and distributes its products directly to consumers through various forms of electronic media and direct-to-consumer mailings. The company's principal electronic media activity is its television home shopping network, which markets brand-name merchandise and proprietary and private-label consumer products at competitive or discount prices. ValueVision's live, 24-hour-a-day home shopping programming operates under the brand name Shop NBC and is distributed through cable affiliation and through its own broadcast television stations to approximately 60 million homes daily. Products sold on the network include jewelry, giftware, collectibles, apparel, electronics, housewares, seasonal items and various other merchandise items. Jewelry represents the company's largest single category of merchandise, representing 39% of television home shopping and Internet sales in 2006. The company's wholly-owned subsidiary, ValueVision Interactive, Inc., complements its television home shopping business with the sale of merchandise through its e-commerce web site, shopnbc.com. Another subsidiary, VVI Fulfillment Center, Inc., provides order fulfillment, warehousing and telemarketing services to Ralph Lauren Media, LLC, the NBC Experience Store in New York City and non-jewelry merchandise sold on the company's television home shopping program and web site. General Electric and its NBC television subsidiary own a 40% stake in ValueVision. In late 2006, ShopNBC and GE Retail Consumer Finance launched a ShopNBC branded MasterCard as well as an improved ShopNBC private label credit card.

FINANCIALS: Sales and profits are in thousands of dollars—add 000 to get the full amount. 2007 Note: Financial information for 2007 was not available for all companies at press time.

2007 Sales: $767,275	2007 Profits: $-2,685	**U.S. Stock Ticker: VVTV**	
2006 Sales: $691,851	2006 Profits: $-16,040	**Int'l Ticker:** Int'l Exchange:	
2005 Sales: $623,634	2005 Profits: $-57,886	Employees: 1,200	
2004 Sales: $591,185	2004 Profits: $-11,675	Fiscal Year Ends: 1/31	
2003 Sales: $554,900	2003 Profits: $-39,100	Parent Company:	

SALARIES/BENEFITS:

Pension Plan:	ESOP Stock Plan:	Profit Sharing:	Top Exec. Salary: $850,000	Bonus: $1,287,024
Savings Plan:	Stock Purch. Plan:		Second Exec. Salary: $375,385	Bonus: $378,536

OTHER THOUGHTS:

Apparent Women Officers or Directors:
Hot Spot for Advancement for Women/Minorities:

LOCATIONS: ("Y" = Yes)

West:	Southwest:	Midwest:	Southeast:	Northeast:	International:
		Y		Y	

VERIZON COMMUNICATIONS   www.verizon.com

Industry Group Code: 513300A Ranks within this company's industry group: Sales: 1   Profits: 2

Print Media/Publishing:	Movies:	Equipment/Supplies:		Broadcast/Cable:	Music/Audio:	Sports/Games/Gambling:
Newspapers:	Movie Theaters:	Equipment/Supplies:	Y	Broadcast TV:	Music Production:	Games/Sports:
Magazines:	Movie Production:	Gambling Equipment:		Cable TV:	Retail Music:	Retail Games Stores:
Books:	TV/Video Prod.:	Special Services:	Y	Satellite Broadcast:	Retail Audio Equip.:	Stadiums/Teams:
Book Stores:	Video Rental:	Advertising Services:		Radio:	Music Print./Dist.:	Gambling/Casinos:
Distribution/Printing:	Video Distribution:	Info. Sys. Software:		Online Information:	Multimedia:	Rides/Theme Parks:

TYPES OF BUSINESS:

Local Telephone Service
Telecommunications Services
Wireless Services
Long-Distance Services
High-Speed Internet Access
Video-on-Demand Services
e-Commerce & Online Services

BRANDS/DIVISIONS/AFFILIATES:

Verizon Wireless
Verizon New York, Inc.
GTE Southwest, Inc.
Verizon New England, Inc.
Verizon South, Inc.
Qwest Wireless
MCI Communications
NextWave

CONTACTS: *Note: Officers with more than one job title may be intentionally listed here more than once.*

Ivan G. Seidenberg, CEO
Dennis F. Strigl, COO
Dennis F. Strigl, Pres.
Doreen A. Toben, CFO/Exec. VP
John G. Stratton, Chief Mktg. Officer/Exec. VP
Marc C. Reed, Exec. VP-Human Resources
Shaygan Kheradpir, CIO/Exec. VP
William P. Barr, General Counsel/Exec. VP
John W. Diercksen, Exec. VP-Strategy, Dev. & Planning
Thomas J. Tauke, Exec. VP-Public Affairs, Policy & Comm.
Ronald H. Lataille, Sr. VP-Investor Rel.
Catherine T. Webster, Treas./Sr. VP
Virginia P. Ruesterholz, Pres., Verizon Telecom
Marianne Drost, Deputy General Counsel/Corp. Sec./Sr. VP
John F. Killian, Pres., Verizon Business
Thomas A. Bartlett, Controller/Sr. VP
Ivan G. Seidenberg, Chmn.

Phone: 212-395-1000	Fax:
Toll-Free: 800-621-9900	
Address: 140 West St., New York, NY 10007 US	

GROWTH PLANS/SPECIAL FEATURES:

Verizon Communications, Inc. and its subsidiaries form one of the world's leading providers of communications services, including wireline, wireless and Internet services. The firm has over 48 million access line equivalents in the U.S. and 5 million internationally; and over 60.7 million U.S. wireless customers. Global operations encompass over 30 countries in the Americas, Europe and Asia Pacific. Verizon operates in two segments, Wireline and Domestic Wireless. Wireline provides telephone services including voice, broadband video and data, network access and nationwide long-distance services. The Wireless segment also owns and operates next generation Internet Protocol (IP) networks in the U.S. and over 150 other countries. The Domestic Wireless segment, which operates under the name Verizon Wireless, provides wireless voice and data products and services as well as equipment sales in the U.S. Verizon spun off its Information Services segment, Idearc, in 2006. Also in 2006, Verizon completed its merger with MCI Communications. In September 2006, the firm officially opened Verizon Center, a new operations facility in New Jersey which employs nearly 2,400 people. In early 2007, the company and Fairpoint Communications agreed to merge Verizon's wireline business in Maine, New Hampshire and Vermont. Verizon is positioning itself as more of a broadband and wireless firm than a traditional landline provider. The firm had nearly 8 million broadband subscribers in mid 2007. Nearly all customers can subscribe to a 3Mbps download speed service at very reasonable cost. Millions more have the option of using the new FiOS 5 Mbps service that can include TV via IP and other entertainment options.

In May 2007, Verizon implemented a new program that provides company employees with secure, 24/7 online access to their medical and prescription history, plus a robust snapshot of their health status that can be shared with health care providers.

FINANCIALS: Sales and profits are in thousands of dollars—add 000 to get the full amount. 2007 Note: Financial information for 2007 was not available for all companies at press time.

2007 Sales: $	2007 Profits: $	**U.S. Stock Ticker: VZ**
2006 Sales: $88,144,000	2006 Profits: $6,197,000	**Int'l Ticker:** Int'l Exchange:
2005 Sales: $69,518,000	2005 Profits: $7,397,000	Employees: 242,000
2004 Sales: $65,751,000	2004 Profits: $7,831,000	Fiscal Year Ends: 12/31
2003 Sales: $67,752,000	2003 Profits: $3,077,000	Parent Company:

SALARIES/BENEFITS:

Pension Plan:	ESOP Stock Plan:	Profit Sharing:	Top Exec. Salary: $2,100,000	Bonus: $4,252,500
Savings Plan: Y	Stock Purch. Plan:		Second Exec. Salary: $1,200,000	Bonus: $1,824,000

OTHER THOUGHTS:

Apparent Women Officers or Directors: 4
Hot Spot for Advancement for Women/Minorities: Y

LOCATIONS: ("Y" = Yes)

West:	Southwest:	Midwest:	Southeast:	Northeast:	International:
Y	Y	Y	Y	Y	Y

Note: Financial information, benefits and other data can change quickly and may vary from those stated here.

VIACOM INC

www.viacom.com

Industry Group Code: 513210 **Ranks within this company's industry group:** Sales: 3   Profits: 3

Print Media/Publishing:	Movies:		Equipment/Supplies:		Broadcast/Cable:		Music/Audio:	Sports/Games/Gambling:	
Newspapers:	Movie Theaters:		Equipment/Supplies:		Broadcast TV:		Music Production:	Games/Sports:	Y
Magazines:	Movie Production:	Y	Gambling Equipment:		Cable TV:	Y	Retail Music:	Retail Games Stores:	
Books:	TV/Video Prod.:	Y	Special Services:	Y	Satellite Broadcast:		Retail Audio Equip.:	Stadiums/Teams:	
Book Stores:	Video Rental:		Advertising Services:		Radio:		Music Print./Dist.:	Gambling/Casinos:	
Distribution/Printing:	Video Distribution:	Y	Info. Sys. Software:		Online Information:		Multimedia:	Rides/Theme Parks:	

TYPES OF BUSINESS:

Cable TV Networks
Television Production/Syndication
Film Production
Online Media
Video Distribution
Video Games

BRANDS/DIVISIONS/AFFILIATES:

National Amusement, Inc.
MTV Networks
Nickelodeon
Comedy Central
CMT: Country Music Television
BET Networks
Paramount Pictures Corp
DreamWorks SKG

CONTACTS: *Note: Officers with more than one job title may be intentionally listed here more than once.*

Philippe Dauman, CEO
Philippe P. Dauman, Pres.
Thomas E. Dooley, CFO
JoAnne A. Griffith, Exec. VP-Human Resources
Thomas E. Dooley, Chief Admin. Officer/Sr. Exec. VP
Michael D. Fricklas, General Counsel/Sec./Exec. VP
Wade Davis, Sr. VP-Strategy, Mergers & Acquisitions
Carl D. Folta, Exec. VP-Corp. Comm.
James Bombassei, Sr. VP-Investor Rel.
Jacques Tortoroli, Chief Acct. Officer/Corp. Controller/Sr. VP
Brad Grey, Chmn./CEO-Paramount Motion Picture Group
Debra Lee, CEO/Pres., BET Networks
Judy McGrath, Chmn./CEO-MTV Networks
DeDe Lea, Exec. VP-Gov't Affairs
Sumner M. Redstone, Exec. Chmn.

Phone: 212-258-6000	**Fax:** 212-258-6464
Toll-Free: 800-516-4399	
Address: 1515 Broadway, New York, NY 10036 US	

GROWTH PLANS/SPECIAL FEATURES:

Viacom, Inc., spun off from now CBS Corp. (formerly Viacom, Inc.) and reorganized in January 2006, is an international media conglomerate. National Amusement, Inc., owned by the Redstone family, owns 73% of Viacom. Viacom is composed of two segments: Media Networks (formerly Cable Networks), generating approximately 63% of 2006 revenues; and Filmed Entertainment, 38%. Media Networks, operating more than 135 television networks, consist of BET Network, which consists of BET, BETJ, BET Gospel and BET Hip Hop, and the MTV Network. MTV owns the cable television program services MTV: Music Television, VH1, CMT: Country Music Television, Logo, Nickelodeon, Nick at Nite, Comedy Central, Spike TV, TV Land and others; and the digital properties MTV.com, URGE, Comedycentral.com, VSPOT, TurboNick, NeoPets, Xfire and iFilm. Media Networks offers its television content via 171 web sites, with plans to offer content to mobile phones. The Filmed Entertainment segment consists of Paramount Pictures Corp. Paramount produces, finances and distributes feature motion pictures; and has a film library of over 3,500 movies and programs. Online gaming communication and community platform Xfire, Inc. was acquired in 2006 for $112 million; Atom Entertainment, Inc., an online game, short film and animation destination, was acquired in September 2006 for $200 million; and it acquired Harmonix Music Systems, Inc., popular videogame title Guitar Hero developer, for $175 million, in October 2006. In 2006, Viacom acquired DreamWorks LLC for $1.53 billion. DreamWorks produces movies and television programming and markets these properties for home entertainment. In May 2006, Viacom sold 51% of DW Funding, LLC, owner of DreamWorks film library, to Soros Strategic Partners LP and Dune Entertainment II, LLC, for $900 million. Other Paramount companies include Paramount Vantage, Paramount Classics, MTV Films and Nickelodeon Movies. In August 2007, Viacom sold its music publishing business, Famous Music Publishing, to Sony/ATV Music Publishing for around $370 million.

FINANCIALS: Sales and profits are in thousands of dollars—add 000 to get the full amount. 2007 Note: Financial information for 2007 was not available for all companies at press time.

2007 Sales: $	2007 Profits: $	**U.S. Stock Ticker:** VIA
2006 Sales: $11,466,500	2006 Profits: $1,592,100	**Int'l Ticker:** Int'l Exchange:
2005 Sales: $9,609,600	2005 Profits: $1,256,900	**Employees:** 32,160
2004 Sales: $8,132,200	2004 Profits: $293,700	**Fiscal Year Ends:** 12/31
2003 Sales: $7,304,400	2003 Profits: $338,500	**Parent Company:**

SALARIES/BENEFITS:

Pension Plan: Y	ESOP Stock Plan:	Profit Sharing:	Top Exec. Salary: $4,101,954	Bonus: $
Savings Plan: Y	Stock Purch. Plan:		Second Exec. Salary: $3,050,000	Bonus: $5,500,000

OTHER THOUGHTS:

Apparent Women Officers or Directors: 6
Hot Spot for Advancement for Women/Minorities: Y

LOCATIONS: ("Y" = Yes)

West:	Southwest:	Midwest:	Southeast:	Northeast:	International:
Y		Y		Y	Y

VINDIGO INC

www.vindigo.com

Industry Group Code: 511208 Ranks within this company's industry group: Sales: Profits:

Print Media/Publishing:	Movies:	Equipment/Supplies:	Broadcast/Cable:	Music/Audio:	Sports/Games/Gambling:	
Newspapers:	Movie Theaters:	Equipment/Supplies:	Broadcast TV:	Music Production:	Games/Sports:	Y
Magazines:	Movie Production:	Gambling Equipment:	Cable TV:	Retail Music:	Retail Games Stores:	
Books:	TV/Video Prod.:	Special Services:	Satellite Broadcast:	Retail Audio Equip.:	Stadiums/Teams:	
Book Stores:	Video Rental:	Advertising Services:	Radio:	Music Print./Dist.:	Gambling/Casinos:	
Distribution/Printing:	Video Distribution:	Info. Sys. Software:	Online Information:	Multimedia:	Rides/Theme Parks:	

TYPES OF BUSINESS:

Mobile Media Content
Mobile Marketing Products
Navigation Tools
Ringtones
Games

BRANDS/DIVISIONS/AFFILIATES:

Vindigo
Vindigo RingMaster
Shadowgate
Upoc
For-Side.com Co. Ltd,
waymobile.com, Inc.
AwayAuction

CONTACTS: Note: Officers with more than one job title may be intentionally listed here more than once.

Jason Devitt, CEO
Samantha Saturn, VP-Mktg.
Dave Hock, VP-Research
Bob Fitterman, CTO
Tricia Han, VP-Product Dev.
Janet Kasdan, VP-Eng.
Marci Weisler, VP-Bus. Dev.
Candace L. Martin, VP-Quality Assurance
Carrie Himelfarb-Seifer, VP-Sales
Greg Genrich, VP-Design

Phone: 212-590-6900	**Fax:** 212-590-6999
Toll-Free:	
Address: 500 7th Ave., 17th Fl., New York, NY 10018 US	

GROWTH PLANS/SPECIAL FEATURES:

Vindigo is a mobile media company that publishes and distributes content for cell phones and other wireless personal devices through a network of partnerships. This network has a combined reach of more than 140 million mobile subscribers. Vindigo's content includes wallpaper, ringtones, local information, maps, news, entertainment and sports information. Vindigo, the service after which the company is named, is a combination navigator and city guide, with information on shopping, restaurants, museums, gas stations and many other things. Vindigo RingMaster is a ringtone shop where wireless subscribers can preview and download ringtones, exclusive celebrity audio material, chart-toppers, voicetones, sound effects, classic hits, theme songs and more. Vindigo recently launched a new fantasy adventure game, developed for QUALCOMM's BREW solution on mobile phones in North America, under the name Shadowgate. Upoc is a bulletin board service that allows instant messaging within groups created to discuss certain topics. The company has created certain marketing partnerships with over 100 advertisers such as Cadillac and MasterCard. Vindigo has been a subsidiary of For-Side.com Co. Ltd., one of Japan's and the world's largest mobile media companies, since August 2004, but continues to operate as an independent entity led by existing management and markets itself under the Vindigo Studios brand. The firm, together with CTIA Wireless IT and Entertainment, owns waymobile.com, Inc., a San Diego-based developer and publisher of advanced mobile content and commerce products, including AwayAuction for eBay.

FINANCIALS: Sales and profits are in thousands of dollars—add 000 to get the full amount. 2007 Note: Financial information for 2007 was not available for all companies at press time.

2007 Sales: $	2007 Profits: $	**U.S. Stock Ticker:** Subsidiary
2006 Sales: $	2006 Profits: $	**Int'l Ticker:** Int'l Exchange:
2005 Sales: $	2005 Profits: $	Employees:
2004 Sales: $	2004 Profits: $	Fiscal Year Ends: 4/30
2003 Sales: $	2003 Profits: $	Parent Company: FOR-SIDE.COM CO LTD

SALARIES/BENEFITS:

Pension Plan:	ESOP Stock Plan:	Profit Sharing:	Top Exec. Salary: $	Bonus: $
Savings Plan:	Stock Purch. Plan:		Second Exec. Salary: $	Bonus: $

OTHER THOUGHTS:

Apparent Women Officers or Directors: 6
Hot Spot for Advancement for Women/Minorities: Y

LOCATIONS: ("Y" = Yes)

West:	Southwest:	Midwest:	Southeast:	Northeast: Y	International:

Note: Financial information, benefits and other data can change quickly and may vary from those stated here.

VIVENDI SA   www.vivendi.com

Industry Group Code: 512230 Ranks within this company's industry group: Sales: 1   Profits: 1

Print Media/Publishing:	Movies:		Equipment/Supplies:		Broadcast/Cable:		Music/Audio:		Sports/Games/Gambling:	
Newspapers:	Movie Theaters:		Equipment/Supplies:		Broadcast TV:	Y	Music Production:	Y	Games/Sports:	Y
Magazines:	Movie Production:	Y	Gambling Equipment:		Cable TV:	Y	Retail Music:		Retail Games Stores:	
Books:	TV/Video Prod.:	Y	Special Services:	Y	Satellite Broadcast:		Retail Audio Equip.:	Y	Stadiums/Teams:	
Book Stores:	Video Rental:		Advertising Services:		Radio:		Music Print./Dist.:	Y	Gambling/Casinos:	
Distribution/Printing:	Video Distribution:	Y	Info. Sys. Software:		Online Information:		Multimedia:		Rides/Theme Parks:	

TYPES OF BUSINESS:

Music Production & Publishing
Cable & Satellite Television
Video Games & Software
Telecommunications Services
Cellular Telephone Service
Film Distribution
Theme Parks

BRANDS/DIVISIONS/AFFILIATES:

Universal Music Group
Group Canal+
StudioCanal
SFR Cegetel
Maroc Telecom
Vivendi Games
NBC Universal

CONTACTS: *Note: Officers with more than one job title may be intentionally listed here more than once.*

Jean-Bernard Levy, CEO
Philippe Capron, CFO
Rene Penisson, Sr. Exec. VP-Human Resources
Jean-Francois Dubos, General Counsel
Robert De Metz, Sr. Exec. VP-Strategy & Dev.
Michel Bourgeois, Exec. VP-Corp. Comm.
Daniel Scolan, Exec. VP-Investor Rel.
Regis Turrini, Exec. VP-Divestitures, Mergers & Acquisitions
Abdeslam Ahizoune, Chmn. Mgt. Board-Maroc Telecom
Frank Esser, Chmn./CEO-SFR
Doug Morris, Chmn./CEO-Universal Music Group
Jean-Bernard Levy, Chmn.

Phone: 33-1-71-71-10-00	Fax: 33-1-71-71-10-01
Toll-Free:	
Address: 42 Ave. de Friedland, Paris, 75380 France	

GROWTH PLANS/SPECIAL FEATURES:

Vivendi SA, formerly Vivendi Universal, is a company focusing on the areas of music, TV, cinema, telecommunications, Internet connectivity and interactive games. The company operates in seven units: Universal Music Group; Canal+ Group; SFR; Maroc Telecom; Vivendi Games; Holding & Corporate; and non-core. The Universal Music Group is a leading supplier of recorded music, music videos, DVDs and music publishing, and it contributes 17% of gross earnings. Universal Music sells one out of every four albums worldwide. Group Canal+, a French company offering pay-TV channels through Canal+ and CanalSat and one of the world's largest film libraries through StudioCanal; as a whole, the group contributes 1.7% of earnings. SFR Cegetel is a leading French telecommunications provider, and it contributes 59.1% of earnings. SFR is France's number two mobile carrier with 17.9 million customers, as well as owning 40.5% of Neuf Cegetel, France's number two fixed-line operator. Maroc Telecom is a Moroccan telecommunications firm, providing mobile, fixed-line and internet access to over 10.7 million mobile customers and 1.3 million fixed lines; it contributes 20.86% of earnings. Vivendi Games is a global developer, publisher and distributor of interactive games, with over 8.5 million players worldwide; it contributes 2.6%. The Holding and Corporate segment provides organizational direction and control for the company's other segments. Over 60% of Vivendi's revenue is generated in France, with the U.S. accounting for the second most at 12.2%. Vivendi Universal and General Electric merged Vivendi Universal Entertainment (comprising the company's film, television, theme park and related holdings) with NBC to create NBC Universal. Currently, GE holds an 80% interest in NBC Universal, with the remaining 20% controlled by Vivendi. In early 2006, the SFR unit exceeded 1 million exclusively 3G cell phone customers. In September 2006, the company acquired the BMG Music Publishing Group from Bertelsmann AG for $2.09 billion. In December 2007, the firm agreed to acquire 68% of Activision, Inc.

FINANCIALS: Sales and profits are in thousands of dollars—add 000 to get the full amount. 2007 Note: Financial information for 2007 was not available for all companies at press time.

2007 Sales: $	2007 Profits: $	**U.S. Stock Ticker:**
2006 Sales: $26,522,143	2006 Profits: $3,458,838	**Int'l Ticker: VIV** Int'l Exchange: Paris-Euronext
2005 Sales: $25,780,500	2005 Profits: $2,934,852	Employees: 34,694
2004 Sales: $29,026,000	2004 Profits: $1,021,000	Fiscal Year Ends: 12/31
2003 Sales: $32,328,900	2003 Profits: $-1,437,000	Parent Company:

SALARIES/BENEFITS:

Pension Plan:	ESOP Stock Plan:	Profit Sharing:	Top Exec. Salary: $	Bonus: $
Savings Plan:	Stock Purch. Plan:		Second Exec. Salary: $	Bonus: $

OTHER THOUGHTS:

Apparent Women Officers or Directors: 1
Hot Spot for Advancement for Women/Minorities:

LOCATIONS: ("Y" = Yes)

West:	Southwest:	Midwest:	Southeast:	Northeast:	International:
Y	Y	Y	Y	Y	Y

VULCAN INC

www.vulcan.com

Industry Group Code: 551110 Ranks within this company's industry group: Sales: Profits:

Print Media/Publishing:	Movies:		Equipment/Supplies:		Broadcast/Cable:	Music/Audio:	Sports/Games/Gambling:
Newspapers:	Movie Theaters:	Y	Equipment/Supplies:		Broadcast TV:	Music Production:	Games/Sports:
Magazines:	Movie Production:	Y	Gambling Equipment:	Y	Cable TV:	Retail Music:	Retail Games Stores:
Books:	TV/Video Prod.:		Special Services:	Y	Satellite Broadcast:	Retail Audio Equip.:	Stadiums/Teams:
Book Stores:	Video Rental:		Advertising Services:		Radio:	Music Print./Dist.:	Gambling/Casinos:
Distribution/Printing:	Video Distribution:		Info. Sys. Software:		Online Information:	Multimedia:	Rides/Theme Parks:

TYPES OF BUSINESS:

Company & Enterprise Management
Film Production
Entertainment Investments
Telecommunications Investments
Sports Teams
Real Estate
Museums

BRANDS/DIVISIONS/AFFILIATES:

Vulcan Productions
Science Fiction Museum & Hall of Fame
Hospital (The)
Seattle Seahawks
Portland Trail Blazers
SpaceShipOne
Wired-World
DreamWorks SKG

CONTACTS: Note: Officers with more than one job title may be intentionally listed here more than once.

Jody Patton, CEO
Jody Patton, Pres.
Nathaniel (Buster) Brown, CFO
Chris Purcell, VP-Tech.
Denise Wolf, VP-Oper.
Denise Wolf, VP-Corp. Dev.
Steven C. Crosby, VP-Corp. Comm.
Denise K. Fletcher, Exec. VP-Finance
Lance Conn, VP-Investment Mgmt.
Ada M. Healey, VP-Real Estate Dev.
Richard E. Hutton, VP-Media Dev.
Nathaniel (Buster) Brown, VP-Bus. Finance & Reporting
Paul G. Allen, Chmn.

Phone: 206-342-2000	Fax: 206-342-3000
Toll-Free:	
Address: 505 5th Ave. S., Ste. 900, Seattle, WA 98104 US	

GROWTH PLANS/SPECIAL FEATURES:

Vulcan, Inc. was founded by Paul Allen, Microsoft's co-founder, to research and implement his investments, and does everything from building museums and making original motion pictures to launching businesses and developing new technologies. It invests heavily in the Pacific Northwest and primarily focuses on projects involving education, preserving history and the arts. Though the company believes that technology can enhance these projects and deliver them to a broader audience, achieving high levels of creativity is its main objective. Its creative projects include Vulcan Productions, several museums and The Hospital. Vulcan Productions is an independent film studio whose recent productions include Hard Candy and several documentaries, including The Blues, executive produced by Martin Scorsese. Vulcan's museums include the Science Fiction Museum and Hall of Fame, the Microcomputer Gallery and the Flying Heritage Collection of rare WWII airplanes. The Hospital is a multi-use venue for international music and film professionals created from the derelict St. Paul's Hospital in the London borough of Camden. The firm owns two major league sports teams, the Seattle Seahawks and Portland Trail Blazers, as well as various real estate properties, including 505 Union Station in Seattle, a 291,860 square foot office building where the company headquarters are located. Vulcan recently won the $10 million X Prize with SpaceShipOne, the first privately built spacecraft to successfully enter outer space. Vulcan invests in companies that fit Allen's Wired-World strategy to contribute to or benefit from the technology of other companies within Vulcan's extensive investment portfolio. Other investments in telecommunications, media, retail, software, hardware and biotechnology, include companies such as DreamWorks SKG, Oxygen Media and RCN Corporation.

Vulcan offers its employees apartment assistance, an employee assistance plan, insurance benefits for domestic partners, tuition reimbursement, up to $100 a month for transportation, an on-premises athletic facility and health club membership.

FINANCIALS: Sales and profits are in thousands of dollars—add 000 to get the full amount. 2007 Note: Financial information for 2007 was not available for all companies at press time.

2007 Sales: $	2007 Profits: $	U.S. Stock Ticker: Private
2006 Sales: $	2006 Profits: $	Int'l Ticker: Int'l Exchange:
2005 Sales: $	2005 Profits: $	Employees:
2004 Sales: $	2004 Profits: $	Fiscal Year Ends: 12/31
2003 Sales: $	2003 Profits: $	Parent Company:

SALARIES/BENEFITS:

Pension Plan:	ESOP Stock Plan:	Profit Sharing:	Top Exec. Salary: $	Bonus: $
Savings Plan: Y	Stock Purch. Plan:		Second Exec. Salary: $	Bonus: $

OTHER THOUGHTS:

Apparent Women Officers or Directors: 4
Hot Spot for Advancement for Women/Minorities: Y

LOCATIONS: ("Y" = Yes)

West:	Southwest:	Midwest:	Southeast:	Northeast:	International:
Y					

WALT DISNEY COMPANY (THE)   www.disney.com

Industry Group Code: 513210 Ranks within this company's industry group: Sales: 1   Profits: 1

Print Media/Publishing:		Movies:		Equipment/Supplies:		Broadcast/Cable:		Music/Audio:		Sports/Games/Gambling:	
Newspapers:		Movie Theaters:		Equipment/Supplies:		Broadcast TV:	Y	Music Production:	Y	Games/Sports:	
Magazines:		Movie Production:	Y	Gambling Equipment:		Cable TV:	Y	Retail Music:		Retail Games Stores:	
Books:	Y	TV/Video Prod.:	Y	Special Services:	Y	Satellite Broadcast:		Retail Audio Equip.:		Stadiums/Teams:	Y
Book Stores:		Video Rental:		Advertising Services:		Radio:		Music Print./Dist.:		Gambling/Casinos:	
Distribution/Printing:		Video Distribution:		Info. Sys. Software:		Online Information:		Multimedia:		Rides/Theme Parks:	

TYPES OF BUSINESS:

Cable TV Networks, Broadcasting & Entertainment
Filmed Entertainment
Professional Hockey Team
Television Networks
Music & Book Publishing
Online Entertainment Programs
Theme Parks, Resorts & Cruise Lines
Merchandising

BRANDS/DIVISIONS/AFFILIATES:

Touchstone Pictures
Hollywood Pictures
Miramax
Dimension
ABC Television Network
Disneyland
ESPN
Pixar

CONTACTS: *Note: Officers with more than one job title may be intentionally listed here more than once.*

Robert A. Iger, CEO
Robert A. Iger, Pres.
Thomas O. Staggs, CFO/Sr. Exec. VP
Wes Coleman, Chief Human Resources Officer/Exec. VP
Andy Mooney, Chmn.-Disney Consumer Prod.
Alan Braverman, General Counsel/Sr. Exec. VP/Sec.
Kevin Mayer, Exec. VP-Corp. Strategy, Bus. Dev. & Tech. Group
Zenia Mucha, Exec. VP-Corp. Comm.
Christine M. McCarthy, Exec. VP-Corp. Finance & Real Estate/Treas.
Ronald L. Iden, Sr. VP-Security
Preston Padden, Exec. VP-Gov't Rel.
George W. Bodenheimer, Pres., ESPN, Inc. & ABC Sports
Walter C. Liss., Pres., ABC Television
John E. Pepper, Jr., Chmn.
Andy Bird, Pres., Walt Disney Int'l

Phone: 818-560-1000	Fax: 818-560-1930
Toll-Free:	
Address: 500 S. Buena Vista St., Burbank, CA 91521-9722 US	

GROWTH PLANS/SPECIAL FEATURES:

The Walt Disney Company, together with its subsidiaries, is an international entertainment company operating in four major business segments: media networks; studio entertainment; consumer products; and parks and resorts. The media networks segment contributes 43% of all revenues. The segment is comprised of domestic broadcast television networks, domestic television stations, cable/satellite networks and international broadcast operations, television production and distribution, domestic broadcast radio networks and stations, as well as Internet and mobile operations. The company also owns and operates cable networks, including ESPN, ABC Family, the History Channel, the Biography Channel, Lifetime Television, E! Entertainment Television, Style and A&E. The studio entertainment segment produces and acquires live action and animated motion pictures, direct-to-video programming, musical recordings and live stage plays. The consumer products segment designs, promotes and sells various merchandise based on the firm's intellectual property. The parks and resorts segment manages the operations of the Walt Disney World Resort and the Disney Cruise Line in Florida, the Disneyland resort in California and ESPN Zone facilities in several states, as well as managing the Disneyland Resort Paris and Hong Kong Disneyland (in which the company has a 51% and a 43% interest, respectively) and licenses the Tokyo Disney Resort in Japan. The Walt Disney World Resort includes the Magic Kingdom, Epcot, Disney-MGM Studios and Disney's Animal Kingdom; hotels; vacation ownership units; a retail, dining and entertainment complex; a sports complex; conference centers; campgrounds; golf courses; water parks and other recreational facilities. Currently Disney operates 8 ESPN Zones, located in California, Georgia, Maryland, Illinois, Colorado, Nevada, New York and Washington, D.C.

Disney employees receive theme park passports, educational reimbursement, access to the Walt Disney Company Foundation Scholarship Program, credit union membership, a personal assistant network and on-site child care services. In addition, the company holds employee and cast member contests.

FINANCIALS: Sales and profits are in thousands of dollars—add 000 to get the full amount. 2007 Note: Financial information for 2007 was not available for all companies at press time.

2007 Sales: $35,510,000	2007 Profits: $4,687,000	**U.S. Stock Ticker: DIS**
2006 Sales: $33,747,000	2006 Profits: $3,374,000	**Int'l Ticker:** Int'l Exchange:
2005 Sales: $31,374,000	2005 Profits: $2,533,000	Employees: 137,000
2004 Sales: $30,752,000	2004 Profits: $2,345,000	Fiscal Year Ends: 9/30
2003 Sales: $27,061,000	2003 Profits: $1,267,000	Parent Company:

SALARIES/BENEFITS:

Pension Plan: Y	ESOP Stock Plan:	Profit Sharing:	Top Exec. Salary: $2,000,000	Bonus: $15,000,000
Savings Plan: Y	Stock Purch. Plan:		Second Exec. Salary: $1,037,500	Bonus: $4,000,000

OTHER THOUGHTS:

Apparent Women Officers or Directors: 4
Hot Spot for Advancement for Women/Minorities: Y

LOCATIONS: ("Y" = Yes)

West:	Southwest:	Midwest:	Southeast:	Northeast:	International:
Y	Y	Y	Y	Y	Y

WALT DISNEY STUDIOS (THE)   studioservices.go.com

Industry Group Code: 512110 Ranks within this company's industry group: Sales: Profits:

Print Media/Publishing:	Movies:		Equipment/Supplies:	Broadcast/Cable:	Music/Audio:		Sports/Games/Gambling:
Newspapers:	Movie Theaters:		Equipment/Supplies:	Broadcast TV:	Music Production:	Y	Games/Sports:
Magazines:	Movie Production:	Y	Gambling Equipment:	Cable TV:	Retail Music:		Retail Games Stores:
Books:	TV/Video Prod.:	Y	Special Services:	Satellite Broadcast:	Retail Audio Equip.:		Stadiums/Teams:
Book Stores:	Video Rental:		Advertising Services:	Radio:	Music Print./Dist.:	Y	Gambling/Casinos:
Distribution/Printing:	Video Distribution:	Y	Info. Sys. Software:	Online Information:	Multimedia:		Rides/Theme Parks:

TYPES OF BUSINESS:
Movie Production & Post-Production Services
Movie Distribution
Theatrical Productions
Music Production
Music Distribution

BRANDS/DIVISIONS/AFFILIATES:
Walt Disney Company (The)
Disney Theatrical Productions
Disney Music Group
Disney Animation Studios

CONTACTS: *Note: Officers with more than one job title may be intentionally listed here more than once.*
Mark Zoradi, Pres-Motion Pictures Group
Oren Aviv, Pres.-Production
Alan Bergman, Pres.
Ed Catmull, Pres.-Pixar & Animation
John Lasseter, Chief Creative Officer
Richard Cook, Chmn.

Phone: 818-560-1000	**Fax:** 818-560-1930
Toll-Free:	
Address: 500 S. Buena Vista St., Burbank, CA 91521-9722 US	

GROWTH PLANS/SPECIAL FEATURES:

Walt Disney Studios, a division of The Walt Disney Company, distributes movies under the Walt Disney Pictures, Touchstone, Pixar, Miramax Films and Hollywood Pictures names.   It operates Walt Disney Studios Home Entertainment, distributing films for rental and sale; Disney Theatrical Productions, producer of Broadway musicals; Disney on Ice; Walt Disney Records; Hollywood Records; and Lyric Street Records. It also offers production and post-production services as well as facilities.   Its production services include six sound stages, used to film the live action sequences for Fantasia in 1940, and, more recently, used to film portions of Pearl Harbor, Pirates of the Caribbean and Armageddon.   They have also been used to film TV shows, such as the Mickey Mouse Club and Sports Night.   The studio's business street features a 1950s facade, and has been used in Ellen, Alias, My Wife & Kids and commercials and print ads.   Lastly, its backlot services include lighting; property (set dressing); costumes; stock and custom moulding; a staff shop for custom fabrications; signs and graphics; a paint shop; craft services; and transportation, including on-site fueling with freeway access, passenger vehicles, heavy duty trucks and various trailers.   Post-production services include five dubbing and one ADR (Automated Dialogue Replacement) stage in the studio, all of which feature advanced sound editing tools and at least some seating.   Its sound editing services include digital and analog editing suites equipped with 140 gigabytes of storage capacity, Pro Tools software, a 4 terabyte sound F/X server and other accoutrement.   The studio's imaging services include digital imaging; title graphics; a black and white film lab; and an optical sound track department.   Lastly, the studio has eight screening rooms on the lot and one in New York City, all of which feature advance audio/visual capabilities.   Facilities include rehearsal rooms, conference rooms, parking, commissaries, production office space, a service station and the Disney store.

FINANCIALS: Sales and profits are in thousands of dollars—add 000 to get the full amount. 2007 Note: Financial information for 2007 was not available for all companies at press time.

2007 Sales: $	2007 Profits: $	**U.S. Stock Ticker: Subsidiary**
2006 Sales: $	2006 Profits: $	**Int'l Ticker:** Int'l Exchange:
2005 Sales: $7,587,000	2005 Profits: $	Employees:
2004 Sales: $	2004 Profits: $	Fiscal Year Ends: 9/30
2003 Sales: $	2003 Profits: $	Parent Company: WALT DISNEY COMPANY (THE)

SALARIES/BENEFITS:

Pension Plan:	ESOP Stock Plan:	Profit Sharing:	Top Exec. Salary: $	Bonus: $
Savings Plan:	Stock Purch. Plan:		Second Exec. Salary: $	Bonus: $

OTHER THOUGHTS:

Apparent Women Officers or Directors:
Hot Spot for Advancement for Women/Minorities:

LOCATIONS: ("Y" = Yes)

West:	Southwest:	Midwest:	Southeast:	Northeast:	International:
Y					

WARNER BROS ENTERTAINMENT INC www.warnerbros.com

Industry Group Code: 512110 Ranks within this company's industry group: Sales: Profits:

Print Media/Publishing:	Movies:		Equipment/Supplies:	Broadcast/Cable:		Music/Audio:	Sports/Games/Gambling:
Newspapers:	Movie Theaters:		Equipment/Supplies:	Broadcast TV:	Y	Music Production:	Games/Sports:
Magazines: Y	Movie Production:	Y	Gambling Equipment:	Cable TV:		Retail Music:	Retail Games Stores:
Books:	TV/Video Prod.:	Y	Special Services:	Satellite Broadcast:		Retail Audio Equip.:	Stadiums/Teams:
Book Stores:	Video Rental:		Advertising Services:	Radio:		Music Print./Dist.:	Gambling/Casinos:
Distribution/Printing:	Video Distribution:	Y	Info. Sys. Software:	Online Information:		Multimedia:	Rides/Theme Parks:

TYPES OF BUSINESS:

Film Production
Television Production & Broadcasting
Video Distribution
Animation
Comic Books
Brand Licensing

BRANDS/DIVISIONS/AFFILIATES:

Time Warner Inc
Jazz Singer (The)
Warner Bros. Pictures
Village Roadshow Pictures
New Line Cinema
Classic MGM
DC Comics
CW Television Network (The)

CONTACTS: *Note: Officers with more than one job title may be intentionally listed here more than once.*

Barry M. Meyer, CEO
Alan F. Horn, COO
Alan F. Horn, Pres.
Edward (Ed) Romano, CFO/Exec. VP
Dawn Taubin, Pres., Domestic Mktg.
Darcy Antonellis, Sr. VP-Worldwide Anti-Piracy Oper. & Tech.
Chris Cookson, CTO/Pres., Tech. Oper.
Brad Globe, Pres., Consumer Prod.
Steve Papazian, Pres., Worldwide Physical Prod.
Gary Credle, Exec. VP-Admin.
John Schulman, General Counsel/Exec. VP
Gary Credle, Exec. VP-Studio Oper.
Steven S. Spira, Pres., Worldwide Bus. Affairs
Susan Nahley Fleishman, Exec. VP-Corp. Comm.
Bruce Rosenblum, Pres., Television Group
Kevin Tsujihara, Pres., Home Entertainment Group
Debra Baker, Sr. VP-Interactive Entertainment Oper.
Polly Cohen, Pres., Warner Independent Pictures
Barry M. Meyer, Chmn.
Richard Fox, Exec. VP-Int'l

Phone: 818-954-6000	Fax: 212-954-7667
Toll-Free:	
Address: 4000 Warner Blvd., Burbank, CA 91522 US	

GROWTH PLANS/SPECIAL FEATURES:

Warner Bros. Entertainment, a subsidiary of Time Warner, creates, produces, distributes, licenses and markets films, television shows, DVDs, animation, comic books, interactive entertainment, international cinema and television broadcasting. In 1927, Warner Bros. was the first production house to release a synchronized-sound feature film, titled The Jazz Singer. Films are produced under the names Warner Bros. Pictures, Warner Bros. Pictures International, Village Roadshow Pictures, Gaylord Films, Alcon Entertainment, New Line Cinema, Castle Rock, Lorimar Pictures, RKO and Classic MGM. Recent hit films have included 300 and the Harry Potter Series. The company's Independent Pictures division produces up to 10 feature films every year, usually budgeted under $20 million, and includes the hit documentary March of the Penguins. The Warner Bros. Television Group oversees the company's television businesses, producing primetime and cable series through Warner Bros. Television and Warner Horizon Television; first-run series through Telepictures productions; and animation series through Warner Bros. Animation. The company is also a partner with CBS in The CW Television Network. The company's primetime series include ER, Smallville, Without A Trace and Nip/Tuck. Warner Bros. Animation's library is comprised of roughly 14,000 animated episodes and shorts, including such brands as Looney Tunes and Hanna-Barbera, as well as such characters as Bugs Bunny; Daffy Duck; Tweety; Tom and Jerry; Popeye; the Flintstones; and Scooby-Doo. The firm owns DC Comics, a leading comic book publisher and the creator of comic book icons such as Superman, Batman and Wonder Woman. The DC Comics line also includes the revamped MAD Magazine. Warner Bros. also owns the marketing rights to classic movies such as Citizen Kane, Casablanca, Gone with the Wind and Wizard of Oz. In September 2007, Warner Bros. formed an alliance with Abu Dhabi Media Company which includes the development of a theme park and a co-finance agreement covering feature film and videogame production.

FINANCIALS: Sales and profits are in thousands of dollars—add 000 to get the full amount. 2007 Note: Financial information for 2007 was not available for all companies at press time.

2007 Sales: $	2007 Profits: $	**U.S. Stock Ticker: Subsidiary**
2006 Sales: $	2006 Profits: $	**Int'l Ticker:** Int'l Exchange:
2005 Sales: $11,850,000	2005 Profits: $	Employees:
2004 Sales: $	2004 Profits: $	Fiscal Year Ends: 12/31
2003 Sales: $	2003 Profits: $	Parent Company: TIME WARNER INC

SALARIES/BENEFITS:

Pension Plan:	ESOP Stock Plan:	Profit Sharing:	Top Exec. Salary: $	Bonus: $
Savings Plan:	Stock Purch. Plan:		Second Exec. Salary: $	Bonus: $

OTHER THOUGHTS:

Apparent Women Officers or Directors: 11
Hot Spot for Advancement for Women/Minorities: Y

LOCATIONS: ("Y" = Yes)

West:	Southwest:	Midwest:	Southeast:	Northeast:	International:
Y					

WARNER MUSIC GROUP

www.wmg.com

Industry Group Code: 512230 Ranks within this company's industry group: Sales: 3   Profits: 3

Print Media/Publishing:	Movies:		Equipment/Supplies:	Broadcast/Cable:	Music/Audio:		Sports/Games/Gambling:	
Newspapers:	Movie Theaters:		Equipment/Supplies:	Broadcast TV:	Music Production:	Y	Games/Sports:	
Magazines:	Movie Production:		Gambling Equipment:	Cable TV:	Retail Music:		Retail Games Stores:	
Books:	TV/Video Prod.:	Y	Special Services:	Satellite Broadcast:	Retail Audio Equip.:		Stadiums/Teams:	
Book Stores:	Video Rental:		Advertising Services:	Radio:	Music Print./Dist.:	Y	Gambling/Casinos:	
Distribution/Printing:	Video Distribution:		Info. Sys. Software:	Online Information:	Multimedia:		Rides/Theme Parks:	

TYPES OF BUSINESS:

Recorded Music Distribution
Music Production
Music Printing
Music Publishing
Soundtracks
Compilations
Digital Music Downloads
Video Production

BRANDS/DIVISIONS/AFFILIATES:

Warner Bros. Records
Atlantic Records Group (The)
Elektra Entertainment
Word Entertainment
Rhino Entertainment
Warner/Chappell Music, Inc.
Warner Music Entertainment
Rykodisc

CONTACTS: Note: Officers with more than one job title may be intentionally listed here more than once.

Edgar Bronfman, Jr., CEO
Michael D. Fleisher, CFO/Exec. VP
Mitchell Imber, Sr. VP-Physical Sales
Caroline Stockdale, Exec. VP-Global Human Resources
Maggie Miller, CIO
Paul M. Robinson, General Counsel/Exec. VP
Alejandro Zubillaga, Exec. VP-Digital Strategy & Bus. Dev.
Susan Mazo, Sr. VP-Corp. Comm.
Lyor Cohen, CEO-U.S. Recorded Music
Caroline Stockdale, Exec. VP-Global Human Resources
Peter Scherr, VP-Interactive Mktg.
Mike Saunter, CFO-Warner Music International
Edgar Bronfman, Jr., Chmn.
Patrick Vien, CEO-Warner International

Phone: 212-484-8000	Fax: 212-333-3987
Toll-Free:	
Address: 75 Rockefeller Plaza, New York, NY 10019 US	

GROWTH PLANS/SPECIAL FEATURES:

Warner Music Group is a global company specializing in Recorded Music and Music Publishing. The recorded music business (conducted through Warner Bros. Records and The Atlantic Records Group among others) markets, sells and licenses recorded music CDs, DVDs, downloads and ringtones. The firm's recording companies include Reprise Records, Maverick Records, Atlantic Group, Rykodisc, Sire, Elektra Entertainment, Word Entertainment and Warner Music International (WMI). WMI distributes American and local music to a network of affiliates and licensees in more than 50 countries. Warner-Elektra-Atlantic Corporation (WEA Corp.) and Ryko Distribution are independent music distributors in the U.S. Warner/Chappell Music, a music publishing company, holds the publishing rights to more than a million songs from over 65,000 songwriters. Warner Strategic Marketing promotes the company's catalog of music and artists, and includes Rhino Entertainment and Warner Music Group Soundtracks among others. In 2007, Warner Music Group acquired a 70% stake in Taisuke, an artist services company in Japan. In the same year, Warner Music extended its digital technology efforts across the globe by forming separate partnerships with two international companies, Orascom Telecom and ACCESS China Media Solutions to deliver music-based content to consumers in North Africa and the Middle East, China and Asian pacific markets. Also in 2007, Warner/Chappel music acquired a licensing agreement with Microsoft to claim, administer and license Microsoft-owned music compositions, as well as develop new music publishing opportunities for Microsoft. The company embarked on several partnerships in 2007 with digital media technology companies to provide its consumers easier access to music and videos via mobile and online technologies. These partners include Joost, a company that combines television and internet services, Dailymotion, a video sharing website; Telenor, a leading mobile operator; and SNOCAP, MySpace's music service. It also partnered with Premium TV to develop a series of online TV sites.

FINANCIALS: Sales and profits are in thousands of dollars—add 000 to get the full amount. 2007 Note: Financial information for 2007 was not available for all companies at press time.

2007 Sales: $3,385,000	2007 Profits: $-21,000	**U.S. Stock Ticker: WMG**
2006 Sales: $3,516,000	2006 Profits: $60,000	**Int'l Ticker:** Int'l Exchange:
2005 Sales: $3,502,000	2005 Profits: $-169,000	Employees: 3,800
2004 Sales: $2,548,000	2004 Profits: $-136,000	Fiscal Year Ends: 9/30
2003 Sales: $3,376,000	2003 Profits: $	Parent Company:

SALARIES/BENEFITS:

Pension Plan:	ESOP Stock Plan:	Profit Sharing:	Top Exec. Salary: $1,000,000	Bonus: $6,250,000
Savings Plan:	Stock Purch. Plan:		Second Exec. Salary: $1,000,000	Bonus: $6,000,000

OTHER THOUGHTS:

Apparent Women Officers or Directors: 5
Hot Spot for Advancement for Women/Minorities: Y

LOCATIONS: ("Y" = Yes)

West:	Southwest:	Midwest:	Southeast:	Northeast:	International:
Y			Y	Y	Y

Note: Financial information, benefits and other data can change quickly and may vary from those stated here.

WASHINGTON POST CO

www.washpostco.com

Industry Group Code: 511110 Ranks within this company's industry group: Sales: 5   Profits: 5

Print Media/Publishing:		Movies:		Equipment/Supplies:		Broadcast/Cable:		Music/Audio:		Sports/Games/Gambling:	
Newspapers:	Y	Movie Theaters:		Equipment/Supplies:		Broadcast TV:	Y	Music Production:		Games/Sports:	
Magazines:	Y	Movie Production:		Gambling Equipment:		Cable TV:	Y	Retail Music:		Retail Games Stores:	
Books:		TV/Video Prod.:		Special Services:	Y	Satellite Broadcast:		Retail Audio Equip.:		Stadiums/Teams:	
Book Stores:		Video Rental:		Advertising Services:	Y	Radio:		Music Print./Dist.:		Gambling/Casinos:	
Distribution/Printing:		Video Distribution:		Info. Sys. Software:		Online Information:		Multimedia:		Rides/Theme Parks:	

TYPES OF BUSINESS:

Newspaper Publishing
Television Broadcasting
Cable Television Systems
Magazine Publishing
Educational Services
Internet Publishing
Printing/Distribution Services
Recycling & Used Paper Sales

BRANDS/DIVISIONS/AFFILIATES:

Washington Post (The)
Daily Herald Company (The)
Gazette Newspapers, Inc.
Newsweek
CableONE
Washingtonpost.Newsweek Interactive Co.
Slate.com
Kaplan, Inc.

CONTACTS:
Note: Officers with more than one job title may be intentionally listed here more than once.

Donald E. Graham, CEO
John B. Morse, Jr., CFO/VP
Ann L. McDaniel, VP-Human Resources
Ralph S. Terkowitz, VP-Tech.
Veronica Dillon, VP/General Counsel/Corp. Sec.
Gerald M. Rosberg, VP-Planning & Dev.
Rima Calderon, Dir.-Corp. Comm.
John B. Morse, Jr., VP-Finance
Patrick Butler, VP-New Bus. Dev., Public Policy & Corp. Projects
Christopher Ma, VP-Planning & Dev. of New Bus. Opportunities
Daniel J. Lynch, Treas.
Wallace R. Cooney, Controller
Donald E. Graham, Chmn.

Phone: 202-334-6000	**Fax:** 202-334-4536
Toll-Free:	
Address: 1150 15th St. NW, Washington, DC 20071 US	

GROWTH PLANS/SPECIAL FEATURES:

Washington Post Co. operates in five core business segments: newspaper publishing, principally The Washington Post; magazine publishing, most notably Newsweek; television broadcasting; cable television networks; and educational services, through subsidiary Kaplan, Inc. The Washington Post is a morning and Sunday newspaper with a daily circulation of over 700,000 and a Sunday circulation of close to 1 million, distributed through newsstands and home delivery in Washington, D.C., Virginia and Maryland. The Post also operates a joint news wire service with the Los Angeles Times and publishes regional newspapers in Maryland (Gazette Newspapers, Inc.) and Everett, Washington (The Daily Herald Company). Washingtonpost.Newsweek Interactive Company (WPNI), part of the newspaper group, develops news and information products for electronic distribution. This includes washingtonpost.com, which features the full editorial text of The Post as well as classified advertising, online advertising and original content, Slate.com and the Newsweek website. Magazines remain a stable source of revenue for the firm, with lead imprint Newsweek maintaining news bureaus in eight U.S. and 11 foreign cities. Internationally, Newsweek is published in a Europe, Middle East and Africa edition; a Korea and Japan edition; and a Latin American edition. The company owns six VHF television-broadcasting stations in Detroit, Houston, Miami, Orlando, San Antonio and Jacksonville through its subsidiary Post-Newsweek Stations, Inc. Five of these stations are affiliated with major networks; the station in Jacksonville, Florida is an independent station. The firm's cable television operations, managed by its CableONE subsidiary, provide service to over 709,000 subscribers and digital video service to over 219,000 subscriptions. Through Kaplan, Inc., the company provides educational services such as test preparation and Federal Student Financial Aid Programs funding. In October2007, the firm acquired CourseAdvisor, Inc., which provides student leads for the post-secondary education market. Over 1.5 million students use the directory to select schools and programs.

FINANCIALS:
Sales and profits are in thousands of dollars—add 000 to get the full amount. 2007 Note: Financial information for 2007 was not available for all companies at press time.

2007 Sales: $	2007 Profits: $	**U.S. Stock Ticker:** WPO
2006 Sales: $3,904,927	2006 Profits: $324,459	**Int'l Ticker:** Int'l Exchange:
2005 Sales: $3,553,887	2005 Profits: $314,344	Employees: 17,100
2004 Sales: $3,300,104	2004 Profits: $332,732	Fiscal Year Ends: 12/31
2003 Sales: $2,838,911	2003 Profits: $241,088	Parent Company:

SALARIES/BENEFITS:

Pension Plan: Y	ESOP Stock Plan:	Profit Sharing:	Top Exec. Salary: $585,000	Bonus: $1,286,170
Savings Plan: Y	Stock Purch. Plan: Y		Second Exec. Salary: $400,000	Bonus: $1,003,048

OTHER THOUGHTS:

Apparent Women Officers or Directors: 5
Hot Spot for Advancement for Women/Minorities: Y

LOCATIONS: ("Y" = Yes)

West:	Southwest:	Midwest:	Southeast:	Northeast:	International:
Y	Y	Y	Y	Y	Y

WASSERMAN MEDIA GROUP LLC

www.wmgllc.com

Industry Group Code: 541800 **Ranks within this company's industry group:** Sales: Profits:

Print Media/Publishing:	Movies:		Equipment/Supplies:	Broadcast/Cable:	Music/Audio:	Sports/Games/Gambling:	
Newspapers:	Movie Theaters:		Equipment/Supplies:	Broadcast TV:	Music Production:	Games/Sports:	
Magazines:	Movie Production:	Y	Gambling Equipment:	Cable TV:	Retail Music:	Retail Games Stores:	
Books:	TV/Video Prod.:		Special Services:	Satellite Broadcast:	Retail Audio Equip.:	Stadiums/Teams:	Y
Book Stores:	Video Rental:		Advertising Services:	Radio:	Music Print./Dist.:	Gambling/Casinos:	
Distribution/Printing:	Video Distribution:	Y	Info. Sys. Software:	Online Information:	Multimedia:	Rides/Theme Parks:	

TYPES OF BUSINESS:

Sports Management Agency
Marketing and Branding Services
Sports Film Production

BRANDS/DIVISIONS/AFFILIATES:

WMG Management
WMG Marketing
Studio411
WMG Investments
411vm.com
motorcross.com
surfspot.com
studio411.com

CONTACTS: *Note: Officers with more than one job title may be intentionally listed here more than once.*

Casey Wasserman, CEO
Josh Swartz, COO
Michael Watts, CFO
Arn Tellem, Pres., WMG Management
Jeff Knapple, Pres., WMG Marketing
Luke McDonough, Pres., Studio411
Eli Lande, Pres., WMG Events
Casey Wasserman, Chmn.

Phone: 310-407-0200	Fax:
Toll-Free:	
Address: 12100 W. Olympic Blvd., Los Angeles, CA 60064 US	

GROWTH PLANS/SPECIAL FEATURES:

Wasserman Media Group LLC (WMG) is an expansive sports marketing agency and the holding company for the Los Angeles Avengers of the Arena Football League. The company is organized into four divisions: WMG Management, WMG Marketing, Studio411 and WMG Investments. WMG Management is a leading sports management company. Its client are among the most recognized and talented athletes across baseball, basketball, BMX, motorcross, skateboarding, snowboarding, soccer and surfing. Clients include Nomar Garciaparra, Jason Giambi, Hideki Matsui, Dmitri Young, Pau Gasol, Ben Wallace, Sue Bird, Mia Hamm and Misty May-Treanor. In addition, the company represented six of the top 30 picks in the 2006 NBA draft. WMG Marketing secures naming rights for sports and entertainment destinations, pursues corporate sponsorships and develops marketing programs for consumer brands. The division was selected to sell the naming rights for the New York Giants and Jets $1 billion stadium after it closed a $178 million deal with Emirates airline to sponsor Arsenal FC's new stadium. WMG Marketing's other clients include Nestle, GMAC, Nascar, Proctor & Gamble, MSN, T-Mobile and Avaya. Studio411 specializes in financing, producing, distributing and marketing action sports content in the surfing, skateboard, snowboard, motorcross and BMX markets. Its distribution network includes 411vm.com, motorcross.com, surfspot.com and studio411.com. In 2006, Studio411 released 37 titles and two photo books for various sports producers and companies, including Quiksilver, Oakley, Vans, Globe and Ice Cream. WMG Investments pursues ancillary business ventures in the media and sports industries; it also manages WMG's mergers and acquisitions. At the end of 2006, WMG acquired the soccer, rugby and marketing divisions of SFX Sports Group, Europe, one of Europe's leading sports management businesses. The acquisition follows closely WMG's acquisition of SportsNet, a leading profession soccer athlete management company.

FINANCIALS: Sales and profits are in thousands of dollars—add 000 to get the full amount. 2007 Note: Financial information for 2007 was not available for all companies at press time.

2007 Sales: $	2007 Profits: $	**U.S. Stock Ticker: Private**
2006 Sales: $	2006 Profits: $	**Int'l Ticker:** Int'l Exchange:
2005 Sales: $	2005 Profits: $	Employees:
2004 Sales: $	2004 Profits: $	Fiscal Year Ends:
2003 Sales: $	2003 Profits: $	Parent Company:

SALARIES/BENEFITS:

Pension Plan:	ESOP Stock Plan:	Profit Sharing:	Top Exec. Salary: $	Bonus: $
Savings Plan:	Stock Purch. Plan:		Second Exec. Salary: $	Bonus: $

OTHER THOUGHTS:

Apparent Women Officers or Directors:
Hot Spot for Advancement for Women/Minorities:

LOCATIONS: ("Y" = Yes)

West:	Southwest:	Midwest:	Southeast:	Northeast:	International:
Y			Y	Y	Y

Note: Financial information, benefits and other data can change quickly and may vary from those stated here.

WENNER MEDIA LLC   www.rollingstone.com

Industry Group Code: 511120 Ranks within this company's industry group: Sales: Profits:

Print Media/Publishing:		Movies:	Equipment/Supplies:	Broadcast/Cable:	Music/Audio:	Sports/Games/Gambling:
Newspapers:		Movie Theaters:	Equipment/Supplies:	Broadcast TV:	Music Production:	Games/Sports:
Magazines:	Y	Movie Production:	Gambling Equipment:	Cable TV:	Retail Music:	Retail Games Stores:
Books:	Y	TV/Video Prod.:	Special Services:	Satellite Broadcast:	Retail Audio Equip.:	Stadiums/Teams:
Book Stores:		Video Rental:	Advertising Services:	Radio:	Music Print./Dist.:	Gambling/Casinos:
Distribution/Printing:		Video Distribution:	Info. Sys. Software:	Online Information:	Multimedia:	Rides/Theme Parks:

TYPES OF BUSINESS:

Magazine Publishing
Online Media
Book Publishing

BRANDS/DIVISIONS/AFFILIATES:

Rolling Stone
Men's Journal
US Weekly
Rolling Stone Online
I'm From Rolling Stone

CONTACTS: *Note: Officers with more than one job title may be intentionally listed here more than once.*

Jann S. Wenner, Pres.
John Gruber, CFO
Gary Armstrong, Chief Mktg. Officer-Rolling Stone
Pamela Fox, Dir.-Human Resources
William Kwan, Dir.-IT
Dana Rosen, General Counsel
Michael Small, Dir.-Rolling Stone Online
Lisa Dallos, Sr. VP-Corp. Comm.
Mark Neschis, Dir.-Publicity
Will Dana, Managing Editor
Ed Hecht, Dir.-Advertising
Timothy Walsh, VP
Jane Wenner, VP
Jann S. Wenner, Chmn.

Phone: 212-484-1616	Fax: 212-484-3435
Toll-Free:	
Address: 1290 Ave. of the Americas, New York, NY 10104-0298 US	

GROWTH PLANS/SPECIAL FEATURES:

Wenner Media LLC runs all the operations for publishing three magazines: Men's Journal, Rolling Stone and US Weekly. The firm also manages websites devoted to each magazine. Rolling Stone, a media icon of the rock-and-roll scene, has a circulation of approximately 1.25 million. Rolling Stone Online offers news and information about the music world, in addition to Rolling Stone radio, personal ads, shopping and ticket sales. Men's Journal, a health, fitness and adventure magazine, has a circulation of about 2.7 million. US Weekly, owned and operated by subsidiary US Weekly LLC, is a joint venture with Walt Disney; it covers celebrity gossip and has a circulation of approximately 1.06 million. Wenner also makes books based on the subject matter of the magazines through a partnership with Hyperion printing. The firm is operated primarily by CEO, Chairman and Editor of Rolling Stone Magazine, Jann Wenner, who has edited Rolling Stone since its inception in 1967. Wenner has teamed up with MTV to launch a new reality-based TV show, I'm From Rolling Stone, in early 2007.

FINANCIALS: Sales and profits are in thousands of dollars—add 000 to get the full amount. 2007 Note: Financial information for 2007 was not available for all companies at press time.

2007 Sales: $	2007 Profits: $	**U.S. Stock Ticker: Private**
2006 Sales: $	2006 Profits: $	**Int'l Ticker:** Int'l Exchange:
2005 Sales: $	2005 Profits: $	Employees:
2004 Sales: $	2004 Profits: $	Fiscal Year Ends: 12/31
2003 Sales: $	2003 Profits: $	Parent Company:

SALARIES/BENEFITS:

Pension Plan:	ESOP Stock Plan:	Profit Sharing:	Top Exec. Salary: $	Bonus: $
Savings Plan: Y	Stock Purch. Plan:		Second Exec. Salary: $	Bonus: $

OTHER THOUGHTS:

Apparent Women Officers or Directors: 22
Hot Spot for Advancement for Women/Minorities: Y

LOCATIONS: ("Y" = Yes)

West:	Southwest:	Midwest:	Southeast:	Northeast:	International:
Y	Y	Y	Y	Y	

WESTWOOD ONE INC
www.westwoodone.com

Industry Group Code: 512110 Ranks within this company's industry group: Sales: 7 Profits: 7

Print Media/Publishing:	Movies:	Equipment/Supplies:		Broadcast/Cable:		Music/Audio:	Sports/Games/Gambling:	
Newspapers:	Movie Theaters:	Equipment/Supplies:		Broadcast TV:	Y	Music Production:	Games/Sports:	Y
Magazines:	Movie Production:	Gambling Equipment:		Cable TV:		Retail Music:	Retail Games Stores:	
Books:	TV/Video Prod.:	Special Services:	Y	Satellite Broadcast:		Retail Audio Equip.:	Stadiums/Teams:	
Book Stores:	Video Rental:	Advertising Services:		Radio:		Music Print./Dist.:	Gambling/Casinos:	
Distribution/Printing:	Video Distribution:	Info. Sys. Software:		Online Information:		Multimedia:	Rides/Theme Parks:	

TYPES OF BUSINESS:
Radio Programming Production & Distribution
Information Services

BRANDS/DIVISIONS/AFFILIATES:
Metro Networks
Shadow Broadcast Services
Infinity Broadcasting Corp.
SmartRoute Systems
Shadow Traffic
AccuWeather.com

CONTACTS: Note: Officers with more than one job title may be intentionally listed here more than once.
Peter Kosann, CEO
Peter Kosann, Pres.
Gary Yusko, CFO
Roby Wiener, Chief Mktg. Officer
Carolyn Jones, VP-Human Resources
Paul Bronstein, VP-Research
Luis Rodriguez, CIO
Patrick Parnham, VP-Technical Services
Beth Robinson, Sr. VP-Eng. & Oper.
David Hillman, Chief Admin. Officer
David Hillman, General Counsel/Sec.
Conrad Trautman, Sr. VP-Oper. & Eng.
David Hillman, Exec.VP-Bus. Affairs
Paul Gregrey, Exec. VP/Dir.-Sales
David Halberstam, Exec. VP/Gen. Mgr.-Westwood One Sports
Bart Tessler, Sr. VP-Network News/Talk Programming

Phone: 212-641-2000	Fax: 212-641-2185
Toll-Free: 800-877-0007	
Address: 40 W. 57th St., 5th Fl., New York, NY 10019 US	

GROWTH PLANS/SPECIAL FEATURES:
Westwood One supplies radio and television stations with information services and programming. The company is one of the largest domestic outsource-providers of traffic reporting services and one of the nation's largest radio networks, producing and distributing national news, sports, talk, music and special event programs, in addition to local news, sports, weather, video news and other information programming. The company has more than 5,000 affiliates. Westwood One's principal source of revenue is the sale of commercial airtime to advertisers through its operating divisions, Metro/Shadow (which is comprised of Metro Networks and Shadow Broadcast Services) and the network division. The company provides local traffic and information broadcast reports in over 95 of the top 100 Metro Survey Area (MSA) markets in the United States. The network division offers radio stations traditional news services, including CBS Radio news and CNN Radio news, in addition to weekday and weekend news and entertainment features and programs. These programs include: major sporting events, including the National Football League, Notre Dame football and other college football and basketball games, the National Hockey League, the Masters and the Olympics, live personality intensive talk shows, live concert broadcasts, countdown shows, music and interview programs and exclusive satellite simulcasts with cable networks. The company also offers traffic reporting to over 200 television stations. CBS Radio (formerly Infinity Broadcasting) manages Westwood One. Westwood One and AccuWeather, Inc. announced in June 2007 an extension of their content and distribution partnership by which Metro Networks traffic content will be added to AccuWeather.com sites on both the wired and mobile web. Beginning in August 2007, visitors to AccuWeather.com have had access to Metro Networks' RealTraffic interactive traffic service offering timely information delivered to mobile device-users accessing AccuWeather.com.

FINANCIALS: Sales and profits are in thousands of dollars—add 000 to get the full amount. 2007 Note: Financial information for 2007 was not available for all companies at press time.

		U.S. Stock Ticker: WON
2007 Sales: $	2007 Profits: $	
2006 Sales: $493,995	2006 Profits: $-469,453	Int'l Ticker: Int'l Exchange:
2005 Sales: $557,830	2005 Profits: $77,886	Employees: 2,400
2004 Sales: $562,246	2004 Profits: $86,955	Fiscal Year Ends: 12/31
2003 Sales: $539,226	2003 Profits: $100,039	Parent Company:

SALARIES/BENEFITS:
Pension Plan:	ESOP Stock Plan:	Profit Sharing: Y	Top Exec. Salary: $600,000	Bonus: $150,000
Savings Plan: Y	Stock Purch. Plan:		Second Exec. Salary: $475,000	Bonus: $120,000

OTHER THOUGHTS:
Apparent Women Officers or Directors: 2
Hot Spot for Advancement for Women/Minorities:

LOCATIONS: ("Y" = Yes)
West:	Southwest:	Midwest:	Southeast:	Northeast:	International:
Y	Y	Y	Y	Y	

Note: Financial information, benefits and other data can change quickly and may vary from those stated here.

WHEREHOUSE ENTERTAINMENT (RECORD TOWN INC)
www.wherehouse.com

Industry Group Code: 451220 Ranks within this company's industry group: Sales: Profits:

Print Media/Publishing:	Movies:	Equipment/Supplies:	Broadcast/Cable:	Music/Audio:		Sports/Games/Gambling:	
Newspapers:	Movie Theaters:	Equipment/Supplies:	Broadcast TV:	Music Production:		Games/Sports:	
Magazines:	Movie Production:	Gambling Equipment:	Cable TV:	Retail Music:	Y	Retail Games Stores:	Y
Books:	TV/Video Prod.:	Special Services:	Satellite Broadcast:	Retail Audio Equip.:	Y	Stadiums/Teams:	
Book Stores:	Video Rental:	Advertising Services:	Radio:	Music Print./Dist.:		Gambling/Casinos:	
Distribution/Printing:	Video Distribution:	Info. Sys. Software:	Online Information:	Multimedia:		Rides/Theme Parks:	

TYPES OF BUSINESS:

Music & Video, Retail
Online Sales
Consumer Electronics Sales
Book Sales

GROWTH PLANS/SPECIAL FEATURES:

Wherehouse Entertainment is a brand name of Record Town, Inc., which is the principal operating division and a wholly-owned subsidiary of Trans World Entertainment Corporation.   Record Town operates music, movie, video game, and other entertainment software retailers across the U.S., operating under the names Waxie Maxie, Planet Music, Camelot Music, The Wall, CD World, Disc Jockey, F.Y.E. (For Your Entertainment), F.Y.E. Games, F.Y.E. Movies, Harmony House, Streetside Records, Specs, Coconuts, Strawberries, Second Spin and Wherehouse Music.   In addition, the firm operates several web sites that retail movies, music, video games and other entertainment software.   The firm's web sites include fye.com, Coconuts.com, Hherehouse.com and SecondSpin.com.   In addition to entertainment software, many of the retailers sell electronics ranging from digital cameras to personal stereo systems.

BRANDS/DIVISIONS/AFFILIATES:

Trans World Entertainment
Wherehouse Music
wherehouse.com
F.Y.E. (For Your Entertainment)
CD World
Second Spin
Camelot Music
Record Town USA, LLC

CONTACTS: *Note: Officers with more than one job title may be intentionally listed here more than once.*

John J. Sullivan, Exec. VP/CFO
Fred L. Fox, Exec. VP-Merch & Mktg
Bruce J. Eisenberg, Exec. VP-Real Estate

Phone: 518-452-1242	Fax:
Toll-Free:	
Address: 38 Corporate Circle, Albany, NY 12203 US	

FINANCIALS: Sales and profits are in thousands of dollars—add 000 to get the full amount. 2007 Note: Financial information for 2007 was not available for all companies at press time.

2007 Sales: $	2007 Profits: $	**U.S. Stock Ticker: Subsidiary**
2006 Sales: $	2006 Profits: $	**Int'l Ticker:** Int'l Exchange:
2005 Sales: $	2005 Profits: $	Employees: 5,260
2004 Sales: $	2004 Profits: $	Fiscal Year Ends: 1/31
2003 Sales: $	2003 Profits: $	Parent Company: TRANS WORLD ENTERTAINMENT CORP

SALARIES/BENEFITS:

Pension Plan:	ESOP Stock Plan:	Profit Sharing:	Top Exec. Salary: $347,884	Bonus: $
Savings Plan:	Stock Purch. Plan:		Second Exec. Salary: $341,250	Bonus: $

OTHER THOUGHTS:

Apparent Women Officers or Directors:
Hot Spot for Advancement for Women/Minorities:

LOCATIONS: ("Y" = Yes)

West:	Southwest:	Midwest:	Southeast:	Northeast:	International:
Y	Y	Y	Y	Y	

WILLIAM MORRIS AGENCY INC

www.wma.com

Industry Group Code: 711410 Ranks within this company's industry group: Sales: Profits:

Print Media/Publishing:		Movies:		Equipment/Supplies:		Broadcast/Cable:		Music/Audio:		Sports/Games/Gambling:	
Newspapers:		Movie Theaters:		Equipment/Supplies:		Broadcast TV:		Music Production:		Games/Sports:	
Magazines:		Movie Production:		Gambling Equipment:		Cable TV:		Retail Music:		Retail Games Stores:	
Books:	Y	TV/Video Prod.:		Special Services:	Y	Satellite Broadcast:		Retail Audio Equip.:		Stadiums/Teams:	
Book Stores:		Video Rental:		Advertising Services:	Y	Radio:		Music Print./Dist.:		Gambling/Casinos:	
Distribution/Printing:		Video Distribution:		Info. Sys. Software:		Online Information:		Multimedia:		Rides/Theme Parks:	

TYPES OF BUSINESS:

Talent Agency
Literary Agency
Sports Marketing & Agents
Media Consulting
Book Publishing

BRANDS/DIVISIONS/AFFILIATES:

William Morris Consulting

CONTACTS: *Note: Officers with more than one job title may be intentionally listed here more than once.*

James A. Wiatt, CEO
David Wirtschafter, Pres.
Irv Weintraub, CFO
Norman Brokaw, Chmn.

Phone: 310-859-4000	Fax: 310-859-4462
Toll-Free:	
Address: 1 William Morris Pl., Beverly Hills, CA 90212 US	

GROWTH PLANS/SPECIAL FEATURES:

The William Morris Agency, Inc. (WMA) is one of the largest and oldest talent and literary agencies in the world. Founded in 1898, WMA represents clients in almost every aspect of the entertainment industry including film, television, commercials, music and theater. In addition, the company is engaged in book publishing, sports marketing and corporate consulting. WMA's book department represents established authors and accepts submissions from prospective writers. The department works closely with the motion picture and television departments to bring books to both large and small screens. The sports marketing department represents athletes both on- and off- the field, with services including contract negotiation, licensing and the pursuit of broadcasting and sponsorship opportunities. WMA's roster of clients includes athletes in sports such as tennis, figure skating, basketball and football, as well as television announcers and commentators. William Morris Consulting offers media expertise to a wide variety of industry segments, including telecommunications, technology, lodging, gaming, publishing, retail, consumer products, apparel and cosmetics. At the end of 2006, WMA began construction on its new eco-friendly headquarters; the new building is expected to open in 2009.

FINANCIALS: Sales and profits are in thousands of dollars—add 000 to get the full amount. 2007 Note: Financial information for 2007 was not available for all companies at press time.

2007 Sales: $	2007 Profits: $	**U.S. Stock Ticker: Private**	
2006 Sales: $	2006 Profits: $	**Int'l Ticker:** Int'l Exchange:	
2005 Sales: $	2005 Profits: $	Employees:	
2004 Sales: $	2004 Profits: $	Fiscal Year Ends: 12/31	
2003 Sales: $	2003 Profits: $	Parent Company:	

SALARIES/BENEFITS:

Pension Plan:	ESOP Stock Plan:	Profit Sharing:	Top Exec. Salary: $	Bonus: $
Savings Plan:	Stock Purch. Plan:		Second Exec. Salary: $	Bonus: $

OTHER THOUGHTS:

Apparent Women Officers or Directors:
Hot Spot for Advancement for Women/Minorities:

LOCATIONS: ("Y" = Yes)

West:	Southwest:	Midwest:	Southeast:	Northeast:	International:
Y			Y	Y	Y

WMS INDUSTRIES INC

www.wms.com

Industry Group Code: 713290 **Ranks within this company's industry group:** Sales: 6   Profits: 4

Print Media/Publishing:	Movies:	Equipment/Supplies:		Broadcast/Cable:	Music/Audio:	Sports/Games/Gambling:
Newspapers:	Movie Theaters:	Equipment/Supplies:		Broadcast TV:	Music Production:	Games/Sports:
Magazines:	Movie Production:	Gambling Equipment:	Y	Cable TV:	Retail Music:	Retail Games Stores:
Books:	TV/Video Prod.:	Special Services:	Y	Satellite Broadcast:	Retail Audio Equip.:	Stadiums/Teams:
Book Stores:	Video Rental:	Advertising Services:		Radio:	Music Print./Dist.:	Gambling/Casinos:
Distribution/Printing:	Video Distribution:	Info. Sys. Software:		Online Information:	Multimedia:	Rides/Theme Parks:

TYPES OF BUSINESS:

Gaming Machines
Video Lottery Terminals
Gaming Operations

BRANDS/DIVISIONS/AFFILIATES:

WMS Gaming, Inc.
Orion Financement Company B.V.

CONTACTS: *Note: Officers with more than one job title may be intentionally listed here more than once.*

Brian R. Gamache, CEO
Orrin J. Edidin, COO/Exec. VP
Brian R. Gamache, Pres.
Scott D. Schweinfurth, CFO/Exec. VP
Kathleen J. McJohn, General Counsel/VP/Sec.
Scott D. Schweinfurth, Treas.
Louis J. Nicastro, Chmn.

Phone: 847-785-3000	Fax: 847-785-3058
Toll-Free:	
Address: 800 S. Northpoint Blvd., Waukegan, IL 60085 US	

GROWTH PLANS/SPECIAL FEATURES:

WMS Industries, Inc. designs, manufactures and markets gaming machines (video and mechanical reel type); video lottery terminals; and gaming operations, which consist of the placement in legal gaming venues of participation games, including gaming machines linked to wide-area progressive jackpot systems, local-are progressive jackpot systems and non-linked, stand-alone gaming machines. The firm conducts its machine business through its subsidiaries, including WMS Gaming, Inc. WMS also develops and sells mechanical reel-spinning gaming machines and poker games. The company's gaming machines include games such as Monopoly, Hollywood Squares, Men in Black, World Series of Poker and Powerball. WMS sells and leases its gaming machines through 31 salespeople in offices in the U.S. and 12 salespeople in its international offices. In 2006, the firm acquired the privately-held Orion Financement Company B.V., a Netherlands-based holding company that designs, manufactures and sells gaming machines.

WMS offers its employees medical, dental, vision and life insurance; a 401(k) plan; and tuition reimbursement.

FINANCIALS: Sales and profits are in thousands of dollars—add 000 to get the full amount. 2007 Note: Financial information for 2007 was not available for all companies at press time.

2007 Sales: $539,800	2007 Profits: $48,900	**U.S. Stock Ticker: WMS**
2006 Sales: $451,200	2006 Profits: $33,300	Int'l Ticker: Int'l Exchange:
2005 Sales: $388,400	2005 Profits: $21,200	Employees: 1,414
2004 Sales: $230,200	2004 Profits: $- 900	Fiscal Year Ends: 6/30
2003 Sales: $178,700	2003 Profits: $-8,300	Parent Company:

SALARIES/BENEFITS:

Pension Plan:	ESOP Stock Plan:	Profit Sharing:	Top Exec. Salary: $737,500	Bonus: $493,670
Savings Plan: Y	Stock Purch. Plan:		Second Exec. Salary: $470,000	Bonus: $248,749

OTHER THOUGHTS:

Apparent Women Officers or Directors: 1
Hot Spot for Advancement for Women/Minorities:

LOCATIONS: ("Y" = Yes)

West:	Southwest:	Midwest:	Southeast:	Northeast:	International:
Y		Y	Y	Y	Y

WPP GROUP PLC

www.wpp.com

Industry Group Code: 541810 Ranks within this company's industry group: Sales: 1 Profits: 1

Print Media/Publishing:	Movies:	Equipment/Supplies:		Broadcast/Cable:	Music/Audio:	Sports/Games/Gambling:
Newspapers:	Movie Theaters:	Equipment/Supplies:		Broadcast TV:	Music Production:	Games/Sports:
Magazines:	Movie Production:	Gambling Equipment:		Cable TV:	Retail Music:	Retail Games Stores:
Books:	TV/Video Prod.:	Special Services:	Y	Satellite Broadcast:	Retail Audio Equip.:	Stadiums/Teams:
Book Stores:	Video Rental:	Advertising Services:	Y	Radio:	Music Print./Dist.:	Gambling/Casinos:
Distribution/Printing:	Video Distribution:	Info. Sys. Software:		Online Information:	Multimedia:	Rides/Theme Parks:

TYPES OF BUSINESS:

Advertising & Marketing Services
Communications Consulting
Human Resources Consulting
IT Consulting
Advertising Consulting
Brand Research & Tools
Public Relations

BRANDS/DIVISIONS/AFFILIATES:

Ogilvy & Mather Worldwide
BRANDZ
BrandAsset Valuator
PRecision
DSG Strategies, Inc.
Black Arc Advertising
Burson-Marsteller
Shaw Marketing Group

CONTACTS: Note: Officers with more than one job title may be intentionally listed here more than once.

Martin Sorrell, CEO
Tro Piliguian, COO/Exec. VP
Marie W. Capes, Corp. Sec.
Mark Read, Dir.-Strategy
Feona McEwan, Group Dir.-Comm.
Fran Butera, Dir.-Investor Rel.
Paul Richardson, Group Dir.-Finance
Richard Oldworth, CEO-Buchanan Comm.
Jon Cook, Pres., VML/Managing Partner
Scott McCormick, Chief Vision Officer
Eric Baumgartne, Chief Creative Officer
Philip Lader, Chmn.
Lee Doyle, CEO-Mediaedge & North American Oper.

Phone: 44-20-7408-2204	Fax: 44-20-7493-6819
Toll-Free:	
Address: 27 Farm St., London, W1J 5RJ UK	

GROWTH PLANS/SPECIAL FEATURES:

WPP Group plc is one of the five largest global management firms for communications consulting and advertising, with more than 2,000 offices in 106 countries. The company's revenue is generated in a variety of industry segments, including advertising and media information; consultancy; public relations; branding and identity; healthcare communications; and direct, promotion and relationship marketing. Through its more than 70 subsidiaries, the group offers assistance in human resources, information technology, public relations, brand development, property management, procurement, practice development and knowledge sharing. Each of the company's subsidiaries is a distinct entity with capabilities and resources of its own, for which WPP provides client and employee aid. The firm serves its subsidiaries through initiatives such as a collection of proprietary products, such as BRANDZ, the world's largest brand research study; BrandAsset Valuator, a tool used for the development of brands and brand names; and PRecision, a toolkit for the measurement of media and delivery impact. In addition, the group manages the Knowledge Bank, a collection of studies, essays and analyses from members of the group. Recent acquisitions include Aqua Online; Blue Interactive Marketing Ltd.; 24/7 Real Media Inc. for $649 million; Schematic; Blast Radius; and Public Strategies, Inc. Additionally, it acquired stakes in PBN Holdings; Dawson International Marketing Communications; OOT S.r.l, an Italian digital interactive agency; Invidi Technologies Corp.; and India-based Quasar Media Private Limited. In December 2007, WPP entered into a $4.5 billion partnership with Dell Inc. to create a new global integrated marketing and communications agency.

FINANCIALS: Sales and profits are in thousands of dollars—add 000 to get the full amount. 2007 Note: Financial information for 2007 was not available for all companies at press time.

2007 Sales: $	2007 Profits: $	**U.S. Stock Ticker: WPPGY**
2006 Sales: $11,436,000	2006 Profits: $934,266	**Int'l Ticker: WPP** Int'l Exchange: London-LSE
2005 Sales: $9,244,400	2005 Profits: $684,700	Employees: 91,000
2004 Sales: $8,243,000	2004 Profits: $560,400	Fiscal Year Ends: 12/31
2003 Sales: $7,542,790	2003 Profits: $564,300	Parent Company:

SALARIES/BENEFITS:

Pension Plan:	ESOP Stock Plan:	Profit Sharing:	Top Exec. Salary: $1,334,010	Bonus: $24,000
Savings Plan:	Stock Purch. Plan:		Second Exec. Salary: $533,990	Bonus: $95,640

OTHER THOUGHTS:

Apparent Women Officers or Directors: 2
Hot Spot for Advancement for Women/Minorities: Y

LOCATIONS: ("Y" = Yes)

West:	Southwest:	Midwest:	Southeast:	Northeast:	International:
Y	Y	Y	Y	Y	Y

Note: Financial information, benefits and other data can change quickly and may vary from those stated here.

WYNN RESORTS LIMITED

www.wynnresorts.com

Industry Group Code: 721120 Ranks within this company's industry group: Sales: 5   Profits: 2

Print Media/Publishing:	Movies:	Equipment/Supplies:	Broadcast/Cable:	Music/Audio:	Sports/Games/Gambling:	
Newspapers:	Movie Theaters:	Equipment/Supplies:	Broadcast TV:	Music Production:	Games/Sports:	
Magazines:	Movie Production:	Gambling Equipment:	Cable TV:	Retail Music:	Retail Games Stores:	
Books:	TV/Video Prod.:	Special Services:	Satellite Broadcast:	Retail Audio Equip.:	Stadiums/Teams:	Y
Book Stores:	Video Rental:	Advertising Services:	Radio:	Music Print./Dist.:	Gambling/Casinos:	
Distribution/Printing:	Video Distribution:	Info. Sys. Software:	Online Information:	Multimedia:	Rides/Theme Parks:	

TYPES OF BUSINESS:

Hotel Casinos

BRANDS/DIVISIONS/AFFILIATES:

Wynn Las Vegas
Wynn Macau

CONTACTS: *Note: Officers with more than one job title may be intentionally listed here more than once.*

Stephen A. Wynn, CEO
Marc D. Schorr, COO
Ronald J. Kramer, Pres.
John Strzemp, CFO/Exec. VP
Kim Sinatra, General Counsel/Sr. VP/Corp. Sec.
Matt Maddox, Sr. VP-Bus. Dev.
Matt Maddox, Treas.
Linda Chen, Pres., Wynn International Mktg., Ltd.
Grant R. Bowie, Pres., Wynn Resorts Macau
Andrew Pascal, Pres./COO-Wynn Las Vegas, LLC
Scott Peterson, CFO-Wynn Resorts Macau
Stephen A. Wynn, Chmn.

Phone: 702-770-7555	Fax: 702-697-5009
Toll-Free:	
Address: 3131 Las Vegas Blvd. S., Las Vegas, NV 89109 US	

GROWTH PLANS/SPECIAL FEATURES:

Wynn Resorts, Ltd. is a leading developer, owner and operator of destination casino resorts. It owns and operates the Wynn Las Vegas, a destination casino resort on the Strip in Las Vegas, Nevada; the company is also constructing and will operate the Wynn Macau, a casino resort development located in the Macau Special Administrative Region of China. Wynn Las Vegas offers 2,716 rooms and suites in its 45-story tower, plus 36 fairway villas and six private-entry villas for its premium guests. The approximately 111,000-square-foot casino features 132 table games, a baccarat salon, private VIP gaming rooms, a poker room, 1,974 slot machines, a race and sports book and a keno lounge. The resort's 22 food and beverage outlets feature six fine dining restaurants, including restaurants helmed by award winning chefs. Wynn Las Vegas also offers a nightclub, an ultra-lounge, a spa and salon, a Ferrari and Maserati automobile dealership, wedding chapels, an 18-hole golf course, approximately 223,000 square feet of meeting space and an approximately 74,000-square-foot retail promenade featuring boutiques from Chanel, Christian Dior, Graff, Manolo Blahnik, Jean-Paul Gaultier and Louis Vuitton. Wynn Las Vegas also has two showrooms, The Wynn Theater and The Broadway Theater. Since opening, Wynn Las Vegas has experienced an overall 94.4% average occupancy and $287 average daily room rate, which compares favorably to the overall 89.7% average occupancy and $120 average daily room rate of the Las Vegas Strip. Wynn Macau opened to the public in September 2006. This first phase of Wynn Macau features approximately 600 hotel rooms and suites, approximately 220 table games and approximately 380 slot machines in approximately 100,000 square feet of casino gaming space, seven restaurants, approximately 26,000 square feet of retail space, a spa and salon, entertainment lounges and meeting facilities.

Wynn Resorts offers its employees financial assistance with continuing education, an employee assistance program, annual social events and athletic team sponsorship.

FINANCIALS: Sales and profits are in thousands of dollars—add 000 to get the full amount. 2007 Note: Financial information for 2007 was not available for all companies at press time.

2007 Sales: $	2007 Profits: $	U.S. Stock Ticker: WYNN
2006 Sales: $1,432,257	2006 Profits: $628,728	Int'l Ticker: Int'l Exchange:
2005 Sales: $721,981	2005 Profits: $-90,836	Employees: 15,500
2004 Sales: $ 195	2004 Profits: $-204,171	Fiscal Year Ends: 12/31
2003 Sales: $1,018	2003 Profits: $-40,099	Parent Company:

SALARIES/BENEFITS:

Pension Plan:	ESOP Stock Plan:	Profit Sharing:	Top Exec. Salary: $2,343,151	Bonus: $3,221,833
Savings Plan: Y	Stock Purch. Plan:		Second Exec. Salary: $1,271,538	Bonus: $1,907,307

OTHER THOUGHTS:

Apparent Women Officers or Directors: 2
Hot Spot for Advancement for Women/Minorities:

LOCATIONS: ("Y" = Yes)

West:	Southwest:	Midwest:	Southeast:	Northeast:	International:
Y					Y

XINHUA FINANCE LIMITED

www.xfn.com

Industry Group Code: 514100   Ranks within this company's industry group: Sales: Profits:

Print Media/Publishing:	Movies:	Equipment/Supplies:	Broadcast/Cable:	Music/Audio:	Sports/Games/Gambling:
Newspapers:	Movie Theaters:	Equipment/Supplies:	Broadcast TV:	Music Production:	Games/Sports:
Magazines:	Movie Production:	Gambling Equipment:	Cable TV:	Retail Music:	Retail Games Stores:
Books:	TV/Video Prod.:	Special Services:	Satellite Broadcast:	Retail Audio Equip.:	Stadiums/Teams:
Book Stores:	Video Rental:	Advertising Services:	Radio:	Music Print./Dist.:	Gambling/Casinos:
Distribution/Printing:	Video Distribution:	Info. Sys. Software:	Online Information:	Multimedia:	Rides/Theme Parks:

TYPES OF BUSINESS:

Financial Data Publishing
Financial News
Financial Research
Advertising Services

BRANDS/DIVISIONS/AFFILIATES:

XFMedia
Xinhua Far East China Rating
Merchant
JCBN Group
Xinhua Finance Media (XFMedia)

CONTACTS: Note: Officers with more than one job title may be intentionally listed here more than once.

Fredy Bush, CEO
Daniel J. Connell, COO
Jae Young Lie, Pres.
Gordon T. Lau, CFO
John Mclean, Dir.-Legal Affairs
Jennifer Chan, Dir.-Investor Rel.
Yoshitaka Yamada, Dir.-Investor Rel., Japan
Jane Hartley, CEO-G7 Group, Inc.
Ji Guang Wu, Chmn.

Phone: 852-31963939	Fax: 852-31010332
Toll-Free:	
Address: 2003-5 Vicwood Plz. 199 Des Voeux Road Central, Hong Kong, China	

GROWTH PLANS/SPECIAL FEATURES:

Xinhua Financial Limited is a leading financial information and media services provider in China. The company operates in five segments: Indices, Ratings, Financial News, Investor Relation (IR) Services and Distribution. The Indices segment offers a broad series of benchmark and tradable indices to track the China and U.S. equity and bond markets. Through its subsidiaries, Merchant and Xinhua Far East China Rating, the company combines research and analytic tools to offer independent, forward-looking ratings assessments & opinions on Chinese companies and sectors. The financial news segment (consisting of 16 news bureaus globally) offers up-to-the-minute economic news and stories affecting the Chinese and world economies. The IR segment offers a full range of investor and public relations services, including the formulation and implementation of strategic capital market and media campaigns. The distribution division provides financial information products to financial institutions and corporations and high net worth individuals mainly in China. Currently, the company is using various financial mediums to build its media distribution capabilities to reach a wider audience in China. The company's subsidiary, Xinhua Finance Media (XFMedia), a leading diversified financial and entertainment media company, targets the growing high net worth population and is a key arm in helping Xinhua Financial Limited build its distribution sector by offering advertising, broadcast, print, production and research services. The firm also offers tailor-made, customized integrated solutions for its clients, encompassing Xinhua Finance's full range of core products and distribution channels. In 2007, the firm's subsidiary XFMedia acquired JCBN Group, an advertising group with operations in Shanghai, Beijing and Hong Kong.

The company hires seasoned employees along with new college graduates and offers all employees a balanced combination of growth, challenge, collegiality and entrepreneurship.

FINANCIALS: Sales and profits are in thousands of dollars—add 000 to get the full amount. 2007 Note: Financial information for 2007 was not available for all companies at press time.

2007 Sales: $	2007 Profits: $	U.S. Stock Ticker: XFML
2006 Sales: $	2006 Profits: $	Int'l Ticker: Int'l Exchange:
2005 Sales: $	2005 Profits: $	Employees:
2004 Sales: $	2004 Profits: $	Fiscal Year Ends:
2003 Sales: $	2003 Profits: $	Parent Company:

SALARIES/BENEFITS:

Pension Plan:	ESOP Stock Plan:	Profit Sharing:	Top Exec. Salary: $	Bonus: $
Savings Plan:	Stock Purch. Plan:		Second Exec. Salary: $	Bonus: $

OTHER THOUGHTS:

Apparent Women Officers or Directors: 3
Hot Spot for Advancement for Women/Minorities: Y

LOCATIONS: ("Y" = Yes)

West:	Southwest:	Midwest:	Southeast:	Northeast:	International: Y

Note: Financial information, benefits and other data can change quickly and may vary from those stated here.

XINHUA FINANCE MEDIA LIMITED
www.xinhuafinancemedia.com
Industry Group Code: 511000 Ranks within this company's industry group: Sales: Profits:

Print Media/Publishing:		Movies:		Equipment/Supplies:		Broadcast/Cable:		Music/Audio:		Sports/Games/Gambling:	
Newspapers:	Y	Movie Theaters:		Equipment/Supplies:		Broadcast TV:	Y	Music Production:		Games/Sports:	
Magazines:	Y	Movie Production:		Gambling Equipment:		Cable TV:		Retail Music:		Retail Games Stores:	
Books:		TV/Video Prod.:	Y	Special Services:		Satellite Broadcast:		Retail Audio Equip.:		Stadiums/Teams:	
Book Stores:		Video Rental:		Advertising Services:	Y	Radio:		Music Print./Dist.:		Gambling/Casinos:	
Distribution/Printing:		Video Distribution:		Info. Sys. Software:		Online Information:		Multimedia:		Rides/Theme Parks:	

TYPES OF BUSINESS:
Entertainment Media
Advertising
Television & Radio Broadcasting
Print Publications
Television Production
Research

BRANDS/DIVISIONS/AFFILIATES:
Small World Television
JCBN Company Limited
Xinhua Finance Limited

CONTACTS: *Note: Officers with more than one job title may be intentionally listed here more than once.*
Fredy Bush, CEO
Zhu Shan, COO
Graham Earnshaw, Pres.
Andrew Chang, CFO
Stephen X. Wei, Pres., Research Group
Jennifer Chan Lyman, Dir.-Investor Rel.
Henry Heung-Ming, Internal Auditor
Teddy L. Weidong, Pres., Advertising Group
Alex F.C. Tak, Pres., Print Group (Magazine)
Zhao Li, Pres., Print Group (Newspaper)
Yu Gang, Pres., Production Group
Fredy Bush, Chmn.

Phone: 86-10-8567-6000	Fax: 86-21-6448-4955
Toll-Free:	
Address: 6A Jian Wai Ave., Tower D, Beijing, 100022 China	

GROWTH PLANS/SPECIAL FEATURES:
Xinhua Finance Media Ltd. (XF Media), a subsidiary of Xinhua Finance, is one of China's leading financial and entertainment media companies, focused on China's expanding high net worth population. The firm utilizes TV, radio, newspapers, magazines and other distribution channels to reach its target audience, and is divided into five business groups: advertising, broadcast, print, production and research. The advertising group utilizes nationwide television, radio, newspaper, magazines, online and outdoor media in China to produce and place integrated advertising campaigns. The broadcast group produces and distributes content for both television and radio; sells advertising and provides consulting services to both TV and radio stations; and organizes financial and economic themed events. This segment also provides mobile value-added services including text messaging, interactive voice response and online gaming, as well as wireless marketing services. The print group contains both magazines and newspapers, having exclusive rights to sell advertising for and provide consulting services to Money Journal; Chinese Venture; Fund Observer; and Economic Observer. The production group creates TV productions, animated content, and graphic design focused on advertising. The research group offers advertisers research data and market information to better understand targeted customer bases. This group also assists XF Media's other business groups in choosing content that is appropriate to the targeted audience. This segment has research partnerships in over 200 cities throughout China, and counts among its customers Wal-Mart, Pepsi (China) and Wrigley. In March 2007, the firm listed on the Nasdaq Global Market, and raised $300 million to support strategic acquisitions of complementary businesses. In August 2007, XF Media acquired a 70% interest in Small World Television, a production and consulting company, for $5 million. In November 2007, the company acquired JCBN Company Ltd., an advertising company with operations in Shanghai, Beijing and Hong Kong, for $43 million.

FINANCIALS: Sales and profits are in thousands of dollars—add 000 to get the full amount. 2007 Note: Financial information for 2007 was not available for all companies at press time.

2007 Sales: $	2007 Profits: $	U.S. Stock Ticker: XFML
2006 Sales: $	2006 Profits: $	Int'l Ticker: Int'l Exchange:
2005 Sales: $	2005 Profits: $	Employees:
2004 Sales: $	2004 Profits: $	Fiscal Year Ends:
2003 Sales: $	2003 Profits: $	Parent Company: XINHUA FINANCE LIMITED

SALARIES/BENEFITS:
Pension Plan:	ESOP Stock Plan:	Profit Sharing:	Top Exec. Salary: $	Bonus: $
Savings Plan:	Stock Purch. Plan:		Second Exec. Salary: $	Bonus: $

OTHER THOUGHTS:
Apparent Women Officers or Directors: 2
Hot Spot for Advancement for Women/Minorities:

LOCATIONS: ("Y" = Yes)
West:	Southwest:	Midwest:	Southeast:	Northeast:	International: Y

XM SATELLITE RADIO HOLDINGS INC   www.xmradio.com

Industry Group Code: 513111A Ranks within this company's industry group: Sales: 1   Profits: 1

Print Media/Publishing:	Movies:	Equipment/Supplies:	Broadcast/Cable:	Music/Audio:	Sports/Games/Gambling:
Newspapers:	Movie Theaters:	Equipment/Supplies:	Broadcast TV:	Music Production:	Games/Sports:
Magazines:	Movie Production:	Gambling Equipment:	Cable TV:	Retail Music:	Retail Games Stores:
Books:	TV/Video Prod.:	Special Services:	Satellite Broadcast:	Retail Audio Equip.:	Stadiums/Teams:
Book Stores:	Video Rental:	Advertising Services:	Radio:	Music Print./Dist.:	Gambling/Casinos:
Distribution/Printing:	Video Distribution:	Info. Sys. Software:	Online Information:	Multimedia:	Rides/Theme Parks:

TYPES OF BUSINESS:

Satellite Radio Broadcasting
Radio Programming

BRANDS/DIVISIONS/AFFILIATES:

XM Satellite Radio, Inc.
XM Originals
XM Canada
XM Public Radio
XM NavTraffic

CONTACTS: *Note: Officers with more than one job title may be intentionally listed here more than once.*

Nate Davis, Interim CEO
Nate Davis, COO
Nate Davis, Pres.
Joseph J. Euteneuer, CFO/Exec. VP
Vernon Irvin, Chief Mktg. Officer
Stell Patsiokas, Exec. VP-Tech.
Eric Logan, Exec. VP-Programming
Stell Patsiokas, Exec. VP-Eng.
Joseph M. Titlebaum, General Counsel
Joe Zarella, Exec. VP-Oper.
Dara F. Altman, Exec. VP-Bus. & Legal Affairs
Steve Cook, Exec. VP-Automotive Mktg.
Dan Murphy, Exec. VP-Retail Aftermarket Dist.
Gary M. Parsons, Chmn.

Phone: 202-380-4000	**Fax:** 202-380-4500
Toll-Free: 866-967-2346	
Address: 1500 Eckington Pl. NE, Washington, DC 20002-2194 US	

GROWTH PLANS/SPECIAL FEATURES:

XM Satellite Radio Holdings, Inc. is a nationwide provider of satellite digital radio service to vehicle, home and portable radios. It serves over 230 million vehicles and 110 million households in the U.S., to which it offers more than 170 channels of which 67 are commercial-free music channels; 34 are news, talk and entertainment channels; 39 are sports coverage channels; 21 are local traffic and weather channels; and one is an emergency alert channel. Customers pay a monthly subscription of $12.95 to access the satellite signal on their XM radio set. As of mid-2007, the company had more than 8.5 million subscribers. Its commercial free music channels span a wide range of genres including country, pop, Christian, rock, hip-hop, jazz/blues, Latin, classical and folk/bluegrass. The sports talk and sports coverage radio channels cover college football, men's and women's basketball, tennis, NASCAR and professional golf. ESPN and FoxSports supplement the company's sports talk lineup. The talk radio channels feature programming that includes Fox News, CNN, ABC News & Talk, BBC Worldservice and C-SPAN, with business news provided by CNBC. Porsche, Toyota and General Motors each have long-term contracts with the company to offer factory-installed XM radios into all of their major models. XM radios are available at national electronics retailers under a variety of brand names including Sony, Delphi, and Alpine. Some of the newer models have customizable stock tickers, sports features and XM NavTraffic, a GPS traffic navigation system. Also, through a music service partnership with Cingular Wireless, cell phone customers are able listen to a variety of XM's commercial-free music channels through the XM Radio Mobile service for $8.99 per month. In February 2007, XM agreed to a merger of equals with Sirius Satellite Radio, Inc. The $13 billion merger is subject to massive regulatory oversight, which may derail the deal.

FINANCIALS: Sales and profits are in thousands of dollars—add 000 to get the full amount. 2007 Note: Financial information for 2007 was not available for all companies at press time.

2007 Sales: $	2007 Profits: $	**U.S. Stock Ticker:** XMSR
2006 Sales: $933,417	2006 Profits: $-718,872	**Int'l Ticker:** Int'l Exchange:
2005 Sales: $558,266	2005 Profits: $-666,715	Employees: 860
2004 Sales: $244,443	2004 Profits: $-642,368	Fiscal Year Ends: 12/31
2003 Sales: $91,781	2003 Profits: $-584,535	Parent Company:

SALARIES/BENEFITS:

Pension Plan:	ESOP Stock Plan:	Profit Sharing: Y	Top Exec. Salary: $620,480	Bonus: $
Savings Plan: Y	Stock Purch. Plan: Y		Second Exec. Salary: $460,336	Bonus: $

OTHER THOUGHTS:

Apparent Women Officers or Directors: 1
Hot Spot for Advancement for Women/Minorities: Y

LOCATIONS: ("Y" = Yes)

West:	Southwest:	Midwest:	Southeast:	Northeast:	International:
		Y	Y	Y	Y

Note: Financial information, benefits and other data can change quickly and may vary from those stated here.

YAHOO! INC

www.yahoo.com

Industry Group Code: 514199B Ranks within this company's industry group: Sales: 2   Profits: 2

Print Media/Publishing:	Movies:	Equipment/Supplies:		Broadcast/Cable:	Music/Audio:	Sports/Games/Gambling:
Newspapers:	Movie Theaters:	Equipment/Supplies:		Broadcast TV:	Music Production:	Games/Sports:
Magazines:	Movie Production:	Gambling Equipment:		Cable TV:	Retail Music:	Retail Games Stores:
Books:	TV/Video Prod.:	Special Services:	Y	Satellite Broadcast:	Retail Audio Equip.:	Stadiums/Teams:
Book Stores:	Video Rental:	Advertising Services:	Y	Radio:	Music Print./Dist.:	Gambling/Casinos:
Distribution/Printing:	Video Distribution:	Info. Sys. Software:		Online Information:	Multimedia:	Rides/Theme Parks:

TYPES OF BUSINESS:

Online Portal-Search Engine
Broadcast Media
Job Placement Services
Paid Positioning Services
Advertising Services
Online Business & Consumer Information
Search Technology Licensing
E-Commerce

BRANDS/DIVISIONS/AFFILIATES:

Yahoo.com
Yahoo! Mail
Yahoo! Messenger
Yahoo! Shopping
Gmarket Inc.
HotJobs.com, Ltd.
BlueLithium
Right Media, Inc.

CONTACTS: *Note: Officers with more than one job title may be intentionally listed here more than once.*

Jerry Yang, CEO
Susan Decker, Pres.
Blake Jorgensen, CFO/Exec. VP
Allen Olivo, Interim Chief Mktg. Officer
Libby Sartain, Chief People Yahoo!
Prabhakar Raghavan, Head-Yahoo! Research
Usama Fayyad, Chief Data Officer
Jeff Weiner, Exec. VP-Networks Div.
Qi Lu, Sr. VP-Eng. for Search & Search Mktg.
Michael Callahan, General Counsel/Sec./Exec. VP
Toby R. Coppel, Sr. VP-Corp. Dev.
Jeff Weiner, Sr. VP-Search & Marketplace
Jill Nash, Chief Comm. Officer
Michael Murray, Chief Acct. Officer/Sr. VP-Finance
Usama Fayyad, Exec. VP-Research & Strategic Data Solutions
Gregory Coleman, Exec. VP-Global Sales
Ash Patel, Exec. VP-Platforms & Infrastructure Div.
Michael Walrath, Sr. VP-Right Media Exchange
Terry Semel, Chmn.

Phone: 408-349-3300	Fax: 408-349-3301
Toll-Free:	
Address: 701 First Ave., Sunnyvale, CA 94089 US	

GROWTH PLANS/SPECIAL FEATURES:

Yahoo!, Inc. is a provider of online products and services to consumers and businesses worldwide. In December 2006, the company announced a reorganization of its structure to align itself with the demands of three key customers: audiences, advertisers and publishers. Under the realigned structure, the company has two main business segments: The Audience Group; and the Advertiser & Publisher Group; both of which will be supported by the Technology Group. The Audience Group focuses on growing and developing the typically free Yahoo! Tools used by everyday consumers, such as Yahoo! Mail, Yahoo! Messenger, Yahoo! Calendar, Yahoo! Chat, Yahoo! Greetings, Yahoo! Clubs and Yahoo! Photos. Commerce services include Yahoo! Shopping, Yahoo! Auctions, Yahoo! Finance and Yahoo! Travel. The Advertisers & Publishers Group was created by combining Yahoo!'s marketing solutions, sales teams and distribution partners to streamline the firm's advertising and marketing offerings. The Technology Group engineers and provides upkeep for the advertising and Internet platforms. Yahoo! is present in 20 markets in Europe, Latin America, the Asia Pacific and Canada; and is available in twenty languages. The company has entered into relationships with business partners that offer content, technology and distribution capabilities, which permit the company to bring Yahoo!-branded, targeted media products to the market more quickly. Yahoo! owns a 10% stake in Gmarket Inc., an e-commerce marketplace provider in Korea. The company also operates HotJobs.com, Ltd., a leading Internet job placement and recruiting company. In September 2007, the company agreed to acquire BlueLithium, a leading online global ad network provider, for $300 million. In July 2007, it acquired Right Media, Inc., which it had already owned 20% of, for $650 million.

Yahoo! offers employees discount movie passes; commuter subsidies; a game room; health club membership and massages; on-site dental care, car washes and haircuts; and tuition reimbursement.

FINANCIALS: Sales and profits are in thousands of dollars—add 000 to get the full amount. 2007 Note: Financial information for 2007 was not available for all companies at press time.

2007 Sales: $	2007 Profits: $	**U.S. Stock Ticker: YHOO**
2006 Sales: $6,425,679	2006 Profits: $751,391	**Int'l Ticker:** Int'l Exchange:
2005 Sales: $5,257,668	2005 Profits: $1,896,230	Employees: 11,400
2004 Sales: $3,575,000	2004 Profits: $839,553	Fiscal Year Ends: 12/31
2003 Sales: $1,625,097	2003 Profits: $237,879	Parent Company:

SALARIES/BENEFITS:

Pension Plan:	ESOP Stock Plan:	Profit Sharing:	Top Exec. Salary: $500,000	Bonus: $900,000
Savings Plan: Y	Stock Purch. Plan: Y		Second Exec. Salary: $500,000	Bonus: $850,000

OTHER THOUGHTS:

Apparent Women Officers or Directors: 5
Hot Spot for Advancement for Women/Minorities: Y

LOCATIONS: ("Y" = Yes)

West:	Southwest:	Midwest:	Southeast:	Northeast:	International:
Y	Y	Y	Y	Y	Y

Note: Financial information, benefits and other data can change quickly and may vary from those stated here.

YAHOO! SEARCH MARKETING GROUP

searchmarketing.yahoo.com

Industry Group Code: 541810A Ranks within this company's industry group: Sales: Profits:

Print Media/Publishing:	Movies:	Equipment/Supplies:		Broadcast/Cable:	Music/Audio:	Sports/Games/Gambling:
Newspapers:	Movie Theaters:	Equipment/Supplies:		Broadcast TV:	Music Production:	Games/Sports:
Magazines:	Movie Production:	Gambling Equipment:		Cable TV:	Retail Music:	Retail Games Stores:
Books:	TV/Video Prod.:	Special Services:		Satellite Broadcast:	Retail Audio Equip.:	Stadiums/Teams:
Book Stores:	Video Rental:	Advertising Services:	Y	Radio:	Music Print./Dist.:	Gambling/Casinos:
Distribution/Printing:	Video Distribution:	Info. Sys. Software:		Online Information:	Multimedia:	Rides/Theme Parks:

TYPES OF BUSINESS:
Online Marketing & Advertising

BRANDS/DIVISIONS/AFFILIATES:
Sponsored Search
Content Match
Ambassador Directory

CONTACTS: Note: Officers with more than one job title may be intentionally listed here more than once.
Qi Lu, Sr. VP-Eng. Search & Search Mktg.
Kristen Wareham, Sr. Mgr.-Comm.
Jeff Winer, Sr. VP-Search & Marketplace, Yahoo!
Steve Mitgang, Sr. VP-Advertising Platforms & Products, Yahoo!

Phone: 818-524-3000	Fax: 818-524-3001
Toll-Free: 888-811-4686	
Address: 3333 Empire Ave., Burbank, CA 91504 US	

GROWTH PLANS/SPECIAL FEATURES:
Yahoo! Search Marketing Group (YSMG), a subsidiary of Yahoo!, offers paid search results advertising services. The Sponsored Search option allows businesses to create ads that appear alongside search results, activated by particular key words. When a Yahoo! user runs a search containing those key words, corresponding advertisements appear alongside the algorithmic search results. The advertising company pays only when a customer clicks their ad. Complementing the Sponsored Search is Content Match, in which company ads appear alongside algorithmic search results that include related content. The firm also offers access to the Ambassador Directory, a list of Yahoo! Search Marketing accredited agencies and search engine marketers that are available to help individual businesses drive targeted sales leads through Sponsored Search. YSMG is headquartered in Burbank, California, with additional offices in New York, New York; Chicago, Illinois; and Palo Alto, California; and international subsidiary offices in Europe, Asia and Australia.

Employee benefits include medical, dental and vision coverage; employee stock purchase plan; 401(k) with company match; tuition reimbursement; and free lattes.

FINANCIALS: Sales and profits are in thousands of dollars—add 000 to get the full amount. 2007 Note: Financial information for 2007 was not available for all companies at press time.

2007 Sales: $	2007 Profits: $	U.S. Stock Ticker: Subsidiary
2006 Sales: $	2006 Profits: $	Int'l Ticker: Int'l Exchange:
2005 Sales: $	2005 Profits: $	Employees: 876
2004 Sales: $	2004 Profits: $	Fiscal Year Ends: 12/31
2003 Sales: $	2003 Profits: $	Parent Company: YAHOO! INC

SALARIES/BENEFITS:

Pension Plan:	ESOP Stock Plan:	Profit Sharing:	Top Exec. Salary: $	Bonus: $37,500
Savings Plan: Y	Stock Purch. Plan: Y		Second Exec. Salary: $85,000	Bonus: $85,000

OTHER THOUGHTS:
Apparent Women Officers or Directors: 1
Hot Spot for Advancement for Women/Minorities:

LOCATIONS: ("Y" = Yes)

West:	Southwest:	Midwest:	Southeast:	Northeast:	International:
Y		Y		Y	Y

YOUBET.COM INC

www.youbet.com

Industry Group Code: 713210 **Ranks within this company's industry group:** Sales: 7 Profits: 9

Print Media/Publishing:	Movies:	Equipment/Supplies:		Broadcast/Cable:	Music/Audio:	Sports/Games/Gambling:	
Newspapers:	Movie Theaters:	Equipment/Supplies:		Broadcast TV:	Music Production:	Games/Sports:	
Magazines:	Movie Production:	Gambling Equipment:		Cable TV:	Retail Music:	Retail Games Stores:	
Books:	TV/Video Prod.:	Special Services:	Y	Satellite Broadcast:	Retail Audio Equip.:	Stadiums/Teams:	
Book Stores:	Video Rental:	Advertising Services:		Radio:	Music Print./Dist.:	Gambling/Casinos:	Y
Distribution/Printing:	Video Distribution:	Info. Sys. Software:		Online Information:	Multimedia:	Rides/Theme Parks:	

TYPES OF BUSINESS:

Online Gambling
Horse Racetrack Wagering
Pari-Mutuel Wagering
Horse Racing Information
mobile wagering

BRANDS/DIVISIONS/AFFILIATES:

You Bet Network
Youbet Advantage
Youbet.com TotalAccess
Youbet Express
Players Trust
International Racing Group
United Tote
Bruen Productions International, Inc.

CONTACTS: *Note: Officers with more than one job title may be intentionally listed here more than once.*

Gary W. Sproule, CEO
Gary W. Sproule, COO
James A. Burk, CFO
Thomas L. Levenick, VP-Mktg. & Sales
Scott Soloman, Corp. Sec.
Victor Gallo, VP-Bus. Dev.
Michael L. Knapp, Dir-New Product Integration
Jeff Franklin, Pres., Youbet Online Services
Todd Galbate, VP-Client Svcs.
Louis J. Tavano, Gen. Mng.-Int'l Racing Corp.

Phone: 818-668-2100	**Fax:** 818-668-2101
Toll-Free: 888-968-2388	
Address: 5901 De Soto Ave., Woodland Hills, CA 91367 US	

GROWTH PLANS/SPECIAL FEATURES:

Youbet.com, Inc. is a leading brand name for online event sports entertainment, pari-mutuel wagering and other types of online gaming. Its principal product, the You Bet Network, allows subscribers to wager on live events online and on all major racetracks in 41 states. To date, the company has processed over $1 billion in wagers. Network members can watch events, access a database of handicapping information and wager on a selection of coast-to-coast thoroughbred and harness horse races via a closed-loop network. You Bet Advantage is the only player incentive program of its kind in the U.S. Virtually 100% of U.S., Canadian and Australian horse racing content is available 24 hours a day. The network is interactive and provides a real-time environment. It also features commingled track pools, live audio and video and up-to-the-minute information from the tracks. Youbet.com operates Youbet.com TotalAccess, an Oregon-based hub for the acceptance and placement of wagers. The company has also developed a web-based application, Youbet Express, to enhance and improve the network. Additionally, Youbet.com features Players Trust, which places players' deposits in the custody of a major U.S. financial institution. Youbet.com is the sole provider of horse racing information for CBS SportsLine.com, an official online wagering platform of Churchill Downs Incorporated and the Kentucky Derby. Youbet.com operates internationally in Australia, Canada, Hong Kong, Japan and South Africa through a wholly-owned subsidiary, International Racing Group. The firm also owns Bruen Productions International, Inc., a full-service broadcast production company, that produces its audio/video marketing content. In 2007, Youbet.com's subsidiary; United Tote, a global manufacturer and operator of pari-mutuel wagering systems; partnered with Phantom Fiber Corporation to offer mobile phone wagering.

Youbet.com's employee benefits include credit union membership, a 401(k) plan, discounted stock options, training and development programs, a wellness program, medical and dental benefits and flexible benefit accounts.

FINANCIALS: Sales and profits are in thousands of dollars—add 000 to get the full amount. 2007 Note: Financial information for 2007 was not available for all companies at press time.

2007 Sales: $	2007 Profits: $	**U.S. Stock Ticker:** UBET
2006 Sales: $136,683	2006 Profits: $-2,031	**Int'l Ticker:** Int'l Exchange:
2005 Sales: $88,837	2005 Profits: $5,691	Employees: 447
2004 Sales: $65,249	2004 Profits: $4,631	Fiscal Year Ends: 12/31
2003 Sales: $53,120	2003 Profits: $-4,003	Parent Company:

SALARIES/BENEFITS:

Pension Plan: Y	ESOP Stock Plan:	Profit Sharing: Y	Top Exec. Salary: $510,470	Bonus: $262,023
Savings Plan: Y	Stock Purch. Plan: Y		Second Exec. Salary: $344,500	Bonus: $137,800

OTHER THOUGHTS:

Apparent Women Officers or Directors:
Hot Spot for Advancement for Women/Minorities:

LOCATIONS: ("Y" = Yes)

West:	Southwest:	Midwest:	Southeast:	Northeast:	International:
Y					

Note: Financial information, benefits and other data can change quickly and may vary from those stated here.

YOUNG BROADCASTING INC   www.youngbroadcasting.com

Industry Group Code: 513120 Ranks within this company's industry group: Sales: 17 Profits: 16

Print Media/Publishing:	Movies:	Equipment/Supplies:		Broadcast/Cable:		Music/Audio:	Sports/Games/Gambling:
Newspapers:	Movie Theaters:	Equipment/Supplies:		Broadcast TV:	Y	Music Production:	Games/Sports:
Magazines:	Movie Production:	Gambling Equipment:		Cable TV:		Retail Music:	Retail Games Stores:
Books:	TV/Video Prod.:	Special Services:		Satellite Broadcast:		Retail Audio Equip.:	Stadiums/Teams:
Book Stores:	Video Rental:	Advertising Services:	Y	Radio:		Music Print./Dist.:	Gambling/Casinos:
Distribution/Printing:	Video Distribution:	Info. Sys. Software:		Online Information:		Multimedia:	Rides/Theme Parks:

TYPES OF BUSINESS:

Television Broadcasting
Advertising Sales

BRANDS/DIVISIONS/AFFILIATES:

Adam Young, Inc.

CONTACTS: *Note: Officers with more than one job title may be intentionally listed here more than once.*

Vincent J. Young, CEO
Deborah A. McDermott, Pres.
James A. Morgan, CFO/Exec. VP
Daniel R. Batchelor, VP-Sales
Peter Grazioli, CIO/VP-IT
James A. Morgan, Sec.
Robert Peterson, VP-Bus. Dev.
Stephen J. Baker, Controller/VP
Brian Greif, VP-News
Vincent J. Young, Chmn.

Phone: 212-754-7070	Fax: 212-758-1229
Toll-Free:	
Address: 599 Lexington Ave., New York, NY 10022 US	

GROWTH PLANS/SPECIAL FEATURES:

Young Broadcasting, Inc. owns and operates 10 television stations in various parts of the country. Five of the stations are ABC affiliates; three are CBS affiliates; one is an affiliate of MyNetworkTV; the last is affiliated with NBC. Its stations are WLNS-TV in Lansing, Michigan; KRON-TV in San Francisco, California; WBAY-TV in Green Bay, Wisconsin; KELO-TV in Sioux Falls, South Dakota; KLFY-TV in Lafayette, Louisiana; WTEN in Albany, New York; WRIC in Richmond, Virginia; WATE in Knoxville, Tennessee; KWQC in the Quad Cities (Davenport and Bettendorf, Iowa and Moline and Rock Island, Illinois); and WKRN in Nashville, Tennessee. Together these stations represent 6.02% of American television household coverage. In addition to national programming, stations owned by Young Broadcasting offer local news and sports programming. While compensation paid by the networks (ABC, etc.) to Young's affiliated stations for broadcasting network programming accounts for some of its revenue, advertising generates approximately 96% of its revenue. Local advertising, which typically runs for only a few weeks, generates 53% of Young's advertising revenue, and is sold by station sales staff. Young also owns and operates a national television advertising sales representation firm, Adam Young, Inc., which generates the remaining 47%. Young's corporate strategy is to acquire stations at below market prices and turn them into more profitable operations by streamlining costs and boosting advertising revenue. To spread its risk, the company has made a point of acquiring stations in geographically diverse areas. It foresees additional growth in television station acquisitions and in targeted marketing techniques. To that end, the company has focused its efforts on working closely with advertisers to target specific television audiences, and on upgrading sales staffs in its local markets. Young recently reached a three year joint sales and shared services agreement with WHTV-TV, a UPN affiliate operating in Jackson and Lansing, Michigan, owned by Spartan TV, LLC.

FINANCIALS: Sales and profits are in thousands of dollars—add 000 to get the full amount. 2007 Note: Financial information for 2007 was not available for all companies at press time.

2007 Sales: $	2007 Profits: $	U.S. Stock Ticker: YBTVA
2006 Sales: $225,153	2006 Profits: $-56,641	Int'l Ticker: Int'l Exchange:
2005 Sales: $197,478	2005 Profits: $-91,346	Employees: 1,265
2004 Sales: $225,524	2004 Profits: $-44,276	Fiscal Year Ends: 12/31
2003 Sales: $132,234	2003 Profits: $-49,117	Parent Company:

SALARIES/BENEFITS:

Pension Plan:	ESOP Stock Plan:	Profit Sharing:	Top Exec. Salary: $1,335,055	Bonus: $1,147,000
Savings Plan: Y	Stock Purch. Plan:		Second Exec. Salary: $701,955	Bonus: $442,000

OTHER THOUGHTS:

Apparent Women Officers or Directors: 1
Hot Spot for Advancement for Women/Minorities:

LOCATIONS: ("Y" = Yes)

West:	Southwest:	Midwest:	Southeast:	Northeast:	International:
Y		Y	Y	Y	

ZIFF DAVIS MEDIA INC   www.ziffdavis.com

Industry Group Code: 511120 Ranks within this company's industry group: Sales: Profits:

Print Media/Publishing:	Movies:	Equipment/Supplies:	Broadcast/Cable:	Music/Audio:	Sports/Games/Gambling:
Newspapers:	Movie Theaters:	Equipment/Supplies:	Broadcast TV:	Music Production:	Games/Sports:
Magazines: Y	Movie Production:	Gambling Equipment:	Cable TV:	Retail Music:	Retail Games Stores:
Books:	TV/Video Prod.:	Special Services: Y	Satellite Broadcast:	Retail Audio Equip.:	Stadiums/Teams:
Book Stores:	Video Rental:	Advertising Services:	Radio:	Music Print./Dist.:	Gambling/Casinos:
Distribution/Printing:	Video Distribution:	Info. Sys. Software:	Online Information:	Multimedia:	Rides/Theme Parks:

TYPES OF BUSINESS:

Online Content & Publishing
Computer & Technology Magazines
Conferences & Events
Custom Publishing
Research Services
Market Intelligence

BRANDS/DIVISIONS/AFFILIATES:

PC Magazine
1up.com
eWEEK
CIO Insight
MacWorld
Electronic Gaming Monthly
Baseline
Ziff Davis Holdings, Inc.

CONTACTS: Note: Officers with more than one job title may be intentionally listed here more than once.

Jason Young, CEO
Mark D. Moyer, CFO/Sr. VP
Ken Beach, Sr. VP-Corp. Sales
Beth Repeta, VP-Human Resources
Elda Vale, Sr. VP-Corp. Mktg. & Research
Norris Boothe, CTO/VP-Product Mktg.
Gregory Barton, General Counsel/Exec. VP-Licensing
Priscilla Ng, VP-e-Events
Randy Zane, VP-Corp. Comm.
Martha Schwartz, Sr. VP-Custom Solutions
Scott McCarthy, Pres., Game Group
Sloan Seymour, Pres., Enterprise Group
Jason Young, Pres., Consumer & Small Business Group
Robert F. Callahan, Chmn.
Suk Park, Managing Dir.-Ziff Davis Media Int'l

Phone: 212-503-3500	Fax: 212-503-4599
Toll-Free:	
Address: 28 E. 28th St., New York, NY 10016-7930 US	

GROWTH PLANS/SPECIAL FEATURES:

Ziff Davis Media, Inc. (ZDMI) is an integrated media company focused on the technology, video game and consumer lifestyle markets. The company is an information services provider of technology media including publications, web sites, conferences, events, e-seminars, e-newsletters, custom publishing, list rental, research and market intelligence. ZDMI's operations are organized into three operating units: Consumer/Small Business, responsible for PC Magazine; the Game Group, which includes 1up.com; and the Enterprise Group, which includes eWEEK. ZDMI licenses its content and brands in over 45 countries and in 13 languages worldwide. The firm's events business is organized under the Enterprise Group through Custom Solutions, which builds targeted events for the business and consumer technology communities. The ZDMI portfolio includes three print magazines and 15 web sites reaching over 26 million people per month in conjunction with event attendees. Its titles include PC Magazine, pcmagnetwork.com, eWEEK, Baseline, CIO Insight, Electronic Gaming Monthly, Computer Gaming World, ExtremeTech.com and GameVideos.com among others. The firm also has a joint venture with International Data Group to publish MacWorld, a magazine providing information about Macintosh products. Ziff Davis Holdings, Inc. indirectly owns 100% of ZDMI through which it conducts all of its business. In early 2007, ZDMI discontinued publication of Official U.S. PlayStation Magazine. Also in 2007, the company launched Ziff Davis IT Link, an online social network for IT professionals. Recently, the firm announced plans to sell its Enterprise Group to an affiliate of Insight Venture Partners, a private equity and venture capital firm, for $150 million.

FINANCIALS: Sales and profits are in thousands of dollars—add 000 to get the full amount. 2007 Note: Financial information for 2007 was not available for all companies at press time.

2007 Sales: $	2007 Profits: $	U.S. Stock Ticker: Subsidiary
2006 Sales: $	2006 Profits: $	Int'l Ticker: Int'l Exchange:
2005 Sales: $187,611	2005 Profits: $-118,075	Employees: 460
2004 Sales: $204,477	2004 Profits: $-85,186	Fiscal Year Ends: 12/31
2003 Sales: $194,107	2003 Profits: $-1,909	Parent Company: ZIFF DAVIS HOLDINGS INC

SALARIES/BENEFITS:

Pension Plan:	ESOP Stock Plan: Y	Profit Sharing:	Top Exec. Salary: $1,000,000	Bonus: $1,000,000
Savings Plan:	Stock Purch. Plan:		Second Exec. Salary: $500,000	Bonus: $500,000

OTHER THOUGHTS:

Apparent Women Officers or Directors: 7
Hot Spot for Advancement for Women/Minorities: Y

LOCATIONS: ("Y" = Yes)

West:	Southwest:	Midwest:	Southeast:	Northeast:	International:
Y				Y	Y

ADDITIONAL INDEXES

<table>
<tr><td colspan="2" align="center">**CONTENTS:**</td></tr>
<tr><td>Index of Firms Noted as "Hot Spots for Advancement" for Women/Minorities</td><td>**536**</td></tr>
<tr><td>Index by Subsidiaries, Brand Names and Selected Affiliations</td><td>**538**</td></tr>
</table>

INDEX OF FIRMS NOTED AS HOT SPOTS FOR ADVANCEMENT FOR WOMEN & MINORITIES

2929 ENTERTAINMENT
ABC INC
ALLIANCE ATLANTIS COMMUNICATIONS INC
AMAZON.COM INC
AMERICAN EXPRESS CO
AMERICAN GREETINGS CORP
AMERISTAR CASINOS INC
ANHEUSER BUSCH COS INC
AOL LLC
ARBITRON INC
ARISTOCRAT LEISURE LTD
ATARI INC
AVID TECHNOLOGY INC
BALLY TOTAL FITNESS HOLDING CORPORATION
BARNES & NOBLE INC
BEASLEY BROADCAST GROUP INC
BELO CORP
BERRY COMPANY (THE)
BERTELSMANN AG
BEST BUY CO INC
BOOTH CREEK SKI HOLDINGS INC
BRITISH BROADCASTING CORPORATION (BBC)
BRITISH SKY BROADCASTING GROUP PLC
CANWEST GLOBAL COMMUNICATIONS
CBS CORP
CBS RADIO
CENTRAL EUROPEAN MEDIA ENTERPRISES LTD
CHARTER COMMUNICATIONS INC
CHURCHILL DOWNS INC
CIRCUIT CITY STORES INC
CLEAR CHANNEL COMMUNICATIONS INC
CLUBCORP INC
COLUMBIA TRISTAR MOTION PICTURE GROUP
COMCAST CORP
CONDE NAST PUBLICATIONS INC
CORUS ENTERTAINMENT INC
COURIER CORP
COX COMMUNICATIONS INC
COX ENTERPRISES INC
COX RADIO INC
CURVES INTERNATIONAL INC
CW NETWORK (THE)
DELAWARE NORTH COMPANIES
DIALOG
DICK CLARK PRODUCTIONS INC
DISCOVERY COMMUNICATIONS INC
DOUBLECLICK INC
DOW JONES & CO INC
DREAMWORKS ANIMATION SKG INC
DREAMWORKS SKG
E W SCRIPPS CO
ELECTRONIC ARTS INC
EMAP PLC
ENTERCOM COMMUNICATIONS CORP

FISHER COMMUNICATIONS INC
FORBES INC
FREEDOM COMMUNICATIONS INC
GAMING PARTNERS INTERNATIONAL CORP
GANNETT CO INC
GATEHOUSE MEDIA INC
GEMSTAR-TV GUIDE INTERNATIONAL INC
GENERAL ELECTRIC CO (GE)
GLAM MEDIA INC
GLU MOBILE INC
GOOGLE INC
GRUPO RADIO CENTRO SA DE CV
HARPO INC
HARRAH'S ENTERTAINMENT INC
HARRIS INTERACTIVE INC
HARTE-HANKS INC
HEARST CORPORATION (THE)
HEARST-ARGYLE TELEVISION INC
HERSHEY CO
HOLLYWOOD MEDIA CORP
HOUGHTON MIFFLIN CO
IAC/INTERACTIVECORP
IMAX CORPORATION
IMG WORLDWIDE INC
INSIGHT COMMUNICATIONS COMPANY INC
INTERACTIVE DATA CORPORATION
INTERNATIONAL GAME TECHNOLOGY
INTERPUBLIC GROUP OF COMPANIES INC
ITV PLC
IVILLAGE INC
JOHN WILEY & SONS INC
JOHNSON PUBLISHING COMPANY INC
JOURNAL COMMUNICATIONS INC
JOURNAL REGISTER CO
JUMPTV INC
LANDMARK COMMUNICATIONS INC
LEE ENTERPRISES INC
LIBERTY GLOBAL INC
LIVE NATION INC
LUCASFILM LTD
MARTHA STEWART LIVING OMNIMEDIA INC
MCCLATCHY COMPANY (THE)
MDI ENTERTAINMENT LLC
MEDIANEWS GROUP INC
MICROSOFT CORP
MIDWAY GAMES INC
MORRIS COMMUNICATIONS COMPANY LLC
MTV NETWORKS
MULTIMEDIA GAMES INC
NASPERS LIMITED
NBC UNIVERSAL
NEW YORK TIMES CO (THE)
NEWS CORP
NTN BUZZTIME INC
OMNICOM GROUP INC
PEARSON PLC
PENTON MEDIA INC
PINNACLE ENTERTAINMENT INC

PIXAR ANIMATION STUDIOS INC
PLAYBOY ENTERPRISES INC
PRIMEDIA INC
R R DONNELLEY & SONS CO
RADIO ONE
RADIOSHACK CORPORATION
RAINBOW MEDIA HOLDINGS LLC
RANK GROUP PLC (THE)
RAYCOM MEDIA INC
READER'S DIGEST ASSOCIATION INC
REUTERS GROUP PLC
RODALE INC
ROGERS COMMUNICATIONS INC
RTL GROUP SA
SAGA COMMUNICATIONS INC
SALON MEDIA GROUP INC
SCHOLASTIC CORP
SCIENTIFIC GAMES CORPORATION
SHANDA INTERACTIVE ENTERTAINMENT
LIMITED
SHARP CORPORATION
SHOP AT HOME NETWORK LLC
SHUN TAK HOLDINGS LIMITED
SIMON & SCHUSTER INC
SIRIUS SATELLITE RADIO
SONY CORPORATION
SONY PICTURES ENTERTAINMENT
SRS LABS INC
SUDDENLINK COMMUNICATIONS
THOMSON CORP (THE)
TIME WARNER CABLE INC
TIME WARNER INC
TIVO INC
TURNER BROADCASTING SYSTEM
UNITED TALENT AGENCY INC
VAIL RESORTS INC
VERIZON COMMUNICATIONS
VIACOM INC
VINDIGO INC
VULCAN INC
WALT DISNEY COMPANY (THE)
WARNER BROS ENTERTAINMENT INC
WARNER MUSIC GROUP
WASHINGTON POST CO
WENNER MEDIA LLC
WPP GROUP PLC
XINHUA FINANCE LIMITED
XM SATELLITE RADIO HOLDINGS INC
YAHOO! INC
ZIFF DAVIS MEDIA INC

INDEX OF SUBSIDIARIES, BRAND NAMES AND AFFILIATIONS

Brand or subsidiary, followed by the name of the related corporation

INDEX OF SUBSIDIARIES, BRAND NAMES AND AFFILIATIONS, CONT.

INDEX OF SUBSIDIARIES, BRAND NAMES AND AFFILIATIONS, CONT.

INDEX OF SUBSIDIARIES, BRAND NAMES AND AFFILIATIONS, CONT.

BET Networks; **VIACOM INC**
BET24.com; **MODERN TIMES GROUP MTG AB**
BetNet; **MULTIMEDIA GAMES INC**
Better Homes and Gardens; **MEREDITH CORP**
Better.tv; **MEREDITH CORP**
Big Kahuna's; **PALACE ENTERTAINMENT**
Big River Resources LLC; **REX STORES CORP**
Big Sky Resort; **BOYNE USA RESORTS**
bigcharts.com; **MARKETWATCH INC**
BillBird; **GTECH HOLDINGS CORP**
Binion's Horseshoe Hotel and Casino; **MTR GAMING GROUP INC**
Binney & Smith; **HALLMARK CARDS INC**
Biography Channel (The); **A&E TELEVISION NETWORKS**
BioITWorld Conference; **INTERNATIONAL DATA GROUP INC**
BioWare Odyssey Engine; **BIOWARE CORP**
Bizarre Creations Ltd.; **ACTIVISION INC**
Black Arc Advertising; **WPP GROUP PLC**
Black Hawk Casino; **RIVIERA HOLDINGS CORP**
BlackAmericaWeb.com; **RADIO ONE**
Blackwell Publishing (Holdings) Ltd.; **JOHN WILEY & SONS INC**
Blazing 7s; **BALLY TECHNOLOGIES INC**
Blitz; **MIDWAY GAMES INC**
Blockbuster Total Access; **BLOCKBUSTER INC**
Blockdot.com; **MEDIA GENERAL INC**
Bloomberg Electronic Trading Systems; **BLOOMBERG LP**
Bloomberg Magazine; **BLOOMBERG LP**
Bloomberg News; **BLOOMBERG LP**
Bloomberg Professional; **BLOOMBERG LP**
Bloomberg Roadshows; **BLOOMBERG LP**
Bloomberg Television; **BLOOMBERG LP**
Bloomberg Terminals; **BLOOMBERG LP**
Bloomberg Tradebook; **BLOOMBERG LP**
Blue Chip Hotel & Casino; **BOYD GAMING CORP**
Blue Note Records; **EMI GROUP PLC**
Blue Square; **RANK GROUP PLC (THE)**
BlueLithium; **YAHOO! INC**
bluemountain.com; **AMERICAN GREETINGS CORP**
Blueprint; **MARTHA STEWART LIVING OMNIMEDIA INC**
Blues Brothers; **BALLY TECHNOLOGIES INC**
Blu-ray Disc Security Technology; **MACROVISION CORP**
BMG Entertainment; **SONY BMG MUSIC ENTERTAINMENT**
Body+Soul Magazine; **MARTHA STEWART LIVING OMNIMEDIA INC**
Bonus Bank; **ARISTOCRAT LEISURE LTD**
Book$mart, Inc.; **BOOKS A MILLION INC**
Bookland; **BOOKS A MILLION INC**
Books & Co.; **BOOKS A MILLION INC**

Books etc.; **BORDERS GROUP INC**
Books, Inc.; **BORDERS GROUP INC**
Boomerang; **TURNER BROADCASTING SYSTEM**
Boomtown Bossier; **PINNACLE ENTERTAINMENT INC**
Boomtown Reno; **PINNACLE ENTERTAINMENT INC**
Booth Creek Resorts; **BOOTH CREEK SKI HOLDINGS INC**
Borders Australia Pty Limited; **BORDERS GROUP INC**
Borders Express; **BORDERS GROUP INC**
Borders UK Limited; **BORDERS GROUP INC**
Borgata Hotel & Casino; **BOYD GAMING CORP**
Borsheim's Jewelry Corp.; **BERKSHIRE HATHAWAY INC**
Boston Bruins; **DELAWARE NORTH COMPANIES**
Boston College Club; **CLUBCORP INC**
Boston Globe (The); **NEW YORK TIMES CO (THE)**
Boulder Station Hotel & Casino; **STATION CASINOS INC**
Bourgogne et Grasset; **GAMING PARTNERS INTERNATIONAL CORP**
Box Office Essentials; **RENTRAK CORP**
Boyne Country Sports; **BOYNE USA RESORTS**
Boyne Highlands; **BOYNE USA RESORTS**
Boyne Mountain; **BOYNE USA RESORTS**
Boyne Realty; **BOYNE USA RESORTS**
BrandAsset Valuator; **WPP GROUP PLC**
BRANDZ; **WPP GROUP PLC**
Brasil Holdings, LLC; **CINEMARK INC**
Breckenridge; **VAIL RESORTS INC**
Bridge Information Systems; **REUTERS GROUP PLC**
Brightcove AdNet; **BRIGHTCOVE INC**
Brightcove Network; **BRIGHTCOVE INC**
Brighton Resort; **BOYNE USA RESORTS**
Brightstar Corp.; **RADIOSHACK CORPORATION**
Brigtcove Platform; **BRIGHTCOVE INC**
Bristol Renaissance Faire; **RENAISSANCE ENTERTAINMENT CORP**
Broadcast Software International, Inc.; **CUMULUS MEDIA INC**
Broadcasting Media Partners, Inc.; **UNIVISION COMMUNICATIONS INC**
Broadview Media; **RAYCOM MEDIA INC**
Broadway.com; **HOLLYWOOD MEDIA CORP**
Broder Webb Chervin Silbermann Agency; **INTERNATIONAL CREATIVE MANAGEMENT (ICM)**
Bruen Productions International, Inc.; **YOUBET.COM INC**
Bud Jones Company (The); **GAMING PARTNERS INTERNATIONAL CORP**
Budweiser; **ANHEUSER BUSCH COS INC**
Buena Vista Home Entertainment; **MIRAMAX FILM CORP**

INDEX OF SUBSIDIARIES, BRAND NAMES AND AFFILIATIONS, CONT.

INDEX OF SUBSIDIARIES, BRAND NAMES AND AFFILIATIONS, CONT.

INDEX OF SUBSIDIARIES, BRAND NAMES AND AFFILIATIONS, CONT.

INDEX OF SUBSIDIARIES, BRAND NAMES AND AFFILIATIONS, CONT.

INDEX OF SUBSIDIARIES, BRAND NAMES AND AFFILIATIONS, CONT.

INDEX OF SUBSIDIARIES, BRAND NAMES AND AFFILIATIONS, CONT.

INDEX OF SUBSIDIARIES, BRAND NAMES AND AFFILIATIONS, CONT.

INDEX OF SUBSIDIARIES, BRAND NAMES AND AFFILIATIONS, CONT.

INDEX OF SUBSIDIARIES, BRAND NAMES AND AFFILIATIONS, CONT.

INDEX OF SUBSIDIARIES, BRAND NAMES AND AFFILIATIONS, CONT.

INDEX OF SUBSIDIARIES, BRAND NAMES AND AFFILIATIONS, CONT.

INDEX OF SUBSIDIARIES, BRAND NAMES AND AFFILIATIONS, CONT.

INDEX OF SUBSIDIARIES, BRAND NAMES AND AFFILIATIONS, CONT.

INDEX OF SUBSIDIARIES, BRAND NAMES AND AFFILIATIONS, CONT.

Maroc Telecom; **VIVENDI SA**
Marquee Holdings, Inc.; **AMC ENTERTAINMENT INC**
Marriott International Inc; **LODGENET ENTERTAINMENT CORP**
Martha Stewart Living; **MARTHA STEWART LIVING OMNIMEDIA INC**
Martha Stewart Radio; **SIRIUS SATELLITE RADIO**
Martha Stewart Radio; **MARTHA STEWART LIVING OMNIMEDIA INC**
Martha Stewart Signature; **MARTHA STEWART LIVING OMNIMEDIA INC**
Martha Stewart Weddings; **MARTHA STEWART LIVING OMNIMEDIA INC**
Martha Stewart: The Catalog For Living; **MARTHA STEWART LIVING OMNIMEDIA INC**
Marvel Comics; **MARVEL ENTERTAINMENT INC**
Marvel Digital Comics Unlimited; **MARVEL ENTERTAINMENT INC**
Marvel: Ultimate Alliance; **ACTIVISION INC**
Mass Effect; **BIOWARE CORP**
MATAV-Cable Systems Media Ltd; **HOT CABLE SYSTEMS MEDIA LTD**
Match.com; **IAC/INTERACTIVECORP**
Material Entertainment; **NEW LINE CINEMA**
Matrix Software; **ALLIANCE ENTERTAINMENT CORP**
Matsushita PDP Company Ltd.; **MATSUSHITA ELECTRIC INDUSTRIAL CO LTD**
Max Trax; **CORUS ENTERTAINMENT INC**
Maxim; **DENNIS PUBLISHING LTD**
McCann Erickson Advertising; **INTERPUBLIC GROUP OF COMPANIES INC**
McCann Healthcare Worldwide; **INTERPUBLIC GROUP OF COMPANIES INC**
McCann Worldgroup; **INTERPUBLIC GROUP OF COMPANIES INC**
McClatchy Interactive; **MCCLATCHY COMPANY (THE)**
McDonald's Corp.; **REDBOX AUTOMATED RETAIL LLC**
McDougal Littell, Inc.; **HOUGHTON MIFFLIN CO**
McGraw-Hill Broadcasting; **MCGRAW HILL COS INC**
McGraw-Hill Construction; **MCGRAW HILL COS INC**
McGraw-Hill Education; **MCGRAW HILL COS INC**
MCI Communications; **VERIZON COMMUNICATIONS**
McIntosh; **HARVEY ELECTRONICS INC**
MD2 Workstation; **SHUFFLE MASTER INC**
Mecca Bingo; **RANK GROUP PLC (THE)**
Mechanicsville Local (The); **MEDIA GENERAL INC**
Media 24; **NASPERS LIMITED**
Mediabistro.com; **JUPITERMEDIA CORP**
Mediabolic, Inc.; **MACROVISION CORP**
Mediacom Online; **MEDIACOM COMMUNICATIONS CORP**
Mediacom OnlineMax; **MEDIACOM COMMUNICATIONS CORP**
Mediacom Phone; **MEDIACOM COMMUNICATIONS CORP**
MediaNews Group Interactive (MNGi); **MEDIANEWS GROUP INC**
Meet the Writers; **BARNESANDNOBLE.COM INC**
Mega Communications; **ENTRAVISION COMMUNICATIONS CORPORATION**
Mega Media Holdings, Inc.; **SPANISH BROADCASTING SYSTEM INC**
Mega TV; **SPANISH BROADCASTING SYSTEM INC**
Megajackpots; **INTERNATIONAL GAME TECHNOLOGY**
MegaMania; **MULTIMEDIA GAMES INC**
MegaModem; **RCN CORP**
MegaModem Mach 20; **RCN CORP**
MegaPanel; **NETRATINGS INC**
Melco International Development Limited; **MELCO PBL ENTERTAINMENT LIMITED**
Melco PBL Gaming; **MELCO PBL ENTERTAINMENT LIMITED**
Meltdown; **MULTIMEDIA GAMES INC**
Mempo; **METRO INTERNATIONAL SA**
Men's Fitness; **DENNIS PUBLISHING LTD**
Men's Journal; **WENNER MEDIA LLC**
Mentv; **CANWEST GLOBAL COMMUNICATIONS**
Merchant; **XINHUA FINANCE LIMITED**
Merchants@; **AMAZON.COM INC**
Mercury Records; **UNIVERSAL MUSIC GROUP**
metails.com; **BUY.COM INC**
Metal Container Corp.; **ANHEUSER BUSCH COS INC**
MetaStories; **BRIGHTCOVE INC**
Metro Boston; **METRO INTERNATIONAL SA**
Metro Networks; **WESTWOOD ONE INC**
Metro USA; **METRO INTERNATIONAL SA**
Metro-Goldwyn-Mayer Inc (MGM); **MGM PICTURES**
Metro-Goldwyn-Mayer Inc (MGM); **UNITED ARTISTS CORPORATION**
Metropolitan Club; **CLUBCORP INC**
MFORMA Group, Inc.; **HANDS-ON MOBILE**
MGM Grand Las Vegas; **MGM MIRAGE**
MGM Networks; **METRO-GOLDWYN-MAYER INC (MGM)**
MGM Studios; **METRO-GOLDWYN-MAYER INC (MGM)**
MGM Television Entertainment; **METRO-GOLDWYN-MAYER INC (MGM)**
Michelob; **ANHEUSER BUSCH COS INC**
Michigan's Adventure; **CEDAR FAIR LP**
Microsoft Dynamics; **MICROSOFT CORP**
Microsoft Live; **MICROSOFT CORP**
Microsoft Office 12; **MICROSOFT CORP**
Microsoft Official Academic Curriculum; **JOHN WILEY & SONS INC**

INDEX OF SUBSIDIARIES, BRAND NAMES AND AFFILIATIONS, CONT.

INDEX OF SUBSIDIARIES, BRAND NAMES AND AFFILIATIONS, CONT.

INDEX OF SUBSIDIARIES, BRAND NAMES AND AFFILIATIONS, CONT.

INDEX OF SUBSIDIARIES, BRAND NAMES AND AFFILIATIONS, CONT.

INDEX OF SUBSIDIARIES, BRAND NAMES AND AFFILIATIONS, CONT.

INDEX OF SUBSIDIARIES, BRAND NAMES AND AFFILIATIONS, CONT.

INDEX OF SUBSIDIARIES, BRAND NAMES AND AFFILIATIONS, CONT.

INDEX OF SUBSIDIARIES, BRAND NAMES AND AFFILIATIONS, CONT.

INDEX OF SUBSIDIARIES, BRAND NAMES AND AFFILIATIONS, CONT.

INDEX OF SUBSIDIARIES, BRAND NAMES AND AFFILIATIONS, CONT.

INDEX OF SUBSIDIARIES, BRAND NAMES AND AFFILIATIONS, CONT.

INDEX OF SUBSIDIARIES, BRAND NAMES AND AFFILIATIONS, CONT.

INDEX OF SUBSIDIARIES, BRAND NAMES AND AFFILIATIONS, CONT.